EMPLOYMENT DISCRIMINATION LAW

CASES AND MATERIALS ON EQUALITY IN THE WORKPLACE

Seventh Edition

By

Robert Belton
Professor of Law
Vanderbilt University Law School

Dianne Avery
Professor of Law
University at Buffalo Law School
The State University of New York

Maria L. Ontiveros
Professor of Law
University of San Francisco School of Law

and

Roberto L. Corrada
Professor of Law
University of Denver College of Law

for
THE LABOR LAW GROUP

AMERICAN CASEBOOK SERIES®

Mat # 40155793

ISBN 0–314–14709–8

 TEXT IS PRINTED ON 10% POST CONSUMER RECYCLED PAPER

To Joy, Keith, and Alaina, and in memory of my mother, Mary Lendon Belton.

R.B.

For my mother and in memory of my father.

D.A.

For Paul, Henry, and Clara, and in memory of my father.

M.L.O.

For Theresa, Maximo, Amelia, and my dear abuelas, Ana Maria and Carmen Luisa.

R.L.C.

*

Foreword

The Labor Law Group is an association of law teachers, most of whom serve on faculties in the United States; others teach in Belgium, Canada, England, and Israel.

At the December 1946 meeting of the Labor Law Roundtable of the Association of American Law Schools, Professor W. Willard Wirtz (who became Secretary of Labor in 1962) delivered a compelling paper criticizing the labor law course books then available. His remarks so impressed those present that the Roundtable Council organized a general conference on the teaching of the subject. At the conference, held in Ann Arbor in 1947, some conferees agreed to exchange proposals for sections of a hoped-for new course book. The late Professor Robert E. Mathews served as coordinator. Beginning in 1948, a preliminary mimeographed version was used in seventeen schools; each user supplied comments and suggestions for change. In 1953, a hard-cover version was published under the title *Labor Relations and the Law*. The thirty-one "cooperating editors" were so convinced of the value of multi-campus collaboration that they gave up any individual claims to royalties. Instead, those royalties were paid to a trust fund to be used to develop and "provide the best possible materials" for training students in labor law and labor relations. The Declaration of Trust memorializing this agreement was executed November 4, 1953, and remains the Group's charter.

Cooperative ventures among legal scholars are often centered around ideological orthodoxies or common experiences or identities. In contrast, the Labor Law Group has tried to expand the scope of perceptions and experiences represented within its membership. Consistent with this goal, it has attained significant diversification in the racial, gender, national, and ideological composition of its participants and, additionally, has drawn its membership and leadership from institutions that are varied in size, styles, status, and geography.

The founding committee's hope that the initial collaboration would bear fruit has been fulfilled. Under Professor Mathews' continuing chairmanship, the Group's members produced *Readings on Labor Law* in 1955 and *The Employment Relation and the Law* in 1957, edited by Robert Mathews and Benjamin Aaron. A second edition of *Labor Relations and the Law* appeared in 1960, with Benjamin Aaron and Donald H. Wollett as co-chairmen, and a third edition was published in 1965, with Jerre Williams at the helm.

In June of 1969, the Group, now chaired by William P. Murphy, sponsored a conference to reexamine the labor law curriculum. The meeting, held at the University of Colorado, was attended by practitioners and by full-time teachers including nonmembers as well as members of the Group. The conference papers and discussion summaries were distributed to law school libraries and to participants. In meetings that followed the conference, the Group decided to reshape its work substantially. It restructured itself into ten task forces, each assigned a unit of no more than two hundred pages on a discrete topic such as employment discrimination or union-member relations. An individual teacher could then choose two or three of these units as the material around which to build a particular course. This multi-unit approach dominated the Group's work throughout much of the 1970s under Professor Murphy and his successor as chairman, Herbert L. Sherman, Jr. As the decade progressed and teachers refined their views about what topics to include and how to address them, some units were dropped from the series while others increased in scope and length. Under Professor Sherman's chairmanship, the Group planned a new series of six enlarged books to cover the full range of topics taught by labor and employment law teachers.

Professor James E. Jones, Jr., was elected chairman in 1978 and shepherded to completion the promised set of six full-size, independent casebooks. In addition, during this period supplements were published for some books. The Group continued to reevaluate its work and eventually decided that it was time to convene another conference of law teachers.

In 1984, the Group, now chaired by Robert Covington, sponsored another general conference to discuss developments in the substance and teaching of labor and employment law, this time at Park City, Utah. (The conference papers were distributed to law school libraries as well as participants.) Those discussions and a subsequent working session led to the conclusion that the Group should devote principal attention to three new conventional length course books, one devoted to employment discrimination, one to union-management relations, and one to the individual employment relationship. In addition, work was planned on more abbreviated course books to serve as successors to the Group's earlier works covering public employment bargaining and labor arbitration.

In 1989, with Alvin Goldman as Chair, the Group met in Breckenridge, Colorado, to assess its most recent effort and develop plans for the future. In addition to outlining new course book projects, the Group discussed ways to assist teachers of labor and employment law in their efforts to expand conceptual horizons and perspectives. In pursuit of the latter goals it co-sponsored, in 1992, a conference held at the University of Toronto Faculty of Law at which legal and nonlegal specialists examined alternative models of corporate governance and their impact on workers.

When Robert J. Rabin became Chair in 1996, the Group and a number of invited guests met in Tucson, Arizona, to celebrate the imminent fiftieth anniversary of the Group. The topics of discussion included the impact of the global economy and of changing forms of representation on the teaching of labor and employment law, and the impact of new technologies of electronic publishing on the preparation of teaching materials. The Group honored three of its members who had been present at the creation of the Group, Willard Wirtz, Ben Aaron, and Clyde Summers.

The Group next met in Scottsdale, Arizona in December, 1999, to discuss the production of materials that would more effectively bring emerging issues of labor and employment law into the classroom. Among the issues discussed were integration of international and comparative materials into the labor and employment curriculum and the pedagogical uses of the World Wide Web.

Laura J. Cooper became Chair of the Group in July, 2001. In June, 2003, the Group met in Alton, Ontario, Canada. The focus there was on labor law on the edge—looking at doctrinal synergies between workplace law and other legal and social-science disciplines, and workers on the edge, exploring the legal issues of highly compensated technology workers, vulnerable immigrant employees, and unionized manufacturing employees threatened by foreign competition. The Group also heard a report from its study of the status of the teaching of labor and employment law in the nation's law schools and discussed the implications of the study for the Group's future projects.

In addition to this book on employment discrimination law, we presently have four other books in print, all published by West Group: *Labor and Employment Law: Problems, Cases and Materials in the Law of Work* (Third Edition), by Robert J. Rabin, Eileen Silverstein, George Schatzki, and Kenneth G. Dau-Schmidt; *ADR in the Workplace*, by Laura J. Cooper, Dennis R. Nolan, and Richard A. Bales (Second Edition forthcoming 2005); *Legal Protection for the Individual Employee* (Third Edition), by Matthew W. Finkin, Alvin L. Goldman, Clyde W. Summers, and Kenneth G. Dau-Schmidt; and *Public Sector Employment*, by Joseph R. Grodin, June M. Weisberger, and Martin H. Malin. The Group is also currently at work on two additional projects. We are creating, for Foundation Press, *Labor Law Stories*, a collection of historical essays about the most significant labor law decisions. We are also at work on an entirely new text on labor issues in the global economy.

At any one time, roughly twenty-five to thirty persons are actively engaged in the Group's work; this has proved a practical size, given problems of communication and logistics. Coordination and editorial review of the projects are the responsibility of the executive committee, whose members are the successor trustees of the Group. Governance is by consensus; votes are taken only to elect trustees and to determine whom to invite to join the Group. Since 1953, more than seventy persons have worked on Group projects; in keeping with the original agreement, none has ever received anything more than reimbursement of expenses.

Employment Discrimination Law: Cases and Materials on Equality in the Workplace is the seventh edition of the Labor Law Group's casebook on employment discrimination. The organizing theme of this edition, like the sixth edition, is an exploration of the laws enacted to make equality in the workplace a reality. The book emphasizes federal protection against discrimination in employment under the major antidiscrimination statutes, such as Title VII of the Civil Rights Act of 1964, the Age Discrimination in Employment Act of 1967, and the Americans with Disabilities Act of 1990. Federal and state constitutional protections, federal regulatory interpretations, executive orders, and state laws on equality are included where appropriate. The materials explore the meaning of discrimination, theories and defenses, problems of proving or disproving claims of discrimination, and remedies. Like previous editions, the seventh edition contains numerous note problems and questions developed from employment discrimination cases. For the seventh edition, Roberto L. Corrada and Maria L. Ontiveros join the authors of the sixth edition, Dianne Avery and Robert Belton.

Robert Belton is Professor of Law at Vanderbilt University School of Law. He received his law degree from Boston University School of Law. Before entering law teaching, Professor Belton served as Assistant Counsel with the NAACP Legal Defense and Educational Fund, Inc. ("Inc. Fund") where he had major responsibility for a national litigation project to enforce, on behalf of plaintiffs, laws prohibiting discrimination in employment. Also, prior to joining the Vanderbilt Law School faculty, he was a partner in one of the first racially integrated law firms in the South. He served as counsel or co-counsel for plaintiffs in a number of landmark employment discrimination cases, some of which are included in this book, e.g., *Griggs v. Duke Power Co.* (1971), *Albemarle Paper Co. v. Moody* (1975), and *Harris v. Forklift Systems* (1993). His scholarly and teaching interests are race and the law, employment discrimination, individual employee rights, and constitutional torts. Professor Belton has been a member of the Labor Law Group since 1984 and has been a co-author of the Group's employment discrimination books and supplements since 1987.

Dianne Avery is Professor of Law at the University at Buffalo Law School, where she served as Vice Dean for Academic Affairs from 1998 to 2002. She has degrees from Duke University, Wesleyan University, and the University at Buffalo Law School. Her scholarly and teaching interests are in labor and employment law—including labor history—property, and feminist legal theory. Professor Avery became a member of the Labor Law Group in 1990 and joined its Executive Committee in 1998.

Maria L. Ontiveros is Professor of Law at the University of San Francisco School of Law. She has earned degrees from the University of California, Harvard Law School, Cornell University, and Stanford Law School. Her research interests focus on workplace issues affecting women of color and organizing immigrant workers. Professor Ontiveros has been a member of the Labor Law Group since 1998 and was a co-author of the 2002 Supplement to the sixth edition of *Employment Discrimination Law*.

Roberto L. Corrada is Professor of Law at the University of Denver College of Law, where he is currently University Sturm Professor for Excellence in Teaching and Learning. He earned his undergraduate degree from George Washington University and his law degree from Catholic University of America's Columbus School of Law. His scholarship and teaching interests include labor and employment law, administrative law, the scholarship of teaching and learning, contracts, and LatCrit theory. He has been a member of the Labor Law Group since 2000.

THE EXECUTIVE COMMITTEE

DIANNE AVERY
LANCE COMPA
LAURA J. COOPER, *CHAIR*
MARION G. CRAIN
KENNETH G. DAU-SCHMIDT
DEBORAH MALAMUD
MARTIN H. MALIN
DENNIS R. NOLAN
ROBERT J. RABIN

May 2004

Preface

This is the seventh edition of the Labor Law Group's casebook on employment discrimination law, which was first published in 1971. The first through the fifth editions were published under the title *Discrimination in Employment: Unit Three of Labor Relations and Social Problems*. Beginning with the sixth edition, a new title, *Employment Discrimination Law: Cases and Materials on Equality in the Workplace*, was adopted to reflect the authors' approach to the materials.

A course on employment discrimination law can be approached from several different and overlapping perspectives: civil rights law, labor relations law, or employment law. Deciding how to treat employment discrimination thus poses a challenge to any author preparing a set of teaching materials.

A study of employment law generally begins with an exploration of the American common law doctrine of employment at will. Originating in the late nineteenth century, the employment-at-will doctrine, broadly interpreted, permits employers to dictate unilaterally the terms and conditions of employment for employees who are not covered by individual contracts or collective bargaining agreements. Since the 1960s, legislation prohibiting discrimination in employment has dramatically limited the traditional common law privileges of employers to discharge employees at will, and, consequently, has fundamentally reshaped the legal framework of the individual employment relationship. The incursions on the employment-at-will doctrine brought about by the antidiscrimination laws are related to a more general erosion of the underlying rationale of employment-at-will through changes in contract and tort doctrine governing the employment relationship, as well as through general employment statutes in many jurisdictions that address issues of procedural and substantive fairness in both public and private employment. These developments began in the 1970s and are ongoing still, but antidiscrimination laws are only a piece, albeit a significant one, of a broader revolution in employment law.

The body of public law that governs labor relations has developed within a framework of antidiscrimination principles that originated in race discrimination cases but ultimately are founded on broader principles of fairness. Thus, unions engaged in collective bargaining have a "duty of fair representation" that shapes their relationships with all of the employees in the bargaining units that they represent. But the concerns of unions and union organizers reach to many topics and many groups of employees; issues such as race and gender relations, or the rights of older or disabled workers, may come to the fore at various times, but they are not central to either the mandates of labor legislation or the social and political functions of labor unions.

On the other hand, statutes that prohibit discrimination in employment are an essential component of our civil rights laws. While employment discrimination law continues to be an important regulatory regime that affects and reflects both the law of individual employment relationships and the law of labor relations, there appears to be a general consensus that a fundamental purpose of laws prohibiting discrimination in employment because of race, color, sex, religion, national origin, age, and disability is to implement the national civil rights policy on equality in the workplace. The dominant theme of the seventh edition of this book is, therefore, equality in the workplace.

The title, *Employment Discrimination Law: Cases and Materials on Equality in the Workplace*, thus reflects the maturation, since the publication of the first edition, of employment discrimination law as a critical development in the broader goal of effectuating equality in society. The cases and materials in the book are organized around an examination of the reach and limits of laws designed to make workplace equality a reality. The book focuses primarily on the federal statutory protection against discrimination in employment, but, when appropriate, the role of constitutional provisions and state laws on equality are explored as well.

The book is divided into five parts. Part I consists of two chapters. Chapter 1 provides a framework for thinking about the problem of discrimination in employment and the various meanings of equality that are or might be embodied in legislative attempts to remedy discrimination. The second chapter surveys the major federal laws that prohibit discrimination in employment and briefly outlines the statutory procedures and enforcement schemes, as well as the statutory definitions of protected individuals or groups and covered entities.

Part II is the core of the book. With a primary focus on Title VII of the Civil Rights Act of 1964, as amended, Chapters 3 and 4 cover the basic theories of discrimination (or meanings of equality), the analytical paradigms for bringing disparate treatment and disparate impact claims, and available defenses. Chapter 5 provides a basis for comparing constitutional and statutory approaches to equality in the workplace through materials on equal protection doctrine and § 1981, the Civil Rights Act of 1866.

Part III provides coverage of discrimination on the basis of specific categories: sex (Chapter 6), sex-based compensation schemes (Chapter 7), harassment (Chapter 8), sexual orientation (Chapter 9), religion (Chapter 10), national origin (Chapter 11), age (Chapter 12), and disability (Chapter 13). The materials on sexual harassment, sexual orientation, national origin, and disability have been extensively revised to reflect significant developments in the law since the sixth edition. The final two chapters in Part III cover the topics of union liability for discrimination (Chapter 14) and retaliation (Chapter 15). Where relevant, the cases and textual materials demonstrate how various laws prohibiting discrimination in employment overlap with other federal statutes affecting the employment relationship, such as the Family and Medical Leave Act, the Immigration Reform and Control Act, and the National Labor Relations Act. The scope and depth of the coverage in Chapter 13 of the Americans with Disabilities Act, the most recent comprehensive federal civil rights law, is necessarily more limited than the coverage of some other subject areas. Many law schools now offer a separate course dealing with the complex and difficult issues that arise under disability law; the materials here are intended to serve as an introduction to a more comprehensive treatment of the subject in other courses.

Part IV on relief consists of two chapters. First, Chapter 16 provides an overview, primarily through textual material, of the forms of relief that discrimination plaintiffs may seek, such as back pay, front pay, reinstatement, and compensatory and punitive damages. The major portion of Chapter 17 examines the legality of affirmative action as a remedy under federal employment discrimination statutes, but materials on the legality of affirmative action under the Constitution are included for comparative purposes.

Part V, consisting of one chapter, explores the use of alternative dispute resolution (ADR) procedures and fora as a means of resolving claims of employment discrimination. In particular, this chapter highlights the legal consequences of predispute agreements in which employees waive their rights to bring federal discrimination claims in court.

A significant feature of the seventh edition, like the sixth edition, is the extensive use of scholarship drawn from the work of critical race theorists and feminist legal scholars, in addition to the more traditional pedagogical materials that form the core of the book. The cases and materials provide a firm grounding in the doctrinal developments of employment discrimination law and the theoretical approaches of rights-based scholarship. But conventional assumptions about the objectivity, neutrality, and universality of law are challenged by the feminist and critical race scholarship that we have incorporated throughout the book. In addition, we include some materials on the law and economics approach to issues in employment discrimination law. This extensive and significant body of scholarship, however, is somewhat less central to the approach we have taken, which focuses more on the ideals of equality of opportunity and fairness to individuals as the motivating purpose behind civil rights legislation in general and employment discrimination statutes in particular. Finally, at several points in the book we have included comparative materials from different societies and cultures to suggest alternative perspectives on the problems of discrimination in employment. Our goal has been to offer a number of different perspectives on the social and historical context in which employment discrimination law has developed, with an emphasis on the voices that have emerged from or been associated with traditionally disenfranchised and victimized groups such as women and people of color.

A word about our editing conventions. The cases and excerpted materials have been edited, sometimes extensively, to suit the requirements of space and our pedagogical purposes. In general, deleted material is indicated by ellipses, and original footnote numbers have been retained. Citations in cases, however, have been omitted without ellipses or parenthetical explanation, unless the context required clarification. Citations in some cases have been altered to conform to Bluebook style.

Our goal has been to produce a casebook that is a readable and teachable introduction to the law of employment discrimination; inevitably, we have produced a book that reflects our own teaching and research interests and strengths. We hope that somewhere between our desires and our abilities we have struck a balance that will suit the needs of many of our colleagues and their students.

ROBERT BELTON
Nashville, Tennessee

DIANNE AVERY
Buffalo, New York

MARIA L. ONTIVEROS
San Francisco, California

ROBERTO L. CORRADA
Denver, Colorado

May 2004

Acknowledgments

As with any project of this magnitude, a number of people whose names do not appear on the title page have made important contributions that we would like to acknowledge here.

At Vanderbilt Law School, special thanks go to Shannon McCoy, Agnes Panwai Leung, and Costin Shamble for research assistance in the preparation of this book. Vanderbilt Law librarian, Emily Urban, was especially helpful in accessing necessary research resources of the Vanderbilt and other libraries. Bob's secretary, Dorothy Kuchinski, has worked faithfully and diligently through another edition of this book. Bob expresses his sincere thanks to Dean Kent Syverud for research support. For Joy, Bob's spouse, many, many thanks again for the patience with and understanding of the maddening work habits endured during this project.

At the University at Buffalo Law School, Dianne wants to acknowledge her appreciation for the excellent work of Joyce Farrell, Barbara Premielewski, Lois Stutzman, Sue Martin, and Suzanne Caruso, who all contributed in various capacities to preparing this edition for publication. Dean Nils Olsen generously provided Dianne with research support for the project. As with the sixth edition, Dianne is grateful for the constant encouragement, good advice, and even better humor offered throughout by her spouse and colleague, Fred Konefsky.

At the University of San Francisco School of Law, excellent research assistance was provided by reference librarians Lee Ryan and John Shafer, as well as law students Yesenia Gallegos and Merritt Quisumbing. Special thanks go to Gabe Madway and Teresa Martinez for working above and beyond the call of duty during the production of the manuscript. Maria, as always, appreciates the support of her Dean, Jeffrey Brand.

At the University of Denver College of Law, a number of people contributed to the preparation of this book. Excellent research assistance was provided by students Jane Ritter and Vanessa Becker. Cie Adams, Hope Kentnor, and Raymond Bailey provided very able assistance with changes to the manuscript and other various types of support. Roberto benefitted heavily from conversations with co-authors and also from conversations with his colleague Professor Martin Katz. Roberto's work on the book was facilitated by summer research support provided by the University of Denver College of Law. Roberto is also indebted to his Dean, Mary Ricketson, for her strong support of his work. For Theresa Corrada, Roberto's spouse, who practices in the employment law area as a shareholder at Isaacson, Rosenbaum, Woods, and Levy in Denver, thanks for your love, friendship, support, and many conversations about the theory and practice of employment discrimination law.

The sixth and seventh editions of this book have attempted to build on the pedagogical foundations laid by the authors of the previous five editions. A stalwart of the earlier editions is James E. Jones, Jr., Professor Emeritus at the University of Wisconsin Law School. Professor Jones was an author on each edition published between 1971 and 1987, as well as a 1990 supplement to the 1987 edition. Other editors of previous editions include Professors Robert N. Covington, Aaron A. Caghan, and William P. Murphy. We are indebted to their work.

Finally, we want to thank the members of the Labor Law Group Editorial Policy Committee—Laura Cooper, Lance Compa, Ken Dau-Schmidt, Deborah Malamud, Dennis Nolan, and Bob Rabin—who have provided comments and suggestions that have made this a better book. (The inevitable mistakes and omissions in a book of this size and complexity are our own.) Few people outside the Labor Law Group can fully appreciate the collaborative efforts that many members of the Group have dedicated, for over half a century, to the mission of producing classroom materials for teaching labor and employment law. It is a privilege to be able to carry that tradition forward in this new edition of *Employment Discrimination Law: Cases and Materials on Equality in the Workplace.*

ROBERT BELTON
DIANNE AVERY
MARIA L. ONTIVEROS
ROBERTO L. CORRADA

Editorial Policy Committee

The Labor Law Group

---

*

The Labor Law Group

———

Currently Participating Members

Steven D. Anderman
University of Essex School of Law

Harry W. Arthurs
Osgoode Hall Law School, York University

James Atleson
University at Buffalo Law School, The State University of New York

Dianne Avery
University at Buffalo Law School, The State University of New York

Richard A. Bales
Northern Kentucky University, Salmon P. Chase College of Law

Robert Belton
Vanderbilt University Law School

Roger Blanpain
Instituut voor Arbeidsrecht

Christopher David Ruiz Cameron
Southwestern University School of Law

Laura J. Cooper
University of Minnesota Law School

Lance Compa
Cornell University, School of Industrial and Labor Relations

Roberto L. Corrada
University of Denver College of Law

Robert N. Covington
Vanderbilt University Law School

Marion G. Crain
University of North Carolina School of Law

Kenneth G. Dau-Schmidt
Indiana University-Bloomington, School of Law

Matthew W. Finkin
University of Illinois College of Law

Lucinda M. Finley
University at Buffalo Law School, The State University of New York

Catherine L. Fisk
University of Southern California Law Center, Los Angeles

Joel W. Friedman
Tulane University School of Law

Julius G. Getman
The University of Texas School of Law

Alvin L. Goldman
University of Kentucky College of Law

Joseph R. Grodin
University of California, Hastings College of Law

Alan Hyde
Rutgers, The State University of New Jersey, S. I. Newhouse Center for Law and Justice

James E. Jones, Jr.
University of Wisconsin Law School

Thomas C. Kohler
Boston College Law School

Brian A. Langille
University of Toronto, Faculty of Law

Deborah C. Malamud
New York University School of Law

Martin H. Malin
Chicago-Kent School of Law, Illinois Institute of Technology

Mordehai Mironi
Haifa University

Robert B. Moberly
Leflar Law Center, University of Arkansas, Fayetteville

Dennis R. Nolan
University of South Carolina School of Law

Maria L. Ontiveros
University of San Francisco School of Law

Robert J. Rabin
Syracuse University College of Law

George Schatzki
Arizona State University College of Law

Calvin W. Sharpe
Case Western Reserve University Law School

Eileen Silverstein
University of Connecticut School of Law

Clyde W. Summers
University of Pennsylvania Law School

Katherine Van Wezel Stone
Cornell Law School

Summary of Contents

*

Table of Contents

Table of Cases

The principal cases are in bold type. Cases cited or discussed in the text are roman type. References are to pages. Cases cited in principal cases and within other quoted materials are not included.

EMPLOYMENT DISCRIMINATION LAW

CASES AND MATERIALS ON EQUALITY IN THE WORKPLACE

Seventh Edition

*

Part I

INTRODUCTION

Chapter 1

THE PROBLEM OF DISCRIMINATION IN EMPLOYMENT: A BRIEF OVERVIEW

The jurisprudence of employment discrimination raises three simply stated but difficult legal and policy questions: what is discrimination, how is it proven, and if proven, what are appropriate remedies? Much of this book is devoted to the way legislators, the courts, and commentators have attempted to address these questions.

In discussing the problem of discrimination, one commentator observed,

> All of us well-socialized Westerners know that discrimination against other human beings is wrong. Yet we also realize, if we think about it at all, that we discriminate against others routinely and inevitably. We all know it is wrong to refuse to hire women as truck drivers, to refuse to let blacks practice law, to bar Moslems from basketball teams, or to refuse to sit next to Rastafarians at lunch counters. At the same time, we also know it is not wrong to refuse to hire the blind as truck drivers, to refuse to admit those who flunk the bar exam to the practice of law, to bar short, slow, uncoordinated persons from the basketball team, or to refuse to sit next to people who haven't bathed recently.
>
> What explains and justifies the distinctions we make between discrimination that is wrongful and discrimination that is not? * * * [A]nswering this question is much more difficult than most people assume.

Larry Alexander, *What Makes Wrongful Discrimination Wrong? Biases, Preferences, Stereotypes, and Proxies*, 141 U.Pa.L.Rev. 149, 151 (1982).

One possible and perhaps simple response to this question, considered in the context of employment, is as stated by one court:

> Every employment decision involves discrimination. An employer, when deciding who to hire, who to promote, and who to fire, must discriminate among persons. Permissible bases for discrimina-

tion include education, experience, and references. Impermissible bases for discrimination, under federal law, include race, sex, and age. * * * Thus, in an employment discrimination suit, the key question usually is: On what basis did the employer discriminate? Put another way, the question is one of causation: What caused the adverse employment action of which the plaintiff complains?

Wright v. Southland Corp., 187 F.3d 1287, 1289 (11th Cir.1999).

Our laws and policies once actually permitted if not encouraged discrimination, rather than simply being silent on the subject. A cause of action for unlawful discrimination was not recognized at common law. *See* Violette v. IBM Corp., 962 F.Supp. 446, 449–50 (D.Vt.1996), *aff'd*, 116 F.3d 466 (2d Cir.1997) (table). Our present-day antidiscrimination statutes and constitutional principles abrogate rights to discriminate in business relations, including in the employment relationship, that were once recognized as part of the fabric of common-law doctrine and constitutional guarantees of freedom of contract. For example, Thomas Cooley, a late-nineteenth-century jurist and legal scholar, articulated the then prevailing view on civil rights in his treatise on tort law: "It is a part of every man's civil rights that he be left at liberty to refuse business relations with any person whomsoever, whether the refusal rests upon reason, or is the result of whim, caprice, prejudice, or malice." Thomas M. Cooley, A Treatise on the Law of Torts 278 (1879). Thus, under the American common-law doctrine of employment at will, an employer could discriminate against any individual on any basis, including race, color, sex, religion, national origin, age, or disability, without incurring legal liability. *See generally* Arthur S. Leonard, *A New Common Law of Employment Termination*, 66 N.C.L.Rev. 631, 632–33 (1988) (explaining that laws prohibiting discrimination in employment laid the foundation for the erosion of the employment-at-will doctrine).

The emergence of a broad-based national policy against discrimination in employment, as well as in other areas such as education, public accommodations, voting, and housing, was grounded in developments that antedate World War II. Blacks were the primary beneficiaries of these early developments. *See* Louis C. Kesselman, The Social Politics of FEPC: A Study in Reform Pressure Movements (1948); Michael I. Sovern, Legal Restraints on Racial Discrimination in Employment, ch. 2 (1966) [hereinafter Sovern, Legal Restraints]. In *Brown v. Board of Education*, 347 U.S. 483, 74 S.Ct. 686, 98 L.Ed. 873 (1954), the Supreme Court rejected the "separate but equal" doctrine that had legitimated governmental policies of racial segregation since *Plessy v. Ferguson*, 163 U.S. 537, 16 S.Ct. 1138, 41 L.Ed. 256 (1896). Although *Brown* enunciated a fundamental principle of racial equality, the decision did little, standing alone, to eradicate the legacy of decades of racial discrimination. Moreover, *Brown v. Board of Education* applied only to public employers and other public institutions. For a documentary film on the continuing significance of racial discrimination in the aftermath of *Brown*, *see* Eyes on the Prize: America's Civil Rights Years (1954–65).

Following World War II, a number of states enacted fair employment practices acts, but the first major piece of modern federal legislation on discrimination in employment was the Equal Pay Act of 1963, 29 U.S.C. § 206(d), an amendment to the Fair Labor Standards Act, which prohibits sex-based wage discrimination. It is widely acknowledged, however, that the major turning point in the development of a national policy on discrimination in employment was the enactment of Title VII of the Civil Rights Act of 1964, 42 U.S.C. § 2000e *et seq.* Title VII prohibits employers (as defined in the Act), employment agencies, and labor organizations from discriminating against applicants and employees on the basis of race, color, sex, religion, and national origin. Title VII is only one of several titles in the Civil Rights Act of 1964; other titles deal with discrimination in public accommodations, education, voting, and federally assisted programs. The Civil Rights Act of 1964 is the most comprehensive federal statute that has been enacted for the purpose of providing individuals with a remedy for unlawful discrimination.

Title VII has become the most significant statute implementing the national policy on equal employment opportunity, and the workplace has become a major focus of efforts to define the meaning of equality. But as Professor James E. Jones, Jr., has argued, "[t]he story of modern efforts of government, particularly at the federal level, to establish equal employment opportunity begins with the issuance of Executive Order 8802 [3 C.F.R. 957 (1941)] by President Roosevelt in 1941." James E. Jones, Jr., *Some Reflections on Title VII of the Civil Rights Act of 1964 at Twenty*, 36 Mercer L.Rev. 813, 815 (1985). Executive Order 8802 prohibited racial discrimination in employment by the federal government, private defense-related industries, and federal contractors. As explained by Professor Michael Sovern, there are historical parallels between the circumstances under which President Roosevelt issued Executive Order 8802 and Congress enacted the Civil Rights Act of 1964:

> It was not the hopes of minorities that brought relief [in the struggle for equal employment opportunity], nor even the horrors of racism elsewhere in the world, although the President was surely moved by them. The disquieting reality is that President Roosevelt was embarrassed into acting by the threat of a demonstration march on Washington. Scheduled for July 1, 1941, the march seemed likely to attract 100,000 [blacks] to the capital to protest against the substantial exclusion of [blacks] from employment in government and defense industries.

Sovern, Legal Restraints, at 9. *See also* Mary L. Dudziak, Cold War Civil Rights: Race and the Image of American Democracy (2000); John Hope Franklin & Alfred A. Moss, Jr., From Slavery to Freedom: A History of African Americans 436–37 (7th ed.1994). The principal organizer of the planned march was A. Philip Randolph, the president of the Brotherhood of Sleeping Car Porters, a black labor organization.

A powerful coalition of blacks and whites, men and women, liberal Democrats and moderate Republicans, labor organizations, Protestants and Jews, played a critical role in the enactment of the Civil Rights Act of 1964. *See* Randall Kennedy, *Persuasion and Distrust: A Comment on the Affirmative Action Debate*, 99 Harv.L.Rev. 1327, 1327 (1986). Even more significant, however, was the impact of the civil rights demonstrations of the early 1960s and the succession of Vice President Lyndon Johnson to the presidency following the assassination of President John F. Kennedy on November 22, 1963. *See generally* Charles Whalen & Barbara Whalen, The Longest Debate: A Legislative History of the 1964 Civil Rights Act (1985). The nation and civil rights advocates were galvanized by two widely publicized events in the spring and summer of 1963: a brutal attack on civil rights demonstrators in Birmingham, Alabama, and the "March on Washington for Jobs and Freedom." The 1963 March on Washington, which was led, in part, by the Reverend Martin Luther King, Jr., was modeled on Randolph's threatened 1941 march that had led to the issuance of President Roosevelt's Executive Order 8802. *See id.* at 20; Eyes on the Prize: America's Civil Rights Years: No Easy Walk (Episode 4, 1961–63) (a chronicle of the 1963 March on Washington). About eight months after Lyndon Johnson became President, he signed into law the Civil Rights Act of 1964.

The United States now has a number of laws, federal executive orders, and regulations prohibiting discrimination in employment because of race, color, sex, religion, age, disability, and national origin. Even before the enactment of Title VII some states had adopted laws on discrimination in employment. *See* Bureau of Nat'l Affairs, State Fair Employment Laws and Their Administration (1964). Other states and municipalities have enacted similar laws since Title VII became law. Section B of Chapter 2 provides a survey of the major federal laws prohibiting discrimination in employment.

The most blatant and overt discriminatory employment practices that were evident at the time Congress enacted the Civil Rights Act of 1964 rarely exist today. There appears to be a general consensus that the broader aim of laws prohibiting discrimination in employment is to effectuate the national policy of equality, and we have now arrived at a point in our effort to remedy discrimination in employment—as well as in other contexts such as public accommodations and housing—when we can acknowledge that progress has been made in implementing the national commitment to the principle of equality. Nevertheless, we continue to disagree about the meaning of "equality" and the nature of "discrimination" as a social, moral, and political problem; we also disagree about the extent to which discrimination on the basis of race, sex, national origin, religion, age and disability continues to shape employment decisions. At least two theories of equality have emerged since *Brown v. Board of Education* and the Civil Rights Act of 1964. *See generally* Robert Belton, *Discrimination and Affirmative Action: An Analysis of Competing Theories of Equality and* Weber, 59 N.C.L.Rev. 531 (1981); Julia Lamber, *Discretionary Decisionmaking: The Application of Title VII's Disparate Impact Theory*, 1985 U.Ill.L.Rev. 869. One theory of equality is *equal treatment*: It embraces the notion of "colorblind" or "sex-blind" decisionmaking. Under this view of equality, similarly qualified individual employees should be treated the same by an employer in the sense that the employee's race, color, religion, sex, national origin, age, or disability should not be a factor in any employment decision. Equal treatment thus focuses on fairness to the individual instead of fairness to the protected group of which he is a member. The Supreme Court found support for the equal treatment concept in the language of § 703(a)(1) of Title VII, 42 U.S.C. § 2000e–2(a)(1), which makes it an unlawful employment practice for an employer to discriminate against *"any individual * * * because of such individual's* race." (Emphasis added.) *See* McDonald v. Santa Fe Trail Transp. Co., 423 U.S. 923, 96 S.Ct. 264, 46 L.Ed.2d 248 (1975), discussed in Chapter 3. Arguably a rigid application of this view of equal treatment would prohibit consideration of statutorily protected criteria in all circumstances, including an affirmative action program intended to mitigate the continuing effects of prior discrimination.

A second conception of equality is *equal opportunity* or *equal achievement*. For example, according to this view of equality, it is sometimes appropriate (and may be necessary) for employers to consider the race or sex of employees in order to remedy the past and continuing effects of race or sex discrimination and to assure that the harmful effects of historical discrimination are not perpetuated in the workplace. Thus, policies and practices that constitute barriers to the employment opportunities of blacks and women are prohibited. Proponents of equal opportunity are also concerned with the quantity and quality of the jobs in which minorities and women are employed, with persisting patterns of job segregation by race and sex, and with the disproportionate underrepresentation of minorities and women in many segments of the workforce, particularly their underrepresentation in high-status, high-income jobs. Those who support equal opportunity criticize equal treatment as an inadequate conception of equality because it fails to provide a remedy for the continuing effects of past discrimination. The Supreme Court found statutory support for the equal opportunity view of equality in § 703(a)(2) of Title VII, 42 U.S.C. § 2000e–2(a)(2), which provides that it is an unlawful employment practice for an employer to "limit, segregate, or classify his employees or applicants for employment in any way which would *deprive or tend to deprive* any individual of employment opportunity or otherwise *adversely affect* his status as an employee, because of such individual's race, color, religion, sex, or national origin." (Emphasis added.) *See* Griggs v. Duke Power Co., 401 U.S. 424, 429–30, 91 S.Ct. 849, 852–53, 28 L.Ed.2d 158 (1971) (finding that the legislative purpose of Title VII was to achieve equality of employment "opportunities" and to remove "barriers" to such equality), reproduced in Chapter 4, and United Steelworkers of America v. Weber, 443 U.S. 193, 204, 99 S.Ct. 2721, 2728, 61 L.Ed.2d 480 (1979) (rejecting an interpretation of Title VII that would forbid "all private, voluntary, race-conscious affirmative action efforts to hasten the elimination of [the] vestiges [of racial discrimination]''), reproduced in Chapter 17.

———

UNDERSTANDING AFFIRMATIVE ACTION*

DAVID BENJAMIN OPPENHEIMER

23 Hastings Const.L.Q. 921, 946–47, 950–52 (1996).

* * *

III. THE PSYCHOLOGY OF DISCRIMINATION

* * * Over the past fifty years, psychologists, sociologists, political scientists, and pollsters have revealed substantial evidence that discrimination is pervasive in our society. Discriminatory attitudes are often unconscious, and unconscious discrimination has an enormous impact on the lives of blacks and other people of color, and on women of all races and ethnicities. There is considerable evidence that because so much discrimination is motivated by unconscious beliefs and stereotypes, minority group members and women will be significantly harmed by unintended, non-malicious discrimination. * * *

Surveys taken during the past fifty years demonstrate that views expressed by whites about racial discrimination have dramatically changed, and that virtually all whites in American society now profess a commitment to non-discrimination, at least in public arenas such as employment. If our society mirrored the expressed viewpoints of its white members, prohibitions of race discrimination would be unnecessary. When more closely examined, however, the surveys demonstrate a continuing high level of general racial prejudice held by whites against blacks, Hispanics and Asians. Although the surveys show that the percentage of whites openly supporting discrimination has dropped considerably, surveys on implementation of civil rights and more sophisticated surveys attempting to measure white stereotypes about blacks demonstrate high levels of covert racism. These surveys support the view that overt racism has lost favor socially, but racist attitudes lie close beneath the surface of our society.

* * *

A. Survey Evidence Regarding Racial Attitudes of White Americans

Three national survey organizations have been conducting regular polls on the racial attitudes and beliefs of white adults over the past five decades: the National Opinion Research Center (NORC) at the University of Chicago, the Institute for Social Research (ISR) at the University of Michigan, and the Gallup Organization (Gallup). A recent comprehensive study examines the trends exhibited by these polls from 1942 through 1987. * * *

* * *

A few surveys, most notably a series of questions asked by NORC between 1942 and 1968, attempted to understand the source of white racism by measuring white stereotypes about black Americans. Beginning in 1942 NORC asked "[i]n general, do you believe that Negroes are as intelligent as white people that is, can they learn things just as well if they are given the same education and training?" In 1942, 53% of respondents answered that blacks were not as intelligent as whites. By 1970, that number had declined to a still very sizable 23%. But here again, the 77% of the whites who responded that they believed blacks to be as intelligent as whites may be overstated, because the contrary response now may be recognized as socially unacceptable even among those whites who continue to believe it to be true.

A 1990 NORC study * * * sheds further light on racial attitudes of whites toward blacks in the areas of intelligence and a number of other topics in which stereotypes abound. White subjects were asked to rate various ethnic groups regarding certain character traits, such as unintelligent/intelligent and hard-working/lazy. The subjects were given a scale of 1 to 7, and asked to place each ethnic group rated on the appropriate point of the scale for each characteristic. Unlike * * * earlier polls * * *, the 1990 NORC study carefully avoided using declarative statements with which the subjects could agree or disagree, thereby reducing the likelihood that people would censor themselves from stating socially unacceptable views. For example, subjects were not asked the 1942–68 question "[d]o you think Negroes are as intelligent as white people?" They were instead asked to generally rate whites in intelligence, and then to do the same for blacks and other minorities.

Several of the resulting comparisons are illustrative of the depth of racial stereotyping in America today. Asked to rate racial groups on the characteristic of intelligence, 53.2% rated blacks less intelligent than whites, with 40.5% stating no difference. An almost identical 53.5% rated Hispanics as less intelligent than whites, with 40.1% rating the groups as the same. A smaller but still significant 36.3% rated Asians less intelligent than whites, with 44.6% rating no difference.

On the question of hard-working/lazy, 62.2% of the subjects rated blacks as less hard-working than whites, while 31.9% rated them equally; 54.1% rated Hispanics less hard-working than whites, while 37.2% rated them equally; and 34.2% said Asians were less hard-working than whites, while 30.3% said they were more hard-working, and 35.8% said there was no difference. * * *

To appreciate the significance of such a high number of whites viewing minority group members as less intelligent and less hard-working than whites, consider the effect in the area of employment discrimination. It is likely that employers selecting employees will choose those whom they view as the most intelligent and hard-working. In matters of employee evaluation, stereotypes may become self-fulfilling prophecies by way of suggestion, since most people are prone to seeing what they expect to see. An employer is thus likely, at the 97% level, to subscribe to a belief in the principle of equal employment opportunity, to articulate that belief, and to believe she is applying it. Yet she is nonetheless far more likely than not to view black and Hispanic employees and applicants, and somewhat more likely to view Asian employees and applicants, as less intelligent and less hard-working than are whites. If she applies these stereotypes in evaluating applicants and employees, the resulting decisions are likely to result in substantial discrimination against the minority employees.

* * *

Notes and Questions

1. How should "discrimination" be defined for purposes of federal antidiscrimination laws? In thinking about the question, consider Professor Oppenheimer's excerpt set out above and the following:

[W]hile white men comprise approximately 43% of the U.S. workforce, in Corporate America, they are disproportionately represented at the highest levels of management. Almost 97% of senior managers at Fortune 1000 industrial and Fortune 500 service firms are white. Between 95% and 97% of senior managers of Fortune 1500 firms are male, and minority women comprise a mere 5% of those 3% to 5% of senior management positions held by women. Even holding constant educational achievement, white men account for a disproportionate share of executive, administrative, and management jobs.

White men have 68 percent more of the executive, administrative, and managerial positions than should be expected * * * all things being equal. * * * [W]hite men are overrepresented in top positions regardless to [sic] educational levels. Black women are the most underrepresented group in executive, administrative, and managerial occupations for each educational level, when compared to Black men and white non-Hispanic men and women. [Quoting 1995 report of Federal Glass Ceiling Commission.]

White men are also disproportionately represented among the ranks of Fortune 500 CEOs (95%), daily newspaper editors (90%), law firm partners (85%), tenured professors (between 70% and 85%), and TV news directors (77%). As of 1993, 86% of federal courts of appeals judges and 88% of federal district court judges were men.

Anne Lawton, *The Meritocracy Myth and the Illusion of Equal Employment Opportunity*, 85 Minn.L.Rev. 587, 600–01 (2000) (citations omitted). Based on similar aggregate statistics, a newspaper commentator stated that white males "dominate just about everything but NOW and the NAACP; even in the NBA, most of the head coaches and general managers are white guys. So now they want underdog status, too, and the moral clout that comes with victimhood?" David Gates, *White Male Paranoia*, Newsweek, Mar. 29, 1993, at 38. Notwithstanding these statistics, the number of claims filed by whites (and males) with the EEOC and in court alleging "reverse discrimination" is increasing. *See* Angela Onwuachi–Willig, *When "Different" Means the Same: Applying a Different Standard of Proof to White Plaintiffs Under the* McDonnell Douglas *Prima Facie Case Test*, 50 Case W.Res.L.Rev. 53, 53–54 (1999) (discussing the trend).

2. What conception of "equality" is or should be embodied in the federal civil rights laws that prohibit discrimination?

3. As you read the following materials on the disparate treatment and disparate impact theories of discrimination, consider whether these two doctrinal developments in discrimination law are in fact founded on competing theories of equality.

4. Can the different goals of equal treatment and equal opportunity be reconciled or accommodated?

5. Can you articulate how your own assumptions about the law and employment relations or your own experience in the workplace might have shaped the way that you think about discrimination and the principles of equality?

6. Congress provided a statutory definition of "discrimination" for the first time in the Americans with Disabilities Act of 1990. Section 102(b) of the ADA, 42 U.S.C. § 12112(b). The ADA is explored in Chapter 13.

Note: The Early "Southern Jurisprudence" of Title VII

Much of the jurisprudence of employment discrimination law was established in early cases arising under Title VII of the Civil Rights Act of 1964. The expansive and liberal interpretation of Title VII during the first decade of its enforcement is perhaps unparalleled in civil rights law. Led in substantial part by the United States Court of Appeals for the Fifth Circuit—before the Fifth Circuit was split into the Fifth and Eleventh Circuits—the federal courts, for the most part, broadly construed Title VII with respect to the three issues identified at the beginning of this chapter: the meaning of discrimination, rules of evidence and procedure, and remedies. *See* Robert Belton, *Title VII of the Civil Rights Act of 1964: A Decade of Private Enforcement and Judicial Developments*, 20 St.L.U.L.J. 225 (1976). *See generally* Jack Greenberg, Crusaders in the Courts: How a Dedicated Band of Lawyers Fought the Civil Rights Revolution 412–29 (1994).

There were a number of reasons for the early liberal construction of Title VII, but two interrelated developments stand out. The first is what has been characterized as the "Southern Jurisprudence" of Title VII. Alfred A. Blumrosen, *The Law Transmission System and the Southern Jurisprudence of Employment Discrimination*, 6 Indus.Rel.L.J. 313, 340, 342 (1984). The "Southern Jurisprudence" refers to a line of landmark Title VII cases decided by the federal courts in the South, and particularly the decisions of several judges on the Court of Appeals for the Fifth Circuit. Central judicial figures in the development of this "Southern Jurisprudence" were Fifth

Circuit Judges Elbert P. Tuttle, John Minor Wisdom, John R. Brown, and Richard Taylor Rives, and District Court Judges J. Skelley Wright of Louisiana, Frank M. Johnson of Alabama, and John Butzner of Virginia. These judges, like other Southern federal judges, had first-hand knowledge of racial discrimination based on their role, during the 1950s, 1960s, and 1970s, in implementing the 1954 *Brown v. Board of Education* school desegregation case and other civil rights cases. *See generally* Jack Bass, Unlikely Heroes (1981), and Frank T. Read & Lucy S. McGough, Let Them Be Judges: The Judicial Integration of the Deep South (1978).

Professor Blumrosen argued that the "Southern Jurisprudence" was "calculated to simplify the attack on segregated employment systems" and that judges from other circuits "seemed to defer informally to their counterparts in the South who had intimately experienced the relationship between racial prejudice and employment practices." Blumrosen, *supra*, at 342. Professor Chamallas, discussing the "Southern Jurisprudence" of Title VII, noted,

> Historically, the Fifth Circuit has been a very important site for the development of anti-discrimination law. The Fifth Circuit cases decided in the first decade after the passage of the Civil Rights Act of 1964 held out the promise of an end to racial segregation and stratification in the workplace. Class actions attacking policies on hiring, promotion and transfer "across-the-board," judicial mistrust of subjective procedures, and a presumption of discrimination in a high percentage of individual cases gave plaintiffs leverage to challenge longstanding traditions of racial segregation. The challenge posed by these early cases was cut short, however, by a retreat by the United States Supreme Court starting in the late 1970s. By the 1980s, patterns of racial segregation were more often defended in the courts as a product of choice or custom, rather than an artifact of discrimination. The class action had all but disappeared from the scene, and high burdens of proof had been imposed on plaintiffs trying to show either intentional discrimination or group-based adverse impact. The focus of Title VII changed from the creation of new opportunities through hiring, promotion, and affirmative action to a far less ambitious emphasis on curtailing dismissals and layoffs of protected groups. When they surfaced, liberal visions of equality were often submerged in dissents.

Martha Chamallas, *Racial Segregation and Cultural Domination: A Rubin Trilogy on Title VII*, 52 La.L.Rev. 1457, 1458–59 (1992).

The second development in Title VII law, which grew out of the "Southern Jurisprudence," was the "present effects of past discrimination" theory of discrimination. Many of the earliest Title VII cases were class actions brought against employers and labor organizations, particularly in Southern states, that had long histories of intentionally limiting the employment opportunities of blacks and women because of race and sex. After Title VII was enacted, these employers and labor unions abandoned such overt discrimination, but the effects of their pre-Act policies and practices continued to be reflected in racial or sexual stratification—blacks and women in lower paying jobs, whites and males in higher paying jobs. Thus, a major issue confronting the courts early in the litigation brought under Title VII was whether the statute reaches the post-Act effects of pre-Act intentional discrimination, even though the specific discriminatory employment practices which caused those effects had been eliminated.

In response to this dilemma, federal courts enunciated the "present effects of past discrimination" theory of discrimination. Judge Butzner laid the foundations for the theory in *Quarles v. Philip Morris, Inc.*, 279 F.Supp. 505 (E.D.Va.1968), and the Fifth Circuit fleshed it out in *Local 189, United Papermakers and Paperworkers v. United States,* 416 F.2d 980 (5th Cir. 1969), *cert. denied,* 397 U.S. 919, 90 S.Ct. 926, 25 L.Ed.2d 100 (1970). *Quarles* and *Local 189* essentially established a two-pronged test for finding unlawful discrimination: (1) were the challenged employment practices that antedated the effective date of Title VII based on a subjective intent to treat applicants and employees differently because of race or sex; and (2) if so, even though the challenged practice is facially neutral, are there present effects—in the post-Act period—of that history of intentional discrimination, such as a workforce that is stratified on the basis of race and sex? Consequently, facially neutral employment practices—such as tests or diploma requirements—adopted before Title VII, but which have the effect of locking blacks and women into race- or sex-stratified jobs in the post-Act period, violate Title VII unless the defendant proves that the practice is mandated by business necessity. (The business necessity defense is covered in Chapter 4.)

Although the "present effects of past discrimination" theory is the doctrinal precursor of the disparate impact theory, the Supreme Court has effectively rejected it as a viable rationale for challenging discrimination in union negotiated seniority systems. International Brotherhood of Teamsters v. United States, 431 U.S. 324, 97 S.Ct. 1843, 52 L.Ed.2d 396 (1977). The disparate impact theory, however, was developed in cases that involved either pen and paper testing by employers or seniority systems negotiated by local unions that were historically segregated on the basis of race or sex in workplaces with a tradition of discriminatory hiring practices. *See generally* George Cooper and Richard Sobol, *Seniority and Testing Under Fair Employment Laws: A General Approach to Objective Criteria of Hiring and Promotion,* 82 Harv.L.Rev. 1598 (1969). In many of the early cases brought under Title VII, the evidence of intentional discrimination was manifest in employment practices. Over time, as employers and unions abandoned overt discriminatory practices, plaintiffs increasingly had to rely upon circumstantial evidence because direct proof of discriminatory intent was not available.

Chapter 2

LAWS PROHIBITING DISCRIMINATION IN EMPLOYMENT: AN OVERVIEW

A. INTRODUCTION

The United States has a number of laws, federal executive orders, and regulations prohibiting discrimination in employment in the public and private sectors because of race, color, sex, religion, national origin, age, and disability. Even before the enactment of Title VII of the Civil Rights Act of 1964, some states had adopted laws prohibiting discrimination in employment, but many of these earlier state laws were limited to discrimination because of race, creed, color, or national origin. *See* Bureau of National Affairs, State Fair Employment Laws and Their Administration (1964). Since Title VII became law, most states and a number of municipalities have enacted laws prohibiting discrimination in employment. Some of these state laws provide broader coverage than analogous federal laws.

The purpose of this chapter is to provide an overview of laws prohibiting discrimination in employment. Section B is a brief survey of federal statutes, constitutional provisions, and executive orders that prohibit discrimination in employment. Section C presents a broad overview of the administrative and judicial enforcement schemes of the major federal laws on employment discrimination. Section D identifies and briefly discusses some of the major issues of coverage that are not clearly defined in federal statutory law. These issues include identifying the individuals and groups who are protected from unlawful discrimination in the workplace (focusing on the meaning of "race" and "color"), determining who is an "employee" and who is an "employer" for purposes of Title VII, defining an "unlawful employment *practice*," and deciding who can be found liable for the acts of an employer's agents.

B. SURVEY OF MAJOR FEDERAL LAWS ON EMPLOYMENT DISCRIMINATION

The following is a survey of major federal laws on employment discrimination. Congress has amended most of the statutory provisions at one time or another since the dates of their original enactment. The laws are listed in the order in which they were enacted.

1. *The Federal Constitution*:

a. *The Fifth Amendment*: The Due Process Clause of the Fifth Amendment is a constitutional provision that prohibits federal employers from, *inter alia*, engaging in discrimination in employment. The Fifth Amendment, ratified in 1791, does not have a specific clause on equal protection as is true with the Fourteenth Amendment, but the Supreme Court has construed its Due Process Clause as embodying an equal protection component. *See, e.g.*, Bolling v. Sharpe, 347 U.S. 497, 499–500, 74 S.Ct. 693, 694–95, 98 L.Ed. 884 (1954); Adarand Constructors, Inc. v. Pena, 515 U.S. 200, 115 S.Ct. 2097, 132 L.Ed.2d 158 (1995) (describing the Court's history of applying identical equal protection standards to state and federal action).

b. *The Fourteenth Amendment*: The Due Process and Equal Protection Clauses of the Fourteenth Amendment, which was ratified in 1868, prohibit states and municipalities from discriminating in employment. Lawful resident aliens are entitled to protection under the constitutional equal protection clauses. *See* Truax v. Raich, 239 U.S. 33, 36 S.Ct. 7, 60 L.Ed. 131 (1915). The protection against discrimination extends to race, sex, alienage, and age, but the level of protection is not the same for all protected classes. Equal protection analysis is covered in Chapter 5.

c. *The First Amendment*: The First Amendment protects public employees against religious discrimination by their governmental employers. Both the Free Exercise and the Establishment Clauses of the First Amendment have been relied upon to regulate discrimination because of religion in the workplace. Public and private employers also have relied upon the free speech provision in the First Amendment as a defense to workplace harassment claims. The role of the First Amendment in employment discrimination law is discussed in Chapters 8 (harassment) and 10 (religion).

2. *The Reconstruction Era Civil Rights Legislation*: Congress enacted a number of civil rights statutes after the Civil War to enforce the rights embodied in the Thirteenth, Fourteenth, and Fifteenth Amendments to the Constitution. Of these Reconstruction Era civil rights statutes, the two most significant for employment discrimination law are 42 U.S.C. §§ 1981 and 1983. Section 1981 was originally § 1 of the Civil Rights Act of 1866, *see* Johnson v. Railway Express Agency, Inc., 421 U.S. 454, 95 S.Ct. 1716, 44 L.Ed.2d 295 (1975), now codified, as amended, as 42 U.S.C. § 1981. The law is now well settled that the clause in § 1981(a) providing that "[a]ll persons within the jurisdiction of the

United States shall have the same right * * * to make and enforce contracts * * * as is enjoyed by white citizens" makes it unlawful for covered entities to discriminate against individuals because of race. See Chapter 5. Whether any other clause of § 1981(a) prohibits discrimination in employment because of race is treated in Chapter 5. Section 1983 was originally § 1 of the Civil Rights Act of 1871. *See* Monroe v. Pape, 365 U.S. 167, 81 S.Ct. 473, 5 L.Ed.2d 492 (1961). Section 1983, unlike § 1981, is not a source of substantive rights, but it provides individuals a cause of action for the deprivation of substantive rights guaranteed under other federal laws or the Constitution. Because of restrictive interpretations adopted by the Supreme Court soon after the enactment of §§ 1981 and 1983, these civil rights statutes remained dormant for many years. One of the major limitations the Court read into the early civil rights legislation was the "state action" doctrine. *See e.g.*, In re Civil Rights Cases, 109 U.S. 3, 3 S.Ct. 18, 27 L.Ed. 835 (1883). The federal courts, including the Supreme Court, revived §§ 1981 and 1983 in a series of cases decided in the 1960s and 1970s. For example, in 1961 the Supreme Court broadly defined the meaning of state action in *Monroe v. Pape* for § 1983 claims. And in *Johnson v. Railway Express*, the Court held that § 1981 prohibits private employers from engaging in racial discrimination in employment. Section 1981 and the relationship between § 1981, equal protection, and § 1983 are covered in Chapter 5.

3. *The Equal Pay Act of 1963*: The Equal Pay Act (EPA), 29 U.S.C. § 206(d), which was enacted in 1963 as an amendment to the Fair Labor Standards Act of 1938, proscribes sex-based wage discrimination in employment. The Equal Pay Act is explored in Chapter 7.

4. *Title VII of the Civil Rights Act of 1964*: Title VII, 42 U.S.C. § 2000e *et seq.*, makes it unlawful for public and private employers, labor organizations, and employment agencies to discriminate against applicants and employees on the basis of their race, color, sex, religion, and national origin. The enactment of Title VII concluded a legislative process that lasted several decades, "during which Congress considered and rejected more than 200 fair employment measures." *See* Herbert Hill, *Black Workers, Organized Labor, and Title VII of the 1964 Civil Rights Act: Legislative History and Litigation Record, in* Race in America: The Struggle for Equality 263, 263 (Herbert Hill & James E. Jones, Jr. eds. 1993). Among the more significant amendments to Title VII are the 1972 amendments extending coverage to federal, state, and local government employers; the 1978 amendment providing that discrimination because of pregnancy is sex discrimination; and the 1991 amendments providing for compensatory and punitive damages, and jury trials in Title VII cases. The pervasive influence of Title VII's jurisprudence is manifest throughout each of the chapters that follow.

5. *Title VI of the Civil Rights Act of 1964*: Like Title VII, Title VI, 42 U.S.C. § 2000d *et seq.*, was enacted as part of the Civil Rights Act of 1964. Title VI prohibits discrimination because of race, color, or national origin in any program or activity receiving federal financial assistance, e.g., grants, loans, or contracts (other than those of insurance guaranty).

Title VI contains a provision limiting the statute's coverage to situations in which the primary objective of the federal assistance is to provide for employment. 42 U.S.C. § 2000d–3. In *Grove City College v. Bell*, 465 U.S. 555, 104 S.Ct. 1211, 79 L.Ed.2d 516 (1984), a case arising under Title IX of the Educational Amendments of 1972, 42 U.S.C. § 1681 *et seq.*, the Supreme Court narrowly construed the phrase "program or activity receiving Federal financial assistance." Title IX, a statute with language similar to Title VI's, is discussed *infra* note 7. The Court in *Grove City* held that the phrase was intended to apply only to the specific program for which federal financial assistance was awarded. In response to *Grove City*, Congress passed the Civil Rights Restoration Act of 1987, Pub. L.No. 100–259, 102 Stat. 28, 20 U.S.C. § 1687 (2000). The Restoration Act amended not only Title IX, but also other statutes like Title VI, by broadly defining the phrase "program or activity" to mean all of the operations of any entity that receives federal funds. 42 U.S.C. § 2000d–4a.

The Supreme Court has recognized that individuals have a private right of action to seek relief from employment discrimination under Title VI. *See* Guardians Ass'n v. Civil Serv. Comm'n of the City of New York, 463 U.S. 582, 103 S.Ct. 3221, 77 L.Ed.2d 866 (1983). In *Guardians*, a deeply divided court issued six opinions on several issues; nevertheless, seven Justices expressed the view that a violation of Title VI requires proof of discriminatory intent. *See id.* at 608 n.1, 103 S.Ct. at 3235 n.1 (Powell, J., concurring). One year later, in *Consolidated Rail Corp. v. Darrone*, 465 U.S. 624, 630 n.9, 104 S.Ct. 1248, 1252 n.9, 79 L.Ed.2d 568 (1984), Justice White stated that a majority of the Court in *Guardians* had agreed that, under Title VI, retroactive relief is available to private parties for both intentional and unintentional discrimination. The extent to which Title VI can be used as a remedy for employment discrimination remains to be resolved by the courts or Congress.

6. *The Age Discrimination in Employment Act of 1967*: The Age Discrimination in Employment Act (ADEA), 29 U.S.C. § 621 *et seq.*, prohibits discrimination on the basis of age, against applicants and employees who are forty years of age and older. The ADEA is covered in Chapter 12. *See also* Note on the Eleventh Amendment in this chapter.

7. *Title IX of the Educational Amendments of 1972*: Title IX, 20 U.S.C. § 1681 *et seq.*, prohibits discrimination on the basis of sex in any educational program or activity that receives federal financial assistance. Congress enacted Title IX for two reasons. "First, Congress wanted to avoid the use of federal resources to support [sex-based] discriminatory practices; second, it wanted to provide individual citizens effective protection against those practices." Cannon v. University of Chicago, 441 U.S. 677, 704, 99 S.Ct. 1946, 1961, 60 L.Ed.2d 560 (1979).

The federal courts have not yet definitively determined whether employees in federally funded programs have a private right of action for sex-based employment discrimination under Title IX, and, if so, whether proof of intentional discrimination is the only theory under which a plaintiff can prevail. The Fifth Circuit is the only court of appeals to directly consider this issue. In *Lakoski v. James*, 66 F.3d 751 (5th Cir.1995), *cert. denied sub nom.* Lakoski v. University of Texas Med. Branch at Galveston, 519 U.S. 947, 117 S.Ct. 357, 136 L.Ed.2d 249 (1996), the Fifth Circuit held that Title VII is the exclusive remedy for individuals seeking damages for sex-based employment discrimination policies in federally funded programs and activities. The court concluded that Title VII preempts Title IX sex-based employment discrimination claims because of the comprehensive remedial scheme Congress adopted in Title VII. *Id.* at 758. Subsequently, in *Lowrey v. Texas A & M University System*, 117 F.3d 242 (5th Cir.1997), the Fifth Circuit limited the reach of its preemption analysis under *Lakoski*. The court held that preemption is inapplicable to claims for retaliation under Title IX. The court reasoned that Title VII does not provide a claim for relief for retaliation against an individual at a federally funded educational institution who complains about its noncompliance with the substantive provisions of Title IX.

8. *The Vocational Rehabilitation Act of 1973*: Prior to the enactment of the Americans with Disabilities Act of 1990, 42 U.S.C. § 12111 (ADA), the Vocational Rehabilitation Act of 1973, 29 U.S.C. §§ 791, 793, 794, was the principal federal statute prohibiting employment discrimination against persons with disabilities. The Rehabilitation Act prohibits the federal government, federal contractors, and federal grantees from discriminating against individuals with disabilities who are otherwise qualified to perform the work. 29 U.S.C. § 791 (federal government); *id.* § 793 (federal contractors); *id.* § 794 (entities receiving federal funds). Employment discrimination on the basis of disabilities and the relationship between the Rehabilitation Act and the ADA are explored in Chapter 13.

9. *The Immigration Reform and Control Act of 1986*: The Immigration Reform and Control Act of 1986 (IRCA), 8 U.S.C. § 1324B, prohibits discrimination in employment on the basis of national origin and citizenship. There is an overlap between Title VII and IRCA because both statutes prohibit discrimination in employment on the basis of an individual's national origin. IRCA is covered briefly in Chapter 11.

10. *Title I of the Americans with Disabilities Act of 1990*: Congress enacted the Americans with Disabilities Act of 1990 (ADA), 42 U.S.C. § 12111 *et seq.*, for the purpose of eliminating discrimination against qualified individuals with disabilities. In addition to covering employment discrimination, this comprehensive statute prohibits discrimination against individuals with disabilities in public accommodations, services provided by state and municipal governments, public and private transportation, and telecommunications. Title I of the ADA prohibits discrimination in employment against qualified individuals with a disability who, with or without reasonable accommodation, can perform the essential functions of the job. Discrimination in employment on the basis of disabilities is covered in Chapter 13. *See also* Note on the Eleventh Amendment in this chapter.

11. *The Civil Rights Act of 1991*: Congress enacted the Civil Rights Act of 1991, Pub.L.No. 102–166, 105 Stat. 1071 (1991) (codified in scattered sections of 2 U.S.C., 16 U.S.C., 29 U.S.C., and in 42 U.S.C. §§ 2000e, 1981, 12111), to overturn or modify a series of statutory employment discrimination decisions that the Supreme Court issued during some of its previous Terms. *See. e.g.,* William P. Murphy, *Supreme Court Review*, 5 Lab.Law. 679, 679–92 (1989) (reviewing and analyzing the labor and employment law decisions of the 1988 Term of the Supreme Court). Congress determined that these decisions had "weakened the scope and effectiveness of Federal civil rights protections." Pub.L.No. 102–166, § 2(2). In addition, Congress wanted to provide for jury trials in Title VII cases and to expand the remedies available to plaintiffs under the civil rights laws by providing for compensatory and punitive damages, with statutory caps, under Title VII, the ADA, and the Rehabilitation Act. Most of the Supreme Court decisions that were modified or overturned by the 1991 Civil Rights Act are covered in the chapters that follow.

The 1991 Civil Rights Act amended five federal statutes: Title VII of the Civil Rights Act of 1964 (Title VII), the Age Discrimination in Employment Act (ADEA), the Americans with Disabilities Act (ADA), § 1 of the Civil Rights Act of 1866 (§ 1981), and the Civil Rights Attorney's Fees Awards Act of 1976. In addition, it created three new statutes: (1) 42 U.S.C. § 1981a, which provides for compensatory and punitive damages under Title VII, the ADA, and the Rehabilitation Act; (2) the Glass Ceiling Act of 1991; and (3) the Government Employee Rights Act of 1991. The substantive provisions of the 1991 Civil Rights Act do not apply retroactively. Landgraf v. USI Film Prods., 511 U.S. 244, 114 S.Ct. 1483, 128 L.Ed.2d 229 (1994); Rivers v. Roadway Express, Inc., 511 U.S. 298, 114 S.Ct. 1510, 128 L.Ed.2d 274 (1994).

12. *The Government Employee Rights Act of 1991*: The Government Employee Rights Act of 1991 (GERA), 2 U.S.C. § 1201 *et seq.*, establishes procedures to protect employees of the United States Senate, the Architect of the Capitol, and the Superintendent of the Senate Office Building; presidential appointees not subject to Senate confirmation; and the staff of elected officials who were previously exempted from Title VII, the ADEA, the ADA, and Rehabilitation Act. The Act establishes the Office of Senate Fair Employment Practices to process administratively the employment discrimination claims of covered employees in the Senate. The EEOC has administrative responsibility over employment discrimination claims of covered presidential appointees. GERA establishes a four-step administrative and judicial process, and covered employees are entitled to judicial review of the final administrative decision under a narrowly defined standard. *See* Johnson v. Office of Senate Fair Employment Practices, 35 F.3d 1566 (Fed.Cir.1994) (judicial review of claim of Senate employee); Guy v. Illinois, 958 F.Supp. 1300 (N.D.Ill. 1997) (judicial review of claim of previously exempt state employee).

13. *Family and Medical Leave Act of 1993*: Congress passed the Family and Medical Leave Act (FMLA) in an effort "to balance the

demands of the workplace with the needs of families, to promote the stability and economic security of families, and to promote national interests in preserving family integrity." FMLA § 2601(b)(1), 29 U.S.C. § 2601(b)(1). The FMLA entitles eligible employees to take up to twelve weeks of unpaid leave "for medical reasons, for the birth or adoption of a child, and for the care of a child, spouse, or parent who has a serious health condition." *Id.* at § 2601(b)(2), 29 U.S.C. § 2601(b)(2). The FMLA is covered in Chapter 6, Section D. *See also* Note on the Eleventh Amendment in this chapter.

14. *The Congressional Accountability Act of 1995*: As a result of the Congressional Accountability Act (CAA), Pub.L.No. 104–1, 109 Stat. 3 (1995) (codified at 2 U.S.C. §§ 1301–1438, and in scattered sections of 2 U.S.C., 5 U.S.C., 29 U.S.C., 40 U.S.C., and 42 U.S.C.), eleven civil rights and labor laws, including Title VII, the ADA, the ADEA, and the Rehabilitation Act, are applicable to the legislative branch of the federal government. 2 U.S.C. § 1302. The CAA also establishes remedies and procedures for aggrieved employees to seek relief from violations of these laws. For a discussion of the procedures for deciding claims arising under the CAA, *see* James T. O'Reilly, *Collision in the Congress: Congressional Accountability, Workplace Conflict, and the Separation of Powers*, 5 Geo. Mason L.Rev. 1, 8–17 (1996). To ensure that existing claims under GERA would not abate with the enactment of the CAA, the CAA has a savings clause which provides that GERA is the exclusive remedy for claims that arose before the effective date of CAA. 2 U.S.C. § 1435. *See* Riggin v. Office of Senate Fair Employment Practices, 61 F.3d 1563 (Fed.Cir.1995). Congress enacted the CAA primarily in response to criticism that Congress, as an employer, frequently exempts itself from coverage of laws that it imposes on private, state, and local government employers.

During the discussions about the CAA, Congress contemplated covering the judiciary. Instead, however, Congress included a provision of the CAA that directed the federal Judicial Conference of the United States to study and report to Congress, not later than December 1996, on the propriety of applying to the federal judiciary civil rights and labor laws comparable to those that now cover the federal legislative branch. 2 U.S.C. § 1434. The Judicial Conference issued its report in December 1996 and concluded, *inter alia*, "in light of current judicial branch policies, * * * legislation is neither necessary nor advisable in order to provide judicial branch employees with protections comparable to those provided to legislative branch employees." Study of Judicial Branch Coverage Pursuant to the Congressional Accountability Act of 1995, at 2. For a treatment of potential gender bias in the judicial clerkship selection process, *see* Lynn K. Rhinehart, Note, *Is There Gender Bias in the Judicial Law Clerk Selection Process?*, 83 Geo.L.J. 575 (1994). For a report on the first-ever demographic profile by race, sex, and national origin of Supreme Court law clerks and potential discrimination against minorities in its selection procedures, *see* Tony Mauro, *Corps of Clerks Lacking in Diversity*, USA Today, Mar. 13, 1998, at A12.

15. *Presidential Executive Orders*: Beginning with Executive Order 8802 issued by President Roosevelt in 1941, 3 C.F.R. § 234 (1941), every president has issued or affirmed an executive order prohibiting discrimination in employment by private employers who contract with the federal government to perform work above a specified dollar amount. In 1965, President Johnson issued Executive Order 11,246, 3 C.F.R. § 339 (1965). Originally limited to prohibiting discrimination by federal contractors on the basis of race, color, national origin, or religion, Executive Order 11,246 was amended by Executive Order 11,375 in 1967 to include sex discrimination, 3 C.F.R. § 684 (1967). Executive Order 11,246, as amended, is implemented by Revised Order No. 4, 41 C.F.R. § 60 (1999), and enforced by the Office of Federal Contract Compliance Programs in the Department of Labor. *See generally* James E. Jones, Jr., *Twenty-One Years of Affirmative Action: The Maturation of the Administrative Enforcement Process Under the Executive Order 11,246 as Amended*, 59 Chi.-Kent L.Rev. 67 (1982).

In 1969, President Nixon issued Executive Order 11,478, prohibiting discrimination in federal employment on the basis of race, color, religion, sex, or national origin. 34 Fed.Reg. 12,985 (1969). President Carter amended Executive Order 11,478 in 1978 to add handicap and age to its categories of prohibited discrimination. Exec. Order No. 12,106, 44 Fed.Reg. 1053 (1978). Executive Order 11,478 was again amended in 1998 when President Clinton added sexual orientation as a prohibited basis for discrimination in federal employment. Exec. Order No. 13,087, 3 C.F.R. § 191(1998), *reprinted as amended in* 42 U.S.C. § 2000e (2000).

16. *The Glass Ceiling Act of 1991*: Congress enacted the Glass Ceiling Act as Title II of the Civil Rights Act of 1991, Pub.L.No. 102–166, 105 Stat. 1081, *reprinted in* 41 U.S.C. § 2000e app. at 535–38 (1994). The term "glass ceiling" is a metaphor for the barriers that keep women and minorities, regardless of their merit, from reaching the highest levels in the business world. Congress found that, "despite a dramatically growing presence in the workplace, women and minorities remain underrepresented in management and decisionmaking positions in business." *Id.* § 202(a)(1). To address this problem, the Act established a twenty-one person Glass Ceiling Commission to prepare recommendations on how to eliminate artificial barriers to the advancement of women and minorities in employment. *Id.* § 203(a)(1)-(b)(1). The Commission issued a report in 1995 entitled *Good for Business: Making Full Use of the Nation's Human Capital*.

Note: The Eleventh Amendment as a Bar to Civil Claims for Damages Against States

The Eleventh Amendment to the Constitution of the United States provides:

> The Judicial power of the United States shall not be construed to extend to any suit in law or equity, commenced or prosecuted against one of the United States by Citizens of another State, or by Citizens or Subjects of any Foreign State.

U.S. Const. amend. XI. The Supreme Court has held that the Eleventh Amendment bars a citizen from bringing suit against the citizen's own state in federal court, even though the express terms of the Eleventh Amendment refer only to suits by citizens of another state. Hans v. Louisiana, 134 U.S. 1, 10 S.Ct. 504, 33 L.Ed. 842 (1890). The Court has recognized several exceptions to the Eleventh Amendment: (1) a state may waive its immunity and consent to suit in federal court, and (2) Congress can abrogate a state's Eleventh Amendment immunity without the state's consent as long as Congress does so pursuant to its power to enforce, by appropriate legislation, the substantive provisions of the Fourteenth Amendment. In *Seminole Tribe of Florida v. Florida*, 517 U.S. 44, 116 S.Ct. 1114, 134 L.Ed.2d 252 (1996), and *Alden v. Maine*, 527 U.S. 706, 119 S.Ct. 2240, 144 L.Ed.2d 636 (1999), the Court held that the Eleventh Amendment bars civil actions for damages brought by private parties under federal laws unless Congress, in enacting the legislation, has both (1) unequivocally expressed its intent to waive a state's Eleventh Amendment immunity, and (2) acted pursuant to a valid exercise of power granted to Congress by the Constitution. Congress can abrogate a state's Eleventh Amendment immunity by means of its enforcement authority under § 5 of the Fourteenth Amendment, but it cannot do so under its Article I Commerce Clause power. *Seminole Tribe*, 517 U.S. at 55, 116 S.Ct. at 1123.

Congress has unequivocally expressed its intent to abrogate states' Eleventh Amendment immunity in many federal laws prohibiting discrimination in employment, e.g., Title VII, the ADEA, the ADA, and the EPA. After the Court's decisions in *Seminole Tribe* and *Alden v. Maine*, states regularly have raised the Eleventh Amendment defense, namely whether Congress has the constitutional authority to abrogate their Eleventh Amendment immunity. The following material briefly reviews developments in this effort by states to invoke Eleventh Amendment immunity in order to avoid employment discrimination suits brought by private parties seeking damages.

ADEA: In *Kimel v. Florida Board of Regents*, 528 U.S. 62, 120 S.Ct. 631, 145 L.Ed.2d 522 (2000), the overarching issue was whether the Eleventh Amendment bars suits for monetary damages brought in federal courts by state employees against nonconsenting states for violations of the ADEA. In a 5–4 decision authored by Justice O'Connor, the Court ruled that the Eleventh Amendment bars such suits because Congress exceeded its authority under § 5 of the Fourteenth Amendment. The Court held that the substantive mandate the ADEA imposes on state governments is disproportionate to any unconstitutional conduct that conceivably could be targeted by the ADEA because age, unlike race, is not a suspect classification and a state may discriminate on the basis of age without offending the Fourteenth Amendment if the age classification is rationally related to a legitimate state interest. The Court found little in the legislative history of the ADEA to confirm that age discrimination was a widespread problem that demanded what the Court termed "the strong remedy" of the ADEA.

ADA: In *Board of Trustees of University of Alabama v. Garrett*, 531 U.S. 356, 121 S.Ct. 955, 148 L.Ed.2d 866 (2001), in a 5–4 decision authored by Chief Justice Rehnquist, the Court held that private ADA suits for employment discrimination brought against nonconsenting states in federal court for money damages are barred by the Eleventh Amendment. Among other reasons, the Court found that the legislative history of the ADA failed to support an identifiable history of irrational employment discrimination against the disabled. The reasoning of the Court in *Garrett* paralleled, in substantial part, the reasoning of the Court in *Kimel*.

The Vocational Rehabilitation Act of 1972: This Act requires states that accept federal funds to waive their Eleventh Amendment immunity to suit in federal court for violations of § 504 of the Rehabilitation Act. 42 U.S.C. § 2000d–7. One limitation of § 504 is that it covers only individual state agencies or departments that accept or distribute federal funds. Most of the courts deciding the issue have held that § 504 constitutes a valid congressional abrogation of a state's Eleventh Amendment immunity to private actions brought in federal courts. Jim C. v. United States, 235 F.3d 1079 (8th Cir.2000), *cert. denied sub nom.* Arkansas Dep't of Educ. v. Jim C., 533 U.S. 949, 121 S.Ct. 2591, 150 L.Ed.2d 750 (2001); Stanley v. Litscher, 213 F.3d 340, 344 (7th Cir.2000) (collecting cases). The courts have distinguished the Rehabilitation Act and ADA cases on the ground that the abrogation of states' Eleventh Amendment immunity in the Rehabilitation Act is a valid exercise of Congress's authority under the spending clause.

Equal Pay Act: Of the eight cases the Court remanded to lower courts for reconsideration in light of *Kimel*, two were Equal Pay Act cases in which the court of appeals rejected the Eleventh Amendment immunity defense in cases brought by private citizens seeking, *inter alia*, monetary damages: Varner v. Illinois State Univ., 150 F.3d 706 (7th Cir.1998), *vacated and remanded*, 528 U.S. 1110, 120 S.Ct. 928, 145 L.Ed.2d 806 (2000); and Anderson v. State Univ. of N.Y., 169 F.3d 117 (2d Cir.1999), *vacated and remanded*, 528 U.S. 1111, 120 S.Ct. 929, 145 L.Ed.2d 807 (2000). On remand, the Seventh Circuit reaffirmed its earlier decision that the Eleventh Amendment does not bar EPA claims against states. Varner v. Illinois State Univ., 226 F.3d 927 (7th Cir.2000), *cert. denied*, 533 U.S. 902, 121 S.Ct. 2241, 150 L.Ed.2d 230 (2001). The court held, *inter alia*, that, in contrast to the ADEA, which was at issue in *Kimel*, the EPA is not aimed at the kind of discrimination that receives only rational basis review. Rather, under the Constitution, gender-based discrimination to which the EPA is directed is subject to an exceedingly more rigorous standard of review—heightened scrutiny—than is true of age discrimination. In *Anderson*, the Second Circuit, in turn, remanded the case back to the district court. After reconsidering the case in light of *Kimel*, the district court held that Congress had satisfied the constitutional standards to abrogate a state's Eleventh Amendment immunity under the EPA, even though the EPA's legislative history is silent on Congress's constitutional source of authority when, in 1972, Congress extended coverage of the EPA to states. Anderson v. State Univ. of N.Y., 107 F.Supp.2d 158 (N.D.N.Y.2000). Other courts that have considered the issue post-*Kimel* also have held that Congress validly abrogated states' immunity in private EPA claims. *See, e.g*, Siler–Khodr v. University of Texas Health Science Ctr. San Antonio, 261 F.3d 542, 550 (5th Cir.2001) (collecting cases); Kovacevich v. Kent State, 224 F.3d 806 (6th Cir.2000). The opposing view, that Congress did not validly abrogate states' Eleventh Amendment immunity under the EPA, is set out in a judge's opinion dissenting from the denial of a petition for an en banc hearing in *Siler-Khodr*, 292 F.3d 221 (5th Cir.2002).

Family and Medical Leave Act: In *Nevada Department of Human Resources v. Hibbs,* 538 U.S. 721, 123 S.Ct. 1972, 155 L.Ed.2d 953 (2003), the Court held that a private party's suit seeking damages under the Family and Medical Leave Act of 1993 (FMLA), 29 U.S.C. § 2612 (2000), is not barred by the Eleventh Amendment. The FMLA and *Hibbs* are covered in Chapter 6. *Hibbs* also strongly supports the view that Congress satisfied the constitutional standards to abrogate states' Eleventh Amendment immunity in private suits for damages under the Equal Pay Act.

Title VII: In *Fitzpatrick v. Bitzer*, 427 U.S. 445, 96 S.Ct. 2666, 49 L.Ed.2d 614 (1976), the Court held that the Eleventh Amendment does not immunize a state from liability for back pay and attorney's fees awards in a Title VII employment discrimination case. *Fitzpatrick* was decided before *Kimel* and *Garrett*. Subsequent to *Kimel* and *Garrett*, the lower courts have continued to rely upon *Fitzpatrick* to hold that the Eleventh Amendment does not bar private suits against states for monetary damages. *See, e.g.*, Nanda v. Board of Trustees of Univ. of Ill., 303 F.3d 817 (7th Cir.2002), *cert. denied*, ___ U.S. ___, 123 S.Ct. 2246, 156 L.Ed.2d 110 (2003); Okruhlik v. University of Ark., Bd. of Trustees, 255 F.3d 615, 622 (8th Cir.2001) (collecting cases). The Supreme Court's decision in *Hibbs* offers strong support that Congress acted constitutionally in abrogating states' Eleventh Amendment immunity in Title VII. In discussing the history of states in limiting employment opportunities of women, the Court in *Hibbs* stated that "Congress responded to this history of discrimination by abrogating States' sovereign immunity in Title VII * * *, and we sustained this abrogation in *Fitzpatrick*." *Hibbs*, 538 U.S. at ___, 123 S.Ct. at 1978

Section 1981: The courts are unanimous in holding that states cannot be sued in federal court for monetary damages under § 1981 because Congress did not unmistakably express its intent in the legislation to waive states' Eleventh Amendment immunity. *See* Freeman v. Michigan Dep't of State, 808 F.2d 1174 (6th Cir.1987), Demuren v. Old Dominion Univ., 33 F.Supp.2d 469, 474 n.5 (E.D.Va.) (collecting cases), *aff'd,* 188 F.3d 501 (4th Cir.1999) (table).

Discrimination Claims Brought by the Federal Government: Although individuals are barred by the Eleventh Amendment from suing states for damages for employment discrimination under the ADEA, the ADA, and § 1981, when the federal government, including the EEOC, prosecutes such cases in federal court, states are not immune from monetary damages, even when damages are sought on behalf of individuals. *See, e.g.*, United States v. Mississippi Dep't of Pub. Safety, 321 F.3d 495 (5th Cir.2003) (citing Supreme Court authority); EEOC v. Board of Regents of the Univ. of Wis. Sys., 288 F.3d 296 (7th Cir.2002). In *EEOC v. Board of Regents*, the Seventh Circuit relied upon *Alden v. Maine*, 527 U.S. 706, 755, 119 S.Ct. 2240, 2267, 144 L.Ed.2d 636 (1999), in which the Supreme Court said that "[in] ratifying the Constitution, the States consented to suits brought by other States or by the Federal Government." Also in *Garrett*, the Court recognized that, even though private suits against states under the ADA are barred by the

Eleventh Amendment, the ADA can nevertheless be enforced by the United States in actions for damages. 531 U.S. 356, 374 n.9, 121 S.Ct. 955, 968 n.9.

The Ex Parte Young *Exception to the Eleventh Amendment*: The Supreme Court endorsed an important exception to the rule that the Eleventh Amendment bars private suits against states for damages in federal courts. In *Ex Parte Young*, 209 U.S. 123, 28 S.Ct. 441, 52 L.Ed. 714 (1908), the Supreme Court held that when a state official acts in violation of the Constitution or federal law, he is acting *ultra vires* and is no longer entitled to the state's immunity from suit. The *Ex Parte Young* doctrine allows civil actions against state officials for prospective injunctive relief only, but it does not allow monetary damages. In *Gibson v. Arkansas Department of Correction*, 265 F.3d 718 (8th Cir.2001), the court held that a private party may sue a state official for prospective injunctive relief under the ADA by relying on the *Ex Parte Young* doctrine. In *Gibson*, the court relied in part on a footnote in *Garrett*, 531 U.S. at 374 n.9, 121 S.Ct. at 968 n.9, in which the Court noted that the *Ex Parte Young* doctrine is available to private individuals seeking injunctive relief. *See also* Kulkarni v. CUNY, 2001 WL 1415200 (S.D.N.Y.2001) (holding that *Ex Parte Young* applies to § 1981 claims).

Local Governments: The Eleventh Amendment immunity does not extend to local government units such as cities and counties. Lincoln County v. Luning, 133 U.S. 529, 10 S.Ct. 363, 33 L.Ed. 766 (1890).

Notes: Other Remedies for Employment Discrimination

1. *State and Local Laws*: Most states and a number of municipalities have laws prohibiting discrimination in employment. State laws frequently extend discrimination protection to categories not covered under federal laws. For example, some states and municipalities prohibit discrimination in employment because of marital status, sexual orientation, or physical appearance. For a detailed accounting of state legislation, see 3 Empl.Prac. Guide (CCH). The efficacy of local legislation in protecting individuals from discrimination in the private sector is explored in Chad A. Readler, *Local Government Anti–Discrimination Laws: Do They Make a Difference?*, 31 U.Mich.J.L. Reform 777 (1998).

2. *Labor Relations Laws*: The Supreme Court has construed the National Labor Relations Act, 29 U.S.C. § 151 *et seq.*, and the Railway Labor Act, 45 U.S.C. § 151 *et seq.*, to impose on labor organizations the obligation to represent the interests of all members of the appropriate bargaining unit fairly and without regard to race, sex, religion, or national origin. This obligation is referred to as the duty of fair representation (DFR). The duty of fair representation, as well as union liability for discrimination under civil rights laws such as Title VII or § 1981, is covered in Chapter 14.

3. *Collective Bargaining Agreements*: In 1995, the Bureau of National Affairs, which maintains a file of about 4,000 private sector collective bargaining agreements, reported the results of a survey of a 400–contract sample of those agreements. Bureau of Nat'l Affairs, Basic Patterns in Union Contracts (14th ed.1995). Ninety-five percent of the agreements had a guarantee against discrimination—by either the union, the employer, or

both; 87 percent of the agreements prohibited discrimination on the basis of race, color, creed, sex, national origin, or age; and 65 percent of these antidiscrimination clauses also prohibited one or more of the following: political activity or affiliation, marital status, mental or physical disability, Vietnam veteran status, or sexual orientation. *Id*. at 126–27. Thirty-nine percent of the agreements had provisions requiring compliance with federal, state, or local laws prohibiting discrimination. *Id*. Public sector collective bargaining agreements have similar antidiscrimination provisions providing broad protection, through grievance and arbitration processes, to public employees.

4. *Veterans' Rights*: Veterans are not only protected from employment discrimination on the basis of their former military status, but they are also provided certain job preferences because of their military service or training. The Uniformed Services and Reemployment Rights Act of 1994 (USERRA), 38 U.S.C. §§ 4301–07, strengthens, replaces, and overhauls the earlier Veterans' Reemployment Rights Act. Courts interpreting USERRA frequently borrow from Title VII jurisprudence. *See* Knowles v. Citicorp Mortgage, Inc., 142 F.3d 1082 (8th Cir.1998). Section 712 of Title VII, 42 U.S.C. § 2000e–11, provides that nothing in Title VII is to be "construed to repeal or modify any Federal, State, territorial, or local law creating special rights or preference for veterans."

C. ENFORCEMENT SCHEMES

Because there is no administrative enforcement scheme for employment discrimination claims based upon § 1981 or the Constitution, plaintiffs bringing such claims are not required to exhaust administrative remedies before filing suit. *See, e.g.*, Johnson v. Railway Express Agency, Inc., 421 U.S. 454, 460, 95 S.Ct. 1716, 1720, 44 L.Ed.2d 295 (1975) (collecting cases noting that "the filing of a Title VII charge and resort to Title VII's administrative machinery are not prerequisites for the institution of a section 1981 action"). Section 1981 claims and constitutional claims are filed directly in the appropriate state or federal court, subject to the applicable statute of limitations. On the other hand, employment discrimination claims brought under Title VII, the ADEA, and the ADA are subject to both administrative processes and adjudication in civil court. Thus, exhaustion of administrative remedies is a prerequisite to a lawsuit brought under these statutes. Administrative resolution of employment discrimination charges is primarily the responsibility of the Equal Employment Opportunity Commission.

The Equal Employment Opportunity Commission: Title VII of the Civil Rights Act of 1964 became effective on July 1, 1965. Congress established the Equal Employment Opportunity Commission (EEOC) to enforce Title VII. Initially, the EEOC had authority only to investigate charges of unlawful discrimination under Title VII. If the EEOC found reasonable cause to believe that a charge was true, it could attempt to resolve the charge only through "informal methods of conference, conciliation, and persuasion." Title VII, § 706(b), 42 U.S.C. § 2000e–5(b). Because Congress declined to provide the EEOC with the "cease and desist" authority given to some other federal agencies, such as the National Labor Relations Board, NLRA § 10(c), the EEOC initially was characterized as a "poor enfeebled thing." Michael I. Sovern, Legal Restraints on Racial Discrimination in Employment 205 (1966). Since 1965, however, several reforms have strengthened the enforcement authority of the EEOC. First, in the 1972 amendments to Title VII, Congress gave the EEOC the authority to seek judicial enforcement of Title VII. 42 U.S.C. § 2000e–5(f). Second, under President Carter's Reorganization Plan No. 1 of 1978, 3 C.F.R. 321 (1979), *reprinted in* 5 U.S.C. app. at 1366, the EEOC is now the major federal agency responsible for the enforcement of laws prohibiting discrimination in employment. Prior to the adoption of the Reorganization Plan, federal antidiscrimination enforcement efforts were distributed among eighteen different federal agencies. The purpose of the Reorganization Plan was to provide a unified, coherent federal structure by making the EEOC the primary federal agency with responsibility for administering and enforcing federal statutory laws prohibiting discrimination in employment. The EEOC now has the major enforcement responsibility for Title VII, the ADEA, the ADA, and the Equal Pay Act. In addition, the EEOC has taken over responsibility from the Civil Service Commission for employment discrimination enforcement in the federal sector.

The EEOC has statutory authority to promulgate procedural regulations to enforce Title VII, 42 U.S.C. § 2000e–12, and the ADA, 42 U.S.C. § 12116. Those regulations are found at 29 C.F.R. § 1601 (Title VII), and 29 C.F.R. § 1630 (ADA). The EEOC also has promulgated procedural regulations for ADEA claims, 29 C.F.R. § 1626, federal sector employment discrimination claims, 29 C.F.R. § 1614, and other statutes over which it has administrative enforcement responsibility. In addition to procedural regulations, the EEOC has issued *Guidelines* on, for example, claims based on discrimination because of sex, religion, national origin, and harassment, and on employment selection procedures. Unlike the procedural regulations, the *Guidelines* are the EEOC's substantive interpretations of the statutes. In appropriate cases, the courts, including the Supreme Court, may defer to the EEOC's substantive interpretations of the law when they find those interpretations to be reasonable and consistent with the purposes of the statute.

The Supreme Court has held that the level of deference it will accord to the EEOC's *Guidelines* "will depend upon the thoroughness evident in its consideration, the validity of its reasoning, it consistency with earlier and later pronouncements, and all those factors which give it power to persuade." General Electric Co. v. Gilbert, 429 U.S. 125, 142, 97 S.Ct. 401, 411, 50 L.Ed.2d 343 (1976) (quoting Skidmore v. Swift & Co., 323 U.S. 134, 140, 65 S.Ct. 161, 89 L.Ed. 124 (1944)). *See, e.g.,* EEOC v. Commercial Office Prod. Co., 486 U.S. 107, 108 S.Ct. 1666, 100 L.Ed.2d 96 (1988). *See generally* John S. Moot, Comment, *An Analysis of Judicial Deference to EEOC Interpretive Guidelines*, 1 Admin.L.J. 213 (1987).

1. ADMINISTRATIVE EXHAUSTION

As one judge has observed, Title VII is "rife with procedural requirements which are sufficiently labyrinthine to baffle the most experienced lawyer, yet its enforcement mechanisms are usually triggered by laymen." Egelston v. State Univ. College at Geneseo, 535 F.2d 752, 754 (2d Cir.1976). Moreover, as Professor Brooks has argued, "[p]rocedural mistakes can effectively nullify substantive rights, and poor remedies can render the pursuit of such rights useless and thereby vitiate the law's effectiveness"; these "propositions" are "[n]owhere* * * better illustrated than in the case of Title VII." Roy L. Brooks, *A Roadmap Through Title VII's Procedural and Remedial Labyrinth*, 24 Sw.U.L.Rev. 511, 511 (1995). The observations by Professor Brooks and the court in *Egelston* are equally applicable to the ADEA and the ADA. *See, e.g.*, Jim Beall, Note, *The Charge–Filing Requirement of the Age Discrimination in Employment Act: Accrual and Equitable Modification*, 91 Mich.L.Rev. 798 (1993). What follows is a brief overview of some of the administrative requirements that plaintiffs must satisfy prior to filing a civil action under Title VII and the ADA.

a. *Basic requirements for Title VII and ADA Claims*: An individual seeking relief from unlawful employment discrimination under Title VII or the ADA may not file a civil suit until she has first exhausted administrative remedies before the EEOC. 42 U.S.C. § 2000e–5. *See* Love v. Pullman Co., 404 U.S. 522, 523, 92 S.Ct. 616, 617, 30 L.Ed.2d 679 (1972). The ADA adopts the same administrative exhaustion requirement applicable to Title VII claims. 42 U.S.C. § 12117. An individual (or the aggrieved or charging party) must satisfy two statutory requirements in order to bring a civil action: she must (1) timely file a charge with the EEOC, and (2) timely file a complaint in federal court within ninety days of receipt of the right-to-sue notice from the EEOC. McDonnell Douglas Corp. v. Green, 411 U.S. 792, 798, 93 S.Ct. 1817, 1822, 36 L.Ed.2d 668 (1973); Alexander v. Gardner–Denver Co., 415 U.S. 36, 47, 94 S.Ct. 1011, 1019, 39 L.Ed.2d 147 (1974). The administrative exhaustion requirement is covered in this section. The timely filing requirement is covered in the next section on judicial enforcement.

To satisfy the administrative filing requirement under Title VII § 706(e)(1), 42 U.S.C. § 2000e–5(e)(1), an aggrieved party must file a charge with the EEOC "within one hundred and eighty days after the alleged unlawful employment practice occurred" or "within three hundred days after the alleged unlawful employment practice occurred" if the aggrieved party has "initially instituted proceedings with a State or local agency with authority to grant or seek relief." As to the second statutory filing requirement, Title VII § 706(f)(1), 42 U.S.C. § 2000e–5(f)(1), provides that an aggrieved person has ninety days within which to file a civil action after receipt of notice-of-right-to-sue from the EEOC. If these two filing requirements have been satisfied, a federal or state court has jurisdiction to hear and decide the case even though the EEOC has not complied with or completed all of its statutory obligations under Title VII, such as (1) serving a copy of the charge on the defendant, *see, e.g.*, Russell v. American Tobacco Co., 528 F.2d 357, 365 (4th Cir.1975), *cert. denied*, 425 U.S. 935, 96 S.Ct. 1666, 48 L.Ed.2d 176 (1976); (2) making a reasonable cause determination; or (3) attempting conciliation, *see, e.g.,* Robinson v. Lorillard Corp., 444 F.2d 791 (4th Cir.), *cert. dismissed,* 404 U.S. 1006, 92 S.Ct. 573, 30 L.Ed.2d 655 (1971). *See also* Baba v. Japan Travel Bureau Int'l, Inc., 111 F.3d 2 (2d Cir.1997) (no implied cause of action to sue EEOC for improper investigation or processing of a charge).

Section 706(b) of Title VII, 42 U.S.C. § 2000e-(5)(b), provides that a charge filed with the EEOC "shall be in writing under oath or affirmation." An EEOC regulation states that "a charge is sufficient when the [EEOC] receives from the person making the charge a written statement sufficiently precise to identify the parties and to describe generally the action or practices complained of." 29 C.F.R. § 1601.12(b). The regulation further provides that "[a] charge may be amended to cure technical defects or omissions, including the failure to verify the charge. * * * Such amendments * * * shall relate back to the date the charge was first received." *Id.* In *Edelman v. Lynchburg College,* 535 U.S. 106, 122 S.Ct. 1145, 152 L.Ed.2d 188 (2002), the Supreme Court resolved a conflict split over whether an unverified EEOC intake questionnaire that is timely filed but not verified within the 180–or 300–day filing period constitutes a timely filed charge. The plaintiff in *Edelman* filed a timely unverified charge with the EEOC within the applicable 300 days of the occurrence of the alleged act of unlawful discrimination, but he did not verify the charge until thirteen days after the expiration of the 300 days. *Edelman* upheld an EEOC regulation permitting a timely filed unverified charge to be verified after the expiration of the charge-filing period. The regulation provides that the verification of a charge relates back to a timely filed unverified charge. The Court upheld the EEOC regulation on the ground that it was a reasonable interpretation of the provision in Title VII governing the filing of charges of discrimination with the EEOC.

b. *Deferral or nondeferral jurisdiction and timely filing*: The time requirement for filing an EEOC charge depends upon whether the claim arises in a deferral or nondeferral jurisdiction. A deferral jurisdiction has a state or local agency that is authorized "to grant or seek relief" from employment discrimination or "to institute criminal proceedings" against such practices. Title VII, § 706(c), 42 U.S.C. § 2000e–5(c). A nondeferral jurisdiction is one which does not satisfy the requirements of § 706(c), 42 U.S.C. § 2000e–5(c). The EEOC determines which jurisdictions qualify as deferral jurisdictions. *See* 29 C.F.R. §§ 1601.70–1601.75. In a deferral jurisdiction, the charge must be filed with the EEOC within 300 days after the alleged unlawful employment practice has occurred, but the charge may not be filed with the EEOC before the expiration of 60 days after proceedings have been commenced under state or local law, unless such proceedings have been terminated earlier. Title VII §§ 706(c), 706(e), 42 U.S.C. §§ 2000e–5(c),–5(e). With respect to claims arising in nondeferral jurisdictions, Title VII provides that a charge shall be filed within 180 days after the alleged unlawful employment practice has occurred. In *New York Gaslight Club, Inc. v. Carey,* 447 U.S. 54, 65, 100 S.Ct. 2024, 2031–32, 64 L.Ed.2d 723 (1980), the Supreme Court held that, in deferral jurisdictions, "initial resort to state and local remedies is mandated." The EEOC cannot proceed with a charge if that charge should have been filed with a state or local agency in the first instance. The EEOC may, however, refer the charge to a state or local agency on behalf of a charging party, defer its own action on the charge, and then assume jurisdiction over the charge when appropriate deference to the state or local agency has been satisfied. *See* Love v. Pullman Co., 404 U.S. 522, 92 S.Ct. 616, 30 L.Ed.2d 679 (1972).

In *Mohasco Corp. v. Silver*, 447 U.S. 807, 100 S.Ct. 2486, 65 L.Ed.2d 532 (1980), the Supreme Court held that Congress intended the term "filed" to have the same meaning in both §§ 706(c) and 706(e) of Title VII, 42 U.S.C. §§ 2000e–5(c),–5(e). In *Mohasco*, the plaintiff alleged that he had been discharged on August 29, 1975, because of his religion. He first filed his charge with the EEOC on June 15, 1976—291 days after his discharge. Because the claim arose in a deferral jurisdiction, the EEOC referred the charge to the state agency, the New York State Division of Human Rights. Under § 706(c), once the proceedings have commenced before the state or local agency, the complainant cannot file an EEOC charge "before the expiration of sixty days." 42 U.S.C. § 2000e–5(c). In *Mohasco*, the EEOC ultimately assumed jurisdiction over the charge 357 days after the plaintiff's discharge. The district court dismissed the plaintiff's complaint on the ground that it had not been filed with the EEOC within the 300–day limitation period of § 706(e)(1). The Supreme Court affirmed the decision. As a general rule, under *Mohasco*, when a claim arises in a deferral jurisdiction, a complainant who initially files a charge with the EEOC must do so within 240 days of the alleged unlawful employment practice. This 240–day time period permits the EEOC to defer the charge to the state agency for 60 days and allows the complainant to satisfy the 300–day limit for filing the charge with the EEOC.

c. *The timely filing requirement:* Section 706(e)(1) of Title VII, 42 U.S.C. § 2000e–5(e)(1), requires the timely filing of a charge with the EEOC within either one hundred and eighty days or three hundred days "after the alleged unlawful employment practice occurred * * *." The question when an "alleged unlawful practice has occurred" so as to trigger the running of the 180–or 300–day filing requirement has been a contentious issue in many cases. The issue most frequently arises in cases in which a plaintiff relies upon a series of alleged adverse employment actions, some of which occurred within and some of which occurred outside of the 180 or 300–day period. The case that follows is the Supreme Court's latest treatment of the issue.

NATIONAL RAILROAD PASSENGER CORP. v. MORGAN

Supreme Court of the United States, 2002.
536 U.S. 101, 122 S.Ct. 2061, 153 L.Ed.2d 106.

JUSTICE THOMAS delivered the opinion of the Court.

* * *

I

On February 27, 1995, Abner J. Morgan, Jr., a black male, filed a charge of discrimination and retaliation against Amtrak with the EEOC and cross-filed with the California Department of Fair Employment and Housing. Morgan alleged that during the time period that he worked for Amtrak he was "consistently harassed and disciplined more harshly than other employees on account of his race."[1] The EEOC issued a "Notice of Right to Sue" on July 3, 1996, and Morgan filed this lawsuit on October 2, 1996. While some of the allegedly discriminatory acts about which Morgan complained occurred within 300 days of the time that he filed his charge with the EEOC, many took place prior to that time period. Amtrak filed a motion, arguing, among other things, that it was entitled to summary judgment on all incidents that occurred more than 300 days before the filing of Morgan's EEOC charge. The District Court granted summary judgment in part to Amtrak, holding that the company could not be liable for conduct occurring before May 3, 1994, because that conduct fell outside of the 300–day filing period. * * * The District Court held that "[b]ecause Morgan believed that he was being discriminated against at the time that all of these acts occurred, it would not be unreasonable to expect that Morgan should have filed an EEOC charge on these acts before the limitations period on these claims ran."

Morgan appealed. The United States Court of Appeals for the Ninth Circuit reversed, relying on its previous articulation of the continuing violation doctrine, which "allows courts to consider conduct that would ordinarily be time barred 'as long as the untimely incidents represent an ongoing unlawful employment practice.' "232 F.3d 1008, 1014 (9th Cir. 2000) (quoting *Anderson v. Reno,* 190 F.3d 930, 936 (9th Cir.1999)). * * *

In the Ninth Circuit's view, a plaintiff can establish a continuing violation that allows recovery for claims filed outside of the statutory period in one of two ways. First, a plaintiff may show "a series of related acts one or more of which are within the limitations period." Such a "serial violation is established if the evidence indicates that the alleged acts of discrimination occurring prior to the limitations period are sufficiently related to those occurring within the limitations period." The alleged incidents, however, "cannot be isolated, sporadic, or discrete." Second, a plaintiff may establish a continuing violation if he shows "a systematic policy or practice of discrimination that operated, in part, within the limitations period—a systemic violation."

* * * Because Morgan alleged three types of Title VII claims, namely, discrimination, hostile environment, and retaliation, the Court of Appeals considered the allegations with respect to each category of

---

1. Such discrimination, he alleges, began when the company hired him in August 1990 as an electrician helper, rather than as an electrician. Subsequent alleged racially motivated discriminatory acts included a termination for refusing to follow orders, Amtrak's refusal to allow him to participate in an apprenticeship program, numerous "written counselings" for absenteeism, as well as the use of racial epithets against him by his managers.

claim separately and found that the pre-limitations conduct was sufficiently related to the post-limitations conduct to invoke the continuing violation doctrine for all three. * * * [T]he Court of Appeals reversed and remanded for a new trial.

We granted certiorari, and now reverse in part and affirm in part.

II

The Courts of Appeals have taken various approaches to the question whether acts that fall outside of the statutory time period for filing charges set forth in 42 U.S.C. § 2000e–5(e) are actionable under Title VII. While the lower courts have offered reasonable, albeit divergent solutions, none are compelled by the text of the statute. * * *

Title 42 U.S.C. § 2000e–5(e)(1) is a charge filing provision that "specifies with precision" the prerequisites that a plaintiff must satisfy before filing suit. *Alexander v. Gardner–Denver Co.*, 415 U.S. 36, 47, 94 S.Ct. 1011, 39 L.Ed.2d 147 (1974). An individual must file a charge within the statutory time period and serve notice upon the person against whom the charge is made. In a State that has an entity with the authority to grant or seek relief with respect to the alleged unlawful practice, an employee who initially files a grievance with that agency must file the charge with the EEOC within 300 days of the employment practice; in all other States, the charge must be filed within 180 days. A claim is time barred if it is not filed within these time limits.

For our purposes, the critical sentence of the charge filing provision is: "A charge under this section *shall be filed* within one hundred and eighty days *after the alleged unlawful employment practice occurred.*" § 2000e–5(e)(1) (emphasis added). The operative terms are "shall," "after * * * occurred," and "unlawful employment practice." "[S]hall" makes the act of filing a charge within the specified time period mandatory. "[O]ccurred" means that the practice took place or happened in the past.[5] The requirement, therefore, that the charge be filed "after" the practice "occurred" tells us that a litigant has up to 180 or 300 days *after* the unlawful practice happened to file a charge with the EEOC.

The critical questions, then, are: What constitutes an "unlawful employment practice" and when has that practice "occurred"? Our task is to answer these questions for both discrete discriminatory acts and hostile work environment claims. The answer varies with the practice.

A

We take the easier question first. A discrete retaliatory or discriminatory act "occurred" on the day that it "happened." A party, therefore, must file a charge within either 180 or 300 days of the date of the act or lose the ability to recover for it.

---

5. * * * Webster's Third New International Dictionary 1561 (1993) defines "occur" as "[t]o present itself: come to pass: take place: HAPPEN." See also Black's Law Dictionary 1080 (6th ed.1990) (defining "[o]ccur" as "[t]o happen; * * * to take place; to arise").

Morgan argues that the statute does not require the filing of a charge within 180 or 300 days of each discrete act, but that the language requires the filing of a charge within the specified number of days after an "unlawful employment *practice.*" "Practice," Morgan contends, connotes an ongoing violation that can endure or recur over a period of time. In Morgan's view, the term "practice" therefore provides a statutory basis for the Ninth Circuit's continuing violation doctrine. This argument is unavailing, however, given that 42 U.S.C. § 2000e–2 explains in great detail the sorts of actions that qualify as "[u]nlawful employment practices" and includes among such practices numerous discrete acts. See, *e.g.,* § 2000e–2(a) ("It shall be an unlawful employment practice for an employer—(1) to fail or refuse to hire or to discharge any individual, or otherwise to discriminate against any individual with respect to his compensation, terms, conditions, or privileges of employment, because of such individual's race, color, religion, sex, or national origin * * * "). There is simply no indication that the term "practice" converts related discrete acts into a single unlawful practice for the purposes of timely filing. *Cf.* § 2000e–6(a) (providing that the Attorney General may bring a civil action in "pattern or practice" cases).

We have repeatedly interpreted the term "practice" to apply to a discrete act or single "occurrence," even when it has a connection to other acts. For example, in *Electrical Workers v. Robbins & Myers, Inc.,* 429 U.S. 229, 234, 97 S.Ct. 441, 50 L.Ed.2d 427 (1976), an employee asserted that his complaint was timely filed because the date "the alleged unlawful employment practice occurred" was the date after the conclusion of a grievance arbitration procedure, rather than the earlier date of his discharge. The discharge, he contended, was "tentative" and "nonfinal" until the grievance and arbitration procedure ended. Not so, the Court concluded, because the discriminatory act *occurred* on the date of discharge—the date that the parties understood the termination to be final. *Id.,* at 234–235, 97 S.Ct. 441. Similarly, in *Bazemore v. Friday,* 478 U.S. 385, 106 S.Ct. 3000, 92 L.Ed.2d 315 (1986) *(per curiam),* a pattern-or-practice case, when considering a discriminatory salary structure, the Court noted that although the salary discrimination began prior to the date that the act was actionable under Title VII, "[e]ach week's paycheck that deliver[ed] less to a black than to a similarly situated white is a wrong actionable under Title VII * * *." *Id.,* at 395, 106 S.Ct. 3000.

This Court has also held that discrete acts that fall within the statutory time period do not make timely acts that fall outside the time period. In *United Air Lines, Inc. v. Evans,* 431 U.S. 553, 97 S.Ct. 1885, 52 L.Ed.2d 571 (1977), United forced Evans to resign after she married because of its policy against married female flight attendants. Although Evans failed to file a timely charge following her initial separation, she nonetheless claimed that United was guilty of a present, continuing violation of Title VII because its seniority system failed to give her credit for her prior service once she was re-hired. The Court disagreed, concluding that "United was entitled to treat [Evans' resignation] as lawful after [she] failed to file a charge of discrimination within the" charge filing period then allowed by the statute. *Id.,* at 558, 97 S.Ct. 1885. At the same time, however, the Court noted that "[i]t may constitute relevant background evidence in a proceeding in which the status of a current practice is at issue." *Ibid.* The emphasis, however, "should not be placed on mere continuity" but on "whether any present *violation* exist[ed]." *Ibid.* (emphasis in original).

In *Delaware State College v. Ricks,* 449 U.S. 250, 101 S.Ct. 498, 66 L.Ed.2d 431 (1980), the Court evaluated the timeliness of an EEOC complaint filed by a professor who argued that he had been denied academic tenure because of his national origin. Following the decision to deny tenure, the employer offered him a " 'terminal' " contract to teach an additional year. *Id.,* at 253, 101 S.Ct. 498. Claiming, in effect, a " 'continuing violation,' " the professor argued that the time period did not begin to run until his actual termination. *Id.,* at 257, 101 S.Ct. 498. The Court rejected this argument: "Mere continuity of employment, without more, is insufficient to prolong the life of a cause of action for employment discrimination." *Ibid.* In order for the time period to commence with the discharge, "he should have identified the alleged discriminatory acts that continued until, or occurred at the time of, the actual termination of his employment." *Ibid.* He could not use a termination that fell within the limitations period to pull in the time-barred discriminatory act. Nor could a time-barred act justify filing a charge concerning a termination that was not independently discriminatory.

We derive several principles from these cases. First, discrete discriminatory acts are not actionable if time barred, even when they are related to acts alleged in timely filed charges. Each discrete discriminatory act starts a new clock for filing charges alleging that act. The charge, therefore, must be filed within the 180–or 300–day time period after the discrete discriminatory act occurred. The existence of past acts and the employee's prior knowledge of their occurrence, however, does not bar employees from filing charges about related discrete acts so long as the acts are independently discriminatory and charges addressing those acts are themselves timely filed. Nor does the statute bar an employee from using the prior acts as background evidence in support of a timely claim.

As we have held, however, this time period for filing a charge is subject to equitable doctrines such as tolling or estoppel. See *Zipes v. Trans World Airlines, Inc.,* 455 U.S. 385, 393, 102 S.Ct. 1127, 71 L.Ed.2d 234 (1982) * * *. Courts may evaluate whether it would be proper to apply such doctrines, although they are to be applied sparingly. * * *

The Court of Appeals applied the continuing violations doctrine to what it termed "serial violations," holding that so long as one act falls within the charge filing period, discriminatory and retaliatory acts that are plausibly or sufficiently related to that act may also be considered for the purposes of liability. With respect to this holding, therefore, we reverse.

Discrete acts such as termination, failure to promote, denial of transfer, or refusal to hire are easy to identify. Each incident of discrimination and each retaliatory adverse employment decision constitutes a separate actionable "unlawful employment practice." Morgan can only file a charge to cover discrete acts that "occurred" within the appropriate time period.[7] While Morgan alleged that he suffered from numerous discriminatory and retaliatory acts from the date that he was hired through March 3, 1995, the date that he was fired, only incidents that took place within the timely filing period are actionable. Because Morgan first filed his charge with an appropriate state agency, only those acts that occurred 300 days before February 27, 1995, the day that Morgan filed his charge, are actionable. During that time period, Morgan contends that he was wrongfully suspended and charged with a violation of Amtrak's "Rule L" for insubordination while failing to complete work assigned to him, denied training, and falsely accused of threatening a manager.[8] All prior discrete discriminatory acts are untimely filed and no longer actionable.[9]

* * *

JUSTICE O'CONNOR, with whom THE CHIEF JUSTICE joins, with whom JUSTICE SCALIA and JUSTICE KENNEDY join as to all but Part I, and with whom Justice BREYER joins as to Part I, concurring in part and dissenting in part.

I join Part II–A of the Court's opinion because I agree that Title VII suits based on discrete discriminatory acts are time barred when the plaintiff fails to file a charge with the Equal Employment Opportunity Commission (EEOC) within the 180–or 300–day time period designated in the statute. * * *

I

The Court today holds that, for discrete discriminatory acts, § 2000e–5(e)(1) serves as a form of statute of limitations, barring recovery for actions that take place outside the charge-filing period. The Court acknowledges, however, that this limitation period may be adjusted by equitable doctrines. * * * Like the Court, I see no need to resolve fully

---

7. Because the Court of Appeals held that the "discrete acts" were actionable as part of a continuing violation, there was no need for it to further contemplate when the time period began to run for each act. The District Court noted that "Morgan believed that he was being discriminated against at the time that all of these acts occurred * * *." There may be circumstances where it will be difficult to determine when the time period should begin to run. One issue that may arise in such circumstances is whether the time begins to run when the injury occurs as opposed to when the injury reasonably should have been discovered. But this case presents no occasion to resolve that issue.

8. The final alleged discriminatory act, he contends, led to his termination on March 3, 1995. Morgan alleges that after the manager reported that Morgan had threatened him, he was ordered into a supervisor's office. Then, after he asked for union representation or the presence of a co-worker as a witness, the supervisor denied both, ordered everyone out of the office, and yelled at Morgan to get his "black ass" into the office. Morgan refused and went home. He was subsequently suspended and charged with violations of two company rules and, following an investigatory hearing, terminated.

9. We have no occasion here to consider the timely filing question with respect to "pattern-or-practice" claims brought by private litigants as none are at issue here.

the application of the discovery rule to claims based on discrete discriminatory acts. I believe, however, that some version of the discovery rule applies to discrete-act claims. See 2 B. Lindemann & P. Grossman, Employment Discrimination Law 1349 (3d ed.1996) ("Although [Supreme Court precedents] seem to establish a relatively simple 'notice' rule as to when discrimination 'occurs' (so as to start the running of the charge-filing period), courts continue to disagree on what the notice must be *of*" (emphasis in original)). In my view, therefore, the charge-filing period precludes recovery based on discrete actions that occurred more than 180 or 300 days after the employee had, or should have had, notice of the discriminatory act.

* * *

[Part II–B of *Morgan*, in which the Court holds that the continuing violation theory is applicable to hostile environment harassment cases is discussed in Chapter 8, Section C.]

Notes and Questions

1. *Morgan* discussed at least four distinct kinds of unlawful employment practices at issue in that case: discrete acts of discrimination, retaliation, hostile work environment claims, and pattern-or-practice claims. The Court specifically rejects the applicability of the continuing violation theory to discrete acts of discrimination and retaliation claims but leaves open the question whether the continuing violation theory is applicable to pattern-or-practice claims. As you read the cases in the chapters that follow, consider whether the unlawful employment practice at issue is based on a discrete act of discrimination, retaliation, a hostile work environment, or a pattern-or-practice claim.

2. What kind of notice is appropriate to inform an applicant or employee that an alleged act of unlawful discrimination has occurred? Actual notice from the employer? *See* Wright v. AmSouth Bancorp., 320 F.3d 1198, 1202 (11th Cir.2003) ("[t]he key determination * * * is when [the plaintiff] received unequivocal notice of his termination"). Should constructive notice be sufficient? Should an applicant's or employee's suspicion be sufficient notice that triggers the onset of the timely filing requirement? *See* Jones v. Dillard's, Inc., 331 F.3d 1259 (11th Cir.2003) (employee made written notes of suspicion of age discrimination). Does *Morgan* impose an obligation on an employee or applicant to use due diligence to discover when and whether he has been the victim of an act of allegedly unlawful employment discrimination? What does Justice Thomas say about the notice issue? How would Justice O'Connor approach this issue?

3. What potential problems do you envision under *Morgan's* discrete acts doctrine? Consider the following. As a general rule, a plaintiff may seek relief in court only from those claims that were alleged in a timely filed charge with the EEOC, and only those respondents named in the EEOC charge can be named as defendants in the civil action. Prior to *Morgan*, the lower courts adopted the "like or related" doctrine to determine which claims can be asserted in a civil action when that particular claim was not

alleged in the EEOC charge. The doctrinal foundation of the "like and related" doctrine was first articulated in *Sanchez v. Standard Brands, Inc.*, 431 F.2d 455 (5th Cir.1970). *Sanchez* held that a plaintiff may raise allegations in a judicial complaint of " 'any kind of discrimination like or related to the allegations contained in the [EEOC] charge and growing out of such allegation during the pendency of the case before the Commission.' " *Id.* at 466 (quoting King v. Georgia Power Co., 295 F.Supp. 943, 947 (N.D.Ga. 1968)). In *Sanchez*, the plaintiff, a female of Hispanic origin, checked the box on the EEOC charge form labeled "Sex," but failed to check the box labeled "National Origin." The Fifth Circuit found that the facts alleged in the "Explanation" section of the charge form were identical for both the plaintiff's claim of national origin and her claim of sex discrimination. Therefore, the court ruled that the plaintiff's lawsuit could go forward on both claims because both arose out of the same facts. Most courts of appeals have followed the *Sanchez* rule. *See, e.g.*, Babrocky v. Jewel Food Co. & Retail Meatcutters, 773 F.2d 857 (7th Cir.1985). Does the "like and related" doctrine survive in light of the *Morgan* discrete acts doctrine?

Also, consider the following: The plaintiff was denied a promotion to the same job on January 30, 1999, January 30, 2001, and January 30, 2002. The job was vacant on each occasion, and the plaintiff applied and was qualified for the position. He believed the employer's action on each occasion was a result of his race. He timely filed three different charges with the EEOC for each occurrence. If each occurrence is considered to be a discrete act, would he have to file three separate lawsuits under *Morgan*?

4. The Court in *Morgan* held that a plaintiff is not barred from using prior acts of discrimination as background evidence in support of a timely claim based on a discrete act. Presumably, this "background evidence" includes time-barred claims. Does this rule provide a gaping loophole that allows plaintiffs to circumvent the Court's pronouncement on discrete acts?

5. *Timely Filing and Equitable Considerations*: In *Zipes v. Trans World Airlines, Inc.*, 455 U.S. 385, 102 S.Ct. 1127, 71 L.Ed.2d 234 (1982), the Supreme Court held that "filing a timely charge of discrimination with the EEOC is not a jurisdictional prerequisite to suit in federal court, but a requirement that, like a statute of limitations, is subject to waiver, estoppel, and equitable tolling." *Id.* at 393, 102 S.Ct. at 1132. Waiver is appropriate in very limited circumstances, such as where the parties have agreed to extend the period in which the plaintiff may file her charge or the defendant has delayed in alleging a timeliness defense. *See, e.g.*, Leake v. University of Cincinnati, 605 F.2d 255 (6th Cir.1979) (defendant waived its right to seek dismissal on timeliness grounds when, in an effort to obtain more time to conduct its own investigation of the charge, defendant told the plaintiff that it would not assert a timeliness defense); Girard v. Rubin, 62 F.3d 1244, 1247 (9th Cir.1995) (failure to contest the timeliness determination in the administrative process constituted waiver of the defense). Estoppel may be raised where an employer affirmatively misleads a claimant or intentionally prevents a claimant from filing a charge with the EEOC in a timely fashion. For example, in *Reeb v. Economic Opportunity Atlanta, Inc.*, 516 F.2d 924 (5th Cir.1975), the employer told the plaintiff, a female, that she was being terminated because the company did not have the funds to continue her position. More than six months later, the plaintiff learned that her job had

not been eliminated. Rather, the position had been refilled by a male who was allegedly less qualified. The district court dismissed the plaintiff's complaint on the ground that she had not satisfied the technical filing requirements of Title VII. The Fifth Circuit reversed, holding that the statutory period for filing a charge was tolled by the inequitable conduct of the employer in lying to the plaintiff. The court held that the Title VII filing period "does not begin to run until the facts which would support a cause of action are apparent or should be apparent to a person with a reasonably prudent regard for his rights." *Id.* at 930. The *Zipes* liberal tolling, estoppel, and waiver rules may not apply when the plaintiff is represented by counsel at all stages of the proceedings. *See* Leite v. Kennecott Copper Corp., 558 F.Supp. 1170 (D.Mass.), *aff'd*, 720 F.2d 658 (1st Cir.1983) (table).

6. *State Judicial Remedies and Claim Preclusion*: Even if a plaintiff files a timely charge with the EEOC, the doctrine of res judicata may preclude a federal court from addressing the claim when a state court has previously addressed the same claim on the merits. The issue before the Supreme Court in *Kremer v. Chemical Construction Corp.*, 456 U.S. 461, 102 S.Ct. 1883, 72 L.Ed.2d 262 (1982), was whether a federal court is required to give preclusive or res judicata effect to a state court judgment when a plaintiff in an employment discrimination case has sought and obtained judicial review in a state court after first exhausting state administrative remedies. Kremer, a Jewish immigrant from Poland, worked for the Chemical Construction Corporation. He filed a timely charge of religious discrimination with the EEOC after he was laid off in 1975. The EEOC referred the charge to the state agency, which investigated and found that the charge was meritless. Kremer then sought review of the state agency's decision in state court; ultimately, the highest state court affirmed the agency's decision. Next the EEOC reviewed the charge and made a no-cause finding. Kremer then filed a civil action in federal court. The Supreme Court affirmed the lower court's ruling dismissing Kremer's claim on the grounds of res judicata. The Court grounded its decision on 28 U.S.C. § 1738, which requires federal courts to grant full faith and credit to state court judgments.

Some courts have held that *Kremer* also applies if the defendant rather than the plaintiff seeks and obtains state judicial review of a state administrative ruling. *E.g.*, Trujillo v. County of Santa Clara, 775 F.2d 1359 (9th Cir.1985); Hickman v. Electronic Keyboarding, Inc., 741 F.2d 230, 232 n.3 (8th Cir.1984). The dilemma posed in cases like *Kremer* led Justice Blackmun to observe in *Kremer* that "a prudent discrimination complainant may make every effort to prevent the state agency from reaching a final decision" because "he runs the risk that his adversary may seek judicial review." *Kremer*, 456 U.S. at 504–05 n.18, 102 S.Ct. at 1909 n.18 (Blackmun, J., dissenting). But *Kremer* does not apply when the state has deprived the plaintiff of a property interest in violation of the Due Process Clause of the Fourteenth Amendment. *See* Logan v. Zimmerman Brush Co., 455 U.S. 422, 102 S.Ct. 1148, 71 L.Ed.2d 265 (1982) (state court refused to review state administrative ruling in employment discrimination case because of procedural errors committed by the agency; claimant had a property interest in the administrative process that the state had established to enforce its antidiscrimination laws).

Under the Court's interpretation of 28 U.S.C. § 1738, unreviewed state administrative proceedings are not entitled to full faith and credit by federal courts and thus have no preclusive effect upon subsequent Title VII litigation in federal courts. University of Tennessee v. Elliott, 478 U.S. 788, 106 S.Ct. 3220, 92 L.Ed.2d 635 (1986).

7. *Exhaustion Requirement in ADEA Actions*: Unlike Title VII and the ADA, which generally requires exhaustion of administrative remedies before the EEOC, the ADEA provides two separate avenues for relief to employees who claim they have been the victims of unlawful employment discrimination. First, federal employees may file an administrative complaint pursuant to the rules and regulations that the ADEA authorizes the EEOC to promulgate. 29 U.S.C. § 633a(b). Second, an employee or applicant may bring a civil action for legal and equitable relief after filing a charge with the EEOC, provided the individual has given the EEOC not less than thirty days notice of an intent to file the civil action and has filed the notice within 180 days after the alleged unlawful practice occurred. 29 U.S.C. § 633a(d).

8. *Administrative Exhaustion for Federal Employees*: The procedures required for exhaustion of administrative remedies in employment discrimination cases against federal employers are generally more complex than in other cases. One of the main reasons for the complexity is that federal employees have a broad range of job protections. Most federal employees are protected from political patronage under the merit system. They are also protected from discrimination on the basis of race, color, religion, sex, national origin, age, and disability. The Office of Personnel Management (OPM), the Merit Systems Protection Board (MSPB), and the EEOC have overlapping jurisdiction for job protection for federal sector employees. The administrative exhaustion requirement for federal employees is explored in detail in John P. Stimson, *Unscrambling Federal Merit Protection*, 150 Mil.L.Rev. 165 (1995). Under the Reorganization Plan of 1978, the EEOC has principal administrative responsibility for employment discrimination claims brought by federal civil service employees; the EEOC has issued detailed regulations on how that responsibility is to be carried out by each federal agency. 29 C.F.R. § 1614. Briefly, as Major Stimson explains, the process works like this: The federal employee must first exhaust the procedures required by the particular federal agency where the charge arose. The second step involves an appeal to the EEOC, at the conclusion of which the charging party may elect to continue to pursue administrative relief or to file a civil action. If the complainant elects to pursue a civil action under Title VII or the ADA, the time period for filing the action depends on the type of charges before the EEOC. ADEA claimants have more "flexibility" than Title VII or ADA claimants in the administrative exhaustion process. Different exhaustion issues arise in a "mixed" case, which is a claim involving allegations of both a general civil service violation and unlawful employment discrimination. *See* Stimson, *supra* at 188–99.

2. JUDICIAL ENFORCEMENT

Section 706(f)(1) of Title VII, 42 U.S.C. § 2000e–5(f)(1), provides that if the EEOC dismisses a charge, or if, within 180 days of the filing of the charge, the EEOC (or the Attorney General in a case involving a governmental employee) has not filed a civil action or entered into a conciliation agreement, the EEOC must notify the aggrieved party who may then file a civil action within ninety days of receiving such notice. This notice is known as the "right-to-sue letter." The Supreme Court has interpreted the phrase "civil action" in Title VII, § 706(f), 42 U.S.C. § 2000e–5(f), to mean a trial *de novo*. *See* Chandler v. Roudebush, 425 U.S. 840, 844–45, 96 S.Ct. 1949, 1952, 48 L.Ed.2d 416 (1976) (federal employees); McDonnell Douglas Corp. v. Green, 411 U.S. 792, 798–99, 93 S.Ct. 1817, 1822, 36 L.Ed.2d 668 (1973) (private employees). Both federal and state courts of competent jurisdiction are authorized to exercise jurisdiction over Title VII and ADA claims. In *Yellow Freight System, Inc. v. Donnelly*, 494 U.S. 820, 821, 110 S.Ct. 1566, 1567, 108 L.Ed.2d 834 (1990), the Supreme Court rejected the argument that federal courts have exclusive jurisdiction over Title VII lawsuits. Federal and state courts also have concurrent jurisdiction over ADEA claims. ADEA, 29 U.S.C. § 626(c)(1).

a.　*Timely filing in court*: Receipt of the right-to-sue letter triggers the beginning of the ninety days within which an aggrieved party must file a civil action in state or federal court. This statutory notice requirement has raised a number of issues. When the EEOC determines that it will probably be unable to process a charge within the 180–day period, a long-standing regulation authorizes sending out a right-to-sue letter prior to the expiration of the 180 days. 29 C.F.R. § 1601.28(a)(2). The courts are divided on the validity of this regulation. Some courts have upheld the regulation on the ground that the practice is not expressly prohibited under Title VII or that it protects aggrieved parties when the EEOC, a perpetually underfunded agency, clearly will not be able to investigate a charge within the 180–day period. *See, e.g.*, Sims v. Trus Joist MacMillan, 22 F.3d 1059 (11th Cir.1994); Bryant v. California Brewers Ass'n, 585 F.2d 421, 425 (9th Cir.1978), *vacated on other grounds*, 444 U.S. 598, 100 S.Ct. 814, 63 L.Ed.2d 55 (1980). Other courts have held that the regulation is invalid on the ground either that it undermines the congressional goal of achieving nonadversarial resolution of employment discrimination claims or that the practice will tend to inundate the federal courts with frivolous discrimination lawsuits. *See, e.g.*, Martini v. Federal Nat'l Mortgage Ass'n, 178 F.3d 1336 (D.C.Cir.1999) (invalidating the regulation and discussing the circuit split), *cert. dismissed*, 528 U.S. 1147, 120 S.Ct. 1155, 145 L.Ed.2d 1065 (2000).

The courts have adopted different rules on when the 90–day filing period begins to run after the EEOC sends the notice-of-right-to-sue letter by certified mail and the Post Office leaves a notice indicating a specified period of time in which the letter must be picked up before it is returned to the EEOC. For example, the Seventh Circuit has adopted an actual notice rule, but the rule does not apply to a plaintiff who fails to receive actual notice through her own fault. *See* Houston v. Sidley & Austin, 185 F.3d 837 (7th Cir.1999) (citing St. Louis v. Alverno College, 744 F.2d 1314, 1316–17 (7th Cir.1984)). In *Harvey v. City of New Bern Police Department*, 813 F.2d 652 (4th Cir.1987), the Fourth Circuit expressly rejected the Seventh Circuit's rule and adopted instead a "reasonable short time" rule within which a plaintiff must pick up the right-to-sue notice after receiving notice from the Post Office that a letter is waiting for her. In *Ebbert v. Daimler–Chrysler Corp.*, 319 F.3d 103 (3d Cir.2003), the court held that oral notice from the EEOC may trigger the 90–day filing rule if it is equivalent to written notice from the EEOC.

The notice requirement also raises questions regarding the circumstances under which "constructive notice" triggers the 90–day filing requirement. In *Franks v. Bowman Transportation Co.*, 495 F.2d 398, 404–06 (5th Cir.1974), *rev'd on other grounds*, 424 U.S. 747, 96 S.Ct. 1251, 47 L.Ed.2d 444 (1976), the EEOC sent the statutory notice to the plaintiff, but the plaintiff's nine-year-old son received and eventually lost it. Approximately one year later, the plaintiff, unaware that his son had lost the first notice, requested a right-to-sue letter. The plaintiff filed suit within ninety days after receipt of the second notice. The court held that the complaint had been timely filed and rejected defendant's argument that, under a constructive receipt theory, the plaintiff should be deemed to have received the first notice. The Eleventh Circuit, formerly the Fifth Circuit, revisited its *Franks* "constructive notice" doctrine in *Zillyette v. Capital One Financial Corp.*, 179 F.3d 1337 (11th Cir.1999). In *Zillyette*, an ADA case, the court held that an employee must retrieve a notice-of-right-to-sue within a reasonable time following notice by the Post Office of its effort to deliver a certified letter from the EEOC. The court deemed a reasonable time to be three days after notice from the Post Office. The three-day rule is based on Fed.R.Civ.P. 6(e), which governs the time for taking action after service by mail. In *Bell v. Eagle Motor Lines, Inc.*, 693 F.2d 1086 (11th Cir.1982), however, the court relied upon the constructive receipt doctrine to dismiss the case when the plaintiff filed his complaint more than ninety days after his wife had received the statutory notice.

The 90–day rule is not jurisdictional, Hill v. John Chezik Imports, 869 F.2d 1122 (8th Cir.1989), and the Supreme Court has stated that equitable tolling of the ninety days may be justified where the notice from the EEOC is inadequate, where a motion for appointment of counsel is pending, where the court has led the plaintiff to believe all statutory requirements for bringing suit have been satisfied, or where the defendant's misconduct has "lulled the plaintiff into inaction." Baldwin County Welcome Ctr. v. Brown, 466 U.S. 147, 151, 104 S.Ct. 1723, 1725–26, 80 L.Ed.2d 196 (1984).

The doctrine of laches may bar suit if an aggrieved party unreasonably delays requesting the right-to-sue notice or the notice is returned to the EEOC because the plaintiff failed to provide the EEOC with a current address and the defendant is prejudiced by the plaintiff's conduct. *See, e.g.*, Jeffries v. Chicago Transit Auth., 770 F.2d 676 (7th Cir.1985) (laches bar suit where plaintiff filed complaint in court more than ten years after filing the charge with the EEOC), *cert. denied*, 475 U.S. 1050, 106 S.Ct. 1273, 89 L.Ed.2d 581 (1986). The EEOC is not subject to the same timely filing requirements as private parties, but in *Occidental Life Insurance Co. v. EEOC*, 432 U.S. 355, 97 S.Ct. 2447, 53 L.Ed.2d 402 (1977), the Supreme Court held that suits filed by the EEOC may be dismissed under the laches doctrine.

A special set of problems arises when the plaintiff is represented by counsel at any time during the course of the administrative proceedings or before the ninety days expire after receipt of the notice of right-to-sue. If an attorney has been designated as the agent of the plaintiff to receive the EEOC notice, the 90–day period begins to run when the attorney receives the notice. *See* Jones v. Madison Serv. Corp., 744 F.2d 1309, 1313–14 (7th Cir.1984); Perez v. Dana Corp., 545 F.Supp. 950 (E.D.Pa. 1982), *aff'd on other grounds*, 718 F.2d 581 (3d Cir.1983).

b. *What constitutes a complaint?*: In *Baldwin County Welcome Center v. Brown*, 466 U.S. 147, 104 S.Ct. 1723, 80 L.Ed.2d 196 (1984) (per curiam), a pro se litigant filed his right-to-sue letter in the district court because he had difficulty obtaining an attorney to represent him. The plaintiff argued that the filing of the right-to-sue letter tolled the running of the 90–day filing period. The Court disagreed, holding that the filing of the notice of right-to-sue does not toll the running of the 90–day filing requirement because the statutory notice, standing alone, fails to satisfy Rule 8(a) of the Federal Rules of Civil Procedure. Under Rule 8(a), a complaint must state the basis of jurisdiction, set forth a short, plain statement of the facts, and a prayer for relief. Because a right-to-sue letter does not contain a statement of the factual basis of the claim, it cannot qualify as a complaint under Rule 8(a). *Id.* at 149, 104 S.Ct. at 1723.

c. *Suits by the EEOC and the Attorney General*: The EEOC has authority to bring civil actions in its own name. Title VII § 706, 42 U.S.C. § 2000e–5. The Court affirmed the authority of the EEOC to bring suits in its own name, independent of the rights or the actions or inactions of alleged discriminatees, in *EEOC v. Waffle House*, 534 U.S. 279, 122 S.Ct. 754, 151 L.Ed.2d 755 (2002), reproduced, in part, in Chapter 18, Section B. Also, the Attorney General is authorized to bring civil actions against governmental employers who are covered by the relevant statutory scheme. Title VII, § 707, 42 U.S.C. § 2000e–6.

D. COVERAGE UNDER LAWS PROHIBITING DISCRIMINATION IN EMPLOYMENT

A fundamental policy objective of laws prohibiting discrimination in employment is to make "equality" a reality in the workplace. To accomplish this objective, the basic mandate of these laws is to make it unlawful for employers, employment agencies, and labor organizations to discriminate against applicants and employees because of such individuals' race, color, religion, sex, national origin, age, or disability. Because Congress left undefined many key terms in these statutes, a recurring issue in employment discrimination law is how to define the boundaries of each category or status that is protected under federal employment discrimination statutes. Of course, determining whether an individual is protected under the Age Discrimination in Employment Act is rarely, if ever, an issue because the protected class is defined as individuals forty years of age and over. The meaning of race, sex, or disability, unlike chronological age, is not as readily ascertained. How these terms are defined is important for several reasons, for example, identifying those who are the beneficiaries of these laws, complying with statutory record-keeping requirements, and collecting and analyzing statistical data as evidence in employment discrimination cases. Congress also failed to provide a meaningful definition of employer, perhaps the most important entity that is subject to the basic mandate of these laws.

The following materials briefly explore some recurring issues that arise because of the absence of statutory definitions of several key terms that are used to establish the coverage of the laws prohibiting discrimination in employment. First, by focusing on the meaning of "race" and "color," we begin to grapple with the problem of identifying the individuals or groups who are protected from unlawful employment discrimination. (The meaning of "sex" is discussed in Chapters 6, 7, 8, and 9; "religion" in Chapter 10; "national origin" in Chapter 11; and "disability" in Chapter 13.) Next, we briefly explore the problem of defining "employee" and the related issue of distinguishing between "employer" and "employee." Another issue is whether an employer's "agent" can be held individually liable for the unlawful employment decisions he makes for his "employer." Finally, we explore the meaning of employment "practice," because unless plaintiff's claim falls within the meaning of "terms, conditions, or privileges of employment" that practice is not unlawful. A key term that also is not defined in federal statutes, other than the ADA, is *discrimination*. The problem of defining the meaning of discrimination is pervasive throughout most of the remaining chapters in this book.

1. THE MEANING OF "RACE" AND "COLOR"

The primary reason Congress enacted Title VII was to provide a remedy for blacks who have been the victims of racial discrimination in employment. The statutory term Congress selected in order to achieve this objective, however, is race-neutral; the term is just plain "race." But what is "race"? And who should decide who belongs to which "race"? In *McDonald v. Santa Fe Trail Transportation Co.*, 427 U.S. 273, 96 S.Ct. 2574, 49 L.Ed.2d 493 (1976), the Supreme Court held that whites as well as blacks are protected from racial discrimination under Title VII and § 1981, even though § 1981 refers to "white citizens." The Supreme Court's most comprehensive exploration of the meaning of the term "race" in employment discrimination law is found in the following decision, which arose under §1981.

ST. FRANCIS COLLEGE v. AL–KHAZRAJI

Supreme Court of the United States, 1987.
481 U.S. 604, 107 S.Ct. 2022, 95 L.Ed.2d 582.

JUSTICE WHITE delivered the opinion of the Court.

[The issue in *Al-Khazraji* was whether the plaintiff, a citizen of the United States who was born in Iraq, could bring a race discrimination claim under § 1981.]

Although § 1981 does not itself use the word "race," the Court has construed the section to forbid all "racial" discrimination in the making of private as well as public contracts. Runyon v. McCrary, 427 U.S. 160, 168, 174–175, 96 S.Ct. 2586, 49 L.Ed.2d 415 (1976). * * *

Petitioners contend that respondent is a Caucasian and cannot allege the kind of discrimination § 1981 forbids. Concededly, *McDonald v. Santa Fe Trail Transportation Co.*, 427 U.S. 273, 96 S.Ct. 2574, 49 L.Ed.2d 493 (1976), held that white persons could maintain a § 1981 suit; but that suit involved alleged discrimination against a white person in favor of a black, and petitioner submits that the section does not encompass claims of discrimination by one Caucasian against another. * * *

Petitioner's submission rests on the assumption that all those who might be deemed Caucasians today were thought to be of the same race when § 1981 became law in the 19th century; and it may be that a variety of ethnic groups, including Arabs, are now considered to be within the Caucasian race.[4] The understanding of "race" in the 19th century, however, was different. Plainly, all those who might be deemed Caucasian today were not thought to be of the same race at the time § 1981 became law.

In the middle years of the 19th century, dictionaries commonly referred to race as a "continued series of descendants from a parent who is called the *stock*," N. Webster, An American Dictionary of the English Language 666 (New York 1830) (emphasis in original), "the lineage of a family," 2 N. Webster, A Dictionary of the English Language 411 (New Haven 1841), or "descendants of a common ancestor," J. Donald, Chambers' Etymological Dictionary of the English Language 415 (London 1871). * * * It was not until the 20th century that dictionaries began

---

4. There is a common popular understanding that there are three major human races—Caucasoid, Mongoloid, and Negroid. Many modern biologists and anthropologists, however, criticize racial classifications as arbitrary and of little use in understanding the variability of human beings. It is said that genetically homogeneous populations do not exist and traits are not discontinuous between populations; therefore, a population can only be described in terms of relative frequencies of various traits. Clear-cut categories do not exist. The particular traits which have generally been chosen to characterize races have been criticized as having little biological significance. It has been found that differences between individuals of the same race are often greater than the differences between the "average" individuals of different races. These observations and others have led some, but not all, scientists to conclude that racial classifications are for the most part sociopolitical, rather than biological, in nature.

referring to the Caucasian, Mongolian, and Negro races, 8 The Century Dictionary and Cyclopedia 4926 (1911), or to race as involving divisions of mankind based upon different physical characteristics. Webster's Collegiate Dictionary 794 (3d ed. 1916). * * *

Encyclopedias of the 19th century also described race in terms of ethnic groups, which is a narrower concept of race than petitioners urge. Encyclopedia Americana in 1858, for example, referred to various races such as Finns, vol. 5, p. 123, Gypsies, 6 *id.*, at 123, Basques, 1 *id.*, at 602, and Hebrews, 6 *id.*, at 209. The 1863 version of the New American Cyclopaedia divided the Arabs into a number of subsidiary races, vol. 1, p. 739; represented the Hebrews as of the Semitic race, 9 *id.*, at 27, and identified numerous other groups as constituting races, including Swedes, 15 *id.*, at 216, Norwegians, 12 *id.*, at 410, Germans, 8 *id.*, at 200, Greeks, 8 *id.*, at 438, Finns, 7 *id.*, at 513, Italians, 9 *id.*, at 644–645 (referring to mixture of different races), Spanish, 14 *id.*, at 804, Mongolians, 11 *id.*, at 651, Russians, 14 *id.*, at 226, and the like. The Ninth edition of the Encyclopedia Britannica also referred to Arabs, vol. 2, p. 245 (1878), Jews, 13 *id.*, at 685 (1881), and other ethnic groups such as Germans, 10 *id.*, at 473 (1879), Hungarians, 12 *id.*, at 365 (1880), and Greeks, 11 *id.*, at 83 (1880), as separate races.

These dictionary and encyclopedic sources are somewhat diverse, but it is clear that they do not support the claim that for the purposes of § 1981, Arabs, Englishmen, Germans, and certain other ethnic groups are to be considered a single race. We would expect the legislative history of § 1981, which the Court held in *Runyon v. McCrary* had its source in the Civil Rights Act of 1866, as well as the Voting Rights Act of 1870, to reflect this common understanding, which it surely does. The debates are replete with references to the Scandinavian races, Cong. Globe, 39th Cong., 1st Sess., 499 (1866) (remarks of Sen. Cowan), as well as the Chinese, *id.*, at 523 (remarks of Sen. Davis), Latin, *id.*, at 238 (remarks of Rep. Kasson during debate of home rule for the District of Columbia), Spanish, *id.*, at 251 (remarks of Sen. Davis during debate of District of Columbia suffrage), and Anglo–Saxon races, *id.*, at 542 (remarks of Rep. Dawson). Jews, *ibid.*, Mexicans, *see ibid.* (remarks of Rep. Dawson), blacks, *passim* , and Mongolians, *id.*, at 498 (remarks of Sen. Cowan), were similarly categorized. Gypsies were referred to as a race. *ibid.* (remarks of Sen. Cowan). * * *

* * *

The history of the 1870 Act reflects similar understanding of what groups Congress intended to protect from intentional discrimination. It is clear, for example, that the civil rights sections of the 1870 Act provided protection for immigrant groups such as the Chinese. This view was expressed in the Senate. Cong. Globe, 41st Cong., 2d Sess., 1536, 3658, 3808 (1870). In the House, Representative Bingham described § 16 of the Act, part of the authority for § 1981, as declaring "that the States shall not hereafter discriminate against the immigrant from China and in favor of the immigrant from Prussia, nor against the immigrant from France and in favor of the immigrant from Ireland."

Based on the history of § 1981, we have little trouble in concluding that Congress intended to protect from discrimination identifiable classes of persons who are subjected to intentional discrimination solely because of their ancestry or ethnic characteristics. Such discrimination is racial discrimination that Congress intended § 1981 to forbid, whether or not it would be classified as racial in terms of modern scientific theory. The Court of Appeals was thus quite right in holding that § 1981, "at a minimum," reaches discrimination against an individual "because he or she is genetically part of an ethnically and physiognomically distinctive subgrouping of homo sapiens." It is clear from our holding, however, that a distinctive physiognomy is not essential to qualify for § 1981 protection.

* * *

Notes and Questions

1.   Should the *Al-Khazraji* definition of "race" apply equally to claims brought under § 1981 and Title VII? For example, should a Jewish employee be allowed to allege race discrimination in a Title VII claim solely on the ground that she is Jewish?

2.   Do the terms "race" and "ethnicity" refer to natural or socially constructed categories, or a combination of both? Consider the following perspective:

> [W]hat constitutes a race and how one recognizes a racial difference are culturally determined. Whether two individuals regard themselves as of the same or of different races depends not on the degree of similarity of their genetic material but on whether history, tradition, and personal training and experiences have brought them to regard themselves as belonging to the same group or to different groups. Since all human beings are of one species and since all populations tend to merge when they exist in contact, group differentiation will be based on cultural behavior and not on genetic difference.

James C. King, The Biology of Race 156–57 (1981). For further discussion of race as being socially constructed, *see* Ian F. Haney Lopez, *The Social Construction of Race: Some Observations on Illusion, Fabrication, and Choice*, 29 Harv.C.R.-C.L.L.Rev. 1 (1994). *See also* Tom Morganthau, *What Color Is Black?*, Newsweek, Feb. 13, 1995, at 62.

3.   What is the race of a person born of a black parent and a white parent? Or a person who has one Asian–American parent and one white parent? Should we adopt separate mixed-race classifications for the offspring of parents of different races, as has been proposed by the Office of Management and Budget? *See* Standards for the Classification of Data on Race and Ethnicity, 59 F.R. 29831 (June 9, 1994); Luther Wright, Jr., Note, *Who's Black, Who's White, and Who Cares: Reconceptualizing the United States's Definition of Race and Racial Classifications*, 48 Vand.L.Rev. 513 (1995).

4. Should an employer be permitted to challenge a plaintiff's characterization of his own racial identity? This has clear implications for the affirmative action debate (see Chapter 17). Consider the following: In 1975, twin brothers, Paul and Philip Malone, took a civil service competitive exam for jobs with the fire department in Boston, Massachusetts. The Malone brothers were fair-haired and light-skinned, and they had Caucasian features; moreover, they listed their race as "white" on their initial job applications. They both performed poorly on the 1975 exam and were denied employment. In 1977, they took the civil service exam again, but this time they identified their race as "black." At the time of the second exam, Boston had agreed to a court-ordered affirmative action plan in order to increase the number of blacks in the fire department, and the Malones wanted to benefit from this affirmative action plan. With the scores the Malones received in 1977, they would not have qualified if they were treated as white candidates, but based on their self-identification as black, they could be hired under the affirmative action program. What factors should be relevant in deciding whether the Malones are white or black: (1) visual observations of their features; (2) appropriate documentation, such as birth certificates, which establish ancestry; or (3) evidence that they or their families hold themselves out to be black and are considered to be black in their community? The Malones' evidence that they are "black" consisted of a questionable and inconclusive photograph of a woman alleged to be the Malones' maternal great grandmother and the Malones' claim that they had been told that she was black. Other evidence, however, showed that Malone family members had consistently held themselves out as white for three generations. Should the Malones have been denied employment on the basis of "racial fraud"? The Malones' case is discussed in the Wright, *supra* Note 3.

5. In *Bennun v. Rutgers State University*, 941 F.2d 154 (3d Cir.1991), *cert. denied*, 502 U.S. 1066, 112 S.Ct. 956, 117 L.Ed.2d 124 (1992), the plaintiff claimed that he had been discriminated against because he was Hispanic. In an affidavit, the plaintiff asserted "that his father was a Sephardic Jew who, like all Sephardic Jews, traced his lineage to those Jews who were expelled from Spain during the Spanish Inquisition." *Id.* at 172. The district court, however, based its finding that the plaintiff was Hispanic on the following facts: the plaintiff was born in Argentina, he believed that he was Hispanic, he had adopted Spanish cultural traditions, and he spoke Spanish at home. The court of appeals rejected the defendant's argument that the plaintiff was not Hispanic because the district court judge, based on his opportunity to observe the plaintiff's "appearance, speech and mannerisms," had ruled in favor of the plaintiff on the issue. *Id.* at 173. On the issue of how plaintiff's status as a protected class member should be determined, the Third Circuit said:

> We think unlawful discrimination must be based on [the plaintiff's] objective appearance to others, not his subjective feeling about his own ethnicity. Discrimination stems from a reliance on immaterial outward appearances that stereotype an individual with imagined, usually undesirable, characteristics thought to be common to members of the group that shares these superficial traits. It results in a stubborn refusal to judge a person on his merits as a human being. Our various statutes against discrimination express the policy that this refusal to judge

people who belong to various groups, particularly disadvantaged, groups is too costly to be tolerated in a society committed to equal individual liberty and opportunity.

Id. Do you agree with the standard adopted by Third Circuit in *Bennun*? Under *Bennun,* is it irrelevant what race the plaintiff considers himself to be?

6.   A white person who was born and lived in an African country moved to the United States and eventually became a United States citizen. He was denied a promotion by his United States employer after he became a United States citizen. He contends that, as an African–American, he was denied the promotion because of his race. What arguments, if any, might be open to his employer that he cannot seek relief on the ground that he is an African–American?

7.   *The Meaning of "Color":* Title VII also prohibits discrimination on the basis of "color." Title VII, § 703(a), 42 U.S.C. § 2000e–2(a). How is "color" different from "race"? Consider the following case: Employees in the Internal Revenue Service (IRS) office in which the plaintiff works are predominantly black. The plaintiff is a light-skinned black person; her supervisor is a dark-skinned black person. Plaintiff sues the IRS under Title VII and § 1981 alleging that her supervisor treats her differently because of her light complexion. Should her claim be treated as an allegation of discrimination based on "race" or based on "color?" *See* Walker v. Secretary of the Treasury, IRS, 713 F.Supp. 403 (N.D.Ga.1989). *See also* Ali v. National Bank of Pakistan, 508 F.Supp. 611 (S.D.N.Y.1981) (plaintiff, a light-skinned individual, whose origins are in Punjab, brought an action under Title VII alleging discrimination on the basis of "color" by other dark-skinned individuals who also were from India). What arguments would you make based on the *Al-Khazraji* case?

8.   In her article, *Shades of Brown: The Law of Skin Color*, 49 Duke L.J. 1487 (2000), Professor Trina Jones argues that because "antidiscrimination efforts have focused primarily on race, the courts have largely ignored discrimination within racial classifications on the basis of skin color," and that " 'colorism' is a present reality" that "will assume increasing significance in the future." *Id.* at 1487. She further argues that "color hierarchy in the U.S. is relatively easy to define at its extremes"—whites at the top and blacks at the bottom. *Id.* at 1555. A fundamental question she raises is whether "there [is] a danger that one segment of the race may move forward while another segment is left behind." *Id.* at 1554. What are the implications of her arguments for the multiracial-categorization movement? For intersectionality? For disability? For affirmative action?

Notes: Intersectionality

1.   Intersectionality theory posits that individuals have multiple identities that are not addressed by legal doctrines based solely on a single identity or status. For example, in a well-known article on the multi-dimensionality of "Black women," Professor Kimberlé Crenshaw criticized the judicial developments under Title VII for requiring "Black women" to seek relief based on either race or sex but not both. Kimberlé Crenshaw, *Demarginaliz-*

ing the Intersection of Race and Sex: A Black Feminist Critique of Antidiscrimination Doctrine, Feminist Theory and Antiracist Politics, 1989 U.Chi. Legal F. 139. She argued that black women should be recognized as a separate protected class under the statute because the discrimination that black women experience is different in kind and degree from the discrimination faced by white women or black men. Professor Crenshaw observed that

> in race discrimination cases, discrimination tends to be viewed in terms of sex-or class-privileged Blacks; in sex discrimination cases, the focus is on race and class-privileged women.

> This focus on the most privileged group members marginalizes those who are multiply-burdened and obscures claims that cannot be understood as resulting from discrete sources of discrimination. I suggest further that this focus on otherwise-privileged group members creates a distorted analysis of racism and sexism because the operative conceptions of race and sex become grounded in experiences that actually represent only a subset of a much more complex phenomenon.

Id. at 140.

2. Several courts have been willing to embrace intersectionality theory in Title VII cases. One of the leading cases is *Jefferies v. Harris County Community Action Association*, 615 F.2d 1025 (5th Cir.1980), a Title VII employment discrimination case brought by a black female. The issue in *Jefferies* was whether the district court erred in refusing to recognize a protected subclass of black females. The district court viewed the plaintiff as having membership in two separate protected classes: race and sex. First, viewing the plaintiff as a member of the black race, the court rejected her race discrimination claim because a black male had been given the at-issue job. Then, viewing the plaintiff as a female, the district court found that statistical evidence showed no discrimination against women. The court of appeals reversed, holding that the plaintiff's claim should have been evaluated on the basis of her status as a *black female*.

> We agree with Jefferies that the district court improperly failed to address her claim of discrimination on the basis of both race and sex. The essence of Jefferies' argument is that an employer should not escape from liability for discrimination against black females by a showing that it does not discriminate against blacks and that it does not discriminate against females. We agree that discrimination against black females can exist even in the absence of discrimination against black men or white women.

* * *

> * * * In the absence of a clear expression by Congress that it did not intend to provide protection against discrimination directed especially toward black women as a class separate and distinct from the class of women and the class of blacks, we cannot condone a result which leaves black women without a viable Title VII remedy.

Id. at 1032.

The *Jefferies* court implicitly recognized that black women throughout American history have worked in subservient roles and have been subjected to adverse conditions that have not been imposed upon either black men or white women. *See id.* at 1034. The Tenth Circuit followed *Jefferies* in *Hicks v. Gates Rubber Co.*, 833 F.2d 1406 (10th Cir.1987).

In *Degraffenreid v. General Motors*, 413 F.Supp. 142 (E.D.Mo.1976), *aff'd in part, rev'd in part on other grounds*, 558 F.2d 480 (8th Cir.1977), the district court declined to recognize black women as a protected subclass. The court reasoned that to do so would create a "super-remedy," which would give black women additional avenues of relief not envisioned by the drafters of Title VII. The court argued that "[t]he prospect of the creation of new classes of protected minorities, governed only by the mathematical principles of permutation and combination, raises the prospect of opening the hackneyed Pandora's box." *Id.* at 145. On appeal, the Eighth Circuit did not reach the intersectionality issue; nevertheless, Judge Bright stated, in dicta, "[w]e do not subscribe entirely to the district court's reasoning in rejecting [plaintiffs'] claims of race and sex discrimination under Title VII." *DeGraffenreid*, 558 F.2d at 484.

3. What is your view on whether recognizing black women as a separate subgroup protected under employment discrimination laws destabilizes or undermines the traditional categories of "race" and "sex"? Consider the following in thinking about the question:

In 1990, commentators noted that "[n]onwhite women, 81 percent of whom are black, have gone a long way toward reducing the occupational gap between themselves and white women. However, *nonwhite women* continue to lag far behind *white men.*" Barbara F. Reskin & Patricia A. Roos, Job Queues, Gender Queues: Explaining Women's Inroads into Male Occupations 5 (1990). Wage and salary data from the Labor Department's Bureau of Labor Statistics showed that while women's wages were 77 percent of men's wages in 1999, black and Hispanic women earned 64 percent and 55 percent, respectively, of white men's wages. Bureau of Labor Statistics, Highlights of Women's Earnings in 1999 (Rep. 943) (2000). In some occupations, black women may experience wage discrimination that is a result of historical patterns of occupational segregation based on both sex and race. Regarding the status of being a black woman, one scholar observed:

> Perhaps the greatest difference in the status of Black and white women is the difference in occupational status. There is an important historical dimension to this occupational status. Before 1940, the majority (60 percent) of Black women worked as private household workers. A third of all Black women were so employed in 1960, but just 6 percent worked in private household jobs in 1980. Partly because of this labor market legacy, Black women have experienced as much or more occupational segregation as white women but in a different set of jobs. Even as Black women's occupational patterns shifted between 1960 and 1980, Black women have been both more heavily represented in "traditionally female" jobs than have white women and until recently more likely to be represented in service than in clerical jobs.

* * *

* * * [Black women] also experience an occupational segregation distinct from the occupational segregation white women experience. In

addition to being employed in jobs that are "typically female," Black women are also employed in jobs that are typically, or disproportionately Black female. If Black women are either deliberately or traditionally crowded into a few low-paying jobs, they lower wages in those jobs where they cluster and reduce competition (or increase wages) in the jobs from which they are excluded. This concept of Black women's crowding explains, in part, why Black women receive lower pay than white women in similar occupations.

Julianne Malveaux, *Gender Difference and Beyond: An Economic Perspective on Diversity and Commonality Among Women, in* Theoretical Perspectives on Sexual Difference 226, 230, 231 (Deborah L. Rhode ed. 1990).

4. Should the courts recognize a subclass of Asian women under the intersectionality theory? Relying on *Jefferies*, the Ninth Circuit in *Lam v. University of Hawai'i*, 40 F.3d 1551, 1562 (9th Cir.1994), held yes, because "[l]ike other subclasses under Title VII, Asian women are subject to a set of stereotypes and assumptions shared neither by Asian men nor by white women," and they may be targeted for discrimination even in the absence of discrimination against Asian men or white women. In support of its decision, the *Lam* court cited J. Hagedorn, *Asian Women in Film: No Joy, No Luck, Ms.*, Jan./Feb. 1994, at 74. *Lam*, 40 F.3d at 1562 n.21.

5. Should black men be recognized as a subgroup that is separate and distinct from black women and white men? Consider the following: In *Bradley v. Pizzaco of Nebraska, Inc.*, 7 F.3d 795 (8th Cir.1993), a black male sued his employer, claiming that he was discharged from his job delivering pizzas for failure to comply with the employer's no-beard policy. The evidence showed that plaintiff suffers from psuedofolliculitis barbae (PFB), a skin condition affecting approximately 50 percent of black males, half of whom cannot shave because of the condition. As a general rule, white males do not suffer from the same medical condition. For arguments why black men should be recognized as a separate subclass protected by Title VII, *see* Floyd D. Weatherspoon, *Remedying Employment Discrimination Against African–American Males: Stereotypical Biases Engender a Case of Race Plus Sex Discrimination*, 36 Washburn L.J. 23 (1996); Note, *Invisible Man: Black and Male Under Title VII*, 104 Harv.L.Rev. 749 (1991).

6. There is a growing body of scholarly literature on intersectionality theory in discrimination law that challenges the traditional binary racial paradigm in the discourse on race and sex. *See, e.g.*, Regina Austin, *Sapphire Bound!*, 1989 Wis.L.Rev. 539; Mary Eaton, *At the Intersection of Gender and Sexual Orientation: Toward Lesbian Jurisprudence*, 3 S.Cal.Rev.L. & Women's Stud. 183 (1994); Trina Grillo, *Anti-Essentialism and Intersectionality: Tools to Dismantle the Master's House*, 10 Berkeley Women's L.J. 16 (1995); Judy Scales–Trent, *Black Women and the Constitution: Finding Our Place, Asserting Our Rights*, 24 Harv.C.R.-C.L.L.Rev. 9 (1989); Virginia W. Wei, Note, *Asian Women and Employment Discrimination: Using Intersectionality Theory to Address Title VII Claims Based on Combined Factors of Race, Gender and National Origin*, 37 B.C.L.Rev. 771 (1996).

2. WHO IS AN "EMPLOYEE"?

Whether a plaintiff is an "employee" generally is not an issue in the majority of employment discrimination cases, but it is now being raised more frequently. For example, a number of cases have addressed the issue of whether partners or other professionals are employees under laws prohibiting discrimination. *See, e.g.,* Cilecek v. Inova Health Sys. Serv., 115 F.3d 256 (4th Cir.1997) (holding that a doctor who contracted to perform medical services at hospital emergency room was not an "employee" but an independent contractor), *cert. denied*, 522 U.S. 1049, 118 S.Ct. 694, 139 L.Ed.2d 639 (1998); Serapion v. Martinez Odell & Calabria, 119 F.3d 982 (1st Cir.1997) (holding that a former law partner who brought a sex discrimination claim was found to be a proprietor, not an "employee," under Title VII), *cert. denied*, 522 U.S. 1047, 118 S.Ct. 690, 139 L.Ed.2d 636 (1998); Simpson v. Ernst & Young, 100 F.3d 436 (6th Cir.1996) (holding that an accountant, who had title of partner but lacked authority usually associated with partnership status, was an "employee"), *cert. denied*, 520 U.S. 1248, 117 S.Ct. 1862, 137 L.Ed.2d 1062 (1997). Lower courts adopted different tests to determine whether an individual was an employee under federal laws prohibiting discrimination in employment. *See, e.g.,* Mares v. Marsh, 777 F.2d 1066, 1067 (5th Cir.1985) (noting the three tests that courts have used to determine whether a plaintiff is an employee under Title VII). In the following case, the Supreme Court granted certiorari to resolve a circuit split on the appropriate test to determine whether an individual is an employee.

CLACKAMAS GASTROENTEROLOGY ASSOCIATES v. WELLS

Supreme Court of the United States, 2003.
538 U.S. 440, 123 S.Ct. 1673, 155 L.Ed.2d 615.

JUSTICE STEVENS delivered the opinion of the Court.

The Americans with Disabilities Act of 1990 (ADA or Act), 104 Stat. 327, as amended, 42 U.S.C. § 12101 *et seq.,* like other federal antidiscrimination legislation, is inapplicable to very small businesses. Under the ADA an "employer" is not covered unless its workforce includes "15 or more employees for each working day in each of 20 or more calendar weeks in the current or preceding calendar year." § 12111(5). The question in this case is whether four physicians actively engaged in medical practice as shareholders and directors of a professional corporation should be counted as "employees ."

I

Petitioner, Clackamas Gastroenterology Associates, P. C., is a medical clinic in Oregon. It employed respondent, Deborah Anne Wells, as a bookkeeper from 1986 until 1997. After her termination, she brought this action against the clinic alleging unlawful discrimination on the basis of disability under Title I of the ADA. Petitioner denied that it was covered by the Act and moved for summary judgment, asserting that it did not have 15 or more employees for the 20 weeks required by the statute. It is undisputed that the accuracy of that assertion depends on whether the four physician-shareholders who own the professional corporation and constitute its board of directors are counted as employees.

* * *

II

"We have often been asked to construe the meaning of 'employee' where the statute containing the term does not helpfully define it." *Nationwide Mut. Ins. Co. v. Darden,* 503 U.S. 318, 322, 112 S.Ct. 1344, 117 L.Ed.2d 581 (1992). The definition of the term in the ADA simply states that an "employee" is "an individual employed by an employer." 42 U.S.C. § 12111(4). That surely qualifies as a mere "nominal definition" that is "completely circular and explains nothing." *Darden,* 503 U.S., at 323, 112 S.Ct. 1344. As we explained in *Darden,* our cases construing similar language give us guidance on how best to fill the gap in the statutory text.

In *Darden* we were faced with the question whether an insurance salesman was an independent contractor or an "employee" covered by the Employee Retirement Income Security Act of 1974 (ERISA). Because ERISA's definition of "employee" was "completely circular," 503 U.S., at 323, 112 S.Ct. 1344, we followed the same general approach that we had previously used in deciding whether a sculptor was an "employee" within the meaning of the Copyright Act of 1976, see Community for Creative Non–Violence v. Reid, 490 U.S. 730 (1989), and we adopted a common-law test for determining who qualifies as an "employee" under ERISA.[5] Quoting *Reid,* 490 U.S., at 739–740, 109 S.Ct. 2166, we explained that " 'when Congress has used the term "employee" without defining it, we have concluded that Congress intended to describe the conventional master-servant relationship as understood by common-law agency doctrine.' " *Darden,* 503 U.S., at 322–323, 112 S.Ct. 1344.

Rather than looking to the common law, petitioner argues that courts should determine whether a shareholder-director of a professional corporation is an "employee" by asking whether the shareholder-di-

---

5. *Darden* described the common-law test for determining whether a hired party is an employee as follows:

" '[W]e consider the hiring party's right to control the manner and means by which the product is accomplished. Among the other factors relevant to this inquiry are the skill required; the source of the instrumentalities and tools; the location of the work; the duration of the relationship between the parties; whether the hiring party has the right to assign additional projects to the hired party; the extent of the hired party's discretion over when and how long to work; the method of payment; the hired party's role in hiring and paying assistants; whether the work is part of the regular business of the

hiring party; whether the hiring party is in business; the provision of employee benefits; and the tax treatment of the hired party.' "503 U.S., at 323–324, 112 S.Ct. 1344 (quoting *Community for Creative Non–Violence v. Reid,* 490 U.S. 730, 751–752, 109 S.Ct. 2166, 104 L.Ed.2d 811 (1989), and citing Restatement (Second) of Agency § 220(2) (1958)).

These particular factors are not directly applicable to this case because we are not faced with drawing a line between independent contractors and employees. Rather, our inquiry is whether a shareholder-director is an employee or, alternatively, the kind of person that the common law would consider an employer.

rector is, in reality, a "partner." * * * The question whether a share-holder-director is an employee, however, cannot be answered by asking whether the shareholder-director appears to be the functional equivalent of a partner. Today there are partnerships that include hundreds of members, some of whom may well qualify as "employees" because control is concentrated in a small number of managing partners. Cf. *Hishon v. King & Spalding,* 467 U.S. 69, 80, n.2, 104 S.Ct. 2229, 81 L.Ed.2d 59 (1984) (Powell, J., concurring) ("[A]n employer may not evade the strictures of Title VII simply by labeling its employees as 'partners' ") * * *. Thus, asking whether shareholder-directors are part-ners—rather than asking whether they are employees—simply begs the question.

* * *

* * * [T]he common law's definition of the master-servant relation-ship does provide helpful guidance. At common law the relevant factors defining the master-servant relationship focus on the master's control over the servant. The general definition of the term "servant" in the Restatement (Second) of Agency § 2(2) (1958), for example, refers to a person whose work is "controlled or is subject to the right to control by the master." See also *id.,* § 220(1) ("A servant is a person employed to perform services in the affairs of another and who with respect to the physical conduct in the performance of the services is subject to the other's control or right to control"). In addition, the Restatement's more specific definition of the term "servant" lists factors to be considered when distinguishing between servants and independent contractors, the first of which is "the extent of control" that one may exercise over the details of the work of the other. *Id.,* § 220(2)(a). We think that the common-law element of control is the principal guidepost that should be followed in this case.

This is the position that is advocated by the Equal Employment Opportunity Commission (EEOC), the agency that has special enforce-ment responsibilities under the ADA and other federal statutes contain-ing similar threshold issues for determining coverage. * * *

* * *

We are persuaded by the EEOC's focus on the common-law touch-stone of control, see *Skidmore v. Swift & Co.,* 323 U.S. 134, 140, 65 S.Ct. 161, 89 L.Ed. 124 (1944) * * *.

As the EEOC's standard reflects, an employer is the person, or group of persons, who owns and manages the enterprise. The employer can hire and fire employees, can assign tasks to employees and supervise their performance, and can decide how the profits and losses of the business are to be distributed. The mere fact that a person has a particular title—such as partner, director, or vice president—should not necessarily be used to determine whether he or she is an employee or a proprietor. Nor should the mere existence of a document styled "employ-ment agreement" lead inexorably to the conclusion that either party is an employee. Rather, as was true in applying common law rules to the independent-contractor-versus-employee issue confronted in *Darden,* the answer to whether a shareholder-director is an employee depends on " 'all of the incidents of the relationship * * * with no one factor being decisive.' "503 U.S., at 324, 112 S.Ct. 1344 (quoting *NLRB v. United Ins. Co. of America,* 390 U.S. 254, 258, 88 S.Ct. 988, 19 L.Ed.2d 1083 (1968)).

[JUSTICE GINSBURG, joined by JUSTICE BRYER, dissented.]

* * *

Notes and Questions

1. The Court remanded *Clackamas* for reconsideration of whether the four physicians were employees under the ADA in light of the right-to-control test because the evidentiary record in the case was dispositive as to whether the plaintiff or the defendant was entitled to prevail on the "employee" issue.

2. *Clackamas* specifically noted that the meaning of the term "employee" is important on two coverage issues. The first issue is whether an individual is an "employee" who may invoke the statutory protections afforded to persons claiming unlawful employment discrimination. The second issue is who is an "employee" for purposes of determining whether an employer satisfies the 15–or 20–employee threshold for coverage of the relevant antidiscrimination statute. Because of the interrelationship between these two issues, the Court was concerned that a broad construction of the term "employee" would unreasonably expand the scope of coverage of these laws: "[A] broad reading of the term 'employee' would—consistent with the statutory purpose of ridding the Nation of discrimination—tend to expand the coverage of [these laws] by enlarging the number of employees entitled to protection and by reducing the number of firms entitled to exemption." *Clackamas*, 538 U.S. at ___ n.6, 123 S.Ct. at 1678 n.6.

3. Although *Clackamas* was an ADA case, the Court specifically noted that the disagreement in the lower courts on the proper test for determining who is an "employee" extended to cases arising under Title VII and the ADEA. *Clackamas*, 538 U.S. at ___ n.3, 123 S.Ct. at 1677 n.3.

4. *Clackamas* directs the parties and the lower courts to give great deference to the EEOC guidelines in determining whether an individual is an "employee" under federal laws prohibiting discrimination in employment. 538 U.S. at ___, 123 S.Ct. 1678–80 (referencing 2 EEOC, Compliance Manual §§ 605.0008–605:00010 (2000)).

5. In *Robinson v. Shell Oil Co.*, 519 U.S. 337, 117 S.Ct. 843, 136 L.Ed.2d 808 (1997), the Court held that the term "employee" under Title VII covers a former employee who claims that his former employer retaliated against him because he had filed a charge of racial discrimination with the EEOC.

6. Should medical interns and residents in graduate medical training programs be considered "employees" under the *Clackmas* test? Should a member of the board of directors of a corporation, who continues to work as

a full-time officer and manager of the corporation, be considered an employee protected under the ADEA? *See* EEOC v. Johnson & Higgins, Inc. 91 F.3d 1529 (2d Cir.1996), *cert. denied*, 522 U.S. 808, 118 S.Ct. 47, 139 L.Ed.2d 13 (1997).

7. Public interest groups and the EEOC may use "testers" who pose as job applicants to determine whether employers engage in discriminatory hiring practices or to gather evidence of discriminatory employment practices. This practice is sometimes called auditing. For example, a black tester and a white tester, both with similar qualifications, are sent at different times to apply for a job for which an employer may be seeking applicants. As a general rule, neither has the intent to accept a job offer if one is made by the employer. The treatment that each tester receives is then compared to evaluate whether the white tester applicant received more favorable treatment than the black tester applicant. Should the black tester have standing to sue if he received less favorable treatment from the employer than the white tester? The courts of appeals are divided on the issue. In *Kyles v. J.K. Guardian Security Services*, 222 F.3d 289, 298 (7th Cir.2000) (collecting cases), the Seventh Circuit held that testers who experience discrimination as job applicants have standing to sue under Title VII. The court held, however, that testers do not have standing under § 1981 because the requisite intent to "make or enforce a contract" is nonexistent. The Fourth Circuit, in *Sledge v. J.P. Stevens & Co.*, 585 F.2d 625 (4th Cir.1978), *cert. denied*, 440 U.S. 981, 99 S.Ct. 1789, 60 L.Ed.2d 241 (1979), held testers do not have standing because they have suffered no cognizable injury as they are not seriously interested in the jobs for which they applied. The EEOC has issued a Policy Guidance supporting the right of testers to sue. *See Kyles*, 222 F.3d at 299 (discussing the EEOC Policy Guidance on testers). Which do you think is the better view?

3. THE MEANING OF "EMPLOYER"

Title VII defines the term "employer" as, *inter alia,* "a person engaged in an industry affecting commerce who has fifteen or more employees for each working day in each of twenty or more calendar weeks in the current or preceding calendar year." Title VII § 701(b), 42 U.S.C. 2000e(b). "Employer" is similarly defined in the ADA, ADA § 101(5)(A), and the ADEA, 29 U.S.C. § 630(b), except that the threshold number of employees under the ADEA is twenty rather than fifteen. Does *Clackamas* help define the meaning of "employer"?

In *Walters v. Metropolitan Educational Enterprises, Inc.*, 519 U.S. 202, 117 S.Ct. 660, 136 L.Ed.2d 644 (1997), the Supreme Court resolved a split among the circuits on the meaning of "employer" under Title VII. Some lower courts had adopted the "compensation" method, holding that an employer is not covered under Title VII unless the employer actually compensated fifteen or more employees on each working day of the relevant twenty or more calendar weeks in the current or preceding calendar year. Other courts had adopted the "payroll" method, holding that an employer is covered under Title VII if it had fifteen or more employees on its payroll on each working day of the relevant twenty or more calendars weeks in the current or preceding year.

The issue before the Supreme Court in *Walters* was whether Title VII's jurisdictional definition of "employer" is satisfied when an employer maintains fifteen or more employees on its payroll for the requisite number of weeks even though fewer than fifteen employees report to work or are on paid leave on each day of such week. In a unanimous decision, the Supreme Court adopted the "payroll" method, which relies on the "ultimate touchstone," i.e., "whether the employer has an employment relationship with the individual on the day in question." *Walters,* 519 U.S. at 211, 117 S.Ct. at 666, 663. In recognizing a broad interpretation of the term "employer," the Court concluded that the payroll method "represents the fair reading of the statutory language," *id.* at 207, 117 S.Ct. at 664, and that the compensation method urged by the employer would lead to "unique peculiarities," *id.* at 210, 117 S.Ct. at 665. For example, the Court stated that under the compensation method, a half-time worker who worked every day but only in the morning would be counted, yet a half-time employee who worked every other day would not. *Id.* at 210, 117 S.Ct. at 665. The Court also believed the compensation method would involve "an incredibly complex and expensive factual inquiry," *id.* at 210, 117 S.Ct. at 665, whereas under the payroll method "all one needs to know about a given employee for a given year is whether the employee started or ended employment during that year and, if so, when." *Id.* at 210, 117 S.Ct. at 665–66. The result of *Walters* may mean that fewer employers will be exempt from these statutes as small employers. *See* Paul M. Barrett, *Job-Bias Rule for Small Firms Will Be Clarified by High Court,* Wall St.J., Mar. 19, 1996, at B9 (referring to a 1991 Census Bureau report that "there were more than 550,000 businesses with 10 to 19 workers and that these enterprises employed about 7.4 million people").

Single employer: The courts have not adopted a uniform test for deciding whether a small employer with fewer than fifteen (or twenty) employees, which falls below the threshold for coverage under Title VII (or the ADA or ADEA), and its larger parent company or other affiliates with fifteen (or twenty) or more employees constitute a single employer. *See* Lyes v. City of Riviera Beach, Fla., 166 F.3d 1332 (11th Cir.1999). Most of the courts deciding the issue have adopted the common law "integrated employer" test, which was initially adopted by, the National Labor Relations Board to decide employer coverage under the National Labor Relations Act. The factors the courts consider under the "integrated employer" test include (1) interrelation of operations, (2) common management, (3) common ownership, (4) and centralized control of labor relations and personnel. *See* Papa v. Katy Indus., Inc., 166 F.3d 937, 940–41 (7th Cir.1999) (collecting cases), *cert. denied,* 528 U.S. 1019, 120 S.Ct. 526, 145 L.Ed.2d 408 (1999). In *Papa,* the Seventh Circuit rejected the "integrated employer" test and, instead, focused on the policy for exempting smaller employers from coverage of laws prohibiting discrimination in employment. The relevant inquiry under the Seventh Circuit test asks: (1) whether a parent company would be liable for the subsidiary employer's debts, torts, or contract breaches under the traditional standards for "piercing the corporate veil"; (2) whether the enterprise split itself into smaller companies, "each with fewer than the statutory minimum of employees, for the express purpose of avoiding liability under the discrimination laws"; and (3) whether "the parent company might have directed the discriminatory act, practice, or policy of which the employee of its subsidiary was complaining." *Id.* at 940–41.

Notes and Questions

1. Who should decide, judge or jury, whether a small employer and its parent corporation are a single employer? The majority in *Scarfo v. Ginsberg*, 175 F.3d 957 (11th Cir.1999), *cert. denied*, 529 U.S. 1003, 120 S.Ct. 1267, 146 L.Ed.2d 217 (2000), held that the judge decides because it is a jurisdictional issue. The dissenting judge adopted the view that the jury should decide because the issue is intertwined with the merits of the plaintiff's claim.

2. Who is the "employer" of "employees" when individuals are leased out by one company to work on a temporary basis for another company? *See* Mark A. Hanley, *Who's the Boss? How Discrimination Law Treats Leased Employees, Independent Contractors, and Consultants*, 48 Lab.L.J. 233 (1997). In its *Enforcement Guidance: The Application of EEO Laws to Contingent Workers Placed by Temporary Employment Agencies and Other Staffing Firms*, 236 DLR E–15 (BNA, Dec. 9, 1997), the EEOC warns employers that using individuals hired and paid by a staffing firm are not automatically relieved of their obligations under federal laws prohibiting discrimination in employment. Rather, Title VII, the ADA, the ADEA, and the Equal Pay Act may apply to temporary or other contingent workers.

3. Coverage of employers, employment agencies, and labor organizations under § 1981 is not subject to the restrictions on employee coverage that are applicable to Title VII, the ADA, and the ADEA. Even a small "mom and pop" grocery store employing only one employee is a covered entity under § 1981.

4. INDIVIDUAL LIABILITY OF AGENTS OF EMPLOYERS

Under Title VII, the ADEA, and the ADA, the term "employer" is statutorily defined to include "any agent" of the employer. Title VII § 701(b), 42 U.S.C. § 2000e-(b); ADEA § 630(b), 29 U.S.C. § 630(b); ADA § 101(5)(A), 42 U.S.C. 12111(5)(A). Courts generally define the term "agent" as a supervisory employee who has the authority to make personnel decisions regarding hiring or firing employees or to otherwise set the terms and conditions of employment for applicants and employees. *See* Paroline v. Unisys Corp., 879 F.2d 100, 104 (4th Cir.1989), *vacated in part on other grounds*, 900 F.2d 27 (4th Cir.1990); Sauers v. Salt Lake County, 1 F.3d 1122, 1125 (10th Cir.1993). The statutes are silent on whether "agents" of "employers" are liable in their individual capacity for any unlawful discriminatory employment decisions that they make. Some of the earlier discrimination cases indicated that agents could be found individually liable. In *Meritor Savings Bank, FSB v. Vinson*, 477 U.S. 57, 106 S.Ct. 2399, 91 L.Ed.2d 49 (1986), covered in

Chapter 8, the Court held that employers are not strictly liable for hostile environment sexual harassment under Title VII. After *Meritor*, the majority of the courts of appeals have held that agents can be held liable only in their representative, not their individual, capacities. As explained by the Tenth Circuit in *Ball v. Renner*, 54 F.3d 664, 666 (1995),

[C]ourts have interpreted the inclusion of "agent" * * * in two distinct ways:

1. as deepening the pool of potential defendants * * * to include supervisory and management personnel who discriminate in the workplace, or

2. as merely broadening the circumstances in which corporations and other organizational employers that otherwise meet the [statutory employee minima] threshold and the industry-affecting-commerce requirement may be liable, by ensuring that the discriminatory acts of individuals are imputed to the employing entity.

The court in *Ball v. Renner* then reviewed the split among the lower courts—both appellate and district—under each of these two views. *Id.* at 666–67.

The Ninth Circuit's decision in *Miller v. Maxwell's International Inc.*, 991 F.2d 583 (1993), *cert. denied sub nom.* Miller v. La Rosa, 510 U.S. 1109, 114 S.Ct. 1049, 127 L.Ed.2d 372 (1994), is one of the leading cases holding that agents are not liable in their individual capacities. In *Miller v. Maxwell's*, the court held that imposing individual liability on agents is inappropriate. The court reasoned that Congress expressed its intent to impose liability only on employers because (1) the term "agent" was included in these statutes only to incorporate respondeat superior liability; (2) the employee limitation in the definition of an employer (fifteen or more employees under Title VII and the ADA, and twenty or more employees under the ADEA) indicates congressional intent not to subject small businesses to the costs of defending employment discrimination claims and makes it "inconceivable that Congress intended to allow civil liability to run against individual employees," *id.* at 587; and (3) the statutory language of the amendments to Title VII in the Civil Rights Act of 1991 indicates that compensatory and punitive damages can be awarded only against employers and not their agents.

Individual liability under § 1981 has been addressed in only a few cases. One of the leading cases holding that agents of employers are liable in their individual capacities is *Faraca v. Clements*, 506 F.2d 956 (5th Cir.) (holding the director of a state agency personally liable for discriminatory action even though the employer was immune from liability), *cert. denied*, 422 U.S. 1006, 95 S.Ct. 2627, 45 L.Ed.2d 668 (1975). *See also* Al–Khazraji v. St. Francis College, 784 F.2d 505, 518 (3d Cir.1986), *aff'd on other grounds*, 481 U.S. 604, 107 S.Ct. 2022, 95 L.Ed.2d 582 (1987); Kolb v. Ohio Dep't of Mental Retardation & Developmental Disabilities, 721 F.Supp. 885, 891 (N.D.Ohio 1989) (individual held liable for intentionally interfering with plaintiff's contractual rights on the basis of race, regardless of whether the employer or anyone else could also be held liable).

5.   THE MEANING OF AN "EMPLOYMENT PRACTICE"

A threshold issue in employment discrimination cases is whether the plaintiff is seeking relief from an "unlawful employment *practice*" or an adverse employment *practice*. To be actionable the "practice" must fall within the statutory phrase, "compensation, terms, conditions, or privileges of employment." *See, e.g.*, Title VII § 703(a)(1), 42 U.S.C § 2000e–2(a)(1); ADEA § 4(a)(1), 29 U.S.C. § 623(a)(1); *see also* ADA § 102(a), 42 U.S.C. § 12112(a). Like the term "discriminate," Congress did not define the phrase "compensation, terms, conditions, or privileges of employment." If the "practice" of an employer does not fall within the meaning of "compensation, terms, conditions, or privileges of employment," then arguably that "practice" is not unlawful even if the employer was motivated by discriminatory intent in taking the action. The Supreme Court has defined the term *practice* to include discrete acts and acts that are continuing in nature. National R.R. Passenger Corp. v. Morgan, 536 U.S. 101, 111, 122 S.Ct. 2061, 2071, 153 L.Ed.2d 106 (2002) ("[w]e have repeatedly interpreted the term 'practice' to apply to a discrete act or single 'occurrence,' even when it has a connection to other acts.").

Some of the most obvious employment practices that fall within the statutory phrase "compensation, terms, conditions, or privileges of employment" are terminations, failures to promote, denials of transfer, or refusals to hire. *See Morgan, id.* at 113, 122 S.Ct. at 2972. Although courts have held that not every employment or personnel decision an employer makes is a "practice," they disagree on the test for deciding which practices of employers do or do not come within the statutory phrase.

In *Ray v. Henderson*, 217 F.3d 1234 (9th Cir.2000), the Ninth Circuit summarized the split in the circuits on the meaning of "compensation, terms, conditions, or privileges of employment":

> We have found that a wide array of disadvantageous changes in the workplace constitute adverse employment actions. While "mere ostracism" by co-workers does not constitute an adverse employment action, *see Strother v. Southern California Permanente Medical Group*, 79 F.3d 859, 869 (9th Cir.1996), a lateral transfer does. In *Yartzoff v. Thomas*, 809 F.2d 1371, 1376 (9th Cir.1987), we held that "[t]ransfers of job duties and undeserved performance ratings, if proven, would constitute 'adverse employment decisions.' " The *Yartzoff* decision was in line with our earlier decision in *St. John v. Employment Development Dept.*, 642 F.2d 273, 274 (9th Cir.1981), where we held that a transfer to another job of the same pay and status may constitute an adverse employment action.

> Similarly, in *Hashimoto v. Dalton*, 118 F.3d 671, 676 (9th Cir.1997), we found that the dissemination of an unfavorable job reference was an adverse employment action "because it was a

'personnel action' motivated by retaliatory animus." We so found even though the defendant proved that the poor job reference did not affect the prospective employer's decision not to hire the plaintiff: "That this unlawful personnel action turned out to be inconsequential goes to the issue of damages, not liability." *Id.*

In *Strother,* we examined the case of an employee who, after complaining of discrimination, was excluded from meetings, seminars and positions that would have made her eligible for salary increases, was denied secretarial support, and was given a more burdensome work schedule. 79 F.3d at 869. We determined that she had suffered from adverse employment actions. *Id.*

These cases place the Ninth Circuit in accord with the First, Seventh, Tenth, Eleventh and D.C. Circuits. These Circuits all take an expansive view of the type of actions that can be considered adverse employment actions. *See Wyatt v. City of Boston,* 35 F.3d 13, 15–16 (1st Cir.1994) (adverse employment actions include "demotions, disadvantageous transfers or assignments, refusals to promote, unwarranted negative job evaluations and toleration of harassment by other employees"); *Knox v. Indiana,* 93 F.3d 1327, 1334 (7th Cir.1996) (employer can be liable for retaliation if it permits "actions like moving the person from a spacious, brightly lit office to a dingy closet, depriving the person of previously available support services * * * or cutting off challenging assignments"); *Corneveaux v. Cuna Mutual Ins. Group,* 76 F.3d 1498, 1507 (10th Cir.1996) (employee demonstrated adverse employment action under the ADEA by showing that her employer "required her to go through several hoops in order to obtain her severance benefits"); *Berry v. Stevinson Chevrolet,* 74 F.3d 980, 986 (10th Cir.1996) (malicious prosecution by former employer can be adverse employment action); *Wideman v. Wal–Mart Stores, Inc.,* 141 F.3d 1453, 1456 (11th Cir.1998) (adverse employment actions include an employer requiring plaintiff to work without lunch break, giving her a one-day suspension, soliciting other employees for negative statements about her, changing her schedule without notification, making negative comments about her, and needlessly delaying authorization for medical treatment); *Passer v. American Chemical Soc.,* 935 F.2d 322, 330–331 (D.C.Cir.1991) (employer's cancellation of a public event honoring an employee can constitute adverse employment action under the ADEA, which has an anti-retaliation provision parallel to that in Title VII).

The Second and Third circuits hold an intermediate position within the circuit split. They have held that an adverse action is something that materially affects the terms and conditions of employment. *See Robinson v. City of Pittsburgh,* 120 F.3d 1286, 1300 (3d Cir.1997) ("retaliatory conduct must be serious and tangible enough to alter an employee's compensation, terms, conditions, or privileges of employment * * * to constitute [an] 'adverse employment action' "); *Torres v. Pisano,* 116 F.3d 625, 640 (2d Cir.1997) (to show an adverse employment action employee must demonstrate "a materially adverse change in the terms and conditions of employment") (quoting *McKenney v. New York City Off–Track Betting Corp.,* 903 F.Supp. 619, 623 (S.D.N.Y.1995)).

The Fifth and Eighth Circuits, adopting the most restrictive test, hold that only "ultimate employment actions" such as hiring, firing, promoting and demoting constitute actionable adverse employment actions. *See Mattern v. Eastman Kodak Co.,* 104 F.3d 702, 707 (5th Cir.1997) (only "ultimate employment decisions" can be adverse employment decisions); *Ledergerber v. Stangler,* 122 F.3d 1142, 1144 (8th Cir.1997) (transfer involving only minor changes in working conditions and no reduction in pay or benefits is not an adverse employment action).

The government urges us to turn from our precedent, and to adopt the Fifth and Eighth Circuit rule that only "ultimate employment actions" such as hiring, firing, promoting and demoting constitute actionable adverse employment actions.[5] But we cannot square such a rule with our prior decisions. Actions that we consider adverse employment actions, such as the lateral transfers in *Yartzoff* and *St. John,* the unfavorable reference that had no affect [sic] on a prospective employer's hiring decisions in *Hashimoto,* and the imposition of a more burdensome work schedule in *Strother* are not ultimate employment actions. Nor, for that matter, does the test adopted by the Second and Third Circuits comport with our precedent. While some actions that we consider to be adverse (such as disadvantageous transfers or changes in work schedule) do "materially affect the terms and conditions of employment," others (such as an unfavorable reference not affecting an employee's job prospects) do not.

Id. at 1240–42 (9th Cir.2000). The Seventh Circuit offered this view of the issue:

Adverse employment action has been defined quite broadly in this circuit. In some cases, for example when an employee is fired, or suffers a reduction in benefits or pay, it is clear that an employee has been the victim of an adverse employment action. But an

---

5. The government relies on *Burlington Industries, Inc. v. Ellerth,* 524 U.S. 742, 761, 118 S.Ct. 2257, 141 L.Ed.2d 633 (1998) for the proposition that only ultimate employment actions such as "hiring, firing, failing to promote, reassignment with significantly different responsibilities [and] a decision causing a significant change in benefits" constitute adverse employment actions. But the discussion in *Burlington Industries* cited by the government concerns the types of employment actions which, if taken by a supervisor, would subject the employer to vicarious liability for harassment. *See* 524 U.S. at 760–761, 118 S.Ct. 2257. Although the Supreme Court cited to circuit-level Title VII cases that defined "adverse employment actions," the Court specifically declined to adopt the holdings of those cases: "Without endorsing the specific results of those decisions, we think it prudent to import the concept of a tangible employment action for resolution of the vicarious liability issue we consider here." *Id.* at 761, 118 S.Ct. 2257. Therefore, we reject the contention that *Burlington Industries* set forth a standard for adverse employment actions in the anti-retaliation context. [*Burlington* is reproduced in Chapter 8, Section C.1.]

employment action does not have to be so easily quantified to be considered adverse for our purposes. "[A]dverse job action is not limited solely to loss or reduction of pay or monetary benefits. It can encompass other forms of adversity as well." *Collins v. State of Illinois*, 830 F.2d 692, 703 (7th Cir.1987). In *Collins* the employee was placed in a new department where her supervisors didn't even know what her job entailed. Her office was taken away from her, and she was assigned to a desk outside her supervisor's office, where a receptionist would typically sit. She also lost her phone, business cards, and listing in professional directories and publications. These changes were found to constitute adverse employment action. Likewise, in *Dahm v. Flynn*, 60 F.3d 253 (7th Cir.1994), we found that "a dramatic downward shift in skill level required to perform job responsibilities can rise to the level of an adverse employment action * * *." *Dahm* at 257.

While adverse employment actions extend beyond readily quantifiable losses, not everything that makes an employee unhappy is an actionable adverse action. Otherwise, minor and even trivial employment actions that "an irritable, chip-on-the-shoulder employee did not like would form the basis of a discrimination suit." *Williams v. Bristol–Myers Squibb Co.*, 85 F.3d 270, 274 (7th Cir.1996). In *Crady v. Liberty National Bank & Trust Co. of Indiana*, 993 F.2d 132 (7th Cir.1993), we found that a change in title from assistant vice-president and manager of one branch of a bank to a loan officer position at a different branch did not by itself constitute an adverse employment action. Another case where adverse employment action was found to be absent is *Spring v. Sheboygan Area School District*, 865 F.2d 883 (7th Cir.1989). In *Spring*, a 65–year-old school principal was offered the choice between retirement and transfer to a different school as part of a school district reorganization plan. The transfer would have afforded the principal a two-year contract and a merit pay increase, but she would have had to share the position with a co-principal. The court found that the "humiliation" she claimed the co-principal arrangement would cause did not constitute an adverse employment action because "public perceptions were not a term or condition of Spring's employment." *Spring*, at 886. The only negative employment-related consequence of the transfer was found to be an increase in the distance she had to travel to work. This alone did not constitute an actionable adverse employer action. Likewise, in *Flaherty v. Gas Research Institute*, 31 F.3d 451 (7th Cir.1994), we found that a lateral transfer, where the employee's existing title would be changed and the employee would report to a former subordinate, may have cause a "bruised ego," but did not constitute an adverse employment action. Most recently, in *Williams*, we found that the strictly lateral transfer of a salesman from one division of a pharmaceutical company to another was not an adverse employment action.

Smart v. Ball State Univ., 89 F.3d 437, 441–42 (7th Cir.1996).

Although most of the cases reported to date on this development have been retaliation claims, see Chapter 15, the tests discussed in *Ray v. Henderson* have been applied as well in a range of disparate treatment cases, as illustrated in the Seventh Circuit's decision in *Smart v. Ball State*. The Supreme Court has not addressed the circuit split identified in *Ray*, and the signals from some of its other cases are mixed. In a race discrimination case, *McDonnell Douglas Corp. v. Green*, 411 U.S. 792, 801, 93 S.Ct. 1817, 1824, 36 L.Ed.2d 668 (1973) the Court observed that "Title VII tolerates no racial discrimination, subtle or otherwise." The Court also said in *Los Angeles Department of Water and Power v. Manhart*, 435 U.S. 702, 707 n.13, 98 S.Ct. 1370, 1384 n.13, 55 L.Ed.2d 657 (1978), that Congress intended "to strike at the entire spectrum of disparate treatment of men and women" in employment (quoting Sprogis v. United Air Lines, Inc., 444 F.2d 1194, 1198 (7th Cir.1971)). On the other hand, the Court held, in *Burlington Industries, Inc. v. Ellerth*, 524 U.S. 742, 118 S.Ct. 2257, 141 L.Ed.2d 633 (1998), and *Faragher v. City of Boca Raton*, 524 U.S. 775, 118 S.Ct. 2275, 141 L.Ed.2d 662 (1998), that employers can be held vicariously liable for their supervisors' sexual harassment of employees that involves a "tangible employment action." The Court then defined *tangible employment action* as a personnel action that "constitutes a significant change in employment status, such as hiring, firing, failing to promote, reassignment with significantly different responsibilities, or a decision causing a significant change in benefits." *Burlington Industries*, 524 U.S. at 760, 118 S.Ct. at 2268.

Notes and Questions

1. What argument would you make in the following cases that the actions at issue either are or are not an ultimate employment decision or a materially adverse employment action:

a. Stockett, a black male, brings a Title VII race discrimination action alleging that he was required to submit to a drug test as a condition of employment. All applicants are required to take the drug test. Would the drug testing requirement constitute an adverse action? Would it make a difference if Stockett could show that he was administered the drug test under conditions designed to humiliate or harass him? *See* Stockett v. Muncie Indiana Transit Sys., 221 F.3d 997 (7th Cir.2000)

b. Sexual harassment is covered in Chapter 8. One theory of sexual harassment is hostile work environment. One of the key elements of this theory is proof that conduct of a sexual nature was severe or pervasive. An employer is not generally liable to an employee for sexual harassment by a co-worker unless the employer knew or should have known about the harassment and failed to take corrective measures. Brooks, a female employee, and a male co-worker were at work one evening. The male came up behind her, reached under her sweater and bra, and fondled her bare breast while she was on the telephone. Assume that the employer saw the male employee engage in this conduct but did nothing about it. Has Brooks suffered an adverse employment practice? An ultimate material adverse action? A tangible employment action? *Cf.* Brooks v. San Mateo, 229 F.3d

917 (9th Cir.2000) (declining to decide whether a single instance of co-worker sexual harassment is actionable under Title VII because the employer took prompt remedial action).

2. Some commentators have criticized the *ultimate employment decision* and *materially adverse employment decision* tests on the ground that they are inconsistent with the statutory language and contravene the purposes and the broad remedial goals of employment discrimination laws. *See* Ernest F. Lidge, III, *The Meaning of Discrimination: Why Courts Have Erred in Requiring Employment Discrimination Plaintiffs to Prove That the Employer's Action Was Materially Adverse or Ultimate*, 47 U.Kan.L.Rev. 333 (1999); Rebecca Hanner White, *De Minimis Discrimination*, 47 Emory L.J. 1121 (1998).

Note: Extraterritorial Application of Discrimination Laws

In *EEOC v. Arabian American Oil Co.*, 499 U.S. 244, 111 S.Ct. 1227, 113 L.Ed.2d 274 (1991), the Supreme Court held that Title VII does not apply extraterritorially. Congress overruled that decision in § 109 of the Civil Rights Act of 1991; thus, Title VII and the ADA, like the ADEA, now apply extraterritorially. Landgraf v. USI Film Prods., 511 U.S. 244, 251, 114 S.Ct. 1483, 1489, 128 L.Ed.2d 229 (1994). For discussion of some of the problems in applying employment discrimination laws to United States employers who do business in foreign countries, see Meredith Poznanski Cook, Note, *The Extraterritorial Application of Title VII: Does the Foreign Compulsion Defense Work?*, 20 Suffolk Transnat'l L.Rev. 133 (1996); Mary Claire St. John, Note, *Extraterritorial Application of Title VII: The Foreign Compulsion Defense and Principles of International Comity*, 27 Vand.J. Transnat'l L. 869 (1994).

For a discussion of some of the problems of applying the extraterritorial provisions to foreign individuals who apply in foreign countries for jobs in the United States, see *Reyes-Gaona v. North Carolina Growers Ass'n, Inc.*, 250 F.3d 861 (4th Cir.), *cert. denied*, 534 U.S. 995, 122 S.Ct. 463, 151 L.Ed.2d 380 (2001); Ruhe C. Wadud, Note, *Allowing Employers to Discriminate in the Hiring Process Under the Age Discrimination in Employment Act: The Case of* Reyes–Gaona, 27 N.C.J. Int'l L. & Com.Reg. 335 (2001).

Part II

THEORIES OF DISCRIMINATION AND ANALYTICAL PARADIGMS

Chapter 3

DISPARATE TREATMENT

A. INTRODUCTION: THE MEANING AND THEORIES OF "DISCRIMINATION"

In this chapter we begin an in-depth study of employment discrimination law by first examining the meaning and theories of discrimination. The two major theories of discrimination are disparate treatment and disparate impact. The disparate treatment theory is covered in this chapter. The disparate impact theory is covered in Chapter 4.

Although federal laws prohibit discrimination in employment because of specific characteristics, federal laws, except for the Americans with Disabilities Act, do not provide a statutory definition of "discriminate." An often-quoted interpretive memorandum entered into the Congressional Record by Senators Case and Clark, the Republican and Democratic floor managers of Title VII in the Senate, states that

> [t]o discriminate is to make a distinction, to make a difference in treatment or favor, and those distinctions or differences in treatment or favor which are prohibited by section 704 are those which are based on any five of the forbidden criteria: race, color, religion, sex, and national origin. Any other criterion or qualification for employment is not affected by this title.

110 Cong.Rec. 7213 (1964). Senator McClellan, concerned that Title VII would become a "dragnet, a catchall," that would reach far beyond the purposes of the statute, proposed an amendment to Title VII that would limit its scope to adverse employment actions based "solely" on race, color, religion, sex, or national origin. *Id.* at 13,837 (1964). The Senate rejected the McClellan proposal. *Id.* at 13,838. A similar amendment, the "Dowdy Amendment," was rejected by the House of Representatives. 110 Cong.Rec. 2728 (1964).

In the end, because most statutes on employment discrimination law are silent on the meaning of "discrimination," Congress left the responsibility for defining discrimination to the federal courts. *Cf.* Alexander v. Gardner–Denver, 415 U.S. 36, 44, 94 S.Ct. 1011, 1017, 39 L.Ed.2d 147 (1974) ("final responsibility for enforcement of Title VII is vested with federal courts"). After more than a decade of judicial developments under Title VII, the Supreme Court in *Teamsters v. United States*, 431 U.S. 324, 335 n.15, 97 S.Ct. 1843, 1854 n.15, 52 L.Ed.2d 396 (1977), summarized the two basic theories of discrimination on which much of the jurisprudence of employment discrimination law is based—disparate treatment and disparate impact:

> "Disparate treatment" * * * is the most easily understood type of discrimination. The employer simply treats some people less favorably than others because of their race, color, sex, religion or national origin. Proof of discriminatory motive is critical, although it can in some situations be inferred from the mere fact of differences in treatment. Undoubtedly disparate treatment was the most obvious evil Congress had in mind when it enacted Title VII. *See, e.g.,* 110 Cong. Rec. 13088 (1964) (remarks of Sen. Humphrey) ("What the bill does * * * is simply make it an illegal practice to use race as a factor in denying employment. It provides that men and women shall be employed on the basis of their qualifications, not as Catholic citizens, not as Protestant citizens, not as Jewish citizens, not as colored citizens, but as citizens of the United States").

> Claims of disparate treatment may be distinguished from disparate impact claims. The latter involves employment practices that are facially neutral in their treatment of different groups but in fact fall more harshly on one group than another and cannot be justified by business necessity. Proof of discriminatory motive * * * is not required under a disparate impact theory.

See also Raytheon Co. v. Hernandez, ___ U.S. ___, ___, 124 S.Ct. 513, 519, 157 L.Ed.2d 357 (2003) (the Supreme Court observed that it "has consistently recognized a distinction between claims of discrimination based on disparate treatment and claims of discrimination based on disparate impact").

The disparate treatment theory is based on judicial construction of § 703(a)(1) of Title VII, 42 U.S.C. § 2000e–2(a)(1). McDonnell Douglas Corp. v. Green, 411 U.S. 792, 93 S.Ct. 1817, 36 L.Ed.2d 668 (1973). The disparate impact theory, which is grounded in the landmark Supreme Court case of *Griggs v. Duke Power Co.*, 401 U.S. 424, 91 S.Ct. 849, 28 L.Ed.2d 158 (1971), is based on judicial construction of § 703(a)(2) of Title VII, 42 U.S.C. § 2000e–2(a)(2). *Connecticut v. Teal*, 457 U.S. 440, 102 S.Ct. 2525, 73 L.Ed.2d 130 (1982). A major difference between the two theories is that discriminatory intent is the key element in a disparate treatment claim, but discriminatory intent is not an element in a disparate impact claim. Most employment discrimination cases are brought under the disparate treatment theory, which is the focus of this chapter and, indeed, most of the materials in this book. *See* John J. Donohue, III & Peter Siegelman, *The Changing Nature of Employment Discrimination Litigation*, 43 Stan.L.Rev. 983, 989 (1991) (noting that in 1989 only 101 of the 7,613 employment discrimination cases were brought under the disparate impact theory).

The two basic theories of discrimination originated in cases arising under Title VII, but both theories are not applicable to all of the laws prohibiting discrimination in employment. For example, the disparate impact theory is not applicable in employment discrimination claims based on the Equal Protection Clause of the Fourteenth Amendment or the Civil Rights Act of 1866, 42 U.S.C. § 1981. See Chapter 5. Congress provided a statutory definition of "discriminate" for the first time in the Americans with Disabilities Act of 1990 (ADA), § 102(b), 42 U.S.C. § 12112(b), which includes additional theories of discrimination. For example, the ADA defines the term "discriminate," *inter alia*, as "not making reasonable accommodations to the known physical and mental limitations of an otherwise qualified individual with a disability who is an applicant or employee." ADA, § 102(b)(5)(A), 42 U.S.C. § 12112(b)(5)(A).

Questions

As you read and study the cases and other materials in this and later chapters, consider the following questions:

1.   What are the implications of the two basic theories of discrimination—disparate treatment and disparate impact—for achieving "equality" in the workplace?

2.   The two theories of discrimination parallel the two conceptions of equality discussed in Chapter 1. Can the goals of equal treatment and equal opportunity be reconciled or accommodated or do they embrace different visions of equality?

3.   To what extent do the experiences and views of judges (and your own experiences and views) influence the rules and doctrines that they (or you) are willing to adopt in interpreting the laws prohibiting discrimination?

B.   DISPARATE TREATMENT CLAIMS

When a plaintiff seeks relief in an employment discrimination case under the disparate treatment theory, the critical issue the factfinder must decide is whether the plaintiff has proven that an adverse employment practice is based upon unlawful discriminatory motivation. As the Supreme Court has said, "[t]he ultimate question in every discrimination case involving a claim of disparate treatment is whether the plaintiff was the victim of intentional discrimination." Reeves v. Sanderson Plumbing Prod., Inc., 530 U.S. 133, 153, 120 S.Ct. 2097, 2111, 147 L.Ed.2d 105 (2000). In *United States Postal Service Board of Governors v. Aikens*, 460 U.S. 711, 103 S.Ct. 1478, 1482, 75 L.Ed.2d 403 (1983), the Court said that the "factual inquiry" in an employment discrimination case based on the disparate treatment theory is whether the defendant was "treating 'some people less favorably than others because of their race, color, religion, sex or national origin.' "*Id.* at 715, 103 S.Ct. at 1482 (citations omitted). Intentional discrimination is an issue of fact to be decided by the factfinder, Pullman–Standard v. Swint, 456 U.S. 273,

287–88, 102 S.Ct. 1781, 1789, 72 L.Ed.2d 66 (1982), and the factfinder's determination on this fact issue will be set aside on appeal only if it is clearly erroneous, Anderson v. City of Bessemer, 470 U.S. 564, 573, 105 S.Ct. 1504, 1511, 84 L.Ed.2d 518 (1985).

Proving intentional discrimination can be difficult in disparate treatment cases, particularly in those cases in which a plaintiff must rely solely upon circumstantial evidence. However, the law is well settled that, as in any civil case, a plaintiff may prove a claim of unlawful employment discrimination, including the ultimate fact of intentional discrimination, by direct or circumstantial evidence. *See, e.g.*, United States Postal Serv. Bd. of Governors v. Aikens, 460 U.S. at 714 n.3, 103 S.Ct. at 1481 n.3; Desert Palace, Inc. v. Costa, 539 U.S. 90, 94, 123 S.Ct. 2148, 2154, 156 L.Ed.2d 84 (2003) (the conventional rule in civil litigation allows a plaintiff in an employment discrimination case to prove a case of intentional discrimination by direct or circumstantial evidence).

We begin the study of the disparate treatment theory of discrimination with the leading case of *McDonnell Douglas Corp. v. Green*, 411 U.S. 792, 93 S.Ct. 1817, 36 L.Ed.2d 668 (1973). Plaintiffs in the overwhelming majority of individual, non-class-action disparate treatment employment discrimination cases must rely solely on circumstantial evidence. *See, e.g.*, Russell v. Microdyno Corp., 65 F.3d 1229, 1237 (4th Cir.1995); Rattray v. City of Nat'l City, 36 F.3d 1480, 1485 (9th Cir.1994), *cert. denied*, 516 U.S. 820, 116 S.Ct. 80, 133 L.Ed.2d 39 (1995); Sims v. Cleland, 813 F.2d 790, 793 (6th Cir.1987). The purpose of the *McDonnell Douglas* framework is to assist the factfinder in deciding the "elusive factual question of intentional discrimination" when a plaintiff uses circumstantial evidence to prove intentional discrimination under the disparate treatment theory. Texas Dep't of Community Affairs v. Burdine, 450 U.S. 248, 255, n.8, 101 S.Ct. 1089, 1094 n.8, 67 L.Ed.2d 207 (1981).

The *McDonnell Douglas* evidentiary and analytical approach assumes that a single motive—either a lawful motive or an unlawful motive, but not both—is the reason for an adverse employment action from which a plaintiff seeks relief. In the classic *McDonnell Douglas* paradigm, the plaintiff, relying upon circumstantial evidence, tries to prove that an unlawful discriminatory motive, rather than the lawful motive articulated by the employer, is the real or true reason the employer made the adverse decision. The employer, on the other hand, seeks to convince the factfinder that its decision was based on a legitimate, nondiscriminatory reason. *See* Haskins v. Department of Army, 808 F.2d 1192, 1197 (6th Cir.), *cert. denied*, 484 U.S. 815, 108 S.Ct. 68, 98 L.Ed.2d 32 (1987). Over time, however, different factual paradigms began to emerge, and the challenge of attempting to fit these new factual paradigms into the *McDonnell Douglas* analytical framework became problematical and frequently produced circuit splits. *See, e.g.*, Russell v. Microdyne Corp., 65 F.3d 1229, 1235–39 (4th Cir.1995) (commenting upon the problems created by the emergence of additional factual paradigms in the post-*McDonnell Douglas* era).

This chapter explores the disparate treatment theory through five factual and analytical schemes: (1) single-motive or pretext cases, (2) mixed-or dual-motive cases, (3) after-acquired evidence cases, (4) pattern-or-practice cases, and (5) affirmative action cases. The materials in Section B.2. of this chapter explore a set of issues on proving discriminatory intent by circumstantial or direct evidence. At the time the complaint is filed, a plaintiff is not required to specify which of these proof and analytical schemes she intends to rely upon, but at some point during the trial the district court must determine which evidentiary scheme is appropriate in order to decide the merits of the case or to instruct the jury, if it is a jury trial. Price Waterhouse v. Hopkins, 490 U.S. 228, 247 n.12, 109 S.Ct. 1775, 1789 n.12, 104 L.Ed.2d 268 (1989).

1. PRETEXT OR SINGLE–MOTIVE CASES

McDONNELL DOUGLAS CORP. v. GREEN

Supreme Court of the United States, 1973.
411 U.S. 792, 93 S.Ct. 1817, 36 L.Ed.2d 668.

JUSTICE POWELL delivered the opinion of the Court.

The case before us raises significant questions as to the proper order and nature of proof in actions under Title VII of the Civil Rights Act of 1964.

Petitioner, McDonnell Douglas Corp., is an aerospace and aircraft manufacturer headquartered in St. Louis, Missouri, where it employs over 30,000 people. Respondent, a black citizen of St. Louis, worked for petitioner as a mechanic and laboratory technician from 1956 until August 28, 1964 when he was laid off in the course of a general reduction in petitioner's work force.

Respondent, a long-time activist in the civil rights movement, protested vigorously that his discharge and the general hiring practices of petitioner were racially motivated. As part of this protest, respondent and other members of the Congress on Racial Equality illegally stalled their cars on the main roads leading to petitioner's plant for the purpose of blocking access to it at the time of the morning shift change. * * *

On July 2, 1965, a "lock-in" took place wherein a chain and padlock were placed on the front door of a building to prevent the occupants, certain of petitioner's employees, from leaving. Though respondent apparently knew beforehand of the "lock-in," the full extent of his involvement remains uncertain.

Some three weeks following the "lock-in," on July 25, 1965, petitioner publicly advertised for qualified mechanics, respondent's trade, and respondent promptly applied for re-employment. Petitioner turned down respondent, basing its rejection on respondent's participation in the "stall-in" and "lock-in." Shortly thereafter, respondent filed a formal complaint with the Equal Employment Opportunity Commission, claiming that petitioner had refused to rehire him because of his race and persistent involvement in the civil rights movement, in violation of § 703(a)(1) * * * of [Title VII].

[The District Court ruled against respondent, but the Court of Appeals reversed.]

* * *

II

The critical issue before us concerns the order and allocation of proof in a private, non-class action challenging employment discrimination. * * * The language of Title VII makes plain the purpose of Congress to assure equality of employment opportunities and to eliminate those discriminatory practices and devices which have fostered racially stratified job environments to the disadvantage of minority citizens. * * *

* * * The broad overriding interest, shared by employers, employees, and the consumer, is efficient and trustworthy workmanship assured through fair and racially neutral employment and personnel decisions. In the implementation of such decisions, it is abundantly clear that Title VII tolerates no racial discrimination, subtle or otherwise.

In this case respondent, the complainant below, charges that he was denied employment "because of his involvement in civil rights activities" and "because of his race and color." Petitioner denied discrimination of any kind, asserting that its failure to re-employ respondent was based upon and justified by his participation in the unlawful conduct against it. Thus, the issue at the trial on remand is framed by those opposing factual contentions. * * *

The complainant in a Title VII trial must carry the initial burden under the statute of establishing a prima facie case of racial discrimination. This may be done by showing (i) that he belongs to a racial minority; (ii) that he applied and was qualified for a job for which the employer was seeking applicants; (iii) that, despite his qualifications, he was rejected; and (iv) that, after his rejection, the position remained open and the employer continued to seek applicants from persons of complainant's qualifications. In the instant case, we agree with the Court of Appeals that respondent proved a prima facie case. Petitioner sought mechanics, respondent's trade, and continued to do so after respondent's rejection. Petitioner, moreover, does not dispute respondent's qualifications and acknowledges that his past work performance in petitioner's employ was "satisfactory."

The burden then must shift to the employer to articulate some legitimate, nondiscriminatory reason for the employee's rejection. We need not attempt in the instant case to detail every matter which fairly could be recognized as a reasonable basis for a refusal to hire. Here petitioner has assigned respondent's participation in unlawful conduct against it as the cause for his rejection. We think that this suffices to discharge petitioner's burden of proof at this stage and to meet respondent's prima facie case of discrimination.

The Court of Appeals intimated, however, that petitioner's stated reason for refusing to rehire respondent was a "subjective" rather than objective criterion which "carr[ies] little weight in rebutting charges of discrimination." This was among the statements which caused the dissenting judge to read the opinion as taking "the position that such unlawful acts as Green committed against McDonnell would not legally entitle McDonnell to refuse to hire him, even though no racial motivation was involved * * *." Regardless of whether this was the intended import of the opinion, we think the court below seriously underestimated the rebuttal weight to which petitioner's reasons were entitled. Respondent admittedly had taken part in a carefully planned "stall-in," designed to tie up access to and egress from petitioner's plant at a peak traffic hour. Nothing in Title VII compels an employer to absolve and rehire one who has engaged in such deliberate, unlawful activity against it. * * *

Petitioner's reason for rejection thus suffices to meet the prima facie case, but the inquiry must not end here. While Title VII does not, without more, compel rehiring of respondent, neither does it permit petitioner to use respondent's conduct as a pretext for the sort of discrimination prohibited by § 703(a)(1). On remand, respondent must * * * be afforded a fair opportunity to show that petitioner's stated reason for respondent's rejection was in fact pretext. Especially relevant to such a showing would be evidence that white employees involved in acts against petitioner of comparable seriousness to the "stall-in" were nevertheless retained or rehired. Petitioner may justifiably refuse to rehire one who was engaged in unlawful, disruptive acts against it, but only if this criterion is applied alike to members of all races.

Other evidence that may be relevant to any showing of pretext includes facts as to the petitioner's treatment of respondent during his prior term of employment; petitioner's reaction, if any, to respondent's legitimate civil rights activities; and petitioner's general policy and practice with respect to minority employment. On the latter point, statistics as to petitioner's employment policy and practice may be helpful to a determination of whether petitioner's refusal to rehire respondent in this case conformed to a general pattern of discrimination against blacks. In short, on the retrial respondent must be given a full and fair opportunity to demonstrate by competent evidence that the presumptively valid reasons for his rejection were in fact a cover-up for a racially discriminatory decision.

* * *

III

In sum, respondent should have been allowed to pursue his claim under § 703(a)(1). If the evidence on retrial is substantially in accord with that before us in this case, we think that respondent carried his burden of establishing a prima facie case of racial discrimination and that petitioner successfully rebutted that case. But this does not end the matter. On retrial, respondent must be afforded a fair opportunity to demonstrate that petitioner's assigned reason for refusing to re-employ was a pretext or discriminatory in its application. If the District Judge so finds, he must order a prompt and appropriate remedy. In the absence of such a finding, petitioner's refusal to rehire must stand.

* * *

FURNCO CONSTRUCTION CORP. v. WATERS

Supreme Court of the United States, 1978.
438 U.S. 567, 98 S.Ct. 2943, 57 L.Ed.2d 957.

JUSTICE REHNQUIST delivered the opinion of the Court.

Respondents are three black bricklayers who sought employment with petitioner Furnco Construction Corp. Two of the three were never offered employment. The third was employed only long after he initially applied. Upon adverse findings entered after a bench trial, the District Court for the Northern District of Illinois held that respondents had not proved a claim under * * * the "disparate treatment" theory * * *. The Court of Appeals for the Seventh Circuit, concluding that under *McDonnell Douglas* respondents had made out a prima facie case which had not been effectively rebutted, reversed the judgment of the District Court. We granted certiorari to consider important questions raised by this case regarding the exact scope of the prima facie case under *McDonnell Douglas* and the nature of the evidence necessary to rebut such a case. Having concluded that the Court of Appeals erred in its treatment of the latter question, we reverse and remand to that court for further proceedings consistent with this opinion.

I

A few facts in this case are not in serious dispute. Petitioner Furnco, an employer within the meaning of §§ 701(b) and (h) of Title VII, specializes in refractory installation in steel mills and, more particularly, the rehabilitation or relining of blast furnaces with what is called in the trade "firebrick." Furnco does not, however, maintain a permanent force of bricklayers. Rather, it hires a superintendent for a specific job and then delegates to him the task of securing a competent work force. In August 1971, Furnco contracted with Interlake, Inc., to reline one of its blast furnaces. Joseph Dacies, who had been a job superintendent for Furnco since 1965, was placed in charge of the job and given the attendant hiring responsibilities. He did not accept applications at the jobsite, but instead hired only persons whom he knew to be experienced and competent in this type of work or persons who had been recommended to him as similarly skilled. * * * Respondents Samuels and Nemhard were not hired, though they were fully qualified and had also attempted to secure employment by appearing at the jobsite gate. Out of the total of 1,819 man-days worked on the Interlake job, 242, or 13.3%, were worked by black bricklayers.

* * * The District Court elaborated at some length as to the "critical" necessity of insuring that only experienced and highly qualified fire-bricklayers were employed. Improper or untimely work would result in substantial losses both to Interlake, which was forced to shut down its furnace and lay off employees during the relining job, and to Furnco, which was paid for this work at a fixed price and for a fixed time period. In addition, not only might shoddy work slow this work process down, but it also might necessitate costly future maintenance work with its attendant loss of production and employee layoffs; diminish Furnco's reputation and ability to secure similar work in the future; and perhaps even create serious safety hazards, leading to explosions and the like. These considerations justified Furnco's refusal to engage in on-the-job training or to hire at the gate, a hiring process which would not provide an adequate method of matching qualified applications to job requirements and assuring that the applicants are sufficiently skilled and capable. * * *

II

A

We agree with the Court of Appeals that the proper approach was the analysis contained in *McDonnell Douglas*. We also think the Court of Appeals was justified in concluding that as a matter of law respondents made out a prima facie case of discrimination under *McDonnell Douglas*. * * *

B

We think the Court of Appeals went awry, however, in apparently equating a prima facie showing under *McDonnell Douglas* with an ultimate finding of fact as to discriminatory refusal to hire under Title VII; the two are quite different and that difference has a direct bearing on the proper resolution of this case. The Court of Appeals, as we read its opinion, thought Furnco's hiring procedures not only must be reasonably related to the achievement of some legitimate purpose, but also must be the method which allows the employer to consider the qualifications of the largest number of minority applicants. We think the imposition of that second requirement simply finds no support either in the nature of the prima facie case or the purpose of Title VII.

The central focus of the inquiry in a case such as this is always whether the employer is treating "some people less favorably than others because of their race, color, religion, sex, or national origin." Teamsters v. United States, 431 U.S. 324, 335 n. 15, 97 S.Ct. 1843, 1854 n. 15, 52 L.Ed.2d 396 (1977). The method suggested in *McDonnell Douglas* for pursuing this inquiry, however, was never intended to be rigid, mechanized, or ritualistic. Rather, it is merely a sensible, orderly way to evaluate the evidence in light of common experience as it bears on the critical question of discrimination. A prima facie case under *McDonnell Douglas* raises an inference of discrimination only because we presume these acts, if otherwise unexplained, are more likely than not based on the consideration of impermissible factors. And we are willing to presume this largely because we know from our experience that more often than not people do not act in a totally arbitrary manner, without any underlying reasons, especially in a business setting. Thus, when all legitimate reasons for rejecting an applicant have been eliminated as possible reasons for the employer's actions, it is more likely than not the employer, who we generally assume acts only with *some* reason, based his decision on an impermissible consideration such as race.

When the prima facie case is understood in the light of the opinion in *McDonnell Douglas*, it is apparent that the burden which shifts to the employer is merely that of proving that he based his employment decision on a legitimate consideration, and not an illegitimate one such as race. To prove that, he need not prove that he pursued the course which would both enable him to achieve his own business goal *and* allow him to consider the *most* employment applications. Title VII prohibits him from having as a goal a work force selected by any proscribed discriminatory practice, but it does not impose a duty to adopt a hiring procedure that maximizes hiring of minority employees. To dispel the adverse inference from a prima facie showing under *McDonnell Douglas*, the employer need only "articulate some legitimate, nondiscriminatory reason for the employee's rejection." 411 U.S. at 802, 93 S.Ct. at 1824.

The dangers of embarking on a course such as that charted by the Court of Appeals here, where the court requires businesses to adopt what it perceives to be the "best" hiring procedures, are nowhere more evident than in the record of this very case. Not only does the record not reveal that the court's suggested hiring procedure would work satisfactorily, but also there is nothing in the record to indicate that it would be any less "haphazard, arbitrary, and subjective" than Furnco's method, which the Court of Appeals criticized as deficient for exactly those reasons. Courts are generally less competent than employers to restructure business practices, and unless mandated to do so by Congress they should not attempt it.

This is not to say, of course, that proof of a justification which is reasonably related to the achievement of some legitimate goal necessarily ends the inquiry. The plaintiff must be given the opportunity to introduce evidence that the proffered justification is merely a pretext for discrimination. And as we noted in *McDonnell Douglas*, this evidence might take a variety of forms. But the Court of Appeals, although stating its disagreement with the District Court's conclusion that the employer's hiring practices were a "legitimate, nondiscriminatory reason" for refusing to hire respondents, premised its disagreement on a view which we have discussed and rejected above. It did not conclude that the practices were a pretext for discrimination, but only that different practices would have enabled the employer to at least consider, and perhaps to hire, more minority employees. But courts may not impose such a remedy on an employer at least until a violation of Title VII has been proved, and here none had been under the reasoning of either the District Court or the Court of Appeals.

C

The Court of Appeals was also critical of petitioner's effort to employ statistics in this type of case. While the matter is not free from doubt, it appears that the court thought that once a *McDonnell Douglas* prima facie showing had been made out, statistics of a racially balanced work force were totally irrelevant to the question of motive. That would undoubtedly be a correct view of the matter if the *McDonnell Douglas* prima facie showing were the equivalent of an ultimate finding by the trier of fact that the original rejection of the applicant was racially motivated: A racially balanced work force cannot immunize an employer from liability for specific acts of discrimination. * * * It is clear beyond cavil that the obligation imposed by Title VII is to provide an equal opportunity for each applicant regardless of race, without regard to whether members of the applicant's race are already proportionately represented in the work force.

A *McDonnell Douglas* prima facie showing is not the equivalent of a factual finding of discrimination, however. Rather, it is simply proof of actions taken by the employer from which we infer discriminatory animus because experience has proved that in the absence of any other explanation it is more likely than not that those actions were bottomed on impermissible considerations. When the prima facie showing is understood in this manner, the employer must be allowed some latitude to introduce evidence which bears on his motive. Proof that his work force was racially balanced or that it contained a disproportionately high percentage of minority employees is not wholly irrelevant on the issue of intent when that issue is yet to be decided. We cannot say that such proof would have absolutely no probative value in determining whether the otherwise unexplained rejection of the minority applicants was discriminatorily motivated. Thus, although we agree with the Court of Appeals that in this case such proof neither was nor could have been sufficient to *conclusively* demonstrate that Furnco's actions were not discriminatorily motivated, the District Court was entitled to *consider* the racial mix of the work force when trying to make the determination as to motivation. The Court of Appeals should likewise give similar consideration to the proffered statistical proof in any further proceedings in this case.

* * *

[The opinion of JUSTICE MARSHALL, with whom JUSTICE BRENNAN joined, concurring in part and dissenting in part, is omitted.]

Notes and Questions

1. Although it is now widely accepted that the disparate treatment theory of discrimination is based on a construction of § 703(a)(1), the Supreme Court has not clearly tied its prima facie case doctrine or order and allocation of the burdens of proof to specific statutory language in Title VII. The genesis of the prima facie case doctrine and the burden-allocation rules probably originated in the Eighth Circuit's decision in *McDonnell Douglas*. In its original decision, the Eighth Circuit stated,

> When a black man demonstrates that he possesses the qualifications to fill a job opening and that he was denied the job, we think he presents a prima facie case of racial discrimination and that the burden passes to the employer to demonstrate a substantial relationship between the reasons offered for denying employment and the requirements of the job. * * *

* * *

> * * * [R]emand is required because the district court did not use the correct standard in determining whether McDonnell's refusal to rehire Green was racially motivated. If McDonnell can demonstrate that Green's participation in the "stall-in" in some objective way reflects adversely upon job performance, McDonnell's refusal to rehire Green will be justified.

Green v. McDonnell Douglas Corp., 463 F.2d 337, 344 (8th Cir.1972), *remanded on other grounds*, 411 U.S. 792, 93 S.Ct. 1817, 36 L.Ed.2d 668 (1973). In a footnote, the Eighth Circuit observed that "the reasons advanced by McDonnell for refusing to hire Green may be found to be pretextual, particularly since McDonnell advanced the unsupported charge that Green had 'actively cooperated' in the 'lock-in.' " *Id.* at 344 n.6.

Nothing in the Eighth Circuit's opinion in *McDonnell Douglas* suggests that the court derived the prima facie case doctrine and the allocations of the burdens of proof from any specific provision or language in Title VII. Rather, the court purportedly found support for its decision in *Griggs v. Duke Power Co.*, 401 U.S. 424, 91 S.Ct. 849, 28 L.Ed.2d 158 (1971), the Supreme Court case that established the doctrinal foundations for the disparate impact theory. (*Griggs* is covered in Chapter 4.) The specific language from *Griggs* on which the Eighth Circuit relied states that "[i]f an employment practice which operates to exclude Negroes cannot be shown to be related to job performance, the practice is prohibited." Green v. McDonnell Douglas Corp., 463 F.2d at 343 (*quoting* Griggs v. Duke Power, 401 U.S. 424, 431, 91 S.Ct. 849, 28 L.Ed.2d 158 (1971)). Later, in denying McDonnell Douglas' petition for rehearing and rehearing en banc, the Eighth Circuit modified the panel's decision as follows:

> When a black man demonstrates that he possesses the qualifications to fill a job opening and he was denied the job which continues to remain open, we think he presents a prima facie case of racial discrimination. However, an applicant's past participation in unlawful conduct

directed at his prospective employer might indicate the applicant's lack of a responsible attitude toward performing work for that employer.

> * * * Green should be given the opportunity to show [the] reasons offered by the Company were pretextual.

Id. at 353. In *McDonnell Douglas*, the Supreme Court modified the Eighth's Circuit's formulation of the prima facie case by substituting "racial minority" for "black man." The Supreme Court's adoption of the phrase "racial minority" has created a conflict in the lower courts on how to apply the *McDonnell Douglas* framework in the affirmative actions cases. The affirmative action cases are covered in Section 5 of this chapter.

2.   The Supreme Court elaborated upon the rationale for the *McDonnell Douglas* analytical framework in *Teamsters v. United States*, 431 U.S. 324, 358 n.44, 97 S.Ct. 1843, 1866 n.44, 52 L.Ed.2d 396 (1977):

> The *McDonnell Douglas* case involved an individual complainant seeking to prove one instance of unlawful discrimination. An employer's isolated decision to reject an applicant who belongs to a racial minority does not show that the rejection was racially based. Although the *McDonnell Douglas* formula does not require direct evidence of discrimination, it does demand that the alleged discriminatee demonstrate at least that his rejection did not result from the two most common legitimate reasons on which an employer might rely to reject a job applicant: an absolute or relative lack of qualifications or the absence of a vacancy in the job sought. Elimination of these two reasons for the refusal to hire is sufficient, absent other explanation, to create an inference that the decision was a discriminatory one.

Is the Court suggesting that employers are rational economic actors?

3.   The *McDonnell Douglas* framework is grounded substantially in the fact that courts are willing to acknowledge that "[d]efendants of even minimal sophistication will neither admit discriminatory animus nor leave a paper trail demonstrating it; and because most employment decisions involve an element of discretion, alternative hypotheses (including that of simple mistake) will always be possible and often plausible." Riordan v. Kempiners, 831 F.2d 690, 697 (7th Cir.1987). Another court has observed that "[u]nless the employer is a latter-day George Washington, employment discrimination is as difficult to prove as who chopped down the cherry tree." Thornbrough v. Columbus & Greenville R.R., 760 F.2d 633, 638 (5th Cir.1985).

4.   In *Furnco*, the Supreme Court cautioned that the *McDonnell Douglas* framework of analysis "was never intended to be rigid, mechanized, or ritualistic," but is rather "merely a sensible, orderly way to evaluate the evidence in light of common experience as it bears on the critical question of discrimination." *Furnco*, 438 U.S. at 577, 98 S.Ct at 2949. Of course, membership in a protected class is a *sine qua non* for proving a prima facie case, but how a plaintiff can satisfy the other elements often raises difficult questions.

5.   Since *McDonnell Douglas*, the Supreme Court in the following cases—*Burdine*, *Hicks*, and *Reeves*—and lower courts have spent a substantial amount of judicial effort to flesh out the single-motive disparate treatment theory in cases in which plaintiffs rely on circumstantial evidence to

prove discriminatory animus. As you read the following materials, attempt to postulate the underlying reason or reasons why the courts have had so much difficulty in developing an appropriate analytical framework for proving or disproving discriminatory intent with circumstantial evidence. A useful starting point for thinking about the problem is the following observation by Professor Tristin Green:

> Traditional disparate treatment theory conceptualizes discrimination as individual, measurable, and static, looking to the state of mind of a particular decisionmaker at a discrete point in time. Disparate treatment doctrine has long been understood to require a showing of intentional discrimination, often defined in terms of conscious motivation to discriminate. This requirement, together with the social reality of blatant racism regularly expressed in the early days of Title VII, led to a conception of discrimination as an adverse decision made by a single actor who holds overtly racist or consciously stereotypical beliefs about members of the victim's group. Like a surgeon with a scalpel, we uncover discrimination through the traditional disparate treatment theory by dissecting the mind of the decisionmaker, searching for signs that discriminatory animus or conscious bias motivated the decisionmaker to take a particular action at a precisely defined moment in time.

Tristin K. Green, *Discrimination in Workplace Dynamics: Toward a Structural Account of Disparate Treatment*, 38 Harv.C.R.-C.L.L.Rev. 91, 112–13 (2003) (footnotes omitted). Consider also the following Note on critical race theory.

Note: Discrimination and Critical Race Theory

Writing at the beginning of the twentieth century, William E. B. DuBois, a distinguished African American scholar, asserted that the problem of the twentieth century is "the problem of the color line." W. E. B. DuBois, The Souls of Black Folk 1 (Candace Press 1996) (1903). The problem of how to eradicate racial discrimination or to remedy "the problem of the color line" remains one of the thorniest issues in American society, and it is even more so today as our society becomes increasingly multiracial and multiethnic. The civil rights movements of the 1950s and 1960s and the civil rights legislation of the 1960s, including the Civil Rights Act of 1964, which includes Title VII, brought about important social reforms. The legal system and traditional liberal discourse and scholarship on civil rights played important roles in producing the civil rights reforms of the 1960s and 1970s. *See generally* Robert Belton, *Title VII of the Civil Rights Act of 1964: A Decade of Private Enforcement and Judicial Development*, 20 St.Louis U.L.J. 225, 304–05 (1976). The dominant discourse on civil rights, however, also undermined the transformative potential of the civil rights movement. The introduction to a collection of essays on critical race theory notes:

> The law's incorporation of what several authors * * * call "formal equality" (prohibitions against explicit racial exclusion, like "white only" signs) marks a decidedly progressive movement in U.S. political and social history. However, the fact that civil rights advocates met with some success in the nation's courts and legislatures ought not obscure the role that the American legal order played in the deradicalization of

racial liberation movements. Along with the suppression of explicit white racism (the widely celebrated aim of civil rights reform), the dominant legal conception of racism as a discrete and identifiable act of "prejudice based on skin color" placed virtually the entire range of everyday social practices—social practices developed and maintained throughout the period of formal American apartheid—beyond the scope of critical examination or remediation.

* * * From its inception, mainstream legal thinking in the U.S. has been characterized by a curiously constricted understanding of race and power. Within this cramped conception of racial domination, the evil of racism exists when—and only when—one can point to specific, discrete acts of racial discrimination, which is in turn narrowly defined as decision-making based on the irrational and irrelevant attribute of race. Given this essentially negative, indeed, dismissive view of racial identity and its social meanings, it was not surprising that mainstream legal thought came to embrace the idea of "color-blindness" as the dominant moral compass of social enlightenment about race.

Introduction to Critical Race Theory: The Key Writing That Formed the Movement xiv-xv (Kimberlé Crenshaw et al., eds.1995).

The debate over the legality of affirmative action helped to slow the earlier pace of racial reform. "Affirmative action endorses the use of race as a socially significant category of perception and representation, but the deepest elements of mainstream civil rights ideology had come to identify such race-consciousness as racism itself." *Id.* at xv. Critical race theory emerged in the wake of concerns about the slow and cyclical nature of racial remediation over the course of many decades, the liberal and conservative discourse about the degree to which racial discrimination continued to exist in American life, and the fact that most of the scholarship on civil rights considered to be significant was written by a small group of white male professors of constitutional law at elite law schools. *See, e.g.*, Richard Delgado, *The Imperial Scholar: Reflections on a Review of Civil Rights Literature*, 132 U.Pa.L.Rev. 561 (1984).

Kimberlé Crenshaw, one of the leading critical race scholars, articulated some of the basic tenets of critical race theory:

While no determinative definition of the work is yet possible, one can generally say that [critical race scholarship] focuses on the relationship between law and racial subordination in American society. It shares with liberal race critique a view that law has provided an area for challenging white supremacy. Critical race theory goes beyond the liberal critiques, however, in that it exposes the facets of law and legal discourse that create racial categories and legitimate racial subordination.

Other broad themes common to critical race theory include the view that racism is endemic to, rather than a deviation from American norms. This developing literature reflects a common skepticism toward dominant claims of meritocracy, neutrality, objectivity, and color blindness. Critical race theory embraces a contextualized historical analysis of racial hierarchy as part of its challenge to the presumptive legitimacy of societal institutions.

Kimberlé Crenshaw, *A Black Feminist Critique of Antidiscrimination Law and Politics, in* Politics of Law: A Progressive Critique 195, 213–14 (David Kairys ed.1990).

Professor Richard Delgado, one of the most prolific critical race scholars, offers this view of critical race theory ("CRT"):

> CRT begins with a number of basic insights. One is that racism is normal, not aberrant in American society. Because racism is an ingrained feature of our landscape, it looks ordinary and natural to persons in the culture. Formal equality—rules and laws that insist on treating blacks and whites (for example) alike—can thus remedy only the most extreme and shocking forms of injustice, the ones that stand out. It can do little about the business-as-usual forms of racism that people of color confront every day and that account for much misery, alienation, and despair.

Introduction, Critical Race Theory: The Cutting Edge xvi (Richard Delgado & Jean Stefancic eds.2000).

In a book assessing more than a decade of critical race jurisprudence, the editors argue that

> CRT [rejects] at least three entrenched, mainstream beliefs about racial injustice. * * *The first * * * is that "blindness" to race will eliminate racism. * * * Critical race theorists have challenged this belief, asserting instead that self-conscious racial identities can be and have been the source of individual fulfillment, collective strength, and incisive policy-making.
>
> The second * * * is that racism is a matter of individuals, not systems. The goal of antidiscrimination law, as understood historically and currently by courts, was to search for perpetrators and victims: perpetrators could be identified through "bad" acts and intentions, while victims were (only) those who could meet shifting, and increasingly elusive, burdens of proof. Instead, critical race theorists have located racism and its everyday operation in the very structures within which the guilty and the innocent were to be identified * * *.
>
>   * * *
>
> The third * * * is that one can fight racism without paying attention to sexism, homophobia, economic exploitation, and other forms of oppression or injustice. From the beginning, CRT has been dedicated to antiracist social transformation through an antisubordination analysis that would be "intersectional" or "multidimensional," taking into account the complex layers of individual and group identity that help to construct social and legal positions.

Fancisco Valdes, Jerome McCristal Culp & Angela P. Harris, *Introduction: Battles Waged, Won, and Lost: Critical Race Theory at the Turn of the Millennium, in* Crossroads, Directions, and a New Critical Race Theory 1–2 (Fancisco Valdes et al. eds., 2002).

One of the major issues of concern to critical race scholars is the role of intent in antidiscrimination law. Critical race scholar, Professor Charles R. Lawrence, III, drew upon both psychoanalytic theory and cognitive psychology in his highly influential article, *The Id, the Ego, and Equal Protection: Reckoning with Unconscious Racism*, 39 Stan.L.Rev. 317 (1987), to expose some of the critical fault lines in the intent theory. Professor Lawrence argued that the Equal Protection Clause, embodying a theory that "seeks to remove racial prejudice from governmental decisionmaking[,] must acknowledge and incorporate * * * unconscious motivation." *Id.* at 327. He wrote:

> There are two explanations for the unconscious nature of our racially discriminatory beliefs and ideas. First, Freudian theory states that the human mind defends itself against discomfort or guilt by denying or refusing to recognize those ideas, wishes, and beliefs that conflict with what the individual has learned is good or right. While our historical experience has made racism an integral part of our culture, our society has more recently embraced an ideal that rejects racism as immoral. When an individual experiences conflict between racist ideas and the societal ethic that condemns those ideas, the mind excludes his racism from consciousness.

> Second, the theory of cognitive psychology states that culture— including for example, the media and an individual's parents, peers, and authority figures—transmits certain beliefs and preferences. Because these beliefs are so much a part of the culture, they are not experienced as explicit lessons. Instead, they seem part of the individual's rational ordering of her perceptions of the world. The individual is unaware, for example, that the ubiquitous presence of a cultural stereotype has influenced her perceptions that blacks are lazy or unintelligent. * * * These tacit understandings, because they have never been articulated, are less likely to be experienced at a conscious level.

Id. at 322–23. *See, e.g.,* Harris v. International Paper Co., 765 F.Supp. 1509, 1515–16 (D.Me.) (a racial harassment case relying, in part, on Professor Lawrence's analysis in ruling for the plaintiff), *vacated in part*, 765 F.Supp. 1529 (D.Me.1991), in Chapter 8, Section D.

Much of the critical race scholarship in the early days was written by black law professors teaching at historically white law schools and focused almost exclusively on the black/white paradigm in race discourse. Professor Derrick A. Bell, the first tenured African–American law professor at Harvard Law School, is considered to be at the center of the emergence of critical race jurisprudence. Over time, however, other historically subordinated groups began to question the limitation of critical race scholarship to the black/white paradigm and to develop a body of scholarship that was responsive to their own analyses of traditional liberal civil rights discourse. For example, Latina/o Critical Theory (LatCrit) endeavors to address the ways in which Latinas/os have been racialized in the United States. *See, e.g.*, Symposium, *LatCrit Theory: Naming and Launching a New Discourse of Critical Legal Scholarship*, 2 Harv. Latino L.Rev. 177 (1997). Some of the central concerns of LatCrits are issues regarding immigration, nativism, language rights, and transnational identities. Critical race feminist scholars combine feminism with critical race theory to challenge liberal theories of racism and civil rights by focusing on the persistence and pervasiveness of racial discrimination. *See, e.g.*, Critical Race Feminism (Adrien Katherine Wing ed.1997). Critical race feminist scholars set out to expose racism in judicial rulings by arguing that women of color may suffer intersectional or multidimensional discrimination that is different from harms inflicted on white women and black men. Asian American scholars have begun to explore issues of race and ethnicity, such as the myth of the "model minority," from a different perspective. *See, e.g.*, Robert Chang, *Toward an Asian American Legal Scholarship: Critical Race Theory, Post–Structuralism, and Narrative Space*, 81 Cal.L.Rev. 1243 (1993). Critical race theory has generated another new category of legal scholarship known as "critical white studies" which focuses on white supremacy and white privilege as a social organizing principle. *See, e.g.*, Critical White Studies: Looking Behind the Mirror (Richard Delgado & Jean Stefancic eds. 1997).

TEXAS DEPARTMENT OF COMMUNITY AFFAIRS v. BURDINE

Supreme Court of the United States, 1981.
450 U.S. 248, 101 S.Ct. 1089, 67 L.Ed.2d 207.

JUSTICE POWELL delivered the opinion of the Court.

This case requires us to address again the nature of the evidentiary burden placed upon the defendant in an employment discrimination suit brought under Title VII of the Civil Rights Act of 1964. The narrow question presented is whether, after the plaintiff has proved a prima facie case of discriminatory treatment, the burden shifts to the defendant to persuade the court by a preponderance of the evidence that legitimate, nondiscriminatory reasons for the challenged employment action existed.

I

Petitioner, the Texas Department of Community Affairs (TDCA), hired respondent, a female, in January 1972, for the position of accounting clerk in the Public Service Careers Division (PSC). PSC provided training and employment opportunities in the public sector for unskilled workers. * * *

* * *

Respondent filed this suit in the United States District Court for the Western District of Texas. She alleged that the failure to promote and the subsequent decision to terminate her had been predicated on gender discrimination in violation of Title VII. After a bench trial, the District Court held that neither decision was based on gender discrimination. The court relied on the testimony of Fuller [the executive director of the department] that the employment decisions necessitated by the commands of the Department of Labor were based on consultation among trusted advisers and a nondiscriminatory evaluation of the relative qualifications of the individuals involved. He testified that the three individuals terminated did not work well together, and that TDCA thought that eliminating this problem would improve PSC's efficiency. The court accepted this explanation as rational and, in effect, found no evidence that the decisions not to promote and to terminate respondent were prompted by gender discrimination.

The Court of Appeals for the Fifth Circuit reversed in part. The court held that the District Court's "implicit evidentiary finding" that the male hired as Project Director was better qualified for that position than respondent was not clearly erroneous. Accordingly, the court affirmed the District Court's finding that respondent was not discriminated against when she was not promoted. The Court of Appeals, however, reversed the District Court's finding that Fuller's testimony sufficiently had rebutted respondent's prima facie case of gender discrimination in the decision to terminate her employment at PSC. The court reaffirmed its previously announced views that the defendant in a Title VII case bears the burden of proving by a preponderance of the evidence the existence of legitimate nondiscriminatory reasons for the employment action and that the defendant also must prove by objective evidence that those hired or promoted were better qualified than the plaintiff. The court found that Fuller's testimony did not carry either of these evidentiary burdens. It, therefore, reversed the judgment of the District Court and remanded the case for computation of backpay. Because the decision of the Court of Appeals as to the burden of proof borne by the defendant conflicts with interpretations of our precedents adopted by other Courts of Appeals, we granted certiorari. We now vacate the Fifth Circuit's decision and remand for application of the correct standard.

II

In *McDonnell Douglas Corp. v. Green*, 411 U.S. 792, 93 S.Ct. 1817, 36 L.Ed.2d 668 (1973), we set forth the basic allocation of burdens and order of presentation of proof in a Title VII case alleging discriminatory treatment. First, the plaintiff has the burden of proving by the preponderance of the evidence a prima facie case of discrimination. Second, if the plaintiff succeeds in proving the prima facie case, the burden shifts to the defendant "to articulate some legitimate, nondiscriminatory reason for the employee's rejection." Third, should the defendant carry this burden, the plaintiff must then have an opportunity to prove by a preponderance of the evidence that the legitimate reasons offered by the defendant were not its true reasons, but were a pretext for discrimination.

The nature of the burden that shifts to the defendant should be understood in light of the plaintiff's ultimate and intermediate burdens. The ultimate burden of persuading the trier of fact that the defendant intentionally discriminated against the plaintiff remains at all times with the plaintiff. *See generally* 9 J. Wigmore, Evidence § 2489 (3d ed. 1940) (the burden of persuasion "never shifts"). The *McDonnell Douglas* division of intermediate evidentiary burdens serves to bring the litigants and the court expeditiously and fairly to this ultimate question.

The burden of establishing a prima facie case of disparate treatment is not onerous. The plaintiff must prove by a preponderance of the evidence that she applied for an available position for which she was qualified, but was rejected under circumstances which give rise to an inference of unlawful discrimination. [The Court acknowledged that the parties did not contest that respondent had proved a prima facie case.] The prima facie case serves an important function in the litigation: it eliminates the most common nondiscriminatory reasons for the plaintiff's rejection. * * * Establishment of the prima facie case in effect creates a presumption that the employer unlawfully discriminated against the employee. If the trier of fact believes the plaintiff's evidence, and if the employer is silent in the face of the presumption, the court must enter judgment for the plaintiff because no issue of fact remains in the case.[7]

The burden that shifts to the defendant, therefore, is to rebut the presumption of discrimination by producing evidence that the plaintiff was rejected, or someone else was preferred, for a legitimate, nondiscriminatory reason. The defendant need not persuade the court that it was actually motivated by the proffered reasons. It is sufficient if the defendant's evidence raises a genuine issue of fact as to whether it discriminated against the plaintiff.[8] To accomplish this, the defendant must clearly set forth, through the introduction of admissible evidence, the reasons for the plaintiff's rejection.[9] The explanation provided must be legally sufficient to justify a judgment for the defendant. If the defendant carries this burden of production, the presumption raised by the prima facie case is rebutted,[10] and the factual inquiry proceeds to a new level of specificity. Placing this burden of production on the defendant thus

7. The phrase "prima facie case" not only may denote the establishment of a legally mandatory, rebuttable presumption, but also may be used by courts to describe the plaintiff's burden of producing enough evidence to permit the trier of fact to infer the fact at issue. 9 J. Wigmore, Evidence § 2494 (3d ed.1940). *McDonnell Douglas* should have made it apparent that in the Title VII context we use "prima facie case" in the former sense.

8. This evidentiary relationship between the presumption created by a prima facie case and the consequential burden of production placed on the defendant is a traditional feature of the common law. "The word 'presumption' properly used refers only to a device for allocating the production burden." F. James & G. Hazard, Civil Procedure § 7.9, at 255 (2d ed.1977) (footnote omitted). *See* Fed. Rule Evid. 301. Usually, assessing the burden of production helps the judge determine whether the litigants have created an issue of fact to be decided by the jury. In a Title VII case, the allocation of burdens and the creation of a presumption by the establishment of a prima facie case is intended progressively to sharpen the inquiry into the elusive factual question of intentional discrimination.

9. An articulation not admitted into evidence will not suffice. Thus, the defendant cannot meet its burden merely through an answer to the complaint or by argument of counsel.

10. In saying that the presumption drops from the case, we do not imply that the trier of fact no longer may consider evidence previously introduced by the plaintiff to establish a prima facie case. A satisfactory explanation by the defendant destroys the legally mandatory inference of discrimination arising from the plaintiff's initial evidence. Nonetheless, this evidence and inferences properly drawn therefrom may be considered by the trier of fact on the issue of whether the defendant's explanation is pretextual. Indeed, there may be some cases where the plaintiff's initial evidence, combined with effective cross-examination of the defendant, will suffice to discredit the defendant's explanation.

serves simultaneously to meet the plaintiff's prima facie case by presenting a legitimate reason for the action and to frame the factual issue with sufficient clarity so that the plaintiff will have a full and fair opportunity to demonstrate pretext. The sufficiency of the defendant's evidence should be evaluated by the extent to which it fulfills these functions.

The plaintiff retains the burden of persuasion. She now must have the opportunity to demonstrate that the proffered reason was not the true reason for the employment decision. This burden now merges with the ultimate burden of persuading the court that she has been the victim of intentional discrimination. She may succeed in this either directly by persuading the court that a discriminatory reason more likely motivated the employer or indirectly by showing that the employer's proffered explanation is unworthy of credence.

III

In reversing the judgment of the District Court that the discharge of respondent from PSC was unrelated to her sex, the Court of Appeals adhered to two rules it had developed to elaborate the defendant's burden of proof. First, the defendant must prove by a preponderance of the evidence that legitimate, nondiscriminatory reasons for the discharge existed. Second, to satisfy this burden, the defendant "must prove that those he hired * * * were somehow better qualified than was plaintiff; in other words, comparative evidence is needed."

A

The Court of Appeals has misconstrued the nature of the burden that *McDonnell Douglas* and its progeny place on the defendant. We stated in [*Board of Trustees of Keene State College v. Sweeney*, 439 U.S. 24, 25 n. 2, 99 S.Ct. 295, 296 n. 2, 58 L.Ed.2d 216 (1978)], that "the employer's burden is satisfied if he simply 'explains what he has done' or 'produc[es] evidence of legitimate nondiscriminatory reasons.' "It is plain that the Court of Appeals required much more: it placed on the defendant the burden of persuading the court that it had convincing, objective reasons for preferring the chosen applicant above the plaintiff.

The Court of Appeals distinguished *Sweeney* on the ground that the case held only that the defendant did not have the burden of proving the absence of discriminatory intent. But this distinction slights the rationale of *Sweeney* and of our other cases. We have stated consistently that the employee's prima facie case of discrimination will be rebutted if the employer articulates lawful reasons for the action; that is, to satisfy this intermediate burden, the employer need only produce admissible evidence which would allow the trier of fact rationally to conclude that the employment decision had not been motivated by discriminatory animus. The Court of Appeals would require the defendant to introduce evidence which, in the absence of any evidence of pretext, would *persuade* the trier of fact that the employment action was lawful. This exceeds what properly can be demanded to satisfy a burden of production.

The court placed the burden of persuasion on the defendant apparently because it feared that "[i]f an employer need only *articulate*—not prove—a legitimate, nondiscriminatory reason for his action, he may compose fictitious, but legitimate, reasons for his actions." Turner v. Texas Instruments, Inc., 555 F.2d 1251, 1255 (5th Cir.1977). We do not believe, however, that limiting the defendant's evidentiary obligation to a burden of production will unduly hinder the plaintiff. First, as noted above, the defendant's explanation of its legitimate reasons must be clear and reasonably specific. This obligation arises both from the necessity of rebutting the inference of discrimination arising from the prima facie case and from the requirement that the plaintiff be afforded "a full and fair opportunity" to demonstrate pretext. Second, although the defendant does not bear a formal burden of persuasion, the defendant nevertheless retains an incentive to persuade the trier of fact that the employment decision was lawful. Thus, the defendant normally will attempt to prove the factual basis for its explanation. Third, the liberal discovery rules applicable to any civil suit in federal court are supplemented in a Title VII suit by the plaintiff's access to the Equal Employment Opportunity Commission's investigatory files concerning her complaint. Given these factors, we are unpersuaded that the plaintiff will find it particularly difficult to prove that a proffered explanation lacking a factual basis is a pretext. We remain confident that the *McDonnell Douglas* framework permits the plaintiff meriting relief to demonstrate intentional discrimination.

B

The Court of Appeals also erred in requiring the defendant to prove by objective evidence that the person hired or promoted was more qualified than the plaintiff. *McDonnell Douglas* teaches that it is the plaintiff's task to demonstrate that similarly situated employees were not treated equally. The Court of Appeals' rule would require the employer to show that the plaintiff's objective qualifications were inferior to those of the person selected. If it cannot, a court would, in effect, conclude that it has discriminated.

The court's procedural rule harbors a substantive error. Title VII prohibits all discrimination in employment based upon race, sex, and national origin. "The broad, overriding interest, shared by employer, employee, and consumer, is efficient and trustworthy workmanship assured through fair and * * * neutral employment and personnel decisions." *McDonnell Douglas*, 411 U.S. at 801, 93 S.Ct. at 1823. Title VII, however, does not demand that an employer give preferential treatment to minorities or women. 42 U.S.C. § 2000e–2(j). *See* Steelworkers v. Weber, 443 U.S. 193, 205–06, 99 S.Ct. 2721, 2728–29, 61 L.Ed.2d 480 (1979). The statute was not intended to "diminish traditional management prerogatives." *Id*. at 207, 99 S.Ct. at 2729. It does not require the employer to restructure his employment practices to maximize the number of minorities and women hired. Furnco Constr. Corp. v.

Waters, 438 U.S. 567, 577–78, 98 S.Ct. 2943, 2949–50, 57 L.Ed.2d 957 (1978).

The views of the Court of Appeals can be read, we think, as requiring the employer to hire the minority or female applicant whenever that person's objective qualifications were equal to those of a white male applicant. But Title VII does not obligate an employer to accord this preference. Rather, the employer has discretion to choose among equally qualified candidates, provided the decision is not based upon unlawful criteria. The fact that a court may think that the employer misjudged the qualifications of the applicants does not in itself expose him to Title VII liability, although this may be probative of whether the employer's reasons are pretexts for discrimination.

IV

In summary, the Court of Appeals erred by requiring the defendant to prove by a preponderance of the evidence the existence of nondiscriminatory reasons for terminating the respondent and that the person retained in her stead had superior objective qualifications for the position. When the plaintiff has proved a prima facie case of discrimination, the defendant bears only the burden of explaining clearly the nondiscriminatory reasons for its actions. * * *

Notes and Questions

1. *Inferences and Presumptions*: Traditionally the prima facie case doctrine refers to the obligation of a plaintiff to shoulder the burden of the production of evidence by introducing enough evidence to permit the factfinder to *infer* the fact at issue. *See* Black's Law Dictionary 1189–90 (6th ed.1991). In statutory employment discrimination cases, however, *Burdine* holds that evidence sufficient to establish a prima facie case creates a legally mandatory, rebuttable *presumption*. 450 U.S. at 254 n.7, 101 S.Ct. at 1094 n.7. *Burdine* uses both "inference" and "presumption" to characterize the prima facie case, but there is a difference between the two terms. A *presumption* is a rule of law that *requires* the factfinder to assume, at least temporarily, the existence of certain facts once a party has proved other—usually logically related—facts. An *inference* is a deduction the factfinder *may* make from established facts on the basis of reason and experience. *See generally* Robert Belton, *Burdens of Pleading and Proof in Discrimination Cases: Toward a Theory of Procedural Justice*, 34 Vand.L.Rev. 1205 (1981).

2. The general rule on the role of a presumption in civil actions is set out in Rule 301 of the Federal Rules of Evidence which provides:

> In all civil actions and proceedings not otherwise provided for by Act of Congress or by these rules, a presumption imposes on the party against whom it is directed the burden of going forward with evidence to rebut or meet the presumption, but does not shift to such party the burden of proof in the sense of the risk of nonpersuasion, which remains throughout the trial upon the party on whom it was originally cast.

In discussing the relationship between a presumption and inference in employment discrimination law, the Eleventh Circuit stated that

> [the "legal presumption of discrimination"] ensures that a plaintiff who cannot establish that the employer harbored a discriminatory animus towards her may still survive a motion for judgment as a matter of law at the close of her case and thus force the employer to articulate its motives for the challenged employment decision so that the plaintiff has an opportunity to raise an inference of intentional discrimination by circumstantial evidence. The presumption, therefore, accounts for the disparity in access to information between employee and employer regarding the employer's true motives for making the challenged employment decision.

Walker v. Mortham, 158 F.3d 1177, 1192 (11th Cir.1998), *cert. denied*, 528 U.S. 809, 120 S.Ct. 39, 145 L.Ed.2d 36 (1999).

3. *Elements of a Prima Facie Case*: Even though the Supreme Court stated in *Burdine* that "the burden of establishing a prima facie case of disparate treatment is not onerous," hard questions are frequently raised about whether the plaintiff has established a prima facie case. Proving membership in a protected class is probably the easiest element to establish.

a. *The application element*: As a general rule, the failure of a plaintiff to apply formally for a job is fatal to establishing a prima facie case of a discriminatory refusal to hire. *See, e.g.*, Lockridge v. Board of Trustees of Univ. of Ark., 315 F.3d 1005 (8th Cir.2003) (en banc). Nevertheless, the failure to apply for a position may be excused. The dissenting opinion in *Lockridge* set out some of the reasons the failure to apply may be excused. These reasons include instances "where the employer has no formal application process, where the employee is unaware of the opportunity, or where the employer's employment promotions policy is 'informal and subjective,' and 'vague or secretive,' " or where the plaintiff has "made every reasonable attempt to convey his interest in the job to the employer," or "the employer has failed to establish a clear personnel procedure for promotions." *Id.* at 1013 (Heaney, J., dissenting)(citations omitted).

i. *The futile gesture doctrine*: The futile gesture doctrine may also excuse a plaintiff's failure to apply. For example, if an employer has a reputation for refusing to employ members of a group protected by Title VII, the failure to apply may be excused. The futile gesture doctrine is grounded in *Teamsters v. United States*, 431 U.S. 324, 365–66, 97 S.Ct. 1843, 1870, 52 L.Ed.2d 396 (1977), where the Court said:

> If an employer should announce his policy of discrimination by a sign reading "Whites Only" on the hiring-office door, his victims would not be limited to the few who ignored the sign and subjected themselves to personal rebuffs. The same message can be communicated to potential applicants more subtly but just as clearly by an employer's actual practices by his consistent discriminatory treatment of actual applicants, by the manner in which he publicizes vacancies, his recruitment techniques, his responses to casual or tentative inquiries, and even by the racial or ethnic composition of that part of his work force from which he has discriminatorily excluded members of [protected] groups. When a person's desire for a job is not translated into a formal application solely

because of his unwillingness to engage in a futile gesture he is as much of a victim of discrimination as is he who goes through the motion of submitting an application.

The Supreme Court also acknowledged the vitality of the futile gesture doctrine in *Dothard v. Rawlinson*, 433 U.S. 321, 97 S.Ct. 2720, 53 L.Ed.2d 786 (1977). *Dothard* involved, *inter alia*, a challenge to a state policy that, on its face, limited the employment opportunities of women in male maximum security prisons. *Dothard* is reproduced in Chapter 4.

ii. Baylor College of Medicine, a medical school in Texas, entered into a contract with the King Faisal Hospital, which is located in Riyadh, Saudia Arabia, and is owned by the Saudi government. Under the contract, Baylor College agreed to send rotating teams of doctors on its faculty to perform surgeries at the hospital. The agreement required doctors who participated in the program to secure entry and exit visas from the Saudi government and to remain in Saudi Arabia for at least three consecutive months. Doctors who participated in the program were paid handsomely: annualized salaries at twice the level of compensation they received from Baylor, plus generous travel and living expenses while in Saudi Arabia. None of the Jewish doctors on the faculty of Baylor were permitted to participate in the program because they would not be allowed entry visas into Saudi Arabia. Could the Jewish doctors on the faculty who want to bring a Title VII claim against Baylor succeed in establishing the application element of a prima facie case if they failed to apply for the program? *See* Abrams v. Baylor College of Med., 581 F.Supp. 1570 (S.D.Tex.1984), *aff'd in part, rev'd in part*, 805 F.2d 528 (5th Cir.1986). On the issue whether Baylor College might be able to defend its practice by raising the bona fide occupational qualification statutory defense found in Title VII, § 703(e), 42 U.S.C. § 2000e–2(e), see Chapter 10, Section D.

b. *The qualification element*: Very often the most critical factual issue in an employment discrimination case is whether the plaintiff is qualified for the job at issue. The law is not entirely clear on the standard a plaintiff must satisfy to establish the qualification element at the prima face stage. In *Teamsters v. United States*, 431 U.S. 324, 358 n.44, 97 S.Ct. 1843, 1866 n.44, 52 L.Ed.2d 396 (1977), the Supreme Court stated that the plaintiff must prove that her rejection for a particular job was not the result of "an absolute or relative lack of qualifications." A plaintiff is *absolutely qualified* for a job when she possesses the minimum qualifications for the position; she is *relatively qualified* when her qualifications compare favorably with those of other persons who were considered for the position. *See* Alisa D. Shudofsky, Note, *Relative Qualifications and the Prima Facie Case in Title VII Litigation*, 82 Colum.L.Rev. 553 (1982).

Relying on the Supreme Court's decisions in *Burdine* and *Patterson v. McLean Credit Union*, 491 U.S. 164, 109 S.Ct. 2363, 105 L.Ed.2d 132 (1989), most courts have adopted the rule that a plaintiff satisfies the qualification element of the prima facie case by proving that she possessed the qualifications established by the employer, usually in a written job description. *See, e.g.*, Walker v. Mortham, 158 F.3d 1177 (11th Cir.1998) (clarifying the law on the qualification element in the prima facie stage in light of *Burdine* and *Patterson*), *cert. denied*, 528 U.S. 809, 120 S.Ct. 39, 145 L.Ed.2d 36 (1999). In

Walker v. Mortham the court held that the trial court erred in "imposing as part of the prima facie case a requirement that [a] plaintiff establish that the successful applicant for his or her coveted position was less than or equally qualified to hold the position." *Id.* at 1193. A plaintiff's relative qualifications is most relevant to pretext analysis if an employer satisfies its burden of production of evidence by simply stating that the person selected had qualifications superior to the plaintiff's. At this point, the plaintiff has the burden of demonstrating that the employer's claim that it awarded the job to a better qualified person is pretextual by showing either that the plaintiff was better qualified than the person chosen for the position or that the employer's claim that the individual selected was better qualified than the plaintiff is not worthy of credence. *See* Manning v. Chevron Chem. Co., 332 F.3d 874, 881 (5th Cir. 2003); Hooks v. Diamond Crystal Specialty Foods, Inc., 997 F.2d 793, 798 (10th Cir.1993); Mitchell v. Baldrige, 759 F.2d 80, 85 (D.C.Cir.1985).

The Fourth Circuit, in *King v. Rumsfeld*, 328 F.3d 145 (4th Cir.2003), has substantially limited the role of the testimony of a co-worker as a fact witness on the qualifications of a plaintiff at the prima facie stage:

> King's own testimony, of course, cannot establish a genuine issue as to whether King was meeting appellee's expectations. * * * Nor can the fact testimony of King's co-workers that his lesson plans were comparable to theirs establish this genuine issue. Proof that King's performance was comparable to his co-workers' is *not* proof that King's performance met appellee's legitimate job performance expectations. It is *only* proof that his work looked like that of his co-workers, a fact that, without more, does not bear on the critical inquiry. For this reason we have long rejected the relevance of such testimony and held it to be insufficient to establish the third required element of a prima facie discrimination case.

> The irrelevance of King's co-workers *as fact witnesses* does not, as King contends, foreclose employees like him from ever proving a prima facie case of race and sex discrimination. King argues that our rule only allows employees to satisfy the prima facie standard in the unique, and employer-controlled, circumstance where the employer either (1) concedes that the employee was performing satisfactorily at the time of discharge, or (2) has previously given the employee positive performance reviews that establish this third element. But such is not the case. For King to establish that his work met appellee's legitimate job performance expectations he had only to offer qualified expert opinion testimony as to (1) appellee's legitimate job performance expectations and (2) analysis and evaluation of King's performance in light of those expectations.

> It is not inconceivable that a plaintiff's co-workers could qualify as expert witnesses to testify as to their employer's legitimate job performance expectations and as to their own analysis and evaluation of the plaintiff's performance in light of those expectations. But King never proffered his co-workers in this capacity. And, even had the co-workers been so proffered, their testimony never touched on either of these two critical inquiries. * * *

Id. at 149–50. Before he was discharged, the plaintiff in *King*, a black male, had been hired as a teacher, subject to a two year probationary period. Has the court in *King* limited its rule on the need for "qualified expert opinion testimony" to professional jobs? As pointed out by the dissent in *King*, Rule 701 of the Federal Rules of Evidence provides that a lay witness in federal court may offer an opinion on the basis of relevant historical or narrative facts that the witness has perceived. *See id.* at 157 (Gregory, J., concurring in part, dissenting, in part).

c. *Must the employment opportunity be awarded to a person outside of plaintiff's protected class?*: The fourth prong of the *McDonnell Douglas* prima facie case provides that in a failure to hire case, the plaintiff needs to put on evidence that "after [plaintiff's] rejection, the position remained open and the employer continued to seek applicants from persons of complainant's qualifications." To satisfy this prong, is it necessary for the plaintiff to present evidence that the individual the employer selected for the vacancy is not in the same protected group as the plaintiff? And if the replacement is a member of the same group, may the employer rely upon the *same-group* defense? *See, e.g.*, Carson v. Bethlehem Steel Corp., 82 F.3d 157 (7th Cir.1996) (per curiam) (white replaced by another white); Barnes v. Humana Health Plans, Inc., 1997 WL 779094 (N.D.Ill.1997) (black replaced by another black).

Prior to the Supreme Court's decision in *O'Connor v. Consolidated Coin Caterers Corp.*, 517 U.S. 308, 116 S.Ct. 1307, 134 L.Ed.2d 433 (1996) the lower courts were divided on these issues. Some courts held that a plaintiff is not required to prove that the vacancy was awarded to an individual who is not in the same protected class as the plaintiff. *See, e.g.*, Diaz v. AT & T, 752 F.2d 1356 (9th Cir.1985); DeLesstine v. Fort Wayne State Hosp. & Training Ctr., 682 F.2d 130 (7th Cir.), *cert. denied sub nom.* Ackerman v. DeLesstine, 459 U.S. 1017, 103 S.Ct. 378, 74 L.Ed.2d 511 (1982). In *Diaz*, the court held that failing to find a prima facie case in this situation would amount to construing Title VII as protecting only groups and not individuals. *Diaz* primarily relied on *Connecticut v. Teal*, 457 U.S. 440, 102 S.Ct. 2525, 73 L.Ed.2d 130 (1982), which held that, in enacting Title VII, Congress did not give employers the "license to discriminate" against some individuals in a protected class merely because other individuals in the same protected class are treated favorably. *Id.* at 454, 102 S.Ct. at 2534. *Teal* is reproduced in Chapter 4. Other courts suggested a *per se* rule that awarding a job to an applicant who is a member of the same protected class as the plaintiff precludes a finding of an inference of intentional discrimination. *See, e.g.*, Hawkins v. Ceco Corp., 883 F.2d 977, 984 (11th Cir.1989), *cert. denied*, 495 U.S. 935, 110 S.Ct. 2180, 109 L.Ed.2d 508 (1990); Jefferies v. Harris County Community Action Ass'n, 615 F.2d 1025, 1030 (5th Cir.1980), *appeal after remand*, 693 F.2d 589 (5th Cir.1982).

In *Consolidated Coin*, an age discrimination case, the employer fired the plaintiff, age 56, and replaced him with a 40–year-old worker. Because the ADEA protects applicants and employees 40 years of age and older, both the plaintiff and his replacement were members of the same protected class. (The ADEA is covered in Chapter 12.) In a unanimous decision, the Court in *Consolidated Coin* held "[t]he fact that one person in the protected class has lost out to another person in the protected class is * * * irrelevant, so long as he has lost *because of* [his status as a protected class member]," and evidence that a "plaintiff was replaced by someone outside the protected class is not a proper element of the *McDonnell Douglas* prima facie case." 517 U.S. at 312, 116 S.Ct. at 1310. Under *Consolidated Coin* a plaintiff in an ADEA case can establish a prima face case under the *McDonnell Douglas* framework even if both the plaintiff and his replacement are protected under the ADEA as long as the replacement is substantially younger than the plaintiff. The Court reaffirmed the *Consolidated Coin* rule in *Olmstead v. L.C.* ex rel. *Zimring*, 527 U.S. 581, 598 n.10, 119 S.Ct. 2176, 2186 n.10, 144 L.Ed.2d 540 (1999), over a dissent by Justice Thomas, who argued that the "traditional" concept of discrimination does not encompass "disparate treatment among members of the same protected class." *Id.* at 616, 119 S.Ct. at 2194 (Thomas, J., dissenting). Do you think there is merit to Justice Thomas's view?

Most of the courts of appeals have applied the *Consolidated Coin* rule to employment discrimination cases other than ADEA cases to hold that an employer is not entitled to judgment as a matter of law by proof that the plaintiff's replacement and the plaintiff are in the same protected class. *See* Stella v. Mineta, 284 F.3d 135, 145–46 (D.C.Cir.2002) (collecting cases); Pivirotto v. Innovative Sys. Inc., 191 F.3d 344, 355 (3d Cir.1999) (applying the *Consolidated Coin* rule to race and sex cases). After *Consolidated Coin* the Fourth Circuit has continued to adhere to its rule that ordinarily a plaintiff must show that the at-issue position was filled by someone who is not a member of the plaintiff's class. But the Fourth Circuit has recognized that exceptions to this general rule include (1) age discrimination cases where a plaintiff is replaced by a younger person who is also protected by the ADEA; (2) cases where there has been a significant period of time between the adverse employment action and the decision to hire a replacement who is also within the protected class; and (3) cases where the hiring of another person within the protected class was calculated to disguise unlawful discrimination against the plaintiff. Brown v. McLean, 159 F.3d 898, 905–06 (4th Cir.1998), *cert. denied sub nom.* Brown v. Mayor & City Council of Baltimore, 526 U.S. 1099, 119 S.Ct. 1577, 143 L.Ed.2d 672 (1999).

In *Perry v. Woodward*, 199 F.3d 1126, 1137 (10th Cir.1999), the Tenth Circuit observed that an inflexible rule

> would preclude suits against employers who replace a terminated employee with an individual who shares her protected attribute only in an attempt to avert a lawsuit. It would preclude suits by [sic] employers who hire and fire minority employees in an attempt to prevent them from vesting in employment benefits or developing a track record to qualify for promotion. It would also preclude a suit against an employer who terminates a woman it negatively perceives as a "feminist" and replaces her with a woman who is willing to be subordinate to her male co-workers or replaces an African–American with an African–American who is perceived to "know his place." * * * Such a result is unacceptable.

Id. at 1137. Should the fact that the employer hired or promoted a person in the same protected class as the plaintiff be totally irrelevant to an ultimate finding of intentional discrimination, particularly under pretext analysis? *See* Edwards v. Wallace Community College, 49 F.3d 1517 (11th Cir.1995).

d. *Post-rejection action of employer*: Assume that the plaintiff was qualified for a particular job, applied for the vacant position, but was rejected. Afterwards, the employer decided either to leave the position vacant or to contract out the work. Should the employer's decision preclude the establishment of a prima facie case? *See* Mitchell v. Worldwide Underwriters Ins. Co., 967 F.2d 565 (11th Cir.1992) (yes, unless plaintiff's evidence shows that the employer, in failing to consider the plaintiff for another open position in the company, intended to discriminate against the plaintiff); *but see* Williams v. 55th St. Theatre Found., 1994 WL 501760, *5 (S.D.N.Y.1994) (no, because "a plaintiff is not required to show that he was actually 'replaced' by a younger employee in order to raise an inference of age discrimination"). Which do you believe is the better view?

4. *McDonnell Douglas* was a refusal to hire case, but the Supreme Court admonished lower courts that "[t]he facts necessarily will vary in Title VII cases, and the specification * * * of the prima facie proof [in hiring cases] is not necessarily applicable in every respect to differing factual situations." 411 U.S. at 802 n.13, 93 S.Ct. at 1824 n.13. The following examples illustrate how the lower courts are attempting to adapt the *McDonnell Douglas* framework to other kinds of employment discrimination claims:

a. *Promotions*: Plaintiff was qualified for the promotion, was rejected despite being qualified, and another applicant with equal or lesser qualifications was promoted. *See* Sprague v. Thorn Americas, Inc., 129 F.3d 1355 (10th Cir.1997). A plaintiff in a failure to promote case must ordinarily prove that she applied for a specific job. However, she may not have to present evidence that she applied for a promotion where she has notified the employer that she is interested in being promoted to a particular *class of jobs* but is unaware of specific promotion opportunities because the employer does not post vacancies. *See* Mauro v. Southern New Eng. Telecomm., Inc., 208 F.3d 384 (2d Cir.2000). In *Paldano v. Althin Medical, Inc.*, 974 F.Supp. 1441, 1446 (S.D.Fla.1996), the court held that, in discriminatory promotion cases, "where an employer does not use a notice procedure for posting available promotions, an employer has a duty to consider all who might be interested in a promotion" because "[o]therwise the lack of a notice procedure could result in vacancy information being available only to one segment of a work force and place no check on individual biases."

b. *Demotions*: At the time of the plaintiff's demotion, she was performing her job at a level that met the employer's legitimate expectations; after the demotion, the employer replaced the plaintiff with someone of comparable or lesser qualifications. *See* Tuck v. Henkel Corp., 973 F.2d 371 (4th Cir.1992), *cert. denied*, 507 U.S. 918, 113 S.Ct. 1276, 122 L.Ed.2d 671 (1993).

c. *Nondisciplinary or wrongful discharges*: Plaintiff was doing her job well enough to establish that she was performing adequately; after discharging her, the employer assigned someone else to do the same work. *See, e.g.,* Reeves v. Sanderson Plumbing Prods. Inc., 530 U.S. 133, 142–43, 120 S.Ct. 2097, 2105–06, 147 L.Ed.2d 105 (2000); Perry v. Woodward, 199 F.3d 1126,

1135 (10th Cir.1999), *cert. denied*, 529 U.S. 1110, 120 S.Ct. 1964, 146 L.Ed.2d 796 (2000). *Reeves* is reproduced in this chapter.

d. *Disciplinary discharges and the test for determining "comparable seriousness"*: In a typical disciplinary discharge case, the plaintiff who has violated a legitimate rule or policy of the employer claims that, in imposing the sanction, the employer has treated him less favorably than other similarly situated employees, not in the same protected group, who have violated company rules. *McDonald v. Santa Fe Trail Transportation Co.*, 427 U.S. 273, 96 S.Ct. 2574, 49 L.Ed.2d 493 (1976), is a leading Supreme Court case involving disciplinary discharges. Two white employees and one black employee were jointly charged with stealing property that belonged to a customer of the employer. The employer discharged the two white employees involved, but retained the black employee. The discharged employees sued the employer under Title VII and § 1981 for a discriminatory discharge on the basis of race. They also sued their union for discrimination in the handling of their grievances. The Court in *Santa Fe* adopted a "comparable seriousness" standard as a critical element in the disciplinary discharge cases:

> [P]recise equivalence in culpability between employees is not the ultimate question: as we indicated in *McDonnell Douglas*, an allegation that other "employees involved in acts against [the employer] of *comparable seriousness* * * * were nevertheless retained * * *" is adequate to plead an inferential case that the employer's reliance on his discharged employee's misconduct as grounds for terminating him was merely a pretext.

427 U.S. at 283 n.11, 96 S.Ct. at 2580 n.11.

Lower courts have been attempting to flesh out the *Santa Fe* "comparable seriousness" standard applicable in the disciplinary discharge cases. In one of the earlier cases in this development, the Sixth Circuit adopted a rather rigorous test in *Mitchell v. Toledo Hospital*, 964 F.2d 577 (6th Cir.1992). In that case, the employer discharged a black female for allegedly concealing some company forms and then lying about whether she had knowledge of their location. The employer's handbook made lying a terminable offense. In attempting to establish the element of comparable seriousness, the plaintiff introduced evidence that one white employee had not been discharged for cursing a supervisor—conduct which arguably constituted insubordination—and another white employee had not been discharged for absenteeism. The Sixth Circuit held that the plaintiff had failed to establish a prima facie case. On the question of the appropriate proof necessary to satisfy the comparable seriousness test, the Sixth Circuit said:

> It is fundamental that to make a comparison of a discrimination plaintiff's treatment to that of non-minority employees, the plaintiff must show that the "comparables" are similarly-situated *in all respects*. Thus, to be deemed "similarly-situated," the individuals with whom the plaintiff seeks to compare his/her treatment must have dealt with the same supervisor, have been subject to the same standards and have engaged in the same conduct without such differentiating or mitigating circumstances that would distinguish their conduct or the employer's treatment of them for it.

964 F.2d at 583 (citations omitted). The Sixth Circuit held that the plaintiff produced no facts to establish that the two white employees she identified as not having been fired were similarly situated in all respects, and that she did not produce evidence that the alleged absenteeism and insubordination were comparable to plaintiff's lying.

Over time, the Sixth Circuit recognized that its "in all respects" test was so rigorous that it had the effect of removing the protective reach of laws prohibiting discrimination from certain categories of employees, for example, employees who occupy unique positions, and that a narrow interpretation of the *Mitchell* test had the potential to "undermine the remedial purpose of antidiscrimination statutes." Ercegovich v. Goodyear Tire & Rubber Co., 154 F.3d 344, 352 (6th Cir.1998). For this reason, the Sixth Circuit retreated from a rigid interpretation of *Mitchell*. *See* Graham v. Long Island R.R., 230 F.3d 34, 40 (2d Cir. 2000) (noting the Sixth Circuit's retreat). After a review of its post-*Mitchell* decisions, the Sixth Circuit, in *Ercegovich* concluded that

> [c]ourts should not assume * * * that the specific factors discussed in *Mitchell* are relevant factors in cases arising under different circumstances, but should make an independent determination as to the relevancy of a particular aspect of the plaintiff's employment status and that of the non-protected employee. The plaintiff need not demonstrate an exact correlation with the employee receiving more favorable treatment for the two to be "similarly situated;" rather as this court held [in one of the post-*Mitchell* decisions], the plaintiff and the employee to whom the plaintiff seeks to compare himself or herself must be similar in "all relevant aspects."

154 F.3d at 352 (citations omitted). *Ercegovich* did not specifically declare that it was abandoning the *Mitchell* "in all respects" test in favor of the "all relevant aspects" test, but post-*Ercegovich* Sixth Circuit cases have focused primarily on the "all relevant aspects" test. *See, e.g.*, Clayton v. Meijer, Inc., 281 F.3d 605, 611 (6th Cir. 2002); Majewski v. Automatic Data Processing, Inc., 274 F.3d 1106, 1116. (6th Cir.2001).

Other formulations of the "comparable seriousness" test include "all material respects," "reasonably close resemblance of the facts and circumstances of the plaintiff's and comparator's cases, rather than showing they are identical," "reasonableness is the touchstone * * * and the plaintiff's case and comparison cases * * * need not be perfect." Graham v. Long Island R.R., 230 F.3d 34, 40 (2d Cir. 2000) (noting tests from other circuits). For a discussion of the similarly situated standard in employment discrimination law and a circuit-by-circuit review, see Ernest F. Lidge, III, *The Courts' Misuse of the Similarly Situated Concept in Employment Discrimination Law*, 67 Mo.L.Rev. 831 (2002). Consider the following:

i. A black male vice president of a bank was discharged after allowing a stripper to perform at a business meeting on the bank's premises in celebration of another employee's birthday. He brought a Title VII action alleging that his discharge was racially motivated. At trial he introduced evidence that two lower-level employees, both white, had hired strippers to perform at functions on the bank's premises and neither was fired for his conduct. What arguments could you make that the *Santa Fe* comparable

seriousness standard was (or was not) met? *See* Hargett v. National West-
minster Bank, 78 F.3d 836 (2d Cir.), *cert. denied*, 519 U.S. 824, 117 S.Ct. 84,
136 L.Ed.2d 41 (1996); Watts v. City of Norman, 270 F.3d 1288 (10th
Cir.2001), *cert. denied*, 535 U.S. 1055, 122 S.Ct. 1912, 152 L.Ed.2d 822
(2002) (holding that nonsupervisory personnel are not similarly situated to
supervisory personnel in disciplinary matters).

ii. A black employee was reprimanded because, on several occasions, he
came to work under the influence of alcohol. A white employee was discharged after the employer learned that he had been criminally charged with
use and possession of cocaine. Have the employees engaged in conduct that
is of comparable seriousness? *See* Wormley v. Arkla, Inc., 871 F.Supp. 1079
(E.D.Ark.1994). *See also* Green v. Armstrong Rubber Co., 612 F.2d 967 (5th
Cir.) (comparing employees who were fighting with knives), *cert. denied*, 449
U.S. 879, 101 S.Ct. 227, 66 L.Ed.2d 102 (1980).

e. *Constructive discharges*: Under the doctrine of constructive discharge, an employer engages in unlawful employment discrimination when
an employee involuntarily resigns in order to escape intolerable working
conditions that she is subjected to because of her race, sex, national origin,
or religion. For example, in one of the leading cases on constructive discharge under Title VII, the plaintiff, an atheist, resigned because the
employer insisted that she attend business meetings which always began
with a prayer or what the court called a "theological appetizer." The court
concluded that the plaintiff had been constructively discharged because she
acted reasonably in light of the employer's mandatory requirements that
amounted to religious discrimination. Young v. Southwestern Sav. & Loan
Ass'n, 509 F.2d 140 (5th Cir.1975).

The Seventh Circuit has offered the following approaches to constructive
discharges:

> Constructive discharge, like actual discharge, is a materially adverse
> employment action. But to demonstrate constructive discharge, the
> plaintiff must show that she was forced to resign because her working
> conditions, from the standpoint of the reasonable employee, had become
> unbearable. We are ordinarily faced with a situation in which the
> employee only alleges that she resigned because of *discriminatory
> harassment*, and in such cases, we require the plaintiff to demonstrate a
> discriminatory work environment "even more egregious than the high
> standard for hostile work environment." *Tutman v. WBBM–TV, Inc.,*
> 209 F.3d 1044, 1050 (7th Cir.2000), *cert. denied*, 531 U.S. 1078, 121
> S.Ct. 777, 148 L.Ed.2d 675 (2001).

> But that is not the only method of demonstrating constructive
> discharge. When an employer acts in a manner so as to have communi-
> cated to a reasonable employee that she will be terminated, and the
> plaintiff employee resigns, the employer's conduct may amount to con-
> structive discharge. *See generally Bragg v. Navistar Int'l Transp. Corp.,*
> 164 F.3d 373, 377 (7th Cir.1998) ("Constructive discharge exists to give
> Title VII protection to a plaintiff who decides to quit rather than wait
> around to be fired."); *cf. Hunt v. City of Markham, Illinois,* 219 F.3d
> 649, 655 (7th Cir.2000) ("A person who is told repeatedly that he is not
> wanted, has no future, and can't count on ever getting another raise

would not be acting unreasonably if he decided that to remain with this employer and would necessarily be inconsistent with even a minimal sense of self-respect, therefore intolerable.'').

In this case, the EEOC has met its burden of showing constructive discharge. It has sufficiently demonstrated that a reasonable employee standing in [the employee's] shoes would have believed that had she not resigned, she would have been terminated. Most significantly, when [the employee] arrived at work, her belongings were packed and her office was being used for storage. That evidence is only underscored by the other evidence pointing to her imminent termination, specifically * * * evidence [of] significant changes in [the employee's] evaluations, repeated accusations of her failure to follow directives, and a general environment in which [a supervisor] was hostile to [the employee's] religious beliefs. To complete the picture, [a supervisor] called [the employee] and stated that her failure to remember the location of several test scores was "the last straw." This environment, in which her employer made reasonably clear to her that she had reached the end of the line—where "the handwriting [was] on the wall" and the axe was about to fall—could have indeed been to a reasonable employee unbearable.

EEOC v. University of Chicago Hosps., 276 F.3d 326, 331–32 (7th Cir.2002).

Although the federal courts universally recognize the constructive discharge doctrine, the circuits are split on the proper standard to apply. *See* Martin v. Cavalier Hotel Corp., 48 F.3d 1343, 1354 (4th Cir.1995) (collecting cases); *see also* Campbell v. Florida Steel Corp., 919 S.W.2d 26, 33–34 (Tenn.1996) (collecting cases). A majority of the courts of appeals have adopted an objective standard that a constructive discharge occurs when a reasonable person would have felt compelled to resign because of intolerable discriminatory working conditions. The rationale for the objective "reasonable person" standard is that it affords employers better protection from frivolous claims than a subjective standard. *See, e.g.,* Irving v. Dubuque Packing Co., 689 F.2d 170 (10th Cir.1982); Bourque v. Powell Elec. Mfg., Co., 617 F.2d 61 (5th Cir.1980). A minority of the courts of appeals have adopted a subjective standard which requires a plaintiff to prove that her employer deliberately engaged in a course of unlawful discriminatory conduct designed to force her to quit. A finding of intentional conduct is critical under the minority view. *See, e.g.,* Bristow v. Daily Press, Inc., 770 F.2d 1251 (4th Cir.1985), *cert. denied,* 475 U.S. 1082, 106 S.Ct. 1461, 89 L.Ed.2d 718 (1986).

i. Which standard on constructive discharge would you endorse? Why? Is there really a difference between the two standards if the court evaluates the defendant's intent under the tort doctrine that an actor must intend the reasonably foreseeable consequences of its actions? *See Martin,* 48 F.3d at 1355.

ii. If the courts are willing to recognize a constructive discharge as a "term or condition" of employment, is there any reason they should not likewise recognize a constructive demotion as a "term or condition" of employment? What factors would be relevant in distinguishing between a constructive discharge and a constructive demotion? *See* Simpson v. Borg–Warner Automotive, Inc., 196 F.3d 873 (7th Cir.1999).

iii. The courts of appeals are split on whether a constructive discharge in harassment cases is a tangible employment action. *See* Suders v. Easton, 325 F.3d 432 (3d Cir.2003), *cert. granted sub nom.* Pennsylvania State Police v. Suders, ___ U.S. ___, 124 S.Ct. 803, 157 L.Ed.2d 692 (2003) (sexual harassment). If it is, then an employer is precluded from asserting an affirmative defense to vicarious liability for harassment by a supervisor, as established by the Supreme Court in *Burlington Industries, Inc. v. Ellerth,* 524 U.S. 742, 118 S.Ct. 2257, 141 L.Ed.2d 633 (1998), and *Faragher v. City of Boca Raton,* 524 U.S. 775, 118 S.Ct. 2275, 141 L.Ed.2d 662 (1998). The affirmative defense in supervisory harassment cases is covered in Chapter 8.

5. *The "Legitimate, Nondiscriminatory Reason" Defense: McDonnell Douglas* imposes an obligation on the employer to introduce evidence of a "legitimate, nondiscriminatory reason" to rebut a plaintiff's prima facie case in circumstantial evidence cases.

a. Is there a substantive difference between the terms "legitimate" and "nondiscriminatory"? In *Hazen Paper Co. v. Biggins,* 507 U.S. 604, 612, 113 S.Ct. 1701, 1707, 123 L.Ed.2d 338 (1993), an age discrimination case reproduced in Chapter 12, the Supreme Court interpreted "legitimate" to mean no more than "nondiscriminatory" when it held that firing the plaintiff to prevent his pension plan from vesting was a legitimate, nondiscriminatory reason.

b. What are some of the more obvious "legitimate, nondiscriminatory" reasons an employer could "articulate" that would readily satisfy the defense in a discharge case? In a refusal to hire case? In a failure to promote case?

c. If McDonnell Douglas had rejected Green because he was a vegetarian, would that reason satisfy the legitimate, nondiscriminatory reason defense? *Cf.* Friedman v. Southern Cal. Permanente Med. Group, 102 Cal.App.4th 39, 125 Cal.Rptr.2d 663 (2002) (holding that where plaintiff, a vegan, was not hired because he refused to be vaccinated with a mumps vaccine grown in chicken embryos, his veganism was not a religious creed protected under state employment discrimination law), *cert. denied,* ___ U.S. ___, 123 S.Ct. 2078, 155 L.Ed.2d 1063 (2003)).

d. If McDonnell Douglas had rejected Green because he wore dreadlocks instead of because of his participation in civil rights demonstrations, would that reason be sufficient to raise the legitimate, nondiscriminatory reason defense? *See, e.g.,* Eatman v. United Parcel Serv., 194 F.Supp.2d 256, 259 (S.D.N.Y.2002) (considering effect of employer's policy that drivers wear hats to cover " 'unconventional' hairstyles, which included 'dreadlocks,' 'braids,' 'corn rolls,' a 'dew rag' and a 'ponytails' "); Rogers v. American Airlines, Inc., 527 F.Supp. 229 (S.D.N.Y.1981) (upholding an employer's policy prohibiting employees in certain types of jobs from wearing all-braided hairstyles). Would it make a difference if Green wore dreadlocks as part of his religious practice as a Rastafarian? *See* Booth v. Maryland, 327 F.3d 377 (4th Cir.2003).

e. Traci is a black female whose hair is naturally black but she has dyed her hair blond. She applied as a housekeeper at a hotel and was rejected because of the hotel's grooming policy prohibiting extremes in hair color. The hotel's argument is that Traci's blond hair violates the grooming policy. What argument would you make that Traci could or could not establish a prima facie case under a disparate treatment theory of discrimination? Assuming she could establish a prima facie case, what argument would you make that the hotel's grooming policy is or is not a legitimate, nondiscriminatory reason? *See* Santee v. Windsor Court Hotel Ltd. Partnership, 2000 WL 1610775 (E.D.La.2000). *See also* Chapter 6, Section F (Dress, Grooming, and Appearance Requirements).

    f. Tom and Jane submit applications for a position the employer is seeking to fill. Both applicants are well-qualified for the job. The employer awards the job to Tom because, in addition to his job qualifications, Tom and the hiring manager are friends who go fishing together on a regular basis. Assuming that Jane could establish a prima facie case of sex discrimination, would evidence that Tom received favorable consideration because he is a fishing buddy of the hiring manager constitute a legitimate, nondiscriminatory reason that rebuts Jane's prima facie case? In other words, should a defense based on cronyism be sufficient? *See* Foster v. Dalton, 71 F.3d 52 (1st Cir.1995). Is unconscious sexism at issue in this case?

    6. In *Burdine*, the Fifth Circuit had required the defendant to bear the burden of persuasion with respect to its rebuttal evidence of a legitimate, nondiscriminatory reason in order to discourage employers from relying on "fictitious, but legitimate reasons." Is the court saying that the burden of persuasion should be placed on the employer to encourage employers to be truthful? If so, are you convinced by the Supreme Court's response to this argument in *Burdine*? In *St. Mary's Honor Center v. Hicks*, 509 U.S. 502, 113 S.Ct. 2742, 125 L.Ed.2d 407 (1993), reproduced below, the Court addressed more specifically the issue whether Title VII should be construed to discourage employers from lying in advancing the legitimate, nondiscriminatory reason defense.

    7. *The Role of Liberal Discovery Rules in Proving Pretext*: The Supreme Court in *Burdine* was convinced that, with effective use of the liberal federal rules of discovery in civil suits, a plaintiff would not "find it particularly difficult to prove that a proffered explanation lacking a factual basis is a pretext." 450 U.S. at 258, 101 S.Ct. at 1096. In *University of Pennsylvania v. EEOC*, 493 U.S. 182, 110 S.Ct. 577, 107 L.Ed.2d 571 (1990), the Supreme Court reaffirmed its views on the significant role of liberal civil discovery rules in employment discrimination cases. In *University of Pennsylvania*, a woman had been denied tenure on the faculty. In the process of investigating her charge of sex discrimination, the EEOC subpoenaed university documents relating to her tenure decision as well as the tenure decisions for five of her male colleagues. The university refused to produce the documents, asserting a special privilege not to disclose confidential peer review materials under both the common law and principles of "academic freedom" protected by the First Amendment. The university argued that its ability to obtain candid assessments of the work of candidates being considered for promotion or tenure in the future would be harmed by compelled disclosure of the documents. The Supreme Court, in a unanimous opinion, rejected the university's arguments and required it to disclose the confidential documents to the EEOC because, for purposes of discovery, the comparative peer review materials were clearly relevant to determining whether sex discrimination had occurred in the university's tenure process.

Even though the *Burdine* and *University of Pennsylvania* cases offer theoretical support for broad discovery in employment discrimination litigation, at a practical level the scope of discovery is committed to the discretion of federal district court judges and federal magistrates with limited oversight by the courts of appeals. For an overview of the problems of discovery in employment discrimination cases and an argument in support of broad discovery in disparate treatment cases, see Susan K. Grebeldinger, *How Can a Plaintiff Prove Intentional Discrimination if She Cannot Explore the Relevant Circumstances: The Need for Broad Workplace and Time Parameters in Discovery*, 74 Denv.U.L.Rev. 159 (1996).

8. *Litigation Strategy*: The courts generally have held that the *McDonnell Douglas–Burdine* analytic scheme is not a three-step "judicial minuet" of procedure—plaintiff's evidence of a prima facie case; defendant's rebuttal evidence of a legitimate, nondiscriminatory reason; and plaintiff's surrebuttal evidence of pretext. *See* Flowers v. Crouch–Walker Corp., 552 F.2d 1277, 1281–82 (7th Cir.1977) (citing Sime v. Trustees of Cal. State Univ. & Colleges, 526 F.2d 1112, 1114 (9th Cir.1975)). In *Sime*, the court held that a motion for dismissal under Rule 41(b)* of the Federal Rules of Civil Procedure was proper at the close of plaintiff's case-in-chief when the defendant had met its burden through the testimony of the plaintiff's witnesses. Plaintiff's trial strategy in *Sime* was to put on only so much evidence as was necessary and sufficient to establish a prima facie case and then to present her evidence of pretext only after the defendant had put on its evidence of a legitimate, nondiscriminatory reason. Defendant, however, was able to present its rebuttal evidence on its legitimate, nondiscriminatory reason by cross-examining—and discrediting—the plaintiff's own witnesses during her case-in-chief. In view of *Sime*, what litigation strategy is suggested?

At the close of the plaintiff's evidence, the defendant can challenge the sufficiency of the plaintiff's prima facie case by a motion for judgment as a matter of law in a jury trial, Fed.R.Civ.P. 50(a), or by a motion for a judgment on partial findings in a nonjury trial, Fed.R.Civ.P. 52(c). However, once a case proceeds to the next stage and the defendant has produced evidence of a legitimate, nondiscriminatory reason, the evidentiary sufficiency of the prima facie case is no longer at issue. In *United States Postal Service Board of Governors v. Aikens*, 460 U.S. 711, 715, 103 S.Ct. 1478, 1482, 75 L.Ed.2d 403 (1983), the Court held that "[w]here the defendant has done everything that would be required of him if the plaintiff had properly made out a *prima facie* case, whether the plaintiff really did is no longer relevant," and that the "district court has before it all the evidence it needs to decide whether 'the defendant intentionally discriminated against the plaintiff.' "

9. *Pretext*: Pretext analysis generally involves an assessment of the totality of the evidence presented by the parties to decide whether it is more probable than not that an employer was motivated by a discriminatory animus in making an adverse employment decision. *McDonnell Douglas*

---

* The 1991 amendments to the Federal Rules of Civil Procedure replaced this part of Rule 41(b) with a new Rule 52(c) (nonjury trials) that parallels Rule 50(a) (jury trials).

equates a finding of pretext with "a cover-up for a racially discriminatory decision." In *Visser v. Packer Engineering Associates*, 924 F.2d 655, 657 (7th Cir.1991), the court defined pretext as a phony reason: "[a] pretext, in employment law, is a reason that the employer offers for the action claimed to be discriminatory and that the court disbelieves, allowing the inference that the employer is trying to conceal a discriminatory reason for his action." The Third Circuit defined pretext as a "fabricated justification" in *Chipollini v. Spencer Gifts, Inc.*, 814 F.2d 893, 898, *cert. denied*, 483 U.S. 1052, 108 S.Ct. 26, 97 L.Ed.2d 815 (1987).

Probably the most common way to show pretext is to demonstrate that similarly situated individuals in a different class received more favorable treatment. On this point, the Court in *McDonnell Douglas* stated that "[e]specially relevant [to the issue of pretext] would be evidence that white employees involved in acts against petitioner of comparable seriousness to the 'stall-in' were nevertheless retained or rehired." 411 U.S. at 804, 93 S.Ct. at 1825. *McDonnell Douglas* also recognized that the following types of evidence are relevant to the issue of pretext: the employer's reactions to Green's legitimate civil rights activities; the employer's general policies and practices on its treatment of minority employees; and statistical evidence that might show a general pattern of discrimination against blacks. *Id.* at 804–05, 93 S.Ct. at 1825–26. In *Johnson v. Kroger Co.*, 319 F.3d 858, 866–87 (6th Cir.2003) (citing Dews v. A.B. Dick Co., 231 F.3d 1016, 1021 (6th Cir.2000)), the court held that a plaintiff can show pretext to refute an employer's evidence of a legitimate, nondiscriminatory reason in three ways: the proffered reason "(1) has no basis in fact; (2) did not actually motivate the defendant's challenged conduct; or (3) was insufficient to warrant the challenged conduct." Weaknesses, implausibilities, or contradictions in the employer's proffered legitimate reason for its adverse action may be sufficient to allow a reasonable factfinder to find them unworthy of credence. *See* Garrett v. Hewlett Packard Co., 305 F.3d 1210, 1217 (10th Cir.2002).

Courts have held that they do not "sit as [a] super-personnel department[] reviewing the wisdom or fairness of the business judgment made by employers, except to the extent that those judgments involve intentional discrimination." Hutson v. McDonnell Douglas Corp., 63 F.3d 771, 781 (8th Cir.1995). *See also* Kralman v. Illinois Dep't of Veterans' Affairs, 23 F.3d 150 (7th Cir.1994) (laws against discrimination in employment do not evaluate the correctness or desirability of an employer's decision, but only whether it is motivated by discriminatory animus). Keeping this in mind, what arguments on pretext could you make on behalf of the plaintiff or employer in the following situations?

a.   Plaintiff in an age discrimination case received good job performance evaluations historically, but received numerous unfavorable job evaluations after filing a charge with the EEOC. *See* Hairston v. Gainesville Sun Publ'g Co., 9 F.3d 913 (11th Cir.1993).

b.   The employer did not follow its own written policy on disciplinary procedures in disciplining a black supervisory employee but did so in disciplining a nonsupervisory white employee engaged in similar misconduct. *See* Kohls v. Beverly Enter. Wis., Inc., 259 F.3d 799 (7th Cir.2001).

c. A female employee was hired as a secretary in February. The following August, she informed her employer that she was pregnant. The employer terminated her in November and told her that she was discharged because of lack of work. The EEOC brought an action on behalf of the terminated employee alleging that she was discharged because of pregnancy, a violation of Title VII. The employer acknowledged that it had made a corporate decision to give her the "lack of work" explanation rather than tell her the "real reason" for her discharge, which was that she lacked the skills needed for the secretarial position she held. *See* EEOC v. Yenkin–Majestic Paint Corp., 112 F.3d 831 (6th Cir.1997).

10. *Pretext and the Honest Belief Defense*: Suppose McDonnell Douglas had rehired Green when he reapplied for his position and then discharged him because it honestly and in good faith—but mistakenly—believed that Green had lied on his application. After McDonnell Douglas hires another black man to replace him, Green files a lawsuit alleging that his discharge was racially motivated. After the lawsuit is filed, McDonnell Douglas discovers that Green had not, in fact, lied on his application and concludes that it had made a bad business judgment in discharging him. Should honest mistake, good faith belief, or the fact that an employer made an adverse employment decision because of poor business judgment be sufficient as a legitimate, nondiscriminatory reason or preclude Green from showing pretext? The courts have adopted an "honest belief" rule for these cases, but have adopted different views on the defense. The different views are set out in the Sixth Circuit's decision in *Smith v. Chrysler Corp.*, 155 F.3d 799 (6th Cir.1998):

> [The "honest belief" rule], as developed in a series of Seventh Circuit decisions, provides that so long as the employer honestly believed in the proffered reason given for its employment action, the employee cannot establish pretext even if the employer's reason is ultimately found to be mistaken, foolish, trivial, or baseless. The rationale behind the rule is that the focus of a discrimination suit is on the intent of the employer. If the employer honestly, albeit mistakenly, believes in the non-discriminatory reason it relied upon in making its employment decision, then the employer arguably lacks the necessary discriminatory intent. * * *

> The Seventh Circuit, however, apparently does not require an employer to demonstrate that its belief was reasonably grounded on particularized facts that were before it at the time of the employment action. Instead, for the rule to apply, the employer need only provide an honest reason for firing the employee, even if that reason had no factual support. * * * To the extent the Seventh Circuit's application of the "honest belief" rule credits an employer's belief without requiring that it be reasonably based on particularized facts rather than on ignorance and mythology, we reject its approach.

> * * * [I]n order for an employer's proffered non-discriminatory basis for its employment action to be considered honestly held, the employer must be able to establish its reasonable reliance on the particularized facts that were before it at the time the decision was

made. If the employer is unable to produce such evidence to support its employment action, then the "honest belief" rule does not apply. Even if the employer is able to make such a showing, the protection afforded by the rule is not automatic. * * * [O]nce the employer is able to point to the particularized facts that motivated its decision, the employee has the opportunity to produce "proof to the contrary. * * *

In deciding whether an employer reasonably relied on the particularized facts then before it, we do not require that the decisional process used by the employer be optimal or that it left no stone unturned. Rather, the key inquiry is whether the employer made a reasonably informed and considered decision before taking an adverse employment action. Although courts should resist attempting to micro-manage the process used by employers in making their employment decisions, neither should they blindly assume that an employer's description of its reasons is honest. When the employee is able to produce sufficient evidence to establish that the employer failed to make a reasonably informed and considered decision before taking its adverse employment action, thereby making its decisional process "unworthy of credence," then any reliance placed by the employer in such a process cannot be said to be honestly held.

Id. at 807–08. *See also* McKnight v. Kimberly Clark Corp., 149 F.3d 1125, 1129 (10th Cir.1998) ("An articulated motivating reason is not converted into pretext merely because, with the benefit of hindsight, it turned out to be poor business judgment. The test is good faith belief."); Dionne v. Shalala, 209 F.3d 705 (8th Cir.2000) (honest mistake insufficient to prove pretext). What arguments might be open to a plaintiff to controvert a good faith, honest mistake or poor judgment defense? Should the good faith defense be tested by an objective reasonable employer standard or a subjective standard for a particular employer? *See* Castille v. Teletech Customer Care Mgmt. (CO), Inc., 56 Fed.App. 895 (10th Cir.), *cert. denied,* ___ U.S. ___, 124 S.Ct. 90, 157 L.Ed.2d 99 (2003).

One commentator has labeled the Seventh Circuit's rule the "pure honest belief regime," and the Sixth Circuit's rule the "honest belief plus reasonableness regime." Rebecca Michaels, Note, *Legitimate Reasons for Firing: Must They Be Reasonable,* 71 Fordham L.Rev. 2643 (2003). Which is the better view?

11. Suppose the factfinder disbelieves the employer's evidence offered as a legitimate, nondiscriminatory reason or, worse yet, believes that the employer actually lied with respect to its rebuttal evidence. Should the plaintiff be entitled to a judgment in her favor on that ground alone? Consider this question as you read the following cases: *St. Mary's Honor Center v. Hicks,* and *Reeves v. Sanderson Plumbing Products, Inc.* Also, consider whether the Court's approaches in these two cases on pretext analysis can be harmonized. If not, what reason or reasons might explain the different outcomes in the cases?

ST. MARY'S HONOR CENTER v. HICKS

Supreme Court of the United States, 1993.
509 U.S. 502, 113 S.Ct. 2742, 125 L.Ed.2d 407.

JUSTICE SCALIA delivered the opinion of the Court.

We granted certiorari to determine whether, in a suit against an employer alleging intentional racial discrimination in violation of § 703(a)(1) of Title VII of the Civil Rights Act of 1964, the trier of fact's rejection of the employer's asserted reasons for its actions mandates a finding for the plaintiff.

I

Petitioner St. Mary's Honor Center (St. Mary's) is a halfway house operated by the Missouri Department of Corrections and Human Resources (MDCHR). Respondent Melvin Hicks, a black man, was hired as a correctional officer at St. Mary's in August 1978 and was promoted to shift commander, one of six supervisory positions, in February 1980.

In 1983 MDCHR conducted an investigation of the administration of St. Mary's, which resulted in extensive supervisory changes in January 1984. Respondent retained his position, but John Powell became the new chief of custody (respondent's immediate supervisor) and petitioner Steve Long the new superintendent. Prior to these personnel changes respondent had enjoyed a satisfactory employment record, but soon thereafter became the subject of repeated, and increasingly severe, disciplinary actions. He was suspended for five days for violations of institutional rules by his subordinates on March 3, 1984. He received a letter of reprimand for alleged failure to conduct an adequate investigation of a brawl between inmates that occurred during his shift on March 21. He was later demoted from shift commander to correctional officer for his failure to ensure that his subordinates entered their use of a St. Mary's vehicle into the official log book on March 19, 1984. Finally, on June 7, 1984, he was discharged for threatening Powell during an exchange of heated words on April 19.

* * *

II

* * * Petitioners do not challenge the District Court's finding that respondent satisfied the minimal requirements of * * * a [*McDonnell Douglas*] prima facie case * * *.

* * *

Respondent does not challenge the District Court's finding that petitioners sustained their burden of production by introducing evidence of two legitimate, nondiscriminatory reasons for their actions: the severity and the accumulation of rules violations committed by respondent. * * *

The District Court, acting as trier of fact in this bench trial, found that the reasons petitioners gave were not the real reasons for respondent's demotion and discharge. It found that respondent was the only supervisor disciplined for violations committed by his subordinates; that similar and even more serious violations committed by respondent's coworkers were either disregarded or treated more leniently; and that Powell manufactured the final verbal confrontation in order to provoke respondent into threatening him. It nonetheless held that respondent had failed to carry his ultimate burden of proving that *his race* was the determining factor in petitioners' decision first to demote and then to dismiss him. In short, the District Court concluded that "although [respondent] has proven the existence of a crusade to terminate him, he has not proven that the crusade was racially rather than personally motivated."

The Court of Appeals set this determination aside on the ground that "[o]nce [respondent] proved all of [petitioners'] proffered reasons for the adverse employment actions to be pretextual, [respondent] was entitled to judgment as a matter of law." The Court of Appeals reasoned:

> Because all of defendants' proffered reasons were discredited, defendants were in a position of having offered no legitimate reason for their actions. In other words, defendants were in no better position than if they had remained silent, offering no rebuttal to an established inference that they had unlawfully discriminated against plaintiff on the basis of his race.

That is not so. By producing *evidence* (whether ultimately persuasive or not) of nondiscriminatory reasons, petitioners sustained their burden of production, and thus placed themselves in a "better position than if they had remained silent."

* * *

If * * * the defendant has succeeded in carrying its burden of production, the *McDonnell Douglas* framework—with its presumptions and burdens—is no longer relevant. To resurrect it later, after the trier of fact has determined that what was "produced" to meet the burden of production is not credible, flies in the face of our holding in *Burdine* that to rebut the presumption "[t]he defendant need not persuade the court that it was actually motivated by the proffered reasons." 450 U.S. at 254, 101 S.Ct. at 1094. The presumption, having fulfilled its role of forcing the defendant to come forward with some response, simply drops out of the picture. The defendant's "production" (whatever its persuasive effect) having been made, the trier of fact proceeds to decide the ultimate question: whether plaintiff has proven "that the defendant intentionally discriminated against [him]" because of his race. *Id.* at 253, 101 S.Ct. at 1093. The factfinder's disbelief of the reasons put forward by the defendant (particularly if disbelief is accompanied by a suspicion of mendacity) may, together with the elements of the prima facie case, suffice to show intentional discrimination. Thus, rejection of the defendant's proffered reasons will *permit* the trier of fact to infer the ultimate fact of intentional discrimination,[4] and the Court of Appeals was correct when it noted that, upon such rejection, "[n]o additional proof of discrimination is *required*," (emphasis added). But the Court of Appeals' holding that rejection of the defendant's proffered reasons *compels* judgment for the plaintiff disregards the fundamental principle of Rule 301 that a presumption does not shift the burden of proof, and ignores our repeated admonition that the Title VII plaintiff at all times bears the "ultimate burden of persuasion."

III

Only one unfamiliar with our case-law will be upset by the dissent's alarum that we are today setting aside "settled precedent," "two decades of stable law in this Court," "a framework carefully crafted in precedents as old as 20 years," which "Congress is [aware]" of and has implicitly approved. * * * We mean to answer the dissent's accusations in detail, by examining our cases, but at the outset it is worth noting the utter implausibility that we would ever have held what the dissent says we held.

* * *

The principal case on which the dissent relies is *Burdine*. While there are some statements in that opinion that could be read to support the dissent's position, all but one of them bear a meaning consistent with our interpretation, and the one exception is simply incompatible with other language in the case. *Burdine* describes the situation that obtains after the employer has met its burden of adducing a nondiscriminatory reason as follows: "Third, should the defendant carry this burden, the plaintiff must then have an opportunity to prove by a preponderance of the evidence that the legitimate reasons offered by the defendant were not its true reasons, but were a pretext for discrimination." 450 U.S. at 253, 101 S.Ct. at 1093. The dissent takes this to mean that if the plaintiff proves the asserted reason to be *false*, the plaintiff wins. But a reason cannot be proved to be "a pretext *for discrimination*" unless it is shown *both* that the reason was false, *and* that discrimination was the real reason. *Burdine*'s later allusions to proving or demonstrating simply "pretext," are reasonably understood to refer to the previously described pretext, *i.e.*, "pretext for discrimination."

[The Court's dissection of *Burdine*, almost sentence by sentence, is omitted.]

* * *

In sum, our interpretation of *Burdine* creates difficulty with one sentence; the dissent's interpretation causes many portions of the opin-

---

4. Contrary to the dissent's confusion-producing analysis, there is nothing whatever inconsistent between this statement and our later statements that (1) the plaintiff must show "*both* that the reason was false, *and* that discrimination was the real reason," and (2) "it is not enough * * * to *dis*believe the employer." Even though (as we say here) rejection of the defendant's proffered reasons is enough at law to *sustain* a finding of discrimination, *there must be a finding of discrimination*.

ion to be incomprehensible or deceptive. But whatever doubt *Burdine* might have created was eliminated by [*United States Postal Serv. Bd. of Governors v. Aikens*, 460 U.S. 711, 103 S.Ct. 1478, 75 L.Ed.2d 403 (1983)]. There we said, in language that cannot reasonably be mistaken, that "the ultimate question [is] discrimination *vel non*." 460 U.S. at 714, 103 S.Ct. at 1481. Once the defendant "responds to the plaintiff's proof by offering evidence of the reason for the plaintiff's rejection, the factfinder must then decide" *not* (as the dissent would have it) whether that evidence is credible, but "whether the rejection was discriminatory within the meaning of Title VII." *Id*. at 714–15, 103 S.Ct. at 1481. * * * It is not enough, in other words, to *dis*believe the employer; the factfinder must *believe* the plaintiff's explanation of intentional discrimination. * * *

IV

We turn, finally, to the dire practical consequences that the respondents and the dissent claim our decision today will produce. What appears to trouble the dissent more than anything is that, in its view, our rule is adopted "for the benefit of employers who have been found to have given false evidence in a court of law," whom we "favo[r]" by "exempting them from responsibility for lies." As we shall explain, our rule in no way gives special favor to those employers whose evidence is disbelieved. But initially we must point out that there is no justification for assuming (as the dissent repeatedly does) that those employers whose evidence is disbelieved are perjurers and liars. * * * To say that the company which in good faith introduces such testimony, or even the testifying employee himself, becomes a liar and a perjurer when the testimony is not believed, is nothing short of absurd.

Undoubtedly some employers (or at least their employees) will be lying. But even if we could readily identify these perjurers, what an extraordinary notion, that we "exempt them from responsibility for their lies" unless we enter Title VII judgments for the plaintiffs! Title VII is not a cause of action for perjury; we have other civil and criminal remedies for that. * * *

* * *

The dissent repeatedly raises a procedural objection that is impressive only to one who mistakes the basic nature of the *McDonnell Douglas* procedure. It asserts that "the Court now holds that the further inquiry [*i.e.*, the inquiry that follows the employer's response to the prima facie case] is wide open, not limited at all by the scope of the employer's proffered explanation." The plaintiff cannot be expected to refute "reasons not articulated by the employer, but discerned in the record by the factfinder." He should not "be saddled with the tremendous disadvantage of having to confront, not the defined task of proving the employer's stated reasons to be false, but the amorphous requirement of disproving all possible nondiscriminatory reasons that a factfinder might find lurking in the record." "Under the scheme announced today, any conceivable explanation for the employer's actions that might be suggested by the evidence, however unrelated to the employer's articulated reasons, must be addressed by [the] plaintiff." These statements imply that the employer's "proffered explanation," his "stated reasons," his "articulated reasons," somehow exist *apart from the record*—in some pleading, or perhaps in some formal, nontestimonial statement made on behalf of the defendant to the factfinder. ("Your honor, pursuant to *McDonnell Douglas* the defendant hereby formally asserts, as *its* reason for the dismissal at issue here, incompetence of the employee.") Of course it does not work like that. The reasons the defendant sets forth are set forth "through the introduction of admissible evidence." *Burdine*, 450 U.S. at 255, 101 S.Ct. at 1094. In other words, the defendant's "articulated reasons" *themselves* are to be found "lurking in the record." It thus makes no sense to contemplate "the employer who is caught in a lie, but succeeds in *injecting* into the trial an *unarticulated* reason for its actions." There is a "lurking-in-the-record" problem, but it exists not for us but for the dissent. *If*, after the employer has met its preliminary burden, the plaintiff need not prove discrimination (and therefore need not disprove *all* other reasons suggested, no matter how vaguely, in the record) there must be some device for determining which particular portions of the record represent "articulated reasons" set forth with sufficient clarity to satisfy *McDonnell Douglas*—since it is only *that* evidence which the plaintiff must refute. But of course our *McDonnell Douglas* framework makes no provision for such a determination, which would have to be made not at the close of the trial but *in medias res*, since otherwise the plaintiff would not know what evidence to offer. It makes no sense.

* * *

Finally, respondent argues that it "would be particularly ill-advised" for us to come forth with the holding we pronounce today "just as Congress has provided a right to jury trials in Title VII" cases. We think quite the opposite is true. Clarity regarding the requisite elements of proof becomes all the more important when a jury must be instructed concerning them, and when detailed factual findings by the trial court will not be available upon review.

* * *

JUSTICE SOUTER, with whom JUSTICE WHITE, JUSTICE BLACKMUN, and JUSTICE STEVENS join, dissenting.

Twenty years ago, in *McDonnell Douglas Corp. v. Green*, 411 U.S. 792, 93 S.Ct. 1817, 36 L.Ed.2d 668 (1973), this Court unanimously prescribed a "sensible, orderly way to evaluate the evidence" in a Title VII disparate-treatment case, giving both plaintiff and defendant fair opportunities to litigate "in light of common experience as it bears on the critical question of discrimination." Furnco Constr. Corp. v. Waters, 438 U.S. 567, 577, 98 S.Ct. 2943, 2949 (1978). We have repeatedly reaffirmed and refined the *McDonnell Douglas* framework, most notably in *Texas Dept. of Community Affairs v. Burdine*, 450 U.S. 248, 101 S.Ct. 1089, 67 L.Ed.2d 207 (1981), another unanimous opinion. But today, after two decades of stable law in this Court and only relatively recent disruption in some of the Circuits, the Court abandons this practical framework together with its central purpose, which is "to sharpen the inquiry into the elusive factual question of intentional discrimination." *Id.* at 255 n.8, 101 S.Ct. at 1095 n.8. Ignoring language to the contrary in both *McDonnell Douglas* and *Burdine*, the Court holds that, once a Title VII plaintiff succeeds in showing at trial that the defendant has come forward with pretextual reasons for its actions in response to a prima facie showing of discrimination, the factfinder still may proceed to roam the record, searching for some nondiscriminatory explanation that the defendant has not raised and that the plaintiff has had no fair opportunity to disprove. Because the majority departs from settled precedent in substituting a scheme of proof for disparate-treatment actions that promises to be unfair and unworkable, I respectfully dissent.

* * *

The majority's scheme greatly disfavors Title VII plaintiffs without the good luck to have direct evidence of discriminatory intent. * * * [U]nder the majority's scheme, a victim of discrimination lacking direct evidence will now be saddled with the tremendous disadvantage of having to confront, not the defined task of proving the employer's stated reasons to be false, but the amorphous requirement of disproving all possible nondiscriminatory reasons that a factfinder might find lurking in the record. In the Court's own words, the plaintiff must "disprove *all* other reasons suggested, no matter how vaguely, in the record."

While the Court appears to acknowledge that a plaintiff will have the task of disproving even vaguely suggested reasons, and while it recognizes the need for "[c]larity regarding the requisite elements of proof," it nonetheless gives conflicting signals about the scope of its holding in this case. In one passage, the Court states that although proof of the falsity of the employer's proffered reasons does not "compe[l] judgment for the plaintiff," such evidence, without more, "will permit the trier of fact to infer the ultimate fact of intentional discrimination." The same view is implicit in the Court's decision to remand this case, keeping Hicks's chance of winning a judgment alive although he has done no more (in addition to proving his prima facie case) than show that the reasons proffered by St. Mary's are unworthy of credence. But other language in the Court's opinion supports a more extreme conclusion, that proof of the falsity of the employer's articulated reasons will not even be sufficient to sustain judgment for the plaintiff. For example, the Court twice states that the plaintiff must show "*both* that the reason was false, *and* that discrimination was the real reason." * * * This "pretext-plus" approach would turn *Burdine* on its head, and it would result in summary judgment for the employer in the many cases where the plaintiff has no evidence beyond that required to prove a prima facie case and to show that the employer's articulated reasons are unworthy of credence. *Cf.* Carter v. Duncan–Huggins, Ltd., 727 F.2d 1225, 1245 (D.C.Cir.1984) (Scalia, J., dissenting) ("In order to get to the jury the plaintiff would * * * have to introduce some evidence * * * that the *basis* for [the] discriminatory treatment was *race*") (emphasis in original).

* * *

Because I see no reason why Title VII interpretation should be driven by concern for employers who are too ashamed to be honest in court, at the expense of victims of discrimination who do not happen to have direct evidence of discriminatory intent, I respectfully dissent.

Notes and Questions

1. Prior to *Hicks*, the federal courts of appeals were divided on what a plaintiff had to prove to show pretext. The split developed primarily over whether the *Burdine* surrebuttal required that the plaintiff prove *only* that the defendant's proffered legitimate, nondiscriminatory reason was not credible or, *in addition*, that the defendant was actually motivated by a discriminatory motive. The circuits thus adopted at least three theories on the issue: "pretext only", "pretext-may" (a version of "pretext-only"), and "pretext-plus." *See* Anderson v. Baxter Healthcare Corp., 13 F.3d 1120, 1122–23 (7th Cir.1994). The circuit split developed in the wake of the rather brief discussion of pretext in *Burdine*.

a. *Pretext-only*: Under the pretext-only rule, if the plaintiff convinced the factfinder that the employer's proffered reasons were not credible or not the real reasons for the adverse employment decision, she was automatically entitled to a judgment in her favor. According to the courts adopting pretext-only before *Hicks*, a finding that the employer's articulated justification was false was equivalent to a finding that the employer intentionally discriminated. This is the position adopted by the Court of Appeals in *Hicks*. The pretext-only jurisdictions relied upon several lines of reasoning. First, *Burdine* had adopted an either/or rule: "[the plaintiff] may succeed [in proving intentional discrimination] either directly by persuading the court that a discriminatory reason more likely motivated the employer or indirectly by showing that the employer's proffered explanation is unworthy of credence." 450 U.S. at 256, 101 S.Ct. at 1095. Second, the rationale of *McDonnell Douglas*, *Furnco*, and *Burdine* was that employers generally act for a reason, and those who cannot advance a legitimate, nondiscriminatory reason for an employment decision more likely than not acted with a discriminatory motive. Third, a finding that the defendant's legitimate, nondiscriminatory reason was pretextual or unworthy of credence revived the presumption of discrimination created by the plaintiff's evidence in the prima facie case.

b. *Pretext-may*: The pretext-may rule—sometimes discussed as being a variant of the pretext-only rule—holds that the prima facie case combined with sufficient evidence for a reasonable factfinder to reject the employer's evidence of a legitimate, nondiscriminatory reason permits, but does not require, the factfinder to find that the employer's decision was based on a discriminatory or unlawful motive.

c. *Pretext-plus*: Court that adopted the pretext-plus rule required evidence sufficient to undermine the credibility of the employer's justifications and some *additional* evidence that the employer's *real reason* was motivated by discriminatory intent. Jurisdictions adopting pretext-plus supported the rule on the ground that laws prohibiting discrimination in employment do not prohibit poor business judgment, arbitrary behavior, or discrimination not based on a prohibited criterion. Thus, under pretext-plus, employers who made decisions motivated by considerations not otherwise prohibited by law could conceal their reasons without violating employment discrimination laws. *See, e.g.*, Medina–Munoz v. R.J. Reynolds Tobacco Co., 896 F.2d 5, 9 (1st Cir.1990) ("In the final round of shifting burdens, it is up to plaintiff, unassisted by the original presumption, to show that the employer's stated reason 'was but a pretext for [unlawful discrimination].' To achieve this plateau, a * * * plaintiff must do more than simply refute or cast doubt on the company's rationale for the adverse action. The plaintiff must also show a discriminatory animus based on [an unlawful reason].").

2. *Hicks* clearly rejected the "pretext-only" rule. But the viability of "pretext-plus" and "pretext-may" depends on whether the following two statements from *Hicks* can be reconciled. Can they be reconciled?

a. "The factfinder's disbelief of the reasons put forward by the defendant (particularly if disbelief is accompanied by a suspicion of mendacity) may, together with the elements of the prima facie case, suffice to show intentional discrimination. Thus, rejection of the defendant's proffered reasons, will *permit* the trier of fact to infer the ultimate fact of intentional discrimination, and the Court of Appeals was correct when it noted that, upon such rejection, '[n]o additional proof of discrimination is *required*.' " 509 U.S. at 511, 113 S.Ct. at 2749.

b. "But a reason cannot be proved to be 'a pretext *for discrimination*' unless it is shown *both* that the reason was false and that discrimination was the real reason." 509 US. at 515, 113 S.Ct. at 2752.

3. Justice Souter's dissent in *Hicks* criticized the majority for adopting a rule that "benefit[s] * * * employers who have been found to have given false evidence" because it allows employers to escape liability for their lies. 509 U.S. at 537, 113 S.Ct. at 2763. Justice Scalia responded to Justice Souter by arguing that Title VII is not "a cause of action for perjury." *Id.* at 521, 113 S.Ct. at 2754. But in *ABF Freight System, Inc. v. NLRB*, 510 U.S. 317, 114 S.Ct. 835, 127 L.Ed.2d 152 (1994), a case decided after *Hicks*, Justice Scalia chastised the NLRB for not adopting a rule that would discourage lying in NLRB proceedings. In *ABF Freight*, the Court upheld a decision of the National Labor Relations Board reinstating, with back pay, an employee who was the victim of anti-union discrimination, even though the employee had lied—to his employer and to the administrative law judge who heard the unfair labor practice claim—concerning the reason he was late for work. The Court held that a contrary ruling might force the Board to divert its attention from its primary duty of enforcing labor relations laws and to devote unnecessary attention to resolving collateral disputes about credibility. Also, the Court held that there are "other civil and criminal remedies" to redress perjury, specifically citing Justice Scalia's statement in *Hicks*. *Id.* at 325, 114 S.Ct. at 840. Although Justice Scalia joined in the judgment in *ABF*

Freight, he expressed his disappointment that the Court did not adopt a rule that would discourage perjury: "I concur in the judgment of the Court that the NLRB did nothing against the law, and regret that it missed an opportunity to do something for the law." *Id.* at 331, 114 S.Ct. at 843. Can Justice Scalia's views in the two cases be reconciled? Would a pretext-only rule discourage lying by employers?

4.   One way to look at the different approaches to pretext advocated by Justices Scalia and Souter in *Hicks* is to characterize the case as a judicial debate about the significance of the continuing effects of discrimination almost thirty years after the enactment of the Civil Right Act of 1964. The question thus becomes: If we have made significant "progress" over the past thirty years or so in achieving equality in our society, then do we need the same level of judicial oversight in the implementation of the national policy against discrimination as we needed at the time Congress enacted Title VII in 1964?

5.   A number of academics have argued that courts have defined basic civil rights by manipulating process, that is by focusing on procedure rather than substance. For example, several commentators argued that

> [p]rocedure now defines unlawful discrimination and determines the outcome of Title VII cases. Thus, without grappling with the nature of discrimination, theories of equality, or the historical or sociological complexities of employment disparities between African–Americans and whites, the courts have rewritten the law and changed the workplace behavior using the language of procedure.

Phyllis Tropper Baumann et al., *Substance in the Shadow of Procedure: The Integration of Substantive and Procedural Law in Title VII Cases*, 33 B.C.L.Rev. 211, 220 (1992). Professor Malamud has argued that *Hicks* presents a formalistic approach to the complex problem of reaching agreement on a workable definition of discrimination and that, after *Hicks*, "the *McDonnell Douglas–Burdine* structure can impoverish courts' understanding of the evidence, and decrease the likelihood that courts will recognize the novel legal issues about the nature of discrimination that are so often presented by the evidence even in seemingly routine cases." Deborah C. Malamud, *The Last Minuet: Disparate Treatment After* Hicks, 93 Mich.L.Rev. 2229, 2301 (1995). Do you agree?

> Professor Calloway has argued that

> [i]n enacting Title VII, Congress was primarily concerned with bringing an end to disparate treatment, the most basic form of discrimination. * * * Because direct evidence of discrimination is rarely available, Title VII's success in rooting out disparate treatment has been due, in large measure, to methods of proof based on the assumption that, absent explanation, adverse treatment of statutorily protected groups is more likely than not the result of discrimination. * * *

> * * * With its decision in [*Hicks*] the Court joined academics, judges, and a growing segment of the American population that has come to believe that discrimination no longer exists. Under this view, the failure of African Americans, women, and other groups protected by Title VII to achieve equal employment opportunities results not from

discrimination, but rather from inadequate motivation or deficient personal and work skills. * * * [T]he Court both questioned the continued prevalence of discrimination and invited lower court judges and juries to do the same. * * * Juries, drawn from a society that believes discrimination has been eliminated, may also view alleged discrimination with skepticism.

Deborah A. Calloway, St. Mary's Honor Center v. Hicks: *Questioning the Basic Assumption*, 26 Conn.L.Rev. 997, 997–98 (1994). Professor Calloway further argues that,

> *Hicks* is significant, not for its narrow legal holding, but for the attitude underlying that holding * * * [T]his is about what evidence is sufficient to meet the plaintiff's burden of persuasion on discriminatory intent. What evidence makes it "more likely than not" that the defendant discriminated? The answer depends on one's belief about the prevalence of discrimination.

Id. at 1008–09. Professor Calloway concludes that "[g]iven the continued operation of discrimination," the Supreme Court's analysis in *Hicks* is "inconsistent with reality and unduly burdens plaintiffs seeking redress under Title VII because it allows judges and juries to act on their unfounded and inaccurate assumptions about discrimination." *Id*. at 998.

How would you evaluate Professor Calloway's criticism of *Hicks*? Are her conclusions capable of empirical verification? In thinking about these questions, consider that in 1883 the Supreme Court concluded:

> When a man has emerged from slavery, and by the aid of beneficent legislation has shaken off the inseparable concomitants of that state, there must be some stage in the progress of his elevation when he takes the rank of mere citizen, and ceases to be the special favorite of the laws, and when his rights as a citizen, or a man, are to be protected in the ordinary modes by which other men's rights are protected.

Civil Rights Cases, 109 U.S. 3, 25, 3 S.Ct. 18, 31, 27 L.Ed. 835 (1883). The *Civil Rights Cases* were an integral part of the judicial dismantling of the civil rights legislation enacted after the Civil War to enforce the Thirteenth, Fourteenth, and Fifteenth Amendments. In *Plessy v. Ferguson*, 163 U.S. 537, 16 S.Ct. 1138, 41 L.Ed. 256 (1896), the Supreme Court legitimated the "separate but equal doctrine." *See* Derrick A. Bell, Race, Racism and American Law 55–63 (4th ed.2000); Eugene Gressman, *The Unhappy History of Civil Rights Legislation*, 50 Mich.L.Rev. 1323 (1952). Decisions such as *Plessy v. Ferguson* and the *Civil Rights Cases* helped to usher in the southern Jim Crow laws.

After *Hicks*, a split developed in the lower courts as to a plaintiff's evidentiary burden in opposing a motion for summary judgment or a motion for judgment as a matter of law after a jury had ruled in favor of a plaintiff. Some courts construed *Hicks* as adopting the pretext-plus rule. Other courts construed *Hicks* as adopting the "pretext-may" rule. Furthermore, some courts adopting the pretext-plus construction of

Hicks held that a plaintiff could not succeed in a *McDonnell Douglas* single-motive case unless the plaintiff presented direct evidence to establish pretext. Consequently, there was a substantial increase in motions for summary judgment filed by employers after *Hicks*. In these motions for a summary judgment, which permits prompt disposition of a case in which there is no genuine issue of material facts, employers argued that the evidence was insufficient, as a matter of law, to prove discriminatory animus under the pretext-plus construction of *Hicks*. In addition, even before *Hicks,* there was an increase in the number of summary judgment motions filed by employers in the wake of the Civil Rights Act of 1991, which provides for jury trials in certain disparate treatment cases. The fact that the Civil Rights Act of 1991 provides for compensatory and punitive damages, created strong incentives for employers to seek to have cases resolved by a judge at an early stage rather than risk the possibility of large jury awards. In the following case, the Court once again attempted to clarify its *McDonnell Douglas* analytical framework for deciding the issue of discriminatory animus based on circumstantial evidence.

REEVES v. SANDERSON PLUMBING PRODUCTS, INC.

Supreme Court of the United States, 2000.
530 U.S. 133, 120 S.Ct. 2097, 147 L.Ed.2d 105.

JUSTICE O'CONNOR delivered the opinion of the Court.

This case concerns the kind and amount of evidence necessary to sustain a jury's verdict that an employer unlawfully discriminated on the basis of age. Specifically, we must resolve whether a defendant is entitled to judgment as a matter of law when the plaintiff's case consists exclusively of a prima facie case of discrimination and sufficient evidence for the trier of fact to disbelieve the defendant's legitimate, nondiscriminatory explanation for its action. We must also decide whether the employer was entitled to judgment as a matter of law under the particular circumstances presented here.

I

In October 1995, petitioner Roger Reeves was 57 years old and had spent 40 years in the employ of respondent, Sanderson Plumbing Products, Inc., a manufacturer of toilet seats and covers. Petitioner worked in a department known as the "Hinge Room," where he supervised the "regular line." Joe Oswalt, in his mid-thirties, supervised the Hinge Room's "special line," and Russell Caldwell, the manager of the Hinge Room and age 45, supervised both petitioner and Oswalt. Petitioner's responsibilities included recording the attendance and hours of those under his supervision, and reviewing a weekly report that listed the hours worked by each employee.

In the summer of 1995, Caldwell informed Powe Chesnut, the director of manufacturing and the husband of company president Sandra Sanderson, that "production was down" in the Hinge Room because employees were often absent and were "coming in late and leaving early." Because the monthly attendance reports did not indicate a problem, Chesnut ordered an audit of the Hinge Room's timesheets for July, August, and September of that year. According to Chesnut's testimony, that investigation revealed "numerous timekeeping errors and misrepresentations on the part of Caldwell, Reeves, and Oswalt." Following the audit, Chesnut, along with Dana Jester, vice president of human resources, and Tom Whitaker, vice president of operations, recommended to company president Sanderson that petitioner and Caldwell be fired. In October 1995, Sanderson followed the recommendation and discharged both petitioner and Caldwell.

In June 1996, petitioner filed suit * * * contending that he had been fired because of his age in violation of the Age Discrimination in Employment Act of 1967 (ADEA). At trial, respondent contended that it had fired petitioner due to his failure to maintain accurate attendance records, while petitioner attempted to demonstrate that respondent's explanation was pretext for age discrimination. Petitioner introduced evidence that he had accurately recorded the attendance and hours of the employees under his supervision, and that Chesnut, whom Oswalt described as wielding "absolute power" within the company, had demonstrated age-based animus in his dealings with petitioner.

[After the district court denied the respondent's motions for judgment as a matter of law], * * * the case went to the jury. * * * [T]he jury returned a verdict in favor of petitioner * * *.

The Court of Appeals for the Fifth Circuit reversed, holding that petitioner had not introduced sufficient evidence to sustain the jury's finding of unlawful discrimination. After noting respondent's proffered justification for petitioner's discharge, the court acknowledged that petitioner "very well may" have offered sufficient evidence for "a reasonable jury [to] have found that [respondent's] explanation for its employment decision was pretextual." The court explained, however, that this was "not dispositive" of the ultimate issue—namely, "whether Reeves presented sufficient evidence that his age motivated [respondent's] employment decision." Addressing this question, the court weighed petitioner's additional evidence of discrimination against other circumstances surrounding his discharge. Specifically, the court noted that Chesnut's age-based comments "were not made in the direct context of Reeves's termination"; there was no allegation that the two other individuals who had recommended that petitioner be fired (Jester and Whitaker) were motivated by age; two of the decisionmakers involved in petitioner's discharge (Jester and Sanderson) were over the age of 50; all three of the Hinge Room supervisors were accused of inaccurate recordkeeping; and several of respondent's management positions were filled by persons over age 50 when petitioner was fired. On this basis, the court concluded that petitioner had not introduced sufficient evidence for a rational jury to conclude that he had been discharged because of his age.

We granted certiorari to resolve a conflict among the Courts of Appeals as to whether a plaintiff's prima facie case of discrimination (as defined in *McDonnell Douglas)*, combined with sufficient evidence for a reasonable factfinder to reject the employer's nondiscriminatory explanation for its decision, is adequate to sustain a finding of liability for intentional discrimination. * * *.

II

* * * This Court has not squarely addressed whether the *McDonnell Douglas* framework, developed to assess claims brought under § 703(a)(1) of Title VII of the Civil Rights Act of 1964 also applies to ADEA actions. Because the parties do not dispute the issue, we shall assume, arguendo, that the *McDonnell Douglas* framework is fully applicable here.

* * * It is undisputed that petitioner satisfied this burden here: (i) at the time he was fired, he was a member of the class protected by the ADEA ("individuals who are at least 40 years of age," 29 U.S.C. § 631(a)), (ii) he was otherwise qualified for the position of Hinge Room supervisor, (iii) he was discharged by respondent, and (iv) respondent successively hired three persons in their thirties to fill petitioner's position. The burden therefore shifted to respondent to "produc[e] evidence that the plaintiff was rejected, or someone else was preferred, for a legitimate, nondiscriminatory reason." *Burdine, supra*, at 254. This burden is one of production, not persuasion; it "can involve no credibility assessment." *St. Mary's Honor Center, supra*, at 509. Respondent met this burden by offering admissible evidence sufficient for the trier of fact to conclude that petitioner was fired because of his failure to maintain accurate attendance records. Accordingly, "the *McDonnell Douglas* framework—with its presumptions and burdens"—disappeared, *St. Mary's Honor Center, supra*, at 510, and the sole remaining issue was "discrimination *vel non*," *Aikens, supra*, at 714.

* * *

In this case, the evidence supporting respondent's explanation for petitioner's discharge consisted primarily of testimony by Chesnut and Sanderson and documentation of petitioner's alleged "shoddy record keeping." Chesnut testified that a 1993 audit of Hinge Room operations revealed "a very lax assembly line" where employees were not adhering to general work rules. As a result of that audit, petitioner was placed on 90 days' probation for unsatisfactory performance. In 1995, Chesnut ordered another investigation of the Hinge Room, which, according to his testimony, revealed that petitioner was not correctly recording the absences and hours of employees. Respondent introduced summaries of that investigation documenting several attendance violations by 12 employees under petitioner's supervision, and noting that each should have been disciplined in some manner. Chesnut testified that this failure to discipline absent and late employees is "extremely important when you are dealing with a union" because uneven enforcement across departments would keep the company "in grievance and arbitration cases, which are costly, all the time." He and Sanderson also stated that petitioner's errors, by failing to adjust for hours not worked, cost the company overpaid wages. Sanderson testified that she accepted the recommendation to discharge petitioner because he had "intentionally falsif[ied] company pay records."

Petitioner, however, made a substantial showing that respondent's explanation was false. First, petitioner offered evidence that he had properly maintained the attendance records. Most of the timekeeping errors cited by respondent involved employees who were not marked late but who were recorded as having arrived at the plant at 7 a.m. for the 7 a.m. shift. Respondent contended that employees arriving at 7 a.m. could not have been at their workstations by 7 a.m., and therefore must have been late. But both petitioner and Oswalt testified that the company's automated timeclock often failed to scan employees' timecards, so that the timesheets would not record any time of arrival. On these occasions, petitioner and Oswalt would visually check the workstations and record whether the employees were present at the start of the shift. They stated that if an employee arrived promptly but the timesheet contained no time of arrival, they would reconcile the two by marking "7 a.m." as the employee's arrival time, even if the employee actually arrived at the plant earlier. On cross-examination, Chesnut acknowledged that the timeclock sometimes malfunctioned, and that if "people were there at their work station[s]" at the start of the shift, the supervisor "would write in seven o'clock." Petitioner also testified that when employees arrived before or stayed after their shifts, he would assign them additional work so they would not be overpaid.

Petitioner similarly cast doubt on whether he was responsible for any failure to discipline late and absent employees. Petitioner testified that his job only included reviewing the daily and weekly attendance reports, and that disciplinary writeups were based on the monthly reports, which were reviewed by Caldwell. Sanderson admitted that Caldwell, and not petitioner, was responsible for citing employees for violations of the company's attendance policy. Further, Chesnut conceded that there had never been a union grievance or employee complaint arising from petitioner's recordkeeping, and that the company had never calculated the amount of overpayments allegedly attributable to petitioner's errors. Petitioner also testified that, on the day he was fired, Chesnut said that his discharge was due to his failure to report as absent one employee, Gina Mae Coley, on two days in September 1995. But petitioner explained that he had spent those days in the hospital, and that Caldwell was therefore responsible for any overpayment of Coley. Finally, petitioner stated that on previous occasions that employees were paid for hours they had not worked, the company had simply adjusted those employees' next paychecks to correct the errors.

Based on this evidence, the Court of Appeals concluded that petitioner "very well may be correct" that "a reasonable jury could have found that [respondent's] explanation for its employment decision was pretextual." Nonetheless, the court held that this showing, standing alone, was insufficient to sustain the jury's finding of liability: "We must, as an essential final step, determine whether Reeves presented sufficient evidence that his age motivated [respondent's] employment decision." And in making this determination, the Court of Appeals ignored the evidence supporting petitioner's prima facie case and challenging respondent's explanation for its decision. The court confined its review of evidence favoring petitioner to that evidence showing that Chesnut had directed derogatory, age-based comments at petitioner, and that Chesnut had singled out petitioner for harsher treatment than younger employees. It is therefore apparent that the court believed that only this additional evidence of discrimination was relevant to whether the jury's verdict should stand. That is, the Court of Appeals proceeded from the assumption that a prima facie case of discrimination, combined with sufficient evidence for the trier of fact to disbelieve the defendant's legitimate, nondiscriminatory reason for its decision, is insufficient as a matter of law to sustain a jury's finding of intentional discrimination.

In so reasoning, the Court of Appeals misconceived the evidentiary burden borne by plaintiffs who attempt to prove intentional discrimination through indirect evidence. This much is evident from our decision in *St. Mary's Honor Center.* There we held that the factfinder's rejection of the employer's legitimate, nondiscriminatory reason for its action does not compel judgment for the plaintiff. The ultimate question is whether the employer intentionally discriminated, and proof that "the employer's proffered reason is unpersuasive, or even obviously contrived, does not necessarily establish that the plaintiff's proffered reason * * * is correct." *Id.*, at 524. In other words, "[i]t is not enough * * * to disbelieve the employer; the factfinder must believe the plaintiff's explanation of intentional discrimination." *Id.*, at 519.

In reaching this conclusion, however, we reasoned that it is permissible for the trier of fact to infer the ultimate fact of discrimination from the falsity of the employer's explanation. Specifically, we stated:

> The factfinder's disbelief of the reasons put forward by the defendant (particularly if disbelief is accompanied by a suspicion of mendacity) may, together with the elements of the prima facie case, suffice to show intentional discrimination. Thus, rejection of the defendant's proffered reasons will permit the trier of fact to infer the ultimate fact of intentional discrimination.

Id., at 511.

Proof that the defendant's explanation is unworthy of credence is simply one form of circumstantial evidence that is probative of intentional discrimination, and it may be quite persuasive. *See id.*, at 517 ("[P]roving the employer's reason false becomes part of (and often considerably assists) the greater enterprise of proving that the real reason was intentional discrimination"). In appropriate circumstances, the trier of fact can reasonably infer from the falsity of the explanation that the employer is dissembling to cover up a discriminatory purpose.

Such an inference is consistent with the general principle of evidence law that the factfinder is entitled to consider a party's dishonesty about a material fact as "affirmative evidence of guilt." Wright v. West, 505 U.S. 277, 296 (1992). Moreover, once the employer's justification has been eliminated, discrimination may well be the most likely alternative explanation, especially since the employer is in the best position to put forth the actual reason for its decision. * * * Thus, a plaintiff's prima facie case, combined with sufficient evidence to find that the employer's asserted justification is false, may permit the trier of fact to conclude that the employer unlawfully discriminated.

This is not to say that such a showing by the plaintiff will always be adequate to sustain a jury's finding of liability. Certainly there will be instances where, although the plaintiff has established a prima facie case and set forth sufficient evidence to reject the defendant's explanation, no rational factfinder could conclude that the action was discriminatory. For instance, an employer would be entitled to judgment as a matter of law if the record conclusively revealed some other, nondiscriminatory reason for the employer's decision, or if the plaintiff created only a weak issue of fact as to whether the employer's reason was untrue and there was abundant and uncontroverted independent evidence that no discrimination had occurred. *See* Aka v. Washington Hosp. Ctr., 156 F.3d, at 1291–1292; *see also* Fisher v. Vassar College, 114 F.3d, at 1338 ("[I]f the circumstances show that the defendant gave the false explanation to conceal something other than discrimination, the inference of discrimination will be weak or nonexistent"). To hold otherwise would be effectively to insulate an entire category of employment discrimination cases from review under Rule 50, and we have reiterated that trial courts should not "treat discrimination differently from other ultimate questions of fact." *St. Mary's Honor Center, supra*, at 524 (quoting *Aikens*, 460 U.S., at 716).

Whether judgment as a matter of law is appropriate in any particular case will depend on a number of factors. Those include the strength of the plaintiff's prima facie case, the probative value of the proof that the employer's explanation is false, and any other evidence that supports the employer's case and that properly may be considered on a motion for judgment as a matter of law. For purposes of this case, we need not—and could not—resolve all of the circumstances in which such factors would entitle an employer to judgment as a matter of law. It suffices to say that, because a prima facie case and sufficient evidence to reject the employer's explanation may permit a finding of liability, the Court of Appeals erred in proceeding from the premise that a plaintiff must always introduce additional, independent evidence of discrimination.

III

A

The remaining question is whether, despite the Court of Appeals' misconception of petitioner's evidentiary burden, respondent was nonetheless entitled to judgment as a matter of law. Under Rule 50, a court should render judgment as a matter of law when "a party has been fully heard on an issue and there is no legally sufficient evidentiary basis for a reasonable jury to find for that party on that issue." Fed. Rule Civ.Proc. 50(a). The Courts of Appeals have articulated differing formulations as to what evidence a court is to consider in ruling on a Rule 50 motion. * * *

* * * [T]he standard for granting summary judgment "mirrors" the standard for judgment as a matter of law, such that "the inquiry under each is the same." Anderson v. Liberty Lobby, Inc., 477 U.S. 242, 250–251 (1986). It therefore follows that, in entertaining a motion for judgment as a matter of law, the court should review all of the evidence in the record.

In doing so, however, the court must draw all reasonable inferences in favor of the nonmoving party, and it may not make credibility determinations or weigh the evidence. "Credibility determinations, the weighing of the evidence, and the drawing of legitimate inferences from the facts are jury functions, not those of a judge." *Liberty Lobby, supra*, at 255. Thus, although the court should review the record as a whole, it must disregard all evidence favorable to the moving party that the jury is not required to believe. *See* Wright & Miller 299. That is, the court should give credence to the evidence favoring the nonmovant as well as that "evidence supporting the moving party that is uncontradicted and unimpeached, at least to the extent that that evidence comes from disinterested witnesses." *Id.*, at 300.

B

Applying this standard here, it is apparent that respondent was not entitled to judgment as a matter of law. In this case, in addition to establishing a prima facie case of discrimination and creating a jury issue as to the falsity of the employer's explanation, petitioner introduced additional evidence that Chesnut was motivated by age-based animus and was principally responsible for petitioner's firing. Petitioner testified that Chesnut had told him that he "was so old [he] must have come over on the Mayflower" and, on one occasion when petitioner was having difficulty starting a machine, that he "was too damn old to do [his] job." According to petitioner, Chesnut would regularly "cuss at me and shake his finger in my face." Oswalt, roughly 24 years younger than petitioner, corroborated that there was an "obvious difference" in how Chesnut treated them. He stated that, although he and Chesnut "had [their] differences," "it was nothing compared to the way [Chesnut] treated Roger." Oswalt explained that Chesnut "tolerated quite a bit" from him even though he "defied" Chesnut "quite often," but that Chesnut treated petitioner "[i]n a manner, as you would * * * treat * * * a child when * * * you're angry with [him]." Petitioner also demonstrated that, according to company records, he and Oswalt had nearly identical rates of productivity in 1993. Yet respondent conducted an efficiency study of only the regular line, supervised by petitioner, and placed only petitioner on probation. Chesnut conducted that efficiency study and, after having testified to the contrary on direct examination, acknowledged on cross-examination that he had recommended that petitioner be placed on probation following the study.

Further, petitioner introduced evidence that Chesnut was the actual decisionmaker behind his firing. Chesnut was married to Sanderson, who made the formal decision to discharge petitioner. Although Sanderson testified that she fired petitioner because he had "intentionally falsif[ied] company pay records," respondent only introduced evidence concerning the inaccuracy of the records, not their falsification. A 1994 letter authored by Chesnut indicated that he berated other company directors, who were supposedly his co-equals, about how to do their jobs. Moreover, Oswalt testified that all of respondent's employees feared Chesnut, and that Chesnut had exercised "absolute power" within the company for "[a]s long as [he] can remember."

In holding that the record contained insufficient evidence to sustain the jury's verdict, the Court of Appeals misapplied the standard of review dictated by Rule 50. Again, the court disregarded critical evidence favorable to petitioner—namely, the evidence supporting petitioner's prima facie case and undermining respondent's nondiscriminatory explanation. The court also failed to draw all reasonable inferences in favor of petitioner. For instance, while acknowledging "the potentially damning nature" of Chesnut's age-related comments, the court discounted them on the ground that they "were not made in the direct context of Reeves's termination." And the court discredited petitioner's evidence that Chesnut was the actual decisionmaker by giving weight to the fact that there was "no evidence to suggest that any of the other decision makers were motivated by age." Moreover, the other evidence on which the court relied—that Caldwell and Oswalt were also cited for poor recordkeeping, and that respondent employed many managers over age 50—although relevant, is certainly not dispositive. *See Furnco*, 438 U. S., at 580 (evidence that employer's work force was racially balanced, while "not wholly irrelevant," was not "sufficient to conclusively demonstrate that [the employer's] actions were not discriminatorily motivated"). In concluding that these circumstances so overwhelmed the evidence favoring petitioner that no rational trier of fact could have found that petitioner was fired because of his age, the Court of Appeals impermissibly substituted its judgment concerning the weight of the evidence for the jury's.

The ultimate question in every employment discrimination case involving a claim of disparate treatment is whether the plaintiff was the victim of intentional discrimination. Given the evidence in the record supporting petitioner, we see no reason to subject the parties to an additional round of litigation before the Court of Appeals rather than to resolve the matter here. * * * Given that petitioner established a prima facie case of discrimination, introduced enough evidence for the jury to reject respondent's explanation, and produced additional evidence of age-based animus, there was sufficient evidence for the jury to find that respondent had intentionally discriminated. The District Court was therefore correct to submit the case to the jury, and the Court of Appeals erred in overturning its verdict.

For these reasons, the judgment of the Court of Appeals is reversed.

JUSTICE GINSBURG, concurring.

The Court today holds that an employment discrimination plaintiff may survive judgment as a matter of law by submitting two categories of evidence: first, evidence establishing a "prima facie case," as that term is used in *McDonnell Douglas*; and second, evidence from which a rational factfinder could conclude that the employer's proffered explanation for its actions was false. Because the Court of Appeals in this case plainly, and erroneously, required the plaintiff to offer some evidence beyond those two categories, no broader holding is necessary to support reversal.

I write separately to note that it may be incumbent on the Court, in an appropriate case, to define more precisely the circumstances in which plaintiffs will be required to submit evidence beyond these two categories in order to survive a motion for judgment as a matter of law. I anticipate that such circumstances will be uncommon. As the Court notes, it is a principle of evidence law that the jury is entitled to treat a party's dishonesty about a material fact as evidence of culpability. Under this commonsense principle, evidence suggesting that a defendant accused of illegal discrimination has chosen to give a false explanation for its actions gives rise to a rational inference that the defendant could be masking its actual, illegal motivation. Whether the defendant was in fact motivated by discrimination is of course for the finder of fact to decide; that is the lesson of *St. Mary's Honor Center v. Hicks*. But the inference remains—unless it is conclusively demonstrated, by evidence the district court is required to credit on a motion for judgment as a matter of law, that discrimination could not have been the defendant's true motivation. If such conclusive demonstrations are (as I suspect) atypical, it follows that the ultimate question of liability ordinarily should not be taken from the jury once the plaintiff has introduced the two categories of evidence described above. Because the Court's opinion leaves room for such further elaboration in an appropriate case, I join it in full.

Notes and Questions

1. One of the main differences between *Hicks* and *Reeves* is that the issue of the role of pretext in disparate treatment cases arose in different postures. In *Hicks*, the issue concerned the kind and amount of evidence necessary to allow a factfinder to find in favor of a plaintiff on the ultimate fact issue of intentional discrimination after all of the evidence has been presented by the parties. The issue in *Reeves*, on the other hand, concerned the kind and amount of evidence necessary to raise a triable fact issue regarding discriminatory animus in the context of either a Rule 50 motion for judgment as a matter of law after the case has been tried or a Rule 56 motion for summary judgment before the case goes to trial. Note how broadly the Court in *Reeves* stated the issue: "We granted certiorari * * * to

resolve a conflict among the Courts of Appeals as to whether a plaintiff's prima facie case of discrimination * * *, combined with sufficient evidence for a reasonable factfinder to reject the employer's nondiscriminatory explanation for its decision, is adequate to sustain a finding of liability for intentional discrimination."

2. Does *Reeves* resolve the conflicting interpretations of pretext in *Hicks*, i.e., pretext-plus and pretext-only? If so, is pretext-plus no longer relevant after *Reeves*? Does it really matter if pretext-plus is dead or alive in view of the fact that the ultimate finding of intentional discrimination is to be made on the "record as a whole"?

3. *Reeves* did not categorically hold that the prima facie case plus sufficient evidence to challenge the believability of an employer's legitimate, nondiscriminatory reason are always sufficient to submit the case to the factfinder. The Court indicated that there may be cases in which additional evidence may be necessary on the issue of intentional discrimination beyond the prima facie case and the falsity of the employer legitimate nondiscriminatory reason. Implicit in Justice Ginsburg's concurring opinion was her concern that the court's "additional evidence" exception would likely lead to the same ambiguous legacy created by *Hicks*. Does the concern raised by Justice Ginsburg leave open the possibility that some version of "pretext-plus" is viable even after *Reeves*?

4. Consider the following excerpt from *Zimmermann v. Associates First Capital Corp.*, 251 F.3d 376, 381–82 (2d Cir.2001), in light of Justice Ginsburg's concern about the "additional evidence" exception in *Reeves*:

> Since *Reeves,* the case law has been developing as to what sort of a record will permit a plaintiff who presents evidence of a *prima facie* case and evidence of a pretext to have a jury consider the ultimate issue of discrimination and what sort of record will entitle a defendant to judgment as a matter of law. The Fifth Circuit appears to understand *Reeves* to mean that a *prima facie* case and evidence of pretext take a case to a jury in the absence of "*unusual circumstances* that would prevent a rational fact-finder from concluding that the employer's reasons for failing to promote her were discriminatory and in violation of Title VII." *Blow v. City of San Antonio,* 236 F.3d 293, 298 (5th Cir.2001) (emphasis added). * * * The Fourth Circuit has observed that if the plaintiff proves a *prima facie* case and pretext, her claim must go to a jury unless "there is evidence that precludes a finding of discrimination." *Rowe v. Marley Co.,* 233 F.3d 825, 830 (4th Cir.2000).

> Our Circuit has not read *Reeves* quite so favorably to Title VII plaintiffs. Without insisting on unusual circumstances or evidence precluding a finding of discrimination, as the Fourth and Fifth Circuits have done, we have simply ruled in several cases that a record that included evidence of a *prima facie* case and evidence permitting a finding of pretext did not suffice to permit a finding of discrimination. The task * * * is to examine the entire record and, in accordance with *Reeves,* make the case-specific assessment as to whether a finding of discrimination may reasonably be made.

Which view of pretext is the most reasonable interpretation of *Reeves*? A circuit-by-circuit analysis is provided in Ryan Vantrease, *The Aftermath of*

St. Mary's Honor Center v. Hicks *and* Reeves v. Sanderson Plumbing Prod., Inc.: *A Call For Clarification*, 39 Brandeis L.J. 747 (2001).

5. What arguments would you make on behalf of the plaintiff or the employer that a triable issue of intentional discrimination is or is not raised in the following situations?

a. Green, a black male, applies for a vacancy at McDonnell Douglas for which he is qualified. McDonnell Douglas rejects Green's application on the ground that he is not qualified for the position. Green brings a Title VII employment discrimination claim against McDonnell Douglas alleging that he was denied the vacancy because of his race. McDonnell Douglas relies on Green's lack of qualifications as its legitimate, nondiscriminatory reason for not hiring him. Green presents evidence that the person McDonnell Douglas hired for the vacancy is substantially less qualified than Green based on the company's own written qualifications for the vacancy. There is also evidence in the record that Green's application was rejected because he wears dreadlocks and that McDonnell Douglas has an unwritten practice of not hiring anyone who wears dreadlocks.

b. Juan Pera, who worked for a bank as an investment banker brings an employment discrimination case against his employer alleging that he was fired because of his national origin. Pera presents evidence that supports a prima facie case of national origin discrimination, including proof that he was qualified to do his job and that his position was filled by someone of a different national origin. The employer's rebuttal evidence is that Pera was fired because of insubordination after he refused to complete an assigned work order. In surrebuttal, Pera testifies that he refused to complete the work assignment because the project would have required him to violate federal banking laws, that he threatened to report this fact to federal banking officials, and that his supervisor told him to "keep his mouth shut" if he ever wanted to work in the banking business again. *See* Rothmeier v. Investment Advisers, Inc., 85 F.3d 1328 (8th Cir.1996).

6. Professor Lanctot has argued that *Reeves* created a "cryptic loophole" and that "[t]he long history of pretext litigation shows that courts will exploit any loopholes provided by the Supreme Court to dismiss what they consider to be unmeritorious discrimination suits." Catherine J. Lanctot, *Secrets and Lies: The Need for a Definitive Rule of Law in Pretext Cases*, 61 La.L.Rev. 539, 544, 546 (2001).

7. Suppose an employer's rebuttal to a prima facie case is that a plaintiff was denied an employment opportunity because it was awarded to a better qualified candidate. How might the plaintiff raise a triable issue of intentional discrimination for pretext analysis? In *Millbrook v. IBP, Inc.*, 280 F.3d 1169 (7th Cir.), *cert. denied*, 573 U.S. 884, 123 S.Ct. 117, 154 L.Ed.2d 143 (2002), the court ruled that

> " * * * a plaintiff's own frequent admonitions about her work performance or qualifications do not sufficiently cast doubt on the legitimacy of her employer's proffered reasons for its employment actions." Similarly * * * "mere submission of materials from a co-worker or supervisor indicating that an employee's performance is satisfactory does not * * * create a material issue of fact." A plaintiff's contention that he is the better candidate for a vacancy constitutes nothing but the employee's

own opinion as to his qualifications. This cannot create an issue of material fact because "[a]n employee's perception of his own performance * * * cannot tell a reasonable factfinder something about what the employer believes about the employee's abilities." "And without proof of a lie [as to what the employer believed] no inference of discriminatory motive can be drawn."

Id. at 1181 (citations omitted).

In *Deines v. Texas Department of Protective & Regulatory Services*, 164 F.3d 277, 279 (5th Cir.1999), the Fifth Circuit reaffirmed its rule that where a claim of discrimination is based on relative qualifications, "disparities in qualifications are not enough in and of themselves to demonstrate discriminatory intent unless those disparities are so apparent as to virtually jump off the page and slap you in the face." The court based its rule on the proposition that

> it is not the function of the jury to scrutinize the employer's judgment as to who is the best qualified to fill the position; nor is it the jury's task to weigh the respective qualifications of the applicants. * * * The single issue for the trier of fact is whether the employer's selection of a particular applicant over the plaintiff was motivated by discrimination.

Id. at 281. Other courts have adopted the Fifth Circuit's "jump off the page" rule. *See Millbrook*, 280 F.3d at 1179–80 (collecting cases). Is *Deines* still good law after *Reeves*? *See* Manning v. Chevron Chem. Co., 332 F.3d 874, 884 (5th Cir.2003) (Dennis, J., concurring) (questioning whether *Deines* remains good law after *Reeves)*.

Note: The Perjurious Client and a Lawyer's Ethical Obligations

Recall that in *Hicks* the Supreme Court said that the term "pretext" provides "no justification for assuming * * * that those employers whose evidence is disbelieved are perjurers and liars," and "[t]o say that the company which in good faith introduces such testimony, or even the testifying employee himself, becomes a liar and a perjurer when the testimony is not believed, is nothing short of absurd." 509 U.S. at 520–21, 113 S.Ct. at 2742. A witness commits perjury if (a) he testifies under oath about a material fact; (b) his testimony is false; (c) he knows it is false; and (d) his testimony is voluntary and intentional and not the result of confusion, mistake, or faulty memory. *Compare* 18 U.S.C. § 1621 (1994) *with* United States v. Dunnigan, 507 U.S. 87, 113 S.Ct. 1111, 122 L.Ed.2d 445 (1993); *and* United States v. Swink, 21 F.3d 852, 857–59 (8th Cir.1994). Federal and state judges, lawyers, and legal academics believe that perjury in some form permeates civil and criminal proceedings, and that perjury is on the rise. Even though there are federal and state laws on perjury, prosecution for perjury occupies a low priority for prosecutors because of lack of adequate resources. In many instances, witnesses lie because they know they will get away with it. *See* Mark Curriden, *The Lies Have It*, 81 A.B.A.J. 68 (May 1995). *See also* Richard C. Wydick, *The Ethics of Witness Coaching*, 17 Cardozo L.Rev. 1 (1995).

A perjurious client (or "Pinocchio" client) can be a problem for an attorney who must ethically and effectively discharge the responsibilities owed to the client, colleagues, the public, the courts, and to himself or herself. The difficulties arise because of two competing imperatives in the ABA Model Rules of Professional Conduct and Disciplinary Rules. Model Rule 3.3 (Candor Toward the Tribunal) provides that a lawyer shall not knowingly "offer evidence that the lawyer knows to be false." Model Rule 3.4(b) states that a lawyer must not "counsel or assist a witness to testify falsely." Model Rule 1.6 (Confidentiality of Information) provides for client confidentiality. Model Rule 3.3 and almost all jurisdictions provide that the rule against false testimony trumps Model Rule 1.6 on confidentiality. Model Code DR 7–102(A)(4) provides that a lawyer must not "knowingly use perjured testimony or false evidence," and Model Code DR 7–102(A)(6) states that a lawyer must not "participate in the creation or preservation of evidence when he knows or it is obvious that the evidence is false."

Another source of concern is procedural. Under Rule 11 of the Federal Rules of Civil Procedure, every pleading, written motion, and similar court document submitted to a federal court by a represented party must be signed by an attorney of record in his or her own name. The signature on the document is deemed to certify that the attorney has made a reasonable inquiry into the facts and that all the allegations or factual assertions are either supported by evidence or likely to be supported by evidence after further investigation or discovery. Denials of fact must be either warranted by the evidence or identified as being reasonably based on a lack of information or belief. Violations of Rule 11 can subject the signing attorney, as well as law firms and parties, to sanctions, including payment of attorney's fees resulting from the violation.

To what extent does *Hicks* compound the legal and ethical difficulties an attorney faces with a perjurious client or witness in employment litigation? Or does the *Hicks* majority's treatment of lying pose any ethical problems for an attorney at all? What is the extent of an attorney's ethical obligation to ensure that his client is truthful in testifying or presenting other kinds of evidence?

EEOC v. CONSOLIDATED SERVICE SYSTEMS

United States Court of Appeals for the Seventh Circuit, 1993.
989 F.2d 233.

POSNER, Circuit Judge.

The Equal Employment Opportunity Commission brought this suit in 1985 against a small company which provides janitorial and cleaning services at a number of buildings in the Chicago area. The owner of the company is a Korean immigrant, as are most of its employees. The suit charges that the company discriminated in favor of persons of Korean origin, in violation of Title VII, * * * by relying mainly on word of mouth to obtain new employees. After a bench trial, the district judge dismissed the suit on the ground that the Commission had failed to prove discrimination * * *.

Between 1983, when Mr. Hwang, the company's owner, bought the company from its previous owner, also a Korean, and the first quarter of 1987, 73 percent of the applicants for jobs with Consolidated, and 81 percent of the hires, were Korean. Less than 1 percent of the work force in Cook County is Korean and at most 3 percent of the janitorial and cleaner work force. It doesn't take a statistician to tell you that the difference between the percentage of Koreans in Consolidated's work force and the percentage of Koreans in the relevant labor market, however exactly that market is defined, is not due to chance. But is it due to discrimination? The district judge found it was not, and we do not think his finding was clearly erroneous.

There is no direct evidence of discrimination. The question is whether the circumstantial evidence compels an inference of discrimination—*intentional* discrimination ("disparate treatment," in the jargon of Title VII cases). * * *

We said that Consolidated is a small company. The EEOC's lawyer told us at argument that the company's annual sales are only $400,000. We mention this fact not to remind the reader of David and Goliath, or to suggest that Consolidated is exempt from Title VII (it is not), or to express wonderment that a firm of this size could litigate in federal court for seven years (and counting) with a federal agency, but to explain why Mr. Hwang relies on word of mouth to obtain employees rather than reaching out to a broader community less heavily Korean. It is the cheapest method of recruitment. Indeed, it is practically costless. Persons approach Hwang or his employees—most of whom are Korean too—at work or at social events, and once or twice Hwang has asked employees whether they know anyone who wants a job. At argument the EEOC's lawyer conceded, perhaps improvidently but if so only slightly so, that Hwang's recruitment posture could be described as totally passive. Hwang did buy newspaper advertisements on three occasions—once in a Korean-language newspaper and twice in the *Chicago Tribune*—but as these ads resulted in zero hires, the experience doubtless only confirmed him in the passive posture. The EEOC argues that the single Korean newspaper ad, which ran for only three days and yielded not a single hire, is evidence of discrimination. If so, it is very weak evidence. The Commission points to the fact that Hwang could have obtained job applicants at no expense from the Illinois Job Service as further evidence of discrimination. But he testified that he had never heard of the Illinois Job Service and the district judge believed him.

If an employer can obtain all the competent workers he wants, at wages no higher than the minimum that he expects to have to pay, without beating the bushes for workers—without in fact spending a cent on recruitment—he can reduce his costs of doing business by adopting just the stance of Mr. Hwang. And this is no mean consideration to a firm whose annual revenues in a highly competitive business are those of a mom and pop grocery store. Of course if the employer is a member of an ethnic community, especially an immigrant one, this stance is likely to result in the perpetuation of an ethnically imbalanced work force.

Members of these communities tend to work and to socialize with each other rather than with people in the larger community. The social and business network of an immigrant community racially and culturally distinct from the majority of Americans is bound to be largely confined to that community, making it inevitable that when the network is used for job recruitment the recruits will be drawn disproportionately from the community.

No inference of *intentional* discrimination can be drawn from the pattern we have described, even if the employer would prefer to employ people drawn predominantly or even entirely from his own ethnic or, here, national-origin community. Discrimination is not preference or aversion; it is acting on the preference or aversion. If the most efficient method of hiring, adopted *because* it is the most efficient (not defended because it is efficient—the statute does not allow an employer to justify intentional discrimination by reference to efficiency, 42 U.S.C. § 2000e–2(k)(2)), just happens to produce a work force whose racial or religious or ethnic or national-origin or gender composition pleases the employer, this is not intentional discrimination. EEOC v. Chicago Miniature Lamp Works, 947 F.2d 292, 299 (7th Cir.1991). The motive is not a discriminatory one. "Knowledge of a disparity is not the same thing as an intent to cause or maintain it." American Nurses' Ass'n v. Illinois, 783 F.2d 716, 722 (7th Cir.1986). Or if, though the motives behind adoption of the method were a mixture of discrimination and efficiency, Mr. Hwang would have adopted the identical method of recruitment even if he had no interest in the national origin of his employees, the fact that he had such an interest would not be a "but for" cause of the discriminatory outcome and again there would be no liability. There is no evidence that Hwang *is* biased in favor of Koreans or prejudiced against any group underrepresented in his work force, except what the Commission asks us to infer from the imbalance in that force and Hwang's passive stance.

We said the passive stance is the cheapest method of recruitment. It may also be highly effective in producing a good work force. There are two reasons. The first is that an applicant referred by an existing employee is likely to get a franker, more accurate, more relevant picture of working conditions than if he learns about the job from an employment agency, a newspaper ad, or a hiring supervisor. The employee can give him the real low-down about the job. The result is a higher probability of a good match, and a lower probability that the new hire will be disappointed or disgruntled, perform badly, and quit. Second, an employee who refers someone for employment may get in trouble with his employer if the person he refers is a dud; so word of mouth recruitment in effect enlists existing employees to help screen new applicants conscientiously.

If this were a disparate-impact case (as it was once, but the Commission has abandoned its claim of disparate impact), and, if, contrary to *EEOC v. Chicago Miniature Lamp Works*, 947 F.2d at 304–05, word of mouth recruitment were deemed an employment practice and hence was subject to review for disparate impact, as assumed in *Clark v. Chrysler*

Corp., 673 F.2d 921, 927 (7th Cir.1982), and held in *Thomas v. Washington County School Board*, 915 F.2d 922, 924–26 (4th Cir.1990), then the advantages of word of mouth recruitment would have to be balanced against its possibly discriminatory effect when the employer's current work force is already skewed along racial or other disfavored lines. But in a case of disparate treatment, the question is different. It is whether word of mouth recruitment gives rise to an inference of intentional discrimination. Unlike an explicit racial or ethnic criterion or, what we may assume without deciding amounts to the same thing, a rule confining hiring to relatives of existing employees in a racially or ethnically skewed work force, as in *Thomas v. Washington County School Board*, word of mouth recruiting does not compel an inference of intentional discrimination. At least it does not do so where, as in the case of Consolidated Service Systems, it is clearly, as we have been at pains to emphasize, the cheapest and most efficient method of recruitment, notwithstanding its discriminatory impact. Of course, Consolidated had some non-Korean applicants for employment, and if it had never hired any this would support, perhaps decisively, an inference of discrimination. Although the respective percentages of Korean and of non-Korean applicants hired were clearly favorable to Koreans (33 percent to 20 percent), the EEOC was unable, as explained more fully below, to find a single person out of the 99 rejected non-Koreans who could show that he or she was interested in a job that Mr. Hwang ever hired for. Many, perhaps most, of these were persons who responded to the ad he placed in the *Chicago Tribune* for a contract that he never got, hence never hired for.

The Commission cites the statement of Consolidated's lawyer that his client took advantage of the fact that the Korean immigrant community offered a ready market of cheap labor as an admission of "active" discrimination on the basis of national origin. It is not discrimination, and it is certainly not active discrimination, for an employer to sit back and wait for people willing to work for low wages to apply to him. The fact that they are ethnically or racially uniform does not impose upon him a duty to spend money advertising in the help-wanted columns of the *Chicago Tribune*. The Commission deemed Consolidated's "admission" corroborated by the testimony of the sociologist William Liu, Consolidated's own expert witness, who explained that it was natural for a recent Korean immigrant such as Hwang to hire other recent Korean immigrants, with whom he shared a common culture, and that the consequence would be a work force disproportionately Korean. Well, of course. People who share a common culture tend to work together as well as marry together and socialize together. That is not evidence of illegal discrimination.

Although the Commission's witness list contained the names of 99 persons whom Hwang had refused to hire allegedly because they were not Korean, at trial it presented only four of these persons as witnesses. One was a woman whose national origin the record does not disclose, but we shall assume that she is not Korean. She applied for a job with

Consolidated in response to one of the ads he had placed in the *Tribune*. She was not hired. Hwang testified that he hired no one who responded to the ad because he failed to receive the contract which he had placed the ad in expectation of receiving. The district judge believed him. The judge also thought it odd that this witness had been a receptionist both before she applied for the job with Consolidated and after she failed to get it. He doubted that she had really wanted a job cleaning buildings.

The next witness had responded to the same ad. His national origin, too, is not of record but we may assume from his name and from the fact that the EEOC offered him as a witness that he is not Korean. Apart from believing Hwang's testimony that the ad had been placed to obtain workers for a job that never materialized, the judge found this witness's testimony "incredible," in part because he gave contradictory evidence. The judge disbelieved the third witness as well, sensing that he had not really wanted a job with Consolidated because he had just quit a higher paying job. The last witness was adamant that he had learned about the job opening at Consolidated from the *Chicago Sun–Times*, in which Consolidated had never advertised. In addition, he had been fired from his previous job because he had been caught stealing from his employer. He also testified that he was seeking a job that paid almost twice what Consolidated was offering.

This was a sorry parade of witnesses, especially when we recall that the Commission culled it from a list of 99. We can hardly fault the district judge for concluding from all the evidence that the Commission had failed to prove that Consolidated was deliberately discriminating in favor of Koreans.

In a nation of immigrants, this must be reckoned an ominous case despite its outcome. The United States has many recent immigrants, and today as historically they tend to cluster in their own communities, united by ties of language, culture, and background. Often they form small businesses composed largely of relatives, friends, and other members of their community, and they obtain new employees by word of mouth. These small businesses—grocery stores, furniture stores, clothing stores, cleaning services, restaurants, gas stations—have been for many immigrant groups, and continue to be, the first rung on the ladder of American success. Derided as clannish, resented for their ambition and hard work, hated or despised for their otherness, recent immigrants are frequent targets of discrimination, some of it violent. It would be a bitter irony if the federal agency dedicated to enforcing the antidiscrimination laws succeeded in using those laws to kick these people off the ladder by compelling them to institute costly systems of hiring. There is equal danger to small black-run businesses in our central cities. Must such businesses undertake in the name of nondiscrimination costly measures to recruit nonblack employees?

* * *

Notes and Questions

1. *The cost justification defense*: A principal issue raised by *Consolidated Service* is whether it is fair to draw an inference of *intentional* discrimination from a selection mechanism that appears to be efficient? If not, should cost or economic justification be recognized as a legitimate, nondiscriminatory reason that is sufficient to rebut a prima facie case of disparate treatment? i.e., a legitimate, nondiscriminatory reason, in employment discrimination law. The cost or economic justification defense can be defined as a "justification offered by an employer other than that related to the ability of persons to efficiently perform the particular job in question. Such justification includes containment of costs in the areas of, for example, personnel administration, training, salaries and fringe benefits, and avoidance of the risk of tort liability arising from workplace hazards." Mark Brodin, *Costs, Profits, and Equal Employment Opportunity*, 62 Notre Dame L.Rev. 318, 320 n.14 (1987).

The Supreme Court rejected the cost or economic justification defense in a Title VII sex discrimination disparate treatment case, *City of Los Angeles Department of Water & Power v. Manhart*, 435 U.S. 702, 716–17, 98 S.Ct. 1370, 1379–80, 55 L.Ed.2d 657 (1978), reproduced in Chapter 7. *Manhart* involved a challenge to an employer's facially discriminatory policy that required females to contribute more to its pension plan than similarly situated males. In rejecting the employer's cost justification for the sex distinction in its policy, the Supreme Court said, "[t]hat argument might prevail if Title VII contained a cost-justification defense comparable to the affirmative defense available in a [Robinson–Patman Act] price discrimination suit. But neither Congress nor the courts have recognized such a defense under Title VII." *Id.* at 716–17, 98 S.Ct. at 1379–80. The Court also rejected a cost justification defense in striking down an employer's policy that limited the employment opportunities of fertile female workers in a hazardous industry. The employer—a battery manufacturer—argued that its policy was necessary to avoid potential tort liability for harm to fetuses that might result from the exposure of fertile females to the occupational hazards of lead used in its manufacturing processes. United Automobile Workers v. Johnson Controls, 499 U.S. 187, 111 S.Ct. 1196, 113 L.Ed.2d 158 (1991), reproduced in Chapter 6. In *Wilson v. Southwest Airlines*, 517 F.Supp. 292, 304 (N.D.Tex.1981), the court held that the "potential loss of profits or possible loss of competitive advantage" was not relevant to an employer's asserted bona fide occupational qualification (BFOQ) defense of its refusal to hire males as flight attendants and ticket agents. The airline had claimed that its marketing campaign focusing on the sex appeal of its female employees was necessary to build up its new business. The BFOQ defense is covered in Chapter 6.

Manhart, *Johnson Controls*, and *Wilson* are disparate treatment cases that involved employer policies that explicitly discriminated between groups of employees on the basis of sex. In *Riley v. Technical and Management Services Corp.*, 872 F.Supp. 1454, 1462 (D.Md.1995), *aff'd*, 79 F.3d 1141 (4th Cir.1996), a Title VII sex discrimination case, the court held that cost-cutting is a legitimate, nondiscriminatory reason in a disparate-treatment single-motive case. In a disparate impact case, *Wards Cove Packing Co. v. Atonio*, 490 U.S. 642, 109 S.Ct. 2115, 104 L.Ed.2d 733 (1989), the Supreme Court ruled that consideration of costs is relevant in evaluating the employer's evidence in support of its defense of business necessity. *Wards Cove* is reproduced in Chapter 4. When you study the disparate impact materials in Chapter 4, consider whether there are justifications for recognizing a cost defense in disparate impact cases but not in disparate treatment cases.

2. Judge Posner, the author of *Consolidated Service Systems*, is a leading law and economics scholar. His analysis in upholding Consolidated Service's word-of-mouth hiring policy is grounded in the efficiency rationale of the neoclassical economic model of labor markets. One commentator has stated:

> Legal theorists with faith in the principles of neoclassical economic models of labor markets assert that antidiscrimination statutes are inefficient and unnecessary. They characterize a statute or regulation that preempts an employer's considered personal choice and directs that some other applicant be hired or promoted as introducing inefficiency into the employment equation. A core belief in market rationality also leads these commentators to deny that state regulation of hiring decisions can be a corrective policy. Instead, addressing imbalances through legislative intercession is seen as a needlessly distributive method that is inferior both to allowing labor market dynamics to restore a nondiscriminatory balance, and to nonregulative incentives, such as job programs or cost-spreading through a tax system.

Michael Ashley Stein, *Labor Markets, Rationality, and Workers with Disabilities*, 21 Berkeley J.Emp. & Lab.L. 314, 314 (2000) (citations omitted).

Another commentator has concluded that the "economic literature offers two basic explanations of why an employer might treat employees differently because of their race": (1) taste for discrimination, and (2) statistical discrimination.

> According to the taste for discrimination model, either the employer itself or someone whose tastes the employer has an incentive to consider—such as employees or customers—dislikes members of a minority group and does not want to associate with them. The effect of this taste is that the employer incurs an additional cost for employing a member of a minority group.

> * * *

> Statistical discrimination can occur in the absence of any taste for discrimination. A rational employer will discriminate, even if no relevant action has any discriminatory animus, if the employer concludes that race is a proxy for job qualifications.

> Discrimination in this form occurs because information about an employee's qualifications is often costly to obtain. An employee's race, however, is cheaply ascertained. Therefore, if a firm concludes that an employee's race correlates with his or her qualifications, and if better information about qualifications is too costly to discover, it will be

rational, profit-maximizing behavior for the firm to offer lower wages to a minority employee than it would offer to a nonminority employee.

* * *

    Both taste-based discrimination and statistical discrimination are illegal under current law.

David A. Strauss, *The Law and Economics of Racial Discrimination in Employment: The Case for Numerical Standards*, 79 Geo.L.J. 1619, 1621, 1622–23 (1991). Statistical discrimination in the law and economics literature is also referred to as "rational discrimination." In his book, Forbidden Grounds: The Case Against Employment Discrimination Laws 59–78 (1992), Richard Epstein relied, in part, on "rational discrimination" in calling for a repeal of laws prohibiting discrimination in employment.

    Which of the two economic rationales for discrimination, if either, did Judge Posner rely upon in *Consolidated Service Systems*: taste for discrimination or statistical discrimination?

    3. In commenting upon the different perspectives of law and economics scholars and critical race scholars on the subject of racial discrimination, Professor Rachel Moran observed,

> [M]any economists believe that racial animus is declining, so that other explanations must be found for the persistence of discrimination. Market theorists have turned to statistical discrimination and social networks to account for continuing racial disparities. * * *
>
>   In contrast to law and economics, critical race theory has concerned itself with how race is constructed through unconscious bias and institutional structures. Race scholars do not presume that rational choice is the sine qua non of human behavior. Instead, they try to unpack the reflexive habits and hidden assumptions that guide racial judgments. Rather than worry about whether statistical discrimination is rational, critical race theorists question whether it is just. In analyzing how privilege is perpetuated, race scholars see social networks as only one example of the patterns and practices that entrench inequality.

Rachel F. Moran, *The Elusive Nature of Discrimination*, 55 Stan.L.Rev. 2365, 2366–67 (2003). Which of these two views of discrimination identified by Professor Moran do you believe is the better view. Or is the rationality of a practice one essential element in determining whether it is just?

    4. Generally a plaintiff can establish a violation under the disparate impact theory when an employer's word-of-mouth recruiting policy results in a predominantly white work force or job category. *See* Barnett v. W.T. Grant Co., 518 F.2d 543 (4th Cir.1975); Grant v. Bethlehem Steel Corp., 635 F.2d 1007 (2d Cir.1980), *cert. denied*, 452 U.S. 940, 101 S.Ct. 3083, 69 L.Ed.2d 954 (1981), *appeal after remand*, 823 F.2d 20 (2d Cir.1987). But in *Consolidated Service Systems*, Judge Posner based his decision on the asserted efficiency and effectiveness of word-of-mouth recruiting for small nonmajority employers. Is there any principled basis to distinguish between large employers, such as IBM or General Motors, and small immigrant-owned or minority-owned businesses or "ethnic economies" in the application of the

Consolidate Service rule? In thinking about this question consider the following:

a. *Consolidated Service Systems* describes an employment practice that is developing in many in inner city communities. A number of inner cities have large black and immigrant populations resulting, in substantial part, from the phenomenon of "white flight." As white small-business owners have moved out of predominantly black city neighborhoods, recent immigrants have often become the new entrepreneurs who provide entry-level, low-paying jobs in small neighborhood businesses, such as corner grocery stores and produce markets. There is evidence that many of these immigrant-employers are reluctant to hire blacks. *See* Jonathan Kaufman, *Help Wanted: Immigrants' Businesses Often Refuse to Hire Inner City Blacks*, Wall St.J., June 6, 1995, at A1. Kaufman, a journalist, noted the following research findings: (1) researchers estimate that immigrant-owned businesses account for one-quarter of all low-wage jobs in New York and Los Angeles; (2) although New York's population is 25% black, only 5% of the employees at Korean-owned stores are black Americans, while more than a third are Mexican and Latin American immigrants; (3) in Los Angeles, which is 17% black, only 2% of small Korean-owned businesses hire blacks, whereas 17% hire Latinos; (4) a survey of Korean store owners in Harlem, a black neighborhood in New York City, found that a large majority believe that blacks are less intelligent, less honest, and more prone to criminal acts than whites. *Id.*

b. The following is an excerpt from Lan Cao, *The Diaspora of Ethnic Economies: Beyond the Pale?*, 44 Wm. & Mary L.Rev. 1521 (2003):

Assume * * * that a black-owned business in Harlem * * * [hires] African American workers from the neighborhood rather than those from other ethnic groups. Or that this black-owned business has successfully established linkages with other clusters of black-owned firms, buying from and selling to one another and generating a positive ripple effect for the black community. Similar stories about ethnic solidarity and "fraternal and communal sentiments" abound throughout the United States and in many countries around the world, sometimes resulting in the establishment of a distinct type of ethnic economy, the ethnic niche—the clustering of ethnic entrepreneurs in the same occupations and industries. Indians and Pakistanis, for example, own a large proportion of gas stations and budget motels in the United States and newsstands in New York City. The diamond industry is dominated by Orthodox Jews who rely on ethnic networks to further economic exchanges. Cambodians and Vietnamese in California own a disproportionate number of doughnut shops and nail salons, respectively. Koreans own a large number of green groceries in New York City and wig stores nationwide. Arabs own grocery stores in Chicago, as do Lebanese Muslims in Detroit and Toledo. Soviet Jews operate half the taxicabs in Los Angeles. * * *

* * * Sociologists have noted the tendency to equate members of one's ethnic group with that "inbred group of near or distant kinsmen whom one knows as intimates and whom therefore one can trust. One intuitively expects fellow ethnics to behave at least somewhat benevo-

lently toward one because of kin selection, reinforced by reciprocity * * *. Fellow ethnics are, in the deepest sense, 'our people.' "

Id. at 1524–27 (citations omitted). If you were employed in the Office of General Counsel of the EEOC, what argument would you make that the EEOC should or should not sue any of the businesses identified in the Cao excerpt?

5. The Americans with Disabilities Act of 1990, covered in Chapter 13, recognizes a cost defense to a claim of disability discrimination. The defense derives from the obligation of an employer to make reasonable accommodations for its disabled employees if doing so will not impose an undue hardship on the employer. 42 U.S.C. § 12111(10)(B). Should the courts recognize a cost defense in discrimination cases in the absence of statutory authority?

Note: The Same-Actor Defense

In a number of situations, the person who initially hired an employee is also the person who later discharged her. If the plaintiff is able to establish a prima facie case of employment discrimination based upon circumstantial evidence, what weight, if any, should be given to the fact that the same supervisor both hired and fired the plaintiff? A majority of the courts deciding this issue have endorsed the same-actor (same supervisor, same decision-maker or common actor) inference defense. *See, e.g.*, Bradley v. Harcourt, Brace & Co., 104 F.3d 267 (9th Cir.1996); Anna Laurie Bryant & Richard Bales, *Using the Same–Actor "Inference" in Employment Discrimination Cases*, 1999 Utah L.Rev. 255. Courts adopting the same-actor defense hold that, where the same supervisor both hired and fired an employee and the period between the hiring and firing is relatively short, the employer is entitled to an inference that the discharge was not motivated by discriminatory animus.

The Court of Appeals for the Fourth Circuit was the first court to endorse the same-actor defense in *Proud v. Stone*, 945 F.2d 796 (4th Cir.1991). The court reasoned that " '[i]t hardly makes sense to hire workers from a group one dislikes (thereby incurring the psychological costs of associating with them), only to fire them once they are on the job.' " *Id.* at 797 (quoting John J. Donohue & Peter Siegelman, *The Changing Nature of Employment Discrimination*, 43 Stan.L.Rev. 983, 1017 (1991)). The courts of appeals do not agree on whether the same-actor defense should be recognized and, if so, whether it should be treated as an inference or a presumption. *See e.g.*, Wexler v. White's Fine Furniture, 317 F.3d 564, (6th Cir.2003) (reviewing the split in the circuits on the amount of weight that should be given to the same-actor inference). *Proud v. Stone* focused on the "relatively short" period between the hiring and firing but the courts have applied the same-actor defense to intervals up to four years or more. See Notes & Comments, Julie Northrop, *The "Same-Actor Inference" in Employment Discrimination: Cheap Justice?*, 73 Wash.L.Rev. 193, 221 (1998) (collecting cases).

The Seventh Circuit in *Johnson v. Zema Systems Corp.*, 170 F.3d 734 (7th Cir.1999), observed:

The psychological assumption underlying the same-actor inference may not hold true on the facts of the particular case. For example, a manager might hire a person of a certain race expecting [him] not to rise to a position in the company where daily contact with the manager would be necessary. Or an employer might hire an employee of a certain gender expecting that person to act, or dress, or talk in a way the employer deems acceptable for that gender and then fire that employee if she fails to comply with the employer's gender stereotype. Similarly, if an employee were the first African–American hired, an employer might be unaware of his own stereotypical views of African–Americans at the time of hiring. If the employer subsequently discovers he does not wish to work with African–Americans and fires the newly hired employee for this reason, the employee would still have a claim of racial discrimination despite the same-actor inference.

Id. at 745.

a. An implicit assumption in the same-actor defense is that discriminatory animus, if it exists, manifests itself in all aspects of the employment relationship from initial hire through termination and all other terms and conditions of employment. Is the assumption flawed? *See, e.g.*, Linda Hamilton Krieger, *Civil Rights Perestroika: Intergroup Relations After Affirmative Action*, 86 Cal.L.Rev. 1251, 1314–16, (1998) (arguing that the same-actor defense is flawed because "[c]ognitive forms of intergroup bias will not operate consistently, even in the same decision maker" because expression of intergroup bias "will vary, according to the specific situation in which the decision maker finds himself").

b. What purpose does evidence on the same-actor inference serve? Is it an attack on the presumption of discriminatory intent that the plaintiff seeks to establish under the *McDonnell Douglas* framework? Is it a legitimate, nondiscriminatory reason? Or should it be relevant only with respect to pretext analysis? *See, e.g.*, Schmidt v. Montgomery Kone, Inc., 69 F.Supp.2d 706, 711 (E.D.Pa.1999). Should it be limited to firing cases, or should it be applicable to other employment actions such as denial of promotions?

c. Does the same-actor inference encourage employers to hire blacks and women, as suggested by the Seventh Circuit in *EEOC v. Our Lady of Resurrection Medical Center*, 77 F.3d 145, 151 (7th Cir.1996)?

2. PROVING DISCRIMINATORY INTENT BY CIRCUMSTANTIAL OR DIRECT EVIDENCE

Conventional rules of civil litigation, which require a plaintiff to prove a claim of unlawful employment discrimination by a preponderance of the evidence, using direct or circumstantial evidence, generally apply in federal employment discrimination cases. Desert Palace, Inc. v. Costa, 539 U.S. 90, 94, 123 S.Ct. 2148, 2154, 156 L.Ed.2d 84 (2003) (*quoting* Price Waterhouse v. Hopkins, 490 U.S. 228, 253, 109 S.Ct. 1775, 1792, 104 L.Ed.2d 268 (1989), and Postal Service Bd. of Governors v. Aikens, 460 U.S. 711, 714 n.3, 103 S.Ct. 1478, 1481 n.3, 75 L.Ed.2d 403 (1983)). Noting that "juries are routinely instructed that '[t]he law makes no distinction between the weight or value to be given to either direct or circumstantial evidence,' " the Supreme Court has held that both circumstantial and direct evidence are equally competent to prove the ultimate fact issue of intentional discrimination. *Desert Palace*, 539 U.S. at 94, 123 S.Ct. at 2154 (*quoting* 1A K. O'Malley, J. Grenig & W. Lee, Federal Jury Practice and Instructions, Criminal § 12.04 (5th ed.2000)). The courts tend to use the terms "direct evidence" and "smoking gun evidence" interchangeably. *See, e.g.*, Holtz v. Rockefeller & Co., 258 F.3d 62, 76 (2d Cir.2001); Santiago–Ramos v. Centennial P.R. Wireless Corp., 217 F.3d 46, 53 (1st Cir.2000).

A fundamental question that is raised by the fact that a plaintiff can prove intentional discrimination with circumstantial or direct evidence is whether a plaintiff who has direct evidence is "better off" than a plaintiff who must rely on circumstantial evidence. The material in this section in included to explore this question.

a. *What is the difference, between "direct" and "circumstantial" evidence?* The lower courts have long recognized that it is difficult to draw a bright line between direct evidence and circumstantial evidence. *See, e.g.*, Dominguez–Cruz v. Suttle Caribe, Inc., 202 F.3d 424, 429 (1st Cir.2000), Bartlik v. Department of Labor, 73 F.3d 100, 103 n.5 (6th Cir.1996). One court has stated that "the various circuit courts have as many definitions of 'direct evidence' as they do employment discrimination cases." Tyler v. Bethlehem Steel Corp., 958 F.2d 1176, 1183 (2d Cir.), *cert.denied*, 506 U.S. 826, 113 S.Ct. 82, 121 L.Ed.2d 46 (1992). The observation by the *Tyler* court is borne out in *Fernandes v. Costa Brothers Masonry, Inc.*, 199 F.3d 572 (1st Cir.1999). In *Fernandes*, after canvassing the state of the law on the meaning of "direct evidence" in employment discrimination cases, Judge Selya concluded that the courts of appeals had adopted three different definitions. The first is the "classic" definition that the term means "evidence which, if believed, suffices to prove the fact of discriminatory animus without inference, presumption, or resort to other evidence." *Id*. at 582. The second is "animus plus," which defines "direct evidence" as "evidence, both direct and circumstantial, of conduct or statements that (1) reflect directly the alleged discriminatory animus and (2) bear squarely on the contested employment decision." *Id*. This definition requires a plaintiff to introduce evidence that is substantially stronger than the kind of evidence that simply raises an inference of discriminatory intent. The third is the "animus" position: "as long as the evidence (whether direct or circumstantial) is tied to the alleged discriminatory animus, it need not bear squarely on the challenged employment decision." *Id. See also* Costa v. Desert Palace, Inc., 299 F.3d 838, 852–53 (9th Cir.2002) (noting other intra-circuit approaches), *aff'd on other grounds*, 539 U.S. 90, 123 S.Ct. 2148, 156 L.Ed.2d 84 (2003).

b. *Reason for the confusion about the meaning of "direct" evidence*: Why is it that the federal courts have had so much difficulty in defining "direct evidence" in employment discrimination law? The major source of the difficulty is Justice O'Connor's concurring opinion in *Price Waterhouse v. Hopkins*, 490 U.S. 228, 109 S.Ct. 1775, 104 L.Ed.2d 268 (1989). *See, e.g.*,

Tyler v. Bethlehem Steel Corp., 958 F.2d 1176, 1183 (2d Cir.), *cert.denied,* 506 U.S. 826, 113 S.Ct. 82, 121 L.Ed.2d 46 (1992); Fernandes v. Costa Bros. Masonry, Inc., 199 F.3d 572, 581–82 (1st Cir.1999). Justice O'Connor took the position that a plaintiff in a mixed-motive case had to introduce direct evidence to prove that discriminatory animus was "a substantial factor" in an adverse employment decision in order to shift the burden of persuasion to the employer on the same-decision defense. *Price Waterhouse,* 490 U.S. at 276, 109 S.Ct. at 1804 (O'Connor, J., concurring in the judgment). (Mixed-motive cases are covered in Section B.3. of this chapter.) The court in *Fernandes* summarized the fallout from Justice O'Connor's concurring opinion:

> Justice O'Connor furnished a trenchant, universally accepted example of what is not direct evidence: stray remarks, such as "statements by nondecisionmakers, or statements by decisionmakers unrelated to the decisional process itself." Since then, * * * jurists have struggled in attempting to define the term affirmatively. This operose task not only has divided the courts of appeals but also has created a patchwork of intra-circuit conflicts.

199 F.3d at 581 (citations omitted). The stray remarks doctrine is discussed in Note 5 below.

Notes and Questions

1. *Facial Discrimination*: The most obvious case of direct evidence is one in which an employer adopts an explicit policy that on its face uses a prohibited criterion such as sex or age to limit the employment opportunities of members of a protected class. For example, in *United Automobile Workers v. Johnson Controls*, 499 U.S. 187, 111 S.Ct. 1196, 113 L.Ed.2d 158 (1991), reproduced in Chapter 6, the employer, a battery manufacturer, had a written policy of refusing to allow fertile female employees to work in jobs involving occupational exposure to lead. The employer justified the policy on the basis of its concern about the potential risks of harm to any fetus that a female employee might conceive. The Supreme Court held that, despite the absence of a malevolent motive, the employer's policy was facially discriminatory under Title VII because it applied only to fertile women and not to fertile men. As the Court said, "the absence of a malevolent motive does not convert a facially discriminatory policy into a neutral policy with a discriminatory effect," and "[w]hether an employment practice involves disparate treatment through explicit facial discrimination does not depend on why the employer discriminates but rather on the explicit terms of the discrimination." *Id.* at 199, 111 S.Ct. at 1203. Likewise, in *Los Angeles Department of Water & Power v. Manhart*, 435 U.S. 702, 98 S.Ct. 1370, 55 L.Ed.2d 657 (1978), the Supreme Court found that the employer's policy of requiring female employees to make larger contributions to a pension fund than male employees was discriminatory on its face. And, in *Trans World Airlines, Inc. v. Thurston*, 469 U.S. 111, 105 S.Ct. 613, 83 L.Ed.2d 523 (1985), the Court found that the employer's written transfer policy based on age was direct evidence of discrimination against the plaintiffs who were in a protected class under the ADEA.

The only defense in the facial or policy discrimination cases is one of the statutory defenses, for example, the bona fide occupational defense (BFOQ) found in § 703(e) of Title VII, 42 U.S.C. § 2000e–2(e). The Title BFOQ defense permits employers to hire and classify employees on the basis of their religion, sex, or national origin, but by statute race and color are not subject to the BFOQ defense. See Chapter 6 (sex), Chapter 11 (national origin), and Chapter 10 (religion). Section 4(f) of the ADEA, 29 U.S.C § 623(f), provides a statutory BFOQ defense in age discrimination cases. See Chapter 12.

2. *Statements of Discriminatory Animus*: In another straightforward case of direct evidence of discriminatory animus, the employer expressly denies an individual a job because of a statutorily prohibited motive at the time the adverse employment decision is made. For example, in *Bell v. Birmingham Linen Service*, 715 F.2d 1552 (11th Cir.), *cert. denied*, 467 U.S. 1204, 104 S.Ct. 2385, 81 L.Ed.2d 344 (1984), the employer's agent denied a female a job in the washroom of a laundry because he believed that if he granted it "every woman in the plant would go into the washroom." *Id*. at 1553. The court found the statement to be direct evidence of discriminatory animus. Likewise, some courts have recognized that remarks to the effect that "I won't hire you because you are a woman," or "I'm firing you because you are not a Christian," or "I'm reassigning you because you are black" are compelling examples of direct evidence of discriminatory animus. *See* Venters v. City of Delphi, 123 F.3d 956, 973 (7th Cir.1997).

In *Heim v. Utah*, 8 F.3d 1541, 1546 (10th Cir.1993), plaintiff filed a sex discrimination claim under Title VII alleging that her male supervisor denied her cross training in other jobs because of her gender. The evidence showed that her supervisor remarked in the context of an alleged problem with plaintiff's job performance: "Fucking women, I hate having fucking women in the office." *Id*. at 1546. Shortly after the statement, the supervisor denied plaintiff an opportunity to work in a temporary job assignment for which she has previously been granted permission. Plaintiff argued that the supervisor's statement was direct evidence of discriminatory intent. The *Heim* court rejected the argument, reasoning that,

> Although the remark by [the supervisor] was certainly inappropriate and boorish, it was on its face a statement of [the supervisor's] personal opinion. The evidence does not show that [the supervisor] acted with discriminatory intent, only that he unprofessionally offered his private negative view of women during a display of bad temper at work.

Id. at 1547. What argument would you make in favor of a finding that the supervisor's statement is direct evidence of discriminatory intent?

3. *Stereotyping as Evidence of Discriminatory Intent*: *Price Waterhouse v. Hopkins*, 490 U.S. 228, 109 S.Ct. 1775, 104 L.Ed.2d 268 (1989), is a landmark case in which the Supreme Court held that an employer's reliance on stereotyping can constitute direct evidence of discriminatory intent in an employment discrimination case. *See id*. at 251, 109 S.Ct. at 1791.

> Ann Hopkins had worked at Price Waterhouse's Office of Government Services in Washington, D.C., for five years when the partners in that office proposed her as a candidate for partnership. Of the 662 partners at the firm at that time, 7 were women. Of the 88 persons

proposed for partnership that year, only 1—Hopkins—was a woman. Forty-seven of these candidates were admitted to the partnership, 21 were rejected, and 20—including Hopkins—were "held" for reconsideration the following year. Thirteen of the 32 partners who had submitted comments on Hopkins supported her bid for partnership. Three partners recommended that her candidacy be placed on hold, eight stated that they did not have an informed opinion about her, and eight recommended that she be denied partnership.

In a jointly prepared statement supporting her candidacy, the partners in Hopkins' office showcased her successful 2–year effort to secure a $25 million contract with the Department of State, labeling it "an outstanding performance" and one that Hopkins carried out "virtually at the partner level." * * *

The partners in Hopkins' office praised her character as well as her accomplishments, describing her in their joint statement as "an outstanding professional" who had a "deft touch," a "strong character, independence and integrity." Clients appear to have agreed with these assessments. At trial, one official from the State Department described her as "extremely competent, intelligent," "strong and forthright, very productive, energetic and creative." Another high-ranking official praised Hopkins' decisiveness, broadmindedness, and "intellectual clarity"; she was, in his words, "a stimulating conversationalist." Evaluations such as these led Judge Gesell to conclude that Hopkins "had no difficulty dealing with clients and her clients appear to have been very pleased with her work" and that she "was generally viewed as a highly competent project leader who worked long hours, pushed vigorously to meet deadlines and demanded much from the multidisciplinary staffs with which she worked."

On too many occasions, however, Hopkins' aggressiveness apparently spilled over into abrasiveness. Staff members seem to have borne the brunt of Hopkins' brusqueness. Long before her bid for partnership, partners evaluating her work had counseled her to improve her relations with staff members. Although later evaluations indicate an improvement, Hopkins' perceived shortcomings in this important area eventually doomed her bid for partnership. Virtually all of the partners' negative remarks about Hopkins—even those of partners supporting her—had to do with her "interpersonal skills." Both "[s]upporters and opponents of her candidacy" * * * "indicated that she was sometimes overly aggressive, unduly harsh, difficult to work with and impatient with staff."

There were clear signs, though, that some of the partners reacted negatively to Hopkins' personality because she was a woman. One partner described her as "macho"; another suggested that she "overcompensated for being a woman"; a third advised her to take "a course at charm school." Several partners criticized her use of profanity; in response, one partner suggested that those partners objected to her swearing only "because it's a lady using foul language." Another supporter explained that Hopkins "ha[d] matured from a tough-talking somewhat masculine hard-nosed mgr to an authoritative, formidable, but much more appealing lady ptr candidate." But it was the man who

* * * bore responsibility for explaining to Hopkins the reasons for the Policy Board's decision to place her candidacy on hold who delivered the *coup de grace*: in order to improve her chances for partnership, Thomas Beyer advised, Hopkins should "walk more femininely, talk more femininely, dress more femininely, wear make-up, have her hair styled, and wear jewelry."

Dr. Susan Fiske, a social psychologist and Associate Professor of Psychology at Carnegie–Mellon University, testified at trial that the partnership selection process at Price Waterhouse was likely influenced by sex stereotyping. Her testimony focused not only on the overtly sex-based comments of partners but also on gender-neutral remarks, made by partners who knew Hopkins only slightly, that were intensely critical of her. One partner, for example, baldly stated that Hopkins was "universally disliked" by staff, and another described her as "consistently annoying and irritating"; yet these were people who had had very little contact with Hopkins. According to Fiske, Hopkins' uniqueness (as the only woman in the pool of candidates) and the subjectivity of the evaluations made it likely that sharply critical remarks such as these were the product of sex stereotyping—although Fiske admitted that she could not say with certainty whether any particular comment was the result of stereotyping. Fiske based her opinion on a review of the submitted comments, explaining that it was commonly accepted practice for social psychologists to reach this kind of conclusion without having met any of the people involved in the decisionmaking process.

In previous years, other female candidates for partnership also had been evaluated in sex-based terms. As a general matter, Judge Gesell concluded, "[c]andidates were viewed favorably if partners believed they maintained their femin[in]ity while becoming effective professional managers"; in this environment, "[t]o be identified as a 'women's lib[b]er' was regarded as [a] negative comment."

490 U.S. at 232–36, 109 S.Ct. at 1781–83.

On the matter of the significance of evidence of decisionmaking based on sex stereotyping, the Court said,

In the specific context of sex stereotyping, an employer who acts on the basis of a belief that a woman cannot be aggressive, or that she must not be, has acted on the basis of gender.

* * * As for the legal relevance of sex stereotyping, we are beyond the day when an employer could evaluate employees by assuming or insisting that they matched the stereotype associated with their group for " '[i]n forbidding employers to discriminate against individuals because of their sex, Congress intended to strike at the entire spectrum of disparate treatment of men and women resulting from sex stereotypes.' " *Los Angeles Dept. of Water and Power v. Manhart*, 435 U.S. 702, 707 n.13, 98 S.Ct. 1370, 1375 n.13, 55 L.Ed.2d 657 (1978) (quoting *Sprogis v. United Air Lines, Inc.*, 444 F.2d 1194, 1198 (CA 7 1971). An employer who objects to aggressiveness in women but whose positions require this trait places women in an intolerable and impermissible catch 22: out of a job if they behave aggressively and out of a job if they do not. Title VII lifts women out of this bind.

Remarks at work that are based on sex stereotypes do not inevitably prove that gender played a part in a particular employer decision. The plaintiff must show that the employer actually relied on her gender in making its decision. In making this showing, stereotyped remarks can certainly be *evidence* that gender played a part.

490 U.S. at 250–51, 109 S.Ct. at 1790–91 (plurality opinion) (original emphasis). *See* Thomas v. Eastman Kodak Co., 183 F.3d 38, 59–62 (1st Cir.1999) (explaining the significance of the Court's recognition of stereotyping evidence as a form of direct evidence of discriminatory intent).

a. Professor Mary F. Radford's article, *Sex Stereotyping and the Promotion of Women to Positions of Power*, 41 Hastings L.J. 471, 494–96 (1990), contains an excellent discussion of the stereotyping of women in the workplace. Radford surveys the literature on sex stereotyping, noting that

[i]n what has been referred to as the "definitive work on sex-role stereotypes," Broverman [Broverman et al., *Sex-Role Stereotypes: A Current Appraisal*, 28 J.Soc.Change 59 (1972)] measured the degree to which various personality traits were perceived as typical of men or women. Adjectives that consistently were viewed as describing "male" traits included the following: aggressive, independent, unemotional, objective, not easily influenced, dominant, calm, active, competitive, logical, worldly, skilled in business, direct, adventurous, self-confident, ambitious. Adjectives representing "female" traits included: talkative, does not use harsh language, tactful, gentle, aware of other's feelings, religious, neat, quiet, easily expresses tender feelings, very strong need for security. * * *

* * *

As these adjectives indicate, and as numerous studies have confirmed, the "masculine" traits generally are associated more strongly in our society with good mental health. Consequently, these traits are viewed (by both males and females) as being those to which a mature adult should aspire.

* * *

Despite the numerous criticisms that may be leveled against the sex stereotyping of personality traits, an important phenomenon is that the "masculine" traits are correlated strongly with success in the workplace.

Id. Although the "work world has changed considerably since employers felt free to tell women they would not be hired for 'men's jobs,'" it has been argued that with the prevalence of gender stereotyping "employers trap female professionals in a 'double bind,' judging them incompetent if they act like women and labeling them 'difficult,' or worse, if they act like men." Kari Aamot–Snapp, Note, *Putting Teeth into Minnesota's Employment Discrimination Law: A Legislative Proposal Defining Gender Stereotyping*, 79 Minn. L.Rev. 211, 211–12 (1994) (footnotes omitted).

b. In *Thomas v. Eastman Kodak Co.*, 183 F.3d 38, 59–61 (1st Cir.1999), the court held that the stereotyping principles of *Price Waterhouse* are equally applicable in race and other kinds of discrimination cases. There are a number of empirical studies that demonstrate the existence of negative stereotyping of blacks in the United States in the employment context. The results of many of these studies are summarized in Judith Olans Brown, Stephen N. Subrin & Phyllis Tropper Bauman, *Some Thoughts About Social Perception and Employment Law: A Modest Proposal for Reopening the Judicial Dialogue*, 46 Emory L.J. 1487, 1497–1504 (1997). For a discussion of different views on subtle discrimination in employment in the context of retaliation, see Terry Smith, *Everyday Indignities: Race, Retaliation, and the Promise of Title VII*, 34 Colum.Hum.Rts.L.Rev. 529 (2003). Professor Smith's concept of "subtle discrimination" embraces notions drawn from the work of Professor Charles Lawrence's classic critical race article, *The Id, the Ego, and Equal Protection: Reckoning with Unconscious Racism*, 39 Stan. L.Rev. 317 (1987); as well as theories developed in Peggy Cooper's *Law as Microaggression*, 98 Yale L.J. 1576 (1989); Barbara Flagg's *Fashioning a Title VII Remedy for Transparently White Subjective Decisionmaking*, 104 Yale L.J. 2009 (1995); and David Oppenheimer's *Negligent Discrimination*, 141 U.Pen.L.Rev. 899 (1993).

4. *Epithets and Derogatory Comments*: Suppose an agent or supervisor of an employer who has authority to make employment decisions calls older employees "little old ladies," "old farts," "old bastards," or "old crows," Castle v. Sangamo Weston, Inc., 837 F.2d 1550, 1553 (11th Cir.1988); or a white employee who works in a position in which the majority of employees are minorities a "white token" or "white fagot," Young v. City of Houston, 906 F.2d 177, 180 (5th Cir.1990); or a black male employee a "nigger" or "boy," Brown v. East Miss. Elec. Power Assoc., 989 F.2d 858, 861 (5th Cir.1993); Ross v. Douglas County, 234 F.3d 391, 393 (8th Cir.2000); or a woman employee a "bitch," or a black female employee a "black bitch," Costa v. Desert Palace, Inc., 238 F.3d 1056, 1060 (9th Cir.2000), *affirmed on other grounds*, 539 U.S. 90, 123 S.Ct. 2148, 156 L.Ed.2d 84 (2003). Suppose Latino employees are told, "[w]etbacks, I wish you would speak where I can understand you," EEOC v. Premier Operator Servs., Inc., 113 F.Supp.2d 1066, 1071 (N.D.Tex. 2000); Ugalde v. W.A. McKenzie Asphalt Co., 990 F.2d 239, 243 (5th Cir.1993); or a female employee is told she needs a good Christian boyfriend to teach her to be submissive, Campos v. City of Blue Springs, 289 F.3d 546, 548–49 (8th Cir.2002). Under what circumstances should theses statements be considered direct evidence of discriminatory animus?

The lower courts have adopted conflicting views on whether discriminatory epithets or derogatory comments used by decisionmakers in reference to an employee's race, sex, age, religion, national origin, or disability constitute direct evidence or circumstantial evidence. *Compare, e.g.,* Hunter v. Allis–Chalmers Corp., 797 F.2d 1417, 1423 (7th Cir.1986) (evidence that supervisor called blacks "niggers" was considered direct evidence of discriminatory intent) *with, e.g.,* Howard v. National Cash Register Co., 388 F.Supp. 603, 606 (S.D.Ohio 1975) (evidence of "disrespect and prejudice" by white employees toward a black co-worker does not establish direct evidence of discrimination because an employer cannot be required to discharge all of the "Archie Bunkers" in its workplace).

In commenting upon both stereotyping and epithets as direct evidence of discriminatory intent, the Eleventh Circuit observed in *Merritt v. Dillard Paper Co.*, 120 F.3d 1181, 1189 (11th Cir.1997), that

> [e]vidence that only suggests discrimination, or that is subject to more than one interpretation, does not constitute direct evidence. In a long line of cases, this Court has found direct evidence where "actions or statements of an employer reflect[] a discriminatory or retaliatory attitude correlating to the discrimination or retaliation complained of by the employee." *Caban-Wheeler v. Elsea,* 904 F.2d 1549, 1555 (11th Cir.1990). *See Haynes v. W.C. Caye & Co., Inc.,* 52 F.3d 928, 930 (11th Cir.1995) (holding that statement questioning whether "sweet little old lady could get tough enough" to do job and statement that "a woman was not competent enough to do this job" constitute direct evidence); *Burns v. Gadsden State Community College,* 908 F.2d 1512, 1518 (11th Cir.1990) (holding that statement that "no woman would be named to a B scheduled job" constitutes direct evidence); *Caban-Wheeler,* 904 F.2d at 1555 (holding that defendant's statement that program needed a black director constitutes direct evidence); *E.E.O.C. v. Alton Packaging Corp.,* 901 F.2d 920, 923 (11th Cir.1990) (holding that general manager's statement that "if it was his company, he wouldn't hire any black people" and production manager's statement that "you people can't do a * * * thing right" constitute direct evidence); *E.E.O.C. v. Beverage Canners, Inc.,* 897 F.2d 1067, 1068 n. 3, 1072 (11th Cir.1990) (holding that plant manager's constant barrage of racial slurs and statements such as "[t]hose niggers out there will not get anywhere in this company" constitute direct evidence); *Sennello v. Reserve Life Ins. Co.,* 872 F.2d 393, 394, 395 (11th Cir.1989) (holding that statement that "we can't have women in management" constitutes direct evidence); *Walters v. City of Atlanta,* 803 F.2d 1135, 1141–42 (11th Cir.1986) (holding that memorandum requesting a new list of candidates because "current register * * * does not include any minority group representation" constitutes direct evidence); *Wilson v. City of Aliceville,* 779 F.2d 631, 633, 636 (11th Cir.1986) (holding that mayor's statement that "he wasn't gonna let no Federal government make him hire no god-dam nigger" constitutes direct evidence); *Thompkins v. Morris Brown College,* 752 F.2d 558, 561, 563 (11th Cir.1985) (holding that college president's statement that he saw no reason for a woman to have a second job and statement that males had families and needs that female plaintiff did not constitute direct evidence); *Miles v. M.N.C. Corp.,* 750 F.2d 867, 874–75 (11th Cir.1985) (holding that plant manager's statement that he wouldn't hire blacks because "[h]alf of them weren't worth a shit" constitutes direct evidence); *Bell v. Birmingham Linen Serv.,* 715 F.2d 1552, 1553, 1557 (11th Cir.1983) (holding that supervisor's statement that he would not put woman in washerman position because "every woman in the plant would want to go into the washroom" constitutes direct evidence); *but see Harris,* 99 F.3d at 1082, 1083 n.2 (holding that statement that "under the circumstances we did not need to employ a black at Thompson High School" open to more than one interpretation and thus not direct evidence).

As we have explained in the age discrimination context, the quintessential example of direct evidence would be "a management memorandum saying, 'Fire Earley—he is too old.'" *Earley,* 907 F.2d at 1081.

In his book entitled *Nigger: The Strange Career of a Troublesome Word* (2002), Randall Kennedy, a black law professor at Harvard Law School, explores questions such as how to define the word "nigger," whether it is more opprobrious than other racial epithets, whether only blacks should be entitled to use the word, whether violent responses to "nigger baiting" should be punished less harshly because they are provoked, whether employees should be discharged for using the word at work, and whether the myriad harms caused by use of the word can be mitigated or remedied. How would you respond to the questions Professor Kennedy raises?

Does the stray remarks doctrine, discussed below, provide a workable approach to determining when stereotyping and epithet evidence constitute direct evidence or circumstantial evidence of discriminatory intent?

5.   *The Stray Remarks Doctrine*: Relying on Justice O'Connor's concurrence in *Price Waterhouse v. Hopkins,* 490 U.S. 228, 109 S.Ct. 1775, 104 L.Ed.2d 268 (1989), the lower courts developed the "stray remarks" doctrine to determine when statements by employers and their agents evincing discriminatory animus are direct or circumstantial evidence of intentional discrimination. In *Price Waterhouse,* Justice O'Connor asserted that "stray remarks" about race and gender cannot constitute direct evidence of unlawful discriminatory intent, but by negative implication, she suggested circumstances may exist when remarks relating to a prohibited criterion are not truly "stray," but are germane to the decisionmaking process:

> [S]tray remarks in the workplace, while perhaps probative of sexual harassment, cannot justify requiring the employer to prove that its hiring and promotion decisions were based on legitimate criteria. Nor can statements by nondecisionmakers, or statements by decisionmakers unrelated to the decisional process itself suffice to satisfy the plaintiff's burden in this regard. * * * Race and gender always "play a role" in an employment decision in the benign sense that these are human characteristics of which decisionmakers are aware and may comment on in a perfectly neutral and nondiscriminatory fashion. For example, in the context of this case, a mere reference to a "lady candidate" might show that gender "played a role" in the decision, but by no means could support a rational factfinder's inference that the decision was made "because of" sex. What is required * * * [is] direct evidence that decisionmakers placed substantial negative reliance on an illegitimate criterion in reaching their decision.

Id. at 277, 109 S.Ct. at 1804–05.

In *Brown v. CSC Logic, Inc.,* 82 F.3d 651 (5th Cir.1996), the court adopted a four-part test to determine whether epithets, stereotyping evidence, or other evidence or remarks made by supervisors are direct evidence or circumstantial evidence. The Fifth Circuit explained the four-part test in *Wallace v. Methodist Hospital System,* 271 F.3d 212 (5th Cir.2001):

> "[F]or comments in the workplace to provide sufficient evidence of discrimination, they must be '1)related [to the protected class of persons

of which the plaintiff is a member]; 2) proximate in time to the terminations; 3) made by an individual with authority over the employment decision at issue; and 4) related to the employment decision at issue.' " Where "[c]omments[] are vague and remote in time [they] are insufficient to establish discrimination. In contrast, specific comments made over a lengthy period of time are sufficient."

Id. at 222 (internal citations omitted). The stray remarks doctrine directs factfinders to examine the relationship between the remarks and the decisionmaking process; the linkage between the prohibited criterion and the substance of the statements; the specificity of the statements with regard to the employment decision at issue, such as hiring, promotion, or termination; the relationship of the remarks to the plaintiff's situation; and the temporal relationship between the statements and the employment decision. *See, e.g.,* Holmes v. Marriott Corp., 831 F.Supp. 691, 704–06 (S.D.Iowa 1993) (commenting on the post-*Price Waterhouse* developments in the "stray remarks" doctrine.).

Statements and other comments found to be stray remarks and thus not direct evidence may constitute circumstantial evidence that is probative of the ultimate fact of intentional discrimination. *See* Hasham v. California State Bd. of Equalization, 200 F.3d 1035, 1049–50 (7th Cir.2000). Justice O'Connor, whose concurring opinion in *Price Waterhouse* is the doctrinal genesis of the stray remarks doctrine, also authored the Court's opinion in *Reeves v. Sanderson Plumbing Products, Inc.*, 530 U.S. 133, 120 S.Ct. 2097, 147 L.Ed.2d 105 (2000). Does *Reeves* have implications for the "stray remarks" doctrine? Recall that in *Reeves*, Justice O'Connor noted that the at-issue age-based comments were not made in the "direct context of Reeves's termination." The Fifth Circuit held that the stray remarks doctrine survives *Reeves* "at least where the plaintiff has failed to produce substantial evidence of pretext." Auguster v. Vermilion Parish Sch. Bd., 249 F.3d 400, 405 (5th Cir.2001). *See also* Laina Rose Reinsmith, Note, *Proving an Employer's Intent: Disparate Treatment Discrimination and the Stray Remarks Doctrine After* Reeves v. Sanderson Plumbing Products, 55 Vand. L.Rev. 219 (2002) (discussing what parts, if any, of the stray remarks doctrine should still be considered good law after *Reeves*).

Judge Posner, in *Shager v. Upjohn Co.*, 913 F.2d 398, 402 (7th Cir. 1990), said that his examination of lower court cases on the stray remarks doctrine led him to the conclusion that "all these cases really stand for is the common sense proposition that a slur is not in and of itself proof of actionable discrimination, even if repeated." What response might the critical race theorists give in response to Judge Posner's characterization of the stray remarks doctrine?

6. *Background Climate and Conduct*: Should a background history and climate of bias toward black and older workers be sufficient to constitute direct evidence or circumstantial evidence of unlawful intent to discriminate on the basis of race and age? In *Estes v. Dick Smith Ford, Inc.*, 856 F.2d 1097 (8th Cir.1988), the court held that it was reversible error for the trial judge to exclude background evidence that showed a climate of racial and age bias in the workplace. The district court had prevented the plaintiff, an older black employee, from presenting evidence to the jury that the company, a car

dealership, had excluded blacks from its workforce; that it had fired two employees because of age; that its service department offered free rides to white customers while black customers were told to rent cars; and that managers referred to blacks as "niggers."

7. *The Cat's Paw Theory of Imputed Intent*: In *Shager v. Upjohn Co.*, 913 F.2d 398 (7th Cir.1990), the plaintiff claimed that he was discharged because of his age. The court first concluded that Shager had presented sufficient evidence to survive a motion for summary judgment on the issue of whether his supervisor intended to discriminate against him because of his age. The supervisor had made statements such as these "older people don't much like or much care for us baby boomers," and "it is refreshing to work with a young man with such a wonderful outlook on life and on his job." *Id.* at 400. The court then dealt with the issue posed by the fact that Shager had been fired not by his supervisor but by a hiring committee that was unaware of Shager's age when it fired him. The Seventh Circuit held that if the committee had "acted as the conduit of [the supervisor's] prejudice—his cat's paw—the innocence of the members would not spare the company from liability." *Id.* at 405. On the other hand, if the committee decision was not "a mere rubber stamp" of the supervisor's bias, the court held there would be no basis for finding that the employer had violated the ADEA. *Id.* at 406. Finding that the supervisor had "set up Shager to fail" in the performance of his job and then portrayed him in the "worst possible light" to the committee, the court concluded that the committee's decision was "tainted" by the supervisor's age-based prejudice and the supervisor's "influence may well have been decisive." *Id.* at 405.

Other courts have adopted the *Shager* "cat's paw" theory under which the discriminatory intent of an employee without the authority to affect terms and conditions of employment may be imputed to the employer. *See, e.g.*, Russell v. McKinney Hosp. Venture, 235 F.3d 219, 227 (5th Cir.2000) (collecting cases). In *Griffin v. Washington Convention Center*, 142 F.3d 1308, 1312 (D.C.Cir.1998), the court stated that "evidence of a subordinate's bias is relevant where the ultimate decision maker is not insulated from the subordinate's influence." The key factual issue under the cat's paw theory is whether the subordinate possessed leverage or exerted influence over the titular decisionmaker. *See* Schreiner v. Caterpillar, Inc., 250 F.3d 1096, 1099 (7th Cir.2001) (ruling that there must be a factual basis in the record for the assertion that the biased individual's prejudice was the motivation for the decision maker's action). The Supreme Court relied upon *Shager's* cat's paw theory in *Burlington Industries, Inc. v. Ellerth*, 524 U.S. 742, 118 S.Ct. 2257, 141 L.Ed.2d 633 (1998), reproduced in Chapter 8, Section C.1, in support of its theory for imposing liability on employers for harassment by supervisors. Did the Court, in effect, apply the cat's paw theory in *Reeves v. Sanderson Plumbing*? Recall that in *Reeves* the supervisor who made the age-based statement was the husband of the company's president, who made the decision to fire Reeves.

8. *Collective Decisionmaking*: Where the employer has a collective decisionmaking process, consisting of input from a number of individuals or agents, and one of the participants is influenced by sexist or racial animus in making his decisions, should his vote against an employee be considered direct evidence or circumstantial evidence of discriminatory intent? *Universi-*

ty of Pennsylvania v. EEOC, 493 U.S. 182, 110 S.Ct. 577, 107 L.Ed.2d 571 (1990), illustrates a typical collective decision-making process in colleges and universities where faculty members act as a body in making hiring, promotion, and tenure decisions. In *Barbano v. Madison County*, 922 F.2d 139, 141 (2d Cir.1990), one member of a hiring committee for a public agency that provided services to veterans and their dependents asked a female candidate for the position of director "whether [her] husband would object to her 'running around the country with men,' and said he would not want his wife to do it." Because other members of the committee acquiesced in this line of questioning, the Second Circuit affirmed the district court's finding of disparate treatment on the basis of sex and held that a "knowing and informed toleration of discriminatory statements by those participating in the interview constitutes evidence of discrimination by all those present." *Id.* at 143.

For a discussion of the problem of determining discriminatory intent in multi-actor employment decisionmaking, see Rebecca Hanner White and Linda Hamilton Krieger, *Whose Motive Matters? Discrimination in Multi–Actor Employment Decision Making*, 61 La.L.Rev. 495 (2001). The authors argue that framing the disparate treatment inquiry as a search for conscious intent results in plaintiffs losing too many employment discrimination claims "in which even conscious, deliberate discrimination by an agent of an employer, acting within the course and scope of his employment, has caused the challenged action to be taken." *Id.* at 499. The authors argue that the focus of the inquiry should be on causation, i.e., "whether there exists an unbroken chain of causation between the employee's [protected trait] and the challenged decision." *Id.*

9. When, if ever, should silence be considered as evidence of discriminatory animus? Consider the following. A hospital hires Christi Smith as a staff nurse. She reports to Dolly Wood, the head nurse. Smith took maternity leave, and shortly after her return from leave a co-worker told her that some of the doctors were upset about her inaccessibility during her maternity leave. The co-worker also told Smith that the doctors had complained to Wood of her inaccessibility as well. The hospital discharged her about two months after she returned from maternity leave. Before she left, however, Smith went to see Wood, and asked her, "Is it true that doctors complained about my maternity leave, and that is the main reason I am being discharged?" Wood never responded to Smith's questions. *See* Weston–Smith v. Cooley Dickinson Hosp., Inc., 282 F.3d 60 (1st Cir.2002).

10. Sue is a black female who was employed by Tempco. Sue's supervisor, Tom, was concerned about her poor job performance and low productivity. As he wrote in a memorandum to her, he believed that her substandard performance was caused in substantial part by the fact that "she was allowing herself to become the black matriarch" at work because a number of black employees sought her advice about issues of race. Sue told Tom that she was offended by his "black matriarch" statement. Tom reported Sue's reaction to his superior, and they decided not to say anything further about her job performance to avoid a potential claim of racial discrimination. Subsequently, Sue was given "satisfactory" annual evaluations and even merit raises, although there were serious concerns about her job performance. Because of economic concerns, Tempco was forced to reduce its

workforce, and it terminated employees solely on the basis of work performance. Sue was terminated under that standard. Some white employees whose work had been unsatisfactory had received counseling which helped them improve their performance and avoid termination. Would Sue have a potential Title VII direct evidence claim based on this evidence? *See* Vaughn v. Edel, 918 F.2d 517 (5th Cir.1990).

3. MIXED–MOTIVE CASES

A mixed-motive case is one in which the employer relies upon both a legitimate, nondiscriminatory reason and an unlawful, discriminatory reason at the moment it makes an adverse employment decision, and both the legitimate and illegitimate reasons are motivating factors in the adverse employment decision.

DESERT PALACE, INC. v. COSTA

Supreme Court of the United States, 2003.
539 U.S. 90, 123 S.Ct. 2148, 156 L.Ed.2d 84.

JUSTICE THOMAS delivered the opinion of the Court.

The question before us in this case is whether a plaintiff must present direct evidence of discrimination in order to obtain a mixed-motive instruction under Title VII of the Civil Rights Act of 1964, as amended by the Civil Rights Act of 1991 (1991 Act). We hold that direct evidence is not required.

I

A

Since 1964, Title VII has made it an "unlawful employment practice for an employer * * * to discriminate against any individual * * *, *because of* such individual's race, color, religion, sex, or national origin." 78 Stat. 255, 42 U.S.C. § 2000e–2(a)(1) (emphasis added). In *Price Waterhouse v. Hopkins,* 490 U.S. 228, 109 S.Ct. 1775, 104 L.Ed.2d 268 (1989), the Court considered whether an employment decision is made "because of" sex in a "mixed-motive" case, *i.e.,* where both legitimate and illegitimate reasons motivated the decision. The Court concluded that, under § 2000e–2(a)(1), an employer could "avoid a finding of liability * * * by proving that it would have made the same decision even if it had not allowed gender to play such a role." *Id.,* at 244, 109 S.Ct. 1775; see *id.,* at 261, 109 S.Ct. 1775, n. (White, J., concurring in judgment); *id.,* at 261, 109 S.Ct. 1775 (O'CONNOR, J., concurring in judgment). The Court was divided, however, over the predicate question of when the burden of proof may be shifted to an employer to prove the affirmative defense.

Justice Brennan, writing for a plurality of four Justices, would have held that "when a plaintiff * * * proves that her gender played a *motivating* part in an employment decision, the defendant may avoid a finding of liability only by proving by a preponderance of the evidence that it would have made the same decision even if it had not taken the plaintiff's gender into account." *Id.,* at 258, 109 S.Ct. 1775 (emphasis added). The plurality did not, however, "suggest a limitation on the possible ways of proving that [gender] stereotyping played a motivating role in an employment decision." *Id.,* at 251–252, 109 S.Ct. 1775.

Justice White and Justice O'Connor both concurred in the judgment. Justice White would have held that the case was governed by *Mt. Healthy City Bd. of Ed. v. Doyle,* 429 U.S. 274, 97 S.Ct. 568, 50 L.Ed.2d 471 (1977), and would have shifted the burden to the employer only when a plaintiff "show[ed] that the unlawful motive was a *substantial* factor in the adverse employment action." *Price Waterhouse, supra,* at 259, 109 S.Ct. 1775. Justice O'Connor, like Justice White, would have required the plaintiff to show that an illegitimate consideration was a "substantial factor" in the employment decision. 490 U.S., at 276, 109 S.Ct. 1775. But, under Justice O'Connor's view, "the burden on the issue of causation" would shift to the employer only where "a disparate treatment plaintiff [could] show by *direct evidence* that an illegitimate criterion was a substantial factor in the decision." *Ibid.* (emphasis added).

Two years after *Price Waterhouse,* Congress passed the 1991 Act "in large part [as] a response to a series of decisions of this Court interpreting the Civil Rights Acts of 1866 and 1964." *Landgraf v. USI Film Products,* 511 U.S. 244, 250, 114 S.Ct. 1483, 128 L.Ed.2d 229 (1994). In particular, § 107 of the 1991 Act, which is at issue in this case, "respond[ed]" to *Price Waterhouse* by "setting forth standards applicable in 'mixed motive' cases" in two new statutory provisions.[1] 511 U.S., at 251, 114 S.Ct. 1483. The first establishes an alternative for proving that an "unlawful employment practice" has occurred:

> Except as otherwise provided in this subchapter, an unlawful employment practice is established when the complaining party demonstrates that race, color, religion, sex, or national origin was a motivating factor for any employment practice, even though other factors also motivated the practice.

42 U.S.C. § 2000e–2(m). The second provides that, with respect to " 'a claim in which an individual proves a violation under section 2000e–2(m),' "the employer has a limited affirmative defense that does not absolve it of liability, but restricts the remedies available to a plaintiff. The available remedies include only declaratory relief, certain types of injunctive relief, and attorney's fees and costs. 42 U.S.C. § 2000e–5(g)(2)(B). In order to avail itself of the affirmative defense, the employer must "demonstrat[e] that [it] would have taken the same action in the absence of the impermissible motivating factor." *Ibid.*

Since the passage of the 1991 Act, the Courts of Appeals have divided over whether a plaintiff must prove by direct evidence that an

---

1. This case does not require us to decide when, if ever, § 107 applies outside of the mixed-motive context.

impermissible consideration was a "motivating factor" in an adverse employment action. See 42 U.S.C. § 2000e–2(m). Relying primarily on Justice O'Connor's concurrence in *Price Waterhouse,* a number of courts have held that direct evidence is required to establish liability under § 2000e–2(m). See, *e.g., Mohr v. Dustrol, Inc.,* 306 F.3d 636, 640–641 (C.A.8 2002); *Fernandes v. Costa Bros. Masonry, Inc.,* 199 F.3d 572, 580 (C.A.1 1999); *Trotter v. Board of Trustees of Univ. of Ala.,* 91 F.3d 1449, 1453–1454 (C.A.11 1996); *Fuller v. Phipps,* 67 F.3d 1137, 1142 (C.A.4 1995). In the decision below, however, the Ninth Circuit concluded otherwise.

B

Petitioner Desert Palace, Inc. * * * employed respondent Catharina Costa as a warehouse worker and heavy equipment operator. Respondent was the only woman in this job and in her local Teamsters bargaining unit.

Respondent experienced a number of problems with management and her co-workers that led to an escalating series of disciplinary sanctions, including informal rebukes, a denial of privileges, and suspension. Petitioner finally terminated respondent after she was involved in a physical altercation in a warehouse elevator with fellow Teamsters member Herbert Gerber. Petitioner disciplined both employees because the facts surrounding the incident were in dispute, but Gerber, who had a clean disciplinary record, received only a 5–day suspension.

Respondent subsequently filed this lawsuit against petitioner in the United States District Court for the District of Nevada, asserting claims of sex discrimination and sexual harassment under Title VII. The District Court dismissed the sexual harassment claim, but allowed the claim for sex discrimination to go to the jury. At trial, respondent presented evidence that (1) she was singled out for "intense 'stalking' "by one of her supervisors, (2) she received harsher discipline than men for the same conduct, (3) she was treated less favorably than men in the assignment of overtime, and (4) supervisors repeatedly "stack[ed]" her disciplinary record and "frequently used or tolerated" sex-based slurs against her.

Based on this evidence, the District Court denied petitioner's motion for judgment as a matter of law, and submitted the case to the jury with instructions, two of which are relevant here. First, without objection from petitioner, the District Court instructed the jury that ' "the plaintiff has the burden of proving * * * by a preponderance of the evidence that she "suffered adverse work conditions" and that her sex was a motivating factor in any such work conditions imposed upon her.'"

Second, the District Court gave the jury the following mixed-motive instruction:

" 'You have heard evidence that the defendant's treatment of the plaintiff was motivated by the plaintiff's sex and also by other lawful reasons. If you find that the plaintiff's sex was a motivating factor in the defendant's treatment of the plaintiff, the plaintiff is entitled to your verdict, even if you find that the defendant's conduct was also motivated by a lawful reason.

" 'However, if you find that the defendant's treatment of the plaintiff was motivated by both gender and lawful reasons, you must decide whether the plaintiff is entitled to damages. The plaintiff is entitled to damages unless the defendant proves by a preponderance of the evidence that the defendant would have treated plaintiff similarly even if the plaintiff's gender had played no role in the employment decision.' "

Petitioner unsuccessfully objected to this instruction, claiming that respondent had failed to adduce "direct evidence" that sex was a motivating factor in her dismissal or in any of the other adverse employment actions taken against her. The jury rendered a verdict for respondent, awarding backpay, compensatory damages, and punitive damages. The District Court denied petitioner's renewed motion for judgment as a matter of law.

The Court of Appeals initially vacated and remanded, holding that the District Court had erred in giving the mixed-motive instruction because respondent had failed to present "substantial evidence of conduct or statements by the employer directly reflecting discriminatory animus." In addition, the panel concluded that petitioner was entitled to judgment as a matter of law on the termination claim because the evidence was insufficient to prove that respondent was "terminated because she was a woman."

The Court of Appeals reinstated the District Court's judgment after rehearing the case en banc. The en banc court saw no need to decide whether Justice O'Connor's concurrence in *Price Waterhouse* controlled because it concluded that Justice O'Connor's references to "direct evidence" had been "wholly abrogated" by the 1991 Act. And, turning "to the language" of § 2000e–2(m), the court observed that the statute "imposes no special [evidentiary] requirement and does not reference 'direct evidence.' " Accordingly, the court concluded that a "plaintiff * * * may establish a violation through a preponderance of evidence (whether direct or circumstantial) that a protected characteristic played 'a motivating factor.' " Based on that standard, the Court of Appeals held that respondent's evidence was sufficient to warrant a mixed-motive instruction and that a reasonable jury could have found that respondent's sex was a "motivating factor in her treatment." Four judges of the en banc panel dissented, relying in large part on "the reasoning of the prior opinion of the three-judge panel."

We granted certiorari.

II

This case provides us with the first opportunity to consider the effects of the 1991 Act on jury instructions in mixed-motive cases. Specifically, we must decide whether a plaintiff must present direct evidence of discrimination in order to obtain a mixed-motive instruction under 42 U.S.C. § 2000e–2(m). Petitioner's argument on this point proceeds in three steps: (1) Justice O'Connor's opinion is the holding of *Price Waterhouse;* (2) Justice O'Connor's *Price Waterhouse* opinion requires direct evidence of discrimination before a mixed-motive instruction can be given; and (3) the 1991 Act does nothing to abrogate that holding. Like the Court of Appeals, we see no need to address which of the opinions in *Price Waterhouse* is controlling: the third step of petitioner's argument is flawed, primarily because it is inconsistent with the text of § 2000e–2(m).

Our precedents make clear that the starting point for our analysis is the statutory text. See *Connecticut Nat. Bank v. Germain,* 503 U.S. 249, 253–254, 112 S.Ct. 1146, 117 L.Ed.2d 391 (1992). And where, as here, the words of the statute are unambiguous, the " 'judicial inquiry is complete.' " *Id.,* at 254, 112 S.Ct. 1146. Section 2000e–2(m) unambiguously states that a plaintiff need only "demonstrat[e]" that an employer used a forbidden consideration with respect to "any employment practice." On its face, the statute does not mention, much less require, that a plaintiff make a heightened showing through direct evidence. Indeed, petitioner concedes as much.

Moreover, Congress explicitly defined the term "demonstrates" in the 1991 Act, leaving little doubt that no special evidentiary showing is required. Title VII defines the term " 'demonstrates' " as to "mee[t] the burdens of production and persuasion." § 2000e(m). If Congress intended the term " 'demonstrates' " to require that the "burdens of production and persuasion" be met by direct evidence or some other heightened showing, it could have made that intent clear by including language to that effect in § 2000e(m). Its failure to do so is significant, for Congress has been unequivocal when imposing heightened proof requirements in other circumstances, including in other provisions of Title 42. See, *e.g.,* 8 U.S.C. § 1158(a)(2)(B) (stating that an asylum application may not be filed unless an alien "demonstrates by clear and convincing evidence" that the application was filed within one year of the alien's arrival in the United States); 42 U.S.C. § 5851(b)(3)(D) (providing that "[r]elief may not be ordered" against an employer in retaliation cases involving whistleblowers under the Atomic Energy Act where the employer is able to "*demonstrat[e] by clear and convincing evidence* that it would have taken the same unfavorable personnel action in the absence of such behavior" (emphasis added)); cf. *Price Waterhouse,* 490 U.S., at 253, 109 S.Ct. 1775 (plurality opinion) ("Only rarely have we required clear and convincing proof where the action defended against seeks only conventional relief").

In addition, Title VII's silence with respect to the type of evidence required in mixed-motive cases also suggests that we should not depart from the "[c]onventional rul[e] of civil litigation [that] generally appl[ies] in Title VII cases." That rule requires a plaintiff to prove his case "by a preponderance of the evidence," using "direct or circumstantial evidence," *Postal Service Bd. of Governors v. Aikens,* 460 U.S. 711,

714, n. 3, 103 S.Ct. 1478, 75 L.Ed.2d 403 (1983). We have often acknowledged the utility of circumstantial evidence in discrimination cases. For instance, in *Reeves v. Sanderson Plumbing Products, Inc.,* 530 U.S. 133, 120 S.Ct. 2097, 147 L.Ed.2d 105 (2000), we recognized that evidence that a defendant's explanation for an employment practice is "unworthy of credence" is "one form of *circumstantial evidence* that is probative of intentional discrimination." *Id.,* at 147, 120 S.Ct. 2097 (emphasis added). The reason for treating circumstantial and direct evidence alike is both clear and deep-rooted: "Circumstantial evidence is not only sufficient, but may also be more certain, satisfying and persuasive than direct evidence." *Rogers v. Missouri Pacific R. Co.,* 352 U.S. 500, 508, n. 17, 77 S.Ct. 443, 1 L.Ed.2d 493 (1957).

The adequacy of circumstantial evidence also extends beyond civil cases; we have never questioned the sufficiency of circumstantial evidence in support of a criminal conviction, even though proof beyond a reasonable doubt is required. See *Holland v. United States,* 348 U.S. 121, 140, 75 S.Ct. 127, 99 L.Ed. 150 (1954) (observing that, in criminal cases, circumstantial evidence is "intrinsically no different from testimonial evidence"). And juries are routinely instructed that "[t]he law makes no distinction between the weight or value to be given to either direct or circumstantial evidence." 1A K. O'Malley, J. Grenig, & W. Lee, Federal Jury Practice and Instructions, Criminal § 12.04 (5th ed.2000); see also 4 L. Sand, J. Siffert, W. Loughlin, S. Reiss, & N. Batterman, Modern Federal Jury Instructions ¶ 74.01 (2002) (model instruction 74–2). It is not surprising, therefore, that neither petitioner nor its *amici curiae* can point to any other circumstance in which we have restricted a litigant to the presentation of direct evidence absent some affirmative directive in a statute.

Finally, the use of the term "demonstrates" in other provisions of Title VII tends to show further that § 2000e2(m) does not incorporate a direct evidence requirement. See, *e.g.,* 42 U.S.C. §§ 2000e–2(k)(1)(A)(i), 2000e-5(g)(2)(B). For instance, § 2000e–5(g)(2)(B) requires an employer to "demonstrat[e] that [it] would have taken the same action in the absence of the impermissible motivating factor" in order to take advantage of the partial affirmative defense. Due to the similarity in structure between that provision and § 2000e–2(m), it would be logical to assume that the term "demonstrates" would carry the same meaning with respect to both provisions. But when pressed at oral argument about whether direct evidence is required before the partial affirmative defense can be invoked, petitioner did not "agree that * * * the defendant or the employer has any heightened standard" to satisfy. Absent some congressional indication to the contrary, we decline to give the same term in the same Act a different meaning depending on whether the rights of the plaintiff or the defendant are at issue. See *Commissioner v. Lundy,* 516 U.S. 235, 250, 116 S.Ct. 647, 133 L.Ed.2d 611 (1996) ("The interrelationship and close proximity of these provisions of the statute 'presents a classic case for application of the "normal rule of statutory construction that identical words used in different parts of the same act are intended to have the same meaning' " (quoting *Sullivan v. Stroop,* 496 U.S. 478, 484, 110 S.Ct. 2499, 110 L.Ed.2d 438 (1990)).

For the reasons stated above, we agree with the Court of Appeals that no heightened showing is required under § 2000e–2(m).[3]

* * *

In order to obtain an instruction under § 2000e–2(m), a plaintiff need only present sufficient evidence for a reasonable jury to conclude, by a preponderance of the evidence, that "race, color, religion, sex, or national origin was a motivating factor for any employment practice." Because direct evidence of discrimination is not required in mixed-motive cases, the Court of Appeals correctly concluded that the District Court did not abuse its discretion in giving a mixed-motive instruction to the jury. Accordingly, the judgment of the Court of Appeals is affirmed.

JUSTICE O'CONNOR, concurring.

I join the Court's opinion. In my view, prior to the Civil Rights Act of 1991, the evidentiary rule we developed to shift the burden of persuasion in mixed-motive cases was appropriately applied only where a disparate treatment plaintiff "demonstrated by direct evidence that an illegitimate factor played a substantial role" in an adverse employment decision. *Price Waterhouse v. Hopkins,* 490 U.S. 228, 275, 109 S.Ct. 1775, 104 L.Ed.2d 268 (1989) (O'CONNOR, J., concurring in judgment). This showing triggered "the deterrent purpose of the statute" and permitted a reasonable factfinder to conclude that "absent further explanation, the employer's discriminatory motivation 'caused' the employment decision." *Id.,* at 265, 109 S.Ct. 1775 (O'CONNOR, J., concurring in judgment).

As the Court's opinion explains, in the Civil Rights Act of 1991, Congress codified a new evidentiary rule for mixed-motive cases arising under Title VII. I therefore agree with the Court that the District Court did not abuse its discretion in giving a mixed-motive instruction to the jury.

Notes and Questions

1. *Mt. Healthy City School District Board of Education v. Doyle,* 429 U.S. 274, 97 S.Ct. 568, 50 L.Ed.2d 471 (1977), is the doctrinal foundation of the "same decision" defense that first the courts and then later Congress incorporated into employment discrimination law. In *Mt. Healthy,* a public school board refused to renew Fred Doyle's teaching contract. The school board justified its action on three grounds: (1) Doyle's lack of skills in professional matters; (2) his use of an obscene gesture while attempting to discipline two students in the school cafeteria; and (3) his disclosure to a local radio station that the school board had suggested the adoption of a

---

3. Of course, in light of our conclusion that direct evidence is not required under § 2000e–2(m), we need not address the second question on which we granted certiora- ri: "What are the appropriate standards for lower courts to follow in making a direct evidence determination in 'mixed-motive' cases under Title VII?"

dress code for teachers. Doyle claimed that the school board's decision violated his free speech rights under the First and Fourteenth Amendments. The lower courts ordered the school board to renew Doyle's contract because his communication to the radio station was protected speech under the First Amendment, which had either "played a role" or was a "substantial factor" in the school board's decision, even though the board would have been justified in not renewing his contract on the other grounds. The Supreme Court vacated the decision:

> Clearly the Board legally *could* have dismissed [Doyle] had the radio station incident never come to its attention. * * * We are thus brought to the issue whether, even if that were the case, the fact that the protected conduct played a "substantial part" in the actual decision not to renew would necessarily amount to a constitutional violation justifying remedial action. We think that it would not.

> A rule of causation which focuses solely on whether protected conduct played a part, "substantial" or otherwise, in a decision not to rehire could place an employee in a better position as a result of the exercise of constitutionally protected conduct than he would have occupied had he done nothing. The difficulty with the rule enunciated by the District Court is that it would require reinstatement in cases where a dramatic and perhaps abrasive incident is inevitably on the minds of those responsible for the decision to rehire, and does indeed play a part in that decision—even if the same decision would have been reached had the incident not occurred. The constitutional principle at stake is sufficiently vindicated if such an employee is placed in no worse position than if he had not engaged in the conduct. A borderline or marginal candidate should not have the employment question resolved against him because of constitutionally protected conduct. But that same candidate ought not be able, by engaging in such conduct, to prevent his employer from assessing his performance record and reaching a decision not to hire on the basis of that record, simply because the protected conduct makes the employer more certain of the correctness of its decision.

429 U.S. at 285–86, 97 S.Ct. at 575.

2. One of the major issues unresolved by *Costa* is whether § 703(m) of Title VII, 42 U.S.C. § 2000e–2(m), abolished the distinction between mixed-motive cases and single-motive pretext cases that are brought under § 703(a)(1). The employer has only the burden of production of evidence on the legitimate, nondiscriminatory reason defense in a *McDonnell Douglas* circumstantial evidence case, but has the burden of persuasion in addition to the burden of production of evidence on the same-decision defense. If the employer carries its burden on the same-decision defense, § 706(g)(2)(b), 42 U.S.C. § 2000e–5(g)(2)(B), adds a "safety valve": "an employer can escape damages and orders of reinstatement, hiring, promotion and the like—but not attorney's fees or declaratory or injunctive relief—by proving the absence of 'but for' causation as an affirmative defense." Costa v. Desert Palace, Inc., 299 F.3d 838, 850 (9th Cir.2002), *aff'd on other grounds*, 539 U.S. 90, 123 S.Ct. 2148, 156 L.Ed.2d 84 (2003). As *Costa* stated, a number of lower courts had drawn a distinction between single-motive pretext cases

and mixed-motive cases on the ground that direct evidence is required in a mixed-motive case. That distinction is no longer good law under *Costa*, but whether *Costa* abolished the distinction between single-motive pretext and mixed-motive cases as a matter of substantive or procedural law is not entirely clear. *See, e.g.*, Dunbar v. Pepsi–Cola General Bottlers of Iowa, 285 F.Supp.2d 1180, 1192 (N.D.Iowa.2003) (discussing the split in the district courts after *Costa* on this issue and noting that "some courts have read *Desert Palace* to apply to 'single-motive' cases as well as 'mixed-motive' cases, some have read it to spell the demise of the *McDonnell Douglas* burden-shifting paradigm, and some has read it to do both."). The Ninth Circuit specifically addressed the issue in its decision in *Costa:*

> In addition to the confusion over "direct evidence," there has been considerable misunderstanding regarding the relationship among the *McDonnell Douglas* burden-shifting analysis (sometimes referred to as "pretext" analysis), which primarily applies to summary judgment proceedings, and the terms single-motive and mixed-motive, which primarily refer to the theory or theories by which the defendant opposes the plaintiff's claim of discrimination. The short answer is that all of these concepts coexist without conflict.

* * *

As the Supreme Court elaborated a few years after *McDonnell Douglas,* the prima facie case "eliminates the most common nondiscriminatory reasons for the plaintiff's rejection." *Burdine,* 450 U.S. at 254, 101 S.Ct. 1089. Therefore, "we presume these acts, if otherwise unexplained, are more likely than not based on the consideration of impermissible factors." *Id. Burdine* clarified, however, that the plaintiff need not rely on this presumption: "She may succeed * * * either directly by persuading the court that a discriminatory reason more likely motivated the employer or indirectly by showing that the employer's proffered explanation is unworthy of credence." *Id.* at 256, 101 S.Ct. 1089.

Throughout these cases and those that followed, the court reaffirmed the canons of proof: the plaintiff retains the "ultimate burden of persuading the court that she has been the victim of intentional discrimination," *id.* at 256, 101 S.Ct. 1089; the question comes down to whether she has made her case.

The plaintiff may make out a prima facie case—which may, admittedly, be a weak showing—that entitles her to a commensurately small benefit, a transitory presumption of discrimination: the burden of *production* only shifts briefly to the employer to explain why it took the challenged action, if not based on the protected characteristic. In practice, employers quickly rebut the presumption and it "drops from the case." *Burdine,* 450 U.S. at 256 n. 10, 101 S.Ct. 1089; *see also* Deborah C. Malamud, *The Last Minuet: Disparate Treatment after Hicks,* 93 Mich. L.Rev. 2229, 2302–04 (1995). The burden of production then shifts back to the plaintiff to introduce evidence from which the factfinder could conclude that the employer's proffered reason was pretextual. The burden of *persuasion* always remains with the employee to prove the ultimate Title VII violation–unlawful discrimination.

It is important to emphasize, however, that nothing compels the parties to invoke the *McDonnell Douglas* presumption. Evidence can be in the form of the *McDonnell Douglas* prima facie case, or other sufficient evidence—direct or circumstantial—of discriminatory intent. Thus, although *McDonnell Douglas* may be used where a single motive is at issue, this proof scheme is not the exclusive means of proof in such a case. Indeed, it also might be invoked in cases in which the defendant asserts a "same decision" defense to certain remedies, a circumstance in which mixed motives are at issue.

Regardless of the method chosen to arrive at trial, it is not normally appropriate to introduce the *McDonnell Douglas* burden-shifting framework to the jury.[6] At that stage, the framework "unnecessarily evade[s] the ultimate question of discrimination *vel non*." *Aikens,* 460 U.S. at 714, 103 S.Ct. 1478.

Once at the trial stage, the plaintiff is required to put forward evidence of discrimination "because of" a protected characteristic.[7] After hearing both parties' evidence, the district court must decide what legal conclusions the evidence could reasonably support and instruct the jury accordingly. This determination is distinct from the question of whether to invoke the *McDonnell Douglas* presumption, which occurs at a separate, earlier stage of proceedings, involves summary judgment rather than jury instructions, and is unrelated to the number of possible motives for the challenged action. Instead, the choice of jury instructions depends simply on a determination of whether the evidence supports a finding that just one—or more than one-factor actually motivated the challenged decision. Justice White, in his concurring opinion in *Price Waterhouse,* succinctly described how the type of evidence presented affects the question facing the jury:

In [single-motive] cases, "the issue is whether either illegal or legal motives, but not both, were the 'true' motives behind the decision." In mixed-motive cases, however, there is no one "true" motive behind the decision. Instead, the decision is a result of multiple factors, at least one of which is legitimate. *Price Waterhouse,* 490 U.S. at 260, 109 S.Ct. 1775 (White, J., concurring in the judgment) (citation omitted). Following the 1991 amendments, characterizing the evidence as mixed-motive instead of single-motive results only in the availability of a different defense, a difference which derives directly from the statutory text, not from judicially created proof structures.

* * *

6. The presumption is thus what has been termed a "bursting bubble" presumption. In one limited circumstance, the presumption retains vitality at trial: where there is no rebuttal by the employer, but the plaintiff's prima facie case is in factual dispute. The jury then determines whether the prima facie case is established. If it is, the jury must find discrimination. *Hicks,* 509 U.S. at 509–10, 113 S.Ct. 2742.

7. As the Supreme Court has observed, a case need not be characterized or labeled at the outset. Rather, the shape will often emerge after discovery or even at trial. Similarly, the complaint itself need not contain more than the allegation that the adverse employment action was taken because of a protected characteristic. *See Price Waterhouse,* 490 U.S. at 247 n. 12, 109 S.Ct. 1775 (plurality opinion).

Regardless of what kind of instructions are given, we emphasize that there are not two fundamentally different types of Title VII cases. In some cases, the employer may be entitled to the "same decision" affirmative defense instruction. In others, it may not. The employee's ultimate burden of proof in all cases remains the same: to show by a preponderance of the evidence that the challenged employment decision was "because of" discrimination.

* * *

To summarize: *McDonnell Douglas* and "mixed-motive" are not two opposing types of cases. Rather, they are separate inquiries that occur at separate stages of the litigation. Nor are "single-motive" and "mixed-motive" cases fundamentally different categories of cases. Both require the employee to prove discrimination; they simply reflect the type of evidence offered. Where the employer asserts that, even if the factfinder determines that a discriminatory motive exists, the employer would in any event have taken the adverse employment action for other reasons, it may take advantage of the "same decision" affirmative defense. The remedies will differ if the employer prevails on that defense. * * *

299 F.3d at 854–57.

3. Is it necessary for the trier of fact to go through the *McDonnell Douglas* analysis—prima facie case, consideration of the employer's same-decision defense and pretext—in a mixed-motive case where the plaintiff relies upon circumstantial evidence to prove discriminatory animus was "a motivating factor"? Consider the Ninth Circuit's discussion of pretext in *Costa*:

Finally, we turn to the question of where the concept of pretext fits in this framework. Although cases in which the *McDonnell Douglas* framework is applied are sometimes referred to as "pretext cases," and we have no wish to change a quarter century of usage, it should be noted that questions of pretext may arise in any Title VII case, regardless of whether it is analyzed under *McDonnell Douglas*. Cases in which the dispute is only over whether or not the employer possessed the discriminatory motive alleged need not involve pretext, although they often do. For example, if the plaintiff chooses not to invoke the *McDonnell Douglas* framework, the employer need not proffer any explanation for the challenged action, but may simply require the plaintiff to prove her case of discrimination. Nor is the concept of pretext alien to cases in which an employer asserts a "same decision" or "but for" defense. For example, one of the employer's purportedly legitimate reasons may be pretextual. On the other hand, another may not. As Justice O'Connor recently explained in writing for the Court: "Proof that the defendant's explanation is unworthy of credence is simply one form of circumstantial evidence that is probative of intentional discrimination * * *." *Reeves*, 530 U.S. at 147, 120 S.Ct. 2097.

299 F.3d at 838, 857, *aff'd on other grounds*, 539 U.S. 90, 123 S.Ct. 2148, 2154, 156 L.Ed.2d 84 (2003).

4. Another issue left unanswered by *Costa* is who decides—judge or jury—whether the case is a mixed-motive or a single-motive case. The courts

are not in agreement on the jury instructions in employment discrimination cases as explained by the Ninth Circuit in *Sanghvi v. City of Claremont*, 328 F.3d 532, 538–40 (9th Cir.2003). The Ninth Circuit in *Costa* suggested the following approach:

> As a practical matter, the question of how many motives the evidence reasonably supports affects the jury instructions as follows:

> If, based on the evidence, the trial court determines that the only reasonable conclusion a jury could reach is that discriminatory animus is the *sole* cause for the challenged employment action or that discrimination played *no* role at all in the employer's decisionmaking, then the jury should be instructed to determine whether the challenged action was taken "because of" the prohibited reason. If the jury determines that the employer acted because of discriminatory intent, the employee prevails and may receive the full remedies available under Title VII; if not, the employer prevails. In such cases the employer does not benefit from the "same decision" defense, which, if successful, significantly limits the employee's remedies.

> In contrast, in cases in which the evidence could support a finding that discrimination is one of two or more reasons for the challenged decision, at least one of which may be legitimate, the jury should be instructed to determine first whether the discriminatory reason was "a motivating factor" in the challenged action. If the jury's answer to this question is in the affirmative, then the employer has violated Title VII. However, if the jury then finds that the employer has proved the "same decision" affirmative defense by a preponderance of the evidence, 42 U.S.C. § 2000e–5(g)(2)(B), the employer will escape the imposition of damages and any order of reinstatement, hiring, promotion, and the like, and is liable solely for attorney's fees, declaratory relief, and an order prohibiting future discriminatory actions.

299 F.3d at 856–57.

5. Because the Supreme Court in *Costa* held that a plaintiff is not *required* to present direct evidence of discriminatory animus in order to receive a mixed-motive instruction, the Court did not need to resolve the split in the circuits on the meaning of direct evidence. The second issue on which the Court had granted certiorari in *Costa* was "[w]hat are the appropriate standards for lower courts to follow in making a direct evidence determination in 'mixed-motive' cases under Title VII?" The parties had fully briefed the issue, but the Court found it unnecessary to address the question in light of its holding that "a motivating factor" can be proven by either direct or circumstantial evidence. *Costa*, 539 U.S. at 94 n.3, 123 S.Ct. at 2155 n.3.

6. After *Costa* are courts more or less likely to grant summary judgments in defendants' favor? Is *Costa* likely to increase pressure on defendants to settle employment discrimination cases? What are the advantages and disadvantages for plaintiffs and defendants if a case is decided as a mixed-motive case? In the Civil Rights Act of 1991, in § 703(m) of Title VII, Congress overturned *Price Waterhouse*, but only insofar as it made the same-decision defense a liability-determining rule in mixed-motive cases. 42 U.S.C. § 2000e–2(m). Also, in § 706(g)(2)(B) of Title VII, 42 U.S.C. § 2000e–

5(g)(2)(B), Congress limited the remedies a plaintiff may receive if the employer prevails on its same-decision defense. (Read § 703(m) and § 706(g)(2)(B) in the Statutory Supplement.)

7. Do the 1991 amendments to the Civil Rights Act strike an appropriate balance between Title VII's goals of eliminating discrimination and employers' preferences for autonomy in making employment decisions? Consider the case of *Stevens v. Gravette Medical Center Hospital*, 998 F.Supp. 1011 (W.D.Ark.1998): Stevens, a nurse, brought a Title VII sex discrimination action claiming that he was denied a promotion to a supervisory position in the OB/GYN department because of his sex. The jury made two findings: (1) plaintiff's sex was a motivating factor in the employer's decision to deny plaintiff the promotion, and (2) the employer would have made the same adverse decision without considering his sex. Proceeding under § 706(g)(2)(B), plaintiff sought a declaratory judgment, nominal damages, an injunction restraining the employer from engaging in sex discrimination in the future, and attorney's fees. The court denied the request for nominal damages on the ground that they are a substitute for compensatory damages and § 706(g)(2)(B) precludes awards of compensatory damages. The court denied the request for a declaratory judgment because, even though plaintiff had presented evidence that the employer had a policy and practice of not assigning male nurses to the OB/GYN section, the jury had not been instructed on the policy and practice claims, and the plaintiff had not objected to the absence of an instruction on that claim. The court also denied the request for injunctive relief because, among other reasons, the plaintiff had resigned and the evidence did not support a finding that the discriminatory conduct was likely to continue in the future. Finally, the court denied plaintiff's request for an award of attorney's fees on the ground that plaintiff had obtained only a "technical or pyrrhic victory." *Id.* at 1020.

8. The general rule on attorney's fees in employment discrimination cases is that a prevailing plaintiff should recover attorney's fees unless special circumstances would render such an award unjust. *See* Christiansburg Garment Co. v. EEOC, 434 U.S. 412, 98 S.Ct. 694, 54 L.Ed.2d 648 (1978), reproduced in Chapter 16. Relying on the Supreme Court's decision in *Farrar v. Hobby*, 506 U.S. 103, 113 S.Ct. 566, 121 L.Ed.2d 494 (1992), the majority of the courts of appeals have adopted a proportionality rule on awards of fees in Title VII mixed-motive cases. *See, e.g.*, Sheppard v. Riverview Nursing Ctr., 88 F.3d 1332 (4th Cir.), *cert. denied*, 519 U.S. 993, 117 S.Ct. 483, 136 L.Ed.2d 377 (1996). In *Farrar*, the Supreme Court held that attorney's fees should be awarded to prevailing parties who have received some relief on the merits of their claims, but that the reasonableness of the fee award should be proportional to the degree to which a plaintiff has been successful. The court in *Sheppard* stated that the *Farrar* proportionality rule was "designed to prevent a situation in which a client receives a pyrrhic victory and the lawyers take a pot of gold." *Id.* at 1338. The *Sheppard* rule appears to be that *Farrar* should be applied in mixed-motive cases to deny all but a nominal fee award simply because a mixed-motive plaintiff cannot recover monetary damages or obtain injunctive relief. The majority of the courts of appeals have followed *Sheppard. See, e.g.*, Norris v. Sysco Corp., 191 F.3d 1043 (9th Cir.1999); *but see* Gudenkauf v. Stauffer Communications, Inc., 158 F.3d 1074 (10th Cir.1998) (holding that

attorney's fees should ordinarily be awarded in mixed-motive cases in all but special circumstances).

4. AFTER–ACQUIRED EVIDENCE CASES

McKENNON v. NASHVILLE BANNER PUBLISHING CO.

Supreme Court of the United States, 1995.
513 U.S. 352, 115 S.Ct. 879, 130 L.Ed.2d 852.

JUSTICE KENNEDY delivered the opinion for a unanimous Court.

The question before us is whether an employee discharged in violation of the Age Discrimination in Employment Act of 1967 is barred from all relief when, after her discharge, the employer discovers evidence of wrongdoing that, in any event, would have led to the employee's termination on lawful and legitimate grounds.

I

For some 30 years, petitioner Christine McKennon worked for respondent Nashville Banner Publishing Company. She was discharged, the Banner claimed, as part of a work force reduction plan necessitated by cost considerations. McKennon, who was 62 years old when she lost her job, thought another reason explained her dismissal: her age. She filed suit in the United States District Court for the Middle District of Tennessee, alleging that her discharge violated the Age Discrimination in Employment Act of 1967 (ADEA). * * *

In preparation of the case, the Banner took McKennon's deposition. She testified that, during her final year of employment, she had copied several confidential documents bearing upon the company's financial condition. She had access to these records as secretary to the Banner's comptroller. McKennon took the copies home and showed them to her husband. Her motivation, she averred, was an apprehension she was about to be fired because of her age. When she became concerned about her job, she removed and copied the documents for "insurance" and "protection." A few days after these deposition disclosures, the Banner sent McKennon a letter declaring that removal and copying of the records was in violation of her job responsibilities and advising her (again) that she was terminated. The Banner's letter also recited that had it known of McKennon's misconduct it would have discharged her at once for that reason.

For purposes of summary judgment, the Banner conceded its discrimination against McKennon. The District Court granted summary judgment for the Banner, holding that McKennon's misconduct was grounds for her termination and that neither backpay nor any other remedy was available to her under the ADEA. The United States Court of Appeals for the Sixth Circuit affirmed on the same rationale. We granted certiorari to resolve conflicting views among the Courts of Appeals on the question whether all relief must be denied when an employee has been discharged in violation of the ADEA and the employer later discovers some wrongful conduct that would have led to discharge if it had been discovered earlier. We now reverse.

II

We shall assume, as summary judgment procedures require us to assume, that the sole reason for McKennon's initial discharge was her age, a discharge violative of the ADEA. Our further premise is that the misconduct revealed by the deposition was so grave that McKennon's immediate discharge would have followed its disclosure in any event. The District Court and the Court of Appeals found no basis for contesting that proposition, and for purposes of our review we need not question it here. We do question the legal conclusion reached by those courts that after-acquired evidence of wrongdoing which would have resulted in discharge bars employees from any relief under the ADEA. That ruling is incorrect.

The Court of Appeals considered McKennon's misconduct, in effect, to be supervening grounds for termination. That may be so, but it does not follow, as the Court of Appeals said in citing one of its own earlier cases, that the misconduct renders it " 'irrelevant whether or not [McKennon] was discriminated against.' " We conclude that a violation of the ADEA cannot be so altogether disregarded.

* * * The substantive, antidiscrimination provisions of the ADEA are modeled upon the prohibitions of Title VII. Its remedial provisions incorporate by reference the provisions of the Fair Labor Standards Act of 1938. 29 U.S.C. § 626(b). When confronted with a violation of the ADEA, a district court is authorized to afford relief by means of reinstatement, backpay, injunctive relief, declaratory judgment, and attorney's fees. In the case of a willful violation of the Act, the ADEA authorizes an award of liquidated damages equal to the backpay award. The Act also gives federal courts the discretion to "grant such legal or equitable relief as may be appropriate to effectuate the purposes of [the Act]." *Id.*

The ADEA and Title VII share common substantive features and also a common purpose: "the elimination of discrimination in the workplace." Oscar Mayer & Co. v. Evans, 441 U.S. 750, 756, 99 S.Ct. 2066, 2071, 60 L.Ed.2d 609 (1979). * * * The private litigant who seeks redress for his or her injuries vindicates both the deterrence and the compensation objectives of the ADEA. *See* Alexander v. Gardner–Denver Co., 415 U.S. 36, 45, 94 S.Ct. 1011, 1018, 39 L.Ed.2d 147 (1974) ("[T]he private litigant [in Title VII] not only redresses his own injury but also vindicates the important congressional policy against discriminatory employment practices"). It would not accord with this scheme if after-acquired evidence of wrongdoing that would have resulted in termination operates, in every instance, to bar all relief for an earlier violation of the Act.

The objectives of the ADEA are furthered when even a single employee establishes that an employer has discriminated against him or her. The disclosure through litigation of incidents or practices which violate national policies respecting nondiscrimination in the work force is itself important, for the occurrence of violations may disclose patterns of noncompliance resulting from a misappreciation of the Act's operation or entrenched resistance to its commands, either of which can be of industry-wide significance. The efficacy of its enforcement mechanisms becomes one measure of the success of the Act.

The Court of Appeals in this case relied upon two of its earlier decisions, *Johnson v. Honeywell Info. Sys., Inc.*, 955 F.2d 409 (6th Cir.1992); *Milligan-Jensen v. Michigan Technological Univ.*, 975 F.2d 302 (6th Cir.1992), and the opinion of the Court of Appeals for the Tenth Circuit in *Summers v. State Farm Mutual Auto. Ins. Co.*, 864 F.2d 700 (1988). Consulting those authorities, it declared that it had "firmly endorsed the principle that after-acquired evidence is a complete bar to any recovery by the former employee where the employer can show it would have fired the employee on the basis of the evidence." *Summers*, in turn, relied upon our decision in *Mt. Healthy City Bd. of Ed. v. Doyle*, 429 U.S. 274, 97 S.Ct. 568, 50 L.Ed.2d 471 (1977), but that decision is inapplicable here.

In *Mt. Healthy* we addressed a mixed-motives case, in which two motives were said to be operative in the employer's decision to fire an employee. One was lawful, the other (an alleged constitutional violation) unlawful. We held that if the lawful reason alone would have sufficed to justify the firing, the employee could not prevail in a suit against the employer. The case was controlled by the difficulty, and what we thought was the lack of necessity, of disentangling the proper motive from the improper one where both played a part in the termination and the former motive would suffice to sustain the employer's action. That is not the problem confronted here. As we have said, the case comes to us on the express assumption that an unlawful motive was the sole basis for the firing. McKennon's misconduct was not discovered until after she had been fired. The employer could not have been motivated by knowledge it did not have and it cannot now claim that the employee was fired for the nondiscriminatory reason. Mixed motive cases are inapposite here, except to the important extent they underscore the necessity of determining the employer's motives in ordering the discharge, an essential element in determining whether the employer violated the federal antidiscrimination law. * * *

Our inquiry is not at an end, however, for even though the employer has violated the Act, we must consider how the after-acquired evidence of the employee's wrongdoing bears on the specific remedy to be ordered. Equity's maxim that a suitor who engaged in his own reprehensible conduct in the course of the transaction at issue must be denied equitable relief because of unclean hands, a rule which in conventional formulation operated *in limine* to bar the suitor from invoking the aid of the equity court, has not been applied where Congress authorizes broad equitable relief to serve important national policies. We have rejected the unclean hands defense "where a private suit serves important public purposes." Perma Life Mufflers, Inc. v. International Parts Corp., 392 U.S. 134, 138, 88 S.Ct. 1981, 1984, 20 L.Ed.2d 982 (1968). That does not mean, however, the employee's own misconduct is irrelevant to all the remedies otherwise available under the statute. The statute controlling this case provides that "the court shall have jurisdiction to grant such legal or equitable relief as may be appropriate to effectuate the purposes of this chapter, including without limitation judgments compelling employment, reinstatement or promotion, or enforcing the liability for [amounts owing to a person as a result of a violation of this chapter]." 29 U.S.C. § 626(b); *see also* § 216(b). In giving effect to the ADEA, we must recognize the duality between the legitimate interests of the employer and the important claims of the employee who invokes the national employment policy mandated by the Act. The employee's wrongdoing must be taken into account, we conclude, lest the employer's legitimate concerns be ignored. The ADEA, like Title VII, is not a general regulation of the workplace but a law which prohibits discrimination. The statute does not constrain employers from exercising significant other prerogatives and discretions in the course of the hiring, promoting, and discharging of their employees. In determining appropriate remedial action, the employee's wrongdoing becomes relevant not to punish the employee, or out of concern "for the relative moral worth of the parties," *Perma Life Mufflers*, 392 U.S. at 139, 88 S.Ct. at 1984, but to take due account of the lawful prerogatives of the employer in the usual course of its business and the corresponding equities that it has arising from the employee's wrongdoing.

The proper boundaries of remedial relief in the general class of cases where, after termination, it is discovered that the employee has engaged in wrongdoing must be addressed by the judicial system in the ordinary course of further decisions, for the factual permutations and the equitable considerations they raise will vary from case to case. We do conclude that here, and as a general rule in cases of this type, neither reinstatement nor front pay is an appropriate remedy. It would be both inequitable and pointless to order the reinstatement of someone the employer would have terminated, and will terminate, in any event and upon lawful grounds.

The proper measure of backpay presents a more difficult problem. Resolution of this question must give proper recognition to the fact that an ADEA violation has occurred which must be deterred and compensated without undue infringement upon the employer's rights and prerogatives. The object of compensation is to restore the employee to the position he or she would have been in absent the discrimination, but that principle is difficult to apply with precision where there is after-acquired evidence of wrongdoing that would have led to termination on legitimate grounds had the employer known about it. Once an employer learns about employee wrongdoing that would lead to a legitimate discharge, we cannot require the employer to ignore the information, even if it is acquired during the course of discovery in a suit against the employer and even if the information might have gone undiscovered absent the suit. The beginning point in the trial court's formulation of a remedy should be calculation of backpay from the date of the unlawful discharge to the date the new information was discovered. In determining the appropriate order for relief, the court can consider taking into further account extraordinary equitable circumstances that affect the legitimate interests of either party. An absolute rule barring any recovery of backpay, however, would undermine the ADEA's objective of forcing employers to consider and examine their motivations, and of penalizing them for employment decisions that spring from age discrimination.

Where an employer seeks to rely upon after-acquired evidence of wrongdoing, it must first establish that the wrongdoing was of such severity that the employee in fact would have been terminated on those grounds alone if the employer had known of it at the time of the discharge. The concern that employers might as a routine matter undertake extensive discovery into an employee's background or performance on the job to resist claims under the Act is not an insubstantial one, but we think the authority of the courts to award attorney's fees, mandated under the statute, 29 U.S.C. §§ 216(b), 626(b), and in appropriate cases to invoke the provisions of Rule 11 of the Federal Rules of Civil Procedure will deter most abuses.

* * *

Notes and Questions

1. An employer's "after-acquired evidence" defense arises in two basic fact situations: when an employee has engaged in either resume fraud or on-the-job misconduct, which the employer first discovers some time after the employee has initiated a discrimination proceeding. Employee misconduct can include theft or misuse of the employer's or a customer's property, conflict of interest, anticompetitive conduct, and also certain off-the-job criminal behavior.

2. A widely cited 1988 study found that three percent of job applicants misrepresented that they had a college degree; three percent listed employers for whom they had never worked; three percent listed nonexistent jobs that they claimed they had worked; four percent misrepresented job titles they had with previous employers; and eleven percent misrepresented the reasons for leaving previous employment. *See* George D. Mesritz, *"After–Acquired" Evidence of Pre–Employment Misrepresentations: An Effective Defense Against Wrongful Discharge Claims*, 18 Emp.Rel.L.J. 215, 222 (1992). *See also* Mitchell H. Rubinstein, *The Use of Predischarge Misconduct Discovered After an Employee's Termination as a Defense in Employment Litigation*, 24 Suffolk U.L.Rev. 1 (1990). The Federal Bureau of Investigation estimates that 500,000 persons nationwide claim they have college degrees they never earned, and a congressional study estimates that one-third of all job applicants commit resume fraud. *See* Renee Haines, *FBI: 500,000 Fudge Facts on Their Resumes*, Houston Chronicle, Oct. 19, 1992, at 11A.

3. Suppose that an associate at a law firm files a Title VII claim that she was denied partnership on the basis of sex. How should the law firm respond to after-acquired evidence that the associate committed resume fraud in seeking a job with the firm? *See* Nancy Millich, *Ethical Integrity in the Legal Profession: Survey Results Regarding Law Students' Veracity on Resumes and Recommendations for Enhancing Legal Ethics Outside the Classroom*, 24 Ariz.St.L.J. 1181 (1992).

4. In what ways, if any, does *Desert Palace v. Costa* affect the analysis in the after-acquired evidence cases?

5. Should the after-acquired evidence defense be characterized as an affirmative defense or a legitimate, nondiscriminatory reason? Does it make a difference?

Although the after-acquired evidence defense is not specifically listed as an affirmative defense in Rule 8(c) of the Federal Rules of Civil Procedure, the court in *Red Deer v. Cherokee County, Iowa*, 183 F.R.D. 642 (N.D.Iowa 1999), held that it is an affirmative defense. The court relied upon a number reasons: *McKennon* imposed the burden of proof on this defense on defendants; the defense does not controvert the plaintiff's proof, but is raised instead to avoid the plaintiff's claim; and notice of the defense is necessary to avoid surprise and undue prejudice to the plaintiff. *Red Deer* held also that, as an affirmative defense, it must be plead by the employer under penalty of waiver or forfeiture, unless an employer obtains leave from a court to amend its answer to raise the defense.

6. After an employee is discharged from his job as a staff physician at a hospital, he claims that he was fired because of age, race, religion, and sex. During the course of pretrial discovery, hospital administrators learn for the first time that he never went to medical school. What should the outcome be under *McKennon*? Does *McKennon* suggest a standard for evaluating the severity of employee misconduct that would permit the employer to prevail on the after-acquired evidence defense under certain circumstances?

In *Herring v. Thomasville Furniture Industries, Inc.*, 1999 WL 1937352 (M.D.N.C.1999), the court held that *McKennon* imposes the burden of proof (production and persuasion) on the employer to convince the factfinder that it was unaware of the plaintiff's misconduct at the time it made the adverse employment decision, the misconduct was serious enough to justify the decision, and the employer would have made the same decision if it had known about the misconduct at the time. *Id* at *3. In *Herring*, the employer's after-acquired evidence defense was based on the claim that the plaintiff had provided false information regarding the dates and amount of time she had worked for two previous employers. Even though the employer pointed to a written policy that falsification may be a ground for disciplinary action, the policy, standing alone, was not sufficient to allow the employer to prevail on the defense. The court rejected the defense on the grounds that the alleged falsifications did not appear to be deliberate but were more likely inadvertent errors. If a court or jury rules against an employer on its after-acquired evidence defense, the plaintiff is entitled to back pay, front pay, reinstatement, and other appropriate forms of relief, including compensatory and punitive damages. See Chapter 16 (Remedies).

7. The plaintiff filed an ADEA claim alleging that his employer discharged him because of his age. On the eve of trial, the employer learned that the plaintiff had falsely stated on his application that he was a college graduate. Relying on *McKennon*, the employer argued that it would not have hired the plaintiff if it had known of the resume fraud. Is the "would not have hired" defense sufficient under *McKennon*? *See* Shattuck v. Kinetic Concepts, Inc., 49 F.3d 1106, 1108–09 (5th Cir.1995).

8. Should an employer's success on the after-acquired evidence defense preclude an award of compensatory damages in a disparate treatment claim under the Civil Rights Act of 1991? What about punitive damages? *See EEOC Guidance on After–Acquired Evidence, reprinted in* 1995 Daily Lab. Rep. (BNA) 241, d29 (Dec. 15, 1995) ("out-of-pocket losses analogous to backpay losses incurred after the date that the discovery of wrongdoing is discovered will typically be excluded," but "[n]othing in *McKennon* suggests that compensatory damages for emotional harm should be time limited"; punitive damages are not barred if the plaintiff's proof meets the "malice or reckless indifference" standard of the Civil Rights Act of 1991 and "are virtually always appropriate where retaliation has been established").

9. Compare the mixed-motive cases brought under the Civil Rights Act of 1991 with the after-acquired evidence cases. The plaintiff in the mixed-motive case would not be entitled to backpay under § 706(g)(2)(B)(ii) of Title VII, but the plaintiff in the after-acquired evidence case may be entitled to some backpay or other damages. Is the difference in the availability of backpay justified as a matter of policy? In both cases the same-decision defense is at work, is it not?

10. Does *McKennon* adequately address the problem that employers now have an incentive to ransack employees' personnel records or to undertake *post hoc* investigations or extensive pretrial discovery to try to find misconduct that supports an after-acquired evidence defense? *See* Susan A. Bocamazo, *Misconduct of Plaintiff Is Now Critical in Employment Discrimination Cases*, 95–26 Law.Wkly.USA 1 (Dec. 16, 1995).

11. *Evidence of Post–Termination Misconduct or "After After–Acquired Evidence"*: Should *McKennon* be limited to employee misconduct that occurs during the course of employment or should it extend to "after-acquired" evidence of post-termination misconduct? In *Sigmon v. Parker Chapin Flattau & Klimpl*, 901 F.Supp. 667 (S.D.N.Y.1995), plaintiff had been an associate for a law firm, but was fired after she alleged that she had been the victim of unlawful sex discrimination. Pursuant to a long-standing firm policy, the plaintiff was provided with an office and a telephone in order to conduct a job search. While in the office, the plaintiff inadvertently found an unsealed, unmarked box that contained a file with evaluations of her work by senior attorneys. She copied the documents in her file, as well as other documents in the box containing evaluations of twenty other associates. Subsequently, she informed the law firm that she had copied the confidential personnel documents, and the firm sought to use this evidence of her post-termination misconduct as a limitation of potential damages. *Sigmon* followed other district courts in holding that *McKennon* does not apply to after-acquired evidence of post-employment conduct. *Id.* at 682–83. Finding that

the defendant was not prejudiced by the plaintiff's "questionable" post-termination conduct, however, the court denied the law firm's summary judgment motion to limit damages based on that conduct. *Id.* at 682. *See* Carr v. Woodbury County Juvenile Detention Ctr., 905 F.Supp. 619, 626–27 (N.D.Iowa 1995) (collecting cases of "after after-acquired evidence"). Do you agree?

The Tenth Circuit, in *Medlock v. Ortho Biotech, Inc.*, 164 F.3d 545 (10th Cir.), *cert. denied*, 528 U.S. 813, 120 S.Ct. 48, 145 L.Ed.2d 42 (1999), left open the question whether the rule of *McKennon* should be construed to permit limitations on relief for post-termination conduct. At least one commentator has argued that egregious post-termination misconduct should ordinarily bar reinstatement and curtail back pay. Christine Neylon O'Brien, *The Law of After–Acquired Evidence in Employment Discrimination Cases: Clarification of the Employer's Burden, Remedial Guidance, and the Enigma of Post–Termination Misconduct*, 65 UMKC L.Rev. 159 (1996). Do you agree?

5. PATTERN–OR–PRACTICE OR SYSTEMIC DISCRIMINATION CASES

Section 707 of Title VII, 42 U.S.C. § 2000e–6, and § 107 of the ADA, 42 U.S.C. § 12117(a), empower the federal government, either the EEOC or the United States Department of Justice, to bring a civil action against an employer charging systemic discrimination against a protected group. In these cases, the federal government has to demonstrate that there exists "a pattern or practice of resistance to the full enjoyment of any of the rights secured by" these Acts. Title VII § 707(a), 42 U.S.C. § 2000e–6(a). The terms "pattern-or-practice" and "systemic discrimination" are often used either alternatively or singly to characterize employment discrimination cases brought by the federal government. *See, e.g.*, EEOC v. Shell Oil Co., 466 U.S. 54, 69, 70, 104 S.Ct. 1621, 1631, 80 L.Ed.2d 41 (1984). The ADEA does not use the phrase pattern-or-practice in connection with the authority of the EEOC to bring civil actions, but the courts have allowed the EEOC to bring pattern-or-practice age cases. *See, e.g.*, EEOC v. Western Elec. Co., Inc., 713 F.2d 1011, 1016 n. 14 (4th Cir.1983).

The *King* case that follows discusses the analytical methodology in pattern-or-practice suits based on the disparate treatment theory, which was enunciated by the Supreme Court in *Teamsters v. United States*, 431 U.S. 324, 336–37 n.16, 97 S.Ct. 1843, 1855 n.16, 52 L.Ed.2d 396 (1977). Although *Teamsters* was brought by the federal government, the Supreme Court implicitly endorsed the application of pattern-or-practice principles and rules of proof to class actions brought by private parties. *Id.* at 357–62, 97 S.Ct. at 1866–68. *See, e.g.*, Cox v. American Cast Iron Pipe Co., 784 F.2d 1546, 1559 (11th Cir.), *cert. denied*, 479 U.S. 883, 107 S.Ct. 274, 93 L.Ed.2d 250 (1986).

KING v. GENERAL ELECTRIC COMPANY

United States Court of Appeals for the Seventh Circuit, 1992.
960 F.2d 617.

BAUER, Chief Judge.

[Two groups of employees brought suits against their employer under the Age Discrimination in Employment Act of 1967 (ADEA), 29 U.S.C. § 621 et seq., and the trial court consolidated them for trial. The trial court entered judgment on behalf of some of the plaintiffs and against other plaintiffs. On appeal, the Seventh Circuit ruled, *inter alia*, that the evidence was insufficient to demonstrate a pattern-or-practice of discrimination.]

* * *

B.   Legal Framework

* * *

A plaintiff in an age discrimination case may prove his claim in two ways. He may try to meet his burden head on by presenting direct or circumstantial evidence that age was the determining factor in his discharge. Or, the plaintiff may use the indirect, burden-shifting method of proof developed in Title VII cases originally outlined in *McDonnell Douglas Corp. v. Green.* Under either method, the ultimate burden of persuasion remains with the plaintiff at all times.

* * *

Title VII provides another enforcement mechanism that played a pivotal role in the resolution of the case below. This is the class-based pattern-or-practice trial. The term pattern-or-practice derives from § 707(a) of the Civil Rights Act of 1964. The section states:

> When the EEOC has reasonable cause to believe that any person or group of persons is engaged in a pattern-or-practice of resistance to the full enjoyment of any rights secured by this subchapter, and that the pattern-or-practice is of such a nature and is intended to deny the full exercise of rights herein described, the EEOC may bring a civil action . * * *

The Supreme Court has stated that "the pattern-or-practice language in § 707(a) of Title VII was not intended as a term of art, and the words reflect only their usual meaning." *Teamsters v. United States*, 431 U.S. 324, 336–37 n. 16, 97 S.Ct. 1843, 1855 n. 16, 52 L.Ed.2d 396 (1977). In making this finding, the Court relied in part upon legislative history.

> "[A] pattern-or-practice would be present only where the denial of rights consists of something more than an isolated, sporadic incident, but is repeated, routine, or of a generalized nature. There would be a pattern-or-practice if, for example, a number of companies or persons in the same industry or line of business discrimi-

nated, if a chain of motels or restaurants practiced racial discrimination throughout all or a significant part of its system, or if a company repeatedly and regularly engaged in acts prohibited by the statute. * * * The point is that single, insignificant, isolated acts of discrimination by a single business would not justify a finding of a pattern-or-practice * * *."

110 Cong. Rec. 14270 (1964) (Statement of Senator Humphrey) (quoted in *Teamsters*, 431 U.S. at 336–37 n.16, 97 S.Ct. at 1855 n.16.). The Court has noted the "manifest" difference between individual claims of discrimination and a class action alleging a general pattern-or-practice. Cooper v. Federal Reserve Bank of Richmond, 467 U.S. 867, 876, 104 S.Ct. 2794, 2799, 81 L.Ed.2d 718 (1984). Proving isolated or sporadic discriminatory acts by the employer is insufficient to establish a prima facie case of a pattern-or-practice of discrimination.

The *Cooper* Court explained this distinction, drawing upon its holding in *General Telephone Co. of Southwest v. Falcon*, 457 U.S. 147, 102 S.Ct. 2364, 72 L.Ed.2d 740 (1982). In *Falcon*, the Court held that an individual's claim that he was not promoted because of racial animus did not necessarily make him an adequate representative of a class composed of persons who had allegedly been refused employment for discriminatory reasons. The Court noted the "wide gap" between individual claims and class claims of discrimination. *Falcon*, 457 U.S. at 157, 102 S.Ct. at 2370.

> "[T]o bridge that gap, [the claimant] must prove much more than the validity of his own claim. Even though evidence that he was passed over for promotion when several less deserving whites were advanced may support the conclusion that respondent was denied the promotion because of his national origin, such evidence would not necessarily justify the additional inferences (1) that this discriminatory treatment is typical of petitioner's promotion practices, (2) that petitioner's promotion practices are motivated by a policy of ethnic discrimination that pervades petitioner's * * * division, or (3) that this policy of ethnic discrimination is reflected in petitioner's other employment practices, such as hiring, in the same way it is manifested in the promotion practices."

Cooper, 467 U.S. at 876–77, 104 S.Ct. at 2800 (quoting *Falcon*, 457 U.S. at 157–58, 102 S.Ct. at 2370–71).

The *Cooper* Court further observed that "a class plaintiff's attempt to prove the existence of a companywide policy [(i.e., a pattern-or-practice)], or even a consistent practice within a given department, may fail even though discrimination against one or two individuals has been proved." 467 U.S. at 878, 104 S.Ct. at 2800. This observation reinforces the distinction between individual and class claims. It is quite proper, the Court noted, to recognize that a "court must be wary of a claim that the true color of a forest is better revealed by reptiles hidden in the weeds than by the foliage of countless freestanding trees." *Id*. at 879–80,

104 S.Ct. at 2801 (quoting NAACP v. Claiborne Hardware Co., 458 U.S. 886, 934, 102 S.Ct. 3409, 3436, 73 L.Ed.2d 1215 (1982)).

In order to prove that the employer has engaged in a pattern-or-practice of discrimination, then, the plaintiff must show that there is regular, purposeful, less-favorable treatment of a protected group. *See, e.g., Teamsters*, 431 U.S. at 335, 97 S.Ct. at 1854 (government's theory was "that the company * * * regularly and purposefully treated Negroes and Spanish-surnamed Americans less favorably than white persons."). We have explained that

> plaintiffs in a pattern-or-practice government or class discrimination claim have the initial burden of showing that the unlawful discrimination was the employer's regular policy. A plaintiff must "establish a prima facie case that such a [discriminatory] policy existed." *Teamsters*, 431 U.S. at 360, 97 S.Ct. at 1867. In other words, a plaintiff would have to prove "by a preponderance of the evidence that [the] discrimination was the company's standard operating procedure—the regular rather than the unusual practice." *Id.* at 336, 97 S.Ct. at 1855.

EEOC v. Sears, Roebuck & Co., 839 F.2d 302, 354–55 (7th Cir.1988). Once plaintiffs establish a broad pattern or policy of discrimination, courts have found it is reasonable to infer that the employer discriminated against particular individuals, unless the employer can prove otherwise. Thus, once the pattern is established, the burden shifts to the defendant to show there was no discrimination. The Court explained the logic of shifting burdens in Title VII cases in *Teamsters*, using *Franks v. Bowman*, 424 U.S. 747, 96 S.Ct. 1251, 47 L.Ed.2d 444 (1976) as an example:

> [In *Franks*, the class] alleged a broad-based policy of employment discrimination; upon proof of that allegation, there were reasonable grounds to infer that individual hiring decisions were made in pursuit of the discriminatory policy and to require the employer to come forth with evidence dispelling that inference.[45]

Teamsters, 431 U.S. at 359, 97 S.Ct. at 1866.

In order to support the "judicial evaluation" (that it is more probable than not that an employer that routinely discriminates, discriminated against a particular individual), there must be significant evidence of the alleged routine. In *Teamsters*, for example, the government first presented statistical evidence showing grave disparities between the percentages of blacks in the population at large, those employed by the defendant, and those employed in particular positions. In fact, no blacks were employed in some positions until after the suit was filed. The government then supported this evidence with individual

---

45. The holding in *Franks* that proof of a discriminatory pattern and practice creates a rebuttable presumption in favor of individual relief is consistent with the manner in which presumptions are created generally. Presumptions shifting the burden of proof are often created to reflect judicial evaluations of probabilities and to conform with a party's superior access to the proof.

testimony recounting over forty specific instances of discrimination. The Court held that this evidence was sufficient to carry the government's burden of proof.

Other courts considering what evidence is necessary to show that an employer routinely and purposely discriminated have also required substantial proof of the practice. Thus, in *Chisholm v. United States Postal Service*, 665 F.2d 482, 495 (4th Cir.1981), twenty class members testified about individual discrimination to support the statistical evidence. Without significant individual testimony to support statistical evidence, courts have refused to find a pattern-or-practice of discrimination. One court has warned that "the definition of a pattern-or-practice is not capable of a mathematical formulation * * *." Ste. Marie v. Eastern Ry. Ass'n, 650 F.2d 395, 406 (2d Cir.1981). In *Ste. Marie*, the court found seven individual discriminatory acts coupled with problematic statistical evidence were insufficient to support a finding of a pattern-or-practice of discrimination. *See also* Cooper v. Federal Reserve Bank of Richmond, 467 U.S. 867, 104 S.Ct. 2794, 81 L.Ed.2d 718 (1984), (citing with approval the opinion of the court below, EEOC v. Federal Reserve Bank of Richmond, 698 F.2d 633, 643–44 (4th Cir.1983), contrasting 20 or 40 class members testifying of class discrimination (sufficient) to three or even seven incidents of discrimination over a period of years (insufficient)); Goff v. Continental Oil Co., 678 F.2d 593, 597 (5th Cir.1982) (even if all three witnesses' accounts of racial discrimination were true, this evidence would not have been enough to prove a pattern-or-practice of company-wide discrimination).

* * * Title VII permits the Attorney General to bring civil actions to stop widespread practices that prevent protected groups from fully exercising their rights. 42 U.S.C. § 2000e–6(a). Individuals harmed by the challenged practice may join the government's suit.

ADEA has no parallel provision, but courts nevertheless have adopted the pattern-or-practice terminology and the shifting burden of persuasion to ADEA actions. EEOC v. Western Electric, 713 F.2d 1011 (4th Cir.1983); EEOC v. Sandia, 639 F.2d 600 (10th Cir.1980). Moreover, in some cases plaintiffs have attempted to prove that the employer engaged in a pattern of discrimination in order to bolster their individual claims. *See, e.g.,* Graefenhain v. Pabst Brewing Co., 827 F.2d 13 (7th Cir.1987). In *Graefenhain*, the two plaintiffs presented evidence intended

> to show that Pabst's reduction in force explanation was merely a pretext for terminating older, higher salaried employees. In other words, [plaintiffs] attempted to show that their termination was part of a plan to cut costs by replacing older, higher salaried employees with inexperienced, younger employees who could be paid less.

Id. at 17. We must reiterate, however, that isolated, sporadic discrimination is not sufficient. Because of the seriousness of the charge, it is essential that plaintiffs adequately support allegations that an employer routinely engages in wide-spread discriminatory practices.

* * *

Notes

1. All of the federal statutes prohibiting discrimination in employment are silent on whether private plaintiffs may bring pattern-or-practice or systemic discrimination suits. The courts, however, have recognized the right of plaintiffs to bring these kinds of claims as class actions under Rule 23 of the Federal Rules of Civil Procedure. *See, e.g.*, Cooper v. Federal Reserve Bank of Richmond, 467 U.S. 867, 104 S.Ct. 2794, 81 L.Ed.2d 718 (1984); Franks v. Bowman Transp. Co., 424 U.S. 747, 96 S.Ct. 1251, 47 L.Ed.2d 444 (1976). *Cooper* and *Franks* are discussed in the *King* case. A pattern-or-practice case brought by the federal government is not subject to the class action requirements of Rule 23 of the Federal Rules of Civil Procedure. General Tel. Co. of the Northwest, Inc. v. EEOC, 446 U.S. 318, 100 S.Ct. 1698, 64 L.Ed.2d 319 (1980). In *In re Bemis Co.*, 279 F.3d 419 (7th Cir.2002), the court held that the EEOC is exempt from the strictures of Rule 23 even if it seeks compensatory and punitive damages under the Civil Rights Act of 1991. In addition to relying on *General Telephone*, the court also relied on the Supreme Court's decision in *EEOC v. Waffle House, Inc.*, 534 U.S. 279, 122 S.Ct. 754, 151 L.Ed.2d 755 (2002), in which the Court held that the EEOC is not barred from seeking judicial relief, including monetary damages, for an employee who had entered into an agreement with his employer to submit his employment discrimination claim to arbitration. *Waffle House* is covered in Chapter 18.

2. Prior to 1977, the lower courts routinely allowed private plaintiffs to bring class action employment discrimination claims in federal courts. The courts allowed these class action cases to go forward based upon three interrelated theories. The first is the "private attorney general" theory, which holds that a class action is more than a claim by a single individual seeking to vindicate purely private rights because, "[w]hether in name or not, the suit is perforce a sort of class action for fellow employees similarly situated." Jenkins v. United Gas Corp., 400 F.2d 28, 33 (5th Cir.1968). Second the courts adopted the "across-the-board" theory under which a single plaintiff or a representative group of plaintiffs is allowed to represent all similarly situated persons affected by an employer's discriminatory practices. The rationale for "across-the-board" class actions was that they were necessary to effectuate the broad remedial purposes of antidiscrimination statutes. *See, e.g.*, Senter v. General Motors Corp., 532 F.2d 511, 524 (6th Cir.), *cert. denied*, 429 U.S. 870, 97 S.Ct. 182, 50 L.Ed.2d 150 (1976). The seminal case adopting the "across-the-board" class action theory is *Johnson v. Georgia Highway Express, Inc.*, 417 F.2d 1122 (5th Cir.1969). Third, the courts held that class actions were appropriate from a policy perspective because class actions promote judicial economy, eliminate the possibility of inconsistent and varying outcomes, and protect the employer from the possible burden of defending multiple lawsuits challenging the same employ-

ment practice. *See, e.g.*, Mack v. General Elec. Co., 329 F.Supp. 72, 75 (E.D.Pa.1971).

Beginning with the its 1977 decision in *East Texas Motor Freight System, Inc. v. Rodriguez*, 431 U.S. 395, 97 S.Ct. 1891, 52 L.Ed.2d 453 (1977), the Supreme Court placed substantial limitations on civil rights class action litigation. *Rodriguez* was a private class action case brought on behalf of Latino and black applicants and employees. The court of appeals had certified the case as a class action, but the Supreme Court reversed on the grounds, *inter alia*, that the named plaintiffs were not proper representatives of the class on whose behalf the case was brought. Five years later, in *General Telephone Company of the Southwest v. Falcon*, 457 U.S. 147, 102 S.Ct. 2364, 72 L.Ed.2d 740 (1982), the Court further limited the use of class actions in employment discrimination (and civil rights) cases. The lower court had certified a class action on behalf of "Mexican–American persons who are employed, or who might be employed or may in the future be employed, and all Mexican–Americans who have applied or who would have applied" but for the employer's discriminatory conduct. *Id.* at 151, 102 S.Ct. at 2367. In holding that the purported class representative must strictly meet the prerequisites of Rule 23 of the Federal Rules of Civil Procedure on numerosity, commonality, typicality, and adequacy of representation, the Court, in *Falcon*, substantially undercut the "across-the-board" theory of class actions that had allowed a plaintiff or a group of plaintiffs to represent broad classes of employees, former employees, discharged employees, employees denied promotions, and applicants in a single lawsuit.

The Civil Rights Act of 1991 provides another potential hurdle to private class action cases. The courts are now split on whether a Rule 23 class action can be brought in a disparate treatment case in which the plaintiffs seek compensatory and punitive damages. Two of the major issues in the circuit split are whether (1) plaintiffs are entitled to recover compensatory and punitive damages in a Rule 23(a)(2) class action, and (2) whether federal courts can create, bifurcate, or modify employment discrimination proceedings in a Rule 23(a)(2) class action. *Compare* Allison v. Citgo Petroleum Corp., 151 F.3d 402 (5th Cir.1998) (adopting a bright-line rule both requiring Rule 23 to be applied to certify a class for damages and making Rule 23 applicable for injunctive relief in class cases) *with* Robinson v. Metro–North Commuter R.R. Co., 267 F.3d 147 (2d Cir.2001) (district court abused its discretion in denying request for certification of a class action under Title VII because the court could have bifurcated the trial on the issues of liability and remedy). The impact of the Civil Rights Act of 1991 on private class action employment discrimination cases is discussed in Daniel Piar, *The Uncertain Future of Title VII Class Action Cases After the Civil Rights Act of 1991*, 2001 BYU L.Rev. 305. For a treatment of employment discrimination class actions in light of the Civil Rights Act of 1991, see Scotty Shively, *Resurgence of the Class Action Lawsuit in Employment Discrimination Cases: New Obstacles Presented by the 1991 Amendments to the Civil Right Act*, 13 U.Ark. Little Rock L.Rev. 925 (2001).

3. As noted in footnote 45 in *King*, the Supreme Court held in *Franks v. Bowman*, that if plaintiffs prevail on the issue of liability in Stage I of a bifurcated trial, each member of the class is the beneficiary of a "presumptive entitlement" rule, i.e., presumptively entitled to appropriate make-

whole and rightful place relief. Also, in *Cooper v. Federal Reserve Bank of Richmond*, 467 U.S. 867, 876, 104 S.Ct. 2794, 81 L.Ed.2d 718 (1984), the Court held that "[w]hile a finding of a pattern and practice itself justifies an award of prospective relief to the class, additional proceedings are ordinarily required to determine the scope of relief for members of the class." The series of "mini-trials" that often accompany bifurcated class action proceedings prompt many employers to settle employment discrimination class action cases.

4. A number of class action pattern-or-practice employment discrimination suits have been resolved through record-breaking settlements including substantial monetary awards. One of the most publicized cases is the Texaco case, which settled for $176 million after public disclosure of a tape-recorded meeting that allegedly indicated that some managerial agents of Texaco used explicit racial ephithets in reference to black employees. Other cases include: Coca–Cola ($192 million); Home Depot ($104 million); Shoney's ($105 million); and State Farm Insurance ($152 million). These and other class action cases are discussed in Michael Selmi, *The Price of Discrimination: The Nature of Class Action Employment Discrimination and Its Effects*, 81 Tex. L.Rev. 1249 (2003). *See also* Bari–Ellen Robert, Roberts v. Texaco: A True Story of Race and Corporate America (1998) (story of the Texaco case); Steve Watkins, The Black O: Racism and Redemptions in an American Corporate Empire (1997) (story of the Shoney's case). One of the incentives employers have to settle class action suits is that jury trials in disparate treatment cases are now available under the Civil Rights Act of 1991. *See, e.g.,* William C. Martucci, Eric Smith & Karen K. Cain, *Class Action Litigation in the Employment Arena—The Corporate Employers' Perspective*, 58 J.Mo.B. 332 (2002) (listing other large settlements in employment discrimination cases).

5. *The Continuing Violation Theory*: In *National Railroad Passenger Corp. v. Morgan*, 536 U.S. 101, 122 S.Ct. 2061, 153 L.Ed.2d 106 (2002), the Supreme Court held that Title VII precludes recovery for discrete acts of discrimination that occur outside the statutory timely filing period. (Portions of *Morgan* are reproduced in Chapters 2 and 8.) Under *Morgan* the continuing violation theory is inapplicable to discrete acts, but it is applicable to hostile work environment claims. The Court expressly reserved judgment on whether the continuing violation theory is applicable to pattern-or-practice claims brought by private litigants." *Id.* at 115 n.9, 122 S.Ct. at 2073 n.9.

Should the continuing violation theory apply to private class-action pattern-or-practice claims? Does the *Teamsters'* definition of a pattern-or-practice claim, as quoted in *King*, fit *Morgan's* definition of a hostile work environment claim: "A hostile work environment claim is comprised of a series of separate acts that collectively constitute one 'unlawful employment practice.'" *Morgan*, 536 U.S. at 117, 122 S.Ct. at 2074. Based upon *Morgan*, the court in *Campbell v. National Railroad Passenger Corp.*, 222 F.Supp.2d 8 (D.D.C.2002), held that the continuing violation theory is applicable to private pattern-or-practice cases because, like hostile work environment cases, they involve a series of separate acts comprising a single unlawful employment practice. The plaintiff in *Campbell* alleged a pattern or practice of racial discrimination in hiring, advancement, training, discipline, work and equipment assignment (in addition to a hostile work environment).

Is there a counter argument that a pattern-or-practice claim is more like a series of discrete acts that occur over time that are related to each other? Consider the case of *Bazemore v. Friday*, 478 U.S. 385, 106 S.Ct. 3000, 92 L.Ed.2d 315 (1986). *Bazemore* was a claim brought as a pattern-or-practice case alleging racial discrimination in pay. Prior to 1965, the state employer maintained a racially segregated system of employment that included paying black employees less than white employees who were doing substantially the same work. The employer integrated its racially discriminatory divisions after it became subject to Title VII but did not eliminate some of the pay inequities between its black and white employees. The Supreme Court rejected the employer's argument that it had no duty to eliminate the pay disparities that originated prior to 1972. The Court held that the fact that the employer discriminated prior to 1972 did not excuse perpetuating the racially discriminatory salary inequities subsequent to the time it was covered by Title VII. The Court also held that "[e]ach week's paycheck that delivers less to a black than to a similarly situated white is a wrong actionable under Title VII regardless of the fact that this pattern was begun prior to the effective date of Title VII." *Bazemore*, 478 U.S. at 395, 106 S.Ct. 3000. Lower courts construed *Bazemore* as endorsing the continuing violation theory for pay discrimination claims. *See* Inglis v. Buena Vista Univ., 235 F.Supp.2d 1009, 1021–22 (N.D.Iowa 2002).

In *Morgan*, the Court recognized that *Bazemore* was a pattern-or-practice case and cited it as an example of an instance in which the Court had "repeatedly interpreted the term 'practice' to apply to a discrete act or a single 'occurrence' even when it has a connection to other acts." In *Delaware State College v. Ricks*, 449 U.S. 250, 257, 101 S.Ct. 498, 66 L.Ed.2d 431 (1980), also cited in *Morgan*, the Court held that "[m]ere continuity of employment, without more, is insufficient to prolong the life of a cause of action for employment discrimination." And, in *United Air Lines, Inc. v. Evans*, 431 U.S. 553, 558, 97 S.Ct. 1885, 52 L.Ed.2d 571 (1977), cited in *Morgan* as well, the Court held that the lingering effects of prior discriminatory conduct are not subject to the continuing violation theory. Relying on *Morgan*, *Bazemore*, *Ricks*, and *Evans*, the district court in *Inglis v. Buena Vista University*, 235 F.Supp.2d 1009 (N.D.Iowa 2002), held that pay discrimination cases under Title VII and the Equal Pay Act are no longer subject to the continuing violation theory where an employer has discontinued the practice. These cases, under *Inglis*, fall within the *Morgan* discrete acts doctrine. Is there a difference between pay equity cases like *Inglis* and discrimination cases like *King* and *Campbell* that suggests that the continuing violation theory should apply in one and not the other? Even if the *Inglis* court is correct that, under *Morgan*, the continuing violation theory is no longer applicable to pay equity cases, the tolling principles of *Morgan* may apply.

6. AFFIRMATIVE ACTION CASES

An affirmative action plan is a race-or sex-specific plan that is designed to provide a remedy for the present and continuing effects of historical overt discrimination against blacks and women, as well as the effects of discrimination motivated by unconscious biases and stereotypical assumptions. Some commentators characterize affirmative action plans as "reverse discrimination" because employers are permitted to take the race or sex of the applicant or employee into consideration as a factor in making employment decisions. The legality of affirmative action plans has been and continues to be one of the more controversial problems in employment discrimination law and, more generally, in civil rights law. *See, e.g.,* Grutter v. Bollinger, 539 U.S. 306, 123 S.Ct. 2325, 156 L.Ed.2d 304 (2003); Gratz v. Bollinger, 539 U.S. 244, 123 S.Ct. 2411, 156 L.Ed.2d 257 (2003). For this reason, the subject is treated more broadly in Chapter 17.

The materials in this section address the relevance of the *McDonnell Douglas* prima facie case doctrine and burden-shifting rules in affirmative action cases. Because race or sex is one of the factors that an employer may rely upon when making an employment decision pursuant to an affirmative action plan, such decisions present paradigmatic direct evidence of disparate treatment. To date, most of the plaintiffs in affirmative action cases have been white males who have claimed that employers specifically considered their race or sex in denying them employment opportunities. *See, e.g.,* Johnson v. Transportation Agency, Santa Clara County, 480 U.S. 616, 107 S.Ct. 1442, 94 L.Ed.2d 615 (1987) (sex), discussed below and in Chapter 17, and United Steelworkers v. Weber, 443 U.S. 193, 99 S.Ct. 2721, 61 L.Ed.2d 480 (1979) (race), discussed below and in Chapter 17.

In *Johnson v. Transportation Agency*, a public employer had voluntarily adopted an affirmative action plan to increase employment opportunities for qualified minorities and women who were underrepresented in certain job categories. The plaintiff—a white male—and a female applied for a vacancy. The employer found both applicants qualified, but awarded the position to the female pursuant to its affirmative action plan. Plaintiff then filed suit under Title VII alleging that he was discriminated against because of his sex. In addressing the allocation of the burdens of proof when a voluntary affirmative action plan is asserted as a defense to an employment decision, the Supreme Court ruled:

> This case * * * fits readily within the analytical framework set forth in *McDonnell Douglas v. Green.* Once the plaintiff establishes a prima facie case that race or sex has been taken into account in an employer's employment decision, the burden shifts to the employer to articulate a nondiscriminatory rationale for its decision. The existence of an affirmative action plan provides such a rationale. If such a plan is articulated as the basis for the employer's decision, the burden shifts to the plaintiff to prove that the employer's justification is pretextual and the plan is invalid. As a practical matter, of course, an employer will generally seek to avoid a charge of pretext by presenting evidence in support of its plan. That does not mean, however, as [plaintiff] suggests, that reliance on an affirmative action plan is to be treated as an affirmative defense, requiring the employer to carry the burden of proving the validity of the plan. The burden of proving its invalidity remains on the plaintiff.

Johnson, 480 U.S. at 626–27, 107 S.Ct. at 1449. *Johnson* and *Steelworkers v. Weber*, 443 U.S. 193, 99 S.Ct. 2721, 61 L.Ed.2d 480 (1979), reproduced in Chapter 17, are the leading Supreme Court cases on the legality of voluntary affirmative action plans that are challenged solely under Title VII. These cases adopt a three-pronged test for upholding the plan: (1) the plan must be designed to break down old patterns of discrimination; (2) the plan must not trammel the interests of white (or male) employees; and (3) the plan must be temporary and not designed to maintain a balanced workforce based on race or sex.

As you read the following materials, consider whether the *McDonnell Douglas/Burdine* analytic scheme should be modified for white or male plaintiffs who challenge employer decisions under affirmative action plans. Does the fact that white males in particular, as a group, have not suffered the history of discrimination experienced by either blacks or women provide an adequate rationale for heightened evidentiary and procedural burdens in "reverse discrimination" challenges to affirmative action plans?

IADIMARCO v. RUNYON

United States Court of Appeals for the Third Circuit, 1999.
190 F.3d 151.

McKEE, Circuit Judge.

We are asked to review the District Court's grant of summary judgment in favor of the United States Postal Service, and against its employee, Charles Iadimarco. Iadimarco filed an action under Title VII of the 1964 Civil Rights Act alleging "reverse discrimination" after he was denied a requested promotion within the Postal Service. The District Court ruled that Iadimarco had not established a prima facie case of illegal discrimination. * * * [W]e hold that Iadimarco established a prima facie case under Title VII. * * *

I. FACTUAL AND PROCEDURAL BACKGROUND

* * * Iadimarco's contention is based upon his belief that [the employer] wanted to hire a minority applicant for the * * * position to diversify the work place. Iadimarco's assertion is based in large part upon a memorandum that [the employer] issued to all plant managers and installation heads in December of 1992 (the "diversity memo"). The memo stated:

> As we proceed to fill vacancies, I want to ensure that very serious consideration is given to the issue of diversity—I cannot emphasize this point more strongly. The management teams in our plants should reflect the composition of our workforce and communities if we are to benefit from the contributions that minorities, women, and ethnic groups can bring to our decision making processes and the social harmony that this will instill in our work environment.

* * *

On May 28, 1993, Iadimarco initiated a proceeding before the Equal Employment Opportunity Commission because he believed that he had been denied the Monmouth position because he is a White male. * * *

II. Discussion

A. *The District Court's Decision.*

The District Court concluded that it had to apply the ever-present burden-shifting analysis announced in *McDonnell Douglas Corp. v. Green*, 411 U.S. 792, 802, 93 S.Ct. 1817, 36 L.Ed.2d 668 (1973). In conducting that analysis, the District Court noted a split among the courts of appeals in "reverse discrimination" cases as to the prerequisites of a prima facie case required of a White male. The court stated that although "the Third Circuit has yet to address this issue, most of the [district] courts in this Circuit have required plaintiffs to first establish background circumstances that support an inference that the defendant employer is 'the unusual employer who discriminates against the majority.'" * * *

* * *

B. *The Prima Facie Case in "Reverse Discrimination" Suits Under Title VII.*

* * * [C]ourts have struggled in attempting to apply the *McDonnell Douglas* burden-shifting framework to Title VII suits by White plaintiffs, and no universally accepted statement of the appropriate standard has emerged. The confusion arises from the wording of the very first prong of the *McDonnell Douglas* test. Obviously, a White plaintiff can not establish "membership in a minority group" in the same way a Black plaintiff can. In an effort to "cram"[6] the "reverse discrimination" cases into the *McDonnell Douglas* framework, most courts of appeals that have considered the issue require White plaintiffs to present evidence of "background circumstances" that establish that the defendant is "that unusual employer who discriminates against the majority," *Parker v. Baltimore & O. R. Co.*, 652 F.2d 1012, 1017 (D.C.Cir.1981), instead of showing minority group status. * * * After *Parker* was decided, the Court of Appeals for the D. C. Circuit amplified its "background circumstances" modification of *McDonnell Douglas*. The court stated:

> The evidence that this Court has found in the past to constitute "background circumstances" can be divided into two categories: (1) evidence indicating the particular employer * * * has some reason or inclination to discriminate invidiously against whites, and (2) evidence indicating that there is something "fishy" about the facts of the case at hand that raises an inference of discrimination.

---

6. *See* Eastridge v. Rhode Island College, 996 F.Supp. 161, 167 (D.R.I.1998) ("attempting to cram a reverse discrimination case into the *McDonnell Douglas* framework is not a reasonable approach * * *."); Cully v. Milliman & Robertson, Inc., 20 F.Supp.2d 636, 641 (S.D.N.Y.1998) (same).

Harding, at 153. The court also cautioned that " 'background circumstances' need not mean 'some circumstances in the employer's background.' ''Rather, the court noted ''[o]n the contrary, other evidence about the 'background' of the case at hand—including an allegation of superior qualifications—can be equally valuable.'' *Id*. The court also insisted that the ''background circumstances'' test ''is not an additional hurdle for white plaintiffs,'' and asserted that it was merely ''a faithful transposition of the *McDonnell Douglas/Burdine* test * * * ''into the context of ''reverse discrimination.'' *Id*. at 154.

Despite that clarification, some courts have concluded that substituting ''background circumstances'' for the first prong of *McDonnell Douglas* does raise the bar, and those courts have rejected the *Parker/Harding* analysis for that reason. For example, in *Eastridge*, the court concluded that the *Parker/Harding* test ''require[s] a reverse discrimination plaintiff to show that the specific employer has displayed a pattern of discrimination against the majority in the past [and therefore] imposes a more onerous burden on such a plaintiff as compared to any plaintiff from any protected group.'' 996 F.Supp. at 161. *See also* Ulrich v. Exxon Co., 824 F.Supp. 677, 683–84 (S.D.Tex.1993) (describing the ''background circumstances'' test as imposing a ''heightened burden'' and citing cases that have criticized it). In *Cully v. Milliman & Robertson, Inc.*, 20 F.Supp.2d 636, 641 (S.D.N.Y.1998), the court invited a comparison between *Parker* and *Lucas v. Dole*, 835 F.2d 532 (4th Cir.1987), and described the former as requiring a ''higher prima facie burden for reverse discrimination plaintiffs'' and the latter as having ''no higher prima facie burden.'' In *Collins v. School District of Kansas City*, 727 F.Supp. 1318, 1320 (W.D.Mo., 1990), the court concluded that the ''background circumstances'' test required a ''special showing'' of White Plaintiffs, and rejected the test for that reason. The court also concluded that the ''unusual employer'' prong of *Parker* established an ''arbitrary barrier which serves only to frustrate those who have legitimate Title VII claims.'' * * * The *Collins* court reasoned that the Court of Appeals for the Eighth Circuit would not * * * adopt the heightened burden the district court believed was endemic in the ''background circumstances'' inquiry. However, when the Court of Appeals was finally called upon to address the issue of the appropriate prima facie standard required in ''reverse discrimination'' cases, it did adopt the *Parker/Harding* requirement of ''background circumstances.'' *See* Duffy v. Wolle, 123 F.3d 1026 (8th Cir.1997). * * *

The ''background circumstances'' test has been adopted by the respective circuit court of appeals in each of the following cases: Mills v. Health Care Serv. Corp., 171 F.3d 450, 457 (7th Cir.1999); *Duffy*, 123 F.3d at 1036–37; Reynolds v. School Dist. No. 1, 69 F.3d 1523, 1534 (10th Cir.1995); Notari v. Denver Water Dept., 971 F.2d 585 (10th Cir.1992); and Murray [v. Thistledown Racing Club, Inc.], 770 F.2d [63] at 66–67 [(6th Cir.1985)]. However, application and interpretation of the test has often proven difficult. * * *

Here, as stated above, the District Court substituted the "background circumstances" requirement for the minority group status otherwise required under the first prong of the *McDonnell Douglas* test. We now reject the "background circumstances" analysis set forth in *Parker*, *Harding*, and their progeny.

The prima facie case under *McDonnell Douglas* merely states "the basic allocation of burdens and order of presentation of proof [under] Title VII * * *." *Burdine*, 450 U.S. at 252, 101 S.Ct. 1089. It raises an inference of discrimination only because we presume these acts, if otherwise unexplained in the context of the prongs of the *McDonnell Douglas* prima facie case, are more likely than not based on the consideration of impermissible factors. See Furnco Const. Corp. v. Waters, 438 U.S. 567, 577, 98 S.Ct. 2943, 57 L.Ed.2d 957 (1978). However, "[t]he central focus of the inquiry * * * is always whether the employer is treating some people less favorably than others because of their race, color, religion, sex, or national origin." *Id.* (internal quotation marks omitted).

Accordingly, all that should be required to establish a prima facie case in the context of "reverse discrimination" is for the plaintiff to present sufficient evidence to allow a fact finder to conclude that the employer is treating some people less favorably than others based upon a trait that is protected under Title VII. * * * Stating the prima facie case in terms of "background circumstances" and the uniqueness of the particular employer is both problematic and unnecessary. As noted above, many of the courts that have tried to apply such an analysis have concluded that it results in a heightened burden for the plaintiff despite the aforementioned proclamations to the contrary by the court that developed the test. The pronouncement in *Harding* that the analysis there did not heighten the plaintiff's burden has not convinced several of the district courts that have had to determine the appropriate analysis.

Moreover, the suggestion that a plaintiff must prove "background circumstances" to establish that the defendant is a "unique employer that discriminates against the majority" has a tendency to force the plaintiff to initially present proof that would otherwise only become relevant to rebut the employer's explanation of the challenged conduct. * * * Thus, the *Parker/Harding* modification can undermine the basic point of the *McDonnell Douglas* burden-shifting regime to make it easier for employees to bring claims that would otherwise be extraordinarily difficult to prove. The Supreme Court imposed the burden-shifting test to eliminate early on some of the most common nondiscriminatory reasons for employment decisions, as well as to place the burden of production on the party with the most access to the employer's decision making process, *i.e.*, the employer itself. *Parker*, *Harding*, and their progeny go too far in amending the prima facie case to include allegations of reverse discrimination.

Moreover, to the extent it might be argued that *Harding* does not go as far as we suggest, we believe that the concept of "background circumstances" is irremediably vague and ill-defined. For example, one of the alleged background circumstances here is that Iadimarco was more qualified than Williams. That can hardly be termed a "background circumstance," unless that term is defined to include anything that suggests discrimination. Indeed, some courts have proclaimed their adoption of the "background circumstances" requirement as suggested by *Parker* and *Harding*, but have further modified that test in a manner that renders the test itself absolutely unnecessary. For example, in *Notari*, 971 F.2d 585 (10th Cir.1992), the court stated:

> we agree that a Title VII disparate treatment plaintiff who pursues a reverse discrimination claim, and seeks to obtain the benefit of the *McDonnell Douglas* presumption, must, in lieu of showing he belongs to a protected group, establish background circumstances that support an inference that the defendant is one of those unusual employers who discriminates against the majority.

971 F.2d at 589. However, the court then held that such a plaintiff could also establish a prima facie case by direct evidence, or by indirect evidence that supported a finding of discriminatory intent.

> We adopt the set of prima facie case alternatives that the Fourth Circuit has outlined. Thus, a plaintiff who presents direct evidence of discrimination *or indirect evidence sufficient to support a reasonable probability, that but for the plaintiff's status the challenged employment decision would have favored the plaintiff* states a prima facie case of intentional discrimination under Title VII.

Id. at 590 (emphasis added). However, it is obvious that this alternative method of indirect proof negates the need to ever present evidence of "background circumstances." All that will ever be required of a White-male plaintiff under this test is that he presents sufficient evidence to support the reasonable probability of discrimination. There is no need to embark upon the problematic detour of showing "background circumstances."

* * *

Moreover, one might contend that a "background circumstance" must be something in the employer's background. Such a requirement does raise the bar for the prospective "reverse discrimination" plaintiff, notwithstanding the denial of this limitation in *Harding*. Moreover, a review of cases addressing this issue illustrates that it is difficult, if not impossible, to come up with a definition of "background circumstances" that is clear, neither under nor over inclusive, and possible to satisfy. In *Stock v. Universal Foods Corp.*, 817 F.Supp. 1300 (D.Md.1993), the court replaced the "background circumstances" requirement with the requirement that plaintiff establish "he belongs to a class." 817 F.Supp. at 1306. In *Wilson v. Bailey*, 934 F.2d 301, 304 (11th Cir.1991), the court also stated Title VII requires a White plaintiff to establish that "he belongs to a class" as the first step in establishing a prima facie case under *McDonnell Douglas*. However, neither court further defined the "class" to which it was referring. The discussion in *Stock* and *Wilson* illustrate just how vague and problematic the *Parker/Harding* approach can be. Inasmuch as everyone belongs to some "class," substituting membership in an undefined class for membership in a minority group is tantamount to eliminating the first prong of the *McDonnell Douglas* framework *sub silentio*.

Moreover, the amorphous nature of "background circumstances" can lead to jury confusion. The Title VII plaintiff needs only to present sufficient evidence to allow a fact finder to conclude that the unexplained decision that forms the basis of the allegation of discrimination was motivated by discriminatory animus. It is at the pretext stage that "background circumstances" would normally be introduced. Courts struggling with "cramming" the "background circumstances" inquiry into the first prong of *McDonnell Douglas* may well require "pretextual" evidence as part of the plaintiff's initial evidence. Such evidence may be relevant to the "background circumstances" surrounding the claim of discrimination or to a finding that defendant is an employer that is likely to discriminate. The result is the "heightened burden" many district courts have criticized and that *Harding* disclaimed.

Accordingly, rather than require "background circumstances" about the uniqueness of the defendant employer, a plaintiff who brings a "reverse discrimination" suit under Title VII should be able to establish a prima facie case in the absence of direct evidence of discrimination by presenting sufficient evidence to allow a reasonable fact finder to conclude (given the totality of the circumstances) that the defendant treated plaintiff "less favorably than others because of [his] race, color, religion, sex, or national origin." *Furnco*, 438 U.S. at 577, 98 S.Ct. 2943.* * *

Notes and Questions

1. In *Iadimarco v. Runyon*, Judge McKee joined in the decision of the court, but he did not view the *Parker/Harding* "background circumstances" rule to be inconsistent with the *McDonnell Douglas* approach. His views were set out in a footnote to the court's decision:

> Judge McKee believes that the approach set forth in *Parker* and *Harding* is merely a restatement of the *McDonnell Douglas* test just as the Court of Appeals for the D.C. Circuit intended it to be. He concludes that "[I]nvidious discrimination against [W]hite [men] is relatively uncommon in our society, and so there is nothing inherently suspicious in an employer's decision to promote a qualified minority [or female] applicant instead of a qualified [W]hite [male] applicant." *Harding*, 9 F.3d at 153. In his view, requiring a White male plaintiff to show certain "background circumstances" merely requires that plaintiff to present some evidence from which a reasonable fact finder could conclude that it is more likely than not that the unfavorable employment decision is the result of discriminatory animus. Judge McKee's belief is based in part upon *Livingston v. Roadway Exp., Inc.*, 802 F.2d 1250, 1252 (10th Cir.1986), * * * wherein the court explained:

the presumptions in the Title VII analysis that are valid when the plaintiff belongs to a disfavored group are not necessarily justified when the plaintiff is a member of a historically favored group. Accordingly, when a plaintiff who is a member of a favored group alleges disparate treatment, the courts have adjusted the prima facie case to reflect this specific context by requiring a showing of background circumstances [which] support the suspicion that the defendant is that unusual employer who discriminated against the majority.

Accordingly, Judge McKee concludes that the Court of Appeals for the D.C. Circuit is correct in stating that the "background circumstances" test "is not an additional hurdle for [W]hite plaintiffs." *Harding*, 9 F.3d at 154. He agrees with that court's belief that the test is merely "a faithful transposition of the *McDonnell Douglas/Burdine* test * * * " into the context of "reverse discrimination," *Id.* at 154, so long as the analysis of "background circumstances" and the "uniqueness" of the employer is undertaken in the manner intended by the Court of Appeals for the D.C. Circuit.

However, even though Judge McKee believes the test to merely be a restatement of *McDonnell Douglas*, he concedes that it is just too vague and too prone to misinterpretation and confusion to apply fairly and consistently. He agrees that the approach the court adopts today allows for less confusion and more consistency than the *Parker/Harding* approach.

Iadimarco, 190 F.3d at 163 n.10.

2. Is the *Parker/Harding* "background circumstances" rule defensible in view of the Court's pronouncement in *Oncale v. Sundowner Offshore Services*, 523 U.S. 75, 118 S.Ct. 998, 140 L.Ed.2d 201 (1998), that

in the * * * context of racial discrimination in the workplace we have rejected any conclusive presumption that an employer will not discriminate against members of his own race. "Because of the many facets of human motivation, it would be unwise to presume as a matter of law that human beings of one identifiable group will not discriminate against other members of that group." *Castaneda v. Partida*, 430 U.S. 482, 499, 97 S.Ct. 1272, 1282, 51 L.Ed.2d 498 (1977).

Id. at 78, 118 S.Ct. at 1001. *Oncale* is reproduced in Chapter 8.

3. Other courts of appeals have adopted the *Parker* "background circumstances" standard. The Sixth Circuit adopted the standard in *Murray v. Thistledown Racing Club, Inc.*, 770 F.2d 63 (6th Cir.1985), but subsequently questioned this holding in *Pierce v. Commonwealth Life Ins. Co.*, 40 F.3d 796, 801 n.7 (6th Cir.1994) ("[w]e have serious misgivings about the soundness" of the *Parker* standard). The Tenth Circuit adopted the *Parker* standard in *Notari v. Denver Water Department*, 971 F.2d 585 (10th Cir. 1992). Unlike other cases, *Notari* applied the *Parker* standard in a case not involving an affirmative action plan.

4. Does the *Parker* "background circumstances" rule adopt, in effect, a prima facie-plus theory in the affirmative action cases, with the "background circumstances" being the plus?

5. Does the data in Chapter 1, note 1 support or undercut the "background circumstances rule"?

6. An employer had two job vacancies, each in a different location. Both positions were essentially identical in terms of pay, responsibility, and status. Plaintiff, a qualified white male, applied first for both positions. Later, a qualified white female applied for only one of the jobs and was hired. The other job was then offered to the plaintiff. Angry that he did not get the job he preferred, the plaintiff has sued under Title VII. Can he establish a prima facie case of sex discrimination? *See* Stoner v. Wisconsin Dep't of Agric., Trade & Consumer Protection, 50 F.3d 481 (7th Cir.1995).

7. Some courts have held that "evidence that an employer violated its own affirmative action plan may be relevant to the question of discriminatory intent." Gonzales v. Police Dep't, San Jose, Cal., 901 F.2d 758, 761 (9th Cir.1990); *see also* Antol v. Perry, 82 F.3d 1291, 1301 (3d Cir.1996) (collecting cases).

8. *Iadimarco* identifies two different analytic approaches to affirmative action cases. There is yet a third approach: § 703(m) of Title VII, 42 U.S.C. § 2000e–2(m), covered in Section B.3 of this chapter. Is § 703(m) the "death knell" for voluntary affirmative action plans? How relevant is the statutory same-decision defense in § 706(g)(2)(B) to the analysis of affirmative action cases in light of § 116 of the 1991 Civil Rights Act, which provides that "[n]othing in the amendments * * * shall be construed to affect court-ordered remedies, *affirmative action*, or conciliation agreements, that are accordance with the law." (Emphasis added). How should the analysis and burden shifting rules apply under a § 703(m) approach to affirmative action in light of *Desert Palace v. Costa*?

Chapter 4

DISPARATE IMPACT

A. INTRODUCTION

The courts developed the disparate impact theory during the first decade of enforcement of Title VII. See Alfred W. Blumrosen, *Strangers in Paradise:* Griggs v. Duke Power Co. *and The Concept of Employment Discrimination*, 71 Mich.L.Rev. 59 (1972). The term "disparate impact" refers to "employment practices that are facially neutral in their treatment of different groups but that in fact fall more harshly on one group than another and cannot be justified by business necessity." Teamsters v. United States, 431 U.S. 324, 335 n. 15, 97 S.Ct. 1843, 1854 n. 15, 52 L.Ed.2d 396 (1977). The theory of disparate impact is sometimes called "adverse impact," "disparate effect," "unintentional discrimination," or "statistical discrimination." Initially, disparate impact theory was a rather straightforward yet important doctrinal development in employment discrimination law, but over the years it has been transformed into a complex and sometimes confusing body of law.

The materials in this chapter explore the basic analytical approaches to disparate impact claims (Section B), the use of statistical evidence in employment discrimination litigation (Section C), the business necessity defense (Section D), and the "bottom line" defense (Section E). Almost two decades after the seminal disparate impact case of *Griggs v. Duke Power Co.*, 401 U.S. 424, 91 S.Ct. 849, 28 L.Ed.2d 158 (1971), the Supreme Court revisited and redefined the law on disparate impact in *Watson v. Fort Worth Bank & Trust*, 487 U.S. 977, 108 S.Ct. 2777, 101 L.Ed.2d 827 (1988), and *Wards Cove Packing Co. v. Atonio*, 490 U.S. 642, 109 S.Ct. 2115, 104 L.Ed.2d 733 (1989). The Court's treatment of disparate impact in *Watson* and *Wards Cove* and Congress' response in the Civil Rights Act of 1991 are covered in Section F.

As you study the materials in this chapter, keep in mind the questions on the meaning of equality that are raised in Chapter 1. Consider also the following: (1) What conception of equality is embraced by the majority and dissenting opinions in the principal cases in this chapter? (2) Does *Griggs* provide a coherent theoretical underpinning for the disparate impact theory? If not, then do *Watson* and *Wards Cove*?

B. THE THEORY OF DISPARATE IMPACT

1. OBJECTIVE CRITERIA

The disparate impact theory was first articulated in Title VII class action cases brought by black job applicants and employees who alleged that their employment opportunities were limited by the pen and paper tests and educational requirements used by employers in hiring and promotion decisions. Both of these practices were challenged in *Griggs v. Duke Power Co.*, reproduced below. Testing and educational requirements in employment, however, are only a part of a larger phenomenon in American life: a preoccupation with objective measurements of ability. In the employment context these practices allegedly cloak employment decisions with objectivity. *See generally* David A. Goslin, The Search for Ability: Standardized Testing in Social Perspective (1963).

The interest in meritocracy, selection of the best qualified employees, improved productivity, and security from claims of unlawful employment discrimination are some of the concerns that motivate employers to rely upon objective criteria in making employment decisions. Objective criteria, so the argument goes, reduce, if they do not entirely eliminate, discriminatory decisionmaking. Perhaps the most accurate way to determine whether an individual can do a particular job is to provide her with an opportunity to do the job for a period of time and then assess her performance; but this process is costly both in human and financial terms. Nevertheless, employment decisions based on objective criteria do not always guarantee that an employer can survive a claim of unlawful discrimination. To what extent could an employer's reliance on objective criteria in employment decisions mask unconscious racial or sexual biases? On the other hand, does the existence of a disparate impact necessarily suggest an underlying intent to discriminate? Consider the following excerpt.

SOCIAL–SCIENTIFIC AND LEGAL CHALLENGES TO EDUCATION AND TEST REQUIREMENTS IN EMPLOYMENT*

PAUL BURSTEIN & SUSAN PITCHFORD
37 Soc.Probs. 243, 244–45 (1990).

For over a hundred years, employers have been requiring more and more education of applicants for more and more jobs. "The explanation for these trends * * * has commonly been treated as obvious. Education prepares students in the skills necessary for work, and skills are the main determinant of occupational success."** Human capital theory formalized this intuitively appealing notion, proposing that acquiring

* Copyright © 1990 by the Society for the Study of Social Problems. Reprinted from *Social Problems*, Vol. 37, No.2, pages 244–45, by permission.

** Randall Collins, The Credential Society: An Historical Sociology of Education and Stratification 7 (1979).

education amounts to investing in improved productivity, which in turn leads to higher income as a return on the money and time invested. The very strong relationship between educational attainment and economic outcomes supported the theory; the rate of return on education was very good compared to that for other investments.

Further research raised doubts about the relationship between education and labor market outcomes, however. The relationship was very strong, but social scientists found it surprisingly difficult to show exactly how knowledge acquired in school improved productivity or income. For example, academic performance (measured by either grades or standardized tests) proved to be only very weakly related to subsequent earnings, leading scholars to ask why those with more education earned more than those with less. These questions in turn led to the development of theories competing with human capital theory to explain the relationship between education and earnings.

Two of these are especially relevant here. The first sees employers making hiring decisions on the basis of very limited information, constrained by the cost of acquiring information about potential employees and of developing models for predicting job performance. Employers use education to screen potential employees inexpensively, relying on educational attainment to indicate which potential employees have characteristics the employer considers desirable, including cognitive skills, strength of character, or capacity to learn quickly on the job.

The second theory sees the labor market seething with conflict among social and cultural groups struggling for economic advantage and political power. From this perspective, groups adopt educational criteria to restrict access to desirable positions; for example, professional groups restrict entry by requiring prospective entrants to acquire highly specialized educations; unions likewise mandate long apprenticeships in programs with few openings, and ethnic, religious, and other groups attempt to manipulate occupations they dominate and educational institutions to preserve and improve their positions.

To the extent that the screening and conflict approaches are correct, it is not efficient free markets that produce the high correlation between educational attainment and income; instead, the correlation is socially constructed by groups that have the power to organize educational and economic institutions to their own advantage.

Similar arguments can be made about employers' use of standardized tests. No one claims that tests increase productivity, but they are widely used to predict it; like those with more education, those with better test scores are believed to be better on the job. This belief is seemingly borne out by studies showing that test scores are correlated with earnings.

As with education, however, social scientists have come to question why test scores are related to earnings. Scores may be related to productivity, but there is little direct evidence for such a conclusion. Employers may use tests either because they are cheap, convenient, and widely accepted, or because they protect the positions of dominant groups. Gould* and others have lent considerable plausibility to this hypothesis by showing how tests were developed and used to justify and preserve the power of high-status, white, Anglo–Saxon, Protestant male elites.

How might these theoretical controversies be resolved? Obtaining evidence on two issues is especially crucial. First, are educational attainment and test scores actually related to productivity on the job? If they are, their use in employment decisions make sense, and human capital theory gains credibility. If they are not, their use in employment decisions is called into question, and alternative theories become more plausible. Second, what are the consequences of educational requirements and test scores in employment decisions for different social groups? If employers' use of such criteria harms some groups, because their members have less education or lower test scores than members of other groups, then the conflict approach to labor market outcomes becomes more plausible. Employers might have adopted such criteria without intending to harm any particular group; but if some groups were harmed, the possibility that the criteria were adopted to benefit some at the expense of others certainly cannot be ruled out.

These issues were very much on the minds of lawyers and black workers involved in EEO litigation after the passage of Title VII of the Civil Rights Act of 1964 * * *. Their efforts and the judicial response made these issues central to the struggle for EEO * * *.

GRIGGS v. DUKE POWER CO.

Supreme Court of the United States, 1971.
401 U.S. 424, 91 S.Ct. 849, 28 L.Ed.2d 158.

CHIEF JUSTICE BURGER delivered the opinion of the Court.

We granted the writ in this case to resolve the question whether an employer is prohibited by the Civil Rights Act of 1964, Title VII, from requiring a high school education or passing of a standardized general intelligence test as a condition of employment in or transfer to jobs when (a) neither standard is shown to be significantly related to successful job performance, (b) both requirements operate to disqualify Negroes at a substantially higher rate than white applicants, and (c) the jobs in question formerly had been filled only by white employees as part of a longstanding practice of giving preference to whites.

* * * All the petitioners are employed at the Company's Dan River Steam Station, a power generating facility located at Draper, North

---

* See Stephen Jay Gould, The Mismeasure of Man (1981).

Carolina. At the time this action was instituted, the Company had 95 employees at the Dan River Station, 14 of whom were Negroes; 13 of these are petitioners here.

The District Court found that prior to July 2, 1965, the effective date of the Civil Rights Act of 1964, the Company openly discriminated on the basis of race in the hiring and assigning of employees at its Dan River plant. The plant was organized into five operating departments: (1) Labor, (2) Coal Handling, (3) Operations, (4) Maintenance, and (5) Laboratory and Test. Negroes were employed only in the Labor Department where the highest paying jobs paid less than the lowest paying jobs in the other four "operating" departments in which only whites were employed. Promotions were normally made within each department on the basis of job seniority. Transferees into a department usually began in the lowest position.

In 1955 the Company instituted a policy of requiring a high school education for initial assignment to any department except Labor, and for transfer from the Coal Handling to any "inside" department (Operations, Maintenance, or Laboratory). When the Company abandoned its policy of restricting Negroes to the Labor Department in 1965, completion of high school also was made a prerequisite to transfer from Labor to any other department. From the time the high school requirement was instituted to the time of trial, however, white employees hired before the time of the high school education requirement continued to perform satisfactorily and achieve promotions in the "operating" departments. Findings on this score are not challenged.

The Company added a further requirement for new employees on July 2, 1965, the date on which Title VII became effective. To qualify for placement in any but the Labor Department it became necessary to register satisfactory scores on two professionally prepared aptitude tests, as well as to have a high school education. Completion of high school alone continued to render employees eligible for transfer to the four desirable departments from which Negroes had been excluded if the incumbent had been employed prior to the time of the new requirement. In September 1965 the Company began to permit incumbent employees who lacked a high school education to qualify for transfer from Labor or Coal Handling to an "inside" job by passing two tests—the Wonderlic Personnel Test, which purports to measure general intelligence, and the Bennett Mechanical Comprehension Test. Neither was directed or intended to measure the ability to learn to perform a particular job or category of jobs. The requisite scores used for both initial hiring and transfer approximated the national median for high school graduates.[3]

The District Court had found that while the Company previously followed a policy of overt racial discrimination in a period prior to the Act, such conduct had ceased. The District Court also concluded that Title VII was intended to be prospective only and, consequently, the

3. The test standards are thus more stringent than the high school requirement, since they would screen out approximately half of all high school graduates.

impact of prior inequities was beyond the reach of corrective action authorized by the Act.

The Court of Appeals was confronted with a question of first impression, as are we, concerning the meaning of Title VII. After careful analysis a majority of that court concluded that a subjective test of the employer's intent should govern, particularly in a close case, and that in this case there was no showing of a discriminatory purpose in the adoption of the diploma and test requirements. On this basis, the Court of Appeals concluded there was no violation of the Act.

The Court of Appeals reversed the District Court in part * * *. The Court of Appeals noted, however, that the District Court was correct in its conclusion that there was no showing of a racial purpose or invidious intent in the adoption of the high school diploma requirement or general intelligence test and that these standards had been applied fairly to whites and Negroes alike. It held that, in the absence of a discriminatory purpose, use of such requirements was permitted by the Act. In so doing, the Court of Appeals rejected the claim that because these two requirements operated to render ineligible a markedly disproportionate number of Negroes, they were unlawful under Title VII unless shown to be job related. We granted the writ on these claims.

The objective of Congress in the enactment of Title VII is plain from the language of the statute. It was to achieve equality of employment opportunities and remove barriers that have operated in the past to favor an identifiable group of white employees over other employees. Under the Act, practices, procedures, or tests neutral on their face, and even neutral in terms of intent, cannot be maintained if they operate to "freeze" the status quo of prior discriminatory employment practices.

The Court of Appeals' opinion, and the partial dissent, agreed that, on the record in the present case, "whites register far better on the Company's alternative requirements" than Negroes.[6] This consequence would appear to be directly traceable to race. Basic intelligence must have the means of articulation to manifest itself fairly in a testing process. Because they are Negroes, petitioners have long received inferior education in segregated schools and this Court expressly recognized these differences in *Gaston County v. United States*, 395 U.S. 285, 89 S.Ct. 1720, 23 L.Ed.2d 309 (1969). There, because of the inferior education received by Negroes in North Carolina, this Court barred the institution of a literacy test for voter registration on the ground that the test would abridge the right to vote indirectly on account of race. Congress did not intend by Title VII, however, to guarantee a job to every person regardless of qualifications. In short, the Act does not

---

6. In North Carolina, 1960 census statistics show that, while 34% of white males had completed high school, only 12% of Negro males had done so. U.S. Bureau of the Census, U.S. Census of Population: 1960, Vol. 1 * * *.

Similarly, with respect to standardized tests, the EEOC in one case found that use of a battery of tests, including the Wonderlic and Bennett tests used by the Company in the instant case, resulted in 58% of whites passing the tests, as compared with only 6% of the blacks.

command that any person be hired simply because he was formerly the subject of discrimination, or because he is a member of a minority group. Discriminatory preference for any group, minority or majority, is precisely and only what Congress has proscribed. What is required by Congress is the removal of artificial, arbitrary, and unnecessary barriers to employment when the barriers operate invidiously to discriminate on the basis of racial or other impermissible classification.

Congress has now provided that tests or criteria for employment or promotion may not provide equality of opportunity merely in the sense of the fabled offer of milk to the stork and the fox. On the contrary, Congress has now required that the posture and condition of the job-seeker be taken into account. It has—to resort again to the fable—provided that the vessel in which the milk is proffered be one all seekers can use. The Act proscribes not only overt discrimination but also practices that are fair in form, but discriminatory in operation. The touchstone is business necessity. If an employment practice which operates to exclude Negroes cannot be shown to be related to job performance, the practice is prohibited.

On the record before us, neither the high school completion requirement nor the general intelligence test is shown to bear a demonstrable relationship to successful performance of the jobs for which it was used. Both were adopted, as the Court of Appeals noted, without meaningful study of their relationship to job-performance ability. Rather, a vice president of the Company testified, the requirements were instituted on the Company's judgment that they generally would improve the overall quality of the work force.

The evidence, however, shows that employees who have not completed high school or taken the tests have continued to perform satisfactorily and make progress in departments for which the high school and test criteria are now used.[7] The promotion record of present employees who would not be able to meet the new criteria thus suggests the possibility that the requirements may not be needed even for the limited purpose of preserving the avowed policy of advancement within the Company. In the context of this case, it is unnecessary to reach the question whether testing requirements that take into account capability for the next succeeding position or related future promotion might be utilized upon a showing that such long-range requirements fulfill a genuine business need. In the present case the Company has made no such showing.

The Court of Appeals held that the Company had adopted the diploma and test requirements without any "intention to discriminate against Negro employees." We do not suggest that either the District Court or the Court of Appeals erred in examining the employer's intent; but good intent or absence of discriminatory intent does not redeem employment procedures or testing mechanisms that operate as "built-in

---

7. For example, between July 2, 1965, and November 14, 1966, the percentage of white employees who were promoted but who were not high school graduates was nearly identical to the percentage of non-graduates in the entire white work force.

headwinds'' for minority groups and are unrelated to measuring job capability.

The Company's lack of discriminatory intent is suggested by special efforts to help the undereducated employees through Company financing of two-thirds the cost of tuition for high school training. But Congress directed the thrust of the Act to the *consequences* of employment practices, not simply the motivation. More than that, Congress has placed on the employer the burden of showing that any given requirement must have a manifest relationship to the employment in question.

The facts of this case demonstrate the inadequacy of broad and general testing devices as well as the infirmity of using diplomas or degrees as fixed measures of capability. History is filled with examples of men and women who rendered highly effective performance without the conventional badges of accomplishment in terms of certificates, diplomas, or degrees. Diplomas and tests are useful servants, but Congress has mandated the commonsense proposition that they are not to become masters of reality.

The Company contends that its general intelligence tests are specifically permitted by § 703(h) of the Act. That section authorizes the use of "any professionally developed ability test" that is not "designed, intended *or used* to discriminate because of race * * *." (Emphasis added.)

The Equal Employment Opportunity Commission, having enforcement responsibility, has issued guidelines interpreting § 703(h) to permit only the use of job-related tests.[9] The administrative interpretation of the Act by the enforcing agency is entitled to great deference. Since the Act and its legislative history support the Commission's construction, this affords good reason to treat the guidelines as expressing the will of Congress.

Section 703(h) was not contained in the House version of the Civil Rights Act but was added in the Senate during extended debate. For a period, debate revolved around claims that the bill as proposed would prohibit all testing and force employers to hire unqualified persons simply because they were part of a group formerly subject to job discrimination. Proponents of Title VII sought throughout the debate to assure the critics that the Act would have no effect on job-related tests. Senators Case of New Jersey and Clark of Pennsylvania, comanagers of the bill on the Senate floor, issued a memorandum explaining that the proposed Title VII "expressly protects the employer's right to insist that any prospective applicant, Negro or white, *must meet the applicable job qualifications.* Indeed, the very purpose of Title VII is to promote hiring

---

9. EEOC Guidelines on Employment Testing Procedures, issued August 24, 1966, provide[d]:

The Commission accordingly interprets "professionally developed ability test" to mean a test which fairly measures the knowledge or skills required by the particular job or class of jobs which the applicant seeks, or which fairly affords the employer a chance to measure the applicant's ability to perform a particular job or class of jobs. The fact that a test was prepared by an individual or organization claiming expertise in test preparation does not, without more, justify its use within the meaning of Title VII. * * *

on the basis of job qualifications, rather than on the basis of race or color." 110 Cong.Rec. 7247. (Emphasis added.) Despite these assurances, Senator Tower of Texas introduced an amendment authorizing "professionally developed ability tests." Proponents of Title VII opposed the amendment because, as written, it would permit an employer to give any test, "whether it was a good test or not, so long as it was professionally designed. Discrimination could actually exist under the guise of compliance with the statute." 110 Cong. Rec. 13504 (remarks of Sen. Case).

The amendment was defeated and two days later Senator Tower offered a substitute amendment which was adopted verbatim and is now the testing provision of § 703(h). Speaking for the supporters of Title VII, Senator Humphrey, who had vigorously opposed the first amendment, endorsed the substitute amendment, stating: "Senators on both sides of the aisle who were deeply interested in title VII have examined the text of this amendment and have found it to be in accord with the intent and purpose of that title." 110 Cong.Rec. 13724. The amendment was then adopted. From the sum of the legislative history relevant in this case, the conclusion is inescapable that the EEOC's construction of § 703(h) to require that employment tests be job related comports with congressional intent.

Nothing in the Act precludes the use of testing or measuring procedures; obviously they are useful. What Congress has forbidden is giving these devices and mechanisms controlling force unless they are demonstrably a reasonable measure of job performance. Congress has not commanded that the less qualified be preferred over the better qualified simply because of minority origins. Far from disparaging job qualifications as such, Congress has made such qualifications the controlling factor, so that race, religion, nationality, and sex become irrelevant. What Congress has commanded is that any tests used must measure the person for the job and not the person in the abstract.

The judgment of the Court of Appeals is, as to that portion of the judgment appealed from, reversed.

Justice Brennan took no part in the consideration or decision of this case.

Notes and Questions

1. *Griggs* was the result of a litigation campaign that was patterned, in substantial part, on the litigation strategy that led to *Brown v. Board of Education*, 347 U.S. 483, 74 S.Ct. 686, 98 L.Ed. 873 (1954). The strategy involved the filing of a large numbers of cases under Title VII and § 1981, a monitoring system—to identify cases, issues, and industries—that suggested a systematic law reform approach, and the use of class actions. *See* Jack Greenberg, Crusaders in the Courts: How a Dedicated Band of Lawyers Fought for the Civil Rights Revolution 412–29 (1994); Robert Belton, *A Comparative Review of Public and Private Enforcement of Title VII of the Civil Rights Act of 1964*, 31 Vand.L.Rev. 905 (1978). *Brown* overturned the

"separate but equal" doctrine that had legitimated racial segregation of public schools, and the decision profoundly altered equal protection jurisprudence. The rationale of *Griggs*, too, had a similarly significant impact on civil rights jurisprudence. *See* Robert Belton, *Title VII of the Civil Rights Act of 1964: A Decade of Private Enforcement and Judicial Developments*, 20 St.Louis U.L.J. 225, 229–30, 305 (1976).

2. The *Griggs* disparate impact theory holds that a facially neutral employment practice that has a substantial adverse effect on the employment opportunities of members of protected classes is unlawful employment discrimination unless justified by business necessity.

3. The issue in *Griggs* was whether discriminatory intent is an element that is required in all employment discrimination claims brought under Title VII. The lower courts in *Griggs* held that it was. 292 F.Supp. 243 (M.D.N.C. 1968); 420 F.2d 1225 (4th Cir.1970). Examine §§ 703(h) and 706(g) of Title VII, 42 U.S.C. §§ 2000e–2(h) and 2000e–5(g). Both provisions contain specific language calling for findings of intentional discrimination: § 703(h) in the case of seniority and testing and § 706(g) as a prerequisite to injunctive relief. What is the significance of these statutory "intent" provisions after *Griggs*?

4. *Section 703(a)(2)*: Contrast the language of § 703(a)(2) with § 703(a)(1). The term "discriminate" is used in § 703(a)(1), but not in § 703(a)(2). The Supreme Court did not articulate its reliance on the language of § 703(a)(2) to support the disparate impact theory until eleven years after *Griggs* in *Connecticut v. Teal*, 457 U.S. 440, 102 S.Ct. 2525, 73 L.Ed.2d 130 (1982), reproduced in this chapter.

> [Section 703(a)(2)] speaks, not in terms of jobs and promotions, but in terms of *limitations* and *classifications* that would deprive any individual of employment *opportunities*. A disparate impact claim reflects the language of § 703(a)(2) and Congress' basic objectives in enacting that statute: "to achieve equality of employment *opportunities* and remove barriers that have operated in the past to favor an identifiable group of white employees over other employees." When an employer uses a nonjob-related barrier in order to deny a minority or woman applicant employment or promotion, and that barrier has a significant adverse effect on minorities or women, then the applicant has been deprived of an employment *opportunity* "because of * * * race, color, religion, sex, or national origin."

Id. at 448, 102 S.Ct. at 2531 (original emphasis) (quoting *Griggs*, 401 U.S. at 429–30, 91 S.Ct. at 852–53).

As pointed out in Chapter 3, an often-quoted interpretive memorandum entered into the Congressional Record by Senators Case and Clark, the respective Republican and Democratic floor managers of Title VII in the Senate, simply states, for example, that

> [t]o discriminate is to make a distinction, to make a difference in treatment or favor, and those distinctions or differences in treatment or favor which are prohibited by section 704 are those which are based on any five of the forbidden criteria: race, color, religion, sex, and national

origin. Any other criterion or qualification for employment is not affected by this title.

110 Cong. Rec. 7213 (1964). However, the legislative history of the 1972 amendments to Title VII cites *Griggs* with approval. The Senate Report states:

> Employment discrimination as viewed today is a * * * complex and pervasive phenomenon. Experts familiar with the subject now generally describe the problem in terms of "systems" and "effects" rather than simply intentional wrongs * * *.

S.Rep.No.92–415, at 5 (1971). *See also* H.R.Rep.No.92–238, at 8 (1971). In addition, the section-by-section analyses of the 1972 amendments submitted to both Houses explicitly stated that in any area not addressed by the amendments, present case law—which, as Congress had already recognized, included the then recent decision in *Griggs*—was intended to continue to govern. 118 Cong.Rec. 7166, 7564 (1972). Should the favorable discussion of *Griggs* in the 1972 legislative history be deemed congressional approval of the disparate impact theory? Congress codified the disparate impact theory in the Civil Rights Act of 1991. The Civil Rights Act of 1991 is covered later in this Chapter.

5. To construe the meaning of "equality of opportunity" and "discrimination," the Court in *Griggs* invoked Aesop's fable about a stork and a fox. 401 U.S. at 431, 91 S.Ct. at 853. The following is a recent translation of the fable:

> The fox is said to have started it by inviting the stork to dinner and serving a liquid broth on a marble slab which the hungry stork could not so much as taste. The stork, in turn, invited the fox to dinner and served a narrow-mouthed jug filled with crumbled food. The stork was able to thrust her beak inside and eat as much as she wanted, while her guest was tormented with hunger. As the fox was licking the neck of the jug in vain, the stork is supposed to have said, "When others follow your example, you have to grin and bear it."

Aesop's Fables 81 (Laura Gibbs trans., Oxford Univ. Press 2002). How does the Court's use of Aesop's fable support the view that prohibiting only intentional discrimination is insufficient as a matter of law (and policy) to achieve equality in the workplace (and perhaps in society at large) for groups that historically have been treated differently because of race or sex? Does the Court's reliance upon the fable support the equal opportunity view of equality, the equal treatment view, or both perspectives? *See, e.g.,* Mary Ellen Maatman, *Listening to Deaf Culture: A Reconceptualization of Difference Analysis Under Title VII,* 13 Hofstra L.J. 269, 320–21 & 320 n.362 (1996).

6. In thinking about the comparison between the disparate impact and disparate treatment theories of discrimination, are both necessary to achieve equality in the workplace, or should one theory be given preference over the other? Does the following excerpt help in responding to the question?:

> Disparate impact theory presents a monumentally different conceptualization of discrimination than that embraced by traditional dispa-

rate treatment jurisprudence. Defining discrimination in terms of consequences rather than purpose, disparate impact theory interprets Title VII to require that members of protected groups not be unnecessarily harmed in employment because of group differences. Under disparate impact theory, use of employment practices that have a disparate impact on groups with protected characteristics is unlawful unless the employer can show that the practices are job related and justified by business necessity. The employer need not show intent to discriminate in these circumstances; it is enough that the employer uses an employment practice that, although facially neutral and neutral in application, disqualifies a disproportionate percentage of a particular group of applicants from consideration. Disparate impact theory marks a significant departure from the purely individualistic conception of discrimination underlying existing disparate treatment doctrine * * *

* * *

As *Griggs* illustrates, the disparate impact theory conceptualizes discrimination in terms of institutional barriers to equal opportunity for women and minorities. Accordingly, disparate impact theory has proven an invaluable tool for reducing employer reliance on job requirements that are unrelated to job performance but that stand in the way of minority progress. Without such a tool, employers would have been free to adopt facially neutral job requirements that maintained the exclusion of blacks and minorities from vast areas of employment. In addition, by recognizing systems as legitimate subjects for legal regulation, the *Griggs* Court opened the door for a structural approach to combating discrimination more broadly. * * * [Disparate impact] recognizes the role that institutional choices, even those that are neutral in design and in application, can play in perpetuating stratification in the workplace.

Tristin K. Green, *Discrimination in the Workplace Dynamics: Toward a Structural Account of Disparate Treatment Theory*, 38 Harv.C.R.-C.L.L.Rev. 91, 136–37 (2003).

7. In addition to providing a theoretical and legal basis for remedying institutional discrimination, does the impact theory also provide a theoretical and legal basis for remedying the effect of societal discrimination? In thinking about this question, it should be noted that the Supreme Court has rejected the rationale of societal discrimination as a compelling state interest to justify affirmative action. See, e.g, Wygant v. Jackson Bd. of Ed., 476 U.S. 267, 276, 106 S.Ct. 1842, 1848, 90 L.Ed.2d 260 (1986) ("Societal discrimination, without more, is too amorphous a basis for imposing a racially classified remedy" because a "court could uphold remedies that are ageless in their reach into the past, and timeless in their ability to affect the future.") (plurality opinion).

8. *Analytical Framework*: The Supreme Court addressed the analytical framework for disparate impact claims in *Albemarle Paper Co. v. Moody*, 422 U.S. 405, 95 S.Ct. 2362, 45 L.Ed.2d 280 (1975). *Albemarle Paper Co.*, like *Griggs*, was a Title VII class action case brought by black employees who challenged the employer's use of professionally developed general ability tests, as well as its high school diploma requirement. The Court relied on professional standards of test validation promulgated by the EEOC to

determine that the employer had not met its burden of proving the "job relatedness" of its testing program. In addition, the Court announced the burden of allocation rules for litigating a disparate impact case:

In *Griggs v. Duke Power Co.*, this Court unanimously held that Title VII forbids the use of employment tests that are discriminatory in effect unless the employer meets "the burden of showing that any given requirement [has] * * * a manifest relationship to the employment in question." This burden arises, of course, only after the complaining party or class has made out a prima facie case of discrimination, *i.e.*, has shown that the tests in question select applicants for hire or promotion in a racial pattern significantly different from that of the pool of applicants. *See* McDonnell Douglas Corp. v. Green, 411 U.S. 792, 802, 93 S.Ct. 1817, 1824, 36 L.Ed.2d 668 (1973). If an employer does then meet the burden of proving that its tests are "job related," it remains open to the complaining party to show that other tests or selection devices, without a similarly undesirable racial effect, would also serve the employer's legitimate interest in "efficient and trustworthy workmanship." *Id.* at 801, 93 S.Ct. at 1823. Such a showing would be evidence that the employer was using its tests merely as a "pretext" for discrimination.

Albemarle Paper Co., 422 U.S. at 425, 95 S.Ct. at 2375.

If a plaintiff proves "pretext" in a disparate treatment case, it means that the plaintiff is entitled to a finding that the employer has intentionally engaged in unlawful discrimination against the plaintiff. What is the purpose of a finding of "pretext" in disparate impact cases, as that term is used in *Albemarle Paper Co.*, when intent is not an element, i.e., need not be proven? Should it be deemed to be the functional "equivalent to intentional discrimination," as stated by Justice O'Connor in *Watson v. Fort Worth Bank & Trust*, 487 U.S. 977, 997, 108 S.Ct. 2777, 2790, 101 L.Ed.2d 827 (1988), reproduced, in part, in Section F of this chapter? If pretext in disparate impact cases is deemed to be the functional equivalent to intent, is there any meaningful distinction left between the theories of disparate treatment and disparate impact?

9. The Supreme Court substantially modified the disparate impact analytical framework in *Wards Cove Packing Co. v. Atonio*, 490 U.S. 642, 109 S.Ct. 2115, 104 L.Ed.2d 733 (1989). In turn, Congress legislatively changed the analytical framework in disparate impact cases in the Civil Rights Act of 1991, Section 703(k) of Title VII. 42 U.S.C. § 2000e–2(k). See Section F of this chapter.

10. *Uniform Guidelines on Employee Selection*: In *Griggs*, the Supreme Court relied upon the EEOC's 1966 and 1970 testing guidelines. Prior to 1978, in addition to the EEOC, the Office of Federal Contract Compliance Programs (which administratively enforces Executive Order 11,246), the federal Civil Service Commission, the Department of Justice, and the Department of Labor had separately issued guidelines on employment selection criteria. These different sets of guidelines were sometimes inconsistent and conflicting. The Equal Employment Opportunity Coordinating Council, created by a 1972 amendment to Title VII, ultimately resolved the conflicts between the federal enforcement authorities. The result was the promul-

gation in 1978 of the *Uniform Guidelines on Employee Selection Procedures*, 29 C.F.R. § 1607 (2003). The *Uniform Guidelines* now govern federal administrative enforcement of laws prohibiting employment discrimination by all of the federal agencies. *See generally* Ronald B. Rubin, Note, *The Uniform Guidelines on Employee Selection Procedures: Compromises and Controversies*, 28 Cath.U.L.Rev. 605 (1979).

The *Uniform Guidelines* adopt a broad definition of "selection procedures" that may be subjected to disparate impact analysis:

> Any measure, combination of measures, or procedures used as a basis for any employment decision. Selection procedures include the full range of assessment techniques from traditional paper and pencil tests, performance tests, training programs, or probationary periods and physical, educational, and work experience requirements through informal or casual interviews and unscored application forms.

29 C.F.R. § 1607.16Q. An "employment decision" includes "hiring, promotion, demotion, membership (for example, in a labor organization), referral, retention, * * * licensing and certification, to the extent that certification is covered by Federal equal employment law[, and o]ther selections decisions, such as selection for training or transfer * * * if they lead to any of the decisions listed above." *Id.* § 1607.2B.

11. Plaintiffs have used the disparate impact theory to challenge a wide range of facially neutral employment practices and policies. *See, e.g.,* Dothard v. Rawlinson, 433 U.S. 321, 97 S.Ct. 2720, 53 L.Ed.2d 786 (1977) (disparate impact on females of height and weight requirements for employment as prison guards); New York City Transit Auth. v. Beazer, 440 U.S. 568, 99 S.Ct. 1355, 59 L.Ed.2d 587 (1979) (disparate impact on minorities of policy limiting employment opportunities of methadone users); Gregory v. Litton Sys., Inc., 316 F.Supp. 401 (C.D.Cal.1970), *aff'd as modified*, 472 F.2d 631 (9th Cir.1972) (disparate impact on blacks of employers' inquiries about arrest records); Wallace v. Debron Corp., 494 F.2d 674 (8th Cir.1974) (disparate impact on blacks of policies limiting employment opportunities of persons subject to wage garnishment proceedings); Johnson v. Pike Corp. of America, 332 F.Supp. 490 (C.D.Cal.1971) (same); Green v. Missouri Pac. R.R., 549 F.2d 1158 (8th Cir.1977) (disparate impact on blacks of policies limiting employment opportunities because of prior criminal convictions); Local 53, Asbestos Workers v. Vogler, 407 F.2d 1047 (5th Cir.1969) (disparate impact on blacks of nepotism rules for union membership in an all-white union); United States v. City of Warren, Mich., 61 Empl.Prac.Dec. (CCH) ¶ 42,271 (E.D.Mich.1993) (disparate impact on blacks of employer's policy of limiting recruitment advertisements to local county newspaper with small black readership).

The applicability of disparate impact analysis to policies on English-only rules, that is, rules requiring employees to speak only English on the job, is treated in the materials on national origin in Chapter 11.

12. A company has a policy against rehiring employees who were terminated for misconduct. Suppose Joel Hernandez who has worked for this company for twenty-five years is discharged because he engaged in off-duty illegal drug use. Illegal drug use, including off-duty use of illegal drugs, is considered employee misconduct under the company's policy. Hernandez

enters a drug rehabilitation program for drug users. He then reapplied for employment with the company, but his application is rejected because he had been discharged for violating the company's workplace misconduct rules. A recovering drug addict is deemed to have a disability under the ADA. Hernandez, after exhausting his administrative remedies before the EEOC, files a claim in state court seeking relief under the ADA claiming that the company's rejection of his application constituted unlawful employment discrimination against him because his disability. He seeks relief only under the disparate treatment theory. Assume that Hernandez establishes a prima facie case of disparate treatment discrimination and the company asserts its facially neutral no-rehire policy as a legitimate nondiscriminatory reason. Assume further that the company's no-rehire policy has a disparate impact on recovering drug users. May a court apply disparate impact analysis to the facially neutral no-rehire policy in determining whether it is a legitimate nondiscriminatory reason under the *McDonnell Douglas* single motive analytical paradigm?

In *Raytheon Co. v. Hernandez*, ___ U.S. ___, 124 S.Ct. 513, 157 L.Ed.2d 357 (2003), the Supreme Court held that a trial court commits legal error when it applies disparate impact analysis to an employer's facially neutral policy asserted as a legitimate nondiscriminatory reason when the plaintiff seeks relief solely under the disparate treatment theory. The Court based its decision on the ground that it has consistently recognized a distinction between disparate treatment and disparate impact claims:

> Because "the factual issues, and therefore the character of the evidence presented, differ when the plaintiff claims that a facially neutral employment policy has a discriminatory impact on a protected class," Texas Dept. of Community Affairs v. Burdine, 450 U.S. 248, 252 n.5, 101 S.Ct. 1089, 67 L.Ed.2d 207 (1981), courts must be careful to distinguish between [disparate impact and disparate treatment] theories."

Id. at ___, 124 S.Ct. at 519. Under *Raytheon*, a facially neutral employment practice is a "quintessential legitimate nondiscriminatory reason" even if it has an adverse impact on a protected class as long as the plaintiff relies solely on the disparate treatment theory. *See id*. at ___, 124 S.Ct. at 520. To challenge such a practice, the plaintiff must also seek relief under the disparate impact theory. *Raytheon* is reproduced in Chapter 13.

13. *The Conversion Doctrine*: In addition to pleading both disparate treatment and disparate impact where the evidence supports a potential finding of the adverse impact of a facially neutral employment practice offered as a legitimate nondiscriminatory reason defense, the conversion doctrine may be an option. Professor Douglas A. Laycock explained the conversion doctrine in *Statistical Proof and Theories of Discrimination*, 49 Law & Contemp.Probs., Autumn 1986, at 97, 97:

> The basic crunch on employers comes from the combination of the disparate treatment and disparate impact theories. Disparate treatment theory requires employers to hire randomly or on some measure of merit. Most choose merit, at least in part. But disparate impact theory is suspicious of all measures of merit; the employer must justify each measure used with prohibitively expensive validation studies. The combination is a great one-two punch for plaintiffs: charge the employer

with disparate treatment, and when he explains the rejection of women or minorities with measures of merit, charge him with disparate impact on the basis of each and every defense. This strategy has been available since *Griggs v. Duke Power Co.*

The District of Columbia Court of Appeals recognized the conversion doctrine in *Segar v. Smith*, 738 F.2d 1249 (D.C.Cir.1984), *cert. denied sub nom.* Meese v. Segar, 471 U.S. 1115, 105 S.Ct. 2357, 86 L.Ed.2d 258 (1985). *See also* Barbara A. Norris, *Multiple Regression Analysis in Title VII Cases: A Structural Approach to Attacks of "Missing Factors" and "Pre–Act Discrimination,"* 49 Law & Contemp.Probs., Autumn 1986, at 63.

14. *Resumé Scanning Software*: The technological "revolution" has introduced resumé scanning software that allows employers to scan resumés into computers and to search those resumés for key words. The use of resumé scanning software is more efficient than manually sifting through and reading each resumé to decide which applicants have the qualifications for vacancies. Does the use of resumé scanning software eliminate the possibility of unlawful employment discrimination? Proponents of resumé scanning software argue that, used properly, this screening method is race- and gender-blind. Their argument is that the technology eliminates unconscious or "unwitting" discrimination that may occur when a personnel manager reviews the resumé since the software program applies identical objective criteria every time. Opponents argue that resumé scanning is "a potential time bomb for employers and a potential mine for plaintiffs lawyers" because, for example, the software may screen out individuals without a high school diploma for a job that does not necessarily require a high school diploma. *See* Mark Hansen, *Critics View Resume–Scanning Software as Newest Form of Employment Discrimination*, 85 A.B.A.J. 36 (March 1999) (quoting James Fadigan, an Orlando, Florida-based consultant on the subject of equal employment opportunity). Scanning for zip codes may have an adverse impact on a protected class. The same is true for persons with arrest or conviction records, or for age. Key words used by some groups may be different from those used by other groups. One of the claims made in an employment discrimination claim against Walt Disney Company is that the use of resumé scanning software discriminated against blacks because black applicants are likely to use different "key words" on resumés than white applicants. *See* Alison B. Marshall, *Learning to E–Manage: Technology Has Created New Pitfalls for Employers*, Legal Times, Feb. 14, 2000, at 42. What advice would you give an employer who uses resumé scanning software in its employee selection process to minimize or eliminate unlawful discrimination with this technology?

15. The courts are split on whether word-of-mouth recruitment of protected class members is subject to disparate impact analysis. United States v. Georgia Power Co., 474 F.2d 906 (5th Cir.1973) (disparate impact theory applies); EEOC v. Chicago Miniature Lamp Works, 947 F.2d 292 (7th Cir.1991) (word-of-mouth recruiting is not a sufficiently affirmative act by the employer to be an "employment practice" for purposes of the disparate impact theory). Re-examine *EEOC v. Consolidated Service Systems*, 989 F.2d 233 (7th Cir.1993), reproduced in Chapter 3, in which the EEOC challenged the employer's word-of-mouth recruiting policy under the disparate treat-

ment theory. How would you analyze the case under the disparate impact theory?

16. A major law firm has a policy of offering employment as first-year associates to third-year law students, but only to those who are either on law review or in the top fifteen percent of their class. Which groups of students are most likely to be adversely affected by the policy? Does the hiring policy have a "demonstrable relationship to successful performance" on the job? *See generally* Richardson v. McFadden, 540 F.2d 744 (4th Cir.1976) (black law school graduates challenge to South Carolina bar exam), 563 F.2d 1130 (4th Cir.1977) (on rehearing), *cert. denied*, 435 U.S. 968, 98 S.Ct. 1606, 56 L.Ed.2d 59 (1978); Garcia v. Colorado State Bd. of Law Examiners, 760 F.2d 239 (10th Cir.) (constitutional challenge to bar exam by Latino graduates), *cert. denied sub nom.* Lucero v. Colorado State Bd. of Law Examiners, 474 U.S. 856, 106 S.Ct. 163, 88 L.Ed.2d 135 (1985); Daniel G. Lupo, *Don't Believe The Hype: Affirmative Action In Large Law Firms*, 11 Law & Ineq. 615 (1993); Stephen L. Carter, Reflections of an Affirmative Action Baby (1991) *See also* Elizabeth K. Ziewacz, Can the Glass Ceiling Be Shattered?: The Decline of Women Partners in Large Law Firms, 57 Ohio St.L.J. 971 (1996).

17. White males are protected from employment discrimination under Title VII. Can you think of any facially neutral employment practices that would have an adverse impact on the employment opportunities of white males and that could be challenged under the disparate impact theory? Testing practices? High school diploma requirements? Social workers at inner-city social institutions must have the ability to relate to inner-city black teenagers? If you cannot readily think of any such practices, what might be the explanation?

Note: The Legitimacy of the Disparate Impact Theory

By any standard, *Griggs v. Duke Power Co.* ranks as the most important civil rights case since *Brown v. Board of Education*. Like *Brown*, the Court's adoption of the disparate impact theory, however, has generated an on-going debate about the legitimacy of the theory and its underlying rationale. The debate among the Justices of the Supreme Court is reflected in cases such as *Connecticut v. Teal*, 457 U.S. 440, 448, 102 S.Ct. 2525, 2531, 73 L.Ed.2d 130 (1982), *Wards Cove Packing Co. v. Atonio*, 490 U.S. 642, 109 S.Ct. 2115, 104 L.Ed.2d 733 (1989), and *United Steelworkers of America v. Weber*, 443 U.S. 193, 99 S.Ct. 2721, 61 L.Ed.2d 480 (1979). *Connecticut v. Teal* and *Wards Cove* are reproduced in this chapter and *Weber* is reproduced in Chapter 17 on affirmative action.

Scholars have criticized the Supreme Court on its failure in *Griggs* to explain the theoretical underpinnings of the disparate impact theory. As one commentator observed,

> Missing from the Burger Court's opinion was a clear explanation of the theory underlying disparate impact law. Was the theory bottomed on the existence of past or present discrimination against minorities? Did the theory—as suggested by the reliance on the "the fabled offer of milk

to the stork and the fox"—assume that prerequisites for employment might validly test the qualifications of persons of one race while excluding qualified members of another race? Was the disparate impact test designed to provide equality of results rather than equality of opportunity? Was the test to erode or promote merit systems of employment?

Brian K. Landsberg, *Race and the Rehnquist Court*, 66 Tul.L.Rev. 1267, 1281 (1992).

Another commentator stated that

[a]lthough *Griggs v. Duke Power Co.*, the seminal disparate impact case, was decided well over a decade ago, there is still disagreement on the underlying theory of the disparate impact model. An acceptable theory must resolve a paradox created by the model: how can an employer who uses only a racially neutral employment criterion be deemed to have made an employment decision based on race? [There are] four approaches to this paradox. The "intent" theory postulates that evidence of adverse impact is evidence of discriminatory intent. Thus, although an employment criterion is facially neutral, its disparate impact exposes race-based decisionmaking. Under the "past discrimination" theory, an employment criterion with a disparate impact on black persons is unlawful if the disparate impact results from past race-based decisionmaking. * * * The "functional equivalence" theory holds that neutral criteria that have an adverse impact on black persons and cannot be justified by any business necessity are the functional equivalents of race and, therefore, should be treated like race. Finally, the "statistical discrimination" theory views the disparate impact model as a mechanism to prohibit discrimination as defined by economic theory.

Steven L. Willborn, *The Disparate Impact Model of Discrimination: Theory and Limits*, 34 Am.U.L.Rev. 799, 804 (1985).

Professor Willborn offers an explanation for and a criticism of each rationale. The intent rationale, he suggests, is structured around the argument that disparate impact is clearly relevant to the issue of discriminatory intent; thus a severe disparate impact may by itself justify a finding of discriminatory motive as the Court held in *Teamsters v. United States*, 431 U.S. 324, 97 S.Ct. 1843, 52 L.Ed.2d 396 (1977). Professor Willborn recognizes, however, as the Supreme Court itself acknowledged in *Griggs*, that the disparate impact theory is not an intent-based standard. A past discrimination rationale does not have much appeal, he argues, because the impact theory does not require a showing of past discrimination. But in *Steelworkers v. Weber*, 443 U.S. 193, 99 S.Ct. 2721, 61 L.Ed.2d 480 (1979), reproduced in Chapter 17, the Court adopted a test for determining the legality of voluntary affirmative action plans under Title VII that recognizes the significance of the continuing and present effects of past societal discrimination. Several of the Supreme Court Justices subscribe to the functional equivalency theory. Justice O'Connor, writing for a plurality in *Watson v. Fort Worth Bank & Trust*, 487 U.S. 977, 987, 108 S.Ct. 2777, 2785, 101 L.Ed.2d 827 (1988), argued that "the necessary premise of the disparate impact approach is that some employment practices, adopted without a deliberately discriminatory motive, may in operation be functionally equivalent to intentional discrimination.'' The statistical discrimination rationale is grounded in an economic analysis of labor markets and assumes that employers take action because they lack sufficient information to make low cost decisions. He argues that the statistical discrimination theory best explains the disparate impact theory. *See* Willborn, *supra*, at 804–26.

Other scholars have advanced other theoretical justifications for the disparate impact theory. Professor Caldwell, a critical race scholar, has argued the disparate impact theory is designed to enhance productivity and efficiency by redistributing employment opportunities. Paulette Caldwell, *Reaffirming the Disproportionate Effects Standard of Liability in Title VII Litigation*, 46 U.Pitt.L.Rev. 555 (1985). Professor Perry has argued that the theory is designed to prevent the perpetuation of past discrimination. Michael J. Perry, *The Disproportionate Theory of Discrimination*, 125 U.Pa. L.Rev 540 (1977). Professor Rutherglen has argued that the theory is designed to prevent disparate treatment in cases where pretextual discrimination is difficult to prove. George Rutherglen, *Disparate Impact Theory Under Title VII: An Objective Theory of Discrimination*, 73 Va.L.Rev. 1297 (1987).

For an argument that *Griggs* was wrongly decided, see Michael Evan Gold, *Griggs' Folly: An Essay on the Theory, Problems, and Origin of the Adverse Impact Definition of Employment Discrimination and a Recommendation for Reform*, 7 Indus.Rel.L.J. 429 (1985). In his book, Forbidden Grounds: The Case Against Employment Discrimination Laws (1992), Professor Richard A. Epstein argues that Title VII and other laws prohibiting discrimination in employment should be repealed because market forces are sufficient to address discriminatory employment practices.

Notwithstanding the lack of consensus among scholars about the legitimacy of disparate impact analysis, the Supreme Court in the following case extended the use of disparate impact theory to employment decisions relying on subjective criteria.

2. SUBJECTIVE CRITERIA

WATSON v. FORT WORTH BANK & TRUST

Supreme Court of the United States, 1988.
487 U.S. 977, 108 S.Ct. 2777, 101 L.Ed.2d 827.

JUSTICE O'CONNOR announced the judgement of the Court.

This case requires us to decide what evidentiary standards should be applied under Title VII of the Civil Rights Act of 1964 * * * in determining whether an employer's practice of committing promotion decisions to the subjective discretion of supervisory employees has led to illegal discrimination.

I

Petitioner Clara Watson, who is black, was hired by respondent Fort Worth Bank and Trust (the Bank) as a proof operator in August 1973. In

January 1976, Watson was promoted to a position as teller in the Bank's drive-in facility. In February 1980, she sought to become supervisor of the tellers in the main lobby; a white male, however, was selected for this job. Watson then sought a position as supervisor of the drive-in bank, but this position was given to a white female. In February 1981, after Watson had served for about a year as a commercial teller in the Bank's main lobby, and informally as assistant to the supervisor of tellers, the man holding that position was promoted. Watson applied for the vacancy, but the white female who was the supervisor of the drive-in bank was selected instead. Watson then applied for the vacancy created at the drive-in; a white male was selected for that job. The Bank, which has about 80 employees, had not developed precise and formal criteria for evaluating candidates for the positions for which Watson unsuccessfully applied. It relied instead on the subjective judgment of supervisors who were acquainted with the candidates and with the nature of the jobs to be filled. All the supervisors involved in denying Watson the four promotions at issue were white.

[The issue before the Court was whether the *Griggs* disparate impact analysis applies to subjective criteria. The Court was unanimous in holding that it does. JUSTICE O'CONNOR delivered the opinion of the Court on this issue.]

* * *

Our decisions have not addressed the question whether disparate impact analysis may be applied to cases in which subjective criteria are used to make employment decisions. * * * [T]he Courts of Appeals are in conflict on the issue. * * *

B

* * *

We are persuaded that our decisions in *Griggs* and succeeding cases could largely be nullified if disparate impact analysis were applied only to standardized selection practices. However one might distinguish "subjective" from "objective" criteria, it is apparent that selection systems that combine both types would generally have to be considered subjective in nature. Thus, for example, if the employer in *Griggs* had consistently preferred applicants who had a high school diploma and who passed the company's general aptitude test, its selection system could nonetheless have been considered "subjective" if it also included brief interviews with the candidates. So long as an employer refrained from making standardized criteria absolutely determinative, it would remain free to give such tests almost as much weight as it chose without risking a disparate impact challenge. If we announced a rule that allowed employers so easily to insulate themselves from liability under *Griggs*, disparate impact analysis might effectively be abolished.

We are also persuaded that disparate impact analysis is in principle no less applicable to subjective employment criteria than to objective or standardized tests. In either case, a facially neutral practice, adopted without discriminatory intent, may have effects that are indistinguishable from intentionally discriminatory practices. It is true, to be sure, that an employer's policy of leaving promotion decisions to the unchecked discretion of lower level supervisors should itself raise no inference of discriminatory conduct. Especially in relatively small businesses like respondent's, it may be customary and quite reasonable simply to delegate employment decisions to those employees who are most familiar with the jobs to be filled and with the candidates for those jobs. It does not follow, however, that the particular supervisors to whom this discretion is delegated always act without discriminatory intent. Furthermore, even if one assumed that any such discrimination can be adequately policed through disparate treatment analysis, the problem of subconscious stereotypes and prejudices would remain. In this case, for example, petitioner was apparently told at one point that the teller position was a big responsibility with "a lot of money * * * for blacks to have to count." Such remarks may not prove discriminatory intent, but they do suggest a lingering form of the problem that Title VII was enacted to combat. If an employer's undisciplined system of subjective decisionmaking has precisely the same effects as a system pervaded by impermissible intentional discrimination, it is difficult to see why Title VII's proscription against discriminatory actions should not apply. In both circumstances, the employer's practices may be said to "adversely affect [an individual's] status as an employee, because of such individual's race, color, religion, sex, or national origin." 42 U.S.C. § 2000e–2(a)(2). We conclude, accordingly, that subjective or discretionary employment practices may be analyzed under the disparate impact approach in appropriate cases.

* * *

Notes and Questions

1. Justice Kennedy took no part in the decision. The remaining Justices issued three separate opinions, but all agreed that the disparate impact theory is applicable in cases challenging subjective job criteria.

2. A plurality in *Watson* blunted the potential efficacy of the application of the *Griggs'* disparate impact theory to subjective decisionmaking in the second part of the opinion by endorsing rigorous evidentiary and procedural constraints to address the employers' argument that extending *Griggs* to subjective criteria would inevitably compel employers to adopt quotas or preferential treatment policies. This part of *Watson* is reproduced in Section F of this chapter.

3. What is subjective decisionmaking in the employment context? Consider the following:

Subjective hiring and promotion systems control access to jobs in both white-collar and blue-collar employment. A subjective system for allocating jobs is characterized by one of more of the following characteristic:

(a) the employer does not widely advertise the job, but instead invites a select few to apply;

(b) the employer makes no thorough analysis of the appropriate criteria (e.g., job skills) on which to select a candidate for the job;

(c) the employer provides no precise, fixed criteria which the evaluator is required to consider with respect to every candidate, or provides criteria which is largely intuitive, such as "ability" and "potential for growth;" or

(d) the employer does not require review of the decision either by the candidate or by the evaluator's supervisor.

Unstructured interviews are an obvious example of a subjective system for allocating jobs. When hiring, employers commonly rely on impression gained from unstructured interviews. In making promotion decisions, employers usually consider a candidate's record of job performance. However, employers also use additional subjective criteria, such as "desire for the promotion," "aptitude," and "common sense," thus reducing the significance of an employee's objective job performance. In addition, the candidate's record of job performance may itself be subjective. For example, the candidate's record may be based on performance ratings by his supervisors who used factors that are no more concrete or objective than those used in the hiring process.

Maurice E.R. Munroe, *The EEOC: Pattern and Practice Imperfect*, 13 Yale L. & Pol'y Rev. 219, 233–35 (1995) (citations omitted).

4. Most job application processes involve an unstructured interview of the applicant at some stage, often after qualified individuals are screened through objective criteria. Does this mean that women and minorities who are rejected from jobs are more likely to bring disparate impact claims against employers who use interviews as part of the hiring process? Are interviews inherently discriminatory? A district judge described one employer's use of interviews to select applicants for unskilled jobs at a steel plant as follows: " '[T]he process by which [the employer] divined who, among its applicants, were the best qualified was wholly subjective, consisting essentially of combining the gut reactions to the applicant of employees in the personnel office and one or more foremen in the plant.' " Green v. USX Corp., 896 F.2d 801, 805 (3d Cir.) (quoting *Green v. U.S. Steel Corp.*, 570 F.Supp. 254, 269 (E.D.Pa.1983)), *cert. denied*, 498 U.S. 814, 111 S.Ct. 53, 112 L.Ed.2d 29 (1990). How can an employer ensure that interviews are more than just "gut reactions"?

5. Other than interviews, what subjective hiring decisions or practices might be found to have a disparate impact on protected classes of individuals? What about an employer's decisions on where and how to publicize information about its open positions? For example, would an employer, whose workforce is predominantly white, face potential liability for discriminating against blacks if it advertises for job openings only in a local newspaper that is distributed in the surrounding racially homogeneous county of white residents? *See* United States v. City of Warren, Michigan, 138 F.3d 1083, 1094 (6th Cir.1998).

6.   In the process of reducing its workforce to save costs, an employer must make decisions regarding which job titles will be cut and how many employees in each title will be cut. If the result of these subjective decisions about workforce reductions is that a disproportionate number of persons over the age of forty is discharged, can the decisions be challenged under *Watson* on the theory that they have a disparate impact on a class of persons protected under the ADEA? *See* District Council 37, American Fed'n of State, County & Mun. Employees v. New York City Dep't of Parks & Recreation, 113 F.3d 347, 351 (2d Cir.1997).

7.   What are some of the stereotypical assumptions about protected class members on which subjective decisionmaking might be based? See Professor Oppenheimer's excerpt in Chapter 1.

8.   For an exploration of some of the difficulties of applying disparate impact analysis to subjective decisionmaking, as well as proposed alternatives to the current doctrine as applied in race discrimination cases, see Barbara J. Flagg, *Fashioning a Title VII Remedy for Transparently White Subjective Decisionmaking*, 104 Yale L.J. 2009 (1995).

9.   One of the challenges facing plaintiffs who wish to rely on evidence of stereotyping to support a finding of discrimination is that the import of that evidence may not be readily recognizable by the judge or jury. See Chapter 3 B. 2. Consider Joe's Stone Crab Club, which is a fourth-generation family-owned nationally known seafood restaurant. During the stone crab season, the restaurant is extremely busy serving up to 1400 patrons each weeknight and 1800 patrons on weekend nights. During the stone crab season, the Club hires approximately 70 food servers, in addition to other workers. To hire new food servers, the Club conducts "roll call" each year on the second Tuesday in October. It rarely advertises for food servers, but attracts substantially more applicants for the few food server slots that open up annually. Historically all of the employees hired as food servers have been male and the Club's explanation is that it wants to maintain an "Old World" European tradition, in which the highest level of food service is performed by men in order to create an ambience of "fine dining" for its customers. The club does not have an express policy of excluding females from the position of food server. Is there an argument for treating this case as one of disparate impact based on subjective decisionmaking? *See* EEOC v. Joe's Stone Crab, Inc., 220 F.3d 1263, 1268–70 (11th Cir.2000).

10.   Would you recommend the following proposed jury instruction to assist a jury in assessing the weight it should give to subjective criteria or stereotyping evidence?

> All of us, no matter how hard we try not to, tend to look at others and weigh what they have to say through the lens of our own experience and background. We each have a tendency to stereotype others and make assumptions about them. Often we see life and evaluate evidence through a clouded filter that tends to favor those like ourselves. I urge you to do the best you can to put aside such stereotypes, for all litigants and witnesses are entitled to a level playing field in which we can do the best we can to put aside our stereotypes and prejudices.

This case, as I have told you, involves Title VII, which is the federal anti-discrimination in employment statute. Congress determined that discrimination against African Americans and others was widespread in our country. Unfortunately, such discrimination is by no means a thing of the past. As you weigh the testimony of witnesses and the other evidence, bear in mind that racial discrimination does in fact exist in our society. Of course, that racial discrimination exists in the United States by no means suggests that this defendant discriminated. You must decide the facts about this defendant on the evidence presented in this case. Evidence does exist, however, in a context; and the context includes the regrettable tendency of all humans to stereotype to some extent and the unfortunate reality of continued employment discrimination in our country.

Judith Olans Brown, Stephen N. Subrin & Phyllis Tropper Baumann, *Some Thoughts About Social Perception and Employment Discrimination Law: A Modest Proposal for Reopening the Judicial Dialogue*, 46 Emory L.J. 1487 app. at 1531 (1997).

C.   STATISTICAL EVIDENCE

The often-cited aphorism from *Alabama v. United States*, 304 F.2d 583, 586 (5th Cir.), *aff'd*, 371 U.S. 37, 83 S.Ct. 145, 9 L.Ed.2d 112 (1962), that "statistics often tell much and Courts listen" is equally applicable in employment discrimination litigation. Although the material on statistical evidence is included in the chapter on disparate impact, statistical evidence and the basic principles covered in this Section are equally applicable to disparate treatment claims. In *McDonnell Douglas v. Green*, for example, reproduced in Chapter 3, the Supreme Court specifically stated that statistical evidence is relevant in disparate treatment cases. 411 U.S. at 804, 93 S.Ct. at 1825. The materials on statistical evidence in this section examine some of the basic, and largely nontechnical, legal rules on the use of statistical evidence in analyzing claims of employment discrimination. For a detailed and technical treatment of statistics in discrimination law, see David C. Baldus & James W. L. Cole, Statistical Proof of Discrimination (1980).

Broadly speaking, the use of statistics is a "scientific" method of drawing inferences from samples; it is a method of attempting to draw valid conclusions from incomplete data. Mathematics is the medium of expression of statistical evidence. Although shrouded in the language of expertise, statistics are merely one form of circumstantial evidence. Statistics in employment discrimination cases are a form of descriptive evidence, because they are offered to describe the factual consequences or adverse impact of facially neutral employment criteria on the employment opportunities of protected classes.

In the following three cases—*Teamsters*, *Hazelwood*, and *Dothard*—decided in 1977, the Supreme Court broadly endorsed the use of statistical evidence in employment discrimination law.

TEAMSTERS v. UNITED STATES

Supreme Court of the United States, 1977.
431 U.S. 324, 97 S.Ct. 1843, 52 L.Ed.2d 396.

JUSTICE STEWART delivered the opinion of the Court.

This litigation brings here several important questions under Title VII of the Civil Rights Act of 1964. The issues grow out of alleged unlawful employment practices engaged in by an employer and a union. The employer is a common carrier of motor freight with nationwide operations, and the union represents a large group of its employees. The District Court and the Court of Appeals held that the employer had violated Title VII by engaging in a pattern and practice of employment discrimination against Negroes and Spanish-surnamed Americans * * *.

I

The United States brought an action in a Tennessee federal court against the petitioner T.I.M.E.-D.C., Inc. (company), pursuant to § 707(a) of the Civil Rights Act of 1964. The complaint charged that the company had followed discriminatory hiring, assignment, and promotion policies against Negroes at its terminal in Nashville, Tenn. The Government brought a second action against the company almost three years later in a Federal District Court in Texas, charging a pattern and practice of employment discrimination against Negroes and Spanish-surnamed persons throughout the company's transportation system. The petitioner International Brotherhood of Teamsters (union) was joined as a defendant in that suit. * * *

The central claim in both lawsuits was that the company had engaged in a pattern or practice of discriminating against minorities in hiring so-called line drivers. Those Negroes and Spanish-surnamed persons who had been hired, the Government alleged, were given lower paying, less desirable jobs as servicemen or local city drivers, and were thereafter discriminated against with respect to promotions and transfers.[3] * * *

The cases went to trial and the District Court found that the Government had shown "by a preponderance of the evidence that T.I.M.E.-D.C. and its predecessor companies were engaged in a plan and practice of discrimination in violation of Title VII * * *." * * *

* * *

* * * We granted both the company's and the union's petitions for certiorari to consider the significant questions presented under the Civil Rights Act of 1964.

---

3. *Line drivers*, also known as over-the-road drivers, engage in long-distance hauling between company terminals. They compose a separate bargaining unit at the company. Other district bargaining units include *servicemen*, who service trucks, unhook tractors and trailers, and perform similar tasks; and *city operations*, composed of dockmen, hostlers, and city drivers who pick up and deliver freight within the immediate area of a particular terminal. All of these employees were represented by the petitioner union.

II

In this Court the company and the union contend that their conduct did not violate Title VII in any respect, asserting first that the evidence introduced at trial was insufficient to show that the company engaged in a "pattern or practice" of employment discrimination. * * *

A

* * *

We agree with the District Court and the Court of Appeals that the Government carried its burden of proof. As of March 31, 1971, shortly after the Government filed its complaint alleging systemwide discrimination, the company had 6,472 employees. Of these, 314 (5%) were Negroes and 257 (4%) were Spanish-surnamed Americans. Of the 1,828 line drivers, however, there were only 8 (0.4%) Negroes and 5 (0.3%) Spanish-surnamed persons, and all of the Negroes had been hired after the litigation had commenced. With one exception—a man who worked as a line driver at the Chicago terminal from 1950 to 1959—the company and its predecessors *did not employ a Negro on a regular basis as a line driver until 1969.* And, as the Government showed, even in 1971 there were terminals in areas of substantial Negro population where all of the company's line drivers were white. A great majority of the Negroes (83%) and Spanish-surnamed Americans (78%) who did work for the company held the lower paying city operations and serviceman jobs, whereas only 39% of the nonminority employees held jobs in those categories.

The Government bolstered its statistical evidence with the testimony of individuals who recounted over 40 specific instances of discrimination. Upon the basis of this testimony the District Court found that "[numerous] qualified black and Spanish-surnamed American applicants who sought line driving jobs at the company over the years, either had their requests ignored, were given false or misleading information about requirements, opportunities, and application procedures, or were not considered and hired on the same basis that whites were considered and hired." Minority employees who wanted to transfer to line-driver jobs met with similar difficulties.

The company's principal response to this evidence is that statistics can never in and of themselves prove the existence of a pattern or practice of discrimination, or even establish a prima facie case shifting to the employer the burden of rebutting the inference raised by the figures. But, as even our brief summary of the evidence shows, this was not a case in which the Government relied on "statistics alone." The individuals who testified about their personal experiences with the company brought the cold numbers convincingly to life.

In any event, our cases make it unmistakably clear that "[s]tatistical analyses have served and will continue to serve an important role" in cases in which the existence of discrimination is a disputed issue. Mayor of Philadelphia v. Educational Equality League, 415 U.S. 605, 620, 94

S.Ct. 1323, 1333, 39 L.Ed.2d 630 (1974). *See also* McDonnell Douglas Corp. v. Green, 411 U.S. 792, 805, 93 S.Ct. 1817, 1825–26, 36 L.Ed.2d 668 (1973). We have repeatedly approved the use of statistical proof, where it reached proportions comparable to those in this case, to establish a prima facie case of racial discrimination in jury selection cases. Statistics are equally competent in proving employment discrimination.[20] We caution only that statistics are not irrefutable; they come in infinite variety and, like any other kind of evidence, they may be rebutted. In short, their usefulness depends on all of the surrounding facts and circumstances.

In addition to its general protest against the use of statistics in Title VII cases, the company claims that in this case the statistics revealing racial imbalance are misleading because they fail to take into account the company's particular business situation as of the effective date of Title VII. The company concedes that its line drivers were virtually all white in July 1965, but it claims that thereafter business conditions were such that its work force dropped. Its argument is that low personnel turnover, rather than post-Act discrimination, accounts for more recent statistical disparities. It points to substantial minority hiring in later years, especially after 1971, as showing that any pre-Act patterns of discrimination were broken.

The argument would be a forceful one if this were an employer who, at the time of suit, had done virtually no new hiring since the effective date of Title VII. But it is not. Although the company's total number of

20. Petitioners argue that statistics, at least those comparing the racial composition of an employer's work force to the composition of the population at large, should never be given decisive weight in a Title VII case because to do so would conflict with § 2000e–2(j). That section provides:

> Nothing contained in this subchapter shall be interpreted to require any employer * * * to grant preferential treatment to any individual or to any group because of the race * * * or national origin of such individual or group on account of an imbalance which may exist with respect to the total number or percentage of persons of any race * * * or national origin employed by any employer * * * in comparison with the total number or percentage of persons of such race * * * or national origin in any community, State, section, or other area, or in the available work force in any community, State, section, or other area.

The argument fails in this case because the statistical evidence was not offered or used to support an erroneous theory that Title VII requires an employer's work force to be racially balanced. Statistics showing racial or ethnic imbalance are probative in a case such as this one only because such imbalance is often a telltale sign of purposeful discrimination; absent explanation, it is ordinarily to be expected that nondiscriminatory hiring practices will in time result in a work force more or less representative of the racial and ethnic composition of the population in the community from which employees are hired. Evidence of long-lasting and gross disparity between the composition of a work force and that of the general population thus may be significant even though § 703(j) makes clear that Title VII imposes no requirement that a work force mirror the general population. Considerations such as small sample size may, of course, detract from the value of such evidence, and evidence showing that the figures for the general population might not accurately reflect the pool of qualified job applicants would also be relevant.

"Since the passage of Civil Rights Act of 1964, the courts have frequently relied upon statistical evidence to prove a violation. * * * In many cases the only available avenue of proof is the use of racial statistics to uncover clandestine and covert discrimination by the employer or union involved." United States v. Ironworkers Local 86, 443 F.2d 544, 551 (9th Cir.1971).

employees apparently dropped somewhat during the late 1960's, the record shows that many line drivers continued to be hired throughout this period, and that almost all of them were white. To be sure, there were improvements in the company's hiring practices. The Court of Appeals commented that "T.I.M.E.-D.C.'s recent minority hiring progress stands as a laudable good faith effort to eradicate the effects of past discrimination in the area of hiring and initial assignment." But the District Court and the Court of Appeals found upon substantial evidence that the company had engaged in a course of discrimination that continued well after the effective date of Title VII. The company's later changes in its hiring and promotion policies could be of little comfort to the victims of the earlier post-Act discrimination, and could not erase its previous illegal conduct or its obligation to afford relief to those who suffered because of it.[23]

The District Court and the Court of Appeals, on the basis of substantial evidence, held that the Government had proved a prima facie case of systematic and purposeful employment discrimination, continuing well beyond the effective date of Title VII. The company's attempts to rebut that conclusion were held to be inadequate.[24] For the reasons we have summarized, there is no warrant for this Court to disturb the findings of the District Court and the Court of Appeals on this basic issue.

* * *

HAZELWOOD SCHOOL DISTRICT v. UNITED STATES

Supreme Court of the United States, 1977.
433 U.S. 299, 97 S.Ct. 2736, 53 L.Ed.2d 768.

JUSTICE STEWART delivered the opinion of the Court.

The petitioner Hazelwood School District covers 78 square miles in the northern part of St. Louis County, Mo. In 1973 the Attorney General

---

23. The company's narrower attacks upon the statistical evidence–that there was no precise delineation of the areas referred to in the general population statistics, that the Government did not demonstrate that minority populations were located close to terminals or that transportation was available, that the statistics failed to show what portion of the minority populations were located close to terminals or that transportation was available, that the statistics failed to show what portion of the minority population was suited by age, health, or other qualifications to hold trucking jobs, etc.–are equally lacking in force. At best, these attacks go only to the accuracy of the comparison between the composition of the company's work force at various terminals and the general population of the surrounding communities. They detract little from the Government's further showing that Negroes and Spanish-surnamed Americans who were hired were overwhelmingly excluded from line-driver jobs. Such employ-ees were willing to work, had access to the terminal, were healthy and of working age, and often were at least sufficiently qualified to hold city-driver jobs. Yet they became line drivers with far less frequency than whites.

In any event, fine tuning of the statistics could not have obscured the glaring absence of minority line drivers. As the Court of Appeals remarked, the company's inability to rebut the inference of discrimination came not from a misuse of statistics but from "the inexorable zero."

24. The company's evidence, apart from the showing of recent changes in hiring and promotion policies, consisted mainly of general statements that it hired only the best qualified applicants. But "affirmations of good faith in making individual selections are insufficient to dispel a prima facie case of systematic exclusion." Alexander v. Louisiana, 405 U.S. 625, 632, 92 S.Ct. 1221, 1226, 31 L.Ed.2d 536 (1972). * * *

brought this lawsuit against Hazelwood and various of its officials, alleging that they were engaged in a "pattern or practice" of employment discrimination in violation of Title VII of the Civil Rights Act of 1964. * * *

Hazelwood was formed from 13 rural school districts between 1949 and 1951 by a process of annexation. By the 1967–1968 school year, 17,550 students were enrolled in the district, of whom only 59 were Negro; the number of Negro pupils increased to 576 of 25,166 in 1972–1973, a total of just over 2%.

From the beginning, Hazelwood followed relatively unstructured procedures in hiring its teachers. * * * The personnel office did not substantively screen the applicants in determining which of them to send for interviews, other than to ascertain that each applicant, it selected, would be eligible for state certification by the time he began the job. Generally, those who had most recently submitted applications were most likely to be chosen for interviews.

Interviews were conducted by a department chairman, program coordinator, or the principal at the school where the teaching vacancy existed. Although those conducting the interviews did fill out forms rating the applicants in a number of respects, it is undisputed that each school principal possessed virtually unlimited discretion in hiring teachers for his school. The only general guidance given to the principals was to hire the "most competent" person available, and such intangibles as "personality, disposition, appearance, poise, voice, articulation, and ability to deal with people" counted heavily. The principal's choice was routinely honored by Hazelwood's Superintendent and the Board of Education.

In the early 1960's Hazelwood found it necessary to recruit new teachers, and for that purpose members of its staff visited a number of colleges and universities in Missouri and bordering States. All the institutions visited were predominantly white, and Hazelwood did not seriously recruit at either of the two predominantly Negro four-year colleges in Missouri. As a buyer's market began to develop for public school teachers, Hazelwood curtailed its recruiting efforts. For the 1971–1972 school year, 3,127 persons applied for only 234 teaching vacancies; for the 1972–1973 school year, there were 2,373 applications for 282 vacancies. A number of the applicants who were not hired were Negroes.

Hazelwood hired its first Negro teacher in 1969. The number of Negro faculty members gradually increased in successive years: 6 of 957 in the 1970 school year; 16 of 1,107 by the end of the 1972 school year; 22 of 1,231 in the 1973 school year. By comparison, according to 1970 census figures, of more than 19,000 teachers employed in that year in the St. Louis area, 15.4% were Negro. That percentage figure included the St. Louis City School District, which in recent years has followed a policy of attempting to maintain a 50% Negro teaching staff. Apart from that school district, 5.7% of the teachers in the county were Negro in 1970.

Drawing upon these historic facts, the Government mounted its "pattern or practice" attack in the District Court upon four different fronts. It adduced evidence of (1) a history of alleged racially discriminatory practices, (2) statistical disparities in hiring, (3) the standardless and largely subjective hiring procedures, and (4) specific instances of alleged discrimination against 55 unsuccessful Negro applicants for teaching jobs. Hazelwood offered virtually no additional evidence in response, relying instead on evidence introduced by the Government, perceived deficiencies in the Government's case, and its own officially promulgated policy "to hire all teachers on the basis of training, preparation and recommendations, regardless of race, color or creed."

The District Court ruled that the Government had failed to establish a pattern or practice of discrimination. * * * The court found nothing illegal or suspect in the teacher-hiring procedures that Hazelwood had followed. * * *

The Court of Appeals for the Eighth Circuit reversed. After suggesting that the District Court had assigned inadequate weight to evidence of discriminatory conduct on the part of Hazelwood before the effective date of Title VII, the Court of Appeals rejected the trial court's analysis of the statistical data as resting on an irrelevant comparison of Negro teachers to Negro pupils in Hazelwood. The proper comparison, in the appellate court's view, was one between Negro teachers in Hazelwood and Negro teachers in the relevant labor market area. Selecting St. Louis County and St. Louis City as the relevant area, the Court of Appeals compared the 1970 census figures, showing that 15.4% of teachers in that area were Negro, to the racial composition of Hazelwood's teaching staff. In the 1972–1973 and 1973–1974 school years, only 1.4% and 1.8%, respectively, of Hazelwood's teachers were Negroes. This statistical disparity, particularly when viewed against the background of the teacher-hiring procedures that Hazelwood had followed, was held to constitute a prima facie case of a pattern or practice or racial discrimination.

In addition, the Court of Appeals reasoned that the trial court had erred in failing to measure the 55 instances in which Negro applicants were denied jobs against the four-part standard for establishing a prima facie case of individual discrimination set out in this Court's opinion in *McDonnell Douglas Corp. v. Green*. Applying that standard, the appellate court found 16 cases of individual discrimination, which "buttressed" the statistical proof. Because Hazelwood had not rebutted the Government's prima facie case of a pattern or practice of racial discrimination, the Court of Appeals directed judgment for the Government and prescribed the remedial order to be entered.

We granted certiorari to consider a substantial question affecting the enforcement of a pervasive federal law.

The petitioners primarily attack the judgment of the Court of Appeals for its reliance on "undifferentiated work force statistics to find an unrebutted prima facie case of employment discrimination." The question they raise, in short, is whether a basic component in the Court of Appeals' finding of a pattern or practice of discrimination—the comparatively small percentage of Negro employees on Hazelwood's teaching staff—was lacking in probative force.

This Court's recent consideration in *Teamsters v. United States* of the role of statistics in pattern-or-practice suits under Title VII provides substantial guidance in evaluating the arguments advanced by the petitioners. * * * We also noted that statistics can be an important source of proof in employment discrimination cases, since

> absent explanation, it is ordinarily to be expected that nondiscriminatory hiring practices will in time result in a work force more or less representative of the racial and ethnic composition of the population in the community from which employees are hired. Evidence of longlasting and gross disparity between the composition of a work force and that of the general population thus may be significant even though § 703(j) makes clear that Title VII imposes no requirement that a work force mirror the general population.

Teamsters v. United States, 431 U.S. 324, 340 n. 20, 97 S.Ct. 1843, 1856 n. 20, 52 L.Ed.2d 396 (1977). Where gross statistical disparities can be shown, they alone may in a proper case constitute prima facie proof of a pattern or practice of discrimination.

There can be no doubt, in light of the *Teamsters* case, that the District Court's comparison of Hazelwood's teacher work force to its student population fundamentally misconceived the role of statistics in employment discrimination cases. The Court of Appeals was correct in the view that a proper comparison was between the racial composition of Hazelwood's teaching staff and the racial composition of the qualified public school teacher population in the relevant labor market.[13] The percentage of Negroes on Hazelwood's teaching staff in 1972–1973 was 1.4%, and in 1973–1974 it was 1.8%. By contrast, the percentage of

---

13. In *Teamsters*, the comparison between the percentage of Negroes on the employer's work force and the percentage in the general areawide population was highly probative, because the job skill there involved—the ability to drive a truck—is one that many persons possess or can fairly readily acquire. When special qualifications are required to fill particular jobs, comparisons to the general population (rather than to the smaller group of individuals who possess the necessary qualifications) may have little probative value. The comparative statistics introduced by the Government in the District Court, however, were properly limited to public school teachers, and therefore this is not a case like *Mayor v. Educational Equality League*, 415 U.S. 605, 94 S.Ct. 1323, 39 L.Ed.2d 630 (1974) in which the racial-composition comparisons failed to take into account special qualifications for the position in question.

Although the petitioners concede as a general matter the probative force of the comparative work-force statistics, they object to the Court of Appeals' heavy reliance on these data on the ground that applicant-flow data, showing the actual percentage of white and Negro applicants for teaching positions at Hazelwood, would be firmer proof. * * * [T]here was no clear evidence of such statistics. We leave it to the District Court on remand to determine whether competent proof of those data can be adduced. If so, it would, of course, be very relevant.

qualified Negro teachers in the area was, according to the 1970 census, at least 5.7%.[14] Although these differences were on their face substantial, the Court of Appeals erred in substituting its judgment for that of the District Court and holding that the Government had conclusively proved its "pattern or practice" lawsuit.

The Court of Appeals totally disregarded the possibility that this prima facie statistical proof in the record might at the trial court level be rebutted by statistics dealing with Hazelwood's hiring after it became subject to Title VII. Racial discrimination by public employers was not made illegal under Title VII until March 24, 1972. A public employer who from that date forward made all its employment decisions in a wholly nondiscriminatory way would not violate Title VII even if it had formerly maintained an all-white work force by purposefully excluding Negroes. For this reason, the Court cautioned in the *Teamsters* opinion that once a prima facie case has been established by statistical workforce disparities, the employer must be given an opportunity to show that "the claimed discriminatory pattern is a product of pre-Act hiring rather than unlawful post-Act discrimination." 431 U.S. at 360, 97 S.Ct. at 1867.

The record in this case showed that for the 1972–1973 school year, Hazelwood hired 282 new teachers, 10 of whom (3.5%) were Negroes; for the following school year it hired 123 new teachers, 5 of whom (4.1%) were Negroes. Over the two-year period, Negroes constituted a total of 15 of the 405 new teachers hired (3.7%). Although the Court of Appeals briefly mentioned these data in reciting the facts, it wholly ignored them in discussing whether the Government had shown a pattern or practice of discrimination. And it gave no consideration at all to the possibility that post-Act data as to the number of Negroes hired compared to the total number of Negro applicants might tell a totally different story.

What the hiring figures prove obviously depends upon the figures to which they are compared. The Court of Appeals accepted the Government's argument that the relevant comparison was to the labor market area of St. Louis County and the city of St. Louis, in which, according to the 1970 census, 15.4% of all teachers were Negro. The propriety of that

14. As is discussed below, the Government contends that a comparative figure of 15.4%, rather than 5.7%, is the appropriate one. But even assuming, *arguendo*, that the 5.7% figure urged by the petitioners is correct, the disparity between that figure and the percentage of Negroes on Hazelwood's teaching staff would be more than fourfold for the 1972–1973 school year, and threefold for the 1973–1974 school year. A precise method of measuring the significance of such statistical disparities was explained in *Castaneda v. Partida*, 430 U.S. 482, 496–97 n. 17, 97 S.Ct. 1272, 1281 n. 17, 51 L.Ed.2d 498 (1977). It involves calculation of the "standard deviation" as a measure of predicted fluctuations from the expected value of a sample. Using the 5.7% figure as the basis for calculating the expected value, the expected number of Negroes on the Hazelwood teaching staff would be roughly 63 in 1972–1973 and 70 in 1973–1974. The observed number in those years was 16 and 22, respectively. The difference between the observed and expected values was more than six standard deviations in 1972–1973 and more than five standard deviations in 1973–1974. The Court in *Castaneda* noted that "[a]s a general rule for such large samples, if the difference between the expected value and the observed number is greater than two or three standard deviations," then the hypothesis that teachers were hired without regard to race would be suspect. 430 U.S. at 496–97 n.17, 97 S.Ct. at 1281 n.17.

comparison was vigorously disputed by the petitioners, who urged that because the city of St. Louis has made special attempts to maintain a 50% Negro teaching staff, inclusion of that school district in the relevant market area distorts the comparison. Were that argument accepted, the percentage of Negro teachers in the relevant labor market area (St. Louis County alone) as shown in the 1970 census would be 5.7% rather than 15.4%.

The difference between these figures may well be important; the disparity between 3.7% (the percentage of Negro teachers hired by Hazelwood in 1972–1973 and 1973–1974) and 5.7% may be sufficiently small to weaken the Government's other proof, while the disparity between 3.7% and 15.4% may be sufficiently large to reinforce it.[17] In determining which of the two figures—or, very possibly, what intermediate figure—provides the most accurate basis for comparison to the hiring figures at Hazelwood, it will be necessary to evaluate such considerations as (i) whether the racially based hiring policies of the St. Louis City School District were in effect as far back as 1970, the year in which the census figures were taken; (ii) to what extent those policies have changed the racial composition of that district's teaching staff from what it would otherwise have been; (iii) to what extent St. Louis' recruitment policies have diverted to the city, teachers who might otherwise have applied to Hazelwood; (iv) to what extent Negro teachers employed by the city would prefer employment in other districts such as Hazelwood; and (v) what the experience in other school districts in St. Louis County indicates about the validity of excluding the City School District from the relevant labor market.

It is thus clear that a determination of the appropriate comparative figures in this case will depend upon further evaluation by the trial

---

17. Indeed, under the statistical methodology explained in *Castaneda v. Partida*, 430 U.S. at 496–97 n.17, 97 S.Ct. at 1281 n.17, involving the calculation of the standard deviation as a measure of predicted fluctuations, the difference between using 15.4% and 5.7% as the areawide figure would be significant. If the 15.4% figure is taken as the basis for comparison, the expected number of Negro teachers hired by Hazelwood in 1972–1973 would be 43 (rather than the actual figure of 10) of a total of 282, a difference of more than five standard deviations; the expected number in 1973–1974 would be 19 (rather than the actual figure 5) of a total of 123, a difference of more than three standard deviations. For the two years combined, the difference between the observed number of 15 Negro teachers hired (of a total of 405) would vary from the expected number of 62 by more than six standard deviations. Because a fluctuation of more than two or three standard deviations would undercut the hypothesis that decisions were being made ran-

domly with respect to race, each of these statistical comparisons would reinforce rather than rebut the Government's other proof. If, however, the 5.7% areawide figure is used, the expected number of Negro teachers hired in 1972–1973 would be roughly 16, less than two standard deviations from the observed number of 10; for 1973–1974, the expected value would be roughly seven, less than one standard deviation from the observed value of 5; and for the two years combined, the expected value of 23 would be less than two standard deviations from the observed total of 15. A more precise method of analyzing these statistics confirms the results of the standard deviation analysis. *See* F. Mosteller, R. Rourke, & G. Thomas, Probability with Statistical Applications 494 (2d ed. 1970).

These observations are not intended to suggest that precise calculations of statistical significance are necessary in employing statistical proof, but merely to highlight the importance of the choice of the relevant labor market area.

court. As this Court admonished in *Teamsters*: "[S]tatistics * * * come in infinite variety. * * * [T]heir usefulness depends on all of the surrounding facts and circumstances." 431 U.S. at 340, 97 S.Ct. at 1856–57. Only the trial court is in a position to make the appropriate determination after further findings. And only after such a determination is made can a foundation be established for deciding whether or not Hazelwood engaged in a pattern or practice of racial discrimination in its employment practices in violation of the law.

We hold, therefore, that the Court of Appeals erred in disregarding the post-Act hiring statistics in the record, and that it should have remanded the case to the District Court for further findings as to the relevant labor market area and for an ultimate determination of whether Hazelwood engaged in a pattern or practice of employment discrimination after March 24, 1972.[15] Accordingly, the judgment is vacated, and the case is remanded to the District Court for further proceedings consistent with this opinion.

JUSTICE BRENNAN, concurring.

I join the Court's opinion. * * * It should be plain, however, that the liberal substantive standards for establishing a Title VII violation, including the usefulness of statistical proof, are reconfirmed.

* * *

[The opinions of JUSTICE WHITE, concurring, and JUSTICE STEVENS, dissenting, are omitted.]

DOTHARD v. RAWLINSON

Supreme Court of the United States, 1977.
433 U.S. 321, 97 S.Ct. 2720, 53 L.Ed.2d 786.

JUSTICE STEWART delivered the opinion of the Court.

Appellee Dianne Rawlinson sought employment with the Alabama Board of Corrections as a prison guard, called in Alabama a "correctional counselor." After her application was rejected, she brought this class suit under Title VII * * * alleging that she had been denied employment because of her sex in violation of federal law. A three-judge Federal District Court for the Middle District of Alabama decided in her favor. We noted probable jurisdiction of this appeal from the District Court's judgment.

I

At the time she applied for a position as correctional counselor trainee, Rawlinson was a 22–year-old college graduate whose major course of study had been correctional psychology. She was refused

15. It will also be open to the District Court on remand to determine whether sufficiently reliable applicant-flow data are available to permit consideration of the petitioners' argument that those data may undercut a statistical analysis dependent upon hirings alone.

employment because she failed to meet the minimum 120–pound weight requirement established by an Alabama statute. The statute also establishes a height minimum of 5 feet 2 inches.

After her application was rejected because of her weight, Rawlinson filed * * * a complaint in the District Court on behalf of herself and other similarly situated women, challenging the statutory height and weight minima as violative of Title VII * * *. A three-judge court was convened. While the suit was pending, the Alabama Board of Corrections adopted Administrative Regulation 204, establishing gender criteria for assigning correctional counselors to maximum-security institutions for "contact positions," that is, positions requiring continual close physical proximity to inmates of the institution. Rawlinson amended her class-action complaint by adding a challenge to Regulation 204 as also violative of Title VII * * *. [The portion of the Court's decision dealing with Regulation 204 is reproduced in Chapter 6.]

Like most correctional facilities in the United States, Alabama's prisons are segregated on the basis of sex. * * *

A correctional counselor's primary duty within these institutions is to maintain security and control of the inmates by continually supervising and observing their activities. To be eligible for consideration as a correctional counselor, an applicant must possess a valid Alabama driver's license, have a high school education or its equivalent, be free from physical defects, be between the ages of 20 1/2 years and 45 years at the time of appointment, and fall between the minimum height and weight requirements of 5 feet 2 inches, and 120 pounds, and the maximum of 6 feet 10 inches, and 300 pounds. Appointment is by merit, with a grade assigned each applicant based on experience and education. No written examination is given.

At the time this litigation was in the District Court, the Board of Corrections employed a total of 435 people in various correctional counselor positions, 56 of whom were women. Of those 56 women, 21 were employed at the Julia Tutwiler Prison for Women, 13 were employed in noncontact positions at the four male maximum-security institutions, and the remaining 22 were employed at the other institutions operated by the Alabama Board of Corrections. Because most of Alabama's prisoners are held at the four maximum-security male penitentiaries, 336 of the 435 correctional counselor jobs were in those institutions, a majority of them concededly in the "contact" classification. Thus, even though meeting the statutory height and weight requirements, women applicants could under Regulation 204 compete equally with men for only about 25% of the correctional counselor jobs available in the Alabama prison system.

II

In enacting Title VII, Congress required "the removal of artificial, arbitrary, and unnecessary barriers to employment when the barriers operate invidiously to discriminate on the basis of racial or other impermissible classification." Griggs v. Duke Power Co., 401 U.S. 424, 431, 91 S.Ct. 849, 853, 28 L.Ed.2d 158 (1971). The District Court found that the minimum statutory height and weight requirements that applicants for employment as correctional counselors must meet constitute the sort of arbitrary barrier to equal employment opportunity that Title VII forbids. The appellants assert that the District Court erred both in finding that the height and weight standards discriminate against women, and in its refusal to find that, even if they do, these standards are justified as "job related."

A

The gist of the claim that the statutory height and weight requirements discriminate against women does not involve an assertion of purposeful discriminatory motive. It is asserted, rather, that these facially neutral qualification standards work in fact disproportionately to exclude women from eligibility for employment by the Alabama Board of Corrections. We dealt in *Griggs v. Duke Power Co.* and *Albemarle Paper Co. v. Moody* with similar allegations that facially neutral employment standards disproportionately excluded Negroes from employment, and those cases guide our approach here.

* * *

Although women 14 years of age or older compose 52.75% of the Alabama population and 36.89% of its total labor force, they hold only 12.9% of its correctional counselor positions. In considering the effect of the minimum height and weight standards on this disparity in rate of hiring between the sexes, the District Court found that the 5'2"— requirement would operate to exclude 33.29% of the women in the United States between the ages of 18–79, while excluding only 1.28% of men between the same ages. The 120–pound weight restriction would exclude 22.29% of the women and 2.35% of the men in this age group. When the height and weight restrictions are combined, Alabama's statutory standards would exclude 41.13% of the female population while excluding less than 1% of the male population. Accordingly, the District Court found that Rawlinson had made out a prima facie case of unlawful sex discrimination.

The appellants argue that a showing of disproportionate impact on women based on generalized national statistics should not suffice to establish a prima facie case. They point in particular to Rawlinson's failure to adduce comparative statistics concerning actual applicants for correctional counselor positions in Alabama. There is no requirement, however, that a statistical showing of disproportionate impact must always be based on analysis of the characteristics of actual applicants. The application process itself might not adequately reflect the actual potential applicant pool, since otherwise qualified people might be discouraged from applying because of a self-recognized inability to meet the very standards challenged as being discriminatory. A potential applicant could easily determine her height and weight and conclude that to make an application would be futile. Moreover, reliance on general population demographic data was not misplaced where there was no reason to suppose that physical height and weight characteristics of Alabama men and women differ markedly from those of the national population.

For these reasons, we cannot say that the District Court was wrong in holding that the statutory height and weight standards had a discriminatory impact on women applicants. The plaintiffs in a case such as this are not required to exhaust every possible source of evidence, if the evidence actually presented on its face conspicuously demonstrates a job requirement's grossly discriminatory impact. If the employer discerns fallacies or deficiencies in the data offered by the plaintiff, he is free to adduce countervailing evidence of his own. In this case no such effort was made.

B

We turn, therefore, to the appellants' argument that they have rebutted the prima facie case of discrimination by showing that the height and weight requirements are job related. These requirements, they say, have a relationship to strength, a sufficient but unspecified amount of which is essential to effective job performance as a correctional counselor. In the District Court, however, the appellants produced no evidence correlating the height and weight requirements with the requisite amount of strength thought essential to good job performance. Indeed, they failed to offer evidence of any kind in specific justification of the statutory standards.[14]

If the job-related quality that the appellants identify is bona fide, their purpose could be achieved by adopting and validating a test for applicants that measures strength directly. Such a test, fairly administered, would fully satisfy the standards of Title VII because it would be one that "measure[s] the person for the job and not the person in the abstract." *Griggs*, 401 U.S. at 436, 91 S.Ct. at 856. But nothing in the present record even approaches such a measurement.

For the reasons we have discussed, the District Court was not in error in holding that Title VII of the Civil Rights Act of 1964, as amended, prohibits application of the statutory height and weight requirements to Rawlinson and the class she represents.

* * *

14. [T]he appellants contend that the establishment of the minimum height and weight standards by statute requires that they be given greater deference than is typically given private employer-established job qualifications. The relevant legislative history of the 1972 amendments extending Title VII to the States as employers does not, however, support such a result. Instead, Congress expressly indicated the intent that the same Title VII principles be applied to governmental and private employers alike. *See* H.R.Rep.No.92–238, at 17 (1971); S.Rep.No.92–415, at 10 (1971). Thus for both private and public employers, "[t]he touchstone is business necessity," *Griggs*, 401 U.S. at 431, 91 S.Ct. at 853; a discriminatory employment practice must be shown to be necessary to safe and efficient job performance to survive a Title VII challenge.

JUSTICE REHNQUIST, with whom THE CHIEF JUSTICE and JUSTICE BLACKMUN join, concurring in the result and concurring in part.

* * * I do not believe—and do not read the Court's opinion as holding—that all or even many of the height and weight requirements imposed by States on applicants for a multitude of law enforcement agency jobs are pretermitted by today's decision.

I agree that the statistics relied upon in this case are sufficient, absent rebuttal, to sustain a finding of a prima facie violation of § 703(a) (2), in that they reveal a significant discrepancy between the numbers of men, as opposed to women, who are automatically disqualified by reason of the height and weight requirements. The fact that these statistics are national figures of height and weight, as opposed to statewide or pool-of-labor-force statistics, does not seem to me to require us to hold that the District Court erred as a matter of law in admitting them into evidence. * * *

* * *

Appellants, in order to rebut the prima facie case under the statute, had the burden placed on them to advance job-related reasons for the qualification. * * * Appellants argued only the job-relatedness of actual physical strength; they did not urge that an equally job-related qualification for prison guards is the *appearance* of strength. As the Court notes, the primary job of correctional counselor in Alabama prisons "is to maintain security and control of the inmates * * * ," a function that I at least would imagine is aided by the psychological impact on prisoners of the presence of tall and heavy guards. If the appearance of strength had been urged upon the District Court here as a reason for the height and weight minima, I think that the District Court would surely have been entitled to reach a different result than it did. For, even if not perfectly correlated, I would think that Title VII would not preclude a State from saying that anyone under 5'2" or 120 pounds, no matter how strong in fact, does not have a sufficient appearance of strength to be a prison guard.

* * * As appellants did not even present the "appearance of strength" contention to the District Court as an asserted job-related reason for the qualification requirements, I agree that their burden was not met. * * *

[The opinion of JUSTICE MARSHALL, with whom JUSTICE BRENNAN joins, concurring in part and dissenting in part, is omitted.]

Notes and Questions

1. In *Teamsters* and *Hazelwood*, the Court rejected the argument that § 703(j) of Title VII, 42 U.S.C. § 2000e–2(j), limits the use of statistical evidence.

a. Has the Court, in effect, nullified the substantive meaning of § 703(j)?

b. If the Court had accepted the employer's argument in *Teamsters* that § 703(j) should be construed to endorse a blanket rule that "statistics can never in and of themselves prove * * * discrimination, or even establish a prima facie case shifting to the employer the burden of rebutting the inference raised by the figures," would such a ruling have sounded the death knell for the disparate impact theory?

2. For a critique of the use of statistical evidence in employment discrimination cases, see Kingsley R. Browne, *Statistical Proof of Discrimination: Beyond "Damned Lies,"* 68 Wash.L.Rev. 477 (1993). Professor Browne argues that courts erroneously discount the role of chance as a cause of workforce disparities and erroneously assume that the workforce of a nondiscriminatory employer will "mirror the racial and sexual composition" of the relevant labor market. *Id.* at 482.

3. *Statistical Significance and Measurement of Adverse Impact*: Because both plaintiffs and defendants will normally submit statistical evidence, the prima facie case depends upon the relative quality of the evidence presented by the opposing parties. Statistical evidence is not probative unless it satisfies the statistical significance rule, that is, unless it supports the inference that a policy or practice has a significant effect on limiting the employment opportunities of a protected class. Statistical significance is a measure of the probability that a disparity is not simply due to chance rather than any other identifiable factor such as race or sex. The courts have allowed the use of a variety of approaches to determine whether a challenged employment practice has a significant adverse impact on the employment opportunities of protected classes.

a. *Gross disparities*: Gross statistical disparities alone, in some cases, may be sufficient to establish a prima facie case. For example, in *Teamsters*, note 23, the Supreme Court noted that the inability of the employer to rebut the inference of discrimination based on statistical evidence was not the result of the misuse of statistics but from the "inexorable zero," that is, the total absence of blacks and Hispanics from the at-issue jobs. Teamsters v. United States, 431 U.S. 324, 342 n. 23, 97 S.Ct. 1843, 1858 n. 23, 52 L.Ed.2d 396 (1977). *See also* EEOC v. American Nat'l Bank, 652 F.2d 1176, 1190 (4th Cir.1981) (focusing on the underrepresentation of blacks in office, clerical, and management jobs), *cert. denied*, 459 U.S. 923, 103 S.Ct. 235, 74 L.Ed.2d 186 (1982).

b. *Standard deviation*: One of the most widely accepted statistical methods of determining disparate impact is through application of the standard deviation formula. Standard deviation analysis is a professionally approved methodology used to determine whether observed differences in the racial or sexual composition of an employer's workforce occurred by chance, or whether an explanation other than chance, for example, race or sex, explains the differences. The Supreme Court sanctioned standard deviation analysis for employment discrimination cases in *Hazelwood*. *Castaneda v. Partida*, 430 U.S. 482, 97 S.Ct. 1272, 51 L.Ed.2d 498 (1977), cited approvingly in *Hazelwood*, was a jury discrimination case in which the Court endorsed standard deviation analysis. Courts often cite *Castaneda* to justify the use of standard deviation analysis in employment discrimination cases.

See Guardians Ass'n v. Civil Serv. Comm'n, 630 F.2d 79, 86 (2d Cir.1980), *cert. denied*, 452 U.S. 940, 101 S.Ct. 3083, 69 L.Ed.2d 954 (1981).

The standard deviation is a measure of spread, dispersion, or variability of a group of numbers. Generally, the fewer the number of standard deviations that separate an observed from a predicted result, the more likely it is that the observed disparity is not really a "disparity" at all, but rather a random or chance fluctuation. Conversely, the greater the number of standard deviations, the less likely it is that chance is the cause of any difference between the expected and observed results. A finding of two standard deviations corresponds approximately to a one in twenty, or five percent, chance that a disparity is merely a random deviation from the norm, and most social scientists accept two deviations as a threshold level of "statistical significance." *See* Cooper v. University of Tex. at Dallas, 482 F.Supp. 187, 194 (N.D.Tex.1979) (citing Norman H. Nie et al., SPSS: Statistical Package for the Social Sciences 222 (2d ed.1975)), *aff'd*, 648 F.2d 1039 (5th Cir.1981) (per curiam).

In *Kadas v. MCI Systemhouse*, 255 F.3d 359 (7th Cir.2001), the court noted that "[s]ome cases suggest that statistical evidence is not admissible to show discrimination unless it is significant at the conventional 5 percent significance level (that is, the coefficient of the relevant correlation is at least two standard deviations away from zero) * * *." Judge Posner explained that this means "unless there is no more than a 5 percent probability that a statistical correlation between the dependent variable * * * and the independent variable having legal significance * * * [which] we would observe even if the variable were uncorrelated in the population from which the sample was drawn." *Id*. Judge Posner also observed that "[t]he 5 percent test is arbitrary," and its acceptance is driven by scholarly concerns unrelated to the realities of litigation. According to Judge Posner, "[l]itigation generally is not fussy about evidence; much eyewitness and other nonquantitative evidence is subject to significant probability of error, yet no effort is made to exclude it if it doesn't satisfy some counterpart to the 5 percent significance test." *Id*. The admissibility of evidence, Judge Posner cautioned, is "different from the weight to be accorded to the significance of a particular correlation found by the study." *Id*.

c. *The four-fifths rule*: The *Uniform Guidelines* adopt a "four-fifths" rule for selection procedures:

> A selection rate for any race, sex, or ethnic group which is less than four-fifths (4/5) (or eighty percent) of the rate for the group with the highest rate will generally be regarded by Federal enforcement agencies as evidence of adverse impact, while a greater than four-fifths rate will generally not be regarded by Federal enforcement agencies as evidence of adverse impact.

29 C.F.R. § 1607.4D. Under the 80% rule, the failure of a protected group, such as blacks or women, to have a success rate which is at least 80% of the most successful group is considered evidence of disparate impact. *See* United States v. City of Chicago, 663 F.2d 1354, 1357 n.8 (7th Cir.1981) (en banc). *See also* Firefighters Inst. for Racial Equality v. City of St. Louis, 616 F.2d 350, 356–57 (8th Cir.1980), *cert. denied*, 452 U.S. 938, 101 S.Ct. 3079, 69 L.Ed.2d 951 (1981) (black selection rate was 7.1%, while the white selection

rate was 16.7%; thus the rate of selection of blacks was only 42.5% of the rate of selection of whites and substantially below the 80% rule established by the *Uniform Guidelines*); Thomas v. City of Evanston, 610 F.Supp. 422, 427–28 (N.D.Ill.1985) (selection rate of 1.18% for women applicants to the police department easily satisfied the 80% rule and proved adverse impact of physical exam). Some courts have applied the 80% rule fairly rigidly. *See, e.g.,* Bigby v. City of Chicago, 38 Fair Empl.Prac.Cas. (BNA) 844, 847 (N.D.Ill.1984) (adverse impact found for selection rates for promotion of black versus white police sergeants of 76% on cumulative scores and 78.5% on performance scores), *aff'd on other grounds,* 766 F.2d 1053 (7th Cir. 1985), *cert.denied sub nom.* Thoele v. City of Chicago, 474 U.S. 1056, 106 S.Ct. 793, 88 L.Ed.2d 771 (1986). Other courts have recognized that the four-fifths rule may lead to absurd results and, for this reason, have held that it is a rule of thumb which must be considered along with the sample size. Wilmore v. City of Wilmington, 533 F.Supp. 844, 853 (D.Del.1982). *See also* Elaine Shoben, *Differential Pass–Fail Rates in Employment Testing: Statistical Proof Under Title VII,* 91 Harv.L.Rev. 793, 805 (1978) (criticizing the 80% rule as ill-conceived because it fails to take account of differences in sample sizes).

d. *Multiple regression:* Multiple regression analysis is a relatively sophisticated statistical technique designed to estimate the effects of several independent variables on a single dependent variable. In the employment discrimination law context, it is used to measure the effect of factors such as race, sex, age, education, and experience on the outcome of an employment decision. *See* David C. Baldus & James W. L. Cole, Statistical Proof of Discrimination 357 (1980). The methodology has been used primarily in salary discrimination cases, especially cases involving professional positions, in which the claim is that blacks or women are paid less than similarly situated whites or males. *See, e.g.,* Sobel v. Yeshiva Univ., 839 F.2d 18, 21–22 (2d Cir.1988); Wilkins v. University of Houston, 654 F.2d 388 (5th Cir.1981). The Supreme Court endorsed the use of multiple regression in *Bazemore v. Friday,* 478 U.S. 385, 390–401, 106 S.Ct. 3000, 3004–09, 92 L.Ed.2d 315 (1986). For a further discussion of multiple regression, see Franklin M. Fisher, *Multiple Regression in Legal Proceedings,* 80 Colum.L.Rev. 702 (1980), and Michael O. Finkelstein, *The Judicial Recognition of Multiple Regression Studies in Race and Sex Discrimination Cases,* 80 Colum.L.Rev. 737 (1980).

4. *Relevant Labor Market: Hazelwood* introduced the notion that relevant labor market analysis is critical to fine-tuning statistical evidence for determining statistical significance. As a general proposition, the relevant labor market includes both the geographical area from which the employer draws its employees and the population in that area which has the qualifications for the at-issue jobs. Parties often disagree over how the relevant labor market should be defined. *See generally* David C. Baldus & James W. L. Cole, Statistical Proof of Discrimination §§ 4.1–.3 (1980). What was the relevant labor market for statistical purposes in *Griggs?* In *Teamsters?* In *Dothard?* Should the mobility of the work force be relevant in defining the relevant labor market? *See* Johnson v. Goodyear Tire & Rubber Co., 491 F.2d 1364 (5th Cir.1974) (yes).

5. *Lack of Interest Defense*: The lack of interest defense to a prima facie case of disparate impact discrimination is based on the argument that a statistically significant disparity in race or sex is not the result of race or sex discrimination, but the lack of interest by minorities or women in jobs in which they are underrepresented. A leading case endorsing the lack of interest defense is *EEOC v. Sears, Roebuck & Co.*, 628 F.Supp. 1264 (N.D.Ill.1986), *aff'd*, 839 F.2d 302 (7th Cir.1988). The case was brought on behalf of a class of women who claimed that Sears had discriminated against them by maintaining a sex-stratified sales force, with men dominating the higher paid, commissioned sales jobs for "big ticket" items such as home improvements, major appliances, furnaces, air conditioners, heating, and plumbing systems. Women, on the other hand, were concentrated in lower paid, noncommissioned jobs selling apparel, linens, towels, paint, and cosmetics. Sears convinced the court that the statistical evidence was not probative of sex discrimination because the sexual disparity was attributable to women's own preferences for noncompetitive work. In affirming the lower court's ruling in favor of Sears, the Seventh Circuit set forth the findings of the trial court:

> The [trial] court found that "[t]he most credible and convincing evidence offered at trial regarding women's interest in commission sales at Sears was the detailed, uncontradicted testimony of numerous men and women who were Sears store managers, personnel managers and other officials, regarding their efforts to recruit women into commission sales." These witnesses testified to their only limited success in affirmative action efforts to persuade women to sell on commission, and testified that women were generally more interested in product lines like clothing, jewelry, and cosmetics that were usually sold on a noncommissioned basis, than they were in product lines involving commission selling like automotive, roofing, and furnaces. The contrary applied to men. Women were also less interested in outside sales which often required night calls on customers than were men, with the exception of selling custom draperies. Various reason for women's lack of interest in commission selling included fear or dislike of what they perceived as cutthroat competition, and increased pressure and risk associated with commission sales. Noncommission selling, on the other hand, was associated with more social contact and friendship, less pressure and less risk. This evidence was confirmed by a study of national surveys and polls from the mid–1930's through 1983 regarding the changing status of women in American society, from which Sears' experts made conclusions regarding women's interest in commission selling; morale surveys of Sears employees, which the court found "demonstrate[] that noncommission saleswomen were generally happier with their present jobs at Sears, and were much less likely than their male counterparts to be interested in other positions, such as commission sales"; a job interest survey taken at Sears in 1976; a survey taken in 1982 of commission and noncommission salespeople at Sears regarding their attitudes, interests, and the personal beliefs and lifestyles of the employees, which the court concluded showed that noncommission salesmen were "far more interested" in commission sales than were noncommission saleswomen; and national labor force data.

Sears, 839 F.2d at 320–21. A detailed examination of *Sears* is found in Ruth Milkman, *Women's History and the* Sears *Case*, 12 Feminist Stud. 375 (1986).

The Supreme Court's decision in *Wards Cove Packing Co. v. Atonio*, 490 U.S. 642, 109 S.Ct. 2115, 104 L.Ed.2d 733 (1989), reproduced in this Chapter, offers support for the lack of interest defense. There, the Court rejected the plaintiffs' reliance upon the employer's workforce as the relevant statistical population because the minority employees on whose behalf the case was brought did not seek the jobs that were held by nonminority workers and because the plaintiffs offered no evidence that minority workers would have applied for jobs other than the ones in which they were employed.

Professors Vicki Schultz and Stephen Petterson, in *Race, Gender, Work, and Choice: An Empirical Study of the Lack of Interest Defense in Title VII Cases Challenging Job Segregation*, 59 U.Chi.L.Rev. 1073 (1992), did an analysis of the judicial treatment of the lack of interest defense in race and sex discrimination cases. The authors concluded that *Sears* was not an atypical case. The courts in almost half of the cases they examined concluded that sex segregation was attributable to women's own work preferences. The authors also found that between 1967 and 1977, the ten year period just after the enactment of Title VII, the courts more often than not rejected the lack of interest defense in race discrimination cases and seemed to assume that racial discrimination was a product of racial inequities in the work place. Since 1977, however, courts have been more apt to attribute racial segregation to the choices of minority workers. *See also* Vicki Schultz, *Telling Stories About Women and Work: Judicial Interpretations of Sex Segregation in the Workplace in Title VII Cases Raising the Lack of Interest Argument*, 103 Harv.L.Rev. 1749 (1990).

a. To what extent might the lack of interest defense be based on stereotypical assumptions about women? About blacks? About other minorities? What are those assumptions?

b. To what extent might unlawful discriminatory practices in the workplace such as sexual harassment, which is treated in Chapter 8, explain why women may be reluctant to seek jobs in traditionally male-dominated positions?

c. The district court in *Stender v. Lucky Stores, Inc.*, 803 F.Supp. 259 (N.D.Cal.1992), held that the lack of interest defense is limited to disparate impact claims and may not be asserted in disparate treatment cases? Do you agree?

6. For a discussion of the use of nonstatistical evidence in disparate impact cases, see Julia Lamber, *Alternatives to Challenged Employee Selection Criteria: The Significance of Nonstatistical Evidence in Disparate Impact Cases Under Title VII*, 1985 Wisc.L.Rev. 1 (1985).

7. The parties in employment discrimination litigation often rely heavily on a battery of expert witnesses on issues of liability (Stage I) and relief (Stage II). These experts may include statisticians, labor economists, sociologists, social psychologists, industrial psychologists, and a range of human relations professionals. Expert witness testimony from statisticians, labor

economists and industrial psychologists is of particular significance in disparate impact cases. What is "expert testimony" and when should a court let "experts" testify? One of the major problems is distinguishing between "expert testimony" and "junk science." One of the concerns about keeping "junk science" away from juries is that juries tend to believe anything a witness offered as an expert says and for that reason judges should protect impressionable jurors from hearing from so-called experts who lack objective credibility.

Until recently, federal (and state) courts deemed the controlling test on the admissibility of expert testimony to be the test set forth in *Frye v. United States*, 293 F. 1013 (D.C.Cir.1923). *Frye* held that scientific evidence must have gained general acceptance in the relevant community to be admissible. In a landmark 1993 case, *Daubert v. Merrell Dow Pharmaceuticals, Inc.*, 509 U.S. 579, 113 S.Ct. 2786, 125 L.Ed.2d 469 (1993), the Supreme Court held that the *Frye* test had been superseded by the Federal Rules of Evidence and that expert testimony could be admitted if the district court deemed it both relevant and reliable. In rejecting the *Frye* test, *Daubert* allows for new and innovative expert testimony to be used that might not yet have gained general acceptance in the relevant community. *Daubert* placed the responsibility on trial courts to distinguish between scientific evidence that is based on flawed methodology and that which is not. This is now called the "gatekeeping function."

After *Daubert*, a split developed in the circuits over whether *Daubert* applies only to scientific testimony or whether it applies to all testimony, regardless of whether it was "scientific" in nature. The Supreme Court resolved the split in *Kumho Tire Co. v. Carmichael*, 526 U.S. 137, 119 S.Ct. 1167 143 L.Ed.2d 238 (1999). *Kumho Tire* announced the general proposition that *Daubert* applies to all expert testimony, not just scientific testimony: " * * * *Daubert*'s general holding—setting forth the trial judge's gatekeeping obligation—applies not only to testimony based on scientific knowledge, but also to testimony based on technical and other specialized knowledge." 119 S.Ct. at 1171. The Court in *Kumho Tire* based its reasoning on Federal Rule of Evidence 702. Rule 702 permits all experts to offer opinion testimony, regardless of whether they are "scientific" opinions, and deems the distinction between "scientific knowledge" and "technical or other specialized knowledge" to be illusory, without support in the federal rules. *See Kumho Tire*, 119 S.Ct. at 1174.

Since *Daubert*, it has become commonplace for the parties in employment discrimination litigation to challenge some or all of the expert witness evidence of the opposing parties at trial or in pre-trial *Daubert* motions. *See generally* John V. Jansonius & Andrew M. Gould, *Expert Testimony in Employment Litigation: The Role of Reliability Addressing Admissibility*, 50 Baylor L.Rev. 267 (1998).

Note: Statistical Evidence and Individual Disparate Treatment Claims

In *McDonnell Douglas v. Green*, the Court held that statistical evidence can be probative in individual disparate treatment cases. And in *Hazelwood*, the Court held that "gross statistical disparities * * * alone may in a proper case constitute prima facie evidence of a pattern or practice of discrimination." 433 U.S. at 307–08, 97 S.Ct. at 2741 (citing *Teamsters*). Suppose a plaintiff brings a disparate treatment employment discrimination case alleging that she was denied a promotion because she is a woman. The employer's promotion decisions are based solely on unwritten subjective criteria. The plaintiff's only evidence of discrimination is statistical proof of a substantial disparity between the percentage of females in high-level salaried positions and the overall percentage of females working in the plaintiff's unit of the company. Should this evidence be sufficient to establish a prima facie case of sex discrimination? *See* Davis v. Califano, 613 F.2d 957 (D.C.Cir.1979) (statistics alone may establish a prima facie case of discrimination in an individual disparate treatment action); *but see* Taylor v. Secretary of the Army, 583 F.Supp. 1503 (D.C.Md.1984) (declining to follow *Davis* for individual claims of disparate treatment).

There is some suggestion in other cases that statistical evidence standing alone may establish a prima facie case in individual disparate treatment cases based on circumstantial evidence. The reasoning is grounded on the view that a plaintiff is not required to produce direct evidence and may rely upon circumstantial evidence. *See, e.g.*, Denison v. Swaco Geolograph Co., 941 F.2d 1416 (10th Cir.1991); Arnold v. United States Postal Serv., 863 F.2d 994 (D.C.Cir.1988); Shidaker v. Tisch, 833 F.2d 627 (7th Cir.1986). The general rule appears to be, however, that gross statistical evidence alone is insufficient; the plaintiff also must put on evidence of a causal connection between the statistics and the particular adverse employment practice from which the plaintiff seeks relief. For example, in *Walls v. Petersburg*, 895 F.2d 188 (4th Cir.1990), the plaintiff, a black female, was discharged for refusing to complete a background questionnaire which asked about arrest and conviction records of members of the employee's family, her marriages and divorces, and homosexual conduct. She presented statistics showing that the questions were more likely to elicit negative answers from blacks than from whites. The court held that the statistical evidence was insufficient to establish a prima facie case because she failed to put on evidence of a causal relationship between the statistical evidence and her discharge. *See also* LeBlanc v. Great Am. Ins. Co., 6 F.3d 836 (1st Cir.1993); Gadson v. Concord Hosp., 966 F.2d 32 (1st Cir.1992); Smith v. Horner, 839 F.2d 1530, 1536 n. 8 (11th Cir.1988) (statistics are relevant but cannot alone establish a prima facie case of individual disparate treatment). *See generally* Ginny Conlan, Comment, *Recent Cases—Davis v. Califano*, 49 U.Cin.L.Rev. 495 (1980).

In *Estes v. Dick Smith Ford, Inc.*, 856 F.2d 1097 (8th Cir.1988), the plaintiff, a black man, brought an individual disparate treatment claim of race discrimination. The trial court excluded the plaintiff's statistical evidence concerning the racial composition of the employer's workforce on the ground that it was not material since the plaintiff was not bringing a disparate impact claim. The Eighth Circuit reversed on the ground that the jury might have evaluated plaintiff's claim of intentional racial discrimination differently had he been allowed to present evidence that, from 1978 to 1983, the 153 new employees hired included no blacks and the workforce of 214 employees previously hired included only four blacks.

D. THE BUSINESS NECESSITY DEFENSE

Although there was no explicit statutory support for the business necessity defense prior to 1991, the legislative history suggests that Congress did not want Title VII to be construed as allowing an undue infringement upon the efficiency and productivity of businesses. In fact, the provision in Title VII on ability testing, § 703(h), 42 U.S.C. § 2000e–2(h), was included in response to a state administrative ruling which had struck down an employment test on the ground that it was culturally biased against blacks. Section 703(h) provides, *inter alia*:

> nor shall it be an unlawful employment practice for an employer to give and act upon the results of any professionally developed ability test provided that such test, its administration or action upon the results is not designed, intended or used to discriminate because of race, color, religion, sex or national origin.

Because of concern about the potential adverse effects of Title VII enforcement on the efficiency and productivity of businesses, Congress did not give the EEOC authority to issue cease and desist orders. *See* Note, *Business Necessity under Title VII of the Civil Rights Act of 1964: A No–Alternative Approach*, 84 Yale L.J. 98, 104–05 & 105 n.33 (1974).

The doctrinal foundations of the business necessity defense were established in the early Title VII seniority discrimination cases. Quarles v. Philip Morris, Inc., 279 F.Supp. 505 (E.D.Va.1968), was among the first cases decided under Title VII and involved a claim challenging a racially segregated seniority system. The plaintiffs, black employees, challenged the continuing effects of a previously segregated seniority and promotion system that the employer and union had adopted prior to the effective date of Title VII. The defendants had ceased their overt racially discriminatory practices in January 1966, but the effects of their previously overtly racially discriminatory seniority and promotion practices continued after that date. The defendants relied upon, *inter alia,* a NLRB case, Whitfield v. United Steelworkers of America, Local No. 2708, 263 F.2d 546 (5th Cir.1959), *cert. denied*, 360 U.S. 902, 79 S.Ct. 1285, 3 L.Ed.2d 1254 (195), in which the Labor Board, on facts similar to *Quarles*, had refused to allow black employees to transfer immediately to previously racially segregated white jobs under a collective bargaining agreement on the grounds that the black employees were not sufficiently qualified, without prior training, to perform the jobs. The court, in *Quarles*, however, ordered the defendants, including the union, to transfer plaintiffs to jobs historically reserved for white employees. The court distinguished *Whitfield* on the ground that, in *Whitfield*, "[b]usiness necessity, not racial discrimination, dictated the limited transfer privileges in *Whitfield*." *Id.* at 518. In an important case decided by the then-Fifth Circuit, Papermakers and Paperworkers Local 189 v. United States, 416 F.2d 980 (5th Cir.1969), *cert. denied*, 397 U.S. 919, 90 S.Ct. 926, 25 L.Ed.2d 100 (1970), the court held that "[w]hen an employer and union have discriminated in the past and when its present policies renew or exaggerate discriminatory effects, those policies must yield, unless there is an overriding legitimate nonracial business purpose." *Id*. at 989. Relying in part on *Quarles*, the court in *Local 189* further held that "facially neutral but needlessly restrictive tests may not be imposed where they perpetuate the effects of previous racial discrimination." *Id*. at 991. The plaintiff, in *Griggs*, relied upon *Local 189* and *Quarles* in their brief in the Supreme Court. Petitioner's Opening Brief, at 16, 26, 26, 28, Griggs v. Duke Power Co., 401 U.S. 424, 91 S.Ct. 849, 28 L.Ed.2d 158 (1971) (No. 124).

Prior to the Supreme Court's 1989 decision in *Wards Cove Packing Co. v. Atonio*, 490 U.S. 642, 109 S.Ct. 2115, 104 L.Ed.2d 733, the courts treated the business necessity defense as an affirmative defense, thus imposing upon the employer both the burden of production of evidence and the burden of persuasion on this issue. *See id*. at 660, 109 S.Ct. at 2126; *id*. at 668 & n.14, 109 S.Ct. at 2131 & n.14 (Stevens, J., dissenting). Assuming the plaintiff has no evidence of an alternative practice that would equally well serve the needs of the employer, when a defendant successfully meets its burden of proving business necessity, its challenged employment practice is not unlawful discrimination even if the practice has a substantial adverse impact on the employment opportunities of a protected class. For example, in *EEOC v. Carolina Freight Carriers Corp.*, 723 F.Supp. 734 (S.D.Fla.1989), the court held that an employer satisfied the business necessity defense in support of its policy of refusing to hire felons convicted of theft-related crimes as full-time drivers. The employer justified the policy on the grounds that the company incurred large annual losses from theft and that it was reasonable to rely upon past histories of employees as a proxy for trustworthiness.

In the eighteen-year period between *Griggs* and *Wards Cove*, the proper interpretation of the business necessity defense became a major issue because the Supreme Court articulated different standards in a series of employment discrimination cases. Re-examine *Griggs*, in which the Court stated that the "touchstone" of an employer's defense of its employment practices is "business necessity." In the same paragraph, the Court also seems to have endorsed a "job relatedness" test: the employer's facially neutral practices must "be shown to be related to job performance."

In the early post-*Griggs* cases, the lower courts adopted a stringent standard on business necessity. For example, the Fourth Circuit required employers to prove that a challenged practice was *essential* to the operation of their businesses:

> Collectively these cases [*Griggs*; Local 189, United Papermakers & Paperworkers v. United States, 416 F.2d 980 (5th Cir.1969), *cert. denied*, 397 U.S. 919, 90 S.Ct. 926, 25 L.Ed.2d 100 (1970); Jones v. Lee Way Motor Freight, 431 F.2d 245 (10th Cir.1970)] conclusively establish that the applicable test is not merely whether there exists

a business purpose for adhering to a challenged practice. The test is whether there exists an overriding legitimate business purpose such that the practice is necessary to the safe and efficient operation of the business. Thus, the business purpose must be sufficiently compelling to override any racial impact; the challenged practice must effectively carry out the business purpose it is alleged to serve; and there must be available no acceptable alternative policies or practices which could better accomplish the business purpose advanced, or accomplish it equally well with a lesser differential racial impact.

Robinson v. Lorillard Corp., 444 F.2d 791, 798 (4th Cir.), *cert. dismissed*, 404 U.S. 1006, 92 S.Ct. 573, 30 L.Ed.2d 655 (1971). Subsequently, in the wake of later Supreme Court decisions, the lower courts began to retreat from a strict test of business necessity, as described in the case that follows.

CONTRERAS v. CITY OF LOS ANGELES

United States Court of Appeals for the Ninth Circuit, 1981.
656 F.2d 1267, *cert. denied*, 455 U.S. 1021, 102 S.Ct. 1719, 72 L.Ed.2d 140 (1982).

WALLACE, Circuit Judge.

Certain former and present city workers (appellants) appeal from the district court's judgment that they are entitled to no relief under Title VII of the Civil Rights Act of 1964 and 42 U.S.C. § 1981, for having lost their jobs by failing allegedly discriminatory civil service examinations. We affirm.

* * *

Statistical disparities alone may constitute prima facie proof of discrimination. Although the prima facie case requirement is not automatically satisfied by statistical evidence of adverse impact, we hold that a prima facie case is established when such evidence of discriminatory impact is completely uncontroverted. Accordingly, we reverse the district court's ruling that Gonzalez failed to establish prima facie discrimination. We must therefore determine whether the City met its burden of proving that the auditor examination was job related.

III

A. The Employer's Burden of Proof Under Title VII

* * * The question before us is: what must an employer show to meet its burden of proving that pre-employment test[s], having a disproportionate, adverse impact on a racial minority, are sufficiently justified by business need to survive a Title VII challenge?

* * *

The Supreme Court first considered an employer's duty under Title VII in *Griggs v. Duke Power Co.* and concluded that "Congress has placed on the employer the burden of showing that any given requirement must have a manifest relationship to the employment in question." 401 U.S. at 432, 91 S.Ct. at 854. *Griggs* suggests that the Court perceived "business necessity" to be the same standard as "job-related," and viewed both as requiring only that an employer prove that his employment practices are legitimately related to job performance * * *. *Id.* at 431, 91 S.Ct. at 853.

Four years after the *Griggs* decision, the Supreme Court answered the very question considered by us today: "What must an employer show to establish that pre-employment tests racially discriminatory in effect, though not in intent, are sufficiently 'job related' to survive challenge under Title VII?" Albemarle Paper Co. v. Moody, 422 U.S. at 408, 95 S. Ct. at 2367. The employer in *Albemarle* attempted to justify its use of aptitude tests that disproportionately excluded blacks by employing an expert to "validate" the tests in terms of job-relatedness. Various defects in the validation study convinced the Supreme Court that the employer had failed to satisfy its burden of proof. Significantly, however, the Court did not interpret Title VII as requiring employer proof of a strong form of "business necessity." Indeed, the Court in *Albemarle* never used the term "business necessity." Rather, the Court "clarified" the "standard of proof for job relatedness," by articulating a standard that is "the same as that of the *Griggs* case—that discriminatory tests are impermissible unless shown, by professionally acceptable methods, to be 'predictive of or significantly correlated with important elements of work behavior which comprise or are relevant to the job or jobs for which the candidates are being evaluated.'" *Id.* at 431, 95 S.Ct. at 2378, *quoting* 29 C.F.R. § 1607.4(c). It was this articulation of an employer's Title VII burden that we relied upon in *Craig.*

We now turn to the troublesome Supreme Court language that appears in *Dothard v. Rawlinson*, 433 U.S. 321, 97 S.Ct. 2720, 53 L.Ed.2d 786 (1977). *Dothard* invalidated a height and weight requirement for prison guards that disproportionately excluded women applicants and was not proven to be "job-related." In doing so, the Court required employer proof identical to that required in its earlier cases: "the employer must meet 'the burden of showing that any given requirement [has] * * * a manifest relationship to the employment in question.'" *Id.* at 329, 97 S.Ct. at 2727 (quoting *Griggs*). Although the holding tracks prior Supreme Court cases, an unnecessary footnote contains the few words that cause our present difficulty: "a discriminatory employment practice must be shown to be necessary to safe and efficient job performance to survive a Title VII challenge." *Id.* at 332 n.14, 97 S.Ct. at 2728 n.14. This footnote formulation is belied by the broader standard applied in the *Dothard* text.

Since *Dothard*, the Court has indicated that the *Griggs/Albemarle* standard, rather than the *Dothard* footnote, controls Title VII inquiries. In *New York Transit Authority v. Beazer*, 440 U.S. 568, 99 S.Ct. 1355, 59 L.Ed.2d 587 (1979), the plaintiffs challenged a Transit Authority (TA) refusal to hire narcotics users, specifically methadone users. The Court stated:

> Respondents recognize, and the findings of the District Court establish, that TA's legitimate employment goals of safety and efficiency require that exclusion of all users of illegal narcotics, barbiturates, and amphetamines, and of a majority of all methadone users. The District Court also held that those goals require the exclusion of all methadone users from the 25% of its positions that are "safety sensitive." Finally, the District Court noted that those goals are significantly served by—*even if they do not require*—TA's rule as it applies to all methadone users including those who are seeking employment in nonsafety-sensitive positions. *The record thus demonstrates that TA's rule bears a "manifest relationship to the employment in question." Griggs*, 401 U.S. at 432, 91 S.Ct. at 854.

Id., 440 U.S. at 587 n.31, 99 S.Ct. at 1366 n.31 (emphasis added). Thus, the Court's most recent application of the employer's Title VII burden of proof not only follows the standards set forth in *Griggs* and *Albemarle*, but implicitly approves employment practices that significantly serve, but are neither required by nor necessary to, the employer's legitimate business interests.

* * * We hold that discriminatory tests are impermissible unless shown, by professionally accepted methods, to be predictive of or significantly correlated with important elements of work behavior that comprise or are relevant to the job or jobs for which candidates are being evaluated.

B. VALIDATION OF THE AUDITOR EXAMINATION

* * *

To satisfy [the business necessity test the court adopts in this case], examinations such as the one used by the City to hire auditors must be " 'validated' in terms of job performance." Washington v. Davis, 426 U.S. 229, 247, 96 S.Ct. 2040, 2051, 48 L.Ed.2d 597 (1976). Title VII requires no single method of examination validation, but only that the method chosen be professionally acceptable. * * *

In [*Craig v. County of Los Angeles, 626 F.2d 659* (9th Cir.1980*)*], we established a three-step procedure for validation of examinations used to select employees from among a group of applicants:

> The employer must first specify the particular trait or characteristic which the selection device is being used to identify or measure. The employer must then determine that that particular trait or characteristic is an important element of work behavior. Finally, the employer must demonstrate by "professionally acceptable methods" that the selection device is "predictive of or significantly correlated" with the element of work behavior identified in the second step.

626 F.2d at 662 (quoting *Albemarle*). Applying the *Craig* procedure to the facts of this case, we conclude that the City successfully validated the auditor examination in terms of job-relatedness.

The City's validation of the auditor examination consisted of two phases: a job-analysis phase and an examination-review phase. In the job-analysis phase, a number of auditors and auditor supervisors employed in various civil service positions throughout the city were organized as a group of job experts for the purpose of determining what skill, knowledge, and ability was essential to the position of auditor. These job experts held four meetings. * * * The final product of these meetings, a compilation of elements critical to the position of auditor, weighted according to their relative importance, was used by the City's examining division to create the 100–question auditor examination.

The examination review phase of the City's validation study occurred after the applicants had taken the examination. In this phase, a new group of job experts was selected from among civil service auditors and supervisors employed by the City. These experts individually reviewed each question and decided if it tested one of the critical elements identified in the first phase. * * * As a result of this procedure, all but five questions were determined to be job related.

This validation study satisfies our three-step procedure set forth in *Craig v. County of Los Angeles*. First, the initial meetings during the job-analysis phase specified the particular trait or characteristic which was to be measured by the examination. Second, the last two meetings during the job-analysis phase determined which characteristics or traits were important elements of the auditor position. Third, the examination-review phase demonstrated that the auditor examination was significantly correlated with those elements of work behavior identified in the job-analysis phase.

As mentioned earlier, a key requirement of this third step, a requirement essential to proof of job relatedness generally, is that the validation method be professionally acceptable. At trial, the City produced expert testimony that its validation procedures met professional standards. Gonzalez produced expert testimony that the procedures were professionally unacceptable. The district judge resolved this conflict of testimony in favor of the City's expert, not only by ruling that the examinations were job related, but also by resolving every testimonial dispute between these experts in favor of the City. We will not disturb such a credibility determination.

* * *

IV

"If an employer [meets] the burden of proving that its tests are 'job related,' it remains open to the complaining party to show that other tests or selection devices, without a similarly undesirable racial effect, would also serve the employer's legitimate interest in 'efficient and trustworthy workmanship.' "*Albemarle Paper Co.*, 422 U.S. at 425, 95 S.Ct. at 2375 (quoting *McDonnell Douglas*). Gonzalez contends that the auditor examination, even if job related, violates Title VII because the City could have effectively screened auditor applicants by use of less discriminatory oral interviews. In making this contention, Gonzalez cites extensively from *Crockett v. Green*, 388 F.Supp. 912, 919–21 (E.D.Wis. 1975), *aff'd*, 534 F.2d 715 (7th Cir.1976), a case which places upon the employer the burden of proving that no alternative screening device was available. The district court opinion in *Crockett*, which was rendered before the Supreme Court's decision in *Albemarle Paper Co. v. Moody*, clearly misallocates the burden of proof. Once an employer has shown a selection device to be job related, it becomes the plaintiff's responsibility to prove that a less discriminatory alternative would satisfy the employer's hiring needs. With the burden of proof properly allocated in this case, we agree with the district court's conclusion that Gonzalez failed to prove the existence of less-discriminatory screening devices that would have satisfied the City's civil service hiring needs.

The only evidence produced by Gonzalez to establish the existence of alternative auditor selection methods was expert testimony that Spanish-surnamed individuals generally do better in oral interviews than on written examinations and that oral examinations could be used to screen applicants. However, even if the district court accepted this testimony as establishing that oral interviews have a less disparate impact on minorities, it does not satisfy Gonzalez' burden of proving that oral interviews, as an alternative to written examinations, would satisfy the City's civil service hiring needs. That oral interviews were used in the past to hire auditors for the Mayor's office, a fact upon which Gonzalez relies, does not prove that such interviews would satisfy the merit hiring requirements of the new civil service division. Evidence in the record reveals that the oral interviews previously used were designed to meet the special needs of the Mayor's office, not those of a civil service classification. Moreover, that oral interviews were used to screen applicants in other job categories transferred out of the Mayor's office at the same time that the auditor position was transferred, another fact upon which Gonzalez relies, does not prove that such interviews would have satisfied the auditor-hiring needs of the new department. As the district court correctly concluded, Gonzalez did not prove that a less discriminatory alternative was available.

* * *

Notes and Questions

1. Based on a review of post-*Griggs* cases, the Ninth Circuit adopted a test of business necessity that is substantially less stringent than the earlier cases, such as *Robinson v. Lorillard*, had enunciated.

2. *Validation*: Validation is a process for determining whether a selection procedure actually predicts successful job performance. There is no single validation methodology. The *Uniform Guidelines*, which are based on professional standards adopted by the American Psychological Association, accept three basic methods of validation: (1) "empirical" or "criterion" validation (demonstrated by identifying criteria that indicate successful job

performance and then correlating test scores to performance criteria); (2) "construct" validation (demonstrated by examinations that measure the degree to which job applicants have identifiable characteristics that have been determined to be important in successful job performance); and (3) "content" validation (demonstrated by tests with contents that closely approximate tasks to be performed on the job). *Uniform Guidelines*, 29 C.F.R. § 1607.5 (1989).

3. *Sliding-Scale Approach*: In *Spurlock v. United Airlines, Inc.*, 475 F.2d 216 (10th Cir.1972), a race discrimination case, the Tenth Circuit held that a college degree is related to the job of airline flight officer. The court adopted a sliding-scale approach to validation:

> When a job requires a small amount of skill and training and the consequences of hiring an unqualified applicant are insignificant, the courts should examine closely any pre-employment standard or criterion which discriminates against minorities. In such a case, the defendant should have a heavy burden to demonstrate to the court's satisfaction that his employment criteria are job-related. On the other hand, when the job clearly requires a high degree of skill and the economic and human risks involved in hiring an unqualified applicant are great, the employer bears a correspondingly lighter burden to show that his employment criteria are job related. * * * The courts, therefore, should proceed with great caution before requiring an employer to lower his pre-employment standards for such a job.

475 F.2d at 219. Other courts have endorsed the *Spurlock* sliding-scale approach. *See* Davis v. City of Dallas, 777 F.2d 205, 213 & n. 7 (5th Cir.1985) (collecting cases), *cert. denied*, 476 U.S. 1116, 106 S.Ct. 1972, 90 L.Ed.2d 656 (1986).

4. *Differential Validation*: The differential validation theory recognizes that a test may accurately predict the probability of successful job performance for one race but may underpredict for another race. The theory is based on the well-documented fact that blacks as a class generally do less well on general ability and other aptitude tests, including those used in employment selection. *See generally* Mark Kelman, *Concepts of Discrimination in "General Ability" Job Testing*, 104 Harv.L.Rev. 1157 (1991). The 1966 and 1970 EEOC *Guidelines on Testing* endorsed differential validation, requiring employers to conduct separate validation studies for minorities and nonminorities. *See* United States v. City of Chicago, 549 F.2d 415, 433 (7th Cir.) (requiring differential validation), *cert. denied sub nom.* Arado v. United States, 434 U.S. 875, 98 S.Ct. 225, 54 L.Ed.2d 155 (1977); Cormier v. PPG Indus., Inc., 519 F.Supp. 211, 262 (W.D.La.1981) (rejecting differential validation). The Supreme Court endorsed differential validation in *Albemarle Paper Co. v. Moody*, 422 U.S. 405, 435, 95 S.Ct. 2362, 2380, 45 L.Ed.2d 280 (1975). The *Uniform Guidelines*, however, eliminated the requirement for differential validation in 1979 and replaced it with a requirement of "unfairness" studies. 29 C.F.R. § 1607.14B(8) (1989).

5. *Race-Norming*: Differential validation is a form of race-norming. A test is race-normed if a black person who scored in the 75th percentile of black test-takers is reported as having received the same score as a white person who scored in the 75th percentile of white test-takers, even though

the white test-taker received a higher raw score. *See* Kelman, *supra,* at 1192 n.91. Congress prohibited race-norming in the Civil Rights Act of 1991 by making it a violation of Title VII to "adjust the scores of employment related tests on the basis of race, color, religion, sex, or national origin." Section 703(*l*), 42 U.S.C. § 2000e–2(*l*). The history leading to Congressional banning of race-norming is discussed in Kelman, *supra,* at 1204–06.

6. *Judicial Notice of Established Presumptions*: In some cases, courts have been willing to take judicial notice that certain employment criteria presumptively satisfy the business necessity defense. For example, in *Aguilera v. Cook County Police and Corrections Merit Board*, 760 F.2d 844 (7th Cir.), *cert. denied*, 474 U.S. 907, 106 S.Ct. 237, 88 L.Ed.2d 238 (1985), the court ruled that "there has been enough judicial and professional experience with educational requirements in law enforcement to establish a presumption in civil rights cases that a high school requirement is an appropriate requirement for anyone who is going to be a [police or corrections] officer," and that employers should not be required to prove "over and over again" that such requirements are necessary for such jobs. *Id.* at 847–48.

7. *Alternative Employment Practices*: *Contreras* is one of the few cases to reach the issue of acceptable alternative employment practices. Most disparate impact cases are decided on the basis of either the sufficiency of the plaintiff's evidence establishing a prima facie case of adverse impact or the sufficiency of the defendant's evidence proving business necessity. In *Gillespie v. State of Wisconsin*, 771 F.2d 1035, 1045 (7th Cir.1985), the court rejected plaintiff's "bare assertion" that the employer could have used a short-answer essay examination, a multiple-choice test, or even a commercially developed test as an alternative to the challenged written examination.

a. Consider the following: Since 1945, the South Carolina Board of Education has based public school teachers' salaries on the scores they receive on the National Teachers Examination (NTE). Teachers are permitted to take the NTE an unlimited number of times. A disproportionate number of black teachers receive low scores on the NTE and as a result receive lower salaries than white teachers. Assume that the disparate impact of the NTE requirement can be shown and that the school board can establish its defense of business necessity. Can the plaintiffs meet their burden of proving a less discriminatory alternative method of establishing teachers' salaries if they show that incumbent teachers are evaluated once every three years in a joint session between the teacher and principal, the evaluations are reduced to writing, the evaluations are entirely subjective, and the conclusions about the teachers' performance range from outstanding to unacceptable? *See* Newman v. Crews, 651 F.2d 222 (4th Cir.1981).

b. The City of Atlanta has adopted a facially neutral policy that requires all fire fighter employees be clean-shaven or a no-beard rule. Many blacks suffer from a bacterial disorder that is aggravated when they shave. If they bring an action under the disparate impact theory, they can easily prove a prima facie case. The City asserts a safety justification for the no-beard rule: one of the pieces of equipment fire fighters must wear over their face when fighting a fire requires the removal of all facial hair in order for the equipment to fit properly. Assume that the City satisfies its obligation with respect to the business necessity defense, what possible reasonable alternative proposal might the black fire fighter advance? See Fitzpatrick v. City of Atlanta, 2 F.3d 1112 (11th Cir.1993).

E. THE BOTTOM–LINE DEFENSE

CONNECTICUT v. TEAL

Supreme Court of the United States, 1982.
457 U.S. 440, 102 S.Ct. 2525, 73 L.Ed.2d 130.

JUSTICE BRENNAN delivered the opinion of the Court.

We consider here whether an employer sued for violation of Title VII of the Civil Rights Act of 1964 may assert a "bottom-line" theory of defense. Under that theory, as asserted in this case, an employer's acts of racial discrimination in promotions—effected by an examination having disparate impact—would not render the employer liable for the racial discrimination suffered by employees barred from promotion if the "bottom-line" result of the promotional process was an appropriate racial balance. We hold that the "bottom line" does not preclude respondent employees from establishing a prima facie case, nor does it provide petitioner employer with a defense to such a case.

I

Four of the respondents, Winnie Teal, Rose Walker, Edith Latney, and Grace Clark, are black employees of the Department of Income Maintenance of the State of Connecticut. Each was promoted provisionally to the position of Welfare Eligibility Supervisor and served in that capacity for almost two years. To attain permanent status as supervisors, however, respondents had to participate in a selection process that required, as the first step, a passing score on a written examination. This written test was administered on December 2, 1978, to 329 candidates. Of these candidates, 48 identified themselves as black and 259 identified themselves as white. The results of the examination were announced in March 1979. With the passing score set at 65,[3] 54.17 percent of the identified black candidates passed. This was approximately 68 percent of the passing rate for the identified white candidates.[4] The four respon-

---

3. The mean score on the examination was 70.4 percent. However, because the black candidates had a mean score 6.7 percentage points lower than the white candidates, the passing score was set at 65, apparently in an attempt to lessen the disparate impact of the examination.

4. The following table shows the passing rates of various candidate groups:

Candidate Group	Number	No. Receiving Passing Score	Passing Rate (%)
Black	48	26	54.17
Hispanic	4	3	75.00
Indian	3	2	66.67
White	259	206	79.54
Unidentified	15	9	60.00
Total	329	246	74.77

dents were among the blacks who failed the examination, and they were thus excluded from further consideration for permanent supervisory positions. In April 1979, respondents instituted this action in the United States District Court for the District of Connecticut against petitioners, the State of Connecticut, two state agencies, and two state officials. Respondents alleged, *inter alia*, that petitioners violated Title VII by imposing, as an absolute condition for consideration for promotion, that applicants pass a written test that excluded blacks in disproportionate numbers and that was not job related.

More than a year after this action was instituted, and approximately one month before trial, petitioners made promotions from the eligibility list generated by the written examination. In choosing persons from that list, petitioners considered past work performance, recommendations of the candidates' supervisors and, to a lesser extent, seniority. Petitioners then applied what the Court of Appeals characterized as an affirmative-action program in order to ensure a significant number of minority supervisors. Forty-six persons were promoted to permanent supervisory positions, 11 of whom were black and 35 of whom were white. The overall result of the selection process was that, of the 48 identified black candidates who participated in the selection process, 22.9 percent were promoted and of the 259 identified white candidates, 13.5 percent were promoted.[6] It is this "bottom-line" result, more favorable to blacks than to whites, that petitioners urge should be adjudged to be a complete defense to respondents' suit.

After trial, the District Court entered judgment for petitioners. The court treated respondents' claim as one of disparate impact. * * * However, the court found that, although the comparative passing rates for the examination indicated a prima facie case of adverse impact upon minorities, the result of the entire hiring process reflected no such adverse impact. Holding that these "bottom-line" percentages precluded the finding of a Title VII violation, the court held that the employer was not required to demonstrate that the promotional examination was job related. The United States Court of Appeals for the Second Circuit reversed, holding that the District Court erred in ruling that the results of the written examination alone were insufficient to support a prima facie case of disparate impact in violation of Title VII. The Court of Appeals stated that where "an identifiable pass-fail barrier denies an employment opportunity to a disproportionately large number of minorities and prevents them from proceeding to the next step in the selection process," that barrier must be shown to be job related. We granted certiorari, and now affirm.

Petitioners do not contest the District Court's implicit finding that the examination itself resulted in disparate impact under the "eighty percent rule" of the Uniform Guidelines on Employee Selection Procedures adopted by the Equal Employment Opportunity Commission. Those guidelines provide that a selection rate that "is less than [80 percent] of the rate for the group with the highest rate will generally be regarded * * * as evidence of adverse impact." 29 C.F.R. § 1607.4D (1981).

6. The actual promotion rate of blacks was thus close to 170 percent that of the actual promotion rate of whites.

II

A

We must first decide whether an examination that bars a disparate number of black employees from consideration for promotion, and that has not been shown to be job related, presents a claim cognizable under Title VII. * * *

Respondents base their claim on * * * *Griggs v. Duke Power Co.* * * *.

* * *

Petitioners' examination, which barred promotion and had a discriminatory impact on black employees, clearly falls within the literal language of § 703(a) (2), as interpreted by *Griggs*. The statute speaks, not in terms of jobs and promotions, but in terms of *limitations* and *classifications* that would deprive any individual of employment *opportunities*.[9] A disparate-impact claim reflects the language of § 703(a) (2) and Congress' basic objectives in enacting that statute: "to achieve equality of employment *opportunities* and remove barriers that have operated in the past to favor an identifiable group of white employees over other employees." *Griggs*, 401 U.S. at 429–30, 91 S.Ct. at 852–53 (emphasis added). When an employer uses a nonjob-related barrier in order to deny a minority or woman applicant employment or promotion, and that barrier has a significant adverse effect on minorities or women, then the applicant has been deprived of an employment *opportunity* "because of * * * race, color, religion, sex, or national origin." In other words, § 703(a) (2) prohibits discriminatory "artificial, arbitrary, and unnecessary barriers to employment," 401 U.S. at 431, 91 S.Ct. at 853, that "limit * * * or classify * * * applicants for employment * * * in any way which would deprive or tend to deprive any individual of employment *opportunities*." (Emphasis added.)

* * *

In short, the District Court's dismissal of respondents' claim cannot be supported on the basis that respondents failed to establish a prima facie case of employment discrimination under the terms of § 703(a) (2). The suggestion that disparate impact should be measured only at the bottom line ignores the fact that Title VII guarantees these individual respondents the *opportunity* to compete equally with white workers on the basis of job-related criteria. Title VII strives to achieve equality of opportunity by rooting out "artificial, arbitrary, and unnecessary" employer-created barriers to professional development that have a discriminatory impact upon individuals. Therefore, respondents' rights under § 703(a) (2) have been violated, unless petitioners can demonstrate that the examination given was not an artificial, arbitrary, or unnecessary

9. In contrast, the language of § 703(a) (1), 42 U.S.C. § 2000e–2(a) (1), if it were the only protection given to employees and applicants under Title VII, might support petitioners' exclusive focus on the overall result. That subsection makes it an unlawful employment practice to fail or refuse to hire or to discharge any individual, or otherwise to discriminate against any individual with respect to his compensation, terms, conditions or privileges of employment, because of such individual's race, color, religion, sex, or national origin.

barrier, because it measured skills related to effective performance in the role of Welfare Eligibility Supervisor.

B

* * *

In sum, respondents' claim of disparate impact from the examination, a pass-fail barrier to employment opportunity, states a prima facie case of employment discrimination under § 703(a) (2), despite their employer's nondiscriminatory "bottom line," and that "bottom line" is no defense to this prima facie case under § 703(h).

III

Having determined that respondents' claim comes within the terms of Title VII, we must address the suggestion of petitioners and some *amici curiae* that we recognize an exception, either in the nature of an additional burden on plaintiffs seeking to establish a prima facie case or in the nature of an affirmative defense, for cases in which an employer has compensated for a discriminatory pass-fail barrier by hiring or promoting a sufficient number of black employees to reach a nondiscriminatory "bottom line." We reject this suggestion, which is in essence nothing more than a request that we redefine the protections guaranteed by Title VII.

Section 703(a) (2) prohibits practices that would deprive or tend to deprive *"any individual* of employment opportunities." The principal focus of the statute is the protection of the individual employee, rather than the protection of the minority group as a whole. Indeed, the entire statute and its legislative history are replete with references to protection for the individual employee.

In suggesting that the "bottom line" may be a defense to a claim of discrimination against an individual employee, petitioners and *amici* appear to confuse unlawful discrimination with discriminatory intent. The Court has stated that a non-discriminatory "bottom line" and an employer's good-faith efforts to achieve a nondiscriminatory work force, might in some cases assist an employer in rebutting the inference that particular action had been intentionally discriminatory: "Proof that [a] work force was racially balanced or that it contained a disproportionately high percentage of minority employees is not wholly irrelevant on the issue of intent when that issue is yet to be decided." Furnco Constr. Corp. v. Waters, 438 U.S. 567, 580, 98 S.Ct. 2943, 2952, 57 L.Ed.2d 957 (1978). But resolution of the factual question of intent is not what is at issue in this case. Rather, petitioners seek simply to justify discrimination against respondents on the basis of their favorable treatment of other members of respondents' racial group. Under Title VII, "[a] racially balanced work force cannot immunize an employer from liability for specific acts of discrimination." *Id.* at 579, 98 S.Ct. at 2950–51. * * *

It is clear that Congress never intended to give an employer license to discriminate against some employees on the basis of race or sex merely because he favorably treats other members of the employees' group. We recognized in *Los Angeles Dept. of Water & Power v. Manhart,*

435 U.S. 702, 708, 98 S.Ct. 1370, 1374, 55 L.Ed.2d 657 (1978), that fairness to the class of women employees as a whole could not justify unfairness to the individual female employee because the "statute's focus on the individual is unambiguous." *Id.* at 708, 98 S.Ct. at 1375. Similarly, in *Phillips v. Martin Marietta Corp.*, 400 U.S. 542, 91 S.Ct. 496, 27 L.Ed.2d 613 (1971) (per curiam), we recognized that a rule barring employment of all married *women* with preschool children, if not a bona fide occupational qualification under § 703(e), violated Title VII, even though female applicants without preschool children were hired in sufficient numbers that they constituted 75 to 80 percent of the persons employed in the position plaintiff sought.

Petitioners point out that *Furnco*, *Manhart*, and *Phillips* involved facially discriminatory policies, while the claim in the instant case is one of discrimination from a facially neutral policy. The fact remains, however, that irrespective of the form taken by the discriminatory practice, an employer's treatment of other members of the plaintiffs' group can be "of little comfort to the victims of * * * discrimination." Teamsters v. United States, 431 U.S. 324, 342, 97 S.Ct. 1843, 1858, 52 L.Ed.2d 396 (1977). Title VII does not permit the victim of a facially discriminatory policy to be told that he has not been wronged because other persons of his or her race or sex were hired. That answer is no more satisfactory when it is given to victims of a policy that is facially neutral but practically discriminatory. Every *individual* employee is protected against both discriminatory treatment and "practices that are fair in form, but discriminatory in operation." *Griggs*, 401 U.S. at 431, 91 S.Ct. at 853. Requirements and tests that have a discriminatory impact are merely some of the more subtle, but also the more pervasive, of the "practices and devices which have fostered racially stratified job environments to the disadvantage of minority citizens." *McDonnell Douglas*, 411 U.S. at 800, 93 S.Ct. at 1823.

* * *

JUSTICE POWELL, with whom THE CHIEF JUSTICE, JUSTICE REHNQUIST, and JUSTICE O'CONNOR join, dissenting.

In past decisions, this Court has been sensitive to the critical difference between cases proving discrimination under Title VII, by a showing of disparate treatment or discriminatory intent and those proving such discrimination by a showing of disparate impact. Because today's decision blurs that distinction and results in a holding inconsistent with the very nature of disparate-impact claims, I dissent.

I

* * *

* * * [W]hile disparate-*treatment* cases focus on the way in which an individual has been treated, disparate-*impact* cases are concerned with the protected group. * * *

In keeping with this distinction, our disparate-impact cases consistently have considered whether the result of an employer's *total selection process* had an adverse impact upon the protected group. If this case were decided by reference to the total process—as our cases suggest that it should be—the result would be clear. Here 22.9% of the blacks who entered the selection process were ultimately promoted, compared with only 13.5% of the whites. To say that this selection process had an unfavorable "disparate impact" on blacks is to ignore reality.

The Court, disregarding the distinction drawn by our cases, repeatedly asserts that Title VII was designed to protect individual, not group, rights. It emphasizes that some individual blacks were eliminated by the disparate impact of the preliminary test. But this argument confuses the *aim* of Title VII with the legal theories through which its aims were intended to be vindicated. It is true that the aim of Title VII is to protect individuals, not groups. But in advancing this commendable objective, Title VII jurisprudence has recognized two distinct methods of proof. In one set of cases—those involving direct proof of discriminatory intent—the plaintiff seeks to establish direct, intentional discrimination against him. In that type of case, the individual is at the forefront throughout the entire presentation of evidence. In disparate-impact cases, by contrast, the plaintiff seeks to carry his burden of proof by way of *inference*—by showing that an employer's selection process results in the rejection of a disproportionate number of members of a protected group to which he belongs. From such a showing a fair inference then may be drawn that the rejected applicant, as a member of that disproportionately excluded group, was himself a victim of that process' " 'built-in headwinds.' " *Griggs*, 401 U.S. at 432, 91 S.Ct. at 854. But this method of proof—which actually *defines* disparate-impact theory under Title VII—invites the plaintiff to prove discrimination by reference to the group rather than to the allegedly affected individual. There can be no violation of Title VII on the basis of disparate impact in the absence of disparate impact on a *group*.

* * *

III

Today's decision takes a long and unhappy step in the direction of confusion. Title VII does not require that employers adopt merit hiring or the procedures most likely to permit the greatest number of minority members to be considered for or to qualify for jobs and promotions. Employers need not develop tests that accurately reflect the skills of every individual candidate; there are few if any tests that do so. Yet the Court seems unaware of this practical reality, and perhaps oblivious to the likely consequences of its decision. By its holding today, the Court may force employers either to eliminate tests or rely on expensive, job-related, testing procedures, the validity of which may or may not be sustained if challenged. For state and local governmental employers with limited funds, the practical effect of today's decision may well be the adoption of simple quota hiring. This arbitrary method of employment is itself unfair to individual applicants, whether or not they are members of minority groups. And it is not likely to produce a competent work force. Moreover, the Court's decision actually may result in employers employing *fewer* minority members. * * *

* * *

Notes and Questions

1. The following is a simple illustration of the bottom-line approach. The employer bases its hiring decisions on the applicant's score on an employment examination and on the results of an interview used to evaluate subjective criteria. The following table shows the results of each step of the hiring process for black and white applicants.

	Blacks	*Whites*
No. of Applicants	100	100
No. Failed the Test	60	10
No. Interviewed	40	90
No. Offered Employment	10	10

Although blacks are disproportionately eliminated by the test, the final selection process, based on the interviews, shows that black applicants are offered employment at a rate equal to white applicants. The bottom-line defense requires that, in determining whether disparate impact has been shown, one must look to the bottom line of the selection process—here the relative proportion of applicants of each race offered employment—rather than the adverse impact of a specific criterion that is used in the course of selection process.

2. Several important developments ushered in the bottom-line defense. First, after *Griggs*, the courts began to develop a coherent body of law on the disparate impact theory. Statistical evidence became an important evidentiary tool because the Supreme Court, in *Teamsters*, had rejected a restrictive interpretation of § 703(j) of Title VII, the so-called anti-preferential treatment provision. *Teamsters*, *Hazelwood*, and *Dothard* endorsed a very liberal view of the use of statistical evidence. The judicially developed defense of business necessity was deemed to be an affirmative defense for which the defendant had both the burden of production of evidence and the burden of persuasion. To carry the burden of persuasion on the business necessity defense, employers were required to validate the employment criteria that caused the adverse impact. As the plurality recognized in *Watson v. Fort Worth Bank & Trust Co.*, 487 U.S. 977, 108 S.Ct. 2777, 101 L.Ed.2d 827 (1988), reproduced in this chapter, validation can be quite difficult, costly, and time-consuming.

Second, in the wake of *Albemarle Paper Co. v. Moody*, 422 U.S. 405, 95 S.Ct. 2362, 45 L.Ed.2d 280 (1975), and *Franks v. Bowman Transportation Co.*, 424 U.S. 747, 96 S.Ct. 1251, 47 L.Ed.2d 444 (1976), the courts began developing a substantial body of law on the various forms of appropriate relief for employment discrimination, such as back pay, front pay, reinstatement, and hiring remedies. In addition, the courts were beginning to develop rules on attorney's fees quite favorable to successful plaintiffs. Thus, the success of plaintiffs in employment discrimination cases was becoming very costly for defendants. These twin developments—the costs of defending and the costs of losing disparate impact cases—sent a clear message to defendants: either affirmatively demonstrate that the challenged employment practice is job related or face a substantial risk of Title VII liability and imposition of a substantial monetary remedy.

In response, in order to minimize the probability that employees could prove violations of Title VII under the disparate impact theory, employers began to adopt voluntary affirmative action plans. Professor Belton has observed:

The *Griggs* disparate impact theory provided both the practical and doctrinal foundations for race-and sex-specific affirmative action plans. * * *

* * *

* * * It was generally agreed that a validation study provided the most probative evidence of business necessity. Validation, however, was commonly known to be difficult, costly, and time-consuming.

Accordingly, many employers sought alternative ways to reduce the likelihood of a disparate impact suit. Primarily, they adopted affirmative action plans, pursuant to which they expressly took race or sex into account in hiring or promoting in order to substantially reduce racial and sexual disparities in their workforce. By reducing these disparities, it became more difficult for plaintiffs to use statistical evidence to establish a prima facie case of disparate impact discrimination. * * *

Robert Belton, *The Dismantling of the* Griggs *Disparate Impact Theory and the Future of Title VII: The Need for a Third Reconstruction*, 8 Yale L. & Pol'y Rev. 223, 231–33 (1990). *See also* Alfred W. Blumrosen, *The Legacy of* Griggs: *Social Progress and Subjective Judgments*, 63 Chi.-Kent L.Rev. 1, 6 (1987); Mack A. Player, *Is* Griggs *Dead? Reflecting (Fearfully) on* Wards Cove Packing Co. v. Atonio, 17 Fla.St.U.L.Rev. 1, 44 n.167 (1989). If an employer adopted an affirmative action plan, however, there was a possibility that a white or male applicant or employee would bring a "reverse discrimination" claim. *See, e.g.*, Steelworkers v. Weber, 443 U.S. 193, 99 S.Ct. 2721, 61 L.Ed.2d 480 (1979). See Chapter 3, Section B.2.

After some initial policy differences on whether to endorse the bottom-line defense, federal agencies with enforcement authority—EEOC, Department of Justice, United States Civil Service Commission, and Office of Federal Contract Compliance Programs—endorsed the defense in the *Uniform Guidelines. See* Alfred Blumrosen, *The Bottom Line in Equal Employment Guidelines: Administering a Polycentric Problem*, 33 Admin.L.Rev. 323 (1981). In the administrative process, the employer could use the bottom-line defense when faced with a charge of disparate impact employment discrimination. Thus, at this stage, particularly in those cases in which the employer used multi-selection criteria, the employer was not required to validate selection criteria that had an adverse impact on protected groups.

3. A fundamental policy issue at stake in *Teal*—an issue that remains largely unresolved—is whether laws against discrimination protect individu-

als or groups. In thinking about this policy issue, can you harmonize *Teal* and *Griggs*? Assume that the policy is that laws against discrimination in employment protect individuals rather than groups, how would this change, if at all, the theory and analysis in the affirmative action cases covered in Chapter 3, Section 6?

F. *GRIGGS* REVISITED

The impact of *Griggs* on the development of employment discrimination law, and more generally on the development of civil rights jurisprudence, has been profound. But neither the courts nor Congress has resolved the fundamental policy question about competing theories of equality—equal treatment versus equal opportunity. And in fact, support for both visions of equality can be found in *Griggs*. As the membership on the Supreme Court and lower federal courts began to change in the 1980s, so did the jurisprudence of employment discrimination law.

WATSON v. FORT WORTH BANK & TRUST

Supreme Court of the United States, 1988.
487 U.S. 977, 108 S.Ct. 2777, 101 L.Ed.2d 827.

[The Court granted certiorari on the question of whether "the racially adverse impact of an employer's practice of simply committing employment decisions to the unchecked discretion of a white supervisory corps [is] subject to the test of *Griggs v. Duke Power Co.*, 401 U.S. 424, 91 S.Ct. 849, 28 L.Ed.2d 158 (1971)?" The Court was unanimous in holding that disparate impact analysis applies to subjective criteria. The facts are set out in *Watson v. Fort Worth Bank & Trust* reproduced in Section B. 2 of this chapter. A plurality of the Court, however, addressed an issue not presented in the petition for certiorari—the proper evidentiary standard to be applied in such cases. CHIEF JUSTICE REHNQUIST, and JUSTICES WHITE and SCALIA, joined with JUSTICE O'CONNOR who wrote the plurality's opinion. JUSTICE KENNEDY took no part in the consideration or decision of the case.]

* * *

The distinguishing features of the factual issues that typically dominate in disparate impact cases do not imply that the ultimate legal issue is different than in cases where disparate treatment analysis is used. Nor do we think it is appropriate to hold a defendant liable for unintentional discrimination on the basis of less evidence than is required to prove intentional discrimination. Rather, the necessary premise of the disparate impact approach is that some employment practices, adopted without a deliberately discriminatory motive, may in operation be functionally equivalent to intentional discrimination.

Perhaps the most obvious examples of such functional equivalence have been found where facially neutral job requirements necessarily operated to perpetuate the effects of intentional discrimination that occurred before Title VII was enacted. In *Griggs* itself, for example, the employer had a history of overt racial discrimination that predated the enactment of the Civil Rights Act of 1964. * * *

* * *

C

Having decided that disparate impact analysis may in principle be applied to subjective as well as to objective practices, we turn to the evidentiary standards that should apply in such cases. It is here that the concerns raised by respondent have their greatest force. Respondent contends that a plaintiff may establish a prima facie case of disparate impact through the use of bare statistics, and that the defendant can rebut this statistical showing only by justifying the challenged practice in terms of "business necessity," or "job relatedness." Standardized tests and criteria, like those at issue in our previous disparate impact cases, can often be justified through formal "validation studies," which seek to determine whether discrete selection criteria predict actual on-the-job performance. Respondent warns, however, that "validating" subjective selection criteria in this way is impracticable. Some qualities—for example, common sense, good judgment, originality, ambition, loyalty, and tact—cannot be measured accurately through standardized testing techniques. Moreover, success at many jobs in which such qualities are crucial cannot itself be measured directly. Opinions often differ when managers and supervisors are evaluated, and the same can be said for many jobs that involve close cooperation with one's co-workers or complex and subtle tasks like the provision of professional services or personal counseling. Because of these difficulties, we are told, employers will find it impossible to eliminate subjective selection criteria and impossibly expensive to defend such practices in litigation. Respondent insists, and the United States agrees, that employers' only alternative will be to adopt surreptitious quota systems in order to ensure that no plaintiff can establish a statistical prima facie case.

We agree that the inevitable focus on statistics in disparate impact cases could put undue pressure on employers to adopt inappropriate prophylactic measures. It is completely unrealistic to assume that unlawful discrimination is the sole cause of people failing to gravitate to jobs and employers in accord with the laws of chance. It would be equally unrealistic to suppose that employers can eliminate, or discover and explain, the myriad of innocent causes that may lead to statistical imbalances in the composition of their work forces. Congress has specifically provided that employers are not required to avoid "disparate impact" as such:

Nothing contained in [Title VII] shall be interpreted to require any employer * * * to grant preferential treatment to any individual or to any group because of the race, color, religion, sex, or national origin of such individual or group on account of an imbalance which may exist with respect to the total number or percentage of persons of any race, color, religion, sex, or national origin employed by any employer * * * in comparison with the total number or percentage of persons of such race, color, religion, sex, or national origin in any community, State, section, or other area, or in the available work force in any community, State, section, or other area.

42 U.S.C. § 2000e–2(j).

Preferential treatment and the use of quotas by public employers subject to Title VII can violate the Constitution, and it has long been recognized that legal rules leaving any class of employers with "little choice" but to adopt such measures would be "far from the intent of Title VII." *Albemarle Paper Co.*, 422 U.S. at 449, 95 S.Ct. at 2390 (Blackmun, J., concurring in judgment). Respondent and the United States are thus correct when they argue that extending disparate impact analysis to subjective employment practices has the potential to create a Hobson's choice for employers and thus to lead in practice to perverse results. If quotas and preferential treatment become the only cost-effective means of avoiding expensive litigation and potentially catastrophic liability, such measures will be widely adopted. The prudent employer will be careful to ensure that its programs are discussed in euphemistic terms, but will be equally careful to ensure that the quotas are met. Allowing the evolution of disparate impact analysis to lead to this result would be contrary to Congress' clearly expressed intent, and it should not be the effect of our decision today.

D

We do not believe that disparate impact theory need have any chilling effect on legitimate business practices. We recognize, however, that today's extension of that theory into the context of subjective selection practices could increase the risk that employers will be given incentives to adopt quotas or to engage in preferential treatment. Because Congress has so clearly and emphatically expressed its intent that Title VII not lead to this result, 42 U.S. C. § 2000e–2(j), we think it imperative to explain in some detail why the evidentiary standards that apply in these cases should serve as adequate safeguards against the danger that Congress recognized. Our previous decisions offer guidance, but today's extension of disparate impact analysis calls for a fresh and somewhat closer examination of the constraints that operate to keep that analysis within its proper bounds.

First, we note that the plaintiff's burden in establishing a prima facie case goes beyond the need to show that there are statistical disparities in the employer's work force. The plaintiff must begin by identifying the specific employment practice that is challenged. Although this has been relatively easy to do in challenges to standardized tests, it may sometimes be more difficult when subjective selection criteria are at issue. Especially in cases where an employer combines subjective criteria with the use of more rigid standardized rules or tests, the plaintiff is in our view responsible for isolating and identifying the specific employment practices that are allegedly responsible for any observed statistical disparities.

Once the employment practice at issue has been identified, causation must be proved; that is, the plaintiff must offer statistical evidence of a kind and degree sufficient to show that the practice in question has caused the exclusion of applicants for jobs or promotions because of their membership in a protected group. Our formulations, which have never been framed in terms of any rigid mathematical formula, have consistently stressed that statistical disparities must be sufficiently substantial that they raise such an inference of causation. In *Griggs*, for example, we examined "requirements [that] operate[d] to disqualify Negroes at a substantially higher rate than white applicants." 401 U.S. at 426, 91 S.Ct. at 851. Similarly, we said in *Albemarle Paper Co.* that plaintiffs are required to show "that the tests in question select applicants for hire or promotion in a racial pattern significantly different from that of the pool of applicants." 422 U.S. at 425, 95 S.Ct. at 2375. Later cases have framed the test in similar terms.

Nor are courts or defendants obliged to assume that plaintiffs' statistical evidence is reliable. "If the employer discerns fallacies or deficiencies in the data offered by the plaintiff, he is free to adduce countervailing evidence of his own." *Dothard*, 433 U.S. at 331, 97 S.Ct. at 2727–28. * * * Without attempting to catalog all the weaknesses that may be found in such evidence, we may note that typical examples include small or incomplete data sets and inadequate statistical techniques. Similarly, statistics based on an applicant pool containing individuals lacking minimal qualifications for the job would be of little probative value.

A second constraint on the application of disparate impact theory lies in the nature of the "business necessity" or "job relatedness" defense. Although we have said that an employer has "the burden of showing that any given requirement must have a manifest relationship to the employment in question," *Griggs*, 401 U.S. at 432, 91 S.Ct. at 854, such a formulation should not be interpreted as implying that the ultimate burden of proof can be shifted to the defendant. * * * Thus, when a plaintiff has made out a prima facie case of disparate impact, and when the defendant has met its burden of producing evidence that its employment practices are based on legitimate business reasons, the plaintiff must "show that other tests or selection devices, without a similarly undesirable racial effect, would also serve the employer's legitimate interest in efficient and trustworthy workmanship." *Albemarle Paper Co.*, 422 U.S. at 425, 95 S.Ct. at 2375. Factors such as the cost or other burdens of proposed alternative selection devices are relevant in determining whether they would be equally as effective as the challenged practice in serving the employer's legitimate business goals. The same factors would also be relevant in determining whether the challenged practice has operated as the functional equivalent of a pretext for discriminatory treatment.

Our cases make it clear that employers are not required, even when defending standardized or objective tests, to introduce formal "validation studies" showing that particular criteria predict actual on-the-job performance. * * *

In the context of subjective or discretionary employment decisions, the employer will often find it easier than in the case of standardized tests to produce evidence of a "manifest relationship to the employment in question." It is self-evident that many jobs, for example those involving managerial responsibilities, require personal qualities that have never been considered amenable to standardized testing. In evaluating claims that discretionary employment practices are insufficiently related to legitimate business purposes, it must be borne in mind that "[c]ourts are generally less competent than employers to restructure business practices, and unless mandated to do so by Congress they should not attempt it." *Furnco*, 438 U.S. at 578, 98 S.Ct. at 2950. In sum, the high standards of proof in disparate impact cases are sufficient in our view to avoid giving employers incentives to modify any normal and legitimate practices by introducing quotas or preferential treatment.

* * *

[The opinions of Justice Blackmun, with whom Justices Brennan and Marshall joined, concurring in part and concurring in the judgment, and the opinion of Justice Stevens, concurring in the judgment are omitted.]

Note

In *Price Waterhouse v. Hopkins*, 490 U.S. 228, 275, 109 S.Ct. 1775, 1803, 104 L.Ed.2d 268 (1989), Justice O'Connor, concurring in the judgment, also expressed her view that § 703(j) of Title VII is relevant in analysis of disparate impact claims:

I believe there are significant differences between shifting the burden of persuasion to the employer in a case resting purely on statistical proof as in the disparate impact setting and shifting the burden of persuasion in a case like this one, where an employee has demonstrated by direct evidence that an illegitimate factor played a substantial role in a particular employment decision. First, the explicit consideration of race, color, religion, sex, or national origin in making employment decisions "was the most obvious evil Congress had in mind when it enacted Title VII." *Teamsters*, 431 U.S. at 335 n.15, 97 S.Ct. at 1854–55 n.15. While the prima facie case under *McDonnell Douglas* and the statistical showing of imbalance involved in a disparate impact case may both be indicators of discrimination or its "functional equivalent," they are not, in and of themselves, the evils Congress sought to eradicate from the employment setting. Second, shifting the burden of persuasion to the employer in a situation like this one creates no incentive to preferential treatment in violation of § 2000e-(2)(j). To avoid bearing the burden of justifying its decision, the employer need not seek racial or sexual balance in its work force; rather, all it need do is avoid substantial reliance on forbidden criteria in making its employment decisions.

WARDS COVE PACKING CO. v. ATONIO

Supreme Court of the United States, 1989.
490 U.S. 642, 109 S.Ct. 2115, 104 L.Ed.2d 733.

JUSTICE WHITE delivered the opinion of the Court.

* * *

I

The claims before us are disparate-impact claims, involving the employment practices of petitioners, two companies that operate salmon canneries in remote and widely separated areas of Alaska. The canneries operate only during the salmon runs in the summer months. They are inoperative and vacant for the rest of the year. In May or June of each year, a few weeks before the salmon runs begin, workers arrive and prepare the equipment and facilities for the canning operation. Most of these workers possess a variety of skills. When salmon runs are about to begin, the workers who will operate the cannery lines arrive, remain as long as there are fish to can, and then depart. The canneries are then closed down, winterized, and left vacant until the next spring. During the off-season, the companies employ only a small number of individuals at their headquarters in Seattle and Astoria, Oregon, plus some employees at the winter shipyard in Seattle.

The length and size of salmon runs vary from year to year, and hence the number of employees needed at each cannery also varies. Estimates are made as early in the winter as possible; the necessary employees are hired, and when the time comes, they are transported to the canneries. Salmon must be processed soon after they are caught, and the work during the canning season is therefore intense. For this reason, and because the canneries are located in remote regions, all workers are housed at the canneries and have their meals in company-owned mess halls.

Jobs at the canneries are of two general types: "cannery jobs" on the cannery line, which are unskilled positions; and "noncannery jobs," which fall into a variety of classifications. Most noncannery jobs are classified as skilled positions. Cannery jobs are filled predominantly by nonwhites: Filipinos and Alaska Natives. The Filipinos are hired through, and dispatched by, Local 37 of the International Longshoremen's and Warehousemen's Union pursuant to a hiring hall agreement with the local. The Alaska Natives primarily reside in villages near the remote cannery locations. Noncannery jobs are filled with predominantly white workers, who are hired during the winter months from the companies' offices in Washington and Oregon. Virtually all of the noncannery jobs pay more than cannery positions. The predominantly white noncannery workers and the predominantly nonwhite cannery employees live in separate dormitories and eat in separate mess halls.

In 1974, respondents, a class of nonwhite cannery workers who were (or had been) employed at the canneries, brought this Title VII action against petitioners. Respondents alleged that a variety of petitioners' hiring/promotion practices—*e.g.*, nepotism, a rehire preference, a lack of objective hiring criteria, separate hiring channels, a practice of not promoting from within—were responsible for the racial stratification of the work force and had denied them and other nonwhites employment as noncannery workers on the basis of race. Respondents also complained of petitioners' racially segregated housing and dining facilities. All of respondents' claims were advanced under both the disparate-treatment and disparate-impact theories of Title VII liability.

The District Court held a bench trial, after which it entered 172 findings of fact. It then rejected all of respondents' disparate-treatment claims. It also rejected the disparate-impact challenges * * *.

* * *

* * * [The Court of Appeals] held that respondents had made out a prima facie case of disparate impact in hiring for both skilled and unskilled noncannery positions. The panel remanded the case for further proceedings, instructing the District Court that it was the employer's burden to prove that any disparate impact caused by its hiring and employment practices was justified by business necessity. Neither the en banc court nor the panel disturbed the District Court's rejection of the disparate-treatment claims.[4]

* * * Because some of the issues raised by the decision below were matters on which this Court was evenly divided in *Watson v. Fort Worth Bank & Trust*, 487 U.S. 977, 108 S.Ct. 2777, 101 L.Ed.2d 827 (1988), we granted certiorari, for the purpose of addressing these disputed questions of the proper application of Title VII's disparate-impact theory of liability.

II

In holding that respondents had made out a prima facie case of disparate impact, the Court of Appeals relied solely on respondents'

---

4. The fact that neither the District Court, nor the Ninth Circuit en banc, nor the subsequent Court of Appeals panel ruled for respondents on their disparate-treatment claims—i.e., their allegations of intentional racial discrimination—warrants particular attention in light of the dissents' comment that the canneries "bear an unsettling resemblance to aspects of a plantation economy." (STEVENS, J., dissenting); (BLACKMUN, J., dissenting).

Whatever the "resemblance," the unanimous view of the lower courts in this litigation has been that respondents did not prove that the canneries practice intentional racial discrimination. Consequently, Justice Blackmun's hyperbolic allegation that our decision in this case indicates that this Court no longer "believes that race discrimination * * * against nonwhites * * * is a problem in our society" is inapt. Of course, it is unfortunately true that race discrimination exists in our country. That does not mean, however, that it exists at the canneries—or more precisely, that it has been proved to exist at the canneries.

* * *

statistics showing a high percentage of nonwhite workers in the cannery jobs and a low percentage of such workers in the noncannery positions. Although statistical proof can alone make out a prima facie case, the Court of Appeals' ruling here misapprehends our precedents and the purposes of Title VII, and we therefore reverse.

"There can be no doubt," as there was when a similar mistaken analysis had been undertaken by the courts below in *Hazelwood School Dist. v. United States*, 433 U.S. 299, 308, 97 S.Ct. 2736, 2741, 53 L.Ed.2d 768 (1977), "that the * * * comparison * * * fundamentally misconceived the role of statistics in employment discrimination cases." The "proper comparison [is] between the racial composition of [the at-issue jobs] and the racial composition of the qualified * * * population in the relevant labor market." *Id.* It is such a comparison—between the racial composition of the qualified persons in the labor market and the persons holding at-issue jobs—that generally forms the proper basis for the initial inquiry in a disparate-impact case. Alternatively, in cases where such labor market statistics will be difficult if not impossible to ascertain, we have recognized that certain other statistics—such as measures indicating the racial composition of "otherwise-qualified applicants" for at-issue jobs—are equally probative for this purpose. *See, e.g.,* New York City Transit Authority v. Beazer, 440 U.S. 568, 585, 99 S.Ct. 1355, 1366, 59 L.Ed.2d 587 (1979).

It is clear to us that the Court of Appeals' acceptance of the comparison between the racial composition of the cannery work force and that of the noncannery work force, as probative of a prima facie case of disparate impact in the selection of the latter group of workers, was flawed for several reasons. Most obviously, with respect to the skilled noncannery jobs at issue here, the cannery work force in no way reflected "the pool of *qualified* job applicants" or the "*qualified* population in the labor force." Measuring alleged discrimination in the selection of accountants, managers, boat captains, electricians, doctors, and engineers—and the long list of other "skilled" noncannery positions found to exist by the District Court, by comparing the number of nonwhites occupying these jobs to the number of nonwhites filling cannery worker positions is nonsensical. If the absence of minorities holding such skilled positions is due to a dearth of qualified nonwhite applicants (for reasons that are not petitioners' fault), petitioners' selection methods or employment practices cannot be said to have had a "disparate impact" on nonwhites.

* * * [U]nder the Court of Appeals' theory, simply because nonwhites comprise 52% of the cannery workers at the cannery in question, respondents would be successful in establishing a prima facie case of racial discrimination under Title VII.

Such a result cannot be squared with our cases or with the goals behind the statute. The Court of Appeals' theory, at the very least, would mean that any employer who had a segment of his work force that was—for some reason—racially imbalanced, could be haled into court and forced to engage in the expensive and time-consuming task of defending the "business necessity" of the methods used to select the other members of his work force. The only practicable option for many employers would be to adopt racial quotas, insuring that no portion of their work forces deviated in racial composition from the other portions thereof; this is a result that Congress expressly rejected in drafting Title VII. *See* 42 U.S.C. § 2000e–2(j); *see also* Watson v. Fort Worth Bank & Trust, 487 U.S. at 992–94 & n.2, 108 S.Ct. at 2787–89 & n.2 (opinion of O'CONNOR, J.). The Court of Appeals' theory would "leave the employer little choice * * * but to engage in a subjective quota system of employment selection. This, of course, is far from the intent of Title VII." Albemarle Paper Co. v. Moody, 422 U.S. 405, 449, 95 S.Ct. 2362, 2387, 45 L.Ed.2d 280 (1975) (BLACKMUN, J., concurring in judgment).

The Court of Appeals also erred with respect to the unskilled noncannery positions. Racial imbalance in one segment of an employer's work force does not, without more, establish a prima facie case of disparate impact with respect to the selection of workers for the employer's other positions, even where workers for the different positions may have somewhat fungible skills (as is arguably the case for cannery and unskilled noncannery workers). As long as there are no barriers or practices deterring qualified nonwhites from applying for noncannery positions, if the percentage of selected applicants who are nonwhite is not significantly less than the percentage of qualified applicants who are nonwhite, the employer's selection mechanism probably does not operate with a disparate impact on minorities. Where this is the case, the percentage of nonwhite workers found in other positions in the employer's labor force is irrelevant to the question of a prima facie statistical case of disparate impact. As noted above, a contrary ruling on this point would almost inexorably lead to the use of numerical quotas in the workplace, a result that Congress and this Court have rejected repeatedly in the past.

Moreover, isolating the cannery workers as the potential "labor force" for unskilled noncannery positions is at once both too broad and too narrow in its focus. It is too broad because the vast majority of these cannery workers did not seek jobs in unskilled noncannery positions; there is no showing that many of them would have done so even if none of the arguably "deterring" practices existed. Thus, the pool of cannery workers cannot be used as a surrogate for the class of qualified job applicants because it contains many persons who have not (and would not) be noncannery job applicants. Conversely, if respondents propose to use the cannery workers for comparison purposes because they represent the "qualified labor population" generally, the group is too narrow because there are obviously many qualified persons in the labor market for noncannery jobs who are not cannery workers.

* * *

Consequently, we reverse the Court of Appeals' ruling that a comparison between the percentage of cannery workers who are nonwhite and the percentage of noncannery workers who are nonwhite makes out a prima facie case of disparate impact. Of course, this leaves unresolved whether the record made in the District Court will support a conclusion that a prima facie case of disparate impact has been established on some basis other than the racial disparity between cannery and noncannery workers. This is an issue that the Court of Appeals or the District Court should address in the first instance.

III

Since the statistical disparity relied on by the Court of Appeals did not suffice to make out a prima facie case, any inquiry by us into whether the specific challenged employment practices of petitioners caused that disparity is pretermitted, as is any inquiry into whether the disparate impact that any employment practice may have had was justified by business considerations. Because we remand for further proceedings, however, on whether a prima facie case of disparate impact has been made in defensible fashion in this case, we address two other challenges petitioners have made to the decision of the Court of Appeals.

A

First is the question of causation in a disparate-impact case. The law in this respect was correctly stated by Justice O'Connor's opinion last Term in *Watson v. Fort Worth Bank & Trust,* 487 U.S. at 994, 108 S.Ct. at 2788 89, * * *.

* * *

Our disparate-impact cases have always focused on the impact of *particular* hiring practices on employment opportunities for minorities. Just as an employer cannot escape liability under Title VII by demonstrating that, "at the bottom line," his work force is racially balanced (where particular hiring practices may operate to deprive minorities of employment opportunities), *see* Connecticut v. Teal, 457 U.S. at 450, 102 S.Ct. at 2532, a Title VII plaintiff does not make out a case of disparate impact simply by showing that, "at the bottom line," there is racial *imbalance* in the work force. As a general matter, a plaintiff must demonstrate that it is the application of a specific or particular employment practice that has created the disparate impact under attack. Such a showing is an integral part of the plaintiff's prima facie case in a disparate-impact suit under Title VII.

Here, respondents have alleged that several "objective" employment practices (e.g., nepotism, separate hiring channels, rehire preferences), as well as the use of "subjective decision making" to select noncannery workers, have had a disparate impact on nonwhites. Respondents base this claim on statistics that allegedly show a disproportionately low percentage of nonwhites in the at-issue positions. However, even if on remand respondents can show that nonwhites are underrepresented in the at-issue jobs in a manner that is acceptable under the standards set forth in Section II, *supra*, this alone will *not* suffice to make out a prima facie case of disparate impact. Respondents will also have to demonstrate that the disparity they complain of is the result of one or more of the employment practices that they are attacking here, specifically showing that each challenged practice has a significantly disparate impact on employment opportunities for whites and nonwhites. To hold otherwise would result in employers being potentially liable for "the myriad of innocent causes that may lead to statistical imbalances in the composition of their work forces." *Watson*, 487 U.S. at 992, 108 S.Ct. at 2787.

* * *

B

If, on remand, respondents meet the proof burdens outlined above, and establish a prima facie case of disparate impact with respect to any of petitioners' employment practices, the case will shift to any business justification petitioners offer for their use of these practices. This phase of the disparate-impact case contains two components: first, a consideration of the justifications an employer offers for his use of these practices; and second, the availability of alternative practices to achieve the same business ends, with less racial impact. We consider these two components in turn.

(1)

Though we have phrased the query differently in different cases, it is generally well established that at the justification stage of such a disparate-impact case, the dispositive issue is whether a challenged practice serves, in a significant way, the legitimate employment goals of the employer. The touchstone of this inquiry is a reasoned review of the employer's justification for his use of the challenged practice. * * * A mere insubstantial justification in this regard will not suffice, because such a low standard of review would permit discrimination to be practiced through the use of spurious, seemingly neutral employment practices. At the same time, though, there is no requirement that the challenged practice be "essential" or "indispensable" to the employer's business for it to pass muster: this degree of scrutiny would be almost impossible for most employers to meet, and would result in a host of evils we have identified above.

In this phase, the employer carries the burden of producing evidence of a business justification for his employment practice. * * * We acknowledge that some of our earlier decisions can be read as suggesting otherwise. But to the extent that those cases speak of an employer's "burden of proof" with respect to a legitimate business justification * * * they should have been understood to mean an employer's production—but not persuasion—burden.

(2)

Finally, if on remand the case reaches this point, and respondents cannot persuade the trier of fact on the question of petitioners' business necessity defense, respondents may still be able to prevail. To do so, respondents will have to persuade the factfinder that "other tests or selection devices, without a similarly undesirable racial effect, would also serve the employer's legitimate [hiring] interest[s]"; by so demonstrating, respondents would prove that "[petitioners were] using [their] tests merely as a 'pretext' for discrimination." *Albemarle Paper Co.*, 422 U.S. at 425, 95 S.Ct. at 2375. If respondents, having established a prima facie case, come forward with alternatives to petitioners' hiring practices that reduce the racially disparate impact of practices currently being used, and petitioners refuse to adopt these alternatives, such a refusal would belie a claim by petitioners that their incumbent practices are being employed for nondiscriminatory reasons.

Of course, any alternative practices which respondents offer up in this respect must be equally effective as petitioners' chosen hiring procedures in achieving petitioners' legitimate employment goals. Moreover, "[f]actors such as the cost or other burdens of proposed alternative selection devices are relevant in determining whether they would be equally as effective as the challenged practice in serving the employer's legitimate business goals." *Watson*, 487 U.S. at 998, 108 S.Ct. at 2790. "Courts are generally less competent than employers to restructure business practices," *Furnco Constr. Corp. v. Waters*, 438 U.S. 567, 578, 98 S.Ct. 2943, 2950, 57 L.Ed.2d 957 (1978); consequently, the judiciary should proceed with care before mandating that an employer must adopt a plaintiff's alternative selection or hiring practice in response to a Title VII suit.

* * *

JUSTICE BLACKMUN, with whom Justice BRENNAN and JUSTICE MARSHALL join, dissenting.

* * *

* * * The salmon industry as described by this record takes us back to a kind of overt and institutionalized discrimination we have not dealt with in years: a total residential and work environment organized on principles of racial stratification and segregation, which, as Justice Stevens points out, resembles a plantation economy. This industry long has been characterized by a taste for discrimination of the old-fashioned sort: a preference for hiring nonwhites to fill its lowest level positions, on the condition that they stay there. The majority's legal rulings essentially immunize these practices from attack under a Title VII disparate-impact analysis.

Sadly, this comes as no surprise. One wonders whether the majority still believes that race discrimination—or, more accurately, race discrimination against nonwhites—is a problem in our society, or even remembers that it ever was.

JUSTICE STEVENS, with whom JUSTICE BRENNAN, JUSTICE MARSHALL, and JUSTICE BLACKMUN join, dissenting.

Fully 18 years ago, this Court unanimously held that Title VII of the Civil Rights Act of 1964 prohibits employment practices that have discriminatory effects as well as those that are intended to discriminate. Federal courts and agencies consistently have enforced that interpretation, thus promoting our national goal of eliminating barriers that define economic opportunity not by aptitude and ability but by race, color, national origin, and other traits that are easily identified but utterly irrelevant to one's qualification for a particular job. Regrettably, the Court retreats from these efforts in its review of an interlocutory judgment respecting the "peculiar facts" of this lawsuit. Turning a blind eye to the meaning and purpose of Title VII, the majority's opinion perfunctorily rejects a longstanding rule of law and underestimates the probative value of evidence of a racially stratified work force. I cannot join this latest sojourn into judicial activism.

* * *

Notes and Questions

1. Does the Supreme Court's interpretation of § 703(j) of Title VII, 42 U.S.C. § 2000e–2(j), in *Wards Cove* overrule its interpretation of that same section in note 20 of *Teamsters*, reproduced in Section C of this chapter?

2. The views of Justice O'Connor in *Watson v. Fort Worth Bank & Trust* formed the basis for the Court's decision in *Wards Cove*. How would you describe her conception of equality? It seems clear, does it not, that Justice O'Connor is unwilling to endorse a rule of law that would legitimate "quotas"? *See* Alfred W. Blumrosen, *Society in Transition III: Justice O'Connor and the Destabilization of the* Griggs *Principle of Employment Discrimination*, 13 Women's Rts.L.Rep. 53, 53 (1991) (arguing that Justice O'Connor's views on employment discrimination "reflect a tension between her respect for the established order * * * and her understanding of the need to eliminate employment discrimination" * * * and suggesting that "[t]his tension may stem from her experience of graduating third in her class from Stanford Law School but not receiving a job offer").

3. Does *Wards Cove* resolve the tension in *Griggs* between competing theories of equality? If so, what theory of equality does *Wards Cove* embrace?

4. In the Civil Rights Act of 1991, Congress codified the theory of disparate impact and specified the analytical framework as follows:

(k) Burden of proof in disparate impact cases

(1)(A) An unlawful employment practice based on disparate impact is established under this subchapter only if–

(i) a complaining party demonstrates that a respondent uses a particular employment practice that causes a disparate impact on the basis of race, color, religion, sex, or national origin and the respondent fails to demonstrate that the challenged practice is job related for the position in question and consistent with business necessity; or

(ii) the complaining party makes the demonstration described in subparagraph (C) with respect to an alternative employment practice and the respondent refuses to adopt such alternative employment practice.

(B)(i) With respect to demonstrating that a particular employment practice causes a disparate impact as described in subparagraph (A)(i), the complaining party shall demonstrate that each particular challenged employment practice causes a disparate impact, except that if the complaining party can demonstrate to the court that the elements of a respondent's decisionmaking process are not capable of separation for analysis, the decisionmaking process may be analyzed as one employment practice.

(ii) if the respondent demonstrates that a specific employment practice does not cause the disparate impact, the respondent shall not be required to demonstrate that such practice is required by business necessity.

(C) The demonstration referred to by subparagraph (A)(ii) shall be in accordance with law as it existed on June 4, 1989, with respect to the concept of "alternative employment practices.

* * *

Title VII, § 703(k), 42 U.S.C. § 2000e–2(k).

As stated in the Findings and Purposes section of the Civil Rights Act of 1991, Congress acted to codify the theory of discrimination found in *Griggs v. Duke Power* and to respond to a variety of Supreme Court cases, including *Wards Cove Packing Co. v. Atonio.* Civil Rights Act of 1991, Sec. 2 and 3, Pub.L.No. 102–166, 105 Stat. 1071 (1991).

5. A defendant can rebut a prima facie case of disparate impact under the Civil Rights Act of 1991 by meeting the burden of production of evidence and the burden of persuasion with proof that a "challenged practice is job related for the position in question and consistent with business necessity." 42 U.S.C. § 2000e–2(k) (1) (A). Is the defense as now provided in the 1991 Act more onerous or less onerous than the business necessity test as it existed before *Wards Cove*? Consider the following case:

LANNING v. SOUTHEASTERN PENNSYLVANIA TRANSPORTATION AUTHORITY

United States Court of Appeals for the Third Circuit, 1999.
181 F.3d 478, *cert. denied*, 528 U.S. 1131, 120 S.Ct. 970, 145 L.Ed.2d 840 (2000).

MANSMANN, Circuit Judge.

In this appeal, we must determine the appropriate legal standard to apply when evaluating an employer's business justification in an action challenging an employer's cutoff score on an employment screening exam as discriminatory under a disparate impact theory of liability. We hold today that under the Civil Rights Act of 1991, a discriminatory cutoff score on an entry level employment examination must be shown to measure the minimum qualifications necessary for successful performance of the job in question in order to survive a disparate impact challenge. * * *

I.

* * *

A.

SEPTA is a regional mass transit authority that operates principally in Philadelphia, Pennsylvania. In 1989, in response to a perceived need to upgrade the quality of its transit police force, SEPTA initiated an extensive program designed to improve the department. * * *

In 1991, SEPTA hired Dr. Paul Davis to develop an appropriate physical fitness test for its police officers. * * *

* * * Ultimately, Dr. Davis recommended a 1.5 mile run within 12 minutes. * * *

Dr. Davis recommended that SEPTA use the 1.5 mile run as an applicant screening test. Dr. Davis understood that SEPTA officers would not be required to run 1.5 miles within 12 minutes in the course of their duties, but he nevertheless recommended this test as an accurate measure of the aerobic capacity necessary to perform the job of SEPTA transit police officer. Based upon Dr. Davis' recommendation, SEPTA adopted a physical fitness screening test for its applicants, which included a 1.5 mile run within 12 minutes. * * *

* * * [R]esearch studies confirm that a cutoff of 12 minutes on a 1.5 mile run will have a disparately adverse impact on women. SEPTA concedes that its 1.5 mile run has a disparate impact on women.

* * *

II.

Because SEPTA concedes that its 1.5 mile run has a disparate impact on women, the first prong of the disparate impact analysis is not at issue in this appeal. Rather, this appeal focuses our attention on the proper standard for evaluating whether SEPTA's 1.5 mile run is "job related for the position in question and consistent with business necessity" under the Civil Rights Act of 1991. Because the Act instructs that this standard incorporates only selected segments of prior Supreme Court jurisprudence on the business necessity doctrine, we examine the history of this doctrine in order to resolve this threshold issue.

A.

[The court examined the same Supreme Court decisions on business necessity that the Ninth Circuit reviewed a pre–1991 Act case on the business necessity defense in *Contreras v. City of Los Angeles*, reproduced in Section D of this chapter. The cases are *Griggs*, *Albemarle Paper Co. v. Moody*, *Dothard v. Rawlinson*, and *New York Transit Authority v. Beazer*.]

* * * After the passage of the Act, proponents of both a strict test for business necessity and a more liberal requirement claimed victory in the standard adopted by the Act.[12]

III.

The Supreme Court has yet to interpret the "job related for the position in question and consistent with business necessity" standard adopted by the Act. In addition, our sister courts of appeals that have applied the Act's standard to a Title VII challenge have done so with little analysis. * * *

Because the Act proscribes resort to legislative history with the exception of one short interpretive memorandum endorsing selective caselaw, our starting point in interpreting the Act's business necessity language must be that interpretive memorandum. The memorandum makes clear that Congress intended to endorse the business necessity standard enunciated in *Griggs* and not the *Wards Cove* interpretation of that standard. By Congress' distinguishing between *Griggs* and *Wards Cove*, we must conclude that Congress viewed *Wards Cove* as a significant departure from *Griggs*. Accordingly, because the Act clearly chooses *Griggs* over *Wards Cove*, the Court's interpretation of the business necessity standard in *Wards Cove* does not survive the Act.[13]

We turn now to articulate the standard for business necessity—one most consistent with *Griggs* and its pre*Wards Cove* progeny. The laudable mission begun by the Court in *Griggs* was the eradication of discrimination through the application of practices fair in form but discriminatory in practice by eliminating *unnecessary* barriers to employment opportunities. In the context of a hiring exam with a cutoff score shown to have a discriminatory effect, the standard that best effectuates this mission is implicit in the Court's application of the business necessity doctrine to the employer in *Griggs*, *i.e.*, that a discriminatory cutoff

---

12. *See* Andrew C. Spiropoulos, *Defining the Business Necessity Defense to the Disparate Impact Cause of Action: Finding the Golden Mean*, 74 N.C. L.Rev. 1479, 1516–20 (1996) (outlining the respective positions of both sides to the debate); *compare also* Michael Carvin, *Disparate Impact Claims Under the New Title VII*, 68 Notre Dame L.Rev. 1153 (1993) (arguing that *Wards Cove* is still good law after Civil Rights Act of 1991) *with* Susan S. Grover, *The Business Necessity Defense in Disparate Impact Discrimination Cases*, 30 Ga.L.Rev. 387 (1996) (arguing for a strict business necessity standard under the Act); Note, *The Civil Rights Act of 1991: The Business Necessity Standard*, 106 Harv.L.Rev. 896 (1993) (asserting that *Wards Cove* does not survive the Act).

13. We are cognizant that a contrary argument has been advanced in which it is asserted that *Wards Cove* remains the controlling standard. *See* Carvin, *supra* note 12, at 1157–64. Pursuant to the argument, the business necessity standard announced in *Wards Cove* simply clarified *Griggs* and therefore is not inconsistent with the Act's command to apply the standard enunciated in *Griggs*. In addition, it is asserted that due to the legislative history of the Act, it would be improper to apply a strict business necessity standard. This argument, however, ignores two important aspects of the Act which constrain our interpretation of the standard adopted. First, the interpretive memorandum's distinction between *Griggs* and *Wards Cove* casts significant doubt on the assertion that Congress read *Wards Cove* as simply a clarification of *Griggs*. Second, the Act precludes us from considering the legislative history upon which this argument relies for support. Accordingly, we find this argument to be devoid of merit.

score is impermissible unless shown to measure the minimum qualifications necessary for successful performance of the job in question. Only this standard can effectuate the mission begun by the Court in *Griggs*; only by requiring employers to demonstrate that their discriminatory cutoff score measures the minimum qualifications necessary for successful performance of the job in question can we be certain to eliminate the use of excessive cutoff scores that have a disparate impact on minorities as a method of imposing unnecessary barriers to employment opportunities.

The evolution of the Court's articulation of the business necessity doctrine in both *Albemarle* and *Dothard* reinforces the conclusion that this standard is both implicit in *Griggs* and central to its mission. In *Albemarle*, the Court explained that discriminatory tests must be validated to show that they are "predictive of * * * important elements of work behavior which comprise * * * the job * * * for which candidates are being evaluated" and that the scores of the higher level employees do not necessarily validate a cutoff score for the minimum qualifications to perform the job at an entry level. *Albemarle*, 422 U.S. at 431, 434, 95 S.Ct. 2362. This is simply another way of saying that discriminatory cutoff scores must be validated to show they measure the minimum qualifications necessary for successful performance of the job. Similarly, in *Dothard*, the Court made clear that "a discriminatory employment practice," such as a discriminatory cutoff score on an entry level exam, "must be shown to be necessary to safe and efficient job performance to survive a Title VII challenge." *Dothard*, 433 U.S. at 332 n.14, 97 S.Ct. 2720.

Taken together, *Griggs, Albemarle* and *Dothard* teach that in order to show the business necessity of a discriminatory cutoff score an employer must demonstrate that its cutoff measures the minimum qualifications necessary for successful performance of the job in question. Furthermore, because the Act instructs us to interpret its business necessity language in conformance with *Griggs* and its pre*Wards Cove* progeny, we must conclude that the Act's business necessity language incorporates this standard.

Our conclusion that the Act incorporates this standard is further supported by the business necessity language adopted by the Act. Congress chose the terms "job related for the position in question" *and* "consistent with business necessity." Judicial application of a standard focusing solely on whether the qualities measured by an entry level exam bear some relationship to the job in question would impermissibly write out the business necessity prong of the Act's chosen standard. With respect to a discriminatory cutoff score, the business necessity prong must be read to demand an inquiry into whether the score reflects the minimum qualifications necessary to perform successfully the job in question.

In addition, Congress' decision to emphasize the importance of the policies underlying the disparate impact theory of discrimination through its codification supports application of this standard to discriminatory cutoff scores. The disparate impact theory of discrimination combats not intentional, obvious discriminatory policies, but a type of covert discrimination in which facially neutral practices are employed to exclude, unnecessarily and disparately, protected groups from employment opportunities. Inherent in the adoption of this theory of discrimination is the recognition that an employer's job requirements may incorporate societal standards based not upon necessity but rather upon historical, discriminatory biases.[14] A business necessity standard that wholly defers to an employer's judgment as to what is desirable in an employee therefore is completely inadequate in combating covert discrimination based upon societal prejudices. Only a business necessity doctrine that examines discriminatory cutoff scores in light of the minimum qualifications that are necessary to perform the job in question successfully can address adequately this subtle form of discrimination.[15]

Accordingly, we hold that the business necessity standard adopted by the Act must be interpreted in accordance with the standards articulated by the Supreme Court in *Griggs* and its pre-*Wards Cove* progeny which demand that a discriminatory cutoff score be shown to measure the minimum qualifications necessary for the successful performance of the job in question in order to survive a disparate impact challenge.[16]

✴ ✴ ✴

14. For an interesting discussion on male-oriented biases in the labor market see Maxine N. Eichner, *Getting Women Work That Isn't Women's Work: Challenging Gender Biases in the Workplace Under Title VII*, 97 Yale L.J. 1397 (1988).

15. We need not be concerned that implementation of this standard will result in forcing employers to adopt quotas, a result that would be inconsistent with the mandates of Title VII. If an employer can demonstrate that its discriminatory cutoff score reflects the minimum qualifications necessary for successful job performance, it will be able to continue to use it. If not, the employer must abandon that cutoff score, but is free to develop either a non-discriminatory practice which furthers its goals, or an equally discriminatory practice that can meet this standard. Nothing in the *Griggs* business necessity standard requires employers to hire employees in numbers to reflect the ethnic, racial or gender make-up of the community.

The following example based upon the facts of this case illustrates this point. Asuming that SEPTA's 1.5 mile rule has a disparate impact on women and that SEPTA can not show that the 12 minute cutoff measures the minimum aerobic capacity necessary to be a successful transit officer,

it does not follow that SEPTA would then be required to hire women in equal proportion to men. Several options would be available to SEPTA. For example, SEPTA could: 1) abandon the test as a hiring requirement but maintain an incentive program to encourage an increase in the officers' aerobic capacities; 2) validate a cutoff score for aerobic capacity that measures the minimum capacity necessary to successfully perform the job and maintain incentive programs to achieve even higher aerobic levels; or 3) institute a non-discriminatory test for excessive levels of aerobic capacity such as a test that would exclude 80% of men as well as 80% of women through separate aerobic capacity cutoffs for the different sexes. Each of these options would help SEPTA achieve its stated goal of increasing aerobic capacity without running afoul of Title VII and none of these options require hiring by quota.

16. Relying upon *Spurlock v. United Airlines, Inc.*, 475 F.2d 216 (10th Cir.1972), and like cases from our sister courts of appeals, the dissent asserts that this standard should not apply to SEPTA because the job of SEPTA transit officer implicates issues of public safety. Under the Act, however, our interpretation of the business ne-

WEIS, Circuit Judge, dissenting:

The "minimum qualifications" criterion of business justification does not apply to all types of employment. When public safety is at stake, a lighter burden is placed on employers to justify their hiring requirements. Because I believe that the latter standard applies in this case, I would affirm.

* * *

III.

* * *

The Courts of Appeals have explicitly recognized the relevance of safety considerations in a series of decisions beginning with *Spurlock v. United Airlines, Inc.*, 475 F.2d 216 (10th Cir.1972). In that case, an airline required that applicants for flight officer positions have a college degree and a minimum of 500 flight hours. The Court, citing *Griggs*, held that where "the job clearly requires a high degree of skill and the economic and human risks involved in hiring an unqualified applicant are great, the employer bears a correspondingly lighter burden to show his employment criteria are job related." *Id.* at 219. Because, in the case of pilots, "[t]he risks involved in hiring an unqualified applicant are staggering * * * [t]he courts * * * should proceed with great caution before requiring an employer to lower his pre-employment standards for such a job." *Id.*

Another leading case, *Davis v. City of Dallas*, 777 F.2d 205 (5th Cir.1985), applied the *Spurlock* doctrine to criteria for hiring police officers. The City required a specific amount of college education, no history of recent marijuana usage, and a negative history of traffic

---

cessity language is limited to "the concepts enunciated by the Supreme Court in *Griggs v. Duke Power Co.*, 401 U.S. 424, 91 S.Ct. 849, 28 L.Ed.2d 158 (1971), and in the other *Supreme Court* decisions prior to *Wards Cove Packing Co. v. Atonio*, 490 U.S. 642, 109 S.Ct. 2115, 104 L.Ed.2d 733 (1989)." *See* 137 Cong. Rec. 28,680 (1991) (emphasis added). Because the Supreme Court never adopted the holding of *Spurlock* prior to *Wards Cove*, its [sic] is clear that, under the Act, we are not to consider *Spurlock* as authoritative. Furthermore, if Congress had intended to endorse the holding of *Spurlock*, it could have done so affirmatively. Accordingly, because the Act limits our interpretation to Supreme Court jurisprudence and does not otherwise endorse *Spurlock*, we are not at liberty to adopt the holding of *Spurlock* at this juncture. Moreover, to the extent that *Spurlock* and other cases from our sister courts of appeals can be read to suggest that minimum qualifications do not apply to certain types of employment, these cases are incon-

sistent with the teachings of *Griggs* and are accordingly uninformative under the Act.

Furthermore, to the limited extent that the Supreme Court's pre-*Wards Cove* jurisprudence instructs that public safety is a legitimate consideration, application of the business necessity standard to SEPTA is consistent with that jurisprudence because the standard itself takes public safety into consideration. If, for example, SEPTA can show on remand that the inability of a SEPTA transit officer to meet a certain aerobic level would significantly jeopardize public safety, this showing would be relevant to determine if that level is necessary for the successful performance of the job. Clearly a SEPTA officer who poses a significant risk to public safety could not be considered to be performing his job successfully. We are accordingly confident that application of the business necessity standard to SEPTA is fully consistent with the Supreme Court's pre-*Wards Cove* jurisprudence as required by the Act.

violations. Despite findings of disparate impact, the Court upheld the requirements. Having reviewed the many cases following *Spurlock*, the Court had "no difficulty * * * equating the position of police officer in a major metropolitan area such as Dallas with other jobs that courts have found to involve the important public interest in safety." *Id.* at 215 (internal quotation marks omitted). The degree of public risk and responsibility alone "would warrant examination of the job relatedness of the * * * education requirement under the lighter standard imposed under *Spurlock* and its progeny." *Id.* at 215.

Observing the nature of the positions at issue in *Griggs* and *Albemarle, Davis* noted that in neither case did the Supreme Court suggest that those jobs "were noteworthy for their dangerousness or importance to the public welfare." *Id.* at 210. In contrast, the employment under consideration in *Davis* directly implicated public safety concerns. *See id.* at 211. It is interesting that Justice Blackmun, in *Watson v. Fort Worth Bank & Trust*, 487 U.S. 977, 108 S.Ct. 2777, 101 L.Ed.2d 827 (1988) (plurality op.), objecting to what he considered to be a tendency to weaken the employer's burden, cited *Davis* favorably, stating that "[t]he proper means of establishing business necessity will vary with the type and size of the business in question, as well as the particular job" in question. *Id.* at 1007, 108 S.Ct. 2777. (Blackmun, J., concurring in part and concurring in the judgment).[5]

In a post-*Wards Cove* case involving firefighters, the Court of Appeals for the Eleventh Circuit noted that such "safety claims would afford the City an affirmative defense, for protecting employees from workplace hazards is a goal that, as a matter of law, has been found to qualify as an important business goal for Title VII purposes." *Fitzpatrick v. City of Atlanta*, 2 F.3d 1112, 1119 (11th Cir.1993) (citing Beazer, 440 U.S. at 587 & n. 31, 99 S.Ct. 1355; *Dothard*, 433 U.S. at 331 n. 14, 97 S.Ct. 2720). Thus, "[m]easures demonstrably necessary to meeting the goal of ensuring worker safety are therefore deemed to be 'required by business necessity' under Title VII." *Id.*

In a similar case, the Court of Appeals for the Eighth Circuit wrote that "the law does not require the city to put the lives of [plaintiff] and his fellow firefighters at risk by taking the chance that he is fit for duty when solid scientific studies indicate that persons with test results similar to his are not." *Smith v. City of Des Moines*, 99 F.3d 1466, 1473 (8th Cir.1996). Other Courts of Appeals have reached similar conclusions in cases involving safety-sensitive positions such as truck drivers, bus drivers, firefighters, and police officers.[6]

---

5. In the analogous context of the defense of bona fide occupational qualification, the Supreme Court has stated: " 'The greater the safety factor, measured by the likelihood of harm and the probable severity of that harm in case of an accident, the more stringent may be the job qualifications * * *.' "*Western Air Lines, Inc. v. Criswell*, 472 U.S. 400, 413, 105 S.Ct. 2743,

86 L.Ed.2d 321 (1985) (quoting with approval *Usery v. Tamiami Trail Tours, Inc.*, 531 F.2d 224, 236 (5th Cir.1976)).

6. *See, e.g., York v. American Telephone & Telegraph Co.*, 95 F.3d 948, 952, 959 (10th Cir.1996) (powerhouse operating engineers); *Zamlen v. City of Cleveland*, 906 F.2d 209, 217 (6th Cir.1990) (firefighters);

IV.

With this in mind, I cannot agree that the majority's standard is the correct one for this case. Reducing standards towards the lowest common denominator is particularly inappropriate for a police force. Undoubtedly, candidates who fail the running test—female or male—may have other qualities of particular value to SEPTA, but they must possess the requisite aerobic capacity as well. No matter how laudable it is to reduce job discrimination, to achieve this goal by lowering important public safety standards presents an unacceptable risk.

Aerobic capacity is an objective, measurable factor which gauges the ability of a human being to perform physical activity. The aerobic demands on the human system are affected by absolutes such as the distance traveled, the speed, the number of steps to be climbed, and similar factors. Governmental agency pronouncements will not shorten distances, reduce the number of steps, or decrease the aerobic capacity of perpetrators to match the reduced standards of officers, male or female. Some males and more females cannot meet the necessary requirements. Based on the facts established at trial, those individuals simply cannot perform the job efficiently. To the extent that they cannot, their hire adversely affects public safety.

* * *

Notes and Questions

1. A legislative interpretive memorandum on the business necessity defense under the Civil Rights Act of 1991, as discussed by the majority in *Lanning*, provides:

> The final compromise on the [Civil Rights Act of 1991] agreed to by several Senate sponsors, including Senators Danforth, Kennedy, and Dole, and the Administration states that with respect to *Wards Cove*— Business necessity/ cumulation/alternative business practice—the exclusive legislative history is as follows:

> > The terms 'business necessity' and 'job related' are intended to reflect the concepts enunciated by the Supreme Court in *Griggs v. Duke Power Co.* and in the other Supreme Court decisions prior to *Wards Cove Packing Co. v. Atonio.*

137 Cong.Rec. S15,276 (daily ed. Oct. 25, 1991).

2. As the *Lanning* case illustrates, the courts have not resolved the issue of the appropriate tests for the business necessity defense. In *Donnelly v. Rhode Island Board of Governors for Higher Education*, 929 F.Supp. 583

Hamer v. City of Atlanta, 872 F.2d 1521, 1535 (11th Cir.1989) (firefighters); *Levin v. Delta Air Lines, Inc.*, 730 F.2d 994, 997–98 (5th Cir.1984) (flight attendants); *Chrisner v. Complete Auto Transit, Inc.*, 645 F.2d 1251, 1261–63 (6th Cir.1981) (truck yard employees); *Harriss v. Pan American World* *Airways, Inc.*, 649 F.2d 670, 676 (9th Cir. 1980) (flight attendants); *McCosh v. City of Grand Forks*, 628 F.2d 1058, 1063 (8th Cir. 1980) (police); *Boyd v. Ozark Air Lines, Inc.*, 568 F.2d 50, 54 (8th Cir.1977) (airline pilots) * * *.

(D.R.I.1996), *aff'd*, 110 F.3d 2 (1st Cir.1997), the court stated that the new business necessity test under the 1991 Act reintroduces some of the confusion that existed in Supreme Court decisions prior to *Wards Cove*. The court ultimately concluded that the test under the 1991 Act only requires proof that the challenged practice is "reasonably necessary to achieve an important business objective." *Donnelly*, 929 F.Supp. at 593. The court adopted its test based on the following rationale: Prior to *Wards Cove* the "business necessity" and "job relatedness" tests embodied two seemingly inconsistent concepts that the courts tended to use interchangeably—"business necessity" required a compelling business need whereas "job relatedness" implied only a connection to job performance. In its response to *Wards Cove*, Congress ultimately rejected an earlier formulation of the test that used the phrase "*required* by business necessity" and substituted instead the phrase, "*consistent* with business necessity." The new test was a compromise between legislators who wanted to retain the more rigorous business necessity test and those who were opposed to a rule that required businesses to prove that a challenged practice was indispensable to the conduct of its business. Thus, the 1991 Act adopts a standard that requires something less than a showing that the challenged practice is essential, but also requires something more than the *Wards Cove* standard of legitimate business purpose. *Id.* at 592–93.

3. For a discussion of the pre-*Wards Cove* confusion in Supreme Court cases on the business necessity test, see Gary A. Moore & Michael K. Braswell, *"Quotas" and the Codification of the Disparate Impact Theory: What Did Griggs Really Say and Not Say?*, 55 Alb.L.Rev. 459 (1991); Note, *The Civil Rights Act of 1991: The Business Necessity Standard*, 106 Harv. L.Rev. 896 (1993).

In her article, Linda Lye, Comment, *Title VII's Tangled Tale: The Erosion and Confusion of Disparate Impact and Business Necessity Defense*, 19 Berkeley J.Emp. & Lab.L. 315 (1998), the author argues that the confusion in the judicial efforts to interpret the test of business necessity codified in the Civil Rights Act of 1991 implicates competing social and individual interests:

> [T]he business necessity standard constitutes the juncture at which competing interests are weighed—society's interest in prohibiting practices shown to have a discriminatory effect and an individual employer's interest in furthering important business goals. To the extent that the state of legal doctrine reflects social values, the stringency of the business necessity standard reveals social priorities: a looser standard reflects an increased tolerance for demonstrated discriminatory practices and an emphasis on individual entrepreneurial objectives.

Id. at 319–20. Lye argues for a stringent test to emphasize the importance of prohibiting discriminatory practices. The test she proposes is that "a challenged practice [must be] a reasonable predictor of effective performance of job duties, and in turn these duties must be defined in light of the employer's important business goals." *Id.* at 358. Her test requires answers to three questions: (1) does the challenged practice reasonably predict an applicant's ability to perform a job duty; (2) has the employer identified an important business goal; and (3) does the job duty effectively further that goal. *Id.* at 356. Is there support for the author's point about competing social values in the several tests of business necessity advocated by the majority and the dissenter in *Lanning*?

4. The concern the Supreme Court expressed in *Wards Cove* about adopting rules that would encourage employers to adopt quotas to thwart the possibility of a disparate impact claim appears also to have influenced the majority in *Lanning* in its formulation of a business necessity test. The concern about quotas is grounded, in substantial part, in Title VII § 703(j), 42 U.S.C. § 2000–2(j), which also was issue in *Teamsters*, reproduced in Section C of this chapter. In footnote 15, the *Lanning* court states that its business necessity test "will [not] result in forcing employers to adopt quotas.

5. Section 703(k) (2), 42 U.S.C. § 2000e–2(k) (2), added by the Civil Rights Act of 1991, provides that the business necessity defense cannot be asserted in a disparate treatment claim. If a defendant is precluded from asserting the business necessity defense in a disparate treatment claim, should a plaintiff also be precluded from introducing similar kind of evidence to prove pretext in a disparate treatment claim? Consider the following: The employer, a tire manufacturer, requires applicants for the position of maintenance mechanic to successfully pass a pen and paper test. A black employee applies for a vacancy as a maintenance mechanic on several occasions; he takes and fails the test on two different occasions. He sues the employer under Title VII claiming racial discrimination and relies upon the disparate treatment theory. Evidence shows that several white applicants who had taken and failed the test nevertheless were promoted to maintenance mechanic; other white employees were advised that they need not complete certain sections of the test but the plaintiff was required to complete all sections; and the employer refused the plaintiff the opportunity to review his tests results. Should the plaintiff be allowed to use this evidence to prove pretext under the theory that the test is neither job related nor consistent with business necessity? *See* Sledge v. Goodyear Dunlop Tires North Am., Ltd., 275 F.3d 1014 (11th Cir.2001).

6. On remand in *Lanning*, the district court found that the employer had satisfied the business necessity test articulated by the court of appeals. Lanning v. Southeastern Pa. Transp. Auth., 84 F.E.P.Cases (BNA) 1012, 2000 WL 1790125 (E.D.Pa.2000). The district court found that the standard for employment was necessary to ensure that persons employed in the position would be able to have the capacity to get to a spot where another office needed help in a timely fashion. Otherwise, the court concluded, the safety of fellow officers and the public at large would be at risk. On appeal, the Third Circuit affirmed. 308 F.3d 286 (3d Cir.2002).

Chapter 5

EQUAL PROTECTION AND SECTION 1981

A. INTRODUCTION: THE LEGACY OF THE RECONSTRUCTION–ERA REFORMS

During Reconstruction, Congress embarked on a program of constitutional and legislative reform to benefit the newly freed slaves that produced three constitutional amendments—the Thirteenth, Fourteenth, and Fifteenth Amendments—and a number of statutory enactments, including civil rights legislation. *See* Eugene Gressman, *The Unhappy History of Civil Rights Legislation*, 50 Mich.L.Rev. 1323 (1952). The Thirteenth Amendment outlaws slavery and involuntary servitude. The Fourteenth Amendment guarantees to all persons the privileges and immunities of United States citizenship, due process of law, and equal protection of the laws. The Fifteenth Amendment prohibits both the federal and state governments from depriving citizens of the right to vote on account of race, color, or previous condition of servitude.

Because of Republican concerns that the Thirteenth Amendment would not support the Civil Rights Act of 1866, which was enacted to enforce that amendment, Congress drafted the Fourteenth Amendment to provide the Act of 1866 with a firmer constitutional foundation. Gressman, *supra* at 1324–35. (The 1866 Act is now codified, as amended, at 42 U.S.C. § 1981(a).) Professor Douglas Colbert described the origins of the 1866 Act:

> Although the states ratified the [Thirteenth] Amendment in December 1865, a wave of brutal, racially motivated violence against African Americans swept the South the following year. Local law enforcement officials generally refused to prosecute offenders, and southern states enacted Black Code laws, which were intended to perpetuate African American slavery. * * *
>
> Northern legislators had anticipated southern resistance to the Thirteenth Amendment. While some suggested providing economic reparations to accompany the constitutional guarantee, a strong consensus developed among moderates and conservatives favoring

273

equal protection of the law for all men. The debates leading to passage of the 1866 Civil Rights Act reveal legislators' broad and developing vision of what Thirteenth Amendment freedom rights meant * * *.

* * *

The Bill's first section guaranteed citizenship to all people, other than Native Americans, who were born in the United States. It specifically identified fundamental rights necessary to make all men equal before the law. These included contract and property rights, access to courts, and equality under the law.

Douglas L. Colbert, *Liberating the Thirteenth Amendment*, 30 Harv.C.R.-C.L.L.Rev. 1, 11–13 (1995) (footnotes omitted). In the Equal Protection Clause, the Fourteenth Amendment embodied the fundamental rights of civil equality under the law that were expressed in the 1866 Act. The ratification of the Fourteenth Amendment was followed by the enactment of the Enforcement Act of 1870, which was, in part, a rewording of the Act of 1866 to protect "all persons," instead of "citizens, of every race and color." The language of the 1870 Act is now codified at 42 U.S.C. § 1981, and racial discrimination actions brought under the statute are known as § 1981 claims.

As historian Eric Foner has observed, "[t]he transformation of slaves into free laborers and equal citizens was the most dramatic example of the social and political changes unleashed by the Civil War and emancipation." Eric Foner, Reconstruction: America's Unfinished Revolution, 1863–1877, at xxv (1988). The reform agenda forced Congress to address the meanings of equality, but, as Foner has noted, this was not a simple undertaking.

[T]he implications of the elusive term "equality" were anything but clear in 1865. At the outset of Reconstruction most Republicans still adhered to a political vocabulary inherited from the antebellum era, which distinguished sharply between natural, civil, political, and social rights. The first could not legitimately be circumscribed by government; slavery had been wrong, fundamentally, because it violated the natural rights—life, liberty, and the pursuit of happiness—common to all humanity. Equality in civil rights—equal treatment by the courts and civil and criminal laws—most Republicans now deemed nearly as essential, for an individual's natural rights could not be secured without it. Although Radicals insisted black suffrage must be part of Reconstruction, the vote was commonly considered a "privilege" rather than a right; requirements varied from state to state, and unequal treatment or even complete exclusion did not compromise one's standing as a citizen. And social relations—the choice of business and personal associates—most Americans deemed a personal matter, outside the purview of government.

Id. at 231.

In a series of early cases, the Supreme Court substantially eviscerated the civil rights legislation enacted by Congress during Reconstruction. In the *Slaughter-House Cases*, 83 U.S. (16 Wall.) 36, 21 L.Ed. 394 (1873), the Court largely gutted the privileges and immunities clause of the Fourteenth Amendment by construing it to protect only those rights incident to national citizenship, such as the right to travel. The Court rejected a construction of the privileges and immunities clause that would offer federal protection to the right to property or the right to freedom of contract. In the *Civil Rights Cases*, 109 U.S. 3, 3 S.Ct. 18, 27 L.Ed. 835 (1883), the Court struck down the public accommodations provisions of the Civil Rights Act of 1875 on the ground that Congress lacked the power under either the Thirteenth or Fourteenth Amendment to prohibit private discrimination. And in the 1896 decision of *Plessy v. Ferguson*, 163 U.S. 537, 16 S.Ct. 1138, 41 L.Ed. 256 (1896), the Court constitutionalized the "separate but equal" doctrine.

The Thirteenth, Fourteenth, and Fifteenth Amendments and the civil rights statutes enacted pursuant to these amendments have raised several questions that the Supreme Court has had to address or readdress over time. Two of the most important of these questions are (1) whether these constitutional amendments and laws apply to discrimination against individuals or groups other than blacks, and (2) whether these constitutional amendments and laws apply to discriminatory conduct by private as well as public entities. The Supreme Court addressed the first question in *St. Francis College v Al–Khazraji*, 481 U.S. 604, 107 S.Ct. 2022, 95 L.Ed.2d 582 (1987), reproduced in Chapter 2, and both of these questions are among the issues covered in this chapter.

In commenting upon the Reconstruction reforms, the Supreme Court observed that "[t]he legislative history of the 1866 Act clearly indicates that Congress intended to protect a limited category of rights, specifically defined in terms of racial equality." General Bldg. Contractors Ass'n v. Pennsylvania, 458 U.S. 375, 386, 102 S.Ct. 3141, 73 L.Ed.2d 835 (1982). The Congress that drafted the Fourteenth Amendment also enacted the Civil Rights Act of 1866, which was designed to enforce the Thirteenth Amendment's prohibition of involuntary servitude by prohibiting racial distinctions in the law. Though they shared a common origin and purpose, the Equal Protection Clause of the Fourteenth Amendment and the Civil Rights Act of 1866 have produced distinct bodies of law that now can provide the basis for employment discrimination claims in certain situations. This development is relatively recent: for nearly one-hundred years, equal protection—whether under the Fourteenth Amendment Equal Protection Clause, the equal protection component of the Fifth Amendment Due Process Clause, or § 1981, the Civil Rights Act of 1866, as amended—had little or no relevance in the context of private employment. As a result of a series of Supreme Court cases beginning in the 1960s, however, they now provide significant sources of antidiscrimination rights.

Although most governmental classifications of persons are subject to a test of reasonableness, classifications on the basis of race, religion, nationality, or alienage are considered "inherently suspect" and are subjected to strict scrutiny. The Supreme Court has held that under the strict scrutiny test, racial classifications are constitutional only if they are narrowly tailored to further some compelling state interest. *See, e.g.,* Grutter v. Bollinger, 539 U.S. 306, ___, 123 S.Ct. 2325, 2337–38, 156 L.Ed.2d 304 (2003). An intermediate level of review is used for classifications based on sex. *See, e.g.,* United States v. Virginia, 518 U.S. 515, 116 S.Ct. 2264, 135 L.Ed.2d 735 (1996).

The Equal Protection Clause of the Fourteenth Amendment permits state and local government employees to challenge a variety of discriminatory policies and practices of their employers in § 1983 actions brought in federal or state court. *See* the Civil Rights Act of 1871, 42 U.S.C. § 1983. In addition, the equal protection component of the Fifth Amendment has long been recognized as a constitutional bar to discrimination in federal employment on the basis of race or other suspect classifications. Bolling v. Sharpe, 347 U.S. 497, 74 S.Ct. 693, 98 L.Ed. 884 (1954). Historically, however, most federal employees primarily relied on the administrative processes of the Civil Service Commission to redress discrimination complaints. When Title VII was amended in 1972 to cover employees of federal, state, and local governments, § 717 was added to provide special procedures for federal employees. Section 717 of Title VII now provides the exclusive judicial remedy for discrimination complaints by federal employees covered by that amendment. Brown v. General Servs. Admin., 425 U.S. 820, 96 S.Ct. 1961, 48 L.Ed.2d 402 (1976). The Civil Rights Act of 1991 extended the antidiscrimination provisions of Title VII to employees of the House of Representatives and the Senate and several other groups of federal employees. Nevertheless, in limited circumstances, federal employees who are not covered under these statutes may pursue equal protection claims under the Fifth Amendment. In Davis v. Passman, 442 U.S. 228, 247, 99 S.Ct. 2264, 60 L.Ed.2d 846 (1979), the Court held that its ruling in *Brown v. GSA,* does not foreclose an implied right of action based on the Fifth Amendment when the complainant is expressly unprotected by Title VII. *See* Kizas v. Webster, 707 F.2d 524, 541–43 (D.C.Cir.1983) (discussing relationship between *Brown* and *Davis*), *cert. denied,* 464 U.S. 1042, 104 S.Ct. 709, 79 L.Ed.2d 173 (1984)).

One advantage of the constitutional equal protection doctrine for plaintiffs is that, unlike the antidiscrimination statutes, it theoretically can reach whatever category of persons the courts deem to be in need of special protection. For example, commentators have urged, and a few lower courts have held, that heightened scrutiny under equal protection should be extended to classifications based on sexual identity. *See generally* Patricia A. Cain, *Litigating for Lesbian and Gay Rights: A Legal History,* 79 Va.L.Rev. 1551 (1993); Cass R. Sunstein, *Sexual Orientation and the Constitution: A Note on the Relationship Between Due Process and Equal Protection,* 55 U.Chi.L.Rev. 1161 (1988). For an analysis of equal protection as a prohibition against the subordination of groups of people, see Ruth Colker, *Anti-Subordination Above All: Sex, Race, and Equal Protection*, 61 N.Y.U.L.Rev. 1003 (1986).

Section B of this chapter covers employment discrimination claims brought against public employers under the equal protection clauses of the Fourteenth and Fifth Amendments of the Constitution. Section C treats the theory of liability and scope of protection in employment discrimination claims brought under 42 U.S.C. § 1981. As you read the following materials, consider the ways in which the courts have defined and redefined the concept of equality.

B. EQUAL PROTECTION: THE FIFTH AND FOURTEENTH AMENDMENTS

In the wake of *Brown v. Board of Education*, 347 U.S. 483, 74 S.Ct. 686, 98 L.Ed. 873 (1954), public employers began to abandon policies that overtly discriminated on the basis of race. The effects of many years of racial discrimination and segregation, however, left the workforces of many public employers just as stratified in terms of race as was the case in the private sector. For this reason, a number of lower courts approved the use of the *Griggs v. Duke Power Co.* disparate impact analysis in cases challenging, on equal protection grounds, certain employment tests and hiring practices used by public employers. *See, e.g.*, Chance v. Board of Examiners, 458 F.2d 1167, 1176–77 (2d Cir.1972). The following case is the Supreme Court's response to that development.

WASHINGTON v. DAVIS

Supreme Court of the United States, 1976.
426 U.S. 229, 96 S.Ct. 2040, 48 L.Ed.2d 597.

JUSTICE WHITE delivered the opinion of the Court.

This case involves the validity of a qualifying test administered to applicants for positions as police officers in the District of Columbia Metropolitan Police Department. The test was sustained by the District Court but invalidated by the Court of Appeals. We are in agreement with the District Court and hence reverse the judgment of the Court of Appeals.

I

This action began on April 10, 1970, when two Negro police officers filed suit against the then Commissioner of the District of Columbia, the Chief of the District's Metropolitan Police Department, and the Commissioners of the United States Civil Service Commission. An amended complaint * * * alleged that the promotion policies of the Department were racially discriminatory and sought a declaratory judgment and an injunction. The respondents * * * were permitted to intervene, their amended complaint asserting that their applications to become officers in the Department had been rejected, and that the Department's recruiting procedures discriminated on the basis of race against black applicants by a series of practices including, but not limited to, a written personnel test which excluded a disproportionately high number of Negro applicants. These practices were asserted to violate respondents' rights "under the due process clause of the Fifth Amendment to the United States Constitution * * *." * * *

According to the findings and conclusions of the District Court, to be accepted by the Department and to enter an intensive 17–week training program, the police recruit was required to satisfy certain physical and character standards, to be a high school graduate or its equivalent, and to receive a grade of at least 40 out of 80 on "Test 21," which is "an examination that is used generally throughout the federal service," which "was developed by the Civil Service Commission, not the Police Department," and which was "designed to test verbal ability, vocabulary, reading and comprehension."

The validity of Test 21 was the sole issue before the court on the motions for summary judgment. The District Court noted that there was no claim of "an intentional discrimination or purposeful discriminatory acts" but only a claim that Test 21 bore no relationship to job performance and "has a highly discriminatory impact in screening out black candidates." Respondents' evidence, the District Court said, warranted three conclusions: "(a) The number of black police officers, while substantial, is not proportionate to the population mix of the city. (b) A higher percentage of blacks fail the Test than whites. (c) The Test has not been validated to establish its reliability for measuring subsequent job performance." This showing was deemed sufficient to shift the burden of proof to the defendants in the action, petitioners here; but the court nevertheless concluded that on the undisputed facts respondents were not entitled to relief. The District Court relied on several factors. Since August 1969, 44% of new police force recruits had been black; that figure also represented the proportion of blacks on the total force and was roughly equivalent to 20–to 29–year-old blacks in the 50–mile radius in which the recruiting efforts of the Police Department had been concentrated. It was undisputed that the Department had systematically and affirmatively sought to enroll black officers many of whom passed the test but failed to report for duty. The District Court rejected the assertion that Test 21 was culturally slanted to favor whites and was "satisfied that the undisputable facts prove the test to be reasonably and directly related to the requirements of the police recruit training program and that it is neither so designed nor operates [sic] to discriminate against otherwise qualified blacks." * * * The District Court ultimately concluded that "[t]he proof is wholly lacking that a police officer qualifies on the color of his skin rather than ability" and that the Department "should not be required on this showing to lower standards or to abandon efforts to achieve excellence."

Having lost * * * in the District Court, respondents brought the case to the Court of Appeals claiming that their summary judgment motion, which rested on purely constitutional grounds, should have been granted. The tendered constitutional issue was whether the use of Test 21 invidiously discriminated against Negroes and hence denied them due process of law contrary to the commands of the Fifth Amendment. The Court of Appeals, addressing that issue, announced that it would be guided by *Griggs v. Duke Power Co.*, 401 U.S. 424, 91 S.Ct. 849, 28 L.Ed.2d 158 (1971), a case involving the interpretation and application of Title VII of the Civil Rights Act of 1964, and held that the statutory standards elucidated in that case were to govern the due process question tendered in this one. The court went on to declare that lack of discriminatory intent in designing and administering Test 21 was irrelevant; the critical fact was rather that a far greater proportion of blacks— four times as many—failed the test than did whites. This disproportionate impact, standing alone and without regard to whether it indicated a discriminatory purpose, was held sufficient to establish a constitutional violation, absent proof by petitioners that the test was an adequate measure of job performance in addition to being an indicator of probable success in the training program, a burden which the court ruled petitioners had failed to discharge. * * * The Court of Appeals, over a dissent, accordingly reversed the judgment of the District Court and directed that respondents' motion for partial summary judgment be granted. * * *

II

Because the Court of Appeals erroneously applied the legal standards applicable to Title VII cases in resolving the constitutional issue before it, we reverse its judgment in respondents' favor. Although the petition for certiorari did not present this ground for reversal,[8] our Rule 40(1)(d)(2) provides that we "may notice a plain error not presented"; and this is an appropriate occasion to invoke the Rule.

As the Court of Appeals understood Title VII,[10] employees or applicants proceeding under it need not concern themselves with the employer's possibly discriminatory purpose but instead may focus solely on the racially differential impact of the challenged hiring or promotion practices. This is not the constitutional rule. We have never held that the constitutional standard for adjudicating claims of invidious racial discrimination is identical to the standards applicable under Title VII, and we decline to do so today.

The central purpose of the Equal Protection Clause of the Fourteenth Amendment is the prevention of official conduct discriminating on the basis of race. It is also true that the Due Process Clause of the Fifth Amendment contains an equal protection component prohibiting

8. Apparently not disputing the applicability of the *Griggs* and Title VII standards in resolving this case, petitioners presented issues going only to whether *Griggs v. Duke Power Co.* had been misapplied by the Court of Appeals.

10. Although Title VII standards have dominated this case, the statute was not applicable to federal employees when the complaint was filed; and although the 1972 amendments extending the Title to reach Government employees were adopted prior to the District Court's judgment, the complaint was not amended to state a claim under that Title, nor did the case thereafter proceed as a Title VII case. * * *

the United States from invidiously discriminating between individuals or groups. But our cases have not embraced the proposition that a law or other official act, without regard to whether it reflects a racially discriminatory purpose, is unconstitutional *solely* because it has a racially disproportionate impact.

Almost 100 years ago, *Strauder v. West Virginia*, 100 U.S. 303, 25 L.Ed. 664 (1880), established that the exclusion of Negroes from grand and petit juries in criminal proceedings violated the Equal Protection Clause, but the fact that a particular jury or a series of juries does not statistically reflect the racial composition of the community does not in itself make out an invidious discrimination forbidden by the Clause. "A purpose to discriminate must be present which may be proven by systematic exclusion of eligible jurymen of the proscribed race or by unequal application of the law to such an extent as to show intentional discrimination." Akins v. Texas, 325 U.S. 398, 403–04, 65 S.Ct. 1276, 1279, 89 L.Ed. 1692, 1696 (1945). * * *

The rule is the same in other contexts. *Wright v. Rockefeller*, 376 U.S. 52, 84 S.Ct. 603, 11 L.Ed.2d 512 (1964) upheld a New York congressional apportionment statute against claims that district lines had been racially gerrymandered. The challenged districts were made up predominantly of whites or of minority races, and their boundaries were irregularly drawn. The challengers did not prevail because they failed to prove that the New York Legislature "was either motivated by racial considerations or in fact drew the districts on racial lines"; the plaintiffs had not shown that the statute "was the product of a state contrivance to segregate on the basis of race or place of origin." *Id*. at 56, 58, 84 S.Ct. at 605, 11 L.Ed.2d at 515. * * *

The school desegregation cases have also adhered to the basic equal protection principle that the invidious quality of a law claimed to be racially discriminatory must ultimately be traced to a racially discriminatory purpose. That there are both predominantly black and predominantly white schools in a community is not alone violative of the Equal Protection Clause. The essential element of *de jure* segregation is "a current condition of segregation resulting from intentional state action." Keyes v. School Dist. No.1, 413 U.S. 189, 205, 93 S.Ct. 2686, 2696, 37 L.Ed.2d 548 (1973). "The differentiating factor between *de jure* segregation and so-called *de facto* segregation * * * is *purpose* or *intent* to segregate." *Id*. at 208, 93 S.Ct. at 2696. The Court has also recently rejected allegations of racial discrimination based solely on the statistically disproportionate racial impact of various provisions of the Social Security Act because "[t]he acceptance of appellants' constitutional theory would render suspect each difference in treatment among the grant classes, however lacking in racial motivation and however otherwise rational the treatment might be." Jefferson v. Hackney, 406 U.S. 535, 548, 92 S.Ct. 1724, 1732, 32 L.Ed.2d 285, 297 (1972).

This is not to say that the necessary discriminatory racial purpose must be express or appear on the face of the statute, or that a law's disproportionate impact is irrelevant in cases involving Constitution-based claims of racial discrimination. A statute, otherwise neutral on its face, must not be applied so as invidiously to discriminate on the basis of race. Yick Wo v. Hopkins, 118 U.S. 356, 6 S.Ct. 1064, 30 L.Ed. 220 (1886). It is also clear from the cases dealing with racial discrimination in the selection of juries that the systematic exclusion of Negroes is itself such an "unequal application of the law * * * as to show intentional discrimination." *Akins*, 325 U.S. at 404, 65 S.Ct. at 1279. A prima facie case of discriminatory purpose may be proved as well by the absence of Negroes on a particular jury combined with the failure of the jury commissioners to be informed of eligible Negro jurors in a community, or with racially non-neutral selection procedures. With a prima facie case made out, "the burden of proof shifts to the State to rebut the presumption of unconstitutional action by showing that permissible racially neutral selection criteria and procedures have produced the monochromatic result." Alexander v. Louisiana, 405 U.S. 625, 632, 92 S.Ct. 1221, 1226, 31 L.Ed.2d 536, 542 (1972).

Necessarily, an invidious discriminatory purpose may often be inferred from the totality of the relevant facts, including the fact, if it is true, that the law bears more heavily on one race than another. It is also not infrequently true that the discriminatory impact—in the jury cases for example, the total or seriously disproportionate exclusion of Negroes from jury venires—may for all practical purposes demonstrate unconstitutionality because in various circumstances the discrimination is very difficult to explain on nonracial grounds. Nevertheless, we have not held that a law, neutral on its face and serving ends otherwise within the power of government to pursue, is invalid under the Equal Protection Clause simply because it may affect a greater proportion of one race than of another. Disproportionate impact is not irrelevant, but it is not the sole touchstone of an invidious racial discrimination forbidden by the Constitution. Standing alone, it does not trigger the rule that racial classifications are to be subjected to the strictest scrutiny and are justifiable only by the weightiest of considerations.

* * *

As an initial matter, we have difficulty understanding how a law establishing a racially neutral qualification for employment is nevertheless racially discriminatory and denies "any person * * * equal protection of the laws" simply because a greater proportion of Negroes fail to qualify than members of other racial or ethnic groups. Had respondents, along with all others who had failed Test 21, whether white or black, brought an action claiming that the test denied each of them equal protection of the laws as compared with those who had passed with high enough scores to qualify them as police recruits, it is most unlikely that their challenge would have been sustained. Test 21, which is administered generally to prospective Government employees, concededly seeks to ascertain whether those who take it have acquired a particular level of verbal skill; and it is untenable that the Constitution prevents the

Government from seeking modestly to upgrade the communicative abilities of its employees rather than to be satisfied with some lower level of competence, particularly where the job requires special ability to communicate orally and in writing. Respondents, as Negroes, could no more successfully claim that the test denied them equal protection than could white applicants who also failed. The conclusion would not be different in the face of proof that more Negroes than whites had been disqualified by Test 21. That other Negroes also failed to score well would, alone, not demonstrate that respondents individually were being denied equal protection of the laws by the application of an otherwise valid qualifying test being administered to prospective police recruits.

Nor on the facts of the case before us would the disproportionate impact of Test 21 warrant the conclusion that it is a purposeful device to discriminate against Negroes and hence an infringement of the constitutional rights of respondents as well as other black applicants. As we have said, the test is neutral on its face and rationally may be said to serve a purpose the Government is constitutionally empowered to pursue. Even agreeing with the District Court that the differential racial effect of Test 21 called for further inquiry, we think the District Court correctly held that the affirmative efforts of the Metropolitan Police Department to recruit black officers, the changing racial composition of the recruit classes and of the force in general, and the relationship of the test to the training program negated any inference that the Department discriminated on the basis of race or that "a police officer qualifies on the color of his skin rather than ability."

Under Title VII, Congress provided that when hiring and promotion practices disqualifying substantially disproportionate numbers of blacks are challenged, discriminatory purpose need not be proved, and that it is an insufficient response to demonstrate some rational basis for the challenged practices. It is necessary, in addition, that they be "validated" in terms of job performance in any one of several ways, perhaps by ascertaining the minimum skill, ability, or potential necessary for the position at issue and determining whether the qualifying tests are appropriate for the selection of qualified applicants for the job in question. However this process proceeds, it involves a more probing judicial review of, and less deference to, the seemingly reasonable acts of administrators and executives than is appropriate under the Constitution where special racial impact, without discriminatory purpose, is claimed. We are not disposed to adopt this more rigorous standard for the purposes of applying the Fifth and the Fourteenth Amendments in cases such as this.

A rule that a statute designed to serve neutral ends is nevertheless invalid, absent compelling justification, if in practice it benefits or burdens one race more than another would be far reaching and would raise serious questions about, and perhaps invalidate, a whole range of tax, welfare, public service, regulatory, and licensing statutes that may be more burdensome to the poor and to the average black than to the more affluent white.[14]

Given that rule, such consequences would perhaps be likely to follow. However, in our view, extension of the rule beyond those areas where it is already applicable by reason of statute, such as in the field of public employment, should await legislative prescription.

* * *

Notes and Questions

1. *Evidence of Discriminatory Purpose*: In *Village of Arlington Heights v. Metropolitan Housing Development Corp.*, 429 U.S. 252, 97 S.Ct. 555, 50 L.Ed.2d 450 (1977), the Supreme Court upheld a facially neutral zoning board decision that had the foreseeable effect of perpetuating racially segregated housing. The Court provided a useful summary of the types of evidence that might be used to prove the existence of an invidious racially discriminatory purpose under the Equal Protection Clause:

> *Davis* does not require a plaintiff to prove that the challenged action rested solely on racially discriminatory purposes. Rarely can it be said that a legislature or administrative body operating under a broad mandate made a decision motivated solely by a single concern, or even that a particular purpose was the "dominant" or "primary" one. In fact, it is because legislators and administrators are properly concerned with balancing numerous competing considerations that courts refrain from reviewing the merits of their decisions, absent a showing of arbitrariness or irrationality. But racial discrimination is not just another competing consideration. When there is a proof that a discriminatory purpose has been a motivating factor in the decision, this judicial deference is no longer justified.
>
> Determining whether invidious discriminatory purpose was a motivating factor demands a sensitive inquiry into such circumstantial and direct evidence of intent as may be available. The impact of the official action—whether it "bears more heavily on one race than another," Washington v. Davis, 426 U.S. 229, 246, 96 S.Ct. 2040, 2049, 48 L.Ed.2d 597 (1976)—may provide an important starting point. Sometimes a clear pattern, unexplainable on grounds other than race, emerges from the effect of the state action even when the governing legislation appears neutral on its face. Yick Wo v. Hopkins, 118 U.S. 356, 6 S.Ct. 1064, 30 L.Ed. 220 (1886); Gomillion v. Lightfoot, 364 U.S. 339, 81 S.Ct. 125, 5 L.Ed.2d 110 (1960). The evidentiary inquiry is then relatively easy. But

14. Goodman, *De Facto School Segregation: A Constitutional and Empirical Analysis*, 60 Calif.L.Rev. 275, 300 (1972), suggests that disproportionate-impact analysis might invalidate "tests and qualifications for voting, draft deferment, public employment, jury service, and other government-conferred benefits and opportunities * * *; [s]ales taxes, bail schedules, utility rates, bridge tolls, license fees, and other state-imposed charges." It has also been argued that minimum wage and usury laws as well as professional licensing requirements would require major modifications in light of the unequal-impact rule. Silverman, *Equal Protection, Economic Legislation, and Racial Discrimination*, 25 Vand.L.Rev. 1183 (1972). *See also* Demsetz, *Minorities in the Market Place*, 43 N.C.L.Rev. 271 (1965).

such cases are rare. Absent a pattern as stark as that in *Gomillion* or *Yick Wo*, impact alone is not determinative, and the Court must look to other evidence.

The historical background of the decision is one evidentiary source, particularly if it reveals a series of official actions taken for invidious purposes. The specific sequence of events leading up to the challenged decision also may shed some light on the decisionmaker's purposes. * * * Departures from the normal procedural sequence also might afford evidence that improper purposes are playing a role. Substantive departures too may be relevant, particularly if the factors usually considered important by the decisionmaker strongly favor a decision contrary to the one reached.

The legislative or administrative history may be highly relevant, especially where there are contemporary statements by members of the decisionmaking body, minutes of its meetings, or reports. In some extraordinary instances the members might be called to the stand at trial to testify concerning the purpose of the official action, although even then such testimony frequently will be barred by privilege.

429 U.S. at 265–68, 97 S.Ct. at 563–65.

2. *Refinement of the* Washington v. Davis *Standard*: In *Personnel Administrator of Massachusetts v. Feeney*, 442 U.S. 256, 99 S.Ct. 2282, 60 L.Ed.2d 870 (1979), the Supreme Court addressed a challenge to the constitutionality of the Massachusetts veterans' preference statute on the ground that it discriminated against women in violation of the Equal Protection Clause of the Fourteenth Amendment. The plaintiff, Helen Feeney, was a female civil service employee of twelve years who had passed a number of open competitive civil service examinations for better jobs. Because of the veterans' preference statute, Feeney, a nonveteran, was ranked in each instance below male veterans who had achieved lower test scores. The statute mandated that all veterans who qualified for state civil service positions had to be considered for appointment ahead of any qualifying nonveterans. The statutory preference was facially neutral because it applied to all honorably discharged veterans, male or female; nevertheless, it "operate[d] overwhelmingly to the advantage of males." *Id.* at 259, 99 S.Ct. at 2286. The plaintiff claimed that the inevitable effect of the law was to exclude women from consideration for the best state civil service jobs: at the commencement of the suit over 98% of the veterans in Massachusetts were male. A three-judge district court declared the statute unconstitutional and enjoined its operation, finding "that the absolute preference afforded by Massachusetts to veterans ha[d] a devastating impact upon the employment opportunities of women." *Id.* at 260, 99 S.Ct. at 2286.

The Supreme Court vacated the judgment and remanded for further consideration in light of *Washington v. Davis*. Massachusetts v. Feeney, 434 U.S. 884, 98 S.Ct. 252, 54 L.Ed.2d 169 (1977). Upon remand, the district court reaffirmed its original judgment, concluding that the absolute veterans' preference was "inherently nonneutral because it favors a class from which women have traditionally been excluded," and that its adverse effects on women's employment opportunities were "too inevitable to have been 'unintended.' " *Feeney*, 442 U.S. at 260–61, 99 S.Ct. at 2286. The Supreme Court reversed a second time:

> The cases of *Washington v. Davis* and *Arlington Heights v. Metropolitan Hous. Dev. Corp.* recognize that when a neutral law has a disparate impact upon a group that has historically been the victim of discrimination, an unconstitutional purpose may still be at work. But those cases signaled no departure from the settled rule that the Fourteenth Amendment guarantees equal laws, not equal results. * * * Those principles apply with equal force to a case involving alleged gender discrimination.

> When a statute gender-neutral on its face is challenged on the ground that its effects upon women are disproportionately adverse, a twofold inquiry is thus appropriate. The first question is whether the statutory classification is indeed neutral in the sense that it is not gender-based. If the classification itself, covert or overt, is not based upon gender, the second question is whether the adverse effect reflects invidious gender-based discrimination. In this second inquiry, impact provides an "important starting point," but purposeful discrimination is "the condition that offends the Constitution." Swann v. Charlotte–Mecklenburg Bd. of Educ., 402 U.S. 1, 16, 91 S.Ct. 1267, 1276, 28 L.Ed.2d 554 (1971).

* * *

> * * * The distinction made by [the Massachusetts veteran's preference statute] is, as it seems to be, quite simply between veterans and nonveterans, not between men and women.

* * *

> The appellee's ultimate argument rests upon the presumption, common to the criminal and civil law, that a person intends the natural and foreseeable consequences of his voluntary actions. Her position was well stated in the concurring opinion in the District Court:

>> Conceding * * * that the goal here was to benefit the veteran, there is no reason to absolve the legislature from awareness that the means chosen to achieve this goal would freeze women out of all those state jobs actively sought by men. To be sure, the legislature did not wish to harm women. But the cutting-off of women's opportunities was an inevitable concomitant of the chosen scheme— as inevitable as the proposition that if tails is up, heads must be down. Where a law's consequences are *that* inevitable, can they meaningfully be described as unintended?

> This rhetorical question implies that a negative answer is obvious, but it is not. The decision to grant a preference to veterans was of course "intentional." So, necessarily, did an adverse impact upon non-veterans follow from that decision. And it cannot seriously be argued that the Legislature of Massachusetts could have been unaware that most veterans are men. It would thus be disingenuous to say that the adverse consequences of this legislation for women were unintended, in

the sense that they were not volitional or in the sense that they were not foreseeable.

"Discriminatory purpose," however, implies more than intent as volition or intent as awareness of consequences. It implies that the decisionmaker, in this case a state legislature, selected or reaffirmed a particular course of action at least in part "because of," not merely "in spite of," its adverse effects upon an identifiable group. Yet nothing in the record demonstrates that this preference for veterans was originally devised or subsequently re-enacted because it would accomplish the collateral goal of keeping women in a stereotypic and predefined place in the Massachusetts Civil Service.

To the contrary, the statutory history shows that the benefit of the preference was consistently offered to "any person" who was a veteran. That benefit has been extended to women under a very broad statutory definition of the term veteran. The preference formula itself, which is the focal point of this challenge, was first adopted—so it appears from this record—out of a perceived need to help a small group of older Civil War veterans. It has since been reaffirmed and extended only to cover new veterans. When the totality of legislative actions establishing and extending the Massachusetts veterans' preference are considered, the law remains what it purports to be: a preference for veterans of either sex over nonveterans of either sex, not for men over women.

442 U.S. at 273–74, 278–80, 99 S.Ct. at 2293, 2295–97.

On the issue of foreseeability of the discriminatory consequences of a practice, the Court noted:

This is not to say that the inevitability or foreseeability of consequences of a neutral rule has no bearing upon the existence of discriminatory intent. Certainly, when the adverse consequences of a law upon an identifiable group are as inevitable as the gender-based consequences of [the Massachusetts veterans' preference statute], a strong inference that the adverse effects were desired can reasonably be drawn. But in this inquiry—made as it is under the Constitution—an inference is a working tool, not a synonym for proof. When, as here, the impact is essentially an unavoidable consequence of a legislative policy that has in itself always been deemed to be legitimate, and when, as here, the statutory history and all of the available evidence affirmatively demonstrate the opposite, the inference simply fails to ripen into proof.

442 U.S. at 279 n.25, 99 S.Ct. at 2296 n.25.

In a later case, the Court, citing *Feeney*, stated that "the law distinguishes between actions taken 'because of' a given end from actions taken 'in spite of' their unintended consequences." Vacco v. Quill, 521 U.S. 793, 802–03, 117 S.Ct. 2293, 138 L.Ed.2d 834 (1997). Although *Feeney* involved a claim of sex discrimination, rather than race discrimination, the *Feeney* refinement of the *Washington v. Davis* purposeful discrimination test is equally applicable to other classifications, such as race and other forms of discrimination. *See, e.g.*, United States v. LULAC, 793 F.2d 636, 646–67 (5th Cir.1986) (race discrimination); Gonzalez v. Connecticut, 151 F.Supp.2d 174 (D.Conn.2001) (race discrimination claim by a Latino employee).

3. What explanation might there be that neither Justice Brennan nor Justice Marshall dissented on the disparate impact issue in *Washington v. Davis?*

4. Is the kind of disparate impact discrimination permitted under the *Washington v. Davis* equal protection standard substantively different from the kind of disparate impact discrimination prohibited under the *Griggs* disparate impact theory? The pre-*Washington v. Davis* lower courts applying disparate impact analysis to equal protection claims did not think so. For example, in *Chance v. Board of Examiners*, 458 F.2d 1167, 1176–77 (2d Cir.1972), the court commented,

> [O]nce discrimination has been found it would be anomalous at best if a public employer could stand back and require racial minorities to prove that its employment tests were inadequate at a time when this nation is demanding that private employers in the same situation come forward and affirmatively demonstrate the validity of such tests. The anomaly would only be emphasized by the recent passage of the Equal Employment Opportunity Act of 1972, which broadened Title VII to include state and public employers.

5. In note 10 of *Washington v. Davis* the Court observed that plaintiffs had failed to amend their complaint to state a claim under Title VII, although they could have done so. The plaintiffs, in fact, intended to use their case to test whether the disparate impact theory is applicable to equal protection employment discrimination claims. Suppose the plaintiffs had amended their complaint to include a race discrimination disparate impact claim under Title VII, in addition to their equal protection race discrimination claim. What result?

6. In a portion of the Court's opinion in *Washington v. Davis* that is not reproduced here, the Court held that it was not clear error for the district court to conclude, on the basis of Title VII standards, "that Test 21 was directly related to the requirements of the police training program and that a positive relationship between the test and training-course performance was sufficient to validate the former, wholly aside from its possible relationship to actual performance as a police officer." 426 U.S. at 250, 96 S.Ct. at 2052.

Note: Analysis and Order and Allocation of the Burdens of Proof in Equal Protection Cases

Employment discrimination claims brought under the Equal Protection Clause are generally brought pursuant to 42 U.S.C. § 1983. The courts have stated that an action under § 1983 has two essential elements. The first is that the plaintiff must prove that the defendant acted under the color of state law. The second is that the plaintiff must prove that as a result of defendant's action or conduct, the plaintiff suffered a denial of her federal statutory or constitutional rights or privileges. A § 1983 plaintiff is denied the rights guaranteed by the Equal Protection Clause when she proves she has been treated differently from other similarly situated employees because of race, gender, or national origin. *See, e.g.*, Annis v. County of Westchester, 136 F.3d 239, 245 (2d Cir.1998) (citing Saulpaugh v. Monroe Community Hosp., 4 F.3d 134, 144 (2d Cir.1993)).

Neither *Washington v. Davis*, *Arlington Heights*, nor *Feeney* provide clear guidance on the order and allocation of the burdens of proof in Equal Protection Clause cases. Nor does the Court in any of these cases discuss whether the "purposeful discrimination" theory now applicable in Equal Protection Clause cases is the same or different from the "intent" theory applicable in Title VII disparate treatment cases. Is the order and allocation of the burdens of proof in Equal Protection Clause and Title VII disparate treatment cases the same or different? Or, how relevant is the *McDonnell Douglas Corp. v. Green* analysis in the Equal Protection employment discrimination cases?

In *St. Mary's Honor Center v. Hicks*, 509 U.S. 502, 113 S.Ct. 2742, 125 L.Ed.2d 407 (1993), the plaintiff, a black male, brought a racial discrimination case against the defendant, a state agency, under Title VII and the Equal Protection Clause. His equal protection claim was based on 42 U.S.C. § 1983, which provides for a claim against a state actor for violation of, among others, rights protected by the Equal Protection Clause. Without deciding specifically whether the *McDonnell Douglas* framework is applicable to Equal Protection Clause claims, the Court stated,

> The Court of Appeals held that the purposeful discrimination element of respondent's § 1983 claim against petitioner Long [a state employee who was Hick's supervisor and who fired Hicks] is the same as the purposeful-discrimination element of his Title VII claim against petitioner St. Mary's. * * * Neither side challenges that proposition, and we shall assume that the *McDonnell Douglas* framework is fully applicable to racial-discrimination-in-employment claims under 42 U.S.C. § 1983. Cf. Patterson v. McLean Credit Union, 491 U.S. 164, 186, 109 S.Ct. 2363, 2377–78, 105 L.Ed.2d 132 (1989) (applying framework to claims under 42 U.S.C. § 1981).

Id. at 506 n.1, 113 S.Ct. at 2756 n.1.

Based on the assumption in note 1 in *Hicks*, lower courts have generally applied the *McDonnell Douglas* framework to employment discrimination cases based on the equal protection § 1983 cases. *See, e.g.*, Hankins v. City of Philadelphia, 189 F.3d 353, 356, 363 (3d Cir.1999) (race discrimination case under Title VII and Equal Protection Clause claim under § 1983), Annis v. County of Westchester, 136 F.3d 239, 245 (2d Cir.1998) (sexual harassment case), Boutros v. Canton Regional Transit Auth., 997 F.2d 198, 202 (1993) (elements for prima facie case of national origin and racial harassment are the same under Title VII and § 1983); Silverman v. City of New York, 216 F.Supp.2d 108, 114–115 (E.D.N.Y 2002) (age, race, and religion case brought by Jewish plaintiff under, inter alia, Equal Protection Clause). Consider the following:

> "To establish a *prima facie* case [of racial discrimination under the fourteenth amendment] a plaintiff must show: 'that he or she is a member of a protected class, that he or she is otherwise similarly situated to members of the unprotected class, and that he or she was treated differently from members of the unprotected class." * * * However, * * * a discrimination plaintiff alleging a violation of the equal protection clause bears a heavier burden of proof than a discrimination plaintiff under Title VII: "Under Title VII, the [plaintiff] must prove

that she was discriminated against through disparate treatment based on an impermissible factor * * *. In an Equal Protection claim, the [plaintiff] faces the tougher standard of proving purposeful and intentional acts of discrimination based on her membership in a particular class not just on an individual basis."

Sims v. Mulcahy, 902 F.2d 524, 538 (7th Cir.) (citing McMillian v. Svetanoff, 878 F.2d 186, 189 (7th Cir.1989)), and Forrester v. White, 846 F.2d 29, 32 (7th Cir.1988)), *cert. denied*, 498 U.S. 897, 111 S.Ct. 249, 112 L.Ed.2d 207 (1990).

[T]his Court established that a plaintiff asserting a Fourteenth Amendment equal protection claim under 42 U.S.C. § 1983 must prove the same elements required to establish a disparate treatment claim under Title VII of the Civil Rights Act of 1964. * * * [I]n order to establish a *prima facie* case, the plaintiff must set forth the following elements: "1) he was a member of a protected class; 2) he was subject to an adverse employment action; 3) he was qualified for the job; and 4) for the same or similar conduct, he was treated differently from similarly situated non-minority employees." * * * It should be noted that the plaintiff's race need only be a motivating factor not necessarily the sole factor—in order for the plaintiff to succeed in his claim.

Perry v. McGinnis, 209 F.3d 597 (6th Cir.2000). In a later case, *Weberg v. Franks*, 229 F.3d 514 (6th Cir.2000), the Sixth Circuit noted that because both Title VII and § 1983 prohibit discriminatory employment practices, it looks to Title VII disparate treatment cases for assistance in analyzing Equal Protection Clause employment discrimination claims.

a. Are the analytical frameworks and the order and allocation of the burdens of proof articulated by the Sixth and Seventh Circuits the same or different? If different, which approach is more consistent with the theory of *Washington v. Davis* and *Feeney*?

b. In the classical *McDonnell Douglas* single-motive circumstantial evidence case, the prima facie case establishes a rebuttable presumption of intentional discrimination, and *Texas Department of Community Affairs v. Burdine*, reproduced in Chapter 2, tells us that this is not an onerous burden. In an equal protection case, must plaintiff's evidence establishing a prima facie case do more than establish a rebuttable presumption of purposeful discrimination in order to shift the burden to the defendant? If not, then what do you think the Seventh Circuit meant in *Sims v. Mulcahy* when it said that a plaintiff faces "a tougher standard of proving purposeful discrimination" in an Equal Protection Clause employment discrimination case?

c. In *Texas v. Lesage*, 528 U.S. 18, 120 S.Ct. 467, 145 L.Ed.2d 347 (1999), the Court held that the *Mt. Healthy* same-decision test is equally applicable in a claim based on the Equal Protection Clause. See Chapter 3, Section B. 3. on mixed-motive cases. Thus, under *Lesage*, it is theoretically possible to bring a mixed-motive equal protection employment discrimination case. Note also that in the excerpt from *Arlington Heights* quoted above, the Court said, "When there is a proof that a discriminatory purpose has been *a motivating factor* in the decision, * * * judicial deference is no longer justified." Is the rule from *Desert Palace, Inc. v. Costa*, reproduced in

Chapter 3, that a plaintiff can prove "a motivating factor" by direct or circumstantial evidence equally applicable in equal protection employment discrimination cases in general and mixed-motive equal protection cases in particular?

d. Among other differences between Title VII and Equal Protection Clause employment discrimination claims is that individuals can be held personally liable under the Equal Protection Clause if they are found to be state actors and they may be liable for damages unless foreclosed by the qualified immunity doctrine. *See, e.g.*, Johnson v. Martin, 195 F.3d 1208 (10th Cir.1999); Cheryl L. Anderson, *"Nothing Personal:" Individual Liability Under 42 U.S.C. § 1983 for Sexual Harassment as an Equal Protection Claim*, 19 Berkeley J.Emp. & Lab.L. 60 (1998). Local government employers are not liable under the theory of respondeat superior; they are liable only if the plaintiff alleges and proves that the alleged discrimination was based on a policy or custom adopted by a policymaker of the government employer. *See* Monell v. New York City Dep't of Soc. Servs., 436 U.S. 658, 98 S.Ct. 2018, 56 L.Ed.2d 611 (1978).

C. THE CIVIL RIGHTS ACT OF 1866, 42 U.S.C. § 1981

Following the ratification of the Thirteenth Amendment, Congress enacted the Civil Rights Act of 1866. As amended in 1870, after the ratification of Fourteenth Amendment, § 1981 contains three clauses that extend to "[a]ll persons within the jurisdiction of the United States" the same three specific sets of rights as are "enjoyed by white citizens." 42 U.S.C. § 1981(a). The three sets of rights are: (1) the right "to make and enforce contracts," (2) the right "to sue, be parties, [and] give evidence," and (3) the right "to the full and equal benefit of all laws and proceedings for the security of persons and property." *Id*. A final clause provides that all such persons "shall be subject to like punishment, pains, penalties, taxes, licenses, and exactions of every kind, and to no other" as are enjoyed by white citizens. The right "to make and enforce contracts" clause of § 1981 is now an integral part of the legal regime prohibiting employment discrimination on the basis of race in both public (except the federal government) and private employment. Yet for almost a century after its enactment, the statute was largely ignored, primarily because the Supreme Court construed most of the major post-Civil War civil rights legislation to apply only to states and state actors. The extension of § 1981 to cover private employment had its genesis in the celebrated case of *Jones v. Alfred H. Mayer Co.*, 392 U.S. 409, 88 S.Ct. 2186, 20 L.Ed.2d 1189 (1968), which held that § 1 of the Civil Rights Act of 1866—now codified at 42 U.S.C. § 1982—"bars *all* racial discrimination, private as well as public, in the sale or rental of property." *Id*. at 413, 88 S.Ct. at 2189 (emphasis in original). Then, in *Johnson v. Railway Express Agency*, 421 U.S. 454, 95 S.Ct. 1716, 44 L.Ed.2d 295 (1975), the Court endorsed the position of the lower courts that the right "to make and enforce contracts" clause of § 1981 prohibits racial discrimination in private employment.

The history of § 1981 is explored in *Runyon v. McCrary*, 427 U.S. 160, 96 S.Ct. 2586, 49 L.Ed.2d 415 (1976), which held that § 1981 prohibits racially discriminatory admission policies at privately operated nonsectarian schools. After oral argument and prior to its decision in *Patterson v. McLean Credit Union*, 491 U.S. 164, 109 S.Ct. 2363, 105 L.Ed.2d 132 (1989), the Supreme Court specifically directed the parties to address the question whether the interpretation of § 1981 adopted in *Runyon*, extending § 1981 to the private sector, should be reconsidered. Patterson v. McLean Credit Union, 485 U.S. 617, 108 S.Ct. 1419, 99 L.Ed.2d 879 (1988). This suggested that the Court might be prepared to overrule *Runyon*, but the Court declined to do so.

1. THEORY OF LIABILITY

GENERAL BUILDING CONTRACTORS ASSOCIATION v. PENNSYLVANIA

Supreme Court of the United States, 1982.
458 U.S. 375, 102 S.Ct. 3141, 73 L.Ed.2d 835.

JUSTICE REHNQUIST delivered the opinion of the Court.

Respondents, the Commonwealth of Pennsylvania and the representatives of a class of racial minorities who are skilled or seek work as operating engineers in the construction industry in Eastern Pennsylvania and Delaware, commenced this action under a variety of federal statutes protecting civil rights, including 42 U.S.C. § 1981. The complaint sought to redress racial discrimination in the operation of an exclusive hiring hall established in contracts between Local 542 of the International Union of Operating Engineers and construction industry employers doing business within the Union's jurisdiction. * * * The question[] we resolve [is] whether liability under 42 U.S.C. § 1981 requires proof of discriminatory intent * * *.

* * *

II

The District Court held that petitioners had violated 42 U.S.C. § 1981 notwithstanding its finding that, as a class, petitioners did not intentionally discriminate against minority workers and neither knew nor had reason to know of the Union's discriminatory practices. The first question we address, therefore, is whether liability may be imposed under § 1981 without proof of intentional discrimination.

Title 42 U.S.C. § 1981 provides:

All persons within the jurisdiction of the United States shall have the same right in every State and Territory to make and enforce contracts, to sue, be parties, give evidence, and to the full and equal benefit of all laws and proceedings for the security of persons and property as is enjoyed by white citizens, and shall be subject to like punishment, pains, penalties, taxes, licenses, and exactions of every kind, and to no other.

We have traced the evolution of this statute and its companion, 42 U.S.C.§ 1982, on more than one occasion, and we will not repeat the narrative again except in broad outline.

The operative language of both laws apparently originated in § 1 of the Civil Rights Act of 1866, 14 Stat. 27, enacted by Congress shortly after ratification of the Thirteenth Amendment. "The legislative history of the 1866 Act clearly indicates that Congress intended to protect a limited category of rights, specifically defined in terms of racial equality." Georgia v. Rachel, 384 U.S. 780, 791, 86 S.Ct. 1783, 1789, 16 L.Ed.2d 925 (1966). The same Congress also passed the Joint Resolution that was later adopted as the Fourteenth Amendment. As we explained in *Hurd v. Hodge*, 334 U.S. 24, 32–33, 68 S.Ct. 847, 851–52, 92 L.Ed. 1187 (1948):

> Frequent references to the Civil Rights Act are to be found in the record of the legislative debates on the adoption of the Amendment. It is clear that in many significant respects the statute and the Amendment were expressions of the same general congressional policy. Indeed, as the legislative debates reveal, one of the primary purposes of many members of Congress in supporting the adoption of the Fourteenth Amendment was to incorporate the guaranties of the Civil Rights Act of 1866 in the organic law of the land. Others supported the adoption of the Amendment in order to eliminate doubt as to the constitutional validity of the Civil Rights Act as applied to the States.

Following ratification of the Fourteenth Amendment, Congress passed what has come to be known as the Enforcement Act of 1870, 16 Stat. 140, pursuant to the power conferred by § 5 of the Amendment. Section 16 of that Act contains essentially the language that now appears in § 1981. Indeed, the present codification is derived from § 1977 of the Revised Statutes of 1874, which in turn codified verbatim § 16 of the 1870 Act. Section 16 differed from § 1 of the 1866 Act in at least two respects. First, where § 1 of the 1866 Act extended its guarantees to "citizens, of every race and color," § 16 of the 1870 Act—and § 1981— protects "all persons." Second, the 1870 Act omitted language contained in the 1866 Act, and eventually codified as § 1982, guaranteeing property rights equivalent to those enjoyed by white citizens. Thus, "[a]lthough the 1866 Act rested only on the Thirteenth Amendment * * * and, indeed, was enacted before the Fourteenth Amendment was formally proposed, * * * the 1870 Act was passed pursuant to the Fourteenth, and changes in wording may have reflected the language of the Fourteenth Amendment." Tillman v. Wheaton–Haven Recreation Ass'n, 410 U.S. 431, 439–40 n. 11, 93 S.Ct. 1090, 1095 n. 11, 35 L.Ed.2d 403 (1973).

In determining whether § 1981 reaches practices that merely result in a disproportionate impact on a particular class, or instead is limited to conduct motivated by a discriminatory purpose, we must be mindful of the "events and passions of the time" in which the law was forged. United States v. Price, 383 U.S. 787, 803, 86 S.Ct. 1152, 1161, 16 L.Ed.2d 267 (1966). The Civil War had ended in April 1865. The First Session of the Thirty-ninth Congress met on December 4, 1865, some six months after the preceding Congress had sent to the States the Thirteenth Amendment and just two weeks before the Secretary of State certified the Amendment's ratification. On January 5, 1866, Senator Trumbull introduced the bill that would become the 1866 Act.

The principal object of the legislation was to eradicate the Black Codes, laws enacted by Southern legislatures imposing a range of civil disabilities on freedmen. Most of these laws embodied express racial classifications and although others, such as those penalizing vagrancy, were facially neutral, Congress plainly perceived all of them as consciously conceived methods of resurrecting the incidents of slavery. Senator Trumbull summarized the paramount aims of his bill:

> Since the abolition of slavery, the Legislatures which have assembled in the insurrectionary States have passed laws relating to the freedmen, and in nearly all the States they have discriminated against them. They deny them certain rights, subject them to severe penalties, and still impose upon them the very restrictions which were imposed upon them in consequence of the existence of slavery, and before it was abolished. The purpose of the bill under consideration is to destroy all these discriminations, and to carry into effect the [Thirteenth] amendment.

Cong.Globe, 39th Cong., 1st Sess., 474 (1866). * * *

Of course, this Court has found in the legislative history of the 1866 Act evidence that Congress sought to accomplish more than the destruction of state-imposed civil disabilities and discriminatory punishments. We have held that both § 1981 and § 1982 "prohibit all racial discrimination, whether or not under color of law, with respect to the rights enumerated therein." Jones v. Alfred H. Mayer Co., 392 U.S. 409, 436, 88 S.Ct. 2186, 2201, 20 L.Ed.2d 1189 (1968). Nevertheless, the fact that the prohibitions of § 1981 encompass private as well as governmental action does not suggest that the statute reaches more than purposeful discrimination, whether public or private. Indeed, the relevant opinions are hostile to such an implication. Thus, although we held in *Jones*, that § 1982 reaches private action, we explained that § 1 of the 1866 Act "was meant to prohibit *all racially motivated* deprivations of the rights enumerated in the statute." 392 U.S. at 426, 88 S.Ct. at 2196 (emphasis on "racially motivated" added). Similarly, in *Runyon v. McCrary*, we stated that § 1981 would be violated "if a private offeror refuses to extend to a Negro, *solely because he is a Negro*, the same opportunity to enter into contracts as he extends to white offerees." 427 U.S. 160, 170–71, 96 S.Ct. 2586, 2594, 49 L.Ed.2d 415 (1976).

The immediate evils with which the Thirty-ninth Congress was concerned simply did not include practices that were "neutral on their face, and even neutral in terms of intent," Griggs v. Duke Power Co.,

401 U.S. 424, 430, 91 S.Ct. 849, 853, 28 L.Ed.2d 158 (1971), but that had the incidental effect of disadvantaging blacks to a greater degree than whites. Congress instead acted to protect the freedmen from intentional discrimination by those whose object was "to make their former slaves dependent serfs, victims of unjust laws, and debarred from all progress and elevation by organized social prejudices." Cong.Globe, 39th Cong., 1st Sess., 1839 (1866) (Rep. Clarke). The supporters of the bill repeatedly emphasized that the legislation was designed to eradicate blatant deprivations of civil rights, clearly fashioned with the purpose of oppressing the former slaves. To infer that Congress sought to accomplish more than this would require stronger evidence in the legislative record than we have been able to discern.

Our conclusion that § 1981 reaches only purposeful discrimination is supported by one final observation about its legislative history. As noted earlier, the origins of the law can be traced to both the Civil Rights Act of 1866 and the Enforcement Act of 1870. Both of these laws, in turn, were legislative cousins of the Fourteenth Amendment. The 1866 Act represented Congress' first attempt to ensure equal rights for the freedmen following the formal abolition of slavery effected by the Thirteenth Amendment. As such, it constituted an initial blueprint of the Fourteenth Amendment, which Congress proposed in part as a means of "incorporat[ing] the guaranties of the Civil Rights Act of 1866 in the organic law of the land." Hurd v. Hodge, 334 U.S. at 32, 68 S.Ct. at 851. The 1870 Act, which contained the language that now appears in § 1981, was enacted as a means of enforcing the recently ratified Fourteenth Amendment. In light of the close connection between these Acts and the Amendment, it would be incongruous to construe the principal object of their successor, § 1981, in a manner markedly different from that of the Amendment itself.[17]

With respect to the latter, "official action will not be held unconstitutional solely because it results in a racially disproportionate impact," Arlington Heights v. Metropolitan Housing Dev. Corp., 429 U.S. 252, 264–65, 97 S.Ct. 555, 562–63, 50 L.Ed.2d 450 (1977). "[E]ven if a neutral law has a disproportionately adverse impact upon a racial minority, it is unconstitutional under the Equal Protection Clause only if that impact can be traced to a discriminatory purpose." Personnel Administrator of Mass. v. Feeney, 442 U.S. 256, 272, 99 S.Ct. 2282, 60 L.Ed.2d 870 (1979). The same Congress that proposed the Fourteenth Amendment also passed the Civil Rights Act of 1866, and the ratification of that Amendment paved the way for the Enforcement Act of 1870. These measures were all products of the same milieu and were directed against the same

---

17. It is true that § 1981, because it is derived in part from the 1866 Act, has roots in the Thirteenth as well as the Fourteenth Amendment. Indeed, we relied on that heritage in holding that Congress could constitutionally enact § 1982, which is also traceable to the 1866 Act, without limiting its reach to "state action." *See* Jones v. Alfred H. Mayer Co., 392 U.S. at 438, 8 S.Ct. at 2202. As we have already intimated, however, the fact that Congress acted in the shadow of the Thirteenth Amendment does not demonstrate that Congress sought to eradicate more than purposeful discrimination when it passed the 1866 Act. * * *

evils. Although Congress might have charted a different course in enacting the predecessors to § 1981 than it did in proposing the Fourteenth Amendment, we have found no convincing evidence that it did so.

We conclude, therefore, that § 1981, like the Equal Protection Clause, can be violated only by purposeful discrimination.

* * *

Notes and Questions

1. *Analytical Framework*: In *Patterson v. McLean Credit Union*, 491 U.S. 164, 186, 109 S.Ct. 2363, 2377–78, 105 L.Ed.2d 132 (1989), the Supreme Court held that, in the absence of direct evidence of discrimination, the *McDonnell Douglas/Burdine* circumstantial evidence analytic scheme is applicable in § 1981 cases to prove purposeful or intentional discrimination:

> We have developed, in analogous areas of civil rights law, a carefully designed framework of proof to determine, in the context of disparate treatment, the ultimate issue whether the defendant intentionally discriminated against the plaintiff. *See* Texas Dep't of Community Affairs v. Burdine, 450 U.S. 248, 101 S.Ct. 1089, 67 L.Ed.2d 207 (1981); McDonnell Douglas Corp. v. Green, 411 U.S. 792, 93 S.Ct. 1817, 36 L.Ed.2d 668 (1973). We agree with the Court of Appeals that this scheme of proof * * * should apply to claims of racial discrimination under § 1981.

The analytical models covered in Chapter 3 are generally applicable to § 1981 claims. At least one court has held, however, that the mixed-motive amendments to Title VII, added under the Civil Rights Act of 1991 (§§ 703(m) and 706(g)(2)(B)), do not apply to mixed-motive cases under § 1981. Mabra v. United Food & Commercial Workers, 176 F.3d 1357 (11th Cir.1999). The reason for the court's holding is that when Congress amended § 1981 in the Civil Rights Act of 1991 it did not specifically include § 1981 in the mixed-motive amendments under Title VII. Under *Mabra*, mixed-motive § 1981 cases are governed by the rule the Supreme Court enunciated in *Price Waterhouse v. Hopkins*, 490 U.S. 228, 109 S.Ct. 1775, 104 L.Ed.2d 268 (1989). In *Price Waterhouse*, the Court held that an employer escapes all liability even if the plaintiff presents sufficient evidence for a jury to conclude that a discriminatory animus was a motivating factor in an adverse employment decision if an employer demonstrates that it would have taken the same action—the same-decision defense—for a legitimate reason alone. What rule of statutory construction do you draw from *Mabra*? Is it a sound rule in light of the fact the same-decision defense adopted in *Price Waterhouse* in 1989 was not statutorily codified until 1991? Can you think of any policy reasons that might justify the *Mabra* rule?

2. Unlike Title VII, claims brought under § 1981 are not limited to employees of an employer having fifteen or more employees. *See* Title VII § 701(b), 42 U.S.C. § 2000e(b). Thus, mom-and-pop corner grocery stores are subject to the reach of § 1981. Section 1981 prohibits racial discrimination in contexts other than employment, but the majority of § 1981 claims involve employment discrimination claims. *See* Theodore Eisenberg & Stew-

art Schwab, *The Importance of Section 1981*, 73 Cornell L.Rev. 596, 601 (1988) (approximately 77% of all § 1981 claims involve employment claims).

3. Does § 1981 reach the attorney-client relationship? A corporation discharged an attorney who was in-house counsel because the client did not want a "New York Jew" as its attorney. Should the attorney, who is Jewish, have a claim for relief under § 1981? *See* Mass v. McClenahan, 893 F.Supp. 225 (S.D.N.Y.1995) (yes, despite the general rule that a client has a right to discharge an attorney at any time).

4. *Section 1981 Claims Cognizable Under the "To Make and Enforce Contract" Clause*:

a. *Prohibited conduct*: Prior to *Patterson v. McLean Credit Union*, 491 U.S. 164, 109 S.Ct. 2363, 105 L.Ed.2d 132 (1989), lower courts were generally in agreement that § 1981 was co-extensive with the kinds of racial discrimination claims that could be brought under Title VII, e.g., hiring, discharge, denial of promotion, and racial harassment. In *Patterson*, the Supreme Court held that § 1981 prohibits racial discrimination only in the making and enforcement of employment contracts, not in other aspects of the contractual relationship. *Patterson* involved a § 1981 suit by a black female who claimed she was harassed, rejected for promotion, and eventually discharged, all because of her race. The Court held that the plaintiff had no claim under § 1981 for racial harassment because the alleged violation involved not the making of a contract but conduct that occurred after the formation of the contract. The Court's limited interpretation of the scope of claims cognizable in § 1981 actions led to a conflict in the lower courts over what claims—other than cases of racially discriminatory hiring—could be brought under § 1981. *See generally* Caroline R. Fredrickson, *The Misreading of* Patterson v. McLean Credit Union: *The Diminishing Scope of Section 1981*, 91 Colum.L.Rev. 891 (1991).

Patterson v. McLean Credit Union was among a number of Supreme Court cases that Congress either overturned or otherwise modified in the Civil Rights Act of 1991. Congress amended § 1981 to overturn *Patterson* by adding, *inter alia,* the following new subsection:

> (b) For purposes of this section, the term "make and enforce contracts" includes the making, performance, modification, and termination of contracts, and the enjoyment of all benefits, privileges, terms, and conditions of the contractual relationship.

105 Stat. 1071, 42 U.S.C. § 1981(b).

b. *Claims by at-will employees*: The 1991 amendments to § 1981 were intended to restore the law on claims that could be brought against private employers prior to *Patterson*. An argument that employers are now advancing is that § 1981 does not apply to at-will employees. The structure of the argument in its broadest form is that § 1981 prohibits discrimination in employment in the making and enforcing of contracts, and that, by definition, at-will employees do not have formal employment contracts. *See* Fadeyi v. Planned Parenthood Ass'n of Lubbock, 160 F.3d 1048, 1049 (5th Cir. 1998). In its narrowest form, the argument is that § 1981 does not encompass a claim for discriminatory discharge because under the at-will doctrine, an employer can discharge an employee for good reason, bad reason, or no reason at all. *See* Perry v. Woodward, 199 F.3d 1126, 1132–33 (10th Cir. 1999). The district courts are divided on the issue. However, the courts of appeals that have addressed the issue have generally agreed that § 1981 protects at-will employees from unlawful racial discrimination in employment, including racially discriminatory discharges, at least where an at-will employment relationship is recognized as a contractual relationship under state law. *See* Spriggs v. Diamond Auto Glass, 165 F.3d 1015, 1020 (4th Cir.1999) (at-will employment is a contractual relationship under Maryland law); *Fadeyi, supra* (same under Texas law); *Perry, supra* (same under New Mexico law). As the court in *Perry* explained, § 1981 somewhat alters the rules of the at-will employment relationship:

> The amendment of section 1981 to include prohibition against racially discriminatory conduct in the termination of contracts effectively altered the at-will relationship. Although the general rule that an employer can discharge an at-will employee for any reason or no reason at all is still valid, an employer can no longer terminate an at-will relationship for a racially discriminatory reason.

199 F.3d at 1133. Courts rejecting the argument that at-will employees cannot sue under § 1981 have relied upon these reasons: (1) the absence of a formal contract does not preclude at-will employees from bringing other kinds of contract or pseudo contract actions such as a claim when an employer fails to pay agreed-upon wages; (2) Congress could not have intended to exclude at-will employees from the reach of § 1981; and (3) allowing at-will employees to sue for racial discrimination under § 1981 furthers the remedial purpose of the statute. *See, e.g.,* Copley v. Bax Global, Inc., 80 F.Supp.2d 1342, 1346 (S.D.Fla.2000) (citations omitted). *See also* Joanna L. Grossman, *Making a Federal Case Out of It: Section 1981 and At–Will Employment*, 67 Brook.L.Rev. 329 (2001).

The Supreme Court's decision in *Haddle v. Garrison*, 525 U.S. 121, 119 S.Ct. 489, 142 L.Ed.2d 502 (1998), lends support to the view that an at-will contractual relationship is sufficient to satisfy § 1981. In *Haddle*, an at-will employee alleged that the defendants conspired to have him fired in retaliation for obeying a federal grand jury subpoena and to deter him from testifying at a federal criminal trial. The plaintiff sued under 42 U.S.C. § 1985(2). Section 1985(2), in relevant part, prohibits conspiracies to deter a witness from testifying in courts, or to injure such person in his person or property on account of having so testified. The Supreme Court rejected the view of the Eleventh Circuit, which had held that the plaintiff had to allege that he suffered an injury to a constitutionally protected property interest to seek relief under § 1985(2). The Supreme Court found that the harm alleged in the case, essentially third-party interference with an at-will employment relationship, was merely a species of the traditional tort of interference with a contractual relationship. Several district courts have found *Haddle* to be persuasive authority that supports the rule that interference with an at-will contractual relationship constitutes interference with an individual's right to "make and enforce contracts" under § 1981, as amended by the Civil Rights Act of 1991. *See, e.g.,* Betts v. Sundstrand Corp., 1999 WL 436579 (N.D.Ill. 1999).

c. *Application to white persons*: The Supreme Court has held that § 1981 prohibits racial discrimination in private employment against whites as well as nonwhites, despite the language in § 1981 providing that "[a]ll persons" covered by the statute shall have the same rights as "white citizens." McDonald v. Santa Fe Trail Transp. Co., 427 U.S. 273, 96 S.Ct. 2574, 49 L.Ed.2d 493 (1976). In this respect, the application of § 1981 is analogous to Title VII, the terms of which are not limited to discrimination against members of any particular race. *See* §§ 703(a)(1) & 703(a)(2) of Title VII, 42 U.S.C. §§ 2000e–2(a)(1) & 2000e–2(a)(2).

d. *Sex and religious discrimination*: Sex discrimination claims cannot be brought under § 1981. *See* Runyon v. McCrary, 427 U.S. 160, 96 S.Ct. 2586, 49 L.Ed.2d 415 (1976) (§ 1981 does not apply to discrimination based on sex or religion); Bobo v. ITT, Continental Baking Co., 662 F.2d 340 (5th Cir.1981), *cert. denied*, 456 U.S. 933, 102 S.Ct. 1985, 72 L.Ed.2d 451 (1982) (same).

e. *Alienage discrimination by private employers*: Whether § 1981 prohibits private employers from discriminating on the basis of alienage is unresolved. *Compare, e.g.*, Duane v. GEICO, 37 F.3d 1036 (4th Cir.1994) (holding that § 1981 prohibits private discrimination against aliens), *cert. granted*, 513 U.S. 1189, 115 S.Ct. 1251, 131 L.Ed.2d 132, *cert. dismissed*, 515 U.S. 1101, 115 S.Ct. 2272, 132 L.Ed.2d 253 (1995), *with* Bhandari v. First Nat'l Bank of Commerce, 829 F.2d 1343 (5th Cir.1987) (en banc) (§ 1981 does not prohibit discrimination against aliens by private parties), *vacated*, 492 U.S. 901, 109 S.Ct. 3207, 106 L.Ed.2d 558, *reinstated on remand*, 887 F.2d 609 (5th Cir.1989) (en banc), *cert. denied*, 494 U.S. 1061, 110 S.Ct. 1539, 108 L.Ed.2d 778 (1990). Justice White dissented from the denial of certiorari in *Bhandari*. *Id.*

In *Anderson v. Conboy*, 156 F.3d 167 (2d Cir.1998), *cert. dismissed sub nom. United Brotherhood of Carpenters & Joiners of America v. Anderson*, 527 U.S. 1030, 119 S.Ct. 2418, 144 L.Ed.2d 789 (1999), the plaintiff, a Jamaican citizen, was working in the United States as a business representative for a labor union. He was subsequently discharged because he was not a United States citizen. He brought an action under § 1981 alleging discrimination because of alienage. In a case of first impression, the Second Circuit held that the plain language of § 1981, as amended by the Civil Rights Act of 1991, prohibits private discrimination because of alienage. The Second Circuit concluded that before the 1991 amendments, § 1981 prohibited states from discrimination because of alienage, but found that with the 1991 Act Congress had broadened the protection to include private discrimination against aliens as well. The union had argued that § 1981 should not be construed to prohibit alienage discrimination by private parties because doing so would conflict with and undermine the Immigration Reform and Control Act of 1986 (IRCA). IRCA is discussed in Chapter 11. Noting that Title VII and § 1981 coexist despite overlapping coverage, the Second Circuit concluded that § 1981 and IRCA likewise could coexist with respect to alienage discrimination. The court also rejected the union's argument that allowing private alienage discrimination claims under § 1981 would endorse this absurd result: Employers would be liable under § 1981 simply by refusing to hire undocumented workers to ensure compliance with IRCA. With respect to the argument that Congress had limited § 1981 claims to race discrimination, the court stated that had Congress intended to do so it could easily have drafted the 1991 amendments to accomplish that result. In granting certiorari, the Supreme Court limited its review to the question whether "[t]aking into account constitutional powers pursuant to which it was enacted, does 42 U.S.C. § 1981 prohibit discrimination against noncitizens on the basis of alienage in private contracts?" 526 U.S. 1086, 119 S.Ct. 1495, 143 L.Ed.2d 650 (1999). The parties subsequently settled the case and the Court dismissed the certiorari petition.

f. *National origin discrimination by private employers*: A plaintiff bringing a discrimination claim under § 1981 against a private employer solely on the basis of national origin is likely to face a motion to dismiss on the authority of *Saint Francis College v. Al–Khazraji*, 481 U.S. 604, 107 S.Ct. 2022, 95 L.Ed.2d 582 (1987), reproduced in Chapter 2. In *Al-Khazraji*, a professor who was a practicing Moslem born in Iraq of Arabian ancestry brought a § 1981 action against a private university claiming discrimination on the basis of "national origin, religion, and/or race." *Id.* at 605, 107 S.Ct. at 2022. The Supreme Court affirmed the Third Circuit's judgment that the plaintiff's § 1981 case could go forward because he had properly alleged racial discrimination on the basis of his Arabian ancestry. The Court, in an opinion by Justice White, made the following distinction between the viability of claims based on race as opposed to national origin or religion:

> Based on the history of § 1981, we have little trouble in concluding that Congress intended to protect from discrimination identifiable classes of persons who are subjected to intentional discrimination solely because of their ancestry or ethnic characteristics. Such discrimination is racial discrimination that Congress intended § 1981 to forbid, whether or not it would be classified as racial in terms of modern scientific theory. * * * If respondent on remand can prove that he was subjected to intentional discrimination based on the fact that he was born an Arab, rather than solely on the place or nation of his origin, or his religion, he will have made out a case under § 1981.

Id. at 613, 107 S.Ct. at 2028.

In a concurring opinion, however, Justice Brennan suggested that the Court's attempt to distinguish between race and national origin claims was problematical:

> Pernicious distinctions among individuals based solely on their ancestry are antithetical to the doctrine of equality upon which this Nation is founded. * * * I write separately only to point out that the line between discrimination based on "ancestry or ethnic characteristics," and discrimination based on "place or nation of * * * origin," is not a bright one. It is true that one's ancestry—the ethnic group from which an individual and his or her ancestors are descended—is not necessarily the same as one's national origin—the country "where a person was *born*, or more broadly, the country from which his or her ancestors *came*." Espinoza v. Farah Manufacturing Co., 414 U.S. 86, 88, 94 S.Ct. 334, 336, 38 L.Ed.2d 287 (1973) (emphasis added). Often, however, the two are identical as a factual matter: one was born in the nation whose primary stock is one's own ethnic group. Moreover, national origin claims have been treated as ancestry or ethnicity claims

in some circumstances. For example, in the Title VII context, the terms overlap as a legal matter. * * * I therefore read the Court's opinion to state only that discrimination based on *birthplace alone* is insufficient to state a claim under § 1981.

Id. at 614, 107 S.Ct. at 2028–29. In light of *Al-Khazraji*, would you argue that a § 1981 claim against a private employer based solely on allegations of "national origin" discrimination can *never* go forward? *See* Aramburu v. Boeing Co., 112 F.3d 1398, 1411 n.10 (10th Cir.1997) (§ 1981 does not protect individuals on the basis of national origin). See the discussion of the meaning of national origin under Title VII in Chapter 11. For a discussion on whether national origin should be recognized under § 1981, see Lorilyn Chamberlin, *National Origin Discrimination Under Section 1981*, 51 Fordham L.Rev. 919 (1983).

5. *Right to Jury Trial*: The courts of appeals are divided on whether either party is entitled to a jury trial in a § 1981 action. *Compare* Setser v. Novack Inv. Co., 657 F.2d 962 (8th Cir.) (§ 1981 back pay suit gives rise to jury trial), *cert. denied*, 454 U.S. 1064, 1066, 102 S.Ct. 615, 616, 70 L.Ed.2d 601 (1981) (White, J., dissenting from denial of certiorari because of conflict in the circuits), *with* Moore v. Sun Oil Co., 636 F.2d 154 (6th Cir.1980) (no right to jury trial); Lynch v. Pan American World Airways, Inc., 475 F.2d 764 (5th Cir.1973) (claim for monetary damages does not mandate jury trial).

6. *Procedural Requirements*: Unlike Title VII claims, a claim brought under § 1981 is not subject to a requirement of exhaustion of administrative remedies. In *Johnson v. Railway Express Agency*, 421 U.S. 454, 461, 95 S.Ct. 1716, 1721, 44 L.Ed.2d 295 (1975), the Supreme Court noted that "the remedies available under Title VII and under § 1981, although related, and although directed to most of the same ends, are separate, distinct, and independent." Although not subject to an exhaustion of administrative remedies requirement, § 1981 claims are subject to statutes of limitations as discussed in the following note.

7. *Statute of Limitations*: Unlike Title VII and the ADEA, § 1981 does not have its own built-in statute of limitations. *See* Title VII, § 706(e), 42 U.S.C. 2000e–5(e); ADEA, § 7(d)(1), 29 U.S.C. § 626(d)(1). Thus, 42 U.S.C. § 1988 requires courts to adopt the most analogous limitations period provided by state law. In *Wilson v. Garcia*, 471 U.S. 261, 105 S.Ct. 1938, 85 L.Ed.2d 254 (1985), the Court held that a state's "personal injury" statute of limitations is the most appropriate limitations period for claims brought under 42 U.S.C. § 1983, and the reasoning of *Wilson* was later applied to § 1981 claims in *Goodman v. Lukens Steel*, 482 U.S. 656, 107 S.Ct. 2617, 96 L.Ed.2d 572 (1987). Where a state has multiple statutes of limitations for personal injuries, the residual or general personal injury statute of limitations applies, not the one for "intentional" torts. Owens v. Okure, 488 U.S. 235, 109 S.Ct. 573, 102 L.Ed.2d 594 (1989).

On December 1, 1990, Congress enacted 28 U.S.C. § 1658 to eliminate some of the confusion regarding the appropriate statute of limitations to be applied in civil actions brought under federal statutes that do not have their own express limitation periods. Section 1658 provides that: "[e]xcept as otherwise provided by law, a civil action arising under an Act of Congress enacted after the date of the enactment of this section may not be commenced later than four years after the cause of action accrues." P.L. 101–650, 104 Stat. 5114. *See generally* Kimberly Jade Norwood, *28 U.S.C. § 1658: A Limitation Period with Real Limitations*, 69 Ind.L.J. 477 (1994).

Section 1981 was enacted long before 1990, but, as discussed above, the Supreme Court limited the substantive reach of § 1981 in *Patterson v. McLean Credit Union*, 491 U.S. 164, 109 S.Ct. 2363, 105 L.Ed.2d 132 (1989). On November 21, 1991, about a year after Congress enacted § 1658, Congress amended § 1981 in the Civil Rights Act of 1991. Lower courts are divided over whether the new four-year statute of limitations in § 1658 applies to § 1981 as amended by Congress in 1991. *See* Zubi v. AT & T Corp., 219 F.3d 220 (3d Cir.2000) (summarizing the three distinct approaches various district courts have adopted). The Supreme Court has granted certiorari in *Jones v. R.R. Donnelley & Sons Co.*, 305 F.3d 717 (7th Cir.2002), *cert. granted*, ___ U.S. ___, 123 S.Ct. 2074, 155 L.Ed.2d 1059 (2003), to decide the issue.

8. *Unions*: In *Daniels v. Pipefitters' Association Local Union No. 597*, 945 F.2d 906 (7th Cir.1991), *cert. denied*, 503 U.S. 951, 112 S.Ct. 1514, 117 L.Ed.2d 651 (1992), the court found a union liable under § 1981 because it had denied a black employee a referral to a job on the basis of race. Because the union's job referral service was the primary process through which employers hired union members, the discriminatory conduct of the union interfered with the plaintiff's ability to enter into an employment contract. In addition, the union was liable under § 1981 for interfering with the employee's ability to enforce a provision of the collective bargaining agreement that required the union to refer its members on a nondiscriminatory basis.

9. *Section 1981 Employment Discrimination Claims Cognizable Under the "Full and Equal Benefits of All Laws" Clause:* Until recently the "make and enforce contracts" clause of § 1981 has been the main focus of claims of racial discrimination against private parties. In a recent development, lower courts are now divided on the issue whether race discrimination claims can be brought against a private party under the right to "the full and equal benefit of all laws" clause. The Sixth Circuit has held that the federal statutory right to "the full and equal benefit of all laws" protects individuals against impairment of such rights by private racial discrimination. Chapman v. Higbee Co., 319 F.3d 825 (6th Cir.2003) (en banc), *petition for cert. filed*, (U.S. May 6, 2003) (U.S. No. 02–1646). One of the grounds on which the Sixth Circuit relied is section (c) of § 1981 which provides that "[t]he rights protected by this section are protected against impairment by nongovernmental discrimination and impairment under color of State law." Other courts hold that private parties cannot be sued under this clause because states not private parties enact "laws," therefore only the state can deny "the full and equal benefit" of "laws." *See id*. at 837–38. (Suhrheinrich, J., dissenting) (collecting cases). Most of the cases to date in which private parties have sued private defendants under the "full and equal benefit of all laws" clause of § 1981 have been consumer racial profiling cases. See cases cited in the majority and dissenting opinions in *Chapman. Id*. at 833 n.6, *id*. at 837–38. (Suhrheinrich, J., dissenting). The courts have not yet addressed the issue whether the "full and equal benefits" clause may be the source of

protection against racial discrimination in employment by private employers. What arguments could you make that the "full and equal benefits" clause of § 1981 should or should not extend to racial discrimination in employment by private employers?

2. SECTION 1981 CLAIMS AGAINST STATE AND LOCAL GOVERNMENT EMPLOYERS

ODEN v. OKTIBBEHA COUNTY, MISSISSIPPI

United States Court of Appeals for the Fifth Circuit.
246 F.3d 458, *cert. denied*, 534 U.S. 948, 122 S.Ct. 341, 151 L.Ed.2d 258 (2001).

PARKER, J., Circuit Judge.

* * *

II. PROPER DEFENDANTS UNDER TITLE VII AND 42 U.S.C. § 1981

A. Defendants and Remedies under § 1981

Plaintiffs may plead causes of action under both Title VII and § 1981 against private employers to remedy discrimination in private employment contracts. *See Runyon v. McCrary,* 427 U.S. 160, 174, 96 S.Ct. 2586, 49 L.Ed.2d 415 (1976); *Johnson v. Railway Express Agency, Inc.,* 421 U.S. 454, 459, 95 S.Ct. 1716, 44 L.Ed.2d 295 (1975). Plaintiffs may also pursue a § 1983 cause of action against persons acting under color of state law in order to assert their substantive rights under § 1981. We must determine whether Oden can assert an independent cause of action under § 1981 against Oktibbeha County and the Sheriff in his official and individual capacities.

1. The County and the Sheriff in His Official Capacity

In 1989, the Supreme Court held in *Jett v. Dallas Independent School District,* 491 U.S. 701, 731, 109 S.Ct. 2702, 105 L.Ed.2d 598 (1989), that § 1981 did not provide a separate cause of action against local government entities. The Court concluded that plaintiffs must assert a cause of action against state actors under § 1983 to remedy violations of civil rights under § 1981. *See id.* Several courts have addressed the continuing significance of the Court's plurality decision after Congress passed the Civil Rights Act of 1991. The Act amended § 1981 by adding subsection (c), which states that the rights protected by § 1981 "are protected against impairment by nongovernmental discrimination and impairment under color of state law." 42 U.S.C. § 1981(c).[2] In order to determine whether Oden could pursue a separate cause of action under § 1981 against Oktibbeha County and the Sheriff

---

2. The circuit courts are split as to the effect of the Civil Rights Act of 1991 upon the Court's holding in *Jett.* The Fourth Circuit and Eleventh Circuit concluded that the 1991 amendment had no affect on the Court's opinion. See Butts v. County of Volusia, 222 F.3d 891, 894 (11th Cir.2000); Dennis v. County of Fairfax, 55 F.3d 151, 156 n. 1 (4th Cir.1995). The Ninth Circuit, however, concluded that the 1991 amendment implicitly created a cause of action against local government entities. See Federation of African American Contractors v. Oakland, 96 F.3d 1204 (9th Cir.1996).

in his official capacity, we must address whether the 1991 amendment abrogated the Court's holding in *Jett* and created a separate cause of action against local government entities.

Subsection (c) does not expressly create a remedial cause of action against local government entities, and we are not persuaded that such a remedy should be implied. In *Jett,* the Court held that Congress intended § 1983 to be the sole remedy for discrimination by persons acting under color of state law. *See Jett,* 491 U.S. at 731, 109 S.Ct. 2702. The Court reasoned that § 1981 implicitly created an independent cause of action against private actors because no other statute created such a remedy. *See id.* at 732, 109 S.Ct. 2702. Because § 1983 provided a remedy against persons acting under color of state law, the Court declined to imply a cause of action under § 1981 independent of § 1983. We are persuaded that the conclusion in *Jett* remains the same after Congress enacted the 1991 amendments. Subsection (c) addresses only substantive rights. Section 1983 remains the only provision to expressly create a remedy against persons acting under color of state law. The addition of subsection (c) creates no more of a need for the judiciary to imply a cause of action under § 1981 against state actors than existed when the Supreme Court decided *Jett.*

The legislative history of the 1991 amendment is supportive of our conclusion. By enacting subsection (c), Congress stated that it intended to codify the Supreme Court's decision in *Runyon v. McCrary. See Butts,* 222 F.3d at 894 (citing H.R. Rep. No. 102–40(I), at 92 (1991), reprinted in 1991 U.S.C.C.A.N. 549, 630; H.R. Rep. No. 102–40(II), at 37 (1991), reprinted in 1991 U.S.C.C.A.N. 694, 731). *See also Anderson v. Conboy,* 156 F.3d 167, 179 (2d Cir.1998). In *Runyon,* the Supreme Court reaffirmed that § 1981 implies a right of action based on racial discrimination against private actors. *See Runyon,* 427 U.S. at 174–75, 96 S.Ct. 2586. There is no congressional statement of intent to overrule *Jett.* By codifying *Runyon,* Congress confirmed that § 1981 implies a cause of action against private actors.

The question follows then why, if Congress only intended to codify *Runyon,* does subsection (c) include language referring to persons acting under color of state law? The Ninth Circuit reasoned that this allusion to persons acting under color of state law implies Congressional intent to create a remedy in addition to § 1983. *See Oakland,* 96 F.3d at 1213. We disagree. "[T]he judicial power to imply or create remedies * * * should not be exercised in the face of an express decision by Congress concerning the scope of remedies available under a particular statute." *Jett,* 491 U.S. at 732, 109 S.Ct. 2702 (citing *National R.R. Passenger Corp. v. National Assn. of R.R. Passengers,* 414 U.S. 453, 458, 94 S.Ct. 690, 38 L.Ed.2d 646 (1974)). Because Congress neither expressed its intent to overrule *Jett,* nor explicitly created a remedy against state actors in addition to § 1983, we are not willing to deviate from the Supreme Court's analysis of § 1981 in *Jett.* Accordingly, Deputy Oden could not maintain an independent cause of action under § 1981 against Oktibbeha County and Sheriff Dolph Bryan in his official capacity.

* * *

Notes and Questions

1. *Oden* represent the majority view of those circuits that have specifically addressed the issue whether the Congress overruled *Jett* in the Civil Rights Act of 1991. Other circuits agreeing with *Oden* are the Fourth Circuit, Dennis v. County of Fairfax, 55 F.3d 151, 156 n.1 (4th Cir.1995); and the Eleventh Circuit, Butts v. County of Volusia, 222 F.3d 891, 894 (11th Cir.2000). No other circuit as of this date has followed the Ninth Circuit's view. Which do you believe is the better view?

2. The "policy or custom" requirement of § 1983 is clearly satisfied when a plaintiff can rely on a legislative enactment or executive order as the basis for a § 1981 claim against a government employer. *See, e.g.*, Monell v. New York City Dep't of Soc. Servs., 436 U.S. 658, 98 S.Ct. 2018, 56 L.Ed.2d 611 (1978). The most difficult cases on "policy or custom" are those involving a single or isolated decision by a municipal official. The Supreme Court has struggled with this issue in a number of cases since *Monell*. In *City of St. Louis v. Praprotnik*, 485 U.S. 112, 124–25, 108 S.Ct. 915, 924–25, 99 L.Ed.2d 107 (1988), the Court said this about identifying policymakers who have authority to bind a municipality:

> We begin by reiterating that the identification of policymaking officials is a question of state law. "Authority to make municipal policy may be granted directly by a legislative enactment or may be delegated by an official who possesses such authority, and of course, whether an official had final policymaking authority is a question of state law." Pembaur v. Cincinnati, 475 U.S. 469, 483, 106 S.Ct. 1292, 1300, 89 L.Ed.2d 452 (1986) (plurality opinion). Thus the identification of policymaking officials is not a question of federal law, and it is not a question of fact in the usual sense. The States have extremely wide latitude in determining the form that local government takes, and local preferences have led to a profusion of distinct forms. * * * Without attempting to canvass the numberless factual scenarios that may come to light in litigation, we can be confident that state law (which may include valid local ordinances and regulations) will always direct a court to some official or body that has the responsibility for making law or setting policy in any given area of a local government's business.

3. *Federal Employees*: Federal employees covered by Title VII may not sue federal agencies under § 1981 because the Supreme Court so held in *Brown v. General Services Administration*, 425 U.S. 820, 96 S.Ct. 1961, 48 L.Ed.2d 402 (1976), when it declared that Title VII is the exclusive remedy for racial discrimination by covered federal government employers. In 1972, Congress extended the protections of Title VII to most federal employees in § 717, 42 U.S.C. § 2000e–16. In addition, § 117 of the Civil Rights Act of 1991 extended the rights and protections of Title VII to employees of the House of Representatives and employees of agencies of Congress. Title III, § 301 *et seq.*, of the 1991 Act, known as the "Government Employee Rights

Act of 1991," created an Office of Senate Fair Employment Practices and established procedures to protect Senate employees from discrimination on the basis of race, color, religion, sex, national origin, age, or disability.

4. *Individual Liability Under § 1981.* State and local employers who satisfy the state action doctrine can be sued for employment discrimination based on race under § 1981, but may nevertheless avoid the obligation to pay monetary damages because of the defense of qualified immunity. Qualified immunity protects government officials performing discretionary functions from civil trials for damages if their conduct does not violate clearly established constitutional or statutory rights of which a reasonable person would have known. *See, e.g.,* Richmond v. Board of Regents of the Univ. of Minn., 957 F.2d 595 (8th Cir.1992); Lambert v. Fulton County, Ga., 253 F.3d 588 (11th Cir.2001).

5. Discrimination by state and local government employers because of alienage is prohibited by § 1981. *See, e.g.,* Graham v. Richardson, 403 U.S. 365, 377, 91 S.Ct. 1848, 1855, 29 L.Ed.2d 534 (1971) (§ 1981 protects aliens from discrimination by state governments).

6. For an empirical study of the relevancy of § 1981 now that Title VII is on the books, see Theodore Eisenbert & Stewart Schwab, *The Importance of Section 1981*, 73 Cornell L.Rev. 596 (1988).

*

Part III

SPECIFIC CATEGORIES OF DISCRIMINATION

Chapter 6

DISCRIMINATION BECAUSE OF SEX

A. INTRODUCTION

On February 8, 1964, two days before the House voted on the Civil Rights Bill, Representative Howard W. Smith, a Southern Democrat who opposed the bill, proposed that "sex" be added as a prohibited category to Title VII. Despite the ensuing "humorous debate, later enshrined as 'Ladies Day in the House,'" the amendment was passed that same day by a vote of 168 to 133. Jo Freeman, *How "Sex" Got into Title VII: Persistent Opportunism as a Maker of Public Policy*, 9 Law & Ineq.J. 163, 163 (1991). Most courts and commentators have viewed this sparse legislative history as evidence that "sex" was included in Title VII as a "joke" or a failed eleventh-hour maneuver to defeat the Civil Rights Bill. *See id.* at 164, 176–77; Robert C. Bird, *More Than a Congressional Joke: A Fresh Look at the Legislative History of Sex Discrimination of the 1964 Civil Rights Act*, 3 Wm. & Mary J. Women & L. 137, 137–40 (1997). More recent interpretations of the context of the passage of the "sex" amendment suggest, however, that the "sex discrimination provision was the result of complex political struggles involving racial issues, presidential politics, and competing factions of the women's rights movement." Bird, *supra*, at 138; *see generally* Freeman, *supra*. According to these revisionist accounts, members of the National Women's Party (NWP), who for years had lobbied Congress for an Equal Rights Amendment (ERA), and a handful of women members of the House, who spoke out in favor of the amendment, were instrumental in assuring its passage. Freeman concluded:

> The civil rights movement, and the various civil rights bills, opened up a window of opportunity of which the activists took advantage. The NWP and women members of Congress lacked the resources to effect major policy changes by themselves; instead they grabbed the coattails of a major social movement which did have these resources. Persistent opportunism forced the federal government to make a major public innovation in an area which it had not previously acknowledged as being very important.

Freeman, *supra*, at 184.

Despite its ambiguous origins, the prohibition of employment discrimination because of sex ultimately has proved to be as significant in many respects as the primary purpose behind Title VII—the elimination and remediation of race-based employment decisions. Initially, Title VII's broad prohibition against sex discrimination in employment was viewed by supporters as an extension of the principles of equality and nondiscrimination found in the Equal Pay Act of 1963. Conservative feminists who had supported an Equal Rights Amendment apparently envisioned Title VII as a "surrogate" for the ERA: a means of removing arbitrary barriers to the economic and social advancement of women, both individually and as a class. *See* Freeman, *supra*, at 183. While Title VII has certainly not eliminated discriminatory employment practices or inequality between the sexes, the thousands of meritorious statutory claims brought by women who were the victims of unlawful employment discrimination have undoubtedly altered the way employers and employees think about sex discrimination in the workplace. Yet, the courts continue to struggle with complex issues raised by the cases, including the most fundamental question of what "sex" means for purposes of the statute.

In 1979, Professor Catharine MacKinnon presented evidence that sex discrimination in employment is, in some respects, an even more intractable and harmful social and economic problem than race discrimination. Catharine A. MacKinnon, Sexual Harassment of Working Women: A Case of Sex Discrimination 14 (1979). After almost forty years of experience with Title VII, few would question the wisdom or necessity of including "sex" as a prohibited basis for employment discrimination, deserving the same statutory protection as the other immutable traits— race, color, and national origin. In a nine-month period ending June 30, 2002, the EEOC filed more than twice as many class actions alleging sex discrimination than alleging race discrimination. *See Sex Discrimination Cases Predominate in Recent Class Actions Filed by EEOC*, 20 Hum. Resources Rep. (BNA) No.34, at 948 (Sept. 2, 2002) (reporting that from Oct. 1, 2001, to June 30, 2002, the EEOC filed twenty-nine class actions alleging sex discrimination and thirteen class actions alleging race discrimination against black employees). Significantly, four of the twenty-nine sex-based class actions involved allegations of discrimination against men. *Id*. Thus, although the inclusion of "sex" as a prohibited basis for employment decisions was initially understood as a women's issue, the statute has long functioned to protect men as well as women from many arbitrary sex-based employment decisions.

Political equality was the acknowledged achievement of the first women's movement in the United States, but attaining the suffrage in 1920 did not ensure women an equal share in political power. Likewise, Title VII promises women equal opportunity in the labor market, but it, alone, can neither eradicate fundamental attitudes about women and work nor alter the underlying structure of the labor market. Historian Patricia Cooper has observed,

Many women in the 1990s enjoy expanded job choices and opportunities and many women's daily experiences on the job contrast sharply with those of most women back in 1920. That year, women constituted about one fifth of the labor force. In 1992, women were almost half of the nation's workers, and three quarters of all U.S. women between ages thirty-five and forty-four worked for pay. But overall, much has not changed. Women are still regarded by many as "outsiders—as visitors to a male labor force."[3] Thousands of women still work in low-paid jobs with no hope of advancement. Men's work and women's work are sill highly segregated— fewer than ten percent of Americans share the same job, employer, and location with someone of the other sex. The United States Census in 1990 listed 503 occupations; one-third of all working women were concentrated in just ten of them, including clerical jobs, retail sales, food preparation, school teaching, and nursing. Despite everything that has happened since World War II, women still are concentrated in the very same occupations that topped the list back in 1940.

Patricia Cooper, *"A Masculinist Vision of Useful Labor"—Popular Ideologies About Women and Work in the United States, 1820 to 1939*, 84 Ky.L.J. 827, 828 (1996) (citations omitted).

Economic and social conditions, as well as personal choices and constraints, and an individual's education, ability, and personality, help determine the job opportunities of both women and men. *See generally* Mitra Toossi, *A Century of Change: The U.S. Labor Force, 1950–2050*, Monthly Lab. Rev., May 2002, at 15. Geography plays a role, too. For example, women who worked full time in 1999, earned on average 72.7 percent of what men earned. *Women Have Not Achieved Economic Equity With Men in Any State, New Report Says*, 20 Hum. Resources Rep. (BNA) No.48, at 1339 (Dec. 9, 2002) (citing Institute for Women's Policy Research, *The Status of Women in the State*s (2002)).Women living in the District of Columbia, however, earned 89 percent of men's earnings; whereas women in Wyoming earned only 64 percent. *Id.* Unionization is also a factor: "female union members earned 38.2 percent more per week than female nonunion workers," and "women of color who are represented by a union earn[ed] 38.6 percent more than their nonunion counterparts." *Id.* Moreover, "workplace inequity * * * is often structurally embedded in the norms and cultural practices of an institution." Susan Sturm, *Lawyers and the Practice of Workplace Equity*, 2002 Wis.L.Rev. 277, 281.

Despite Title VII, the ADEA, and the ADA, the "protected" traits— sex, race, color, religion, national origin, age, and disability—often continue to play a role, directly or indirectly, in the availability of job opportunities. Other institutional actors, besides employers, can also

---

3. Alice Kessler–Harris, Working Women: Myths and Realities, N.Y. Times, Aug.   18, 1982, at A21.

affect the culture and practices of the workplace. The courts, for example, have significant responsibility for filling in the details in any outline of legislative reform—for determining in many individual cases how capacious or narrow the legislative vision of statutes like Title VII will ultimately prove to be. Are courts partly responsible for perpetuating workplace sex discrimination when they fail to challenge underlying assumptions about gender and work? Professor Vicki Schultz wrote:

> Title VII promised working women change. But, consciously or unconsciously, courts have interpreted the statute with some of the same assumptions that have historically legitimated women's economic disadvantage. Most centrally, courts have assumed that women's aspirations and identities as workers are shaped exclusively in private realms that are independent of and prior to the workworld. By assuming that women form stable job aspirations before they begin working, courts have missed the ways in which employers contribute to creating women workers in their images of who "women" are supposed to be. Judges have placed beyond the law's reach the structural features of the workplace that gender jobs and people, and disempower women from aspiring to higher-paying nontraditional employment.

Vicki Schultz, *Telling Stories About Women and Work: Judicial Interpretations of Sex Segregation in the Workplace in Title VII Cases Raising the Lack of Interest Argument*, 103 Harv.L.Rev. 1749, 1756 (1990). For additional perspectives on societal, governmental, and internal barriers to the advancement of women and minorities in American businesses, see Federal Glass Ceiling Commission, Good for Business: Making Full Use of the Nation's Human Capital (1995).

As you read the cases and materials in this chapter, evaluate them as a basis for developing your own ideas about the relationship of legislative reform and judicial decisionmaking to social change. Is the existing framework of civil rights statutes and judge-made law adequate now to address the problems of sex discrimination in employment? Do you anticipate that this framework can adapt to employment patterns that may occur in the next decades? Consider the following demographic trends: According to a 1997 study, women made up 46% of the American workforce in 1994, and will comprise 48% of the workforce in 2005 and about 50% in 2020. Richard W. Judy & Carol D'Amico, Workforce 2020: Work and Workers in the 21st Century 112–13, 110 (Hudson Institute 1997). Women will account for 50% of the total of new entrants to the labor force between 1994 and 2005 and almost two-thirds (62%) of the *net* new entrants for this period. *Id. See also* William B. Johnston, Workforce 2000: Work and Workers for the 21st Century (Hudson Institute 1987).

Is sex discrimination still a problem? This question may seem relevant only to individuals contemplating careers in jobs that continue to be highly sex-segregated: women who want to be firefighters, men who want to be nurses. Some jobs may have physical requirements that few women can satisfy without additional training. *See, e.g.*, Lanning v. Southeastern Pennsylvania Transp. Auth. (SEPTA), 308 F.3d 286 (3d Cir.2002) (*Lanning II*) (upholding an aerobic test for applicants to a transit police training program that disqualifies 90% of female applicants), discussed in Chapter 4. Other jobs, such as nursing or the legal profession, may have more subtle barriers to entry by individuals who do not match the gender role historically associated with those careers.

Consider your own career aspirations. Most law students are by now familiar with the case of *Bradwell v. Illinois*, 83 U.S. (16 Wall.) 130, 21 L.Ed. 442 (1873), in which the Supreme Court upheld the decision of the Illinois Supreme Court denying Myra Bradwell admittance to the bar solely because she was a woman. Justice Bradley concurred in the opinion, observing that the Court's ruling was justified because women's "natural and proper timidity and delicacy" and their "paramount destiny and mission * * * to fulfill the noble and benign offices of wife and mother" made them inherently unsuited for the demands of the legal profession. *Id.* at 141. Looking at the gender composition of your law school class, you might conclude that the gender bias and stereotyping typified by Justice Bradley's concurrence in *Bradwell* is a relic of ancient history. The year 2001 marked the first time that the number of women entering law school in the United States exceeded the number of men. Joe G. Baker, *The Influx of Women into Legal Professions: An Economic Analysis*, Monthly Lab.Rev., Aug. 2002, at 14, 14.

As law students, you can examine your own assumptions about whether or to what extent gender discrimination is still a problem in the workplace generally or in the workplace you are about to enter—the legal profession. As you think about these issues, consider the following observations by Professor Deborah Rhode:

> In law as in other traditionally male-dominated occupations, women have made dramatic progress. Since the 1960s, female representation among new entrants to the bar has increased from about 3 percent to 45 percent. However, women still account for only about 16 percent of full professors in law schools, 13 percent of the partners in the nation's 250 largest law firms, and 8 percent of judges in the federal courts. Disparities in the pool of eligible candidates cannot explain the extent of this underrepresentation. Female lawyers are less than half as likely as similarly qualified male colleagues to become partners, and pay gaps range from 10 to 35 percent between men and women in comparable positions. The disparities are even greater for women of color.

Deborah L. Rhode, Speaking of Sex: The Denial of Gender Inequality 141 (1997) (citation omitted); *see also* Paul W. Mattessich & Cheryl W. Heilman, *The Career Paths of Minnesota Law School Graduates: Does Gender Make a Difference?*, 9 Law & Ineq.J. 59 (1990).

If sex discrimination continues to limit women's employment opportunities (even in the legal profession), what is the explanation? *See* Federal Glass Ceiling Commission, *supra*, at 26–27; *see also* Ramona L.

Paetzold & Rafael Gelu, *Through the Looking Glass: Can Title VII Help Women and Minorities Shatter the Glass Ceiling?*, 31 Hous.L.Rev. 1517, 1520 (1995) (arguing that "[t]he courts' interpretation of Title VII has not been sufficiently sensitive to the subtle ways in which women and minorities come to be excluded from mid-level and upper level positions within organizations—ways so subtle that employers themselves are not always aware of them"). Are the theories of liability developed under Title VII adequate to explain these persistent disparities in employment opportunities for men and women? How can we know for sure whether the disparities are caused by unlawful discrimination or by other factors? *See* Christine Jolls, *Is There a Glass Ceiling?*, 25 Harv.Women's L.J. 1 (2002) (arguing that the "glass ceiling" exists and is significantly explained by unlawful sex discrimination). A 2001 American Bar Association report stated: "On average, female lawyers earn about $20,000 less than male lawyers, and significant disparities persist even between those with similar qualifications, experience, and positions." *ABA Study Finds That Female Lawyers Earn Less Than Men, Face Bias, Harassment*, 19 Hum. Resources Rep. (BNA) No.18, at 498 (May 7, 2001) (quoting *The Unfinished Agenda, Women and the Legal Profession* (ABA) Apr. 26, 2001, available at <*http://www.abanet.org*>. Moreover, "men are at least twice as likely as similarly qualified women to obtain partnership." *Id.* In light of these facts, why do increasing numbers of women choose the legal profession? *See generally* Baker, *supra*, at 23 (arguing that "the legal profession is very attractive to women compared with other professional fields in terms of labor force participation, career re-entry, earnings, and returns to schooling").

A number of issues arising out of claims of sex discrimination in private or public employment are addressed in other chapters. This chapter focuses on several selected topics and cases that raise concerns that are unique in sex discrimination cases. After a brief introduction in Section B to the analytical paradigms and theories of liability used in sex discrimination cases, Section C examines the case law interpreting the Pregnancy Discrimination Act (PDA), a 1978 amendment to Title VII. Section D addresses the role of the Family and Medical Leave Act (FMLA) of 1993 in buttressing Title VII's antidiscrimination principles and in attempting to insure that childbirth and family care-giving responsibilities are not a barrier to employment opportunities of both men and women. Next, Section E explores the sex-based bona fide occupational qualification (BFOQ) defense. Finally, Section F discusses how the theories of liability and defenses developed in sex discrimination cases have been applied in the context of challenges to sex-based dress, grooming, and appearance requirements. The Equal Pay Act (EPA) and the interplay between Title VII and the EPA will be discussed in Chapter 7 and sexual harassment will be covered in Chapter 8. The contested meanings of the term "sex" in Title VII law is further examined in Chapter 9, which deals with discrimination on the basis of sexual orientation.

B. THEORETICAL AND ANALYTICAL APPROACHES TO SEX DISCRIMINATION

1. WHAT IS "SEX" DISCRIMINATION?

Title VII has proved to be remarkably adaptable in addressing a range of difficult questions about the meaning of discrimination. As Professor Kathryn Abrams commented, "[t]his flexibility is particularly evident with respect to women." Kathryn Abrams, *Title VII and the Complex Female Subject*, 92 Mich.L.Rev. 2479, 2497 (1994). Over the course of more than three decades, the courts have accepted several distinct theories of liability in gender discrimination cases. Professor Abrams described three of these theories:

> The most recurrent, and most influential, theory has been an "equality" or "sameness" theory of discrimination. This theory describes women as substantially similar to men in most respects germane to employment; it describes discrimination as the prejudiced or erroneous failure to recognize this similarity, resulting in treatment of women as inferior, unable, or otherwise different from the paradigmatic male denizens of the workplace. A second theory, which has surfaced in cases involving pregnancy or gender-role expectations, highlights ways in which women differ from men. It notes that women's participation in the workforce is shaped by biological differences related to gestation and childbirth and by gender-role expectations that affect behavior in the workplace and require the integration of conflicting responsibilities of work and family. According to the "difference" theory, discrimination results from the failure to recognize these differences, to anticipate the devaluative light in which employers may view them, or to accommodate them in structuring the demands of workplaces. A third theory, which has been particularly influential in cases involving sexual harassment, characterizes discrimination as the devaluative sexualization or derogation of women in the workplace. Whether employers are expressing overt hostility or manifesting "sex role spillover,"[3] harassment characterizes women primarily as sexual objects, or as objects of sex-based derision, rather than as competent workers.

Id. at 2479–80.

Abrams identifies a fourth theoretical approach to gender discrimination "that emphasize[s] the complex, intersectional character of the female subject and the variability of the discriminatory animus that subject encounters." *Id.* at 2481. According to Abrams, cases that require an understanding of "the complex female subject," fall into two

---

3. This term is taken from Barbara A.   (1985).
Gutek, Sex and the Workplace 15–16

broad categories. In the first category, plaintiffs allege "intersectional" or "sex-plus" theories of discrimination against certain subgroups. *See generally id.* at 2493–2502 (discussing discrimination and "intersectionality"). Intersectional claims, discussed in Chapter 2, rely on the intersection of two or more prohibited categories, such as sex and race (e.g., black women, Asian women, black men) or sex and age (e.g., women over forty). *See, e.g.,* Lam v. University of Hawai'i, 40 F.3d 1551, 1562 (9th Cir.1994) (sex and race); Arnett v. Aspin, 846 F.Supp. 1234, 1239–41 (E.D.Pa.1994) (sex and age). *See generally* Kimberlé Crenshaw, *Demarginalizing the Intersection of Race and Sex: A Black Feminist Critique of Antidiscrimination Doctrine, Feminist Theory and Antiracist Politics,* 1989 U.Chi. Legal F. 139.

"Sex-plus" claims are based on discrimination "against subclasses of women, distinguished not simply by gender but by an additional characteristic such as weight or marital or parental status." Abrams, *supra,* at 2495. The Supreme Court's first case to address sex discrimination recognized the viability of a "sex-plus" claim. In *Phillips v. Martin Marietta Corp.,* 400 U.S. 542, 91 S.Ct. 496, 27 L.Ed.2d 613 (1971), the Court held that an employer's rule that prohibited mothers of preschool-aged children from holding certain positions was a prima facie violation of Title VII. Because mothers of very young children were treated differently from fathers of young children, the company policy discriminated on the basis of sex. *See also* Sprogis v. United Air Lines, 444 F.2d 1194 (7th Cir.1971) (holding that a rule excluding married women from positions as airline flight attendants violates Title VII); Coleman v. B–G Maintenance Management of Colorado, Inc., 108 F.3d 1199, 1203–04 (10th Cir.1997) (to prevail on sex-plus-marriage discrimination claim, plaintiff must prove that the subclass of married women was treated differently from the corresponding subclass of married men). Moreover, a plaintiff can be in a subclass characterized as raising a combination of "intersectional" and "sex-plus" claims. *See, e.g.,* Chambers v. Omaha Girls Club, 834 F.2d 697 (8th Cir.1987) (single black pregnant women); Fisher v. Vassar College, 114 F.3d 1332 (2d Cir.1997) (en banc) (older married women), *cert. denied,* 522 U.S. 1041, 118 S.Ct. 851, 139 L.Ed.2d 752, (1998); *see also* Wendi Barish, Comment, *"Sex–Plus" Discrimination: A Discussion of* Fisher v. Vassar College, 13 Hofstra Lab.L.J. 239 (1995).

Professor Abrams describes the second category of cases dealing with the "complex, female subject" as demonstrating

> a different kind of complex subjectivity: it is produced, not by the intersection of two categorical traits, but by the juxtaposition of qualities thought to occupy polar positions within the same categorical dichotomy. Plaintiffs may be blacks with light skin, men who behave in "socially female" ways, women who respond to sexual harassment in a manner more typical of men.

Abrams, *supra,* at 2502; *see generally id.* at 2502–17 (discussing discrimination and "categorical ambivalence"). For an exploration of the legal and social dilemmas faced by white blacks, see Judy Scales–Trent, Notes of a White Black Woman: Race, Color, Community (1995); Judy Scales–Trent, *Commonalities: On Being Black and White, Different and the Same*, 2 Yale J.L. & Feminism 305 (1990); for effeminate men, see Mary Anne Case, *Disaggregating Gender from Sex and Sexual Orientation: The Effeminate Man in the Law and Feminist Jurisprudence*, 105 Yale L.J. 1 (1991). Do the theoretical approaches identified by Professor Abrams help to clarify the meaning of sex discrimination? Or do they introduce unnecessary complexity?

2.   ANALYTICAL PARADIGMS: DISPARATE TREATMENT AND DISPARATE IMPACT CLAIMS

Sex discrimination claims brought under Title VII can be analyzed under both the disparate treatment and disparate impact paradigms covered in Chapters 3 and 4. One scholar has argued that

> the disparate impact approach provides an effective way of answering the important critique that a formal equality approach only aids women who can and want to be like men. It is an approach that is exquisitely group sensitive. Combined with the formal equality approach, it challenges both individual and institutional barriers to equal advancement. Moreover, because it seeks to correct society's male tilt, it does so in a way which promises to benefit all, not only women.

Nadine Taub, *The Relevance of Disparate Impact Analysis in Reaching for Gender Equality*, 6 Constitutional L.J. 941, 948 (1996). Using Title VII law to attempt to "correct society's male tilt," however, has inherent limitations in challenging many subtle barriers to equal employment opportunities for women. For example, a restaurant with an "Old World" ambience may have a reputation for hiring only men as food servers through word-of-mouth recruitment. If women are discouraged from applying for, or even seriously considering, these jobs, a disappointed applicant with a viable claim of disparate treatment may never come forward as a potential plaintiff. Only if the EEOC should decide to challenge the restaurant's hiring polices under §§ 706 and 707 of Title VII, will the employer have an incentive to change its hiring practices, and, indeed, the hiring practices may ultimately be found unlawful under a disparate treatment or disparate impact theory. While such a finding will benefit women who seek these high-paying food server positions in the future, only women who had a "real and present interest in applying during the actionable period," and "effectively were deterred by [the employer's] reputation for discriminatory hiring practices" will be entitled to relief under the "futile act" doctrine. EEOC v. Joe's Stone Crabs, Inc., 296 F.3d 1265, 1275 (11th Cir.2002), *cert. denied*, ___ U.S. ___, 123 S.Ct. 2606, 156 L.Ed.2d 627 (2003). How many qualified women who cannot meet this "futile act" test might have applied if the discriminatory practices had not existed in the first place? Are their lost opportunities any less significant or costly than those experienced by the few women who may be entitled to relief? The "futile act" or "futile gesture" doctrine is discussed in Chapter 3, Section B.1, following the *Burdine* case.

Consider how disparate treatment or disparate impact analysis might be applied to the following problems:

a. Lynch, a woman, was hired by a construction company as a carpenter's apprentice. All construction workers were required to use the same portable toilets. The toilets were dirty, had no running water or sanitary napkins, and often had no toilet paper or the paper was soiled. The employer owned a building near the construction site that had fully equipped restroom facilities for men and women. Company policy, however, prohibited construction workers from using these indoor restrooms. After she developed several urinary tract infections as a result of using the unsanitary portable toilets, Lynch began to use the company's indoor women's restroom. When she continued to use this restroom despite a warning from her employer, Lynch was discharged for violating a company rule. Does Lynch have a claim under Title VII for sex discrimination if the evidence shows that none of the male construction workers had ever used the company's indoor restroom facilities? If so, under what theory? *See* Lynch v. Freeman, 817 F.2d 380 (6th Cir.1987). *Compare* DeClue v. Central Ill. Light Co., 223 F.3d 434 (7th Cir.2000), *with id.* at 437 (Rovner, J., dissenting).

b. Sal and Robin, husband and wife, worked for the same bank branch—Sal as the manager and Robin as an assistant cashier. Sal was discharged after he pleaded guilty to federal bank fraud charges for misappropriating a substantial amount of money belonging to an elderly client. The bank also discharged Robin because the officers and directors feared that customers would question Robin's credibility because of her husband's criminal conduct. Robin sues under Title VII alleging sex discrimination on the theory that she is a victim of a sexual stereotype that a woman's character mirrors her husband's. Does Robin have a viable sex discrimination claim? *See* Panis v. Mission Hills Bank, 60 F.3d 1486 (10th Cir.1995), *cert. denied*, 516 U.S. 1160, 116 S.Ct. 1045, 134 L.Ed.2d 192 (1996).

c. For five years, Elaine Smith was an executive secretary to Robert Connally, the executive vice president and chief operating officer of a sports broadcasting network. Under the network's staffing policy, Smith's job grade was based on the rank of her "boss" in the company's corporate hierarchy. As executive secretary to Connally, Smith worked in a luxurious environment and enjoyed privileges not enjoyed by most of the other secretaries, all of whom are female. As a result of a corporate reorganization, Connally was removed from his position, and he eventually left the network. Because Connally's replacement, a male, selected another woman as his executive secretary, Smith was downgraded to a less prestigious and lower-paid secretarial position with fewer responsibilities. Assuming that her qualifications are not at issue, does Smith have a viable claim that the network's staffing policy for its secretaries, which resulted in her reduction in grade, constitutes sex discrimination under Title VII? *See* Truskoski v. ESPN, Inc., 823 F.Supp. 1007 (D.Conn.1993).

d.　Darlene was employed as a bartender at a hotel casino for over twenty years. Last month she was fired because she refused to conform to the casino's new dress and grooming code for female employees who serve beverages. Under the "Personal Best" policy, women are required to wear makeup, defined as "foundation or powder, blush, lipstick, and mascara." They must have their hair "teased, curled, or styled," and may use only "clear, white, pink or red" nail polish. In addition, they must wear only "nude or natural color stockings." Men who worked in the casino bar are required only to "keep their hair cut above the collar, finger nails trimmed, and their face free of makeup." Does Darlene have a viable claim for sex discrimination under Title VII? *See* Lambda Legal Appeals Federal Sex Discrimination Case on Behalf of Woman Fired from Harrah's Casino (June 16, 2003), <*http://www.lambdalegal.org/cgi-bin/iowa/documents/record?record=1275*>.

e.　Sarah was employed as a dispatcher for United Parcel Service. She was denied a promotion to the position of dispatcher supervisor, and the position was later filled by a male. The division manager told her she was not recommended for the position "because of her inability to handle confrontational situations" that were likely to arise in the job. In particular, her immediate supervisor said he was "scared that [she] might cry if [she] got into a confrontation * * * with a driver" or "if [she] ever got a good ass chewing." Does Sarah have a claim for sex discrimination? *See* Crone v. United Parcel Serv., Inc., 301 F.3d 942 (2002). What if the facts involved John, a male substitute teacher in a public school system who is told he will not be called to substitute again. At a meeting with the school principal, she told him he was "too macho." Is this statement evidence of actionable sex discrimination under Title VII? What else would you want to know? *See* Lautermilch v. Findlay City Sch., 314 F.3d 271 (2003).

C.　DISCRIMINATION ON THE BASIS OF PREGNANCY

1.　THE PREGNANCY DISCRIMINATION ACT OF 1978

Women of childbearing age work and work in great numbers. In nonagricultural industries in 1988, approximately 45% of workers were female. Seventy-two percent of all women who worked in nonagricultural industries were under age 45. Sixty-three percent of working men and 55% of working women were married and living with their spouses. Eighty-five percent of all working women are expected to become pregnant at least one time during their working life. Thus, the workplace has a significant percentage of women of childbearing age who work and who will become pregnant while they work.

Maureen E. Lally–Green, *The Implications of Inadequate Maternity Leave Policies Under Title VII,* 16 Vt.L.Rev. 223, 226 (1991) (citations omitted).

In 1978, Congress amended Title VII, adding a new definition, § 701(k), known as the Pregnancy Discrimination Act of 1978 (PDA). 42 U.S.C. § 2000e(k). The amendment provided a definition of the terms "because of sex" and "on the basis of sex." One court noted,

> In 1978, Congress had the opportunity to expound on its view of sex discrimination by amending Title VII to make clear that discrimination because of "pregnancy, childbirth, or related medical conditions" is discrimination on the basis of sex. The amendment * * * was not meant to alter the contours of Title VII: rather, Congress intended to correct what it felt was an erroneous interpretation of Title VII by the United States Supreme Court in *General Electric Co. v. Gilbert,* 429 U.S. 125, 97 S.Ct. 401, 50 L.Ed.2d 343 (1976). In *Gilbert,* the Supreme Court held that an otherwise comprehensive short-term disability policy that excluded pregnancy-related disabilities from coverage did not discriminate on the basis of sex. The *Gilbert* majority based it decision on two findings: (a) pregnancy discrimination does not adversely impact all women and therefore is not the same thing as gender discrimination; and (b) disability insurance which covers the same illnesses and conditions for both men and women is equal coverage. To the *Gilbert* majority, the fact that pregnancy-related disabilities were an uncovered risk unique to women did not destroy the facial parity of the coverage. The dissenting justices, Justice Brennan, Justice Marshall, and Justice Stevens, took issue with these findings, arguing that: (a) women, as the only sex at risk for pregnancy, were being subjected to unlawful discrimination; and (b) in determining whether an employment policy treats the sexes equally, the court must look at the comprehensiveness of the coverage provided to each sex. It was the dissenters interpretation of Title VII which ultimately prevailed in Congress.

Erickson v. Bartell Drug Co., 141 F.Supp.2d 1266, 1269–70 (W.D.Wash. 2001).

Nashville Gas Co. v. Satty, 434 U.S. 136, 98 S.Ct. 347, 54 L.Ed.2d 356 (1977) was the Supreme Court's next Title VII pregnancy discrimination case after *Gilbert* and before Congress enacted the Pregnancy Discrimination Act (PDA). Two issues were involved in *Satty*. The first was whether an employer's policy of terminating employees' accrued seniority during pregnancy-related absences violated Title VII. The second issue was whether a policy of refusing to grant disability pay to pregnant employees on leave violated Title VII. Based on a benefit/detriment analysis, the Court held that the policy of denying accumulated seniority violated Title VII, but based on *Gilbert*, the Court held that the policy of denying disability pay did not violate the Act.

The following case was the first opportunity the Supreme Court had to interpret the Pregnancy Discrimination Act. Ironically, like several significant sex discrimination cases that have reached the Supreme Court, the case was brought by male employees.

NEWPORT NEWS SHIPBUILDING & DRY DOCK CO. v. EEOC

Supreme Court of the United States, 1983.
462 U.S. 669, 103 S.Ct. 2622, 77 L.Ed.2d 89.

JUSTICE STEVENS delivered the opinion of the Court.

[When the Pregnancy Discrimination Act became effective, "the petitioner amended its health insurance plan to provide its female employees with hospitalization benefits for pregnancy-related conditions to the same extent as for other medical conditions. The plan continued, however, to provide less favorable pregnancy benefits for spouses of male employees." The male employees challenged the new plan under Title VII.]

* * *

Ultimately the question we must decide is whether petitioner has discriminated against its male employees with respect to their compensation, terms, conditions, or privileges of employment because of their sex within the meaning of § 703(a)(1) of Title VII. Although the Pregnancy Discrimination Act has clarified the meaning of certain terms in this section, neither that Act nor the underlying statute contains a definition of the word "discriminate." In order to decide whether petitioner's plan discriminates against male employees because of *their* sex, we must therefore go beyond the bare statutory language. Accordingly, we shall consider whether Congress, by enacting the Pregnancy Discrimination Act, not only overturned the specific holding in *General Electric v. Gilbert*, but also rejected the test of discrimination employed by the Court in that case. We believe it did. Under the proper test petitioner's plan is unlawful, because the protection it affords to married male employees is less comprehensive than the protection it affords to married female employees.

* * *

Section 703(a) makes it an unlawful employment practice for an employer to "discriminate against any individual with respect to his compensation, terms, conditions, or privileges of employment, because of such individual's race, color, religion, sex, or national origin * * *." Health insurance and other fringe benefits are "compensation, terms, conditions, or privileges of employment." Male as well as female employees are protected against discrimination. Thus, if a private employer were to provide complete health insurance coverage for the dependents of its female employees, and no coverage at all for the dependents of its male employees, it would violate Title VII.[22] Such a practice would not

---

22. Consistently since 1970 the EEOC has considered it unlawful under Title VII for an employer to provide different insurance coverage for spouses of male and female employees. *See* Guidelines On Discrimination Because of Sex, 29 C.F.R. 1604.9(d).

pass the simple test of Title VII discrimination that we enunciated in *Los Angeles Dept. of Water & Power v. Manhart*, 435 U.S. 702, 711, 98 S.Ct. 1370, 1377, 55 L.Ed.2d 657 (1978), for it would treat a male employee with dependents "in a manner which but for that person's sex would be different."[23] The same result would be reached even if the magnitude of the discrimination were smaller. For example, a plan that provided complete hospitalization coverage for the spouses of female employees but did not cover spouses of male employees when they had broken bones would violate Title VII by discriminating against male employees.

Petitioner's practice is just as unlawful. Its plan provides limited pregnancy-related benefits for employees' wives, and affords more extensive coverage for employees' spouses for all other medical conditions requiring hospitalization. Thus the husbands of female employees receive a specified level of hospitalization coverage for all conditions; the wives of male employees receive such coverage except for pregnancy-related conditions.[24] Although *Gilbert* concluded that an otherwise inclusive plan that singled out pregnancy-related benefits for exclusion was nondiscriminatory on its face, because only women can become pregnant, Congress has unequivocally rejected that reasoning. The 1978 Act makes clear that it is discriminatory to treat pregnancy-related conditions less favorably than other medical conditions. Thus petitioner's plan unlawfully gives married male employees a benefit package for their dependents that is less inclusive than the dependency coverage provided to married female employees.

There is no merit to petitioner's argument that the prohibitions of Title VII do not extend to discrimination against pregnant spouses because the statute applies only to discrimination in employment. A two-step analysis demonstrates the fallacy in this contention. The Pregnancy Discrimination Act has now made clear that, for all Title VII purposes, discrimination based on a woman's pregnancy is, on its face, discrimination because of her sex. And since the sex of the spouse is always the opposite of the sex of the employee, it follows inexorably that discrimination against female spouses in the provision of fringe benefits is also

Similarly, in our Equal Protection Clause cases we have repeatedly held that, if the spouses of female employees receive less favorable treatment in the provision of benefits, the practice discriminates not only against the spouses but also against the female employees on the basis of sex. *See, e.g.,* Frontiero v. Richardson, 411 U.S. 677, 688, 93 S.Ct. 1764, 1771, 36 L.Ed.2d 583 (1973).

23. The *Manhart* case was decided several months before the Pregnancy Discrimination Act was passed. Although it was not expressly discussed in the legislative history, it set forth some of the "existing title VII principles" on which Congress relied. In *Manhart* the Court struck down the employer's policy of requiring female employees to make larger contributions to its pension fund than male employees, because women as a class tend to live longer than men. * * *

24. This policy is analogous to the exclusion of broken bones for the wives of male employees, except that both employees' wives and employees' husbands may suffer broken bones, but only employees' wives can become pregnant.

discrimination against male employees.[25] By making clear that an employer could not discriminate on the basis of an employee's pregnancy, Congress did not erase the original prohibition against discrimination on the basis of an employee's sex.

In short, Congress' rejection of the premises of *General Electric v. Gilbert* forecloses any claim that an insurance program excluding pregnancy coverage for female beneficiaries and providing complete coverage to similarly situated male beneficiaries does not discriminate on the basis of sex. Petitioner's plan is the mirror image of the plan at issue in *Gilbert*. The pregnancy limitation in this case violates Title VII by discriminating against male employees.

The judgment of the Court of Appeals is affirmed.

[JUSTICE REHNQUIST, joined by JUSTICE POWELL, filed a dissenting opinion.]

Notes and Questions

1. *Pregnancy and Disparate Treatment—The Prima Facie Case:* Many cases of individual disparate treatment under the PDA will be analyzed under the burden-shifting scheme of *McDonnell Douglas–Burdine–Hicks,* which is covered in Chapter 3. *See, e.g.*, Templet v. Hard Rock Constr. Co., 2003 WL 181363, at *2–3 (E.D.La.2003). For example, in a case alleging discharge on the basis of pregnancy, the plaintiff can establish a prima facie case by showing that "(1) she is a member of a protected class; (2) she satisfactorily performed the duties required by the position; (3) she was discharged; and (4) her position remained open and was ultimately filled by a non-pregnant employee." Flores v. Buy Buy Baby, Inc., 118 F.Supp.2d 425, 430 (S.D.N.Y.2000). To prevail in a pregnancy discrimination case under a disparate treatment theory, however, does a plaintiff have to establish as part of her prima facie case that the employer knew that she was pregnant at the time of the adverse employment decision? *See* Prebilich–Holland v. Gaylord Ent'mt Co., 297 F.3d 438 (6th Cir.2002). If this is part of a plaintiff's burden, what is required—evidence of the employer's actual knowledge or evidence that the employer reasonably should have known that she was pregnant?

2. *Standing*: A husband and wife were employed as vice presidents in the same company. Shortly after the company president learned that the wife was pregnant, he terminated both employees. They filed a lawsuit alleging that they were both discharged because of the wife's pregnancy. Would the husband have standing to sue under Title VII? Under the PDA?

---

25. *See* n.22, *supra*. This reasoning does not require that a medical insurance plan treat the pregnancies of employees' wives the same as the pregnancies of female employees. For example, as the EEOC recognizes, an employer might provide full coverage for employees and no coverage at all for dependents. Similarly, a disability plan covering employees' children may exclude or limit maternity benefits. Although the distinction between pregnancy and other conditions is, according to the 1978 Act, discrimination "on the basis of sex," the exclusion affects male and female *employees* equally since both may have pregnant dependent daughters. The EEOC's guidelines permit differential treatment of the pregnancies of dependents who are not spouses. *See* 44 Fed.Reg. 23804, 23805, 23807 (1979).

On what theory? *See* Nicol v. Imagematrix, Inc., 773 F.Supp. 802 (E.D.Va. 1991).

If an employer discharges an employee because it believes that she is pregnant, but it turns out that the employee was not actually pregnant at the time she was fired, can she seek relief under the PDA? *See* Jolley v. Phillips Educ. Group of Central Florida, Inc., 71 Fair Empl.Prac.Cas. (BNA) 916 (M.D.Fla.1996). What if the employee is not pregnant at the time of the adverse employment decision, but is attempting to become pregnant? *See* Pacourek v. Inland Steel Co., 858 F.Supp. 1393 (N.D.Ill.1994).

3. *Mandatory Maternity Leave Policies*: With the advent of the PDA, most employers have abandoned restrictive maternity leave policies—mandatory leave at a specified point in the pregnancy and specific dates for returning to work. In *Cleveland Board of Education v. LaFleur*, 414 U.S. 632, 94 S.Ct. 791, 39 L.Ed.2d 52 (1974), the Supreme Court held that a public employer's mandatory leave policy based on a conclusive, irrebuttable presumption about the ability of pregnant women to work during the last four or five months before the anticipated birth of a child violates the Fourteenth Amendment due process rights of public employees. Before the enactment of the PDA, courts generally relied on *LaFleur* to strike down mandatory leave and mandatory return policies challenged under Title VII. *See, e.g., In re* National Airlines, Inc., 434 F.Supp. 249, 257 (1977) ("to hold that mandatory leave requirements, without regard to individual ability to work, does not create a prima facie case under Title VII would result in the constitutional standard promulgated in *LaFleur* being less restrictive than the one in Title VII"); *but see disagreement recognized in* deLaurier v. San Diego Unified Sch. Dist., 588 F.2d 674 (9th Cir.1978) (upholding a mandatory leave policy requiring employees to leave work at the beginning of the ninth month of pregnancy); *id.* at 690 (Hufstedler, J., dissenting) ("Although *LaFleur* rested on constitutional grounds, it is nevertheless instructive because a mandatory leave policy that cannot pass due process muster necessarily fails to meet the more stringent standard of Title VII.").

4. *Pregnancy and Disparate Impact*: The courts have experienced some difficulty in analyzing PDA claims that are based on the interaction of pregnancy-leave policies with other employer policies that provide leaves of absence. One issue is whether it is more appropriate to apply disparate treatment or disparate impact analysis. *Scherr v. Woodland School Community Consolidated District No. 50*, 867 F.2d 974 (7th Cir.1988), is one of the leading cases holding that pregnancy discrimination claims may be subject to disparate impact analysis under these circumstances. In *Scherr*, two female school teachers—Susan Scherr and Rebecca Maganuco—brought separate actions challenging their employers' maternity leave policies under both disparate treatment and disparate impact theories.

In consolidated proceedings, the Seventh Circuit in *Scherr* rejected the argument of the defendant school districts that "the PDA is a sweeping mandate of equal treatment, but does not contemplate disparate impact claims." *Id.* at 978; *see also id.* at 980. Both school districts permitted three types of leave: paid sick leave, unpaid maternity leave, and unpaid general leave. Sherr, a tenured teacher, became pregnant and sought to take paid sick leave from Woodland for the time that she was disabled by her pregnancy and unpaid maternity leave for the remainder of the school year. Woodland argued that it had an unwritten policy precluding all teachers from combining their paid and unpaid leave, although the applicable collective bargaining agreement only prohibited combining unpaid maternity leave with paid leave. Scherr sued Woodland under Title VII when the school denied her request to combine paid and unpaid leave and required her to take unpaid maternity leave for the period of her disability. The Seventh Circuit remanded Scherr's case for trial on both her disparate treatment and disparate impact claims. *Id.* at 982, 983.

In Maganuco's case, the court rejected the plaintiff's disparate treatment claim that her school's sick-leave policy barred women from using accumulated sick leave for a period of pregnancy-related disability if they also want to take personal leave to care for a newborn child. In effect, Leyden's policy required women to take unpaid maternity leave rather than sick pay if they wanted to provide child care after their pregnancy-related disability was over. The court distinguished Maganuco's situation from Scherr's on the grounds that the terms of Leyden's leave-of-absence policy "would not allow any teacher to use paid sick leave immediately prior to taking a leave of absence." *Id.* at 983. Nevertheless, the court remanded Maganuco's disparate impact claim. *Id.* at 984. Following remand, the court held that Leyden's leave policies did not have a disparate impact on women on the basis of pregnancy. Maganuco v. Leyden Community High Sch. Dist. 212, 939 F.2d 440 (7th Cir.1991). *See also* Barrash v. Bowen, 846 F.2d 927 (4th Cir.1988) (denial of leave to breast-feed did not give rise to a disparate impact claim). Does *Newport News* suggest a resolution to these conflicting analyses?

In *EEOC v. Warshawsky and Co.*, 768 F.Supp. 647 (N.D.Ill.1991), the court held that a policy requiring a one-year waiting period before employees could take paid sick leave violated Title VII because of its impact on pregnant women. According to the employer's written leave policy, employees had to be employed for one year before they became eligible for paid sick leave. The employer also had a consistent policy of discharging employees who took unpaid sick leave for two or more weeks before completing their first year on the job. Statistics showed that from January 1985 to March 1989, Warshawsky employed 1,105 female first-year employees and 773 male first-year employees. Under the sick-leave policy, fifty-three first-year employees were discharged during this period. Fifty women were discharged and only three men. Of the women discharged, twenty were discharged because of pregnancy or related medical conditions. Assuming a disparate impact claim could be brought, how should the protected group be defined? All pregnant first-year employees? All first-year employees who required sick leave?

If, as the PDA states and the courts have held, discrimination on the basis of pregnancy is sex discrimination, then does it make sense to use disparate impact analysis? What is the facially neutral policy in *Scherr*? In *Maganuco*? In *Warshawsky*? Under *Wards Cove* or the Civil Rights Act of 1991, see Chapter 4, what are the relevant comparison groups? *See* Garcia v. Woman's Hosp. of Texas, 97 F.3d 810 (5th Cir.1996); EEOC v. Ackerman, Hood & McQueen, 956 F.2d 944 (10th Cir.), *cert. denied*, 506 U.S. 817, 113 S.Ct. 60, 121 L.Ed.2d 28 (1992).

5.　*Discharges on the Basis of Pregnancy–Related Absenteeism or Leave*:
Would it be a violation of the PDA if an employer discharged a pregnant
employee whose excessive absenteeism was caused by morning sickness?
Isn't morning sickness quite clearly a "condition" related to pregnancy? In
Troupe v. May Department Stores, 20 F.3d 734 (7th Cir.1994), a pregnant
saleswoman at a Lord & Taylor department store was discharged one day
before her maternity leave was to begin. Troupe's severe morning sickness
during the first trimester of pregnancy caused her chronic tardiness at work.
Despite accommodations in her work schedule, repeated warnings, and a
probationary period, the tardiness continued. On the day of her discharge,
the company's human resources manager told Troupe that she did not
believe Troupe would return to work after her maternity leave. Judge
Posner decided that "a termination so motivated" does not violate Title VII
because it "implies that [Lord & Taylor] fired Ms. Troupe not because she
was pregnant but because she cost the company more than she was worth to
it." *Troupe*, 20 F.3d at 737, 738.

In affirming the district court's grant of defendant's motion for summary judgment, Judge Posner observed that Troupe had

> made no effort to show that if all the pertinent facts were as they are
> except for the fact of her pregnancy, she would not have been fired.
> * * * The Pregnancy Discrimination Act requires the employer to
> ignore an employee's pregnancy, but * * * not her absence from work,
> unless the employer overlooks the comparable absences of nonpregnant
> employees in which event it would not be ignoring pregnancy after all.

Id. at 738. Judge Posner discussed the reach of the PDA:

> The Pregnancy Discrimination Act does not, despite the urgings of
> feminist scholars, e.g., Herma Kay Hill, *Equality and Difference: The
> Case of Pregnancy*, 1 Berkeley Women's L.J. 1, 30–31 (1985), require
> employers to offer maternity leave or take other steps to make it easier
> for pregnant women to work, to make it as easy, say, as it is for their
> spouses to continue working during pregnancy. Employers can treat
> pregnant women as badly as they treat similarly affected but nonpreg-
> nant employees, even to the point of "conditioning the availability of an
> employment benefit on an employee's decision to return to work after
> the end of the medical disability that pregnancy causes."

Id. at 738.

Judge Posner analyzed the facts of *Troupe* under a strict disparate
treatment paradigm. Would a disparate impact analysis have been warranted? *Compare Troupe with* Raytheon v. Hernandez, ___ U.S. ___, 124 S.Ct.
513, 157 L.Ed.2d 357 (2003), which is covered in Chapter 13. Is Judge
Posner's view of the PDA consistent with the purposes of the statute? The
facts in *Troupe* occurred before the effective date of the Family and Medical
Leave Act of 1993 (FMLA), discussed in Section D of this chapter. Would the
FMLA have made any difference in Troupe's rights? Or in Judge Posner's
analysis of those rights? Posner's analysis in *Troupe* has been followed in the
Third Circuit case *In re Carnegie Center Associates*, 129 F.3d 290, 297 (3rd
Cir.1997) (the plain language of the PDA compels the view, adopted in
Troupe, "that an employer legitimately can consider an employee's absence
on maternity leave in making an adverse employment decision"), *cert. denied*

sub nom. Rhett v. Carnegie Ctr. Assocs., 524 U.S. 938, 118 S.Ct. 2342, 141 L.Ed.2d 714 (1998). *See also* Smith v. F.W. Morse & Co., 76 F.3d 413, 424 (1st Cir.1996) ("Title VII mandates that an employer must put an employee's pregnancy (including her departure on maternity leave) to one side in making its employment decisions—but the statute does not command that an employer bury its head in the sand and struthiously refrain from implementing business judgments simply because they affect a parturient employee"). *See generally* David C. Wyld, *Morning Sickness: Testing the Proper Bounds of Employee Protection and Employer Prerogative Under the Pregnancy Discrimination Act*, 46 Lab.L.J. 88 (1995).

6.   What if an employee does not have an attendance problem because of pregnancy, but the employer assumes that, because the employee is pregnant, she is likely to be absent in the future? Will the employer violate Title VII if it discharges her in anticipation of her possible future absences? The Seventh Circuit, in such a case, observed,

> There might be some limited circumstances in which an employer could be justified in taking anticipatory adverse action against a pregnant employee. Although the PDA was designed to allow individual women to make independent choices about whether to continue to work while pregnant, it was not designed to handcuff employers by forcing them to wait until an employee's pregnancy causes a special economic disadvantage. The PDA does not create such an artificial divide between pregnancy, childbirth and related medical conditions and the secondary effects of a pregnancy which might affect job performance. Pregnancy causes normal inconveniences that might "interrupt the workplace's daily routines," including, for example, the need to take more frequent snack and restroom breaks and the need to take some time off, at the very least, to give birth. Judith G. Greenberg, *The Pregnancy Discrimination Act: Legitimating Discrimination Against Pregnant Women in the Workforce*, 50 Me.L.Rev. 225, 250 (1998); *see also* In re Carnegie Center Associates, 129 F.3d 290, 306 (3d Cir.1997) (McKee, J., dissenting) (describing "the absence [from work] endemic to pregnancy"). An employer may, under narrow circumstances * * * project the normal inconveniences of pregnancy and their secondary effects into the future and take actions in accordance with and in proportion to those predictions. Of course, it will rarely be one hundred percent demonstrable that a pregnant woman will be unable to meet a BFOQ sometime in the future. Cases such as *Marshall v. American Hospital Association,* 157 F.3d 520, 522–23 (7th Cir.1998), in which an employee announces that she will be unavailable to work in the future and thus explicitly requests special treatment, are exceptional. It is not merely a question whether the pregnant employee asks for special treatment, however; other evidence might also be probative of the employee's ability to continue to meet the employer's legitimate job expectations. But an employer cannot take anticipatory action unless it has a good faith basis, supported by sufficiently strong evidence, that the normal inconveniences of an employee's pregnancy will require special treatment.

Maldonado v. U.S. Bank, 186 F.3d 759, 767 (7th Cir.1999).

Consider the following: The plaintiff had previously been a full-time employee of a political campaign committee. Following the birth of her second child she began working for the committee on a part-time schedule— three days a week. In January, she informed her employer that she was again pregnant and expecting the birth of her third child the following August. In February, the committee began a new "off-year" program and hired five new employees. In March, the plaintiff was asked to resume full-time work. When she refused, her supervisor told her that she would be fired if she did not agree to work full-time. The plaintiff again refused and was fired. She then brought a claim against her employer under the PDA. Does the plaintiff have a viable claim of pregnancy discrimination under Title VII? *See* Gleklen v. Democratic Congressional Campaign Comm., Inc., 199 F.3d 1365 (D.C.Cir.2000).

How would your analysis be affected if the plaintiff presented credible evidence supporting the following allegations? (1) When the plaintiff first returned to work following the birth of her second child, she complained about the volume of work and said, "Maybe I should go home and have another baby." Her supervisor responded, "If you have another baby, I'll invite you to stay home." (2) At the time the plaintiff told her supervisor that she was pregnant again, the supervisor said to the department head, "Oh, my God, she's pregnant again." (3) At the time the plaintiff was fired, her supervisor said, "Hopefully this will give you some time to spend at home with your children." (4) Although the employer has hired and retained several employees who became pregnant, it has previously fired only one other employee—and she was pregnant. *See* Sheehan v. Donlen Corp., 173 F.3d 1039 (7th Cir.1999). *See also* Laxton v. Gap, Inc., 333 F.3d 572, (5th Cir.2003); Wallace v. Methodist Hosp. Sys., 271 F.3d 212, 223 (5th Cir.2001), *cert. denied*, 535 U.S. 1078, 122 S.Ct. 1961, 152 L.Ed.2d 1022 (2002).

7. *The Scope of "Related Medical Conditions"*: The "related medical conditions" provision of the PDA has been construed to cover only those disabilities or illnesses that are incapacitating for the employee. One court noted,

> Admittedly, the [PDA] does not define what constitute "related medical conditions." However, the substantive references to "related medical conditions" within [the] legislative history are all in the context of the extent to which female employees can be denied medical benefits, such as sick leave and health insurance coverage, arising from pregnancy and childbirth. Further, Congress' express intent was to codify the pre-*Gilbert* EEOC guidelines that required "employers to treat *disabilities* caused or contributed to by pregnancy, miscarriage, abortion, childbirth and recovery therefrom as all other temporary disabilities." We believe these factors indicate Congress' intent that "related medical conditions" be limited to incapacitating conditions for which medical care or treatment is usual and normal. Neither breast-feeding and weaning, nor difficulties arising therefrom, constitute such a condition.

> * * * "[I]f a woman wants to stay home to take care of a child, no benefits must be paid because this is not a medically determined condition related to pregnancy."

Wallace v. Pyro Mining Co., 789 F.Supp. 867, 869 (W.D.Ky.1990) (citations omitted), *aff'd*, 951 F.2d 351 (6th Cir.1991). In *Fleming v. Ayers & Assocs.*, 948 F.2d 993 (6th Cir.1991), the court held that an employer who refused to hire a female because of the cost of insurance associated with her child's illness did not violate the PDA.

8. *Unwed Pregnancy*: In *Jacobs v. Martin Sweets Co.*, 550 F.2d 364 (6th Cir.), *cert. denied*, 431 U.S. 917, 97 S.Ct. 2180, 53 L.Ed.2d 227 (1977), the court held that transfer of an unwed pregnant woman against her wishes to an inferior position constituted a constructive discharge in violation of Title VII. Could an adverse employment practice based on a policy against unwed pregnancy be justified under a bona fide occupational qualification or business necessity defense? *See* Chambers v. Omaha Girls Club, 834 F.2d 697 (8th Cir.1987), discussed in Section E of this chapter.

Title VII contains two exemptions for religious entities in § 702(a) and § 703(e)(2), discussed in Chapter 10. Can an employer that is a religious school discharge an unmarried librarian for her pregnancy which the church considers evidence of her sinfulness? *See* Vigars v. Valley Christian Ctr. of Dublin, 805 F.Supp. 802 (N.D.Cal.1992) (discussed in Chapter 10). What if the employer is not a "religious entity" but merely has religious or moral scruples about employing women who are pregnant and not married?

9.   How would you analyze the following case? The plaintiff was employed as a teacher in an elementary school operated by a religious entity. In the middle of the school year, the plaintiff got married. Shortly thereafter, when she was visibly pregnant, she began wearing maternity clothes at school. Her supervisor, a member of the religious order that ran the school, correctly concluded from the plaintiff's appearance that she had engaged in premarital sex. Subsequently, the plaintiff's teaching contract was not renewed. The letter terminating her contract stated, "We expect our teachers to be good, strong role models for our children. * * * [P]arents in the community have serious concerns about a teacher who marries and is expecting a child 5 months after the wedding date. * * * The Church does not uphold sexual intercourse outside of marriage. We consider this a breach of contract * * *." The plaintiff has brought a Title VII claim that her nonrenewal was because of her pregnancy. The employer claims that her contract was not renewed because she had engaged in premarital sex in violation of both her contract and the promises that she had made "to exemplify the moral values taught by the Church." Does the plaintiff have a prima facie case of discrimination under the PDA? Is she qualified for the position? If she has established a prima facie case, has the employer articulated a legitimate, nondiscriminatory reason for its employment decision? Could the plaintiff get to a jury to establish pretext on the basis of evidence that the school (1) gave her a "glowing" performance evaluation after learning of her pregnancy, (2) permitted her to continue teaching until the end of the school year, and (3) made no attempt to discover whether its male teachers engaged in premarital sex? *See* Cline v. Catholic Diocese of Toledo, 206 F.3d 651 (6th Cir.2000).

10.   *Abortion*: Is abortion a pregnancy-related "medical condition" that affects women? Congress indicated that it is. Following the broad statutory mandate that "women affected by pregnancy, childbirth, or related medical

conditions shall be treated the same for all employment-related purposes, including receipt of benefits under fringe benefit programs, as other persons not so affected but similar in their ability or inability to work," the PDA provides the following exclusion and a proviso regarding abortion:

> This subsection shall not require an employer to pay for health insurance benefits for abortion, except where the life of the mother would be endangered if the fetus were carried to term, or except where medical complications have arisen from an abortion: *Provided*, That nothing herein shall preclude an employer from providing abortion benefits or otherwise affect bargaining agreements with regard to abortion.

42 U.S.C. § 2000e(k). The EEOC Guidelines interpret this statutory language to mean that

> [t]he basic principle of the [PDA] is that women affected by pregnancy and related conditions must be treated the same as other applicants and employees on the basis of their ability or inability to work. A woman is therefore protected against such practices as being fired * * * merely because she is pregnant or has had an abortion.

29 C.F.R. app. § 1604 (1986). Finally, the legislative history of § 2000e(k) provides:

> Because [the PDA] applies to all situations in which women are "affected by pregnancy, childbirth, and related medical conditions," its basic language covers women who chose to terminate their pregnancies. Thus, no employer may, for example, fire or refuse to hire a woman simply because she has exercised her right to have an abortion.

H.R.Conf.Rep. No. 95–1786, 95th Cong., 2d Sess. 4. Thus, Title VII protects the status of being pregnant and indicates that abortion is a "medical condition" related to pregnancy. The EEOC guidelines and legislative history assert that the PDA protects the status of having had an abortion.

11. Consider the applicability of the PDA in the following case: A restaurant employee was a young, unwed mother who discovered that she was pregnant for a second time. Her pregnancy and the fact that she was contemplating having an abortion became a subject of controversy among her co-workers. Ultimately, she decided not to terminate her pregnancy and carried to term. In the meantime, however, her employer discharged her on the ground that the uproar caused by her "contemplated" abortion interfered with her ability to perform her job. Does the employee have a viable claim under Title VII? *See* Turic v. Holland Hospitality, Inc., 85 F.3d 1211 (6th Cir.1996) (holding that, as a matter of law, "[a] woman's right to have an abortion encompasses more than simply the act of having an abortion; it includes the contemplation of an abortion, as well"). Are you persuaded by the reasoning of the court in *Turic* that "[s]ince an employer cannot take adverse employment action against a female employee for her decision to have an abortion, it follows that the same employer also cannot take adverse employment action against a female employee for merely thinking about what she has a right to do." *Id.* at 1214.

The district court in *Turic* found that the employee was discharged because she merely thought about having an abortion. But what about the employer's argument that her thoughts were communicated to her co-workers and disrupted the workplace? Is it ever reasonable for employment decisions to hinge on the subjective responses of fellow employees? Would the employer in *Turic* have a legitimate, nondiscriminatory reason for its action on the basis that it would discharge any employee who disrupts the work environment by discussing his or her private plans for controversial elective medical procedures? For example, can an employee be disciplined for disrupting the workplace by talking about her plans to have liposuction? Or body piercing? What about a man discussing a planned vasectomy or a woman discussing her planned breast implants? *Turic* suggests that employers must treat a female employee's on-the-job "contemplation"—and discussion—of having an abortion with greater deference than her contemplation and discussion of a medical procedure not related to pregnancy. Is this what the PDA requires?

12. *Preferential Treatment of Pregnant Workers*: In *California Federal Savings & Loan Association v. Guerra*, 479 U.S. 272, 107 S.Ct. 683, 93 L.Ed.2d 613 (1987), the Supreme Court held that a California statute that requires employers to grant unpaid maternity leave and reinstatement rights to pregnant employees is not preempted by the PDA. The employer's challenge to the statute was based on the second clause of the PDA which provides that "childbirth, or related medical conditions shall be treated the same for all employment-related purposes, including receipt of benefits under fringe benefits programs, as other persons not so affected but similar in their ability or inability to work * * *." 42 U.S.C. § 2000e(k). The challenger argued that the second clause of the PDA embraced the equal treatment theory of equality; thus, the California statute was preempted under the PDA because it granted preferential treatment to pregnant workers.

The Court, in an opinion written by Justice Marshall, agreed with the court of appeal's conclusion that Congress intended the PDA to be "a floor beneath which pregnancy disability benefits may not drop—not a ceiling above which they may not rise," *Guerra*, 479 U.S. at 285, 107 S.Ct. at 691, and that "[t]he entire thrust behind this legislation is to guarantee women the basic right to participate fully and equally in the workforce, without denying them the fundamental right to full participation in family life." *Id.* at 289, 107 S.Ct. at 693–94. On the question of the theory of equality the PDA endorsed, the Court said the state law "promotes equal employment opportunity" because "[b]y 'taking pregnancy into account,' California's pregnancy disability leave statute allows women, as well as men, to have families without losing their jobs." *Id.*, 107 S.Ct. at 694. Justice White, joined by Chief Justice Rehnquist and Justice Powell, dissented on the ground that the state law singled out pregnancy for preferential treatment and thus squarely conflicted with the second clause of the PDA.

Is it clear that the Supreme Court has endorsed preferential treatment of pregnant workers in *Guerra*? Suppose that a private employer in California adopts a policy that provides female employees with *paid* leave for the period of any pregnancy-related disability, while all other employees who are disabled for other reasons must take *unpaid* leave. Would the employer be able to defend the policy on the basis of the rationale in *Guerra*? Now that the federal government has enacted the Family and Medical Leave Act of 1993 (discussed in Section D of this chapter), which is federal legislation similar to the California statute discussed in *Guerra*, are the issues raised in *Guerra* still relevant?

13. Plaintiff's job as an airline ticket agent involves assisting customers with their baggage at check-in; consequently, she frequently lifts loads weighing more than twenty pounds. Shortly after the plaintiff became pregnant, she began to experience disabling pain in her lower back, and her doctor ordered her not to lift loads in excess of twenty pounds for the remaining months of her pregnancy. The airline has a policy of providing "light duty" assignments to all employees who suffer occupational injuries. When plaintiff applied for a light duty assignment, the airline refused because her back pain did not result from an on-the-job injury. Does the plaintiff have a prima facie case of discrimination under the PDA? If so, under what theory—disparate treatment or disparate impact? How would Judge Posner apply the PDA to these facts? *See* the discussion of the *Troupe* case, *supra* Note 5. What analysis is suggested by *Guerra? Compare* Urbano v. Continental Airlines, Inc., 138 F.3d 204 (5th Cir.1998) (finding no PDA liability), *with* Ensley–Gaines v. Runyon, 100 F.3d 1220 (6th Cir.1996) (finding PDA liability). *See also* Spivey v. Beverly Enter., Inc., 196 F.3d 1309, 1313 (11th Cir.1999) (agreeing with the analysis in *Urbano* and holding that "an employer does not violate the PDA when it offers modified duty solely to employees who are injured on the job and not to employees who suffer from a non-occupational injury"); EEOC v. Horizon/CMS Healthcare Corp., 220 F.3d 1184, 1195–96 (10th Cir.2000) (ruling that claim for liability under PDA may go forward on evidence that employer offered modified duty to employees injured off the job but not to pregnant employees). *See also* Jamie L. Clanton, Note, *Toward Eradicating Pregnancy Discrimination at Work: Interpreting the PDA to "Mean What It Says,"* 86 Iowa L.Rev. 703 (2001) (discussing *Ensley–Gaines, Urbano,* and *Spivey* cases and arguing that under the PDA employers are required to provide the same accommodations to pregnant workers that they provide to other employees injured on the job).

14. *Unemployment Compensation*: The Federal Unemployment Tax Act (FUTA), 26 U.S.C. § 3301, is a cooperative federal-state program to benefit unemployed workers. FUTA establishes certain minimum standards that states must adopt in order to participate in the program. Specifically, § 3304(a)(12) mandates that "no person shall be denied compensation under such State law solely on the basis of pregnancy or termination of pregnancy." Consider the following case: An employer refused to rehire a female employee, who had taken maternity leave, because no positions were available when she wanted to return to work. When the employee filed for unemployment compensation, Missouri denied her claim pursuant to a state statute disqualifying workers who had "left work voluntarily without good cause attributable to his work or to his employer." In *Wimberly v. Labor & Industrial Relations Commission*, 479 U.S. 511, 107 S.Ct. 821, 93 L.Ed.2d 909 (1987), decided eight days after *Guerra*, Justice O'Connor, writing for a unanimous Court, upheld the denial of unemployment benefits. The Court construed § 3304(a)(12) as prohibiting states from singling out pregnancy for unfavorable treatment, but not mandating that states provide pregnant employees with preferential treatment. Because the state Division of Employment Security had found that the female employee in *Wimberly* left work

" 'voluntarily and without good cause attributable to [her] work or to [her] employer,' " *id.* at 513, 107 S.Ct. at 823, the Court found that the plaintiff was not being denied compensation "solely on the basis of pregnancy." Are you persuaded by the Court's rationale in *Wimberly*? Does the analysis of *General Electric v. Gilbert*, discussed in *Newport News*, support the result?

2. FRINGE BENEFITS AND THE PREGNANCY DISCRIMINATION ACT

The topic of sex-based fringe benefits is addressed in Chapter 7, Sex–Based Compensation Schemes. In the first-generation of sex-based fringe benefit cases, the Supreme Court issued two significant decisions dealing with employer reliance on sex-based actuarial tables in determining employee benefits. First, in *City of Los Angeles Department of Water & Power v. Manhart*, 435 U.S. 702, 98 S.Ct. 1370, 55 L.Ed.2d 657 (1978), in Chapter 7, Section E, the Court held that an employer pension plan that requires female employees to make larger contributions than male employees violates Title VII. Then, in *Arizona Governing Committee v. Norris*, 463 U.S. 1073, 103 S.Ct. 3492, 77 L.Ed.2d 1236 (1983), discussed in Chapter 7, Section E, Note 1, the Court extended the rationale of *Manhart* to find that deferred-compensation plans providing employees the option of purchasing private annuities that pay women contributors lower benefits than their male counterparts also violate Title VII. At issue in both *Manhart* and *Norris* was the question of whether employers could rely on expressly sex-based actuarial tables to determine employees' fringe benefits. *Manhart* was decided shortly before the Pregnancy Discrimination Act was passed. As the following case shows, the next generation of Title VII sex discrimination cases dealing with fringe benefits has required courts to revisit *Gilbert* and *Newport News* in interpreting the meaning of the Pregnancy Discrimination Act.

ERICKSON v. BARTELL DRUG CO.

United States District Court, Western District of Washington, 2001.
141 F.Supp.2d 1266.

LASNIK, District Judge.

* * * [T]his case raise[s] an issue of first impression in the federal courts' whether the selective exclusion of prescription contraceptives from defendant's generally comprehensive prescription plan constitutes discrimination on the basis of sex. In particular, plaintiffs assert that Bartell's decision not to cover prescription contraceptives such as birth control pills, Norplant, Depo–Provera, intra-uterine devices, and diaphragms under its Prescription Benefit Plan for non-union employees violates Title VII, as amended by the Pregnancy Discrimination Act, 42 U.S.C. § 2000e(k).

A.   APPLICATION OF TITLE VII

* * *

The language of the PDA was chosen in response to the factual situation presented in *Gilbert*, namely a case of overt discrimination toward pregnant employees. Not surprisingly, the amendment makes no reference whatsoever to prescription contraceptives. Of critical importance to this case, however, is the fact that, in enacting the PDA, Congress embraced the dissent's broader interpretation of Title VII which not only recognized that there are sex-based differences between men and women employees, but also required employers to provide women-only benefits or otherwise incur additional expenses on behalf of women in order to treat the sexes the same.

Although this litigation involves an exclusion for prescription contraceptives rather than an exclusion for pregnancy-related disability costs, the legal principles established by *Gilbert* and its legislative reversal govern the outcome of this case. An employer has chosen to offer an employment benefit which excludes from its scope of coverage services which are available only to women. All of the services covered by the policy are available to both men and women, so, as was the case in *Gilbert*, "[t]here is no risk from which men are protected and women are not. Likewise, there is no risk from which women are protected and men are not." *Gilbert*, 429 U.S. at 135, 97 S.Ct. 401. Nevertheless, the intent of Congress in enacting the PDA, even if not the exact language used in the amendment, shows that mere facial parity of coverage does not excuse or justify an exclusion which carves out benefits that are uniquely designed for women.

The fact that equality under Title VII is measured by evaluating the relative comprehensiveness of coverage offered to the sexes has been accepted and amplified by the Supreme Court. In *Newport News Shipbuilding & Dry Dock Co. v. EEOC*, 462 U.S. 669, 103 S.Ct. 2622, 77 L.Ed.2d 89 (1983), the Supreme Court found that a health insurance plan which covered pregnancy-related costs for female employees, but not for the spouses of male employees, violated Title VII and the PDA. * * * Thus, a policy which provided complete coverage to the male spouses of female employees but only partial coverage for the female spouses of male employees discriminated against the male employees.

The other tenet reaffirmed by the PDA (*i.e.*, that discrimination based on any sex-based characteristic is sex discrimination) has also been considered by the courts. The Supreme Court has found that classifying employees on the basis of their childbearing capacity, regardless of whether they are, in fact, pregnant, is sex-based discrimination. International Union, United Automobile, Aerospace and Agricultural Implement Workers of Am. v. Johnson Controls, Inc., 499 U.S. 187, 197–98, 111 S.Ct. 1196, 113 L.Ed.2d 158 (1991). The court's analysis turned primarily on Title VII's prohibition on sex-based classifications, using the PDA merely to bolster a conclusion that had already been reached. To the extent that a woman's ability to get pregnant may not fall within the literal language of the PDA, the court was not overly concerned. Rather, the court focused on the fact that disparate treatment based on unique, sex-based characteristics, such as the capacity to bear children, is sex discrimination prohibited by Title VII. Having reviewed the legislative history of Title VII and the PDA, the language of the statute itself, and the relevant case law, the Court finds that Bartell's exclusion of prescription contraception from its prescription plan is inconsistent with the requirements of federal law. The PDA is not a begrudging recognition of a limited grant of rights to a strictly defined group of women who happen to be pregnant. Read in the context of Title VII as a whole, it is a broad acknowledgment of the intent of Congress to outlaw any and all discrimination against any and all women in the terms and conditions of their employment, including the benefits an employer provides to its employees. Male and female employees have different, sex-based disability and healthcare needs, and the law is no longer blind to the fact that only women can get pregnant, bear children, or use prescription contraception. The special or increased healthcare needs associated with a woman's unique sex-based characteristics must be met to the same extent, and on the same terms, as other healthcare needs. Even if one were to assume that Bartell's prescription plan was not the result of intentional discrimination,[7] the exclusion of women-only benefits from a generally comprehensive prescription plan is sex discrimination under Title VII.

Title VII does not require employers to offer any particular type or category of benefit. However, when an employer decides to offer a prescription plan covering everything except a few specifically excluded drugs and devices, it has a legal obligation to make sure that the resulting plan does not discriminate based on sex-based characteristics and that it provides equally comprehensive coverage for both sexes. * * * In light of the fact that prescription contraceptives are used only by women, Bartell's choice to exclude that particular benefit from its generally applicable benefit plan is discriminatory.[8]

B.   Specific Arguments Raised by Defendant–Employer

Bartell argues that opting not to provide coverage for prescription contraceptive devices is not a violation of Title VII because: (1) treating contraceptives differently from other prescription drugs is reasonable in that contraceptives are voluntary, preventative, do not treat or prevent

---

7. There is no evidence or indication that Bartell's coverage decisions were intended to hinder women in their ability to participate in the workforce or to deprive them of equal treatment in employment or benefits. The most reasonable explanation for the current state of affairs is that the exclusion of women-only benefits is merely an unquestioned holdover from a time when employment-related benefits were doled out less equitably than they are today. The lack of evidence of bad faith or malice toward women does not affect the validity of plaintiffs' Title VII claim. Where a benefit plan is discriminatory on its face, no inquiry into subjective intent is necessary. See Norris, 463 U.S. at 1080–86, 103 S.Ct. 3492.

8. Bartell's argument that its prescription plan is not discriminatory because the female dependants of male employees are subject to the same exclusions as are female employees is unavailing First, discriminating against a protected class cannot be justified through consistency. Second, Bartell ignores the clear import of Congress' repudiation of Gilbert: a policy which uses sex-based characteristics to limit benefits, thereby creating a plan which is less comprehensive for one sex than the other, violates Title VII.

an illness or disease, and are not truly a "healthcare" issue; (2) control of one's fertility is not "pregnancy, childbirth, or related medical conditions" as those terms are used in the PDA; (3) employers must be permitted to control the costs of employment benefits by limiting the scope of coverage; (4) the exclusion of all "family planning" drugs and devices is facially neutral; (5) in the thirty-seven years Title VII has been on the books, no court has found that excluding contraceptives constitutes sex discrimination; and (6) this issue should be determined by the legislature, rather than the courts. Each of these arguments is considered in turn.

(1) *Contraceptives as a Health Care Need*

An underlying theme in Bartell's argument is that a woman's ability to control her fertility differs from the type of illness and disease normally treated with prescription drugs in such significant respects that it is permissible to treat prescription contraceptives differently than all other prescription medicines. The evidence submitted by plaintiffs shows, however, that the availability of affordable and effective contraceptives is of great importance to the health of women and children because it can help to prevent a litany of physical, emotional, economic, and social consequences. *See* Sylvia A. Law, *Sex Discrimination and Insurance for Contraception,* 73 Wash.L.Rev. 363, 364–68 (1998).

Unintended pregnancies, the condition which prescription contraceptives are designed to prevent, are shockingly common in the United States and carry enormous costs and health consequences for the mother, the child, and society as a whole. Over half of all pregnancies in this country are unintended. Committee on Unintended Pregnancy, Institute of Medicine, *The Best Intentions Unintended Pregnancy and the Well–Being of Children and Families* 1 (Sarah S. Brown & Leon Eisenberg eds., 1995). A woman with an unintended pregnancy is less likely to seek prenatal care, more likely to engage in unhealthy activities, more likely to have an abortion, and more likely to deliver a low birthweight, ill, or unwanted baby. Unintended pregnancies impose significant financial burdens on the parents in the best of circumstances. If the pregnancy results in a distressed newborn, the costs increase by tens of thousands of dollars. Office of Technology Assessment, *Healthy Children: Investing in the Future* 85 (1988). In addition, the adverse economic and social consequences of unintended pregnancies fall most harshly on women and interfere with their choice to participate fully and equally in the "marketplace and the world of ideas." Stanton v. Stanton, 421 U.S. 7, 14–15, 95 S.Ct. 1373, 43 L.Ed.2d 688 (1975).

The availability of a reliable, affordable way to prevent unintended pregnancies would go a long way toward ameliorating the ills described above. Although there are many factors which help explain the unusually high rate of unintended pregnancies in the United States, an important cause is the failure to use effective forms of birth control. Alan Guttmacher Institute, *Contraception Counts: State-by-State Information* 1 (May 1997). Insurance policies and employee benefit plans which exclude coverage for effective forms of contraception contribute to the failure of at-risk women to seek a physician's assistance in avoiding unwanted pregnancies. Law, 73 Wash.L.Rev. at 364, 368–72.

The fact that prescription contraceptives are preventative appears to be an irrelevant distinction in this case: Bartell covers a number of preventative drugs under its plan. The fact that pregnancy is a "natural" state and is not considered a disease or illness is also a distinction without a difference. Being pregnant, though natural, is not a state that is desired by all women or at all points in a woman's life. Prescription contraceptives, like all other preventative drugs, help the recipient avoid unwanted physical changes. As discussed above, identifying and obtaining an effective method of contraception is a primary healthcare issue throughout much of a woman's life and is, in many instances, of more immediate importance to her daily healthcare situation than most other medical needs. Although there are some distinctions that can be drawn between prescription contraceptives and the other prescription drugs covered by Bartell's plan, none of them is substantive or otherwise justifies the exclusion of contraceptives from a generally comprehensive healthcare plan.

(2) *Pregnancy Discrimination Act*

Defendant argues that the exclusion of prescription contraceptives from defendant's prescription benefit plan does not run afoul of the PDA and is not, therefore, unlawful. Under the express terms of the PDA, discrimination because of "pregnancy, childbirth, or related medical conditions" is a form of prohibited sex discrimination. When Congress enacted the PDA, it clearly had in mind the obvious and then-commonplace practice of discriminating against women in all aspects of employment, from hiring to the provision of fringe benefits, based on an assumption that women would get pregnant and leave the workforce. This perception relegated women to the role of marginal, temporary workers who had no need to participate in seniority programs, no hope of promotion, and no claim to the full panoply of employment benefits.

Having reviewed the legislative history of the PDA, it is clear that in 1978 Congress had no specific intent regarding coverage for prescription contraceptives. The relevant issue, however, is whether the decision to exclude drugs made for women from a generally comprehensive prescription plan is sex discrimination under Title VII, with or without the clarification provided by the PDA. The Court finds that, regardless of whether the prevention of pregnancy falls within the phrase "pregnancy, childbirth, or related medical conditions," Congress' decisive overruling of *Gilbert* evidences an interpretation of Title VII which necessarily precludes the choices Bartell has made in this case.

(3) *Business Decision to Control Costs*

Bartell also suggests that it should be permitted to limit the scope of its employee benefit programs in order to control costs. Cost is not, however, a defense to allegations of discrimination under Title VII. *See Manhart*; 29 C.F.R. § 1604.9(e). While it is undoubtedly true that employers may cut benefits, raise deductibles, or otherwise alter coverage options to comply with budgetary constraints, the method by which the employer seeks to curb costs must not be discriminatory. Bartell offers its employees an admittedly generous package of healthcare benefits, including both third-party healthcare plans and an in-house prescription program. It cannot, however, penalize female employees in an effort to keep its benefit costs low. The cost savings Bartell realizes by excluding prescription contraceptives from its healthcare plans are being directly borne by only one sex in violation of Title VII. Although Bartell is permitted, under the law, to use non-discriminatory cuts in benefits to control costs, it cannot balance its benefit books at the expense of its female employees.

(4) *Neutrality of Exclusions*

Prescription contraceptives are not the only drugs or devices excluded from coverage under Bartell's benefit plan. Bartell argues that it has chosen to exclude from coverage all drugs for "family planning," and that this exclusion is neutral and non-discriminatory. There is no "family planning" exclusion in the benefit plan, however, and the contours of such a theoretical exclusion are not clear. On the list of excluded drugs and devices, contraceptive devices and infertility drugs are the two categories which might be considered "family planning" measures. Contrary to defendant's explanation, there appear to be some drugs which fall under the "family planning" rubric which are covered by the plan. Prenatal vitamins, for example, are frequently prescribed in anticipation of a woman becoming pregnant and are expressly covered under the plan. And although both parties agree that Bartell's plan excludes coverage for Viagra, an impotency drug, it is not clear that it falls into any of the excluded categories.

Even if the Court were able to identify a consistent theory to explain the various exclusions and inclusions in Bartell's plan, the exclusion of prescription contraceptives, alone or in combination with the exclusion of infertility drugs, is in no way neutral or equal. Although the issue is not before the Court, there is at least an argument that the exclusion of infertility drugs applies equally to male and female employees, making the coverage offered to all employees less comprehensive in roughly the same amount and manner. The additional exclusion of prescription contraceptives, however, reduces the comprehensiveness of the coverage offered to female employees while leaving the coverage offered to male employees unchanged. As discussed above, such inequities are discriminatory and violate Title VII.

(5) *New Interpretation of an Old Law*

Employers in general, and Bartell in particular, might justifiably wonder why, when Title VII has been on the books for thirty-seven years, this Court is only now holding that it includes a right to prescription contraceptives in certain circumstances. The answer, of course, is that until this case, no court had been asked to evaluate the common practice of excluding contraceptives from a generally comprehensive health plan under Title VII. While there are a number of possible explanations for the lack of litigation over this issue, none of them changes the fact that, having now been properly raised as a matter of statutory construction, this Court is constitutionally required to rule on the issue before it.

Although the Court's decision is a matter of first impression for the judiciary, it is not the first tribunal to consider the lawfulness of a contraception exclusion. On December 14, 2000, the EEOC made a finding of reasonable cause on the same issue which is entitled to some deference. * * * Most importantly, * * * the enforcing agency's overall interpretation of Title VII comports with this Court's construction of the Act and led the Commission to the same conclusion reached by this Court. * * *

(6) *Legislative Issue*

Although this litigation involves politically charged issues with far-reaching social consequences, the parties' dispute turns on the interpretation of an existing federal statute. The Court must determine whether, given the facts of this case and the scope of the coverage offered by defendant, the exclusion of prescription contraceptives from Bartell's prescription plan constitutes discrimination because of sex under Title VII. The normal rules of statutory construction, not the give and take of a legislative body, will guide this determination. Contrary to defendant's suggestion, it is the role of the judiciary, not the legislature, to interpret existing laws and determine whether they apply to a particular set of facts. * * * While it is interesting to note that Congress and some state legislatures are considering proposals to require insurance plans to cover prescription contraceptives, that fact does not alter this Court's constitutional role in interpreting Congress' legislative enactments in order to resolve private disputes.

C. Conclusion

* * * For all of the foregoing reasons, the Court finds that Bartell's prescription drug plan discriminates against Bartell's female employees by providing less complete coverage than that offered to male employees. Although the plan covers almost all drugs and devices used by men, the exclusion of prescription contraceptives creates a gaping hole in the coverage offered to female employees, leaving a fundamental and immediate healthcare need uncovered. Pursuant to the analysis in the *Gilbert* dissents, *Newport News,* and *Johnson Controls,* Title VII requires employers to recognize the differences between the sexes and provide equally comprehensive coverage, even if that means providing additional benefits to cover women-only expenses.

* * *

Notes and Questions

1. Because the plaintiffs in *Erickson* prevailed under a disparate treatment theory, the court did not need to address the merits of its disparate impact claim. In *EEOC v. United Parcel Service, Inc.*, 141 F.Supp.2d 1216 (D.Minn.2001), the EEOC sued UPS on behalf of a male employee whose wife was denied coverage of her prescription for oral contraceptives. The UPS prescription plan for its employees denied coverage of oral contraceptives, regardless of the reason they had been prescribed. The employee's wife had an hormonal disorder which was treatable with oral contraceptives. The court denied the company's motion to dismiss on the grounds that the EEOC had alleged facts that, if true, established both a disparate treatment and a disparate impact claim of sex discrimination under Title VII. The court noted: "UPS's Plan does not provide the same benefits and exclusions to male and female employees and their dependent spouses. The Plan excludes oral contraceptives for any reason, including treatment for female hormonale disorders, while medically necessary treatments for male hormonal disorders are not excluded." *Id.* at 1219. Are cases like *Erickson* and *UPS* best analyzed as disparate treatment or disparate impact cases? Is the *UPS* case like *Erickson* or *Newport News*?

2. In October 2001, the National Women's Law Center, which had been involved in the *Erickson* lawsuit, assisted Lisa Mauldin, a Wal–Mart employee, in bringing a similar claim against the retail giant, challenging its exclusion of contraceptives from its prescription drug plan. 19 Hum. Resources Rep. (BNA) No.41, at 1130 (Oct. 22, 2001); 19 Hum. Resources Rep. (BNA) No.29, at 808 (July 23, 2001). In August 2002, the district court granted Mauldin class-action status representing a class of all Wal–Mart's female employees nationwide who were covered by the insurance plan and who purchased prescription contraceptives after March 8, 2001. Mauldin v. Wal–Mart Stores, Inc., No. 1–101–CV–2755, 2002 WL 2022334 (N.D.Ga. Aug. 23, 2002). The class includes thousands of Wal–Mart employees. *See* 20 Hum. Resources Rep. (BNA) No.36, at 987 (Sept. 16, 2002).

D. THE FAMILY AND MEDICAL LEAVE ACT AS ANTIDISCRIMINATION LAW

NEVADA DEPARTMENT OF HUMAN RESOURCES v. HIBBS

Supreme Court of the United States, 2003.
538 U.S. 721, 123 S.Ct. 1972, 155 L.Ed.2d 953.

Chief Justice REHNQUIST delivered the opinion of the Court.

The Family and Medical Leave Act of 1993 (FMLA or Act) entitles eligible employees to take up to 12 work weeks of unpaid leave annually for any of several reasons, including the onset of a "serious health condition" in an employee's spouse, child, or parent. 29 U.S.C. § 2612(a)(1)(C). The Act creates a private right of action to seek both equitable relief and money damages "against any employer (including a public agency) in any Federal or State court of competent jurisdiction,"

§ 2617(a)(2), should that employer "interfere with, restrain, or deny the exercise of" FMLA rights, § 2615(a)(1). We hold that employees of the State of Nevada may recover money damages in the event of the State's failure to comply with the family-care provision of the Act.

Petitioners include the Nevada Department of Human Resources (Department) and two of its officers. Respondent William Hibbs (hereinafter respondent) worked for the Department's Welfare Division. In April and May 1997, he sought leave under the FMLA to care for his ailing wife, who was recovering from a car accident and neck surgery. The Department granted his request for the full 12 weeks of FMLA leave and authorized him to use the leave intermittently as needed between May and December 1997. Respondent did so until August 5, 1997, after which he did not return to work. In October 1997, the Department informed respondent that he had exhausted his FMLA leave, that no further leave would be granted, and that he must report to work by November 12, 1997. Respondent failed to do so and was terminated.

[Hibbs sued the Department in district court "seeking damages and injunctive and declaratory relief for, *inter alia,* violations of 29 U.S.C. § 2612(a)(1)(C)." The Department was awarded summary judgment "on the grounds that the FMLA claim was barred by the Eleventh Amendment." The Ninth Circuit reversed, and the Supreme Court granted certiorari "to resolve a split among the Courts of Appeals on the question whether an individual may sue a State for money damages in federal court for violation of § 2612(a)(1)(C)."]

For over a century now, we have made clear that the Constitution does not provide for federal jurisdiction over suits against nonconsenting States. * * *

Congress may, however, abrogate such immunity in federal court if it makes its intention to abrogate unmistakably clear in the language of the statute and acts pursuant to a valid exercise of its power under § 5 of the Fourteenth Amendment. The clarity of Congress' intent here is not fairly debatable. * * * This case turns, then, on whether Congress acted within its constitutional authority when it sought to abrogate the States' immunity for purposes of the FMLA's family-leave provision.

In enacting the FMLA, Congress relied on two of the powers vested in it by the Constitution: its Article I commerce power and its power under § 5 of the Fourteenth Amendment to enforce that Amendment's guarantees.[1] Congress may not abrogate the States' sovereign immunity pursuant to its Article I power over commerce. Congress may, however,

---

1. Compare 29 U.S.C. § 2601(b)(1) ("It is the purpose of this Act * * * to balance the demands of the workplace with the needs of families, to promote the stability and economic security of families, and to promote national interests in preserving family integrity") with § 2601(b)(5) ("to promote the goal of equal employment op-portunity for women and men, pursuant to [the Equal Protection C]lause") and § 2601(b)(4) ("to accomplish [the Act's other purposes] in a manner that, consistent with the Equal Protection Clause * * *, minimizes the potential for employment discrimination on the basis of sex").

abrogate States' sovereign immunity through a valid exercise of its § 5 power * * *.

* * *

* * * Valid § 5 legislation must exhibit "congruence and proportionality between the injury to be prevented or remedied and the means adopted to that end." *City of Boerne v. Flores,* 521 U.S. 507, 520, 117 S.Ct. 2157, 2164, 138 L.Ed.2d 624 (1997).

The FMLA aims to protect the right to be free from gender-based discrimination in the workplace.[2] We have held that statutory classifications that distinguish between males and females are subject to heightened scrutiny. See, *e.g., Craig v. Boren,* 429 U.S. 190, 197–199, 97 S.Ct. 451, 50 L.Ed.2d 397 (1976). For a gender-based classification to withstand such scrutiny, it must "serv[e] important governmental objectives," and "the discriminatory means employed [must be] substantially related to the achievement of those objectives." *United States v. Virginia,* 518 U.S. 515, 533, 116 S.Ct. 2264, 135 L.Ed.2d 735 (1996) (citations and internal quotation marks omitted). The State's justification for such a classification "must not rely on overbroad generalizations about the different talents, capacities, or preferences of males and females." *Ibid.* We now inquire whether Congress had evidence of a pattern of constitutional violations on the part of the States in this area.

The history of the many state laws limiting women's employment opportunities is chronicled in—and, until relatively recently, was sanctioned by—this Court's own opinions. For example, in *Bradwell v. State,* 16 Wall. 130, 21 L.Ed. 442 (1873) (Illinois), and *Goesaert v. Cleary,* 335 U.S. 464, 466, 69 S.Ct. 198, 93 L.Ed. 163 (1948) (Michigan), the Court upheld state laws prohibiting women from practicing law and tending bar, respectively. State laws frequently subjected women to distinctive restrictions, terms, conditions, and benefits for those jobs they could take. In *Muller v. Oregon,* 208 U.S. 412, 419, n. 1, 28 S.Ct. 324, 52 L.Ed. 551 (1908), for example, this Court approved a state law limiting the hours that women could work for wages, and observed that 19 States had such laws at the time. Such laws were based on the related beliefs that (1) woman is, and should remain, "the center of home and family life," *Hoyt v. Florida,* 368 U.S. 57, 62, 82 S.Ct. 159, 7 L.Ed.2d 118 (1961), and (2) "a proper discharge of [a woman's] maternal functions— having in view not merely her own health, but the well-being of the race—justif[ies] legislation to protect her from the greed as well as the passion of man," *Muller, supra,* at 422, 28 S.Ct. 324. Until our decision

---

2. The text of the Act makes this clear. Congress found that, "due to the nature of the roles of men and women in our society, the primary responsibility for family caretaking often falls on women, and such responsibility affects the working lives of women more than it affects the working lives of men." 29 U.S.C. § 2601(a)(5). In response to this finding, Congress sought "to accomplish the [Act's other] purposes * * * in a manner that * * * minimizes the potential for employment discrimination *on the basis of sex* by ensuring generally that leave is available * * * *on a gender-neutral basis*[,] and to promote the goal of equal employment opportunity for women and men (4)" §§ 2601(b)(4) and (5) (emphasis added).

in *Reed v. Reed,* 404 U.S. 71, 92 S.Ct. 251, 30 L.Ed.2d 225 (1971), "it remained the prevailing doctrine that government, both federal and state, could withhold from women opportunities accorded men so long as any 'basis in reason' "—such as the above beliefs—"could be conceived for the discrimination." *Virginia, supra,* at 531, 116 S.Ct. 2264 (quoting *Goesaert, supra,* at 467, 69 S.Ct. 198).

Congress responded to this history of discrimination by abrogating States' sovereign immunity in Title VII of the Civil Rights Act of 1964, and we sustained this abrogation in *Fitzpatrick v. Bitzer,* 427 U.S. 445, 96 S.Ct. 2666, 49 L.Ed.2d 614 (1976). But state gender discrimination did not cease. "[I]t can hardly be doubted that * * * women still face pervasive, although at times more subtle, discrimination * * * in the job market." *Frontiero v. Richardson,* 411 U.S. 677, 686, 93 S.Ct. 1764, 36 L.Ed.2d 583 (1973). According to evidence that was before Congress when it enacted the FMLA, States continue to rely on invalid gender stereotypes in the employment context, specifically in the administration of leave benefits. Reliance on such stereotypes cannot justify the States' gender discrimination in this area. *Virginia, supra,* at 533, 116 S.Ct. 2264. The long and extensive history of sex discrimination prompted us to hold that measures that differentiate on the basis of gender warrant heightened scrutiny; here, as in *Fitzpatrick,* the persistence of such unconstitutional discrimination by the States justifies Congress' passage of prophylactic § 5 legislation.

As the FMLA's legislative record reflects, a 1990 Bureau of Labor Statistics (BLS) survey stated that 37 percent of surveyed private-sector employees were covered by maternity leave policies, while only 18 percent were covered by paternity leave policies. S.Rep. No. 103–3, pp. 14–15 (1993), U.S.Code Cong. & Admin.News 1993, p. 3. The corresponding numbers from a similar BLS survey the previous year were 33 percent and 16 percent, respectively. *Ibid.* While these data show an increase in the percentage of employees eligible for such leave, they also show a widening of the gender gap during the same period. Thus, stereotype-based beliefs about the allocation of family duties remained firmly rooted, and employers' reliance on them in establishing discriminatory leave policies remained widespread.

Congress also heard testimony that "[p]arental leave for fathers * * * is rare. Even * * * [w]here child-care leave policies do exist, men, *both in the public and private sectors,* receive notoriously discriminatory treatment in their requests for such leave." *Id.,* at 147 (Washington Council of Lawyers) (emphasis added). Many States offered women extended "maternity" leave that far exceeded the typical 4–to 8–week period of physical disability due to pregnancy and childbirth, but very few States granted men a parallel benefit: Fifteen States provided women up to one year of extended maternity leave, while only four provided men with the same. M. Lord & M. King, The State Reference Guide to Work–Family Programs for State Employees 30 (1991). This and other differential leave policies were not attributable to any differential physical needs of men and women, but rather to the pervasive sex-role stereotype that caring for family members is women's work.[5]

Finally, Congress had evidence that, even where state laws and policies were not facially discriminatory, they were applied in discriminatory ways. It was aware of the "serious problems with the discretionary nature of family leave," because when "the authority to grant leave and to arrange the length of that leave rests with individual supervisors," it leaves "employees open to discretionary and possibly unequal treatment." H.R.Rep. No. 103–8, pt. 2, pp. 10–11 (1993). Testimony supported that conclusion, explaining that "[t]he lack of uniform parental and medical leave policies in the work place has created an environment where [sex] discrimination is rampant." 1987 Senate Labor Hearings, pt. 2, at 170 (testimony of Peggy Montes, Mayor's Commission on Women's Affairs, City of Chicago).

In spite of all of the above evidence, Justice KENNEDY argues in dissent that Congress' passage of the FMLA was unnecessary because "the States appear to have been ahead of Congress in providing gender-neutral family leave benefits," and points to Nevada's leave policies in particular. However, it was only "[s]ince Federal family leave legislation was first introduced" that the States had even "begun to consider similar family leave initiatives." S.Rep. No. 103–3, at 20, U.S.Code Cong. & Admin.News 1993, pp. 3, 22.

Furthermore, the dissent's statement that some States "had adopted some form of family-care leave" before the FMLA's enactment, glosses over important shortcomings of some state policies. First, seven States had childcare leave provisions that applied to women only. Indeed, Massachusetts required that notice of its leave provisions be posted only in "establishment[s] in which females are employed." These laws reinforced the very stereotypes that Congress sought to remedy through the FMLA. Second, 12 States provided their employees no family leave, beyond an initial childbirth or adoption, to care for a seriously ill child or family member. Third, many States provided no statutorily guaranteed right to family leave, offering instead only voluntary or discretionary leave programs. Three States left the amount of leave time primarily in employers' hands. Congress could reasonably conclude that such discretionary family-leave programs would do little to combat the stereotypes about the roles of male and female employees that Congress sought to eliminate. Finally, four States provided leave only through administrative regulations or personnel policies, which Congress could reasonably

---

5. For example, state employers' collective-bargaining agreements often granted extended "maternity" leave of six months to a year to women only. * * * In addition, state leave laws often specified that catchall leave-without-pay provisions could be used for extended maternity leave, but did not authorize such leave for paternity purposes. * * *

Evidence pertaining to parenting leave is relevant here because state discrimination in the provision of both types of benefits is based on the same gender stereotype: that women's family duties trump those of the workplace. * * * [B]ecause parenting and family leave address very similar situations in which work and family responsibilities conflict, they implicate the same stereotypes.

conclude offered significantly less firm protection than a federal law. Against the above backdrop of limited state leave policies, no matter how generous petitioner's own may have been, Congress was justified in enacting the FMLA as remedial legislation.

In sum, the States' record of unconstitutional participation in, and fostering of, gender-based discrimination in the administration of leave benefits is weighty enough to justify the enactment of prophylactic § 5 legislation.

* * *

The impact of the discrimination targeted by the FMLA is significant. Congress determined:

> Historically, denial or curtailment of women's employment opportunities has been traceable directly to the pervasive presumption that women are mothers first, and workers second. This prevailing ideology about women's roles has in turn justified discrimination against women when they are mothers or mothers-to-be.

Joint Hearing 100. Stereotypes about women's domestic roles are reinforced by parallel stereotypes presuming a lack of domestic responsibilities for men. Because employers continued to regard the family as the woman's domain, they often denied men similar accommodations or discouraged them from taking leave. These mutually reinforcing stereotypes created a self-fulfilling cycle of discrimination that forced women to continue to assume the role of primary family caregiver, and fostered employers' stereotypical views about women's commitment to work and their value as employees. Those perceptions, in turn, Congress reasoned, lead to subtle discrimination that may be difficult to detect on a case-by-case basis.

We believe that Congress' chosen remedy, the family-care leave provision of the FMLA, is "congruent and proportional to the targeted violation." Congress had already tried unsuccessfully to address this problem through Title VII and the amendment of Title VII by the Pregnancy Discrimination Act. * * *

By creating an across-the-board, routine employment benefit for all eligible employees, Congress sought to ensure that family-care leave would no longer be stigmatized as an inordinate drain on the workplace caused by female employees, and that employers could not evade leave obligations simply by hiring men. By setting a minimum standard of family leave for *all* eligible employees, irrespective of gender, the FMLA attacks the formerly state-sanctioned stereotype that only women are responsible for family caregiving, thereby reducing employers' incentives to engage in discrimination by basing hiring and promotion decisions on stereotypes.

The dissent characterizes the FMLA as a "substantive entitlement program" rather than a remedial statute because it establishes a floor of 12 weeks' leave. In the dissent's view, in the face of evidence of gender-based discrimination by the States in the provision of leave benefits,

Congress could do no more in exercising its § 5 power than simply proscribe such discrimination. But this position cannot be squared with our recognition that Congress "is not confined to the enactment of legislation that merely parrots the precise wording of the Fourteenth Amendment," but may prohibit "a somewhat broader swath of conduct, including that which is not itself forbidden by the Amendment's text." *Kimel v. Florida Bd. of Regents,* 528 U.S. 62, 82, 120 S.Ct. 631, 145 L.Ed.2d 522 (2000). * * *

Indeed, in light of the evidence before Congress, a statute mirroring Title VII, that simply mandated gender equality in the administration of leave benefits, would not have achieved Congress' remedial object. Such a law would allow States to provide for no family leave at all. Where "[t]wo-thirds of the nonprofessional caregivers for older, chronically ill, or disabled persons are working women," H.R.Rep. No. 103–8, pt. 1, p. 24 (1993); S.Rep. No. 103–3, at 7, U.S.Code Cong. & Admin.News 1993, pp. 3, 9, and state practices continue to reinforce the stereotype of women as caregivers, such a policy would exclude far more women than men from the workplace.

* * * [T]he FMLA is narrowly targeted at the fault line between work and family—precisely where sex-based overgeneralization has been and remains strongest—and affects only one aspect of the employment relationship. * * *

We also find significant the many other limitations that Congress placed on the scope of this measure. The FMLA requires only unpaid leave, and applies only to employees who have worked for the employer for at least one year and provided 1,250 hours of service within the last 12 months. Employees in high-ranking or sensitive positions are simply ineligible for FMLA leave; of particular importance to the States, the FMLA expressly excludes from coverage state elected officials, their staffs, and appointed policymakers. Employees must give advance notice of foreseeable leave, and employers may require certification by a health care provider of the need for leave. In choosing 12 weeks as the appropriate leave floor, Congress chose "a middle ground, a period long enough to serve 'the needs of families' but not so long that it would upset 'the legitimate interests of employers.'" *Ragsdale v. Wolverine World Wide, Inc.,* 535 U.S. 81, 94, 122 S.Ct. 1155, 152 L.Ed.2d 167 (2002) (quoting 29 U.S.C. § 2601(b)).[12] Moreover, the cause of action under the FMLA is a restricted one: The damages recoverable are strictly defined and measured by actual monetary losses, and the accrual period for backpay is limited by the Act's 2–year statute of limitations (extended to three years only for willful violations).

---

12. Congress established 12 weeks as a floor, thus leaving States free to provide their employees with more family leave time if they so choose. * * * The dissent faults Congress for giving States this choice, arguing that the FMLA's terms do not bar States from granting more family leave time to women than to men. But Justice KENNEDY effectively counters his own argument in his very next breath, recognizing that such gender-based discrimination would "run afoul of the Equal Protection Clause or Title VII." * * *

For the above reasons, we conclude that § 2612(a)(1)(C) is congruent and proportional to its remedial object, and can "be understood as responsive to, or designed to prevent, unconstitutional behavior." *City of Boerne, supra,* at 532, 117 S.Ct. 2157.

* * *

[SOUTER, J., filed a concurring opinion, in which Ginsburg and Breyer, JJ., joined. STEVENS, J., filed an opinion concurring in the judgment. SCALIA, J., filed a dissenting opinion. KENNEDY, J., filed a dissenting opinion, in which Scalia and Thomas, JJ., joined.]

In general, the FMLA guarantees certain employees at least twelve weeks of leave for childbirth or adoption and related childcare and to attend to serious personal or family health problems. By its ten-year anniversary, over 35 million employees had taken FMLA leaves. *10 Years After It Was Enacted, FMLA Needs Makeover, Advocates Contend,* 21 Hum. Resources Rep. (BNA) No.5, at 117 (Feb. 10, 2003). The FMLA requires covered employers to provide an eligible employee with up to twelve workweeks of leave during any twelve-month period because of (1) the birth of the employee's child and attendant child care; (2) the placement of a child with the employee for adoption or foster care; (3) a serious health condition of the employee's spouse, son, daughter or parent requiring the employee's care; or (4) a serious health condition that makes the employee unable to perform the functions of the job. 29 U.S.C. § 2612(a). The courts interpreting the term "serious health condition" have consistently required a showing of incapacity. *See e.g.,* Martyszenko v. Safeway, Inc., 120 F.3d 120, 122–23 (8th Cir.1997) (discussing incapacity requirement and collecting cases). Should the rationale and holding of *Hibbs* apply to a case where a state employee alleges that she was improperly denied FMLA leave that she sought because of her own serious health condition rather than the health condition of a family member? *See* Brockman v. Wyoming Dep't of Family Servs., 342 F.3d 1159, 1165 (10th Cir.2003) (holding that Congress did not abrogate state sovereign immunity in the FMLA provision for leave for self-care).

The FMLA benefits both women and men with family responsibilities, but women seeking leave for pregnancy and maternity leave and to care for their seriously ill young children or elderly parents are the most obvious beneficiaries of this new federal policy. Women who are mothers are the fastest growing cohort of workers in the United States: between 1976 and 1992 women with children under the age of one increased their participation in the labor force from 31 percent to 54 percent. *Mothers Are Fastest Growing Part of Wage Force, Still Face Wage Gap,* 9 Nat'l Rep. Work & Fam. 190 (Dec. 3, 1996) (citing Institute for Women's Policy Research, The Status of Women in the States). Three-fifths of all women with children under the age of six work for wages. *Id.* By 1998,

59 percent of new mothers with infants participated in the labor force, although this rate dropped to 55 percent in 2000. *Employers Can Take a Number of Steps to Get New Mothers Back to the Workplace*, 20 Hum. Resources Rep. (BNA) No. 31, at 845 (Aug. 5, 2002) (citing Kristin Smith, Maternity Leave and Employment Patterns, 1961–1995 (Census Bureau Report)). According to the Census Bureau, "[b]etween 1991 and 1994, over half (52 percent) of new mothers went back to work within six months of giving birth, as compared to only 14 percent between 1961 and 1965." *Id.* An AFL–CIO survey reported that in 2002

> [s]ixty-three percent of women work 40 or more hours per week * * *. Contrary to conventional assumptions, married mothers who work are not part-timers. Sixty-eight percent of married working mothers put in 40 or more hours per week—compared with 60 percent of women without children.

AFL–CIO, Ask a Working Woman: Survey 2002, 1 (May 7, 2002), *available in <http://www.aflcio.org>.*

Although the FMLA provides for unpaid leave, the employee may elect, or the employer may require, that paid leave be substituted for all or part of FMLA leave. The employee must provide the employer with thirty days notice if leave is foreseeable; otherwise the employee must provide such notice as is practicable. *See, e.g.,* Gay v. Gilman Paper Co., 125 F.3d 1432 (11th Cir.1997) (limited information in employee's spouse's phone call to employee's supervisor was insufficient notice); Manuel v. Westlake Polymers Corp., 66 F.3d 758 (5th Cir.1995) (employee does not need to mention FMLA statute in requesting leave); *see generally* Timothy Stewart Bland, *The Required Content of Employees' Notice to Employers of the Need for Leave Under the FMLA*, 12 Lab.Law. 235 (1996). When both spouses are employed by the same employer, they are entitled to a combined total of twelve weeks of leave for birth or placement of a child or to care for parents with a serious health condition.

An employee on FMLA leave cannot lose benefits accrued prior to the start of leave, and the employer must maintain the employee's benefits under a properly recognized group health plan at the same level and under the same terms as though the employee had continued to work. If the employee does not return to work at the completion of the leave, the employer may recover any health plan premium costs paid during the leave. The general rule, with some exceptions, is that an employee returning from leave is entitled to reinstatement to her former job or an equivalent position if the former job is no longer available.

The FMLA is enforced through either a private civil action for damages or equitable relief, or through administrative action by filing a complaint with the Secretary of Labor. The FMLA does not modify or affect any state or federal law prohibiting discrimination, nor does it preempt state or local laws providing greater leave rights than those found in the FMLA. Title II of the FMLA provides coverage to federal employees. The Department of Labor, which enforces the Act, has issued final regulations. *See* 29 C.F.R. §§ 825.100–825.800; *see also* Cheryl R. Saban & Dena Sacco, *An FMLA Compliance Update: What Every Employer Should Know About the Final Rules*, 21 Empl.Rel.L.J. 145 (1995).

The FMLA covers employees who have worked for at least one year for an employer who employs at least fifty workers. Proposed legislation to extend coverage to employers with at least 25 employees would, if enacted, bring another 13 million employees under the FMLA. 21 Hum. Resources Rep. (BNA) No.5, at 119 (Feb. 10, 2003) (citing S.304, which was introduced by Senator Christopher J. Dodd on Feb. 10, 2003). Nearly half of all private sector employees, however, are not covered by the federal law. Thus, state laws providing for preferential treatment of workers on the basis of family leave continue to play a significant role in this area. A number of complex issues arise when rights created under the FMLA overlap or conflict with rights provided under state laws dealing with family and medical leave or workers compensation, or with other federal statutes covering these rights or benefits. *See, e.g.*, Martin W. Aron & Richard M. De Aguizio, *The Four–Headed Monster: ADA, FMLA, OSHA and Workers' Compensation*, 46 Lab.L.J. 48 (1995).

Notes and Questions

1. *Antidiscrimination or Accommodation?* Is the FMLA an extension of the antidiscrimination principles embodied in Title VII and the PDA? Or does the FMLA require preferential treatment of some groups of employees? Can nondiscrimination and selective preferences or accommodation be reconciled? *See generally* Lucinda M. Finley, *Transcending Equality Theory: A Way Out of the Maternity and the Workplace Debate*, 86 Colum.L.Rev. 1118 (1986). Several years before the enactment of the FMLA, Professor Dowd wrote:

> [I]t is essential that we recognize this fundamental paradox about work and family: that the structure of work and family, and the nature of the conflict between work and family, is not just a women's issue and a gender issue. We must constantly take women and gender into account because they are inseparable from the existing structure and assumptions of family and work. We otherwise risk ignoring, perpetuating or recreating the gendered structure of work and family. At the same time, however, we must get beyond gender, to redefining the relationship between work and family. We must take account of gender in order to transform the workplace, and get beyond gender in order to imagine a world where gender is not a primary determinant of our choices and our vision.

Nancy E. Dowd, *Work and Family: The Gender Paradox and the Limitations of Discrimination Analysis in Restructuring the Workplace*, 24 Harv.C.R.-C.L.L.Rev. 79, 80–81 (1989). To what extent does the FMLA resolve the "paradox" noted by Dowd? More recently, Professor Malin observed:

> Largely missing from the debate over maternal work-family conflicts is any discussion of paternal work-family conflicts. The two, however, are linked to a significant extent. Just as the absence of

adequate maternal leave policies has been a barrier to women's roles in the workplace, the absence of adequate paternal leave policies has been a barrier to men's roles in the home. Furthermore, as long as parental leave remains de facto maternal leave, work-family conflicts will remain a significant barrier to women's employment and a significant source of discrimination against women.

Martin H. Malin, *Fathers and Parental Leave*, 72 Tex.L.Rev. 1047, 1052 (1994). Does the FMLA currently create incentives for working men to increase their involvement in family responsibilities?

Professor Michael Selmi has argued "that the FMLA [should] be amended so as to create greater incentives for men to take leave around the birth or adoption of a child," because "the disproportionate burden of child rearing that falls on women explains a substantial portion of their labor market inequality." Michael Selmi, *Family Leave and the Gender Wage Gap*, 78 N.C.L.Rev. 707, 712, 713 (2000). Selmi explores a range of incentives, "from forcing men to take six weeks of paid leave to the less drastic measure of creating a governmental contract set-aside program aimed at rewarding employers who succeed in encouraging their employees to take family leave. *Id.* at 712–13. Would you support or oppose such amendments to the FMLA? Explain why. In the aftermath of *Hibbs*, will state employers be more likely or less likely to want to hire and retain women of childbearing age?

2. Like the dissenters in *Hibbs*, lower courts have argued that the FMLA is not an antidiscrimination statute like Title VII, but a statute providing "substantive entitlements," like the Fair Labor Standards Act. *See* Diaz v. Fort Wayne Foundry Corp., 131 F.3d 711, 712 (7th Cir.1997) (distinguishing the FMLA from Title VII by noting that "claims under the FLMA do not depend on discrimination" and comparing the FMLA to the NLRA, FLSA, and ERISA). Nevertheless, the FMLA complements and reinforces Title VII's prohibition against discrimination on the basis of pregnancy, childbirth, and related medical conditions by assuring that many women who seek or take leaves for these reasons have legal protections for their jobs and employee benefits. But do the PDA and the FMLA go far enough? Consider the following critique:

If working women are to have the prospect of both having children and career-term employment on an equal basis with men, * * * some form of accommodation must be made. Unlike the incomplete models of the PDA and the FMLA, our proposal attempts to address directly the difficult issue of costs associated with the unique role that women have in bearing children. This biological role creates a foreseeable period of disability for working women at relatively early stages of their working lives which, if unaccommodated, has lasting effects throughout their time in the labor force. If social equality for working women is the goal, then neither of the two current statutory models will achieve that objective. The simple antidiscrimination model does not account for the real difference, nor does it provide for any level of benefits at all. The Family and Medical Leave Act, by contrast does provide for the right of return to the work force for a limited sector of working women. Unfortunately the FMLA is incomplete, not just because it makes women the primary cost bearers of their period of separation from the work force, but because it creates paradoxical incentives for employers to discriminate against women in the initial hiring of employees.

Samuel Issacharoff & Elyse Rosenblum, *Women and the Workplace: Accommodating the Demands of Pregnancy*, 94 Colum.L.Rev. 2154, 2220 (1994).

3. Who are the primary beneficiaries of the FMLA? Professor Crain observed that

[t]he hard-won Family and Medical Leave Act * * * is limited to the protection of workers' jobs and maintenance of existing health benefits (if any) during an unpaid leave of up to twelve weeks to accommodate the birth or adoption of a child, or for care of a seriously ill child, spouse, or parent. The absence of wage replacement in the Act continues the assumption of female dependence on a male breadwinner. Notwithstanding the statute's gender-neutral language, only those who share expenses with a wage earner whose income is sufficient to support the family will be able to take advantage of the limited right to job security that the Act affords. From the perspective of single mothers and working class women whose wages are an essential part of the family income, the Act confers a hollow right. Most working class women will not be able to afford to take unpaid leave, whether or not they are part of a two-earner household, and many have no health benefits to extend during the leave. Moreover, part-time and temporary employees, who are disproportionately female, are not covered by the statute. Finally, the lack of wage replacement ensures that the statutory right is skewed disproportionately towards white women. Women of color are both more likely to be functioning as single heads-of-households and likely to derive a lesser economic benefit (relative to white women) from their associations with men because of the wage disparities between white men and men of color.

Marion Crain, *Confronting the Structural Character of Working Women's Economic Subordination: Collective Action vs. Individual Rights Strategies*, 3–Spring Kan.J.L. & Pub.Pol'y 26, 27–28 (1994).

4. *Pregnancy and the Interplay Between Title VII, the PDA, the FMLA, and the ADA*: The FMLA requires employers to provide unpaid leave for employees with serious medical conditions; Title VII, as amended by the PDA, requires employers to treat pregnant employees the same as other employees who are similar in their ability or inability to perform the job; and the Americans with Disabilities Act of 1991 (ADA), covered in Chapter 13, requires employers to make reasonable accommodations for employees with disabilities who are otherwise qualified to do the job. Often these statutes will address very different situations, but occasions will arise where the provisions of the statutes and agency regulations may provide overlapping, conflicting, or alternative theories of employee rights and employer liability. *See, e.g.*, Smith v. Diffee Ford–Lincoln–Mercury, Inc., 298 F.3d 955 (10th Cir.2002) (finding that an FMLA leave is a reasonable accommodation under the ADA); Navarro v. Pfizer Corp., 261 F.3d 90 (1st Cir.2001) (holding that EEOC's interpretation of a regulation issued under the ADA is not entitled to deference in interpreting the identical regulation adopted by the Secretary of Labor under the FMLA). For example, if a pregnant employee who experiences persistent, disabling morning sickness is denied part-time leave

and then is fired when she cannot perform her job adequately due to recurrent bouts of nausea, does she have a viable claim under Title VII, the PDA, the FMLA, the ADA, or under all of them? *See generally* Deborah A. Calloway, *Accommodating Pregnancy in the Workplace*, 25 Stetson L.Rev. 1 (1995).

EEOC regulations interpreting the ADA state that "conditions, such as pregnancy, that are not the result of a physiological disorder are not impairments." 29 C.F.R.App. § 1630.2(h)(1) (1996). Relying on this regulation, a number of courts have denied ADA claims of pregnant workers. *See* Gudenkauf v. Stauffer Communications, Inc., 922 F.Supp. 465, 473 (D.Kan. 1996) (collecting cases); *see also* Gabriel v. City of Chicago, 9 F.Supp.2d 974 (N.D.Ill.1998) (relying on the Supreme Court's 1998 decision in *Bragdon v. Abbott*, 524 U.S. 624, 118 S.Ct. 2196, 141 L.Ed.2d 540 (1998), and the EEOC's Interpretive Guidance, to hold that pregnancy is not a disability per se under the ADA). For example, in *Gudenkauf*, the plaintiff, during her pregnancy, had complained of "morning sickness, stress, nausea, back pain, swelling and headaches." *Id.* at 469. When she was fired for "poor performance," she brought claims under Title VII, the PDA, ADA, and FMLA. The court permitted the Title VII and PDA claims to go to trial, but dismissed the ADA and FMLA claims. Regarding the ADA claim, the court concluded that "[p]regnancy is a physiological condition, but it is not a disorder. Being the natural consequence of a properly functioning reproductive system, pregnancy cannot be called an impairment." *Id.* at 473. *See also* Lehmuller v. Incorporated Village of Sag Harbor, 944 F.Supp. 1087, 1093 (E.D.N.Y. 1996) (agreeing with the reasoning of *Gudenkauf*); Richards v. City of Topeka, 934 F.Supp. 378, 382 (1996) (same).

A few courts, however, have been critical of the *Gudenkauf* approach to the ADA and have "applied a more refined analysis" of the EEOC regulation that "distinguishe[s] between a normal, uncomplicated pregnancy itself and a complication or condition arising out of the pregnancy." Cerrato v. Durham, 941 F.Supp. 388, 392 (S.D.N.Y.1996); *see also id.* (collecting and discussing cases). For example, following *Cerrato*, the court in *Hernandez v. City of Hartford*, 959 F.Supp. 125 (D.Conn.1997), held that premature labor is a physical impairment under the Rehabilitation Act and the ADA. Chief Judge Dorsey wrote that the EEOC regulation, 29 C.F.R.app. § 1630.2(h)(1), "does not explicitly exclude pregnancy-related impairments, provided they are the result of a physiological disorder." *Id.* at 130.

The EEOC's interpretation of the ADA has been criticized by some scholars. *See* Calloway, *supra*, at 28–29; *see generally* Collette G. Matzzie, *Substantive Equality and Antidiscrimination: Accommodating Pregnancy Under the Americans with Disabilities Act*, 82 Geo.L.J. 193 (1993); Laura Schlictmann, *Accommodation of Pregnancy–Related Disabilities on the Job*, 15 Berkeley J.Emp. & Lab.L. 335 (1994). Professor Calloway, for example, argues that the legislative history of the PDA supports her view that the PDA should be interpreted "to require employers to accommodate pregnant women in the same way they accommodate disabled individuals under the ADA." Calloway, *supra*, at 32.

In contrast to the EEOC's treatment of pregnancy under the ADA, the Labor Department regulations interpreting the FMLA provide that pregnancy is a "serious health condition." See 29 C.F.R. § 825.114(a)(2)(ii) (defining "serious health condition" as "[a]ny period of incapacity due to pregnancy, or for prenatal care"). In general, intermittent or reduced-schedule leaves under the FMLA may be taken only for medical necessity. However, the burden of proving "incapacity" may bar many pregnancy-related FMLA claims. For example, in *Gudenkauf*, the plaintiff's FMLA claim failed because there was insufficient evidence that her "pregnancy and related conditions kept her from performing the functions of her job for more than one-half day." 922 F.Supp. at 475–76.

How would you advise an employer who has received a request for part-time leave from a pregnant employee who is experiencing severe morning sickness? Or from an employee who has requested no overtime work solely because she is pregnant? *See* Whitaker v. Bosch Braking Sys., 180 F.Supp.2d 922, 926–31 (2001). What evidence does an employee need to present to the employer to establish entitlement to a pregnancy-related FMLA leave? *See* Pendarvis v. Xerox Corp., 3 F.Supp.2d 53 (D.D.C.1998) (concluding that the FMLA and federal regulations, "when read as a whole, do not require medical evidence in cases of pregnancy-related severe morning sickness").

5. *Timing of Pregnancy–Related FMLA Leaves:* Can an employer unilaterally determine the timing of a twelve-week FMLA leave for a pregnant employee once the conditions for such a leave have been satisfied? Consider the following scenario: An employee whose job as a laboratory technician involves working with toxic chemicals learns that she is pregnant. Hoping to be given an alternative working assignment for the duration of her pregnancy, she submits to her employer a letter from her doctor stating that she should not be exposed to certain chemicals in the lab while she is pregnant. At the time, she is in her second month of pregnancy. The employer, who has no alternative positions available, immediately places the employee on a twelve-week leave that it designates as FMLA leave. In addition, the employer notifies the employee that if she is unable to return to her position as a lab technician at the end of the twelve-week period, she will be deemed to have voluntarily quit her job. When the FMLA leave ends, the employee—who is then almost six months pregnant—chooses not to return to work at that time, and the employer terminates her employment. Does the employee have a viable claim that the employer violated the FMLA by unilaterally placing her on FMLA leave, at a time when she did not request such a leave, but only sought an alternative job assignment? *See* Harvender v. Norton Co., No. 96–CV–653 (LEK/RWS), 1997 WL 793085, at *7 (N.D.N.Y. 1997) (noting that "[n]owhere in the [FMLA] does it provide that FMLA leave must be granted only when the employee wishes it to be granted"). If the employer has not violated the FMLA, has it violated the Pregnancy Discrimination Act? *See* Carney v. Martin Luther Home, Inc., 824 F.2d 643 (8th Cir.1987) (holding that an employer violated the PDA when it required a pregnant employee to take an unpaid medical leave). Can the purposes of the FMLA and PDA be reconciled if employers are free to determine the timing of FMLA leaves?

6. In its first case interpreting the FMLA, *Ragsdale v. Wolverine World Wide, Inc.*, 535 U.S. 81, 122 S.Ct. 1155, 152 L.Ed.2d 167 (2002), the Supreme Court considered the validity of a FMLA regulation, 29 C.F.R. § 825.700(a), providing that if an employee is absent from work on medical leave and "and

the employer does not designate the leave as FMLA leave, the leave does not count against an employee's FMLA entitlement." In a 5–4 decision, the Court held that the penalty imposed on the employer by the regulation was contrary to the remedial scheme embodied in the FMLA and exceeded the authority of the Secretary of Labor under the Act. After *Ragsdale*, an employer who has provided an employee with paid or unpaid FMLA compliant leave without notice that it is designated as FMLA leave will be able to count that leave time toward the employee's twelve weeks of FMLA leave, unless the employee can show that she was harmed by the lack of notice.

7. *Comparative Perspectives on Family and Medical Leave Policies*: Guaranteed leave that permits employees to address family needs and other personal matters has long been the right of employees in most European countries. Until 1993, the United States and South Africa were the only industrialized countries without family and personal leave policies at the national level. *See generally* Carol Daugherty Rasnic, *The United States' 1993 Family and Medical Leave Act: How Does It Compare with Work Leave Laws in European Countries?*, 10 Conn.J.Int'l L. 105 (1994). The prevailing European model for treating maternity leave goes much further than either the PDA or the FMLA:

> [A]ll women in the European Community nations receive at least seventy-five percent of their salary, save those in Portugal and Britain.
>
> * * * [I]n all European countries that provide pregnancy benefits, with the partial exception of Britain, the prime source of payment is out of general revenues or general social insurance funds. In other words, society as a whole rather than the individual employer assumes the burden for pregnancy leave.
>
> The rejection of the antidiscrimination model for pregnancy-related workplace matters and the direct confrontation with the cost of accommodation establish the critical disparities between European and American law in this area.

Samuel Issacharoff & Elyse Rosenblum, *Women and the Workplace: Accommodating the Demands of Pregnancy*, 94 Colum.L.Rev. 2154, 2213–14 (1994). For a pre-FMLA comparative perspective on work-family policies in the U.S. and other countries, including Third World nations, see Nancy E. Dowd, *Envisioning Work and Family: A Critical Perspective on International Models*, 26 Harv.J. on Legis. 311 (1989). For a comparison of mandatory maternity benefits in Australia and countries in Europe, Asia, and the Americas, see Mercer Human Resource Consulting, Worldwide Benefit & Employment Guidelines 2002/2003. *See also* Cara A. McCaffrey & Austin Graff, Note, *European Union Directive on Parental Leave: Will the European Union Face the Same Problems as Those Faced by the United States Under the 1993 Family and Medical Leave Act?*, 17 Hofstra Lab. & Emp.L.J. 229 (1999).

8. In 2002, California became the first state to enact legislation that will, when it becomes effective, provide employees up to six weeks of partially paid family leave. The legislation (S.B. 1661) increases employee contributions to the State Disability Insurance (SDI) fund; employees who take family leave under the California Family Rights Act (CFRA) will be eligible for a weekly benefit based on California's workers compensation

benefits. *See California Becomes First to Authorize Six Weeks of Partially Paid Family Leave*, 20 Hum. Resources Rep. (BNA) No.38, at 1043 (Sept. 30, 2002). As of 2003, twenty-seven states were considering legislation to provide for paid family leave. *See* 21 Hum. Resources Rep. (BNA) No.5, at 117 (Feb. 10, 2003). Will the fact that California's paid family leave will be funded by employees reduce employers' incentives to discriminate against employees who take family leave or are likely to request family leave?

9. On May 2, 2000, President Clinton signed Executive Order 13152 prohibiting federal employers from discriminating against employees based on their "status as a parent." How does this provision add to existing statutory protections of family care-givers?

10. For further reading, see Joan Williams, Unbending Gender: Why Family and Work Conflict and What to Do About It (1999); Laura T. Kessler, *The Attachment Gap: Employment Discrimination Law, Women's Cultural Caregiving, and the Limits of Economic and Liberal Legal Theory*, 34 U. Mich.J.L.Reform 371 (2001); Peggie R. Smith, *Accommodating Routine Parental Obligations in an Era of Work–Family Conflict: Lessons from Religious Accommodations*, 2001 Wis.L.Rev. 1443; Joan C. Williams & Nancy Segal, *Beyond the Maternal Wall: Relief for Family Caregivers Who Are Discriminated Against on the Job*, 26 Harv. Women's L.J. 77 (2003).

E. BONA FIDE OCCUPATIONAL QUALIFICATION

Should we have a law that permits an employer to defend an employment policy that treats women differently from men if it can establish that the policy is based on a benevolent motive or biological differences and is required to "protect" women or third parties? The assumption that women are in need of special protection by employers or the government has long stood as a barrier to women's full participation in the labor market. Since the enactment of Title VII, however, the courts have struggled to determine under what circumstances employer paternalism towards women workers—which denies women freedom of choice of employment opportunities—constitutes sex discrimination. The statutory loophole that employers, and the courts, turned to in order to justify—and preserve—sex-based practices that limited women's employment opportunities is § 703(e)(1) of Title VII, the "bona fide occupational qualification" or BFOQ defense:

> Notwithstanding any other provision of this title * * * it shall not be an unlawful employment practice for an employer to hire and employ employees * * * on the basis of religion, sex, or national origin in those certain instances where religion, sex, or national origin is a bona fide occupational qualification reasonably necessary to the normal operation of that particular business or enterprise * * *.

42 U.S.C. § 2000e–2(e)(1). Note that "race" and "color" are not included in § 703(e)(1). Can you think of reasons why Congress determined that employment decisions based on race or color could not be defended as a BFOQ?

Professor Calloway has observed:

> Feminists have long struggled with the problem of developing a legal theory capable of promoting employment opportunities for women, without either ignoring women's inherent biological differences or demanding special treatment or accommodation for those differences. The early vision of equality for women, based on equal treatment, has been criticized for failing to acknowledge that women's differences place them at a disadvantage when the law requires only that women be treated the same as men. The strict equality approach fails to question the assumptions underlying gender-neutral social institutions that severely disadvantage women and fails to protect women when they are victimized by those institutions. On the other hand, achieving employment opportunities for women by requiring special treatment or accommodation for women's differences has its own dangers. Highlighting differences stereotypes gender roles and provides a justification for imposing harmful limitations on women. The history of gender discrimination in the United States is littered with cases of "protective" legislation and policies that, in reality, served primarily to limit the rights and opportunities of women.

Deborah A. Calloway, *Accommodating Pregnancy in the Workplace*, 25 Stetson L.Rev. 1, 22 (1995). *See generally* Mary E. Becker, *From* Muller v. Oregon *to Fetal Vulnerability Policies*, 53 U.Chi.L.Rev. 1219 (1986).

In the 1970s, the Supreme Court had two occasions to discuss the merits of employer "benevolent" paternalism versus employee autonomy in the context of sex discrimination cases that raised BFOQ defenses. First, in *Phillips v. Martin Marietta Corp.*, 400 U.S. 542, 91 S.Ct. 496, 27 L.Ed.2d 613 (1971) (per curiam), discussed in Section B.1 of this chapter, the Court discussed whether a BFOQ defense arguably could insulate an employer's practice of denying certain jobs to mothers—but not fathers—of preschool-aged children. The issue on appeal in *Martin Marietta* was whether the plaintiff had made out a prima facie case of sex discrimination under that particular set of facts. Deciding in the affirmative and remanding the case, the Court was not required to reach the substantive merits of the employer's BFOQ defense. Nevertheless, the Court's opinion included speculation about the possibility that a sex-based BFOQ defense might be satisfied with proof that "[t]he existence of such conflicting family obligations" are "demonstrably more relevant to job performance for a woman than for a man." *Id.* at 544, 91 S.Ct. at 498. Justice Marshall, in dissent, objected to the Court's discussion of the BFOQ issue:

> I fear that in this case, where the issue is not squarely before us, the Court has fallen into the trap of assuming the Act permits ancient canards about the proper role of women to be a basis for discrimination. Congress, however, sought just the opposite result.
>
> * * * Even characterizations of the proper domestic roles of the sexes were not to serve as predicates for restricting employment

opportunity. The exception for a "bona fide occupational qualification" was not intended to swallow the rule.

Id. at 545, 91 S.Ct. at 498.

Six years later, in *Dothard v. Rawlinson*, 433 U.S. 321, 97 S.Ct. 2720, 53 L.Ed.2d 786 (1977), reproduced in part in Chapter 4, the Court directly confronted the merits of a sex-based BFOQ defense. In *Dothard*, a female plaintiff claimed that Alabama's height and weight requirements for correctional counselors in the state's prison system violated Title VII because of their disparate impact on women. The Court upheld the district court's finding of a prima facie case based on disparate impact analysis and ruled that Alabama had failed to present any evidence that its height/weight requirements were job-related. In the portion of the *Dothard* opinion reproduced below, the Court considered the plaintiff's challenge to Regulation 204 which required that guards who worked with inmates in the state's sex-segregated correctional facilities had to be the same gender as the inmates. Alabama defended its sex-based job classification as a bona fide occupational qualification under § 703(e) of Title VII. The Supreme Court concluded "that the District Court erred in rejecting the State's contention that Regulation 204 falls within the narrow ambit of the bfoq exception." *Id.* at 334, 97 S.Ct. at 2729. The Court continued:

> The environment in Alabama's penitentiaries is a peculiarly inhospitable one for human beings of whatever sex. Indeed, a Federal District Court has held that the conditions of confinement in the prisons of the State, characterized by "rampant violence" and a "jungle atmosphere," are constitutionally intolerable. Pugh v. Locke, 406 F.Supp. 318, 325 (M.D.Ala.1976). * * *

> In this environment of violence and disorganization, it would be an oversimplification to characterize Regulation 204 as an exercise in "romantic paternalism." In the usual case, the argument that a particular job is too dangerous for women may appropriately be met by the rejoinder that it is the purpose of Title VII to allow the individual woman to make that choice for herself. More is at stake in this case, however, than an individual woman's decision to weigh and accept the risks of employment in a "contact" position in a maximum-security male prison.

> The essence of a correctional counselor's job is to maintain prison security. A woman's relative ability to maintain order in a male, maximum-security, unclassified penitentiary of the type Alabama now runs could be directly reduced by her womanhood. There is a basis in fact for expecting that sex offenders who have criminally assaulted women in the past would be moved to do so again if access to women were established within the prison. There would also be a real risk that other inmates, deprived of a normal heterosexual environment, would assault women guards because they were women. In a prison system where violence is the order of the day, where inmate access to guards is facilitated by dormitory living

arrangements, where every institution is understaffed, and where a substantial portion of the inmate population is composed of sex offenders mixed at random with other prisoners, there are few visible deterrents to inmate assaults on women custodians.

> * * * The likelihood that inmates would assault a woman because she was a woman would pose a real threat not only to the victim of the assault but also to the basic control of the penitentiary and protection of its inmates and the other security personnel. The employee's very womanhood would thus directly undermine her capacity to provide the security that is the essence of a correctional counselor's responsibility.

Id. at 334–36, 97 S.Ct. at 2729–30.

Justices Marshall and Brennan concurred in the Court's conclusion "that the bfoq exception was in fact meant to be an extremely narrow exception to the general prohibition of discrimination on the basis of sex." Their objection was that the Court improperly concluded that the bfoq exception applied to the facts of this case. Justice Marshall wrote in partial dissent:

> It appears that the real disqualifying factor in the Court's view is "[t]he employee's very womanhood." * * * In short, the fundamental justification for the Court's decision is that women as guards will generate sexual assaults. With all respect, this rationale regrettably perpetuates one of the most insidious of the old myths about women—that women, wittingly or not, are seductive sexual objects. The effect of the decision, made I am sure with the best of intentions, is to punish women because their very presence might provoke sexual assaults. It is women who are made to pay the price in lost job opportunities for the threat of depraved conduct by prison inmates. Once again, "[t]he pedestal upon which women have been placed has * * *, upon closer inspection, been revealed as a cage." Sail'er Inn, Inc. v. Kirby, 5 Cal.3d 1, 20, 95 Cal.Rptr. 329, 485 P.2d 529, 541 (1971). It is particularly ironic that the cage is erected here in response to feared misbehavior by imprisoned criminals.

> * * *

> The proper response to inevitable attacks on both female and male guards is not to limit the employment opportunities of law-abiding women who wish to contribute to their community, but to take swift and sure punitive action against the inmate offenders. Presumably, one of the goals of the Alabama prison system is the eradication of inmates' antisocial behavior patterns so that prisoners will be able to live one day in free society. Sex offenders can begin this process by learning to relate to women guards in a socially acceptable manner. To deprive women of job opportunities because of the threatened behavior of convicted criminals is to turn our social priorities upside down.

Id. at 345–46, 97 S.Ct. at 2734–35 (Marshall, J., dissenting).

Underlying the asserted BFOQ defenses in both *Martin Marietta* and *Dothard* were assumptions about women's nature—their reproductive functions and their sexuality. Although *Dothard* purported to adopt a "narrow ambit" constraining an employer's safety justification for its BFOQ defense, the Court's rationale provided limited guidance for lower courts. In a subsequent case, brought under the Age Discrimination in Employment Act (ADEA), the Court refined its test for establishing a BFOQ defense by relying on a safety rationale. In *Western Air Lines, Inc. v. Criswell*, 472 U.S. 400, 105 S.Ct. 2743, 86 L.Ed.2d 321 (1985), discussed in Chapter 12, the Court considered whether an airline's policy of imposing mandatory retirement on flight engineers at age sixty could be justified as an age-based BFOQ. The *Criswell* test emphasized the importance of making employment decisions based on the actual capabilities of individual employees rather than on stereotyped assumptions about the workers in the protected class.

In the following case, *Johnson Controls*, the Court had the opportunity to evaluate a sex-based BFOQ defense to a claim of sex discrimination brought under Title VII and the PDA. As you read the case, evaluate carefully the Court's rationale for the procedural and substantive choices that it made. The Court relies on *Dothard* and *Criswell* for its BFOQ analysis in *Johnson Controls*, but does Justice Blackmun's majority opinion implicitly draw some of its central insights about women and work from Justice Marshall's dissent in *Dothard*?

INTERNATIONAL UNION, UNITED AUTOMOBILE WORKERS v. JOHNSON CONTROLS

Supreme Court of the United States, 1991.
499 U.S. 187, 111 S.Ct. 1196, 113 L.Ed.2d 158.

JUSTICE BLACKMUN delivered the opinion of the Court.

In this case we are concerned with an employer's gender-based fetal-protection policy. May an employer exclude a fertile female employee from certain jobs because of its concern for the health of the fetus the woman might conceive?

I

Respondent Johnson Controls, Inc., manufactures batteries. In the manufacturing process, the element lead is a primary ingredient. Occupational exposure to lead entails health risks, including the risk of harm to any fetus carried by a female employee.

Before the Civil Rights Act of 1964 became law, Johnson Controls did not employ any woman in a battery-manufacturing job. In June 1977, however, it announced its first official policy concerning its employment of women in lead-exposure work:

[P]rotection of the health of the unborn child is the immediate and direct responsibility of the prospective parents. While the medical profession and the company can support them in the exercise of this responsibility, it cannot assume it for them without simultaneously infringing their rights as persons.

* * * Since not all women who can become mothers wish to become mothers (or will become mothers), it would appear to be illegal discrimination to treat all who are capable of pregnancy as though they will become pregnant.

Consistent with that view, Johnson Controls "stopped short of excluding women capable of bearing children from lead exposure," but emphasized that a woman who expected to have a child should not choose a job in which she would have such exposure. The company also required a woman who wished to be considered for employment to sign a statement that she had been advised of the risk of having a child while she was exposed to lead. The statement informed the woman that although there was evidence "that women exposed to lead have a higher rate of abortion," this evidence was "not as clear * * * as the relationship between cigarette smoking and cancer," but that it was, "medically speaking, just good sense not to run that risk if you want children and do not want to expose the unborn child to risk, however small. * * * "

Five years later, in 1982, Johnson Controls shifted from a policy of warning to a policy of exclusion. Between 1979 and 1983, eight employees became pregnant while maintaining blood lead levels in excess of 30 micrograms per deciliter. This appeared to be the critical level noted by the Occupational Safety and Health Administration (OSHA) for a worker who was planning to have a family. See 29 C.F.R. § 1910.1025 (1989). The company responded by announcing a broad exclusion of women from jobs that exposed them to lead:

> [I]t is [Johnson Controls'] policy that women who are pregnant or who are capable of bearing children will not be placed into jobs involving lead exposure or which could expose them to lead through the exercise of job bidding, bumping, transfer or promotion rights.

The policy defined "women * * * capable of bearing children" as "all women except those whose inability to bear children is medically documented." It further stated that an unacceptable work station was one where, "over the past year," an employee had recorded a blood lead level of more than 30 micrograms per deciliter or the work site had yielded an air sample containing a lead level in excess of 30 micrograms per cubic meter.

II

In April 1984, petitioners filed * * * a class action challenging Johnson Controls' fetal-protection policy as sex discrimination that violated Title VII of the Civil Rights Act of 1964. Among the individual plaintiffs were petitioners Mary Craig, who had chosen to be sterilized in order to avoid losing her job, Elsie Nason, a 50–year-old divorcee, who had suffered a loss in compensation when she was transferred out of a job where she was exposed to lead, and Donald Penney, who had been denied a request for a leave of absence for the purpose of lowering his lead level because he intended to become a father. * * *

The District Court granted summary judgment for * * * Johnson Controls[,] [a]pplying a three-part business necessity defense * * *. * * *

The Court of Appeals for the Seventh Circuit, sitting *en banc*, affirmed the summary judgment by a 7–to–4 vote. The majority held that the proper standard for evaluating the fetal-protection policy was the defense of business necessity; that Johnson Controls was entitled to summary judgment under that defense; and that even if the proper standard was a BFOQ, Johnson Controls still was entitled to summary judgment.

* * *

III

The bias in Johnson Controls' policy is obvious. Fertile men, but not fertile women, are given a choice as to whether they wish to risk their reproductive health for a particular job. Section 703(a) of the Civil Rights Act of 1964 prohibits sex-based classifications in terms and conditions of employment, in hiring and discharging decisions, and in other employment decisions that adversely affect an employee's status. Respondent's fetal-protection policy explicitly discriminates against women on the basis of their sex. The policy excludes women with childbearing capacity from lead-exposed jobs and so creates a facial classification based on gender. Respondent assumes as much in its brief before this Court.

Nevertheless, the Court of Appeals assumed, as did the two appellate courts that already had confronted the issue, that sex-specific fetal-protection policies do not involve facial discrimination. These courts analyzed the policies as though they were facially neutral and had only a discriminatory effect upon the employment opportunities of women. Consequently, the courts looked to see if each employer in question had established that its policy was justified as a business necessity. The business necessity standard is more lenient for the employer than the statutory BFOQ defense. The Court of Appeals * * * assumed that because the asserted reason for the sex-based exclusion (protecting women's unconceived offspring) was ostensibly benign, the policy was not sex-based discrimination. That assumption, however, was incorrect.

First, Johnson Controls' policy classifies on the basis of gender and childbearing capacity, rather than fertility alone. Respondent does not seek to protect the unconceived children of all its employees. Despite evidence in the record about the debilitating effect of lead exposure on the male reproductive system, Johnson Controls is concerned only with the harms that may befall the unborn offspring of its female employees. * * * This Court faced a conceptually similar situation in *Phillips v. Martin Marietta Corp.*, 400 U.S. 542, 91 S.Ct. 496, 27 L.Ed.2d 613

(1971), and found sex discrimination because the policy established "one hiring policy for women and another for men—each having pre-school-age children." *Id.* at 544, 91 S.Ct. at 498. Johnson Controls' policy is facially discriminatory because it requires only a female employee to produce proof that she is not capable of reproducing.

Our conclusion is bolstered by the Pregnancy Discrimination Act (PDA), 42 U.S.C. § 2000e(k), in which Congress explicitly provided that, for purposes of Title VII, discrimination " 'on the basis of sex' " includes discrimination "because of or on the basis of pregnancy, childbirth, or related medical conditions." "The Pregnancy Discrimination Act has now made clear that, for all Title VII purposes, discrimination based on a woman's pregnancy is, on its face, discrimination because of her sex." In its use of the words "capable of bearing children" in the 1982 policy statement as the criterion for exclusion, Johnson Controls explicitly classifies on the basis of potential for pregnancy. Under the PDA, such a classification must be regarded, for Title VII purposes, in the same light as explicit sex discrimination. Respondent has chosen to treat all its female employees as potentially pregnant; that choice evinces discrimination on the basis of sex.

We concluded above that Johnson Controls' policy is not neutral because it does not apply to the reproductive capacity of the company's male employees in the same way as it applies to that of the females. Moreover, the absence of a malevolent motive does not convert a facially discriminatory policy into a neutral policy with a discriminatory effect. Whether an employment practice involves disparate treatment through explicit facial discrimination does not depend on why the employer discriminates but rather on the explicit terms of the discrimination. In *Martin Marietta*, the motives underlying the employers' express exclusion of women did not alter the intentionally discriminatory character of the policy. Nor did the arguably benign motives lead to consideration of a business necessity defense. The question in that case was whether the discrimination in question could be justified under § 703(e) as a BFOQ. The beneficence of an employer's purpose does not undermine the conclusion that an explicit gender-based policy is sex discrimination under § 703(a) and thus may be defended only as a BFOQ.

The enforcement policy of the Equal Employment Opportunity Commission accords with this conclusion. On January 24, 1990, the EEOC issued a Policy Guidance in the light of the Seventh Circuit's decision in the present case. The document noted: "For the plaintiff to bear the burden of proof in a case in which there is direct evidence of a facially discriminatory policy is wholly inconsistent with settled Title VII law." The Commission concluded: "[W]e now think BFOQ is the better approach."

In sum, Johnson Controls' policy "does not pass the simple test of whether the evidence shows 'treatment of a person in a manner which but for that person's sex would be different.' " Los Angeles Dept. of Water and Power v. Manhart, 435 U.S. 702, 711, 98 S.Ct. 1370, 55

L.Ed.2d 657 (1978). We hold that Johnson Controls' fetal-protection policy is sex discrimination forbidden under Title VII unless respondent can establish that sex is a "bona fide occupational qualification."

IV

Under § 703(e)(1) of Title VII, an employer may discriminate on the basis of "religion, sex, or national origin in those certain instances where religion, sex, or national origin is a bona fide occupational qualification reasonably necessary to the normal operation of that particular business or enterprise." We therefore turn to the question whether Johnson Controls' fetal-protection policy is one of those "certain instances" that come within the BFOQ exception.

The BFOQ defense is written narrowly, and this Court has read it narrowly. *See, e.g.*, Dothard v. Rawlinson, 433 U.S. 321, 332–37, 97 S.Ct. 2720, 2728–30, 53 L.Ed.2d 786 (1977); Trans World Airlines, Inc. v. Thurston, 469 U.S. 111, 122–25, 105 S.Ct. 613, 622–23, 83 L.Ed.2d 523 (1985). We have read the BFOQ language of § 4(f) of the Age Discrimination in Employment Act of 1967 (ADEA), 29 U.S.C. § 623(f)(1), which tracks the BFOQ provision in Title VII, just as narrowly. *See* Western Air Lines, Inc. v. Criswell, 472 U.S. 400, 105 S.Ct. 2743, 86 L.Ed.2d 321 (1985). Our emphasis on the restrictive scope of the BFOQ defense is grounded on both the language and the legislative history of § 703.

The wording of the BFOQ defense contains several terms of restriction that indicate that the exception reaches only special situations. The statute thus limits the situations in which discrimination is permissible to "certain instances" where sex discrimination is "reasonably necessary" to the "normal operation" of the "particular" business. Each one of these terms—certain, normal, particular—prevents the use of general subjective standards and favors an objective, verifiable requirement. But the most telling term is "occupational"; this indicates that these objective, verifiable requirements must concern job-related skills and aptitudes.

Justice White [in concurrence] defines "occupational" as meaning related to a job. According to Justice White, any discriminatory requirement imposed by an employer is "job-related" simply because the employer has chosen to make the requirement a condition of employment. In effect, Justice White argues that sterility may be an occupational qualification for women because Johnson Controls has chosen to require it. This reading of "occupational" renders the word mere surplusage. "Qualification" by itself would encompass an employer's idiosyncratic requirements. By modifying "qualification" with "occupational," Congress narrowed the term to qualifications that affect an employee's ability to do the job.

Johnson Controls argues that its fetal-protection policy falls within the so-called safety exception to the BFOQ. Our cases have stressed that discrimination on the basis of sex because of safety concerns is allowed only in narrow circumstances. In *Dothard v. Rawlinson*, 433 U.S. 321, 97

S.Ct. 2730, 53 L.Ed.2d 786 (1997), this Court indicated that danger to a woman herself does not justify discrimination. We there allowed the employer to hire only male guards in contact areas of maximum-security male penitentiaries only because more was at stake than the "individual woman's decision to weigh and accept the risks of employment." We found sex to be a BFOQ inasmuch as the employment of a female guard would create real risks of safety to others if violence broke out because the guard was a woman. Sex discrimination was tolerated because sex was related to the guard's ability to do the job—maintaining prison security. We also required in *Dothard* a high correlation between sex and ability to perform job functions and refused to allow employers to use sex as a proxy for strength although it might be a fairly accurate one.

Similarly, some courts have approved airlines' layoffs of pregnant flight attendants at different points during the first five months of pregnancy on the ground that the employer's policy was necessary to ensure the safety of passengers. *[See, e.g.,]* Burwell v. Eastern Air Lines, Inc., 633 F.2d 361 (4th Cir.1980), *cert. denied*, 450 U.S. 965, 101 S.Ct. 1480, 67 L.Ed.2d 613 (1981). In two * * * cases, the courts pointedly indicated that fetal, as opposed to passenger, safety was best left to the mother.

We considered safety to third parties in *Western Airlines, Inc. v. Criswell*, in the context of the ADEA. We focused upon "the nature of the flight engineer's tasks," and the "actual capabilities of persons over age 60" in relation to those tasks. Our safety concerns were not independent of the individual's ability to perform the assigned tasks, but rather involved the possibility that, because of age-connected debility, a flight engineer might not properly assist the pilot, and might thereby cause a safety emergency. Furthermore, although we considered the safety of third parties in *Dothard* and *Criswell*, those third parties were indispensable to the particular business at issue. In *Dothard*, the third parties were the inmates; in *Criswell*, the third parties were the passengers on the plane. We stressed that in order to qualify as a BFOQ, a job qualification must relate to the " 'essence' " or to the "central mission of the employer's business."

Justice White [in concurrence] ignores the "essence of the business" test and so concludes that "protecting fetal safety while carrying out the duties of battery manufacturing is as much a legitimate concern as is safety to third parties in guarding prisons (*Dothard*) or flying airplanes (*Criswell*)." By limiting its discussion to cost and safety concerns and rejecting the "essence of the business" test that our case law has established, he seeks to expand what is now the narrow BFOQ defense. Third-party safety considerations properly entered into the BFOQ analysis in *Dothard* and *Criswell* because they went to the core of the employee's job performance. Moreover, that performance involved the central purpose of the enterprise. Justice White attempts to transform this case into one of customer safety. The unconceived fetuses of Johnson Controls' female employees, however, are neither customers nor third parties whose safety is essential to the business of battery manufacturing. No one can disregard the possibility of injury to future children; the BFOQ, however, is not so broad that it transforms this deep social concern into an essential aspect of battery making.

Our case law, therefore, makes clear that the safety exception is limited to instances in which sex or pregnancy actually interferes with the employee's ability to perform the job. This approach is consistent with the language of the BFOQ provision itself, for it suggests that permissible distinctions based on sex must relate to ability to perform the duties of the job. Johnson Controls suggests, however, that we expand the exception to allow fetal-protection policies that mandate particular standards for pregnant or fertile women. We decline to do so. Such an expansion contradicts not only the language of the BFOQ and the narrowness of its exception, but also the plain language and history of the PDA.

The PDA's amendment to Title VII contains a BFOQ standard of its own: Unless pregnant employees differ from others "in their ability or inability to work," they must be "treated the same" as other employees "for all employment-related purposes." 42 U.S.C. § 2000e(k). This language clearly sets forth Congress' remedy for discrimination on the basis of pregnancy and potential pregnancy. Women who are either pregnant or potentially pregnant must be treated like others "similar in their ability * * * to work." In other words, women as capable of doing their jobs as their male counterparts may not be forced to choose between having a child and having a job.

Justice White asserts that the PDA did not alter the BFOQ defense. He arrives at this conclusion by ignoring the second clause of the Act, which states that "women affected by pregnancy, childbirth, or related medical conditions shall be treated the same for all employment-related purposes * * * as other persons not so affected but similar in their ability or inability to work." 42 U.S.C. § 2000e(k). * * * Justice White now seeks to read the second clause out of the Act.

The legislative history confirms what the language of the PDA compels. Both the House and Senate Reports accompanying the legislation indicate that this statutory standard was chosen to protect female workers from being treated differently from other employees simply because of their capacity to bear children. *See* Amending Title VII, Civil Rights Act of 1964, S. Rep. No. 95–331, pp. 4–6 (1977):

> Under this bill, the treatment of pregnant women in covered employment must focus not on their condition alone but on the actual effects of that condition on their ability to work. Pregnant women who are able to work must be permitted to work on the same conditions as other employees. * * *

> * * *

> [U]nder this bill, employers will no longer be permitted to force women who become pregnant to stop working regardless of their ability to continue.

This history counsels against expanding the BFOQ to allow fetal-protection policies. The Senate Report quoted above states that employers may not require a pregnant woman to stop working at any time during her pregnancy unless she is unable to do her work. Employment late in pregnancy often imposes risks on the unborn child, but Congress indicated that the employer may take into account only the woman's ability to get her job done. With the PDA, Congress made clear that the decision to become pregnant or to work while being either pregnant or capable of becoming pregnant was reserved for each individual woman to make for herself.

We conclude that the language of both the BFOQ provision and the PDA which amended it, as well as the legislative history and the case law, prohibit an employer from discriminating against a woman because of her capacity to become pregnant unless her reproductive potential prevents her from performing the duties of her job. We reiterate our holdings in *Criswell* and *Dothard* that an employer must direct its concerns about a woman's ability to perform her job safely and efficiently to those aspects of the woman's job-related activities that fall within the "essence" of the particular business.[4]

V

We have no difficulty concluding that Johnson Controls cannot establish a BFOQ. Fertile women, as far as appears in the record, participate in the manufacture of batteries as efficiently as anyone else. Johnson Controls' professed moral and ethical concerns about the welfare of the next generation do not suffice to establish a BFOQ of female sterility. Decisions about the welfare of future children must be left to the parents who conceive, bear, support, and raise them rather than to the employers who hire those parents. Congress has mandated this choice through Title VII, as amended by the PDA. Johnson Controls has attempted to exclude women because of their reproductive capacity. Title VII and the PDA simply do not allow a woman's dismissal because of her failure to submit to sterilization.

Nor can concerns about the welfare of the next generation be considered a part of the "essence" of Johnson Controls' business. Judge Easterbrook in this case pertinently observed: "It is word play to say that 'the job' at Johnson [Controls] is to make batteries without risk to fetuses in the same way 'the job' at Western Air Lines is to fly planes without crashing."

---

4. Justice White predicts that our reaffirmation of the narrowness of the BFOQ defense will preclude considerations of privacy as a basis for sex-based discrimination. We have never addressed privacy-based sex discrimination and shall not do so here because the sex-based discrimination at issue today does not involve the privacy interests of Johnson Controls' customers. Nothing in our discussion of the "essence of the business test," however, suggests that sex could not constitute a BFOQ when privacy interests are implicated. *See, e.g.*, Backus v. Baptist Medical Center, 510 F.Supp. 1191 (E.D.Ark.1981) (essence of obstetrics nurse's business is to provide sensitive care for patient's intimate and private concerns), *vacated as moot*, 671 F.2d 1100 (8th Cir. 1982).

Johnson Controls argues that it must exclude all fertile women because it is impossible to tell which women will become pregnant while working with lead. This argument is somewhat academic in light of our conclusion that the company may not exclude fertile women at all; it perhaps is worth noting, however, that Johnson Controls has shown no "factual basis for believing that all or substantially all women would be unable to perform safely and efficiently the duties of the job involved." Weeks v. Southern Bell Tel. & Tel. Co., 408 F.2d 228, 235 (5th Cir.1969), quoted with approval in *Dothard*. Even on this sparse record, it is apparent that Johnson Controls is concerned about only a small minority of women. Of the eight pregnancies reported among the female employees, it has not been shown that any of the babies have birth defects or other abnormalities. The record does not reveal the birth rate for Johnson Controls' female workers, but national statistics show that approximately nine percent of all fertile women become pregnant each year. The birthrate drops to two percent for blue collar workers over age 30. Johnson Controls' fear of prenatal injury, no matter how sincere, does not begin to show that substantially all of its fertile women employees are incapable of doing their jobs.

VI

A word about tort liability and the increased cost of fertile women in the workplace is perhaps necessary. One of the dissenting judges in this case expressed concern about an employer's tort liability and concluded that liability for a potential injury to a fetus is a social cost that Title VII does not require a company to ignore. It is correct to say that Title VII does not prevent the employer from having a conscience. The statute, however, does prevent sex-specific fetal-protection policies. These two aspects of Title VII do not conflict.

More than 40 States currently recognize a right to recover for a prenatal injury based either on negligence or on wrongful death. According to Johnson Controls, however, the company complies with the lead standard developed by OSHA and warns its female employees about the damaging effects of lead. It is worth noting that OSHA gave the problem of lead lengthy consideration and concluded that "there is no basis whatsoever for the claim that women of childbearing age should be excluded from the workplace in order to protect the fetus or the course of pregnancy." 43 Fed. Reg. 52952, 52966 (1978). Instead, OSHA established a series of mandatory protections which, taken together, "should effectively minimize any risk to the fetus and newborn child." *Id.* at 52966. *See* 29 C.F.R. § 1910.1025(k)(ii) (1990). Without negligence, it would be difficult for a court to find liability on the part of the employer. If, under general tort principles, Title VII bans sex-specific fetal-protection policies, the employer fully informs the woman of the risk, and the employer has not acted negligently, the basis for holding an employer liable seems remote at best.

Although the issue is not before us, Justice White observes that "it is far from clear that compliance with Title VII will pre-empt state tort liability." The cases relied upon by him to support his prediction, however, are inapposite. For example, in *California Federal Savings and Loan Assn. v. Guerra*, 479 U.S. 272, 107 S.Ct. 683, 93 L.Ed.2d 613 (1987), we considered a California statute that expanded upon the requirements of the PDA and concluded that the statute was not preempted by Title VII because it was not inconsistent with the purposes of the federal statute and did not require an act that was unlawful under Title VII. Here, in contrast, the tort liability that Justice White fears will punish employers for complying with Title VII's clear command. When it is impossible for an employer to comply with both state and federal requirements, this Court has ruled that federal law pre-empts that of the States.

* * *

If state tort law furthers discrimination in the workplace and prevents employers from hiring women who are capable of manufacturing the product as efficiently as men, then it will impede the accomplishment of Congress' goals in enacting Title VII. Because Johnson Controls has not argued that it faces any costs from tort liability, not to mention crippling ones, the pre-emption question is not before us. We therefore say no more than that the concurrence's speculation appears unfounded as well as premature.

The tort-liability argument reduces to two equally unpersuasive propositions. First, Johnson Controls attempts to solve the problem of reproductive health hazards by resorting to an exclusionary policy. Title VII plainly forbids illegal sex discrimination as a method of diverting attention from an employer's obligation to police the workplace. Second, the specter of an award of damages reflects a fear that hiring fertile women will cost more. The extra cost of employing members of one sex, however, does not provide an affirmative Title VII defense for a discriminatory refusal to hire members of that gender. *See Manhart*. Indeed, in passing the PDA, Congress considered at length the considerable cost of providing equal treatment of pregnancy and related conditions, but made the "decision to forbid special treatment of pregnancy despite the social costs associated therewith." Arizona Governing Comm. for Tax Deferred Annuity and Deferred Compensation Plans v. Norris, 463 U.S. 1073, 1085 n. 14, 103 S.Ct. 3492, 3499 n. 14, 77 L.Ed.2d 1236 (1983).

We, of course, are not presented with, nor do we decide, a case in which costs would be so prohibitive as to threaten the survival of the employer's business. We merely reiterate our prior holdings that the incremental cost of hiring women cannot justify discriminating against them.

VII

Our holding today that Title VII, as so amended, forbids sex-specific fetal-protection policies is neither remarkable nor unprecedented. Concern for a woman's existing or potential offspring historically has been the excuse for denying women equal employment opportunities. *See, e.g.,*

Muller v. Oregon, 208 U.S. 412 (1908). Congress in the PDA prohibited discrimination on the basis of a woman's ability to become pregnant. We do no more than hold that the PDA means what it says.

It is no more appropriate for the courts than it is for individual employers to decide whether a woman's reproductive role is more important to herself and her family than her economic role. Congress has left this choice to the woman as hers to make.

The judgment of the Court of Appeals is reversed, and the case is remanded for further proceedings consistent with this opinion.

JUSTICE WHITE, with whom THE CHIEF JUSTICE and JUSTICE KENNEDY join, concurring in part and concurring in the judgment.

* * *

* * * For the fetal-protection policy involved in this case to be a BFOQ, * * * the policy must be "reasonably necessary" to the "normal operation" of making batteries, which is Johnson Controls' "particular business." Although that is a difficult standard to satisfy, nothing in the statute's language indicates that it could *never* support a sex-specific fetal-protection policy.

On the contrary, a fetal-protection policy would be justified under the terms of the statute if, for example, an employer could show that exclusion of women from certain jobs was reasonably necessary to avoid substantial tort liability. * * *

The Court dismisses the possibility of tort liability by no more than speculating that if "Title VII bans sex-specific fetal-protection policies, the employer fully informs the woman of the risk, and the employer has not acted negligently, the basis for holding an employer liable seems remote at best." Such speculation will be small comfort to employers. First, it is far from clear that compliance with Title VII will pre-empt state tort liability, and the Court offers no support for that proposition. Second, although warnings may preclude claims by injured employees, they will not preclude claims by injured children because the general rule is that parents cannot waive causes of action on behalf of their children, and the parents' negligence will not be imputed to the children. Finally, although state tort liability for prenatal injuries generally requires negligence, it will be difficult for employers to determine in advance what will constitute negligence. Compliance with OSHA standards, for example, has been held not to be a defense to state tort or criminal liability. Moreover, it is possible that employers will be held strictly liable, if, for example, their manufacturing process is considered "abnormally dangerous." *See* Restatement (Second) of Torts § 869, Comment *b* (1979).

* * *

Despite my disagreement with the Court concerning the scope of the BFOQ defense, I concur in reversing the Court of Appeals because that court erred in affirming the District Court's grant of summary judgment in favor of Johnson Controls. * * *

* * *

JUSTICE SCALIA, concurring in the judgment.

I generally agree with the Court's analysis, but have some reservations, several of which bear mention.

First, I think it irrelevant that there was "evidence in the record about the debilitating effect of lead exposure on the male reproductive system." Even without such evidence, treating women differently "on the basis of pregnancy" constitutes discrimination "on the basis of sex," because Congress has unequivocally said so.

Second, the Court points out that "Johnson Controls has shown no factual basis for believing that all or substantially all women would be unable to perform safely * * * the duties of the job involved." In my view, this is not only "somewhat academic in light of our conclusion that the company may not exclude fertile women at all," it is entirely irrelevant. By reason of the Pregnancy Discrimination Act, it would not matter if all pregnant women placed their children at risk in taking these jobs, just as it does not matter if no men do so. As Judge Easterbrook put it in his dissent below: "Title VII gives parents the power to make occupational decisions affecting their families. A legislative forum is available to those who believe that such decisions should be made elsewhere."

Third, I am willing to assume, as the Court intimates, that any action required by Title VII cannot give rise to liability under state tort law. That assumption, however, does not answer the question whether an action *is* required by Title VII (including the BFOQ provision) even if it is subject to liability under state tort law. It is perfectly reasonable to believe that Title VII has *accommodated* state tort law through the BFOQ exception. However, all that need be said in the present case is that Johnson has not demonstrated a substantial risk of tort liability— which is alone enough to defeat a tort-based assertion of the BFOQ exception.

Last, the Court goes far afield, it seems to me, in suggesting that increased cost alone—short of "costs * * * so prohibitive as to threaten the survival of the employer's business,"—cannot support a BFOQ defense. I agree with Justice White's concurrence, that nothing in our prior cases suggests this, and in my view it is wrong. I think, for example, that a shipping company may refuse to hire pregnant women as crew members on long voyages because the on-board facilities for foreseeable emergencies, though quite feasible, would be inordinately expensive. In the present case, however, Johnson has not asserted a cost-based BFOQ.

* * *

Notes and Questions

1. Fetal protection policies were developed because of the well-known fact that exposure to toxins in the workplace can adversely affect the reproductive health of employees. According to one report, there are fifteen to twenty million jobs in the United States that may expose workers to toxins in the workplace that cause reproductive harm. Bureau of National Affairs, Special Report, Pregnancy and Employment: The Complete Handbook on Discrimination, Maternity Leave, and Health and Safety 57 (1987). According to a 1979 estimate, at least 100,000 jobs in the United States excluded women because of potential exposure to toxins that might affect reproductivity. *See* Wendy W. Williams, *Firing the Woman to Protect the Fetus: The Reconciliation of Fetal Protection with Employment Opportunity Goals Under Title VII*, 69 Geo.L.J. 641, 647 n.30 (1981).

Even though *Johnson Controls* addresses employers' sex discrimination on the basis of toxins in the workplace, does it leave unresolved the problem of reproductive harms that such toxins may cause? One commentator observed:

> The controversy surrounding fetal protection policies touches on political and philosophical questions regarding the very definitions of gender equality and gender difference. Feminists are faced with a paradox: To ignore difference is to risk placing women in a workplace designed by and for men, with all of its hazards and lack of concern for the preservation of health and life. On the other hand, to treat women differently from men in the workplace is to reinforce those assumptions and economic structures which form the foundation of women's inequality.

Cynthia R. Daniels, At Women's Expense: State Power and the Politics of Fetal Rights 93 (1993). In requiring that employers treat fertile men and women the same, does the Court in *Johnson Controls* ignore the risks of "placing women in a workplace designed by and for men"? Is there any way to resolve the paradox? Does the Family and Medical Leave Act (FMLA), discussed in Section D of this chapter, provide a solution or just create another paradox?

2. The primary reason that courts had adopted the disparate impact/business necessity analytic scheme for the fetal protection polices before *Johnson Controls* is because they accepted the view that the policies served an important social purpose of protecting unborn fetuses and they did not consider this laudable result to be achievable under a direct evidence/BFOQ analytic scheme. Until 1990, the EEOC had endorsed the disparate impact/business necessity approach to fetal protection policies. Then, in response to the Seventh Circuit's 7–4 en banc decision in *International Union, UAW v. Johnson Controls*, 886 F.2d 871 (7th Cir.1989), the EEOC issued a new Policy Guidance that adopted the direct evidence/BFOQ approach. *See Johnson Controls*, 499 U.S. at 200, 111 S.Ct. at 1204.

3. Out of concern for the health of her fetus, a pregnant nurse refuses to treat a patient with AIDS (Acquired Immune Deficiency Syndrome). The hospital where she works does not require pregnant employees to work with

patients who have herpes or hepatitis B, or to work in areas exposed to radiation. These are the only exceptions to the general rule that all nurses must provide care to all patients. If the nurse is discharged for refusing to treat the AIDS patient, can she establish a violation of the PDA under either a disparate treatment or disparate impact theory? How does *Johnson Controls* affect your analysis? *See* Armstrong v. Flowers Hosp., Inc., 33 F.3d 1308 (11th Cir.1994).

If a pregnant nurse or doctor works in the radiology department of a hospital that offers no special accommodations to pregnant employees, such as temporary transfer to another department during the pregnancy, what are her options after *Johnson Controls* if she wants to avoid exposing her fetus to radiation? *See* Duncan v. Children's Nat'l Med. Ctr., 702 A.2d 207 (D.C.1997). *See generally* Suzanne U. Samuels, *The Fetal Protection Debate Revisited: The Impact of* U.A.W. v. Johnson Controls *on the Federal and State Courts*, 17 Women's Rts.L.Rep. 209 (1996); Suzanne U. Samuels, *The Lasting Legacy of* International Union, U.A.W. v. Johnson Controls: *Equal Employment and Workplace Health and Safety Five Years Later*, 12 Wis. Women's L.J. 1 (1997).

4. What options are open to the employer in a *Johnson Controls*-type case now that the Supreme Court has rejected all of its defenses to the fetal protection plan? *See generally* Mary Becker, *Reproductive Hazards After* Johnson Controls, 31 Hous.L.Rev. 43 (1994); Susan S. Grover, *Employer's Fetal Injury Quandary After* Johnson Controls, 81 Ky.L.J. 639 (1993). Could an employer protect itself from future tort claims by requesting a signed waiver of liability from pregnant employees whose jobs place their fetuses at risk? *See* Mitchell v. RJK of Gloucester, Inc., 899 F.Supp. 246 (E.D.Va.1995).

5. Professor Lucinda Finley has noted that scientific studies done on the effects of toxins exposure have "focused far more on reproductive harm to women" than to men; that the lack of studies on men reflects "the pervasive assumption that women, as the actual childbearers, are uniquely susceptible to harm, and that the health of fetuses can be affected only through the mother"; and that "the male's role in the reproductive process has been too frequently ignored by scientific research" because "paternal effects are harder to trace and to ascertain" than maternal effects. Lucinda M. Finley, *The Exclusion of Fertile Women from the Hazardous Workplace: The Latest Example of Discriminatory Protective Polices, or a Legitimate, Neutral Response to an Emerging Social Problem?*, 38 N.Y.U.Nat'l Conf. on Lab. 16–1, 16–6 (1985).

6. One court observed that Johnson Controls based its fetal-protection policy on the following "unfounded assumptions": fertile women are or will be sexually active; they will become involved with fertile men; they cannot be trusted to employ adequate birth control methods; and they are incapable of weighing the risks involved. Johnson Controls, Inc. v. Fair Emp. & Housing Comm'n, 267 Cal.Rptr. 158, 177 (Cal.App.4th 1990).

7. *The Safety Element of the BFOQ*: In formulating its test of BFOQ, the Supreme Court in *Johnson Controls* relied heavily on its decisions in *Dothard v. Rawlinson* and *Western Air Lines, Inc. v. Criswell*. Should the concern for the health of fetuses be just as strong if not stronger than the concern for inmates in *Dothard* and airline passengers in *Criswell*? Are you

persuaded by the distinctions that the Court makes between safety of fetuses and safety of inmates or passengers?

The Fourth Circuit's decision in *Burwell v. Eastern Airlines*, 633 F.2d 361 (4th Cir.1980), *cert. denied*, 450 U.S. 965, 101 S.Ct. 1480, 67 L.Ed.2d 613 (1981), is one of the leading cases cited by the court in *Johnson Controls* in support of the safety element of the BFOQ. The employer policy at issue in *Burwell* of requiring flight attendants to take a job on the ground after the thirteenth week of pregnancy was based in substantial part on a business necessity rationale. In order to establish the safety-based defense under either the BFOQ or the business necessity defense, the defendant must present convincing expert testimony demonstrating that the challenged practice is required to protect employees or third parties from documented hazards. *See e.g.*, Fitzpatrick v. City of Atlanta, 2 F.3d 1112 (11th Cir.1993).

8. *Morality as an Element of the BFOQ*: In *Johnson Controls*, the Supreme Court rejected the employer's argument that its fetal protection policy was justified on the grounds of morality. Consider the following: Crystal Chambers, an adult, single black female, was employed as an arts and crafts instructor at the Omaha Girls Club, a private, nonprofit corporation. The Club offered young girls from eight to eighteen years old a number of activities, including programs aimed at preventing pregnancies. At the facility where Chambers worked, 90 percent of the members were black, and all of the instructors were black. The Club encouraged close relationships between the girls and the adult staff members who were "trained and expected to act as role models for the girls, with the intent that the girls [would] seek to emulate their behavior." The Club adopted a rule against employing single women who are pregnant because of its view that such women would be negative role models to teenage girls and would frustrate one of the Club's goals—preventing teenage pregnancies. After Chambers became pregnant and informed her supervisor, the Club discharged her pursuant to its policy against single-parent pregnancies. Chambers then filed a claim under Title VII alleging discrimination on the basis of sex. The primary issue before the court of appeals was whether the Club's "role-model" rule was justifiable as a business necessity or a bona fide occupational qualification. The court in *Chambers v. Omaha Girls Club, Inc.*, 834 F.2d 697 (8th Cir.1987), found the rule was justifiable under both defenses: the rule's disparate impact on black females was justified as a business necessity, and the rule's disparate treatment of Chambers because of her pregnancy was justified as a BFOQ.

Could *Chambers* survive analysis under the reasoning in *Johnson Controls* in light of the Court's rejection of the morality defense? Professor Regina Austin, in *Sapphire Bound!*, 1989 Wis.L.Rev. 539, argued that the judges and the employer in *Chambers* imposed their own personal perspectives on morality—"white, male, and middle class"—on a group of inner-city, black teenage girls, without justifying that perspective or determining the perspective of the black teenage members of the Club. *Id.* at 555. Professor Austin, a critical race scholar, also challenged the assumptions of decisionmakers that affect their ability to deal with individuals of different genders, ethnicities, and social status. How would you critique Professor Austin's argument?

9. *The Cost Justification Defense*: *Johnson Controls* rejects a cost justification defense—tort liability, reducing workers' compensation claims, or decreasing insurance costs—for the fetal protection policy. Is the Court's analysis consistent with the court's treatment of the cost justification defense in *EEOC v. Consolidated Service Systems*, reproduced in Chapter 3, and in *Wards Cove*, reproduced in Chapter 4? Note that the Court leaves open the possibility that cost may be a defense in a case in which costs are so prohibitive as to threaten the survival of the business. Consider the following case:

Wilson v. Southwest Airlines, 517 F.Supp. 292 (N.D.Tex.1981), raised a cost justification defense as a rationale for hiring only women as flight attendants and airline ticket agents. By 1971, when its first planes finally began to fly, the fledgling Southwest Airlines had barely survived the four years of litigation that it had taken to obtain permission from the Texas Aeronautics Commission to enter the short-haul airline commuter market of Texas. Facing financial ruin and hoping to gain a competitive advantage quickly in the intrastate market, Southwest adopted a "catchy" advertising campaign based on "an image of feminine spirit, fun and sex appeal" that it believed would appeal to "its predominantly male, business passengers." *Id.* at 294. For example, in its television commercials, "while an alluring feminine voice promise[d] inflight love," attractive female attendants in skimpy outfits served male passengers " 'love bites' (toasted almonds) and 'love potions' (cocktails.) Even [its] ticketing system feature[d] a 'quickie machine' to provide 'instant gratification.' " *Id.* at 294 n.3. Southwest's "Love" campaign was extremely successful, but it entailed hiring only women for its flight attendant and ticket agent positions even though courts and the EEOC had found by then that female-only hiring policies in the airline industry violate Title VII. *See, e.g.*, Diaz v. Pan Am. World Airways, Inc., 442 F.2d 385 (5th Cir.), *cert. denied*, 404 U.S. 950, 92 S.Ct. 275, 30 L.Ed.2d 267 (1971); EEOC Opinion, "Flight Cabin Attendant," 33 Fed.Reg. 3361 (1968).

When Gregory Wilson brought a class action challenging the Southwest's hiring policy, the company defended it as a BFOQ that was "crucial to the airline's continued financial success." *Wilson*, 517 F.Supp. at 293. Southwest argued that the central mission of its business was to make a profit and that its "Love" campaign was an essential marketing tool used to increase profits. How would this argument fare under the Court's analysis in *Johnson Controls*? Consider how the district court responded in *Wilson*:

[T]he fact that a vibrant marketing campaign was necessary to distinguish Southwest in its early years does not lead to the conclusion that sex discrimination was then, or is now, a business necessity. * * *

* * * [S]ex does not become a BFOQ merely because an employer chooses to exploit female sexuality as a marketing tool, or to better insure profitability.

Id. at 303.

10. *Customer Preferences*: The courts have consistently held that customer preferences do not satisfy the BFOQ. In *Diaz v. Pan American World Airways, Inc.*, 442 F.2d 385 (5th Cir.1971), *cert. denied*, 404 U.S. 950, 92 S.Ct. 275, 30 L.Ed.2d 267 (1971), the district court had concluded that being

female was a BFOQ for the position of airline attendant because it found that women were better than men at "providing reassurance to anxious passengers, giving courteous personalized service and, in general, making flights as pleasurable as possible within the limitations imposed by aircraft operations." *Id.* at 387 (citing 311 F.Supp. 559, 563 (S.D.Fla.1970)). The Fifth Circuit reversed, without disturbing the lower court's findings, on the ground that ministering to the psychological needs of passengers was "tangential" to the airline's "primary function" of safely transporting passengers. *Id.* at 388. The court observed:

> While a pleasant environment, enhanced by the obvious cosmetic effect that female stewardesses provide as well as, according to the findings of the trial court, their apparent ability to perform the non-mechanical functions of the job in a more effective manner than most men, may all be important, they are tangential to the essence of the business involved. No one has suggested that having male stewards will so seriously affect the operation of the airline as to jeopardize or even minimize its ability to provide safe transportation from one place to another.

Id.

The court in *Wilson v. Southwest Airlines*, discussed *supra* Note 9, acknowledged the "very narrow standard for weighing customer preference" that courts following *Diaz* had adopted. 517 F.Supp. at 302 n.24. Furthermore, the court acknowledged the EEOC's "authenticity and genuineness" exception to this narrow standard. *Id.* at 301 & 301 n.20 (citing C.F.R. § 1604.2(a)(2) as amended by 45 Fed.Reg. 74676). Where "the primary function of the position, its essence, is to fulfill the audience's expectation and desire for a particular role, characterized by particular physical or emotional traits," the EEOC's regulation would permit male actors to fill male roles. *Id.* at 301. Also, where "sex or vicarious sexual recreation is the primary service provided" such that "the employee's sex and the service provided are inseparable," the regulation would permit employment of a female as "a social escort or topless dancer." *Id.* Can you think of any other jobs that would fit into the EEOC's "authenticity and genuineness" exception? In *Wilson*, the court ruled that Southwest Airlines "is not a business where vicarious sex entertainment is the primary service provided." *Id.* at 302.

11.   What is the difference, if any, between the business necessity and bona fide occupational qualification defenses? Between the BFOQ and the legitimate, nondiscriminatory reason defense? *See* Johnson v. Uncle Ben's, Inc., 657 F.2d 750 (5th Cir.1981); Saunders v. Hercules, Inc., 510 F.Supp. 1137, 1141–42 (W.D.Va.1981).

12.   What conception of equality does the Court endorse in *Johnson Controls*? Can you reconcile the conceptions of equality in *Johnson Controls* and *Guerra*? Samuel Issacharoff and Elyse Rosenblum, in *Women and the Workplace: Accommodating the Demands of Pregnancy*, 94 Colum.L.Rev. 2154 (1994), address the "paradoxical view of pregnancy discrimination evidenced by the conflicting rationales of *Guerra* and *Johnson Controls*." *Id.* at 2158. The authors note that "[t]he same disagreement exists even among feminists who, united in their support for women's equality in the workplace, disagree as to whether equality means equal opportunity for men and

women, as in *Guerra*, or rather, equal treatment of the sexes, as in *Johnson Controls*." *Id.* Issacharoff and Rosenblum argue that "[t]he antidiscrimination model is at best a clumsy vehicle for addressing the difficult questions of resource allocation that are necessarily implicated in accommodating employees who face specific and predictable obstacles to achieving security in the workplace." *Id.* at 2158.

13. *Customs of Foreign Corporations*: In *Sumitomo Shoji America v. Avagliano*, 457 U.S. 176, 102 S.Ct. 2374, 72 L.Ed.2d 765 (1982), a United States-based, wholly-owned subsidiary of a Japanese corporation allegedly refused to promote females to executive, managerial, and sales positions in order to conform to Japanese customary employment practices. A group of past and present female secretarial employees sued Sumitomo on several grounds, including a Title VII claim alleging sex-based discrimination. One of the grounds on which Sumitomo defended was Article VIII(1) of the Treaty of Friendship, Commerce and Navigation between Japan and the United States, which allows companies of each party to hire, among others, "personnel * * * of their choice." Sumitomo argued that it was allowed to limit management positions to males under the terms of the treaty. One issue before the Supreme Court was whether the Japanese subsidiary was exempted from Title VII. The Court held that the treaty defense was inapplicable because the Sumitomo subsidiary, an independent entity, was a company of the United States, not of Japan. The Court, however, did state in a footnote:

> There can be little doubt that some positions in a Japanese controlled company doing business in the United States call for great familiarity with not only the language of Japan, but also the culture, customs, and business practices of that country. * * * Whether Sumitomo can support its assertion of a bona fide occupational qualification or a business necessity defense is not before us.

Id. at 189 n.19, 102 S.Ct. at 2382 n.19. Does this dictum suggest that there may be circumstances where being a male could be a BFOQ for certain positions in a Japanese subsidiary doing business in the United States?

14. *Customs of Foreign Nations*: Can an American company rely on the customs of a foreign country to justify a sex-based BFOQ for jobs that its employees—who are United States citizens—perform in that country? Title VII clearly covers such employees. *See* § 701(f), 42 U.S.C. § 2000e(f). Thus, explicit sex-based hiring and promotion decisions regarding such employees could only be defended as a BFOQ. Should the courts adopt a broader BFOQ analysis for American corporations doing business in foreign countries in which the prevailing social customs and practices discriminate on the basis of gender?

In *Fernandez v. Wynn Oil Co.*, 20 Fair Empl.Prac.Cas. (BNA) 1162 (C.D.Cal.1979), *aff'd*, 653 F.2d 1273 (9th Cir.1981), the employer asserted an alternative defense to its failure to promote the female plaintiff to Director of International Operations—that being male was a BFOQ for a job that involved spending time in South American countries, cultivating new clients and doing business with its customers there. The company argued that the customs and mores of its South American clientele would make it impossible for a woman to succeed in the position. For example, it argued that, because of their attitudes about the proper roles of men and women, South Americans would be offended if a woman held meetings with business clients in her hotel room. Applying the *Diaz* BFOQ analysis (discussed *supra* Note 9), the district court found that employing a man for the position went to the "essence" of the business since hiring a female as Director of International Operations "would have totally subverted any business [the company] hoped to accomplish in those areas of the world." *Id.* at 1165. The district court entered judgment for the employer on several grounds, including the BFOQ defense.

When the plaintiff appealed to the Ninth Circuit, the employer disavowed reliance on the district court's BFOQ analysis, and the plaintiff lost on grounds unrelated to her challenge of the employer's BFOQ defense. *See* 653 F.2d at 1275–76. Nevertheless, the Ninth Circuit, in dictum, rejected the district court's factual findings and legal conclusions pertaining to the employer's BFOQ defense. *Id.* at 1276. The court noted that no evidence was presented that the plaintiff would be required to conduct business from her hotel room in South America, and no evidence supported the district court's findings that hiring a female for the job would " 'destroy the essence' of the [employer's] business or 'create serious safety and efficacy problems.' " *Id.*

The court stressed that neither "stereotypic impressions of male and female roles" nor "stereotyped customer preference[s]" can make gender a BFOQ. *Id.* at 1276–77. In addition, the court cited the EEOC regulation limiting the customer preference BFOQ to "one necessary for the purpose of genuineness or authenticity," *id.* at 1277 (citing 29 C.F.R. § 1604.2(a)(2) (1972)), as well as a 1971 EEOC decision "that the need to accommodate racially discriminatory policies of other nations cannot be the basis of a valid BFOQ exception." *Id.* The court concluded:

> [The employer] attempts to distinguish *Diaz* by asserting that a separate rule applies in international contexts. Such a distinction is unfounded. Though the United States cannot impose standards of nondiscriminatory conduct on other nations through its legal system, the district court's rule would allow other nations to dictate discrimination in this country. No foreign nation can compel the non-enforcement of Title VII here.

Id.

Note: A Privacy–Based BFOQ

The notion that a BFOQ could be based on the privacy interests of clients or customers was raised in the floor debates on the Civil Rights Act of 1964. The House of Representatives briefly considered the BFOQ exception to Title VII on the last day of debate on the bill. Because "sex" had been proposed as a prohibited category under Title VII, Representative Goodell suggested why it should also be included under the BFOQ exception:

> There are so many instances where the matter of sex is a bona fide occupational qualification. For instance, I think of an elderly woman who wants a female nurse. There are many things of this nature which are bona fide occupational qualifications, and it seems to me they would be properly considered here as an exception.

110 Cong.Rec. 2718 (1964).

Courts, before and after *Johnson Controls*, have recognized sex as a BFOQ where health care providers have defended hiring employees of only one sex on the basis of the privacy interests of their patients. These cases have relied on preferences of patients for sexual privacy—as well as assumptions by courts and employers about patient preferences—in situations where the patients have to undress, bathe, or perform toileting functions in the presence of employees. *See, e.g.*, Jennings v. New York State Office of Mental Health, 786 F.Supp. 376 (S.D.N.Y.) (holding that sex is a BFOQ for aides in a psychiatric hospital who feed, clothe, and bathe patients), *aff'd*, 977 F.2d 731 (2d Cir.1992); EEOC v. Mercy Health Ctr., 29 Fair Empl. Prac.Cas. (BNA) 159 (W.D.Okla.1982) (relying, in part, on patient surveys to uphold the exclusion of male nurses from a maternity center); Fesel v. Masonic Home of Del., Inc., 447 F.Supp. 1346 (D.Del.1978) (relying on affidavits of female patients to uphold the exclusion of male nurses and aides in a nursing home), *aff'd mem.*, 591 F.2d 1334 (3d Cir.1979).

As Professor Katherine Bartlett has observed, these preferences "are themselves based on gender-role stereotypes" since "patients who object to male nurses helping them perform their toileting functions are unlikely to object to—and, in fact, may prefer—male doctors." Katherine T. Bartlett, *Only Girls Wear Barrettes: Dress and Appearance Standards, Community Norms, and Workplace Equality*, 92 Mich.L.Rev. 2541, 2542 & n.8 (1994). A number of commentators have criticized the privacy-based BFOQ. *See, e.g.*, Caroline S. Bratt, *Privacy and the Sex BFOQ: An Immodest Proposal*, 48 Alb.L.Rev. 923 (1984); Deborah A. Calloway, *Equal Employment and Third Party Privacy Interests: An Analytical Framework for Reconciling Competing Rights*, 54 Fordham L.Rev. 327 (1985); Elsa M. Shartsis, *Privacy as Rationale for the Sex–Based BFOQ*, 1985 Det.C.L.Rev. 865. Did the Supreme Court in *Johnson Controls* implicitly recognize that privacy concerns could justify sex as a BFOQ in certain circumstances? *See* Bartlett, *supra*, at 2542 n.8 (noting that there are "hints" in *Johnson Controls* "that the Supreme Court is inclined, at the moment at least, to endorse it").

The privacy-based BFOQ has also been raised in cases involving single-sex health clubs and gymnasiums. For example, in *EEOC v. Sedita*, 816 F.Supp. 1291 (N.D.Ill.1993), Women's Workout World (WWW), a company that owned fifteen health clubs, defended its policy of hiring only women as managers, assistant managers, and instructors as a BFOQ justified by the privacy interests of its exclusively female membership. The district judge, Ann Claire Williams, adopted the following analysis:

> An employer asserting a privacy based BFOQ defense must satisfy a three part test: the employer must establish that 1) there is a factual basis for believing that hiring any members of one sex would undermine the essence of its business, 2) the asserted privacy interest is entitled to protection under the law, and 3) no reasonable alternatives exist to protect the privacy interests other than the gender based hiring policy.

Id. at 1295.

Although previous privacy BFOQ cases had involved "exposure to nudity, touching of genitals, and observance of private bodily functions," WWW offered evidence that "a significant part of [its] business involve[d] touching clients on their breasts, inner thighs, buttocks, and crotch area when taking measurements and instructing members on the use of equipment and proper exercise form." *Id.* at 1296. Based on this evidence, the court assumed, for purposes of a summary judgment motion, "that defendants have implicated protectible privacy interests," thus satisfying the second element of the privacy BFOQ defense. *Id.*

To bolster its argument that the privacy interests of its clients went to the "essence" of its business serving an "older, overweight clientele," WWW relied on petitions signed by more than 10,000 of its members that stated that they had joined WWW "to receive personalized exercise instruction" and that they would not patronize WWW if it hired males to perform functions that they would consider an "invasion of [their] privacy rights." *Id.* at 1297. Under the first prong of its privacy BFOQ analysis, the court accepted these petitions, along with affidavits of club managers and the owner's deposition testimony, as factual support for the inferences that "nudity and touching concern the essence of the jobs" and that women would refuse to patronize the clubs if men were employed in those jobs. *Id.* at 1296. Finally, the court agreed that the defendant's concerns about the costs of hiring males, including the cost of "substantially restructur[ing] their exercise facilities by putting in bathroom facilities for men and doors on the locker rooms, * * * are relevant to the reasonableness of the suggested alternatives, and to the ultimate legitimacy of the BFOQ defense." *Id.* at 1297. The court vacated its prior summary judgment in favor of the EEOC and ordered a trial on the merits.

Notes and Questions

1.   Several states now have public accommodation statutes or court rulings that legalize all-male and all-female health clubs and gyms. *See* Patricia Wen, *Single-Sex Health Clubs Get Protection: Celucci Calls Law "Narrowly Crafted,"* Boston Globe, Feb. 7, 1998, at B1 (discussing the new Massachusetts statute). Some of these clubs may consider adopting single-sex hiring policies. Should such discriminatory hiring policies be legitimated under rationales based on customer preferences and cost considerations, arguments that have been rejected in BFOQ cases that are not based on privacy interests? What evidence would an employer need to prevail at trial under a *Sedita* analysis? Should affidavits or petitions signed by the employer's clients or customers be deemed probative or admissible evidence? *See* Spragg v. Shore Care & Shore Mem'l Hosp., 293 N.J.Super. 33, 679 A.2d 685 (1996). Is it sufficient that the members of these clubs subjectively believe that their privacy interests are affected? Or should their beliefs be objectively reasonable as well? Should the age or physical condition of the club members be taken into consideration? *See generally* Miriam A. Cherry, *Exercising the Right to Public Accommodations: The Debate Over Singlesex Health Clubs*, 52 Me.L.Rev. 97 (2000); Michael R. Evans, *The Case for All–Female Health Clubs: Creating a Compensatory Purpose Exception to State Public Accommodation Laws*, 11 Yale J.L. & Feminism 307 (1999).

In *Sedita*, the court quoted the following from an earlier privacy case:

"It is necessary to stress that the purpose of the sex provisions of the Civil Rights Act is to eliminate sex discrimination in employment, not to make over the accepted mores and personal sensitivities of the American people in the more uninhibited image favored by any particular commission or court or commentator."

816 F.Supp. at 1296 (quoting Backus v. Baptist Med. Ctr., 510 F.Supp. 1191, 1195 (E.D.Ark.1981). Do you agree? In 1994 the *Sedita* case settled before it went to trial. While the EEOC and Women's Workout World were in the process of negotiating the settlement, WWW began to hire male instructors at its health clubs. Under the final agreement, WWW agreed to hire qualified male employees in the future and to set aside $30,000 to compensate any men who were discriminated against under its sex-based hiring policy. *See* Mary Ellen Podmolik, *Women's Workout World Agrees to Hire Male Workers*, Chi. Sun–Times, June 15, 1994. Does WWW's willingness to settle on these terms undercut their factual assertions that hiring men would be too costly and would drive away their all-female clients?

2.   Ralph Olsen applied for a position as a massage therapist at the spa of a luxury resort hotel. Although the hotel employed both male and female massage therapists in its spa, the hotel refused to hire Olsen because he is male. Olsen sued the hotel under Title VII, alleging disparate treatment on the basis of sex. The hotel asserted a privacy-based BFOQ defense, claiming that the hotel needed females for a certain percentage of its massage therapist positions in order to satisfy customer demand for female therapists. Customers did not necessarily ask for therapists of their same sex. In fact, many men preferred female therapists and some women preferred male therapists. In addition, some women who requested female therapists, were willing to accept appointments with male therapists if no female therapists were available. Does the hotel have a legitimate privacy-based BFOQ defense to its hiring policy? Is privacy of the customers the "essence of the business" of massage therapy? Or is this a case of a BFOQ defense based on customer preferences or cost justification? *See* Olsen v. Marriott Int'l, Inc., 75 F.Supp.2d 1052 (D.Ariz.1999). *See generally* Amy Kapczynski, Note, *Same-Sex Privacy and the Limits of Antidiscrimination Law*, 112 Yale L.J. 1257 (2003).

3.   In *Torres v. Wisconsin Department of Health and Social Services*, 859 F.2d 1523 (7th Cir.1988), *cert. denied*, 489 U.S. 1017, 109 S.Ct. 1133, 103 L.Ed.2d 194 (1989), plaintiffs, male prison guards at a maximum security prison for women, brought a sex discrimination claim challenging a prison policy providing that correctional officer positions in the prison's living quarters would be staffed only by female correctional officers. As a result, the male officers who had worked in the living quarters were required to accept lower-grade positions. The superintendent of the prison, a female, promulgated the policy based only on her "professional judgment" that removing men from the area was "necessary to foster the goal of rehabilitation" and on the fact that sixty percent of the inmates had been abused by males at some point in her their lives. *Id.* at 1530. The parties and the trial court agreed that empirical studies that might validate the policy did not exist. The district court found that the prison failed to satisfy the BFOQ because it " 'offered no objective evidence, either from empirical studies or otherwise' "that supported the policy. *Id.* at 1531. How should the case be analyzed under *Johnson Controls* and *Sedita*? Would your analysis be different if the policy was tested under a business necessity defense?

4.   A group of female employees brings a Title VII challenge to a policy of a men's prison that requires female employees to obtain the consent of the male inmates before the employees perform "pat down" searches of the inmates. The basic rationale for the policy is to protect the privacy of the inmates. Could the policy survive analysis under the rationale of *Johnson Controls*? *See* Timm v. Gunter, 917 F.2d 1093 (8th Cir.1990), *cert. denied*, 501 U.S. 1209, 111 S.Ct. 2807, 115 L.Ed.2d 979 (1991). In *Robino v. Iranon*, 145 F.3d 1109 (9th Cir.1998), the court upheld a BFOQ defense of the policy of a women's correctional facility which designated six guard positions as female-only. The court held that "these six female-only posts are a reasonable response to the [defendants'] concerns about inmate privacy and allegations of abuse by male [corrections officers]." *Id.* at 1111. The court observed that the plaintiffs—male corrections officers—

> contend a BFOQ defense cannot be based on the privacy rights of the inmates and they correctly note that inmates' privacy rights are limited. However, a person's interest in not being viewed unclothed by members of the opposite sex survives incarceration. Whether or not the inmates could successfully assert their own right to privacy is immaterial in this case. We are concerned here with a considered prison policy that takes into account security, rehabilitation, and morale.

Id.

F.   DRESS, GROOMING, AND APPEARANCE REQUIREMENTS

Once on the job, many employees accept without question the legitimacy of employer rules regarding workplace dress, grooming, and appearance. Indeed, the pressure to conform to informal "dress codes" in some workplaces—such as law offices and courtrooms—may obviate the need for formal rules. But what if an employer's formal rules impose greater burdens on women than on men or, for that matter, on members of a particular race or religion? In deciding whether an employee is suited for a particular job, does an employer violate Title VII when it relies on gender-based assumptions about how men and women should appear? Professor Katharine Bartlett has observed:

> [e]mployers have traditionally assumed substantial prerogatives with respect to the dress and appearance of their employees, imposing burdens on women that are different from those imposed on men. For example, women may be required to wear skirts of a certain length or high-heeled shoes, to conform to different weight criteria than men, or to wear makeup. They may be fired if they have unladylike facial hair or if they wear their hair in a style that may offend customers. They may be required to have sexually alluring figures or to wear sexually provocative clothing, or they may be made to downplay their sexuality. Men, in turn, may be required to wear ties or to keep their hair cut short, or may be prohibited from wearing "women's" jewelry. These requirements pose a special challenge to conventional equality concepts and illus-

trate especially well the difficulties of rooting out workplace rules and practices that are based on well-settled community norms.

Katharine T. Bartlett, *Only Girls Wear Barrettes: Dress and Appearance Standards, Community Norms, and Workplace Equality*, 92 Mich.L.Rev. 2541, 2543–44 (1994) (citations omitted).

Although the EEOC was initially receptive to the argument that gender-based dress and grooming codes constitute sex discrimination in violation of Title VII, the courts, with a few limited exceptions, have consistently rejected challenges to employer rules and informal practices regarding employee workplace attire, grooming standards, and personal appearance. *See, e.g.*, Bartlett, *supra*, at 2556 n.70 (citing EEOC administrative decisions from the early 1970s that "invalidated hair-length requirements or no-beard rules, which applied to men but not women"); *see generally id.* at 2556–68 (discussing the rationales that courts have adopted to deny Title VII claims based on sex-based dress and grooming requirements). The EEOC Compliance Manual now expressly permits different dress codes for men and women, requiring only that the employers impose "equivalent" standards or burdens on both male and female employees. EEOC Compliance Manual § 619.4(d).

The Title VII cases tend to fall into two general fact patterns: (1) challenges to employer dress or grooming codes that are based on gender-linked assumptions and community norms regarding appropriate appearance or attire for men and women, and (2) challenges to employer decisions to employ or retain only employees who have an "attractive" appearance. *See generally* Karl E. Klare, *Power/Dressing: Regulation of Employee Appearance*, 26 New Eng.L.Rev. 1395, 1414–25 (1992) (discussing employer dress codes and attractiveness requirements). In addition, as Professor Klare notes, "[a] cross-cutting set of cases involves the question whether employers can force women to appear in a manner that exploits their sexuality for business purposes, for example, by requiring a revealing uniform." *Id.* at 1415.

In the first category of cases, courts have consistently upheld employer rules that require men, but not women, to have short hair, or that prohibit men from wearing skirts or dresses and women from wearing pants. *Id.* at 1418. For example, when a male reporter of trades on the New York Mercantile Exchange was terminated for violating its requirement that male—but not female—employees have short hair, the court agreed that he did not have a cause of action under Title VII. Tavora v. New York Mercantile Exch., 101 F.3d 907 (2d Cir.1996). After citing the general principle that " 'requiring short hair on men and not on women does not violate Title VII,' " the court observed that "[e]very court of appeals that has considered this issue has agreed." *Id.* at 908 (citing Longo v. Carlisle DeCoppet & Co., 537 F.2d 685 (2d Cir.1976); *see also id.* (collecting cases). *See also* Harper v. Blockbuster Ent. Corp., 139 F.3d 1385 (11th Cir.1998) (different hair length rules for men and women do not violate Title VII), *cert. denied*, 525 U.S. 1000, 119 S.Ct. 509, 142 L.Ed.2d 422 (1998).

In the cases upholding dress and grooming codes that are explicitly based on gender, the courts have adopted several rationales. First is that these types of policies, which do no more than reflect reasonable community norms of appearance, have only a trivial or de minimus impact on employees' working condition. *See, e.g.,* Dodge v. Giant Food, Inc., 488 F.2d 1333, 1337 (D.C.Cir.1973) ("Title VII was never intended to encompass sexual classifications having only an insignificant effect on employment opportunities"); *see also* Klare, *supra* at 1419. Second, many courts consider dress and grooming codes to be outside the legitimate scope of Title VII's statutory objectives and firmly within the lawful prerogatives of the employer.

> Equal employment *opportunity* may be secured only when employers are barred from discriminating against employees on the basis of immutable characteristics, such as race and national origin. Similarly, an employer cannot have one hiring policy for men and another for women *if* the distinction is based on some fundamental right. But a hiring policy that distinguishes on some other ground, such as grooming codes or length of hair, is related more closely to the employer's choice of how to run a business than to equality of employment opportunity.

Willingham v. Macon Tel. Publ'g Co., 507 F.2d 1084, 1092 (5th Cir.1975) (en banc); *see also* Klare, *supra* at 1419.

Finally, some courts accept the argument that the only way to treat men and women equally with regard to appearance is to adopt disparate rules that reflect "the standard of what the community expects of each sex, respectively." Klare, *supra* at 1419. *See, e.g.,* Fagan v. National Cash Register Co., 481 F.2d 1115, 1117 n.3 (D.C.Cir.1973) ("reasonable regulations prescribing good grooming standards are not at all uncommon in the business world, indeed, taking account of basic differences in male and female physiques and common differences in customary dress of male and female employees, it is not usually thought that there is unlawful discrimination 'because of sex' "). From this perspective, equal treatment requires that the employer take gender into account for both male and female employees in promulgating dress and grooming codes.

Not all dress codes, however, can be described as "trivial in their impact on employees, or neutral in affecting men and women alike, or essential to the employer's lawful business objectives." Bartlett, *supra,* at 2544. *Carroll v. Talman Federal Savings & Loan Association of Chicago,* 604 F.2d 1028 (7th Cir.1979), *cert. denied,* 445 U.S. 929, 100 S.Ct. 1316, 63 L.Ed.2d 762 (1980), is a leading case striking down an employer's dress code. In *Carroll,* the employer required female office and managerial employees to wear two-piece, color-coordinated uniforms. The bank supplied the uniforms, but the cost of the uniforms was treated as additional income to the employees. Male employees working in comparable jobs were required to wear "customary business attire" which could "consist of a suit, a sport jacket and pants, or even a 'leisure suit,' as long as it [was] worn with a shirt and tie." *Id.* at 1029. The court found that

> two sets of employees performing the same functions are subjected on the basis of sex to two entirely separate dress codes[,] one including a variety of normal business attire and the other requiring a clearly identifiable uniform. This different treatment in the conditions of employment for female employees cannot be justified by business necessity, since * * * the employer had a variety of non-discriminatory alternative means of assuring good grooming. Moreover, the disparate treatment is demeaning to women. While there is nothing offensive about uniforms *per se*, when some employees are uniformed and others not there is a natural tendency to assume that the uniformed women have a lesser professional status than their male colleagues attired in normal business clothes.

Id. at 1032–33.

To justify its sex-based uniform requirement, the bank asserted two concerns: (1) that female employees would engage in "dress competition," and (2) that if they were permitted to exercise their own judgment regarding their clothing, the women would "follow the fashion" rather than wearing proper "business attire." *Id.* at 1033. The court responded: "Clearly these justifications for the rule reveal that it is based on offensive stereotypes prohibited by Title VII." *Id.* But, if "offensive stereotypes" are a legitimate basis for striking down the dress code in *Carroll*, why do short-hair rules for men, or no-pants rules for women, routinely survive judicial scrutiny? Is it perhaps because these particular grooming norms are so widely accepted that we would not characterize them as "offensive" even though we might agree they are based on stereotypes of what it means to be masculine and feminine? As Karl Klare observed, "[i]t is not obvious why a statute intended to loosen the grip of sexist stereotypes should so powerfully sanctify patriarchal and heterosexist sensibilities." Klare, *supra*, at 1421.

The second category of Title VII cases deals with "facially neutral" appearance requirements that might be an implicit barrier at the time of the hiring decision or could arise later, leading to a demotion or termination. According to one study of the economic effects of employees' appearance, "people with above-average looks receive a pay premium of up to thirteen percent, while those with below-average looks receive a pay penalty as large as fifteen percent." Bartlett, *supra*, at 2565 (citing Daniel S. Hamermesh & Jeff E. Biddle, Beauty and the Labour Market 13 & tbls. 3–5 (National Bureau of Economic Research Working Paper No. 4518, 1993)). At least in theory, such appearance requirements benefit or harm men and women equally, and thus do not discriminate on the basis of sex.

But what if there is evidence that appearance standards are based on stereotypes about men and women? Or that women's appearance is judged more critically than men's? Would the relevance of such evidence depend on whether attractive appearance is an essential aspect of the job? Some of these questions were raised in *Craft v. Metromedia, Inc.*, 766 F.2d 1205 (8th Cir.1985), *cert. denied*, 475 U.S. 1058, 106 S.Ct. 1285, 89 L.Ed.2d 592 (1986), the leading case challenging an employer's use of appearance standards. *See generally* Rhonda Blond–Rosen, *Christine— The Craft Without an Anchor*: Craft v. Metromedia, 3 Cardozo Arts & Ent.L.J. 181 (1984). After hiring news co-anchor, Christine Craft, a Kansas City television station received viewer survey results that were critical of her on-air appearance. The station gave her advice about her make-up and brought in a fashion consultant to select and supervise her wardrobe for each broadcast. When a new survey ranking all the female co-anchors at competing stations in the area showed that Craft lagged behind her peers in "good looks," the station demoted her and took her off the air. Craft brought a Title VII action alleging that the station's "appearance standards were based on stereotyped characterizations of the sexes and were applied to women more constantly and vigorously than they were applied to men." *Id.* at 1210.

In support of her argument that the station "enforced appearance standards more strictly as to female than as to male on-air personnel," Craft presented evidence that only the clothing of females was scrutinized on a daily basis before broadcasts and that "no male was ever directed to take time from his journalistic duties" in order to meet with clothing consultants and to pretest clothing in videotaped sessions. *Id.* at 1212–13. The Eighth Circuit, however, accepted the finding of the district court that "such facts, in light of other evidence, showed only that [the station] was concerned with the appearance of all its on-air personnel and that it took measures appropriate to individual situations, characteristics, and shortcomings." *Id.* at 1213. The other evidence showed that one male news anchor had been "told to lose weight, to get better-fitting clothes, to refrain from wearing sweaters under jackets, and to tie his necktie in a certain manner"; a second "had been told to lose weight and to pay more attention to his wardrobe and hairstyle"; and a third "had been told to try wearing contact lenses and to get a hair piece and had been given a makeup chart on a form similar to that used with Craft." *Id.*

Craft's second argument, that "she was forced to conform to a stereotypical image of how a woman anchor should appear," *id.* at 1214, also failed to persuade the court. In upholding the findings of the district court "that [the station's] appearance standards were based * * * on permissible factors," the Eighth Circuit observed:

> While there may have been some emphasis on the feminine stereo-type of "softness" and bows and ruffles and on the fashionableness of female anchors, the evidence suggests such concerns were incidental to a true focus on consistency of appearance, proper coordination of colors and textures, the effects of studio lighting on clothing and makeup, and the greater degree of conservatism thought necessary in the Kansas City market. The "dos" and "don'ts" for female anchors addressed the need to avoid, for example, tight sweaters or overly "sexy" clothing and extreme "high fashion" or "sporty"

outfits while the male "dos" and "don't" similarly cautioned against "frivolous" colors and "extreme" textures and styles as damaging to the "authority" of newscasters. These criteria do not implicate the primary thrust of Title VII, which is to prompt employers to "discard outmoded sex stereotypes posing distinct employment disadvantages for one sex." Knott v. Missouri Pacific Railroad, 527 F.2d 1249, 1251 (8th Cir.1975); see generally Note, Title VII Limits on Discrimination Against Television Anchorwomen on the Basis of Age–Related Appearance, 85 Colum.L.Rev. 190, 201 (1985).

Courts have recognized that the appearance of a company's employees may contribute greatly to the company's image and success with the public and thus that a reasonable dress or grooming code is a proper management prerogative. Evidence showed a particular concern with appearance in television; the district court stated that reasonable appearance requirements were "obviously critical" to [the station's] economic well-being; and even Craft admitted she recognized that television was a visual medium and that on-air personnel would need to wear appropriate clothes and makeup.

Id. at 1215.

Professor Klare argues that "[t]he categories of 'attractiveness' and 'pleasing appearance' are not and cannot be gender-neutral in our culture. When utilized as a criterion of personnel action, personal appearance necessarily incorporates stereotyped expectations and judgments about women's behavior and worth." Klare, *supra*, at 1425. Do you think that the court in *Craft* would agree? Is the court saying that some stereotypes are fine, as long as they are not "outmoded" and do not pose a "distinct employment disadvantage for one sex"? Were bows and ruffles "outmoded" for professional women in the early 1980s? Or were the "conservative" fashion tastes of Kansas City viewers "outmoded" by comparison with the rest of the country? Whose judgments or perspectives should be taken into account in an employment decision? Or in a court's review of an employment decision? How would the *Craft* court's analysis hold up in light of Justice Brennan's analysis of the role of sexual stereotypes in the partnership selection process at Price Waterhouse? *See* Price Waterhouse v. Hopkins, 490 U.S. 228, 235, 109 S.Ct. 1775, 1782, 104 L.Ed.2d 268 (1989), in Chapter 3 (holding that evidence that a partner of the accounting firm told Ann Hopkins that she could "improve her chances for partnership" if she would " 'walk more femininely, talk more femininely, dress more femininely, wear make-up, have her hair styled, and wear jewelry' " was sufficient to establish that sexual stereotyping played a role in the partnership decision).

Is there any greater "employment disadvantage" than a discharge or demotion? Or is the *Craft* court just suggesting that both male and female newscasters run the same risks? A male newscaster, too, can be taken off the air because of his unacceptable appearance—a balding head, a protruding belly, or a necktie always askew. Consider the following commentary:

> Where the marketing of sexual attractiveness is more subtle, [Title VII] challenges by women employees have been less successful. The courts have often failed to expose the gender discrimination embedded in "facially neutral" socially constructed appearance gender norms, instead relying on sexual mythologies of how women behave, how they should appear, and how they are most valued, to insulate adverse employment decisions from judicial scrutiny. Provided that the employment policy applies at least in theory to both men and women, the legal fiction of gender neutrality is satisfied.

Judith Olans Brown, Lucy A. Williams & Phyllis Tropper Baumann, *The Mythogenesis of Gender: Judicial Images of Women in Paid and Unpaid Labor*, 6 UCLA Women's L.J. 457, 511 (1996). Do you agree that the evidence in *Craft* was sufficient to prove that the TV station's gender-based appearance requirements were equally disadvantageous to the career prospects of both male and female newscasters?

Should a different analysis be required when an employer requires its female (or male) employees to be young and physically attractive, and to wear sexually provocative clothing, in order to market the employer's products or services? Does the answer depend on whether the employer is just using sexual allure as a marketing gimmick or is primarily selling sex—such as where the business is a night club featuring female (or male) strippers or scantily clad "show girls"? *Cf.*, Wilson v. Southwest Airlines Co., 517 F.Supp. 292, 301 (N.D.Tex.1981), discussed *supra* Note 8 following *Johnson Controls* in Section E of this chapter.

Where a gender-based requirement of sexually provocative dress or uniforms exposes females to "unwelcome" sexual harassment from other employees or customers, the courts have been more willing to find the policy discriminatory. For example, in *EEOC v. Sage Realty Corp.*, 507 F.Supp. 599 (S.D.N.Y.1981), Margaret Hasselman was hired as a lobby attendant at an office building to perform "security, safety, maintenance and information functions." *Id.* at 603. She was fired when she refused to continue wearing a "Bicentennial uniform" that consisted of a poncho resembling the American flag worn "open at the sides" over "blue dancer pants and sheer stockings," exposing her "thighs and portions of her buttocks." *Id.* at 604. Another female lobby attendant commented that "if she had wanted to wear a uniform like the Bicentennial outfit * * *, she would have sought work as a cocktail waitress." *Id.* at 605. The court noted that "[w]hile wearing the Bicentennial uniform and as a result of wearing it, Hasselman was subjected to repeated harassment. She received a number of sexual propositions and endured lewd comments and gestures." *Id.* The court held that the defendant's uniform requirement, "when they knew that the wearing of this uniform on the job subjected her to sexual harassment, constituted sex discrimination," *id.* at 609, and ruled that, on these facts, "it is beyond dispute that the wearing of sexually revealing garments does not constitute a bfoq," *id.* at 611.

It may not always be easy to draw the line between cases where sex is the employer's business and cases where sex is used to enhance the profitability of the employer's business. In the former, sexually provocative clothing requirements for women would be an expected and legitimate part of the job; in the latter, such attire might be demeaning to the female employees and nonessential to the employer, and thus discriminatory under Title VII. The controversial dress code and sex-based hiring practices of the Hooters restaurant chain demonstrate the dilemma. The "Hooters Girls"—female employees who work as hosts, servers, and bartenders—must be attractive and buxom in order to be hired and are required to wear T-shirts or tank tops, and very skimpy shorts on the job. Bartlett, *supra*, at 2578. Since the early 1990s, Hooters has been sued several times by men over its practice of hiring only women for its "front-of-the-house" positions. *See id.* at 2578 & n.175. Many restaurant workers, both male and female, prefer working in customer contact positions where they can earn substantial tips. In the fall of 1997, Hooters paid several million dollars to settle a class-action lawsuit brought by men who had been denied jobs as waiters. The settlement, however, "preserves the job category of Hooters Girl, but makes certain positions available to men." Darryl Van Duch, *Bad PR Spurs Cave–Ins: Some Companies Are Settling to Contain Harm from Negative Publicity,* Nat'l L.J., Oct. 13, 1997, at A1.

As Professor Bartlett noted, "to defend its hiring practice of hiring only females for its front-of-the-house positions, and to justify its dress code if that should also be challenged, Hooters would need to establish that its business is, at its essence, the service of sexual excitement." Bartlett, *supra*, at 2578. Arguably Hooters succeeded in doing just that through a public relations maneuver that, according to one reporter, was

> widely believed to have badly embarrassed the EEOC for bringing charges against the restaurant chain. * * * It dressed up a burly, mustachioed male in the same scanty garb adorning its female serving staff and got pictures of the hairy sight on the front pages of newspapers in nearly every big city in which they did business.

Van Duch, *supra*. If Hooters is really in the business of selling "vicarious sexual recreation," and preparing and serving food is not the essence of the business, can Hooters be liable under Title VII if customers sexually harass its scantily clad Hooters Girls? Does the analysis in *EEOC v. Sage Realty Corp.* provide helpful guidance, or is it distinguishable on the facts? For a discussion of these issues, see Jeannie Sclafani Rhee, *Redressing for Success: The Liability of Hooters Restaurant for Customer Harassment of Waitresses,* 20 Harv.Women's L.J. 163 (1997).

Notes and Questions

1. *Sex-Based Weight Requirements*: Many airlines require applicants for flight attendant positions to meet specified height and weight standards. The maximum weight limits are generally set according to insurance industry charts showing average heights and weights for men and women by age. Courts tend to treat these dual weight standards with the same deference they give to sex-based dress and grooming codes that are designed to assure that employees who come in contact with the public have a pleasing, attractive appearance. *See, e.g.*, Jarrell v. Eastern Airlines, 430 F.Supp. 884 (E.D.Va.1977), *aff'd*, 577 F.2d 869 (4th Cir.1978) (rejecting disparate treatment and disparate impact claims in upholding dual weight maximums for male and female flight attendants). An airline cannot refuse to hire men as flight attendants simply because it believes its passengers prefer female attendants. *See, e.g.*, Diaz v. Pan Am. World Airways, Inc., 442 F.2d 385 (5th Cir.), *cert. denied*, 404 U.S. 950, 92 S.Ct. 275, 30 L.Ed.2d 267 (1971). See Note 10 following *Johnson Controls* in Section E of this chapter. But an airline can refuse to hire women who are a few pounds over its weight maximum for females because of an asserted customer preference for "thin" women. Why should customer preferences fail as a justification for a bona fide occupational qualification in the first situation and effectively shield the employer's managerial discretion in the second? Is it because a rule against hiring all men denies employment opportunities to all males, whereas a rule against hiring "overweight" women has a more limited impact on women's opportunities? Or is weight considered a mutable characteristic, unlike sex? Does *Johnson Controls* permit an employer to make employment decisions on the basis of dual, gender-based weight charts? There the Supreme Court concluded that "an explicit gender-based policy is sex discrimination under § 703(a) and thus may be defended only as a BFOQ." International Union, UAW v. Johnson Controls, Inc., 499 U.S. 187, 200, 111 S.Ct. 1196, 1204, 113 L.Ed.2d 158 (1991).

In 1997, the New York Court of Appeals ruled that Delta Airlines did not violate the New York Human Rights Law's prohibition against sex discrimination when it "permitted male applicants [for flight attendant and purser positions] to weigh more than female applicants of the same height and age." Delta Air Lines v. New York State Div. of Human Rights, 91 N.Y.2d 65, 666 N.Y.S.2d 1004, 689 N.E.2d 898, 902 (N.Y.1997). The court stated:

> [T]here is no basis to find as a matter of legal theory that weight limitations in these circumstances must be the same for both men and women.

> * * * Delta demonstrates that it utilized separate weight charts to ensure that males and females were treated relatively equally, based on real physiological differences. It shows that its standards recognized the statistically established norms that males tend to weigh more than females of the same height.

Id.

Do you agree with this analysis in light of the fact that the New York Human Rights Law, like Title VII, protects the rights of *individuals* to equal employment opportunity? A female who regularly lifts weights will have more muscle tissue and less body fat than the "statistically established norm" for women of her height and age. In other words, she may have a body type more typical of a man of her height and age. Is it fair or rational that she can be denied a position as a flight attendant if she satisfies the weight standard for men, but not for women? Is this equal treatment? On the other hand, would an airline violate Title VII if it required all flight attendants to have the same proportion of body fat to body weight that is the statistical norm for males? Consider the following observation by Professor Bartlett:

> Whether women can conform to societal weight standards without compromising their health is * * * increasingly a highly debatable proposition. The medical evidence is overwhelming that women require more body fat as a percentage of their body weight than men do. Without sufficient fat, women will not begin or continue, to menstruate, sustain a successful pregnancy, or breastfeed a child. Even with the pressures girls receive to keep their weight "under control," at puberty girls generally have ten to fifteen percent more body fat than boys. When faced with such medical evidence, however, courts * * * find a way to associate health hazards only with some females, such as those who make the voluntary, individual decision to take birth control pills. Some opinions acknowledge the rather radical methods many flight attendants have used to maintain their weight, including fasts, water shots, diet pills, water pills, and laxatives. At the extreme, these methods can lead to diet pill addictions and eating disorders such as bulimia and anorexia, which is associated with severe physical consequences, including bradycardia (impaired heartbeat), kidney failure, osteoporosis, tooth erosion, seizures, and infertility. Alternatives such as liposuction— the surgical removal of body fat—also carry risks that have no medical justification. That the contemporary community ideal of the thin woman can be viewed as natural and medically well grounded in the face of these health consequences is a testament to the strength and pervasiveness of this ideal.

Bartlett, *supra*, at 2562–63 (citations omitted).

The airline weight cases indicate that, for purposes of regulating employee appearance, an employer can use dual gender-based weight standards that have a proportionally greater adverse impact on employment opportunities of women without being required to show that the standards are job related. Recall that in *Dothard v. Rawlinson*, 433 U.S. 321, 97 S.Ct. 2720, 53 L.Ed.2d 786 (1977), reproduced, in part, in Chapter 4, the Supreme Court held that evidence of the discriminatory impact of Alabama's facially neutral height and weight requirements—a single standard applied to both men and women—established a prima facie case of sex discrimination and the state employer was required to show the requirements were job related—a burden it failed to meet. How do you explain the different outcomes?

Consider the following: An airline adopted dual gender-based weight charts for its male and female flight attendants. The charts were derived from insurance company height and weight tables for men and women. According to the airline's policy, female attendants could not exceed the weight range for a medium-frame woman, and male attendants could not exceed the weight range for a large-frame man. The female attendants would like to challenge the weight limits as discriminatory on the basis of sex under Title VII. Is this a case of disparate impact or disparate treatment? If it is disparate treatment, can the weight standards be justified as a BFOQ? *See* Frank v. United Airlines, Inc., 216 F.3d 845 (9th Cir.2000), *cert. denied,* 532 U.S. 914, 121 S.Ct. 1247, 149 L.Ed.2d 154 (2001).

2. *"Gender–Plus" Claims*: In *Marks v. National Communications Association, Inc.*, 72 F.Supp.2d 322 (S.D.N.Y.1999), the court dismissed the "gender-plus" claim of a plaintiff who alleged that her employer violated Title VII because it refused to hire or promote overweight women for sales positions. The plaintiff, who weighed about 270 pounds, had received outstanding performance evaluations for her work as a telemarketer. A manager told her that if she lost weight she would be promoted to an "outside" sales position. The court stated that "discrimination based on weight alone, or on any other physical characteristic for that matter, does not violate Title VII, unless issues of race, religion, sex, or national origin are intertwined." *Id.* at 330. Plaintiff's inability to identify any overweight male sales representatives was fatal to her "gender-plus" claim that she was treated differently from "similarly situated" males.

What evidence would be sufficient to make out a "gender-plus-weight" claim? If a female plaintiff is considered obese by medical standards, would she have to find an obese male sales representative to show that overweight males were treated differently from overweight females? How do we define "overweight" anyway? Would it suffice to show that one or more male sales representatives are somewhat overweight, although not obese? If the plaintiff were just slightly overweight for her height and body build—but not obese—would there be much of a possibility of prevailing on a "gender-plus-weight" claim? In the *Marks* case, the plaintiff had abandoned her ADA claims. Could an individual who is fired for being overweight seek relief under the Americans with Disabilities Act? *See, e.g.*, Cook v. Rhode Island Dep't of Mental Health, Retardation & Hosps., 10 F.3d 17 (1st Cir.1993); Murray v. John D. Archbold Mem'l Hosp., 50 F.Supp.2d 1368 (M.D.Ga.1999); Hazeldine v. Beverage Media, Ltd., 954 F.Supp. 697 (S.D.N.Y.1997). *See also* Elizabeth Kristen, Comment, *Addressing the Problem of Weight Discrimination in Employment,* 90 Cal.L.Rev. 57 (2002). The ADA is covered in Chapter 13.

3. *Intersecting Claims of Sex, Age, Race, and Disability Discrimination in Dress, Grooming, and Appearance Cases*: The *Delta Air Lines* case, like many employment discrimination cases, involved multiple claims of sex, age, and disability discrimination. The complainants in *Delta Air Lines* argued that in setting weight standards, "Delta should be required to take into consideration that older people may generally tend to heavier weight development." 689 N.E.2d at 902. Finding no evidence that older flight attendants had been subjected to disparate treatment, the court rejected the age claim. In fact, the airline's seniority rules favored older employees overall and its flight attendants were, on average, over 40 years old.

Similarly the court rejected the disability claim on the ground that the complainants were not "medically impaired members of a protected class defined under the New York Human Rights Law." *Id.* at 901. The case of *State Division of Human Rights v. Xerox Corp.*, 65 N.Y.2d 213, 491 N.Y.S.2d 106, 480 N.E.2d 695 (N.Y.1985), which held that clinically diagnosed obesity is a "disability" under the New York Human Rights Law, was distinguishable because the *Delta Air Lines* complainants did not claim or prove that they failed to satisfy Delta's weight requirements because they were obese.

By separating the discrimination claims, the court discounted the potential effects of age on women's weight and the potential effects of excess weight on women's job opportunities. How might you have analyzed these intersecting claims of sex, age, and disability discrimination differently? Are older, slightly "overweight" (but not obese) women denied employment at Delta because they cannot do the job or because they do not satisfy a stereotype of how female flight attendants should appear? Is the *Delta Air Lines* court saying that flight attendants, whether male or female, cannot do the job effectively if they do not meet the stereotypical youthful appearance norms for their gender? Or is the weight requirement not a "stereotype" because it is based on statistical data?

Another airline case involved the intersection of race and gender. In *Rogers v. American Airlines, Inc.*, 527 F.Supp. 229, 231 (S.D.N.Y.1981), an airline grooming rule prohibited all employees who dealt with the public "from wearing an all-braided hairstyle." A female African–American employee who wanted to wear her hair braided in "corn rows" unsuccessfully challenged the rule under Title VII on the grounds of sex and race discrimination. As in *Delta Air Lines*, the court reached the conclusion that there was no discrimination by analyzing the sex and race claims separately, rather than viewing them as an "interdependent and mutually reinforcing relationship of sexism and racism (and other forms of invidious discrimination) that together constitute the existing system of hierarchy and domination." Klare, *supra*, at 1413; *see generally* Paulette Caldwell, *A Hair Piece: Perspectives on the Intersection of Race and Gender*, 1991 Duke L.J. 365. Professor Klare concluded that the court's analysis in *Rogers* was based on a "value judgment that American Airlines is entitled to enforce its view that it might lose sales if some flight attendants or ticket agents wear corn rows, despite the consequences to African–American women in hurt, shame, and impaired employment opportunity." *Id.* at 1414. Should it matter whether this "value judgment" could be verified empirically? Or is Klare's point that employers ought to bear market losses when necessary to preserve the dignity and autonomy of their employees? Is this what Title VII requires?

4. *State and Local Laws Prohibiting Appearance Discrimination*: Although Congress has not enacted a statutory prohibition against appearance discrimination in employment, other government entities have passed such laws. For example, the District of Columbia Human Rights Act prohibits discrimination on the basis of "appearance." D.C. Code § 1–2502(22) defines "appearance" as

> the outward appearance of any person, irrespective of sex, with regard to bodily condition or characteristics, manner or style of dress, and manner or style of personal grooming, including, but not limited to, hair

style and beards. It shall not relate, however, to the requirement of * * * prescribed standards * * * when uniformly applied to a class of employees for a reasonable business purpose * * *.

If a female office worker employed by a lobbying firm in Washington, D.C., is criticized by her supervisor for her "low cut and tight blouses" and her "disheveled hair," would she have a viable appearance discrimination claim under the D.C. Human Rights Act? *See* Atlantic Richfield Co. v. District of Colum. Comm'n on Human Rights, 515 A.2d 1095 (D.C.1986). How would you analyze her claim and the employer's potential defenses? For a perceptive analysis of appearance discrimination laws, see Robert Post, *Prejudicial Appearances: The Logic of American Antidiscrimination Law*, 88 Cal.L.Rev. 1 (2000).

5. Consider the following: Wandra, an African–American woman, was hired to work as an administrative assistant in the Washington, D.C., office of a public relations firm. She generally dressed for work in "African-styled attire" and wore her hair in "dreadlocks, braids, twists, and cornrows." Her manager, a white male, often complimented Wandra on her hair, jewelry, and clothing. Once he said, "You look like an African princess." On another occasion he told her that her "African-styled dress would make nice pillows for a room in his house with African artifacts and pictures." Shortly after these comments, Wandra was terminated and her position was later filled by another African–American woman. Wandra asserts that "the comments made about her appearance offended her personal dignity and were offensive to her heritage as African–American woman." She also argues that she was replaced by an "African–American whose dress more typically reflects corporate America." Would Wandra have a claim for appearance discrimination under D.C. Code § 1–2502(22)? Would she have a claim for discrimination on the basis of "race plus appearance" under Title VII? *See* McManus v. MCI Comm. Corp., 748 A.2d 949 (D.C.2000). Or is this a case of sex-plus-race-plus appearance? According to Professors Carbado and Gulati, "[t]he social meaning of being a black woman is not monolithic and static but contextual and dynamic. An important way in which it is shaped is by performance. In other words, how black women present their identity can (and often does) affect whether and how they are discriminated against." Devon W. Carbado & Mitu Gulati, *The Fifth Black Woman*, 11 J.Contemp. Legal Issues 701, 717 (2001). Should the courts view Wandra as "the victim of an intra-racial (or intra-gender) distinction based not simply on her identity status as a black woman but on her performance of that identity"? *Id.*

6. *Sexual Attractiveness*: Is it unlawful sex discrimination for a male manager to base an employment decision on a female employee's sexual attractiveness? Consider the following: Sandra is employed to sell men's fragrances in a large up-scale department store. In her first year, Sandra's sales record was one of the best of all sales associates for men's fragrances in the store's regional division. At the end of the year, during a tour of the men's fragrance department, Jack, the new manager of the Designer Fragrance Division, observed Sandra working at her counter. He later told Sandra's supervisor, Elysa, that she should fire Sandra because she was "not good looking enough." Jack said, "Get me somebody hot." *See* Yanowitz v. L'Oreal USA, Inc., 131 Cal.Rptr.2d 575, 582 (2003). If Sandra is fired, does she have a claim for sex discrimination? What if Elysa refuses to carry out

Jack's order to fire Sandra because she believes that it is discriminatory to fire a female employee simply because she is not sufficiently sexually attractive to a male manager? Then Elysa is fired for refusing to carry out the manager's order. Would she have a claim for retaliation under Title VII? *See id.* Retaliation claims under Title VII are discussed in Chapter 15. *See also* Steven Greenhouse, *Going for the Look, But Risking Discrimination*, N.Y.Times, July 13, 2003, at 10 (describing hiring practices at Abercrombie & Fitch).

Should discrimination based on physical appearance be treated differently from dress and grooming codes because it is immutable? Is it unfair to discriminate against people because of bodily or facial characteristics that they cannot change? Professor Robert Post observed that

> American antidiscrimination law singles out for special scrutiny specific categories like race, gender, or appearance precisely because in our world these categories are socially salient and meaningful. We treat people differently depending upon whether they are men or women, black or white, beautiful or ugly. We do so because we have been socialized into a culture in which these differences matter, and matter in systematic ways.

Post, *supra* Note 4, at 17.

7. Employer dress and grooming rules, whether formal or informal, have been the subject of much scholarly criticism. For example, critical legal scholar Karl Klare, who finds such rules "intolerable," has argued that

> [t]he primary social function of appearance law is to empower employers, school officials, judges, and other authority figures to enforce the dominant expectations about appearance and to discipline deviance from the approved social norms. Generally speaking, these official appearance standards denigrate cultural and religious diversity and enforce conformity to white, heterosexual, Christian images of beauty and proper grooming. The rules and standards both exploit and repress female sexuality and punish women who depart from (largely) male-created expectations about proper female behavior and roles. Perhaps the central social function of appearance regulation is to maintain the sexual subordination of women to men.

Karl E. Klare, *Power/Dressing: Regulation of Employee Appearance*, 26 New Eng.L.Rev. 1395, 1398 (1992). For a similar perspective, see generally Mary Whisner, *Gender-Specific Clothing Regulation: A Study in Patriarchy*, 5 Harv.Women's L.J. 73 (1982).

Professor Marc Linder, on the other hand, believes workplace dress requirements should reflect "materialistically pedestrian" concerns for worker health rather than the personal, "self-realizing" goals of "cultural diversity" and "autonomy" that Klare proposes. Marc Linder, *Smart Women, Stupid Shoes, and Cynical Employers: The Unlawfulness and Adverse Health Consequences of Sexually Discriminatory Workplace Footwear Requirements for Female Employees*, 22 J.Corp.L. 295, 298 (1997). In his broad-ranging critique of employers' discriminatory footwear rules, Linder focuses on the serious health effects on female flight attendants of airline requirements that they wear high-heel shoes. Linder notes the "pernicious" disabilities caused by high-heeled shoes ("ninety percent of all forefoot surgery [is performed] on women," *id.* at 296) and proposes that "working women should be permitted, in fact strongly encouraged, to dress in comfortable shoes that resemble the shape of their feet all day long." *Id.* at 329. Despite the difficulty of changing "shoe law" when there has been "virtually no litigation under Title VII over this issue," *id.* at 324, Linder argues that flight attendants could use Title VII sex discrimination law to challenge airline sex-based high-heeled shoe rules.

Professor Katharine Bartlett questions whether the legal concept of equality can "transcend the norms of the community that has produced it." Bartlett, *supra*, at 2545. She urges an approach that, rather than rejecting prevailing sex-based community norms of appearance entirely, deliberately takes them into account

> as an important reference point both for determining whether workplace rules and practices disadvantage women and for defining which discriminatory rules—for strategic as well as legal reasons—might have to be allowed as essential to businesses that, however objectionable from a sex-equality perspective they might be, society is not yet prepared to prohibit.

Id. Which of these approaches, if any, would you endorse? *See also* Karen Engle, *The Persistence of Neutrality: The Failure of the Religious Accommodation Provision to Redeem Title VII*, 76 Tex.L.Rev. 317, 340–52 (1997) (contrasting the "separationist" approach of sex discrimination challenges to dress and grooming codes to the "integrationist" approach found in race and national origin cases and the "accommodationist" approach found in the religious accommodation provision of Title VII). How should employers (or courts) respond to the conflicting claims of autonomy, equality, diversity, discipline, uniformity, and conformity raised in these cases? *See* Marc A. Koonin, *Avoiding Claims of Discrimination Based on Personal Appearance, Grooming, and Hygiene Standards*, 15 Lab.Law. 19 (2000).

Chapter 7

SEX–BASED COMPENSATION SCHEMES

A. INTRODUCTION: WAGE DISCRIMINATION

The two principal federal statutes prohibiting sex-based compensation schemes are Title VII and the Equal Pay Act. In 1963 Congress enacted the Equal Pay Act (EPA), 29 U.S.C. § 206(d), an amendment to the Fair Labor Standards Act that requires covered employers to pay women the same rate of pay as men who perform equal work in the same establishment. The concept of equal pay for equal work was not new, nor was the underlying social and economic problem that the EPA addressed: the gender-based dual wage structure. The disparity between the average wages of men and women—the so-called wage gap—has always been related to a separate phenomenon—the sex-segregation of jobs. Indeed, a sociologist has described pay inequality and the sex-segregation of work as "the twin pillars of women's subordination in the workplace." Ruth Milkman, Gender at Work: The Dynamics of Job Segregation by Sex During World War II, at 153 (1987). For example, a Census Bureau report based on data from the March 2002 Current Population Survey found that "[i]n March 2002, 60 percent of women and 74 percent of men were in the labor force, but the proportions of men and women working in certain occupations differed greatly." U.S. Census Bureau, Women and Men in the United States: March 2002, at 3 (Mar.2003). The report concluded:

> Even though women have made progress in entering occupations predominantly held by men (especially executive and professional specialty occupations), the majority of women were still in traditional "female" occupations [in 2002]. For example, of the 18 million people in administrative support occupations (including clerical), 79 percent were women. In contrast, 91 percent of the 14 million people in precision production, craft, and repair occupations were men.

Id.

The sexual division of labor—and the hierarchical assumptions about gender roles and work that have provided the rationale for sex-based dual wage scales—have long been a feature of American society. In the colonial economy, although many agrarian and commodity production tasks were shared by men and women, the religious and social customs and legal rules defining relations in the patriarchal family encouraged a division of labor along gender lines. These gender divisions persisted as women entered the market for wage labor. Between 1820 and 1860, as America developed from a preindustrial to an industrial society, economic and social changes, as well as attitudes about women's roles, reinforced the gender divisions of wage work. During and after the Civil War, however, a number of traditional male jobs were "feminized." For example, wartime labor shortages created new opportunities for women to work as school teachers, secretaries, bookkeepers, clerks, and retail sales clerks—jobs that had formerly been almost exclusively male occupations. Notably, during the Civil War, the United States Treasury began to employ women as clerks, assigning them to low-level tasks previously performed by men. *See* Margery W. Davies, Woman's Place Is at the Typewriter: Office Work and Office Workers, 1870–1930, at 51–52 (1982). At the time, Congress imposed a statutory sex-based dual wage scale by setting maximum annual salaries for female clerks. *See* Act of Mar. 14, 1864, ch. 30, § 6, 13 Stat. 22 (1864) ($600 maximum); Act of July 23, 1866, ch. 208, §§ 6–7, 14 Stat. 191 (1866) ($900 maximum). As one commentator noted in discussing this legislation, "the federal service from its earliest days marked women as a special class, which by law could be utilized as a cheap labor pool." Cathryn L. Claussen, *Gendered Merit: Women and the Merit Concept in Federal Employment, 1864–1944*, 40 Am.J. Legal Hist. 229, 230 (1996).

The Senate first considered the merits of a proposal for equal pay for women in the federal service in 1870. One senator argued in support of the proposal:

> The question is whether when we are advocating equality of rights, equality of labor, equality of wages, universal equality everywhere, we shall say that a person on account of his or her sex shall not receive equal compensation with a person of the other sex. I trust there will be no such distinction made.
>
> * * * I cannot conceive that a man has one particle of gallantry, to say nothing of love of liberty, who will say that a lady who can do equal service with a man and perform the same labor, standing over a counter or a desk, should not have equal compensation. * * * I have voted to bring up the African to my level, to my standard of equality; and now, sir, surely I will not vote against bringing up the female portion of our citizens to an equal level with ourselves.

Cong.Globe, 41st Cong., 2d Sess.3891 (1870) (statement of Sen. Yates), *quoted in* Claussen, *supra*, at 232. A compromise bill was enacted that gave the heads of federal government departments the authority "to appoint female clerks, who may be found to be competent and worthy, to any of the grades of clerkship known to the law * * * with the compensation belonging to the class to which they may be appointed * * *.'' Act of July 12, 1870, ch. 251, § 2, 16 Stat. 230 (1870), *quoted in* Claussen *supra*, at 233.

With the 1870 legislation, statutory wage ceilings for female clerks in the federal civil service were formally abandoned, but the discretionary authority of department heads, in effect, permitted informal dual wage scales and ultimately led to the sex-segregation of many government jobs. The Pendleton Act—the Civil Service Act of 1883—introduced merit hiring on the basis of competitive examinations, opening some new government jobs to women and increasing the proportion of women in the federal civil service. Claussen, *supra*, at 237–38. But occupational sex-segregation was by then firmly established. For example, by the first part of the twentieth century, women dominated clerical work in both the public and private sector. *Id.* at 239. During World War I, "women poured into jobs vacated by men, as well as many of the 100,000 newly created war preparation jobs,'' and "by the war's end, overwhelming occupational segregation had evolved, and wage disparities between the sexes persisted.'' *Id.* at 239–40. *See generally* Valerie Jean Conner, The National War Labor Board: Stability, Social Justice, and the Voluntary State in World War I, at 142–57 (1983); Maurine Weiner Greenwald, Women, War, and Work: The Impact of World War I on Women Workers in the United States 3–45 (1980).

Formal recognition of the concept of equal pay for equal work followed women's suffrage and active reform efforts by women's organizations. Claussen, *supra*, at 241. By 1919, two states—Michigan and Montana—had adopted equal pay statutes that reached private employers. *See* Carin Ann Clauss, *Comparable Worth—The Theory, Its Legal Foundation, and the Feasibility of Implementation*, 20 U.Mich.J.L.Ref. 7, 12 (1986). In 1923, Congress enacted legislation that classified jobs and pay scales in the federal civil service and acknowledged the merit principle by mandating equal pay for equal work. *Id.* (discussing the Classification Act of 1923, ch. 265, 42 Stat. 954 (repealed 1949)). The 1923 Act provided that "[i]n determining the rate of compensation which an employee shall receive, the principle of equal compensation for equal work irrespective of sex shall be followed.'' Classification Act of 1923, § 4, 42 Stat. 1488. "[A]lthough [the Act] theoretically ended the practice of sex-typing of jobs, by the time of its enactment, occupational segregation and the corollary wage disparities had become entrenched in the federal workplace, with over ninety percent of all women in clerical positions.'' Claussen, *supra*, at 242.

While World War I had "primarily occasioned a shift within the female labor force, rather than a movement of non-wage earning women into categories of paid labor,'' during World War II, the number of women in the workforce grew by six million, a 50 percent increase. Greenwald, *supra*, at 13. In her study of the electrical and automobile industries during the second world war, Professor Milkman commented:

World War II was a major turning point in the history of America's working women. Wartime mobilization swept aside the traditional sexual division of labor, and women entered "men's jobs" in basic industry on a massive scale. Women showed that they were fully capable of performing such work. Yet after the war, they were forced back into traditionally female occupations, or out of the labor market altogether. This was no mere temporary setback. Although the number of women has increased rapidly in recent decades, the vast majority are confined to "pink-collar" jobs, while men continue to predominate in the better-paid manufacturing jobs from which women were expelled during demobilization.

Ruth Milkman, Gender at Work: The Dynamics of Job Segregation by Sex During World War II, at 1 (1987).

During World War II, the goal of equal pay was significant for some unions concerned with "protecting the wages of 'men's jobs' in the face of wartime female substitution." *Id.* at 9. In 1942, in carrying out its function to stabilize wages and avert labor strife, the National War Labor Board—concerned with the effects of pay disparities based on both race and gender—formally adopted the principle that " '[i]ncreases which equalize the wage or salary rates paid to females with the rates paid to males for comparable quality and quantity of work on the same or similar operations * * * may be made without approval of the National War Labor Board * * *.' " National War Labor Board, General Order No. 16, Nov. 24, 1942, *quoted in* Clauss, *supra*, at 13; *see also*, Milkman, *supra*, at 65–84 (discussing War Labor Board equal pay decisions in the auto and electrical industries). The experiences of the War Labor Board with setting wartime wage ceilings and adjusting private wage disputes, prompted Congress to propose the first federal equal pay law in 1945. S. 1178, 79th Cong., 1st Sess. (1945); *see* Clauss, *supra*, at 13–14.

Equal pay bills were introduced in every session of Congress over the next eighteen years. In 1963, after changing the language of the bill from "work of *comparable* character on jobs the performance of which requires *comparable* skills" to "*equal* work on jobs the performance of which requires *equal* skills," Congress finally approved the Equal Pay Act. *See* Clauss, *supra*, at 14 (emphasis added). President Kennedy signed the Act on June 10, 1963. Equal Pay Act of 1963, Pub. L. No. 88–38, 77 Stat. 56. The relevant language of the statute provides:

(1) No employer having employees subject to any provisions of this section shall discriminate, within any establishment in which such employees are employed, between employees on the basis of sex by paying wages to employees in such establishment at a rate less than the rate at which he pays wages to employees of the opposite sex in such establishment for equal work on jobs the performance of which requires equal skill, effort, and responsibility, and which are performed under similar working conditions, except where such payment is made pursuant to (i) a seniority system; (ii) a merit

system; (iii) a system which measures earnings by quantity or quality of production; or (iv) a differential based on any other factor other than sex: *Provided*, That an employer who is paying a wage rate differential in violation of this subsection shall not, in order to comply with the provisions of this subsection, reduce the wage rate of any employee.

29 U.S.C. § 206(d)(1). Shortly after the Equal Pay Act went effect on June 11, 1964, Congress enacted Title VII, including language in § 703(h)—the Bennett Amendment—that refers to the Equal Pay Act. The two statutes now offer alternative, but complementary, bases for challenging sex-based disparities in employers' compensation schemes.

Section B of this chapter examines doctrines that have developed in claims brought solely under the Equal Pay Act. Section C discusses the Bennett Amendment to Title VII and explores the difficulties the courts face in attempting to harmonize the relationship between Title VII and the Equal Pay Act. Section D addresses the significance of theories of comparable worth in Title VII wage discrimination cases. Finally, Section E deals with employer liability and defenses under Title VII for sex-based fringe benefits.

B. THE EQUAL PAY ACT OF 1963

CORNING GLASS WORKS v. BRENNAN

Supreme Court of the United States, 1974.
417 U.S. 188, 94 S.Ct. 2223, 41 L.Ed.2d 1.

JUSTICE MARSHALL delivered the opinion of the Court.

These cases arise under the Equal Pay Act of 1963, 29 U.S.C. § 206(d)(1), which added to § 6 of the Fair Labor Standards Act of 1938 the principle of equal pay for equal work regardless of sex. The principal question posed is whether Corning Glass Works violated the Act by paying a higher base wage to male night shift inspectors than it paid to female inspectors performing the same tasks on the day shift, where the higher wage was paid in addition to a separate night shift differential paid to all employees for night work. * * *

I

Prior to 1925, Corning operated its plants in Wellsboro and Corning only during the day, and all inspection work was performed by women. Between 1925 and 1930, the company began to introduce automatic production equipment which made it desirable to institute a night shift. During this period, however, both New York and Pennsylvania law prohibited women from working at night. As a result, in order to fill inspector positions on the new night shift, the company had to recruit male employees from among its male dayworkers. The male employees so transferred demanded and received wages substantially higher than those paid to women inspectors engaged on the two day shifts.[3] During this same period, however, no plant-wide shift differential existed and male employees working at night, other than inspectors, received the same wages as their day shift counterparts. Thus a situation developed where the night inspectors were all male,[4] the day inspectors all female, and the male inspectors received significantly higher wages.

In 1944, Corning plants at both locations were organized by a labor union and a collective-bargaining agreement was negotiated for all production and maintenance employees. This agreement for the first time established a plant-wide shift differential, but this change did not eliminate the higher base wage paid to male night inspectors. Rather, the shift differential was superimposed on the existing difference in base wages between male night inspectors and female day inspectors.

Prior to June 11, 1964, the effective date of the Equal Pay Act, the law in both Pennsylvania and New York was amended to permit women to work at night. It was not until some time after the effective date of the Act, however, that Corning initiated efforts to eliminate the differential rates for male and female inspectors. Beginning in June 1966, Corning started to open up jobs on the night shift to women. Previously separate male and female seniority lists were consolidated and women became eligible to exercise their seniority, on the same basis as men, to bid for the higher paid night inspection jobs as vacancies occurred.

On January 20, 1969, a new collective-bargaining agreement went into effect, establishing a new "job evaluation" system for setting wage rates. The new agreement abolished for the future the separate base wages for day and night shift inspectors and imposed a uniform base wage for inspectors exceeding the wage rate for the night shift previously in effect. All inspectors hired after January 20, 1969, were to receive the same base wage, whatever their sex or shift. The collective-bargaining agreement further provided, however, for a higher "red circle" rate for employees hired prior to January 20, 1969, when working as inspectors on the night shift. This "red circle" rate served essentially to perpetuate the differential in base wages between day and night inspectors.

The Secretary of Labor brought these cases to enjoin Corning from violating the Equal Pay Act and to collect back wages allegedly due female employees because of past violations. Three distinct questions are presented: (1) Did Corning ever violate the Equal Pay Act by paying male night shift inspectors more than female day shift inspectors? (2) If so, did Corning cure its violation of the Act in 1966 by permitting women to work as night shift inspectors? (3) Finally, if the violation was not

3. Higher wages were demanded in part because the men had been earning more money on their day shift jobs than women were paid for inspection work. * * * There is also some evidence in the record that additional compensation was necessary because the men viewed inspection jobs as "demeaning" and as "women's work."

4. A temporary exception was made during World War II when manpower shortages caused Corning to be permitted to employ women on the steady night shift inspection jobs at both locations. It appears that women night inspectors during this period were paid the same higher night shift wages earned by men.

remedied in 1966, did Corning cure its violation in 1969 by equalizing day and night inspector wage rates but establishing higher "red circle" rates for existing employees working on the night shift?

II

Congress' purpose in enacting the Equal Pay Act was to remedy what was perceived to be a serious and endemic problem of employment discrimination in private industry—the fact that the wage structure of "many segments of American industry has been based on an ancient but outmoded belief that a man, because of his role in society, should be paid more than a woman even though his duties are the same." S.Rep. No. 176, 88th Cong., 1st Sess., 1 (1963). The solution adopted was quite simple in principle: to require that "equal work will be rewarded by equal wages." *Id.*

The Act's basic structure and operation are similarly straightforward. In order to make out a case under the Act, the Secretary must show that an employer pays different wages to employees of opposite sexes "for equal work on jobs the performance of which requires equal skill, effort, and responsibility, and which are performed under similar working conditions." Although the Act is silent on this point, its legislative history makes plain that the Secretary has the burden of proof on this issue, as both of the courts below recognized.

The Act also establishes four exceptions—three specific and one a general catchall provision—where different payment to employees of opposite sexes "is made pursuant to (i) a seniority system; (ii) a merit system; (iii) a system which measures earnings by quantity or quality of production; or (iv) a differential based on any other factor other than sex." Again, while the Act is silent on this question, its structure and history also suggest that once the Secretary has carried his burden of showing that the employer pays workers of one sex more than workers of the opposite sex for equal work, the burden shifts to the employer to show that the differential is justified under one of the Act's four exceptions. All of the many lower courts that have considered this question have so held, and this view is consistent with the general rule that the application of an exemption under the Fair Labor Standards Act is a matter of affirmative defense on which the employer has the burden of proof.

The contentions of the parties in this case reflect the Act's underlying framework. Corning argues that the Secretary has failed to prove that Corning ever violated the Act because day shift work is not "performed under similar working conditions" as night shift work. The Secretary maintains that day shift and night shift work are performed under "similar working conditions" within the meaning of the Act. Although the Secretary recognizes that higher wages may be paid for night shift work, the Secretary contends that such a shift differential would be based upon a "factor other than sex" within the catchall exception to the Act and that Corning has failed to carry its burden of proof that its higher base wage for male night inspectors was in fact based on any factor other than sex.

* * *

The most notable feature of the history of the Equal Pay Act is that Congress recognized early in the legislative process that the concept of equal pay for equal work was more readily stated in principle than reduced to statutory language which would be meaningful to employers and workable across the broad range of industries covered by the Act. * * *

* * *

In comparison to the rather complex job evaluation plans used by industry, the definition of equal work used in the first drafts of the Equal Pay bill was criticized as unduly vague and incomplete. * * * [Industry representatives] repeatedly urged that the bill be amended to include an exception for job classification systems, or otherwise to incorporate the language of job evaluation into the bill. * * *

We think it plain that in amending the bill's definition of equal work to its present form, the Congress acted in direct response to these pleas. * * *

Indeed, the most telling evidence of congressional intent is the fact that the Act's amended definition of equal work incorporated the specific language of the job evaluation plan described at the hearings by Corning's own representative—that is, the concepts of "skill," "effort," "responsibility," and "working conditions."

Congress' intent, as manifested in this history, was to use these terms to incorporate into the new federal Act the well-defined and well-accepted principles of job evaluation so as to ensure that wage differentials based upon bona fide job evaluation plans would be outside the purview of the Act. * * *

While a layman might well assume that time of day worked reflects one aspect of a job's "working conditions," the term has a different and much more specific meaning in the language of industrial relations. As Corning's own representative testified at the hearings, the element of working conditions encompasses two subfactors: "surroundings" and "hazards." "Surroundings" measures the elements, such as toxic chemicals or fumes, regularly encountered by a worker, their intensity, and their frequency. "Hazards" takes into account the physical hazards regularly encountered, their frequency, and the severity of injury they can cause. This definition of "working conditions" is not only manifested in Corning's own job evaluation plans but is also well accepted across a wide range of American industry.

Nowhere in any of these definitions is time of day worked mentioned as a relevant criterion. The fact of the matter is that the concept of "working conditions," as used in the specialized language of job evaluation systems, simply does not encompass shift differentials. Indeed, while

Corning now argues that night inspection work is not equal to day inspection work, all of its own job evaluation plans, including the one now in effect, have consistently treated them as equal in all respects, including working conditions. And Corning's Manager of Job Evaluation testified * * * that time of day worked was not considered to be a "working condition." Significantly, it is not the Secretary in this case who is trying to look behind Corning's bona fide job evaluation system to require equal pay for jobs which Corning has historically viewed as unequal work. Rather, it is Corning which asks us to differentiate between jobs which the company itself has always equated. We agree with the Second Circuit that the inspection work at issue in this case, whether performed during the day or night, is "equal work" as that term is defined in the Act.[24]

This does not mean, of course, that there is no room in the Equal Pay Act for nondiscriminatory shift differentials. Work on a steady night shift no doubt has psychological and physiological impacts making it less attractive than work on a day shift. The Act contemplates that a male night worker may receive a higher wage than a female day worker, just as it contemplates that a male employee with 20 years' seniority can receive a higher wage than a woman with two years' seniority. Factors such as these play a role under the Act's four exceptions the seniority differential under the specific seniority exception, the shift differential under the catchall exception for differentials "based on any other factor other than sex."[25]

The question remains, however, whether Corning carried its burden of proving that the higher rate paid for night inspection work, until 1966 performed solely by men, was in fact intended to serve as compensation for night work, or rather constituted an added payment based upon sex. We agree that the record amply supports the District Court's conclusion that Corning had not sustained its burden of proof. As its history revealed, "the higher night rate was in large part the product of the generally higher wage level of male workers and the need to compensate them for performing what were regarded as demeaning tasks." The differential in base wages originated at a time when no other night employees received higher pay than corresponding day workers, and it was maintained long after the company instituted a separate plant-wide shift differential which was thought to compensate adequately for the additional burdens of night work. The differential arose simply because men would not work at the low rates paid women inspectors, and it

---

24. In [the Second Circuit case], Corning also claimed that the night inspection work was not equal to day shift inspection work because night shift inspectors had to do a certain amount of packing, lifting, and cleaning which was not performed by day shift inspectors. Noting that it is now well settled that jobs need not be identical in every respect before the Equal Pay Act is applicable, the Court of Appeals concluded that the extra work performed by night inspectors was of so little consequence that the jobs remained substantially equal. The company has not pursued this issue here.

25. An administrative interpretation by the Wage and Hour Administrator recognizes the legitimacy of night shift differentials shown to be based on a factor other than sex. See 29 C.F.R. § 800.145 (1973).

reflected a job market in which Corning could pay women less than men for the same work. That the company took advantage of such a situation may be understandable as a matter of economics, but its differential nevertheless became illegal once Congress enacted into law the principle of equal pay for equal work.

III

We now must consider whether Corning continued to remain in violation of the Act after 1966 when, without changing the base wage rates for day and night inspectors, it began to permit women to bid for jobs on the night shift as vacancies occurred. It is evident that this was more than a token gesture to end discrimination, as turnover in the night shift inspection jobs was rapid. * * * Relying on these facts, the company argues that it ceased discriminating against women in 1966, and was no longer in violation of the Equal Pay Act.

But the issue before us is not whether the company, in some abstract sense, can be said to have treated men the same as women after 1966. Rather, the question is whether the company remedied the specific violation of the Act which the Secretary proved. We agree with the Second Circuit, as well as with all other circuits that have had occasion to consider this issue, that the company could not cure its violation except by equalizing the base wages of female day inspectors with the higher rates paid the night inspectors. This result is implicit in the Act's language, its statement of purpose, and its legislative history.

As the Second Circuit noted, Congress enacted the Equal Pay Act "[r]ecognizing the weaker bargaining position of many women and believing that discrimination in wage rates represented unfair employer exploitation of this source of cheap labor." In response to evidence of the many families dependent on the income of working women, Congress included in the Act's statement of purpose a finding that "the existence * * * of wage differentials based on sex * * * depresses wages and living standards for employees necessary for their health and efficiency." Pub.L. 88—38, § 2(a) (1), 77 Stat. 56 (1963). And Congress declared it to be the policy of the Act to correct this condition. § 2(b).

To achieve this end, Congress required that employers pay equal pay for equal work and then specified:

> *Provided*, That an employer who is paying a wage rate differential in violation of this subsection shall not, in order to comply with the provisions of this subsection, reduce the wage rate of any employee. 29 U.S.C. § 206(d)(1).

The purpose of this proviso was to ensure that to remedy violations of the Act, "[t]he lower wage rate must be increased to the level of the higher." H.R.Rep. No. 309, 88th Cong., 1st Sess., 3 (1963). Comments of individual legislators are all consistent with this view. Representative Dwyer remarked, for example, "The objective of equal pay legislation * * * is not to drag down men workers to the wage levels of women, but to raise women to the levels enjoyed by men in cases where discrimination is still practiced." 109 Cong.Rec. 2714 (1963). * * *

By proving that after the effective date of the Equal Pay Act, Corning paid female day inspectors less than male night inspectors for equal work, the Secretary implicitly demonstrated that the wages of female day shift inspectors were unlawfully depressed and that the fair wage for inspection work was the base wage paid to male inspectors on the night shift. The whole purpose of the Act was to require that these depressed wages be raised, in part as a matter of simple justice to the employees themselves, but also as a matter of market economics, since Congress recognized as well that discrimination in wages on the basis of sex "constitutes an unfair method of competition." Pub.L. 88–38, § 2(a)(5).

We agree with Judge Friendly [in the Second Circuit case below] that

> In light of this apparent congressional understanding, we cannot hold that Corning, by allowing some—or even many—women to move into the higher paid night jobs, achieved full compliance with the Act. Corning's action still left the inspectors on the day shift— virtually all women—earning a lower base wage than the night shift inspectors because of a differential initially based on sex and still not justified by any other consideration; in effect, Corning was still taking advantage of the availability of female labor to fill its day shift at a differentially low wage rate not justified by any factor other than sex. 474 F.2d 226, 235 (1973).

The Equal Pay Act is broadly remedial, and it should be construed and applied so as to fulfill the underlying purposes which Congress sought to achieve. If, as the Secretary proved, the work performed by women on the day shift was equal to that performed by men on the night shift, the company became obligated to pay the women the same base wage as their male counterparts on the effective date of the Act. To permit the company to escape that obligation by agreeing to allow some women to work on the night shift at a higher rate of pay as vacancies occurred would frustrate, not serve, Congress' ends.

The company's final contention—that it cured its violation of the Act when a new collective-bargaining agreement went into effect on January 20, 1969—need not detain us long. While the new agreement provided for equal base wages for night or day inspectors hired after that date, it continued to provide unequal base wages for employees hired before that date, a discrimination likely to continue for some time into the future because of a large number of laid-off employees who had to be offered re-employment before new inspectors could be hired. * * * We therefore conclude that on the facts of this case, the company's continued discrimination in base wages between night and day workers, though phrased in terms of a neutral factor other than sex, nevertheless operated to perpetuate the effects of the company's prior illegal practice of paying women less than men for equal work.

* * *

JUSTICE STEWART took no part in the consideration or decision of these cases.

[CHIEF JUSTICE BURGER and JUSTICES BLACKMUN and REHNQUIST dissented and filed a statement.]

Notes and Questions

1. *The Elements of a Prima Facie Case Under the Equal Pay Act*: To make out a prima facie EPA case against a covered employer, a plaintiff must establish that (1) in the same establishment, (2) the employer pays different wages to employees of the opposite sex, (3) who perform equal work on jobs requiring equal skill, effort, and responsibility, and (4) the jobs are performed under similar working conditions. Unlike a Title VII case of disparate treatment, "proof of discriminatory intent is not required to establish a prima facie case under the Equal Pay Act." Peters v. City of Shreveport, 818 F.2d 1148, 1153 (5th Cir.1987), *cert. dismissed*, 485 U.S. 930, 108 S.Ct. 1101, 99 L.Ed.2d 264 (1988).

2. *The "Establishment" Requirement*: The term "establishment" is not defined in the Fair Labor Standards Act (FLSA), but in an early case construing the FLSA, the Supreme Court held that the term means what it "normally [means] in business and government"—"a distinct physical place of business." A. H. Phillips, Inc. v. Walling, 324 U.S. 490, 496, 65 S.Ct. 807, 810, 89 L.Ed. 1095 (1945). Under the Equal Pay Act, however, courts have tended to construe broadly the requirement that the EPA violation occur "within any establishment." Thus, where the employer maintains centralized control and administration of separate job sites, it will generally be deemed a single establishment under the EPA. *See* Mulhall v. Advance Security, Inc., 19 F.3d 586, 591–92 & 591 n.11 (11th Cir.) (collecting cases), *cert. denied*, 513 U.S. 919, 115 S.Ct. 298, 130 L.Ed.2d 212 (1994); Marshall v. Dallas Indep. Sch. Dist., 605 F.2d 191, 194 (5th Cir.1979) (holding that, for purposes of an EPA claim, all the schools in a school district are a single establishment). Unless the plaintiff presents evidence of "unusual circumstances," however, the EEOC presumes the term "establishment" means "a distinct physical place of business rather than * * * an entire business or 'enterprise' which may include several separate places of business." 29 C.F.R. § 1620.9(a). The EEOC Interpretive Guidelines continue:

(b) Unusual circumstances may call for two or more distinct physical portions of a business enterprise being treated as a single establishment. For example, a central administrative unit may hire all employees, set wages, and assign the location of employment; employees may frequently interchange work location; and daily duties may be virtually identical and performed under similar working conditions.

29 C.F.R. § 1620.9(b).

In many situations, a broad reading of the establishment requirement will permit a plaintiff who works in a small branch office of a larger enterprise to find in another branch office an appropriate opposite-sex comparator who receives higher wages. A large corporation with many offices or factories throughout the nation generally would not want its employees in low-wage areas of the country to be able to compare their wage rates with the premium wages paid to opposite-sex employees in high-wage areas—such as Boston, New York City, or San Francisco. But this may not always be the case. In *Meeks v. Computer Associates International*, 15 F.3d 1013, 1017 (11th Cir.1994), the employer urged the court to adopt a broad, functional definition of "establishment" that would require the plaintiff, a technical writer, to compare her salary to the company's 116 technical writers—36 male and 80 female—who were located throughout the nation. The company's evidence that it maintained centralized control of personnel, salary, and work assignments, however, was not sufficient to overcome the presumption against treating multiple offices as a single establishment. The court ruled that plaintiff's wages should be compared to those of one higher paid male co-worker in her Florida office. In this situation, the court's narrow reading of the establishment requirement permitted the plaintiff's case to go forward. Do you believe that the court would have adopted this view of the employer's evidence if there had been no male technical writers working in the plaintiff's small-town Florida office?

3   *Equal Work*: To establish a prima facie case under the Equal Pay Act, a female plaintiff does not need to demonstrate that the job she performs is identical to a higher paid job held by a male in the same establishment. Rather, she has to establish only that the two jobs are "substantially equal." *See, e.g.*, Tomka v. Seiler Corp. 66 F.3d 1295, 1310 (2d Cir.1995); Sprague v. Thorn Americas, Inc., 129 F.3d 1355, 1364 (10th Cir.1997) (requiring an EPA plaintiff to show that the jobs at issue are "substantially equal" in terms of "skill," "effort," "responsibility," and "working conditions"). Courts consider the duties actually performed in each job, not the title or job description used by the employer. *See, e.g.*, EEOC v. Grinnell Corp., 881 F.Supp. 406, 410 (S.D.Ind.1995). In determining whether two jobs are substantially equal, courts generally will make an "overall comparison of the work" rather than examining the "individual segments." Buntin v. Breathitt County Bd. of Educ., 134 F.3d 796, 799 (6th Cir.1998). But one court stressed that the equal work comparison should be made "factor by factor with the male comparator." Houck v. Virginia Polytech. Inst., 10 F.3d 204, 206 (4th Cir.1993). Should the level of scrutiny that a court uses in making the equal work comparison depend on the nature of the job? Would you expect courts to be more exacting in comparing jobs in professional occupations as opposed to semi-skilled or technical jobs?

Is a job as a mathematics instructor at a community college substantially equal to the job of an instructor in the college's biology department? What additional information about the two positions would you like to know in order to reach a decision? *See* Strag v. Board of Trustees, 55 F.3d 943 (4th Cir.1995). Are there any special concerns that courts should consider in Equal Pay Act cases involving academic institutions as employers? *See generally* Laura Woodworth Keohane, *Universities, Colleges and the Equal Pay Act: The Fourth Circuit Analyzes a Salary Dispute in* Strag v. Board of Trustees, 19 Campbell L.Rev. 333 (1997).

4. *The Opposite–Sex Comparator(s)*: Selecting an appropriate opposite-sex comparator (or comparators) is an important part of a plaintiff's prima facie case under the Equal Pay Act. An individual female plaintiff can use a single male comparator, although, as one court noted, "it is generally unwise to rely on such a small number of comparater[s] [sic]." Mullenix v. Forsyth Dental Infirmary for Children, 965 F.Supp. 120, 139 (D.Mass.1996). If the plaintiff fails to select a sufficient number of appropriate comparators, the employer may be able to show that, while the plaintiff is paid marginally less than the male comparator or comparators she selected, she also earns marginally more than others who should have been included. *See* Brousard–Norcross v. Augustana College Assoc., 935 F.2d 974, 979 (8th Cir.1991); Sigmon v. Parker Chapin Flattau & Klimpl, 901 F.Supp. 667, 679 (S.D.N.Y. 1995) (plaintiff, an attorney, failed to make out a prima facie case under the Equal Pay Act where she was paid more than some male associates with equal experience, even though one male associate with less experience received a higher salary). For a discussion of the conflicting rulings regarding the appropriate number of opposite-sex comparators needed to establish a prima facie case under the Equal Pay Act, see *Hennick v. Schwans Sales Enterprises*, 168 F.Supp.2d 938, 947–50 (N.D.Iowa 2001) (holding that a sex-based wage discrimination case could be established with proof that at least one opposite-sex comparator was paid more than the plaintiff for equal work).

If there are no appropriate opposite-sex comparators currently employed in the same establishment, a female plaintiff can use evidence that a male predecessor or successor in her present job received higher wages. *See* Gandy v. Sullivan County, Tenn., 24 F.3d 861 (6th Cir.1994). For example, a plaintiff can establish a prima facie wage discrimination case with evidence that, without receiving a raise or a promotion, she assumed the duties of her former supervisor when he retired. Hunt v. Nebraska Pub. Power, 282 F.3d 1021, 1030–31 (8th Cir.2002). Class comparisons may also be made based on the sex-based wage differentials of groups of employees who perform the same job. In these cases, "perfect diversity" of the sexes between the two groups is not necessary. Peters v. City of Shreveport, 818 F.2d 1148, 1164 (5th Cir.1987). In *Corning Glass Works*, the fact that a few women were employed on the higher-paid night shift did not bar the Equal Pay Act claims of the lower-paid women on the day shift.

5. *Unequal Pay*: "Compensation," of course, is a much broader concept than just wages and would include fringe benefits such as insurance and pensions. Moreover, a plaintiff's prima facie case requires only proof of an unequal *rate* of pay, not unequal *total remuneration*. Bence v. Detroit Health Corp., 712 F.2d 1024 (6th cir.1983), *cert. denied*, 465 U.S. 1025, 104 S.Ct. 1281, 79 L.Ed.2d 685 (1984). Consistent with regulations and judicial decisions interpreting the term "wages" under the Fair Labor Standards Act, courts have similarly interpreted "wages" under the Equal Pay Act to include the value of goods or services that employees receive, such as uniforms or lodging that are not provided "primarily for the benefit or convenience of the employer." Laffey v. Northwest Airlines, 642 F.2d 578,

588 (D.C.Cir.1980). Should the concept of compensation also include the value of job security—such as academic tenure—or status within the company hierarchy? Should the "intrinsic rewards" of a job such as "a sense of accomplishment attained from the job, its challenge, variety, and degree of autonomy" be valued as part of an employee's compensation? Nicholas J. Mathys & Laura B. Pincus, *Is Pay Equity Equitable? A Perspective that Looks Beyond Pay*, 44 Lab.L.J. 351, 352 (1993). Or are these factors considered part of the job content or working conditions?

6. *Similar Working Conditions*: In *Corning Glass Works,* the Supreme Court adopted a narrow definition of "working conditions" based on the technical "language of industrial relations" that Congress utilized in drafting the Equal Pay Act. Under the facts of *Corning*, this construction of the term permitted the day-shift plaintiffs to compare their wages to the wages paid to the predominantly male night-shift inspectors for purposes of establishing a prima facie case under the Equal Pay Act. Should Congress amend the Act to include "psychological and physiological impacts" as well as physical "surroundings" and "hazards" within the definition of "working conditions"? Does the *Corning* definition accurately account for the significant similarities and differences between the working conditions of many jobs in post-industrial society? Would a broader definition make it easier or more difficult for plaintiffs to make out a prima facie Equal Pay Act case?

7. *The Equal Pay Act's Four Affirmative Defenses*: The Equal Pay Act allows an employer to pay employees of the opposite sex unequal wages "pursuant to (i) a seniority system; (ii) a merit system; (iii) a system which measures earnings by quantity or quality of production; or (iv) a differential based on any other factor other than sex * * *." 29 U.S.C. § 206(d).

a. *The "Merit System" Defense:* How is merit different from seniority? How can an employer insure that "merit" raises are actually based on merit and not on factors unrelated to merit, such as nepotism or sex? One court has defined a merit system that meets the EPA affirmative defense as "an organized and structured procedure whereby employees are evaluated systematically according to predetermined criteria." EEOC v. Aetna Ins. Co., 616 F.2d 719, 725 (4th Cir.1980) What advice would you give to an employer regarding its implementation and administration of a merit system in order to be sure that it can satisfy a "merit system" affirmative defense under the EPA? *See* Ryduchowski v. Port Auth. of N.Y. & N.J., 203 F.3d 135, 142–43 (2d Cir.2000) (collecting cases that rely on the "merit system" defense).

b. *A "Factor Other Than Sex"*: The "catch-all" fourth affirmative defense under the Equal Pay Act, "any other factor other than sex," is susceptible to varying interpretations, and the courts have found it difficult to develop appropriate standards for the defense. For discussion of the developments in the case law, see Ellen M. Bowden, *Closing the Pay Gap: Redefining the Equal Pay Act's Fourth Affirmative Defense*, 27 Colum.J.L. & Soc.Probs. 225 (1994). The Supreme Court has dealt with the defense in two cases other than *Corning Glass*, but has yet to articulate a comprehensive theory of the defense. In *City of Los Angeles Department of Water & Power v. Manhart*, 435 U.S. 702, 98 S.Ct. 1370, 55 L.Ed.2d 657 (1978), reproduced in Section E of this chapter, the Court indicated that the relative average greater costs of employing one sex would not qualify as a factor other than sex. See also the discussion of the cost justification defense under Title VII in *EEOC v. Consolidated Service Systems* in Chapter 3, in *Wards Cove* in Chapter 4, and in *Southwest Airlines* in Note 9 following *Johnson Controls* in Chapter 6. Also, in *County of Washington v. Gunther*, 452 U.S. 161, 101 S.Ct. 2242, 68 L.Ed.2d 751 (1981), discussed in Section C of this chapter, the Court held that the Equal Pay Act defenses are applicable to a sex-based wage discrimination claim brought solely under Title VII.

8.   *Salary Policies*: As discussed in the following four notes, the lower courts have attempted to develop theories of the EPA's fourth affirmative defense in cases involving sex-based pay disparities resulting from prior salary or salary retention policies.

a.   *Prior Salary*: In *Kouba v. Allstate Insurance Co.*, 691 F.2d 873 (9th Cir.1982), the employer used each new employee's "ability, education, experience, and prior salary" to determine her minimum wage guarantee. *Id.* at 874. This minimum salary was the only compensation paid until an eight-to-thirteen week training period was completed. Then new agents earned the minimum guaranteed wage or sales commissions, whichever was greater. The court found that, because of this compensation scheme, female sales agents were paid less, on average, than male agents. Although the case was brought under Title VII rather than the Equal Pay Act, the employer defended its use of prior salary to determine wages as a "factor other than sex" under the EPA. (In the Bennett Amendment, discussed *infra* Section C, the affirmative defenses of the Equal Pay Act were incorporated into Title VII.)

The court in *Kouba* considered several possible interpretations of the "factor other than sex" defense. One theory would allow the defense only when the challenged practice is facially discriminatory on the basis of sex. A second approach would also permit the defense in cases where all the women employees in a particular establishment are paid less than the men. The court rejected these two theories on the ground that "they would tolerate all but the most blatant" forms of sex-based wage discrimination. *Id.* at 876. A third interpretation, urged by the female sales agents in *Kouba*, would allow the defense only if the employer could show that the wage structure did not perpetuate a history of sex discrimination. The court rejected this approach because it would deny an employer the opportunity to base wages on clearly legitimate factors. In addition, the court observed that "[w]hile Congress fashioned the Equal Pay Act to help cure long-standing societal ills, it also intended to exempt factors such as training and experience that may reflect opportunities denied to women in the past." *Id.*

The court proceeded to articulate a theory that is analogous to a legitimate business necessity defense under Title VII:

> The Equal Pay Act concerns business practices. It would be nonsensical to sanction the use of a factor that rests on some consideration unrelated to business. An employer thus cannot use a factor which causes a wage differential between male and female employees absent an acceptable business reason. Conversely, a factor used to effectuate some business policy is not prohibited simply because a wage differential results.

Even with a business-related requirement, an employer might assert some business reason as a pretext for a discriminatory objective. This possibility is especially great with a factor like prior salary which can easily be used to capitalize on the unfairly low salaries historically paid to women. The ability of courts to protect against such abuse is somewhat limited, however. The Equal Pay Act entrusts employers, not judges, with making the often uncertain decision of how to accomplish business objectives. We have found no authority giving guidance on the proper judicial inquiry absent direct evidence of discriminatory intent. A pragmatic standard, which protects against abuse yet accommodates employer discretion, is that the employer must use the factor reasonably in light of the employer's stated purpose as well as its other practices. The specific relevant considerations will of course vary with the situation.

Kouba, 691 F.2d at 876–77.

In remanding the case, the Ninth Circuit explained how the district court should use this test to evaluate the two business reasons that Allstate claimed were the basis for its use of prior salary to set wages:

Allstate asserts that it ties the guaranteed monthly minimum to prior salary as part of a sales-incentive program. If the monthly minimum far exceeds the amount that the agent earned previously, the agent might become complacent and not fulfill his or her selling potential. By limiting the monthly minimum according to prior salary, Allstate hopes to motivate the agent to make sales, earn commissions, and thus improve his or her financial position. Presumably, Allstate cannot set a uniform monthly minimum so low that it motivates all sales agents, because then prospective agents with substantially higher prior salaries might not risk taking a job with Allstate.

This reasoning does not explain Allstate's use of prior salary during the initial training period. Because the agents cannot earn commissions at that time, there is no potential reward to motivate them to make sales.

* * *

Reasoning that salary corresponds roughly to an employee's ability, Allstate also claims that it uses prior salary to predict a new employee's performance as a sales agent. Relevant considerations in evaluating the reasonableness of this practice include (1) whether the employer also uses other available predictors of the new employee's performance, (2) whether the employer attributes less significance to prior salary once the employee has proven himself or herself on the job, and (3) whether the employer relies more heavily on salary when the prior job resembles the job of sales agent.

Id. at 877–78.

b. *Prior Salary and Market Demand*: A third business reason advanced by the employer in *Kouba* was that "an individual with a higher prior salary can demand more in the marketplace." *Kouba*, 691 F.2d at 877 n.7. The court noted that "[c]ourts disagree whether market demand can ever justify a wage differential." *Id.*; *see id. comparing* Horner v. Mary Inst., 613 F.2d

706, 714 (8th Cir.1980) (allowing the market-demand defense in limited situations), *with* Futran v. RING Radio Co., 501 F.Supp. 734, 739 (N.D.Ga. 1980) (disallowing the market-demand defense in all circumstances). In any event, in *Kouba*, the employer had failed to present any evidence in support of a market-demand defense.

Could a university defend its decision to pay a higher salary to a female chemistry professor than to a similarly qualified male chemistry professor using a market demand argument that because of the shortage of qualified female chemistry Ph.D.'s they are able to command premium pay in the market? *See* University & Community College Sys. of Nev. v. Farmer, 113 Nev. 90, 930 P.2d 730, 737 (1997); Brinkley v. Harbour Recreation Club, 180 F.3d 598, 619 (4th Cir.1999) (Motz, J., dissenting) (noting that the "fact that a woman has less bargaining power to demand a higher salary than a man does not constitute a valid factor 'other than sex' under the Equal Pay Act," and collecting cases rejecting market defense as a "factor other than sex"). Is a university's desire "to diversify its faculty and provide a female role model" for its chemistry students a legitimate reason to offer premium pay to the female chemistry professor? *See id.* Or would it violate Title VII? See the discussion of *Taxman v. Board of Education of the Township of Piscataway*, 91 F.3d 1547 (3d Cir.1996) (en banc), *cert. dismissed*, 522 U.S. 1010, 118 S.Ct. 595, 139 L.Ed.2d 431 (1997), in Chapter 17. Can these sex-based diversity or role model rationales be separated from the reasons the market demand for female chemistry professors was created in the first place?

c.   *Salary Retention or "Red Circling"*: Under a salary retention or "red circling" policy, an employer transfers an employee from a higher-paid skilled job to a less demanding position but continues to pay the employee his same salary. An employer might red circle an employee for economic reasons—to keep him available if his particular services are needed in the future or to keep him from going to work for a competitor, or for more altruistic reasons—to retain a loyal older or disabled worker in a less demanding job. Because the employee retains his former salary, he may earn more than a woman whose job is substantially equal to his new job. Courts have found employer reliance on a salary retention policy to be a legitimate affirmative defense under the Equal Pay Act. *See, e.g.*, Taylor v. White, 321 F.3d 710, 717–20 (8th Cir.2003) (analyzing cases and legislative history on salary retention policies); Mulhall v. Advance Security, Inc., 19 F.3d 586, 595–96 (11th Cir.) (collecting cases), *cert. denied*, 513 U.S. 919, 115 S.Ct. 298, 130 L.Ed.2d 212 (1994). Can you explain why red circling might be upheld as an affirmative defense but a pay disparity based on prior salary with another employer might be considered suspect?

d.   The courts of appeals are in conflict regarding whether the EPA's affirmative defense of a "factor other than sex" must be supported by a legitimate, business-related reason. *See, e.g.,* Aldrich v. Randolph Central Sch. Dist., 963 F.2d 520, 525 (2d Cir.) (holding that gender-neutral job classification systems "may qualify under the factor-other-than-sex defense only when they are based on legitimate business-related considerations"), *cert. denied,* 506 U.S. 965, 113 S.Ct. 440, 121 L.Ed.2d 359 (1992). One commentator has observed that different circuits have adopted one of three tests of the "any other factor other than sex" defense: (1) whether the employer's wage classification system is "gender-neutral" and "applied equally without regard to gender," (2) whether the employer can "show that a legitimate business reason is reasonably related to its wage system," or (3) "whether the employer classifie[s] its employees with criteria reasonably related to the performance of the employee's specific job duties." Jack A. Friedman, *Real Gender–Neutrality for the Factor–Other–Than–Sex Defense*, 11 N.Y.L.Sch.J.Hum.Rts. 241, 248, 251, 252 (1994). *Kouba* adopted the second—"intermediate"—approach. *See id.* at 251. What would be the likely outcome of using each of these three tests in the following situations? (a) An employer adopts a health insurance plan that provides family coverage only for employees who have the status of "head of the household." (b) An employer relies on an employee's previous work experience or level of education to determine salary. (c) An employer reorganizes its departments and adopts a new pay scale to reconcile salaries with job functions and status in the company hierarchy. (d) An employer gives job preferences to war veterans using a system of points established under state law. *See id.* at 254–58.

9. *Equal Pay Act Claims by State Employees.* All the courts of appeals that have addressed the question of Eleventh Amendment immunity under the Equal Pay Act since the Supreme Court's decision in *Kimel v. Florida Board of Regents*, 528 U.S. 62, 120 S.Ct. 631, 145 L.Ed.2d 522 (2000), have held that the Eleventh Amendment does not bar state employees from suing their employers in federal court under the Equal Pay Act. *See, e.g.*, Hundertmark v. Florida Dep't of Transp., 205 F.3d 1272 (11th Cir.2000). *See also* Siler–Khodr v. University of Texas Health Science Ctr. San Antonio, 261 F.3d 542, 550 (5th Cir.2001) (collecting post-*Kimel* cases), *cert. denied*, 537 U.S. 1087, 123 S.Ct. 694, 154 L.Ed.2d 631 (2002). These developments are discussed in Chapter 2. In *Nevada Department of Human Resources v. Hibbs*, 538 U.S. 721, 123 S.Ct. 1972, 155 L.Ed.2d 953 (2003), in Chapter 6, Section D, the Supreme Court held that state employees may recover money damages from state employers that violate the Family and Medical Leave Act. In light of the rationale and holding of *Hibbs*, how do you think the Supreme Court would rule on the issue of Eleventh Amendment immunity to Equal Pay Act claims brought in federal court by state employees?

C. THE BENNETT AMENDMENT TO TITLE VII: RECONCILING THE EQUAL PAY ACT AND TITLE VII

To date, *Corning Glass Works v. Brennan* is the only Supreme Court decision addressing a claim brought solely under the Equal Pay Act. In 1974, at the time that *Corning Glass* was decided, the Equal Pay Act (EPA) had been—for ten years—the exclusive basis for lawsuits challenging sex-based wage disparities. *See* Carin Ann Clauss, *Comparable Worth—The Theory, Its Legal Foundation, and the Feasibility of Implementation*, 20 U.Mich.J.L.Ref. 7, 16 (1986). There were several reasons why the EPA was used during this decade instead of Title VII: the EPA contains fewer procedural hurdles for plaintiffs and the EEOC had issued guidelines in 1965 (that were later withdrawn in 1972) requiring Title VII sex-based wage claims to satisfy the substantive standards under the EPA of "equal pay for equal work." *Id.* at 16 & nn.44–45, 46 n.167. Professor Clauss observed that

> the Equal Pay Act no matter how broadly the courts construed the phrase "equal work," did not apply to jobs that were dissimilar from any of those performed by men. * * * Because the great majority of women were employed in female jobs, the Equal Pay Act had very little effect on the discriminatory undervaluation of women's work.

Id. at 16.

By the mid–1970s, women began to use the broader substantive provisions of Title VII, to challenge wage differentials in jobs of "comparable" worth, as well as sex-based discriminatory practices in the hiring, promotion and compensation of women. *Id.* Comparable worth is discussed in Section D of this chapter. Plaintiffs' attempts to use Title VII to articulate a theory of liability for sex-based discriminatory compensation that was broader than the Equal Pay Act's "equivalence" requirement forced the courts to interpret the meaning of the so-called Bennett Amendment to Title VII. During consideration of the House proposal to add "sex" as a prohibited category to Title VII, the Senate had approved the following amendment proposed by Senator Bennett:

> It shall not be an unlawful employment practice under [Title VII] for any employer to differentiate upon the basis of sex in determining the amount of the wages or compensation paid or to be paid to employees of such employer if such differentiation is authorized by the provisions of section 6(d) of the [Equal Pay Act].

Title VII, § 703(h), 42 U.S.C. § 2000e–2(h). By the end of the 1970s, a conflict had developed in the circuits over whether the Bennett Amendment imposed the "equal work" requirement of the Equal Pay Act in Title VII sex-based wage claims. *See* Clauss, *supra*, at 16, 7 n.2 (collecting cases).

The Supreme Court addressed the effect of the Bennett Amendment in *County of Washington v. Gunther*, 452 U.S. 161, 101 S.Ct. 2242, 68 L.Ed.2d 751 (1981). In *Gunther*, four women brought a Title VII sex discrimination claim against a county in Oregon that paid female guards in the women's section of the county jail substantially less than the male guards in the men's section. The plaintiffs

> alleged that they were paid unequal wages for work substantially equal to that performed by male guards, and in the alternative, that part of the pay differential was attributable to intentional sex discrimination * * * because * * * the county set the pay scale for female guards, but not for male guards, at a level lower than that warranted by its own survey of outside markets and the worth of the jobs.

Id. at 164–65, 101 S.Ct. at 2245. Under Oregon law, only females were permitted to guard women prisoners, and, at the time, no women were employed to guard male inmates. *See id.* at 164 n.2, 101 S.Ct. at 2245 n.2. The plaintiffs conceded that "gender is a bona fide occupation qualification for some of the female guard positions." *Id.* Because the Equal Pay Act did not apply to municipal employees until the enactment of the Fair Labor Standards Amendments of 1974, the plaintiffs had to base their claim solely on Title VII, which has covered municipal employees since 1972. *See id.* at 164 n.3, 101 S.Ct. at 2245 n.3.

The trial court in *Gunther* held that the female guard jobs were not "substantially equal" to the jobs of the male guards because "male guards supervised more than 10 time as many prisoners per guard as did the female guards, and * * * the females devoted much of their time to less valuable clerical duties." *Id.* at 165, 101 S.Ct. at 2245. In addition, the district court refused to permit evidence regarding the plaintiffs' claim that the sex-based disparities in the pay scale were the result of intentional sex discrimination. In dismissing the case, the district court held that "a sex-based wage discrimination claim cannot be brought under Title VII unless it would satisfy the equal work standard of the Equal Pay Act of 1963." *Id.* at 165, 101 S.Ct. at 2246. The Court of Appeals reversed and the Supreme Court affirmed in an opinion by Justice Brennan.

The Court held that a Title VII plaintiff is not required to satisfy the Equal Pay Act's standard of "equal or substantially equal work" in order to proceed with a claim of sex-based wage discrimination under Title VII. The Court cautioned:

> We emphasize at the outset the narrowness of the question before us in this case. Respondents' claim is not based on the controversial concept of "comparable worth," under which plaintiffs might claim increased compensation on the basis of a comparison of the intrinsic worth or difficulty of their job with that of other jobs in the same organization or community. Rather, respondents seek to prove, by direct evidence, that their wages were depressed because of intentional sex discrimination, consisting of setting the wage scale for female guards, but not for male guards, at a level lower than its own survey of outside markets and the worth of the jobs warranted. The narrow question in this case is whether such a claim is precluded by the last sentence of § 703 (h) of Title VII, called the "Bennett Amendment."

Id. at 166, 101 S.Ct. at 2246.

The Court then proceeded to interpret the Bennett Amendment:

> To discover what practices are exempted from Title VII's prohibitions by the Bennett Amendment, we must turn to § 206 (d) of * * * the Equal Pay Act * * *. On its face, the Equal Pay Act contains three restrictions pertinent to this case. First, its coverage is limited to those employers subject to the Fair Labor Standards Act. Thus, the Act does not apply, for example, to certain businesses engaged in retail sales, fishing, agriculture, and newspaper publishing. Second, the Act is restricted to cases involving "equal work on

jobs the performance of which requires equal skill, effort, and responsibility, and which are performed under similar working conditions." Third, the Act's four affirmative defenses exempt any wage differentials attributable to seniority, merit, quantity or quality of production, or "any other factor other than sex."

* * *

The language of the Bennett Amendment suggests an intention to incorporate only the affirmative defenses of the Equal Pay Act into Title VII. The Amendment bars sex-based wage discrimination claims under Title VII where the pay differential is "authorized" by the Equal Pay Act. Although the word "authorize" sometimes means simply "to permit," it ordinarily denotes affirmative enabling action. Black's Law Dictionary 122 (5th ed.1979) defines "authorize" as "[t]o empower; to give a right or authority to act." The question, then, is what wage practices have been affirmatively authorized by the Equal Pay Act.

The Equal Pay Act is divided into two parts: a definition of the violation, followed by four affirmative defenses. The first part can hardly be said to "authorize" anything at all: it is purely prohibitory. The second part, however, in essence "authorizes" employers to differentiate in pay on the basis of seniority, merit, quantity or quality of production, or any other factor other than sex, even though such differentiation might otherwise violate the Act. It is to these provisions, therefore, that the Bennett Amendment must refer.

* * *

* * * The Bennett Amendment was offered as a "technical amendment" designed to resolve any potential conflicts between Title VII and the Equal Pay Act. Thus, with respect to the first three defenses, the Bennett Amendment has the effect of guaranteeing that courts and administrative agencies adopt a consistent interpretation of like provisions in both statutes. Otherwise, they might develop inconsistent bodies of case law interpreting two sets of nearly identical language.

More importantly, incorporation of the fourth affirmative defense could have significant consequences for Title VII litigation. Title VII's prohibition of discriminatory employment practices was intended to be broadly inclusive, proscribing "not only overt discrimination but also practices that are fair in form, but discriminatory in operation." Griggs v. Duke Power Co., 401 U.S. 424, 431, 91 S.Ct. 849, 853, 28 L.Ed.2d 158 (1971). The structure of Title VII litigation, including presumptions, burdens of proof, and defenses, has been designed to reflect this approach. The fourth affirmative defense of the Equal Pay Act, however, was designed differently, to confine the application of the Act to wage differentials attributable to sex discrimination. Equal Pay Act litigation, therefore, has been structured to permit employers to defend against charges of discrimination where their pay differentials are based on a bona fide use of "other factors other than sex." Under the Equal Pay Act, the courts and administrative agencies are not permitted to "substitute their judgment for the judgment of the employer * * * who [has] established and applied a bona fide job rating system," so long as it does not discriminate on the basis of sex. 109 Cong.Rec. 9209 (statement of Rep. Goodell). Although we do not decide in this case how sex-based wage discrimination litigation under Title VII should be structured to accommodate the fourth affirmative defense of the Equal Pay Act, we consider it clear that the Bennett Amendment, under this interpretation, is not rendered superfluous.

We therefore conclude that only differentials attributable to the four affirmative defenses of the Equal Pay Act are "authorized" by that Act within the meaning of § 703 (h) of Title VII.

* * *

Under petitioners' reading of the Bennett Amendment, only those sex-based wage discrimination claims that satisfy the "equal work" standard of the Equal Pay Act could be brought under Title VII. In practical terms, this means that a woman who is discriminatorily underpaid could obtain no relief—no matter how egregious the discrimination might be—unless her employer also employed a man in an equal job in the same establishment, at a higher rate of pay. Thus, if an employer hired a woman for a unique position in the company and then admitted that her salary would have been higher had she been male, the woman would be unable to obtain legal redress under petitioners' interpretation. Similarly, if an employer used a transparently sex-biased system for wage determination, women holding jobs not equal to those held by men would be denied the right to prove that the system is a pretext for discrimination. Moreover, to cite an example arising from a recent case, *Los Angeles Dept. of Water & Power v. Manhart*, 435 U.S. 702, 98 S.Ct. 1370, 55 L.Ed.2d 657 (1978), if the employer required its female workers to pay more into its pension program than male workers were required to pay, the only women who could bring a Title VII action under petitioners' interpretation would be those who could establish that a man performed equal work: a female auditor thus might have a cause of action while a female secretary might not. Congress surely did not intend the Bennett Amendment to insulate such blatantly discriminatory practices from judicial redress under Title VII.

Moreover, petitioners' interpretation would have other far-reaching consequences. Since it rests on the proposition that any wage differentials not prohibited by the Equal Pay Act are "authorized" by it, petitioners' interpretation would lead to the conclusion that discriminatory compensation by employers not covered by the Fair Labor Standards Act is "authorized"—since not prohibited—by the Equal Pay Act. Thus it would deny Title VII protection against sex-based wage discrimination by those employers not subject to the Fair Labor Standards Act but covered by Title VII. There is no persuasive evidence that Congress intended such a result, and the EEOC has rejected it since at least 1965. *See* 29 C.F.R. § 1604.7 (1966). * * *

Id. at 167–80, 101 S.Ct. at 2247–53.

Notes and Questions

1. *Proving "Similar" Work Under Title VII*: If *Gunther* requires only proof of similar—not "substantially equal"—work to make out a prima facie case of wage discrimination under Title VII, what is the difference between the two standards? *See* Sprague v. Thorn Americas, Inc., 129 F.3d 1355, 1363 (10th Cir.1997) (because the pay disparity between a female plaintiff and male assistant product managers was "consistent with the different levels of importance, value, and depth of responsibility between the respective departments," the plaintiff failed to make out a prima facie case under either Title VII or the Equal Pay Act).

2. *The Role of Intent*: The courts have consistently held that discriminatory intent is not an element of the plaintiff's prima facie case under the Equal Pay Act. *See* Fallon v. Illinois, 882 F.2d 1206, 1217 (7th Cir.1989) (collecting cases). But intent is an element of a Title VII case of sex-based wage discrimination. In a Title VII pretext case, once the defendant has articulated a legitimate, nondiscriminatory reason for a pay disparity, what type of evidence would a plaintiff need in order to prove that the employer's explanation is pretextual and that sex discrimination is the reason for the disparity? *See* Knight v. G.W. Plastics, Inc., 903 F.Supp. 674, 679 (D.Vt. 1995). If a plaintiff challenges a sex-based pay disparity under both the EPA and Title VII, will her evidence supporting a prima facie EPA case necessarily support a prima facie Title VII case? *See* Belfi v. Prendergast, 191 F.3d 129, 137 (2d Cir.1999) (recognizing that, "[u]nder the EPA, proof of the employer's discriminatory intent is not necessary for the plaintiff to prevail on her claim," and finding that plaintiff failed to prove intent under her Title VII claim); Tidwell v. Fort Howard Corp., 989 F.2d 406 (10th Cir.1993) (holding that evidence supporting a jury verdict for the plaintiff on her EPA claim did not establish the element of intent for her Title VII claim).

3. *Burdens of Proof*: The Equal Pay Act and Title VII have different burdens of proof. The Eleventh Circuit summarized the significance of the differences in these burdens:

> In contrast to Title VII, the EPA establishes a form of "strict liability":
>
> > Once the disparity in pay between substantially similar jobs is demonstrated, the burden shifts to the defendant to prove that a "factor other than sex" is responsible for the differential. If the defendant fails, the plaintiff wins. The plaintiff is not required to prove discriminatory intent on the part of the defendant.

Miranda v. B & B Cash Grocery Store, Inc., 975 F.2d 1518, 1533 (11th Cir.1992). Thus, there is a significant difference between Title VII and the EPA as to both elements and burdens of proof. Under the EPA, the onus is on the employer to establish that the pay differential was premised on a factor other than sex. Under Title VII, however, the plaintiff must prove that the employer had discriminatory intent. If the evidence is in equipoise on the issue of whether a salary differential is based on a "factor other than sex," the plaintiff is entitled to judgment on her EPA claim. However the employer prevails on the Title VII claim. Under Title VII, the risk of nonpersuasion always remains with the plaintiff.

Meeks v. Computer Assoc. Internat'l, 15 F.3d 1013, 1019 (11th Cir.1994). The courts are divided on whether a violation of the Equal Pay Act automatically establishes Title VII liability in a sex-based wage discrimination case even if the claim is based on the same evidence. The majority of the courts of appeals that have decided the issue "have not abandoned the distinctions between Title VII and the Equal Pay Act, choosing instead to analyze each claim independently, even if brought together on the same underlying facts." Fallon v. Illinois, 882 F.2d 1206, 1214 (7th Cir.1989) (adopting this approach in the Seventh Circuit and collecting cases in the Fifth and Seventh Circuits); *Meeks*, 15 F.3d at 1013 (collecting cases in the Fourth, Fifth, Tenth, and Eleventh Circuits); Belfi v. Prendergast, 191 F.3d 129 (2d Cir.1999) (adopting this approach in the Second Circuit). The Sixth, Eighth, and Ninth Circuits disregard the differences between the proof schemes of the two statutes and hold that liability under the Equal Pay Act automatically establishes Title VII liability. *See Meeks*, 15 F.3d at 1020; *Fallon*, 882 F.2d at 1213–14.

Which approach makes the most sense to you? The EEOC has adopted the view that a finding of a violation of the Equal Pay Act is sufficient to establish a violation of Title VII. 29 C.F.R. § 1620.27. Should the fact that Title VII disparate treatment claims are now triable before juries make a difference, or must the juries be separately instructed on Title VII and Equal Pay Act claims? *See* Korte v. Diemer, 909 F.2d 954 (6th Cir.1990) (a pre–1991 Civil Rights Act case holding that a jury's finding under the Equal Pay Act that an employer discriminated in pay on the basis of sex is binding on a district court judge, sitting without a jury on the Title VII case, when the claim is based on the same set of facts).

4. *After-Acquired Evidence*: Should an employer's evidence of an employee's fraud or other wrongdoing, acquired after the employee has filed suit, bar her Equal Pay Act claim? *See* Boyd v. Rubbermaid Commercial Prod., Inc., 1992 WL 404398 (W.D.Va.1992) (no, because the statutory scheme set out in the Equal Pay Act is distinct from that applicable in Title VII claims); Miller v. Beneficial Mgmt. Corp., 855 F.Supp. 691 (D.N.J.1994) (yes, because monetary awards in Equal Pay Act claims serve the same equitable purposes as back pay under Title VII, there is no logical reason not to allow the after-acquired-evidence defense in Equal Pay Act claims). Both *Boyd* and *Miller* were decided before the Supreme Court's decision in *McKennon v. Nashville Banner Publishing Co.*, 513 U.S. 352, 115 S.Ct. 879, 130 L.Ed.2d 852 (1995), in Chapter 3. Does *McKennon* strongly support either view?

5. *Statute of Limitations:* Before the Supreme Court decision in *National Railroad Passenger Corp. v. Morgan,* 536 U.S. 101, 122 S.Ct. 2061,

153 L.Ed.2d 106 (2002) (discussed in Chapters 2 and 8), most courts had held that discriminatory wage payments are "continuing violations of Title VII, regardless of whether the plaintiff challenged a single act of wage discrimination or a discriminatory wage policy." Inglis v. Buena Vista Univ., 235 F.Supp.2d 1009, 1021 (N.D.Iowa 2002). *See, e.g.,* Goodwin v. General Motors Corp. 275 F.3d 1005, 1010 (10th Cir.) (collecting cases), *cert. denied,* 537 U.S. 941, 123 S.Ct. 340, 154 L.Ed.2d 248 (2002); Calloway v. Partners Nat'l Health Plans, 986 F.2d 446, 449 (11th Cir.1993) (holding that "race-based discriminatory wage payments constitute a continuing violation of Title VII)"); Mitchell v. Jefferson County Bd. of Ed., 936 F.2d 539, 548 (11th Cir.1991) ("The theory of continuing violations has been applied consistently to actions under the Equal Pay Act."); *but see* Dasgupta v. University of Wis. Bd. of Regents, 121 F.3d 1138 (7th Cir.1997) (rejecting the continuing violation theory for a discriminatory wage claim under Title VII).

The rationale for applying the continuing violation theory to discriminatory wage payments derives from *Bazemore v. Friday,* 478 U.S. 385, 106 S.Ct. 3000, 92 L.Ed.2d 315 (1986) (per curiam), a Title VII pattern-and-practice case of race-based wage discrimination in which the Supreme Court observed that "[e]ach week's paycheck that delivers less to a black than to a similarly situated white is a wrong actionable under Title VII * * *." *Id.* at 395, 106 S.Ct. at 3006 (Brennan, J., concurring). In *Morgan,* the Court quoted this passage from *Bazemore* as an example of the Court's use of "the term 'practice' to apply to a discrete act or single 'occurrence,' even when it has a connection to other acts." *Morgan,* 536 U.S. at 111–12, 122 S.Ct. at 2071. In light of your understanding of *Morgan* and *Bazemore,* do you agree that *"Morgan* will likely halt the previous trend of analyzing pay claims under a continuing violations theory without distinguishing between discriminatory pay policies and discrete discriminatory acts"? *Inglis,* 235 F.Supp.2d at 1024. *Compare* Elmenayer v. ABF Freight Sys., Inc., 318 F.3d 130, 134–35 (2d Cir.2003) (a post-*Morgan* case applying the reasoning of *Bazemore* to describe each discriminatory wage payment as "a separate unlawful employment practice," that "give[s] rise to a new claim of an unlawful employment practice" even if the wage payment is "simply a periodic implementation of an adverse decision previously made"); *with Inglis,* 235 F.Supp.2d at 1019–29 (relying on *Morgan* to hold that the continuing violations doctrine does not apply to plaintiffs' Title VII and Equal Pay Act claims of sex-based wage disparities resulting from discriminatory starting salaries).

6. *Sex–Plus–Race Claims of Wage Discrimination*: Plaintiff, a black woman, claims that her employer is discriminating against her on the basis of sex and race by paying her less than certain other employees who perform substantially the same work. She sues her employer under the Equal Pay Act, Title VII, and § 1981, as amended by the Civil Rights Act of 1991. The Equal Pay Act will permit her to challenge sex-based, but not race-based, wage discrimination. Title VII prohibits discrimination in an employee's "compensation" because of race, color, religion, and national origin, as well as sex. Section 1981 may be used to challenge race-based, but not sex-based, wage discrimination in the performance of an employment contract.

Plaintiff's evidence shows that one white female, three white males, and three black males are paid more than she is; although one black male is paid the same salary and one white female is paid less. The employer concedes that the positions of all ten employees are essentially identical, but has evidence that salary decisions are determined on the basis of each employee's experience and longevity of service. Each of the employees who is paid more than the plaintiff has a longer employment history with the employer. The plaintiff took a break of several years in her employment to earn a doctorate in her field of work, and she is now the only employee in her position with a Ph.D. The employer contends that a Ph.D. is not a requirement for the job and has refused to give the plaintiff credit for her years away from employment to earn her advanced degree. Given these facts, how would the plaintiff's and the defendant's evidentiary burdens be satisfied under each of these three statutes? *See* Blount v. Alabama Coop. Extension Serv., 869 F.Supp. 1543 (M.D.Ala.1994).

As the *Blount* case demonstrates, the litigation structure of a wage discrimination suit brought by a black woman requires that the plaintiff disaggregate sex and race and, in effect, treat them as separate statuses for purposes of Title VII, § 1981, and the Equal Pay Act. Only under Title VII can the plaintiff attempt to make out a prima facie case based on the "sex-plus-race" paradigm of wage discrimination. The theory is that

> the combination of her membership in both a minority race and minority gender place her in a special protected class—in this case the class of black females. The effect of utilizing this line of analysis is that a defendant cannot rebut a prima facia [sic] case of intentional discrimination against a black female by showing that female employees as a whole were treated the same as all male employees or that black employees as a whole were treated the same as white employees. The purpose is to focus specifically on the treatment of black females as compared to every other employee outside the class of black females.

Daniel v. Church's Chicken, 942 F.Supp. 533, 538 (S.D.Ala.1996). See the discussion of intersectionality in Chapter 2.

D. COMPARABLE WORTH

Scholars studying the demographics of the labor market have observed:

Occupational *sex* segregation has been more resistant to change than race segregation. Despite revolutionary transformations in the industrial and occupational structures, and changes in the composition of the labor force, the degree of occupational sex segregation among whites remained essentially constant between 1940 and 1970. During the same period, with black women's movement out of domestic work, occupational sex segregation among blacks declined to the level of whites.

    * * * [T]he 1970s represented a watershed for sex segregation. For the first time in this century women made notable gains in some occupations in which men had typically predominated. However, the level of occupational sex segregation at the end of the decade remained high. In 1980 almost half of all women and 53 percent of

men worked in occupations that were at least 80 percent women and men, respectively.

Barbara F. Reskin & Patricia A. Roos, Job Queues, Gender Queues: Explaining Women's Inroads into Male Occupations 5–6 (1990).

A decade later, women's wages in relation to men's had increased, but disparities still remained. In 1994, Heidi Hartmann and Stephanie Aaronson reported on the results of a pay equity study conducted by the Institute for Women's Policy Research and the Urban Institute:

> An American woman working full-time year-round in 1992 earned only 71 percent as much as her male counterpart. This represents a substantial increase since 1982 when the wage ratio of female to male earnings was 62 percent. Approximately half of this increase is due to an increase in women's real wages, while the other half is due to a decrease in men's real wages. Despite this considerable advance, the wage gap remains; women still earn less then men even in the same occupations. When different jobs of comparable worth—those requiring similar levels of skill, effort, responsibility, or knowledge—are compared it is even more common to find pay inequities.

Heidi I. Hartmann & Stephanie Aaronson, *Pay Equity and Women's Wage Increases: Success in the States, A Model for the Nation*, 1 Duke J. Gender L. & Pol'y 69, 69–70 (1994). In August 2001, *Working Women* magazine reported that, on average, women in the United States earn 76 percent of what men earn. *See Some Women Gain Ground in Compensation, But 24 Percent Gap Persists, Survey Shows*, 19 Hum.Resources Rep. (BNA) No. 34, at 937 (Sept. 3, 2001) (summarizing results of the *Working Women* survey).

To understand the sex-based pay equity issues that arise in comparing jobs of "comparable worth," consider the following examples:

> In the state of Washington * * * an evaluation study found the job of legal secretary to be comparable in worth to the job of heavy equipment operator, but it paid $400 less per month. A noted court case in Denver featured nurses suing the city because it was paying them less than, for example, tree trimmers and sign painters, despite the lower educational requirements of those male jobs. In San Jose city government, a study showed that nurses made $9,120 per year less than fire truck mechanics, and that secretaries generally earned less than workers in male jobs that required no more than an eighth-grade education. Women in the California School Employees Association complained that school librarians with master's degrees were paid less than custodians and groundskeepers.

Paula England, *The Pay Gap Between Male and Female Jobs: Organizational Realities*, 25 L. & Soc. Inquiry 913, 915 (2000) (reviewing Robert Nelson & William Bridges, Legalizing Gender Inequality (1999)). Professor England notes that "one is hard-pressed to come up with any examples in which a male job that reasonable people would find comparable in skill, effort, or difficulty of working conditions pays less than a female job." *Id.*

In *County of Washington v. Gunther*, 452 U.S. 161, 166, 101 S.Ct. 2242, 2246, 68 L.Ed.2d 751 (1981), discussed in Section C of this chapter, the Supreme Court was careful to note that the plaintiffs' claim was "not based on the controversial concept of 'comparable worth,' under which plaintiffs might claim increased compensation on the basis of a comparison of the intrinsic worth or difficulty of their job with that of other jobs in the same organization or community." The Court held only that a Title VII sex-based wage discrimination claim did not require proof that the plaintiff and an opposite-sex comparator received disparate pay for "substantially equal" jobs. Although *Gunther* thus significantly broadened the reach of Title VII sex discrimination law beyond the Equal Pay Act's narrow "equivalence" standard, the court did not endorse the use of a generalized theory of "comparable worth." The Court observed:

> Petitioners [the employer] argue strenuously that the approach of the Court of Appeals places "the pay structure of virtually every employer and the entire economy * * * at risk and subject to scrutiny by the federal courts." They raise the specter that "Title VII plaintiffs could draw any type of comparison imaginable concerning job duties and pay between any job predominantly performed by women and any job predominantly performed by men." But whatever the merit of petitioners' arguments in other contexts, they are inapplicable here, for claims based on the type of job comparisons petitioners describe are manifestly different from respondents' claim. Respondents contend that the County of Washington evaluated the worth of their jobs; that the county determined that they should be paid approximately 95% as much as the male correctional officers; that it paid them only about 70% as much, while paying the male officers the full evaluated worth of their jobs; and that the failure of the county to pay respondents the full evaluated worth of their jobs can be proved to be attributable to intentional sex discrimination. Thus, respondents' suit does not require a court to make its own subjective assessment of the value of the male and female guard jobs, or to attempt by statistical technique or other method to quantify the effect of sex discrimination on the wage rates.

Id. at 180–81, 101 S.Ct. at 2253–54.

Gunther was a 5–4 decision, with a dissent by then-Justice Rhenquist that emphasized the narrowness of the Court's holding:

> Even though today's opinion reaches what I believe to be the wrong result, its narrow holding is perhaps its saving feature. The opinion does not endorse the so-called "comparable worth" theory: though the Court does not indicate how a plaintiff might establish a prima facie case under Title VII, the Court does suggest that allegations of unequal pay for unequal, but comparable, work will

not state a claim on which relief may be granted. The Court, for example, repeatedly emphasizes that this is not a case where plaintiffs ask the court to compare the value of dissimilar jobs or to quantify the effect of sex discrimination on wage rates. Indeed, the Court relates, without criticism, respondents' contention that *Lemons v. City and County of Denver*, 620 F.2d 228 (10th Cir.), *cert. denied*, 449 U.S. 888, 101 S.Ct. 244, 66 L.Ed.2d 114 (1980), is distinguishable. There the court found that Title VII did not provide a remedy to nurses who sought increased compensation based on a comparison of their jobs to dissimilar jobs of "comparable" value in the community. *See also* Christensen v. Iowa, 563 F.2d 353 (8th Cir.1977) (no prima facie case under Title VII when plaintiffs, women clerical employees of a university, sought to compare their wages to the employees in the physical plant).

* * *

Because there are no logical underpinnings to the Court's opinion, all we may conclude is that even absent a showing of equal work, there is a cause of action under Title VII where there is direct evidence that an employer has *intentionally* depressed a woman's salary because she is a woman. The decision today does not approve a cause of action based on a *comparison* of the wage rates of dissimilar jobs.

Id. at 203–04, 101 S.Ct. at 2265–66 (Rhenquist, J., dissenting). In the following court of appeals decision interpreting *Gunther*, the analysis by then-Judge Kennedy, effectively foreclosed Title VII litigation as a means of achieving pay equity between sex-segregated occupations under a theory of "comparable worth."

AMERICAN FEDERATION OF STATE, COUNTY, AND MUNICIPAL EMPLOYEES, AFL-CIO (AFSCME) v. STATE OF WASHINGTON

United States Court of Appeals, Ninth Circuit, 1985.
770 F.2d 1401.

KENNEDY, Circuit Judge.

[In 1982, AFSCME brought a Title VII class action suit against the state of Washington on behalf of approximately 15,500 state employees. The class consisted of "state employees who have worked or do work in job categories that are or have been at least seventy percent female." The district court held that "the State discriminated on the basis of sex in violation of Title VII * * * by compensating employees in jobs where females predominate at lower rates than employees in jobs where males predominate, if these jobs, though dissimilar, were identified by certain studies to be of comparable worth."]

The State of Washington has required salaries of state employees to reflect prevailing market rates. Throughout the period in question, comprehensive biennial salary surveys were conducted to assess prevailing market rates. * * * Salaries were fixed by enactment of the budget.

In 1974 the State commissioned a study by management consultant Norman Willis to determine whether a wage disparity existed between employees in jobs held predominantly by women and jobs held predominantly by men. The study examined sixty-two classifications in which at least seventy percent of the employees were women, and fifty-nine job classifications in which at least seventy percent of the employees were men. It found a wage disparity of about twenty percent, to the disadvantage of employees in jobs held mostly by women, for jobs considered of comparable worth. Comparable worth was calculated by evaluating jobs under four criteria: knowledge and skills, mental demands, accountability, and working conditions. A maximum number of points was allotted to each category: 280 for knowledge and skills, 140 for mental demands, 160 for accountability, and 20 for working conditions; and every job was assigned a numerical value under each of the four criteria. The State of Washington conducted similar studies in 1976 and 1980, and in 1983 the State enacted legislation providing for a compensation scheme based on comparable worth. The scheme is to take effect over a ten-year period.

* * *

AFSCME alleges sex-based wage discrimination throughout the state system, but its explanation and proof of the violation is, in essence, Washington's failure as early as 1979 to adopt and implement at once a comparable worth compensation program. The trial court adopted this theory as well. The comparable worth theory, as developed in the case before us, postulates that sex-based wage discrimination exists if employees in job classifications occupied primarily by women are paid less than employees in job classifications filled primarily by men, if the jobs are of equal value to the employer, though otherwise dissimilar. We must determine whether comparable worth, as presented in this case, affords AFSCME a basis for recovery under Title VII.

* * *

* * * It is evident from the legislative history of the Equal Pay Act that Congress, after explicit consideration, rejected proposals that would have prohibited lower wages for comparable work, as contrasted with equal work. The legislative history of the Civil Rights Act of 1964 and the Bennett Amendment, however, is inconclusive regarding the intended coverage of Title VII's prohibition against sex discrimination, and contains no explicit discussion of compensation for either comparable or equal work. The Supreme Court in *Gunther*, stressing the broad remedial purposes of Title VII, construed the Bennett Amendment to incorporate into Title VII the four affirmative defenses of the Equal Pay Act, but not to limit discrimination suits involving pay to the cause of action provided in the Equal Pay Act. The Court noted, however, that the case before it did not involve the concept of comparable worth, and declined

to define "the precise contours of lawsuits challenging sex discrimination in compensation under Title VII." 452 U.S. at 181, 101 S.Ct. at 2254.

In the instant case, the district court found a violation of Title VII, premised upon both the disparate impact and the disparate treatment theories of discrimination. * * *

The trial court erred in ruling that liability was established under a disparate impact analysis. * * * AFSCME's disparate impact argument is based on the contention that the State of Washington's practice of taking prevailing market rates into account in setting wages has an adverse impact on women, who, historically, have received lower wages than men in the labor market. Disparate impact analysis is confined to cases which challenge a specific, clearly delineated employment practice applied at a single point in the job selection process. The instant case does not involve an employment practice that yields to disparate impact analysis. As we noted in an earlier case, the decision to base compensation on the competitive market, rather than on a theory of comparable worth, involves the assessment of a number of complex factors not easily ascertainable, an assessment too multifaceted to be appropriate for disparate impact analysis. Spaulding v. University of Washington, 740 F.2d 686, 708 (9th Cir.), *cert. denied*, 469 U.S. 1036, 105 S.Ct. 511, 83 L.Ed.2d 401 (1984). In the case before us, the compensation system in question resulted from surveys, agency hearings, administrative recommendations, budget proposals, executive actions, and legislative enactments. A compensation system that is responsive to supply and demand and other market forces is not the type of specific, clearly delineated employment policy contemplated by *Dothard* and *Griggs*; such a compensation system, the result of a complex of market forces, does not constitute a single practice that suffices to support a claim under disparate impact theory. Such cases are controlled by disparate treatment analysis. Under these principles and precedents, we must reverse the district court's determination of liability under the disparate impact theory of discrimination.

We consider next the allegations of disparate treatment. Under the disparate treatment theory, AFSCME was required to prove a prima facie case of sex discrimination by a preponderance of the evidence. * * * In an appropriate case, the necessary discriminatory animus may be inferred from circumstantial evidence. Our review of the record, however, indicates failure by AFSCME to establish the requisite element of intent by either circumstantial or direct evidence.

AFSCME contends discriminatory motive may be inferred from the Willis study, which finds the State's practice of setting salaries in reliance on market rates creates a sex-based wage disparity for jobs deemed of comparable worth. AFSCME argues from the study that the market reflects a historical pattern of lower wages to employees in positions staffed predominantly by women; and it contends the State of Washington perpetuates that disparity, in violation of Title VII, by using market rates in the compensation system. The inference of discriminatory motive which AFSCME seeks to draw from the State's participation in the market system fails, as the State did not create the market disparity and has not been shown to have been motivated by impermissible sex-based considerations in setting salaries.

The requirement of intent is linked at least in part to culpability. That concept would be undermined if we were to hold that payment of wages according to prevailing rates in the public and private sectors is an act which, in itself, supports the inference of a purpose to discriminate. Neither law nor logic deems the free market system a suspect enterprise. Economic reality is that the value of a particular job to an employer is but one factor influencing the rate of compensation for that job. Other considerations may include the availability of workers willing to do the job and the effectiveness of collective bargaining in a particular industry. We recognized in *Spalding* that employers may be constrained by market forces to set salaries under prevailing wage rates for different job classifications, 740 F.2d at 708. We find nothing in the language of Title VII or its legislative history to indicate Congress intended to abrogate fundamental economic principles such as the laws of supply and demand or to prevent employers from competing in the labor market.

While the Washington legislature may have the discretion to enact a comparable worth plan if it chooses to do so, Title VII does not obligate it to eliminate an economic inequality which it did not create. Title VII was enacted to ensure equal opportunity in employment to covered individuals, and the State of Washington is not charged here with barring access to particular job classifications on the basis of sex.

We have recognized that in certain cases an inference of intent may be drawn from statistical evidence. *Spalding*, 740 F.2d at 703. We have admonished, however, that statistics must be relied on with caution. *Id.* Though the comparability of wage rates in dissimilar jobs may be relevant to a determination of discriminatory animus, job evaluation studies and comparable worth statistics alone are insufficient to establish the requisite inference of discriminatory motive critical to the disparate treatment theory. The weight to be accorded such statistics is determined by the existence of independent corroborative evidence of discrimination. We conclude the independent evidence of discrimination presented by AFSCME is insufficient to support an inference of the requisite discriminatory motive under the disparate treatment theory.

AFSCME offered proof of isolated incidents of sex segregation as evidence of a history of sex-based wage discrimination. The evidence * * * consists of "help wanted" advertisements restricting various jobs to members of a particular sex. These advertisements were often placed in separate "help wanted—male" and "help wanted—female" columns in state newspapers between 1960 and 1973, though most were discontinued when Title VII became applicable to the states in 1972. At trial, AFSCME called expert witnesses to testify that a causal relationship exists between sex segregation practices and sex-based wage discrimination, and that the effects of sex segregation practices may persist even after the practices are discontinued. However, none of the individually named plaintiffs in the action ever testified regarding specific incidents of discrimination. The isolated incidents alleged by AFSCME are insufficient to corroborate the results of the Willis study and do not justify an inference of discriminatory motive by the State in the setting of salaries for its system as a whole. Given the scope of the alleged intentional act, given the attempt to show the core principle of the State's market-based compensation system was adopted or maintained with a discriminatory purpose, more is required to support the finding of liability than these isolated acts, which had only an indirect relation to the compensation principle itself.

We also reject AFSCME's contention that, having commissioned the Willis study, the State of Washington was committed to implement a new system of compensation based on comparable worth as defined by the study. Whether comparable worth is a feasible approach to employee compensation is a matter of debate. Assuming, however, that like other job evaluation studies it may be useful as a diagnostic tool, we reject a rule that would penalize rather than commend employers for their effort and innovation in undertaking such a study. *See* American Nurses' Ass'n v. Illinois, 606 F.Supp. 1313, 1317–18 (N.D.Ill.1985) (mem.) (a rule requiring implementation of results of job evaluation studies would deter employers from conducting such studies). The results of comparable worth studies will vary depending on the number and types of factors measured and the maximum number of points allotted to each factor. A study which indicates a particular wage structure might be more equitable should not categorically bind the employer who commissioned it. The employer should also be able to take into account market conditions, bargaining demands, and the possibility that another study will yield different results. *Id.* at 1318. *Cf. Gunther*, 452 U.S. at 180–81, 101 S.Ct. at 2253–54 (once an employer decided to adopt a particular job evaluation system, it could not be applied inconsistently).

We hold there was a failure to establish a violation of Title VII under the disparate treatment theory of discrimination, and reverse the district court on this aspect of the case as well. The State of Washington's initial reliance on a free market system in which employees in male-dominated jobs are compensated at a higher rate than employees in dissimilar female-dominated jobs is not in and of itself a violation of Title VII, notwithstanding that the Willis study deemed the positions of comparable worth. Absent a showing of discriminatory motive, which has not been made here, the law does not permit the federal courts to interfere in the market-based system for the compensation of Washington's employees.

* * *

Notes and Questions

1. *Defining "Comparable Worth"*: "Comparable worth" refers to a number of different concepts. Professor Clauss has observed:

> Comparable worth may mean (1) a requirement that compensation be proportional to the intrinsic worth of the job, (2) a pay system under which all jobs of equal value are paid the same, (3) a procedure that permits the comparison of job content and compensation across job families (i.e., work that is dissimilar), (4) evidence used in a wage discrimination case to demonstrate that the difference in wages is due to sex and not to any difference in job value, (5) a requirement that female-dominated jobs be paid the same as male-dominated jobs of equal value, (6) a requirement that the wage rates for female-dominated jobs be established using the same criteria as are used in establishing the wage rates for male-dominated jobs, and (7) a requirement that wage disparities based on sex (or race) be eliminated.

Carin Ann Clauss, *Comparable Worth—The Theory, Its Legal Foundation, and the Feasibility of Implementation*, 20 U.Mich.J.L.Ref. 7, 18 (1986) (citations omitted). *See generally* Paula England, Comparable Worth: Theories and Evidence (1992). Which meaning or meanings of "comparable worth" were at issue in the *AFSCME* case?

2. *Critiques of Comparable Worth*: Many arguments for and against comparable worth have been articulated. Consider the following four perspectives:

> The persistence of the wage gap compels attention for two reasons. First, there is the simple issue of justice; women deserve to be paid fairly for what they do. Second, and perhaps more important for many women, is the need for commensurately higher earnings as their role in supporting their families grows. The proportion of two earner families has increased from 36 percent of all families with children in 1975 to 47 percent of all such families in 1993. The proportion of single female earner families with children has also been rising; they now comprise eighteen percent of all families with children. In 1991, 13.7 million families with children were living below the poverty level; 8.1 million of those families were female-headed.

Heidi I. Hartmann & Stephanie Aaronson, *Pay Equity and Women's Wage Increases: Success in the States, A Model for the Nation*, 1 Duke J. Gender L. & Pol'y 69, 70 (1994) (citations omitted).

> [T]he attempt to justify comparable worth on moral grounds only serves to obscure the effects of comparable worth on various groups. In fact, many women may be hurt by comparable worth. If a consensus exists that women should be compensated for the effects of past discrimination, such compensation should be in the form of a direct public subsidy rather than comparable worth.
>
> * * * Because comparable worth imposes a minimum wage but does nothing about discrimination in the economy, * * * it is fundamentally

inconsistent with, rather than an extension of, existing anti-discrimination legislation.

Daniel R. Fischel & Edward P Lazear, *Comparable Worth and Discrimination in Labor Markets*, 53 U.Chi.L.Rev. 891, 894–95 (1986).

> [F]eminists have argued that a theory of sexual equality will have to take into account the differences between men and women as groups. Applied to the labor market, a model of "equality of difference" recognizes the existence of sex roles in society * * *. Because men have historically dominated the labor market, it overwhelmingly reflects values consistent with male roles and rewards "masculine" choices while ignoring "feminine" concerns and penalizing choices consistent with female roles. To the extent, however, that society considers many traditionally female values not only legitimate but salutary, prices set by the market should incorporate them and, ideally, a theory of labor market discrimination should rectify their exclusion.

Mark Seidenfeld, *Some Jurisprudential Perspectives on Employment Sex Discrimination Law and Comparable Worth*, 21 Rutgers L.J. 269, 271–72 (1990) (citations omitted).

> An employer (private or public) that simply pays the going wage in each of the different types of job[s] in its establishment, and makes no effort to discourage women from applying for particular jobs or to steer them toward particular jobs, would be justifiably surprised to discover that it may be violating federal law because each wage rate and therefore the ratio between them have been found to be determined by cultural and psychological factors attributable to the history of male domination of society.

American Nurses Ass'n v. Illinois, 783 F.2d 716, 720 (7th Cir.1986) (Posner, J.).

3.   After *Gunther* and *AFSCME*, it became clear that courts would not be hospitable to comparable worth theories used in Title VII cases for the purpose of mandating pay equity across sex-segregated jobs. *See, e.g.*, International Union, UAW v. Michigan, 886 F.2d 766 (6th Cir.1989); American Nurses Ass'n v. Illinois, 783 F.2d 716 (7th Cir.1986). Can comparable worth concepts nevertheless still play a role in Title VII cases? For example, can a plaintiff use "comparable worth" statistics comparing pay rates for sex-segregated jobs within a company as indirect evidence of disparate treatment? Or in awarding a backpay remedy to a woman in a case based on evidence of intentional sex-based wage discrimination, would it be appropriate for a court to consider evidence regarding higher pay rates given to employees in "male" jobs of "comparable worth" when there are no comparators working for the same employer who have "similar" or "substantially equal" jobs?

4.   *Disparate Impact*: *AFSCME* rejected disparate impact analysis because (1) disparate impact "is confined to cases that challenge a specific, clearly delineated employment practice applied at a single point in the job selection process," and (2) "the decision to base compensation on the competitive market * * * involves the assessment of a number of complex factors not easily ascertainable, an assessment too multifaceted to be appro-

priate for disparate impact analysis." How would you evaluate these statements of the law on disparate impact today in light of *Watson v. Fort Worth Bank & Trust*, 487 U.S. 977, 108 S.Ct. 2777, 101 L.Ed.2d 827 (1988), in Chapter 4, and the Civil Rights Act of 1991? Professor Perry has written:

> The disparate impact theory under Title VII provides the legal tool to challenge pay-setting practices that cause disparities between wages for women's work and men's work, regardless of whether the jobs in question are similar in content and regardless of the employer's conscious intent. Wherever an employer's facially neutral pay-setting practices are proved to be consequentially preferential to men, disparate impact doctrine requires the courts to examine the business justification for those policies.

Pamela L. Perry, *Let Them Become Professionals: An Analysis of the Failure to Enforce Title VII's Pay Equity Mandate*, 14 Harv. Women's L.J. 127, 136 (1991). Do you agree? Why have courts apparently been so reluctant to accept disparate impact analysis in Title VII sex-based pay disparity cases?

5. *Disparate Treatment*: Are you satisfied that the employer in *AFSCME* did not intend to discriminate on the basis of sex in setting wages? The court observed that "[t]he requirement of intent is linked at least in part to culpability. * * * Neither law nor logic deems the free market system a suspect enterprise." Were discriminatory practices that were once legal under the free market responsible for creating a sex-segregated (as well as a racially segregated) workforce in the first place? Consider the evidence in *AFSCME* that the existing sex-based wage disparity in certain jobs resulted from years of hiring practices that deliberately segregated occupations on the basis of sex. See, for example, the *Hibbs* case in Chapter 6, Section D. Once the state of Washington was aware of the results of its pay equity study, was it intentional discrimination for it to continue to rely on market rates? *See, e.g.*, American Nurses' Ass'n v. Illinois, 783 F.2d 716, 722 (7th Cir.1986) (dicta that intent under Title VII requires more than an "awareness of consequences"). How did the Court in *Corning Glass Works* deal with the post-Equal Pay Act perpetuation of historical pay differentials based on sex? Professor Perry observed:

> Congress * * * rejected the notion that the market is always the preferable way to set wages by enacting Title VII. Congress made the policy decision to intervene and, absent business necessity, to correct the discriminatory effects of the market. The decision to intervene was appropriate because the market is not value neutral. Rather, an employer's demand for workers necessarily incorporates notions of value. To the extent employers value female workers less than male workers, either because of their tastes for discrimination or because of their perceptions regarding productivity of the two groups, use of the market manifests precisely the type of practice Title VII was designed to regulate.

Perry, *supra* Note 4, at 178. For analyses of the use of disparate treatment theory in Title VII sex-based pay cases, see Clauss, *supra* Note 1; Mack A. Player, *Exorcising the Bugaboo of "Comparable Worth": Disparate Treatment Analysis of Compensation Differences Under Title VII*, 41 Ala.L.Rev. 321 (1990).

6. *Legislating Pay Equity in State and Local Governments*: Both before and after the *AFSCME* litigation, a number of state and local public employers—in the United States and in other countries—began to undertake pay equity studies similar to the study commissioned by the State of Washington in *AFSCME*. A number of these studies ultimately led to implementation of comparable worth schemes. Perhaps the most far-reaching state comparable worth legislation is the State Employees Pay Equity Law enacted in Minnesota in 1982. Minn.Stat. § 43A.01–3,–14a,–22a (1994). More than twenty states and a number of municipalities have adopted some form of comparable worth law for public employers. Some of these laws, however, have been construed narrowly by the courts. *See, e.g.*, Alaska State Comm'n for Human Rights v. Alaska Dep't of Admin., 796 P.2d 458 (Alaska 1990) (holding that "work of comparable character" means work that is substantially equal). For an analysis of the labor market effects of Minnesota's pay equity plan, see Elaine Sorensen, Comparable Worth: Is It a Worthy Policy? (1994).

7. *Federal Pay Equity Proposals*: In 1985 Congress authorized a study of the pay classification scheme for over 1.5 million federal employees to determine if federal pay practices discriminate on the basis of sex, race, or Hispanic origin. H.R. 3008, 99th Cong., 1st Sess. (1985); *see House Approval of Pay Equity Bill*, 120 Lab.Rel.Rep. (BNA) 162 (Oct. 21, 1985). Opponents of the bill believed that the study would prompt "immediate litigation" like the *AFSCME* lawsuit that was then still being litigated. *Id.* Federal legislation mandating pay equity in the private sector has been proposed, but never enacted. *See, e.g.*, Fair Pay Act of 1994, H.R. 4803, 103d Cong., 2d Sess. (1994). The Fair Pay Act of 1994 would have required employers to pay "the same wage to workers who hold jobs that are equivalent in some combination of skill, effort, responsibility, and working conditions." Even in the absence of broad federal pay equity legislation, the wage rates of private employers who contract with the federal government are subject to federal oversight through regulations implementing Executive Order No. 11,246. 30 Fed.Reg. 12,319 (1965). Would you recommend federal legislation mandating comparable worth? Or would more vigorous enforcement of the existing equal pay laws be adequate to deal with sex-based pay disparities?

8. *Negotiating Pay Equity:* Unions played a significant role in advocating the comparable worth theory at the state legislative level. In particular, union-initiated litigation, such as the *AFSCME* case, often led to the development of legislated or negotiated pay equity schemes. *See* Winn Newman & Lisa Newell, *The Lessons of* AFSCME v. State of Washington, 13 N.Y.U.Rev.L. & Soc. Change 475 (1984–1985). A number of state and local governments that have undertaken pay equity studies have adopted comparable worth schemes as a result of collective bargaining with public sector unions. One of the more well known plans was adopted in 1981 in San Jose, California, to settle a strike called by AFSCME Local 101 to protest the city's failure to remedy pay disparities revealed by its own wage study. *See* Shulamit Kahn, *Economic Implications of Public–Sector Comparable Worth: The Case of San Jose, California*, 31 Ind.Rel. 270 (1992).

9. *Reverse Discrimination—Title VII Challenges to Pay Equity Schemes*: An employer's salary adjustment scheme that is voluntarily adopted in response to its own pay equity study may be vulnerable to a sex-

based "reverse" wage discrimination challenge under Title VII. *See, e.g.,* Maitland v. University of Minn., 155 F.3d 1013 (8th Cir.1998), *on remand* 260 F.3d 959 (2001), *cert. denied*, 535 U.S. 929, 122 S.Ct. 1300, 152 L.Ed.2d 212 (2002); Smith v. Virginia Commonwealth Univ., 84 F.3d 672 (4th Cir.1996) (en banc).

10. *Comparative Perspectives*: Federal pay equity legislation could be modeled on comparable worth legislation adopted in other nations. *See generally* Richard Perlman & Maureen Pike, Sex Discrimination in the Labor Market: The Case for Comparable Worth (1994) (comparing comparable worth policies in the United States, the United Kingdom, and Australia). For example, the most comprehensive comparable worth statute is the 1990 Ontario Pay Equity Act which covers both public and private employers in Ontario, Canada. *See* Nancy K. Kubasek, Jennifer Johnson & M. Neil Browne, *Comparable Worth in Ontario: Lessons the United States Can Learn*, 17 Harv. Women's L.J. 103 (1994).

E. FRINGE BENEFITS

CITY OF LOS ANGELES DEPARTMENT OF WATER & POWER v. MANHART

Supreme Court of the United States, 1978.
435 U.S. 702, 98 S.Ct. 1370, 55 L.Ed.2d 657.

JUSTICE STEVENS delivered the opinion of the Court.

As a class, women live longer than men. For this reason, the Los Angeles Department of Water and Power required its female employees to make larger contributions to its pension fund than its male employees. We granted certiorari to decide whether this practice discriminated against individual female employees because of their sex in violation of § 703(a)(1) of the Civil Rights Act of 1964, as amended.

For many years the Department has administered retirement, disability, and death-benefit programs for its employees. Upon retirement each employee is eligible for a monthly retirement benefit computed as a fraction of his or her salary multiplied by years of service. The monthly benefits for men and women of the same age, seniority, and salary are equal. Benefits are funded entirely by contributions from the employees and the Department, augmented by the income earned on those contributions. No private insurance company is involved in the administration or payment of benefits.

Based on a study of mortality tables and its own experience, the Department determined that its 2,000 female employees, on the average, will live a few years longer than its 10,000 male employees. The cost of a pension for the average retired female is greater than for the average male retiree because more monthly payments must be made to the average woman. The Department therefore required female employees to make monthly contributions to the fund which were 14.84% higher than the contributions required of comparable male employees. Because employee contributions were withheld from paychecks, a female employee took home less pay than a male employee earning the same salary.[5]

[In 1973, plaintiffs sued the Department on behalf of a class of female employees and former employees, seeking injunctive relief and a refund of their excess contributions. The district court granted summary judgment for the plaintiffs, and the Ninth Circuit affirmed.]

* * *

The Department and various *amici curiae* contend that: (1) the differential in take-home pay between men and women was not discrimination within the meaning of § 703(a)(1) because it was offset by a difference in the value of the pension benefits provided to the two classes of employees; (2) the differential was based on a factor "other than sex" within the meaning of the Equal Pay Act of 1963 and was therefore protected by the so-called Bennett Amendment * * *. We consider these contentions in turn.

I

There are both real and fictional differences between women and men. It is true that the average man is taller than the average woman; it is not true that the average woman driver is more accident prone than the average man. Before the Civil Rights Act of 1964 was enacted, an employer could fashion his personnel policies on the basis of assumptions about the differences between men and women, whether or not the assumptions were valid.

It is now well recognized that employment decisions cannot be predicated on mere "stereotyped" impressions about the characteristics of males or females. Myths and purely habitual assumptions about a woman's inability to perform certain kinds of work are no longer acceptable reasons for refusing to employ qualified individuals, or for paying them less. This case does not, however, involve a fictional difference between men and women. It involves a generalization that the parties accept as unquestionably true: Women, as a class, do live longer than men. The Department treated its women employees differently from its men employees because the two classes are in fact different. It is equally true, however, that all individuals in the respective classes do not share the characteristic that differentiates the average class representatives. Many women do not live as long as the average man and many men outlive the average woman. The question, therefore, is whether the existence or nonexistence of "discrimination" is to be determined by comparison of class characteristics or individual characteristics. A "stereotyped" answer to that question may not be the same as the answer that the language and purpose of the statute command.

---

5. The significance of the disparity is illustrated by the record of one woman whose contributions to the fund (including interest on the amount withheld each month) amounted to $18,171.40; a similarly situated male would have contributed only $12,843.53.

The statute makes it unlawful "to discriminate against any *individual* with respect to his compensation, terms, conditions, or privileges of employment, because of such *individual's* race, color, religion, sex, or national origin." 42 U.S.C. § 2000e–2(a)(1) (emphasis added). The statute's focus on the individual is unambiguous. It precludes treatment of individuals as simply components of a racial, religious, sexual, or national class. If height is required for a job, a tall woman may not be refused employment merely because, on the average, women are too short. Even a true generalization about the class is an insufficient reason for disqualifying an individual to whom the generalization does not apply.

That proposition is of critical importance in this case because there is no assurance that any individual woman working for the Department will actually fit the generalization on which the Department's policy is based. Many of those individuals will not live as long as the average man. While they were working, those individuals received smaller paychecks because of their sex, but they will receive no compensating advantage when they retire.

It is true, of course, that while contributions are being collected from the employees, the Department cannot know which individuals will predecease the average woman. Therefore, unless women as a class are assessed an extra charge, they will be subsidized, to some extent, by the class of male employees.[14] It follows, according to the Department, that fairness to its class of male employees justifies the extra assessment against all of its female employees.

But the question of fairness to various classes affected by the statute is essentially a matter of policy for the legislature to address. Congress has decided that classifications based on sex, like those based on national origin or race, are unlawful. Actuarial studies could unquestionably identify differences in life expectancy based on race or national origin, as well as sex.[15] But a statute that was designed to make race irrelevant in the employment market, could not reasonably be construed to permit a take-home-pay differential based on a racial classification.[16]

Even if the statutory language were less clear, the basic policy of the statute requires that we focus on fairness to individuals rather than fairness to classes. Practices that classify employees in terms of religion, race, or sex tend to preserve traditional assumptions about groups rather than thoughtful scrutiny of individuals. The generalization involved in

---

14. The size of the subsidy involved in this case is open to doubt, because the Department's plan provides for survivors' benefits. Since female spouses of male employees are likely to have greater life expectancies than the male spouses of female employees, whatever benefits men lose in "primary" coverage for themselves, they may regain in "secondary" coverage for their wives.

15. For example, the life expectancy of a white baby in 1973 was 72.2 years; a non-white baby could expect to live 65.9 years, a difference of 6.3 years. See Public Health Service, IIA Vital Statistics of the United States, 1973, Table 5–3.

16. Fortifying this conclusion is the fact that some States have banned higher life insurance rates for blacks since the 19th century. *See generally* M. James, The Metropolitan Life—A Study in Business Growth 338–39 (1947).

this case illustrates the point. Separate mortality tables are easily interpreted as reflecting innate differences between the sexes; but a significant part of the longevity differential may be explained by the social fact that men are heavier smokers than women.[17]

Finally, there is no reason to believe that Congress intended a special definition of discrimination in the context of employee group insurance coverage. It is true that insurance is concerned with events that are individually unpredictable, but that is characteristic of many employment decisions. Individual risks, like individual performance, may not be predicted by resort to classifications proscribed by Title VII. Indeed, the fact that this case involves a group insurance program highlights a basic flaw in the Department's fairness argument. For when insurance risks are grouped, the better risks always subsidize the poorer risks. Healthy persons subsidize medical benefits for the less healthy; unmarried workers subsidize the pensions of married workers;[18] persons who eat, drink, or smoke to excess may subsidize pension benefits for persons whose habits are more temperate. Treating different classes of risks as though they were the same for purposes of group insurance is a common practice that has never been considered inherently unfair. To insure the flabby and the fit as though they were equivalent risks may be more common than treating men and women alike;[19] but nothing more than habit makes one "subsidy" seem less fair than the other.[20]

An employment practice that requires 2,000 individuals to contribute more money into a fund than 10,000 other employees simply because each of them is a woman, rather than a man, is in direct conflict with both the language and the policy of the Act. Such a practice does not pass the simple test of whether the evidence shows "treatment of a person in a manner which but for that person's sex would be different."[21]

---

17. *See* R. Retherford, The Changing Sex Differential in Mortality 71–82 (1975). Other social causes, such as drinking or eating habits—perhaps even the lingering effects of past employment discrimination—may also affect the mortality differential.

18. A study of life expectancy in the United States for 1949–1951 showed that 20-year-old men could expect to live to 60.6 years of age if they were divorced. If married, they could expect to reach 70.9 years of age, a difference of more than 10 years. *Id.* at 93.

19. The record indicates, however, that the Department has funded its death-benefit plan by equal contributions from male and female employees. A death benefit—unlike a pension benefit—has less value for persons with longer life expectancies. Under the Department's concept of fairness, then, this neutral funding of death benefits is unfair to women as a class.

20. A variation on the Department's fairness theme is the suggestion that a gender-neutral pension plan would itself violate Title VII because of its disproportionately heavy impact on male employees. This suggestion has no force in the sex discrimination context because each retiree's total pension benefits are ultimately determined by his actual life span; any differential in benefits paid to men and women in the aggregate is thus "based on [a] factor other than sex," and consequently immune from challenge under the Equal Pay Act, 29 U.S.C. § 206(d). Even under Title VII itself—assuming disparate-impact analysis applies to fringe benefits—the male employees would not prevail. Even a completely neutral practice will inevitably have some disproportionate impact on one group or another. *Griggs* does not imply, and this Court has never held, that discrimination must always be inferred from such consequences.

21. *Employment Discrimination and Title VII of the Civil Rights Act of 1964*, 84 Harv.L.Rev. 1109, 1170 (1971).

It constitutes discrimination and is unlawful unless exempted by the Equal Pay Act of 1963 or some other affirmative justification.

II

Shortly before the enactment of Title VII in 1964, Senator Bennett proposed an amendment providing that a compensation differential based on sex would not be unlawful if it was authorized by the Equal Pay Act, which had been passed a year earlier. The Equal Pay Act requires employers to pay members of both sexes the same wages for equivalent work, except when the differential is pursuant to one of four specified exceptions.[23] The Department contends that the fourth exception applies here. That exception authorizes a "differential based on any other factor other than sex."

The Department argues that the different contributions exacted from men and women were based on the factor of longevity rather than sex. It is plain, however, that any individual's life expectancy is based on a number of factors, of which sex is only one. The record contains no evidence that any factor other than the employee's sex was taken into account in calculating the 14.84% differential between the respective contributions by men and women. We agree with Judge Duniway's observation that one cannot "say that an actuarial distinction based entirely on sex is 'based on any other factor other than sex.' Sex is exactly what it is based on." 553 F.2d 581, 588 (1976).[24]

* * *

III

* * *

In essence, the Department is arguing that the prima facie showing of discrimination based on evidence of different contributions for the respective sexes is rebutted by its demonstration that there is a like difference in the cost of providing benefits for the respective classes. That argument might prevail if Title VII, contained a cost justification defense comparable to the affirmative defense available in a price discrimination suit. But neither Congress nor the courts have recognized such a defense under Title VII.

23. * * * We need not decide whether retirement benefits or contributions to benefit plans are "wages" under the Act, because the Bennett Amendment extends the Act's four exceptions to all forms of "compensation" covered by Title VII. The Department's pension benefits, and the contributions that maintain them, are "compensation" under Title VII.

24. The Department's argument is specious because its contribution schedule distinguished only imperfectly between long-lived and short-lived employees, while distinguishing precisely between male and female employees. In contrast, an entirely gender-neutral system of contributions and benefits would result in differing retirement benefits precisely "based on" longevity, for retirees with long lives would always receive more money than comparable employees with short lives. Such a plan would also distinguish in a crude way between male and female pensioners, because of the difference in their average life spans. It is this sort of disparity—and not an explicitly gender-based differential—that the Equal Pay Act intended to authorize.

Although we conclude that the Department's practice violated Title VII, we do not suggest that the statute was intended to revolutionize the insurance and pension industries. All that is at issue today is a requirement that men and women make unequal contributions to an employer-operated pension fund. Nothing in our holding implies that it would be unlawful for an employer to set aside equal retirement contributions for each employee and let each retiree purchase the largest benefit which his or her accumulated contributions could command in the open market. Nor does it call into question the insurance industry practice of considering the composition of an employer's work force in determining the probable cost of a retirement or death benefit plan. Finally, we recognize that in a case of this kind it may be necessary to take special care in fashioning appropriate relief.

* * *

[JUSTICE BLACKMAN concurred in part and concurred in the judgment. CHIEF JUSTICE BURGER, joined by JUSTICE RHENQUIST, concurred in part and dissented in part. JUSTICE MARSHALL concurred in the parts of the Court's opinion reprinted here and dissented in an omitted part regarding relief. JUSTICE BRENNAN took no part in the consideration or decision of this case.]

Notes and Questions

1. In *Arizona Governing Committee v. Norris*, 463 U.S. 1073, 103 S.Ct. 3492, 77 L.Ed.2d 1236 (1983), the Court extended the reach of *Manhart*'s prohibition of using sex-based actuarial tables to determine employees' fringe benefits. The Court held that an employer violates Title VII when its deferred compensation plan provides employees the option of purchasing— from one of several participating private insurance companies—retirement annuities that pay a woman lower benefits than a man who has contributed the same amount in deferred compensation.

2. During the 1980s, *Manhart* and *Norris* provoked a "highly polarized" debate about the use of sex-based statistical differences in employment benefits as well as in the insurance industry generally. Jill Gaulding, Note, *Race, Sex, and Genetic Discrimination in Insurance: What's Fair?*, 80 Cornell L.Rev. 1646, 1661 (1995); *see id.* at 1661 n.100 (citing relevant articles). On one side of the debate, scholars utilized efficiency arguments to "demonstrate that employee pension, annuity, and life insurance plans that do not use sex-distinct mortality tables in fact violate the Equal Pay Act and Title VII." George J. Benston, *The Economics of Gender Discrimination in Employee Fringe Benefits*: Manhart *Revisited*, 49 U.Chi.L.Rev. 489, 492–93 (1982); *see generally* Spencer Kimball, *Reverse Sex Discrimination*: Manhart, 1979 Am.B.Found.Res.J. 83. On the other side, scholars argued that an employer's use of sex-based actuarial tables in providing fringe benefits violates Title VII because the purpose of the statute is to assure equal treatment of individuals, not groups. *See generally* Lea Brilmayer, Richard W. Hekeler, Douglas Laycock & Teresa A. Sullivan, *Sex Discrimination in*

Employer–Sponsored Insurance Plans: A Legal and Demographic Analysis, 47 U.Chi.L.Rev. 505 (1980).

3. Individuals who purchase insurance or annuities on the "open market"—not through their employers—will very likely discover that their premium or contribution rates and benefits are calculated using sex-based actuarial tables. Would you support an amendment to Title VII that would permit employers to rely on sex-based statistical data in addition to other factors—such as lifestyle and other risk factors in the employee's medical history—to determine the rates or coverage of employee pension or insurance benefits? Consider the following observation, based on data from the private insurance industry:

> The effect of sex discrimination in insurance can be quite dramatic. Disability insurance provides an example. After offering unisex pricing in the early 1980s, all four of the nation's major disability insurers have now returned to sex-distinct pricing, in response to the statistics showing that women tend to file a higher number of claims. As a result, the cost of disability insurance for women rose thirty-nine percent in 1994, and women today may need to pay fifty percent more than men to get the same coverage.

Gaulding, *supra* Note 2, at 1663. As Gaulding asks, "What's fair?" *Id.* at 1647. If this type of discrimination is fair in the open market, why is it not fair when an employer contracts to provide the disability plan to employees? Conversely, if it is not allowed in the employment context because Title VII prohibits it as unlawful sex discrimination, why is it tolerated in the insurance market outside of employment?

4. In his 1992 book, *Forbidden Grounds: The Case Against Employment Discrimination Laws*, Professor Richard A. Epstein criticizes *Manhart* because he believes that the effects of the decision will make everyone, men and women, economically worse off than they were when employers could rely on sex-based statistical data in providing fringe benefits. *Id.* at 326; *see generally id.* at 313–28. Can you think of arguments for and against this proposition?

5. How can a descriptive statement about longevity of women be both a fact and a stereotype? Professor Ramona Paetzold has written that "[i]t is through *Manhart* that one learns that 'fact' or 'statistical truths' can still be the basis for illegal stereotypes when their use disadvantages a protected class, as when all women are asked to pay higher pension premiums because as a class, women tend to live longer than men." Ramona L. Paetzold, *Commentary: Feminism and Business Law: The Essential Interconnection,* 31 Am.Bus.L.J. 699, 710 (1994). What if a "statistical truth" is used to advantage a protected class? Would that make it a "legal" stereotype?

Chapter 8

HARASSMENT

A. INTRODUCTION

Employees covered by Title VII, the ADEA, and the ADA have a right to work in an environment free of discriminatory harassment that adversely affects their "terms, conditions, or privileges of employment." But not all workplace harassment is actionable discrimination under these statutes, and, in certain circumstances, employers may have defenses that limit their liability for discriminatory harassment. Because workplace harassment is not directly addressed by federal antidiscrimination laws, federal courts have articulated the elements of a plaintiff's claim of discriminatory harassment, a defendant's defenses, and the burdens of proof each party bears in litigation.

Although most of the Supreme Court cases dealing with discriminatory workplace harassment have arisen from claims of sexual harassment, the doctrinal foundations of harassment claims under Title VII originated in cases of racial and ethnic harassment dating from the early 1970s. *Rogers v. EEOC*, 454 F.2d 234 (5th Cir.1971), *cert. denied*, 406 U.S. 957, 92 S.Ct. 2058, 32 L.Ed.2d 343 (1972), was the first case to recognize that "a working environment heavily charged with discrimination may constitute an unlawful practice" under Title VII, despite the absence of discrete employment actions such as hiring or firing. *Id.* at 239. *Rogers* held that a doctor's practice of segregating his Hispanic patients from his non-Hispanic patients constituted discrimination in "the terms, conditions, or privileges of employment" of a Spanish-surnamed employee, Josephine Chavez, who worked in his office. In *Rogers*, Judge Goldberg wrote:

> We must be acutely conscious of the fact that Title VII of the Civil Rights Act of 1964 should be accorded a liberal interpretation in order to effectuate the purpose of Congress to eliminate the inconvenience, unfairness, and humiliation of ethnic discrimination. Furthermore, I regard this broad-gauged innovation [sic] legislation as a charter of principles which are to be elucidated and explicated by experience, time, and expertise. Therefore, it is my belief that employees' psychological as well as economic fringes are statutorily

entitled to protection from employer abuse, and that the phrase "terms, conditions, or privileges of employment" in Section 703 is an expansive concept which sweeps within its protective ambit the practice of creating a working environment heavily charged with ethnic or racial discrimination. I do not wish to be interpreted as holding that an employer's mere utterance of an ethnic or racial epithet which engenders offensive feelings in an employee falls within the proscription of Section 703. But by the same token I am simply not willing to hold that a discriminatory atmosphere could under no set of circumstances ever constitute an unlawful employment practice. One can readily envision working environments so heavily polluted with discrimination as to destroy completely the emotional and psychological stability of minority group workers, and I think Section 703 of Title VII was aimed at the eradication of such noxious practices.

Id. at 238.

Following *Rogers,* other federal courts recognized hostile work environment claims based on race, religion, and national origin. The federal courts, however, were initially reluctant to extend the rationale underlying racial harassment claims to women's claims of sexual harassment. Judicial decisions in the decade between 1976 and 1986, changed the face of harassment law, eventually placing sexual harassment law at the forefront in the Supreme Court case of *Meritor Savings Bank, FSB v. Vinson,* 477 U.S. 57, 106 S.Ct. 2399, 91 L.Ed.2d 49 (1986), reproduced in Section B.2 of this chapter. Citing the *Rogers* case and its progeny, *Meritor* acknowledged that discriminatory sexual harassment that creates a hostile work environment for the complainant violates Title VII.

The Title VII jurisprudence of harassment as a form of employment discrimination has developed largely in the context of sexual harassment, and this topic is the primary focus of this chapter. Section B.1 briefly introduces *quid pro quo* harassment, the first type of sexual harassment to be recognized as a violation of Title VII; quid pro quo harassment is explored more fully in Section C.1. Section B.2 explores *hostile work environment* sexual harassment through the two Supreme Court cases— *Meritor Savings Bank, FSB v. Vinson* and *Harris v. Forklift Systems, Inc.*—that recognized and defined the elements of sex-based hostile environment claims under Title VII. Section B.3 demonstrates the continuing evolution of the concept of sexual harassment as manifested in the Supreme Court's 1998 decision in *Oncale v. Sundowner Offshore Services, Inc.,* which held that same-sex sexual harassment may be actionable under Title VII. Finally, in Section C, two more 1998 Supreme Court decisions—*Burlington Industries, Inc. v. Ellerth* and *Faragher v. City of Boca Raton*—clarified the standards for employer liability for discriminatory harassment by supervisory employees. The chapter concludes, in Section D, with racial and ethnic harassment, the paradigmatic form of Title VII harassment. Workplace harassment based on other categories is discussed in Chapter 9 (sexual orientation), Chapter 10 (religion), Chapter 11 (national origin), Chapter 12 (age), and Chapter 13 (disability).

B. SEXUAL HARASSMENT

Numerous studies have documented the pervasiveness of sexual harassment in the workplace. *See, e.g.*, Barbara Gutek, Sex and the Workplace: The Impact of Sexual Behavior and Harassment on Women, Men, and Organizations (1985); *see also* B. Glenn George, *The Back Door: Legitimizing Sexual Harassment Claims*, 73 B.U.L.Rev. 1, 2 n.3 (1993) (listing surveys of sexual harassment). In one of the first surveys, published in *Redbook* magazine in 1976, 92% of the 9,000 respondents listed sexual harassment as a "serious" problem, and nine out of ten respondents reported personal experiences with sexual harassment in the workplace. Claire Safran, *What Men Do to Women on the Job: A Shocking Look at Sexual Harassment*, Redbook, Nov. 1976, at 149, 149, 217. *See* Catharine A. MacKinnon, Sexual Harassment of Working Women: A Case of Sex Discrimination 25–29 (1979). A 1987 survey of federal government employees reported that 42% of women and 14% of men experienced some form of workplace sexual harassment. Merit System Protection Board, Sexual Harassment in the Federal Government: An Update 2 (1988). The most likely victims of sexual harassment were single or divorced women between the ages of 20 and 44 who had some college education, worked in a nontraditional job, or worked in a predominantly male environment or for a male supervisor. *Id.* at 3. From May 1985 to May 1987, sexual harassment cost the federal government $267 million for replacement workers, sick leave, and reduced productivity. *Id.* at 4.

In 1988, *Working Woman* magazine reported that almost 90% of the Fortune 500 companies surveyed had acknowledged receiving complaints of sexual harassment from employees. Ronni Sandroff, *Sexual Harassment in the Fortune 500*, Working Woman, Dec. 1988, at 69. Sexual harassment then cost a typical Fortune 500 company about $7 million a year due to absenteeism, low morale, low productivity, and employee turnover. *Id.* This estimate, however, did not include the costs of defending sexual harassment lawsuits or the negative publicity from cases that went to trial. A telephone survey of 1,000 American adults released on February 5, 2002, by the Employment Law Alliance, found that 21 percent of women and 7 percent of men said that they had experienced sexual harassment in the workplace. 20 Human Resources Rep. (BNA), No. 7 at 191 (Feb. 18, 2002); *see also http://www.employmentlawalliance.com.* The full extent of sexual harassment in the workplace is difficult to measure; many incidents may never be reported. Professor MacKinnon observed, "Like women who are raped, sexually harassed women feel humiliated, degraded, ashamed, embarrassed, and cheap, as well as angry." MacKinnon, *supra*, at 47. *See generally* Ellen Bravo & Ellen Cassedy, The 9 to 5 Guide to Combatting Sexual Harassment (1992).

The courts rejected the early Title VII claims of women that sexual harassment constituted sex discrimination "in essence because the acts complained of were not seen to be sufficiently tied to the workplace context." Catharine A. MacKinnon, Sexual Harassment of Working Women: A Case of Sex Discrimination 59 (1979); *see generally id.* at 59–77 (discussing the early sexual harassment cases). By the mid–1970s, however, judicial decisions began to reflect a different understanding of the legality of sexual harassment. The decision of Judge Richey in *Williams v. Saxbe*, 413 F.Supp. 654 (D.D.C.1976), is generally acknowledged as the first to recognize that sexual harassment is cognizable under Title VII. *Williams* involved the claim by a woman that her male supervisor had retaliated against her when she rejected his sexual advances. She alleged that he "engaged in a continuing pattern and practice of harassment and humiliation"—including "unwarranted reprimands"—that culminated in dismissal. *Id.* at 655. In finding a violation of Title VII, Judge Richey held that "the conduct of the plaintiff's supervisor created an artificial barrier to employment which was placed before one gender and not the other, despite the fact that both genders were similarly situated." *Id.* at 657–58.

The following year, in *Barnes v. Costle*, 561 F.2d 983 (D.C.Cir.1977), the Court of Appeals for the District of Columbia Circuit held that an employer was liable for sex discrimination under Title VII when a male supervisor abolished a female plaintiff's job after she refused his sexual advances. The plaintiff had asserted that "retention of her job was conditioned upon submission to sexual relations—an exaction which the supervisor would not have sought from any male." *Id.* at 989. Moreover, "[b]ut for her womanhood, * * * her participation in sexual activity would never have been solicited." *Id.* at 990.

In 1979, Professor MacKinnon wrote:

> Women's experiences of sexual harassment can be divided into two forms which merge at the edges and in the world. The first I term the *quid pro quo*, in which sexual compliance is exchanged, or proposed to be exchanged, for an employment opportunity. The second arises when sexual harassment is a persistent *condition of work*.

MacKinnon, *supra*, at 32. By the late 1970s and early 1980s, the federal courts and the EEOC had begun to adopt the framework—and often the terminology—that Professor MacKinnon had used for analyzing sexual harassment cases. *See, e.g.*, Henson v. Dundee, 682 F.2d 897, 908, 909 n.18 (11th Cir.1982). Both the *Williams* and *Barnes* cases fell within the quid pro quo paradigm, and *Bundy v. Jackson*, 641 F.2d 934 (D.C.Cir. 1981), is considered the first case to endorse the hostile work environment theory of sexual harassment, which is discussed *infra*, in Section B.2. For an analysis of these early sexual harassment cases, see Catharine A. MacKinnon, *The Logic of Experience: Reflections on the Development of Sexual Harassment Law*, 90 Geo.L.J. 813 (2002).

In 1980, the EEOC promulgated guidelines on "Sexual Harassment," 29 C.F.R. § 1604.11, as part of its *Guidelines on Discrimination Because of Sex*. The Guidelines specifically recognized sexual harassment as a violation of Title VII and adopted the two judicially developed theories of sexual harassment: quid pro quo and hostile work environment.

> Harassment on the basis of sex is a violation of Sec. 703 of Title VII. Unwelcome sexual advances, requests for sexual favors, and other verbal or physical conduct of a sexual nature constitute sexual harassment when (1) submission to such conduct is made either explicitly or impliedly a term or condition of an individual's employment, (2) submission to or rejection of such conduct by an individual is used as the basis for employment decisions affecting such individual, or (3) such conduct has the purpose or effect of unreasonably interfering with an individual's work performance or creating an intimidating, hostile, or offensive environment.

29 C.F.R. § 1604.11(a). In 1986, the Supreme Court used the terms "quid pro quo" and "hostile work environment" to describe the two categories of sexual harassment actionable under Title VII. *See* Meritor Savings Bank, FSB v. Vinson, 477 U.S. 57, 65, 106 S.Ct. 2399, 2404–05, 91 L.Ed.2d 49 (1986), in Section B.2 of this chapter.

1. QUID PRO QUO

In *Nichols v. Frank*, 42 F.3d 503 (9th Cir.1994), in an opinion by Judge Reinhardt, the Ninth Circuit relied on the 1980 EEOC Guidelines on Sexual Harassment to find that a supervisor's conduct constituted sexual harassment under Title VII. *Nichols* was a paradigmatic case of quid pro quo sexual harassment. The plaintiff was a deaf-mute female who read at a fifth-grade level and could communicate only through writing and sign language. While she was employed as a mail sorter at a United States postal facility, her supervisor on the night shift repeatedly demanded that she perform oral sex on him. He was the highest ranking manager on her shift and the only supervisor who could use sign language. All of his requests for sexual favors occurred at the work site in the context of discussions about her sick leave, attendance record, job evaluations, and requests for leaves-of-absence. Because the plaintiff feared she would lose her job or job benefits if she refused the supervisor's sexual demands, she "repeatedly but unwillingly performed oral sex on him over a period of approximately six months." *Id.* at 506. After these sex acts, the supervisor would grant the plaintiff certain job benefits. Although she did not report the supervisor's harassing conduct at the time, she subsequently reported the harassment and filed complaints with the Postal Service, the EEOC, and her union, and then brought a Title VII action against the Postal Service. On appeal, the Ninth Circuit held that "quid pro quo sexual harassment occurs whenever an individual explicitly or implicitly conditions a job, a job benefit, or the absence of a job detriment upon an employee's acceptance of sexual conduct." *Id.* at 511.

Using the facts and holding in *Nichols v. Frank* for guidance, can you articulate the elements of a prima facie case of quid pro quo sexual harassment? Which part or parts of the 1980 EEOC Guidelines on Sexual Harassment, reproduced before Section B.1, were violated by the supervisor's conduct in *Nichols*? Would the plaintiff's claim for Title VII relief in *Nichols* have been less compelling if she had not been physically impaired? If she had had a high school education? Should she have complained sooner? Do you think these factors should make a difference in your analysis of a plaintiff's right to relief for quid pro quo sexual harassment? Why or why not? Will Title VII "chill the incidence of legitimate romance" in the workplace? *Nichols,* 42 F.3d at 510. Was the supervisor in *Nichols* interested in a romantic relationship with the plaintiff? Or was he using sex and his position of authority to humiliate her? Does it matter what his intentions were if his sexual advances were not welcomed by the plaintiff? Should a simple quid pro quo threat be sufficient to impose Title VII liability on an employer for the conduct of its supervisor? Judge Reinhardt in *Nichols* implies that in some circumstances a supervisor's "pursuit" of a subordinate might be "forbidden," whereas an employee's pursuit of a co-worker might be "proper"? *Id.* Do you agree?

These and other questions on the topic of quid pro quo sexual harassment will be explored further in Section C, Employer Liability for Harassment. In the following two cases, the Supreme Court articulated the theory supporting Title VII claims for a sexually hostile work environment.

2. HOSTILE WORK ENVIRONMENT

MERITOR SAVINGS BANK, FSB v. VINSON

Supreme Court of the United States, 1986.
477 U.S. 57, 106 S.Ct. 2399, 91 L.Ed.2d 49.

JUSTICE REHNQUIST delivered the opinion of the Court.

* * *

I

[In 1974, Sidney Taylor, a vice president and branch manager of Meritor Savings Bank, hired respondent Mechelle Vinson as a teller-trainee. Under Taylor's supervision, Vinson was promoted from trainee to teller, head teller, and finally assistant branch manager. Vinson "worked at the same branch for four years, and it is undisputed that her advancement there was based on merit alone." In the fall of 1978, Vinson took sick leave "for an indefinite period," and was subsequently discharged for excessive use of that leave. Vinson sued both Taylor and the bank under Title VII, claiming that during her employment she had "constantly been subjected to sexual harassment" by Taylor.]

At the 11–day bench trial, the parties presented conflicting testimony about Taylor's behavior during respondent's employment. Respondent testified that during her probationary period as a teller-trainee, Taylor treated her in a fatherly way and made no sexual advances. Shortly thereafter, however, he invited her out to dinner and, during the course of the meal, suggested that they go to a motel to have sexual relations. At first she refused, but out of what she described as fear of losing her job she eventually agreed. According to respondent, Taylor thereafter made repeated demands upon her for sexual favors, usually at the branch, both during and after business hours; she estimated that over the next several years she had intercourse with him some 40 or 50 times. In addition, respondent testified that Taylor fondled her in front of other employees, followed her into the women's restroom when she went there alone, exposed himself to her, and even forcibly raped her on several occasions. These activities ceased after 1977, respondent stated, when she started going with a steady boyfriend.

Respondent also testified that Taylor touched and fondled other women employees of the bank, and she attempted to call witnesses to support this charge. But while some supporting testimony apparently was admitted without objection, the District Court did not allow her "to present wholesale evidence of a pattern and practice relating to sexual advances to other female employees in her case in chief, but advised her that she might well be able to present such evidence in rebuttal to the defendants' cases." Respondent did not offer such evidence in rebuttal. Finally, respondent testified that because she was afraid of Taylor she never reported his harassment to any of his supervisors and never attempted to use the bank's complaint procedure.

Taylor denied respondent's allegations of sexual activity, testifying that he never fondled her, never made suggestive remarks to her, never engaged in sexual intercourse with her, and never asked her to do so. He contended instead that respondent made her accusations in response to a business-related dispute. The bank also denied respondent's allegations and asserted that any sexual harassment by Taylor was unknown to the bank and engaged in without its consent or approval.

The District Court denied relief, but did not resolve the conflicting testimony about the existence of a sexual relationship between respondent and Taylor. It found instead that

> [i]f [respondent] and Taylor did engage in an intimate or sexual relationship during the time of [respondent's] employment with [the bank], that relationship was a voluntary one having nothing to do with her continued employment at [the bank] or her advancement or promotions at that institution.

The court ultimately found that respondent "was not the victim of sexual harassment and was not the victim of sexual discrimination" while employed at the bank.

* * *

II

Title VII of the Civil Rights Act of 1964 makes it "an unlawful employment practice for an employer * * * to discriminate against any individual with respect to his compensation, terms, conditions, or privileges of employment, because of such individual's race, color, religion, sex, or national origin." 42 U.S.C. § 2000e–2(a)(1). * * *

Respondent argues, and the Court of Appeals held, that unwelcome sexual advances that create an offensive or hostile working environment violate Title VII. Without question, when a supervisor sexually harasses a subordinate because of the subordinate's sex, that supervisor "discriminate[s]" on the basis of sex. Petitioner apparently does not challenge this proposition. It contends instead that in prohibiting discrimination with respect to "compensation, terms, conditions, or privileges" of employment, Congress was concerned with what petitioner describes as "tangible loss" of "an economic character," not "purely psychological aspects of the workplace environment." In support of this claim petitioner observes that in both the legislative history of Title VII and this Court's Title VII decisions, the focus has been on tangible, economic barriers erected by discrimination.

We reject petitioner's view. First, the language of Title VII is not limited to "economic" or "tangible" discrimination. The phrase "terms, conditions, or privileges of employment" evinces a congressional intent " 'to strike at the entire spectrum of disparate treatment of men and women' "in employment. Los Angeles Dept. of Water and Power v. Manhart, 435 U.S. 702, 707 n.13, 98 S.Ct. 1370, 1375 n.13, 55 L.Ed.2d 657 (1978). Petitioner has pointed to nothing in the Act to suggest that Congress contemplated the limitation urged here.

Second, in 1980 the EEOC issued Guidelines specifying that "sexual harassment," as there defined, is a form of sex discrimination prohibited by Title VII. As an "administrative interpretation of the Act by the enforcing agency," Griggs v. Duke Power Co., 401 U.S. 424, 433–34, 91 S.Ct. 849, 855, 28 L.Ed.2d 158 (1971), these Guidelines, " 'while not controlling upon the courts by reason of their authority, do constitute a body of experience and informed judgment to which courts and litigants may properly resort for guidance.' " General Electric Co. v. Gilbert, 429 U.S. 125, 141–42, 97 S.Ct. 401, 411, 50 L.Ed.2d 343 (1976). The EEOC Guidelines fully support the view that harassment leading to noneconomic injury can violate Title VII.

In defining "sexual harassment," the Guidelines first describe the kinds of workplace conduct that may be actionable under Title VII. These include "[u]nwelcome sexual advances, requests for sexual favors, and other verbal or physical conduct of a sexual nature." 29 C.F.R § 1604.11(a) (1985). Relevant to the charges at issue in this case, the Guidelines provide that such sexual misconduct constitutes prohibited "sexual harassment," whether or not it is directly linked to the grant or denial of an economic *quid pro quo*, where "such conduct has the purpose or effect of unreasonably interfering with an individual's work performance or creating an intimidating, hostile, or offensive working environment." § 1604.11(a)(3).

In concluding that so-called "hostile environment" (*i.e.*, non *quid pro quo*) harassment violates Title VII, the EEOC drew upon a substantial body of judicial decisions and EEOC precedent holding that Title VII affords employees the right to work in an environment free from discriminatory intimidation, ridicule, and insult. *Rogers v. EEOC*, 454 F.2d 234 (5th Cir.1971), *cert. denied*, 406 U.S. 957, 92 S.Ct. 2058, 32 L.Ed.2d 343 (1972), was apparently the first case to recognize a cause of action based upon a discriminatory work environment. * * * Courts applied this principle to harassment based on race, religion, and national origin. Nothing in Title VII suggests that a hostile environment based on discriminatory *sexual* harassment should not be likewise prohibited. The Guidelines thus appropriately drew from, and were fully consistent with, the existing case law.

Since the Guidelines were issued, courts have uniformly held, and we agree, that a plaintiff may establish a violation of Title VII by proving that discrimination based on sex has created a hostile or abusive work environment. As the Court of Appeals for the Eleventh Circuit wrote in *Henson v. Dundee*, 682 F.2d 897, 902 (1982):

> Sexual harassment which creates a hostile or offensive environment for members of one sex is every bit the arbitrary barrier to sexual equality at the workplace that racial harassment is to racial equality. Surely, a requirement that a man or woman run a gauntlet of sexual abuse in return for the privilege of being allowed to work and make a living can be as demeaning and disconcerting as the harshest of racial epithets.

Of course, as the courts in both *Rogers* and *Henson* recognized, not all workplace conduct that may be described as "harassment" affects a "term, condition, or privilege" of employment within the meaning of Title VII. For sexual harassment to be actionable, it must be sufficiently severe or pervasive "to alter the conditions of [the victim's] employment and create an abusive working environment." *Rogers*, 454 F.2d at 238; *Henson*, 682 F.2d at 904. Respondent's allegations in this case—which include not only pervasive harassment but also criminal conduct of the most serious nature—are plainly sufficient to state a claim for "hostile environment" sexual harassment.

The question remains, however, whether the District Court's ultimate finding that respondent "was not the victim of sexual harassment," effectively disposed of respondent's claim. The Court of Appeals recognized, we think correctly, that this ultimate finding was likely based on one or both of two erroneous views of the law. First, the District Court apparently believed that a claim for sexual harassment will not lie absent an *economic* effect on the complainant's employment. Since it appears that the District Court made its findings without ever considering the "hostile environment" theory of sexual harassment, the Court of Appeals' decision to remand was correct.

Second, the District Court's conclusion that no actionable harassment occurred might have rested on its earlier "finding" that "[i]f [respondent] and Taylor did engage in an intimate or sexual relationship * * *, that relationship was a voluntary one." But the fact that sex-related conduct was "voluntary," in the sense that the complainant was not forced to participate against her will, is not a defense to a sexual harassment suit brought under Title VII. The gravamen of any sexual harassment claim is that the alleged sexual advances were "unwelcome." 29 C.F.R. § 1604.11(a) (1985). While the question whether particular conduct was indeed unwelcome presents difficult problems of proof and turns largely on credibility determinations committed to the trier of fact, the District Court in this case erroneously focused on the "voluntariness" of respondent's participation in the claimed sexual episodes. The correct inquiry is whether respondent by her conduct indicated that the alleged sexual advances were unwelcome, not whether her actual participation in sexual intercourse was voluntary.

Petitioner contends that even if this case must be remanded to the District Court, the Court of Appeals erred in one of the terms of its remand. Specifically, the Court of Appeals stated that testimony about respondent's "dress and personal fantasies," which the District Court apparently admitted into evidence, "had no place in this litigation." The apparent ground for this conclusion was that respondent's voluntariness *vel non* in submitting to Taylor's advances was immaterial to her sexual harassment claim. While "voluntariness" in the sense of consent is not a defense to such a claim, it does not follow that a complainant's sexually provocative speech or dress is irrelevant as a matter of law in determining whether he or she found particular sexual advances unwelcome. To the contrary, such evidence is obviously relevant. The EEOC Guidelines emphasize that the trier of fact must determine the existence of sexual harassment in light of "the record as a whole" and "the totality of circumstances, such as the nature of the sexual advances and the context in which the alleged incidents occurred." 29 C.F.R. § 1604.11(b) (1985). Respondent's claim that any marginal relevance of the evidence in question was outweighed by the potential for unfair prejudice is the sort of argument properly addressed to the District Court. In this case the District Court concluded that the evidence should be admitted, and the Court of Appeals' contrary conclusion was based upon the erroneous, categorical view that testimony about provocative dress and publicly expressed sexual fantasies "had no place in this litigation." While the District Court must carefully weigh the applicable considerations in deciding whether to admit evidence of this kind, there is no *per se* rule against its admissibility.

* * *

HARRIS v. FORKLIFT SYSTEMS, INC.

Supreme Court of the United States, 1993.
510 U.S. 17, 114 S.Ct. 367, 126 L.Ed.2d 295.

JUSTICE O'CONNOR delivered the opinion of the Court.

* * *

I

Teresa Harris worked as a manager at Forklift Systems, Inc., an equipment rental company, from April 1985 until October 1987. Charles Hardy was Forklift's president.

The Magistrate found that, throughout Harris' time at Forklift, Hardy often insulted her because of her gender and often made her the target of unwanted sexual innuendos. Hardy told Harris on several occasions, in the presence of other employees, "You're a woman, what do you know" and "We need a man as the rental manager"; at least once, he told her she was "a dumb ass woman." Again in front of others, he suggested that the two of them "go to the Holiday Inn to negotiate [Harris'] raise." Hardy occasionally asked Harris and other female employees to get coins from his front pants pocket. He threw objects on the ground in front of Harris and other women, and asked them to pick the objects up. He made sexual innuendos about Harris' and other women's clothing.

In mid-August 1987, Harris complained to Hardy about his conduct. Hardy said he was surprised that Harris was offended, claimed he was only joking, and apologized. He also promised he would stop, and based on this assurance Harris stayed on the job. But in early September, Hardy began anew: While Harris was arranging a deal with one of Forklift's customers, he asked her, again in front of other employees, "What did you do, promise the guy * * * some [sex] Saturday night?" On October 1, Harris collected her paycheck and quit.

Harris then sued Forklift, claiming that Hardy's conduct had created an abusive work environment for her because of her gender. The [district court] * * * found this to be "a close case," but held that Hardy's conduct did not create an abusive environment. The court found that some of Hardy's comments "offended [Harris], and would offend the reasonable woman," but that they were not

> so severe as to be expected to seriously affect [Harris'] psychological well-being. A reasonable woman manager under like circumstances would have been offended by Hardy, but his conduct would not have risen to the level of interfering with that person's work performance.
>
> Neither do I believe that [Harris] was subjectively so offended that she suffered injury * * *. Although Hardy may at times have genuinely offended [Harris], I do not believe that he created a

working environment so poisoned as to be intimidating or abusive to [Harris].

* * *

We granted certiorari, to resolve a conflict among the Circuits on whether conduct, to be actionable as "abusive work environment" harassment (no *quid pro quo* harassment issue is present here), must "seriously affect [an employee's] psychological well-being" or lead the plaintiff to "suffe[r] injury."

II

* * * When the workplace is permeated with "discriminatory intimidation, ridicule, and insult," that is "sufficiently severe or pervasive to alter the conditions of the victim's employment and create an abusive working environment," Title VII is violated.

This standard, which we reaffirm today, takes a middle path between making actionable any conduct that is merely offensive and requiring the conduct to cause a tangible psychological injury. As we pointed out in *Meritor*, "mere utterance of an * * * epithet which engenders offensive feelings in a [sic] employee," does not sufficiently affect the conditions of employment to implicate Title VII. Conduct that is not severe or pervasive enough to create an objectively hostile or abusive work environment—an environment that a reasonable person would find hostile or abusive—is beyond Title VII's purview. Likewise, if the victim does not subjectively perceive the environment to be abusive, the conduct has not actually altered the conditions of the victim's employment, and there is no Title VII violation.

But Title VII comes into play before the harassing conduct leads to a nervous breakdown. A discriminatorily abusive work environment, even one that does not seriously affect employees' psychological well-being, can and often will detract from employees' job performance, discourage employees from remaining on the job, or keep them from advancing in their careers. Moreover, even without regard to these tangible effects, the very fact that the discriminatory conduct was so severe or pervasive that it created a work environment abusive to employees because of their race, gender, religion, or national origin offends Title VII's broad rule of workplace equality. The appalling conduct alleged in *Meritor*, and the reference in that case to environments " 'so heavily polluted with discrimination as to destroy completely the emotional and psychological stability of minority group workers,' " (quoting *Rogers v. EEOC*), merely present some especially egregious examples of harassment. They do not mark the boundary of what is actionable.

We therefore believe the District Court erred in relying on whether the conduct "seriously affected plaintiff's psychological well-being" or led her to "suffe[r] injury." Such an inquiry may needlessly focus the factfinder's attention on concrete psychological harm, an element Title VII does not require. Certainly Title VII bars conduct that would seriously affect a reasonable person's psychological well-being, but the statute is not limited to such conduct. So long as the environment would reasonably be perceived, and is perceived, as hostile or abusive, there is no need for it also to be psychologically injurious.

This is not, and by its nature cannot be, a mathematically precise test. We need not answer today all the potential questions it raises, nor specifically address the [EEOC's] new regulations on this subject. But we can say that whether an environment is "hostile" or "abusive" can be determined only by looking at all the circumstances. These may include the frequency of the discriminatory conduct; its severity; whether it is physically threatening or humiliating, or a mere offensive utterance; and whether it unreasonably interferes with an employee's work performance. The effect on the employee's psychological well-being is, of course, relevant to determining whether the plaintiff actually found the environment abusive. But while psychological harm, like any other relevant factor, may be taken into account, no single factor is required.

III

Forklift, while conceding that a requirement that the conduct seriously affect psychological well-being is unfounded, argues that the District Court nonetheless correctly applied the *Meritor* standard. We disagree. Though the District Court did conclude that the work environment was not "intimidating or abusive to [Harris]," it did so only after finding that the conduct was not "so severe as to be expected to seriously affect plaintiff's psychological well-being," and that Harris was not "subjectively so offended that she suffered injury." The District Court's application of these incorrect standards may well have influenced its ultimate conclusion, especially given that the court found this to be a "close case."

We therefore reverse the judgment of the Court of Appeals, and remand the case for further proceedings consistent with this opinion.

JUSTICE SCALIA, concurring.

* * *

"Abusive" (or "hostile," which in this context I take to mean the same thing) does not seem to me a very clear standard—and I do not think clarity is at all increased by adding the adverb "objectively" or by appealing to a "reasonable person['s]" notion of what the vague word means. Today's opinion does list a number of factors that contribute to abusiveness, but since it neither says how much of each is necessary (an impossible task) nor identifies any single factor as determinative, it thereby adds little certitude. As a practical matter, today's holding lets virtually unguided juries decide whether sex-related conduct engaged in (or permitted by) an employer is egregious enough to warrant an award of damages. One might say that what constitutes "negligence" (a traditional jury question) is not much more clear and certain than what constitutes "abusiveness." Perhaps so. But the class of plaintiffs seeking to recover for negligence is limited to those who have suffered harm, whereas under this statute "abusiveness" is to be the test of whether legal harm has been suffered, opening more expansive vistas of litigation.

Be that as it may, I know of no alternative to the course the Court today has taken. One of the factors mentioned in the Court's nonexhaustive list—whether the conduct unreasonably interferes with an employee's work performance—would, if it were made an absolute test, provide greater guidance to juries and employers. But I see no basis for such a limitation in the language of the statute. Accepting *Meritor*'s interpretation of the term "conditions of employment" as the law, the test is not whether work has been impaired, but whether working conditions have been discriminatorily altered. I know of no test more faithful to the inherently vague statutory language than the one the Court today adopts. For these reasons, I join the opinion of the Court.

JUSTICE GINSBURG, concurring.

Today the Court reaffirms the holding of *Meritor Savings Bank v. Vinson*: "[A] plaintiff may establish a violation of Title VII by proving that discrimination based on sex has created a hostile or abusive work environment." The critical issue, Title VII's text indicates, is whether members of one sex are exposed to disadvantageous terms or conditions of employment to which members of the other sex are not exposed. As the Equal Employment Opportunity Commission emphasized, the adjudicator's inquiry should center, dominantly, on whether the discriminatory conduct has unreasonably interfered with the plaintiff's work performance. To show such interference, "the plaintiff need not prove that his or her tangible productivity has declined as a result of the harassment." Davis v. Monsanto Chemical Co., 858 F.2d 345, 349 (6th Cir. 1988). It suffices to prove that a reasonable person subjected to the discriminatory conduct would find, as the plaintiff did, that the harassment so altered working conditions as to "ma[k]e it more difficult to do the job." *See id. Davis* concerned race-based discrimination, but that difference does not alter the analysis; except in the rare case in which a bona fide occupational qualification is shown, Title VII declares discriminatory practices based on race, gender, religion, or national origin equally unlawful.

* * *

Notes and Questions

1. *The Prima Facie Case*: *Henson v. City of Dundee*, 682 F.2d 897, 902 (11th Cir.1982), cited by the Court in *Meritor*, is considered the leading case establishing the elements necessary to make a prima facie case of hostile work environment claim: (1) that the employee belongs to a protected class; (2) that the employee was subjected to unwelcome sexual harassment, including sexual advances, requests for sexual favors, or other verbal or physical conduct of a sexual nature; (3) that the harassment was based on sex; (4) that the harassment affected a term, condition, or privilege of

employment; and (5) that the doctrine of respondeat superior applies. Does the Supreme Court in *Meritor* and *Harris* adopt or reject all or part of the *Henson* analytical approach to hostile environmental claims?

2. *Proving Unwelcomeness*: *Henson v. City of Dundee* defined the element of "unwelcomeness" as requiring proof that the plaintiff did not solicit or invite the conduct. The element of unwelcomeness is applicable only in sexual harassment cases. Why should that be so? In its amicus brief in *Meritor*, the EEOC argued for inclusion of this element on the ground that it was needed to "ensure that sexual harassment charges do not become the tool by which one party to a consensual relationship may punish the other." Brief for EEOC as Amicus Curiae, *Meritor* (No.84–1979). Do you believe there is merit to this concern? Is it consistent with the *Harris* "totality of the circumstances" test? What obligations does the requirement of "unwelcomeness" impose upon the plaintiff?

What purpose does the "unwelcomeness" requirement serve? Professor Henry Chambers offers the following "working theory" of the requirement of proof of "unwelcomeness" in sexual harassment cases: "[U]nwelcomeness stems from the notions that welcome conduct does not tend to cause harm and that harassers and employers need affirmative notice that conduct is harassing before the employer is deemed responsible for subsequent similar conduct." Professor Henry L. Chambers, Jr., *(Un)Welcome Conduct and the Sexually Hostile Environment*, 53 Ala.L.Rev. 733, 750 (2002). Should plaintiffs be required to "express" unwelcomeness? If so, how? Should a simple request to "stop" be sufficient? Or necessary? Is this too much of a burden? As you read the sexual harassment materials in this chapter, consider whether you would agree with Professor Chambers' conclusion that "[t]he unwelcomeness requirement should be eliminated because it no longer serves any useful purpose that is not already served by another feature of sexual harassment law and is at odds with Title VII's goals." *Id.* at 787. *See generally* Mary F. Radford, *By Invitation Only: The Proof of Welcomeness in Sexual Harassment Cases*, 72 N.C.L.Rev. 499 (1994); Ann C. Juliano, Note, *Did She Ask for It? The "Unwelcome" Requirement in Sexual Harassment Cases*, 77 Cornell L.Rev. 1558 (1992).

a. *The plaintiff's provocative speech and dress*: In *Meritor*, the Supreme Court agreed that evidence of the plaintiff's "sexually provocative speech or dress" could be relevant to the question of whether the plaintiff welcomed conduct of a sexual nature. One commentator criticizing this "welcomed conduct" defense argued that the *Meritor* evidentiary standard (1) "implies that the primary motivation for sexual harassment is sexual attraction" and "ignores that harassment is often a manifestation of power"; (2) "mischaracterizes female sexuality" by "categoriz[ing] female sexual conduct according to conventional, passive sex roles"; and (3) "is reminiscent of defense tactics in rape cases that attempt to blame the victim for the crime." Christina A. Bull, Comment, *The Implications of Admitting Evidence of a Sexual Harassment Plaintiff's Speech and Dress in the Aftermath of* Meritor Savings Bank v. Vinson, 41 UCLA L.Rev. 117, 119 (1993). Are these valid criticisms? When is harassment ever "welcome"? One commentator has argued that "a separate finding of welcomeness by the court is an unneeded and redundant step in sexual harassment cases." Casey J. Wood, *"Inviting Sexual Harass-*

ment": The Absurdity of the Welcomeness Requirement in Sexual Harassment Law, 38 Brandeis L.J. 423, 430 (1999–2000). Would you agree?

b. *Employer policies on appearance and behavior*: Some management attorneys recommend that employers adopt policies on personal appearance and behavior. For example, two commentators recently suggested the following policy:

> Please avoid extremes in dress and behavior. Flashy, skimpy, or revealing outfits and other non-business-like clothing are unacceptable. Likewise, unprofessional behavior in the workplace, such as sexually related conversations, inappropriate touching (*i.e.*, kissing, hugging, massaging, sitting on laps) of another employee, and any other behavior of a sexual nature is prohibited. Employees who fail to observe these standards will be subject to disciplinary action, up to and including termination.

James J. McDonald, Jr. & Daniel S. Fellner, *A Plaintiff's Obligation to "Avoid Harm Otherwise": New Life for the Welcomeness Defense*, 25 Employee Rel.L.J. 17, 32 (1999). What are the advantages for an employer in adopting and implementing such a policy? Would it constitute sexual discrimination under Title VII to fire a female employee who wears sexually provocative clothing at work in violation of such a rule? Or would it be sexual harassment for a supervisor to "badger" her about her inappropriate dress? *See, e.g.,* Schmitz v. ING Securities, Futures & Options, Inc., 10 F.Supp.2d 982 (N.D.Ill.1998), *aff'd*, 191 F.3d 456 (7th Cir.1999). Why should the employee who is not a harasser have to change her behavior? Why should the limitation be visited upon the person without fault? If a female employee wears a skimpy dress, is she suddenly an open target for harassment?

c. *The plaintiff's use of vulgar language*: Is a male supervisor's offensive and vulgar language "unwelcome" if his female subordinate also occasionally uses swear words on the job? *See* Hocevar v. Purdue Fredcrick Co., 223 F.3d 721, 736–37 (8th Cir.2000). Does a female who uses crude, profane language "welcome" the sexually degrading language that is directed at her by her male co-workers? *See* Carr v. Allison Gas Turbine Div., 32 F.3d 1007, 1011–12 (7th Cir.1994). What if the female employee never swears?

d. *The adolescent plaintiff*: Are there special concerns about the "welcomeness" of sexual advances when the victim of workplace harassment is an adolescent? *See generally* Seymour Moskowitz, *Adolescent Workers and Sexual Harassment,* 51 Lab.L.J., Fall 2000, at 78. In 1997, nearly one-half million teenagers from fifteen to seventeen years old were reported to have been employed at some time during the year. *Id.* at 85 n.1 (citing U.S. Dep't of Labor, Bureau of Labor Statistics, *Employment Earnings* [January, 1997]). Can a 16–year-old have a truly "consensual" sexual relationship with an older co-worker? With a supervisor?

3. *Severity or Pervasiveness*: *Harris v. Forklift* requires a plaintiff to satisfy both an objective and subjective test in proving that sexual harassment was sufficiently "severe or pervasive" to affect "the conditions of the victim's employment." What is the difference, if any, between proving that conduct was severe or pervasive, according to both objective and subjective perspectives, and proving that it was "unwelcome" to the plaintiff? How can

employees distinguish between legitimate flirtation or teasing and illegal harassment? *See generally* Richard L. Wiener & Linda E. Hurt, *Social Sexual Conduct at Work: How Do Workers Know When It Is Harassment and When It Is Not?*, 34 Cal.W.L.Rev. 53 (1997).

In his concurrence in *Harris v. Forklift*, Justice Scalia expresses concern that the terms "abusive" or "hostile" do not provide "a very clear standard" and that "virtually unguided juries" will decide whether conduct is "egregious enough to warrant an award of damages." Is this concern warranted? Many sexual harassment claims result in dismissal or summary judgment for the defendant, so the plaintiff never reaches either a bench trial or a jury trial. *See* Ann Juliano & Stewart J. Schwab, *The Sweep of Sexual Harassment Cases*, 86 Cornell L.Rev. 548, 568 (2001) (reporting on the significant increase in the percentage of sexual harassment cases resulting in dismissal or summary judgment from 1986 to 1995). Following the Civil Rights Act of 1991, even when a hostile work environment case goes to jury trial, a jury verdict based on a finding of "severe or pervasive" conduct may be overturned on appeal. *See, e.g.,* Duncan v. General Motors Corp., 300 F.3d 928, 935 (8th Cir.2002) (2–1 decision reversing a $1 million jury verdict on the ground that "as a matter of law * * * [the plaintiff] did not show a sexually harassing hostile environment sufficiently severe or pervasive so as to alter the conditions of her employment"), *cert. denied*, 538 U.S. 994, 123 S.Ct. 1789, 155 L.Ed.2d 695 (2003). Is the real danger that judges will improperly substitute their view of the facts for the jury's findings? *See id.* at 936, 938 (Arnold, J., dissenting). *See generally* Theresa M. Beiner, *Let the Jury Decide: The Gap Between What Judges and Reasonable People Believe Is Sexually Harassing*, 75 S.Cal.L.Rev. 791 (2002) (reviewing social science research on what conduct is perceived as "severe or pervasive" sexual harassment); M. Isabel Medina, *A Matter of Fact: Hostile Environments and Summary Judgments*, 8 S.Cal.Rev.L. & Women's Stud. 311 (1999) (arguing that courts are usurping the role of the jury in sexual harassment cases).

a. *What is "severe"?* Can a single incident of harassment, such as a physical assault, violate Title VII? *See* Smith v. Sheahan, 189 F.3d 529, 533 (7th Cir.1999) (yes). What if the assault is not sexual? *See id.* (holding that an assault based on "sex-based animus" rather than "misdirected sexual desire" is actionable). Courts have found that a single incident that is a serious sexual assault, such as rape, is objectively "severe." *See* Ferris v. Delta Air Lines, Inc., 277 F.3d 128, 136 (2d Cir.2001), *cert. denied*, 537 U.S. 824, 123 S.Ct. 110, 154 L.Ed.2d 34 (2002) (finding that a single act of rape is "sufficiently egregious" to "satisfy the first prong of employer liability under a hostile work environment theory"); Little v. Windermere Relocation, Inc., 301 F.3d 958 (9th Cir.2002) (finding that multiple rapes of an employee in one night was "severe"). When should one or two incidents of forcible sexual touching be considered "severe"? *Compare* Hostetler v. Quality Dining, Inc., 218 F.3d 798, 809 (7th Cir.2000) (finding that plaintiff's allegations that her male coworker forced his tongue down her throat one day and the next day tried to unfasten her bra were sufficiently severe to support a jury finding of a hostile work environment), *with* Brooks v. City of San Mateo, 229 F.3d 917 (9th Cir.2000) (finding that, where a male co-worker forcibly fondled the breast of a female dispatcher, the single incident was not sufficiently severe to impose liability on the employer for hostile work environment). What about unwelcome touching that is not clearly sexual? *See* Meriwether v. Caraustar Packaging Co., 326 F.3d 990 (8th Cir.2003) (finding that a single incident where a co-worker squeezed the plaintiff's buttocks followed by an encounter where the co-worker "joked about the incident" was not severe or pervasive). What if there is no physical touching, but only a single verbal attack? *See* Howley v. Town of Stratford, 217 F.3d 141, 154 (2d Cir.2000) (finding that "an extended barrage of obscene verbal abuse" of the plaintiff, delivered "at length, loudly, and in a large group in which the [plaintiff] was the only female and many of the men were her subordinates," was severe enough to support a jury finding of hostile work environment).

Is a single sexual proposition from a high-ranking manager "severe"? Or does a sexual proposition become "severe" only after the subordinate has made it clear that sexual relations would be "unwelcome" and the sexual proposition is repeated? *See* Quantock v. Shared Marketing Servs., Inc., 312 F.3d 899, 904 (7th Cir.2002) (finding that when a company president made three propositions for sex to his subordinate in a single business meeting the conduct was sufficiently severe to be actionable). In *Jones v. Clinton*, 990 F.Supp. 657 (E.D.Ark.1998), *appeal dismissed*, 161 F.3d 528 (8th Cir.1998), a § 1983 action, plaintiff Paula Jones, a state employee, alleged that President Clinton had invited her to his hotel room while he was governor of Arkansas. While she was alone with him in his room, he allegedly made unwelcome sexual advances toward her, stroked her leg, attempted to kiss her, and exposed his penis and asked her to kiss it, after which she fled the room. *Id.* at 664. Relying on Title VII sexual harassment case law for her analysis, Judge Susan Webber Wright ruled that the alleged conduct was not *quid pro quo* sexual harassment, nor was it sufficiently severe or pervasive to support a claim of hostile work environment sexual harassment. *Id.* at 674, 676. Can *Quantock* and *Jones* be reconciled?

b. *What is "pervasive"?* Can a "pervasive" series of offensive incidents—no one of which taken alone could reasonably be considered "severe" sexual harassment—violate Title VII? Because the terms "severe or pervasive" appear in the disjunctive, the plaintiff should be able to satisfy this element of a sexual harassment case by evidence that the harassing conduct is either severe or pervasive or both. But what is necessary to establish that nonsevere—but offensive and unwelcome—conduct is "pervasive" enough to be actionable? *Compare* Smith v. First Union Nat'l Bank, 202 F.3d 234, 242–43 (4th Cir.2000) ("repeated remarks that belittled [the plaintiff] because she was a woman," along with physical threats, are "severe or pervasive"), *with* Shepherd v. Comptroller of Pub. Accounts of Tex., 168 F.3d 871, 874–75 (5th Cir.) (finding that co-worker's "boorish and offensive" comments, staring, and touching plaintiff's arm, which occurred "intermittently for a period of time" were "not severe" and did not "undermine" the plaintiff's "workplace competence"), *cert. denied*, 528 U.S. 963, 120 S.Ct. 395, 145 L.Ed.2d 308 (1999). How do courts determine when, as a matter of law, repeated conduct is sufficiently frequent to be actionable? *Compare* Burnett v. Tyco Corp., 203 F.3d 980, 984 (6th Cir.) (finding that three alleged offensive incidents, only one of which was considered "severe," "spread out at the beginning and at the end of a six-month period [were] not commonplace, ongoing, or continuing," and were, therefore, not severe or pervasive), *cert. denied*, 531 U.S. 928, 121 S.Ct. 307, 148 L.Ed.2d 246 (2000), *with id.* at

985, 986–87 (Martin, C.J., dissenting) (criticizing the majority's "method of computation," which "fails to examine the aggregate effects of the incidents"). What if a male employee merely stares at a female co-worker? Can the act of staring, repeated on a daily basis over a long period of time, ever be actionable sexual harassment? *See* Birchtein v. New United Motor Mfg., 92 Cal.App.4th 994, 112 Cal.Rptr.2d 347, 353 (2001) (finding that a co-worker's repeated acts of staring at the plaintiff are actionable under California's Fair Employment and Housing Act).

4.   *The Problem of Perspective*: In *Ellison v. Brady*, 924 F.2d 872 (1991), the Ninth Circuit used an analytic approach to hostile environment claims that is based on the victim's perspective:

> [W]e believe that in evaluating the severity and pervasiveness of sexual harassment, we should focus on the perspective of the victim. If we only examined whether a reasonable person would engage in allegedly harassing conduct, we would run the risk of reinforcing the prevailing level of discrimination. * * *
>
> We * * * prefer to analyze harassment from the victim's perspective. A complete understanding of the victim's view requires, among other things, an analysis of the different perspectives of men and women. Conduct that many men consider unobjectionable may offend many women. *See, e.g.*, Lipsett v. University of Puerto Rico, 864 F.2d 881, 898 (1st Cir.1988) ("A male supervisor might believe, for example, that it is legitimate for him to tell a female subordinate that she has a 'great figure' or 'nice legs.' The female subordinate, however, may find such comments offensive") * * *. *See also* Ehrenreich, *Pluralist Myths and Powerless Men: The Ideology of Reasonableness in Sexual Harassment Law*, 99 Yale L.J. 1177, 1207–08 (1990) (men tend to view some forms of sexual harassment as "harmless social interactions to which only overly-sensitive women would object"); Abrams, *Gender Discrimination and the Transformation of Workplace Norms*, 42 Vand.L.Rev. 1183, 1203 (1989) (the characteristically male view depicts sexual harassment as comparatively harmless amusement).
>
> We realize that there is a broad range of viewpoints among women as a group, but we believe that many women share common concerns which men do not necessarily share. For example, because women are disproportionately victims of rape and sexual assault, women have a stronger incentive to be concerned with sexual behavior. Women who are victims of mild forms of sexual harassment may understandably worry whether a harasser's conduct is merely a prelude to violent sexual assault. Men, who are rarely victims of sexual assault, may view sexual conduct in a vacuum without a full appreciation of the social setting or the underlying threat of violence that a woman may perceive.
>
> In order to shield employers from having to accommodate the idiosyncratic concerns of the rare hyper-sensitive employee, we hold that a female plaintiff states a prima facie case of hostile environment sexual harassment when she alleges conduct which a reasonable woman would consider sufficiently severe or pervasive to alter the conditions of employment and create an abusive working environment.

We adopt the perspective of a reasonable woman primarily because we believe that a sex-blind reasonable person standard tends to be male-biased and tends to systematically ignore the experiences of women. The reasonable woman standard does not establish a higher level of protection for women than men. Instead, a gender-conscious examination of sexual harassment enables women to participate in the workplace on an equal footing with men. By acknowledging and not trivializing the effects of sexual harassment on reasonable women, courts can work towards ensuring that neither men nor women will have to "run a gauntlet of sexual abuse in return for the privilege of being allowed to work and make a living." Henson v. Dundee, 682 F.2d 897, 902 (11th Cir.1982).

We note that the reasonable victim standard we adopt today classifies conduct as unlawful sexual harassment even when harassers do not realize that their conduct creates a hostile working environment. Well-intentioned compliments by co-workers or supervisors can form the basis of a sexual harassment cause of action if a reasonable victim of the same sex as the plaintiff would consider the comments sufficiently severe or pervasive to alter a condition of employment and create an abusive working environment. That is because Title VII is not a fault-based tort scheme. "Title VII is aimed at the consequences or effects of an employment practice and not at the " " " motivation" of co-workers or employers.

Id. at 878–80.

In a footnote, the *Ellison* court further explained that "[w]e realize that the reasonable woman standard will not address conduct which some women find offensive. Conduct considered harmless by many today may be considered discriminatory in the future. Fortunately, the reasonableness inquiry which we adopt today is not static. As the views of reasonable women change, so too does the Title VII standard of acceptable behavior." 924 F.2d at 879 n.12.

The Juliano and Schwab survey of all federal sexual harassment cases between 1986 and 1995 reports that they "found more articles discussing the reasonable woman standard than courts adopting the standard"—only 25 opinions out of 502. Ann Juliano & Stewart J. Schwab, *The Sweep of Sexual Harassment Cases*, 86 Cornell L.Rev. 548, 584 (2001). In accepting the use of a "reasonable person" standard to determine whether a work environment is hostile or abusive, does the Supreme Court in *Harris v. Forklift* necessarily reject a "reasonable woman" standard? If so, does the objective component of the "reasonable person" standard reflect a legal system and a work environment that privileges male experiences, values, and views? For further analysis of the "reasonable woman" standard in sexual harassment cases, see Caroline A. Forell & Donna M. Matthews, A Law of Her Own: The Reasonable Woman as a Measure of Man 21–120 (2000); Juliano & Schwab, *supra*, at 582–85 & 583 n.140 (citing commentary on the standard).

5. *The "Reasonableness" of Employees' Beliefs—The* Breeden *Retaliation Case*: In *Clark County School District v. Breeden*, 532 U.S. 268, 121 S.Ct. 1508, 149 L.Ed.2d 509 (2001) (per curiam), the Supreme Court held that, because an employee's belief that her supervisor's explicit sexual

comment was "sexual harassment" was not reasonable, her Title VII claim that her employer had retaliated against her for complaining about the comment was not actionable. The female plaintiff in *Breeden* attended a meeting with a male supervisor and a male co-worker for the purpose of reviewing psychological evaluations of several job applicants. One report revealed that the applicant had told a co-worker, "I hear making love to you is like making love to the Grand Canyon." While he was looking at her, the plaintiff's supervisor read this portion of the report out loud and commented, "I don't know what that means." The two men then "chuckled" after the plaintiff's co-worker responded, "Well, I'll tell you later." Subsequently, the plaintiff complained about this incident to the supervisor involved, as well as to other supervisors in the school district. *See Breeden,* 532 U.S. at 269, 121 S.Ct. at 1509.

In her lawsuit, the plaintiff claimed that the employer had punished her for making these complaints and that the employer's acts constituted unlawful retaliation under Title VII. Title VII provides remedies for employees who suffer adverse job consequences because they have "opposed" employer practices that are unlawful under the statute. *See* 42 U.S.C. § 2000–e3(a). The elements of Title VII retaliation claims are addressed in Chapter 15. The Ninth Circuit held that the plaintiff's complaints were protected "opposition" conduct under Title VII "if she had a reasonable, good faith belief that the incident involving the sexually explicit remark constituted unlawful harassment." *Id.* at 270, 121 S.Ct. at 1509. Without ruling "on the propriety of this interpretation," the Supreme Court held that "even assuming it is correct, no one could reasonably believe that the incident recounted above violated Title VII." Although *Breeden* is a retaliation case, its discussion of the objective standard for determining whether harassing conduct is sufficiently severe to be actionable under Title VII has implications for hostile work environment cases generally.

Relying on language in *Harris v. Forklift*, the Court emphasized that

> "A recurring point in [our] opinions is that simple teasing, offhand comments, and isolated incidents (unless extremely serious) will not amount to discriminatory changes in the 'terms and conditions of employment.'"

> No reasonable person could have believed that the single incident recounted above violated Title VII's standard. The ordinary terms and conditions of respondent's job required her to review the sexually explicit statement in the course of screening job applicants. Her co-workers who participated in the hiring process were subject to the same requirement, and indeed, in the District Court respondent "conceded that it did not bother or upset her" to read the statement in the file. Her supervisor's comment, made at a meeting to review the application, that he did not know what the statement meant; her co-worker's responding comment; and the chuckling of both are at worst an "isolated inciden[t]" that cannot remotely be considered "extremely serious," as our cases require.

Id. at 270–71, 121 S.Ct. at 1509–10 (citations omitted). Does *Breeden* add clarity to the requirements of a prima facie case of hostile work environment? Has the Court implicitly rejected the "reasonable woman" perspective adopted in *Ellison v. Brady*? See *supra* Note 4.

6. *Claims for Psychological or Mental Distress*: *Harris v. Forklift* rejected the view that psychological harm is an indispensable element of a hostile work environment claim. A plaintiff may nevertheless seek damages for mental anguish or emotional distress caused by sexual harassment. If a plaintiff alleges that sexual harassment caused psychological, emotional, or mental distress, should the defendant be allowed, through discovery, to compel the plaintiff to submit to psychological testing or other mental examinations? Discovery requests for such evidence are controlled by a "good cause" provision in Rule 35 of the Federal Rules of Civil Procedure. See Jansen v. Packaging Corp. of Am., 158 F.R.D. 409 (N.D.Ill.1994) (appointment of an independent expert in the field of mental health approved); Thompson v. Haskell Co., 65 Fair Empl.Prac.Cas. (BNA) 1088 (M.D.Fla. 1994) (plaintiff required to disclose psychological records when she claimed that she became severely depressed and her employment was terminated when she did not agree to the sexual favors requested). As a general rule, discovery of psychological evidence is likely to be allowed only when a plaintiff places her mental or emotional condition in controversy. See Schlagenhauf v. Holder, 379 U.S. 104, 85 S.Ct. 234, 13 L.Ed.2d 152 (1964). *Compare* Schoffstall v. Henderson, 223 F.3d 818, 823 (8th Cir.2000) (holding that because the plaintiff had placed her mental state in issue, she had waived the psychotherapist-patient privilege), *with* Bridges v. Eastman Kodak Co., 850 F.Supp. 216 (S.D.N.Y.1994) (discovery denied because plaintiff alleged past and not ongoing mental injury), *and* Robinson v. Jacksonville Shipyards, Inc., 118 F.R.D. 525 (M.D.Fla.1988) (mental examination denied because plaintiff's psychological well-being not placed in issue in a sexual harassment case).

7. *Standing*: Some courts require that the harassing conduct be directed specifically at the plaintiff in order to be actionable. For example, in *Childress v. City of Richmond*, 134 F.3d 1205 (4th Cir.1998) (en banc), the court affirmed a district court ruling that seven white male police officers did not have standing to bring a Title VII hostile work environment claim based on racial and sexual harassment directed at black and female officers by their immediate supervisor. *See also id.* at 1208 (Luttig, J. concurring) (discussing standing requirements under Title VII); Leibovitz v. New York City Trans. Auth., 252 F.3d 179 (2d Cir.2001) (discussing standing under Title VII and the Constitution). *See generally* N. Morrison Torrey, *Indirect Discrimination Under Title VII: Expanding Male Standing to Sue for Injuries Received as a Result of Employer Discrimination Against Females*, 64 Wash.L.Rev. 365 (1989).

8. *Class Actions and Pattern-or-Practice Cases:* Class actions brought by individual plaintiffs under Rule 23 of the Federal Rules of Civil Procedure and pattern-or-practice cases brought by the EEOC under § 707 of Title VII, 42 U.S.C. § 2000e–6, have long been considered significant in employment discrimination litigation because of the inherent power of collective representation and broad injunctive relief. But what role should they play in challenging sexual harassment? *See* Michael Selmi, *The Price of Discrimination: The Nature of Class Action Employment Discrimination and Its Effects*, 81 Tex.L.Rev. 1249, 1249–50 (2003) (calling into question "whether [class

action] lawsuits produce substantial benefits to the plaintiff class, prompt any changes in corporate culture, or exact costs sufficient to serve as an adequate deterrent against discrimination").

Consider the case of *Jenson v. Eveleth*. In 1988, two women filed a class action sex discrimination suit against their employer, Eveleth Mines; it was the first Title VII hostile environment class action case. The class was certified by the district court in 1991. Jenson v. Eveleth Taconite Co., 139 F.R.D. 657 (D.Minn.1991) ("Jenson I"). In 1993, the district court ruled that Eveleth was liable to the class of plaintiffs for claims of hostile work environment. Jenson v. Eveleth Taconite Co., 824 F.Supp. 847 (D.Minn. 1993) ("Jenson II"). The court found that "a sexualized, male-oriented, and anti-female atmosphere" prevailed at two of the company's mines. *Id.* at 880. "[V]isual references to sex and to women as sex objects" in graffiti, photographs, and cartoons, as well as male employees' verbal references to women's "body parts" and female employees' "sex lives," pervaded the workplace. *Id.* at 879–80. Subsequently, in the remedial phase of the trial, the district court denied punitive damages and awarded compensatory damages for mental anguish to some members of the plaintiffs' class. The Eighth Circuit affirmed in part and vacated and remanded for a new trial on damages. Jenson v. Eveleth Taconite Co., 130 F.3d 1287 (8th Cir.1997) ("Jenson III"), *cert. denied sub nom.* Oglebay Norton Co. v. Jenson, 524 U.S. 953, 118 S.Ct. 2370, 141 L.Ed.2d 738 (1998). In early 1999, eleven years after the case was filed, the parties reached a settlement. In light of this history, would you encourage plaintiffs to pursue private class action lawsuits to remedy hostile environment sexual harassment? For a detailed account of the *Jenson v. Eveleth* litigation from the perspective of the plaintiffs and their lawyers, see Clara Bingham & Laura Leedy Gansler, Class Action: The Story of Lois Jenson and the Landmark Case that Changed Sexual Harassment Law (2002). *See also* Melissa Hart, *Litigation Narratives: Why* Jenson v. Eveleth *Didn't Change Sexual Harassment Law, But Still Has a Story Worth Telling*, 18 Berkeley Women's L.J. 282 (2003) (reviewing *Class Action*).

Consider the potential impact of a major pattern-or-practice case brought by the EEOC, *EEOC v. Mitsubishi Motor Manufacturing*, 990 F.Supp. 1059 (C.D.Ill.1998) (authorizing the EEOC to bring a pattern-or-practice case based on allegations of sexual harassment). In June of 1998, Mitsubishi Motor Manufacturing of America agreed to pay $34 million to a class of 350 current and former female employees in order to settle the class action sexual harassment suit that the EEOC filed in 1996. Michael Bologna, *Mitsubishi Settles EEOC Suit for $34 Million; Agency Says Class and Amount Largest Ever*, Legal News, 66 U.S.L.W. 2781, 2782 (June 23, 1998). In the EEOC lawsuit,

> the EEOC charged that between 1988 and 1993 Mitsubishi had tolerated boorish, even terrifying behavior by some 400 men who resented the women's presence. Men allegedly used air guns to shoot painful blasts at women's chests and crotches. Others frequently grabbed women by their breasts, simulated masturbation or exposed themselves. One worker allegedly forced a woman's legs apart and threatened to sodomize her. The EEOC said the company had "discouraged complaints and permitted retaliation against women who dared to complain." Among the most

chilling allegations: as supervisors idly listened, one man said he would force a woman to have sex with him—before he killed her.

Peter Annin & John McCormick, *More Than a Tune–Up: Tough Going in a Fight Against Sexual Harassment*, Newsweek, Nov. 24, 1997, at 50, 50–51. For a discussion of the role of the EEOC, the company, and the union in the *Mitsubishi* case, *see* Marion Crain & Ken Matheny, *"Labor's Divided Ranks": Privilege and the United Front Ideology*, 84 Cornell L.Rev. 1542, 1545–53, 1602–05 (1999).

9. *Defenses*: Typically a first-line defense to any claim of sexual harassment (whether quid pro quo or hostile work environment) is the alleged harasser's assertion that "I didn't do it." *Meritor* and *Harris* also endorse the defense to hostile work environment claims that the conduct at issue was either isolated or generally trivial. *See* Johnson v. Tower Air, Inc., 149 F.R.D. 461, 463, 469–70 (E.D.N.Y.1993) (allegations that, during a two-week period, a supervisor once brushed against the plaintiff "in a sexual manner," " 'grabbed his [own] crotch' " as a sexual gesture, and shouted vulgar and offensive comments at the plaintiff and other employees indicated "immature, nasty, and annoying" behavior, but, "without more," was not sufficient evidence of sexual harassment); *see also id.* at 470 (collecting cases). Some courts have summarily rejected the "boys will be boys" defense. *See* Andrews v. City of Philadelphia, 895 F.2d 1469 (3d Cir.1990); Atwood v. Biondi Mitsubishi, 61 Fair Empl.Prac.Cas. (BNA) 1357 (W.D.Pa.1993). From a litigation perspective, what are the differences between a defense that the alleged harassing conduct did not occur and a defense that, even if the conduct did occur as alleged, it did not constitute severe or pervasive sexual harassment?

a. *Discovery and admissibility of evidence of plaintiff's prior sexual history*: Defendants in Title VII cases have sought discovery of a plaintiff's prior sexual behavior to show that a plaintiff either welcomed the alleged sexually harassing conduct or to show that she was not subjectively offended by the conduct. For example, in *Priest v. Rotary*, 98 F.R.D. 755 (N.D.Cal. 1983), a waitress brought a Title VII action alleging that over several months her employer sexually harassed her, demanded sexual favors, and discharged her when she refused to comply with his demands. The employer claimed that the plaintiff was the "sexual aggressor" and that he discharged her because "she was trying to meet and 'pick up' male customers in his bar." *Id.* at 756. In support of this defense, the employer attempted to discover "detailed information about plaintiff's sexual history, including the name of each person which whom she had had sexual relations in the past ten years." *Id.* The magistrate denied the defendant's motion to compel discovery on this issue pursuant to Fed.R.Civ.P. 26(b) and granted the plaintiff's cross-motion for a protective order under Fed.R.Civ.P. 26(c).

The district judge affirmed the magistrate's order on two grounds. First, whether characterized as evidence of motive or "habit," the information sought was not within the then-current broad scope of Rule 26(b), which permits discovery of "any matter, not privileged, * * * relevant to the subject matter," or that "appears reasonably calculated to lead to the discovery of admissible evidence." Second, even if the information were within the scope of Rule 26(b), the plaintiff had demonstrated "good cause" for issuance of a protective order under Rule 26(c) barring discovery into her past sexual history. The district judge observed:

> Discovery of intimate aspects of plaintiffs' lives, as well as those of their past and current friends and acquaintances, has the clear potential to discourage sexual harassment litigants from prosecuting lawsuits such as the instant one. For those more hearty souls who are determined to have their day in court, it has the potential to annoy and harass them significantly. This Court has read excerpts from the transcript of plaintiff's deposition in which defendant sought to elicit information about plaintiff's prior sexual relationships, and finds the annoyance and discomfort which the plaintiff obviously suffered as a result of defendant's inquiries unnecessary and deplorable.

> * * *

> * * * Sexual harassment plaintiffs would appear to require particular protection for this sort of intimidation and discouragement if the statutory cause of action for such claims is to have meaning. Without such protection from the courts, employees whose intimate lives are unjustifiably and offensively intruded upon in the workplace might face the "Catch–22" of invoking their statutory remedy only at the risk of enduring further intrusions into irrelevant details of their personal lives in discovery, and, presumably, in open court.

> The Court is not unmindful that a similar state of affairs once confronted victims in criminal prosecutions for rape, who often ran the risk of finding their own moral characters on trial during the prosecution of their assailants.

> * * *

> This Court is deeply concerned that civil complaints based on sexual harassment in the workplace will be similarly inhibited, if discovery tactics such as the one used by defendant herein are allowed to flourish.

> It is often said, that those who do not learn from history are condemned to repeat it. By carefully examining our experience with rape prosecutions, however, the courts and bar can avoid repeating in this new field of civil sexual harassment suits the same mistakes that are now being corrected in the rape context. The courts and Congress have concluded that even in the criminal context, the use of evidence of a complainant's past sexual behavior is more often harassing and intimidating than genuinely probative, and the potential for prejudice outweighs whatever probative value such evidence may have. Certainly, then, in the context of civil suits for sexual harassment, and absent extraordinary circumstances, inquiry into such areas should not be permitted, either in discovery or at trial.

Priest, 98 F.R.D. at 761–62. Since discovery in federal courts is effectively insulated from judicial review by the "final order" rule for judicial review, plaintiffs have little recourse in cases of abusive discovery if it is permitted by federal magistrates and judges. For examples of intrusive discovery in a sexual harassment lawsuit, see Bingham & Gansler, Class Action, *supra* Note 8, at 283–303.

The Violent Crime Control and Law Enforcement Act of 1994, Pub. L.No. 103–322, 108 Stat. 1919, may limit discovery of the past sexual history of sexual harassment claimants. With respect to civil proceedings, Rule 412 of the Federal Rules of Evidence now provides:

(a) Evidence generally inadmissible. The following evidence is not admissible in any civil or criminal proceeding involving alleged sexual misconduct except as provided in subdivisions (b) and (c):

(1) Evidence offered to prove that any alleged victim engaged in other sexual behavior.

(2) Evidence to prove any alleged victim's sexual pre-disposition.

(b) Exceptions.

* * *

(2) In a civil case, evidence offered to prove the sexual behavior or sexual predisposition of any alleged victim is admissible if it is otherwise admissible under these rules and its probative value substantially outweighs the danger of harm to any victim and of unfair prejudice to any party. Evidence of an alleged victim's reputation is admissible only if it has been placed in controversy by the alleged victim.

(c) Procedure to determine admissibility.

* * *

(2) Before admitting evidence under this rule the court must conduct a hearing in camera and afford the victim and parties a right to attend and be heard. The motion, related papers, and the record of the hearing must be sealed and remain under seal unless the court orders otherwise.

In *Wolak v. Spucci*, 217 F.3d 157 (2d Cir.2000), the court held that Rule 412 applies to the admissibility of evidence of a plaintiff's sexual behavior in a sexual harassment lawsuit. The court observed that "[w]hether a sexual advance was welcome, or whether an alleged victim in fact perceived an environment to be sexually offensive does not turn on the private sexual behavior of the alleged victim, because a woman's expectations about her work environment cannot be said to change depending upon her sexual sophistication." *Id.* at 160. For a discussion of Rule 412 and the circumstances under which evidence of a plaintiff's sexual behavior and sexual predisposition might be admissible in sexual harassment claims, see Paul Nicholas Monnin, *Proving Welcomeness: The Admissibility of Evidence of Sexual History in Sexual Harassment Claims Under the 1994 Amendments to Federal Rule of Evidence 412*, in Special Project: Current Issues in Sexual Harassment Law, 48 Vand.L.Rev. 1155 (1995).

b. Which of the following should be considered relevant evidence in defending a claim of hostile work environment brought by a female plaintiff?

(1) Plaintiff posed nude for *Playboy* magazine on her own time after working hours. She became the subject of sexual harassment after a male co-worker saw the *Playboy* issue and brought it into the workplace. *See* Burns v. McGregor Elec. Indus., 989 F.2d 959 (8th Cir.1993). Should it make a

difference if the plaintiff brought the magazine to the workplace and showed it to her co-workers?

(2) In response to crude and provocative sexual teasing, and sexually oriented crude jokes, the plaintiff responds in kind. *See* Loftin–Boggs v. City of Meridian, 633 F.Supp. 1323 (S.D.Miss.1986), *aff'd*, 824 F.2d 971 (1987), *cert. denied*, 484 U.S. 1063, 108 S.Ct. 1021, 98 L.Ed.2d 986 (1988).

(3) Plaintiff wrote her boss at least one personal, affectionate letter, often ate lunch with him, and participated in mutual kissing and petting with him. *See* Kresko v. Rulli, 432 N.W.2d 764 (Minn.Ct.App.1988).

(4) Plaintiff presents credible evidence that she is hypersensitive to conduct of a sexual nature. *See* Ellison v. Brady, 924 F.2d 872, 879–80 (9th Cir.1991).

c. *Free speech*: Biased, derogatory comments may be ubiquitous in many workplaces, and sex-based comments are particularly prevalent. A 2003 survey of 685 American employees reported that 33.7 percent of the respondents had heard sexually inappropriate comments in the workplace, 29.5 percent heard racial slurs, and 29.3 percent heard ethnic slurs. In addition, 24.4 percent of the respondents reported hearing biased remarks regarding sexual orientation, 22.9 percent heard such statements about another employee's age, and 7.9 percent heard insults targeting disabled individuals. *Equal Opportunity Offense: Biased Comments Cover Array of Groups*, 21 Hum. Resources Rep. (BNA) No.9, at 24 (Mar. 10, 2003). Even though a co-worker's or supervisor's speech may be offensive, it may not be sufficiently "severe or pervasive" to constitute a hostile work environment. But if the speech is sufficiently abusive to be actionable, government restraint of workplace speech raises significant constitutional concerns.

The defense of constitutionally protected free speech has been raised in some of the sexual harassment cases, particularly where the nature of the offensive conduct was primarily verbal or where pornographic pictures were prevalent in the workplace. A leading case rejecting the free speech defense is *Robinson v. Jacksonville Shipyards, Inc.*, 760 F.Supp. 1486 (M.D.Fla. 1991). The court held that injunctive relief limiting discriminatory workplace speech did not violate the First Amendment because (1) the employer did not intend "to express itself" by allowing workplace displays of sexually explicit pictures or employee use of sexually offensive language, and the employer could ban such displays and language without violating the employees' rights of free speech; (2) the offensive pictures and language were not protected speech, but "discriminatory conduct" that caused a hostile work environment—a harm distinguishable from the "communicative impact" of the speech; (3) the court's order limiting discriminatory speech was "nothing more than a time, place, and manner regulation of speech"; (4) the female workers at the shipyard were a "captive audience" subjected to the discriminatory speech, and the First Amendment "admits great latitude in protecting captive audiences from offensive speech"; (5) even if the discriminatory speech were protected speech, any governmental infringement must be analyzed under a balancing approach, and "the governmental interest in cleansing the workplace of impediments to the equality of women" is a "compelling interest" and "the regulation is narrowly drawn to serve this interest"; and (6) by analogy to public employee free speech cases—which balance "the interests of the employee in commenting on protected matters * * * against the employer's interests in maintaining discipline and order in the workplace"—the courts may "without violating the first amendment, require that a private employer curtail the free expression in the workplace of some employees in order to remedy the demonstrated harm inflicted on other employees." *Id.* at 1534–36.

Can you think of any circumstances where an employer might intend "to express itself" through sexually offensive language and pictures? What type of "narrowly drawn" injunction regulating speech would you want (or expect) for a shipyard? What about a poultry factory or an insurance office? Why should the women in any particular workplace be considered a "captive audience"? Don't employees always have the freedom to leave undesirable jobs? Is it realistic to expect that courts will be able to alter deeply entrenched workplace cultures through the use of injunctions that restrain employee speech? If not, what other remedies would serve the goals of Title VII? In any event, is it fair to say that employees in some work settings should just expect that part of the job includes exposure to offensive language, crude jokes, and displays of pornographic material?

In *DeAngelis v. El Paso Municipal Police Officers Association*, 51 F.3d 591 (5th Cir.), *cert. denied*, 516 U.S. 974, 116 S.Ct. 473, 133 L.Ed.2d 403 (1995), the plaintiff, a female police officer, alleged that her fellow police officers wrote and published in a police association newsletter certain articles that sexually harassed her and other newly hired female officers. The police department had no control over the publication and dissemination of the newsletter. The district court ruled in favor of the plaintiff, but the court of appeals reversed on the grounds that the facts did not support a claim of hostile work environment. Nevertheless, the court cautioned that "where pure expression is involved [such as verbal insults, pictorial, or literary matter], Title VII steers into the territory of the First Amendment." *Id.* at 596.

In *Johnson v. County of Los Angeles Fire Department*, 865 F.Supp. 1430 (C.D.Cal.1994), the court held that the First Amendment protects the right of public employees to possess, read, and share *Playboy* magazine at the workplace on their own time. Although *Johnson* was not a Title VII case, what are its implications for female public employees who want to bring a sexual harassment claim because they are offended that their male co-workers read and discuss *Playboy* at work in their free time?

Consider the following: Plaintiff, a female, worked as an Assistant Stage Director at the Metropolitan Opera Association in New York City, where she shared an office with several other stage directors. One of her co-workers, a male, posted seven post-card sized photographs of nude men on a bulletin board in the office they shared. Plaintiff found the pictures offensive, and one day she removed them from the bulletin board and handed them to her co-worker. He immediately put them back up on the bulletin board, where they remained for nearly two years—up until the time that the plaintiff's employment was terminated. Plaintiff brought a Title VII claim that the photographs created a sexually hostile work environment. Does the plaintiff have a viable Title VII claim? If so, does the employer have a free speech defense? *See* Brennan v. Metropolitan Opera Ass'n, Inc., 192 F.3d 310 (2d

Cir.1999); *see also* Brennan v. Metropolitan Opera Ass'n, Inc., 284 A.D.2d 66, 729 N.Y.S.2d 77 (N.Y.App.Div.2001).

The free speech defense has generated a lively debate among legal scholars. In *Title VII as Censorship: Hostile–Environment Harassment and the First Amendment*, 52 Ohio St.L.J. 481 (1991), Kingsley R. Browne, a strong supporter of the defense, argued that Title VII fails to protect core "political" speech in the workplace. *See also* Kingsley R. Browne, *Workplace Censorship: A Response to Professor Sangree*, 47 Rutgers L.Rev. 579, 580–82 (1995). For some opposing views, see Mary Becker, *How Free Is Speech at Work?*, 29 U.C. Davis L.Rev. 815 (1996); Cynthia L. Estlund, *The Architecture of the First Amendment and the Case of Workplace Harassment*, 75 Notre Dame L.Rev. 1361 (1997); Cynthia L. Estlund, *Freedom of Expression in the Workplace and the Problem of Discriminatory Harassment*, 75 Tex. L.Rev. 687 (1997); Keith R. Fentonmiller, Note, *Verbal Sexual Harassment as Equality–Depriving Conduct*, 27 U.Mich.J.L.Reform 565 (1994). *See also* Thomas C. Berg, *Religious Speech in the Workplace: Harassment or Protected Speech?*, 22 Harv.J.L. & Pub. Pol'y 959 (1999); Charles R. Calleros, Aguilar v. Avis Rent A Car System, Inc.: *The California Supreme Court Takes a Divided Freeway to Content–Oriented Regulation of Workplace Speech*, 34 U.S.F.L.Rev. 237 (2000) (discussing *Aguilar v. Avis Rent A Car System, Inc.*, 21 Cal.4th 121, 87 Cal.Rptr.2d 132, 980 P.2d 846 (Cal.1999), *cert. denied*, 529 U.S. 1138, 120 S.Ct. 2029, 146 L.Ed.2d 971).

10. *Computer Harassment*: In the age of the Internet and computer bulletin boards, employees have ready access to a large number of databases, including those containing pornographic literature and digitized pornographic photographs. Through e-mail, employees can send and receive sexually offensive jokes and rumors, as well as highly personal information about co-workers. *See, e.g.,* Owens v. Morgan Stanley & Co., 1997 WL 793004 (S.D.N.Y.1997) (black employees sued employer because of its discriminatory response to the dissemination of racist jokes over company's electronic mail system). Suppose a female employee alleges that she is subjected to hostile work environment harassment because male co-workers repeatedly send sexually explicit e-mail messages to her and display pornographic pictures on their workplace computers. Should she have a claim under Title VII? What steps would you recommend that an employer take to limit its liability? Is this situation any different from the cases where women have claimed that nude photographs and crude sexual language in the workplace create a hostile work environment? For example, if a male employee installs a screen saver with a pornographic image on a computer that he knows will be used on a daily basis by a female co-worker, will she have a viable claim that this is "severe or pervasive" sexual harassment? *See* Duncan v. General Motors Corp., 300 F.3d 928 (8th Cir.2002), *cert. denied*, 538 U.S. 994, 123 S.Ct. 1789, 155 L.Ed.2d 695 (2003).

Could the transmission over an employer's computer system of a single offensive e-mail message ever satisfy the threshold for a prima facie hostile environment claim? Would repeated transmissions of insensitive jokes and comments meet the threshold? Does it matter whether the sender has directed the e-mail at a particular individual or group of individuals as opposed to a general audience? *See* Curtis v. DiMaio, 46 F.Supp.2d 206 (E.D.N.Y.1999) (holding that sending a single offensive e-mail message does not establish an actionable hostile work environment claim for racial and ethnic harassment under § 1981, particularly where the e-mail message was not directed at the plaintiff), *aff'd*, 205 F.3d 1322 (2d Cir.2000). The New Jersey Supreme Court has unanimously ruled that, under the state "Law Against Discrimination," co-workers' insulting e-mail messages on an electronic bulletin board maintained by the employer may create a hostile work environment for the plaintiff who received the e-mail. Blakey v. Continental Airlines, Inc., 164 N.J. 38, 751 A.2d 538 (2000).

If a female employee complains that her co-worker is using the employer's computers in her work area to view pornographic images, how should the employer respond? In *Stuart v. General Motors Corp.*, 217 F.3d 621 (8th Cir.2000), the court ruled that, even if the display of pornographic images on a computer would be actionable sexual harassment, the employer was not liable for harassment when it immediately removed the co-worker's computer, offered to move the plaintiff to another part of the plant, and within days checked all of the company's computers on site for pornographic software. Do employees have any rights in the privacy of the contents of their workplace computers? After surveying the law on workplace privacy, Professor Dennis Nolan concludes,

> Every branch of the law—constitutional, common, and statutory; federal and state—allows employers wide discretion to monitor, restrict, and inspect their employees' electronic communications and files. At the same time, several branches of the law, particularly federal financial regulations, intellectual property doctrines, and anti-discrimination laws, impose at least some risk of liability on employers for their employees' misuse of the employers' communications systems. Given the state of the law, it would be a strange employer indeed that opted to protect employee privacy rather than to invade it.

Dennis R. Nolan, *Privacy and Profitability in the Technological Workplace*, 24 J.Lab.Res., Spring 2003, at 208, 225.

If employees receive pornographic spam on their workplace computers from third parties, can the employer be found liable for a hostile work environment? What if the technology does not exist to filter all spam? *See Failing to Address Pornographic Spam Could Lead to Hostile Environment Claims*, 71 U.S.L.W. No. 48, at 2787 (June 17, 2003). For analyses of workplace computer harassment, see Sally Greenberg, *Threats, Harassment, and Hate On–Line: Recent Developments*, 6 B.U.Pub.Int.L.J. 673, 676–77 (1997); Eugene Volokh, *Freedom of Speech, Cyberspace, and Harassment Law*, 2001 Stan.Tech.L.Rev. 3, 5–24 (arguing that the "Hidden Communications Decency Act" implicit in workplace sexual harassment law has led "many employers rightly [to] fear that politically offensive e-mail or pornographic images glimpsed on co-workers' computers will lead to liability," *id.* at 5, 24); David K. McGraw, Note, *Sexual Harassment in Cyberspace: The Problem of Unwelcome E–Mail*, 21 Rutgers Computer & Tech.L.J. 491, 506–07 (1995).

11. *First Amendment Freedom of Religion and the Ministerial Exception to Title VII*: A novice alleges that he was sexually harassed by priests while he was being trained for the priesthood. He has brought a sexual harassment claim under Title VII. The order of priests has defended on the

grounds that the "ministerial exception" to Title VII permits it the freedom to make its own employment decisions about its ministerial employees. Should religious entities be able to avoid sexual harassment liability on the basis of the ministerial exception? *See* Bollard v. California Province of the Soc'y of Jesus, 196 F.3d 940 (9th Cir.1999). For discussion of the "ministerial exception" to Title VII, see the Note in Chapter 10, Section C.

12.   *Off-Site, After–Hours Harassment*: Can an employer defend against a sexual harassment claim on the grounds that the alleged conduct occurred off-site and after working hours? How can an employer control or monitor the behavior of employees who are not at work? Where is the workplace anyway? *See* Moring v. Arkansas Dep't of Corr., 243 F.3d 452 (8th Cir.2001) (holding employer liable for supervisor's unwelcome sexual advances toward a subordinate which occurred in a hotel room during a business trip). If an employee is raped by the employer's client following a business dinner, should the employer be liable for sexual harassment under Title VII? Does your answer depend on what the employer does when it learns about the sexual assault? *See* Little v. Windermere Relocation, Inc., 301 F.3d 958 (9th Cir.2002) (finding that summary judgment was improperly granted where plaintiff alleged her pay was substantially reduced and she was then discharged after she was allegedly raped by the employer's client). If a female flight attendant is raped by a male airline pilot at a hotel where flight crews are booked for stopovers between flights, should the airline be liable for sexual harassment if it immediately fires the pilot? What if the pilot had a reputation for making unwanted sexual advances toward female flight attendants? *See* Ferris v. Delta Air Lines, Inc., 277 F.3d 128 (2d Cir.2001), *cert. denied*, 537 U.S. 824, 123 S.Ct. 110, 154 L.Ed.2d 34 (2002).

13.   *Disparate Treatment or Disparate Impact:* A female lineman for a utility company complained that her employer's failure to provide "civilized bathroom facilities" for her during work constituted sexual harassment. The plaintiff was the only female lineman working for the company. While on the job site, her male co-workers urinated outdoors, often near where she was working. Because the company failed to provide her with private toilet facilities on the lineman's trucks, she was frequently embarrassed by having to urinate in public within sight of her co-workers. Is this sexual harassment? Or is it just plain sex discrimination? If so, under what theory? Disparate treatment or disparate impact? *See* DeClue v. Central Ill. Light Co., 223 F.3d 434 (7th Cir.2000) (rejecting sexual harassment claim and disparate treatment sex discrimination claim, but noting that plaintiff might have prevailed if she had brought the claim under a disparate impact theory of sex discrimination).

Note: Claims Arising Out of Paramour Preferential Treatment and the Termination of Consensual Sexual Relationships

Plaintiffs have brought "reverse discrimination" or "paramour preference" claims under Title VII based on one employee's allegations that a supervisor has given preferential treatment to another employee with whom he has a sexual relationship. In 1980, the EEOC indicated that personal, social workplace relationships are outside the ambit of Title VII. Preamble to Interim Guidelines on Sex Discrimination, 45 Fed.Reg. 25024 (1980). In

King v. Palmer, 778 F.2d 878 (D.C.Cir.1985), however, the D.C. Circuit suggested that Title VII would permit a discrimination action based on the consensual sexual relationship of third-parties. Subsequently, most courts have disagreed with the implications of *King v. Palmer*. For example, in *DeCintio v. Westchester County Medical Center*, 807 F.2d 304, 307 (2d Cir.1986), *cert. denied*, 484 U.S. 825, 108 S.Ct. 89, 98 L.Ed.2d 50 (1987), the court concluded that "[w]e can adduce no justification for defining 'sex,' for Title VII purposes, so broadly as to include an ongoing, voluntary, romantic engagement." *See also* Taken v. Oklahoma Corp. Comm'n, 125 F.3d 1366, 1370 (10th Cir.1997) (claims based on "a voluntary romantic affiliation, and not on any gender differences" are not actionable under Title VII); Drinkwater v. Union Carbide Corp., 904 F.2d 853, 862 (3d Cir.1990) ("A sexual relationship between a supervisor and a co-employee could adversely affect the workplace without creating a hostile sexual environment."). For a proposal to treat workplace sexual favoritism as actionable sexual harassment under Title VII, see Joan E. Van Tol, *Eros Gone Awry: Liability Under Title VII for Workplace Sexual Favoritism*, 13 Indus.Rel.L.J. 153 (1992).

What if the plaintiff had been involved in a consensual sexual relationship with her alleged harasser? Does this situation raise the same kinds of concerns as allegations of a supervisor's favoritism toward a paramour? In *Nichols v. Frank*, 42 F.3d 503 (9th Cir.1994), the quid pro quo case discussed in Section B.1 of this chapter, Judge Reinhardt observed:

> [C]ourts are understandably reluctant to chill the incidence of legitimate romance. People who work closely together and share common interests often find that sexual attraction ensues. It is not surprising that those feelings arise even when one of the persons is a superior and the other a subordinate. As our workforce grows, and more and more of us find it necessary, or desirable, to earn our own living, we spend an increasing amount of our time at work. Sexual barriers to employment have lessened. We tend these days, far more than in earlier times, to find our friends, lovers, and even mates in the workplace. We spend longer hours at the office or traveling for job-related purposes, and often discover that our interests and values are closer to those of our colleagues or fellow employees than to those of people we meet in connection with other activities. In short, increased proximity breeds increased volitional sexual activity.

Id. at 510. Although courts and the EEOC may be reluctant to interfere with "legitimate" office romance, employers may not be so restrained. Because workplace romances that end may cause disruptions in working relationships or lead to sexual harassment claims, many employers have adopted nonfraternization policies that apply to sexual relationships between co-workers, as well as to the potentially more troublesome relationships between supervisors and their subordinates. As you think about the following situations, consider the potential effect of the "unwelcomeness" requirement of a prima facie case of sexual harassment. See *supra* Section B.2, Note 2, following *Harris v. Forklift*.

　　a.　If a subordinate terminates a sexual relationship with her supervisor, and the supervisor then fires the subordinate, does the fired employee have a claim of sexual harassment? *See* Smith v. Cashland, Inc., 193 F.3d 1158 (10th Cir.1999).

b. What if a subordinate is fired for refusing to resume a consensual lesbian relationship with her supervisor? *See* Llampallas v. Mini–Circuits, Lab, Inc., 163 F.3d 1236 (11th Cir.1998); *cert. denied*, 528 U.S. 930, 120 S.Ct. 327, 145 L.Ed.2d 255 (1999).

c. Suppose that a supervisor, to retaliate against a subordinate for breaking off their consensual sexual relationship, reports to high-level managers that the subordinate's work is unsatisfactory. Based on this (erroneous) report, the company fires the employee. Is this discrimination on the basis of sex? Or actionable sexual harassment? *See Llampallas, id.*

d. If a supervisor terminates a consensual relationship with a subordinate and then fires the subordinate, is the employment decision "because of sex"? Is it actionable under Title VII? *See* Mauro v. Orville, 259 A.D.2d 89, 697 N.Y.S.2d 704 (1999), *leave to appeal denied*, 94 N.Y.2d 759, 705 N.Y.S.2d 6, 726 N.E.2d 483 (2000). Would your analysis be affected by knowing that the supervisor's wife insisted that he end the relationship and fire his employee, and he agreed in order to save his marriage? *See id. See also* Pipkins v. Temple Terrace, Fla., 267 F.3d 1197, 1200 (11th Cir.2001).

e. If an employee sexually harasses a co-worker to retaliate against the co-worker for breaking up their consensual sexual relationship, is the employer—who has notice of the harassment and fails to end it—liable for co-worker hostile environment sexual harassment? *Compare* Succar v. Dade County Sch. Bd., 229 F.3d 1343 (11th Cir.2000), *with* Green v. Administrators of Tulane Educ. Fund, 284 F.3d 642, 656–57 (5th Cir.2002). Does it matter whether the harassment is sexual or nonsexual in nature? *See* Lipphardt v. Durango Steakhouse of Brandon, Inc., 267 F.3d 1183, 1189 (11th Cir.2001). What if the employer retaliates against an employee for complaining about the unwelcome sexual harassment by a co-worker with whom she had a prior intimate relationship? *Id.* at 1188.

f. If an employer fires a supervisor for violating company policy by engaging in a consensual sexual relationship with a subordinate, can the supervisor bring an action for sex discrimination under Title VII? *See* Malone v. Eaton Corp., 187 F.3d 960 (8th Cir.1999).

g. One court asserted that "after a longtime sexual relationship * * * goes sour, it will be only the unusual case that can escape summary judgment." Mosher v. Dollar Tree Stores, 240 F.3d 662, 668 (7th Cir.), *cert. denied*, 534 U.S. 1041, 122 S.Ct. 617, 151 L.Ed.2d 539 (2001). What would be an "unusual case"? If harassment in the workplace follows a failed consensual relationship, is it necessarily true that the harasser is motivated by personal animosity and, therefore, the harassment cannot be because of the victim's gender? *See e.g.,* Kaminski v. Freight–A–Ranger, Inc., 2002 WL 31174461 (N.D.Ill.2002).

Note: Alternative Theories of Liability for Sexual Harassment

Sexual and racial harassment in the workplace became actionable "only because of Title VII," since historically such conduct "was not a tort at common law." Griggs v. National R.R. Passenger Corp., 900 F.2d 74, 75 (6th Cir.1990). As the federal law of sexual harassment developed, however, courts began to uphold a number of common law claims that plaintiffs asserted in order to obtain effective remedies for workplace sexual harassment. Victims of workplace sexual harassment may now sue their employers and harassers under state tort law in addition to bringing claims under state or federal antidiscrimination statutes. Tort theories asserted in sexual harassment cases include assault, battery, intentional or negligent infliction of emotional distress, defamation, invasion of privacy, loss of consortium, negligent hiring and retention, and failure to provide a safe workplace. *See, e.g.,* Maksimovic v. Tsogalis, 177 Ill.2d 511, 227 Ill.Dec. 98, 687 N.E.2d 21 (1997) (permitting claims of assault, battery, and false imprisonment to go forward in case involving coworker sexual harassment). In many jurisdictions, however, tort claims based on sexual harassment will be preempted by state civil rights laws. *See, e.g.,* Jansen v. Packaging Corp. of America, 123 F.3d 490 (7th Cir.1997) (en banc) (holding that a tort claim of intentional infliction of emotional distress was preempted by Illinois Human Rights Act), *cert. denied sub nom.* Ellerth v. Burlington Indus., 524 U.S. 951, 118 S.Ct. 2365, 141 L.Ed.2d 734 (1998); Thomas v. L'Eggs Prods., Inc., 13 F.Supp.2d 806 (C.D.Ill.1998) (holding that a tort claim of negligent retention was preempted by the Illinois Human Rights Act). *See* Martha S. Davis, *Rape in the Workplace,* 41 S.D.L.Rev. 411 (1996) (comparing the treatment of rape under workers' compensations systems, Title VII, and common law tort actions); Pamela J White & Susan R. Matluck, *Conduct Unbecoming a Lawyer: Expanding Tort Remedies for Sexual Harassment,* Brief, Summer 1995, at 16 (discussing the use of tort law to remedy sexual harassment in law firms); Clay Mahaffey, Case Note, 33 Land & Water L.Rev. 731 (1998) (discussing *Kanzler v. Renner,* 937 P.2d 1337 (Wyo.1997), which recognized a cause of action for intentional infliction of emotional distress on the basis of sexual harassment in the workplace).

From the perspective of a victim of workplace sexual harassment, what are some of the advantages and disadvantages of tort law as compared to discrimination law? What about the employer's perspective? Consider the following: (1) tort law can impose liability on small employers, regardless of their size, whereas Title VII coverage is limited to employers of fifteen or more employees; (2) there is no statutory limit on tort damages, whereas Title VII imposes statutory caps on damages depending on the size of the employer (see Chapter 16); and (3) a plaintiff can sue an employer's agent in his individual capacity under tort law, whereas the majority of courts do not recognize individual liability of agents under Title VII (see Chapter 2, Section D.4, and Section C.1, Note 9 following *Faragher*). Can you think of other substantive or procedural advantages or disadvantages for plaintiffs or defendants? For an argument that tort suits against harassers would remedy and deter sexual harassment in the workplace better than discrimination suits against employers, see Mark McLaughlin Hager, *Harassment as a Tort: Why Title VII Hostile Environment Liability Should Be Curtailed,* 30 Conn. L.Rev. 375 (1998). *See also* Rosa Ehrenreich, *Dignity and Discrimination: Toward a Pluralistic Understanding of Workplace Harassment,* 88 Geo.L.J. 1

(1999) (arguing that common law tort actions are a good way to deal with the dignitary harms of "classic" cases of male on female sexual harassment). For an example of tort remedies, see *Hoffman-La Roche, Inc. v. Zeltwanger*, 69 S.W.3d 634 (Tex.App.2002) (upholding a jury award of $8 million in exemplary damages and $1 million in compensatory damages for mental anguish in a sexual harassment case).

Many tort suits against employers based on theories of negligence will be barred by the exclusivity provisions of state workers' compensation laws. *See, e.g.*, Chatman v. Gentle Dental Center of Waltham, 973 F.Supp. 228 (D.Mass.1997). Victims of workplace harassment who seek recovery of medical expenses and lost wages, may choose to file a workers' compensation claim; however, such a claim may bar a subsequent lawsuit for the same injuries under state antidiscrimination law. *See, e.g.*, Jefferson v. California Dep't of Youth Auth., 28 Cal.4th 299, 121 Cal.Rptr.2d 391, 48 P.3d 423 (2002).

Other possible tort claims for sexual harassment include breach of the implied covenant of good faith and fair dealing and wrongful discharge in violation of public policy. *See, e.g.*, Schuster v. Derocili, 775 A.2d 1029, 1036 (Del.2001) (recognizing a claim for breach of the implied covenant of good faith and fair dealing where the plaintiff alleged that she was discharged for refusing to submit to the sexual advances of her supervisor). Generally a public policy discharge suit based on sexual harassment will be preempted by a state antidiscrimination statute or other state law that prohibits the same conduct, although there are exceptions. *Compare* Makovi v. Sherwin–Williams Co., 316 Md. 603, 561 A.2d 179 (1989) (finding preemption), *with* Insignia Residential Corp. v. Ashton, 359 Md. 560, 755 A.2d 1080, 1087 (2000) (ruling that the plaintiff could bring a common law wrongful discharge suit based on the allegation that her supervisor solicited sexual favors from her in violation of a state law prohibiting prostitution, which lacked a remedial scheme), *and* Rojo v. Kliger, 52 Cal.3d 65, 276 Cal.Rptr. 130, 801 P.2d 373 (1990) (holding that California antidiscrimination statute does not preclude common law actions arising out of employment discrimination and that workplace sexual harassment can support a claim for wrongful discharge in violation of public policy).

State employees may seek relief from sexual harassment under the Equal Protection Clause of the Fourteenth Amendment or state constitutional law. For example, see Chapter 5, Section B, and the discussion of § 1983 claims of sexual harassment, *infra* Section C.1, Note 13, following *Faragher*. Moreover, states may enact laws that criminalize sexual harassment in public employment. *See* Sanchez v. State, 995 S.W.2d 677 (Tex.Crim.App. 1999), *cert. denied*, 528 U.S. 1021, 120 S.Ct. 531, 145 L.Ed.2d 411 (1999) (upholding the conviction of a high-level manager of a metropolitan transit board for violating a state criminal law, Tex. Penal Code § 39.03(a)(3), that prohibits public servants, under color of law, from subjecting other persons to sexual harassment).

3. SAME–SEX SEXUAL HARASSMENT: THE MEANING OF "BECAUSE OF SEX"

ONCALE v. SUNDOWNER OFFSHORE SERVICES, INC.

Supreme Court of the United States, 1998.
523 U.S. 75, 118 S.Ct. 998, 140 L.Ed.2d 201.

JUSTICE SCALIA delivered the opinion of the Court.

This case presents the question whether workplace harassment can violate Title VII's prohibition against "discriminat[ion] * * * because of * * * sex," 42 U.S.C. § 2000e–2(a)(1), when the harasser and the harassed employee are of the same sex.

I

The District Court having granted summary judgment for respondent, we must assume the facts to be as alleged by petitioner Joseph Oncale. The precise details are irrelevant to the legal point we must decide, and in the interest of both brevity and dignity we shall describe them only generally. In late October 1991, Oncale was working for respondent Sundowner Offshore Services on a Chevron U.S.A., Inc., oil platform in the Gulf of Mexico. He was employed as a roustabout on an eight-man crew which included respondents John Lyons, Danny Pippen, and Brandon Johnson. Lyons, the crane operator, and Pippen, the driller, had supervisory authority. On several occasions, Oncale was forcibly subjected to sex-related, humiliating actions against him by Lyons, Pippen and Johnson in the presence of the rest of the crew. Pippen and Lyons also physically assaulted Oncale in a sexual manner, and Lyons threatened him with rape.

Oncale's complaints to supervisory personnel produced no remedial action; in fact, the company's Safety Compliance Clerk, Valent Hohen, told Oncale that Lyons and Pippen "picked [on] him all the time too," and called him a name suggesting homosexuality. Oncale eventually quit—asking that his pink slip reflect that he "voluntarily left due to sexual harassment and verbal abuse." When asked at his deposition why he left Sundowner, Oncale stated "I felt that if I didn't leave my job, that I would be raped or forced to have sex."

Oncale filed a complaint against Sundowner * * * alleging that he was discriminated against in his employment because of his sex. * * * [T]he district court held that "Mr. Oncale, a male, has no cause of action under Title VII for harassment by male co-workers." [The Fifth Circuit affirmed.]

II

* * *

Title VII's prohibition of discrimination "because of * * * sex" protects men as well as women, and in the related context of racial discrimination in the workplace we have rejected any conclusive presumption that an employer will not discriminate against members of his own race. "Because of the many facets of human motivation, it would be unwise to presume as a matter of law that human beings of one definable group will not discriminate against other members of that group." Castaneda v. Partida, 430 U.S. 482, 499, 97 S.Ct. 1272, 1282, 51 L.Ed.2d 498 (1977). In *Johnson v. Transportation Agency, Santa Clara Cty.*, 480 U.S. 616, 107 S.Ct. 1442, 94 L.Ed.2d 615 (1987), a male employee claimed that his employer discriminated against him because of his sex when it preferred a female employee for promotion. Although we ultimately rejected the claim on other grounds, we did not consider it significant that the supervisor who made that decision was also a man. If our precedents leave any doubt on the question, we hold today that nothing in Title VII necessarily bars a claim of discrimination "because of * * * sex" merely because the plaintiff and the defendant (or the person charged with acting on behalf of the defendant) are of the same sex.

Courts have had little trouble with that principle in cases like *Johnson*, where an employee claims to have been passed over for a job or promotion. But when the issue arises in the context of a "hostile environment" sexual harassment claim, the state and federal courts have taken a bewildering variety of stances. Some, like the Fifth Circuit in this case, have held that same-sex sexual harassment claims are never cognizable under Title VII. Other decisions say that such claims are actionable only if the plaintiff can prove that the harasser is homosexual (and thus presumably motivated by sexual desire). *Compare* McWilliams v. Fairfax County Board of Supervisors, 72 F.3d 1191 (4th Cir.1996), *with* Wrightson v. Pizza Hut of America, 99 F.3d 138 (4th Cir.1996). Still others suggest that workplace harassment that is sexual in content is always actionable, regardless of the harasser's sex, sexual orientation, or motivations. *See* Doe v. Belleville, 119 F.3d 563 (7th Cir.1997).

We see no justification in the statutory language or our precedents for a categorical rule excluding same-sex harassment claims from the coverage of Title VII. As some courts have observed, male-on-male sexual harassment in the workplace was assuredly not the principal evil Congress was concerned with when it enacted Title VII. But statutory prohibitions often go beyond the principal evil to cover reasonably comparable evils, and it is ultimately the provisions of our laws rather than the principal concerns of our legislators by which we are governed. Title VII prohibits "discriminat[ion] * * * because of * * * sex" in the "terms" or "conditions" of employment. Our holding that this includes sexual harassment must extend to sexual harassment of any kind that meets the statutory requirements.

Respondents and their *amici* contend that recognizing liability for same-sex harassment will transform Title VII into a general civility code for the American workplace. But that risk is no greater for same-sex than for opposite-sex harassment, and is adequately met by careful attention to the requirements of the statute. Title VII does not prohibit all verbal or physical harassment in the workplace; it is directed only at "*discriminat[ion]* * * * because of * * * sex." We have never held that workplace harassment, even harassment between men and women, is automatically discrimination because of sex merely because the words used have sexual content or connotations. "The critical issue, Title VII's text indicates, is whether members of one sex are exposed to disadvantageous terms or conditions of employment to which members of the other sex are not exposed." *Harris*, 510 U.S. at 25, 114 S.Ct. at 372 (Ginsburg, J., concurring).

Courts and juries have found the inference of discrimination easy to draw in most male-female sexual harassment situations, because the challenged conduct typically involves explicit or implicit proposals of sexual activity; it is reasonable to assume those proposals would not have been made to someone of the same sex. The same chain of inference would be available to a plaintiff alleging same-sex harassment, if there were credible evidence that the harasser was homosexual. But harassing conduct need not be motivated by sexual desire to support an inference of discrimination on the basis of sex. A trier of fact might reasonably find such discrimination, for example, if a female victim is harassed in such sex-specific and derogatory terms by another woman as to make it clear that the harasser is motivated by general hostility to the presence of women in the workplace. A same-sex harassment plaintiff may also, of course, offer direct comparative evidence about how the alleged harasser treated members of both sexes in a mixed-sex workplace. Whatever evidentiary route the plaintiff chooses to follow, he or she must always prove that the conduct at issue was not merely tinged with offensive sexual connotations, but actually constituted "*discrimina[tion]* * * * because of * * * sex."

And there is another requirement that prevents Title VII from expanding into a general civility code: As we emphasized in *Meritor* and *Harris*, the statute does not reach genuine but innocuous differences in the ways men and women routinely interact with members of the same sex and of the opposite sex. The prohibition of harassment on the basis of sex requires neither asexuality nor androgyny in the workplace; it forbids only behavior so objectively offensive as to alter the "conditions" of the victim's employment. "Conduct that is not severe or pervasive enough to create an objectively hostile or abusive work environment—an environment that a reasonable person would find hostile or abusive—is beyond Title VII's purview." *Harris*, 510 U.S. at 21, 114 S.Ct. at 370, *citing Meritor*, 477 U.S. at 67, 106 S.Ct. at 2405–06. We have always regarded that requirement as crucial, and as sufficient to ensure that courts and juries do not mistake ordinary socializing in the workplace—such as male-on-male horseplay or intersexual flirtation—for discriminatory "conditions of employment."

We have emphasized, moreover, that the objective severity of harassment should be judged from the perspective of a reasonable person in the plaintiff's position, considering "all the circumstances." *Harris*, 510 U.S. at 23, 114 S.Ct. at 371. In same-sex (as in all) harassment cases, that inquiry requires careful consideration of the social context in which particular behavior occurs and is experienced by its target. A professional football player's working environment is not severely or pervasively abusive, for example, if the coach smacks him on the buttocks as he heads onto the field—even if the same behavior would reasonably be experienced as abusive by the coach's secretary (male or female) back at the office. The real social impact of workplace behavior often depends on a constellation of surrounding circumstances, expectations, and relationships which are not fully captured by a simple recitation of the words used or the physical acts performed. Common sense, and an appropriate sensitivity to social context, will enable courts and juries to distinguish between simple teasing or roughhousing among members of the same sex, and conduct which a reasonable person in the plaintiff's position would find severely hostile or abusive.

III

Because we conclude that sex discrimination consisting of same-sex sexual harassment is actionable under Title VII, the judgment of the Court of Appeals for the Fifth Circuit is reversed, and the case is remanded for further proceedings consistent with this opinion.

Notes and Questions

1. By the 1980s, individuals began to bring Title VII claims alleging that they had been sexually harassed by persons of the same sex. Because these claims did not fit the paradigm of sexual harassment cases—a male harassing a female—the courts adopted a variety of approaches, from denying all same-sex claims, to permitting them only if the harasser was a homosexual, to permitting them only if the conduct was sexual. What does Justice Scalia say about each of these approaches to same-sex harassment? For a survey of the conflicting same-sex harassment cases decided before *Oncale*, see Ramona L. Paetzold, *Same-Sex Sexual Harassment: Can It Be Sex–Related for Purposes of Title VII?*, 1 Emp.Rts. & Emp. Pol'y J. 25, 29–44 (1997).

2. Not long before the Supreme Court granted certiorari in *Oncale*, Professor Katherine Franke classified male-on-male same-sex harassment cases into three categories:

> The first set of cases involve [sic] a gay male supervisor who seeks sexual favors from or creates a sexually hostile environment for his male subordinates or coworkers. * * *

> The second set of cases involve [sic] nongay same-sex harassment. Here, the defendant is either heterosexual, or at least not alleged to be gay, and is charged with exhibiting sexual behavior in the workplace in such a way that another male employee regards as both unwelcome and offensive. * * * [T]he harasser engages in sexual behavior that is designed to or has the effect of making the plaintiff annoyed, uncomfortable, offended, humiliated, intimidated, or otherwise victimized by the defendant's conduct. * * *

> The third set of same-sex sexual harassment cases are [sic] similar to those just described but differ from them in one significant way: the

harassing conduct of a sexual nature was undertaken because of the plaintiff's gender identity. That is, the plaintiff was not sufficiently masculine according to the individual defendant's standards of proper masculine presentation, the gender rules of the particular workplace, or according to masculine gender normativity as defined by the culture more generally.

Katherine M. Franke, *What's Wrong with Sexual Harassment?*, 49 Stan. L.Rev. 691, 696–98 (1997); *see also id.* at 696–98 nn. 16–17 (collecting same-sex harassment cases in each of the three categories).

Which category of same-sex harassment cases best describes the facts alleged in *Oncale*? What additional facts would you want to know to answer this question? Consider the following allegations, which are not presented in the Court's opinion: Joseph Oncale was the youngest member of an eight-man crew on a drilling platform off the coast of Louisiana. As described in the Petitioner's Brief to the Supreme Court, Oncale alleged that "his immediate supervisors * * * and another supervisor * * * physically re-strained him on two occasions while [one of the supervisor's] placed his penis on Mr. Oncale's head and arm." Brief for Petitioner at 5, 1997 WL 458826 (U.S.1997). The same men allegedly attacked Oncale in the shower and "forced a bar of soap into [his] anus." *Id.* They "repeatedly assur[ed] Oncale that they desired and intended sexual intercourse." *Id. See also* Catharine A. MacKinnon, *Amicus Brief: Oncale v. Sundowner Offshore Services, Inc.*, 96–568, *Amici Curiae Brief in Support of Petitioner*, 8 UCLA Women's L.J. 9, 13–14 (1997).

3. *Evidence of Discrimination "Because of Sex"*: Justice Scalia suggest-ed three possible "evidentiary route[s]" that a plaintiff might follow to show that same-sex sexual harassment constitutes discrimination "because of sex." What are they? Do the alleged facts of *Oncale* fit any of these three evidentiary paradigms? If not, how would you suggest that Oncale attempt to prove that he was a victim of *discrimination* "because of sex"? Oncale did not allege that his harassers were homosexuals acting out of sexual desire, and the drilling rig where Oncale worked was a single-sex, not a mixed-sex, workplace. Thus, Oncale would not be able to establish his case through either the first or third evidentiary paradigms suggested by Justice Scalia. Would Oncale's claim fit into Justice Scalia's second suggested evidentiary paradigm? *See* David S. Schwartz, *When Is Sex Because of Sex? The Causa-tion Problem in Sexual Harassment Law*, 150 U.Pa.L.Rev. 1697, 1734 (2002). *See id.* at 1734–36 (discussing the outcome of the remand in *Oncale*.)

4. *Causation—The "But For" Formulation*: In 1997, Professor Franke summarized three major justifications that feminist scholars and the lower federal courts had used to find that sexual harassment is prohibited sex discrimination under Title VII: "(1) it is conduct that would not have been undertaken but for the plaintiff's sex; (2) it is conduct that violates Title VII precisely because it is sexual in nature; and (3) it is conduct that sexually subordinates women to men." Katherine N. Franke, *What's Wrong with Sexual Harassment?*, 49 Stan. L. Rev. 691, 693 (1997). In an attempt to synthesize same-sex harassment with *Meritor* and *Harris*, has the Supreme Court in *Oncale* adopted the first justification described by Professor Franke? Has the Court necessarily rejected the second and third justifica-

tions? In *Oncale*, Justice Scalia's three suggested "evidentiary route[s]" to proving that the same-sex harassment was discrimination "because of sex" share a requirement that the plaintiff establish that the conduct would not have occurred "but for" the plaintiff's sex. The use of the "but for" formulation in sexual harassment cases has been criticized by legal scholars. *See, e.g.*, Franke, *supra*, at 730–47. Causation is an element in all discrimination cases. Is it more difficult to prove causation in same-sex harassment cases than in other types of employment discrimination cases? The next two notes examine some of the problems of using the "but for" formulation in sexual harassment cases.

5. *The Equal Opportunity or Bisexual Harasser Defense*: In the frequently cited dicta in footnote 55 of *Barnes v. Costle*, 561 F.2d 983, 990 n.55 (D.C.Cir.1977), the court concluded that "[i]n the case of the bisexual superior, the insistence upon sexual favors would not constitute gender discrimination because it would apply to male and female employees alike." *See also* Rabidue v. Osceola Ref. Co., 805 F.2d 611, 620 (6th Cir.1986) (conduct offensive to both sexes does not constitute sexual harassment), *cert. denied*, 481 U.S. 1041, 107 S.Ct. 1983, 95 L.Ed.2d 823 (1987); *but see* Hutchison v. Amateur Elec. Supply, Inc., 42 F.3d 1037 (7th Cir.1994) (an employer's boorish behavior is actionable, and it is not relevant nor a defense that such behavior would be as offensive to men as it is to women). Several courts after *Oncale* have recognized the "equal opportunity harasser" or "bisexual harasser" defense. For example, in *Holman v. Indiana*, 211 F.3d 399 (7th Cir.), *cert. denied,* 531 U.S. 880, 121 S.Ct. 191, 148 L.Ed.2d 132 (2000), the court held that when a male supervisor solicited sex from two employees, a married couple, the harassment was not "because of sex." Relying on *Oncale*, the court ruled that "Title VII does not cover the 'equal opportunity' or 'bisexual' harasser * * * because such person is not *discriminating* on the basis of sex. He is not treating one sex better (or worse) than the other; he is treating both sexes the same (albeit badly)." *Id.* at 403. *See also* Lack v. Wal–Mart Stores, Inc., 240 F.3d 255, 262 (4th Cir.2001) (relying on *Oncale* to conclude that that there could be no sexual harassment under the West Virginia Human Rights Act when the alleged harasser was "just an indiscriminately vulgar and offensive supervisor, obnoxious to men and women alike"). The court in *Brown v. Henderson*, 257 F.3d 246, 256 (2d Cir.2001), however, held that "there is no *per se* bar to maintaining a claim of sex discrimination where a person of another sex has been similarly treated."

One commentator observed, "[t]he case of the individual who harasses both sexes sends the entire sexual harassment logic structure crashing to the ground." Steven S. Locke, *The Equal Opportunity Harasser as a Paradigm for Recognizing Sexual Harassment of Homosexuals Under Title VII*, 27 Rutgers L.J. 383, 406 (1996). Can it ever be said that a bisexual harasser "discriminates" between the sexes in selecting his or her object of sexual desire? As Locke noted, "[t]he archetypal bisexual harasser chooses his victims regardless of their gender—he is happy with either. His choice of actual target is determined by his own personal sexual tastes, such as the physical and social characteristics of his prey." *Id.* at 408. Like the bisexual harasser, "[t]he equal opportunity harasser also does not discriminate by gender." *Id.* at 409. Locke argues that this type of harasser "chooses his victims and then crafts his harassment to demean. Both [the bisexual and equal opportunity harasser] root their harassment in sexual conduct, either by demanding sexual favors or by demeaning with sex-based vitriol." *Id.*

In the case of an "equal opportunity harasser," does Justice Scalia's analysis of the "because of sex" requirement mean that a female plaintiff must prove that her female harasser harbored animosity toward "the presence of women in the workplace," but not toward the presence of men? If the harasser treated both sexes in an equally demeaning manner using "sex-specific and derogatory terms," would this evidence negate one of the elements of the plaintiff's claim or provide the employer with a potential defense? Locke concluded that "[u]nder a rigid interpretation of 'because of sex' it would be impossible to find liability when a harasser takes on both sexes." *Id.* at 411. *See also* Walker v. National Revenue Corp., 43 Fed.Appx. 800, 804 (6th Cir.2002) (female supervisor's abusive treatment of her gay subordinate, which included sexual propositions and sexual touching, was not actionable harassment because of sex where she treated all of her subordinates in a "juvenile," "irrational," and "cruel" manner). Do you think that *Oncale* dictates such a "rigid interpretation" of Title VII?

Drawing on the analysis of the district court in *Chiapuzio v. BLT Operating Corp.*, 826 F.Supp. 1334 (D.Wyo.1993), Locke resolved the bisexual/equal opportunity harasser conundrum by adopting a broad definition of "sex":

> Rather than asking if the plaintiff was harassed because of his or her sex, the court should ask whether the vehicle of harassment was sex-based (i.e., was the harassment rooted in sex, sexuality, sex roles, or sex stereotypes). * * * This factor, combined with an emphasis on the harm suffered by the victim, will provide a test which properly focuses on the conduct rather than the motive of the perpetrator.

Id. at 414; *see also* Charles R. Calleros, *The Meaning of "Sex": Homosexual and Bisexual Harassment Under Title VII*, 20 Vt.L.Rev. 55 (1995). In *Chiapuzio*, a husband and wife were employed by the same employer. Their supervisor constantly subjected them both to verbal sexual harassment. The court held that the fact that the supervisor harassed employees of both sexes was not a defense to a claim of sexual harassment. Is *Chiapuzio* still good law after *Oncale*?

6. *Harassment That Is "Sexual" in Nature*: Before *Oncale*, some scholars had argued that same-sex harassing conduct that is "sexual" in nature should violate Title VII regardless of the sex of the perpetrator and victim. For example, Professor Paetzold had proposed that "sexual conduct—sexualized language, sexual innuendo, sexual touchings, sexual displays—in same-sex cases should always be actionable under Title VII, to the same extent that it is in male-female cases. Further, * * * the same presumptions and inferences should apply in same-sex cases as in male-female harassment cases." Paetzold, *supra* note 1, at 47. In *Oncale*, the Court appeared to reject the argument, which had been adopted in one case in the Seventh Circuit, that "workplace harassment that is sexual in content is always actionable, regardless of the harasser's sex, sexual orientation, or motivations." *Oncale*, 118 S.Ct. at 1002 (discussing *Doe v. Belleville*, 119 F.3d 563 (7th Cir.1997),

cert. granted, judgment vacated, 523 U.S. 1001, 118 S.Ct. 1183 140 L.Ed.2d 313 (1998)).

After *Oncale*, if the harassment is sexual in nature, should it matter whether the harasser(s) and victim are of the same sex? *See, e.g.,* Davis v. Coastal Internat'l Sec., 275 F.3d 1119, 1123 (D.C.Cir.2002) (finding that same-sex harassment that is sexual in nature is not actionable under Title VII where conduct of harassers was motivated by a grudge against the plaintiff and was not related to his sex or gender); E.E.O.C. v. Harbert–Yeargin, Inc., 266 F.3d 498, 520 (6th Cir.2001) (Guy, Circuit Judge, concurring in part and dissenting in part, for a majority of the court) (observing, in a same-sex harassment case, that "if the environment is just sexually hostile without an element of gender discrimination, it is not actionable"). If the harasser and victim are of the opposite sex, is harassment necessarily "because of sex" when the harassing behavior and language is sexual in nature? See, *e.g.,* Brown v. Henderson, 257 F.3d 246, 255–56 (2d Cir.2001) (finding that harassment with sexual content is not sex-based harassment where both men and women are harassed and female plaintiff was targeted because of a dispute with her union).

In a study of all sexual harassment cases that resulted in reported opinions from federal district and appellate courts between 1986 and 1995, Juliano and Schwab found that

> [p]laintiffs alleging "harassment as sexualized behavior" have significantly higher win rates than other sexual harassment plaintiffs. Plaintiffs who alleged harassment based on comments of a sexual or physical nature were more successful than plaintiffs who alleged comments that devalued women as women (such as "honey" or "babe"). Further, harassment claims premised upon physical contact of a sexual nature met greater success than physical conduct of a nonsexual nature.

Ann Juliano & Stewart J. Schwab, *The Sweep of Sexual Harassment Cases,* 86 Cornell L. Rev. 548, 580–81 (2001). Do these results suggest that, even before *Oncale*, the federal courts were not interpreting Title VII as a "civility code," but were policing sexualized conduct at the margins of socially tolerable behavior? Are courts more likely to uphold claims of harassment that involve sexualized conduct when the plaintiff and the harasser are of the opposite sex?

After *Oncale,* what is the relevance of explicitly sexual language or conduct in hostile work environment cases? For example, if a male truck driver repeatedly complains about explicit, graphic homophobic graffiti on the walls of the trailers of the distribution center where he is assigned, will he have an actionable claim of a same-sex hostile work environment? *See* Beach v. Yellow Freight Sys., 312 F.3d 391 (8th Cir.2002). After *Oncale,* should it matter whether the plaintiff is a male being harassed by male co-workers or a female being harassed by male co-workers? Will the conduct of a male supervisor who repeatedly yells at and belittles his female subordinate be actionable only if he uses sexually explicit conduct or language? *See* Gregory v. Daly, 243 F.3d 687 (2d Cir.2001). What if he uses sexually explicit language with a male subordinate? Same result?

7. *Harassment Based on Gender Animus:* After *Oncale,* is a hostile work environment "because of sex" established if female employees re-

peatedly taunt their female co-worker, calling her "bitch" and, in effect, accusing her of being sexually promiscuous? *See* Bailey v. Henderson, 94 F.Supp.2d 68, 70 (D.D.C.2000). What if male computer programmers ostracize a female co-worker and refuse to provide her with the system passwords and other information that she needs to perform her job? Is this evidence of a hostile work environment based on gender animus or just a workplace personality conflict? *See* O'Shea v. Yellow Technology Servs., 185 F.3d 1093 (10th Cir.1999). Marrero v. Goya of Puerto Rico, Inc., 304 F.3d 7, 20 (1st Cir.2002) ("Our cases make clear that, 'where a plaintiff endures harassing conduct, although not explicitly sexual in nature, which undermines her ability to succeed at her job, those acts should be considered along with overtly sexually abusive conduct in assessing a hostile work environment claim.' ").

8. *The Social Context of Harassment*: How does the "social context" in *Oncale* affect the question of whether Joseph Oncale experienced "simple teasing or roughhousing among members of the same sex" or an actionable hostile work environment? What is the "social context" of work in an all-male crew that is isolated for long periods of time on a drilling rig in the Gulf of Mexico? Do you think that consideration of "social context" will expand or limit the circumstances under which hostile work environment will be found? Will it matter whether the facts involve allegations of same-sex or opposite-sex harassment?

In *Pirolli v. World Flavors, Inc.*, 1999 WL 1065214 (E.D.Pa.1999), *aff'd in part, rev'd in part*, 263 F.3d 159 (3d Cir.2001) (unpublished table decision), the court relied on the reasoning of *Oncale* to deny the hostile environment claim of a mentally retarded factory worker who alleged that his co-workers twice attempted to sodomize him, physically assaulted him, stuffed him in a garbage container, and threw things at him. After discounting the evidence of attempted sodomy, the court concluded,

> It appears to me that the context in which the alleged harassment took place in this case is one in which the employees engaged in physical horseplay and roughhousing, as well as occasionally offensive banter, as a matter of course. * * * Plaintiff's evidence shows that he was treated no differently than his co-workers were. In light of the rowdy context of plaintiff's workplace, I cannot conclude that a reasonable jury could find that the conduct for which plaintiff has produced evidentiary support rose to a level of severity, offensiveness, or abusiveness that altered the conditions of the workplace.

Id. at *4–5. Would you agree that the facts in *Pirolli* distinguish it from the *Oncale*? *See generally* Hilary S. Axam & Deborah Zalesne, *Simulated Sodomy and Other Forms of Heterosexual "Horseplay": Same Sex Sexual Harassment, Workplace Gender Hierarchies, and the Myth of the Gender Monolith Before and After* Oncale, 11 Yale J.L. & Feminism 155 (1999).

How does consideration of "social context" affect sexual harassment claims generally? For example, after *Oncale,* if a female plaintiff works in a factory, where the work is strenuous, noisy, and dirty, does the "inhospitable" physical work environment prevent her from asserting a sexual harassment claim for a hostile work environment? *See* Conner v. Schrader–Bridgeport Int'l, Inc., 227 F.3d 179, 194 (4th Cir.2000). If a woman starts a job at a small factory where her all-male co-workers and supervisors continue their practice of exchanging vulgar sexual banter throughout the work day, can she prevail on a complaint that their language, which she finds offensive, constitutes sexual harassment? *See* Ocheltree v. Scollon Prods., Inc., 335 F.3d 325 (4th Cir.2003) (en banc), *petition for cert. filed,* 72 U.S.L.W. 3309 (U.S. Oct. 16, 2003) (No. 03–617). For an exploration of the political, social, and cultural complexity of challenging male workplace norms through sexual harassment law, see Nancy S. Ehrenreich, *Pluralist Myths and Powerless Men: The Ideology of Reasonableness in Sexual Harassment Law,* 99 Yale L.J. 1177, 1193–1214 (1990) (discussing *Rabidue v. Osceola Refining Co.,* 805 F.2d 611 (6th Cir.1986), *cert. denied,* 481 U.S. 1041, 107 S.Ct. 1983, 95 L.Ed.2d 823 (1987)).

    9. *The "Totality of Circumstances" After* Oncale: The *Harris v. Forklift* threshold determination of whether hostile environment sexual harassment is severe or pervasive is determined in light of the "totality of circumstances." In *Oncale,* Justice Scalia reaffirmed the significance of viewing the harasser's conduct in light of the "surrounding circumstances, expectations, and relationships." Since *Oncale,* the lower courts have adopted differing approaches to assessing the "totality of circumstances." *Compare* Williams v. General Motors, Corp., 187 F.3d 553, 562 (6th Cir.1999) (holding that the district court had failed to consider properly the "totality of circumstances" when it divided the allegedly harassing conduct into four types and considered each separately); *with* Penry v. Federal Home Loan Bank of Topeka, 155 F.3d 1257, 1262–1263 (10th Cir.1998) (concluding that the supervisor's "gender-neutral antics" over a four year period made the plaintiffs' work environment merely "unpleasant," and the "gender-based" incidents were "too few and far between" to meet the threshold of "severe or pervasive" sexual harassment), *cert. denied,* 526 U.S. 1039, 119 S.Ct. 1334, 143 L.Ed.2d 498 (1999); Mendoza v. Borden, 195 F.3d 1238, 1246 (11th Cir.1999) (en banc) (holding that, considered "in context, not as isolated acts," a supervisor's conduct, which included constantly following and staring at employee, was not severe or pervasive under Title VII), *cert. denied,* 529 U.S. 1068, 120 S.Ct. 1674, 146 L.Ed.2d 483 (2000).

    Recall *Clark County School District v. Breeden,* discussed *supra* Section B.2, Note 5, following *Harris v. Forklift.* Does *Breeden* re-emphasize the point made by Justice Scalia in *Oncale* that Title VII is not "a general civility code for the American workplace"? In other words, will employees— regardless of their gender—have to tolerate a "reasonable" level of incivility at work, including being required on occasion to hear their supervisors and co-workers make crude, sexually explicit comments and jokes. What about "isolated incidents" involving racial epithets or jokes? *See* Schatzman v. Martin Newark Dealership, 158 F.Supp.2d 392, 403 (D.Del.2001) (concluding that "referring to African–Americans as 'monkeys' is more reasonably deemed derogatory than was the interaction in *Breeden*").

    10. *The "Reasonable Person" Standard After* Oncale: Has *Oncale* clarified the "reasonable person" standard in sexual harassment law? Citing *Harris,* the Court in *Oncale* held that the standard is that of "a reasonable person in the plaintiff's position, considering 'all the circumstances.' " Would the following jury instruction be consistent with *Oncale?* "[W]hen you're considering whether the conduct was severe or pervasive, you are to consider

* * * the view of * * * an objectively reasonable woman of lesbian orientation." *See* Muzzy v. Cahillane Motors, Inc., 434 Mass. 409, 749 N.E.2d 691,
696–97 (2001).

11. *Bullying in the Workplace.* In *Oncale,* Justice Scalia made it clear
that recognizing that same-sex harassment claims may be actionable did not
"transform Title VII into a general civility code for the American workplace." A recent survey conducted by researchers at Wayne State University
found that, in the United States, one in six employees is victimized by
bullying at work and about half of the bullies are women. *Bullying in the
Workplace, While Legal, Hurts Productivity, Recruitment and Retention,* 19
Hum. Resources Rep. (BNA) No.42, at 1153, 1153–54 (Oct. 29, 2001) (citing
results of survey). In light of the fact that bullying may be ubiquitous in
American workplaces, how can courts distinguish between harassment that
is actionable on the basis of a protected status such as sex or race and
bullying that is not actionable? In other words, how can courts and juries tell
whether a bully is targeting his or her victim "because of sex" or because of
"personal animosity" or just because that is how the bully treats everyone?
See, e.g., Bowman v. Shawnee St. Univ., 220 F.3d 456, 464 (6th Cir.2000)
(finding that female dean's "intimidation, ridicule, and mistreatment" of
male physical education instructor was not actionable sexual harassment
where her conduct was not of a "sexual" nature and her comments were not
"anti male"). Do we need a new legal theory and a new statute to protect
employees against bullies as well as against sexual harassers? *See Bullying
in the Workplace, supra* (discussing the Campaign Against Workplace Bullying). Professor Fisk has observed that

> [w]ithout a legal theory built around workplace humiliation, it is diffi-
> cult to respond to charges that only women and people of color can sue if
> they are humiliated at work. Without an accepted theory, the "equal
> opportunity harasser"—the supervisor who is abusive to employees
> irrespective of race, sex, or gender—is, at best, a problem for equal
> rights theorists and, at worst, a poster child for the excesses of antidis-
> crimination law.

Catherine L. Fisk, *Humiliation at Work,* 8 Wm. & Mary J. Women & L. 73,
75 (2001). *See also* David C. Yamada, *The Phenomenon of "Workplace
Bullying" and the Need for Status–Blind Hostile Work Environment Protection,"* 88 Geo.L.J. 475 (2000) (proposing a statutory cause of action to
redress the harms of workplace bullying).

12. After the Supreme Court issued its 1998 sexual harassment cases—
Oncale, Ellerth, and *Faragher*—the Court of Appeals for the Fifth Circuit, in
Butler v. Ysleta Independent School District, 161 F.3d 263, 267 (5th Cir.
1998), commented that "[w]e are witnesses to the birth of a second generation of sexual harassment law." Citing the scholarly work of Professors
Kathryn Abrams, Anita Bernstein, Katherine Franke, and Vicki Schultz, the
court concluded that "[w]hile the nuances of these writers' approaches to
sexual harassment differ, all emphasize that sexual harassment is discrimination based on sex, not merely workplace behavior with sexual overtones."
Id. at 267–68. The *Butler* court cites *Oncale* for the proposition that "sexual
content is not the Title VII talisman." *Id.* at 270. Would you agree? Consider
the following perspectives:

a. Professor Franke would define sexual harassment as follows:

[S]exual harassment—between any two people of whatever sex—is a form of sex discrimination when it reflects or perpetuates gender stereotypes in the workplace. I suggest a reconceptualization of sexual harassment as *gender harassment*. Understood in this way, sexual harassment is a kind of sex discrimination not because the conduct would not have been undertaken if the victim had been a different sex, not because it is sexual, and not because men do it to women, but precisely because it is a technology of sexism. That is, it perpetuates, enforces, and polices a set of gender norms that seek to feminize women and masculinize men.

Katherine Franke, *What's Wrong with Sexual Harassment?*, 49 Stan.L.Rev. 691, 696 (1997).

b. Professor Schultz offers the following framework for understanding sexual harassment:

Because many heterosexual men regard any failure to conform to their own preconceived notion of masculinity as a sign of homosexuality—and homosexuality as a failure to conform to their preconceived notion of masculinity—such harassment frequently includes antigay sentiments. * * * Simply because hostile work environment harassment may include some antigay expression, however, does not mean that it is not based on gender. Regardless of whether the harassee's sexuality is placed at issue, such harassment is gender-based if it denigrates the harassee's manhood or otherwise prescribes how the harassee should be or should behave on the job. As the Supreme Court's decision in *Price Waterhouse v. Hopkins* instructs, imposing pressure to conform to preconceived notions of appropriate manhood or womanhood at work is the essence of differential treatment "because of sex" within the meaning of Title VII.

Vicki Schultz, *Reconceptualizing Sexual Harassment*, 107 Yale L.J. 1683, 1776–77 (1998).

c. Not long before *Oncale* was decided, Professor Bernstein argued that a "respectful person" standard should replace reliance on standards of "reasonableness" in sexual harassment law. She wrote,

Hostile environment sexual harassment * * * is a type of incivility or * * * disrespect. * * * [A]ccordingly, hostile environment complaints should refer to respect; the plaintiff should be required to prove that the defendant—a man, or a woman, or a business entity—did not conform to the standard of a respectful person. This respectful person standard would rightly supplant references to reason and reasonableness; respect is integral to the understanding and remedying of sexual harassment, whereas reason is not.

Anita Bernstein, *Treating Sexual Harassment with Respect*, 111 Harv.L.Rev. 445, 450 (1997). Does *Oncale* reject this approach? For a critique of Professor Bernstein's theory of sexual harassment, see Kathryn Abrams, *The New Jurisprudence of Sexual Harassment*, 83 Cornell L.Rev. 1169 (1998); for Professor Bernstein's response, see Anita Bernstein, *An Old Jurisprudence: Respect in Retrospect*, 83 Cornell L.Rev. 1231 (1998); and a rejoinder,

Kathryn Abrams, *Postscript, Spring 1998: A Response to Professors Bernstein and Franke*, 83 Cornell L.Rev. 1257 (1998).

    d.   Professor Abrams observed,

> *Oncale* is in many respects an enigma. In an effort to give a conclusive answer to a case that, by all appearances, he would have preferred not to have had to consider, Justice Scalia skirted the "what," the "how" and the "why" of sexual harassment. He declined to discuss all but the most basic outline of the facts, offered no theory of the wrong that purports to explain why same-sex cases should be included in Title VII's ambit, and provided only a few hints as to how decision-making in these cases should occur. Yet in other respects the case is implausibly promising. Scalia's invocation of the "reasonable person in the plaintiff's position, considering 'all the circumstances' " has a greater potential for group-based specificity than even the much-lauded opinion in *Harris v. Forklift*. The *Oncale* opinion contains a remarkable call for contextualization in the assessment of sexual harassment, tempered only by Scalia's confident and perhaps solipsistic suggestion that one can resolve these cases with a healthy dose of common sense. Most importantly, the opinion throws the door open to an entirely new—and heretofore almost entirely marginalized—group of claimants.

Kathryn Abrams, *Postscript, Spring 1998: A Response to Professors Bernstein and Franke*, 83 Cornell L.Rev. 1257, 1258–59 (1998).

C.   EMPLOYER LIABILITY FOR DISCRIMINATORY HARASSMENT

    Although the Supreme Court in *Meritor* held that "workplace sexual harassment is illegal," the Court "le[ft] open the circumstances in which an employer is responsible under Title VII for such conduct." 477 U.S. 57, 74, 106 S.Ct. 2399, 2409, 91 L.Ed.2d 49 (1986) (Marshall, J., concurring). After reviewing the conflicting standards for employer liability that had been raised by the parties and *amici* in *Meritor*, the Court concluded that

> Congress' decision to define "employer" to include any "agent" of an employer, 42 U.S.C. § 2000e(b), surely evinces an intent to place some limits on the acts of employees for which employers under Title VII are to be held responsible. For this reason, we hold that the Court of Appeals erred in concluding that employers are always automatically liable for sexual harassment by their supervisors. For the same reason, absence of notice to an employer does not necessarily insulate that employer from liability.
>
>   * * * [W]e reject petitioner's view that the mere existence of a grievance procedure and a policy against discrimination, coupled with respondent's failure to invoke that procedure, must insulate petitioner from liability. While those facts are plainly relevant, the situation before us demonstrates why they are not necessarily dispositive. Petitioner's general nondiscrimination policy did not address sexual harassment in particular, and thus did not alert em-

ployees to their employer's interest in correcting that form of discrimination. Moreover, the bank's grievance procedure apparently required an employee to complain first to her supervisor, in this case Taylor. Since Taylor was the alleged perpetrator, it is not altogether surprising that respondent failed to invoke the procedure and report her grievance to him. Petitioner's contention that respondent's failure should insulate it from liability might be substantially stronger if its procedures were better calculated to encourage victims of harassment to come forward.

Meritor, 477 U.S. at 72–73, 106 S.Ct. at 2408.

The then-current EEOC Guidelines, which were discussed in the *Meritor* majority opinion, provided:

> (c) Applying general Title VII principles, an employer * * * is responsible for its acts and those of its agents and supervisory employees with respect to sexual harassment regardless of whether the specific acts complained of were authorized or even forbidden by the employer and regardless of whether the employer knew or should have known of their occurrence. The Commission will examine the circumstances of the particular employment relationship and the job functions performed by the individual in determining whether an individual acts in either a supervisory or agency capacity.

> (d) With respect to conduct between fellow employees, an employer is responsible for acts of sexual harassment in the workplace where the employer (or its agents or supervisory employees) knows or should have known of the conduct, unless it can show that it took immediate and appropriate corrective action.

29 C.F.R. § 1604.11(c)-(d) (1997).

After *Meritor*, the courts of appeals adopted several different standards for imposing liability on employers for the sexual harassment of their supervisors. *See* Frederick J. Lewis & Thomas L. Henderson, *Employer Liability for "Hostile Work Environment" Sexual Harassment Created by Supervisors: The Search for an Appropriate Standard*, 25 U.Mem.L.Rev. 667, 673–86 (1995) (collecting and analyzing the post-*Meritor* cases). These standards included (1) whether the employer "knew or should have known" of the harassment, (2) whether the employer had an effective grievance procedure, and (3) whether the supervisor was acting within the scope of employment. *See id.* at 673–86. In addition, several courts imposed strict liability on employers for the conduct of employees who possessed authority to hire, fire, promote, discharge, or determine other terms and conditions of employment. *Id.* at 683. With respect to nonsupervisory employees, the employer was liable only when it had "actual or constructive notice of the harassment." *Id.* Employer liability for harassment by co-workers is covered in Section C.2 of this chapter. In 1998, in the following two cases, the Supreme Court resolved the conflicting approaches of the circuit courts and the EEOC to the issue of employer liability for supervisory sexual harassment.

1. VICARIOUS LIABILITY: HARASSMENT BY SUPERVISORS

BURLINGTON INDUSTRIES, INC. v. ELLERTH

Supreme Court of the United States, 1998.
524 U.S. 742, 118 S.Ct. 2257, 141 L.Ed.2d 633.

JUSTICE KENNEDY delivered the opinion of the Court.

We decide whether, under Title VII of the Civil Rights Act of 1964, an employee who refuses the unwelcome and threatening sexual advances of a supervisor, yet suffers no adverse, tangible job consequences, can recover against the employer without showing the employer is negligent or otherwise at fault for the supervisor's actions.

I

Summary judgment was granted for the employer, so we must take the facts alleged by the employee to be true. The employer is Burlington Industries, the petitioner. The employee is Kimberly Ellerth, the respondent. From March 1993 until May 1994, Ellerth worked as a salesperson in one of Burlington's divisions in Chicago, Illinois. During her employment, she alleges, she was subjected to constant sexual harassment by her supervisor, one Ted Slowik.

In the hierarchy of Burlington's management structure, Slowik was a mid-level manager. Burlington has eight divisions, employing more than 22,000 people in some 50 plants around the United States. Slowik was a vice president in one of five business units within one of the divisions. He had authority to make hiring and promotion decisions subject to the approval of his supervisor, who signed the paperwork. According to Slowik's supervisor, his position was "not considered an upper-level management position," and he was "not amongst the decision-making or policy-making hierarchy." Slowik was not Ellerth's immediate supervisor. Ellerth worked in a two-person office in Chicago, and she answered to her office colleague, who in turn answered to Slowik in New York.

Against a background of repeated boorish and offensive remarks and gestures which Slowik allegedly made, Ellerth places particular emphasis on three alleged incidents where Slowik's comments could be construed as threats to deny her tangible job benefits. In the summer of 1993, while on a business trip, Slowik invited Ellerth to the hotel lounge, an invitation Ellerth felt compelled to accept because Slowik was her boss. When Ellerth gave no encouragement to remarks Slowik made about her breasts, he told her to "loosen up" and warned, "[y]ou know, Kim, I could make your life very hard or very easy at Burlington."

In March 1994, when Ellerth was being considered for a promotion, Slowik expressed reservations during the promotion interview because she was not "loose enough." The comment was followed by his reaching over and rubbing her knee. Ellerth did receive the promotion; but when Slowik called to announce it, he told Ellerth, "you're gonna be out there with men who work in factories, and they certainly like women with pretty butts/legs."

In May 1994, Ellerth called Slowik, asking permission to insert a customer's logo into a fabric sample. Slowik responded, "I don't have time for you right now, Kim—unless you want to tell me what you're wearing." Ellerth told Slowik she had to go and ended the call. A day or two later, Ellerth called Slowik to ask permission again. This time he denied her request, but added something along the lines of, "are you wearing shorter skirts yet, Kim, because it would make your job a whole heck of a lot easier."

A short time later, Ellerth's immediate supervisor cautioned her about returning telephone calls to customers in a prompt fashion. In response, Ellerth quit. She faxed a letter giving reasons unrelated to the alleged sexual harassment we have described. About three weeks later, however, she sent a letter explaining she quit because of Slowik's behavior.

During her tenure at Burlington, Ellerth did not inform anyone in authority about Slowik's conduct, despite knowing Burlington had a policy against sexual harassment. In fact, she chose not to inform her immediate supervisor (not Slowik) because " 'it would be his duty as my supervisor to report any incidents of sexual harassment.' " On one occasion, she told Slowik a comment he made was inappropriate.

In October 1994, * * * Ellerth filed suit * * * alleging Burlington engaged in sexual harassment and forced her constructive discharge, in violation of Title VII. The District Court granted summary judgment to Burlington. The Court found Slowik's behavior, as described by Ellerth, severe and pervasive enough to create a hostile work environment, but found Burlington neither knew nor should have known about the conduct. * * *

The Court of Appeals en banc reversed in a decision which produced eight separate opinions and no consensus for a controlling rationale. * * * The disagreement revealed in the careful opinions of the judges of the Court of Appeals reflects the fact that Congress has left it to the courts to determine controlling agency law principles in a new and difficult area of federal law. We granted certiorari to assist in defining the relevant standards of employer liability.

II

At the outset, we assume an important proposition yet to be established before a trier of fact. It is a premise assumed as well, in explicit or implicit terms, in the various opinions by the judges of the Court of Appeals. The premise is: a trier of fact could find in Slowik's remarks numerous threats to retaliate against Ellerth if she denied some sexual liberties. The threats, however, were not carried out or fulfilled. Cases based on threats which are carried out are referred to often as *quid pro quo* cases, as distinct from bothersome attentions or sexual remarks that are sufficiently severe or pervasive to create a hostile work environment.

The terms *quid pro quo* and hostile work environment are helpful, perhaps, in making a rough demarcation between cases in which threats are carried out and those where they are not or are absent altogether, but beyond this are of limited utility.

Section 703(a) of Title VII forbids "an employer"—

(1) to fail or refuse to hire or to discharge any individual, or otherwise to discriminate against any individual with respect to his compensation, terms, conditions or privileges of employment, because of such individual's * * * sex.

"*Quid pro quo*" and "hostile work environment" do not appear in the statutory text. The terms appeared first in the academic literature, found their way into decisions of the Courts of Appeals, and were mentioned in this Court's decision in *Meritor.*

* * *

* * * [A]s use of the terms grew in the wake of *Meritor*, they acquired their own significance. The standard of employer responsibility turned on which type of harassment occurred. If the plaintiff established a *quid pro quo* claim, the Courts of Appeals held, the employer was subject to vicarious liability. The rule encouraged Title VII plaintiffs to state their claims as *quid pro quo* claims, which in turn put expansive pressure on the definition. * * *

We do not suggest the terms *quid pro quo* and hostile work environment are irrelevant to Title VII litigation. To the extent they illustrate the distinction between cases involving a threat which is carried out and offensive conduct in general, the terms are relevant when there is a threshold question whether a plaintiff can prove discrimination in violation of Title VII. When a plaintiff proves that a tangible employment action resulted from a refusal to submit to a supervisor's sexual demands, he or she establishes that the employment decision itself constitutes a change in the terms and conditions of employment that is actionable under Title VII. For any sexual harassment preceding the employment decision to be actionable, however, the conduct must be severe or pervasive. Because Ellerth's claim involves only unfulfilled threats, it should be categorized as a hostile work environment claim which requires a showing of severe or pervasive conduct. For purposes of this case, we accept the District Court's finding that the alleged conduct was severe or pervasive. The case before us involves numerous alleged threats, and we express no opinion as to whether a single unfulfilled threat is sufficient to constitute discrimination in the terms or conditions of employment.

When we assume discrimination can be proved, however, the factors we discuss below, and not the categories *quid pro quo* and hostile work environment, will be controlling on the issue of vicarious liability. That is the question we must resolve.

III

We must decide, then, whether an employer has vicarious liability when a supervisor creates a hostile work environment by making explicit threats to alter a subordinate's terms or conditions of employment, based on sex, but does not fulfill the threat. We turn to principles of agency law, for the term "employer" is defined under Title VII to include "agents." 42 U.S.C. § 2000e(b). * * *

As *Meritor* acknowledged, the Restatement (Second) of Agency (1957) (hereinafter Restatement), is a useful beginning point for a discussion of general agency principles. * * *

A

Section 219(1) of the Restatement sets out a central principle of agency law:

> A master is subject to liability for the torts of his servants committed while acting in the scope of their employment.

An employer may be liable for both negligent and intentional torts committed by an employee within the scope of his or her employment. Sexual harassment under Title VII presupposes intentional conduct. While early decisions absolved employers of liability for the intentional torts of their employees, the law now imposes liability where the employee's "purpose, however misguided, is wholly or in part to further the master's business." W. Keeton, D. Dobbs, R. Keeton, & D. Owen, Prosser and Keeton on Law of Torts § 70, at 505 (5th ed.1984). In applying scope of employment principles to intentional torts, however, it is accepted that "it is less likely that a willful tort will properly be held to be in the course of employment and that the liability of the master for such torts will naturally be more limited." F. Mechem, Outlines of the Law of Agency § 394, at 266 (P. Mechem 4th ed.1952). The Restatement defines conduct, including an intentional tort, to be within the scope of employment when "actuated, at least in part, by a purpose to serve the [employer]," even if it is forbidden by the employer. Restatement §§ 228(1)(c), 230. * * *

As Courts of Appeals have recognized, a supervisor acting out of gender-based animus or a desire to fulfill sexual urges may not be actuated by a purpose to serve the employer. The harassing supervisor often acts for personal motives, motives unrelated and even antithetical to the objectives of the employer. There are instances, of course, where a supervisor engages in unlawful discrimination with the purpose, mistaken or otherwise, to serve the employer.

* * *

The general rule is that sexual harassment by a supervisor is not conduct within the scope of employment.

B

Scope of employment does not define the only basis for employer liability under agency principles. In limited circumstances, agency principles impose liability on employers even where employees commit torts outside the scope of employment. The principles are set forth in the much-cited § 219(2) of the Restatement:

(2) A master is not subject to liability for the torts of his servants acting outside the scope of their employment, unless:

(a) the master intended the conduct or the consequences, or

(b) the master was negligent or reckless, or

(c) the conduct violated a non-delegable duty of the master, or

(d) the servant purported to act or to speak on behalf of the principal and there was reliance upon apparent authority, or he was aided in accomplishing the tort by the existence of the agency relation.

Subsection (a) addresses direct liability, where the employer acts with tortious intent, and indirect liability, where the agent's high rank in the company makes him or her the employer's alter ego. None of the parties contend Slowik's rank imputes liability under this principle. There is no contention, furthermore, that a nondelegable duty is involved. *See* § 219(2)(c). So, for our purposes here, subsections (a) and (c) can be put aside.

Subsections (b) and (d) are possible grounds for imposing employer liability on account of a supervisor's acts and must be considered. Under subsection (b), an employer is liable when the tort is attributable to the employer's own negligence. § 219(2)(b). Thus, although a supervisor's sexual harassment is outside the scope of employment because the conduct was for personal motives, an employer can be liable, nonetheless, where its own negligence is a cause of the harassment. An employer is negligent with respect to sexual harassment if it knew or should have known about the conduct and failed to stop it. Negligence sets a minimum standard for employer liability under Title VII; but Ellerth seeks to invoke the more stringent standard of vicarious liability.

Subsection 219(2)(d) concerns vicarious liability for intentional torts committed by an employee when the employee uses apparent authority (the apparent authority standard), or when the employee "was aided in accomplishing the tort by the existence of the agency relation" (the aided in the agency relation standard). As other federal decisions have done in discussing vicarious liability for supervisor harassment, we begin with § 219(2)(d).

C

As a general rule, apparent authority is relevant where the agent purports to exercise a power which he or she does not have, as distinct from where the agent threatens to misuse actual power. In the usual case, a supervisor's harassment involves misuse of actual power, not the false impression of its existence. Apparent authority analysis therefore is inappropriate in this context. If, in the unusual case, it is alleged there is a false impression that the actor was a supervisor, when he in fact was not, the victim's mistaken conclusion must be a reasonable one. When a party seeks to impose vicarious liability based on an agent's misuse of delegated authority, the Restatement's aided in the agency relation rule, rather than the apparent authority rule, appears to be the appropriate form of analysis.

D

We turn to the aided in the agency relation standard. In a sense, most workplace tortfeasors are aided in accomplishing their objective by the existence of the agency relation: Proximity and regular contact may afford a captive pool of potential victims. Were this to satisfy the aided in the agency relation standard, an employer would be subject to vicarious liability not only for all supervisor harassment, but also for all co-worker harassment, a result enforced by neither the EEOC nor any court of appeals to have considered the issue. The aided in the agency relation standard, therefore, requires the existence of something more than the employment relation itself.

At the outset, we can identify a class of cases where, beyond question, more than the mere existence of the employment relation aids in commission of the harassment: when a supervisor takes a tangible employment action against the subordinate. Every Federal Court of Appeals to have considered the question has found vicarious liability when a discriminatory act results in a tangible employment action. In *Meritor*, we acknowledged this consensus. Although few courts have elaborated how agency principles support this rule, we think it reflects a correct application of the aided in the agency relation standard.

In the context of this case, a tangible employment action would have taken the form of a denial of a raise or a promotion. The concept of a tangible employment action appears in numerous cases in the Courts of Appeals discussing claims involving race, age, and national origin discrimination, as well as sex discrimination. Without endorsing the specific results of those decisions, we think it prudent to import the concept of a tangible employment action for resolution of the vicarious liability issue we consider here. A tangible employment action constitutes a significant change in employment status, such as hiring, firing, failing to promote, reassignment with significantly different responsibilities, or a decision causing a significant change in benefits. *Compare* Crady v. Liberty Nat. Bank & Trust Co. of Ind., 993 F.2d 132, 136 (7th Cir.1993) ("A materially adverse change might be indicated by a termination of employment, a demotion evidenced by a decrease in wage or salary, a less distinguished title, a material loss of benefits, significantly diminished material responsibilities, or other indices that might be unique to a particular situation"), *with* Flaherty v. Gas Research Institute, 31 F.3d 451, 456 (7th Cir.1994) (a "bruised ego" is not enough); Kocsis v. Multi-

Care Management, Inc., 97 F.3d 876, 887 (6th Cir.1996) (demotion without change in pay, benefits, duties, or prestige insufficient) and Harlston v. McDonnell Douglas Corp., 37 F.3d 379, 382 (8th Cir.1994) (reassignment to more inconvenient job insufficient).

When a supervisor makes a tangible employment decision, there is assurance the injury could not have been inflicted absent the agency relation. A tangible employment action in most cases inflicts direct economic harm. As a general proposition, only a supervisor, or other person acting with the authority of the company, can cause this sort of injury. A co-worker can break a co-worker's arm as easily as a supervisor, and anyone who has regular contact with an employee can inflict psychological injuries by his or her offensive conduct. But one co-worker (absent some elaborate scheme) cannot dock another's pay, nor can one co-worker demote another. Tangible employment actions fall within the special province of the supervisor. The supervisor has been empowered by the company as a distinct class of agent to make economic decisions affecting other employees under his or her control.

Tangible employment actions are the means by which the supervisor brings the official power of the enterprise to bear on subordinates. A tangible employment decision requires an official act of the enterprise, a company act. The decision in most cases is documented in official company records, and may be subject to review by higher level supervisors. The supervisor often must obtain the imprimatur of the enterprise and use its internal processes.

For these reasons, a tangible employment action taken by the supervisor becomes for Title VII purposes the act of the employer. Whatever the exact contours of the aided in the agency relation standard, its requirements will always be met when a supervisor takes a tangible employment action against a subordinate. In that instance, it would be implausible to interpret agency principles to allow an employer to escape liability, as *Meritor* itself appeared to acknowledge.

Whether the agency relation aids in commission of supervisor harassment which does not culminate in a tangible employment action is less obvious. Application of the standard is made difficult by its malleable terminology, which can be read to either expand or limit liability in the context of supervisor harassment. On the one hand, a supervisor's power and authority invests his or her harassing conduct with a particular threatening character, and in this sense, a supervisor always is aided by the agency relation. *See Meritor*, 477 U.S. at 77, 106 S.Ct. at 2410–11 (Marshall, J., concurring in judgment) ("[I]t is precisely because the supervisor is understood to be clothed with the employer's authority that he is able to impose unwelcome sexual conduct on subordinates"). On the other hand, there are acts of harassment a supervisor might commit which might be the same acts a co-employee would commit, and there may be some circumstances where the supervisor's status makes little difference.

* * *

Although *Meritor* suggested the limitation on employer liability stemmed from agency principles, the Court acknowledged other considerations might be relevant as well. For example, Title VII is designed to encourage the creation of antiharassment policies and effective grievance mechanisms. Were employer liability to depend in part on an employer's effort to create such procedures, it would effect Congress' intention to promote conciliation rather than litigation in the Title VII context and the EEOC's policy of encouraging the development of grievance procedures. *See* 29 C.F.R. § 1604.11(f) (1997); EEOC Policy Guidance on Sexual Harassment, 8 BNA F.E.P. Manual 405:6699 (Mar. 19, 1990). To the extent limiting employer liability could encourage employees to report harassing conduct before it becomes severe or pervasive, it would also serve Title VII's deterrent purpose. As we have observed, Title VII borrows from tort law the avoidable consequences doctrine, and the considerations which animate that doctrine would also support the limitation of employer liability in certain circumstances.

In order to accommodate the agency principles of vicarious liability for harm caused by misuse of supervisory authority, as well as Title VII's equally basic policies of encouraging forethought by employers and saving action by objecting employees, we adopt the following holding in this case and in *Faragher v. Boca Raton,* 524 U.S. 775, 118 S.Ct. 2275, 141 L.Ed.2d 662 (1998), also decided today. An employer is subject to vicarious liability to a victimized employee for an actionable hostile environment created by a supervisor with immediate (or successively higher) authority over the employee. When no tangible employment action is taken, a defending employer may raise an affirmative defense to liability or damages, subject to proof by a preponderance of the evidence, *see* Fed.Rule Civ.Proc. 8(c). The defense comprises two necessary elements: (a) that the employer exercised reasonable care to prevent and correct promptly any sexually harassing behavior, and (b) that the plaintiff employee unreasonably failed to take advantage of any preventive or corrective opportunities provided by the employer or to avoid harm otherwise. While proof that an employer had promulgated an antiharassment policy with complaint procedure is not necessary in every instance as a matter of law, the need for a stated policy suitable to the employment circumstances may appropriately be addressed in any case when litigating the first element of the defense. And while proof that an employee failed to fulfill the corresponding obligation of reasonable care to avoid harm is not limited to showing any unreasonable failure to use any complaint procedure provided by the employer, a demonstration of such failure will normally suffice to satisfy the employer's burden under the second element of the defense. No affirmative defense is available, however, when the supervisor's harassment culminates in a tangible employment action, such as discharge, demotion, or undesirable reassignment.

IV

Relying on existing case law which held out the promise of vicarious liability for all *quid pro quo* claims, Ellerth focused all her attention in the Court of Appeals on proving her claim fit within that category. Given our explanation that the labels *quid pro quo* and hostile work environment are not controlling for purposes of establishing employer liability, Ellerth should have an adequate opportunity to prove she has a claim for which Burlington is liable.

Although Ellerth has not alleged she suffered a tangible employment action at the hands of Slowik, which would deprive Burlington of the availability of the affirmative defense, this is not dispositive. In light of our decision, Burlington is still subject to vicarious liability for Slowik's activity, but Burlington should have an opportunity to assert and prove the affirmative defense to liability. * * *

[JUSTICE GINSBURG concurred in the judgment of the Court.]

JUSTICE THOMAS, with whom JUSTICE SCALIA joins, dissenting.

* * *

Sexual harassment is simply not something that employers can wholly prevent without taking extraordinary measures—constant video and audio surveillance, for example—that would revolutionize the workplace in a manner incompatible with a free society. Indeed, such measures could not even detect incidents of harassment such as the comments Slowick allegedly made to respondent in a hotel bar. The most that employers can be charged with, therefore, is a duty to act reasonably under the circumstances.

* * *

Popular misconceptions notwithstanding, sexual harassment is not a freestanding federal tort, but a form of employment discrimination. As such, it should be treated no differently (and certainly no better) than the other forms of harassment that are illegal under Title VII. I would restore parallel treatment of employer liability for racial and sexual harassment and hold an employer liable for a hostile work environment only if the employer is truly at fault. * * *

Notes and Questions

1. *The EEOC 1999 Enforcement Guidance*: After the Supreme Court issued its opinions in *Ellerth* and *Faragher*, the EEOC rescinded 29 C.F.R. § 1604.11(c), the standard for employer liability for sexual harassment in the Guidelines on Sexual Harassment, and issued a new policy entitled Enforcement Guidance: Vicarious Employer Liability for Unlawful Harassment by Supervisors (6/18/99), EEOC Compliance Manual (BNA), N:4075 [Binder 3]. *See also www.eeoc.gov/docs/harassment.html*. The 1999 Enforcement Guidance discusses the Supreme Court's *Ellerth* and *Faragher* decisions and offers guidance on the vicarious liability issues that arise in cases involving harassment by supervisors. The Enforcement Guidance does not affect the EEOC Guidelines on employer liability for harassment by coworkers, 29 C.F.R. § 1604.11(d). See the EEOC Guidelines at the beginning of this section.

2. By holding that employers are vicariously liable when their supervisors engage in sexual harassment, regardless of whether the conduct is characterized as quid pro quo or hostile work environment, the Supreme Court avoids some but not all aspects of the difficult evidentiary issues that courts previously had to resolve when vicarious liability depended on the plaintiff's ability to fit the facts of her claim into a quid pro quo fact pattern. For example, before *Ellerth*, a finding of quid pro quo harassment, and therefore an employer's vicarious liability, could turn on whether the supervisor's threats or promises and sexual demands were explicit or implicit, regardless of whether the threats were fulfilled. The evidentiary problem was clearly identified by Judge Reinhardt in *Nichols v. Frank*, 42 F.3d 503, 512 (9th Cir.1994):

> We note that difficult factual and legal questions will almost always arise whenever either the conditioning of benefits (or absence of detriment) or the request for favors is not explicit, but is instead *implicit* in the harasser's communications or dealings with his prey. For example, *quid pro quo* harassment is clear if a manager explicitly tells his subordinate "I will fire you unless you sleep with me." However, it is much less clear whether a violation has occurred if a manager simply asks the subordinate whether she would like to have a drink after work to talk about a possible promotion and then sometime after she refuses, awards the position to another employee. It is even less clear if the manager merely invites the employee out for a drink on one or more occasions but does not suggest that he wishes to discuss work-related matters; if the manager is spurned and subsequently withholds anticipated benefits, it may set off alarm bells, but further evidence would be required before a charge of sexual harassment could be sustained.

Consider how the analysis and holding in *Ellerth* potentially change the legal consequences and evidentiary issues for the fact patterns Judge Reinhardt described in *Nichols v. Frank*. In the first scenario, the explicit threat and demand is not quid pro quo harassment if the threat is not fulfilled, i.e., if there are no adverse, tangible job consequences. A single, explicit threat, may not even be sufficient evidence of "severe" harassment to impose liability under a hostile environment analysis. The second scenario, which Judge Reinhardt found "much less clear" as evidence that a violation has occurred, more easily fits within the *Ellerth* quid pro quo paradigm. There is a tangible harm—a failure to receive a promotion. But the sexual advance is not explicit, thus raising proof problems. Was this an implicit quid pro quo or a completely innocuous event?

In the last scenario, is the invitation for a drink a precursor to a consensual social or even sexual relationship, an attempt to be collegial, or an implicit sexual advance? The evidence of a withheld benefit certainly meets the *Ellerth* requirement for tangible economic harm, but was the supervisor's invitation an implicit sexual advance? Is an employee likely to perceive such an invitation as a sexual advance in the absence of other conduct with sexual connotations? Is it only clear that a sexual advance was implicitly intended after the job benefit is withdrawn? Do the facts warrant making such an inference?

3. *The Relevance of a "Tangible Employment Action"*: After *Ellerth,* for purposes of employer liability, the key distinction between sexual harassment claims based on the conduct of a supervisor is not the label—"quid pro quo" or "hostile work environment"—that the plaintiff applies to the claim, but the presence or absence of a "tangible employment action." Thus, in all sexual harassment cases involving conduct of certain supervisors, the plaintiff's ability to prove (or the employer's ability to disprove or discount) evidence of a "tangible employment action" will be critical in establishing employer liability and in determining whether the defendant is entitled to present an affirmative defense. Vicarious liability for hostile work environment will be discussed further in the notes following the next principal case, *Faragher v. City of Boca Raton*, 524 U.S. 775, 118 S.Ct. 2275, 141 L.Ed.2d 662 (1998), which was decided by the Court on the same day as *Ellerth.*

4. *Defining a "Tangible Employment Action"*: *Ellerth* defines a "tangible employment action" as "a significant change in employment status, such as hiring, firing, failing to promote, reassignment with significantly different responsibilities, or a decision causing a significant change in benefits." 524 U.S. at 761, 118 S.Ct. at 2268. Consider the following:

a. *Fulfilled promises of job benefits*: Suppose a supervisor promises a subordinate a job benefit, such as a promotion, if she complies with his sexual demands. The employee complies, and the promise is fulfilled—she is promoted. On these facts, is the employer vicariously liable for sexual harassment? Will the employer be permitted to present an affirmative defense? Note that the Court states in *Ellerth*, "We assumed [in *Meritor*], and with adequate reason, that if an employer demanded sexual favors from an employee in return for a job benefit, discrimination with respect to terms or condition of employment was explicit." *Id.* at 752, 118 S.Ct. at 2264.

What if the supervisor grants benefits that are not expressly linked to sexual demands, as in the following scenario? Over a period of months a female employee endured her male supervisor's repeated invitations to have sex, without ever complying or complaining. The sexual advances were not accompanied by explicit threats or promises. Meanwhile, she received a raise, a favorable job evaluation, and a promotion from the same supervisor. Is the employer vicariously liable for sexual harassment? If so, does the employer have an affirmative defense that she failed to take advantage of its sexual harassment policy? How can she establish a nexus between the sexual advances and the job benefits if the benefits were routine, expected, or earned? *See* Matvia v. Bald Head Island Mgmt., Inc., 259 F.3d 261, 267 (4th Cir.2001).

b. *Unfulfilled promises of job benefits*: Suppose a supervisor orally (and privately) promised an employee a job benefit, such as a promotion, and subsequently made a sexual advance toward the employee that was implicitly linked to fulfillment of the promised promotion. Then, when the employee refused to comply with the sexual demand, the supervisor failed to promote the employee. Does the supervisor's failure to act under these circumstances constitute a "tangible employment action"? If the supervisor's promise does not appear on the company records and was not witnessed by any other employees, and the employee's status has not changed, how can the employee prove there has been a "tangible employment action" consisting of a failure to promote?

c. *Unfulfilled threats of adverse job consequences—submission cases*: Do claims involving tangible employment action adequately describe the universe of potential harms where a supervisor's authority "aids in commission of the harassment"? Is the definition of "tangible employment action" necessarily limited to economic harm? The Court of Appeals for the Second Circuit held that an employee had suffered a tangible employment action when her supervisor forced her to submit to his sexual demands as a condition of keeping her job. Jin v. Metropolitan Life Ins., 310 F.3d 84 (2d Cir.2002). *Jin* held that "[r]equiring an employee to engage in unwanted sex acts is one of the most pernicious and oppressive forms of sexual harassment that can occur in the workplace" and "this type of conduct—a classic quid pro quo for which courts have traditionally held employers liable—fits squarely within the definition of 'tangible employment action.' " *Id.* at 94. Is this holding consistent with *Ellerth*? *See also* Holly D. v. California Inst. of Tech., 339 F.3d 1158, 1170–72 (9th Cir.2003) (following *Jin* and the 1999 EEOC Enforcement Guidance). Does an employee suffer an injury by complying with a supervisor's unwanted sexual demand, regardless of whether the supervisor's economic threat is eventually fulfilled? Are supervisors able to condition sexual demands on credible threats of economic harm in a way no co-worker can? Shortly before *Ellerth* and *Faragher* were decided, Eugene Scalia wrote: "Treating the submission case as actionable quid pro quo harassment is consistent with the term's original definition." Eugene Scalia, *The Strange Career of Quid Pro Quo Sexual Harassment,* 21 Harv.J.L. & Pub. Pol'y 307, 314 (1998). Do you agree?

d. *A single unfulfilled threat*: The Supreme Court accepted the district court's finding that the "numerous alleged threats" of Ellerth's supervisor were "severe or pervasive" sexual harassment. But, the Court "express[ed] no opinion as to whether a single unfulfilled threat is sufficient to constitute discrimination in the terms or conditions of employment." *Ellerth,* 524 U.S. at 754, 118 S.Ct. at 2265. How would you resolve the question that the Supreme Court has left open in *Ellerth*? Professor Joanna Grossman suggests that "a single unfulfilled threat likely will not be sufficiently severe or pervasive to mount a hostile work environment claim." Joanna L. Grossman, *The First Bite Is Free: Employer Liability for Sexual Harassment,* 61 U.Pitt.L.Rev. 671, 681 (2000).

e. *Aggregating job detriments*: After *Ellerth*, can a victim of quid pro quo harassment establish that she suffered adverse employment action by aggregating evidence of a series of minor job detriments, none of which, standing alone, would be considered a "tangible job detriment" or "ultimate employment decision"? *See* Reinhold v. Virginia, 151 F.3d 172, 175 (4th Cir.1998) (holding that plaintiff's evidence that "she was assigned extra work and suffered other harm as a result of her rejection of [her supervisor's] sexual advances" does not establish that she suffered a "tangible employment action").

f. *Constructive discharge as a "tangible employment action"*: If an employee can aggregate a series of relatively minor job detriments, will they be considered a tangible employment action only if they would satisfy the requirements of a constructive discharge? *See* Mallinson–Montague v. Pocrnick, 224 F.3d 1224, 1231 (10th Cir.2000). For that matter, should a constructive discharge ever be considered a tangible employment action under *Ellerth*? The courts are divided on this issue, and in 2003 the Supreme Court granted a petition for certiori in *Suders v. Easton*, 325 F.3d 432 (3rd Cir.2003), *cert. granted sub nom.* Pennsylvania State Police v. Suders, 124 S.Ct. 803, 157 L.Ed.2d 692 (2003). In *Suders*, the Third Circuit held that a constructive discharge is a tangible employment action under *Ellerth* and *Faragher. See id.* at 452–54 (analyzing cases). *Compare* Caridad v. Metro–North Commuter R.R., 191 F.3d 283, 293 (2d Cir.1999) (holding that constructive discharge is not a tangible employment action); *with* Cherry v. Menard, Inc., 101 F.Supp.2d 1160, 1171–77 (N.D.Iowa 2000) (holding that constructive discharge is a tangible employment action and critiquing the *Caridad* opinion).

5. In her 1979 book, *Sexual Harassment of Working Women*, cited in *Ellerth*, 524 U.S. at 751, 118 S.Ct. at 2264, Professor MacKinnon described several scenarios that she believed could be classified as quid pro quo situations:

> Assuming there has been an unwanted sexual advance, a resulting quid pro quo can take one of three possible shapes. In situation one, the woman declines the advance and forfeits an employment opportunity. If the connections are shown, this raises the clearest pattern: sexual advance, noncompliance, employment retaliation. In situation two, the woman complies and does not receive a job benefit. This is complex: was the job benefit denied independently of the sexual involvement? Is employment-coerced sex an injury in itself or does compliance mean consent? Should the woman in effect forfeit the job opportunity as relief *because* she complied sexually? In situation three, the woman complies and receives a job benefit. Does she have an injury to complain of? Do her competitors? In a fourth logical possibility, which does not require further discussion, the woman refuses to comply, receives completely fair treatment on the job, and is never harassed again (and is, no doubt, immensely relieved). In this one turn of events, there truly is "no harm in asking."

Catharine A. MacKinnon, Sexual Harassment of Working Women: A Case of Sex Discrimination 32–33 (1979).

In light of the Supreme Court's holding in *Ellerth*, what are the potential legal consequences of these four factual scenarios today? Would the first three situations impose vicarious liability on the employer under *Ellerth*'s analysis because they all appear to involve tangible job consequences? In answering these questions, assume that the unwelcome sexual advance was made by a "supervisor with immediate (or successively higher) authority over the employee." Do the facts of *Ellerth* fit into the fourth "logical possibility" suggested by Professor MacKinnon? If not, is there a fifth "logical possibility" that Professor MacKinnon implied, but did not state?

6. *Fulfilled Versus Unfulfilled Threats*: Why has the Supreme Court made a distinction in *Ellerth* between fulfilled and unfulfilled threats of supervisors? Professor MacKinnon's first "situation," *supra* Note 5, de-

scribed the "clearest pattern" of quid pro quo—"sexual advance, noncompliance, retaliation." But at the time that a supervisor makes an "unwelcome sexual advance" toward a subordinate in the context of a "threat" of "adverse, tangible job consequences," how is the subordinate able to know, for sure, whether the supervisor is serious about the threat or just bluffing? What are the subordinate's options?

a. First, she can "call his bluff" by refusing his sexual advance. If it turns out that the supervisor was not bluffing, and she suffers adverse, tangible job consequences, the employer is strictly liable and has no affirmative defense. On the other hand, if he was bluffing, and she suffers no adverse job consequences, the subordinate can establish Title VII liability only by showing that the threat (or threats) was sufficiently "severe or pervasive" to constitute a hostile work environment. And the employer has an opportunity to prove its affirmative defense. Many employees might conclude that a one-time unfulfilled threat may not even be worth complaining about.

Consider the classic case of quid pro quo harassment where a supervisor makes a sexual advance, without an explicit threat of adverse job consequences, the employee rejects the advance, and subsequently suffers an adverse "tangible employment action." The timing of events may determine whether the employer is strictly liable or permitted to raise an affirmative defense. For example, if there is a delay of three or four weeks between the employee's rejection of the supervisor's sexual advance and her subsequent discharge, and the supervisor shows no hostility and makes no further advances toward the employee in the interim, can the plaintiff establish a causal link to prove quid pro quo harassment? *See* Farrell v. Planters Lifesavers, 206 F.3d 271, 281 (3d Cir.2000) (finding that causation could be established in these circumstances based on the timing and "other evidence gleaned from the record as a whole from which causation may be inferred"). What if the rejected supervisor waits several months to retaliate against the employee with an adverse employment decision?

b. Second, if the subordinate believes the supervisor is serious and is afraid to "call his bluff," she might comply with the sexual demand. If, as a result of her compliance, the supervisor imposes no adverse job consequences, does *Ellerth* dictate that she has not suffered a "tangible employment action" as a matter of law? If there is no "tangible employment action," can the employer nevertheless be found liable under a hostile work environment theory in this situation? Is sexual conduct coerced by means of a threat necessarily "severe" and "unwelcome" harassment? Does this depend on the nature of the sexual conduct? Or whether the threat was objectively credible? Or perceived by the victim as credible? As long as the employer has a reasonably effective antiharassment policy and complaint procedure, under what circumstances would an employee be "unreasonable," as a matter of law, if she complied first and then complained later?

c. When a supervisor promises an employment benefit to a subordinate in exchange for sexual favors, and the employee subsequently complies and receives the promised job benefit, the scenario fits the third quid pro quo fact pattern described by Professor MacKinnon. Professor MacKinnon wondered whether the employee or her competitors have been harmed. *See also*

MacKinnon, *supra*, at 37–40 (discussing situations "in which women who comply with sexual conditions are advantaged in employment over men or over women who refuse," *id.* at 37). The Supreme Court sees this pattern as explicit quid pro quo harassment. But would the same analysis apply if the subordinate "called the bluff," rejected the sexual demand, and was promoted anyway? Would the employee be likely to complain of sexual harassment under either quid pro quo or hostile work environment theory? Does this suggest that sexual demands conditioned on promises of job benefits ought to be analyzed differently from those that are conditioned on threats of adverse job consequences?

d. Professor MacKinnon's "fourth logical possibility" involves a single unwanted sexual advance by a supervisor, the subordinate's refusal to comply, followed by fair treatment and no further sexual harassment. Could this situation ever result in employer liability under *Ellerth*? In other words, what if a supervisor makes a single sexual advance toward a subordinate, which is implicitly or explicitly linked to employment conditions, but which is rebuffed with no tangible job consequences? Is there "no harm in asking" as Professor MacKinnon suggested?

7. A "notice liability" approach would impose liability on an employer only if it had actual notice of harassment and failed to act. Has the Supreme Court incorporated "notice liability" into the elements of the affirmative defense for supervisory hostile work environment? Before *Ellerth* and *Faragher*, the significance of notice in sexual harassment cases was debated. For example, in 1995, Professor Verkerke had proposed that the courts adopt "notice liability" for all claims of sexual harassment brought by individuals. J. Hoult Verkerke, *Notice Liability in Employment Discrimination Law*, 81 Va.L.Rev. 273 (1995). Under this approach, an employer that had a procedure for handling complaints of sexual harassment would not be liable unless the victim had complained about the harassment and the employer had failed to make an adequate response. *Id.* at 279. Quid pro quo and hostile work environment claims would be treated the same, and no distinctions would be made between harassment by supervisors and by co-workers. Professor David Oppenheimer criticized notice liability on the grounds that it "would turn Title VII on its head," because "[u]nder such a system, employers would effectively get one free act of discrimination or harassment, regardless of the status of the perpetrator." David Benjamin Oppenheimer, *Exacerbating the Exasperating: Title VII Liability of Employers for Sexual Harassment Committed by Their Supervisors*, 81 Cornell L.Rev. 66, 144 (1995). Does *Ellerth* permit "one free act" for quid pro quo harassment when a supervisor's threat of tangible employment action is not fulfilled?

8. *The Serial Harasser*: After reading *Ellerth*, would you conclude that a supervisor can make one "free" sexual request of a subordinate as long as it is polite, nonthreatening—i.e., not expressly or implicitly linked to tangible job consequences—and does not involve any physical touching? Is this what Professor MacKinnon may have had in mind when she suggested there is "no harm in asking"? Does this lead to the possibility that supervisors can politely ask subordinates, one after another, for sexual favors in the hopes that one or more will eventually comply? *See generally* Joanna L. Grossman, *The First Bite Is Free: Employer Liability for Sexual Harassment*, 61 U.Pitt.L.Rev. 671 (2000). Could a pattern of such polite requests of different

employees over a long period of time be considered evidence of "pervasive" sexual harassment? Once the employer is on notice that a supervisor repeats the same unwelcome harassing conduct with successive victims, does the employer have an obligation to remedy the serial harassment permanently? *See* Brooks v. H.J. Russell & Co., 66 F.Supp.2d 1349, 1353–54 (N.D.Ga.1999) (plaintiff's evidence that a supervisor had sexually harassed other employees, long before the alleged harassment of plaintiff, raised an issue of material fact regarding whether the employer knew or should have known about the supervisor's propensities before the plaintiff made her complaint).

Would it ever be reasonable for an employee to comply with such a one-time request by a supervisor if the employer has adopted and disseminated antiharassment policies and complaint procedures that the employee is aware of? If a subordinate did comply, would this necessarily imply the solicitation for sex was welcomed? Or, could compliance indicate that the subordinate felt coerced or intimidated by the supervisor's implicit power and authority over job consequences? Would your answer depend on whether there was an express or implicit threat of job consequences linked to each request for sexual favors?

FARAGHER v. CITY OF BOCA RATON

Supreme Court of the United States, 1998.
524 U.S. 775, 118 S.Ct. 2275, 141 L.Ed.2d 662.

JUSTICE SOUTER delivered the opinion of the Court.

This case calls for identification of the circumstances under which an employer may be held liable under Title VII of the Civil Rights Act of 1964, for the acts of a supervisory employee whose sexual harassment of subordinates has created a hostile work environment amounting to employment discrimination. We hold that an employer is vicariously liable for actionable discrimination caused by a supervisor, but subject to an affirmative defense looking to the reasonableness of the employer's conduct as well as that of a plaintiff victim.

I

Between 1985 and 1990, while attending college, petitioner Beth Ann Faragher worked part time and during the summers as an ocean lifeguard for the Marine Safety Section of the Parks and Recreation Department of respondent, the City of Boca Raton, Florida (City). During this period, Faragher's immediate supervisors were Bill Terry, David Silverman, and Robert Gordon. In June 1990, Faragher resigned.

In 1992, Faragher brought an action against Terry, Silverman, and the City, asserting claims under Title VII, 42 U.S.C. § 1983, and Florida law. So far as it concerns the Title VII claim, the complaint alleged that Terry and Silverman created a "sexually hostile atmosphere" at the beach by repeatedly subjecting Faragher and other female lifeguards to "uninvited and offensive touching," by making lewd remarks, and by speaking of women in offensive terms. The complaint contained specific allegations that Terry once said that he would never promote a woman to the rank of lieutenant, and that Silverman had said to Faragher, "Date me or clean the toilets for a year." Asserting that Terry and Silverman were agents of the City, and that their conduct amounted to discrimination in the "terms, conditions, and privileges" of her employment, 42 U.S.C. § 2000e–2(a)(1), Faragher sought a judgment against the City for nominal damages, costs, and attorney's fees.

Following a bench trial, the United States District Court for the Southern District of Florida found that throughout Faragher's employment with the City, Terry served as Chief of the Marine Safety Division, with authority to hire new lifeguards (subject to the approval of higher management), to supervise all aspects of the lifeguards' work assignments, to engage in counseling, to deliver oral reprimands, and to make a record of any such discipline. Silverman was a Marine Safety lieutenant from 1985 until June 1989, when he became a captain. Gordon began the employment period as a lieutenant and at some point was promoted to the position of training captain. In these positions, Silverman and Gordon were responsible for making the lifeguards' daily assignments, and for supervising their work and fitness training.

The lifeguards and supervisors were stationed at the city beach and worked out of the Marine Safety Headquarters, a small one-story building containing an office, a meeting room, and a single, unisex locker room with a shower. Their work routine was structured in a "paramilitary configuration," with a clear chain of command. Lifeguards reported to lieutenants and captains, who reported to Terry. He was supervised by the Recreation Superintendent, who in turn reported to a Director of Parks and Recreation, answerable to the City Manager. The lifeguards had no significant contact with higher city officials like the Recreation Superintendent.

In February 1986, the City adopted a sexual harassment policy, which it stated in a memorandum from the City Manager addressed to all employees. In May 1990, the City revised the policy and reissued a statement of it. Although the City may actually have circulated the memos and statements to some employees, it completely failed to disseminate its policy among employees of the Marine Safety Section, with the result that Terry, Silverman, Gordon, and many lifeguards were unaware of it.

From time to time over the course of Faragher's tenure at the Marine Safety Section, between 4 and 6 of the 40 to 50 lifeguards were women. During that 5–year period, Terry repeatedly touched the bodies of female employees without invitation, would put his arm around Faragher, with his hand on her buttocks, and once made contact with another female lifeguard in a motion of sexual simulation. He made crudely demeaning references to women generally, and once commented disparagingly on Faragher's shape. During a job interview with a woman he hired as a lifeguard, Terry said that the female lifeguards had sex with their male counterparts and asked whether she would do the same.

Silverman behaved in similar ways. He once tackled Faragher and remarked that, but for a physical characteristic he found unattractive, he would readily have had sexual relations with her. Another time, he pantomimed an act of oral sex. Within earshot of the female lifeguards, Silverman made frequent, vulgar references to women and sexual matters, commented on the bodies of female lifeguards and beachgoers, and at least twice told female lifeguards that he would like to engage in sex with them.

Faragher did not complain to higher management about Terry or Silverman. Although she spoke of their behavior to Gordon, she did not regard these discussions as formal complaints to a supervisor but as conversations with a person she held in high esteem. Other female lifeguards had similarly informal talks with Gordon, but because Gordon did not feel that it was his place to do so, he did not report these complaints to Terry, his own supervisor, or to any other city official. Gordon responded to the complaints of one lifeguard by saying that "the City just [doesn't] care."

In April 1990, however, two months before Faragher's resignation, Nancy Ewanchew, a former lifeguard, wrote to Richard Bender, the City's Personnel Director, complaining that Terry and Silverman had harassed her and other female lifeguards. Following investigation of this complaint, the City found that Terry and Silverman had behaved improperly, reprimanded them, and required them to choose between a suspension without pay or the forfeiture of annual leave.

On the basis of these findings, the District Court concluded that the conduct of Terry and Silverman was discriminatory harassment sufficiently serious to alter the conditions of Faragher's employment and constitute an abusive working environment. The District Court then ruled that there were three justifications for holding the City liable for the harassment of its supervisory employees. * * * The District Court then awarded Faragher one dollar in nominal damages on her Title VII claim.

A panel of the Court of Appeals for the Eleventh Circuit reversed the judgment against the City. Although the panel had "no trouble concluding that Terry's and Silverman's conduct * * * was severe and pervasive enough to create an objectively abusive work environment," it overturned the District Court's conclusion that the City was liable. The panel ruled that Terry and Silverman were not acting within the scope of their employment when they engaged in the harassment, that they were not aided in their actions by the agency relationship, and that the City had no constructive knowledge of the harassment by virtue of its pervasiveness or Gordon's actual knowledge.

In a 7–to–5 decision, the full Court of Appeals, sitting en banc, adopted the panel's conclusion. * * * We * * * now reverse the judgment of the Eleventh Circuit and remand for entry of judgment in Faragher's favor.

II

A

* * *

While indicating the substantive contours of the hostile environments forbidden by Title VII, our cases have established few definite rules for determining when an employer will be liable for a discriminatory environment that is otherwise actionably abusive. Given the circumstances of many of the litigated cases, including some that have come to us, it is not surprising that in many of them, the issue has been joined over the sufficiency of the abusive conditions, not the standards for determining an employer's liability for them. There have, for example, been myriad cases in which District Courts and Courts of Appeals have held employers liable on account of actual knowledge by the employer, or high-echelon officials of an employer organization, of sufficiently harassing action by subordinates, which the employer or its informed officers have done nothing to stop. In such instances, the combined knowledge and inaction may be seen as demonstrable negligence, or as the employer's adoption of the offending conduct and its results, quite as if they had been authorized affirmatively as the employer's policy.

Nor was it exceptional that standards for binding the employer were not in issue in *Harris*. In that case of discrimination by hostile environment, the individual charged with creating the abusive atmosphere was the president of the corporate employer, who was indisputably within that class of an employer organization's officials who may be treated as the organization's proxy.

Finally, there is nothing remarkable in the fact that claims against employers for discriminatory employment actions with tangible results, like hiring, firing, promotion, compensation, and work assignment, have resulted in employer liability once the discrimination was shown. * * *

* * *

The soundness of the results in these cases (and their continuing vitality), in light of basic agency principles, was confirmed by this Court's only discussion to date of standards of employer liability, in *Meritor* * * *.

* * *

B

The Court of Appeals identified, and rejected, three possible grounds drawn from agency law for holding the City vicariously liable for the hostile environment created by the supervisors. It considered whether the two supervisors were acting within the scope of their employment when they engaged in the harassing conduct. The court then enquired whether they were significantly aided by the agency relationship in committing the harassment, and also considered the possibility of imputing Gordon's knowledge of the harassment to the City. Finally, the Court of Appeals ruled out liability for negligence in failing to prevent the harassment. Faragher relies principally on the latter three theories of liability.

1

* * *

Courts of Appeals have typically held, or assumed, that conduct similar to the subject of this complaint falls outside the scope of employment. In so doing, the courts have emphasized that harassment consisting of unwelcome remarks and touching is motivated solely by individual desires and serves no purpose of the employer. For this reason, courts have likened hostile environment sexual harassment to the classic "frolic and detour" for which an employer has no vicarious liability.

* * *

In the case before us, a justification for holding the offensive behavior within the scope of Terry's and Silverman's employment was well put in Judge Barkett's dissent: "[A] pervasively hostile work environment of sexual harassment is never (one would hope) authorized, but the supervisor is clearly charged with maintaining a productive, safe work environment. The supervisor directs and controls the conduct of the employees, and the manner of doing so may inure to the employer's benefit or detriment, including subjecting the employer to Title VII liability." 111 F.3d at 1542. It is by now well recognized that hostile environment sexual harassment by supervisors (and, for that matter, co-employees) is a persistent problem in the workplace. An employer can, in a general sense, reasonably anticipate the possibility of such conduct occurring in its workplace, and one might justify the assignment of the burden of the untoward behavior to the employer as one of the costs of doing business, to be charged to the enterprise rather than the victim. * * *

Two things counsel us to draw the contrary conclusion. First, there is no reason to suppose that Congress wished courts to ignore the traditional distinction between acts falling within the scope and acts amounting to what the older law called frolics or detours from the course of employment. * * *

The second reason goes to an even broader unanimity of views among the holdings of District Courts and Courts of Appeals thus far. Those courts have held not only that the sort of harassment at issue here was outside the scope of supervisors' authority, but, by uniformly judging employer liability for co-worker harassment under a negligence standard, they have also implicitly treated such harassment as outside the scope of common employees' duties as well.

* * * The rationale for placing harassment within the scope of supervisory authority would be the fairness of requiring the employer to bear the burden of foreseeable social behavior, and the same rationale would apply when the behavior was that of co-employees.

The answer to this argument might well be to point out that the scope of supervisory employment may be treated separately by recognizing that supervisors have special authority enhancing their capacity to harass, and that the employer can guard against their misbehavior more easily because their numbers are by definition fewer than the numbers of regular employees. But this answer happens to implicate an entirely separate category of agency law (to be considered in the next section) * * *.

2

The Court of Appeals also rejected vicarious liability on the part of the City insofar as it might rest on the concluding principle set forth in § 219(2)(d) of the Restatement, that an employer "is not subject to liability for the torts of his servants acting outside the scope of their employment unless * * * the servant purported to act or speak on behalf of the principal and there was reliance on apparent authority, or he was aided in accomplishing the tort by the existence of the agency relation." Faragher points to several ways in which the agency relationship aided Terry and Silverman in carrying out their harassment. She argues that in general offending supervisors can abuse their authority to keep subordinates in their presence while they make offensive statements, and that they implicitly threaten to misuse their supervisory powers to deter any resistance or complaint. Thus, she maintains that power conferred on Terry and Silverman by the City enabled them to act for so long without provoking defiance or complaint.

* * *

We therefore agree with Faragher that in implementing Title VII it makes sense to hold an employer vicariously liable for some tortious conduct of a supervisor made possible by abuse of his supervisory authority, and that the aided-by-agency-relation principle embodied in § 219(2)(d) of the Restatement provides an appropriate starting point for determining liability for the kind of harassment presented here. Several courts, indeed, have noted what Faragher has argued, that there is a sense in which a harassing supervisor is always assisted in his misconduct by the supervisory relationship. The agency relationship affords contact with an employee subjected to a supervisor's sexual harassment, and the victim may well be reluctant to accept the risks of blowing the whistle on a superior. When a person with supervisory authority discriminates in the terms and conditions of subordinates' employment, his actions necessarily draw upon his superior position over the people who report to him, or those under them, whereas an employee generally cannot check a supervisor's abusive conduct the same way that she might deal with abuse from a co-worker. When a fellow employee harasses, the victim can walk away or tell the offender where to go, but it may be difficult to offer such responses to a supervisor, whose "power to supervise—[which may be] to hire and fire, and to set work schedules and pay rates—does not disappear * * * when he chooses to harass through insults and offensive gestures rather than directly with threats of firing or promises of promotion." Estrich, *Sex at Work*, 43 Stan.L.Rev. 813, 854 (1991). Recognition of employer liability when discriminatory misuse of supervisory authority alters the terms and conditions of a victim's employment is underscored by the fact that the employer has a greater opportunity to guard against misconduct by supervisors than by common workers; employers have greater opportunity and incentive to screen them, train them, and monitor their performance.

In sum, there are good reasons for vicarious liability for misuse of supervisory authority. That rationale must, however, satisfy one more condition. We are not entitled to recognize this theory under Title VII unless we can square it with *Meritor*'s holding that an employer is not "automatically" liable for harassment by a supervisor who creates the requisite degree of discrimination * * *. [W]e think there are two basic alternatives, one being to require proof of some affirmative invocation of that authority by the harassing supervisor, the other to recognize an affirmative defense to liability in some circumstances, even when a supervisor has created the actionable environment.

There is certainly some authority for requiring active or affirmative, as distinct from passive or implicit, misuse of supervisory authority before liability may be imputed. * * *

But neat examples illustrating the line between the affirmative and merely implicit uses of power are not easy to come by in considering management behavior. * * * Judgment calls would often be close, the results would often seem disparate even if not demonstrably contradictory, and the temptation to litigate would be hard to resist. We think plaintiffs and defendants alike would be poorly served by an active-use rule.

The other basic alternative to automatic liability would avoid this particular temptation to litigate, but allow an employer to show as an affirmative defense to liability that the employer had exercised reasonable care to avoid harassment and to eliminate it when it might occur, and that the complaining employee had failed to act with like reasonable care to take advantage of the employer's safeguards and otherwise to prevent harm that could have been avoided. This composite defense would, we think, implement the statute sensibly, for reasons that are not hard to fathom.

* * * It would * * * implement clear statutory policy and complement the Government's Title VII enforcement efforts to recognize the employer's affirmative obligation to prevent violations and give credit here to employers who make reasonable efforts to discharge their duty. Indeed, a theory of vicarious liability for misuse of supervisory power would be at odds with the statutory policy if it failed to provide employers with some such incentive.

The requirement to show that the employee has failed in a coordinate duty to avoid or mitigate harm reflects an equally obvious policy imported from the general theory of damages, that a victim has a duty "to use such means as are reasonable under the circumstances to avoid or minimize the damages" that result from violations of the statute. Ford Motor Co. v. EEOC, 458 U.S. 219, 231, n. 15, 102 S.Ct. 3057, 73 L.Ed.2d 721 (1982). An employer may, for example, have provided a proven, effective mechanism for reporting and resolving complaints of sexual harassment, available to the employee without undue risk or expense. If the plaintiff unreasonably failed to avail herself of the employer's preventive or remedial apparatus, she should not recover damages that could have been avoided if she had done so. If the victim could have avoided harm, no liability should be found against the employer who had taken reasonable care, and if damages could reasonably have been mitigated no award against a liable employer should reward a plaintiff for what her own efforts could have avoided.

In order to accommodate the principle of vicarious liability for harm caused by misuse of supervisory authority, as well as Title VII's equally basic policies of encouraging forethought by employers and saving action by objecting employees, we adopt the following holding in this case and in *Burlington Industries, Inc. v. Ellerth,* also decided today. * * * [The Court here repeats verbatim the holding in *Ellerth.* See the concluding paragraph in Part III.D of *Ellerth.*]

Applying these rules here, we believe that the judgment of the Court of Appeals must be reversed. The District Court found that the degree of hostility in the work environment rose to the actionable level and was attributable to Silverman and Terry. It is undisputed that these supervisors "were granted virtually unchecked authority" over their subordinates, "directly controll[ing] and supervis[ing] all aspects of [Faragher's] day-to-day activities." It is also clear that Faragher and her colleagues were "completely isolated from the City's higher management." The City did not seek review of these findings.

While the City would have an opportunity to raise an affirmative defense if there were any serious prospect of its presenting one, it appears from the record that any such avenue is closed. The District Court found that the City had entirely failed to disseminate its policy against sexual harassment among the beach employees and that its officials made no attempt to keep track of the conduct of supervisors like Terry and Silverman. The record also makes clear that the City's policy did not include any assurance that the harassing supervisors could be bypassed in registering complaints. Under such circumstances, we hold as a matter of law that the City could not be found to have exercised reasonable care to prevent the supervisors' harassing conduct. Unlike the employer of a small workforce, who might expect that sufficient care to prevent tortious behavior could be exercised informally, those responsible for city operations could not reasonably have thought that precautions against hostile environments in any one of many departments in far-flung locations could be effective without communicating some formal policy against harassment, with a sensible complaint procedure.

* * *

The City points to nothing that might justify a conclusion by the District Court on remand that the City had exercised reasonable care. Nor is there any reason to remand for consideration of Faragher's efforts to mitigate her own damages, since the award to her was solely nominal.

* * *

[JUSTICE THOMAS, joined by JUSTICE SCALIA, dissented for the reasons presented in his dissent in *Ellerth*.]

Notes and Questions

1. The notes following *Ellerth* explored the Court's treatment of employer vicarious liability for harassment resulting in a "tangible employment action." The primary focus of the following notes and questions is the elements of an employer's affirmative defense to a claim of supervisory sexual harassment. For a "Supervisor Sexual Harassment Road Map," demonstrating the steps involved in analyzing cases of supervisory sexual harassment, see *Casiano v. AT & T Corp.*, 213 F.3d 278, 283 n.5, 288 (5th Cir.2000) (Appendix).

2. *Distinguishing "Supervisors" from "Nonsupervisors"*: Under *Ellerth* and *Faragher*, vicarious liability for workplace sexual harassment can be established only where the harasser was "a supervisor with immediate (or successively higher) authority over the employee." Harassment by a supervisor who does not meet this definition will be treated as co-worker harassment, and the plaintiff will have to demonstrate that the employer was negligent in permitting the harassment to continue after actual or constructive notice of the conduct. See Section C.2 of this chapter. Thus, as one court observed, "[t]he starting point for analyzing employer vicarious liability in a Title VII hostile work environment action is to determine whether the person who allegedly created that environment is properly characterized as having been the plaintiff's 'supervisor.'" Mack v. Otis Elevator Co., 326 F.3d 116, 123 (2d Cir.2003). The term "supervisor," however, does not appear in Title VII. In the absence of a statutory definition, the courts will continue to address the issue on a case-by-case basis in light of the *Ellerth* and *Faragher* decisions. *See, e.g.,* Hall v Bodine Elec. Co., 276 F.3d 345, 355 (7th Cir.2002); Joens v. John Morrell & Co., 243 F.Supp.2d 920, 934–41 (N.D.Iowa 2003) (collecting and analyzing cases).

a. In *Faragher,* there was no question that defendants Terry and Silverman had immediate supervisory authority over Faragher and the other lifeguards. The job functions and titles in the Marine Safety Division were organized in "a 'paramilitary configuration' with a clear chain of command." *Faragher*, 118 S.Ct. at 2280. Imagine an organizational structure at the opposite extreme: What if an employer abolishes job titles and other job status distinctions, allocates job functions in a nonhierachical structure, and delegates decisions about salary, promotions, discharges, and job assignments to a collective body? Assume that the harasser has contributed to an actionable hostile work environment of another employee. Both the harasser and the victim work on the same "team" that shares collective decision-making authority. Will the victim be required to prove negligence—that the employer knew or should have known about the harassment—or can the victim show that the harasser has supervisory authority and the employer is responsible under a theory of vicarious liability? Will your answer depend, at least in part, on the degree to which the harasser can effectively recommend to the team changes in working conditions for the victim?

b. In 1947, Congress amended the National Labor Relations Act (NLRA) for the purpose of excluding supervisory employees from coverage under the NLRA. The amendment provides a statutory definition of a "supervisor" as:

> [a]ny individual having authority, in the interest of the employer, to hire, transfer, suspend, lay off, recall, promote, discharge, assign, reward, or discipline other employees, or responsibly to direct them, or to adjust their grievances, or effectively to recommend such action, if in connection with the foregoing the exercise of such authority is not of a merely routine or clerical nature, but requires the use of independent judgment.

29 U.S.C. § 152(11). The EEOC Guidelines on Sexual Harassment, adopted before *Meritor*, state that "[t]he [EEOC] will examine the circumstances of the particular employment relationship and the job functions performed by the individual in determining whether an individual acts in either a supervisory or agency capacity." 29 C.F.R. § 1604.11(c). As Professor Oppenheimer observed, "[a]lthough the EEOC Guidelines did not explicitly adopt the NLRA definition of 'supervisor,' and although the NLRA definition cannot be applied in every instance to Title VII, the definition is nevertheless a useful starting point in distinguishing supervisors from nonsupervisors." David Benjamin Oppenheimer, *Exacerbating the Exasperating: Title VII Liability of Employers for Sexual Harassment Committed by Their Supervisors*, 81 Cornell L.Rev. 66, 118–19 (1995).

c. Should "supervisors" only include individuals with authority to take tangible employment actions against the harassment victim? For example, should a foreman who has no authority to make or recommend a promotion, demotion, suspension, or discharge be treated as a "supervisor" under *Ellerth* and *Faragher*? Compare *Mack*, 326 F.3d at 123–27, *with Joens*, 243 F.Supp.2d 920, 941–42. Are all partners in a law firm "supervisors" of all associates? Are all tenured faculty members "supervisors" of all nontenured faculty members?

3. *Direct Liability—Employer Acquiescence in Harassment*: *Ellerth* and *Faragher* acknowledge that an employer may be directly liable for harassment where it "acts with tortious intent." *Ellerth*, 524 U.S. at 758, 118 S.Ct. at 2267; *Faragher*, 524 U.S. at 789–90, 118 S.Ct. at 2284. When does an employer ever *intend* "the conduct or the consequences" of harassment by supervisors? Professor Oppenheimer has queried: "If middle-management employees acquiesced in the harassment, why should it matter that they thereafter took appropriate action? They had already, as agents of the employer, ratified the improper behavior." Oppenheimer, *supra* Note 2.b, at

133. Was the same-sex harassment in *Oncale* a case of employer acquiescence in sexual harassment? See Section B.3 of this chapter. How do you determine whether an employer's knowledge of harassment and inaction is "demonstrable negligence" or "adoption of the offending conduct"? If the employer acquiesces in harassment, should it be permitted to raise an affirmative defense? If so, does acquiescence mean that, as a matter of law, the employer cannot satisfy the first element of the *Ellerth/Faragher* affirmative defense?

4. *Imputed Liability—The High–Ranking Harasser as a "Proxy" or "Alter Ego" for the Employer*: Why was employer liability not an issue in *Harris v. Forklift*? In *Faragher*, the Court elaborated on the concept of imputing liability to an employer by citing cases where harassers were treated as the proxy or alter ego for the employer under Title VII. In the cases cited, the harasser was the president or other high corporate officer of a corporate employer, or the proprietor, a partner, or owner of a firm. Recall that in *Ellerth*, the alleged harasser, Slowik, was not Ellerth's immediate supervisor, but a corporate officer higher in the corporate hierarchy—the supervisor of Ellerth's supervisor. Why was Slowik not considered a proxy for the employer? For a post-*Ellerth/Faragher* case finding that a bank vice president can be considered the "alter ego" of the bank for purpose of its liability for his alleged sexual harassment of two former employees, see *Mallinson-Montague v. Pocrnick*, 224 F.3d 1224, 1232–33 (10th Cir.2000).

5. *Liability for Punitive Damages*: In *Kolstad v. American Dental Association*, 527 U.S. 526, 119 S.Ct. 2118, 144 L.Ed.2d 494 (1999), discussed in Chapter 16, Section F.2, the Supreme Court relied on the Civil Rights Act of 1991, 42 U.S.C. § 1981a(b)(1), and the agency principles developed in *Ellerth* and *Faragher* to determine when liability for punitive damages should be imputed to the employer. Section 1981a(b)(1) permits awards of punitive damages when the employer acts "with malice or with reckless indifference to the federally protected rights of an aggrieved individual." *See Kolstad*, 527 U.S. at 530, 119 S.Ct. at 2121. Relying on the Restatement (Second) of Agency § 217(C)(c), the *Kolstad* Court ruled that an employer may be held liable for punitive damages where an agent is acting in a "managerial capacity" and is "acting in the scope of employment." *Id.* at 543, 119 S.Ct. at 2128. For example, in *Deters v. Equifax Credit Information Services, Inc.*, 202 F.3d 1262 (10th Cir.2000), the court applied *Kolstad* to uphold an award of punitive damages in a sexual harassment case. The court in *Deters* concluded that "recklessness and malice are to be inferred when a manager responsible for setting or enforcing policy in the area of discrimination does not respond to complaints, despite knowledge of serious harassment." *Id.* at 1269.

Kolstad also recognized that employers could not be vicariously liable for the manager's unlawful discrimination that is "contrary to the employer's 'good faith efforts to comply with Title VII.'" 527 U.S. at 545, 119 S. Ct. at 2129. For example, an employer was permitted to assert a good-faith defense to liability for punitive damages under *Kolstad* where the employer was not aware that its restaurant manager was harassing his subordinate, a bartender, and it had made a "good faith attempt" to establish and enforce an antidiscrimination policy. Cooke v. Stefani Mgmt. Serv., Inc., 250 F.3d 564, 568 (7th Cir.2001). *Kolstad* also cited the Restatement (Second) of Agency

§ 217(C)(a): "Punitive damages can properly be awarded against a master or other principal * * *, if (a) the principal authorized the doing and manner of the act * * *." 527 U.S. at 542, 119 S.Ct. at 2128. After *Kolstad*, if the harassing manager is a high-level employee who can be considered a proxy for the company, can the employer defend against punitive damages regardless of its good faith efforts to comply with Title VII? *See* Passantino v. Johnson & Johnson Consumer Prods., Inc., 212 F.3d 493, 517 (9th Cir.2000).

6. *The First Prong of the Employer's Affirmative Defense to Vicarious Liability*: In cases of employer vicarious liability for supervisory harassment that do not involve a tangible employment action, the employer will have an opportunity to establish its affirmative defense under *Ellerth* and *Faragher*. In considering whether an employer has met its burden of proving the first prong of its affirmative defense—that it "exercised reasonable care to prevent and correct promptly any sexually harassing behavior"—a number of factors may be relevant. What do the facts and holding in *Faragher* suggest that employers should and should not do as a matter of law? If you were advising an employer on how to avoid vicarious liability for supervisory hostile work environment, what information about the firm would you want to know? Is it possible to devise a one-size-fits-all, generic anti-harassment policy and grievance procedure that will—without fail—satisfy the first element of an employer's affirmative defense? Can you imagine any circumstances when an informal policy and procedures would suffice to meet the first element of an employer's affirmative defense under *Ellerth* and *Faragher*?

a. *Antiharassment policies.* While *Ellerth* and *Faragher* create incentives for employers to adopt sexual harassment policies, they also have made it clear that, as a matter of law, Title VII does not actually require employers to have formal sexual harassment policies. Thus, in determining whether an employer can satisfy the first part of the first prong of the *Ellerth/Faragher* affirmative defense, the lack of a formal policy is not necessarily fatal to the employer's defense. *See, e.g.,* Hall v. Bodine Elec. Co., 276 F.3d 345, 356 (7th Cir.2002) (finding that an employer with no formal policy was not liable where it had other channels for reporting sexual harassment by a coworker). On the other hand, even if the employer has instituted a formal sexual harassment policy, it will not automatically meet its burden on this part of its affirmative defense. Frederick v. Sprint/United Mgmt. Co., 246 F.3d 1305, 1313 (11th Cir.2001). Employer practices in implementing the policy may be determinative. For example, what if the employer keeps the written policy in the human resources department where potential complainants can go to get a copy? *See id.* Would it be sufficient if the employer kept the written policy in unmarked binders in public areas in each branch office, which were readily accessible to all employees? Hill v. American Gen. Fin., Inc., 218 F.3d 639, 644–45 (7th Cir.2000). *See also id.* at 645, 646 (Wood, J., dissenting in part) (finding that "[e]mployees cannot be expected to go around opening up all sorts of unmarked binders to see if by any chance they might contain the company's harassment policy"). If an employer's practice is to distribute its formal policy to each employee, can it meet its burden on this portion of its defense if the employee claims never to have received it and the company has no record that it was distributed to her? *See* Montero v. Agco Corp., 192 F.3d 856 (9th Cir.1999).

b. *Delegating authority for handling complaints*: Which individuals in a company should be delegated the authority—and given the responsibility—to report incidents of sexual harassment that come to their attention? Suppose that a relatively low-level employee, an "office co-ordinator," either actually has been given—or is reasonably believed to have—the delegated authority to deal with complaints of sexual harassment. The office co-ordinator learns about a supervisor's harassment of another employee and fails to notify anyone else in the company who is in a position of authority. In addition, the victim of the harassment makes no formal internal complaints despite the existence of a clear complaint procedure. Some time later, after the harassment has continued, the victim finally files a formal internal grievance with the company. The supervisor is immediately reprimanded, and he resigns. Will the employer fail to satisfy the first prong of its defense because it is held to have had notice of the harassment and has failed to correct the harassing behavior? *See* Sims v. Health Midwest Physician Serv. Corp., 196 F.3d 915 (8th Cir.1999).

c. *Employer responses to complaints:* Once an employer receives a complaint of a hostile work environment created by a supervisor, it must take affirmative steps to investigate and, if necessary, take corrective action in order to avoid liability. *See* Haugerud v. Amery School Dist., 259 F.3d 678, 700 (7th Cir.2001) (holding that school district was not entitled to affirmative defense to hostile work environment claim when it "simply did not act" in response to custodian's complaints about supervisor's conduct). On the other hand, even if the employer takes corrective action, a jury or court may second-guess its decisions. For example, when is discipline short of discharge appropriate in cases of supervisory sexual harassment? *See* Beard v. Flying J., Inc., 266 F.3d 792, 799 (8th Cir.2001) (finding that it was a jury question whether a written warning and suspension without pay were sufficient to establish an affirmative defense to a restaurant manager's sexual harassment of his assistant manager). Is it sufficient if the employer transfers the employee who brings the complaint and tells the alleged harasser to leave the complaining employee alone? What if the transfer is to a different department? A different shift? Another division of the company in a different location? Should the alleged harasser be moved instead? Would your analysis be any different if the harasser were a co-worker instead of a supervisor? *See* Skidmore v. Precision Printing & Pkg., Inc., 188 F.3d 606 (5th Cir.1999). Under the *Ellerth/Faragher* vicarious liability rules, can an employer successfully defend a claim of supervisory hostile environment if it responds to harassment with prompt remedial action? Or will the employer merely limit its damages? *See* Curry v. District of Columbia, 195 F.3d 654 (D.C.Cir.1999), *cert. denied*, 530 U.S. 1215, 120 S.Ct. 2219, 147 L.Ed.2d 251 (2000); Webb v. Cardiothoracic Surgery Assocs. of N. Tex., 139 F.3d 532 (5th Cir.1998).

d. *Investigating sexual harassment claims—the Fair Credit Reporting Act: Ellerth* and *Faragher* have increased the incentives for employers to undertake careful and thorough investigations of workplace harassment claims. Under a current Federal Trade Commission letter ruling, employers who contract with third parties, such as outside investigators or consultants, to conduct such investigations must comply with certain notice and reporting provisions of the Fair Credit Reporting Act (FCRA), 15 U.S.C. § 1681 *et seq. See FTC's "Vail Letter" Faces Opposition; Critics Call It Impediment to*

Employer Investigations, 71 U.S.L.W. No. 34, at 2573 (Mar. 11, 2003). The FCRA requires that the employer provide the employee who is the target of the investigation with prior notice of the nature of the inquiry, obtain the employee's consent to the investigation, and disclose to the employee all investigative reports. Can an employer who needs to hire third-party investigators conduct an effective investigation of a sexual harassment complaint if it has to meet the FCRA requirements? Does it help that any attorneys that an employer retains to investigate harassment should be considered agents of the employer, not third parties covered by the FCRA? *See generally* Amy Payne, Note, *Protecting the Accused in Sexual Harassment Investigations: Is the Fair Credit Reporting Act an Answer?,* 87 Va.L.Rev. 381, 402–13 (2001).

    e. *Sexual harassment training programs*: Employer concerns about sexual harassment lawsuits have "spawned a multi-billion dollar sexual harassment training industry staffed by attorneys, consultants, and human resource professionals who offer programs aimed at litigation prevention." Susan Bisom–Rapp, *Fixing Watches with Sledgehammers: The Questionable Embrace of Employee Sexual Harassment Training by the Legal Profession,* 24 T.Jefferson L.Rev. 125, 126 (2002). Professor Bisom–Rapp argues that, although there is "absolutely no empirical support" for the efficacy of such training, the federal courts consider the existence of training programs "as favorable evidence for employers that reasonable steps had been taken to prevent or correct harassment" and to limit liability for punitive damages. *Id.* at 126–27. *See also* Joanna L. Grossman, *The Culture of Compliance: The Final Triumph of Form over Substance in Sexual Harassment Law,* 26 Harv. Women's L.J. 3, 27–49 (2003) (analyzing social science research on preventative measures such as sexual harassment policies and procedures and training programs and concluding that "current preventative efforts employers take may help, but are not sufficient to effect a meaningful reduction in the level of harassment," *id.* at 49).

    7. *The Second Prong of the Employer's Affirmative Defense to Vicarious Liability*: Consider the employer's burden of proof on the second prong of its affirmative defense: "that the plaintiff employee unreasonably failed to take advantage of any preventive or corrective opportunities provided by the employer or to avoid harm otherwise."

    a. *Failure to use the employer's complaint procedure*: The employee's unreasonable failure to use the employer's complaint procedure "will normally suffice to satisfy the employer's burden under the second element of the defense." *Faragher,* 524 U.S. at 808, 118 S.Ct. at 2293. Under what circumstances would a plaintiff's failure to use a complaint procedure be "reasonable"? What about the case of a "serial harasser"? *See supra* Section C.1, Note 8, following *Ellerth.* Could a complaint procedure be so cumbersome or intimidating that it would be reasonable not to use it? Is it unreasonable for an employee to complain about harassment by using the grievance procedure provided under the union's collective bargaining agreement instead of the employer's internal reporting procedures? *See* Watts v. Kroger Co., 170 F.3d 505 (5th Cir.1999). What if the victim complains to the union steward and then fails to follow the steward's advice to report to the employer? What if the employee's complaints to the union steward do not mention the sexual nature of the harassing conduct? *See* Casiano v. AT & T, Corp., 213 F.3d 278 (5th Cir.2000).

b. *Failure to take advantage of "corrective opportunities"*: When is it reasonable for an employee to fail to "take advantage of * * * corrective opportunities provided by the employer"? What if the employer offers to transfer the victim to a different department in order to keep her out of daily contact with her harasser? When would it be reasonable to refuse such an offer?

c. *Failure to "avoid harm otherwise"*: How can an employer prove that a plaintiff has unreasonably failed "to avoid harm otherwise"? Is it reasonable for an employee on a business trip to go out to dinner with her supervisor? Is it reasonable for her to accept his invitation to have drinks with him after dinner while they continue their discussion of business matters? If the supervisor gets drunk and makes crude sexual comments and attempts to touch her in a sexual manner, has she unreasonably failed "to avoid harm otherwise"? Was the sexually harassing conduct foreseeable? If the subordinate subsequently reports the supervisor's harassing conduct through the appropriate channels, the company disciplines him, and the conduct ceases, will the company escape liability entirely, or merely limit its damages? Consider the following:

i. Can a defendant prove that a plaintiff has "failed to avoid harm otherwise" by introducing evidence that the conduct was welcome? *See* James J. McDonald, Jr. & Daniel S. Fellner, *A Plaintiff's Obligation to "Avoid Harm Otherwise": New Life for the Welcomeness Defense*, 25 Employee Rel.L.J. 17 (1999). Suppose a male supervisor invites a female subordinate to a "personal, private" lunch. The female perceives the request, in context, to have a "sexual undertone" and declines the invitation. Was this an implicit sexual proposition? Was this evidence of hostile environment sexual harassment? *See* Pfeil v. Intecom Telecomm., 90 F.Supp.2d 742 (N.D.Tex.2000). If not, is this what is meant by there is "no harm in asking," as discussed *supra* Section C.1, Note 8, following *Ellerth*? If the employee, despite her misgivings, accepts her supervisor's lunch invitation and explicit, unwelcome sexually harassing conduct ensues, has she unreasonably "failed to avoid harm otherwise"? *See generally* Steven H. Aden, *"Harm in Asking": A Reply to Eugene Scalia and An Analysis of the Paradigm Shift in the Supreme Court's Title VII Sexual Harassment Jurisprudence*, 8 Temp.Pol. & Civ.Rts. L.Rev. 477 (1999); Eugene Scalia, *The Strange Career of Quid Pro Quo Sexual Harassment*, 21 Harv.J.L. & Pub. Pol'y 307 (1998).

ii. A female employee, on an out-of-town business trip with her male supervisor, was working on a project in his hotel room late at night when he made sexual advances toward her. She successfully rebuffed him, left his room immediately, and reported the incident to the company the next day. The supervisor was reprimanded and no other incidents occurred until another business trip six months later. At this time, following a day of conference meetings, the employee accepted her supervisor's invitation to go "bar-hopping." Afterwards, around midnight, he invited her to his room to talk and assured her that his intentions were innocent. She agreed on those terms, but once she was in his room, he sexually assaulted her. She managed to flee the room and subsequently filed a Title VII claim against the employer. Assuming that the employer can satisfy the first prong of its affirmative defense, can it satisfy the second prong? Has the plaintiff unreasonably "failed to avoid harm otherwise"? *See* Brown v. Perry 184 F.3d 388 (4th Cir.1999).

iii. A male supervisor in a restaurant made several isolated but unwelcome and offensive sexual remarks to a female employee. She told him that his comments were offensive, but she failed to report his conduct to her employer, despite the existence of a widely disseminated antiharassment policy with effective procedures. The offensive conduct ceased for eight months. Then the supervisor allegedly exposed his genitals to the employee, and she immediately reported the incident to her employer. The employer promptly confronted the supervisor, who then resigned. In response to the employee's Title VII claim of vicarious liability for sexual harassment, can the employer satisfy the second prong of its affirmative defense? *See* Corcoran v. Shoney's Colonial, Inc., 24 F.Supp.2d 601 (W.D.Va.1998).

d. *Delay in complaining*: Assume that an employer has a widely disseminated policy against sexual harassment that (1) defines sexual harassment, (2) identifies employees with authority to deal with harassment complaints, (3) describes the discipline that the company may impose on harassers, and (4) prohibits retaliation for making harassment complaints. The plaintiff, a female employee, who received a copy of the antiharassment policy when she began her employment, was subjected to harassment by her immediate supervisors for over two years before she reported the conduct to the company's Human Resources Department. Within eleven days of receiving her complaint, the company investigated the allegations and terminated the managers. The plaintiff alleges that she worked in an isolated environment, like the plaintiff in *Faragher*, and that the harassing supervisors were the only managers that she reported to in her state. Assuming that the employer has satisfied the first prong of its affirmative defense on these facts, has it also satisfied the second prong? What additional facts would you want to explore? *See* Montero v. AGCO Corp., 192 F.3d 856 (9th Cir.1999). *See also* Matvia v. Bald Head Island Mgmt., Inc., 259 F.3d 261, 269–70 (4th Cir.2001) (a three-month delay in reporting harassment, while plaintiff tried to determine whether her supervisor was a "predator" or merely an "interested man" and to collect evidence against him, was unreasonable); Gawley v. Indiana Univ., 276 F.3d 301, 312 (7th Cir.2001) (a seven-month delay in reporting harassment is unreasonable); Jackson v. Arkansas Dep't of Educ., 272 F.3d 1020, 1026 (8th Cir.2001) (a nine-month delay in reporting harassment is unreasonable), *cert. denied*, 536 U.S. 908, 122 S.Ct. 2366, 153 L.Ed.2d 186 (2002).

e. *Futility of complaining*: An employee who was subjected to hostile environment sexual harassment by her supervisor failed to report the conduct because she believed the following: (1) that her employer has been unresponsive to complaints of sexual harassment brought by other employees, (2) that employees who complained were subjected to subtle forms of workplace retaliation by their supervisors, and (3) that her supervisor is a close friend of several high-level managers in the company. Assuming that the employer can meet the first prong of its affirmative defense, can it satisfy the second prong? Was the plaintiff's failure to report unreasonable? Would it have been "futile" for her to report the harassing conduct when it began? *See* Barrett v. Applied Radiant Energy Corp., 240 F.3d 262, 267–69

(4th Cir.2001). Is it reasonable for an employee not to use the employer's formal sexual harassment policy when it requires that the employee report to her supervisor who is the alleged harasser? If so, does the employer have an effective policy? Does the employer fail to satisfy both prongs of the *Ellerth/Faragher* affirmative defense in this situation? *See* Hare v. H & R Indus., Inc., 2001 WL 1382504, at *3 (E.D.Pa.2001) (yes).

8. *The Catch–22 of the Ellerth/Faragher Affirmative Defense.* A conflict is developing among the courts of appeals on the question of what an employer must prove in order to satisfy the requirements of the *Ellerth/Faragher* affirmative defense. *See* Harrison v. Eddy Potash, Inc., 248 F.3d 1014, 1024–25 (10th Cir.) (collecting cases), *cert. denied,* 534 U.S. 1019, 122 S.Ct. 543, 151 L.Ed.2d 421 (2001). What do you think of the following statement?

> *Ellerth/Faragher* results in a regrettable situation where employers are held liable when they do all that they can to prevent sexual harassment, which nonetheless occurs and the employee reports it. They are liability free, however, when they do a lesser job of preventing harassment, and they happen be fortuitous enough to employ someone who fails to take reasonable steps to report his or her claim.

Brief for Eddy Potash, Inc., *quoted in* Victoria Roberts, *High Court Refuses to Consider Question of Vicarious Liability for Sexual Harassment,* 218 Daily Lab.Rep. (BNA) at AA–3 (Nov. 14, 2000).

Professor John Marks observes a "pro-employer" trend in lower federal court cases decided since *Ellerth* and *Faragher.* John Marks, *Smoke, Mirrors, and the Disappearance of "Vicarious" Liability: The Emergence of a Dubious Summary–Judgment Safe Harbor for Employers Whose Supervisory Personnel Commit Hostile Environment Workplace Harassment,* 38 Hous.L.Rev. 1401 (2002). He argues that in one line of cases, the courts are treating the two prongs of the employer's affirmative defense as if they are written in the disjunctive—that "and" means "or"—particularly in cases of "rapid-onset harassment." *Id.* at 1404. In a second line of cases, the courts are treating the victim's "purportedly unreasonable" delay in complaining about "a more gradual pattern of abuses" as "a total bar to recovery"—"akin to contributory negligence"—rather than as a limitation on damages. *Id.* at 1404–05. *See also* Martha S. West, *Preventing Sexual Harassment: The Federal Courts' Wake-up Call for Women,* 68 Brook.L.Rev. 457 (2002) (criticizing federal court treatment of the *Ellerth/Faragher* affirmative defense).

9. *Individual Liability of Agents for Harassment:* The majority of the courts of appeals have held that supervisors are not individually liable under either Title VII or the ADEA. *See* Wathen v. General Elec. Co., 115 F.3d 400, 404 (6th Cir.1997) (collecting cases); Tomka v. Seiler Corp., 66 F.3d 1295, 1314 (2d Cir.1995). Individual liability of agents was discussed in Chapter 2, Section D.4. What arguments would you make that imposing individual liability on agents of employers, particularly in the sexual harassment cases, would further the objectives of eliminating discrimination in the workplace? Are employer's agents generally individually liable for their workplace torts? In light of the vicarious liability rules for supervisory harassment that the Supreme Court has formulated in *Ellerth* and *Faragher,* would you want to see any changes in the majority rule on agent liability? *See* Chatman v.

Gentle Dental Ctr. of Waltham, 973 F.Supp. 228, 236–38 (D.Mass.1997) (listing and discussing holdings of district and circuit courts).

A number of state courts, interpreting state human rights statutes, have held that supervisors can be found personally liable for their own acts of sexual harassment. *See, e.g.*, Vivian v. Madison, 601 N.W.2d 872 (Iowa 1999) (holding that supervisors can be held individually liable under the Iowa Civil Rights Act and discussing the development of individual liability in other jurisdictions); Brown v. Scott Paper Worldwide Co., 143 Wash.2d 349, 20 P.3d 921, 926 (2001) (finding that a supervisor acting in the interest of an employer covered by the state antidiscrimination statute can be held individually liable for sexual harassment). In addition, professionals who sexually harass their subordinates may risk discipline from licensing bodies. For example, in February 2003, a Chicago attorney received a one-year suspension from the Illinois Attorney Registration and Disciplinary Commission for sexually harassing an associate in his law firm. The female victim had previously won a $1.4 million jury verdict in a lawsuit she brought against the attorney and his law firm. *See Chicago Attorney Loses License to Practice for One Year in Wake of Harassment Verdict*, 21 Hum. Resources Rep. 21 (BNA) No.11, at 301 (Mar. 24, 2003) (citing *In re: Gerald Fishman*, Ill. ARDC, No. 01 CH 109, 2/24/03).

10. *Rights of Alleged Harassers*: Employers may hesitate to discipline or discharge alleged harassers because of concerns about their legal rights to fair treatment. For example, high-level professional employees may be protected by individual contracts, unionized employees may be covered by just cause protections in a collective bargaining agreement, college and university teachers may have academic tenure, and public school teachers may have statutory tenure. Public sector employees may have civil service protections or constitutional rights to due process. At-will employees may have common law or statutory protections against wrongful discharge. *See generally* Hannah Katherine Vorwerk, *The Forgotten Interest Group: Reforming Title VII to Address the Concerns of Workers While Eliminating Sexual Harassment*, 48 Vand.L.Rev. 1019 (1995); Sara Needleman Kline, Comment, *Sexual Harassment, Wrongful Discharge, and Employer Liability: The Employer's Dilemma*, 43 Am.U.L.Rev. 191 (1993); *Stuck in the Middle: Employers Can Face Lawsuits from Accused as Well as Accusers*, 69 U.S.L.W. 2539 (Mar. 13, 2001).

a. Unionized employees who are discharged for sexual harassment may seek reinstatement by filing a grievance under their collective bargaining agreement. If an employer discharges an alleged harasser and an arbitrator subsequently reinstates him or her, the employer may be involved in lengthy litigation attempting to have the decision vacated. *Compare* Chrysler Motors Corp. v. International Union Allied Indus. Workers of Am., 959 F.2d 685 (7th Cir.) (upholding arbitration award of reinstatement for grievant who was terminated for sexually assaulting a female worker), *cert. denied*, 506 U.S. 908, 113 S.Ct. 304, 121 L.Ed.2d 227 (1992); *with* Newsday, Inc. v. Long Island Typographical Union, 915 F.2d 840 (2d Cir.1990) (vacating labor arbitrator's award of reinstatement of alleged harasser as contrary to public policy), *cert. denied*, 499 U.S. 922, 111 S.Ct. 1314, 113 L.Ed.2d 247 (1991). There are limited grounds for vacating arbitral awards, but the potentially broadest ground is that the award is contrary to public policy. *See* Eastern

Associated Coal Corp. v. UMW, 531 U.S. 57, 121 S.Ct. 462, 148 L.Ed.2d 354 (2000) (ruling that an arbitrator's decision reinstating an equipment operator who failed a drug test did not violate public policy). Is sexual harassment contrary to public policy? *See, e.g.,* Weber Aircraft, Inc. v. General Warehousemen & Helpers Union Local 767, 253 F.3d 821, 825–27 (5th Cir.2001) (relying on *Eastern Associated Coal* to find that an arbitrator did not violate public policy by reinstating an employee discharged for sexual harassment). *See generally* Judith Stilz Ogden, *Do Public Policy Grounds Still Exist for Vacating Arbitration Awards?*, 20 Hofstra Lab. & Emp.L.J. 87, 113–15 (2002) (analyzing the effect of *Eastern Associated Coal* on sexual harassment cases).

b. At-will employees accused of harassment may have rights to fair procedures under theories of implied contract or the obligation of good faith and fair dealing. *See* Cotran v. Rollins Hudig Hall Int'l, Inc., 17 Cal.4th 93, 69 Cal.Rptr.2d 900, 948 P.2d 412 (1998) (holding that, when an employee under an implied contract of employment is discharged for sexual harassment, the employer has an obligation to conduct a reasonable investigation and provide the employee with notice of the alleged misconduct and an opportunity to respond). Moreover, employees who are discharged for sexual harassment may bring claims against their employers for torts such as defamation, Meloff v. New York Life Ins. Co., 240 F.3d 138 (2d Cir.2001), and intentional or negligent infliction of mental distress, Malik v. Carrier Corp., 202 F.3d 97 (2d Cir.2000). An employee who is fired for sexual harassment may also have a cause of action against his former co-workers who reported his conduct to the employer during its investigation. Theories of liability might include intentional infliction of mental distress, invasion of privacy, defamation, and interference with advantageous economic relations. *See, e.g.,* Cole v. Chandler, 752 A.2d 1189 (Me.2000).

11. How does the Supreme Court's analysis in *Ellerth* and *Faragher* relate to its per curiam decision in *Clark County School District v. Breeden?* (*Breedon* is discussed *supra* Section B.2, Note 5, following *Harris v. Forklift.*) In light of *Breeden,* how would you advise an *employee* who tells you that she is uncomfortable with her supervisor's occasional sexual jokes or comments, which she sincerely perceives to be offensive and embarrassing? At what point is it reasonable for your client to complain about her supervisor's conduct? If your client complains too early, after only one or two incidents, she may be disciplined for being a "complainer." If, under *Breeden,* no reasonable person would believe that the conduct was severe or pervasive under Title VII, she cannot succeed on a retaliation claim if her employer disciplines or discharges her for her subjectively sincere but objectively unreasonable complaint about her supervisor's conduct. If she waits to complain, how long should she wait? If the employer has an adequate complaint procedure, which she unreasonably delays in using, the employer should be able to prevail on both prongs of its *Ellerth/Faragher* affirmative defense. Employees, unskilled in the intricacies of sexual harassment law, may lose the protections of Title VII if they misjudge the objective severity of the conduct and "unreasonably" complain too early or too late.

How would you advise an *employer* after *Breeden?* When an employee complains about a supervisor's sexually harassing conduct, how can the employer determine whether the employee's perceptions are sincere or reasonable? If the employer determines after an investigation that the employee's beliefs were sincere but unreasonable under *Breeden* and, therefore, chooses not to take corrective action, what are the possible consequences? The supervisor may continue his offensive behavior, and the employee may file a charge of discrimination and then bring a Title VII action. If a judge or jury then determines that the supervisor's conduct was "severe or pervasive" from the perspective of a reasonable person, the employer will not be able to establish either prong of its affirmative defense under *Ellerth* and *Faragher*. Employers, unskilled in the intricacies of sexual harassment law, may lose their defenses under Title VII if they misjudge the objective severity of their supervisor's conduct.

Breeden demonstrates the importance for both plaintiffs and defendants of correctly assessing whether language or conduct is objectively "severe or pervasive" harassment. Does *Breeden* create incentives for employers to discipline or discharge an employee the first time that he or she complains about isolated and trivial harassment, rather than to attempt to respond to the complaint? Do *Ellerth* and *Faragher* similarly create incentives for employers to discipline or discharge alleged harassers, even for complaints of isolated trivial harassment, just to avoid the costs of investigation and the potential of misjudging the reasonableness of the complaint?

12. *State Antidiscrimination Laws and Title VII:* In the aftermath of the 1998 Supreme Court cases of *Oncale, Ellerth,* and *Faragher,* state courts have been addressing the question of whether and how these decisions interpreting federal law affect state antidiscrimination laws. For example, in *Hampel v. Food Ingredients Specialties, Inc.,* 89 Ohio St.3d 169, 729 N.E.2d 726, 733–34 (2000), the Supreme Court of Ohio relied on *Oncale* to find that same-sex sexual harassment is actionable under the state civil rights law. In a diversity case, a federal district court subsequently interpreted *Hampel* as having adopted the *Ellerth/ Faragher* standard for imposing vicarious liability on employers in cases of sexual harassment by supervisors. McCormick v. Kmart Distrib. Ctr., 163 F.Supp.2d 807, 825 (N.D.Ohio 2001). The Michigan Supreme Court has rejected the approach taken in *Ellerth* and *Faragher* for sexual harassment claims brought under the Michigan Civil Rights Act. Chambers v. Trettco, Inc., 463 Mich. 297, 614 N.W.2d 910, 915–16 (Mich. 2000) (holding that employers are vicariously liable for harassment by supervisors only if they are aware of the conduct and fail to take prompt, effective corrective action). The California Supreme Court held that employers are strictly liable under the Fair Employment and Housing Act (FEHA) for sexual harassment by supervisors, but that the "avoidable consequences doctrine" may limit the damages that a plaintiff can recover under a FEHA claim. State Dep't of Health Servs. v. Superior Court, 31 Cal.4th 1026, 6 Cal.Rptr.3d 441, 79 P.3d 556 (2003). Thus, for assessing damages, California has adopted the reasoning of the *Ellerth/Faragher* affirmative defense, which "encourages preventive action by both the employer and employee." 79 P.3d at 564. *Ellerth/Faragher* holding, however, the California rule affects only damages and does not limit liability. *Id.* at 565. States also may issue guidelines on sexual harassment for employers covered by state antidiscrimination statutes. For example, in 2002 the Massachusetts Commission Against Discrimination issued detailed sexual harassment guidelines, which are available at the agency Web site, *http://www.state.ma.us/mcad/*

shguide.html. What are the advantages and disadvantages of having different rules of liability for sexual harassment under state and federal antidiscrimination law?

13.   *Section 1983 Liability for Sexual Harassment:* The lower federal courts have ruled that intentional sexual harassment of employees by government officials acting "under color of state law" is actionable under § 1983 as a violation of equal protection or substantive due process under the Fourteenth Amendment. *See, e.g.,* Jones v. Clinton, 990 F.Supp. 657, 668 (E.D.Ark.1998) (collecting sexual harassment cases brought under Equal Protection Clause); Hawkins v. Holloway, 316 F.3d 777, 785 (8th Cir.2003) (finding that a male sheriff's repeated unwelcome sexual touching of his female subordinate constituted "a violation of her bodily integrity sufficient to support a substantive due process claim" under § 1983). In general, the courts will look to Title VII cases to determine whether the conduct was "unwelcome" and "severe or pervasive." *See* Cross v. Alabama, 49 F.3d 1490 (11th Cir.1995) (holding that the elements of a Title VII and equal protection claim are identical); *Jones,* 990 F.Supp.2d at 668–69 (comparing sexual harassment claims brought under Title VII and § 1983). Section 1983 claims are discussed in Chapter 5.

Because a public official sued in his or her individual capacity under § 1983 can assert a defense of qualified immunity, the threshold of actionable harassment in a substantive due process claim has been held to be "whether conduct amounts to an abuse of governmental power that is so brutal and offensive that it was conscience shocking." *Hawkins,* 316 F.3d at 784 (internal quotation marks omitted). It did not shock the conscience of the court for a male sheriff to grab or touch the "clothed erogenous zones or other sensitive areas" of the bodies of his male subordinates while he made "sexually suggestive comments." *Id.* at 784–85 (finding no § 1983 substantive due process violation on these facts because "the sheriff engaged in his offensive behavior in the context of junior high locker room style male horseplay"). How can you explain a contrary result in *Hawkins* when the victim of the same male sheriff's sexual touching was female? Would the results have been the same under Title VII? Or under an equal protection analysis? *Compare Hawkins with* Downing v. Board of Trustees of Univ. of Ala., 321 F.3d 1017 (11th Cir.2003) (relying on *Oncale* to hold that the Equal Protection Clause protects state employees from same-sex discrimination). Do state employers enjoy Eleventh Amendment immunity from sexual harassment suits brought under the Equal Protection Clause of the Fourteenth Amendment? *See Downing, supra* (holding state university was not immune to private suit for damages under Fourteenth Amendment alleging discrimination on the basis of sex).

Consider the following: A city manager raped a female employee who then sued the municipality for sexual harassment under § 1983. Following a trial on her sexual harassment claim, the jury awarded $2 million to the victim. On appeal, the Court of Appeals for the Eleventh Circuit ruled that the manager was acting under color of law when he raped the employee in her home following a Rotary Club meeting attended by city officials. Although the municipality did have a workplace culture that "tolerated and condoned" sexual harassment of women, it did not have a custom or policy that tolerated rape. Griffin v. City of Opa–Locka, 261 F.3d 1295, 1311–12

(11th Cir.2001), *cert. denied*, 535 U.S. 1033 & 1034, 122 S.Ct. 1789, 152 L.Ed.2d 648 (2002). Thus, the court of appeals reduced the jury award by $1.5 million because the municipality could not be held liable for the rape but only for its custom of tolerating a sexually hostile work environment. In light of *Griffin* and *Faragher,* what steps would you advise a state or municipal employer to take to avoid potential liability for sexual harassment under § 1983 or Title VII?

2. LIABILITY FOR NEGLIGENCE: HARASSMENT BY CO-WORKERS AND NONEMPLOYEES

Proof of employer negligence will continue to be required in order to establish employer liability in Title VII cases dealing with harassment by nonsupervisory employees. Subsection 219(2)(b) of the Restatement (Second) of Agency imposes tort liability on employers for their own negligence. The Court in *Ellerth* acknowledged that this is the general standard for employer liability in sexual harassment cases: "Negligence sets a minimum standard for employer liability under Title VII"; therefore, "[a]n employer is negligent with respect to sexual harassment if it knew or should have known about the conduct and failed to stop it." *Ellerth*, 524 U.S. at 758, 118 S.Ct. at 2267. The federal courts have uniformly adopted the negligence standard to impose employer liability in cases of co-worker harassment. *See Faragher*, 524 U.S. at 799–800, 118 S.Ct. at 2289 (collecting cases and other authority). In the wake of *Ellerth* and *Faragher*, are there any circumstances when a plaintiff will have the burden of proving employer negligence in a case involving a hostile work environment attributed to a supervisor? What if the harassing "supervisor" has no authority over the plaintiff? For example, a harasser might have daily contact with the plaintiff but be a supervisor in a different department in the firm.

Professor Oppenheimer summarized of the relevant principles of employer liability for co-worker harassment from the common law of agency:

> Properly applied, agency law should impose direct liability when an employer: (1) unreasonably fails to instruct its employees to refrain from sexual harassment; (2) unreasonably fails to adopt rules, policies, and regulations designed to prevent harassment from occurring; (3) unreasonably employs people it knows or should know to be engaged in sexual harassment of other employees; (4) fails to properly supervise its employees to prevent harassment from occurring; (5) stands by and does nothing when it knows, or should know, that harassment is occurring; or (6) fails to prevent harassment that it could have reasonably prevented. In such cases, the law of master and servant holds the employer directly liable for the harm caused by the employer's breach of duty. Moreover, when an employer ratifies an act of harassment, it adopts the act as its own. Thus, when an employer fails to disapprove of harassment in an appropriate manner, it may be held directly liable.

David Benjamin Oppenheimer, *Exacerbating the Exasperating: Title VII Liability of Employers for Sexual Harassment Committed by Their Supervisors*, 81 Cornell L.Rev. 66, 98 (1995).

Notice plays an important role in claims of co-worker harassment. Employers are held liable for co-worker sexual harassment that they knew or should have known was occurring and failed to stop. But exactly what is constructive notice? One court defined it as "where an employee provides management level personnel with enough information to raise a probability of sexual harassment in the mind of a reasonable employer, or where the harassment is so pervasive and open that a reasonable employer would have had to be aware of it." Kunin v. Sears Roebuck & Co., 175 F.3d 289 (3d Cir.), *cert. denied*, 528 U.S. 964, 120 S.Ct. 398, 145 L.Ed.2d 310 (1999). If an employee complains to a manager that she is being harassed by co-workers, but fails to describe the sexual nature of the conduct, has the employer received constructive notice of co-worker sexual harassment? *See id. See generally* Note, *Notice in Hostile Environment Discrimination Law*, 112 Harv.L.Rev. 1977 (1999). If an employer designates a manager to whom employees should complain under its sexual harassment policy, does that person have actual authority to handle such complaints? Or apparent authority? If an employee complains about co-worker sexual harassment to the designated manager, will the employer be found to have actual notice of the complaint or constructive notice? *See* Breda v. Wolf Camera & Video, 222 F.3d 886, 889–90 (11th Cir.2000) (finding that employer had actual notice of co-worker sexual harassment when employee complained to the manager who was designated by the employer's policy to handle complaints).

Under a negligence standard, an employer will not be liable for co-worker sexual harassment if it responds to the harassment with "immediate and appropriate corrective action." *See, e.g.,* Stuart v. General Motors Corp., 217 F.3d 621 (8th Cir.2000); Fleming v. Boeing Co., 120 F.3d 242 (11th Cir.1997). What is "appropriate corrective action"? *See, e.g.,* Swenson v. Potter, 271 F.3d 1184, 1192 (9th Cir.2001) (finding that the employer took appropriate corrective action where it relocated the alleged harasser to a different work site in its facility pending completion of its investigation of the complaint).

Notes and Questions

1. What is appropriate corrective action in dealing with a serial harasser? In 1997, three women were awarded a jury verdict of $1.2 million (later reduced to $655,000) based, in part, on evidence that their co-worker sexually harassed eighteen women over a period of twenty years before harassing them. The Court of Appeals for the Seventh Circuit initially vacated the award in 2000 on the grounds that the lower court had improperly excluded evidence regarding the employer's reasons for delaying firing the harasser. EEOC v. Indiana Bell Tel. (Ameritech), 214 F.3d 813 (7th Cir.2000), *reh'g on banc*, 256 F.3d 516 (7th Cir.2001). In her dissent in the now-vacated 2000 opinion, Judge Ilana Diamond Rovner wrote that the

employer had "allowed the equivalent of an armed torpedo to wander about the workplace for years wreaking havoc upon its female employees." *Id.* at 825, 827. Is anything short of discharge appropriate discipline for a "repeat offender"? In dealing with allegations that an employer did not do enough to stop a "repeat offender," the Court of Appeals for the Tenth Circuit held: "The test is whether the employer's response to each incident of harassment is proportional to the incident and reasonably calculated to end the harassment and prevent future harassing behavior." Scarberry v. Exxonmobil Oil Corp., 328 F.3d 1255, 1259–60 (10th Cir.2003). In cases where an employer "cannot predict when an employee will take another approach to harassment designed to avoid detection and discipline," the employer will not be liable for negligence. *Id.* at 1259. Does this make sense? Is sexual harassment ever rational or predictable?

2.   Can employers use the *Ellerth/Faragher* affirmative defense in co-worker harassment cases? In *Swinton v. Potomac Corp.,* 270 F.3d 794 (9th Cir.2001), *cert. denied,* 535 U.S. 1018, 122 S.Ct. 1609, 152 L.Ed.2d 623 (2002), a § 1981 case, the Ninth Circuit ruled that an employer could not use the *Ellerth/Faragher* affirmative defense in a case involving co-worker racial harassment of an African–American employee. In *Swinton,* the plaintiff's co-workers, and a company supervisor who had no direct authority over him, had subjected the plaintiff to racially offensive comments over a period of six months. During this time, his direct supervisor allegedly observed the harassment and did nothing. The employee won a jury verdict, including $1 million in punitive damages, as well as $30,000 for emotional distress. The district judge instructed the jury that the *Ellerth/Faragher* vicarious liability standard and affirmative defense applies only when the supervisor with direct authority over the plaintiff is the harasser, and the negligence standard applies to harassment by co-workers, which includes supervisors without direct authority over the plaintiff. The Ninth Circuit affirmed, agreeing that an employer cannot use an affirmative defense to claims of co-worker harassment, but can nevertheless avoid liability by showing it was not negligent, i.e., that it promptly remedied the harassment once it was on notice that it was occurring.

In its petition for certiorari, the employer noted the circuit split on the issue of the availability of the affirmative defense when a supervisor fails to promptly correct co-worker harassment. To date, the courts of appeals that have considered the issue have applied a negligence standard in these circumstances. In its brief seeking Supreme Court review, the employer had challenged the logic of permitting the employer an affirmative defense when its supervisor harasses a direct subordinate and not when he or she fails to act when a co-worker harasses that same individual. *High Court Lets Stand Ruling Blocking Employer's Use of Affirmative Defense,* 20 Hum. Resources Rep. (BNA) No.17, at 463 (Apr. 29, 2002). Should the same rule for employer liability apply regardless of whether the harassment occurs because of the supervisor's act of harassing a subordinate or his failure to stop co-workers from harassing the subordinate?

3.   When can an employer be found liable for the actionable harassment caused by third parties such as clients or customers? The EEOC guidelines provide that an

employer may also be responsible for the acts of non-employees, with respect to sexual harassment of employees in the workplace, where the employer (or its agents or supervisory employees) knows or should have known of the conduct and fails to take immediate and appropriate corrective action.

29 C.F.R. § 1604.11(e). The First, Eighth, Ninth, and Tenth Circuits have followed the EEOC's guidelines on sexual harassment of employees by nonemployees. *See* Lockard v. Pizza Hut, Inc., 162 F.3d 1062 (10th Cir. 1998); Rodriguez–Hernandez v. Miranda–Velez, 132 F.3d 848 (1st Cir.1998); Crist v. Focus Homes, Inc., 122 F.3d 1107 (8th Cir.1997); Folkerson v. Circus Circus Enter., Inc., 107 F.3d 754 (9th Cir.1997). The courts have applied a negligence theory of liability in these cases because hostile work environment sexual harassment by clients, customers, or suppliers is considered "more analogous to harassment by co-workers than by supervisors." *Lockard*, 162 F.3d at 1074. What should employers do to avoid employees' claims of harassment by customers?

Should sexual harassment of prison guards by inmates be treated the same as employee harassment by customers? Would it make a difference if the guard's co-workers or supervisors encouraged or instigated the inmates' offensive conduct? *Compare* Slayton v. Ohio Dep't of Youth Serv., 206 F.3d 669 (6th Cir.2000), *with* Powell v. Morris, 37 F.Supp.2d 1011 (S.D.Ohio 1999). Can employees who are sexually harassed by their mentally or developmentally disabled clients or patients sue their employers under Title VII? *Compare* Turnbull v. Topeka State Hosp., 255 F.3d 1238 (10th Cir. 2001) (finding that a mental hospital could be held liable for a hostile work environment under Title VII for a patient's sexual assault of a staff psychologist), *cert. denied*, 535 U.S. 970, 122 S.Ct. 1435, 152 L.Ed.2d 380 (2002); *with* Cain v. Blackwell, 246 F.3d 758 (5th Cir.2001) (rejecting the hostile environment claim brought by a female home health nurse who was sexually harassed by an elderly male patient who suffered from Alzheimer's).

In *Salazar v. Diversified Paratransit Inc.*, 126 Cal.Rptr.2d 475 (2002), *review granted & opinion superseded by* 130 Cal.Rptr.2d 656, 63 P.3d 215 (2003), *cause transferred by* 7 Cal.Rptr.3d 1, 79 P.3d 1199 (2003), the court held that an employer that provides transportation for developmentally disabled clients is not liable under the California Fair Employment and Housing Act (FEHA) for its failure to take "all reasonable steps" to prevent a rider's sexual assault on its employee bus driver who claimed that other drivers had repeatedly complained about the client's sexually offensive behavior. In response to *Salazar*, the California Legislature enacted a law imposing liability on employers for sexual harassment of their employees by nonemployees under a negligence standard. Cal.Gov.Code § 12940 (West 2003), 2003 Cal.Legis.Serv. Ch.671 (A.B.76) (West).

Note: Timely Filing of Harassment Charges—The Morgan Case

If an employee files a charge with the EEOC alleging she was subjected to a hostile work environment in violation of Title VII, at what point has the "unlawful employment practice" occurred for purposes of determining whether the charge is timely? If a charge is filed "too early," the conduct may not be actionable because it is not objectively severe or pervasive. When is it "too late" to file a hostile work environment claim? If an employee waits to file a hostile work environment charge until the conduct has escalated in severity, can she recover damages for harassment that occurred outside the statutory 300–day or 180–day period for filing a charge? The Supreme Court addressed this last question in *National Railroad Passenger Corp. v. Morgan,* 536 U.S. 101, 122 S.Ct. 2061, 153 L.Ed.2d 106 (2002), which is reproduced, in part, in Chapter 2. Recall that *Morgan* involved, *inter alia*, a claim of a racially hostile work environment brought against AmTrack by a black male employee. Writing for the Court, Justice Thomas concluded:

> Hostile environment claims are different in kind from discrete acts. Their very nature involves repeated conduct. * * * The "unlawful employment practice" therefore cannot be said to occur on any particular day. It occurs over a series of days or perhaps years and, in direct contrast to discrete acts, a single act of harassment may not be actionable on its own. * * * Such claims are based on the cumulative affect [sic] of individual acts.

* * *

> In determining whether an actionable hostile work environment claim exists, we look to "all the circumstances," including "the frequency of the discriminatory conduct; its severity; whether it is physically threatening or humiliating, or a mere offensive utterance; and whether it unreasonably interferes with an employee's work performance." *Harris.* To assess whether a court may, for the purposes of determining liability, review all such conduct, including those acts that occur outside the filing period, we again look to the statute. It provides that a charge must be filed within 180 or 300 days "after the alleged unlawful employment practice occurred." A hostile work environment claim is comprised of a series of separate acts that collectively constitute one "unlawful employment practice." 42 U.S.C. § 2000e–5(e)(1). The timely filing provision only requires that a Title VII plaintiff file a charge within a certain number of days after the unlawful practice happened. It does not matter, for purposes of the statute, that some of the component acts of the hostile work environment fall outside the statutory time period. Provided that an act contributing to the claim occurs within the filing period, the entire time period of the hostile environment may be considered by a court for the purposes of determining liability.

> * * * Given, therefore, that the incidents comprising a hostile work environment are part of one unlawful employment practice, the employer may be liable for all acts that are part of this single claim. In order for the charge to be timely, the employee need only file a charge within 180 or 300 days of any act that is part of the hostile work environment.

* * *

> Our holding does not leave employers defenseless against employees who bring hostile work environment claims that extend over long periods of time. Employers have recourse when a plaintiff unreasonably delays filing a charge. * * * [T]he filing period is not a jurisdictional

prerequisite to filing a Title VII suit. Rather, it is a requirement subject to waiver, estoppel, and equitable tolling "when equity so requires."

536 U.S. at 115–21, 122 S.Ct. at 2073–76.

Does *Morgan,* along with the doctrines of waiver, equitable estoppel, and equitable tolling, provide a workable rule on timely filing of an EEOC charge of hostile work environment? Suppose an employee has a colorable claim that her supervisor has created a hostile work environment. The employee pursues relief under the employer's sexual harassment policy. After some time passes, the employee believes she has not obtained appropriate relief under the employer's policy. Is the employee required to bring an EEOC charge within 180 or 300 days of the date of the last act of actionable harassment or the date when it is reasonable to believe that the employer has failed to take appropriate action? *See* Frazier v. Delco Elec. Corp., 263 F.3d 663, 666 (7th Cir.2001). Can an employee treat harassing conduct as one "unlawful employment practice" if an employer's "intervening action" effectively stopped the conduct for a period of time before it began again? *See* Watson v. Blue Circle, Inc., 324 F.3d 1252 (11th Cir.2003). If an employer tells an employee not to talk to anyone other than managers about her allegations of sexual harassment, is it reasonable for her not to talk to a lawyer or file a complaint with the EEOC? *See* Beckel v. Wal–Mart Assocs., 301 F.3d 621 (7th Cir.2002).

D. RACIAL AND ETHNIC HARASSMENT

HARRIS v. INTERNATIONAL PAPER CO.

United States District Court for the District of Maine, 1991.
765 F.Supp. 1509, *vacated in part*, 765 F.Supp. 1529.

CARTER, Chief Judge.

[Plaintiff Isom Harris was one of three black men who alleged that International Paper Company had permitted supervisors and co-workers to subject the plaintiffs to a racially hostile work environment in violation of the Maine Human Rights Act (MHRA) . The elements of a prima facie case of racial hostile work environment under MHRA are essentially the same as under Title VII, requiring proof that the conduct was "unwelcome" and "severe or pervasive."]

* * *

* * * The first question which must be answered * * * is what standard is applied by a fact finder to assess whether particular conduct or speech is "unwelcome," and whether that harassment is sufficiently severe and pervasive to violate antidiscrimination law. * * *

In *Lipsett v. University of Puerto Rico*, 864 F.2d 881 (1st Cir.1988), the First Circuit recognized that there may be two different perspectives on the questions of unwelcomeness and pervasiveness: the perpetrator's perspective and the victim's perspective. When considering allegations of sexual harassment, therefore, "the fact finder keeps both the man's and woman's perspective in mind" so that defendants and courts will not

" 'sustain ingrained notions of reasonable behavior fashioned by the offenders.' " *Id.* at 898 (quoting Rabidue v. Osceola Refining Co., 805 F.2d 611, 626 (6th Cir.1986) (Keith, J., dissenting)).

* * *

Black Americans are regularly faced with negative racial attitudes, many unconsciously held and acted upon, which are the natural consequences of a society ingrained with cultural stereotypes and race-based beliefs and preferences. *See generally* Charles H. Lawrence, *The Id, the Ego, and Equal Protection: Reckoning with Unconscious Racism*, 39 Stan.L.Rev. 317 (1987).[11] As a result, instances of racial violence or threatened violence which might appear to white observers as mere "pranks" are, to black observers, evidence of threatening, pervasive attitudes closely associated with racial jokes, comments or nonviolent conduct which white observers are also more likely to dismiss as non-threatening isolated incidents. Mari Matsuda, *Public Response to Racist Speech: Considering the Victim's Story*, 87 Mich.L.Rev. 2320, 2326–35 (1989). The omnipresence of race-based attitudes and experiences in the lives of black Americans causes even nonviolent events to be interpreted as degrading, threatening, and offensive. *See, e.g.,* D. Bell, And We Are Not Saved (1987) 181–85 (describing a fictional encounter with a state trooper); Patricia Williams, *Alchemical Notes: Reconstructing Ideals from Deconstructed Rights*, 22 Harv.C.R.-C.L.L.Rev. 401, 406–13 (1987) (explaining why black and white apartment-seekers assume different perspectives on the formalities of renting an apartment). Even an inadvertent racial slight unnoticed either by its white speaker or white bystanders will reverberate in the memory of its black victim. Lawrence, *supra* at 339–41. Since the concern of Title VII and the MHRA is to redress the effects of conduct and speech on their victims, the fact finder must "walk a mile in the victim's shoes" to understand those effects and how they should be remedied. In sum, the appropriate standard to be applied in this hostile environment racial harassment case is that of a "reasonable black person."[12]

* * *

Plaintiff Harris was forced to run a gauntlet of racial abuse from the time of his arrival at the Jay mill. Harris's principal harassers were

---

11. Because these racial beliefs and stereotypes pervade our society, employing a "reasonable person" standard would permit discriminatory conduct and speech constructed on the foundation of these beliefs and stereotypes to stand unremedied. *See Lipsett,* 864 F.2d at 898 (quoting *Rabidue,* 805 F.2d at 626 (Keith, J. dissenting)).

12. The Court does not mean to imply that there is unanimity of perspective among black Americans. *See, e.g.,* Judy Scales–Trent, *Black Women and the Constitution: Finding Our Place, Asserting Our Rights,* 24 Harv.C.R.-C.L.L.Rev. 9 (1989)

(discussing how black women suffer discrimination of a different form, quality, and intensity than that experienced either by black men or white women). The appropriate standard to be applied in hostile environment harassment cases is that of a reasonable person from the protected group of which the alleged victim is a member. In this instance, because Plaintiffs are black, the appropriate standard is that of a reasonable black person, as that can be best understood and given meaning by a white judge.

Dwight Goff, a "loaned supervisor" brought to Maine from one of Defendant's southern mills to assist during the strike, and Birchard and Kip Brooks, who were permanent replacement workers. Goff's racist views, including the use of epithets like "lazy nigger" and "black son-of-a-bitch," were well known to other workers in the mill. Goff regularly expressed his hatred of black people in Harris's presence, and sabotaged Harris's work. * * *

Harris's problems with the Brooks brothers were even more serious. Birchard and Kip Brooks were equally free with racially derogatory comments aimed at Harris, and complained about Harris's work performance in racial terms. Their racist views were also widely known. One notable incident of public harassment involved the Brooks brothers donning white suits and white hats, ordinarily used while cleaning the paper machines but on this occasion clearly intended to recall the Ku Klux Klan, and "prancing" around Harris at his work station. This incident occurred in the presence of Foreman Parker, who considered it to be merely a joke. On another occasion, Birchard and Kip Brooks threatened to fight with Harris and warned him to get the other black workers who had accompanied Harris from Mobile to Jay for the fight. Even after Harris notified Foreman Richard Parker of the problem, Birchard Brooks continued to threaten Harris.

As a matter of course, Birchard Brooks ignored work directives from Harris, even though he was subordinate to Harris on the Number 2 machine, and he attempted to get others to join in his racist insubordination. This conduct was known to Foreman Parker, who spoke with Brooks at one point. But Birchard Brooks did not limit his racial attacks to Harris. White co-workers considered by Brooks to be too friendly with Harris were titled "nigger lovers," and were physically harassed.

Harris was also subjected to epithets from other workers and supervisors like "black nigger," "goddamn nigger," "black ass," "watermelon man," and "Buckwheat." These incidents were known, in most cases, to supervisors and foremen. "KKK" appeared on rolls of paper with which Harris worked, on a steel support near Harris's work station, and on a picture of a former employee posted in the mill who had himself engaged in racist name-calling.[20] While there may not have been a means by which a supervisor could have seen the graffiti on the paper rolls, the graffiti on the steel support and on the picture was large, enduring, and occurred in an area supervisors visited daily; thus, a supervisor could have and should have seen it. There was also racist graffiti, such as "nigger go back south," in the bathrooms used by workers and supervisors alike. Harris also felt that he was ignored by supervisors who would not even respond to Harris's normal and polite greetings in the morning. He classified his relationships with all the supervisors as "very negative."

20. There was testimony that Harris did not himself remove this cartoon from the bulletin board, even though he had the opportunity. The Court notes that there is no affirmative duty on the part of an employee to act to remove unwelcome racial speech or conduct from the workplace. That burden rests squarely with the employer.

Finally, a picture postcard from the "Our Gang" television series was posted next to the time clock with an added caption reading: "The new generation of papermakers." The postcard was posted within one week of Harris's arrival at the Jay Mill, and depicted the "Little Rascals" in confusion attempting to wash a dog. The character "Buckwheat" was set apart from the other, white children. Harris testified that he perceived this postcard to be racially derogatory and directed at him. When taken in tandem with the use of "Buckwheat" as a racist epithet in the mill, the Court finds that this postcard could be viewed by a reasonable black person to be an unwelcome racial statement.[22]

The Court finds that the quality and quantity of the racial speech and conduct described above and experienced by Plaintiff Harris rises to the level of racial harassment by creating an intimidating, hostile and offensive work environment so severe and pervasive that it substantially altered Harris's working conditions. The Court also finds that there is abundant evidence that Defendant's agents, supervisors, and foremen had actual knowledge of this racial harassment in most circumstances, and in the remaining instances would have had knowledge of the harassment being suffered by Harris had Defendant exercised reasonable care. The Court holds that Plaintiff Harris satisfied his burden of establishing a *prima facie* case of hostile environment racial harassment.

* * *

CERROS v. STEEL TECHNOLOGIES, INC.

United States Court of Appeals for the Seventh Circuit, 2002.
288 F.3d 1040.

DIANE P. WOOD, Circuit Judge.

Hispanic employees were few and far between at the Porter County, Indiana, facility operated by defendant Steel Technologies, Inc. ("Steel"). Plaintiff Tony Cerros was one, and he found the environment at Steel to be exceedingly hostile. He filed this suit under Title VII, alleging that Steel * * * created a hostile work environment because of his national origin and race. * * *

I

Cerros began his employment as a full time employee at Steel in October 1995. By July 1996, he had risen to the position of slitter operator. Although one might think that Cerros's various promotions were evidence of a positive work environment, that was far from true. The district court found that some of the supervisors as well as other employees overtly espoused the offensive philosophy "if it ain't white it ain't right." Cerros himself was frequently subjected to verbal harass-

---

22. There was testimony that the person who posted the postcard on the bulletin board did not intend a racial slight, however, as the Court has already noted, the intent of the speaker is not relevant to the question of the unwelcomeness of the speech.

ment. During 1996 and 1997, employees, including supervisors, referred to him by such racialized derogatory names as "brown boy," "spic," "wetback," "Julio" and "Javier" (these are not Cerros's given or nicknames), talked down to him and muttered comments under their breath. Among the supervisors using racial epithets was Jeff Colvin. In October 1996, Cerros transferred to the first shift to avoid Colvin's harassment. His respite was short-lived: over his protests, Colvin also transferred to the first shift, and the epithets continued.

In addition to the verbal harassment, racist graffiti was painted on the bathroom walls. It included racial remarks and symbols such as "spic," "Go Back to Mexico," "Tony Cerros is a Spic," "KKK," and "White Power." Although the graffiti was cleaned off the walls, Steel never conducted any investigation, nor did it attempt to ascertain who was responsible for the defacement of the room. On another occasion, the tires on Cerros's car were slashed. This severe harassment continued until December 1997, and even beyond.

* * *

Steel's official policy encourages employees who feel discriminated against first to inform their supervisor of inappropriate behavior. If an employee does not receive a response from her immediate supervisor, she is then encouraged to make an appointment with the Plant Manager. If the problem still remains unresolved, a Step Three procedure is available under which the employee may submit a written summary of the situation to the Plant Manager. The Plant Manager submits his own report to the General Manager, who reviews the situation, discusses it with the employee, and renders a decision within seven days. Last is Step Four, under which there is a final appeal to the Vice President if the employee remains dissatisfied.

Cerros began by informing not only his own supervisor, Colvin, but also other supervisors * * * of the harassment. Later, * * * Cerros discussed the situation with * * * the General Manager. There is no evidence that Cerros sought to appeal * * * to the Vice President. In any event, the epithets continued and nothing was done. It was not until Cerros filed a charge of discrimination with the EEOC that there was an investigation into the harassment * * *.

II

* * *

[Cerros claimed that he was subjected to "a working environment made hostile by racial and ethnic slurs and harassment."] * * *

* * * There is no doubt that Cerros subjectively believed that he was a victim of harassment based upon his race or national origin. Nor is there any question that a reasonable person would perceive that the graffiti, remarks, and other harassing conduct were based upon his race and ethnicity. Cerros made efforts to use the complaint mechanisms that were available even though his supervisor was a big part of the problem.

The district court did not consider Steel's affirmative defenses based on *Ellerth* and *Faragher* (relating to the adequacy of its complaint mechanism and Cerros's efforts to use it). At this stage, therefore, the question is only whether the district court committed clear error in concluding that the harassment from which Cerros suffered was not severe or pervasive enough to meet the statutory standard.

The Supreme Court established the rules for deciding this issue in its decision in *Harris v. Forklift.* * * *

The importance of considering the entire context of the workplace was later underscored by the Supreme Court in *Oncale v. Sundowner Offshore Services.* * * *.

The district court acknowledged that it had to consider the totality of the circumstances, but its findings of fact fell short of what *Harris*, *Oncale*, and *Breeden* require * * *. * * *

The district court never explained why [the] appalling litany of misconduct [in this case] was merely "offensive, unenlightened, and inappropriate"—the terms it used in the section of the opinion with the ultimate conclusion that Cerros's claim failed. It characterized the incidents as "relatively isolated," and thus as insufficient to show a hostile work environment. We believe that such a finding may have resulted from a misunderstanding about the legal threshold for harassment cases; like the lower courts in *Harris*, the district court here may well have set the bar too high as a matter of law. This court has found severe verbal harassment of the sort identified by the district court to be prohibited harassment, even when it did not occur every day. In *Shanoff*, the plaintiff alleged he was repeatedly harassed with remarks directed towards his race and his religion. The remarks included referring to Shanoff as a "haughty Jew," and stating "I know how to put you Jews in your place." Shanoff v. Illinois Dept. of Human Serv., 258 F.3d 696, 698–99 (7th Cir.2001). In all, Shanoff was subjected to six severe instances of harassment by his supervisor. Despite Shanoff's objections to the harassment, the supervisor demonstrated her "direct, unambiguous hostility to Shanoff because of his race and religion." *Id.* at 706. We found that this behavior rose to an objectively hostile work environment. *See also* Rodgers v. Western–Southern Life Ins. Co., 12 F.3d 668, 673 (7th Cir.1993) (finding an actionable hostile work environment when supervisors and employees referred to an employee by the term "nigger" between five and ten times while he was employed).

This is not a case where Cerros was a recipient of insults because of a workplace altercation, *cf.* Spearman v. Ford Motor Co., 231 F.3d 1080, 1086 (7th Cir.2000); this also is not a case where there were only a few verbal utterances made in the context of office banter, *Logan v. Kautex Textron N. Am.*, 259 F.3d 635, 639; and this case is nothing like *Sanders v. Vill. of Dixmoor*, 178 F.3d 869, 870 (7th Cir.1999), where there was one isolated racial epithet, in response to the plaintiff's already inappropriate conduct. It appears that the epithets at Steel continued for many months * * *. Adding up all of the derogatory names directed at Cerros as well as all of the graffiti on the bathroom walls, and coupling that with more information about how frequently or how long the abuse endured, the court might well find that both the pervasiveness and the severity measures are high. These are, to a certain degree, inversely related; a sufficiently severe episode may occur as rarely as once, while a relentless pattern of lesser harassment that extends over a long period of time also violates the statute. While there is no "magic number" of slurs that indicate a hostile work environment, we have recognized before that an unambiguously racial epithet falls on the "more severe" end of the spectrum. *See Rodgers,* 12 F.3d at 675 ("Perhaps no single act can more quickly 'alter the conditions of employment and create an abusive working environment' than the use of an unambiguously racial epithet such as 'nigger' by a supervisor in the presence of his subordinates.").

When Cerros attempted to escape the comments by transferring shifts, the offending supervisor followed him to the new shift. Although, as the district court noted, Cerros was not subject to physical threats, *Harris* makes it clear that such a showing is not a *sine qua non* for a harassment claim. Cerros endured a workplace environment filled with slurs and graffiti based on his race and national origin. Steel not only tolerated the harassment, but even worse, according to the facts found by the district court, its supervisors contributed to the harassment. If severe enough, or pervasive enough, this is exactly the sort of conduct Title VII prohibits.

III

Although Title VII does not guarantee a happy workplace, it does provide protection for employees who suffer from discriminatory terms and conditions of employment through a work environment that is permeated with racial epithets that are tolerated by the employer. Cerros has shown enough here to have the opportunity on remand to demonstrate that he has met the standards established in *Harris, Oncale,* and *Breeden.* * * * We VACATE the judgment on his hostile environment harassment claim and REMAND that part of the case for further proceedings. As noted above, because the district court resolved the case in Steel's favor on the basis that no actionable harassment had occurred, it never reached Steel's *Ellerth/Faragher* affirmative defenses. While Cerros is entitled to more precise findings of fact, Steel is by the same token entitled to have its affirmative defenses considered by the court. * * *

Notes and Questions

1. Should the courts treat racial and sexual hostile work environment claims the same? Are the elements of a prima facie case the same, as Chief Judge Carter says in *International Paper?* Are there any significant differences between the two types of claims? Should proof of "unwelcomeness" be an element of a racial hostile work environment case? How is race as a protected status different from sex? Can you think of a case in which a quid pro quo claim of racial or ethnic harassment could be made?

2. *Racial Animus*: Both *International Paper* and *Cerros* involve language and conduct that is explicitly racial. After *Oncale,* is "racial" language or conduct essential to establishing a claim of racial harassment? The Court of Appeals for the First Circuit has adopted an approach to defining "racial" harassment that is similar to the "gender animus" or "gender hostility" approach to defining "sexual" harassment that has been adopted by some courts. *See, e.g.*, O'Shea v. Yellow Tech. Servs., Inc., 185 F.3d 1093 (1999). *See also* Landrau–Romero v. Banco Popular De Puerto Rico, 212 F.3d 607, 614 (1st Cir.2000) ("Alleged conduct that is not explicitly racial in nature may, in appropriate circumstances, be considered along with more overtly discriminatory conduct in assessing a Title VII harassment claim."). *Compare* Aguilera v. Village of Hazel Crest, 234 F.Supp.2d 840, 847 (N.D.Ill. 2002) (finding that statements that plaintiff's "English was bad and he was a bad communicator," in absence of "profane language or racial/ethnic epithets," did not show a hostile work environment), *with* Diaz v. Swift–Eckrich, Inc., 318 F.3d 796, 799 (8th Cir.2003) (statements that "Hispanics should be cleaning" and Hispanics are "stupid" combined with "rude noises," laughter, and general derogatory comments directed at plaintiff are sufficient to show a hostile work environment based on national origin).

3. *The Victim's Perspective*: Does *International Paper* support a variety of "reasonable victim" standards, for example, "reasonable Asian American," "reasonable Rastafarian," "reasonable Muslim," "reasonable nonadherent"? *See, e.g.*, Torres v. Pisano, 116 F.3d 625, 632–33 (2d Cir. 1997) ("a reasonable Puerto Rican would find a workplace in which her boss repeatedly called her a 'dumb spic' and told her that she should stay home, go on welfare, and collect food stamps like the rest of the 'spics' to be hostile"), *cert. denied*, 522 U.S. 997, 118 S.Ct. 563, 139 L.Ed.2d 404 (1997). Can a white judge in a bench trial understand the perspective of a "reasonable black person"? See footnote 12 of *International Paper*. Would the Supreme Court endorse a "reasonable black person perspective"?

4. How would you evaluate the workplace environment in *International Paper*? How was the workplace context affected by the fact that a bitter strike was ongoing? The sixteen-month strike at the International Paper Mill is described in Julius Getman, The Betrayal of Local 14: Paperworkers, Politics, and Permanent Replacements (1998). How about the environment in *Cerros*? Was Cerros the target of all the racist graffiti at the plant? If the "entire context" of the workplace is relevant, can an employee who is a member of a racial minority recover for workplace racial harassment targeted at other members of the plaintiff's protected class or at other racial minorities? *See* Cruz v. Coach Stores, 202 F.3d 560, 570 (2d Cir.2000). Can employees recover for incidents of racial harassment that occur when they are not at work and which they hear about second-hand? *See* Whidbee v. Garzarelli Food Specialties, Inc., 223 F.3d 62, 71 (2d Cir.2000).

5. *Liability for Facially Neutral Language*: Consider the following: Plaintiff, a black woman, alleged that she was subjected to a racially hostile work environment on the basis of the following facts: White supervisors and white co-workers repeatedly referred to the plaintiff and other black workers as "another one," "one of them," and "poor people." In addition, while discussing a personnel dispute about another black worker, a manager told the plaintiff that "if this continues we're going to have to come up there and

get rid of all of you." When the plaintiff asked the manager what he meant by "all of you," he refused to elaborate. Plaintiff perceived the comments to be racially motivated. Would such comments be considered "hostile" or "abusive" under *Harris v. Forklift Systems*? Would they be considered discriminatory "because of race" under *Oncale*? On these facts, in *Aman v. Cort Furniture Rental Corp.*, 85 F.3d 1074 (1996), the Court of Appeals for the Third Circuit reversed the district court's finding that such "racially-neutral" language "demonstrated only rudeness, and not racial animus." *Id.* at 1080 & n.2. The court observed,

> Anti-discrimination laws and lawsuits have "educated" would-be violators such that extreme manifestations of discrimination are thankfully rare. Though they still happen, the instances in which employers and employees openly use derogatory epithets to refer to fellow employees appear to be declining. Regrettably, however, this in no way suggests that discrimination based upon an individual's race, gender, or age is near an end. Discrimination continues to pollute the social and economic mainstream of American life, and is often simply masked in more subtle forms. It has become easier to coat various forms of discrimination with the appearance of propriety, or to ascribe some other less odious intention to what is in reality discriminatory behavior. In other words, while discriminatory conduct persists, violators have learned not to leave the proverbial "smoking gun" behind. As one court has recognized, "defendants of even minimal sophistication will neither admit discriminatory animus or leave a paper trail demonstrating it." Riordan v. Kempiners, 831 F.2d 690, 697 (7th Cir.1987). But regardless of the form that discrimination takes, the impermissible impact remains the same, and the law's prohibition remains unchanged. "Title VII tolerates no racial discrimination, subtle or otherwise." McDonnell Douglas Corp. v. Green, 411 U.S. 792, 801, 93 S.Ct. 1817, 36 L.Ed.2d 668 (1973).

> * * * [T]he use of "code words" can, under circumstances such as we encounter here, violate Title VII. Indeed, a reasonable jury could conclude that the intent to discriminate is implicit in these comments. There are no talismanic expressions which must be invoked as a condition-precedent to the application of laws designed to protect against discrimination. The words themselves are only relevant for what they reveal—the intent of the speaker. A reasonable jury could find that statements like the ones allegedly made in this case send a clear message and carry the distinct tone of racial motivations and implications. They could be seen as conveying the message that members of a particular race are disfavored and that members of that race are, therefore, not full and equal members of the workplace. * * * [T]he pervasive use of derogatory and insulting terms directed at members of a protected class generally, and addressed to those employees personally, may serve as evidence of a hostile environment.

Aman, 85 F.3d at 1081, 1083. Will potential Title VII liability for facially neutral "code words" chill speech between workers of different races in the workplace? On the other hand, if such verbal harassment is not actionable, is there a risk that the harmful effects of racial hostility in the workplace will go unremedied more often than not?

6. *Intersectionality*: Hostile work environment cases often involve the intersection of two or more protected statuses. For example, *Cerros* is described as a case of discriminatory harassment because of race and national origin and because of race and ethnicity. How should the courts treat hostile environment claims based on the intersection of race and sex? Are those "intersecting" claims any different from claims based solely on either racial harassment or sexual harassment? See the discussions of intersectionality in Chapter 2, Section D.1, and Chapter 6, Section B.1 and Section E, Note 3. For an exploration of some of these issues, see L. Camille Hébert, *Analogizing Race and Sex in Workplace Harassment Claims*, 58 Ohio St.L.J. 819 (1997).

7. A black male employee who has been dating a white female co-worker is accused by his supervisors of sexually harassing her. Two white managers summon the black employee to a "counseling session" in a small storage room where they accuse him of sexual harassment and demand that he break off the relationship. When the employee denies that he has harassed his co-worker, one of the managers yells at him, pounds on a desk, and threatens him with physical injury if he does not "leave that white girl alone." Does the employee have a claim for racial harassment under Title VII? *See* Jasmin v. New York State Dep't of Labor, 1999 WL 1225249 (S.D.N.Y.1999).

8. *The Impact of* Ellerth *and* Faragher *on the Courts and the EEOC*: *Cerros* was remanded with instructions to permit the employer to present its "*Ellerth/Faragher* affirmative defenses." Based on the facts provided, do you think the employer is likely to prevail on its affirmative defense? After *Ellerth* and *Faragher,* the federal courts have applied the vicarious liability principles and affirmative defenses for supervisory sexual harassment to cases of supervisory harassment based on race, national origin, age, and disability. *See, e.g.,* Wright–Simmons v. City of Oklahoma City, 155 F.3d 1264 (10th Cir.1998) (racial harassment case remanded for consideration of *Ellerth/Faragher* affirmative defense). The EEOC's proposed Guidelines on Harassment Based on Race, Color, Religion, Gender, National Origin, Age, or Disability in October 1993, 58 F.R. 51266 (October 1, 1993), were later withdrawn after extensive criticism of the religion guidelines by some members of Congress and the public. *See* 59 F.R. 51396 (Oct. 11, 1994). The controversy over the proposed guidelines on religion is discussed in the Note on religious harassment in Chapter 10. On June 18, 1999, the EEOC released a new policy guidance outlining standards for employer liability for harassment by supervisors. *See* EEOC Enforcement Guidance: Vicarious Employer Liability for Unlawful Harassment by Supervisors, 29 C.F.R. § 1604.11, app.A. The guidance extends the *Ellerth/Faragher* employer liability standards to cases of harassment based on race, national origin, age, disability—but not religion—and "on opposition to discrimination or participation in complaint proceedings." The enforcement guidance can be obtained on the EEOC's Web site: *www.eeoc.gov/docs/harassment.html. See also* Timothy S. Bland & David P. Knox, *EEOC's Guidance on Vicarious Liability for Supervisory Harassment: Are the Courts Following the EEOC's Lead?*, 30 U.Mem.L.Rev. 793 (2000).

9. *Section 1981 Claims of Racial Harassment*: Since the enactment of the Civil Rights Act of 1991, employees have been able to bring race-based

hostile work environment claims under both Title VII and 42 U.S.C. § 1981. *See* Jackson v. Motel 6 Multipurpose, Inc., 130 F.3d 999, 1008 n.17 (11th Cir.1997) (collecting cases). For discussion of § 1981 claims generally, see Chapter 5, Section C. In *Danco, Inc. v. Wal–Mart Stores, Inc.*, 178 F.3d 8 (1st Cir.1999), *cert. denied*, 528 U.S. 1105, 120 S.Ct. 843, 145 L.Ed.2d 712 (2000), the court held that independent contractors could also bring claims of hostile work environment racial harassment under § 1981. *See also* Spriggs v. Diamond Auto Glass, 242 F.3d 179 (4th Cir.2001) (Title VII and § 1981 claims of racially hostile work environment based on supervisor's daily use of racial epithets raise a jury question).

10.   *Same-Race Harassment*: In *Ross v. Douglas County, Nebraska*, 234 F.3d 391, 396 (8th Cir.2000), the court relied on *Oncale* to recognize a same-race hostile work environment claim brought by a black correctional officer who alleged that his black supervisor had called him "black boy" and "nigger." Is it the same for a black supervisor to call a black subordinate racial epithets as for a white supervisor to do so? *See* Randall Kennedy, *Nigger: The Strange Career of a Troublesome Word* (2002), and the discussion of epithets in Chapter 3, Section B.2.

11.   *Reverse Racial Harassment*: What kind of evidence would a white plaintiff need to prevail on a claim that a black supervisor or co-worker has created a racially hostile work environment? *See, e.g.,* Bowen v. Missouri Dep't of Soc. Servs., 311 F.3d 878, 884 (8th Cir.2002) (ruling that evidence presented by white employee whose supervisor called her "white bitch" and other epithets that "carried clear racial overtones" is sufficient to defeat a summary judgment motion).

Chapter 9

DISCRIMINATION BECAUSE OF SEXUAL ORIENTATION

A. INTRODUCTION

Although bills to extend federal antidiscrimination laws to include sexual orientation have been introduced in Congress for over a quarter century, no federal statute prohibits employment discrimination based on an employee's sexual orientation. Nevertheless, an increasing number of state and local governments include sexual orientation as a protected status in their civil rights laws and ordinances, and executive orders prohibit sexual orientation discrimination in many state and federal government jobs. While the federal courts and the EEOC agree that Title VII does not protect individuals from employment discrimination on the basis of their sexual orientation, preference, or identity, recent federal cases have challenged the distinction between "sex" and "sexual orientation" in Title VII jurisprudence.

The Supreme Court's 2003 decision in *Lawrence v. Texas*, 539 U.S. 558, 123 S.Ct. 2472, 156 L.Ed.2d 508 (2003), may have a significant impact on gay civil rights generally, including the employment rights of gays and lesbians. *Lawrence* held that a Texas statute criminalizing "intimate sexual conduct" between consenting adults of the same sex was unconstitutional. *Id*. at ___, 123 S.Ct. at 2475. The sweeping rationale of the decision—that "[l]iberty presumes an autonomy of self that includes freedom of thought, belief, expressions, and certain intimate conduct," *id*.—may lead to expanded protections for homosexuals in a variety of areas of law, such as adoption, marriage, and employment, *see, e.g.*, Goodridge v. Department of Public Health, 440 Mass. 309, 798 N.E.2d 941 (2003) (relying, in part, on the reasoning of *Lawrence v. Texas* as support for holding that two same-sex individuals cannot be denied a Massachusetts marriage license under the state constitution), but it also may result in legislative or constitutional backlash.

Proposals to extend civil rights laws to prohibit discrimination on the basis of sexual orientation invoke some of the most deeply held beliefs and assumptions in our culture. *See* Jane S. Schacter, *Skepticism, Culture and the Gay Civil Rights Debate in a Post–Civil–Rights Era*, 110

Harv.L.Rev. 684 (1997) (reviewing Andrew Sullivan, Virtually Normal: An Argument About Homosexuality (1995) and Urvashi Vaid, Virtual Equality: The Mainstreaming of Gay and Lesbian Liberation (1995)). For example, the policy debate over whether to enact laws prohibiting discrimination in employment on the basis of sexual orientation has, in part, been played out in the context of an ongoing controversy about the underlying cause of homosexuality—nature or nurture or some combination of biological and social factors. This larger debate among gay and lesbian activists, health care professionals, scientists, legal scholars, politicians, theologians, and others has spilled into the mass media as well. *See, e.g.*, David Gelman, *Born or Bred?: The Origins of Homosexuality*, Newsweek, Feb. 24, 1992, at 46. *See generally* James Button et al, The Politics of Gay Rights in American Communities (1994); Andrew Koppelman, The Gay Rights Question in American Law (2002).

What is the nature of homosexuality? Is it conduct or identity? *See, e.g., Lawrence*, 539 U.S. at ___, 123 S.Ct. at 2487 (O'Connor, J., concurring) (arguing that the Texas sodomy law "is targeted at more than conduct," but is "instead directed toward gay persons as a class"). One argument for protecting homosexuality is based on the theory that an individual's sexual orientation, like her race, color, or sex, is an immutable trait, not a matter of choice. Others argue that sexuality is socially constructed, not biologically determined. Although some evidence of a genetic basis to homosexuality among men has been suggested from several scientific studies, "instead of resolving the debate, the studies may well have intensified it." Gelman, *supra* at 48. Indeed, nearly all "facts" regarding homosexuality—including the extent of homosexual behavior and homosexual orientation among men and women in the United States—are hotly contested. *Compare* Richard A. Posner, Sex and Reason 294–95 (1992) (noting that "most estimates of male homosexuality are lower than Kinsey's [10 percent]"—ranging from 2 to 5 percent—and concluding that "the percentage of homosexuals in the population as a whole might be little more than 1 percent"), *with* Charles R. Colbert III & John G. Wofford, *Sexual Orientation in the Workplace: The Strategic Challenge*, 9 Compensation & Benefits Mgmt., Summer 1993, at 1, 2 (noting that "[a]pproximately five percent to ten percent of the general population is estimated to be gay or lesbian in fundamental sexual orientation"). *See generally* Edward O. Laumann et al., The Social Organization of Sexuality: Sexual Practices in the United States 283–320 (1994).

In light of this ongoing debate about homosexuality, consider the following findings of fact made by a federal district court judge:

1. Homosexuals comprise between 5% and 13% of the population.

2. Sexual orientation is a characteristic which exists separately and independently from sexual conduct or behavior.

3. Sexual orientation is a deeply rooted, complex combination of factors including a predisposition towards affiliation, affection, or bonding with members of the opposite and/or the same gender.

5. [sic] Sexual behavior is not necessarily a good predictor of a person's sexual orientation.

6. Gender non-conformity such as cross-dressing is not indicative of homosexuality.

8. [sic] Sexual orientation is set in at a very early age—3 to 5 years—and is not only involuntary, but is unamenable to change.

9. Sexual orientation bears no relation to an individual's ability to perform, contribute to, or participate in, society.

* * *

12. Homosexuality is not a mental illness.

13. Homosexuals have suffered a history of pervasive irrational and invidious discrimination in government and private employment, in political organization and in all facets of society in general, based on their sexual orientation.

14. Pervasive private and institutional discrimination against gays, lesbians and bisexuals often has a profound negative psychological impact on gays, lesbians and bisexuals.

15. Gays, lesbians and bisexuals are an identifiable group based on their sexual orientation and their shared history of discrimination based on that characteristic.

16. Gays, lesbians and bisexuals are often the target of violence by heterosexuals due to their sexual orientation.

Equality Found. of Greater Cincinnati, Inc. v. City of Cincinnati (Equality II), 860 F.Supp. 417, 426–27 (S.D.Ohio 1994), *quoted in* Equality Found. of Greater Cincinnati, Inc. v. City of Cincinnati, 54 F.3d 261, 264 n.1 (6th Cir.1995), *cert. denied*, 525 U.S. 943, 119 S.Ct. 365, 142 L.Ed.2d 302 (1998). Would you take issue with any of these judicial findings? If so, what evidence or arguments would be most persuasive? What "facts" regarding homosexuality would you want a legislature to consider in deciding whether to prohibit employment discrimination on the basis of sexual orientation?

Section B.1 of this chapter discusses the leading federal court cases dealing with claims of employment discrimination based on sexual orientation. Section B.2 explores sexual harassment claims brought by employees who are homosexual or perceived to be homosexual. Section C examines constitutional claims brought by individuals—homosexual government employees or military personnel challenging discriminatory government policies or decisions based on sexual orientation—and by gay and lesbian organizations seeking broad civil rights protections. Section D addresses alternative sources of laws that may provide remedies for employment discrimination against homosexuals.

B. SEXUAL ORIENTATION CLAIMS UNDER TITLE VII

1. SEXUAL ORIENTATION DISCRIMINATION AS "SEX" DISCRIMINATION

DeSANTIS v. PACIFIC TELEPHONE & TELEGRAPH CO.

United States Court of Appeals for the Ninth Circuit, 1979.
608 F.2d 327.

CHOY, Circuit Judge.

Male and female homosexuals brought three separate federal district court actions claiming that their employers or former employers discriminated against them in employment decisions because of their homosexuality. They alleged that such discrimination violated Title VII of the Civil Rights Act of 1964 * * *. The district courts dismissed the complaints as failing to state claims under [the] statute. Plaintiffs below appealed. Because of the similarity of issues involved, this court consolidated the appeals at the request of counsel for appellants. We affirm.

I. STATEMENT OF THE CASE

A. Strailey v. Happy Times Nursery School, Inc.

Appellant Strailey, a male, was fired by the Happy Times Nursery School after two years' service as a teacher. He alleged that he was fired because he wore a small gold ear-loop to school prior to the commencement of the school year. * * *

B. DeSantis v. Pacific Telephone & Telegraph Co.

DeSantis, Boyle, and Simard, all males, claimed that Pacific Telephone & Telegraph Co. (PT & T) impermissibly discriminated against them because of their homosexuality. DeSantis alleged that he was not hired when a PT & T supervisor concluded that he was a homosexual. According to appellants' brief, "BOYLE was continually harassed by his co-workers and had to quit to preserve his health after only three months because his supervisors did nothing to alleviate this condition." Finally, "SIMARD was forced to quit under similar conditions after almost four years of employment with PT & T, but he was harassed by his supervisors [as well] * * *. In addition, his personnel file has been marked as not eligible for rehire, and his applications for employment were rejected by PT & T in 1974 and 1976." Appellants DeSantis, Boyle, and Simard also alleged that PT & T officials have publicly stated that they would not hire homosexuals.

* * *

C. Lundin v. Pacific Telephone & Telegraph

Lundin and Buckley, both females, were operators with PT & T. They filed suit in federal court alleging that PT & T discriminated against them because of their known lesbian relationship and eventually fired them. They also alleged that they endured numerous insults by PT & T employees because of their relationship. Finally, Lundin alleged that the union that represented her as a PT & T operator failed adequately to represent her interests and failed adequately to present her grievance regarding her treatment. * * *

II.   Title VII Claim

Appellants argue first that the district courts erred in holding that Title VII does not prohibit discrimination on the basis of sexual preference. They claim that in prohibiting certain employment discrimination on the basis of "sex," Congress meant to include discrimination on the basis of sexual orientation. They add that in a trial they could establish that discrimination against homosexuals disproportionately affects men and that this disproportionate impact and correlation between discrimination on the basis of sexual preference and discrimination on the basis of "sex" requires that sexual preference be considered a subcategory of the "sex" category of Title VII. *See* 42 U.S.C. § 2000e–2.

A.   *Congressional Intent in Prohibiting "Sex" Discrimination*

In *Holloway v. Arthur Andersen & Co.*, 566 F.2d 659 (9th Cir.1977), plaintiff argued that her employer had discriminated against her because she was undergoing a sex transformation and that this discrimination violated Title VII's prohibition on sex discrimination. This court rejected that claim, writing:

> The cases interpreting Title VII sex discrimination provisions agree that they were intended to place women on an equal footing with men. [Citations omitted.]
>
> Giving the statute its plain meaning, this court concludes that Congress had only the traditional notions of "sex" in mind. Later legislative activity makes this narrow definition even more evident. Several bills have been introduced to *amend* the Civil Rights Act to prohibit discrimination against "sexual preference." None have [*sic*] been enacted into law.
>
> Congress has not shown any intent other than to restrict the term "sex" to its traditional meaning. Therefore, this court will not expand Title VII's application in the absence of Congressional mandate. The manifest purpose of Title VII's prohibition against sex discrimination in employment is to ensure that men and women are treated equally, absent a bona fide relationship between the qualifications for the job and the person's sex.

Id. at 662–63.

Following *Holloway*, we conclude that Title VII's prohibition of "sex" discrimination applies only to discrimination on the basis of gender and should not be judicially extended to include sexual preference such as homosexuality. *See* Smith v. Liberty Mutual Insurance Co., 569 F.2d 325, 326–27 (5th Cir.1978); *Holloway*, 566 F.2d at 662–63.

B. Disproportionate Impact

Appellants argue that recent decisions dealing with disproportionate impact require that discrimination against homosexuals fall within the purview of Title VII. They contend that these recent decisions, like *Griggs v. Duke Power Co.*, 401 U.S. 424, 91 S.Ct. 849, 28 L.Ed.2d 158 (1971), establish that any employment criterion that affects one sex more than the other violates Title VII. They quote from *Griggs*:

> What is required by Congress [under Title VII] is the removal of artificial, arbitrary, and unnecessary barriers to employment when the barriers operate invidiously to discriminate on the basis of racial or other impermissible classifications.

401 U.S. at 431, 91 S.Ct. at 853. They claim that in a trial they could prove that discrimination against homosexuals disproportionately affects men both because of the greater incidence of homosexuality in the male population and because of the greater likelihood of an employer's discovering male homosexuals compared to female homosexuals.

Assuming that appellants can otherwise satisfy the requirement of *Griggs*, we do not believe that *Griggs* can be applied to extend Title VII protection to homosexuals. In finding that the disproportionate impact of educational tests on blacks violated Title VII, the Supreme Court in *Griggs* sought to effectuate a major congressional purpose in enacting Title VII: protection of blacks from employment discrimination. For as the Supreme Court noted in *Philbrook v. Glodgett*, 421 U.S. 707, 95 S.Ct. 1893, 44 L.Ed.2d 525 (1975), in construing a statute, "[o]ur objective * * * is to ascertain the congressional intent and give effect to the legislative will." *Id.* at 713, 95 S.Ct. at 1898.

The *Holloway* court noted that in passing Title VII Congress did not intend to protect sexual orientation and has repeatedly refused to extend such protection. Appellants now ask us to employ the disproportionate impact decisions as an artifice to "bootstrap" Title VII protection for homosexuals under the guise of protecting men generally.

This we are not free to do. Adoption of this bootstrap device would frustrate congressional objectives as explicated in *Holloway*, not effectuate congressional goals as in *Griggs*. It would achieve by judicial "construction" what Congress did not do and has consistently refused to do on many occasions. It would violate the rule that our duty in construing a statute is to "ascertain * * * and give effect to the legislative will." *Philbrook*, 421 U.S. at 713, 95 S.Ct. at 1898. We conclude that the *Griggs* disproportionate impact theory may not be applied to extend Title VII protection to homosexuals.

C. Differences in Employment Criteria

Appellants next contend that recent decisions have held that an employer generally may not use different employment criteria for men and women. They claim that if a male employee prefers males as sexual partners, he will be treated differently from a female who prefers male partners. They conclude that the employer thus uses different employment criteria for men and women and violates the Supreme Court's warning in *Phillips v. Martin Marietta Corp.*, 400 U.S. 542, 91 S.Ct. 496, 27 L.Ed.2d 613 (1971):

> The Court of Appeals therefore erred in reading this section as permitting one hiring policy for women and another for men * * *.

Id. at 544, 91 S.Ct. at 497.

We must again reject appellants' efforts to "bootstrap" Title VII protection for homosexuals. While we do not express approval of an employment policy that differentiates according to sexual preference, we note that whether dealing with men or women the employer is using the same criterion: it will not hire or promote a person who prefers sexual partners of the same sex. Thus this policy does not involve different decisional criteria for the sexes.

D.   Interference with Association

Appellants argue that the EEOC has held that discrimination against an employee because of the race of the employee's friends may constitute discrimination based on race in violation of Title VII. See EEOC Dec. No. 71–1902, [1972] Empl.Prac.Guide (CCH) ¶ 6281; EEOC Dec. No. 71–969, [1972] Empl.Prac.Guide (CCH) ¶ 6193. They contend that analogously discrimination because of the sex of the employees' sexual partner should constitute discrimination based on sex.

Appellants, however, have not alleged that appellees have policies of discriminating against employees because of the gender of their friends. That is, they do not claim that the appellees will terminate anyone with a male (or female) friend. They claim instead that the appellees discriminate against employees who have a certain type of relationship—*i.e.*, homosexual relationship—with certain friends. As noted earlier, that relationship is not protected by Title VII. Thus, assuming that it would violate Title VII for an employer to discriminate against employees because of the gender of their friends, appellants' claims do not fall within this purported rule.

E.   Effeminacy

Appellant Strailey contends that he was terminated by the Happy Times Nursery School because that school felt that it was inappropriate for a male teacher to wear an earring to school. He claims that the school's reliance on a stereotype—that a male should have a virile rather than an effeminate appearance—violates Title VII.

In *Holloway* this court noted that Congress intended Title VII's ban on sex discrimination in employment to prevent discrimination because of gender, not because of sexual orientation or preference. Recently the Fifth Circuit similarly read the legislative history of Title VII and concluded that Title VII thus does not protect against discrimination because of effeminacy. Smith v. Liberty Mutual Insurance Co., 569 F.2d 325, 326–27 (5th Cir.1978). We agree and hold that discrimination because of effeminacy, like discrimination because of homosexuality or transsexualism (*Holloway*), does not fall within the purview of Title VII.

Conclusion as to Title VII Claim

Having determined that appellants' allegations do not implicate Title VII's prohibition on sex discrimination, we affirm the district court's dismissals of the Title VII claims.

* * *

Notes and Questions

1. *Sex Stereotyping:* In *Price Waterhouse v. Hopkins*, 490 U.S. 228, 251, 109 S.Ct. 1775, 1791, 104 L.Ed.2d 268 (1989), the Supreme Court recognized that sex stereotyping can be evidence of sex discrimination within the meaning of Title VII. See Chapter 3, Section B.2. Does this support the plaintiffs' argument made in *DeSantis* that discrimination on the basis of sexual orientation can be prohibited sex discrimination under Title VII? Does the portion of the *DeSantis* opinion regarding plaintiff Strailey's effeminate appearance survive *Price Waterhouse*? Consider the following hypothetical in I. Bennet Capers, Note, *Sex(ual Orientation) and Title VII*, 91 Colum.L.Rev. 1158, 1158 (1991) (italics omitted):

> Alice, Bob, and Calvin are sixth year associates at a prestigious Wall Street law firm. All three are up for partnership, along with seven other candidates. The three have stellar records, and rank in the top of their associate class in terms of billable hours and the generation of business. After speaking with the candidates' colleagues and examining the candidates' records, the senior partners conclude that Alice, Bob, and Calvin are superior candidates. Yet the partners decide to vote against their admission to the partnership. Instead, the partners admit the other seven candidates.

> Alice, Bob, and Calvin each inquire as to the basis for the rejection. Alice is told her "tough, macho" behavior, "lack of social graces," and "unladylike language" contributed substantially to her failure to attain acceptance into the partnership. Bob, on the other hand, learns that though his work is superior, the senior partners thought him "too soft," and wondered if he "has lace on his jockcy shorts." Finally, Calvin is told that he was denied partnership for the simple reason that he is gay.

Although Alice, Bob, and Calvin would each receive very different treatment under Title VII, Capers argues that "Title VII can be read as prohibiting employment discrimination based on sexual orientation without a drastic rereading of Title VII, or an imaginary inclusion of the words 'sexual orientation' after the word 'sex' in the statute." *Id.* at 1186. Do you agree? Consider the following perspective offered by Judge Posner:

> I think it worth recording my conviction that the case law has gone off the tracks in the matter of "sex stereotyping" * * *.

> The case law as it has evolved holds * * * that although Title VII does not protect homosexuals from discrimination on the basis of their

sexual orientation, it protects heterosexuals who are victims of "sex stereotyping" or "gender stereotyping."

The origin of this curious distinction * * * is the Supreme Court's decision in *Price Waterhouse v. Hopkins*. Part of the evidence that the plaintiff in that case had been denied promotion because she was a woman was that her male superiors hadn't liked her failure to conform to their expectations regarding feminine dress and deportment. That was indeed a reason to suspect that the firm discriminated against women. But there is a difference that subsequent cases have ignored between, on the one hand, using evidence of the plaintiff's failure to wear nail polish (or, if the plaintiff is a man, his using nail polish) to show that her sex played a role in the adverse employment action of which she complains, and, on the other hand, creating a subtype of sexual discrimination called "sex stereotyping," as if there were a federally protected right for male workers to wear nail polish and dresses and speak in falsetto and mince about in high heels, or for female ditchdiggers to strip to the waist in hot weather. If a court of appeals requires lawyers presenting oral argument to wear conservative business dress, should a male lawyer have a legal right to argue in drag provided that the court does not believe that he is a homosexual, against whom it is free to discriminate? That seems to me a very strange extension of the *Hopkins* case.

The "logic" of the extension is that if an employer disapproves of conduct by a man that it would not disapprove of in a woman, or conduct by a woman that it would not disapprove of in a man, the disapproval is "because of" sex. What is true, as I have said, is that this asymmetry of response may be evidence of sex discrimination; but to equate it to sex discrimination is a mistake. If an employer refuses to hire unfeminine women, its refusal bears more heavily on women than men, and is therefore discriminatory. That was the *Hopkins* case. But if, as in this case, an employer *whom no woman wants to work for* (at least in the plaintiff's job classification) discriminates against effeminate men, there is no discrimination against men, just against a subclass of men. They are discriminated against not because they are men, but because they are effeminate.

If this analysis is rejected, the absurd conclusion follows that the law protects effeminate men from employment discrimination, but only if they are (or are believed to be) heterosexuals. * * * To suppose courts capable of disentangling the motives for disliking the nonstereotypical man or woman is a fantasy.

* * *

"Sex stereotyping" should not be regarded as a form of sex discrimination, though it will sometimes, as in the *Hopkins* case, be evidence of sex discrimination. In most cases * * * the "discrimination" that results from such stereotyping is discrimination among members of the same sex. The distinction can be illustrated by a pair of examples. If the producer of *Antony and Cleopatra* refuses to cast an effeminate man as Antony or a mannish woman as Cleopatra, he is not discriminating against men in the first case and women in the second, although he is catering to the audience's sex stereotypes. But if a fire department refused to hire mannish women to be firefighters, this would be evidence that it was discriminating against women, because mannish women are more likely than stereotypically feminine women to meet the demanding physical criteria for a firefighter.

Hamm v. Weyauwega Milk Prods., Inc. 332 F.3d 1058, 1066–68 (7th Cir. 2003) (Posner, J., concurring). How would Strailey's claim in *DeSantis* fare under Posner's analysis?

2. *Defining "Sex" as "Sexual Orientation"*: Could the term "sex" in Title VII be read broadly to encompass sexual identity, sexual orientation, or sexual preference? In other words, is bias against homosexuals just another form of sex discrimination? *See* Sylvia A. Law, *Homosexuality and the Social Meaning of Gender*, 1988 Wis.L.Rev. 187 (1988). In resolving this issue, the courts and the EEOC had to address a fundamental question: What does "sex" mean for purposes of interpreting the statute? "Sex as a basis of discrimination was added as a floor amendment one day before the House approved Title VII, without prior hearing or debate." Holloway v. Arthur Andersen & Co., 566 F.2d 659, 662 (9th Cir.1977). This "last-ditch effort by opponents of the statute to thwart passage of the Act" failed, and " 'the bill quickly passed as amended, and we are left with little legislative history to guide us in interpreting the Act's prohibition against discrimination based on sex.' " Torres v. National Precision Blanking, 943 F.Supp. 952, 954 (N.D.Ill.1996) (quoting Meritor Savings Bank v. Vinson, 477 U.S. 57, 64, 106 S.Ct. 2399, 2404, 91 L.Ed.2d 49 (1986)). *See also* Marie Elena Peluso, Note, *Tempering Title VII's Straight Arrow Approach: Recognizing and Protecting Gay Victims of Employment Discrimination*, 46 Vand.L.Rev. 1533, 1537–38 (1993) (discussing the history of the amendment).

If there is no clear legislative history, why have courts adopted a traditional, heterosexist notion of "sex"? Is it sufficient to assert that Congress could not possibly have conceived of extending the Act's remedial scheme to homosexuals in 1964? The supporters of the "sex" amendment clearly believed that women were its intended beneficiaries; but nearly two decades after its enactment, the Supreme Court held that Title VII also protects men from employment discrimination. Newport News Shipbuilding & Dry Dock Co. v. EEOC, 462 U.S. 669, 676, 103 S.Ct. 2622, 2627, 77 L.Ed.2d 89 (1983). Furthermore, as discussed in Chapter 8, the Supreme Court has held that same-sex sexual harassment is unlawful discrimination under Title VII. Oncale v. Sundowner Offshore Services, Inc., 523 U.S. 75, 118 S.Ct. 998, 140 L.Ed.2d 201 (1998).

3. *The Relationship Between "Sex," "Gender," and "Sexual Orientation"*: Does "sex" as used in Title VII mean *sex*—a biological classification of males and females based on differences in reproductive organs—or *gender*— a social construct of attributes of psychology, appearance, and behavior that are assumed to be possessed by persons of a particular sex? The Supreme Court, like many courts and commentators, uses the terms "sex" and "gender" interchangeably. *See* Price Waterhouse v. Hopkins, 490 U.S. 228, 239–41, 109 S.Ct. 1775, 1784–86, 104 L.Ed.2d 268 (1989). *DeSantis* concluded that the term "sex" in Title VII means "gender" and not "sexual preference." Similarly, the EEOC in 1976 defined the word "sex" in Title

VII as "a person's gender, an immutable characteristic with which a person is born." EEOC Dec. No. 76–75, [1976] Emp.Prac.Guide (CCH) ¶ 6495, at 4266. Homosexuality, by contrast, is defined as a "condition * * * relate[d] to a person's sexual proclivities or practices, not to his or her gender." *Id.* Professor Mary Anne Case observed:

> The word "gender" has come to be used synonymously with the word "sex" in the law of discrimination. In women's studies and related disciplines, however, the two terms have long had distinct meanings, with gender being to sex what masculine and feminine are to male and female. Were that distinct meaning of gender to be recaptured in the law, great gains both in analytic clarity and in human liberty and equality might well result. For, as things now stand, the concept of gender has been imperfectly disaggregated in the law from sex on the one hand and sexual orientation on the other. Sex and orientation exert the following differential pull on gender in current life and law: When individuals diverge from the gender expectations for their sex—when a woman displays masculine characteristics or a man feminine ones— discrimination against her is now treated as sex discrimination while his behavior is generally viewed as a marker for homosexual orientation and may not receive protection from discrimination.

Mary Anne C. Case, *Disaggregating Gender from Sex and Sexual Orientation: The Effeminate Man in the Law and Feminist Jurisprudence*, 105 Yale L.J. 1, 2 (1995); *see also* Taylor Flynn, *Transforming the Debate, Why We Need to Include Transgender*, 101 Colum.L.Rev. 392 (2001) (essay). In his article on the historical origins of the Euro–American sex/gender system, Professor Francisco Valdes argues that, in contrast to the sex/gender systems of the ancient Greeks and Native Americans, the Euro–American system alone "constructs gender as if it were immutable[,] * * * deduces gender exclusively from sex, and * * * views the deduction as unassailable." Francisco Valdes, *Unpacking Hetero–Patriarchy: Tracing the Conflation of Sex, Gender & Sexual Orientation to Its Origins*, 8 Yale J.L. & Human. 161, 161 (1996). For an exploration of how judicial decisions and cultural forms interact to transform the meanings of sex and gender, see Kenneth L. Karst, *Constitutional Equality as a Cultural Form: The Courts and the Meanings of Sex and Gender*, 38 Wake Forest L.Rev. 513 (2003).

4. *Transsexuals*: In *Ulane v. Eastern Airlines, Inc.*, 742 F.2d 1081 (7th Cir.1984), the court held that Title VII does not protect employees from being discriminated against because they are transsexuals. A former Army pilot decorated for combat service in Vietnam, Kenneth Ulane worked for Eastern Airlines for over a decade before undergoing psychiatric counseling, hormone treatments, and finally sex reassignment surgery in order to become a female named Karen Frances Ulane. When Eastern discovered the "sex" change, it fired Ulane. The district court ruled that Eastern had violated Title VII, but the Seventh Circuit reversed, holding that "Title VII does not protect transsexuals * * *." 742 F.2d at 1084. Because "the operation would not create a biological female in the sense that Ulane would 'have a uterus and ovaries and be able to bear babies[,]' " and because "Ulane's chromosomes * * * are unaffected by the hormones and surgery[,]" *id.* at 1083, the court rejected the argument that Ulane was discriminated against on the basis of "sex." Agreeing with rulings of two

other circuits, the court concluded that "if the term 'sex' as it is used in Title VII is to mean more than biological male or biological female, the new definition must come from Congress." *Id.* at 1087; *see also id.* at 1087 n.12 (citing cases).

In response to the argument that Ulane was discriminated against because she is now a female, the court observed:

> Ulane is entitled to any personal belief about her sexual identity she desires. After the surgery, hormones, appearance changes, and a new Illinois birth certificate and FAA pilot's certificate, it may be that society, as the trial judge found, considers Ulane to be female. But even if one believes that a woman can be so easily created from what remains of a man, that does not decide this case. If Eastern had considered Ulane to be female and had discriminated against her because she was female * * *, then the argument might be made that Title VII applied, but that is not this case. It is clear from the evidence that if Eastern did discriminate against Ulane, it was not because she is female, but because Ulane is a transsexual—a biological male who takes female hormones, cross-dresses, and has surgically altered parts of her body to make it appear to be female.

Id. at 1087. The Seventh Circuit recently reiterated that the "the record [in *Ulane*] suggested that [Karen Ulane's] discharge was not triggered by her gender per se, but by her change in (anatomical) gender." Doe v. City of Belleville, 119 F.3d 563, 592 (7th Cir.1997), *cert. granted, judgment vacated*, 523 U.S. 1001, 118 S.Ct. 1183, 140 L.Ed.2d 313 (1998). Does this distinction make sense to you? *See generally* David M. Neff, *Denial of Title VII Protection to Transsexuals:* Ulane v. Eastern Airlines, Inc., 34 DePaul L.Rev. 553 (1985).

Although all federal courts that have considered claims of transsexual discrimination under Title VII have agreed with *Ulane*, state courts construing state or local antidiscrimination laws are not bound by *Ulane*. *See* Maffei v. Kolaeton Industry, Inc., 164 Misc.2d 547, 626 N.Y.S.2d 391, 394–95 (N.Y.Sup.1995) (discussing *Ulane* and citing federal cases). For example in *Maffei*, the plaintiff, formerly a female, argued that he was subjected to a hostile work environment because he had undergone surgery to change into a male "based on his identity and outward anatomy." *Id.* at 396. Finding "a clear distinction between homosexuals and transsexuals," *id.* at 395, the court refused to find that the plaintiff was protected by a 1991 amendment that added "sexual orientation" to the New York City antidiscrimination law. *Id.* at 396 (citing N.Y. Administrative Code § 8–107). Rather, because "the antidiscrimination statutes are remedial," the court found that

> the creation of a hostile work environment as a result of derogatory comments relating to the fact that as a result of an operation an employee changed his or her sexual status, creates discrimination based on "sex," just as would comments based on the secondary sexual characteristics of a person. * * * In other words, an employee who has fulfilled a sexual identity urge by changing sex and is harassed because of such fulfillment is entitled to the law's protection against employer harassment.

Id.

Which statutory interpretation of the term "sex" in antidiscrimination law do you find more persuasive—*Ulane*'s or *Maffei*'s? *See generally* Joanne Meyerowitz, How Sex Changed: A History of Transsexuality in the United States (2002). For commentary on transsexualism and the law, see Richard Green, *Spelling "Relief" for Transsexuals: Employment Discrimination and the Criteria of Sex*, 4 Yale L. & Pol'y Rev. 125 (1985); Anna Kirkland, *Victorious Transsexuals in the Courtroom: A Challenge for Feminist Legal Theory*, 28 L. & Soc. Inquiry 1 (2003); Leslie Pearlman, Comment, *Transsexualism as Metaphor: The Collision of Sex and Gender*, 43 Buff.L.Rev. 835 (1995). For a listing of state statutes permitting an individual to change the designation of his sex on his birth certificate following sex-reassignment surgery, see Pearlman, *supra*, at 851–52 n.75.

5. *Transvestites*: Transvestites should be distinguished from transsexuals and homosexuals: "transvestites * * * are generally male heterosexuals who cross-dress, i.e., dress as females, for sexual arousal rather than social comfort; [unlike transsexuals] both homosexuals and transvestites are content with the sex into which they were born." Ulane v. Eastern Airlines, Inc., 742 F.2d 1081, 1083 n.3 (7th Cir.1984). If Title VII were amended to prohibit discrimination on the basis of "sexual orientation," would transvestites be protected from employment discrimination under such a statute?

6. Is the fact that Congress explicitly excluded homosexuality and bisexuality, as well as transsexuality and transvestitism, from the definitions of a "disability" under the Americans with Disabilities Act relevant to the question of whether the ban on "sex" discrimination in Title VII includes discrimination on the basis of sexual orientation? *See* 42 U.S.C. § 12211(a) (providing that "homosexuality and bisexuality are not impairments and as such are not disabilities under [the ADA]"); 42 U.S.C § 12211(b)(1) (providing that "under [the ADA], the term 'disability' shall not include—transvestism, transsexualism, * * * gender disorders not resulting from physical impairments, or other sexual behavior disorders; * * * "); 42 U.S.C. § 12208 (providing that "[f]or the purposes [of the ADA], the term 'disabled' or 'disability' shall not apply to an individual solely because that individual is a transvestite").

7. *Recent Developments in Rights of Transgendered Employees.* An estimated 1,000 to 2,000 Americans have sex-change operations each year and many of these transsexuals try to continue working for the same employer while going through the transition. *When Harry Becomes Sally: Transgender Issues Increasingly Confront Employers,* 19 Hum. Resources Rep. (BNA) No. 48, at 1321 (Dec. 10, 2001) (citing Janis Walworth, *Transsexual Workers: An Employer's Guide).* This phenomenon has presented employers, employees, and the courts with some unique questions. For example, when workplace restrooms are designated as men's or women's, which restroom should a transsexual use while at work? Does it matter if the employee has completed the transsexual surgery or is just preparing for the operation—by taking hormones and dressing like the opposite sex? What if the employee is not a transsexual but a transvestite who cross-dresses for work?

If the employer designates restrooms according to biological sex, can a formerly male transsexual claim that she was discriminated against when she was not permitted to use the women's restroom? *See* Goins v. West Group, 635 N.W.2d 717 (Minn.2001) (holding that a formerly male transsexual denied use of women's restroom at work had no cause of action under state law prohibiting sexual orientation discrimination). If the employer permits a formerly male transsexual to use the women's restroom at work, do female employees using the same restroom have any basis to complain under discrimination laws? *See* Cruzan v. Special School Dist., #1, 294 F.3d 981 (8th Cir.2002) (holding that a female employee who objected to sharing the employer's women's restroom with a formerly male transsexual had no claim under Title VII for sexual harassment based on a hostile work environment). If the employer requires a formerly male transsexual to use the men's restroom—because it designates restrooms according to biological sex—would male employees have any basis to complain? In this situation, the male employees would be sharing a restroom with an individual who is biologically male but appears to be female, including having female physical characteristics produced by surgery and a regimen of hormones. For an exploration of these issues, see Richard F. Storrow, *Gender Typing in Stereo: The Transgender Dilemma in Employment Discrimination*, 55 Me.L.Rev. 117 (2003).

These sex discrimination claims involving restroom facilities highlight the limitations of existing laws in dealing with the discrimination claims of transgendered employees. As discussed *supra*, Notes 4 and 5, neither Title VII nor the ADA protects transsexuals or transvestites from employment discrimination. Some jurisdictions, however, may allow claims of transgender discrimination to be brought under existing state or local laws prohibiting discrimination on the basis of sex or disability. *See, e.g., Transgendered Employees Are Protected Under Sex, Disability Bias Laws, Agency Says,* 19 Hum. Resources Rep. (BNA) No. 42, at 1164 (Oct. 29, 2001) (reporting that the Massachusetts Commission Against Discrimination interprets state law to permit claims of male-to-female transsexuals to go forward on the basis of sex discrimination—based on nonconformance with sexual stereotypes—and disability discrimination—based on a diagnosis of gender dysphoria).

Some jurisdictions have enacted civil rights statutes and ordinances explicitly directed at transgendered individuals. For example, in 1993 Minnesota enacted civil rights legislation expressly prohibiting discrimination against transgendered individuals, and more than thirty jurisdictions, including Denver, Seattle, Atlanta, and New Orleans have adopted local ordinances that protect transgendered persons from discrimination. *See* 19 Hum. Resources Rep. (BNA) No. 48, at 1322 (Dec. 10, 2001); 19 Hum. Resources Rep. (BNA) No. 44, at 1214 (Nov. 12, 2001). Under a statute enacted in 2001, Rhode Island now prohibits discrimination in employment, housing, credit, and public accommodation on the basis of "gender identity or expression," which is defined as "[a] person's actual or perceived gender, as well as a person's gender identity, gender-related self image, gender-related appearance, or gender-related expression; whether or not that gender identity, gender-related self image, gender-related appearance or gender-related expression is different from that traditionally associated with the person's sex at birth." R.I. Stat. § 28–5–6(14) (2001) (defining protected status in state employment law). How is this different from a law prohibiting discrimination on the basis of sexual orientation? For further discussion of these issues, see Marvin Dunson III, Comment, *Sex, Gender, and Transgender: The Present and Future of Employment Discrimination Law*, 22 Berkeley J.Emp. & Lab.L. 456 (2001).

8. *Federal Legislative Reform Proposals—The Employment Non–Discrimination Act (ENDA)*: Since 1975, Congress has considered—but failed to enact—a number of bills that would amend Title VII to prohibit employment discrimination on the basis of "affectional or sexual orientation." Ulane v. Eastern Airlines, Inc., 742 F.2d 1081, 1085 & 1085 n.11 (7th Cir.1984). *See* Civil Rights Amendments of 1975, H.R. 5452, 94th Cong., 1st Sess. (1975); *see also* Regina L. Stone–Harris, Comment, *Same-Sex Harassment—The Next Step in the Evolution of Sexual Harassment Law Under Title VII*, 28 St.Mary's L.J. 269, 315–24 (1996) (discussing the Employment Non–Discrimination Act). Indeed, federal courts have often used this fact to support the conclusion that Congress did not intend "sex" in Title VII to include "sexual orientation," *see, e.g.*, DeSantis v. Pacific Tel. & Tel. Co., 608 F.2d 327, 329 (9th Cir.1979), or "transsexualism," *see, e.g., Ulane*, 742 F.2d at 1085. To support its view that Title VII does not cover discrimination on the basis of sexual orientation, the EEOC, like the courts, has relied on the lack of any evidence in the legislative history that Congress intended that the term "sex" include "sexual practices." *See* EEOC Dec. 76–75, 19 Fair Empl. Prac.Cas. (BNA) 1823, 1824 (1975). In an attempt to defuse conservative opposition, ENDA would prohibit employers from using quotas to hire or promote homosexuals, or otherwise give homosexuals preferential treatment in employment. *See* Nadya Aswad, *Federal Gay Rights Legislation Is Reintroduced in House, Senate*, 66 U.S.L.W. 2009 (July 1, 1997). Would extending Title VII protection to homosexuals, even without permitting quotas or preferences, encourage more gays, lesbians, and bisexuals to be open, at work, about their sexual orientation?

9. One commentator has argued that "to ensure true equality of opportunity for lesbians and gay men, employers must create a workplace environment free of antigay discrimination and harassment, in which gay and lesbian employees can feel free to come out and be out of the closet." Jeffrey S. Byrne, *Affirmative Action for Lesbians and Gay Men: A Proposal for True Equality of Opportunity and Workforce Diversity*, 11 Yale L. & Pol'y Rev. 47, 47 (1993). Why should identification or expression of one's sexual orientation ever be an issue in the workplace if it is not a requirement of the job? Can we expect an employee to shed her sexuality and sexual identity when she walks into the office or factory? If not, is it fair to require a homosexual employee to remain "in the closet"—to outwardly conform to the dominant culture of heterosexist behavior and values—as a condition of keeping her job? For discussion of some of the costs of concealment of homosexual identity, see Marc A. Fajer, *Can Two Real Men Eat Quiche Together? Storytelling, Gender–Role Stereotypes, and Legal Protection for Lesbians and Gay Men*, 46 U.Miami L.Rev. 511, 591–602 (1992).

10. *Race or Sex Plus Homosexuality:* If a homosexual black male sues his employer under Title VII on the basis of circumstantial evidence of a racially motivated discharge, can the employer successfully rebut a prima facie case with evidence that the discharge was based solely on the employee's homosexuality? In other words, is homophobia a "legitimate, nondiscriminatory reason" for adverse employment action? In *Doe v. City of*

Belleville, 119 F.3d 563 (7th Cir.1997), *cert. granted, judgment vacated*, 523 U.S. 1001, 118 S.Ct. 1183, 140 L.Ed.2d 313 (1998), the employer argued that the evidence showed that the plaintiff was harassed because of his perceived homosexuality, not his sex. The Seventh Circuit, in reviewing the district court's grant of a summary judgment for the employer, refused to "make a definitive finding as to why [the plaintiff's] co-workers harassed him." *Id.* at 594. The court observed:

> The possibility that [the plaintiff's] harassers may have been motivated by more than one type of animus renders this case no different from one in which the employer may have had mixed motives in treating the plaintiff adversely—one motive proscribed by law, another not. The fact that one motive was permissible does not exonerate the employer from liability under Title VII; the employee can still prevail so long as she shows that her sex played a motivating role in the employer's decision. *See* 42 U.S.C. § 2000e–2(m). The same is true here—all that [the plaintiff] need show is that sex was a motivating (not the sole) factor in the harassment. The evidence before us permits that inference, and we cannot just declare that a case is about sexual orientation, rather than sex, simply because homophobia has reared its head along with sexism.

Id.

What evidence would a gay black male need in order to prove that he was treated differently, at least in part, because of his race (a violation of Title VII) rather than solely because of his sexual orientation (not a violation of Title VII)? Or could the plaintiff claim that he was discriminated against because he was both black and gay? *See* Williamson v. A.G. Edwards & Sons, Inc., 876 F.2d 69, 70 (8th Cir.1989) (per curiam) (to survive summary judgment, plaintiff, a black homosexual male, would have to allege facts adequate to show that "similarly situated" white male homosexual employees were treated more favorably), *cert. denied*, 493 U.S. 1089, 110 S.Ct. 1158, 107 L.Ed.2d 1061 (1990).

If discrimination on the basis of sexual orientation were to be prohibited under Title VII, should gay black males constitute a subclass that is protected on the basis that they belong to two minority groups—black and gay? *See generally* Stephen Holden, *In the Margins of Two Minority Cultures*, New York Times, August 23, 1993, at B1. What about lesbians? Should black, homosexual females be considered a subclass of blacks, or of females? Or are they a subclass of homosexuals? How should these types of multiple categories, constructed around different aspects of an individual's identity, affect the analysis of a Title VII case? For an exploration of these issues, see Mary Eaton, *At the Intersection of Gender and Sexual Orientation: Toward Lesbian Jurisprudence*, 3 S.Cal.Rev.L. & Women's Stud. 183 (1994); Francisco Valdes, *Sex and Race in Queer Legal Culture: Ruminations on Identities & Inter-connectivities*, 5 S.Cal.Rev.L. & Women's Stud. 25 (1995). *See also* Note: Intersectionality, in Chapter 2.

11. In his 1992 book *Sex and Reason*, Judge Richard Posner examines the history and regulation of human sexual behavior from the perspective of economic theory. Homosexuality is addressed throughout the book, but at the conclusion of his chapter on "Homosexuality: The Policy Questions," Posner briefly discusses "whether the laws against racial and sexual and

related forms of discrimination perceived as invidious, laws such as Title VII of the Civil Right Act of 1964, should be extended to cover homosexuals." Richard A. Posner, Sex and Reason 322 (1992). Posner suggests that discrimination against homosexuals is not "less, or less harmful, or less irrational" than discrimination against individuals whose status is currently protected by federal antidiscrimination laws. *Id.* at 323. Nevertheless, he concludes that "the question whether to provide legal protection to homosexuals against discrimination in employment and other areas of life is part of a much larger question having little to do with anything special to sexual preference." *Id.* His solution would be to reject all laws prohibiting discrimination in the private workplace. *Id.* Would no antidiscrimination laws be fairer or more efficient than the existing federal statutory scheme which excludes homosexuals from protection? For a critique of Posner's views, see William N. Eskridge, Jr., *A Social Constructionist Critique of Posner's* Sex and Reason: *Steps Toward a Gaylegal Agenda*, 102 Yale L.J. 333, 335–36 (1992) (review essay).

12.   For some comparative perspectives on workplace discrimination on the basis of sexual orientation, see Ronnie Cohen, Shannon O'Byrne & Patricia Maxwell, *Employment Discrimination Based on Sexual Orientation: The American, Canadian and U.K. Responses*, 17 Law & Ineq. 1 (1999).

2.   SEXUAL HARASSMENT BECAUSE OF SEXUAL ORIENTATION

Although homosexuality is not a protected status under Title VII, homosexuals as a class or as individuals are not denied the general protections of the civil rights laws—prohibiting discrimination on the basis of race, color, religion, national origin, sex, age, or disability. *See* Romer v. Evans, 517 U.S. 620, 116 S.Ct. 1620, 1629, 134 L.Ed.2d 855 (1996). Like heterosexual employees, homosexual employees may be victimized in the workplace by quid pro quo or hostile environment sexual harassment; but such harassment is actionable under Title VII only if it occurs "because of sex," not because of sexual orientation. As one court noted:

> People who are harassed *because* they are homosexual (or are perceived as homosexual) are not protected by Title VII any more than are people who are harassed for having brown eyes. However, it is imperative to note that being homosexual does not deprive someone of protection from sexual harassment under Title VII, it is merely irrelevant to it. The issue is and remains whether one is discriminated against because of one's *gender*.

Vandeventer v. Wabash Nat'l Corp., 887 F.Supp. 1178, 1180 (N.D.Ind. 1995). Thus, for example, if a male supervisor discharges a female employee because she refuses to engage in sexual relations, she should have a viable Title VII quid pro quo sexual harassment claim regardless of whether she is heterosexual or homosexual, or even bisexual. Similarly, a lesbian or gay employee who experiences sexual harassment by same-sex co-workers may have a viable hostile environment claim if the harassment occurred because of the plaintiff's sex. *See Oncale v. Sun-*

downer Offshore Services, Inc., 523 U.S. 75, 118 S.Ct. 998, 140 L.Ed.2d 201 (1998), reproduced in Chapter 8, Section B.3.

In many cases of same-sex harassment before *Oncale*, the sexual orientation of the perpetrator or the victim had been a relevant evidentiary issue. *See* Doe v. City of Belleville, 119 F.3d 563, 585–86 (7th Cir.1997) (rejecting the relevance of the harasser's sexual orientation in same-sex harassment cases, and discussing cases from other circuits that relied on evidence that the harasser was homosexual as part of plaintiff's prima facie case), *cert. granted, judgment vacated*, 523 U.S. 1001, 118 S.Ct. 1183, 140 L.Ed.2d 313 (1998). Although the sexual orientation of the plaintiff should be irrelevant in same-sex quid quo pro harassment cases, pre-*Oncale* courts had relied on the sexual orientation of the supervisor to determine whether the harassment would not have occurred "but for" the plaintiff's sex. For example, in *EEOC v. Walden Book Co.*, 885 F.Supp. 1100, 1103–04 (M.D.Tenn.1995), the court held:

> When a homosexual supervisor is making offensive sexual advances to a subordinate of the same sex, and not doing so to employees of the opposite sex, it absolutely is a situation where, but for the subordinate's sex, he would not be subjected to that treatment.

Professor Katherine Franke observed that "in most of the same-sex sexual harassment cases [before *Oncale*] involving a gay harasser, whether quid pro quo or hostile environment cases, courts have held that the conduct violated Title VII because the harasser's sexual orientation provided conclusive evidence of 'but for' causation." Katherine M. Franke, *What's Wrong With Sexual Harassment?* 49 Stan.L.Rev. 691, 713 (1997). The EEOC, too, had taken the position in same-sex sexual harassment cases that "[t]he crucial inquiry is whether the harasser treats a member or members of one sex differently from members of the other sex." 2 EEOC Compl.Man. (CCH) ¶ 13–1, § 615.2(b)(3).

When same-sex harassment appeared to have occurred because of the plaintiff's homosexuality or perceived homosexuality, courts before *Oncale* uniformly dismissed Title VII claims. *See* Dillon v. Frank, 952 F.2d 403 (6th Cir.1992) (unpublished table decision); Carreno v. Local Union No. 226, Int'l Bhd. of Elec. Workers, 1991 WL 261751 (D.Kan. 1991); *but see* Doe v. City of Belleville, 119 F.3d 563 (7th Cir.1997), *cert. granted, judgment vacated,* 523 U.S. 1001, 118 S.Ct. 1183, 140 L.Ed.2d 313 (1998). The EEOC Compliance Manual provides the following example of same-sex harassment that is not subject to Title VII: "If a male supervisor harasses a male employee because of the employee's homosexuality, then the supervisor's conduct would *not* be sexual harassment since it is based on the employee's sexual preference, not on his gender." 2 EEOC Compl.Man. (CCH) ¶ 13–1, § 615.2 example 2.

One consequence of the current federal case law on same-sex harassment is that employers may have an incentive to avoid hiring employees who are openly gay or lesbian or are perceived to be gay or lesbian. Homosexuals who are hired may have an incentive to stay "in the closet" because, as Professor Franke notes:

Gay people in the workplace are caught in a double bind: when a gay male employee is sexually harassed because he is gay, courts feel compelled to hold that Title VII is limited to discrimination on account of sex, not sexual orientation. Yet when a gay male employee is doing the harassing, courts have been inclined to hold that the offensive conduct *is* sex discrimination because of the defendant's sexual orientation; that is, he or she would not have engaged in the conduct but for the sex of the plaintiff. Therefore, the principle that sex is a concept distinct from sexual orientation is invoked to deny protection to targets who are gay, yet the conflation of these two terms is necessary to find a harasser liable under current Title VII doctrine. As such, gay men and lesbians are subject to all of the law's prohibitions and penalties, yet enjoy none of its protections and remedies. * * *

Franke, *supra*, at 733–34 n.215 (citations omitted).

The case of *Dillon v. Frank*, 952 F.2d 403 (6th Cir.1992) (Table), an unpublished table decision available in unofficial reporting services, *see, e.g.*, 1992 WL 5436 (6th Cir. (Mich.)), has been the subject of much commentary. *See, e.g.*, Jo Bennet, *Same-Sex Sexual Harassment*, 6 Law & Sex. 1 (1996); Samuel A. Marcosson, *Harassment on the Basis of Sexual Orientation: A Claim of Sex Discrimination Under Title VII*, 81 Geo.L.J. 1 (1992); Marie Elena Peluso, Note, *Tempering Title VII's Straight Arrow Approach: Recognizing and Protecting Gay Victims of Employment Discrimination*, 46 Vand.L.Rev. 1533, 1540–42 (1993). Dillon was a postal worker who "was taunted, ostracized, and physically beaten by his co-workers because of their belief that he was a homosexual." *Dillon*, 1992 WL 5436, at **1. One coworker called him "fag," said that he "sucks dicks," and eventually assaulted and seriously injured him. *Id.* Circuit Judge Boggs wrote: "What had begun as a one-man band expanded into a full orchestral assault of verbal abuse. Other employees used similar epithets. Graffiti, the last refuge of the courageous, appeared on conveyor belts and Dillon's loading trucks informing the mail center that 'Dillon sucks dicks' and 'Dillon gives head.' "*Id.* Although Dillon's supervisors and union representatives knew about the harassment, no effective action was taken to abate it, and Dillon eventually resigned "upon advice from his psychiatrist." *Id.*

Dillon made two arguments that were rejected by the court. First, he asserted that, under existing Title VII case law,

all extremely unpleasant working environments that arise because of verbal and other abuse regarding sex are proscribed, and that therefore the fact that the harassment in his case was predicated upon a belief that he is a homosexual, rather than specifically on his being male is irrelevant. * * * [H]e was subjected to this abuse relating to homosexuality solely because he was a man, and therefore has stated a claim under Title VII.

Id. at **5. Second, relying on the Court's ruling in *Price Waterhouse v. Hopkins*, 490 U.S. 228, 251, 109 S.Ct. 1775, 1791, 104 L.Ed.2d 268

(1989), "that evidence of * * * sex stereotyping is admissible to prove sex discrimination," Dillon "contended that he was subject to such stereotyping in that he was not deemed 'macho' enough by his co-workers for a man, and that the verbal abuse resulted from this stereotyping." *Dillon*, 1992 WL 5436, at **5. The court concluded that

> Dillon cannot escape our holding, and those of the other circuits, that homosexuality is not an impermissible criteria on which to discriminate with regard to terms and conditions of employment. Dillon's co-workers deprived him of a proper work environment because they believed him to be homosexual. Their comments, graffiti, and assaults were all directed at demeaning him solely because they disapproved vehemently of his alleged homosexuality. These actions, although cruel, are not made illegal by Title VII.

Id. at **8.

Notes and Questions

1. In *Dillon v. Frank*, Circuit Judge Boggs described some alternative legal remedies available to employees in Dillon's position:

> In a perfect world, the "right" to dignified treatment by one's employer and co-workers would be absolute: all workers of the world would unite in being "nice" toward one another. In our less than perfect world, both criminal and tort law may provide workers with protection against cruel harassment by their co-workers. Indeed, some of the actions Dillon complains of seem capable of remedy under both tort and criminal law, such as [the] beating (battery) and his co-workers [sic] taunting and graffiti-writing (intentional infliction of emotional distress). If Dillon can prove that the harassment ever caused him to be immediately apprehensive of another physical assault * * * he can also sue for assault. In fact to the extent that his co-workers and employer wanted to see Dillon quit, he could even sue for tortious interference with contract or employment relationship. The base result, however, is undisturbed; our decision today does not leave those in Dillon's situation without a legal remedy.

1992 WL 5436, at **8. In addition, the court noted that Dillon alleged that "[m]anagement * * * did nothing more than admonish the harassers, and hold meetings detailing the policy against sexual harassment in place at the center. * * * [They] finally threw up their hands in despair, telling Dillon not to waste their time with his complaints and to fight back when taunted." *Id.* at **1. If you were advising an employee in a situation like Dillon's, what course of action would you recommend—suing co-workers or supervisors, appealing (again) to management or the union, fighting back, or resigning? What about Title VII? Is *Dillon* still good law in light of *Oncale v. Sundowner Offshore Services, Inc.* 523 U.S. 75, 118 S.Ct. 998, 140 L.Ed.2d 201 (1998), reproduced in Chapter 8, Section B.3?

2. The Supreme Court in *Oncale* addressed some of the issues that have divided the circuit courts in their analysis of same-sex sexual harassment cases. The Fifth Circuit in *Oncale*, 83 F.3d 118 (5th Cir.1996), did not

rely on the sexual orientation status (actual or perceived) of either the plaintiff or his same-sex harassers; instead the court focused on the fact that both the harassers and victim were the same sex. The Fifth Circuit also did not rely on a rationale that had been adopted in the Fourth Circuit: that the heterosexual status of the harasser could be used as a basis for rejecting the plaintiff's claim. *See, e.g.,* McWilliams v. Fairfax County Bd. of Supervisors, 72 F.3d 1191 (4th Cir.) (holding that proof that the harassers are homosexual is a required element of a same-sex harassment claim under Title VII), *cert. denied,* 519 U.S. 819, 117 S.Ct. 72, 136 L.Ed.2d 32 (1996); Hopkins v. Baltimore Gas & Elec. Co., 77 F.3d 745 (4th Cir.) (same), *cert. denied,* 519 U.S. 818, 117 S.Ct. 70, 136 L.Ed.2d 30 (1996). Instead, the Fifth Circuit rejected the possibility of same-sex harassment claims under any circumstances. The Supreme Court in *Oncale* reversed, holding that sexual harassment of same-sex employees is actionable under Title VII. Do the facts alleged in *Oncale* suggest that the plaintiff—a married man—was harassed because he was perceived to be gay? Or that the harassers were homosexual? Or do the allegations suggest that the harassment occurred because of the harassers' "vulgarity and insensitivity and meanness of spirit." *McWilliams,* 72 F.3d 1191. Is *Oncale* distinguishable from *Dillon*? What effect, if any, should *Oncale* have on claims of a hostile work environment brought by gay or lesbian employees against co-workers or supervisors who harass all homosexuals, male and female, equally?

3. *Post-*Oncale *Developments*: In *Higgins v. New Balance Athletic Shoe, Inc.,* 194 F.3d 252 (1st Cir.1999), the plaintiff alleged that his supervisor and co-workers harassed him because of his homosexuality. The abusive conduct included sexually derogatory remarks and gestures, as well as physical abuse. Although the court acknowledged that the plaintiff "toiled in a wretchedly hostile environment," summary judgment was warranted because the plaintiff presented no legal theory based on probative evidence that the co-workers harassed him because of sex. The court observed,

> We hold no brief for harassment because of sexual orientation; it is a noxious practice, deserving of censure and opprobrium, but we are called upon here to construe a statute as glossed by the Supreme Court, not to make a moral judgment—and we regard it as settled law that, as drafted and authoritatively construed, Title VII does not proscribe harassment simply because of sexual orientation.

Id. at 259. *See also* Bibby v. Philadelphia Coca Cola Bottling Co., 260 F.3d 257, 261 (3d Cir.2001) (holding that Title VII does not prohibit discrimination on the basis of sexual orientation), *cert. denied,* 534 U.S. 1155, 122 S.Ct. 1126, 151 L.Ed.2d 1018 (2002); Simonton v. Runyon, 232 F.3d 33, 35 (2d Cir.2000) (same).

Two theories of Title VII discrimination that the plaintiff in *Higgins* raised for the first time on appeal were deemed forfeited because they had not been presented to the district court. These two theories were (1) the "sex-plus" theory—that the employer treated men who were sexually attracted to other men differently from women who were attracted to other women—and (2) gender stereotyping—that the harassment occurred because the plaintiff did not conform to stereotyped assumptions about masculine behavior. *See supra* Section B.1, Notes 1 and 10. Although the court rejected the plaintiff's "eleventh-hour" arguments as being untimely, the court acknowledged that, with adequate evidence, the theories could establish liability for discrimination for a homosexual plaintiff who suffers workplace harassment. In particular, the court admonished the district court that after the Supreme Court's holding in *Oncale v. Sundowner Offshore Services, Inc.*,

> the standards of liability under Title VII * * * apply to same-sex plaintiffs just as they do to opposite-sex plaintiffs. In other words, just as a woman can ground an action on a claim that men discriminated against her because she did not meet stereotyped expectations of femininity, a man can ground a claim on evidence that other men discriminated against him because he did not meet stereotyped expectations of masculinity.

Id. at 261 n.4. *See also* Spearman v. Ford Motor Co., 231 F.3d 1080 (7th Cir.2000), *cert. denied*, 532 U.S. 995, 121 S.Ct. 1656, 149 L.Ed.2d 638 (2001) (recognizing that a Title VII same-sex harassment case might be brought on the basis of gender stereotyping).

What do you think of the "sex-plus" claim in *Higgins?* Judge Posner observed that "men are more hostile to male homosexuality than they are to lesbianism." Hamm v. Weyauwega Milk Prods., Inc., 332 F.3d 1058, 1067 (7th Cir.2003) (Posner, J., concurring). Would you agree? Do employers and co-workers treat gay men and lesbians differently? The same? Are the similarities or differences based on "gender," "sexuality," or "sex"?

In *Schmedding v. Tnemec Company, Inc.*, 187 F.3d 862 (8th Cir.1999), the Eighth Circuit Court of Appeals relied on *Oncale* to reverse the dismissal of a same-sex sexual harassment claim brought by a plaintiff who alleged that he was "perceived" as being homosexual. The plaintiff alleged that he was

> patted on the buttocks; asked to perform sexual acts; given derogatory notes referring to his anatomy; called names such as "homo" and "jerk off"; and was subject to the exhibition of sexually inappropriate behavior by others including unbuttoning of clothing, scratching of crotches and buttocks; and humping the door frame of [his] office.

Id. at 865. The district court had dismissed the complaint because it alleged discrimination because of "perceived sexual preference," which is not a violation of Title VII. The plaintiff argued on appeal that he had used the phrase "perceived sexual preference" to indicate that "the harassment included rumors that falsely labeled him as homosexual in an effort to debase his masculinity * * *." *Id.* The court concluded,

> We do not think that, simply because some of the harassment alleged by [the plaintiff] includes taunts of being homosexual or other epithets connoting homosexuality, the complaint is thereby transformed from one alleging harassment based on sex to one alleging harassment based on sexual orientation. We note that in *Oncale* * * * which dealt with claims of same-sex harassment by heterosexual males against a heterosexual male plaintiff, the alleged harassment included the fact that plaintiff was taunted as being homosexual.

Id.

Is the court in *Schmedding* saying that homophobic harassment of heterosexuals by heterosexuals is harassment because of sex? Or that homophobic harassment—as a form of gender-stereotyping—is "sexual" harassment, regardless of the identity of the harasser and victim? Does the case appear to provide Title VII protection from homophobic harassment only to heterosexuals who are falsely perceived as being homosexuals? Or does the case permit a broader adoption of a gender-stereotyping approach that would protect all employees who suffer severe and pervasive homophobic harassment? *See generally* Jennifer A. Drobac, *The* Oncale *Opinion: A Pansexual Response*, 30 McGeorge L.Rev. 1269 (1999); Toni Lester, *Protecting the Gender Nonconformist from the Gender Police—Why the Harassment of Gays and Other Gender Nonconformists Is a Form of Sex Discrimination in Light of the Supreme Court's Decision in* Oncale v. Sundowner, 92 N.M.L.Rev. 89 (1999).

4.   In *Nichols v. Azteca Restaurant Enterprises*, 256 F.3d 864 (9th Cir.2001), the court applied the rationale of *Price Waterhouse v. Hopkins*, 490 U.S. at 250–51, 109 S.Ct. at 1790–91, to find that same-sex harassment based on the plaintiff's failure to conform to gender stereotypes is actionable under Title VII. Although the *Nichols* case does not indicate whether the plaintiff was homosexual, his male coworkers and a male supervisor "mocked [him] for walking and carrying his serving tray 'like a woman,' " and called him names such as "faggot" and "fucking female whore." 256 F.3d at 870. The court ruled that the reasoning of *Hopkins*—which held that it was sex discrimination for an accounting firm to deny partnership to a woman because her dress and behavior was too masculine—"applies with equal force to a man who is discriminated against for acting too feminine." *Id.* at 874. The *Nichols* court concluded that the male-on-male harassment experienced by the plaintiff was harassment "because of sex"—and thus actionable—since it was based on an assumption that he "did not act as a man should act." *Id. See also* Centola v. Potter, 183 F.Supp.2d 403, 408–11 (D.Mass.2002) (ruling that gay postal worker, who never disclosed his sexual orientation at work, can sue for sexual harassment where offensive homophobic conduct was allegedly based on harassers' beliefs that plaintiff was "impermissibly feminine for a man").

Nichols would appear to provide Title VII protection to some gay men and lesbians, as well as to straight men and women who defy gender stereotypes in their dress and conduct while in the workplace. But does it, in effect, extend Title VII protection to homosexuals generally, or to individuals—regardless of their sexual orientation—who are perceived to be homosexual, or just to heterosexuals who do not conform to gender stereotypes at work? *See* Recent Case, 115 Harv.L.Rev. 2074 (2002). Even where courts have recognized claims based on a gender stereotype theory, plaintiffs have had difficulty surviving a motion for summary judgment. *See, e.g.,* Hamm v. Weyauwega Milk Prods., 199 F.Supp.2d 878, 888–91 (E.D.Wis.2002) (analyzing cases of same-sex homophobic hostile work environment brought under a theory of perceived nonconformance with gender stereotypes and finding that plaintiff did not have sufficient evidence to survive a motion for summary judgment); Ianetta v. Putnam Investments, Inc., 183 F.Supp.2d 415, 420–23 (D.Mass.2002) (same).

5. Should there be a legal distinction between verbal gay-baiting—verbal taunting—and a sexual assault? Should it matter whether the victim is an openly declared homosexual? For example, if the victim is openly gay and is subjected to repeated physical sexual abuse from male heterosexual co-workers and supervisors, is the employer liable for hostile work environment under Title VII? After *Oncale*, does it matter that the nature of the physical abuse was sexual? Should the employer be able to defeat the claim on the ground that the conduct was because of the victim's sexual orientation, not because of his sex? Is this case different from *Oncale?* If, unlike the situation in *Oncale,* both men and women were present in the workplace, could the victim successfully argue that he was subjected to working conditions that his female co-workers did not have to endure? For conflicting perspectives on these issues, see the plurality, concurring, and dissenting opinions in *Rene v. MGM Grand Hotel*, 305 F.3d 1061 (9th Cir.2002) (en banc), *cert. denied*, 538 U.S. 922, 123 S.Ct. 1573, 155 L.Ed.2d 313 (2003). *See also* Recent Case, 116 Harv.L.Rev. 1889 (2003) (critiquing *Rene*).

6. *Retaliation*: If an employee, who is perceived to be a lesbian, is fired for complaining about homophobic workplace harassment by her same-sex co-workers, can she bring a Title VII claim for retaliation even though she may not have been entitled to bring a Title VII claim based on the underlying harassing conduct? Title VII retaliation claims are discussed in Chapter 15. In *Bianchi v. Philadelphia*, 183 F.Supp.2d 726 (E.D.Pa.2002), a city firefighter complained to his superiors when he experienced harassment with homophobic content from same-sex subordinates who perceived that he was gay. The court held that, under the rationale of *Oncale*, the plaintiff could not establish an actionable sex-based harassment claim under Title VII because he could not show that his harassers were either (1) motivated by sexual desire, (2) motivated by hostility toward the presence of men in the workplace, or (3) motivated by a belief that he failed to conform to masculine stereotypes. *Id.* at 734–35 (discussing *Oncale* and citing Bibby v. Philadelphia Coca Cola Bottling Co., 260 F.3d 257, 262–63 (3d Cir.2001), *cert. denied*, 534 U.S. 1155, 122 S.Ct. 1126, 151 L.Ed.2d 1018 (2002)). Nevertheless, despite losing his sexual harassment claim, the plaintiff was permitted to go to the jury on his Title VII retaliation claim and a First Amendment claim. The jury awarded him $1.2 million in back pay, front pay, and compensatory damages for being fired in retaliation for his complaints about harassment. *Philadelphia Fireman Perceived as Gay Wins $1.2 Million for Firing Linked to Complaints,* 20 Human Resources Rep. (BNA) No. 11, at 299 (Mar. 18, 2002).

A similar retaliation claim was rejected by the Court of Appeals for the Seventh Circuit in *Hamner v. St. Vincent Hospital & Health Care Center,* 224 F.3d 701 (7th Cir.2000). The plaintiff in *Hamner* was a homosexual who claimed that he was discharged from his job as a nurse in retaliation for filing a grievance complaining about sexual harassment by a male supervisor who was a doctor in his unit. At the close of trial, the magistrate judge granted the hospital's motion for judgment as a matter of law. On appeal, the Seventh Circuit affirmed on the ground that, while the plaintiff had a sincere, good faith belief that he had suffered harassment because of sex, his belief was not objectively reasonable as a matter of law: "The reality is that there is a distinction between one's sex and one's sexuality under Title VII, and that statute only prohibits employers from harassing employees because of their sex." *Id.* at 707. The fact that the plaintiff perceived the harassment as homophobic was fatal to his retaliation claim. How can you explain the different outcomes in *Bianchi* and *Hamner*?

7. One commentator, who supports extending workplace protections to homosexuals, has argued that "Title VII as it currently stands is not the appropriate vehicle for remedying same-sex sexual harassment." Carolyn Grose, *Same-Sex Sexual Harassment: Subverting the Heterosexist Paradigm of Title VII*, 7 Yale J.L. & Feminism 375, 377 (1995). In urging that new legislation is necessary to "provide[] protection for lesbians and gay men because they are lesbians and gay men, not because they have been harassed by lesbians and gay men," Professor Grose observed that

> [a]s long as Title VII excludes homosexuality as a protected category, any attempt to use Title VII to regulate some same-sex interaction in the workplace will send a dangerous mixed message: It is okay to make a workplace miserable for a dyke or a faggot, or for someone who looks or acts like a dyke or a faggot, but it is not okay to make a workplace miserable for a straight man or woman, or for someone who looks or act like a straight man or woman.

Id. at 397, 388. Do you think that Title VII, interpreted in this way, would be constitutional as applied?

8. Another commentator asserts that the cases on sexual orientation discrimination "exemplif[y] a heterosexist judiciary subjectively and discriminatorily applying the law in a manner that disadvantages gay people." E. Gary Spitko, *He Said, He Said: Same–Sex Sexual Harassment Under Title VII and the "Reasonable Heterosexist" Standard*, 18 Berkeley J.Emp. & Lab.L. 56, 76 (1997). Professor Spitko concludes, therefore, that "proscription of same-sex sexual harassment should come only after Congress expressly prohibits employment discrimination on the basis of sexual orientation, [thus] removing an employer's financial incentive to discriminate on the basis of sexual orientation." *Id.* at 96. If it is true that judges (or juries) have heterosexist biases that affect their decisions involving homosexual plaintiffs and defendants, will a new federal statute prohibiting sexual orientation discrimination make much difference in the adjudication of these types of cases? To what extent are the decisions Spitko criticizes sound applications of principles of statutory interpretation and to what extent are they a measure of homophobia? As you read the next section, consider whether they would have come out differently if they were first decided now, after *Lawrence v. Texas*, 539 U.S. 558, 123 S.Ct. 2472, 156 L.Ed.2d 508 (2003). What about Justice Scalia's assertion in *Lawrence* that there is a "law-profession culture" removed from American culture? *Id.* at ___, 123 S.Ct. at 2496–97 (Scalia, J., concurring). Would Professor Spitko be likely to agree with Justice Scalia's claim that the legal profession "has largely signed on to the so-called homosexual agenda"? *Id.* at 2496.

C. PROTECTION OF HOMOSEXUAL CONDUCT AND STATUS UNDER THE CONSTITUTION

Gay men and lesbians employed in government jobs have sometimes relied on the Constitution to challenge adverse employment decisions based on sexual orientation. These § 1983 claims, primarily based on the Equal Protection Clause, but also asserting other constitutional bases such as the First Amendment, have had mixed success. In 2003, in *Lawrence v. Texas,* 539 U.S. 558, 123 S.Ct. 2472, 156 L.Ed.2d 508 (2003), the Supreme Court decided a constitutional issue with symbolic importance for proponents of gay civil rights laws generally, as well as with potential legal ramifications for § 1983 discrimination claims brought by homosexuals in government employment. In *Lawrence,* the Court struck down, by a 6–3 majority, a Texas sodomy statute that criminalized intimate sexual conduct between consenting same-sex adults. Five justices joined Justice Kennedy's opinion to overrule the Court's decision in *Bowers v. Hardwick,* 478 U.S. 186, 106 S.Ct. 2841, 92 L.Ed.2d 140 (1986), on substantive due process grounds. Justice O'Connor concurred in the judgment in *Lawrence* on equal protection grounds, and Justice Scalia and Justice Thomas wrote dissenting opinions. *Lawrence,* 539 U.S. at ___, ___, ___, 123 S.Ct. at 2484 (O'Connor, J., concurring), 2488 (Scalia, J., dissenting), 2498 (Thomas, J., dissenting).

In *Bowers,* the Supreme Court had held that the Due Process Clause of the Fourteenth Amendment did not prohibit states from criminalizing homosexual sodomy. The Court had refused to extend constitutional privacy rights, previously recognized in abortion and contraception cases, among others, to strike down a Georgia criminal statute prohibiting oral or anal intercourse between consenting adults. The holding of *Bowers,* however, was expressly limited to conduct between same-sex partners. *Id.* at 188 n.2, 106 S.Ct. 2842 n.2. In overruling *Bowers,* the Court acknowledged that in the seventeen years between *Bowers* and *Lawrence,* the *Bowers* case had received "substantial and continuing" criticism, "disapproving of its reasoning in all respects, not just as to its historical assumptions." *Lawrence,* 359 U.S. at ___, 123 S.Ct. at 2483. The *Lawrence* Court recognized, "an emerging awareness that liberty gives substantial protection to adult persons in deciding how to conduct their private lives in matters pertaining to sex." *Id.* at ___, 123 S.Ct. at 2480. According to the majority, this "substantive guarantee of liberty" under the Due Process Clause "presumes an autonomy of self that includes freedom of thought, belief, expression, and certain intimate conduct." *Id.* at ___, 123 S.Ct. at 2482, 2475. The potential significance of *Lawrence v. Texas* for antidiscrimination law is suggested by the Court's observation that

> [w]hen homosexual conduct is made criminal by the law of the State, that declaration in and of itself is an invitation to subject homosexual persons to discrimination both in the public and in the private spheres. The central holding of *Bowers* has been brought in question

by this case * * *. Its continuance as precedent demeans the lives of homosexual persons.

Id. at ___, 123 S.Ct. at 2482.

Before *Lawrence v. Texas*, and despite the apparent antihomosexual significance of *Bowers v. Hardwick*, some federal judges were receptive to employment discrimination claims by public employees who alleged a denial of equal protection on the basis of their status as homosexuals. *See, e.g.*, Jantz v. Muci, 759 F.Supp. 1543, 1551 (D.Kan.1991) (holding that, under equal protection analysis, "a governmental classification based on an individual's sexual orientation is inherently suspect"), *rev'd on other grounds*, 976 F.2d 623 (10th Cir.1992), *cert. denied*, 508 U.S. 952, 113 S.Ct. 2445, 124 L.Ed.2d 662 (1993); *see also* Nabozny v. Podlesny, 92 F.3d 446 (7th Cir.1996) (applying rational basis review to hold that a student can proceed with his claim that he was denied equal protection when school administrators permitted other students continually to harass and assault him on the basis of his sexual orientation). *See generally* Nan D. Hunter, *Life After* Hardwick, 27 Harv.C.R.-C.L.L.Rev. 531, 531–32 (1992).

In 1996, a federal jury found that Iowa State University had denied a professor's right to equal protection under the Fourteenth Amendment by denying him tenure because he was gay. The jury awarded the plaintiff $325,000 for back pay, future pay, benefits, and emotional distress. Higginson v. Haggard, No.4–92–CV–30751 (D.C.S.Iowa 1996), 15 Empl.Rel.Wkly. (BNA) 109 (1997).

The equal protection jurisprudence in this area was influenced by several widely publicized equal protection cases involving homosexuals discharged from the military or the military academies. *See* Steffan v. Perry, 41 F.3d 677 (D.C.Cir.1994) (equal protection challenge brought by cadet discharged from the Naval Academy for admitting he was a homosexual); Watkins v. United States Army, 847 F.2d 1329 (9th Cir. 1988) (opinion withdrawn), *aff'd en banc*, 875 F.2d 699 (9th Cir.1989), *cert. denied*, 498 U.S. 957, 111 S.Ct. 384, 112 L.Ed.2d 395 (1990). In *Watkins*, in a (subsequently withdrawn) majority opinion, Circuit Judge Norris found that the Army's exclusionary policy for homosexuals as applied to Perry Watkins—a fourteen-year veteran who openly acknowledged his homosexuality—violated his right to equal protection. Although the Ninth Circuit's subsequent *en banc* decision relied on the doctrine of equitable estoppel to keep the Army from denying Watkins the right to re-enlist, Judge Norris concurred in the result because, he argued, "Watkins is entitled to relief because the Army denied him the equal protection of the laws by discharging and refusing to reenlist him solely on the basis of his homosexuality." 875 F.2d at 711.

In arguing that Perry Watkins belonged to a suspect class deserving heightened scrutiny under equal protection analysis, Judge Norris wrote,

I have no trouble concluding that sexual orientation is immutable for the purposes of equal protection doctrine. Although the causes of homosexuality are not fully understood, scientific research indicates that we have little control over our sexual orientation and that, once acquired, our sexual orientation is largely impervious to change. Scientific proof aside, it seems appropriate to ask whether heterosexuals feel capable of changing their sexual orientation. Would heterosexuals living in a city that passed an ordinance burdening those who engaged in or desired to engage in sex with persons of the opposite sex find it easy not only to abstain from heterosexual activity but also to shift the object of their sexual desires to persons of the same sex? It may be that some heterosexuals and homosexuals can change their sexual orientation through extensive therapy, neurosurgery or shock treatment. But the possibility of such a difficult and traumatic change does not make sexual orientation "mutable" for equal protection purposes. To express the same idea under the alternative formulation, I conclude that allowing the government to penalize the failure to change such a central aspect of individual and group identity would be abhorrent to the values animating the constitutional ideal of equal protection of the laws.

Watkins, 875 F.2d at 726 (Norris, J., concurring). For a perceptive discussion of the social and political significance of the Perry Watkins' story as an example of the relevance of narrative scholarship for expanding the rights of gays and lesbians, see William N. Eskridge, Jr., *Gaylegal Narratives*, 46 Stan.L.Rev. 607 (1994). For further discussion of the treatment of gays and lesbians in the military, *see* Martha Chamallas, *The New Gender Panic: Reflections on Sex Scandals and the Military*, 83 Minn.L.Rev. 305, 364–73 (1998).

The status of homosexuals in public employment, as well as in the military, was constantly contested in the courts and the executive branches of government in the years following *Bowers v. Hardwick*. For example, in *Padula v. Webster*, 822 F.2d 97 (D.C.Cir.1987), the court relied on *Bowers* to reject an equal protection challenge to the FBI's exclusionary policy regarding "practicing homosexuals." In 1993, President Clinton adopted a "Don't ask, don't tell" policy for homosexuals in the armed forces, which was subsequently codified in "a more antihomosexual version of the 'don't tell' part of the administration's policy." Eskridge, *supra*, 46 Stan.L.Rev. at 610 n.13 (citing 10 U.S.C. § 654(b)). Perceptions about the growing political power of gay and lesbian activists provoked a backlash in some communities, resulting in the enactment and judicial approval of laws intended to prohibit extending additional legal protections or preferential treatment to homosexuals. *See, e.g.*, Equality Found. of Greater Cincinnati, Inc., v. City of Cincinnati, 128 F.3d 289 (6th Cir.1997), *cert. denied*, 525 U.S. 943, 119 S.Ct. 365, 142 L.Ed.2d 302 (1998).

This clash between those who wanted expanded civil rights for homosexuals and those who wanted to limit them or deny them entirely, resulted in another significant constitutional challenge before the Supreme Court addressing the status of homosexuals in American social and political life. In *Romer v. Evans*, 517 U.S. 620, 116 S.Ct. 1620, 134 L.Ed.2d 855 (1996), in a 6–3 decision, the Supreme Court struck down, on equal protection grounds, a 1992 Colorado constitutional amendment, adopted by statewide referendum, that "prohibit[ed] all legislative, executive or judicial action at any level of state or local government designed to protect the named class * * * [of] homosexual persons or gays and lesbians." *Id.* at 624, 116 S.Ct. at 1623. Writing for the majority, Justice Kennedy found that the law—Amendment 2—produced a "[s]weeping and comprehensive * * * change in legal status" of homosexuals:

> Homosexuals, by state decree, are put in a solitary class with respect to transactions and relations in both the private and governmental spheres. The amendment withdraws from homosexuals, but no others, specific legal protection from the injuries caused by discrimination, and it forbids reinstatement of these laws and policies.

Id. at 627, 116 S.Ct. at 1625.

The Court ruled that "Amendment 2 fails, indeed defies, even [the] conventional inquiry" for upholding a legislative classification under the Equal Protection Clause:

> First, the amendment has the peculiar property of imposing a broad and undifferentiated disability on a single named group, an exceptional and * * * invalid form of legislation. Second, its sheer breadth is so discontinuous with the reasons offered for it that the amendment seems inexplicable by anything but animus toward the class that it affects; it lacks a rational relationship to legitimate state interests.

Id. at 632, 116 S.Ct. at 1627. By relying on rational basis review, however, the Court in *Romer* avoided addressing whether Amendment 2 "burdens a fundamental right [or] targets a suspect class." *Id.* In his dissent in *Romer,* Justice Scalia relied on *Bowers v. Hardwick* to argue that "[i]f it is constitutionally permissible for a State to make homosexual conduct criminal, surely it is constitutionally permissible for a State to enact other laws merely disfavoring homosexual conduct." *Id.* at 641, 116 S.Ct. at 1631. Now that *Bowers v. Hardwick* has been overruled by *Lawrence v. Texas,* the premise for this particular argument by Justice Scalia is no longer valid. In *Lawrence,* consistent with the rationale of his dissent in *Romer,* Justice Scalia chastised the Court for "tak[ing] sides in the culture war," *Lawrence,* 539 U.S. at ___, 123 S.Ct. at 2497 (Scalia, J., dissenting), and he asserted that "I would no more *require* a State to criminalize homosexual acts—or, for that matter, display *any* moral disapprobation of them—than I would *forbid* it to do so." *Id.* at ___, 123 S.Ct. at 2497 (Scalia, J., dissenting).

Although homosexuals are not protected under Title VII from employment discrimination on the basis of their sexual orientation, under *Romer v. Evans,* the Constitution will not allow states—out of a " 'bare * * * desire to harm a politically unpopular group' "—to pass laws or constitutional amendments that make it "more difficult" for homosexuals as a class "to seek aid from the government." *Id.* at 634, 635, 116 S.Ct. at 1628 (citing U.S. Dep't of Agric. v. Moreno, 413 U.S. 528, 534, 93 S.Ct. 2821, 2826, 37 L.Ed.2d 782 (1973)). As one commentator observed, "[a]lthough the Supreme Court's landmark decision in *Romer v. Evans* should remove one formidable obstacle in the path of gay civil rights legislation, the decision itself does not guarantee the enactment of new antidiscrimination laws; the battle for gay civil rights thus continues." Jane S. Schacter, *Skepticism, Culture and the Gay Civil Rights Debate in a Post–Civil–Rights Era*, 110 Harv.L.Rev. 684, 684 (1997) (book review).

Romer clearly has had an impact on employment discrimination claims brought by gay public employees. For example, in *Quinn v. Nassau County Police Department*, 53 F.Supp.2d 347 (E.D.N.Y.1999), the court ruled that the Equal Protection Clause of the Fourteenth Amendment protects public employees from sexual harassment on the basis of their sexual orientation. The plaintiff, a police officer who was gay, had experienced over nine years of anti-gay abuse by his co-workers— conduct that he claimed his supervisors were aware of and either failed to stop or participated in. The plaintiff brought a claim under 42 U.S.C. § 1983. Relying on the Supreme Court's equal protection analysis in *Romer v. Evans*, the court upheld a $380,000 verdict for the plaintiff and denied the defendants' motion for judgment as a matter of law. Significantly, the court distinguished both Title VII cases and the cases involving equal protection challenges to sexual orientation discrimination in the military. *Id.* at 357–59. Applying the "rational basis test" from *Romer*, the court noted that "government action in a civil rather than a military setting cannot survive a rational basis review when it is motivated by irrational fear and prejudice towards homosexuals." *Id.* at 357. The court concluded that "the Equal Protection Clause protects similarly situated individuals from invidious and irrational discrimination based on sexual orientation." *Id.* at 359.

Does Justice O'Connor's concurring opinion in *Lawrence v. Texas,* 539 U.S. at ___, 123 S.Ct. at 2484, lend support to the court's equal protection analysis in *Quinn?* In *Lawrence,* Justice O'Connor declined to join the majority in overruling *Bowers v. Hardwick,* a case in which she had joined in the opinion of the Court. *See id.* at ___, 123 S.Ct. at 2484. Nevertheless, she concurred in the judgment of the Court in *Lawrence,* finding the Texas sodomy statute unconstitutional under the Equal Protection Clause. Justice O'Connor noted that, unlike the criminal statute at issue in *Bowers,* the Texas statute criminalized only homosexual sodomy and not heterosexual sodomy as well. *See id.* at ___, 123 S.Ct. at 2485–86. She reasoned, "While it is true that the law applies only to conduct, the conduct targeted by this law is conduct that is closely correlated with being homosexual. Under such circumstances, Texas' sodomy law is targeted at more than conduct. It is instead directed toward gay persons as a class." *Id.* at ___, 123 S.Ct. at 2486–87. Relying in part on *Romer v. Evans,* she concluded that "[m]oral disapproval of this group [homosexuals], like a bare desire to harm the group, is an interest that is insufficient to satisfy rational basis review under the Equal Protection Clause." *Id.* at ___, 123 S.Ct. at 2486. The Court in *Lawrence,* however, did not rely on the Equal Protection Clause to strike down the Texas sodomy statute, choosing instead a broader rationale under the Due Process Clause. *Id.* at ___, 123 S.Ct. at 2482. Considering the significance of the equal protection analysis of *Romer v. Evans* for gay rights antidiscrimination claims in public employment, does the substantive due process rationale of the Court in *Lawrence v. Texas* provide additional legitimacy to arguments in support of such claims? Or are there any limits to the "liberty" interest articulated in *Lawrence?*

Public employees discriminated against because of their homosexual status have also brought First Amendment claims. In *Shahar v. Bowers,* 114 F.3d 1097 (11th Cir.1997) (en banc) (8–4 decision), *cert. denied,* 522 U.S. 1049, 118 S.Ct. 693, 139 L.Ed.2d 638 (1998), the attorney general of Georgia withdrew a job offer to a lesbian attorney when he learned that she planned to be "married" to her same-sex partner in a ceremony she described as a "Jewish, lesbian-feminist out-door wedding." *Id.* at 1100. After lengthy litigation over Shahar's First Amendment rights as a public employee to engage in intimate association or expressive association free from employer interference, the Eleventh Circuit concluded:

> Particularly considering this Attorney General's many years of experience and Georgia's recent legal history [with *Bowers v. Hardwick*], we cannot say that he was unreasonable to think that Shahar's acts were likely to cause the public to be confused and to question the Law Department's credibility; to interfere with the Law Department's ability to handle certain controversial matters, including enforcing the law against homosexual sodomy; and to endanger working relationships inside the Department. We also cannot say that the Attorney General was unreasonable to lose confidence in Shahar's ability to make good judgments as a lawyer with the Law Department.

> We stress in this case the sensitive nature of the pertinent professional employment. And we hold that the Attorney General's interest—that is, the State of Georgia's interest—as an employer in promoting the efficiency of the Law Department's important public service does outweigh Shahar's personal associational interests.

Id. at 1110. Is *Shahar* still good law after *Lawrence v. Texas?*

D. ALTERNATIVE SOURCES OF EMPLOYMENT RIGHTS FOR HOMOSEXUALS

A growing number of states and municipalities have passed legislation prohibiting discrimination on the basis of sexual orientation in both public and private employment. In addition, some governors have issued executive orders, and other state officers have implemented policies, that prohibit sexual orientation discrimination in state employment or in certain state agencies. Union contracts and employer policies are other potential sources of rights for gay and lesbian employees. These and other sources of rights are discussed in the notes and questions that follow.

Notes and Questions

1. *State Constitutional Protections*: States may interpret their own constitutional guarantees of due process, equal protection, and freedom of association to provide broader rights than are afforded under the United States Constitution. *See, e.g.*, Gay Law Students Ass'n v. Pacific Tel. & Tel. Co., 24 Cal.3d 458, 474–75, 156 Cal.Rptr. 14, 24, 595 P.2d 592, 602 (Cal. 1979) (holding that "the California Constitution precludes a public utility's management from automatically excluding all homosexuals from consideration for employment positions"). In addition, some states may have additional protections not found in the federal constitution. For example, the California Constitution has an expansive right of privacy that has been interpreted to bar a private employer from using questions regarding an applicant's sexual orientation on a job screening test. Soroka v. Dayton Hudson Corp., 1 Cal.Rptr.2d 77 (Cal.App.1991), *review dismissed as moot*, 24 Cal.Rptr.2d 587, 862 P.2d 148 (Cal.1993).

2. *General State and Local Nondiscrimination Laws:* By 2003, the District of Columbia and fourteen states, more than 100 municipalities, and over 20 counties, had enacted laws or ordinances that protect individuals from discrimination in public and private employment on the basis of sexual orientation. Human Rights Campaign, Equality in the States: Gay, Lesbian, Bisexual and Transgender Americans and State Laws and Legislation in 2003, 8 (June 27, 2003); Human Rights Campaign, The State of the Workplace: For Lesbian, Gay, Bisexual and Transgender Americans 2002 (cited in 21 Hum. Resources Rep. (BNA) No. 20, at 554 (May 26, 2003). Many of these enactments are part of comprehensive laws prohibiting discrimination in employment, housing, public accommodations, education, and other essential services. The states that had adopted some form of statutory protection against discrimination in employment on the basis of sexual orientation by 2003 were California, Connecticut, Hawaii, Maryland, Massachusetts, Minnesota, Nevada, New Hampshire, New Jersey, New Mexico, New York, Rhode Island, Vermont, and Wisconsin. *See* Equality in the States, *supra* at 8. *See generally* Thomas H. Barnard & Timothy J. Downing, *Emerging Law on Sexual Orientation and Employment*, 29 U.Mem.L.Rev. 555 (1999); Jane S. Schacter, *The Gay Civil Rights Debate in the States: Decoding the Discourse of Equivalents*, 29 Harv.C.R.-C.L.L.Rev. 283 (1994). For a report on the effects of state gay rights laws, see Government Accounting Office, Sexual Orientation Based Employment Discrimination: States' Experience With Statutory Prohibitions. Since 1997 (2000) (finding that sexual orientation complaints were a small percentage of the employment discrimination claims brought in the District of Columbia and the eleven states that then had laws prohibiting employment discrimination on the basis of sexual orientation) (cited in 18 Hum. Resources Rep. (BNA) No.18, at 499 (May 8, 2000).

If an employer refuses to hire an individual who is openly gay, and the applicant brings a claim under a state civil rights statute that prohibits employment discrimination on the basis of sexual orientation, can the employer defend its decision on First Amendment grounds? Suppose the employer is the sole proprietor of a small business who asserts that homosexuality is morally repugnant to her and she does not wish to associate with homosexuals in her work. Would *Boy Scouts of America v. Dale*, 530 U.S. 640, 120 S.Ct. 2446, 147 L.Ed.2d 554 (2000), provide a potential constitutional argument for the employer? *Dale* held that the application of New Jersey's public accommodation law to require the Boy Scouts to accept a gay activist as a scoutmaster violated the group's First Amendment right of "expressive association." How is an employer's freedom to select its employees different from a private association's freedom to select its members and leaders? Do employment discrimination laws regulate conduct or speech? *See, e.g.,* Boy Scouts of America v. Wyman, 335 F.3d 80, 93 (2d Cir.2003) (finding that "Connecticut's Gay Rights Law regulates membership and employment policies as conduct, not as expression and, as such, is not obviously viewpoint discriminatory"). *See also* Dale Carpenter, *Expressive Association and Anti–Discrimination Law After* Dale: *A Tripartite Approach*, 85 Minn.L.Rev. 1515 (2001).

3. *"Reverse" Sexual Orientation Discrimination:* In a novel claim for sexual orientation discrimination brought under the New York City Human Rights Law, the court agreed that a heterosexual plaintiff failed to prove that she had experienced a hostile work environment on the basis of her sexual orientation. Brennan v. Metropolitan Opera Ass'n, 284 A.D.2d 66, 729 N.Y.S.2d 77 (2001). The female plaintiff had objected to the workplace display of photographs of nude men and the sexual banter among gay co-workers at the opera house. The court rejected her hostile environment claim under the local ordinance, which prohibited discrimination on the basis of sexual orientation, because the offending conduct was neither severe enough to be actionable harassment nor was it based on her heterosexual orientation. The plaintiff had previously failed to prove actionable sexual harassment under Title VII. *See* Brennan v. Metropolitan Opera Ass'n, 192 F.3d 310 (2d Cir.1999). What arguments could you make that heterosexual employees should or should not be protected under laws enacted to prohibit discrimination on the basis of "sexual orientation"?

4. *Government Employment Nondiscrimination Policies:* In 1973—the year that the American Psychiatric Association formally acknowledged that homosexuality was not a mental disease—the United States Civil Service Commission ruled that homosexuality could not be used as the sole basis for denying a person employment with the federal government. *See* Nan D. Hunter, *Life After* Hardwick, 27 Harv.C.R.-C.L.L.Rev. 531, 539 (1992) (citing Ashton v. Civiletti, 613 F.2d 923, 927 (D.C.Cir.1979)). On May 28, 1998, President Clinton amended Executive Order 11478, Equal Employment Opportunity in Federal Government, "to prohibit discrimination based on sexual orientation" in federal employment. Exec. Order No. 13,087, 63 Fed.Reg. 30,097 (1998). On June 23, 2000, President Clinton issued Executive Order 13,160, which prohibits "discrimination on the basis of race, sex, color, national origin, disability, religion, age, sexual orientation, and status as a parent" in "a Federally conducted education or training program or activity." Exec. Order No. 13,160, 65 Fed.Reg. 39,773 (2000). The order excludes members of the armed forces and students in military academies.

Many employers, both public and private, now offer health and other employment benefits to spouses and domestic partners of employees. Would it be constitutional under the Equal Protection Clause for a public employer to extend spousal health benefits to the same-sex domestic partners of its employees but not to unmarried opposite-sex domestic partners? *See* Irizarry v. Board of Educ., City of Chicago, 251 F.3d 604 (7th Cir.2001).

5. *Collective Bargaining Agreements*: Homosexual employees can have broader procedural and substantive protections under collective bargaining agreements than under Title VII. For example, an employee covered by a collective bargaining agreement can secure the support of the union in processing grievances, thus avoiding court costs and attorney's fees. The grievant can obtain relief in a considerably shorter time than is possible in a Title VII lawsuit, and she does not have to face the technical requirements of a Title VII action or defeat her employer's summary judgment motion. If the harasser is also covered by the agreement, both the victim and the harasser are protected by the duty of fair representation.

Collective bargaining agreements and grievance procedures can protect employees from antigay harassment as well as from adverse employment actions such as hiring and firing. *See, e.g.*, Charter Communications Ent. 1, L.P. v. International Bhd. of Elec. Workers, Local 399, 114 Lab.Arb. (BNA) 769 (2000) (Kelly, Arb.) (finding that an employer had just cause in discharging an employee accused of harassing a gay co-worker in violation of a sexual harassment policy in the company handbook). Although unions initially faced employer resistance to incorporating protections for homosexual employees in collective bargaining agreements, more recently major unions in both the public and private sectors have succeeded in obtaining provisions in collective bargaining agreements that go beyond nondiscrimination to extend employment benefits to same-sex domestic partners. *Compare* James B. Stewart, *Coming Out at Chrysler*, New Yorker, July 21, 1997, at 38 (describing the early, failed efforts of a gay electrician to get a nondiscrimination provision protecting homosexuals included in a three-year contract between Chrysler and the United Auto Workers), *with UAW, Automakers Agree on Extending Health Benefits to Domestic Partners*, 18 Hum. Resources Rep. (BNA) No. 23, at 622 (June 12, 2000) (describing the agreement between the UAW and the Big Three automakers to extend coverage of health care benefits to same-sex domestic partners). In many unionized workplaces, gay caucuses now play a significant role in union negotiating processes. *See, e.g.*, Ruben J. Garcia, *New Voices at Work: Race and Gender Identity Caucuses in the U.S. Labor Movement*, 54 Hastings L.J. 79 (2002).

6. *Corporate Nondiscrimination Policies*: Since as early as the mid–1970s, some private employers—particularly in white-collar, high-tech industries—have promulgated internal nondiscrimination policies protecting their gay and lesbian employees. *See* Stewart, *supra* Note 5, at 40. By the end of 2002, approximately 60 percent of Fortune 500 companies had nondiscrimination policies that prohibited employment discrimination based on sexual orientation. 21 Hum. Resources Rep. (BNA) No. 20, at 554 (May 26, 2003) (citing Human Rights Campaign, The State of the Workplace: For Lesbian, Gay, Bisexual, and Transgender Americans 2002). On July 2, 2003, Wal–Mart Stores announced that it had decided to extend antidiscrimination protection to its gay and lesbian employees. Sarah Kershaw, *New Wal–Mart Policy Protects Gay Workers*, N.Y. Times, July 2, 2003. Wal–Mart is the largest private employer in the United States, with 3,500 stores and more than one million employees. *Id.* Unlike collective bargaining agreements,

such policies would provide some protection for managers and supervisors—who are not covered by the National Labor Relations Act. The so-called smoke-stack, or blue-collar, industries of the Midwest have been much more resistant to both voluntary policies, as well as to union negotiated provisions. *Id.* What might account for these differences in corporate policies? Different community norms in different geographical locations? Different corporate philosophies in different types of workplaces? Distinctions in social class? Different levels of education within the workplace?

7.   In addition to tort and criminal law as a means of approaching harassment of homosexuals, *see supra* Section B.2, discussing *Dillon v. Frank*, other general developments in employment law, such as implied contracts, or the duty of good faith and fair dealing, may provide homosexuals protection from discrimination in employment. For example, in *Ozer v. Borquez*, 940 P.2d 371 (Colo.1997), an associate attorney sued a law firm on two grounds: wrongful discharge on the basis of sexual orientation and invasion of privacy for revealing his HIV-positive status. The court rejected the wrongful discharge claim, but recognized "a tort claim for invasion of privacy in the nature of unreasonable publicity given to one's private life." *Id.* at 378.

8.   *Nondiscrimination Policies of Professional and Academic Associations*: Some associations that regulate entry into the professions and accreditation of professional schools have adopted policies barring discrimination on the basis of sexual orientation. For example, in his dissent in *Romer v. Evans*, 517 U.S. 620, 116 S.Ct. 1620, 134 L.Ed.2d 855 (1996), Justice Scalia distinguished "the views and values of the lawyer class from which the Court's Members are drawn" from the "more plebeian attitudes that apparently still prevail in the United States Congress," by observing that

> [h]ow [the lawyer] class feels about homosexuality will be evident to anyone who wishes to interview job applicants at virtually any of the Nation's law schools. The interviewer may refuse to offer a job because the applicant is a Republican; because he is an adulterer; because he went to the wrong prep school or belongs to the wrong country club; because he eats snails; because he is a womanizer; because she wears real-animal fur; or even because he hates the Chicago Cubs. But if the interviewer should wish not to be an associate or partner of an applicant because he disapproves of the applicant's homosexuality, then he will have violated the pledge which the Association of American Law Schools requires all its member-schools to exact from job interviewers: "assurance of the employer's willingness" to hire homosexuals. Bylaws of the Association of American Law Schools, Inc. § 6–4(b); Executive Committee Regulations of the Association of American Law Schools § 6.19, in 1995 Handbook, Association of American Law Schools.

Id. at 652, 116 S.Ct. at 1637. *See also Lawrence v. Texas*, 539 U.S. 558, ___, 123 S.Ct. 2472, 2496, 156 L.Ed.2d 508 (2003) (Scalia, J., dissenting). Do you believe that this policy of the Association of American Law Schools (AALS) provides effective antidiscrimination protection for gay and lesbian law students seeking jobs in the legal profession?

The Solomon Amendment, 10 U.S.C. § 983(b) (2003), permits the Secretary of Defense to deny federal funding to an institution of higher education that prohibits or prevents military recruiting on campus. In light of the military's prohibition against engaging in homosexual conduct, 10 U.S.C. § 654, can an AALS approved law school comply with both the Solomon Amendment and AALS Bylaw § 6–4(b), which provides for nondiscrimination on the basis of sexual orientation? *See* Forum for Academic & Inst. Rights, Inc. v. Rumsfeld, 291 F.Supp.2d 269 (D.N.J.2003) (a challenge to the constitutionality of the Solomon Amendment brought by, *inter alia*, associations of law schools, law faculty, and law students).

By 2001, the rules of professional conduct for lawyers of nearly one-third of the states included some form of prohibition of discrimination on the basis of sexual orientation. See William C. Duncan, *Sexual Orientation Bias: The Substantive Limits of Ethics Rules*, 11 Am.U.J. Gender Soc. Pol'y & L. 85, 88–89 (2002). Canon 3 of the Model Code of Judicial Conduct admonishes judges to avoid "bias or prejudice" on the basis of "sexual orientation" in "the performance of judicial duties." Model Code of Jud. Conduct, Canon 3(B)(5) (1999). For a discussion of how this professional standard might affect judicial decisionmaking as well as how judges treat lawyers, litigants, and staff members, see Jennifer Gerarda Brown, *Sweeping Reform for Small Rules? Anti–Bias Canons as a Substitute for Heightened Scrutiny,* 85 Minn. L.Rev. 363 (2000). For a critique, see Duncan, *supra.*

9. *Sexual Orientation as an International Human Right:* Outside of the United States, a potential source of antidiscrimination protection for gays and lesbians can be found in international human rights laws. Two commentators observed that

> [a]lthough no international human rights treaties expressly mention homosexuality or sexual orientation, human rights monitoring institutions, both judicial and political, have recently begun to interpret these treaties to protect certain aspects of lesbian and gay identity and conduct. Similarly, legal scholars and human rights activists have argued with increased frequency that governments may not discriminate on the basis of sexual orientation when upholding individual rights and freedoms.

Laurence R. Helfer & Alice M. Miller, *Sexual Orientation and Human Rights: Toward a United States and Transnational Jurisprudence*, 9 Harv. Hum.Rts.J. 61, 61–62 (1996). Is it appropriate or necessary for legislators in the United States to acknowledge these developments in international human rights law when they are considering proposals to extend employment discrimination laws to homosexuals? What about courts? Helfer and Miller comment that

> [c]ourts in the United States have regularly used human rights treaties to inform state and federal constitutional standards even where the treaties do not create an independent cause of action. That these international human rights instruments may not have been ratified by the United States or may be non-self-executing need not dissuade courts from using their rights-protective principles to infuse federal and state constitutional guarantees with meaning.

Id. at 82. In *Lawrence v. Texas,* 539 U.S. 558, ___, 123 S.Ct. 2472, 2481, 2483, 156 L.Ed.2d 508 (2003), the Supreme Court cited cases decided by the European Court of Human Rights as support for overruling *Bowers v.*

Hardwick, observing that "[t]he [constitutional] right the petitioners seek in this case has been accepted as an integral part of human freedom in many other countries." *Id.* at ___, 123 S.Ct. at 2483. *Compare id.* at ___, 123 S.Ct. at 2494–95 (Scalia, J., dissenting) (arguing that the Court's reliance on "foreign views" to support "[c]onstitutional entitlements" in *Lawrence* is "meaningless dicta"). If you were representing a homosexual plaintiff in an employment discrimination case in a court in the United States, what arguments could you make for or against reliance on principles drawn from international human rights cases or treaties? *See generally* Robert Wintemute, Sexual Orientation and Human Rights: The United States Constitution, The European Convention, and the Canadian Charter (1995).

On September 27, 1999, the European Court of Human Rights, in a 7–0 decision, ruled that Britain's policy of prohibiting homosexuals from serving in the military violated the fundamental human right to privacy under Article 8 of the European Convention on Human Rights. *See* Sarah Lyall, *European Court Tells British to Let Gay Soldiers Serve*, N.Y. Times, Sept. 28, 1999, at A8. Because Britain is a signatory to the European Convention on Human Rights, it is bound by the court's judgments. As discussed at the beginning of this section, much of the public debate about rights of homosexuals in the United States has surrounded the issues of the rights of gays and lesbians to serve in the military. What is the relevance, if any, of this particular ruling of the European Court of Human Rights to the policy debate on this issue in the United States?

Chapter 10

DISCRIMINATION BECAUSE
OF RELIGION

A. INTRODUCTION: STATUTORY OVERVIEW

The legislative history of Title VII provides little insight into the reason that Congress included religion among the prohibited criteria in § 703(a); 42 U.S.C. § 2000e–2(a). Nonetheless, prohibiting employment discrimination on the basis of religion is clearly consistent with the basic concept of religious freedom that is embodied in the First Amendment to the Constitution: in a democratic society people should tolerate the religious beliefs and practices of others. Unlike a person's race, color, sex, national origin, or age, however, an individual's religious beliefs and practices are based on matters of choice rather than on an immutable characteristic or status.

As enacted in 1964, Title VII prohibited discrimination on the basis of religion, but imposed no affirmative obligation on employers to accommodate the religious beliefs of their employees. Without congressional guidance on the scope of the employer's duty not to discriminate, the courts and the EEOC adopted different interpretations of the statute. In its first guidelines on religious discrimination, issued in 1966, the EEOC took the view that Title VII required a covered employer to accommodate the religious practices of its employees or prospective employees unless doing so would create a "serious inconvenience to the conduct of the business." 29 C.F.R. § 1605.1(a)(2) (effective June 15, 1966). Subsection (3)(b)(3) of the guidelines, however, permitted the employer to disregard the religious needs of particular employees when establishing requirements for workweek and overtime schedules, as long as the schedules were adopted in a neutral manner, without an intent to discriminate on the basis of religion. *Id.* § 1605.1(a)(3)(b)(3).

After receiving numerous objections from Sabbatarians, the EEOC revised its guidelines in 1967 by omitting subsection (3)(b)(3) and rewording (and renumbering) subsection (2) to provide that

> the duty not to discriminate on religious grounds * * * includes an
> obligation on the part of the employer to make reasonable accommo-

578

dations to the religious needs of employees * * * where such accommodations can be made without undue hardship on the conduct of the employer's business. Such undue hardship, for example, may exist where the employee's needed work cannot be performed by another employee of substantially similar qualifications during the period of absence of the Sabbath observer.

29 C.F.R. § 1605.1(b) (effective July 10, 1967). *See* Appendix A to EEOC, Guidelines on Discrimination Because of Religion, 29 C.F.R. § 1605.1(b) (1997). Initially some employers defended religious discrimination claims by challenging the validity of the 1967 guidelines on the ground that they were unconstitutional or were inconsistent with Title VII. Consequently, some courts narrowly construed the EEOC guidelines because of concern that compelling employers to accommodate the religious beliefs and practices of all their employees would violate the Establishment Clause of the First Amendment, which requires governmental neutrality in matters of religion. A narrow construction also avoided confronting whether the EEOC exceeded its rulemaking authority in issuing the guidelines.

For example, in *Dewey v. Reynolds Metals Co.*, 429 F.2d 324 (6th Cir.1970), *aff'd by an equally divided Court*, 402 U.S. 689, 91 S.Ct. 2186, 29 L.Ed.2d 267 (1971), the Sixth Circuit, in a divided opinion, held that an employer made a reasonable accommodation of an employee's religious practices by permitting him to arrange for his own replacement on Saturdays, despite his religious belief that it would be a sin for him to induce other employees to work on his Sabbath. *Dewey* thus avoided addressing the "grave constitutional questions" that the court believed would have been raised by adopting the EEOC's interpretation of Title VII. *Id.* at 334. In addition, the court expressed doubt whether the 1967 guidelines were consistent with the statute. *Id.*

In 1972, Congress confirmed the EEOC's authority to interpret Title VII according to the 1967 guidelines. Acting largely in response to *Dewey*, Congress added § 701(j), 42 U.S.C. § 2000e(j), in the 1972 amendments to Title VII. *See* 118 Cong.Rec., §§ 227–53 (1972); *see also* Cooper v. General Dynamics, 533 F.2d 163, 167–68 & 168 n.9 (5th Cir.1976) (discussing legislative history of § 701(j)), *cert. denied sub nom.* International Ass'n of Machinists v. Hopkins, 433 U.S. 908, 97 S.Ct. 2972, 53 L.Ed.2d 1091 (1977). Section 701(j) essentially codified the "reasonable accommodation" and "undue hardship" language found in the EEOC's 1966 and 1967 guidelines:

The term "religion" includes all aspects of religious observance and practice, as well as belief, unless an employer demonstrates that he is unable to reasonably accommodate to an employee's or prospective employee's religious observance or practice without undue hardship on the conduct of the employer's business.

Title VII, § 701(j), 42 U.S.C. § 2000e(j).

Any doubts that the EEOC had the authority from Congress to issue its 1967 guidelines on religion were resolved by the 1972 amendment.

See, e.g., *Reid v. Memphis Publ'g Co.*, 468 F.2d 346 (6th Cir.1972) *(holding that the 1967 EEOC guidelines were consistent with pre–1972 Title VII). But doubts about the constitutionality of the "reasonable accommodation" law persisted. Following the enactment of § 701(j), the Sixth Circuit revisited the constitutionality of Title VII's prohibition against religious discrimination in employment in* Cummins v. Parker Seal Co., *516 F.2d 544 (6th Cir.1975),* aff'd by an equally divided Court, 429 U.S. 65, 97 S.Ct. 342, 50 L.Ed.2d 223 (1976), vacated on other grounds unrelated to constitutionality and remanded for reconsideration, 433 U.S. 903, 97 S.Ct. 2965, 53 L.Ed.2d 1087 (1977), decided on remand, 561 F.2d 658 (6th Cir.1977). *After joining the World Wide Church of God, the plaintiff in* Cummins *refused to work on his church's Sabbath—from Friday sundown to Saturday sundown—or on certain holy days. He was discharged following complaints by other supervisors who had to cover his shift on Saturdays. The employer defended its conduct on the ground that it had reasonably accommodated the plaintiff's religious practices under Title VII and that, in any event, the requirement under § 701(j) of accommodating the religious observances and practices of employees violates the Establishment Clause of the First Amendment because it "fosters religion by requiring private employers to defer to their employee's religious idiosyncrasies." 516 F.2d at 551.*

This time the Sixth Circuit, in a divided opinion, rejected the constitutional challenge to § 701(j), as well as to its precursor EEOC regulation—29 C.F.R. § 1605.1. Applying the three standards established by the Supreme Court in *Committee for Public Education v. Nyquist*, 413 U.S. 756, 93 S.Ct. 2955, 37 L.Ed.2d 948 (1973), the circuit court concluded that the statute and regulation passed constitutional muster; they "(1) ' * * * reflect a clearly secular legislative purpose,' (2) ' * * * have a primary effect that neither advances nor inhibits religion,' and (3) ' * * * avoid excessive government entanglement with religion.' " *Cummins*, 516 F.2d at 551–52 (quoting *Nyquist*, 413 U.S. at 772–73, 93 S.Ct. at 2965). Other courts followed *Cummins* in upholding the constitutionality of § 701(j) and the EEOC guidelines from which the amendment to Title VII was derived. *See* McDaniel v. Essex Int'l, Inc., 696 F.2d 34, 37 (6th Cir.1982) (discussing *Cummins* and collecting cases affirming the constitutionality of § 701(j)); EEOC v. Ithaca Indus., Inc., 849 F.2d 116, 119 (4th Cir.1988) (collecting cases).

At first blush § 701(j), when construed in conjunction with § 703(a), 42 U.S.C. § 2000e–2(a), seems to be a straightforward application of a widely recognized and time-honored policy imperative embodied in the First Amendment. But many difficult questions are raised in attempting to implement this policy of tolerance of religious diversity. For example, what constitutes a religious belief or practice that is entitled to some protection? How should a balance be struck of tolerance protected religious practices or beliefs that conflict with other deeply held societal values? Some religious discrimination cases involve interests, dynamics, and problems not found in race and sex discrimination cases. For example, the implementation of the equality principle is a major goal of laws prohibiting discrimination on the basis of race and sex in the workplace, but prohibiting discrimination because of religion seeks to preserve diversity, albeit of religious beliefs and practices. What deference, if any, should be given to an employer's religious beliefs and practices when they conflict with those of an employee's on topics such as abortion? If the prohibition against religious discrimination is intended to preserve diversity of religious beliefs and practices, does it mean that the *Griggs* disparate impact theory (see Chapter 4) should not be applied in the religious discrimination cases? In addition, government employers are subject to both the Free Exercise and Establishment Clauses of the First Amendment, as well as to Title VII's prohibition against religious discrimination. What accommodation, if any, should be made between the First Amendment and Title VII in cases against governmental employers?

The materials in this chapter explore some of these questions. Section B treats the meaning of "religion." Section C covers the religious entity exceptions. Section D covers the prima facie case of religious discrimination and includes a note on the applicability of the bona fide occupational qualification defense to religious discrimination claims. Section E examines the statutory obligation of the employer to "reasonably accommodate" the religious beliefs and practices of employees and applicants unless "undue hardship" is shown and includes notes on the charity substitution rule for unionized workplaces, sexual orientation discrimination, religious harassment, and disparate impact. Finally, Section F explores religious discrimination claims against government employers.

B.   THE MEANING OF "RELIGION"

Congress did not define the meaning of the term "religion" in Title VII, as originally enacted in 1964. The 1972 amendments, adding "religion" to Title VII definitions in § 701(j), fails to adequately address the meaning of "religion" as well because the offered attempt at a definition is circular: "The term *'religion'* includes all aspects of *religious* observance and practice, as well as belief, * * *." (Emphasis added.) The courts thus generally have relied upon definitions of religion adopted by the Supreme Court and the EEOC. The Supreme Court has stated that "[a]lthough a determination of what is a 'religious' belief or practice entitled to constitutional protection may present a most delicate question, the very concept of ordered liberty precludes allowing every person to make his own standards on matters of conduct in which society as a whole has important interests." Wisconsin v. Yoder, 406 U.S. 205, 215–16, 92 S.Ct. 1526, 1533, 32 L.Ed.2d 15 (1972). The Court has also observed that a religious belief or practice, unlike "a matter of personal preference," is characterized by a "deep religious conviction, shared by an organized group, and intimately related to daily living." *Id.* at 216, 92 S.Ct. at 1533. But in *Frazee v. Illinois Department of Employment Security*, 489 U.S. 829, 833, 109 S.Ct. 1514, 1517–18, 103 L.Ed.2d 914

(1989), the Court rejected the view that "to claim the protection of the Free Exercise Clause [of the First Amendment], one must be responding to the commands of a particular religious organization." After Frazee had rejected a temporary retail job that would have required him to violate his personal religious beliefs by working on Sundays, the state of Illinois denied him unemployment benefits. Although he did not belong to any particular Christian denomination, Frazee claimed that he was a Christian. The Court accepted the finding of the lower court that Frazee's refusal to work on Sundays was based on a sincerely held "personal professed religious belief," *id.* at 833, 109 S.Ct. at 1517, and held that his beliefs were protected under the First Amendment.

A number of courts have endorsed or deferred to the definition of "religious practices or beliefs" the EEOC has adopted in its *Guidelines on Discrimination Because of Religion,* 29 C.F.R. § 1605.1:

> In most cases whether or not a practice or belief is religious is not at issue. However, in those cases in which the issue does exist, the [EEOC] will define religious practices to include moral or ethical beliefs as to what is right or wrong which are sincerely held with the strength of traditional religious views. This standard was developed in *United States v. Seeger,* 380 U.S. 163, 85 S.Ct. 850, 13 L.Ed.2d 733 (1965), and *Welsh v. United States,* 398 U.S. 333, 90 S.Ct. 1792, 26 L.Ed.2d 308 (1970). * * * The fact that no religious group espouses such beliefs or the fact that the religious group to which the individual professes to belong may not accept such belief will not determine whether the belief is a religious belief of the employee or prospective employee. The phrase "religious practice" as used in these Guidelines includes both religious observances and practices, as stated in Section 701(j), 42 U.S.C. § 2000e(j).

Courts have, however, continued to struggle with the expansiveness of the *Seeger/Welsh* definition. *See* Rebecca Redwood French, *From Yoder to Yoda: Models of Traditional, Modern, and Postmodern Religion in U.S. Constitutional Law,* 41 Ariz.L.Rev. 49 (1999) (analyzing inconsistency and diversity of approaches to defining religion after *Seeger* and *Welsh*). As a result, judicial approaches to the definition of religion have been inconsistent and other tests have emerged. For example, a number of circuit courts have adopted a test taken from Judge Arlin Adams's concurring opinion in a constitutional case, *Malnak v. Yogi,* 592 F.2d 197, 198 (3d Cir.1979). *See, e.g.,* DeHart v. Horn, 227 F.3d 47 (3d Cir.2000); Love v. Reed, 216 F.3d 682 (8th Cir.2000); United States v. Meyers, 95 F.3d 1475 (10th Cir.1996); Alvarado v. City of San Jose, 94 F.3d 1223 (9th Cir.1996). Judge Adams proposed defining religion using three indicia: first, examine "the nature of the ideas in question"—not to examine truth or orthodoxy, but to determine whether the subject matter is consistent with religion; second, examine the comprehensiveness of the religious belief—a religion does not answer only one question, it has a broader scope; third, examine whether the ideas comprising the religious belief have "any formal, external, or surface signs that may be analogized to accepted religions," including "formal services, ceremonial functions, the existence of clergy, structure and organization, efforts at propagation, observation of holidays," etc. *Malnak*, 592 F.2d at 208–09. The last criterion is not determinative, but can lend support to a claim of religion. *See also* Friedman v. Southern Cal. Permanente Med. Group, 102 Cal.App.4th 39, 125 Cal.Rptr.2d 663 (2002) (adopting Judge Adams's test and criticizing the expansiveness of the EEOC definition).

Notes and Questions

Consider whether any of the following would or should qualify as religious observances, practices, or beliefs:

1.   An employee was discharged after his employer learned that he claims he has a " 'personal religious creed' " that he must ingest Kozy Kitten Cat Food because it " 'contribute[s] significantly to his state of well being.' " Brown v. Pena, 441 F.Supp. 1382, 1384 (S.D.Fla.1977) (quoting Plaintiff's E.E.O.C. Affidavit), *aff'd without opinion*, 589 F.2d 1113 (5th Cir.1979).

2.   An Internal Revenue Service employee refuses to process applications from abortion clinics for tax exempt status as charitable organizations because to do so would "offend his conscience." *See* Haring v. Blumenthal, 471 F.Supp. 1172 (D.D.C.1979), *cert. denied sub nom.* Haring v. Regan, 452 U.S. 939, 101 S.Ct. 3082, 69 L.Ed.2d 953 (1981).

3.   An employee was dismissed from employment because of his membership in the Ku Klux Klan (KKK). He alleges that the Klan is a religion because its meetings are full of "religious pomp and ceremony." *See* Bellamy v. Mason's Stores, Inc., 508 F.2d 504, 505 (4th Cir.1974), *aff'g*, 368 F.Supp. 1025, 1026 (E.D.Va.1973) ("[T]he proclaimed racist and anti-semitic ideology of the organization to which [plaintiff] belongs takes on * * * a narrow, temporal and political character inconsistent with the meaning of 'religion' as used in [Title VII]."). The history and purpose of the KKK are reviewed extensively in EEOC Decision No. 79–06, 26 Fair Empl.Prac.Cas. 1758 (October 18, 1978) (ruling that the KKK is not a religion for purposes of Title VII). What if an employee is dismissed for being a member and minister of a church that promulgates a belief in white supremacy, including the belief that people of color are "savage," that African Americans are subhuman and should be "ship[ped] back to Africa," that Jews control the nation and have instigated the wars in this century and should be driven from power and that the Holocaust never occurred, and also requiring allegiance to the "White Race" and to the "White Man's Bible"? *See* Peterson v. Wilmur Communications, Inc., 205 F.Supp.2d 1014, 1015, 1022 (E.D.Wis.2002) ("Creativity" is a religion despite its white supremacist tenets; the fact that a religious belief is not subjectively moral or ethical does not mean it fails under the EEOC definition of religion).

4.   Ali X is a member of Nation of Islam, otherwise known as the Black Muslims. His employer refuses to permit him to wear the traditional Muslim "Kuffi"—a small skull cap—at work. *See* Calloway v. Gimbel Bros., 19 Fair Empl.Prac.Cas. (BNA) 705 (E.D.Pa.1979); Ali v. Southeast Neighborhood House, 519 F.Supp. 489 (D.D.C.1981).

5. An employer has a workplace dress code that requires all employees to wear pants as part of a uniform. Lois Lane, a female, applied for and was offered a job. She told her employer that her religion prohibits females from wearing pants and asked that she be permitted to substitute a dress or skirt for the uniform. The employer refused her request and then withdrew its offer of employment. *See* Reid v. Kraft Gen. Foods, Inc., 67 Fair Empl. Prac.Cas. (BNA) 1367 (E.D.Pa.1995); Holly M. Bastian, Comment, *Religious Garb Statutes and Title VII: An Uneasy Coexistence*, 80 Geo.L.J. 211 (1991).

6. Employer, a trucking firm, refuses to hire drivers who have used illegal drugs during the previous two years. To implement this policy, the company requires all applicants for truck driving jobs to take a polygraph test to evaluate their responses to questions about their use of illegal drugs. Plaintiff, a Native American who is a member of the Native American Church, applied for a truck driving job. Upon learning the purpose of the polygraph test, he told the interviewer that several times in previous months he had used peyote as a part of his church's religious ceremonies. For this reason, he was denied employment. Use of peyote, a cactus that contains the hallucinogen mescaline, is unlawful under the criminal law of the state in which the employer does business. However, sacramental use of peyote is considered "the central and most sacred practice of the Native American church." Toledo v. Nobel–Sysco, Inc., 892 F.2d 1481, 1484 (10th Cir.1989), *cert. denied*, 495 U.S. 948, 110 S.Ct. 2208, 109 L.Ed.2d 535 (1990); *see also* 21 C.F.R. § 1307.31 (1997); Employment Div., Dep't of Human Resources v. Smith, 485 U.S. 660, 672 n. 15, 108 S.Ct. 1444, 1451 n. 15, 99 L.Ed.2d 753 (1988).

7. An employee is required, as a condition of employment, to attend monthly staff meetings at which business matters pertaining to her job are discussed. All employees are paid to attend these mandatory meetings. A local minister always begins the meetings with a "theological appetizer" consisting of a brief religious message and a prayer. The employee, who is an Atheist, claims that the requirement that she attend these meetings amounts to constructive discharge. *See* Young v. Southwestern Sav. & Loan Ass'n, 509 F.2d 140 (5th Cir.1975); *see also* Kolodziej v. Smith, 425 Mass. 518, 682 N.E.2d 604, *cert. denied*, 522 U.S. 1029, 118 S.Ct. 628, 139 L.Ed.2d 608 (1997).

8. Would an Atheist have a claim for religious discrimination where her employer gave employees a day off on Good Friday as a spring holiday? Good Friday makes it easier for some Christians to observe their religious beliefs and practices. Is a policy of giving employees Good Friday off as a holiday different from giving employees time off for Thanksgiving? *See* Bridenbaugh v. O'Bannon, 185 F.3d 796 (7th Cir.1999), *cert.denied*, 529 U.S. 1003, 120 S.Ct. 1267, 146 L.Ed.2d 217 (2000).

9. Plaintiff, a lesbian, is a member of the Reconstructionist Movement of Judaism. The Movement views same-sex marriages as acceptable and desirable in preference to couples living together without benefit of marriage. When the plaintiff advised her prospective employer that she intended to marry her female partner in a religious ceremony, the employer withdrew its job offer. *See* Shahar v. Bowers, 114 F.3d 1097 (11th Cir.1997) (en banc), *cert. denied* 522 U.S. 1049, 118 S.Ct. 693, 139 L.Ed.2d 638 (1998).

C. THE RELIGIOUS ENTITY EXEMPTIONS

Title VII provides two broad exemptions for religious employers. The first exemption is found in § 702(a), 42 U.S.C. § 2000e–1(a). The original version of § 702(a) provided only that Title VII does not apply to "a religious corporation, association, or society with respect to the employment of individuals of a particular religion to perform work connected with the carrying on by such corporation, association, or society of its *religious activities* * * *." 42 U.S.C. § 2000e–1 (1970)(emphasis added.) Section 702(a), as amended in 1972, now provides that Title VII

> shall not apply to * * * a religious corporation, association, educational institution, or society with respect to the employment of individuals of a particular religion to perform work connected with the carrying on by such corporation, association, educational institution, or society of its *activities*.

42 U.S.C. § 2000e–1(a) (emphasis added). The 1972 amendment removed the "religious" qualifier on "activities" that was included in the original version.

The second exemption, found in § 703(e)(2), 42 U.S.C. § 2000e–2(e)(2), applies only to religious educational institutions. Section 703(e)(2) provides, in relevant part, that

> it shall not be an unlawful employment practice for a school, college, university, or other educational institution or institution of learning to hire and employ employees of a particular religion if such [institution] is, in whole or in substantial part, owned, supported, controlled, or managed by a particular religion or by a particular religious corporation, association, or society, or if the curriculum of such [institution] is directed toward the propagation of a particular religion.

For "religious education institutions" or educational institutions that are "owned, supported, controlled or managed" by a "religious association," there is an obvious overlap between §§ 702(a) and 703(e)(2). For this reason religious schools typically invoke both provisions. For example, in *Little v. Wuerl*, 929 F.2d 944 (3d Cir.1991), the court held that both exemptions to Title VII covered a Catholic school's decision not to rehire a Protestant teacher for conduct that violated Catholic canon law. *See also*, Killinger v. Samford University, 113 F.3d 196 (11th Cir.1997) (applying the two exemptions to Title VII to deny the religious discrimination claim of a professor who was removed from his position at the divinity school of a Baptist university). The courts, however, are split over how broadly or narrowly the exemptions for religious employers should be construed in light of the constitutional protection afforded by the Free Exercise and Establishment Clauses of the First Amendment. *See* Vigars v. Valley Christian Ctr. of Dublin, Cal., 805 F.Supp. 802, 807 n.3 (N.D.Cal.1992). The problem is compounded further by the fact that neither the 1964 nor 1972 version of § 702(a), nor § 703(e)(2), contains an express exemption for discrimination on the basis of race or sex.

Corporation of the Presiding Bishop v. Amos, 483 U.S. 327, 107 S.Ct. 2862, 97 L.Ed.2d 273 (1987), is the leading Supreme Court case interpreting § 702 (Section 702 is now codified as § 702(a), 42 U.S.C. § 2000e–1(a)). The issue in *Amos* was whether it was unconstitutional under the Establishment Clause of the First Amendment to apply the § 702 exemption to the secular nonprofit activities of a religious organization. The Church of Jesus Christ of Latter-day Saints, an unincorporated religious association sometimes referred to as the Mormon or LDS Church, operated a nonprofit gymnasium in Salt Lake City, Utah, that was open to the public. Plaintiff Mayson had worked at the gym as a building engineer for sixteen years when the church discharged him because he did not qualify for a "temple recommend"—a certificate showing that, as a member of the church in full compliance with its standards and practices, the holder is eligible to enter its temples. Mayson and other class plaintiffs argued that if Title VII were construed to permit religious employers to discriminate on religious grounds in obviously nonreligious, secular jobs, then § 702 would violate the Establishment Clause of the First Amendment. The church argued that it was completely exempt from Title VII under § 702. The Supreme Court ruled in favor of the church.

The *Amos* decision turned largely on the application of the three-part test the Supreme Court enunciated in *Lemon v. Kurtzman*, 403 U.S. 602, 91 S.Ct. 2105, 29 L.Ed.2d 745 (1971), to evaluate alleged violations of the Establishment Clause. First, the law must have been enacted for a "secular legislative purpose"; second, the regulation's "principal or primary effect" must be one that "neither advances nor inhibits religion"; and third, the regulation must not involve the government in undue entanglement with religion. *See Amos*, 483 U.S. at 335–39, 107 S.Ct. at 2868–70 (quoting from *Lemon* and applying the *Lemon* test to the facts in *Amos*). Concluding that § 702 did not satisfy the second prong of the *Lemon* test because it had a primary effect of benefitting religious entities, the lower court in *Amos* had ruled in favor of the plaintiff. The Supreme Court reversed, holding that § 702 passed all three parts of the *Lemon* test. The *Amos* decision can also be viewed as an "accommodation" case in that § 702 serves to lift a burden on religious entities imposed by the general requirements of Title VII. It has been suggested that the Supreme Court applies the *Lemon* test less rigidly when the governmental provision at issue seeks to lift a governmental burden, like § 702 does (easing the burden imposed by Title VII's religious nondiscrimination requirement), and *Amos* has been cited as supporting such a view. *See, e.g.,* Roberto L. Corrada, *Religious Accommodation and the National Labor Relations Act*, 17 Berkeley J.Emp. & Lab.L. 185, 254–63 (1996); Michael W. McConnell, *Accommodation of Religion: An Update and Response to Critics*, 60 Geo.Wash.L.Rev. 685,

696 (1992); Mark Tushnet, *The Emerging Principle of Accommodation of Religion (Dubitante)*, 76 Geo.L.J. 1691, 1704 (1988).

Further, the *Amos* Court rejected the appellees' equal protection challenge, holding that "as applied to the nonprofit activities of religious employers, § 702 is rationally related to the legitimate purpose of alleviating significant governmental interference with the ability of religious organizations to define and carry out their religious missions." *Amos*, 483 U.S. at 339, 107 S.Ct. at 2870. Under *Amos*, nonprofit enterprises operated by religious organizations may discriminate on the basis of religion in making employment decisions. However, the Supreme Court left open the issue whether for-profit enterprises operated by religious organizations are similarly exempt from Title VII. Should for-profit operations of religious institutions be exempt from the mandate of Title VII?

Questions

What arguments can you make for or against applying the religious entity exemptions under Title VII in the following cases?

a.   Christian School requires all of its employees to be "born-again believers living a consistent and practical Christian life." Dana Ross, a female, worked at the school as a librarian, where she dealt with students on a daily basis. On occasion she taught physical education or worked as a teacher's aide, but she had no responsibility for the school's religious or secular courses. Before Ross's annulment of her marriage to her first husband was formalized, she conceived a child with the man who later became her second husband. After learning that she was pregnant, the school fired Ross. At the time of the discharge, the school informed Ross that she was being terminated because of her "sin" of being "pregnant without benefit of marriage." Later, however, the school sought to defend the discharge in court on the sole ground that Ross had committed adultery by having "sexual relations with her 'new' husband before she was divorced from her 'old' husband." *See* Vigars v. Valley Christian Ctr. of Dublin, Cal., 805 F.Supp. 802, 804–05 (N.D.Cal.1992).

b.   A church-operated school has a policy that limits health insurance coverage to teachers who are "heads of the household." The school sincerely believes that only males can be heads of households, so female teachers similarly situated to male teachers are denied health insurance coverage. *See* EEOC v. Fremont Christian Sch., 781 F.2d 1362 (9th Cir.1986).

c.   A female secretary to a male pastor of a church claims that the pastor subjected her to hostile work environment sexual harassment. She wants to sue the church and pastor under Title VII. Should she be allowed to go forward with her claim against the church? What if the plaintiff is an associate pastor? *See* Black v. Snyder, 471 N.W.2d 715, 721 (Minn.App.1991) (permitting the sexual harassment claim of an associate pastor to go forward "presents no greater conflict with the church's disciplinary authority than that presented in cases enforcing child abuse laws"). Should a sex discrimination claim be treated any differently than a sexual harassment claim? *See* Geary v. Visitation of the Blessed Virgin Mary Parish Sch., 7 F.3d 324, 331

(3d Cir.1993) (age discrimination claim brought by a lay teacher at a parochial school can proceed "[b]ecause application of the ADEA does not present a significant risk of government entanglement in religion").

Note: The "Ministerial Exception" to Title VII Discrimination Claims Against Religious Institutions

Courts have interpreted Title VII and the ADEA to bar discrimination by religious employers on the basis of race, color, sex, national origin, and age. *See* Geary v. Visitation of the Blessed Virgin Mary Parish Sch., 7 F.3d 324, 331 (3d Cir.1993). They are divided, however, over how broadly or narrowly the exceptions in §§ 702(a) and 703(e)(2) should be construed in sex and race discrimination claims brought against religious employers. *See generally* Treaver Hodson, Comment, *The Religious Employer Exemption Under Title VII: Should a Church Define Its Own Activities?*, 1994 B.Y.U.L.Rev. 571.

The Fifth Circuit carved out a "ministerial exception" to Title VII in *McClure v. Salvation Army*, 460 F.2d 553, *cert. denied*, 409 U.S. 896, 92 S.Ct. 132, 34 L.Ed.2d 153 (1972). Plaintiff, a female minister, brought a Title VII sex discrimination claim alleging that she received lower wages than similarly situated male ministers. Limiting its decision solely to the relationships between a church and its ministers, the court found that the Free Exercise Clause would preclude judicial review of decisions by religious entities concerning the terms and conditions of employment of their ministers because "[t]he relationship between an organized church and its ministers is its lifeblood." *Id.* at 558. In order to avoid reaching this constitutional question, however, *McClure* held that "Congress did not intend, through the nonspecific wording of the applicable provisions of Title VII, to regulate the employment relationship between church and minister." *Id.* at 560. The ministerial exception is grounded in two constitutional rationales. The first is that the imposition of secular standards on a church's employment of its ministers will burden the free exercise of religion; the second is that "the state's interest in eliminating employment discrimination" is outweighed by the church's constitutional right of autonomy in its own domain. Hodson, *supra*, at 599. *See* EEOC v. Catholic Univ. of Am., 83 F.3d 455, 467 (D.C.Cir.1996). For a treatment of sex discrimination experienced by clergywomen, *see* Elisabeth S. Wendorff, *Employment Discrimination and Clergywomen: Where the Law Has Feared to Tread*, 3 S.Cal.Rev.L. & Women's Stud. 136 (1993).

The ministerial exception is not limited to members of the clergy. It has been applied to lay employees of religious institutions whose jobs are "important to the spiritual and pastoral mission of the church." Rayburn v. General Conference of Seventh-day Adventists, 772 F.2d 1164, 1169 (4th Cir.1985), *cert. denied*, 478 U.S. 1020, 106 S.Ct. 3333, 92 L.Ed.2d 739 (1986). The court in *Rayburn* adopted a functional analysis: "As a general rule, if the employee's primary duties consist of teaching, spreading the faith, church governance, supervision of a religious order, or supervision of or participation in religious ritual or worship, he or she should be considered 'clergy.'" B. Bagni, *Discrimination in the Name of the Lord: A Critical Evaluation of Discrimination by Religious Organizations*, 79 Colum.L.Rev.

1514, 1545 (1979) (quoted in *Rayburn,* 772 F.2d at 1169). *See also* EEOC v. Catholic Univ. of Am., 83 F.3d 455, 467 (D.C.Cir.1996).

If a member of the clergy brings a claim of sexual or racial harassment that is likely to require a court to consider the church's decisions in selecting its clergy, the First Amendment may bar the claim. *See, e.g.,* Van Osdol v. Vogt, 908 P.2d 1122 (Colo.1996). *Van Osdol* held that both religion clauses of the First Amendment bar judicial review of a female minister's Title VII claim that her church had retaliated against her by revoking her minister's license after she reported that another minister had sexually harassed several female church employees, as well as several female church members. The court ruled that when a clergy member claims the church has violated Title VII in its decision to appoint or retain her, "the church's interest in free exercise [of religion] outweighs the government's interest in enforcing the particular statute." *Id.* at 1127. Secular courts cannot review such claims because "[t]he decision to hire or discharge a minister is itself inextricable from religious doctrine." *Id.* at 1128. The court also held that the Establishment Clause "insulates a religious institution's choice of minister from judicial review," *id.* at 1133, because "the core ecclesiastical nature of the decision would require excessive government entanglement with the church." *Id.* at 1132. *See* Serbian Eastern Orthodox Diocese for the U.S. & Can. v. Milivojevich, 426 U.S. 696, 717, 96 S.Ct. 2372, 2384, 2386, 49 L.Ed.2d 151 (1976) (the Supreme Court case relied on by *Van Osdol* and other cases for the principle that secular courts have no jurisdiction over "core" issues of church governance, including the selection of ministers). Should a religious entity at least have to claim that a particular offensive practice like sexual harassment is consistent with its religious doctrine or belief system prior to claiming the protections or immunities afforded under the First Amendment or Title VII? *See* Bollard v. California Province of Soc'y of Jesus, 196 F.3d 940, 947 (9th Cir. 1999) ("The Jesuits do not offer a religious justification for the harassment Bollard alleges; indeed, they condemn it as inconsistent with their values and beliefs. There is thus no danger that, by allowing this suit to proceed, we will thrust the secular courts into the constitutionally untenable position of passing judgment on questions of religious faith or doctrine.")

In *Employment Division, Department of Human Resources of Oregon v. Smith,* discussed in Section F of this chapter, the Supreme Court held that religious beliefs do not excuse noncompliance with generally applicable state law. The courts had carved out the "ministerial exception" prior to *Smith.* Based on *Smith,* the plaintiff in *Gellington v. Christian Methodist Episcopal Church,* 203 F.3d 1299 (11th Cir.2000), argued that the "ministerial exception" is no longer good law because Title VII is a neutral law of general applicability and a church cannot avoid compliance with Title VII even where its application would burden the free exercise of religion. The plaintiff in *Gellington* was a minister who had helped a female co-worker, also a minister, to prepare a Title VII sexual harassment complaint against her immediate supervisor at the church. The Eleventh Circuit rejected Gellington's argument that the "ministerial exception" did not survive *Smith.* Following two other circuits that also had held that the "ministerial exception" survives *Smith—EEOC v. Catholic University of America,* 83 F.3d 455 (D.C.Cir.1996), and *Combs v. Central Texas Annual Conference of United*

Methodist Church, 173 F.3d 343 (5th Cir.1999)—the Eleventh Circuit noted that *Smith* recognized two types of government action that can burden the free exercise of religion. The first is interfering with a believer's ability to observe the commands or practices of her faith. The second is encroaching on the ability of a church to manage its internal affairs. *Gellington* held that *Smith* focused on the first type of government action. The "ministerial exception" was developed, in part, to protect churches from the second type. The second type was not an issue in *Smith,* under the reasoning of *Gellington,* and for that reason it does not affect the continuing vitality of the "ministerial exception." (*Gellington* also collects courts of appeals cases that have recognized the "ministerial exception."). For an in-depth treatment of the "ministerial exception," see Laura L. Coon, Note, *Employment Discrimination by Religious Institutions: Limiting the Sanctuary of the Constitutional Ministerial Exception to Religion–Based Employment Decisions,* 54 Vand. L.Rev. 481 (2001).

D. ESTABLISHING A PRIMA FACIE CASE

HELLER v. EBB AUTO CO.

United States Court of Appeals for the Ninth Circuit, 1993.
8 F.3d 1433.

CYNTHIA HOLCOMB HALL, Circuit Judge.

* * *

In late 1984, EBB Auto Company hired Jerrold S. Heller, who is Jewish, as a used-car salesperson. At that time, Heller's wife, Katherine, was studying to convert from Catholicism to Judaism in anticipation of their oldest son's bar mitzvah. Because Jewish law mandates that children take their mother's religion, the bar mitzvah could not take place until Katherine's conversion.[1]

Katherine completed her course of study in early May 1985. On Saturday, May 10, EBB notified Heller that due to an upcoming "tent sale" all vacations and leaves were cancelled for the weekend of May 17–19. On Tuesday, May 14, Rabbi Yonah Geller telephoned Heller at work and told him that the conversion ceremony for Katherine and her study group could take place on the morning of either the upcoming Friday (May 17) or Sunday (May 19). Because he assumed that the dates could not be changed, Heller never attempted to reschedule the ceremony.

Heller telephoned his immediate supervisor, Collyer Young, explained his situation, and asked for two hours off on either Friday or Sunday morning. Young asked if there was any way to hold the ceremony at another time. Upon Heller's negative response, Young gave him permission to miss a Friday morning sales meeting. Heller then tele-

---

1. Conversion to Judaism requires a six- to twelve-month course of study that culminates in a conversion ceremony. * * * For convenience, the rabbis generally convert several persons at the same time. If neces- sary, however, the [rabbinical] court can conduct the ceremony on an individual ba- sis. Absent extraordinary circumstances, the father of children who undergo conver- sion must be present for the ceremony.

phoned Geller and informed the rabbi that he would be able to attend a ceremony on Friday morning. Geller subsequently informed the other members of Katherine's study group and made arrangements for the ceremony.

The next day (Wednesday, May 15), Young's superior, Greg Bowman, learned of Heller's leave of absence and countermanded it. Bowman instructed Young to inform Heller that he was required to attend the meeting and that, if he failed to do so, he would be fired. When Heller insisted on attending the ceremony, Young fired him.

That night, Young telephoned Heller's home, spoke to Katherine, and left word that he wanted to discuss the matter. The following day (Thursday, May 16), Heller went to EBB to pick up his final paycheck and Young attempted to talk things over with him. Heller refused and the parties had no further contact. Heller attended the conversion ceremony on Friday, May 17.

Heller filed suit claiming that his dismissal violated Title VII * * *. Heller's [claim was] tried by the court, which granted summary judgment for EBB * * *. Heller appeals the judgment * * *.

* * *

We analyze Title VII religious discrimination claims under a two-part framework. *First*, the employee must establish a prima facie case by proving that (1) he had a bona fide religious belief, the practice of which conflicted with an employment duty; (2) he informed his employer of the belief and conflict; and (3) the employer threatened him with or subjected him to discriminatory treatment, including discharge, because of his inability to fulfill the job requirements. The prima facie case does *not* include a showing that the employee made any efforts to compromise his or her religious beliefs or practices before seeking an accommodation from the employer. *Second*, if the employee proves a prima facie case, the employer must establish that it initiated good faith efforts to accommodate the employee's religious practices.

The district court concluded that Heller failed to establish a prima facie case * * *. We disagree.

* * *

EBB first suggests that the conversion ceremony is not a religious practice within the protection of Title VII and cites *Wessling v. Kroger Co.*, 554 F.Supp. 548 (E.D.Mich.1982), as support. In *Wessling*, the district court held that an employee's voluntary participation in preparations for a Christmas play at her church was not within the scope of Title VII. The court noted that the employee's early arrival to decorate and receive children was essentially "social in nature" and found that her participation "was family oriented, a family obligation, not a religious obligation." *Id.* at 552.

EBB's reliance on *Wessling* is misplaced. Title VII protects more than the observance of Sabbath or practices specifically mandated by an employee's religion:

> [T]he very words of the statute ("*all aspects* of religious observance and practice * * * ") leave little room for such a limited interpretation * * *. [T]o restrict the act to those practices which are mandated or prohibited by a tenet of the religion, would involve the court in determining not only what are the tenets of a particular religion, * * * but would frequently require the courts to decide whether a particular practice is or is not required by the tenets of the religion. * * * [S]uch a judicial determination [would] be irreconcilable with the warning issued by the Supreme Court in *Fowler v. Rhode Island*, 345 U.S. 67, 70, 73 S.Ct. 526, 527, 97 L.Ed. 828 (1953), "[I]t is no business of courts to say * * * what is a religious practice or activity."

Redmond v. GAF Corp., 574 F.2d 897, 900 (7th Cir.1978) (Title VII protects an employee's participation in regularly-scheduled Bible classes). *Accord* McDaniel v. Essex Int'l, Inc., 571 F.2d 338, 342 (6th Cir.1978) (Title VII "applies to all religious observances and is not limited to claims of discrimination based on requirements of Sabbath work"); Cooper v. General Dynamics, 533 F.2d 163, 168 (5th Cir.1976) ("The language chosen is broad—broader can hardly be imagined—and entirely extravagant to a mere concern for Sabbatarianism or any other particular doctrine or observance"), *cert. denied*, 433 U.S. 908, 97 S.Ct. 2972, 53 L.Ed.2d 1091 (1977); Weitkenaut v. Goodyear Tire & Rubber Co., 381 F.Supp. 1284, 1288–89 (D.Vt.1974) (Title VII protects a minister's attendance at monthly church organizational meetings).

Under this broad framework, Title VII's protections clearly encompass Heller's participation in the conversion ceremony. Geller testified that the ceremony, and the role of the father and husband in it, are part of the basic teachings of Judaism. By sacrificing his job to attend, Heller demonstrated that he attached the utmost religious significance to the ceremony. Either fact is sufficient to invoke the statute.

EBB next asserts that the ceremony did not conflict with Heller's employment duties because Heller could have rescheduled it to a date when he was not working. We disagree.

An inflexible duty to reschedule would impose too great a burden on employees who desire to attend religious ceremonies for which they might be able to change the date or time, such as baptisms, confirmations, or weddings. Although Heller never requested a change of date for the ceremony, his lack of action did not stem from a disregard for his employment duties. Rather, he thought the dates were fixed because the ceremony involved other converts and because his son's bar mitzvah was less than a month away. Given this good faith and the fact that Geller acted in reliance upon Heller's assured availability after Young gave him permission to attend, there was a conflict between Heller's religious practices and his employment obligations.

EBB lastly argues that, because Heller never explained the nature of the ceremony to EBB, he did not give notice of his conflict. The district court in *Wessling* is the only court to find an employee's Title VII notice to be insufficient to establish a prima facie case. There, the plaintiff told her employer only that she wanted to miss work in order to set up for her daughter's Christmas play. The court, in *dicta*, concluded that such notice "was not in terms of a request for an accommodation of her religious practices." *Wessling*, 554 F.Supp. at 552.

A sensible approach would require only enough information about an employee's religious needs to permit the employer to understand the existence of a conflict between the employee's religious practices and the employer's job requirements. *See Redmond*, 574 F.2d at 902 (informing employer that "I [am] not able to work on Saturday because of my religious obligation" is sufficient); Chrysler Corp. v. Mann, 561 F.2d 1282, 1286 (8th Cir.1977) (employee must, at least, "inform[ ] his employer of his religious needs"), *cert. denied*, 434 U.S. 1039, 98 S.Ct. 778, 54 L.Ed.2d 788 (1978). Under such a standard, Heller's notice to EBB was satisfactory. Young and Bowman knew that Heller was Jewish. Young knew that Heller's wife was studying for conversion. And, when Heller requested the time off, he informed Young why he needed to miss work.

Any greater notice requirement would permit an employer to delve into the religious practices of an employee in order to determine whether religion mandates the employee's adherence. If courts may not make such an inquiry, then neither should employers.

The district court therefore erred in holding that Heller did not establish a prima facie Title VII case. Heller demonstrated that his employment duties conflicted with a bona fide religious practice, notified EBB of that conflict, and was discharged because of his refusal to comply with the employment requirements.

* * *

Notes and Questions

1. Should an employer be allowed to challenge the veracity of a plaintiff's asserted "religious" belief or practice that is alleged to conflict with an employer's job requirement? An inquiry into veracity focuses on whether an asserted religious practice or belief falls within the statutory meaning of "religion" under Title VII. Does *Heller* impose a flat ban on an inquiry into the veracity of the religious belief or practice? If so, is it a good rule? Recall the Kozy Kitten Cat Food case, in Section B of this chapter, in which the plaintiff claimed that he was discriminated against because of his "personal religious creed" that eating that brand of cat food "contributed significantly to his state of well being." Recall also *Bellamy v. Mason's Stores, Inc.*, 508 F.2d 504 (4th Cir.1974), in Section B, in which the plaintiff alleged that the Ku Klux Klan is a religion because its rites are full of "religious pomp and ceremony."

2. Should an employer be permitted to challenge the bona fides or sincerity of a plaintiff's religious beliefs or practices? What is the response of the court in *Heller* to this question? In *Philbrook v. Ansonia Board of Education*, 757 F.2d 476, 481–82 (2d Cir.1985), *rev'd on other grounds*, 479 U.S. 60, 107 S.Ct. 367, 93 L.Ed.2d 305 (1986), the Second Circuit made a distinction between inquiries into the verity—or the veracity—and the sincerity of a plaintiff's asserted beliefs or practices.

> We acknowledge that it is entirely appropriate, indeed necessary for a court to engage in analysis of the sincerity—as opposed, of course, to verity—of someone's religious beliefs in both the free exercise context and the Title VII context. We see no reason for not regarding the standard for sincerity under Title VII as that used in Free Exercise cases. * * * This court has recently held that a sincerity analysis is necessary in order to "differentiat[e] between those beliefs that are held as a matter of conscience and those that are animated by motives of deception and fraud."

Patrick v. LeFevre, 745 F.2d 153, 157 (2d Cir.1984).

3. If an inquiry into sincerity is appropriate, should an objective or subjective test control? In *Smith v. Pyro Mining Co.*, 827 F.2d 1081, 1086 (6th Cir.1987), *cert. denied*, 485 U.S. 989, 108 S.Ct. 1293, 99 L.Ed.2d 503 (1988), the majority adopted a subjective test of sincerity, i.e., what the employee actually believed was required by his religious beliefs. The majority's apparent rejection of an objective test was consistent with the Supreme Court's admonishment in *Fowler v. Rhode Island*, 345 U.S. 67, 70, 73 S.Ct. 526, 527, 97 L.Ed. 828 (1953), that "it is no business of courts to say that what is a religious practice or activity for one group is not religion under the protections of the First Amendment." *See Heller*, 8 F.3d at 1438 (quoting *Fowler*). The dissent in *Pyro Mining* argued for the adoption of an objective test on the ground that it would ferret out "purely personal" preferences that are not entitled to constitutional protection. *See id.* at 1096–97 (Krupansky, J., dissenting). Which is the better view? *See* EEOC v. READS, Inc., 759 F.Supp. 1150 (E.D. Pa. 1991) (head covering request by Muslim employee, though not required by religion, protected anyway based on personal religious belief).

4. An employee claims that his religious beliefs and observances require that he should not work on Saturdays but should instead engage in religious activities on that day. The employer hires a private investigator to "tail" the employee for a couple of weeks. The private investigator discovers that the employee regularly plays golf at the local golf course on Saturdays. Should the employer be allowed to introduce the facts uncovered by the private investigator to challenge both the veracity and sincerity of the employee's religious beliefs? What if the employee's adherence to the religious practice or belief is inconsistent? *See* EEOC v. Ilona of Hungary, Inc., 108 F.3d 1569 (7th Cir. 1997) (en banc) (religious observance of Yom Kippur protected although employee inconsistently observed Yom Kippur in the past).

5. Suppose that an employee's religious beliefs conflict with some legitimate work rule of the employer, but the employee has not notified the employer of the conflict. If the employer nevertheless has actual knowledge

of the employee's belief and the conflict, is the employer required to attempt to make an accommodation to resolve the conflict? Should knowledge of the employee's religious beliefs ever be imputed to the employer in order to satisfy the notice requirement of a prima facie case? If so, what facts should be sufficient to be considered constructive notice? *See* Chalmers v. Tulon Co. of Richmond, 101 F.3d 1012, 1019–1021 (4th Cir.1996), *cert. denied*, 522 U.S. 813, 118 S.Ct. 58, 139 L.Ed.2d 21 (1997); Van Koten v. Family Health Mgmt., Inc., 955 F.Supp. 898 (N.D.Ill.1997) (employee failed to present sufficient evidence that employer had knowledge that he followed the "Wiccian" religion which considers Halloween to be its most holy day).

6. Even though the employer has the burdens of production of evidence and persuasion on the reasonable accommodation and undue hardship defenses, should an employee nevertheless be required to prove as an element of the prima facie case that the employer "consciously" failed to make an accommodation to her religious beliefs or practices? *See* EEOC v. UPS, 94 F.3d 314, 317 n.3 (7th Cir.1996) (suggesting an affirmative answer).

7. *Reverse Religious Discrimination Claims*: What must an employee prove to establish a prima facie case when he claims that he was discharged not because of his own religious beliefs but because he did not hold the same religious views as his supervisor? In *Shapolia v. Los Alamos National Laboratory*, 992 F.2d 1033 (10th Cir.1993), plaintiff alleged that he received negative performance evaluations from his supervisor because he was not of the same religious faith as his supervisor, who was a bishop in the Church of Jesus Christ of Latter Day Saints ("Mormon" Church). The negative evaluation eventually led to the plaintiff's discharge. *Shapolia* held that to establish a prima facie case where the plaintiff alleges that he was discriminated against because he did not share his supervisor's religious beliefs, the plaintiff must show "(1) that he was subjected to some adverse employment action; (2) that, at the time the employment action was taken, the employee's job performance was satisfactory; and (3) some additional evidence to support the inference that the employment actions were taken because of a discriminatory motive based upon the employee's failure to hold or follow his or her employer's religious beliefs." *Id.* at 1038. If these elements are satisfied, only then is the plaintiff "entitled to the benefit of the *McDonnell* burden-shifting scheme and its presumption." *Id.* The Tenth Circuit considered this class of cases to be analogous to affirmative action or "reverse discrimination" cases, which are discussed in Chapter 3, Section B.5. *Id.* at 1038 n.6. *See also* Venters v. City of Delphi, 123 F.3d 956, 972 (7th Cir.1997) (citing *Shapolia* with approval for the proposition that a prima facie case of religious discrimination is satisfied when a plaintiff's claim is "not that the [employer] refused to accommodate her religious practices in some way, but that she was discharged because she did not measure up to the * * * religious expectations" of her supervisor, a born-again Christian who wanted to "save her soul").

Note: The Bona Fide Occupational Qualification Defense

Section 703(e) of Title VII, 42 U.S.C. § 2000e–2(e), provides that it is not an unlawful employment practice for an employer to discriminate "on the basis of * * * religion * * * in those certain instances where religion

* * * is a bona fide occupational qualification reasonably necessary to the normal operation of that particular business or enterprise * * * ." The classic cases in which the BFOQ applies are those in which a religious institution limits employment to individuals who are members of the religious order. Most of these cases can be decided under either the religious entity exception or the BFOQ provision. *See, e.g.,* Pime v. Loyola Univ. of Chi., 803 F.2d 351 (7th Cir.1986) (upholding a university's decision to deny a tenure track position to a Jewish professor who was not a Jesuit, on the ground that being a Jesuit was a BFOQ for the available position in the Philosophy Department, even though the district court had rejected the employer's defense that it qualified for the religious employer exemption under § 703(e)(2), because it was not "supported, controlled or managed" by the Society of Jesus). But *EEOC v. Kamehameha Schools/Bishop Estate,* 990 F.2d 458 (9th Cir.), *cert. denied,* 510 U.S. 963, 114 S.Ct. 439, 126 L.Ed.2d 372 (1993), suggests that courts are willing to examine critically whether employment must be limited to persons of the same religious order. In *Kamehameha,* the court found that "adherence to the Protestant faith" was not a BFOQ for a teaching position at private schools that were not controlled or supported by a religious organization even though the will creating the schools required that all teachers be Protestant in order to create a "Protestant presence" at the schools. *Id.* at 465–67, 465 n.15.

Consider the following:

a. Pursuant to state law, a school district provides bus service to students living in the district who attend either public or private schools. A number of male students in the district attend an all-male private religious school operated by a sect of Hasidic Jews. Because religious tenets of the Hasidim prohibit any social interactions between the sexes, Hasidic parents object to having their male children ride on school buses driven by female bus drivers. In response to demands of the Hasidic community, the school board has adopted a policy that bars female bus drivers from driving bus routes on which male Hasidic Jewish students live. All female bus drivers are thus denied the opportunity to bid for these routes, even if they would be entitled to them under seniority rules in the collective bargaining agreement. A group of female school bus drivers brings a class action suit against the school board challenging its policy under Title VII. Is this a case of disparate treatment or disparate impact? In *Bollenbach v. Board of Education of Monroe–Woodbury Central School District,* 659 F.Supp. 1450, 1472 (S.D.N.Y. 1987), the court first relied upon the *McDonnell Douglas* circumstantial evidence paradigm of disparate treatment analysis to find that the plaintiffs had made out a prima facie case of sex discrimination; then, adopting the disparate impact paradigm, the court rejected the defendant's asserted business necessity defense on the ground that its policy was not neutral. Should this case more properly have been analyzed as a direct evidence disparate treatment case rather than an amalgam of a circumstantial evidence and disparate impact case? And if it were analyzed as a direct evidence case, could the school board's policy have been justified as a BFOQ?

b. Baylor College of Medicine, in cooperation with the government of Saudi Arabia, has a rotation program that sends surgical teams from its prestigious cardiovascular unit in Houston, Texas, to King Faisal Specialist Hospital and Research Hospital in Riyadh, Saudi Arabia. The surgeons who participate in the program receive twice the salary of the surgeons at Baylor's Texas facility. Even though Baylor has never had an express agreement with the Saudi government that it would not send Jewish doctors, the college has never permitted any of its Jewish doctors to participate in the program because it believes that the Saudi government would not grant them entry visas. In addition, the college has expressed concerns for the safety of its Jewish doctors if they were allowed to go. *See* Abrams v. Baylor College of Med., 581 F.Supp. 1570 (S.D.Tex.1984) (finding on these facts that plaintiffs had met their burden of proving religious discrimination, and rejecting the employer's business necessity and BFOQ defenses), *aff'd in relevant part*, 805 F.2d 528 (5th Cir.1986). In *Kern v. Dynalectron Corp.*, 577 F.Supp. 1196 (N.D.Tex.1983), *aff'd*, 746 F.2d 810 (5th Cir.1984) (mem.), the district court found that being Moslem was a BFOQ for a position as a pilot who would be required to fly helicopters in Saudi Arabia from Jeddah to the holy area, Mecca. Under Saudi Arabian law, which is based on Islamic principles, any non-Moslem who enters Mecca must be beheaded. What rationale might explain the different outcomes in these two cases?

   c.   The Supreme Court's acknowledgment, in *UAW v. Johnson Controls*, 499 U.S. 187, 111 S.Ct. 1196, 113 L.Ed.2d 158 (1991), in Chapter 6, Section E, that safety concerns can, in limited circumstances, provide a rationale for a BFOQ defense in sex discrimination cases may also be relevant in the religious discrimination cases. *See id.* at 201, 111 S.Ct. at 1204 ("Our cases have stressed that discrimination on the basis of sex because of safety concerns is allowed only in narrow circumstances."). For example, in *Bhatia v. Chevron USA, Inc.*, 734 F.2d 1382 (9th Cir.1984), the court upheld an employer's rule that any employee whose job as a machinist might involve exposure to toxic gases was required to shave any facial hair that might interfere with the gas-tight seals on respirators worn as a safety measure to comply with OSHA standards. Plaintiff was a member of the Sikh religion which prohibits its followers from shaving any body hair. *Bhatia* found that although the plaintiff had made out a prima facie case of religious discrimination, the employer could not retain him without undue hardship on the operation of its business. Under *Johnson Controls* and the rationale of *Bhatia* and *Kern*, could an employer adopt a policy, defensible as a BFOQ, prohibiting Sikhs from working as machinists?

E.   REASONABLE ACCOMMODATION AND UNDUE HARDSHIP

TRANS WORLD AIRLINES, INC. v. HARDISON

Supreme Court of the United States, 1977.
432 U.S. 63, 97 S.Ct. 2264, 53 L.Ed.2d 113.

JUSTICE WHITE delivered the opinion of the Court.

   * * * The issue in this case is the extent of the employer's obligation under Title VII to accommodate an employee whose religious beliefs prohibit him from working on Saturdays.

I

* * *

Petitioner Trans World Airlines (TWA) operates a large maintenance and overhaul base in Kansas City, Mo. On June 5, 1967, respondent Larry G. Hardison was hired by TWA to work as a clerk in the Stores Department at its Kansas City base. Because of its essential role in the Kansas City operation, the Stores Department must operate 24 hours per day, 365 days per year, and whenever an employee's job in that department is not filled, an employee must be shifted from another department, or a supervisor must cover the job, even if the work in other areas may suffer.

Hardison, like other employees at the Kansas City base, was subject to a seniority system contained in a collective-bargaining agreement that TWA maintains with petitioner International Association of Machinists and Aerospace Workers (IAM). The seniority system is implemented by the union steward through a system of bidding by employees for particular shift assignments as they become available. The most senior employees have first choice for job and shift assignments, and the most junior employees are required to work when the union steward is unable to find enough people willing to work at a particular time or in a particular job to fill TWA's needs.

In the spring of 1968 Hardison began to study the religion known as the Worldwide Church of God. One of the tenets of that religion is that one must observe the Sabbath by refraining from performing any work from sunset on Friday until sunset on Saturday. The religion also proscribes work on certain specified religious holidays.

When Hardison informed Everett Kussman, the manager of the Stores Department, of his religious conviction regarding observance of the Sabbath, Kussman agreed that the union steward should seek a job swap for Hardison or a change of days off; that Hardison would have his religious holidays off whenever possible if Hardison agreed to work the traditional holidays when asked; and that Kussman would try to find Hardison another job that would be more compatible with his religious beliefs. The problem was temporarily solved when Hardison transferred to the 11 p.m.–7 a.m. shift. Working this shift permitted Hardison to observe his Sabbath.

The problem soon reappeared when Hardison bid for and received a transfer from Building 1, where he had been employed, to Building 2, where he would work the day shift. The two buildings had entirely separate seniority lists; and while in Building 1 Hardison had sufficient seniority to observe the Sabbath regularly, he was second from the bottom on the Building 2 seniority list.

In Building 2 Hardison was asked to work Saturdays when a fellow employee went on vacation. TWA agreed to permit the union to seek a change of work assignments for Hardison, but the union was not willing to violate the seniority provisions set out in the collective-bargaining contract, and Hardison had insufficient seniority to bid for a shift having Saturdays off.

A proposal that Hardison work only four days a week was rejected by the company. Hardison's job was essential, and on weekends he was the only available person on his shift to perform it. To leave the position empty would have impaired supply shop functions, which were critical to airline operations; to fill Hardison's position with a supervisor or an employee from another area would simply have undermanned another operation; and to employ someone not regularly assigned to work Saturdays would have required TWA to pay premium wages.

When an accommodation was not reached, Hardison refused to report for work on Saturdays. A transfer to the twilight shift proved unavailing since that schedule still required Hardison to work past sundown on Fridays. After a hearing, Hardison was discharged on grounds of insubordination for refusing to work during his designated shift.

Hardison * * * brought this action * * * against TWA and IAM, claiming that his discharge by TWA constituted religious discrimination in violation of Title VII. * * *

[After a bench trial, the district court ruled in favor of TWA and the union. The Eighth Circuit affirmed the judgment for the union, but reversed the judgment for TWA.]

* * *

III

The Court of Appeals held that TWA had not made reasonable efforts to accommodate Hardison's religious needs under the 1967 EEOC guidelines in effect at the time the relevant events occurred. In its view, TWA had rejected three reasonable alternatives, any one of which would have satisfied its obligation without undue hardship. * * *

We disagree with the Court of Appeals in all relevant respects. It is our view that TWA made reasonable efforts to accommodate and that each of the Court of Appeals' suggested alternatives would have been an undue hardship within the meaning of the statute as construed by the EEOC guidelines.

A

It might be inferred from the Court of Appeals' opinion and from the brief of the EEOC in this Court that TWA's efforts to accommodate were no more than negligible. The findings of the District Court, supported by the record, are to the contrary. In summarizing its more detailed findings, the District Court observed:

TWA established as a matter of fact that it did take appropriate action to accommodate as required by Title VII. It held several meetings with plaintiff at which it attempted to find a solution to plaintiff's problems. It did accommodate plaintiff's observance of his special religious holidays. It authorized the union steward to search for someone who would swap shifts, which apparently was normal procedure.

It is also true that TWA itself attempted without success to find Hardison another job. The District Court's view was that TWA had done all that could reasonably be expected within the bounds of the seniority system.

* * *

We shall say more about the seniority system, but at this juncture it appears to us that the system itself represented a significant accommodation to the needs, both religious and secular, of all of TWA's employees. As will become apparent, the seniority system represents a neutral way of minimizing the number of occasions when an employee must work on a day that he would prefer to have off. Additionally, recognizing that weekend work schedules are the least popular, the company made further accommodation by reducing its work force to a bare minimum on those days.

B

We are also convinced, contrary to the Court of Appeals, that TWA itself cannot be faulted for having failed to work out a shift or job swap for Hardison. Both the union and TWA had agreed to the seniority system; the union was unwilling to entertain a variance over the objections of men senior to Hardison; and for TWA to have arranged unilaterally for a swap would have amounted to a breach of the collective-bargaining agreement.

(1)

Hardison and the EEOC insist that the statutory obligation to accommodate religious needs takes precedence over both the collective-bargaining contract and the seniority rights of TWA's other employees. We agree that neither a collective-bargaining contract nor a seniority system may be employed to violate the statute, but we do not believe that the duty to accommodate requires TWA to take steps inconsistent with the otherwise valid agreement. Collective bargaining, aimed at effecting workable and enforceable agreements between management and labor, lies at the core of our national labor policy, and seniority provisions are universally included in these contracts. Without a clear and express indication from Congress, we cannot agree with Hardison and the EEOC that an agreed-upon seniority system must give way when necessary to accommodate religious observances. The issue is important and warrants some discussion.

Any employer who, like TWA, conducts an around-the-clock operation is presented with the choice of allocating work schedules either in accordance with the preferences of its employees or by involuntary assignment. Insofar as the varying shift preferences of its employees complement each other, TWA could meet its manpower needs through voluntary work scheduling. In the present case, for example, Hardison's supervisor foresaw little difficulty in giving Hardison his religious holidays off since they fell on days that most other employees preferred to work, while Hardison was willing to work on the traditional holidays that most other employees preferred to have off.

Whenever there are not enough employees who choose to work a particular shift, however, some employees must be assigned to that shift even though it is not their first choice. Such was evidently the case with regard to Saturday work; even though TWA cut back its weekend work force to a skeleton crew, not enough employees chose those days off to staff the Stores Department through voluntary scheduling. In these circumstances, TWA and IAM agreed to give first preference to employees who had worked in a particular department the longest.

Had TWA nevertheless circumvented the seniority system by relieving Hardison of Saturday work and ordering a senior employee to replace him, it would have denied the latter his shift preference so that Hardison could be given his. The senior employee would also have been deprived of his contractual rights under the collective-bargaining agreement.

It was essential to TWA's business to require Saturday and Sunday work from at least a few employees even though most employees preferred those days off. Allocating the burdens of weekend work was a matter for collective bargaining. In considering criteria to govern this allocation, TWA and the union had two alternatives: adopt a neutral system, such as seniority, a lottery, or rotating shifts; or allocate days off in accordance with the religious needs of its employees. TWA would have had to adopt the latter in order to assure Hardison and others like him of getting the days off necessary for strict observance of their religion, but it could have done so only at the expense of others who had strong, but perhaps nonreligious, reasons for not working on weekends. There were no volunteers to relieve Hardison on Saturdays, and to give Hardison Saturdays off, TWA would have had to deprive another employee of his shift preference at least in part because he did not adhere to a religion that observed the Saturday Sabbath.

Title VII does not contemplate such unequal treatment. The repeated, unequivocal emphasis of both the language and the legislative history of Title VII is on eliminating discrimination in employment, and such discrimination is proscribed when it is directed against majorities as well as minorities. Indeed, the foundation of Hardison's claim is that TWA and IAM engaged in religious *discrimination* in violation of § 703(a)(1) when they failed to arrange for him to have Saturdays off. It would be anomalous to conclude that by "reasonable accommodation" Congress meant that an employer must deny the shift and job preference of some employees, as well as deprive them of their contractual rights, in order to accommodate or prefer the religious needs of others, and we conclude that Title VII does not require an employer to go that far.

(2)

Our conclusion is supported by the fact that seniority systems are afforded special treatment under Title VII itself. Section 703(h) provides in pertinent part:

Notwithstanding any other provision of this subchapter, it shall not be an unlawful employment practice for an employer to apply different standards of compensation, or different terms, conditions, or privileges of employment pursuant to a bona fide seniority or merit system * * * provided that such differences are not the result of an intention to discriminate because of race, color, religion, sex, or national origin. * * *

"[T]he unmistakable purpose of § 703(h) was to make clear that the routine application of a bona fide seniority system would not be unlawful under Title VII." Teamsters v. United States, 431 U.S. 324, 352, 97 S.Ct. 1843, 1863, 52 L.Ed.2d 396 (1977). Section 703(h) is "a definitional provision; as with the other provisions of § 703, subsection (h) delineates which employment practices are illegal and thereby prohibited and which are not." Franks v. Bowman Transp. Co., 424 U.S. 747, 758, 96 S.Ct. 1251, 1261, 47 L.Ed.2d 444 (1976). Thus, absent a discriminatory purpose, the operation of a seniority system cannot be an unlawful employment practice even if the system has some discriminatory consequences.

There has been no suggestion of discriminatory intent in this case. "The seniority system was not designed with the intention to discriminate against religion nor did it act to lock members of any religion into a pattern wherein their freedom to exercise their religion was limited. It was coincidental that in plaintiff's case the seniority system acted to compound his problems in exercising his religion." The Court of Appeals' conclusion that TWA was not limited by the terms of its seniority system was in substance nothing more than a ruling that operation of the seniority system was itself an unlawful employment practice even though no discriminatory purpose had been shown. That ruling is plainly inconsistent with the dictates of § 703(h), both on its face and as interpreted in the recent decisions of this Court.

As we have said, TWA was not required by Title VII to carve out a special exception to its seniority system in order to help Hardison to meet his religious obligations.

C

The Court of Appeals also suggested that TWA could have permitted Hardison to work a four-day week if necessary in order to avoid working on his Sabbath. Recognizing that this might have left TWA short-handed on the one shift each week that Hardison did not work, the court still concluded that TWA would suffer no undue hardship if it were required to replace Hardison either with supervisory personnel or with qualified personnel from other departments. Alternatively, the Court of Appeals suggested that TWA could have replaced Hardison on his Saturday shift with other available employees through the payment of premium wages. Both of these alternatives would involve costs to TWA, either in the form of lost efficiency in other jobs or higher wages.

To require TWA to bear more than a *de minimis* cost in order to give Hardison Saturdays off is an undue hardship.[15] Like abandonment of the seniority system, to require TWA to bear additional costs when no such costs are incurred to give other employees the days off that they want would involve unequal treatment of employees on the basis of their religion. By suggesting that TWA should incur certain costs in order to give Hardison Saturdays off the Court of Appeals would in effect require TWA to finance an additional Saturday off and then to choose the employee who will enjoy it on the basis of his religious beliefs. While incurring extra costs to secure a replacement for Hardison might remove the necessity of compelling another employee to work involuntarily in Hardison's place, it would not change the fact that the privilege of having Saturdays off would be allocated according to religious beliefs.

As we have seen, the paramount concern of Congress in enacting Title VII was the elimination of discrimination in employment. In the absence of clear statutory language or legislative history to the contrary, we will not readily construe the statute to require an employer to discriminate against some employees in order to enable others to observe their Sabbath.

JUSTICE MARSHALL, with whom JUSTICE BRENNAN joins, dissenting.

* * *

Today's decision deals a fatal blow to all efforts under Title VII to accommodate work requirements to religious practices. The Court holds, in essence, that although the EEOC regulations and the Act state that an employer must make reasonable adjustments in his work demands to take account of religious observances, the regulation and Act do not really mean what they say. An employer, the Court concludes, need not grant even the most minor special privilege to religious observers to enable them to follow their faith. As a question of social policy, this result is deeply troubling, for a society that truly values religious pluralism cannot compel adherents of minority religions to make the cruel choice of surrendering their religion or their job. And as a matter of law today's result is intolerable, for the Court adopts the very position that Congress expressly rejected in 1972, as if we were free to disregard congressional choices that a majority of this Court thinks unwise. I therefore dissent.

With respect to each of the proposed accommodations to respondent Hardison's religious observances that the Court discusses, it ultimately notes that the accommodation would have required "unequal treat-

---

15. The dissent argues that "the costs to TWA of either paying overtime or not replacing respondent would [not] have been more than *de minimis*." This ignores, however, the express finding of the District Court that "[b]oth of these solutions would have created an undue burden on the conduct of TWA's business" and it fails to take account of the likelihood that a company as large as TWA may have many employees whose religious observances, like Hardison's, prohibit them from working on Saturdays or Sundays.

ment," in favor of the religious observer. That is quite true. But if an accommodation can be rejected simply because it involves preferential treatment, then the regulation and the statute, while brimming with "sound and fury," ultimately "signif[y] nothing."

* * *

What makes today's decision most tragic, however, is not that respondent Hardison has been needlessly deprived of his livelihood simply because he chose to follow the dictates of his conscience. Nor is the tragedy exhausted by the impact it will have on thousands of Americans like Hardison who could be forced to live on welfare as the price they must pay for worshiping their God. The ultimate tragedy is that despite Congress' best efforts, one of this Nation's pillars of strength—our hospitality to religious diversity—has been seriously eroded. All Americans will be a little poorer until today's decision is erased.

ANSONIA BOARD OF EDUCATION v. PHILBROOK

Supreme Court of the United States, 1986.
479 U.S. 60, 107 S.Ct. 367, 93 L.Ed.2d 305.

CHIEF JUSTICE REHNQUIST delivered the opinion of the Court.

Petitioner Ansonia Board of Education has employed respondent Ronald Philbrook since 1962 to teach high school business and typing classes in Ansonia, Connecticut. In 1968, Philbrook was baptized into the Worldwide Church of God. The tenets of the church require members to refrain from secular employment during designated holy days, a practice that has caused respondent to miss approximately six schooldays each year. We are asked to determine whether the employer's efforts to adjust respondent's work schedule in light of his belief fulfill its obligation under § 701(j) of the Civil Rights Act of 1964, 42 U.S.C. § 2000e(j), to "reasonably accommodate to an employee's * * * religious observance or practice without undue hardship on the conduct of the employer's business."

Since the 1967–1968 school year, the school board's collective-bargaining agreements with the Ansonia Federation of Teachers have granted to each teacher 18 days of leave per year for illness, cumulative to 150 and later to 180 days. Accumulated leave may be used for purposes other than illness as specified in the agreement. A teacher may accordingly use five days' leave for a death in the immediate family, one day for attendance at a wedding, three days per year for attendance as an official delegate to a national veterans organization, and the like. With the exception of the agreement covering the 1967–1968 school year, each contract has specifically provided three days' annual leave for observance of mandatory religious holidays, as defined in the contract. Unlike other categories for which leave is permitted, absences for religious holidays are not charged against the teacher's annual or accumulated leave.

The school board has also agreed that teachers may use up to three days of accumulated leave each school year for "necessary personal business." Recent contracts limited permissible personal leave to those uses not otherwise specified in the contract. This limitation dictated, for example, that an employee who wanted more than three leave days to attend the convention of a national veterans organization could not use personal leave to gain extra days for that purpose. Likewise, an employee already absent three days for mandatory religious observances could not later use personal leave for "[a]ny religious activity," or "[a]ny religious observance." Since the 1978–1979 school year, teachers have been allowed to take one of the three personal days without prior approval; use of the remaining two days requires advance approval by the school principal.

The limitations on the use of personal business leave spawned this litigation. Until the 1976–1977 year, Philbrook observed mandatory holy days by using the three days granted in the contract and then taking unauthorized leave. His pay was reduced accordingly. In 1976, however, respondent stopped taking unauthorized leave for religious reasons, and began scheduling required hospital visits on church holy days. He also worked on several holy days. Dissatisfied with this arrangement, Philbrook repeatedly asked the school board to adopt one of two alternatives. His preferred alternative would allow use of personal business leave for religious observance, effectively giving him three additional days of paid leave for that purpose. Short of this arrangement, respondent suggested that he pay the cost of a substitute and receive full pay for additional days off for religious observances.[3] Petitioner has consistently rejected both proposals.

* * *

[After a bench trial, the district court found that Philbrook had failed to prove his claim of religious discrimination against the school board and the union. The Second Circuit reversed and remanded.]

We granted certiorari to consider the important questions of federal law presented by the decision of the Court of Appeals. Specifically, we are asked to address whether the Court of Appeals erred in finding that Philbrook established a prima facie case of religious discrimination and in opining that an employer must accept the employee's preferred accommodation absent proof of undue hardship. We find little support in the statute for the approach adopted by the Court of Appeals, but we agree that the ultimate issue of reasonable accommodation cannot be resolved without further factual inquiry. We accordingly affirm the judgment of the Court of Appeals remanding the case to the District Court for additional findings.

* * *

3. The suggested accommodation would reduce the financial costs to Philbrook of unauthorized absences. In 1984, for example, a substitute cost $30 per day, and respondent's loss in pay from an unauthorized absence was over $130.

* * * [T]he Court of Appeals assumed that the employer had offered a reasonable accommodation of Philbrook's religious beliefs. This alone, however, was insufficient in that court's view to allow resolution of the dispute. The court observed that the duty to accommodate "cannot be defined without reference to undue hardship." It accordingly determined that the accommodation obligation includes a duty to accept "the proposal the employee prefers unless that accommodation causes undue hardship on the employer's conduct of his business." * * *

We find no basis in either the statute or its legislative history for requiring an employer to choose any particular reasonable accommodation. By its very terms the statute directs that any reasonable accommodation by the employer is sufficient to meet its accommodation obligation. The employer violates the statute unless it "demonstrates that [it] is unable to reasonably accommodate * * * an employee's * * * religious observance or practice without undue hardship on the conduct of the employer's business." 42 U.S.C. § 2000e(j). Thus, where the employer has already reasonably accommodated the employee's religious needs, the statutory inquiry is at an end. The employer need not further show that each of the employee's alternative accommodations would result in undue hardship. * * * [T]he extent of undue hardship on the employer's business is at issue only where the employer claims that it is unable to offer any reasonable accommodation without such hardship. Once the Court of Appeals assumed that the school board had offered to Philbrook a reasonable alternative, it erred by requiring the Board to nonetheless demonstrate the hardship of Philbrook's alternatives.

The legislative history of § 701(j) * * * is of little help in defining the employer's accommodation obligation. To the extent it provides any indication of congressional intent, however, we think that the history supports our conclusion. Senator Randolph, the sponsor of the amendment that became § 701(j), expressed his hope that accommodation would be made with "flexibility" and "a desire to achieve an adjustment." 118 Cong. Rec. 706 (1972). Consistent with these goals, courts have noted that "bilateral cooperation is appropriate in the search for an acceptable reconciliation of the needs of the employee's religion and the exigencies of the employer's business." Brener v. Diagnostic Center Hosp., 671 F.2d 141, 145–46 (5th Cir.1982). Under the approach articulated by the Court of Appeals, however, the employee is given every incentive to hold out for the most beneficial accommodation, despite the fact that an employer offers a reasonable resolution of the conflict. This approach, we think, conflicts with both the language of the statute and the views that led to its enactment. We accordingly hold that an employer has met its obligation under § 701(j) when it demonstrates that it has offered a reasonable accommodation to the employee.[6]

6. The Court of Appeals found support for its decision in the EEOC's guidelines on religious discrimination. * * * To the extent that the guideline, like the approach of the Court of Appeals, requires the employer to accept any alternative favored by the employee short of undue hardship, we find the guideline simply inconsistent with the plain meaning of the statute. * * *

The remaining issue in the case is whether the school board's leave policy constitutes a reasonable accommodation of Philbrook's religious beliefs. * * * We think that the school board's policy in this case, requiring respondent to take unpaid leave for holy day observance that exceeded the amount allowed by the collective-bargaining agreement, would generally be a reasonable one. In enacting § 701(j), Congress was understandably motivated by a desire to assure the individual additional opportunity to observe religious practices, but it did not impose a duty on the employer to accommodate at all costs. The provision of unpaid leave eliminates the conflict between employment requirements and religious practices by allowing the individual to observe fully religious holy days and requires him only to give up compensation for a day that he did not in fact work. Generally speaking, "[t]he direct effect of [unpaid leave] is merely a loss of income for the period the employee is not at work; such an exclusion has no direct effect upon either employment opportunities or job status." Nashville Gas Co. v. Satty, 434 U.S. 136, 145, 98 S.Ct. 347, 353, 54 L.Ed.2d 356 (1977).

But unpaid leave is not a reasonable accommodation when paid leave is provided for all purposes *except* religious ones. A provision for paid leave "that is part and parcel of the employment relationship may not be doled out in a discriminatory fashion, even if the employer would be free * * * not to provide the benefit at all." Hishon v. King & Spalding, 467 U.S. 69, 75, 104 S.Ct. 2229, 2233–34, 81 L.Ed.2d 59 (1984). Such an arrangement would display a discrimination against religious practices that is the antithesis of reasonableness. Whether the policy here violates this teaching turns on factual inquiry into past and present administration of the personal business leave provisions of the collective-bargaining agreement. The school board contends that the necessary personal business category in the agreement, like other leave provisions, defines a limited purpose leave. Philbrook, on the other hand, asserts that the necessary personal leave category is not so limited, operating as an open-ended leave provision that may be used for a wide range of secular purposes in addition to those specifically provided for in the contract, but not for similar religious purposes. We do not think that the record is sufficiently clear on this point for us to make the necessary factual findings, and we therefore affirm the judgment of the Court of Appeals remanding the case to the District Court. The latter court on remand should make the necessary findings as to past and existing practice in the administration of the collective-bargaining agreements.

[JUSTICES MARSHALL and STEVENS separately concurred in part and dissented in part. A portion of Justice Marshall's dissent follows.]

* * *

The Court's analysis in *Trans World Airlines, Inc. v. Hardison*, 432 U.S. 63, 97 S.Ct. 2264, 53 L.Ed.2d 113 (1977), is difficult to reconcile with its holding today. In *Hardison*, the Court held that the employer's chosen work schedule was a reasonable accommodation but nonetheless went on to consider and reject each of the alternative suggested accommodations. The course followed in *Hardison* should have been adopted here as well. "Once it is determined that the duty to accommodate sometimes requires that an employee be exempted from an otherwise valid work requirement, the only remaining question is * * * : Did [the employer] prove that *it exhausted all reasonable accommodations*, and that the *only remaining alternatives would have caused undue hardship* on [the employer's] business?" *Id.*, at 91, 97 S.Ct. at 2280 (Marshall, J., dissenting) (emphasis added).

Notes and Questions

1. *Hardison* suggests a two-step analysis on the defense of inability to reasonably accommodate without undue hardship. Does *Philbrook* modify the *Hardison* analysis? If so, how?

2. Do *Hardison* and *Philbrook* endorse a per se rule that provisions in a collective bargaining agreement dealing with competing interests of the employees whom the union represents constitute reasonable accommodations? The Supreme Court, in an ADA case involving a non-collectively bargained seniority system, found that while ordinarily a disabled employee will not be entitled to an accommodation that places the employee above the requirements of a seniority system, an employee may show special circumstances that make just such an accommodation reasonable. *See* US Airways v. Barnett, 535 U.S. 391, 122 S.Ct. 1516, 152 L.E.2d 589 (2002). Similarly, in *Balint v. Carson City, Nevada,* 180 F.3d 1047 (9th Cir.1999) (en banc), the Ninth Circuit held that a bona fide seniority system does not relieve an employer of the duty to attempt to reasonably accommodate an employee's religious beliefs and practices if an accommodation can be accomplished without violating the seniority rights of other employees. Should it matter for accommodation whether a seniority system arises out of a collective bargaining agreement? *Compare* Beadle v. Hillsborough County Sheriff's Dep't, 29 F.3d 589, 593 (11th Cir. 1994) ("While we recognize that *Hardison* specifically concerned the sufficiency of a seniority system under Title VII to determine employee eligibility for weekends off, we are not persuaded that the Court intended its holding apply only to those systems.") *with* Opuku–Boateng v. State of Cal., 95 F.3d 1461, 1470 (9th Cir. 1996) ("In *Hardison,* the proposed accommodation would have conflicted with the contractually-established seniority system * * *. By contrast, in this case, the scheduling of shifts was not governed by any collective bargaining agreement, and the proposed accommodation would not have deprived any employee of any contractually-established seniority rights or privileges, or indeed of any contractually-established rights or privileges of any kind.").

3. If an employee simply refuses to engage in "bilateral cooperation" with the employer in order to arrange an accommodation for her religious beliefs and practices, should the employer nevertheless be required to propose an accommodation for the employee? *See* Smith v. Pyro Mining Co., 827 F.2d 1081, 1085 (6th Cir.1987) ("Although the burden is on the employer to accommodate the employee's religious needs, the employee must make some effort to cooperate with an employer's attempt at accommodation."), *cert. denied*, 485 U.S. 989, 108 S.Ct. 1293, 99 L.Ed.2d 503 (1988);

EEOC v. Ithaca Indus., Inc., 849 F.2d 116 (4th Cir.1988) (en banc) (where an employee absolutely refuses to work on his Sabbath, the burden is on the employer to attempt to accommodate the employee's religious beliefs by offering alternatives), *cert. denied*, 488 U.S. 924, 109 S.Ct. 306, 102 L.Ed.2d 325 (1988).

4.   In the following situations, what accommodations, if any, could an employer offer to make in order to satisfy its burden under Title VII?

a.   An evangelical Christian employee believes that she should share the gospel with her co-workers. Pursuant to her beliefs, she sends letters to the homes of two employees. First, because she believes that her supervisor has engaged in un-Christian conduct in managing the employer's business, she sends him a letter urging him to confess his "sins" to God. His wife reads the letter and mistakenly believes her husband is having an adulterous affair with someone at work. The employee then sends a letter to a co-worker who has just had a child out-of-wedlock and is convalescing at home with an unspecified illness. The letter states that God "doesn't like when people commit adultery" and insinuates that her illness is God's punishment for her adultery. The recipient of the letter finds it "cruel." *See* Chalmers v. Tulon Co. of Richmond, 101 F.3d 1012 (4th Cir.1996), *cert. denied*, 522 U.S. 813, 118 S.Ct. 58, 139 L.Ed.2d 21 (1997).

b.   Employees of a fast food establishment tell their employer that, according to their "sincerely held Christian religious beliefs," they feel compelled to greet customers with phrases such as "God bless you" and "Praise the Lord." Not all of the customers find the greetings to be "positive, uplifting, and inspirational," and some co-workers tell the employer that they consider the greetings to be "inappropriate for the workplace." *See* Banks v. Service Am. Corp., 952 F.Supp. 703 (D.Kan.1996).

c.   Employee, a police officer, objects on religious grounds to being assigned to police duties at abortion clinics. *Compare* Parrott v. District of Columbia, 58 Empl.Prac.Dec. (CCH) ¶ 41,369, 1991 WL 126020, at *3 (D.D.C.1991) (Title VII's guarantee of reasonable accommodation does not require a police department to exempt a police officer from an assignment that requires policing abortion "rescues," because he has a "duty as a law enforcement officer to protect individuals inside abortion clinics from others' interference with their legally protected rights"), *with* Rodriguez v. Chicago, 69 Fair Empl.Prac.Cas. (BNA) 993 (N.D.Ill.1996) (city's refusal to excuse a Roman Catholic police officer from duty assignments at abortion clinics, despite his strong religious objections, is actionable under Title VII).

d.   Employer proposes that an employee who objects to working on her Sabbath, which is Saturday, first use all of her accrued vacation days before alternative accommodations are considered. *See* Cooper v. Oak Rubber Co., 15 F.3d 1375 (6th Cir.1994).

e.   A female employee has made a private religious vow to wear an anti-abortion button at all times until a national policy is adopted banning all abortions. The button has a color photograph of an aborted fetus and the words "Stop Abortion." Some of her co-workers object to her wearing the pin in the workplace because of the disruption it causes; others do not object because they agree with the button's message. *See* Wilson v. U.S. West Communications, 58 F.3d 1337 (8th Cir.1995).

f. A Jewish salesman informs his company that his religion requires that he must live in an area with an active synagogue. The community he chooses is outside of his sales territory. The company responds that its salespeople must live in communities within their sales area. The salesman tells the company that he is willing to pay all costs related to commuting from and living within his new community. *See* Vetter v. Farmland Indust., 901 F.Supp. 1446 (N.D.Iowa 1995), *rev'd on other grounds,* 120 F.3d 749 (8th Cir. 1997).

5. Noting that the "precise reach" of the employer's duty to accommodate its employees' religious beliefs is not clear, the court in *Brown v. Polk*, 61 F.3d 650, 655 (8th Cir.1995), *cert. denied,* 516 U.S. 1158, 116 S.Ct. 1042, 134 L.Ed.2d 189 (1996), discussed in Section F of this Chapter, concluded that the issue must be resolved on a case-by-case basis. The court summarized some of the rules on undue hardship that the courts have articulated: (1) "[t]he cost of hiring an additional worker or the loss of production that results from not replacing a worker who is unavailable due to a religious conflict can amount to undue hardship"; (2) *"[d]e minimis* cost * * * entails not only monetary concerns, but also the employer's burden in conducting its business"; (3) asserted hardships must be "real" rather than "speculative," "merely conceivable," or "hypothetical"; (4) an employer "stands on weak ground when advancing hypothetical hardships in a factual vacuum"; (5) "[u]ndue hardship cannot be proved by assumptions nor by opinions based on hypothetical facts"; (6) "[u]ndue hardship requires more than proof of some fellow-worker's grumbling," and "[a]n employer * * * would have to show * * * actual imposition on co-workers or disruption of the work routine." *Id.* (citations omitted). Based on these guidelines, which of the following, if any, constitutes an undue hardship:

a. Lynn Weber, a truck driver, is a Jehovah's Witness whose religious beliefs prevent him from accepting long-haul overnight runs with a female partner who is not his wife. The company assigns two-person overnight runs on a seniority basis and informs Weber that "working with women is a part of the job and that he would have to work with women or would not receive any driving assignment." *See* Weber v. Roadway Express, Inc., 199 F.3d 270 (5th Cir.2000).

b. Brenda Enlow, a member of the Conservative Holiness faith, applies to work in a factory manufacturing metal parts. The factory's safety policy includes a requirement that all employees are prohibited from wearing sleeveless shirts and thin-soled shoes, and must wear pants. The policy is intended to reduce exposure of skin to sharp metal parts and the risk of loose clothing becoming stuck on parts and machinery. The policy applies to all employees given that everyone is required to be able to operate all the machines of the plant due to changing production demands on customer orders. However, according to Brenda, her faith has a dress code requiring women and girls to wear dresses that extend below the knee. Brenda also cites the Bible, which states "a woman shall not wear anything that pertains to a man." *See* EEOC v. Oak–Rite Mfg. Corp., 88 Fair Empl.Prac.Cas. (BNA) 126 (S.D.Ind.2001).

6. Employee files a charge with the EEOC alleging that he was discharged because the employer failed to accommodate his religious beliefs

and practices. If the employer makes a settlement offer while the claim is pending before the EEOC, does the offer cure the alleged violation? *See* Toledo v. Nobel–Sysco, Inc., 892 F.2d 1481 (10th Cir.1989), *cert. denied*, 495 U.S. 948, 110 S.Ct. 2208, 109 L.Ed.2d 535 (1990).

7. An employee claims that he was discharged because he refused to remove religious items from his desk although another employee was not disciplined for keeping a Bible on her desk. The employer claims the employee was discharged based on a reduction in force and that he was the lowest ranked employee in the jobs in which the reduction took place. Should this case be analyzed as a circumstantial evidence case in which the defense of a legitimate, nondiscriminatory reason could be raised? *See* Arvin–Thornton v. Philip Morris Prod. Inc., 64 F.3d 655 (4th Cir.1995) (unpublished table decision), *cert. denied*, 516 U.S. 1126, 116 S.Ct. 943, 133 L.Ed.2d 868 (1996).

8. In 1997, the Senate Committee on Labor and Human Resources held hearings on a bill, the Workplace Religious Freedom Act, to amend Title VII to provide that undue hardship shall mean "significant difficulty and expense," reversing *Hardison*'s *de minimus* standard, and to provide that general leave shall always be available for religious observance, reversing *Ansonia*. The bill requires that employers must weigh "significant difficulty and expense" in the context of 1) the essential functions of a job, 2) the identifiable cost of accommodation, 3) the impact of an accommodation precedent on a particular workplace, and 4) the size of, and geographic distance between, the employer's business and facilities. Should *Hardison* and *Ansonia* be reversed? What are the pro's and con's of such a measure? Would such an amendment violate the Constitution's Establishment Clause? *See generally* The Workplace Religious Freedom Act of 1997: Hearings on S. 1124, Senate Committee on Labor and Human Resources, 105th Cong., 1st Sess. 31–57 (statements of Richard Foltin, Lawrence Lorber, Roberto Corrada) (Oct. 21,1997).

Note: Unions, Religious Discrimination Claims, and the Charity Substitution Rule

The liability of labor unions for unlawful discrimination, both as employers and as labor organizations, is covered in Chapter 14. Section 701(j) of Title VII, 42 U.S.C. § 2000e(j), specifically imposes an obligation on employers to reasonably accommodate the religious beliefs and practices of employees unless undue hardship on the conduct of the employer's business is shown. Although § 701(j) is silent with respect to a labor union's obligation to reasonably accommodate the religious beliefs and practices of its members, the courts have nevertheless held that § 701(j) is equally applicable to unions. *See, e.g.*, Tooley v. Martin–Marietta Corp., 648 F.2d 1239 (9th Cir.), *cert. denied*, 454 U.S. 1098, 102 S.Ct. 671, 70 L.Ed.2d 639 (1981).

The National Labor Relations Act (NLRA) and the Railway Labor Act (RLA) both authorize union security agreements. 29 U.S.C. § 158(a)(3); 45 U.S.C. § 142, Eleventh. Generally a security agreement imposes an obligation on members of a bargaining unit to pay the union a fee that is equivalent to the union's initiation fee and dues even if they choose not to become union members and even if they are ideologically opposed to unionism. Under a typical agreement containing a dues "check-off" provision, every member of the bargaining unit is asked to sign a card authorizing the employer to deduct dues and initiation fees from her wages and forward the money to the union. The funds collected go into the union's treasury and are used for a variety of activities such as the negotiation and administration of collective bargaining agreements, grievance and arbitration proceedings, strike funds, and pension funds. Also, some of the funds may be used for other activities such as political activities, lobbying for labor-related legislation, and contributions to charities. *See generally* Norman L. Cantor, *Uses and Abuses of the Agency Shop*, 59 Notre Dame L.Rev. 61 (1983). One of the rationales for union security clauses is avoidance of the "free rider" situation, that is, allowing nonunion members of a bargaining union to reap the benefits of a collective bargaining agreement without contributing to the operating costs of the union.

Some employees have relied upon the reasonable accommodation provision of § 701(j) of Title VII to challenge union security provisions when they have religious scruples against joining unions or paying union dues. A typical situation in which this issue arises is when an employee objects, on religious grounds, to joining the union or paying union dues. In response, the union seeks, pursuant to the union security provision in the collective bargaining agreement, to have the employee discharged for the nonpayment of union dues or their equivalent in mandatory fees. Relying in substantial part on *Trans World Airlines, Inc. v. Hardison*, 432 U.S. 63, 97 S.Ct. 2264, 53 L.Ed.2d 113 (1977), in Section E of this chapter, courts have endorsed the "substitute charity contribution rule" in an attempt to reconcile the tension between a union's legitimate interest in having all of its member participate in the financial costs of collective bargaining, an employee's religious objections to paying union dues, and a union's obligation to reasonably accommodate the religious objections of an employee to the mandatory payment of union dues. The substitute charity contribution rule allows a religious objector to pay to a charity the equivalent amount that is paid to the union by other employees in the bargaining unit who do not have religious objections to paying union dues. In explaining the substitute charitable contribution rule, the court in *Tooley v. Martin–Marietta Corp.* stated that

> [t]he substituted charity contribution is consistent with the balancing of interests promoted by section 701(j). Under this accommodation, the union is entitled to enjoy the benefits of the union agreement while the [employees] are entitled to practice in accordance with their religious convictions. To the extent that the substituted charity accommodation effects this balance, it is reasonable under section 701(j).

648 F.2d at 1242. In rejecting the union's argument that under *Hardison* the loss of dues imposes an undue hardship on the union, *Tooley* held that

> [a] "wide-spread refusal to pay union dues" is sufficient to establish undue hardship, but that is not the contention here. The [union has] not established that the "substituted charity" accommodation, as applied here, will deprive the union of monies necessary for its maintenance or operation.

Id. at 1243–44 (citation omitted).

Prior to 1980, the courts were more sympathetic to unions in cases in which employees had religious objections to paying union dues. Although employing the same balancing test generally used in Title VII cases, the courts were more likely to tip the balance in favor of unions in the enforcement of union security clauses. *See* Steven C. Schwab, *Union Security Agreements and Title VII: The Scope and Effect of the New Section 19 of the National Labor Relations Act*, 17 Gonz.L.Rev. 329 (1981); Charleston C.K. Wang, Comment, *Religious Accommodation Versus Union Security: A Tale of Two Statutes*, 9 No.Ky.L.Rev. 331 (1982). In 1980 Congress enacted § 19 of the NLRA, 29 U.S.C. § 169, in an attempt to reconcile the inconsistency between § 701(j) of Title VII and the NLRA. The scope of the charity substitution rule under § 19 of the NLRA, however, is much narrower than under Title VII. Section 19 affords protection only to "employees who are members of a bona fide religion, body, or sect which has historically held conscientious objections to joining or financially supporting labor organizations." In *International Association of Machinists & Aerospace Workers, Lodge 751 v. Boeing Co.*, 833 F.2d 165, 169 (9th Cir.1987), *cert. denied*, 485 U.S. 1014, 108 S.Ct. 1488, 99 L.Ed.2d 715 (1988), the union argued that the more recent specific protection of § 19 supersedes and limits the broader protection of § 701(j). The Ninth Circuit rejected this statutory construction argument on the ground that the two statutes are not irreconcilable because they "serve independent and separate purposes." *Id.* The Sixth Circuit found § 19 to be unconstitutional in *Wilson v. National Labor Relations Board*, 920 F.2d 1282 (6th Cir.1990), *cert. denied*, 505 U.S. 1218, 112 S.Ct. 3025, 120 L.Ed.2d 896 (1992). For a more extensive discussion of the balance between union security and religious freedom, see Roberto L. Corrada, *Religious Accommodation and the National Labor Relations Act,* 17 Berkeley J.Emp. & Lab.L. 185 (1996).

Consider the following questions:

a.   Suppose an employee does not have any religious objections to labor unions but does, on religious grounds, object to the lobbying efforts of the union in support of abortion rights. What accommodation would be reasonable in such a case if the employee works in a bargaining unit covered by a collective bargaining agreement with a union security provision? *See* EEOC v. University of Detroit, 904 F.2d 331 (6th Cir.1990).

b.   Who should decide which charity should be the recipient of the funds under the substituted charity contribution rule? The employee? The union? A charity that is mutually agreeable to both? *See* Tooley v. Martin–Marietta Corp., 648 F.2d 1239 (9th Cir.), *cert. denied*, 454 U.S. 1098, 102 S.Ct. 671, 70 L.Ed.2d 639 (1981) (employee offered to pay to charity that was mutually agreeable to union and employee).

Note: Religious Freedom and Sexual Orientation Discrimination

The evolving interest at both the federal and state level in prohibiting discrimination against gays and lesbians and the current laws prohibiting discrimination in employment because of religion raise significant issues for employers. *See, e.g.,* Debra Baker, *Acting on One's Belief: Clash Between Gay*

Rights and Religious Freedom Spills Over into the Workplace, 86 A.B.A.J. 18 (Jan.2000). A number of employers have instituted diversity training or diversity awareness programs to educate their employees about federal and state laws that prohibit discrimination in employment because of race, color, sex, religion, age, national origin, and sexual orientation. *See, e.g.,* Sara Rynes & Benson Rosen, *A Field Survey of Factors Affecting the Adoption and Perceived Success of Diversity Training Programs,* 48 Personnel Psychol. 247 (1995); Jack Gordon, *Different from What? Diversity as a Performance Issue,* 32 Training 25 (May 1995); Frederick R. Lynch, The Diversity Machine: The Drive to Change the "White Male Workplace" (1997). The rules enunciated by the Supreme Court on employer liability for harassment in *Ellerth* and *Faragher* (Chapter 8, Section C.1), on same-sex harassment in *Oncale* (Chapter 8, Section B.3), and on punitive damages in *Kolstad* (Chapter 16, Section F.2), impose some obligation on employers to educate their employees about the prohibition against discrimination in the workplace. Because many states and local governments now prohibit discrimination because of sexual orientation, see Chapter 9, education about discrimination against gays and lesbians is often included in employer diversity training or education programs. There is also a growing trend among public and private employers to extend employee benefits to same-sex couples or domestic partners. *See, e.g.,* Foray v. Bell Atlantic, 56 F.Supp.2d 327 (S.D.N.Y.1999) (plaintiff, an unmarried male, who was co-habitating with a female domestic partner, sued his employer under Title VII claiming unlawful sex discrimination because the employer provided certain employee benefits to same-sex partners but did not provide similar benefits to opposite-sex partners).

The tension between laws prohibiting discrimination in employment because of religion and the employers' efforts to protect gays and lesbians from discrimination in the workplace is illustrated in *Altman v. Minnesota Department of Corrections*, 251 F.3d 1199 (8th Cir.2001). There, three public employees were directed to participate in a mandatory diversity education program on discrimination against gays and lesbians in the work force. They alleged that the materials presented at the program caused them discomfort because of their religious beliefs. They attended the session, but read silently from their Bibles at various points. As a result, the employer issued each a written reprimand and one of the plaintiffs was denied a promotion as a result of the reprimand. The reprimands were issued pursuant to an employer policy and there was no evidence that the employer singled out the plaintiffs solely because of their Bible-reading conduct. They sued their employer alleging violations of their rights under, *inter alia*, the Free Speech and Free Exercise Clauses of the First Amendment and Title VII. Analyzing the case solely on Title VII grounds, what argument would you make in favor of the plaintiffs? What defense would you advance in support of the employer's action?

Note: Religious Harassment

Compston v. Borden, Inc., 424 F.Supp. 157 (S.D.Ohio 1976), is one of the earliest cases to recognize that harassment on the basis of religion is actionable under Title VII. *Compston* held that "[w]hen a person vested with managerial responsibilities embarks upon a course of conduct calculated to demean an employee before his fellows because of the employee's professed religious views, such activity necessarily will have the effect of altering the conditions of his employment." *Id.* at 160–61. The Supreme Court approvingly cited *Compston* in its landmark sexual harassment case of *Meritor Savings Bank v. Vinson*, 477 U.S. 57, 66, 106 S.Ct. 2399, 2405, 91 L.Ed.2d 49 (1986), Chapter 8, Section B.2. The courts generally have applied the analytical framework, burden-shifting, and other rules developed in the sexual harassment cases to claims of religious harassment. For example, relying on *Harris v. Forklift Systems*, 510 U.S. 17, 114 S.Ct. 367, 126 L.Ed.2d 295 (1993), and *Henson v. City of Dundee*, 682 F.2d 897 (11th Cir.1982), the court in *Ellis v. Wal–Mart Stores, Inc.*, 952 F.Supp. 1513, 1518 (M.D.Ala.1996), held that to prevail in a religious harassment case, the plaintiff must prove that (1) she belongs to a protected class; (2) she was subjected to unwelcome religious harassment; (3) the harassment was based on religion; and (4) the harassment was sufficiently severe or pervasive to alter or otherwise adversely affect a term, condition, or privilege of her employment. (*Harris* and *Henson* are covered in Chapter 8, Section B.2.) In addition, to establish employer liability, "the plaintiff must show either that: (1) the harasser is the employer or one of its agents; or (2) the employer knew or should have known of the harassment caused by co-workers, but failed to take corrective action." *Id.* The *Harris v. Forklift* totality of circumstances standard was deemed to be equally applicable in the religious discrimination cases. *Id.* In light of the 1998 Supreme Court cases on employer liability for sexual harassment by supervisors, is the *Ellis* rule on employer liability for religious harassment still good law? See *Burlington Industries, Inc. v. Ellerth*, 524 U.S. 742, 118 S.Ct. 2257, 141 L.Ed.2d 633 (1998), *Faragher v. City of Boca Raton*, 524 U.S. 775, 118 S.Ct. 2275, 141 L.Ed.2d 662 (1998) in Chapter 8, Section C.1. Recall that *Harris v. Forklift* adopted a reasonable person standard—consisting of both objective and subjective standards—to determine whether the harassment was sufficiently severe or pervasive. Recall also that some courts have adopted a *reasonable woman* standard in sexual harassment cases or a *reasonable black person* standard in racial harassment cases. Is the *Harris v. Forklift* "reasonable person" standard applicable in the religious harassment cases? How would a court apply a "reasonable religious person" standard?

In July 1993, the EEOC issued proposed guidelines in an effort to clarify the line between protected speech and unlawful harassment. 29 C.F.R. § 1609 (proposed Oct. 1, 1993). Opponents of the proposed guidelines, who were very vocal and apparently well organized, focused on the inclusion of religion in the guidelines. A number of groups and individuals, particularly religious groups, expressed concerns that some employees and employers might use the guidelines to justify suppression of a variety of forms of religious expression in the workplace. For example, requiring removal of a religious symbol from a person's desk or prohibiting any discussion of religion around the water cooler. The furor over the proposed guidelines eventually led to a congressional hearing and ultimately to the EEOC's withdrawal of the guidelines in 1994. *See* 59 Fed.Reg. 58,312 (1994). The debate over the proposed guidelines on religious harassment is treated in Betty L. Dunkum, *Where to Draw the Line: Handling Religious Harassment*

Issues in the Wake of the Failed EEOC Guidelines, 71 Notre Dame L.Rev. 953 (1996).

A portion of the proposed EEOC guidelines provided:

(b)(1) Harassment is verbal or physical conduct that denigrates or shows hostility or aversion toward an individual because of his/her * * * religion * * * or that of his/her relatives, friends, or associates, and that:

(i) Has the purpose or effect of creating an intimidating, hostile, or offensive work environment;

(ii) Has the purpose or effect of unreasonably interfering with an individual's work performance; or

(iii) Otherwise adversely affects an individual's employment opportunities.

(c) The standard for determining whether verbal or physical conduct relating to * * * religion * * * is sufficiently severe to create a hostile or abusive work environment is whether a reasonable person in the same or similar circumstances would find the conduct intimidating, hostile, or abusive.

58 Fed.Reg. 51,266 (proposed Oct. 1, 1993).

The proposed guidelines tracked, in substantial part, the EEOC guidelines on sexual harassment. See Chapter 8, Section B. Should there be guidelines on religious harassment at all? Is there an argument for having guidelines on racial and sexual harassment but not on religious harassment?

The tension between Title VII's prohibition of harassment because of religion and the First Amendment's protection of religious freedom in light of *Ellerth* and *Faragher* is explored in Kimball E. Gilmer & Jeffrey M. Anderson, *Zero Tolerance for God? Religious Expression in the Workplace After* Ellerth *and* Faragher, 42 How.L.J. 327 (1999).

Note: Disparate Impact Religious Discrimination Claims Under Title VII

Most religious discrimination claims are brought under the disparate treatment theory. When plaintiffs have asserted disparate impact claims, the courts have tended to reject them; for example, in *EEOC v. Sambo's of Georgia*, 530 F.Supp. 86, 92–93 (N.D.Ga.1981), the court held that the disparate impact theory is unavailable to challenge a practice allegedly burdening individuals because of their religious beliefs and practices. Some courts, however, have entertained disparate impact religious discrimination claims without questioning whether these cases are even amenable to disparate impact analysis. *See, e.g.*, Tagatz v. Marquette Univ., 681 F.Supp. 1344, 1357–58 (E.D.Wis.1988) (holding that plaintiff's evidence of salary disparities between Catholic and non-Catholic professors failed to establish a prima facie case of disparate impact based on his religion), *aff'd on other grounds*, 861 F.2d 1040 (7th Cir.1988). More recently, the Seventh Circuit has questioned whether the disparate impact theory is appropriate in religious discrimination cases. In *EEOC v. UPS*, 94 F.3d 314 (7th Cir.1996), the employer had a rule that required employees holding jobs that involved contact with the public to be clean-shaven. Plaintiff, a member of an Islamic sect that forbids men from shaving, was denied a job that required contact with the public or customers of the employer. The Seventh Circuit acknowledged that the clean-shaven rule was facially neutral but suggested that the religious discrimination cases "differ from the traditional disparate impact claims in that the discriminatory effect can often be alleviated by some reasonable accommodation of the employment requirement to the employee's particular religious needs," as required by § 701(j) of Title VII. *Id.* at 317 n.3. If disparate impact analysis is appropriate in some religious discrimination cases, should business necessity or reasonable accommodation be the appropriate defense?

F.   CLAIMS AGAINST GOVERNMENT EMPLOYERS

BROWN v. POLK COUNTY, IOWA

United States Court of Appeals for the Eighth Circuit, 1995 (en banc).
61 F.3d 650, *cert. denied*, 516 U.S. 1158, 116 S.Ct. 1042, 134 L.Ed.2d 189 (1996).

MORRIS SHEPPARD ARNOLD, Circuit Judge.

In mid–1986, Isaiah Brown, a black man who identifies himself as a born-again Christian, became the director of the information services (data processing) department for Polk County, Iowa. He reported directly to the county administrator and supervised approximately 50 employees.

In mid–1990, an internal investigation into religious activities conducted on government time by employees in Mr. Brown's department revealed that Mr. Brown had directed a secretary to type Bible study notes for him, that several employees had said prayers in Mr. Brown's office before the beginning of some workdays, that several employees had said prayers in Mr. Brown's office in department meetings held during the day, and that in addressing one meeting of employees, Mr. Brown had affirmed his Christianity and had referred to Bible passages related to slothfulness and "work ethics." Subsequently, the county administrator reprimanded Mr. Brown in writing for a "lack of judgment pertaining to his personal participation in and/or his knowledge of employees participating in activities that could be construed as the direct support of or the promotion of a religious organization or religious activities utilizing the resources of Polk County Government." The reprimand directed Mr. Brown "immediately [to] cease any activities that could be considered to be religious proselytizing, witnessing, or counseling and * * * further [to] cease to utilize County resources that in any way could be perceived as to be supporting a religious activity or religious organization." * * * Subsequently, on a separate occasion, the county administrator directed Mr. Brown to remove from his office all items with a religious connotation, including a Bible in his desk.

In late 1990, the county administrator again reprimanded Mr. Brown in writing, on that occasion for a "lack of judgment" related to financial constraints in the county's budget. Two weeks later, after an internal investigation into personal use of county computers by employees in Mr. Brown's department, the county administrator asked Mr. Brown to resign; when he refused, the county administrator fired him.

In late 1991, Mr. Brown sued the county, its board of supervisors, and the county administrator. Mr. Brown alleged, under 42 U.S.C. § 1983, that the first reprimand and the order to remove from his office all items with a religious connotation violated constitutional guarantees of free exercise of religion, free speech, and equal protection. He also alleged, under * * * [Title VII] * * * that he was fired because of his * * * religion.

* * *

After a five-day bench trial, the district court found for the defendants in all respects. * * * On rehearing *en banc*, however, we affirm in part and reverse in part.

* * *

II

* * *

The district court made the factual finding that religious animus played no part in the decision to fire Mr. Brown. The district court found, instead, that the reason for Mr. Brown's discharge was inadequate performance, specifically, the inability to supervise and administer his department. Because we find that religious activities played a part in the decision to fire Mr. Brown, and that the proof was inadequate to show that Mr. Brown would have been fired if those activities had not been considered, we reverse the district court judgment with respect to the statutory religious discrimination claims.

In most of the cases alleging religious discrimination under Title VII, the employer is a private entity rather than a government, and the First Amendment to the Constitution is therefore not applicable to the employment relationship. In cases such as this one, however, where a government is the employer, we must consider both the First Amendment and Title VII in determining the legitimacy of the county administrator's action. The First Amendment is, of course, applicable to state-created government units by virtue of the Fourteenth Amendment.

With specific reference to the Free Exercise Clause, we hold that in the governmental employment context, the First Amendment protects at least as much religious activity as Title VII does. *See, e.g.,* United States v. Board of Educ., 911 F.2d 882, 890 (3d Cir.1990) ("at the very least, undue hardship is a lower standard than compelling state interest"). Another way of framing that holding is to say that any religious activities of employees that can be accommodated without undue hardship to the governmental employer are also protected by the First Amendment. In other words, if a governmental employer has violated

Title VII, it has also violated the guarantees of the First Amendment. We turn, then, to a more detailed examination of the requirements of Title VII.

III

The county administrator testified that he fired Mr. Brown "because of [a] culmination of incidents" that led him to conclude that Mr. Brown "had lost control of his department and was no longer in a position to manage effectively." The county administrator also testified, moreover, that the reprimand for "religious activities" was "a factor" in the decision to fire Mr. Brown. The labor relations manager for the county testified as well that, in asking for Mr. Brown's resignation and then firing him, the county administrator told Mr. Brown that the first reprimand was among the "concerns" prompting his discharge. Finally, Mr. Brown himself testified that the reasons given for his discharge by the county administrator were "the problems that [had] centered around [Mr. Brown's] department for [the] last two years, primarily religion." Unfortunately, none of the witnesses specified with any more particularity the exact actions to which the county administrator was alluding. We must, therefore, consider what activities were covered by the first reprimand and which, if any, of those activities were protected by Title VII.

* * *

It is undisputed that the defendants made no attempt to accommodate any of Mr. Brown's religious activities. In those circumstances, the defendants may prevail only if they can show that allowing those activities "could not be accomplished without undue hardship." United States v. Board of Educ., 911 F.2d 882, 887 (3d Cir.1990). * * *

* * *

The first reprimand to Mr. Brown was precipitated by the internal investigation into religious activities conducted in mid–1990. The investigation revealed four actions attributed to him—directing a secretary to type his Bible study notes, allowing prayers in his office before the start of the workday, allowing prayers in his office during department meetings, and affirming his Christianity and referring to Bible passages about slothfulness and "work ethics" during one department meeting. We consider each of those activities in light of the commands of Title VII.

The defendants argue that allowing Mr. Brown to direct a county employee to type his Bible study notes would amount to an undue hardship on the conduct of county business, since the work that that employee would otherwise be doing would have to be postponed, done by another employee, or not done at all. We agree that such an activity creates more than a *de minimis* cost to the defendants. We conclude, therefore, that the defendants may not be held liable under Title VII for their actions in relation to that activity.

Nor, by the way, do we believe that the defendants' actions with respect to that activity violate the Free Exercise Clause. That is because we do not consider precluding Mr. Brown from directing a county employee to type his Bible study notes to be a "substantial[] burden" upon his religious practices. Employment Div. v. Smith, 494 U.S. 872, 883, 110 S.Ct. 1595, 1602–03, 108 L.Ed.2d 876 (1990). We would be surprised if directing a county employee to type Bible study notes is "conduct mandated by religious belief," Thomas v. Review Bd., 450 U.S. 707, 718, 101 S.Ct. 1425, 1432, 67 L.Ed.2d 624 (1981), and, indeed, Mr. Brown does not so contend. We conclude, therefore, that Mr. Brown's directing a county employee to type his Bible study notes was not an activity protected at all under the law in this case and, accordingly, that the defendants may not be held liable for their actions with respect to that activity.

With respect to Mr. Brown's allowing prayers in his office before the start of the workday, nothing in Title VII requires that an employer open its premises for use before the start of the workday. Nor, incidentally, would the First Amendment so require in this case, since no proof was offered that Mr. Brown's office was a public forum or a limited public forum or that the defendants allowed employees to use their offices for personal purposes before the start of the workday (indeed, the defendants' position was that once an employee arrived at the office, the workday began, regardless of the actual time, and the defendants' policy manual directed that no personal use of county resources was permitted). We conclude, therefore, that Mr. Brown's allowing prayers in his office before the start of the workday was not an activity protected at all under the law in this case and, accordingly, that the defendants may not be held liable for their actions in relation to that activity.

Mr. Brown also allowed prayers in his office during several department meetings and affirmed his Christianity and referred to Bible passages related to slothfulness and "work ethics" during one department meeting. All of the testimony was that the prayers were entirely voluntary and "spontaneous," "did not occur regularly," and dealt with "matters related to Polk County business," and that Mr. Brown's affirmation of Christianity and reference to Bible passages on slothfulness and "work ethics" occurred during only one meeting. Given their context, all of those actions may well have been impolitic on Mr. Brown's part, but we think that they were inconsequential as a legal matter, especially since they were apparently spontaneous and infrequent.

* * *

In our view, the defendants' examples of the burden that they would have to bear by tolerating trifling instances such as those complained of are insufficiently "real" and too "hypothetical" to satisfy the standard required to show undue hardship. The defendants showed no "actual imposition on co-workers or disruption of the work routine" Burns v. Southern Pac. Transp. Co., 589 F.2d 403, 407, (9th Cir.1978), *cert. denied*, 439 U.S. 1072, 99 S.Ct. 843, 59 L.Ed.2d 38 (1979), generated by occasional spontaneous prayers and isolated references to Christian belief. On this record, we hold that the defendants failed to prove that accommodating such instances as they objected to would lead to undue hardship. The defendants may be held liable, therefore, for firing Mr. Brown on account of those activities unless the defendants can prove that they would have fired him regardless of those activities. *See, e.g.,* Price Waterhouse v. Hopkins, 490 U.S. 228, 242, 244–46, 252–53, 258, 109 S.Ct. 1775, 1786 1787–88, 1791–92, 1794–95, 104 L.Ed.2d 268 (1989) (plurality opinion).

The district court held that Mr. Brown had offered no direct evidence that he was fired on account of his religious activities. We do not understand that conclusion, since, as we have already noted, the county administrator himself testified that the first reprimand, which was based on religious activities, was "a factor" in his decision to fire Mr. Brown. We believe that Mr. Brown presented enough evidence to require the application of a "mixed-motives" analysis instead.

In these circumstances, we could remand to the district court for findings on the question of whether the defendants proved that they would have fired Mr. Brown even if they had not considered his religious activities. In this case, however, we hold that it would be futile to do so, since no reasonable person could conclude from the evidence presented that the defendants proved that they would have fired Mr. Brown anyway. Indeed, when asked specifically at trial if Mr. Brown would have been fired absent the first reprimand, the county administrator responded, "I wouldn't want to speculate on that. * * * I just don't know." * * * We therefore reverse the judgment on the statutory religious discrimination claims and remand the case to the district court for consideration of the appropriate relief on those claims.

IV

We last consider constitutional claims that Mr. Brown did not link to his termination. We reverse the district court with respect to those claims and remand the case for consideration of the appropriate relief.

We are mindful (as the dissenting judges are) that our cases, and First Amendment jurisprudence in general, require that plaintiffs in cases like this must show that the governmental action complained of substantially burdened their religious activities. (We take this to mean that Mr. Brown must show that the burdens placed on him were not inconsiderable.) We have already said as much in a previous section of this opinion. But Mr. Brown has carried that burden. From Mr. Brown's testimony, there can be no doubt that his religious beliefs are extremely important to him and play a central role in his life. He testified that in 1986 or early 1987 he underwent a personal spiritual revival that was "a life-changing experience" for him. He stated, in addition, that prayer was "something that's part of [his] being," that prayer "leads [him] and * * * guides [him]," and that he uses prayer in his life "on a daily basis." He believes, according to his testimony, that prayer "changes things" and, furthermore, that his God expects him to pray "for governments, our nation, our schools, our children, all the pandemic problems inherent in our society." There was no challenge to this testimony then or now, and all of the evidence points to a conclusion that Mr. Brown found the defendants' prohibitions oppressive and vexatious.

In these circumstances, the district court's observation that Mr. Brown did not show "that the removal of religious items from his office inhibited his ability to freely exercise his religion," either proceeds from a misunderstanding of what a substantial burden is, or is a clearly erroneous finding of fact. Our observation above that some of Mr. Brown's religious activities were inconsequential was, of course, meant to indicate that they did not produce even an insignificant external effect in the workplace, not that they were not significant to him.

Mr. Brown first asserts that his First Amendment right to the free exercise of his religion was violated when the county administrator ordered him to "cease any activities that could be considered to be religious proselytizing, witnessing, or counseling" while he was on the job. Although the free exercise of religion is certainly a fundamental constitutional right, we believe that the Supreme Court might well adopt, for Free Exercise cases that arise in the context of public employment, an analysis like the one enunciated in *Pickering v. Board of Education*, 391 U.S. 563, 88 S.Ct. 1731, 20 L.Ed.2d 811 (1968). That case dealt with free speech rather than the Free Exercise of religion, but because the analogy is such a close one, and because we see no essential relevant differences between those rights, we shall endeavor to apply the principles of *Pickering* to the case at hand.

Pickering recognizes a public employee's right to speak on matters that lie at the core of the First Amendment, that is, matters of public concern, so long as "the effective functioning of the public employer's enterprise" is not interfered with. The kind of speech that Polk County prohibited in this case lies right at the core of the Free Exercise Clause. We have, moreover, already indicated at some length our belief that the record reveals no diminution whatever in the effectiveness of governmental functions fairly attributable to anything that Mr. Brown did that is forbidden by the order. The order therefore fails to find any justification under well-settled principles governing the constitutional rights of public employees.

We may concede for the sake of argument that Polk County has a legal right to ensure that its workplace is free from religious activity that harasses or intimidates. But any interference with religious activity that the exercise of that right entails must be reasonably related to the exercise of that right and must be narrowly tailored to its achievement. Here, there was not the least attempt to confine the prohibition to harassing or intimidating speech. Instead, Polk County baldly directed Mr. Brown to "cease any activities that *could be considered* to be religious proselytizing, witnessing, or counseling" (emphasis supplied). That order exhibited a hostility to religion that our Constitution simply prohibits. It would seem to require no argument that to forbid speech "that could be considered" religious is not narrowly tailored to the aim of prohibiting harassment, although it is certainly capable of doing that. If Mr. Brown asked someone to attend his church, for instance, we suppose that that "could be considered" proselytizing, but its prohibition runs afoul of the Free Exercise Clause. Similarly, a statement to the effect that one's religion was important in one's life "could be considered" witnessing, yet for the government to forbid it would be unconstitutional.

The defendants would have us hold that their "interest" in avoiding a claim against them that they have violated the Establishment Clause allows them to prohibit religious expression altogether in their workplaces. Such a position is too extravagant to maintain, for it gives a dominance to the Establishment Clause that it does not have and that would allow it to trump the Free Exercise Clause. One might just as well justify erecting a cross and a creche on county property at Christmas as a means of avoiding a claim that employees had been denied their Free Exercise rights. The clauses cannot, in the nature of things, make conflicting demands on a government, and government is charged with making sure that its activities are confined to the ample and well-defined space that separates them.

Mr. Brown also complains about the directive to remove from his office all items with a religious connotation, including a Bible that was in his desk. It is here, perhaps, that the zealotry of the county administrator is most clearly revealed. Mr. Brown had to remove a plaque containing the serenity prayer ("God, grant me the serenity to accept the things I cannot change, the courage to change the things I can, and the wisdom to know the difference"), another that said, "God be in my life and in my commitment," and a third containing the Lord's Prayer. Most intrusive of all was the order to take down a poster that proclaimed some non-religious inspirational commonplaces that were deemed inappropriate because their author, although he occupied no religious office, had "Cardinal" in his name. Mr. Brown testified that he was told that these items had to go because they might be considered "offensive to employees." Our observations above with reference to the application of the principles of *Pickering* apply with equal force to this second portion of Mr. Brown's claim. There was no showing of disruption of work or any interference with the efficient performance of governmental functions sufficient to allow for this extraordinary action on the part of Polk County. We emphasize, moreover, that even if employees found Mr. Brown's displays "offensive," Polk County could not legally remove them if their "offensiveness" was based on the content of their message. In that case, the county would be taking sides in a religious dispute, which, of course, it cannot do under either the Establishment Clause or the Equal protection Clause. If the "offensive" character of the display ran to a well-grounded apprehension among employees of discriminatory treatment by Mr. Brown, then this case might be entirely different. But the evidence will not support such a finding here. We emphasize, too, that fear alone, even fear of discrimination or other illegal activity, is not enough to justify such a mobilization of governmental force against Mr. Brown. The fear must be substantial and, above all, objectively reasonable. A phobia of religion, for instance, no matter how real subjectively, will not do. As Justice Brandeis has said, rather starkly, "Men feared witches and burnt women." Whitney v. California, 274 U.S. 357, 376, 47 S.Ct. 641, 71 L.Ed. 1095 (1927) (Brandeis, J., concurring).

V

For the reasons indicated, we affirm the judgment of the district court in part, we reverse it in part, and we remand for further proceedings consistent with this opinion.

FAGG, Circuit Judge, dissenting, joined by LOKEN, HANSEN, and MURPHY, Circuit Judges.

* * *

Although the Court recognizes the substantial burden requirement, the Court ignores Brown's failure to show the County's actions rose to the level of a substantial burden on his religious practices. The record lacks any evidence that Brown's born-again Christianity required him to display religious items in his office or to engage in the religious activities restricted by the reprimand. Indeed, the district court found Brown did not prove the removal of the items from his office inhibited his ability to exercise his religion freely. * * * The district court's finding is not clearly erroneous anyway. As for the religious activity restrictions, the Court recognizes the prayers at departmental meetings were spontaneous, infrequent, and inconsequential. The evidence about the change in Brown's religious practices after the reprimand shows the restrictions merely inconvenienced Brown. Rather than engaging in group prayers during work, Brown simply went across the street to the library at lunchtime to read his Bible and pray with others. The reprimand did not restrict Brown's private prayers. Brown has not shown any substantial, concrete harm to his religious practice resulted from Polk County's actions. The Court misplaces reliance on evidence that Brown's "religious beliefs are extremely important to him and play a central role in his life." The fact that Brown sincerely held his religious beliefs does not mean the County's actions substantially burdened Brown's exercise of those beliefs. Because Brown failed to show the County's actions substantially burdened his religious practices, the Court should not even reach the *Pickering* analysis on Brown's Free Exercise claim. * * * I would hold the balance of interests tips in the County's favor in this case, primarily given Brown's status as a supervisor of fifty employees.

* * *

Notes and Questions

1.   The court in *Brown v. Polk County* applies the *Pickering* free speech balancing test to the employee's claim of religious freedom. Is free speech

just like free exercise of religion? In addition to the governmental interest, freedom of religion must be weighed with a constitutional prohibition against establishment of religion. Is this distinction sufficient to make *Pickering* analysis inapplicable? The court also considers the employee's Title VII claim coequally with his Free Exercise claim. Yet, the Supreme Court often refuses to create constitutional precedents when claims can be decided on nonconstitutional grounds. *See, e.g.,* NLRB v. Catholic Bishop of Chicago, 440 U.S. 490, 507, 99 S.Ct. 1313, 59 L.E.2d 533 (1979). Should the *Brown* court decide the constitutional claim when it can rule in the employee's favor based on Title VII's religious discrimination provision?

2. *The Religious Freedom Restoration Act:* The *Brown* court found that the governmental employer's actions substantially burdened the employee's religion, yet in *Employment Division, Department of Human Resources of Oregon v. Smith*, 494 U.S. 872, 110 S.Ct. 1595, 108 L.Ed.2d 876 (1990), the Supreme Court ruled that the Free Exercise Clause permits Oregon to include the sacramental use of peyote within the reach of the state's general criminal law prohibiting the use of certain proscribed drugs. The Court upheld the state statute on the ground that the right of free exercise of religion does not relieve an individual of the general obligation of a citizen to comply with a valid and neutral law of general applicability simply because the law proscribes conduct that his religion sanctions. Prior to *Smith*, the Court had adopted a balancing test set forth in *Sherbert v. Verner*, 374 U.S. 398, 83 S.Ct. 1790, 10 L.Ed.2d 965 (1963), to decide Free Exercise Clause claims. The balancing test requires a court to determine first whether a challenged practice substantially burdens a religious practice or belief, and if it does, then to determine whether the burden is justified by a compelling state interest. The *Smith* Court refused to apply the *Sherbert v. Verner* balancing test in the context of an "across-the-board criminal prohibition on a particular form of conduct." *Smith*, 494 U.S. at 873, 110 S.Ct. at 1597. Should Title VII be viewed as a statute of general applicability for purposes of using the *Smith* case to limit employee Free Exercise protection? How does the *Brown* court rule on this question? Note that Title VII has been viewed as a general antidiscrimination law for purposes of surviving Establishment Clause challenges. *See, e.g.,* Estate of Thornton v. Caldor, 472 U.S. 703, 712, 105 S.Ct. 2914, 86 L.Ed.2d 557 (1985). If the *Smith* case serves to weaken Free Exercise protection should the court's ruling in *Brown* be reconsidered?

In response to *Smith*, Congress enacted the Religious Freedom Restoration Act (RFRA), 42 U.S.C. § 2000bb, to overturn *Smith* and to restore the compelling interest test. The RFRA provided that the "[g]overnment may substantially burden a person's exercise of religion only if it demonstrates that the application of the burden is in furtherance of a compelling governmental interest." In *City of Boerne v. Flores*, 521 U.S. 507, 117 S.Ct. 2157, 138 L.Ed.2d 624 (1997), in a 6–3 decision written by Justice Kennedy, the Supreme Court struck down RFRA on the ground that, in enacting RFRA, Congress had exceeded the scope of its enforcement authority under § 5 of the Fourteenth Amendment. The Court held that the statute violated the separation of powers doctrine and offended the principles of federalism. Some employees had relied upon RFRA as an alternative to Title VII, *see, e.g.,* Helland v. South Bend Community Sch. Corp., 93 F.3d 327, 330–32 (7th

Cir.1996). Also some employers had relied upon RFRA to defend religious discrimination claims. *See, e.g.*, EEOC v. Catholic Univ. of Am., 83 F.3d 455, 467 (D.C.Cir.1996). Under *Boerne v. Flores*, RFRA claims or defenses are now generally unavailable to either employees or employers, but RFRA may have survived *City of Boerne* for employees of the federal government. *See* Young v. Crystal Evangelical Free Church, 141 F.3d 854 (8th Cir. 1998) (holding that RFRA is constitutional as applied to federal employers).

3. *Guidelines on Religious Exercise and Religious Expression in the Federal Workplace*: On August 14, 1997, President Clinton issued guidelines designed to protect religious expression in the workplace for federal civilian employees. *See* 1997 WL 464857 (White House). Under the guidelines,

> [f]ederal employees may keep Bibles or Korans on their desks, tell colleagues how important religion is in their lives and put wreaths on office doors at Christmas time.
>
> They can argue about religion at the water cooler (just as they can argue about baseball or politics), or they can proclaim their atheism if they so choose. They can try to convert co-workers to their religion, but must cease and desist upon request.

David Stout, *Religion and Federal Workers: What Thou Shalt and Shalt Not Do*, N.Y. Times, Aug. 14, 1997, at A14. The guidelines were drafted by a committee representing several religious and civil liberties groups who were responding, in part, to the controversy surrounding the EEOC's failed 1993 effort to adopt guidelines on religious harassment in the workplace. In addition, to avoid potential constitutional challenges, the drafters took into account the reasons that the Supreme Court, in *Boerne v. Flores*, had found the Religious Freedom Restoration Act to be unconstitutional. *See* Susan McInerney, *President Clinton Unveils Religion Guidelines on Expression, Exercise in Federal Workplace*, Legal News, 66 U.S.L.W. 2120, 2121 (Aug. 26, 1997). The guidelines continue to be followed by the federal government. Some observers predict that state and local governments, as well as private employers, will ultimately use the federal guidelines as a model for dealing with issues involving religion in the workplace. *Id.*

4. *Religious Harassment in Public Employment:* In *Venters v. City of Delphi*, 123 F.3d 956 (7th Cir.1997), the plaintiff, Jennifer Venters, claimed that her supervisor, Police Chief Larry Ives, a born-again Christian, subjected her to both quid pro quo and hostile environment religious harassment. The Seventh Circuit reversed a summary judgment in favor of the employer, and remanded for a trial on Venter's Title VII claims, noting that, according to the plaintiff,

> Ives repeatedly subjected her to lectures (at work, during working hours) about her prospects for salvation, made highly personal inquiries into her private life (whether there was truth to purported rumors that she entertained guests in her home with pornography, for example), and ultimately went so far as to tell her that she led a sinful life, that he was certain she had had sex with family members and possibly animals, that she had sacrificed animals in Satan's name, and that committing suicide would be preferable to the life he believed Venters was living. * * * Ives' remarks were uninvited, were intrusive, touched upon the most private aspects of her life, were delivered in an intimidating manner, in

some cases were on their face scandalous, and were unrelenting throughout the entire period post-dating [Ives'] appointment as chief of police, continuing even after she had informed him that his comments to her were inappropriate.

Id. at 976.

With regard to the quid pro quo claim, the court observed that "this type of harassment is not limited to gender discrimination." *Id.* The court continued,

Ives did not, by Venters' account, simply share his religious beliefs with her, but instead he made it clear to her that if she did [not] conform to those views, she would be discharged. * * * Ives told Venters that in order to be a good employee, one had to be spiritually whole, and to meet that criterion one had to be "saved"; he described the police station as "God's house," and warned her that he would "trade" her if she did not play by "God's rules," if she did not embrace "God's way" over "Satan's"; * * * eventually Ives concluded that an "evil spirit had taken [her] soul," and he admonished her that he would not allow that "evil spirit" to reside in the police department.

Id. at 976–77.

Venters demonstrates the potential conflicts between rights arising under Title VII and the First Amendment that may occur in government employment when one employee attempts to communicate deeply held religious beliefs to another employee who wishes "to be left alone to exercise her own thoughts on the subject of religion in private, free of interference from her governmental employer." *Id.* at 977. The 1997 Guidelines on Religious Exercise and Religious Expression in the Federal Workplace, discussed *supra,* Note 3, deal with this dilemma by permitting the speaker's communication on religious topics, until the listener asks him to stop, at which time his First Amendment protections cease. In light of the facts alleged in *Venters*, would such a rule in the City of Delphi have effectively protected the constitutional and statutory rights of all parties?

5. *Federal Employees:* By virtue of congressional enactment, federal agencies are subject to Title VII, age, disability, and equal pay laws, just as are state and government employers and private employers. However, there are some meaningful differences in the way that these laws are applied to federal employees. Section 717 of Title VII provides the basis for federal employee Title VII claims, which can be handled through the Merit Systems Protection Board or through the separate EEO processes of the various federal agencies and then the EEOC. Importantly, in *Brown v. General Services Administration,* 425 U.S. 820, 835, 96 S.Ct. 1961, 1969, 48 L.Ed.2d 402, 413 (1976), the Supreme Court held that § 717 of Title VII was the exclusive remedy for discrimination by a federal agency. As a result, federal employees may not proceed under § 1981 or the Constitution for discrimination on claims that are otherwise covered by Title VII. If the *Polk County* case had been brought by a federal employee against a federal agency, the Title VII religious discrimination claim would likely have superseded the constitutional challenge under the *Brown v. GSA* mandate.

Chapter 11

DISCRIMINATION BECAUSE OF NATIONAL ORIGIN

A. INTRODUCTION

When Congress enacted Title VII, it provided a scanty record of its reasons for including a prohibition against national origin discrimination. *See* U.S. Equal Employment Opportunity Commission, Legislative History of Titles VII and IX, at 3179–81 (1968). Professor Juan F. Perea has offered the following explanation of the history behind the inclusion of national origin in Title VII:

> Prior to the enactment of the Civil Rights Act of 1964, the phrase "national origin" long had been the subject of federal executive and legislative action. In the immigration laws, national origin had been the explicit basis for discrimination because of country of origin by the federal government for approximately four decades, until 1965. With respect to fair employment practices, the phrase appears to have become part of the standard "boilerplate" language of executive orders prohibiting discrimination in employment. This context gave the term its basic meaning, country of birth, at the time of the passage of the Civil Rights Act of 1964.

> In 1924 * * * Congress passed * * * legislation creating national origin quotas for immigration. These quotas, defined by the countries of origin of prospective immigrants, attempted to limit immigration so that the demographic composition of immigrants matched the predominantly white, northern European composition of the extant American population. As a result of these quotas, the federal government discriminated explicitly against prospective immigrants based on their countries of birth.

Juan F. Perea, *Ethnicity and Prejudice: Reevaluating "National Origin" Discrimination Under Title VII*, 35 Wm. & Mary L.Rev. 805, 810–12 (1994). Congress amended the Immigration and Nationality Act, 8 U.S.C. § 1151, in 1965 to replace the national origin quotas with new standards for admission to citizenship in the United States.

In studying and analyzing national origin discrimination claims, it is essential to recognize the historical fact that the United States is essentially a nation of immigrants. Except for the descendants of Native Americans who inhabited North America before it was "discovered" by Europeans and the descendants of slaves who were forcibly brought here, every citizen of the United States is either an immigrant or has descended from immigrants. At the beginning of the current century, about 10% of the population of the United States is foreign born. EEOC Compliance Manual Section 13–I (2002). Regardless of where they were born, about 13% of the United States identified as Hispanic and over 4% identified as Asian. *Id*. Even though the United States is a nation of immigrants, nativism, that is, an intense opposition to immigrants, has been deeply embedded in the American character from the early days of the country. In fiscal year 2002, the EEOC witnessed a 13% increase in charges filed alleging national origin discrimination. EEOC, *Pakistani-American Workers to Share $1.1 Million in Harassment Settlement with Stock Steel* (Mar. 19, 2003), viewed at *www.eeoc.gov/press/3–19–03.html*.

In *Paths to Belonging: The Constitution and Cultural Identity*, 64 N.C.L.Rev. 303, 311 (1986), Professor Kenneth L. Karst stated that

[i]n America hostility among cultural groups * * * is properly seen as a threat to [national unity] * * *. Those who react to cultural differences with fear or anger generally espouse nativist policies designed to repress the differences by excluding the "others" from the country, by forcing them to conform to the norms of the dominant culture, or by relegating them to a subordinate status in society.

Examples of nativism include the Chinese Exclusion Act of 1881, 22 Stat. 58, which suspended Chinese immigration into the United States for ten years; the national origin quotas in immigration laws that favored Anglo–European individuals; the internment of Japanese–American citizens during World War II; and the "No Irish Need Apply" and "No Japs Wanted" employment policies that some employers adopted in the past. *See, e.g.*, President's Committee on Civil Rights, To Secure These Rights 78 (1947). A contemporary illustration of nativism is Proposition 187, a ballot initiative approved by California voters in 1994 that prohibited illegal aliens from receiving public education, social welfare benefits, and nonemergency health services. Nancy Cervantes, Sasha Khokha & Bobbie Murray, *Hate Unleashed: Los Angeles in the Aftermath of Proposition 187*, 17 Chicano–Latino L.Rev. 1 (1995) (documenting complaints about the discriminatory impact of Proposition 187 on the Latino community in Los Angeles). Although most provisions of the initiative were never enforced, "Proposition 187 introduced a new chapter into the history of nativism in California and the nation." *Id.* at 3. *See* League of United Latin American Citizens v. Wilson, 908 F.Supp. 755 (C.D.Cal.1995) (holding most of the initiative unconstitutional because it was preempted by federal immigration law), *on reconsideration in part*, 997 F.Supp. 1244 (C.D.Cal.1997) (same); Nicole E. Lucy, *Mediation of Proposition 187: Creative Solution to an Old Problem? Or Quiet*

Death for Initiatives? 1 Pepp.Disp.Resol.L.J. 123, 141–49, 169–70 (2001) (tracing the history of the Proposition 187 litigation).

One scholar has identified four common themes that nativists have expressed throughout the history of the United States:

> One common complaint is that certain "races" are intellectually and culturally inferior and should not be allowed into the [United States], at least not in substantial numbers. Nativists have often regarded immigrant groups as racial "others" quite different from the Euro–American majority. A second and related theme views those who have immigrated from racially and culturally inferior groups as problematical in terms of their complete assimilation to the dominant Anglo culture. A third theme, articulated most often in troubled economic times, is that "inferior" immigrants are taking the jobs and disrupting the economic conditions of native-born Americans. A fourth notion, also heard most often in times of fiscal crisis, is that immigrants are creating serious government crises, such as by corrupting the voting system or overloading school and welfare systems.

Joe R. Feagin, *Old Poison in New Bottles: The Deep Roots of Modern Nativism, in* Immigrants Out! The New Nativism and the Anti–Immigrant Impulse in the United States 13–14 (Juan F. Perea ed., 1997). *See generally* Berta Esperanza Hernández-Truyol, *Natives, Newcomers and Nativism: A Human Rights Model for the Twenty–First Century*, 23 Fordham Urb.L.J. 1075 (1996).

A fifth theme has emerged during wartime—a fear that "foreigners" pose a threat to national security. During World War II, for example, Japanese Americans were imprisoned in internment camps and German immigrants were targeted as well. Since the terrorist attacks on New York City and Washington, D.C., on September 11, 2001, concerns about terrorism have been raised predominantly with respect to people with Middle Eastern ancestry. *See* Mary Ann Weston & Marda Dunsky, *One Culture, Two Frameworks: U.S. Media Coverage of Arabs at Home and Abroad*, 7 J. Islamic L. & Culture 129, 133 (2002) (noting that Arabs and Arab–Americans are currently stereotyped as terrorists); Lori Sachs, *September 11, 2001: The Constitution During Crisis: A New Perspective*, 29 Fordham Urb.L.J. 1715, 1736–37 (2002) (reporting that the public favors racial profiling of terrorists, mainly targeted at Arab–Americans, to increase security); Susan Akram & Kevin Johnson, *Race, Civil Rights, and Immigration Law After September 11, 2001: The Targeting of Arabs and Muslims*, 58 N.Y.U. Ann.Surv.Am.L. 295, 311–614, 348–49 (observing that antiterrorism fear leads to hostility and discrimination against a variety of ethnic groups).

Discriminatory polices and practices because of national origin are not as open and flagrant today as they have been in past years. Nowadays, national origin discrimination is

> more likely to occur against persons because of the perceptible manifestations of ethnic distinction, ethnic traits, than because of

the often imperceptible fact of national origin. As Professor Allport wrote, "perceptible differences are of basic importance in distinguishing between out-group and in-group members." The perceptible differences that mark out-groups include, among others, skin color, cast of features, gestures, prevalent facial expression, speech or accent, dress, mannerisms, religious practices, food habits, names, place of residence, and insignia.

Juan F. Perea, *Ethnicity and the Constitution: Beyond the Black and White Binary Constitution*, 36 Wm. & Mary L.Rev. 571, 576 (1995) (quoting Gordon Allport, The Nature of Prejudice 9 (25th Ann.ed.1979)).

As a general rule, the theories, defenses, and analyses treated in Chapter 3 on disparate treatment and Chapter 4 on disparate impact are equally applicable to national origin discrimination claims. *See, e.g.*, Odima v. Westin Tucson Hotel, 53 F.3d 1484 (9th Cir.1995) (disparate treatment); Association of Mexican–American Educators v. California, 937 F.Supp. 1397 (N.D.Cal.1996) (disparate impact). The materials in this chapter focus on selected issues involving national origin discrimination in the workplace. The meaning of national origin is covered in Section B, which also includes notes on the BFOQ defense and national origin harassment. Section C discusses the relationship between discrimination based on citizenship status and discrimination based on national origin. It also discusses the interplay between the Immigration Reform and Control Act of 1986 and Title VII. Language discrimination is treated in Section D.

B. THE MEANING OF "NATIONAL ORIGIN"

In the legislative debates on Title VII, Congressman Roosevelt stated: "May I just make very clear that 'national origin' means national. It means the country from which your forebears came. You may be from Poland, Czechoslovakia, England, France or any other country." 110 Cong.Rec. 2549 (1964). An earlier version of Title VII included "ancestry" as one of the prohibited criteria. H.R.Rep. N. 914, 88th Cong., 1st Sess. 87 (1963), but Congress excluded it from the final version. Does the exclusion of "ancestry" from the statute suggest that Congress thought that "national origin" included "ancestry" or that "ancestry" was a broader concept?

The EEOC has adopted a very expansive definition of national origin:

> The [EEOC] defines national origin discrimination broadly as including, but not limited to, the denial of equal employment opportunity because of an individual's, or his or her ancestor's, place of origin; or because an individual has the physical, cultural or linguistic characteristics of a national origin group. The [EEOC] will examine with particular concern charges alleging that individuals within the jurisdiction of the [EEOC] have been denied equal employment opportunity for reasons which are grounded in national

origin considerations, such as (a) marriage to or association with persons of a national origin group; (b) membership in, or association with an organization identified with or seeking to promote the interests of national origin groups; (c) attendance or participation in schools, churches, temples, or mosques, generally used by persons of a national origin group; and (d) because an individual's name or spouse's name is associated with a national origin group. In examining these charges for unlawful national origin discrimination, the [EEOC] will apply general title VII principles, such as disparate treatment and adverse impact.

EEOC, Guidelines on Discrimination Because of National Origin, 29 C.F.R. § 1606.1 (1997).

DAWAVENDEWA v. SALT RIVER PROJECT AGRICULTURAL IMPROVEMENT & POWER DISTRICT

United States Court of Appeals for the Ninth Circuit, 1998.
154 F.3d 1117, *cert. denied*, 528 U.S. 1098, 120 S.Ct. 843, 145 L.Ed.2d 708 (2000).

REINHARDT, Circuit Judge.

Harold Dawavendewa, a Native American, alleges that because he is a Hopi and not a Navajo, he was not considered for a position with a private employer operating a facility on the Navajo reservation. He contends that the employer's conduct constitutes unlawful employment discrimination under Title VII of the Civil Rights Act of 1964. To determine whether Dawavendewa's Title VII complaint may proceed, we address, first, whether discrimination based on tribal affiliation constitutes "national origin" discrimination, and, second, whether such discrimination is permitted under a Title VII provision that allows preferential treatment of Indians in certain specified circumstances.[1] [The portion of the opinion addressing the second issue is omitted.]

Salt River Project Agricultural Improvement and Power District ("Salt River"), an Arizona corporation, entered into a lease agreement with the Navajo Nation in 1969. The agreement allows Salt River to operate a generating station on Navajo land provided that it, among other things, grants employment preferences to members of the Navajo tribe living on the reservation, or, if none are available, to other members of the Navajo tribe.[2] This preference policy is consistent with Navajo tribal law. *See* 15 Navajo Nation Code § 604 (1995).

---

1. We use the terms Indian and Native American interchangeably throughout this opinion. While it is generally desirable for language to retain a fixed meaning, and while unnecessary changes in terminology exacerbate the problems we ordinarily have in understanding each other and in avoiding legal disputes, we recognize that the term Native American has become a part of the common parlance. Nevertheless, the statutes and opinions we examine use the term Indian, which was the appropriate word not so long ago.

2. The employment provision reads as follows:

Lessees agree to give preference in employment to qualified local Navajos, it being understood that "local Navajos" means members of the Navajo Tribe liv-

Dawavendewa, a member of the Hopi tribe, lives in Arizona less than three miles from the Navajo Reservation. In 1991 he unsuccessfully applied for one of seven Operator Trainee positions at the Salt River generating station. He then filed a complaint alleging that Salt River was engaging in national origin discrimination in violation of Title VII. The complaint alleges that he took and passed a test for the position, ranking ninth out of the top twenty applicants, but was neither interviewed nor considered further for it because he was not a member of, or married to a member of, the Navajo Nation.

Salt River moved to dismiss the complaint on the grounds that discrimination on the basis of tribal membership (as opposed to discrimination on the basis of status as a Native American) does not constitute "national origin" discrimination and that Title VII expressly exempts tribal preferences under § 703(i), 42 U.S.C. § 2000e–2 (i) (the "Indian Preferences exemption"). The district court granted the motion to dismiss. It held that Title VII exempts tribal preference policies, and therefore found it unnecessary to decide whether discrimination on the basis of tribal membership constitutes national origin discrimination under Title VII. Dawavendewa appeals.

I

We first address the issue whether discrimination on the basis of tribal membership constitutes "national origin" discrimination for purposes of Title VII. Title VII prohibits employers from discriminating on the basis of "race, color, religion, sex, or national origin." Civil Rights Act of 1964, § 703 (a), 42 U.S.C. § 2000e–2 (a).[4] Although Title VII fails to define "national origin," we have observed that "the legislative history and the Supreme Court both recognize that 'national origin' includes the country of one's ancestors." *Pejic v. Hughes Helicopters, Inc.*, 840 F.2d 667, 673 (9th Cir.1988); *see Espinoza v. Farah Mfg. Co.*, 414 U.S. 86, 88, 38 L.Ed.2d 287, 94 S.Ct. 334 (1973). Further, the regulations implementing Title VII provide that discrimination on the basis of one's ancestor's "place of origin" not nation of origin is sufficient to come within the scope of the statute. *See* 29 C.F.R. § 1606.1. Accordingly, a claim arises when discriminatory practices are based on the place in which one's ancestors lived.

ing on land within the jurisdiction of the Navajo Tribe. All unskilled labor shall be employed from "local Navajos," if available, providing that applicants for employment as unskilled laborers meet the general employment qualifications established by Lessees. Qualified semi-skilled and skilled labor shall be recruited and employed from among "local Navajos." In the event sufficient qualified unskilled, semi-skilled and skilled local Navajo labor is not available, or the quality of work of available skilled or semi-skilled workmen is not acceptable to Lessees, Lessees may then employ, in order of preference, first qualified non-local Navajos, and second, non-Navajos.

4. We note that claims of discrimination on the basis of one's status as a Native American are often brought as race discrimination claims, *see, e.g.,* Weahkee v. Perry, 190 U.S.App.D.C. 359, 587 F.2d 1256 (D.C.Cir.1978), although they have also been brought as national origin claims, *see* Perkins v. Lake County Dep't of Utilities, 860 F.Supp. 1262 (N.D.Ohio 1994).

Consistent with the regulations, we have held that the current political status of the nation or "place" at issue makes no difference for Title VII purposes. In *Pejic v. Hughes Helicopters, Inc.*, we considered the issue whether discrimination against Serbians constituted "national origin" discrimination. 840 F.2d 667, 673 (9th Cir.1988). The employer in *Pejic* contended that a Serbian employee could not bring a discrimination claim because Serbia as a nation had long been extinct. We rejected this argument and held that Serbians were a protected class:

> Unless historical reality is ignored, the term "national origin" must include countries no longer in existence * * *. Given world history, Title VII cannot be read to limit "countries" to those with modern boundaries, or to require their existence for a certain time length before it will prohibit discrimination. Animus based on national origin can persist long after new political structures and boundaries are established.

Id.; *see Roach v. Dresser Indus. Valve & Instr. Div.*, 494 F.Supp. 215, 218 (W.D.La.1980) (recognizing discrimination against "Cajuns" as national origin discrimination under Title VII although colony of Acadia no longer exists).

Under the principles set forth in *Pejic* and the Code of Federal Regulations, we have no trouble concluding that discrimination against Hopis constitutes national origin discrimination under Title VII. The status of Indian tribes among the international community and in relation to the United States has, of course, a complicated history that cannot be summarized briefly, and we will not attempt to do so. It is elementary, however, that the different tribes were at one time considered to be nations by the both the colonizing countries and later the United States. *See* William C. Canby, Jr., *American Indian Law* 68 (1998). In 1832 Chief Justice Marshall wrote:

> The Indian nations had always been considered as distinct, independent, political communities, retaining their original natural rights, as the undisputed possessors of the soil, from time immemorial. * * *

> The Cherokee nation, then is a distinct community, occupying its own territory, with boundaries accurately described. * * *

Worcester v. State of Georgia, 1832, 31 U.S. (6 Pet.) 515, 559–61, 8 L.Ed. 483. The Court has in more recent times recognized the erosion of the Indian tribes' "nation" status. *See Organized Village of Kake v. Egan*, 369 U.S. 60, 72, 7 L.Ed.2d 573, 82 S.Ct. 562 (1962) (Frankfurter, J.) (noting that "by 1880 the Court no longer viewed reservations as distinct nations"). Currently, the different Indian tribes are generally treated as domestic dependent nations that retain limited powers of sovereignty. *See* William C. Canby, *American Indian Law* 72–87 (1998).

Because the different Indian tribes were at one time considered nations, and indeed still are to a certain extent, discrimination on the basis of tribal affiliation can give rise to a "national origin" claim under

Title VII. The fact that "new political structures and boundaries" now exist has no significance. Further, even if the various tribes never enjoyed formal "nation" status, Section 1606.1 of the regulations makes clear that discrimination based on one's ancestor's "place of origin" is sufficient to state a cause of action. Accordingly, under the case law and the regulations interpreting Title VII, tribal affiliation easily falls within the definition of "national origin."

Salt River does not contend that the different Indian tribes are not "nations" for Title VII purposes. Rather, it relies on *Morton v. Mancari,* 417 U.S. 535, 552 554, 41 L.Ed.2d 290, 94 S.Ct. 2474 (1974), for the proposition that employment preferences based on tribal affiliation are based on *political affiliation* rather than national origin and are thus outside the realm of Title VII. *Morton* involved a Due Process challenge to the Bureau of Indian Affair's policy hiring Indian applicants over non-Indian applicants. The Court found that the policy did not constitute an impermissible racial classification because it was "reasonably designed to further the cause of Indian self-government and to make the BIA more responsive to the needs of its constituent groups." *Id.* at 554. However, *Morton* did not involve a claim of discrimination on the basis of membership in a particular tribe. In fact, in *Morton* no claim was made of any violation of Title VII. *Morton* simply held that the employment preference at issue, though based on a racial classification, did not violate the Due Process clause because there was a legitimate non-racial purpose underlying the preference: the unique interest the Bureau of Indian Affairs had in employing Native Americans, or more generally, Native Americans' interests in self-governance interests not present in this case. For these reasons, *Morton* does not affect our conclusion that discrimination in employment on the basis of membership in a particular tribe constitutes national origin discrimination. We therefore conclude that differential employment treatment based on tribal affiliation is actionable as "national origin" discrimination under Title VII.

* * *

Notes and Questions

1. As the *Dawavendewa* court notes in footnote 4, Title VII claims of discrimination against Native Americans have been brought as either race or national origin claims. Does the expansive definition of race for § 1981 claims that was adopted by the Supreme Court in *St. Francis College v. Al–Khazraji*, 481 U.S. 604, 107 S.Ct. 2022, 95 L.Ed.2d 582 (1987), reproduced in Chapter 2, blur the distinction between race, national origin, ancestry, and ethnicity? One professor argued, with regard to Latinos, that

> discrimination based on race and ethnicity may substantively mean two different things. For example, racial discrimination against Latino–Americans may mean discriminatory reactions to Latino–Americans who have Mestizo or Afro–Latino features. On the other hand, ethnic discrimination may mean discriminatory reactions to evidence of Latino–American culture, including language, accent, behavior and clothing.

Yxta Maya Murray, *The Latino–American Crisis of Citizenship*, 31 U.C. Davis L.Rev. 503, 575 (1998). Is that a sound distinction? *See also* Enriquez v. Honeywell, Inc., 431 F.Supp. 901, 904 (E.D.Okla.1977) (observing that "the line between discrimination on account of race and discrimination on account of national origin may be so thin as to be indiscernible").

In what ways does it matter whether the claim is characterized as based on race or national origin? *See* Gloria Sandrino–Glasser, *Los Confundidos: De–Conflating Latino/as' Race and Ethnicity*, 19 Chicano–Latino L.Rev. 69, 142–57 (1998) (arguing that conflation of race and national origin obscures the unique nature of national origin discrimination suffered by Latina/os.); john a. powell, *Legal Implications of the Census: A Minority–Majority Nation: Racing the Population in the Twenty–First Century*, 29 Fordham Urb.L.J. 1395, 1412 (2002) (asserting that treating Latina/o's as "white" for racial purposes separates them from blacks in the civil rights movement and forces them to prove national origin discrimination, which is factually harder to prove than racial discrimination).

2. What is the distinction between national origin, ancestry, and ethnicity under Title VII? Consider the following analysis of these terms:

National origin is the most simply defined and most easily understood. * * * "National origin" under Title VII means both one's national origin and the national origin characteristic of one's ancestry.

Ancestry may be defined as "family descent or lineage." Ancestry, therefore, is a somewhat broader concept than national origin, since it may encompass more than one ancestor and more than one national origin. Although ancestry overlaps with national origin, one's ancestors may not have a single or a strict national origin. Acadians, for example, have a specific ancestry, but no national origin, since Acadia has never been a nation. Gypsies, too, have specific ancestry, but claim no particular national origin.

Ancestry may also be distinct from national origin. Consider the situation of a Cuban-born member of a Chinese community in Cuba who emigrates to the United States. Suppose this person becomes a victim of discrimination because he looks Chinese, speaks Chinese, and speaks English with an obvious Chinese accent. While this example may involve discrimination because of ancestry (his Chinese parents and other ancestors) and because of race and ethnic traits (Chinese physical features, color, language, accent), there is no discrimination because of national origin (Cuban birthplace).

Of the three concepts, ethnicity is the most complex and the most difficult to define because it is a varying mix of different traits. Under a broad definition, ethnicity refers to physical and cultural characteristics that make a social group distinctive, either in group members' eyes or in the view of outsiders. Thus ethnicity consists of a set of ethnic traits that may include, but are not limited to: race, national origin, ancestry, language, religion, shared history, traditions, values, and symbols, all of which contribute to a sense of distinctiveness among members of the group. These traits also may engender a perception of group distinctiveness in persons who are not members of that group. It is the perception of difference, often based on ethnic traits, that results in discrimination.

Juan F. Perea, *Ethnicity and Prejudice: Reevaluating "National Origin" Discrimination Under Title VII*, 35 Wm. & Mary L.Rev. 805, 832–34 (1994). Would a prohibition of discrimination because of ethnicity rather than national origin be more compatible with the goals of Title VII? *See* Eugenio Abellera Cruz, *Unprotected Identities: Recognizing Cultural Ethnic Divergence in Interpreting Title VII's "National Origin" Classification*, 9 Hastings Women's L.J. 161, 186 (1998) (critiquing strictly geographic approach to defining national origin as ignoring the true nature of ethnicity.)

3. What is the "national origin" of multiracial and/or multiethnic applicants and employees? Consider the status of Tiger Woods, a popular professional golfer, whose father had one white, one Native American, and two black grandparents, and whose mother's parents were Chinese and Thai. Woods has adopted the term "Cablinasian," a mix of Caucasian, black, American Indian, and Asian, to describe his own mixed ancestry. *See* George Archibald, *Panel Rejects Census–Form Change*, The Washington Times, July 9, 1997, at A–1.

Suppose an applicant—whose mother is an African–American born in Africa and whose father is an American Jew born in Israel—is denied employment for a job for which she is otherwise qualified. Could the applicant make a Title VII claim based on "national origin"?

4. Beginning in 1977, individuals filling out federal forms, particularly census questionnaires, have been required to identify themselves as belonging to one of four racial groups: (1) white, (2) black, (3) American Indian, Eskimo, Aleut or (4) Asian or Pacific Islander. The Census Bureau included the term "other" for those persons who did not want to check one of these four categories. In the 1990 Census, almost ten million individuals checked off "other" to describe their identity. *See* Barbara Vobejda, *Census Expands Options for Multiracial Families; After Long Debate, Americans Can Choose More Than One Category on Federal Forms*, Wash. Post, Oct. 30, 1997, at A11. But racial self-identification is problematic for multiracial individuals:

> In the situation in which the mother is white and the father is some other race, compared to all the other groups, blacks have a much higher retention of being black—69.1% of the children are black. Another 8% are reported "other" and 22% are reported as white. In contrast 50% of the offspring of white mothers and Native American fathers are reported to be white, 43% of Japanese-white children are reported as white, 35% of Chinese-white children are reported white and 58% of Korean-white children are reported by their parents to be white. In sharp contrast, when the father is Asian Indian and the mother is white only 20% of the children stay Asian Indian. A much lower percentage of children of Japanese, Chinese and Filipino fathers married to white mothers remain identified with their father's Asian origins. While these Asian groups do show a large proportion of the children as "other" race (11.56% for children of Japanese fathers, 15.25% for children of Chinese fathers, and 10.53% for children of Korean fathers), even if one ignores those high percentages, there still are far more children identifying with their white mother's race.

Testimony of Professor Mary C. Waters, Department of Sociology, Harvard University, Before the Subcommittee on Government Management, Information and Technology of the House Committee on Government Reform and Oversight, *reprinted* in Federal News Service, May 22, 1997 (reported in LEXIS, Legis Library, CNGTST file). Professor Waters concluded that "[t]here is no socially meaningful group now that is 'multiracial' in terms of having a culture, a phenotype, a residential or occupational profile, or even of being subject to discrimination." *Id.*

On October 29, 1997, the Census Bureau announced a new federal policy that permits Americans filling out census and other federal forms to select multiple racial categories to describe their racial identity. As one journalist reported,

> In the 2000 census, * * * people can check off as many categories as they like, yielding a much more complex picture of diversity across the American population, but also creating a somewhat unwieldy combination of numbers.

> Ultimately * * * the government would publish population totals for each category and for every possible combination. The Census Bureau, for example, would release the number of Americans identifying themselves as white only, a separate number of those considering themselves both white and black and a third tally of those checking white, black and Asian.

Vobejda, *supra*, at A11.

What are the implications for the enforcement of laws such as Title VII and § 1981—that prohibit discrimination in employment on the basis of race and national origin—of this change in federal census policy? Vobejda reported that the "preliminary analysis" of the acting assistant attorney general for civil rights was that "Americans would be covered by anti-discrimination laws if they considered themselves wholly or partly a member of the protected group." *Id.* In light of this, can you anticipate any particular new problems that employers might face in terms of compliance with antidiscrimination laws? For further discussion of the movement to adopt a multiracial category in the decennial census and its potential effects on discrimination law, see Tanya Katerí Hernández, *"Multiracial" Discourse: Racial Classifications in an Era of Color–Blind Jurisprudence*, 57 Md.L.Rev. 97 (1998).

5.   Should an applicant or employee have to identify a particular "country" or "nation" in which she or her parents were born to make a claim based upon national origin? Palestinians do not have a country, as such. Should they be excluded from coverage? What about Gypsies? *See* Hamdan v. JF Guardian Security Servs., 66 Empl.Prac.Dec. (CCH) ¶ 43,551 (N.D.Ill.1994) (Palestinians); Janko v. Illinois State Toll Highway Auth., 704 F.Supp. 1531 (N.D.Ill.1989) (Gypsies). What about countries no longer in existence? *See* Pejic v. Hughes Helicopters, 840 F.2d 667 (9th Cir.1988) (Serbian employees).

6.   National origin may also overlap with religion, especially when a particular religion is closely associated with a particular national origin. The analysis for discrimination based on religion varies from the analytical model used in other Title VII categories because the statute prohibits discrimination against religious *practice* and requires an employer to accommodate religious practices in certain circumstances.

Notes: Native Americans

1. Native Americans are not a class specifically protected by Title VII. As a group, however, they have suffered a variety of different types of discrimination and harm. See generally the cases and materials assembled in Juan Perea, Richard Delgado, Angela Harris & Stephanie Wildman, Race and Races: Cases and Resources for a Multiracial America 173–245 (2000). As illustrated by *Morton v. Mancari,* discussed in *Dawavendewa,* Native American status is not considered racial for Equal Protection Clause analysis. Instead, Native Americans tribes have been considered sovereign states, subject by conquest to the legislative power of the United States, while retaining powers of self-government. See Felix S. Cohen, Handbook of Federal Indian Law 122–23 (1945). See Rodolfo Acuna, Occupied America: A History of Chicanos (3d ed.1988). In *Rice v. Cayetano,* 528 U.S. 495, 120 S.Ct. 1044, 145 L.Ed.2d 1007 (2000), a voting rights case, the Supreme Court distinguished the Native American experience from that of Native Hawaiians in finding that the latter group, consisting of "any descendant of the aboriginal peoples inhabiting the Hawaiian Islands, which exercised sovereignty and subsisted in the Hawaiian Islands in 1778, and which people thereafter have continued to reside in Hawaii," was a "proxy for race." 528 U.S. at 120 S.Ct. at 1056, 1055. How does this distinguish Native Americans from other groups we have studied? Are Native Americans comparable to Latinos in the Southwest, whose land was occupied and annexed from Mexico in the nineteenth century?

2. As the *Dawavendewa* court noted, Title VII specifically exempts "Indian tribes" from the scope of the definition of employer as used in the statute, 42 U.S.C. § 2000e(b). Courts have construed this exemption broadly, to include entities in addition to tribes. In *Pink v. Modoc Indian Health Project, Inc.,* 157 F.3d 1185 (9th Cir.1998), the court considered whether to grant an exemption to "a nonprofit corporation created and controlled by the Alturas and Cedarville Rancherias, both federally recognized tribes." *Id.* at 1187. The tribes organized Modoc for "charitable, educational, and scientific purposes" in order to deliver health services to their members. The court concluded:

> Although the Ninth Circuit has not specifically addressed whether a nonprofit organization incorporated by two Indian tribes is a "tribe" for purposes of Title VII exemption, the Tenth Circuit has addressed a similar question. In *Dille v. Council of Energy Resource Tribes,* 801 F.2d 373 (10th Cir.1986), the court held that a council comprised of thirty-nine Indian tribes that had joined together to collectively manage energy resources was a "tribe" within the scope of Title VII's Indian tribe exemption. The *Dille* Court held that Congress intended to exempt individual Indian tribes as well as collective efforts by Indian tribes. The court reasoned that the purpose of the tribal exemption, like the purpose of sovereign immunity itself, was to promote the ability of Indian tribes to control their own enterprises. * * *

> Here, Modoc served as an arm of the sovereign tribes, acting as more than a mere business. Modoc's board of directors consisted of two representatives from each Rancheria tribal government. Like the collec-

tion of tribes in *Dille*, Modoc was organized to control a collective enterprise and therefore falls within the scope of the Indian Tribe exemption of Title VII.

Id. at 1188.

3. One commentator has critiqued the *Dawavendewa* opinion as follows:

> It seems that in this era of Indian affairs, many in power have sought ways to erode tribal sovereignty. Any benefit or advantage that a tribe may have is subject to attack. With this case, the Ninth Circuit has found a way to chip away at what little power remains with the Navajo Nation.
>
> This case also opens avenues of attack that no reasonable person would accept. If an Oklahoman denies employment to a Texan, Texas having been a sovereign nation, the Texan would have a "national origin" claim. This would also be true for other citizens of states that were formally nations such as California and Hawaii.

Recent Developments, 23 Am. Indian L.Rev 459, 461 (1998–99).

Note: National Origin and the Bona Fide Occupational Qualification Defense

Neither race nor color is included in Title VII, § 703(e)(1), 42 U.S.C. § 2000e–2(e)(1), which permits discrimination "where religion, sex, or national origin is a bona fide occupational qualification reasonably necessary to the normal operation of that particular business or enterprise." The legislative history suggests that this provision should be liberally construed. For example, Senators Clark and Case, the floor managers of the Civil Rights Act of 1964, submitted an "Interpretive Memorandum" to the Senate which stated, in part,

> This exception [to Title VII] is a limited right to discriminate on the basis of religion, sex, or national origin where the reason for the discrimination is a bona fide occupational qualification. Examples of such legitimate discrimination would be the preference of a French restaurant for a French cook, the preference of a professional baseball team for male players, and the preference of a business which seeks the patronage of members of particular religious groups for a salesman of that religion.

110 Cong. Rec. 7212, 7213 (1964). During the debate in the House of Representatives, Representative Rodino suggested that the owner of a pizzeria "would probably seek as a chef a person of Italian origin. He would do this because pizza pie is something he believes * * * people of Italian national origin are able to make better than others—and is reasonably necessary to the operation of his particular business." 110 Cong. Rec. 2549 (1964). What is the purpose in treating national origin differently than race?

The Supreme Court in *International Union, UAW v. Johnson Controls*, 499 U.S. 187, 111 S.Ct. 1196, 113 L.Ed.2d 158 (1991), covered in Chapter 6, adopted a very narrow interpretation of § 703(e)(1) in a sex discrimination case involving the BFOQ exception. Should courts similarly apply *Johnson*

Controls' narrow interpretation of the BFOQ defense in national origin discrimination cases, or should they adopt a more liberal interpretation as suggested by the legislative history of Title VII?

Note: Harassment Because of National Origin

Cases such as *Meritor Savings Bank v. Vinson*, 477 U.S. 57, 106 S.Ct. 2399, 91 L.Ed.2d 49 (1986), and *Harris v. Forklift Systems*, 510 U.S. 17, 114 S.Ct. 367, 126 L.Ed.2d 295 (1993), covered in Chapter 8, are equally applicable in the Title VII national origin cases. *See, e.g.,* Cerros v. Steel Tech., Inc., 288 F.3d 1040 (7th Cir.2002); Miller v. Kenworth of Dothan, Inc., 277 F.3d 1269 (11th Cir.2002); Aguilera v. Village of Hazel Crest, 234 F.Supp.2d 840 (N.D.Ill.2002); Amirmokri v. Baltimore Gas & Elec. Co., 60 F.3d 1126 (4th Cir.1995). *Rogers v. EEOC*, 454 F.2d 234 (5th Cir.1971), *cert. denied*, 406 U.S. 957, 92 S.Ct. 2058, 32 L.Ed.2d 343 (1972), a national origin harassment case cited with approval by the Supreme Court in *Meritor*, was the first case to recognize a Title VII claim of hostile work environment discrimination.

In the course of an extended discussion of the nature and effect of ethnic epithets, the court in *Howard v. National Cash Register*, 388 F.Supp. 603, 605B06 (S.D.Ohio 1975), stated,

> It is a fact of life that social, ethnic, religious and racial distinctions are frequently drawn. There are Irish who dislike English; English who dislike French; French who despise Germans, Germans who hate Poles; and Poles who loathe Russians. For almost 100 years as waves of immigration have settled this country, there has been a succession of jokes regarding immigrants and classical comic characters poking fun at national groups. "Pat and Mike" jokes were as derogatory of Irish 100 years ago as "Polack" jokes are today. Stupid German comedians were long a staple of vaudeville, and the sly, grasping, money-hungry Jew has been a classic figure of historical literature. To this number was added the ignorant, lazy, shiftless, caricature of a Black, as portrayed by Stephan Fetchit, Amos and Andy, and Eddie "Rochester" Anderson. That these portrayals were degrading, humiliating, and offensive to the ethnic groups they purported to represent has only recently been recognized. The damage, however, to persons of sensitivity was nonetheless deep, nonetheless real.

> The language of the factory and the language of the street have long included words such as "Greaser", "Dago", and "Spick", and "Kike" and "Chink" as well as "Nigger." In the past three years we have even adopted as a part of our folk lore a character who is prejudiced and biased against all persons other than of his own neighborhood, religion and nationality. We refer to such people now as "Archie Bunkers" [after a character in the 1970's television show "All in the Family"]. The Archie Bunkers of this world, within limitations, still may assert their biased view. We have not yet reached the point where we have taken from individuals the right to be prejudiced, so long as such prejudice did not evidence itself in discrimination. This Court will secure plaintiff against discrimination; no court can secure him against prejudice.

If, as the court in *National Cash Register* observed, harassing conduct in the workplace (as in society at large) is the natural historical consequence of a society ingrained with negative attitudes and stereotypes of groups of different national origins, then is the *Harris v. Forklift* "reasonable person" standard likely to be meaningful in "securing" to victims of unlawful harassment freedom from national origin discrimination? *Compare, e.g.,* Richard Delgado, *Words That Wound: A Tort Action for Racial Insults, Epithets, and Name–Calling,* 17 Harv.C.R.-C.L.L.Rev 133 (1982) (advocating civil tort remedy for racial insults as a means of protecting citizens' rights to equality), *with* Kingsley R. Browne, *Title VII as Censorship: Hostile–Environment Harassment and the First Amendment,* 52 Ohio St.L.J. 481 (1991) (arguing that all speech in the workplace is inherently free speech and should be protected).

To what extent should the perspective of the victim in national origin cases be taken into account in determining whether the conduct is deemed to be severe or pervasive under the *Harris v. Forklift* standard? *See generally* Mari J. Matsuda, *Public Response to Racist Speech: Considering the Victim's Story,* 87 Mich.L.Rev. 2320 (1989). The court in *Harris v. International Paper Co.,* 765 F.Supp. 1509, 1515–16 (D.Me.1991) in adopting a "reasonable black person" standard and relying upon the views of several critical race theorists, deemed it appropriate to "walk a mile in the shoes" of the victim in assessing whether the claimed conduct was severe or pervasive. Should the reasonableness standard be adapted depending upon the national origin or ethnicity of the plaintiff?

C. NATIONAL ORIGIN AND CITIZENSHIP

Individuals within the United States generally fit into one of four categories:

    1.   A citizen (a person born here or "naturalized" through a legal process);

    2.   A noncitizen, legal entrant with authorization to work here;

    3.   A noncitizen, legal entrant who does not have authorization to work here; or

    4.   A noncitizen, illegal entrant who lacks the legal right to be here or work here.

Consider to what extent an employer is discriminating on the basis of national origin when it bases an employment decision on membership in any of these categories.

Espinoza v. Farah Manufacturing Co., 414 U.S. 86, 94 S.Ct. 334, 38 L.Ed.2d 287 (1973), is the leading Supreme Court decision addressing the relationship between discrimination based on national origin and discrimination based on citizenship. Espinoza, a citizen of Mexico living in San Antonio, Texas, with her husband, applied for a position as a seamstress at Farah Manufacturing. She was in the country legally and had the legal right to work here. Her husband was a citizen of the United States. Farah rejected her application because of its long-standing policy against hiring noncitizens. The Supreme Court held that Farah's refusal to hire Espinoza did not constitute national origin discrimination.

The Court concluded that Congress did not contemplate that "national origin" should include citizenship because of the legislative history of Title VII and the practice of the federal government's civil service regulations of requiring its employees to be United States citizens. Second, the EEOC *Guidelines on Discrimination Because of National Origin*, 29 C.F.R. § 1606.1(d) (1972), which provide that lawful alien residents cannot be discriminated against based on citizenship because it is tantamount to national origin discrimination, were found inapplicable because more than 96% of Farah's employees were of Mexican ancestry. Finally, the Supreme Court cautioned that "there may be many situations where discrimination on the basis of citizenship would have the effect of discriminating on the basis of national origin." 414 U.S. at 92, 94 S.Ct. at 338. "[F]or example, a citizenship requirement might be but one part of a wider scheme of unlawful national-origin discrimination. In other cases, an employer might use a citizenship test as a pretext to disguise what is in fact national-origin discrimination." *Id.* In those circumstances, the Supreme Court concluded that Title VII "prohibits discrimination on the basis of citizenship whenever it has the purpose of discriminating on the basis of national origin." *Id.* The Supreme Court found that no such purpose or effect had been proven by Espinoza. *Id.* at 93 & n.5, 94 S.Ct. at 339 & n.5. *Espinoza* also made a distinction between discrimination on the basis of citizenship or alienage and discrimination *against* aliens *because of* race, color, religion, sex, or national origin. *Id.* at 95, 94 S.Ct. at 340. The Supreme Court held that "[a]liens are protected from illegal discrimination under [Title VII], but nothing in the Act makes it illegal to discriminate on the basis of citizenship or alienage." *Id. See also* EEOC v. Switching Sys. Div. of Rockwell Int'l Corp., 783 F.Supp. 369 (N.D.Ill.1992).

In the following case, the court considered whether a citizenship requirement may be a pretext for prohibited national origin discrimination:

ANDERSON v. ZUBIETA

United States Court of Appeals for the District of Columbia, 1999.
180 F.3d 329.

Plaintiffs are black American citizens of Panamanian or Hispanic national origin who have long worked for the Panama Canal Commission and its predecessor, the Panama Canal Company (together, the "PCC" or "Canal Commission"). The PCC pays them substantially less in salary and benefits than it pays other American citizens working at the same jobs—the overwhelming majority of whom are white, non-Panamanians. The plaintiffs allege this pay differential constitutes race and national origin discrimination in violation of Title VII of the Civil Rights Act of 1964. * * *

I

The Canal Commission is a wholly-owned United States government corporation. The thirteen plaintiffs were hired by the PCC before 1979, and all but two before 1976. One has since retired. All the plaintiffs are currently United States citizens: eleven were naturalized between 1987 and 1994; one became a citizen in 1977 following his service in the military; and the remaining plaintiff is the son of a United States citizen whose citizenship was not registered with the U.S. Embassy until 1991. The PCC denies plaintiffs three types of benefits [including the so-called "tropical differential"] that it grants to other employees, which generated the pay differential of which they complain. [The pay differential resulted from requirements that employees receiving these benefits must either have been a citizen before a certain date (ranging from 1976–1984) or be an employee recruited from outside Panama.]

* * *

[Plaintiffs] contended that the date-of-citizenship requirements were mere pretext, guaranteeing continued benefits to white non-Panamanians while denying them to black Panamanian employees, the vast majority of whom did not become citizens until after the cut-off dates. They also proffered evidence of what they contended was the Panama Canal's "longstanding history of discriminating against employees from the West Indies in every aspect of Canal life and employment," symbolized, they said, by a racially-based payroll system in which white Canal workers were paid in gold from a "gold roll," while black Panamanians were paid in less-valuable Panamanian silver. "[P]ayment of the tropical differential to some employees and not others," they contended, reflected nothing more than "a continuation of the 'gold' and 'silver' roll wage differentials which were based on race."

The district court granted summary judgment in favor of the Commission and dismissed the case. The court rejected plaintiffs' disparate treatment claim, concluding they were denied benefits because of their "citizenship, not because of membership in a Title VII protected class."
* * *

II

B

* * *

Plaintiffs receive a 15% lower salary than their white, non-Panamanian counterparts and are not given the equity package and vacation benefits. This is sufficient to establish a prima facie case of wage discrimination. There is no dispute that race and national origin are protected classes. Nor is there any dispute that the work plaintiffs perform is substantially the same as that of the white non-Panamanians: the PCC awards the wage differential and benefits as an increment above an employee's base salary regardless of the kind of work he or she performs or the level of skill it requires.

In addition to this comparison of their personal situations, plaintiffs offered statistics showing a wide disparity between the percentages of black versus white U.S. citizens who receive the higher salary and benefits, as well as between the percentages of U.S. citizens of American versus Panamanian or Hispanic national origin who receive them. * * *

C

As the plaintiffs have established a prima facie case of disparate treatment, under the second step of *McDonnell Douglas* "[t]he burden then must shift to the employer to articulate some legitimate, nondiscriminatory reason" for the challenged employment practice. * * *

The district court, however, pretermitted any further analysis * * * after the prima facie stage. Although it agreed that Title VII protects against discrimination "because of [an] individual's race * * * or national origin," the court cut off the analysis of plaintiffs' disparate treatment claim on the ground that the discrimination here was " 'because of' citizenship, not because of membership in a Title VII protected class." Stating that "the Supreme Court held in *Espinoza v. Farah,* that * * * [Title VII] does not offer protection from discrimination on the basis of citizenship," the district court held that plaintiffs had failed as a matter of law to make out a prima facie case of disparate treatment.

The district court's reliance on *Espinoza* was misplaced for two reasons. First, although the Supreme Court did hold that citizenship is not a facially-unlawful criterion for employment decisions, *see* 414 U.S. 86, 91, 94 S.Ct. 334, 38 L. Ed. 2d 287 (1973), it also recognized that "an employer might use a citizenship test as a pretext to disguise what is in fact national-origin discrimination." *Id.* at 92. Title VII, the Court said, "prohibits discrimination on the basis of citizenship whenever it has the purpose or effect of discriminating on the basis of national origin." *Id.* That principle was of no assistance to the *Espinoza* plaintiffs, who alleged discrimination based on Mexican national origin: notwithstanding the employer's citizens-only policy, there was no evidence of discriminatory purpose or effect since more than 96% of its employees were of Mexican descent. Here, however, plaintiffs' claims of pretext and disparate effect are not as easily brushed aside: the overwhelming majority of those who receive the pay differential are whites of non-Panamanian origin. * * * If, as *Espinoza* proclaimed, Title VII truly does "prohibit[ ] discrimination on the basis of citizenship whenever it has the purpose or effect of discriminating on the basis of national origin," then courts must afford plaintiffs an opportunity to prove such a purpose or effect. *See also* 29 C.F.R. § 1606.5(a) (EEOC regulation) ("[W]here citizenship requirements have the purpose or effect of discriminating against an individual on the basis of national origin, they are prohibited by [T]itle VII.").

Second, "citizenship" is simply not the basis upon which the PCC differentiates, or even contends that it differentiates, among its employees. All of the plaintiffs are, in fact, American citizens. Nor is the issue whether it was lawful for the PCC to prefer citizens over noncitizens in 1976, the year the tropical differential policy was announced, or to prefer them in 1989, the year the equity package was cut off. As discussed above, the limitations period has run on those kinds of claims. Instead, the plaintiffs' core contention is that the PCC is engaged in a current, continuing violation of Title VII, because today and every day it pays them less than it pays others who are similarly situated. The question in this case, then, is whether the PCC is unlawfully discriminating against American citizens today, by maintaining a system of preferences based on whether they were citizens at an earlier time. As the PCC itself describes its policies, it differentiates among its employees based on the timing of their citizenship. For that reason, *Espinoza,* a case in which the employer simply preferred citizens over noncitizens is not controlling.

* * *

Notes and Questions

1. Is the distinction that the courts draw between discrimination based on national origin and discrimination based on citizenship convincing? Alternately, is *Anderson v. Zubieta* an example of race discrimination being justified by the use of a citizenship criterion? Articulate the difference in what an employer is seeking to accomplish in citizenship discrimination that is different from what it is seeking to accomplish when discriminating on the basis of national origin and on the basis of race.

2. Suppose a Swiss-owned company incorporated in New York, whose corporate officers are Swiss citizens, discharged several employees, all born in the United States, and replaced them with individuals born in Switzerland. Could the discharged employees claim they were discriminated against because of national origin? *See* Chaiffetz v. Robertson Research Holding, Ltd., 798 F.2d 731 (5th Cir.1986); Thomas v. Rohner–Gehrig & Co., 582 F.Supp. 669 (N.D.Ill.1984).

3. Although citizenship status, in and of itself, may not be the basis for a national origin claim under Title VII, it may be the basis for a constitutional claim under the Equal Protection Clause. Following the terrorist attacks on New York City and Washington, D.C., on September 11, 2001, Congress enacted the Aviation and Transportation Security Act (ATSA), 49 U.S.C. § 40101, which requires that all airport security screening personnel be United States citizens. On behalf of plaintiffs, the American Civil Liberties Union and the Service Employees International Union filed a lawsuit challenging the citizenship requirement. The complaint alleges that at many major airports, a large number of the screeners are legal residents but not citizens (80% of the screeners at San Francisco; 40% at Los Angeles; 70% at Miami; and 80% at Dulles). The complaint further alleges that the citizenship requirement serves no rational purpose because thousands of other employees (pilots, flight attendants, baggage handlers, mechanics, etc.) have access to secure areas and are not required to be citizens; because noncitizens serve in the National Guard, which performed security duties at screening stations; that the best qualified, most experienced screeners will be

fired and replaced by inexperienced screeners; and because no government report has ever identified the citizenship or nationality of screeners as having any connection to the ongoing problems with security. In dismissing the government's motion to dismiss the complaint, the court found that this categorical exclusion of noncitizens can only be upheld if the government can prove it is a narrowly tailored measure that furthers a compelling governmental interest. Gebin v. Mineta, 231 F.Supp.2d 971 (C.D.Cal.2002); Gebin v. Mineta, 239 F.Supp.2d 967 (C.D.Cal.2002) (granting preliminary injunction). What interests are served by the citizenship requirement? How are they related to discrimination based on national origin? Congress later amended Section III of the ATSA to allow nationals to serve as screeners. Pub.L. No. 107–296, § 1603; Gebin v. Mineta, 328 F.3d 1211 (9th Cir.2003) (vacating preliminary injunction).

Note: The Relationship Between the Immigration Reform and Control Act of 1986 and Title VII

In 1986, Congress enacted the Immigration Reform and Control Act (IRCA), 8 U.S.C. § 1324(b)(a)(1), an amendment to the Immigration and Nationality Act of 1952, 8 U.S.C. § 1101 *et seq.* The goals of IRCA are to curtail the large number of illegal immigrants entering the United States by reducing the opportunities for employment and to secure national borders. To achieve these goals, Congress, for the first time, subjected employers to sanctions for knowingly hiring, recruiting, or employing unauthorized aliens. An "unauthorized alien" is defined as an alien who, at the time of employment, has not been admitted for permanent residence in the United States or who lacks authorization for employment from IRCA or the Attorney General. 8 U.S.C. § 1324a(h)(3).

In addition, IRCA prohibits four types of discrimination for employers with four or more employees: national origin discrimination, citizenship discrimination, document abuse, and intimidation/coercion/retaliation. This provision of IRCA duplicates and expands Title VII's protections against national origin discrimination. For example, IRCA makes it an unlawful employment practice for some employers not covered by Title VII—that is, employers with four to fourteen employees who are not covered by § 701(b) of Title VII because they do not have "fifteen or more employees," 42 U.S.C. § 2000e(b)—to discriminate on the basis of national origin in decisions to hire, discharge, or recruit employees or to refer employees for a fee. 8 U.S.C. § 1324b(1)(A). These are fewer employer actions than those reached by Title VII. *See generally* Sarah M. Kendall, Comment, *America's Minorities Are Shown the "Back Door" * * * Again: The Discriminatory Impact of the Immigration Reform and Control Act,* 18 Hous. J. Int'l L. 899 (1996). With respect to citizenship status, IRCA prohibits a covered employer from discriminating against United States citizens, or other protected individuals—generally, immigrants with work authorization cards who are intending to become citizens—on the basis of citizenship in hiring, discharging, or recruiting, or in referring for a fee. *Id.* § 1324b(1)(B). IRCA also protects employees from document abuse by prohibiting covered employers from requiring "more or different documents" than are specified by IRCA for purposes of verifying an individual's employment eligibility, or refusing to honor documents that "on their face reasonably appear to be genuine." 8 U.S.C. § 1324b(a)(6).

ICRA's prohibition on the employment of undocumented workers raises two questions for Title VII plaintiffs: coverage and remedies. *Espinoza v. Farah Manufacturing Co.*, 414 U.S. 86, 95, 94 S.Ct. 334, 340, 38 L.Ed.2d 287 (1973), held that aliens, like citizens, are protected from employment discrimination under Title VII on the basis of all the grounds prohibited under the statute. Does ICRA affect this outcome? In *Egbuna v. Time–Life Libraries, Inc.*, 153 F.3d 184 (4th Cir.1998) (en banc), *cert. denied*, 525 U.S. 1142, 119 S.Ct. 1034, 143 L.Ed.2d 43 (1999), the issue was whether a Title VII plaintiff must prove that he is eligible to work in the United States under IRCA in order to establish a prima facie case of disparate treatment under Title VII. The district court dismissed plaintiff's claim on the ground that because he lacked a "green card," that is, INS authorization to work in the United States, he could not show that he was qualified for the position. A divided panel of the Fourth Circuit reversed, holding that undocumented aliens are protected under Title VII despite the provisions of IRCA, and that, to make out a prima facie case under Title VII, a plaintiff need not prove his or her eligibility under IRCA to work in the United States. The panel adopted the reasoning of the only other court that had faced the issue, *EEOC v. Tortilleria "La Mejor"*, 758 F.Supp. 585 (E.D.Cal.1991). *Tortilleria* held that Congress did not intend for IRCA to amend or repeal any of the previous legislated protection of federal labor and employment laws accorded to aliens, documented or undocumented, including the protection under Title VII. The panel in *Egbuna* expressed its concern that a contrary ruling would provide an incentive for employers to hire illegal aliens, mistreat them, and then argue that the worker has no remedy because of his unauthorized status.

In a 9–4 en banc decision, the Fourth Circuit reversed the panel's decision and affirmed the decision of the district court. The en banc court held that an undocumented alien has no claim under Title VII "because his undocumented status render[s] him ineligible both for the remedies he seeks and for employment within the United States." Egbuna, 153 F.3d at 186. The Fourth Circuit relied upon the following reasons in support of its decision: First, "[w]hen the applicant is an alien, being 'qualified' for the position is not determined by the applicant's capacity to perform the job— rather, it is determined by whether the applicant was an alien authorized for employment in the United States at the time in question." *Id.* at 187. Second, "IRCA effected a monumental change in our country's immigration policy by criminalizing the hiring of unauthorized aliens." *Id.* at 188. Third, "to order [an employer] to hire an undocumented alien would nullify IRCA, which declares it illegal to hire or to continue to employ unauthorized aliens." *Id* at 188. Which view, the panel's decision or the en banc court's decision, best accommodates the mandates of Title VII and IRCA?

In deciding a claim brought under a different federal statute, the Supreme Court reviewed the ability of the National Labor Relations Board to award reinstatement backpay and other remedies to undocumented workers under the National Labor Relations Act in *Hoffman Plastic Compounds, Inc. v. National Labor Relations Board*, 535 U.S. 137, 122 S.Ct. 1275, 152 L.Ed.2d 271 (2002). In a 5–4 decision, the Court found that such relief is foreclosed by federal immigration policy, as found in IRCA. The Court concluded that the Board's authority to select remedies was necessarily circumscribed by federal immigration policy. The Court stated:

> Under the IRCA regime, it is impossible for an undocumented alien to obtain employment in the United States without some party directly contravening explicit congressional policies. Either the undocumented alien tenders fraudulent identification, which subverts the cornerstone of IRCA's enforcement mechanism, or the employer knowingly hires the undocumented alien in direct contradiction of its IRCA obligations. The Board asks that we overlook this fact and allow it to award backpay to an illegal alien for years of work not performed, for wages that could not lawfully have been earned, and for a job obtained in the first instance by a criminal fraud. We find, however, that awarding backpay to illegal aliens runs counter to policies underlying IRCA, policies the Board has no authority to enforce or administer. Therefore, as we have consistently held in like circumstances, the award lies beyond the bounds of the Board's remedial discretion.

* * *

> Lack of authority to award backpay does not mean that the employer gets off scot-free. The Board here has already imposed other significant sanctions against Hoffman—sanctions Hoffman does not challenge. These include orders that Hoffman cease and desist its violations of the NLRA, and that it conspicuously post a notice to employees setting forth their rights under the NLRA and detailing its prior unfair practices. * * * We have deemed such "traditional remedies" sufficient to effectuate national labor policy * * *.

Id. at 152, 122 S.Ct. at 1283, 1285. The Court did find that undocumented workers were still covered by the NLRA, even though IRCA limited their remedies. *Id.* at 122 S.Ct. 1275, 1283 n.4. What are the implications of the *Hoffman* decision to cases brought under Title VII? *See* Escobar v. Spartan Sec. Serv., 281 F.Supp.2d 895 (S.D.Tex.2003) (plaintiff subsequently attained legal status). A discussion of remedies for undocumented aliens under Title VII can be found in Maria L. Ontiveros, *To Help Those Most in Need: Undocumented Workers' Rights and Remedies Under Title VII*, 20 N.Y.U.Rev.L. & Soc. Change 607 (1993–94). *See also* EEOC, *Enforcement Guidance on Remedies Available to Undocumented Workers Under Federal Discrimination Laws* (Oct. 25, 1999).

D. NATIONAL ORIGIN DISCRIMINATION BASED ON LANGUAGE AND ACCENT

The number of non-English-speaking and accented employees in the United States workforce has grown due to recent increases in the number of immigrants entering the country from non-English-speaking countries. In 2000, almost 20% of the United States population (45 million people) spoke a language other than English at home, and over 4% (10.3 million people) spoke little or no English at all. Section 13V: *National Origin Discrimination*, EEOC Compliance Manual (2002). The employment of these individuals has given rise to three different claims based on national origin discrimination: challenges to English proficiency as a job qualification; challenges to policies that require bilingual employees to speak only English at the workplace; and lawsuits alleging discrimination based on an accent.

1. ENGLISH PROFICIENCY AS A JOB REQUIREMENT

An employer that requires its employees to be able to speak English well as a condition of employment may face a claim of discrimination based on national origin. If the requirement is applied to a non-English-speaking employee as opposed to a bilingual employee, most courts suggest applying a disparate impact model because the requirement will have a disparate impact based on national origin. *See* Garcia v. Gloor, 618 F.2d 264, 270 (5th Cir. 1980); Garcia v. Spun Steak Co., 998 F.2d 1480, *cert. denied*, 512 U.S. 1228, 114 S.Ct. 2726, 129 L.Ed.2d 849 (1994); EEOC v. Synchro–Start Prods., Inc., 29 F.Supp.2d 911 (N.D.Ill. 1999). *But see* Chavez v. Hydril Co., 2003 WL 22075740 (N.D.Tex.2003) (utilizing circumstantial disparate treatment model); Dercach v. Indiana Dep't of Highways, 1987 WL 46837 (N.D.Ind.1987) (relying on circumstantial disparate treatment model). Recall that under a disparate impact model, in order to prevail the employer must prove that the language requirement is job related for the position in question and consistent with business necessity. Edward M. Chen, *Speech: Labor Law and Language Discrimination*, 6 Asian L.J. 223, 228–29 (1999); Section 13V B1: *National Origin Discrimination,* EEOC Compliance Manual (2002).

At least one commentator has argued that the federal courts have "set up a false dichotomy by distinguishing 'fully' bilingual from monolingual national origin minorities, including in the latter group those plaintiffs with limited English-language proficiency." Mark Colon, *Line Drawing, Code Switching, and Spanish as Second–Hand Smoke: English–Only Workplace Rules and Bilingual Employees*, 20 Yale L. & Pol'y Rev. 227, 229 (2002). What arguments can be made that a disparate impact model should apply to both monolingual and bilingual employees confronting an English language requirement?

2. ENGLISH-ONLY REQUIREMENT FOR BILINGUAL EMPLOYEES

GARCIA v. SPUN STEAK CO.

United States Court of Appeals for the Ninth Circuit, 1993.
998 F.2d 1480, *cert. denied*, 512 U.S. 1228, 114 S.Ct. 2726, 129 L.Ed.2d 849 (1994).

O'SCANNLAIN, Circuit Judge:

We are called upon to decide whether an employer violates Title VII of the Civil Rights Act of 1964 in requiring its bilingual workers to speak only English while working on the job.

I

Spun Steak Company ("Spun Steak") is a California corporation that produces poultry and meat products in South San Francisco for wholesale distribution. Spun Steak employs thirty-three workers, twenty-four of whom are Spanish-speaking. Virtually all of the Spanish-speaking employees are Hispanic. While two employees speak no English, the others have varying degrees of proficiency in English. Spun Steak has never required job applicants to speak or to understand English as a condition of employment.

Approximately two-thirds of Spun Steak's employees are production line workers or otherwise involved in the production process. Appellees Garcia and Buitrago are production line workers; they stand before a conveyor belt, remove poultry or other meat products from the belt and place the product into cases or trays for resale. Their work is done individually. Both Garcia and Buitrago are fully bilingual, speaking both English and Spanish.

* * *

Prior to September 1990, these Spun Steak employees spoke Spanish freely to their co-workers during work hours. After receiving complaints that some workers were using their bilingual capabilities to harass and to insult other workers in a language they could not understand, Spun Steak began to investigate the possibility of requiring its employees to speak only English in the workplace. Specifically, Spun Steak received complaints that Garcia and Buitrago made derogatory, racist comments in Spanish about two co-workers, one of whom is African–American and the other Chinese–American.

The company's president, Kenneth Bertelson, concluded that an English-only rule would promote racial harmony in the workplace. In addition, he concluded that the English-only rule would enhance worker safety because some employees who did not understand Spanish claimed that the use of Spanish distracted them while they were operating machinery, and would enhance product quality because the U.S.D.A. inspector in the plant spoke only English and thus could not understand if a product-related concern was raised in Spanish. Accordingly, the following rule was adopted:

> [I]t is hereafter the policy of this Company that only English will be spoken in connection with work. During lunch, breaks, and employees' own time, they are obviously free to speak Spanish if they wish. However, we urge all of you not to use your fluency in Spanish in a fashion which may lead other employees to suffer humiliation.

In addition to the English-only policy, Spun Steak adopted a rule forbidding offensive racial, sexual, or personal remarks of any kind.

> It is unclear from the record whether Spun Steak strictly enforced the English-only rule. According to the plaintiffs-appellees, some workers continued to speak Spanish without incident. Spun Steak issued written exceptions to the policy allowing its clean-up crew to

speak Spanish, allowing its foreman to speak Spanish, and authorizing certain workers to speak Spanish to the foreman at the foreman's discretion. One of the two employees who speak only Spanish is a member of the clean-up crew and thus is unaffected by the policy.

* * *

Garcia, Buitrago, and Local 115, on behalf of all Spanish-speaking employees of Spun Steak (collectively, "the Spanish-speaking employees"), filed suit, alleging that the English-only policy violated Title VII. On September 6, 1991, the parties filed cross-motions for summary judgment. The district court denied Spun Steak's motion and granted the Spanish-speaking employees' motion for summary judgment, concluding that the English-only policy disparately impacted Hispanic workers without sufficient business justification, and thus violated Title VII. * * *

* * *

III

* * *

A

The Spanish-speaking employees do not contend that Spun Steak intentionally discriminated against them in enacting the English-only policy. Rather, they contend that the policy had a discriminatory impact on them because it imposes a burdensome term or condition of employment exclusively upon Hispanic workers and denies them a privilege of employment that non-Spanish-speaking workers enjoy. Because their claim focuses on disparities in the terms, conditions, and privileges of employment, and not on barriers to hiring or promotion, it is outside the mainstream of disparate impact cases decided thus far. As a threshold matter, therefore, we must determine whether the disparate impact theory can be made applicable at all.

* * *

* * * We are satisfied that a disparate impact claim may be based upon a challenge to a practice or policy that has a significant adverse impact on the "terms, conditions, or privileges" of the employment of a protected group under section 703(a)(1).

B

* * * In this case, the district court granted summary judgment in favor of the Spanish-speaking employees, concluding that, as a matter of law, the employees had made out the prima facie case and the justifications offered by the employer were inadequate.

1

We first consider whether the Spanish-speaking employees have made out the prima facie case. * * *

It is beyond dispute that, in this case, if the English-only policy causes any adverse effects, those effects will be suffered disproportionately by those of Hispanic origin. The vast majority of those workers at Spun Steak who speak a language other than English—and virtually all those employees for whom English is not a first language—are Hispanic. It is of no consequence that not all Hispanic employees of Spun Steak speak Spanish; nor is it relevant that some non-Hispanic workers may speak Spanish. If the adverse effects are proved, it is enough under Title VII that Hispanics are disproportionately impacted.

The crux of the dispute between Spun Steak and the Spanish-speaking employees, however, is not over whether Hispanic workers will disproportionately bear any adverse effects of the policy; rather, the dispute centers on whether the policy causes any adverse effects at all, and if it does, whether the effects are significant. The Spanish-speaking employees argue that the policy adversely affects them in the following ways: (1) it denies them the ability to express their cultural heritage on the job; (2) it denies them a privilege of employment that is enjoyed by monolingual speakers of English; and (3) it creates an atmosphere of inferiority, isolation, and intimidation. We discuss each of these contentions in turn.

a

The employees argue that denying them the ability to speak Spanish on the job denies them the right to cultural expression. It cannot be gainsaid that an individual's primary language can be an important link to his ethnic culture and identity. Title VII, however, does not protect the ability of workers to express their cultural heritage at the workplace. Title VII is concerned only with disparities in the treatment of workers; it does not confer substantive privileges. It is axiomatic that an employee must often sacrifice individual self-expression during working hours. Just as a private employer is not required to allow other types of self-expression, there is nothing in Title VII which requires an employer to allow employees to express their cultural identity.

b

Next, the Spanish-speaking employees argue that the English-only policy has a disparate impact on them because it deprives them of a privilege given by the employer to native-English speakers: the ability to converse on the job in the language with which they feel most comfortable. It is undisputed that Spun Steak allows its employees to converse on the job. The ability to converse—especially to make small talk—is a privilege of employment, and may in fact be a significant privilege of employment in an assembly-line job. It is inaccurate, however, to describe the privilege as broadly as the Spanish-speaking employees urge us to do.

The employees have attempted to define the privilege as the ability to speak in the language of their choice. A privilege, however, is by definition given at the employer's discretion; an employer has the right to define its contours. Thus, an employer may allow employees to converse on the job, but only during certain times of the day or during the performance of certain tasks. The employer may proscribe certain topics as inappropriate during working hours or may even forbid the use of certain words, such as profanity.

Here, as is its prerogative, the employer has defined the privilege narrowly. When the privilege is defined at its narrowest (as merely the ability to speak on the job), we cannot conclude that those employees fluent in both English and Spanish are adversely impacted by the policy. Because they are able to speak English, bilingual employees can engage in conversation on the job. It is axiomatic that "the language a person who is multi-lingual elects to speak at a particular time is * * * a matter of choice." Garcia v. Gloor, 618 F.2d 264, 270, (5th Cir.1980), *cert. denied*, 449 U.S. 1113, 101 S.Ct. 923, 66 L.Ed.2d 842 (1981). The bilingual employee can readily comply with the English-only rule and still enjoy the privilege of speaking on the job. "There is no disparate impact" with respect to a privilege of employment "if the rule is one that the affected employee can readily observe and nonobservance is a matter of individual preference." *Id.*

* * *

The Spanish-speaking employees argue that fully bilingual employees are hampered in the enjoyment of the privilege because for them, switching from one language to another is not fully volitional. Whether a bilingual speaker can control which language is used in a given circumstance is a factual issue that cannot be resolved at the summary judgment stage. However, we fail to see the relevance of the assertion, even assuming that it can be proved. Title VII is not meant to protect against rules that merely inconvenience some employees, even if the inconvenience falls regularly on a protected class. Rather, Title VII protects against only those policies that have a *significant* impact. The fact that an employee may have to catch himself or herself from occasionally slipping into Spanish does not impose a burden significant enough to amount to the denial of equal opportunity. This is not a case in which the employees have alleged that the company is enforcing the policy in such a way as to impose penalties for minor slips of the tongue. The fact that a bilingual employee may, on occasion, unconsciously substitute a Spanish word in the place of an English one does not override our conclusion that the bilingual employee can easily comply with the rule. In short, we conclude that a bilingual employee is not denied a privilege of employment by the English-only policy.

* * *

c

Finally, the Spanish-speaking employees argue that the policy creates an atmosphere of inferiority, isolation, and intimidation. Under this theory, the employees do not assert that the policy directly affects a term, condition, or privilege of employment. Instead, the argument must be that the policy causes the work environment to become infused with ethnic tensions. The tense environment, the argument goes, itself amounts to a condition of employment.

i

* * *

Here, the employees urge us to adopt a per se rule that English-only policies always infect the working environment to such a degree as to amount to a hostile or abusive work environment. This we cannot do. Whether a working environment is infused with discrimination is a factual question, one for which a per se rule is particularly inappropriate. The dynamics of an individual workplace are enormously complex; we cannot conclude, as a matter of law, that the introduction of an English-only policy, in every workplace, will always have the same effect.

The Spanish-speaking employees in this case have presented no evidence other than conclusory statements that the policy has contributed to an atmosphere of "isolation, inferiority or intimidation." The bilingual employees are able to comply with the rule, and there is no evidence to show that the atmosphere at Spun Steak in general is infused with hostility toward Hispanic workers. Indeed, there is substantial evidence in the record demonstrating that the policy was enacted to prevent the employees from intentionally using their fluency in Spanish to isolate and to intimidate members of other ethnic groups. In light of the specific factual context of this case, we conclude that the bilingual employees have not raised a genuine issue of material fact that the effect is so pronounced as to amount to a hostile environment.

ii

We do not foreclose the prospect that in some circumstances English-only rules can exacerbate existing tensions, or, when combined with other discriminatory behavior, contribute to an overall environment of discrimination. Likewise, we can envision a case in which such rules are enforced in such a draconian manner that the enforcement itself amounts to harassment. In evaluating such a claim, however, a court must look to the totality of the circumstances in the particular factual context in which the claim arises.

In holding that the enactment of an English-only while working policy does not inexorably lead to an abusive environment for those whose primary language is not English, we reach a conclusion opposite to the EEOC's long-standing position. The EEOC Guidelines provide that an employee meets the prima facie case in a disparate impact cause of action merely by proving the existence of the English-only policy. *See*

29 C.F.R. § 1606.7 (a) & (b) (1991). Under the EEOC's scheme, an employer must always provide a business justification for such a rule. The EEOC enacted this scheme in part because of its conclusion that English-only rules may "create an atmosphere of inferiority, isolation and intimidation based on national origin which could result in a discriminatory working environment." 29 C.F.R. § 1606.7(a).

We do not reject the English-only rule Guideline lightly. * * *

* * * Nothing in the plain language of section 703(a)(1) supports EEOC's English-only rule Guideline. * * * It is clear that Congress intended a balance to be struck in preventing discrimination and preserving the independence of the employer. In striking that balance, the Supreme Court has held that a plaintiff in a disparate impact case must prove the alleged discriminatory effect before the burden shifts to the employer. The EEOC Guideline at issue here contravenes that policy by presuming that an English-only policy has a disparate impact in the absence of proof. We are not aware of, nor has counsel shown us, anything in the legislative history to Title VII that indicates that English-only policies are to be presumed discriminatory. Indeed, nowhere in the legislative history is there a discussion of English-only policies at all.

2

Because the bilingual employees have failed to make out a prima facie case, we need not consider the business justifications offered for the policy as applied to them. On remand, if Local 115 is able to make out a prima facie case with regard to employees with limited proficiency in English, the district court could then consider any business justification offered by Spun Steak.

* * *

BOOCHEVER, Circuit Judge, dissenting in part:

I agree with most of the majority's carefully crafted opinion. I dissent, however, from the majority's rejection of the EEOC guidelines. The guidelines provide that an employee establishes a prima facie case in a disparate impact claim by proving the existence of an English-only policy, thereby shifting the burden to the employer to show a business necessity for the rule. See 29 C.F.R. § 1606.7(b) (1991) ("An employer may have a rule requiring that employees speak only in English at certain times where the employer can show that the rule is justified by business necessity."). I would defer to the Commission's expertise in construing the Act, by virtue of which it concluded that English-only rules may "create an atmosphere of inferiority, isolation and intimidation based on national origin which could result in a discriminatory working environment." Id. § 1606.7(a).

As the majority indicates, proof of such an effect of English-only rules requires analysis of subjective factors. It is hard to envision how the burden of proving such an effect would be met other than by conclusory self-serving statements of the Spanish-speaking employees or possibly by expert testimony of psychologists. The difficulty of meeting such a burden may well have been one of the reasons for the promulgation of the guideline. On the other hand, it should not be difficult for an employer to give specific reasons for the policy, such as the safety reasons advanced in this case.

* * *

I conclude that if appropriate deference is given to the administrative interpretation of the Act, we should follow the guideline and uphold the district court's decision that a prima facie case was established. I believe, however, that triable issues were presented whether Spun Steak established a business justification for the rule, and I would remand for trial of that issue.

Notes and Questions

1. The denial of en banc reconsideration in *Spun Steak* evoked a powerful dissent from Judge Reinhardt who argued, in part,:

> Language is intimately tied to national origin and cultural identity; its discriminatory suppression cannot be dismissed as an "inconvenience" to the affected employees, as *Spun Steak* asserts. Even when an individual learns English and becomes assimilated into American society, his native language remains an important manifestation of his ethnic identity and a means of affirming links to his original culture. English-only rules not only symbolize a rejection of the excluded language and the culture it embodies, but also that denial of a side of an individual's personality.

> Thus, the *Spun Steak* majority's emphasis on the *practical* effects of English-only rules is misplaced. Whether or not an individual is, in practice, capable of speaking only English is not the important consideration here by any means. What is far more important is the impact of the prohibition itself. As the EEOC correctly determined, being forbidden under penalty of perjury to speak one's native tongue generally has a pernicious effect on national origin minorities.

> Finally, it should be noted that the imposition of an English-only rule may mask intentional discrimination on the basis of national origin. Even those who support the majority's view acknowledge that "language can be a potent source of racial and ethnic discrimination." Gutierrez v. Municipal Court, 861 F.2d 1187, 1192 (9th Cir.1988) (Kozinski, J., dissenting from denial of rehearing en banc). History is replete with language conflicts that attest, not only to the crucial importance of language to its speakers, but also to the widespread tactic of using language as a surrogate for attacks on ethnic identity. As these examples reveal, the urge to repress another's language is rarely, if ever, driven by benevolent impulses.

> * * * *Spun Steak*'s misguided removal of [the protection the EEOC attempts to provide in its *Guidelines*], based largely on two judges' subjective judgment that the discriminatory impact of English-only rules

is "not significant" seriously undermines one of the basic goals of Title VII.

Garcia v. Spun Steak, 13 F.3d 296, 298–99 (9th Cir.1993) (Reinhardt, J., dissenting from denial of rehearing en banc).

2. In *Spun Steak*, the Ninth Circuit refused to follow its previous decision in *Gutierrez v. Municipal Court*, 838 F.2d 1031 (9th Cir.1988), *vacated as moot*, 490 U.S. 1016, 109 S.Ct. 1736, 104 L.Ed.2d 174 (1989). In *Gutierrez*, the first court of appeals to consider the legality of an employer's English-only rule in light of the EEOC Guidelines struck down an employer's rule that prohibited employees from speaking any language other than English, except when translating official business or during lunch breaks. *Gutierrez* held that an English-only rule in the workplace generally has an adverse impact on non-English speaking employees and for that reason constitutes a discriminatory condition of employment because it has "a direct effect on the general atmosphere and environment of the work place." *Id.* at 1041. *Gutierrez* also held that an employee's ability to comply with a English-only rule was not relevant and could not preclude a finding of disparate impact discrimination. Adopting business necessity as the appropriate defense, *Gutierrez* rejected each of the justifications proffered by the defendant. The employer argued that (1) the rule was necessary because the United States is an English-speaking country and California is an English-speaking state; (2) the use of Spanish is disruptive and creates a "Tower of Babel"; (3) the rule promotes racial harmony; and (4) the rule is required for effective supervision because supervisors do not speak Spanish. *Id.* at 1042–43. *Spun Steak* rejected *Gutierrez* as binding precedent because *Gutierrez* had been vacated as moot by the Supreme Court.

All of the challenged English-only rules that have been upheld have involved bilingual employees and the employers have been able to convince the courts that they have a legitimate business reason for adopting the rule. *See* Roman v. Cornell Univ., 53 F.Supp.2d 223, 236 (N.D.N.Y.1999) (collecting cases); Kania v. Archdiocese of Phila., 14 F.Supp.2d 730 (E.D.Pa.1998) (Polish-speaking plaintiff; court reviews English-only rule cases).

3. The EEOC Guidelines rejected by the majority in *Spun Steak* provide:

Speak-English-only rules.

(a) *When applied at all times.* A rule requiring employees to speak only English at all times in the workplace is a burdensome term and condition of employment. The primary language of an individual is often an essential national origin characteristic. Prohibiting employees at all times, in the workplace, from speaking their primary language or the language they speak most comfortably, disadvantages an individual's employment opportunities on the basis of national origin. It may also create an atmosphere of inferiority, isolation and intimidation based on national origin which could result in a discriminatory working environment. Therefore, the [EEOC] will presume that such a rule violates title VII and will closely scrutinize it.

EEOC, Guidelines on Discrimination Because of National Origin, 29 C.F.R. § 1606.7(a) (2003).

The EEOC's presumption applies only to a rule that requires employees to speak only English *at all times* in the workplace. The presumption is inapplicable when the English-only rule is applied only at certain times. The EEOC Guidelines continue:

> (b) *When applied only at certain times.* An employer may have a rule requiring that employees speak only in English at certain times where the employer can show that the rule is justified by business necessity.

Id. § 1606.7(b) (2003).

Do *Spun Steak* and the EEOC Guidelines suggest the same or different conceptions of national origin? Which of the two views on English-only policies—*Spun Steak* or the EEOC Guidelines—is more consistent with the equality rationale for Title VII?

4.   A number of sociologists and legal scholars argue that language is an important aspect of national origin or ethnicity because it sets a cultural group apart from others. *See, e.g.,* Mark Colon, *Line Drawing, Code Switching, and Spanish as Second–Hand Smoke: English–Only Workplace Rules and Bilingual Employees,* 20 Yale L. & Pol'y Rev. 227, 246–50 (2002); Juan F. Perea, *Demography and Distrust: An Essay on American Languages, Cultural Pluralism, and Official English,* 77 Minn.L.Rev. 269, 276–79 (1992); Bill Piatt, *Toward Domestic Recognition of a Human Right to Language,* 23 Hous.L.Rev. 885, 896 (1986). Assuming that language is an important aspect of national origin, is it an immutable characteristic like race or sex, or is it a mutable characteristic like the grooming standards which courts generally have held are not protected under Title VII? *See* Colon, *supra,* at 250–57 (discussing the dynamics of "code-switching," the unconscious alternation of two languages in one conversation). Should it make a difference whether it is immutable or mutable? *See, e.g.,* Willingham v. Macon Tel. Publ'g Co., 507 F.2d 1084, 1091 (5th Cir.1975) (holding that a rule regulating hair length for males is not prohibited sex discrimination under Title VII because hair length is not an immutable characteristic). See the discussion of grooming standards in Chapter 6, section F.

5.   As the number of non-English-speaking residents in the United States has increased, the number of states attempting to establish English as the official language has grown, provoking constitutional challenges to English-only policies for state employees. For example, in *Arizonans for Official English v. Arizona,* 520 U.S. 43, 117 S.Ct. 1055, 137 L.Ed.2d 170 (1997), the Supreme Court was asked to consider the constitutionality of an Arizona state constitutional provision, adopted by a state referendum, that generally prohibited state employees from using any language other than English in conducting state business. The plaintiffs challenged the Arizona law on the ground that it violated the employees' federal constitutional free speech rights and was facially overbroad. The district court agreed with the plaintiffs' First Amendment free speech challenge and struck down the law. The Ninth Circuit affirmed. The Supreme Court did not reach the merits of the issue on the grounds of standing and mootness. Briefs submitted in the Supreme Court indicated that at least twenty-one states have adopted similar English-only provisions. *See generally* Juan F. Perea, *Demography and Distrust: An Essay on American Languages, Cultural Pluralism, and*

Official English, 77 Minn.L.Rev. 269 (1992); Cecilia Wong, Note, *Language Is Speech: The Illegitimacy of Official English After* Yniguez v. Arizonans for Official English, 30 U.C. Davis L.Rev. 277 (1996).

The English-only campaigns are grounded, in substantial part, on the current debate over multiculturalism. *See generally* Henry L. Gates, Jr., Loose Canons: Notes on the Culture Wars (1992); Yxta Maya Murray, *The Latino–American Crisis of Citizenship*, 31 U.C. Davis L.Rev. 503, 546–59 (1998); *also compare* Doriane Lambelet Coleman, *Individualizing Justice Through Multiculturalism: The Liberal's Dilemma*, 96 Colum.L.Rev. 1093 (1996), *with* Leti Volpp, *Talking "Culture": Gender, Race, Nation, and the Politics of Multiculturalism*, 96 Colum.L.Rev. 1573 (1996). Employment, like education, has become a major sphere in which the controversy over multiculturalism and English-only policies is being waged. *See generally* Mark L. Adams, *Fear of Foreigners: Nativism and Workplace Language Restrictions*, 74 Or.L.Rev. 849 (1995). For a critique of multiculturalism in education, see Arthur M. Schlesinger, Jr., The Disuniting of America: Reflections on a Multicultural Society 67 (1991) (asserting that multiculturalism can lead to "disintegration of the national community, apartheid, Balkanization, tribalization," and that schools and colleges have a responsibility to transmit the core Anglo–Saxon ideas and traditions that form the unique "American synthesis").

6. *Spun Steak* stands alone in allowing a disparate impact claim to be brought under § 703(a)(1). Does *Spun Steak* provide meaningful guidelines on which disparate impact cases should be grounded in § 703(a)(1) of Title VII and which should be grounded in § 703(a)(2)? If so, what other kinds of employment discrimination claims are subject to disparate impact analysis under § 703(a)(1)? Assuming that the *Spun Steak* is correct in holding that under some circumstances a disparate impact claim can be based upon § 703(a)(1), then would the provisions on disparate impact analysis under the Civil Rights Act of 1991, e.g., § 702(k)(1)(A), 42 U.S.C. § 2000e–2(k)(1)(A), also apply? If so, then how would the analysis and allocation of the burdens of proof proceed?

7. Evaluate the following six common business justifications for English-only rules in the workplace that have been examined by one commentator: (1) ensuring worker safety, (2) assuring effective supervision, (3) increasing productivity and efficiency, (4) promoting worker harmony, (5) improving customer relations and satisfaction, and (6) improving employees' English proficiency. Jeanne M. Jorgensen, Comment, *"English-Only" in the Workplace and Title VII Disparate Impact: The Ninth Circuit's Misplaced Application of "Ability to Comply" Should Be Rejected in Favor of the EEOC's Business Necessity Test*, 25 Sw.U.L.Rev. 407, 422–27 (1996).

8. A police department has a policy that requires bilingual Spanish-speaking police officers and employees to use their Spanish-speaking skills when necessary to carry out the duties of the police department. They do not receive additional compensation when called upon to speak Spanish in the course of doing their work. Statistics show that more Latino/Latina* employ-

---

* There appears to be a general preference for the nomenclature "Latino" over "Hispanic." The Supreme Court has used the term "Latino." *See* Hernandez v. New York, 500 U.S. 352, 355, 111 S.Ct. 1859, 1864, 114 L.Ed.2d 395 (1991). " 'Latino' is

ees than non-Latino/Latina employees are affected by this policy. Would the Spanish-speaking employees have an argument that the policy violates Title VII prohibition against discrimination because of national origin? Should these be analyzed as disparate impact or disparate treatment claims? *See* Cota v. Tucson Police Dep't, 783 F.Supp. 458 (D.Ariz.1992); Morales v. Human Rights Div., 878 F.Supp. 653 (S.D.N.Y.1995).

9. *Reverse English–Only Claims*: In *McNeil v. Aguilos*, 831 F.Supp. 1079 (S.D.N.Y.1993), the plaintiff, a black female, brought a pro se claim under Title VII and § 1981 alleging that Filipino nurses, including her supervisor, spoke Tagalog on the job in order to isolate and harass her. Tagalog is the main language of the Philippines. The plaintiff also alleged that the use of Tagalog by her co-workers impeded her ability to perform her job effectively and that, as a result, she was not promoted. Plaintiff cited as a specific example of her difficulty the fact that her supervisor gave the unit report in Tagalog and that, when she asked the supervisor a specific question, her supervisor failed to respond. What argument would you make in support of plaintiff's claim? What defense on behalf of the employer? The trial court dismissed the case on the ground that the plaintiff willfully disregarded discovery orders and failed to prosecute her claim. McNeil v. Aguilos, 1996 WL 219637 (S.D.N.Y.1996), *aff'd*, 107 F.3d 3 (2d Cir.1996) (unpublished table decision), *cert. denied*, 520 U.S. 1223, 117 S.Ct. 1721, 137 L.Ed.2d 843 (1997).

10. For a discussion of the Canadian experience in recognizing language rights of its French-and English-speaking citizens and Canada's commitment to equal rights, *see* Terrence Meyerhoff, Note & Comment, *Multiculturalism and Language Rights in Canada: Problems and Prospects for Equality and Unity*, 9 Am.U.J. Int'l L. & Pol'y 913 (1994).

3. ACCENT DISCRIMINATION AS NATIONAL ORIGIN DISCRIMINATION

Another class of cases involving language discrimination arises out of accent discrimination claims. The courts have recognized that discrimination on the basis of a foreign accent can violate the prohibition against national origin discrimination under Title VII. In *Carino v. University of Oklahoma*, 750 F.2d 815 (10th Cir.1984), plaintiff brought an action alleging that he had been demoted from his position as a dental laboratory supervisor because of his Filipino accent. The court of appeals affirmed a decision in favor of the plaintiff and established the basic rule that other courts have followed: "A foreign accent that does not interfere with a Title VII claimant's ability to perform duties of the position he has been denied is not a legitimate justification for adverse

an abbreviated version of the Spanish word *latinoamericano*, or Latin American. 'Hispanic' is the English translation of *hispano*, a word commonly used to describe all peoples of Spanish-speaking origin." Manuel Peréz-Rivas, *Hispanic, Latino: Which?*, N.Y. Newsday, Oct. 13, 1991, at 6, 6. Though the two terms are roughly synonymous, many prefer the word "Latino" because "Hispanic" is thought to have colonial and assimila-tive overtones. *See* Paul Brest & Miranda Oshige, *Affirmative Action for Whom?*, 47 Stan.L.Rev. 855, 883 n.148 (1995). The term "Latino" is also suggestive of Latin America's indigenous culture apart from its Spanish origins. Deborah Ramirez, *Multiculture Empowerment: It's Not Just Black and White Anymore*, 47 Stan.L.Rev. 957, 959 n.9 (1995).

employment decisions." *Id.* at 819. *See* Berke v. Ohio Dep't of Pub. Welfare, 628 F.2d 980 (6th Cir.1980) (finding national origin discrimination against an employee demoted because of his Filipino accent).

A case on accent discrimination that has been the subject of a great deal of critical commentary is *Fragante v. City & County of Honolulu*, 888 F.2d 591 (9th Cir.1989), *cert. denied*, 494 U.S. 1081, 110 S.Ct. 1811, 108 L.Ed.2d 942 (1990). The plaintiff, Manuel Fragante, had received the highest score for a clerk's position out of over 700 applicants who had taken the test for that position. After a brief interview, which was part of the screening process, he was rejected because of a perceived deficiency in oral communication skills caused by his heavy Filipino accent. The district court ruled for the employer, finding that the decision to deny Fragante the job was justified based on the BFOQ defense, even though the interview lacked formality such as standards, instructions, guidelines, or criteria, and the rating sheet for interviews was inadequate. The Ninth Circuit, in its original decision, affirmed on the basis of the BFOQ defense. In a later amended opinion, the court disregarded its original decision grounded in the BFOQ defense, but nevertheless again ruled in favor of the employer. 888 F.2d 591 (9th Cir.1989). In the course of its analysis, the court said:

> Preliminarily, we do well to remember that this country was founded and has been built in large measure by people from other lands, many of whom came here—especially after our earlier beginnings—with a limited knowledge of English. This flow of immigrants has continued and has been encouraged over the years. * * * We hold out promises of freedom, equality, and economic opportunity to many who only know these words as concepts. It would be more than ironic if we followed up our invitation to people such as Manuel Fragante with a closed economic door based on national origin discrimination. It is no surprise that Title VII speaks to this issue and clearly articulates the policy of our nation: unlawful discrimination based on national origin shall not be permitted to exist in the workplace. But, it is also true that there is another important aspect of Title VII: the preservation of an employer's remaining freedom of choice. Price Waterhouse v. Hopkins, 490 U.S. 228, 109 S.Ct. 1775, 104 L.Ed.2d 268 (1989).

Id. at 596. The court then reaffirmed its ruling in favor of the employer on the ground that the employer had articulated a legitimate, nondiscriminatory reason for its rejection of Fragante, namely, that those selected had communication skills superior to Fragante's and that Fragante had failed to show that the employer's explanation was pretext for invidious discrimination on the basis of national origin. *Id.* at 596–99.

Several critical race scholars have criticized *Fragante* on the ground that the equality principle on which Title VII is based is conceptually flawed because it requires plaintiffs to introduce direct evidence of discriminatory bias or intent by an employer when in fact discrimination is often based on unconscious bias. For example, Professor Mari Matsuda characterized the defense that the court accepted as the "can't understand" defense. She argued that the courts have failed to address the question whether an employer should be free to choose the "best" accent in view of the fact that everyone has an accent. Mari J. Matsuda, *Voices of America: Accent, Antidiscrimination Law, and a Jurisprudence for the Last Reconstruction*, 100 Yale L.J. 1329, 1333–40, 1350 (1991). She wrote:

> A major complicating factor in applying Title VII to accent cases is the difficulty in sorting out accents that actually impede job performance from accents that are simply different from some preferred norm imposed, whether consciously or subconsciously, by the employer. The reality that accent discrimination is often unconscious, renders the judicial search for pretext pointless. Pretext by definition involves a conscious choice to discriminate.

Id. at 1352. Professor Matsuda relies on the influential article by Professor Charles R. Lawrence, *The Id, the Ego, and Equal Protection: Reckoning with Unconscious Racism*, 39 Stan.L.Rev. 317 (1987), in developing her argument that unconscious bias, "prejudice and status are tied inextricably to speech evaluation" in the accent discrimination cases. Matsuda, *supra*, at 1332. She advocates a four-part inquiry for analyzing accent discrimination cases:

1. What level of communication is required for the job?

2. Was the candidate's speech fairly evaluated?

3. Is the candidate intelligible to the pool of relevant, nonprejudiced listeners, such that job performance is not unreasonably impeded?

4. What accommodations are reasonable given the job and any limitations in intelligibility?

Id. at 1368.

For other critical race analyses of *Fragante*, see Roy L. Brooks & Mary Jo Newborn, *Critical Race Theory and Classical–Liberal Civil Rights Scholarship: A Distinction Without a Difference?*, 82 Cal.L.Rev. 787, 824–32 (1994). *See also* Linda M. Mealey, Note, *English-Only and "Innocent" Employers: Clarifying National Origin Discrimination and Disparate Impact Theory Under Title VII*, 74 Minn.L.Rev. 387 (1989).

In the absence of a distinct proof structure for accent discrimination, such as that suggested by Matsuda, how are judges and juries left to evaluate these cases? In the following case, the court considered a hiring supervisor's comments about an applicant's accent, as well as the applicant's relative qualifications, in affirming the plaintiff Hasham's national origin (Pakistani) claim. Consider to what extent this approach serves the purposes of Title VII.

HASHAM v. CALIFORNIA STATE BOARD OF EQUALIZATION

United States Court of Appeals for the Seventh Circuit, 2000.
200 F.3d 1035.

COFFEY, Circuit Judge:

* * *

I. BACKGROUND

* * *

A. *Qualifications of Hasham and Smith*

Hasham scored an 87 on the Supervisor I exam while Smith scored an 83. Hasham has a Bachelor of Arts degree from the University of Karachi, Pakistan, and a Bachelor of Science degree in Business Administration and a Masters of Science degree in Accounting from Roosevelt University in Chicago. At the time of the promotion at issue, Hasham had informed Zigelman that he was a certified public accountant ("CPA"), while Smith on the other hand, had a Bachelor's degree in accounting but was not qualified as a CPA.

According to Zigelman's testimony at trial, prior to his promotion of Smith, every supervisor in the Houston office was a CPA. Further, as of September 1993, Hasham had twelve and one-half years of tax auditing out-of-district accounts experience in contrast to Smith's six years. Moreover, Hasham had completed several difficult and large "mega" audits (audits of large multi-national corporations) for CBOE, while Smith had yet to complete even one as of September 1993 and had more aged audits than Hasham. Also, prior to recommending Smith for the promotion, Zigelman contacted Lynn Thompson, Hasham's supervisor at the time, and received a favorable reference.

* * *

III. DISCUSSION

A. *Intentional National Origin Discrimination*

* * *

1. *Discriminatory Comments*

It was revealed at trial that sometime around the month of August 1993, Zigelman [the person responsible for the promotion decision] made a comment to one of the auditors in the Houston office about the foreign accent of an auditor from the New York office named D. Patel. Zigelman said that Patel was difficult to understand and then remarked about Hasham, "If you want to hear something difficult, you should have heard that guy from Chicago. He was extremely difficult to understand. In fact, how did he expect to be a supervisor if he can't communicate with people." Another Houston auditor also testified that he heard Zigelman on another occasion state in a demeaning tone that he could not understand Hasham. However, Zigelman did testify at trial that there was "absolutely" no reason to believe that Hasham's accent would interfere with his ability to supervise. Also, in February 1992, Ruth Malloy and Pamela Hartman, two auditors in the Houston office, testified that they heard Zigelman say that he did "not want to hire any more foreigners" after he was told that an Asian applicant was waiting to be interviewed. We are of the opinion that a reasonable jury could have concluded that, in conjunction with Zigelman's contradictory testimony, his comments about Hasham's accent and comment about the hiring of foreigners demonstrated a discriminatory animus that governed his promotional decision, which we are in no position, "particularly * * * in employment discrimination cases[,] to * * * supplant [ ] our view of the credibility or weight of the evidence for that of * * * the jury." Hybert v. Hearst Corp., 900 F.2d 1050, 1054 (7th Cir.1990).

2.   *Evidence of Pretext*

Defendant argues that Smith was promoted for the following reasons: Zigelman believed that Smith was the most qualified candidate; to continue promoting in-house employees; and to accommodate Carol Cross's voluntary demotion. Obviously, it is the prerogative of the jury to weigh and balance the credibility of each and every witness and disbelieve or believe any or all reasonable testimony and evidence offered to support an employment decision." " "

* * *

* * *[W]hen considering Zigelman's testimony in its totality, the jury might very well have considered his proffered reasons for his promotion decision suspect and thus, unreliable.

* * *

B.   *The District Court's Evidentiary Rulings*

Defendant CBOE contends that the district court committed reversible error when it made the following evidentiary rulings: * * * (3) admitted Zigelman's alleged comments regarding the "hiring of foreigners" and Hasham's accent. * * *

* * *

3.   *Prejudicial Comments*

CBOE * * * also alleges that the testimony by Houston employees about Zigelman's alleged discriminatory comments were inadmissible stray remarks. Zigelman's two comments at issue, occurring on different occasions, are that he did "not want to hire anymore foreigners" and, stated in a demeaning tone, he couldn't understand Hasham's accent.

In relation to the statement about foreigners, Defendant contends that the statement occurred 18 months prior to the promotion at issue and thus, was too remote in time and bore no relationship to Hasham because it dealt with hiring and not promoting. CBOE also asserts that Zigelman's comment that he couldn't understand Hasham's accent, allegedly stated in a demeaning tone, is too ambiguous to prove intentional discrimination. Defendant's argument might have some merit if this was solely a direct proof case because remarks must indeed be related to the employment promotion decision to evidence discriminatory intent. However, because Hasham presents his case through "indirect" evidence, remarks relied upon need only be probative of discriminatory bias when determining, along with other evidence, if Zigelman's proffered reasons for promotion were pretextual. Further, when evaluating the probative value of Zigelman's statements, his remarks do not stand alone; in an indirect proof case, "no one piece of evidence need support a finding of discrimination," but rather the court must take "the facts as a whole." Futrell v. J.I. Case, 38 F.3d 342, 350 (7th Cir.1994). The remark is only but a part of a pattern of falsehoods, contradictions and discriminatory statements by Zigelman that, as a whole, convincingly demonstrate intentional discrimination. Thus, Defendant's distinctions between "hiring" and "promoting" and the 18 months separating the "foreigners" remark and the promotion in question are unpersuasive when considering the remark in conjunction with the aforementioned evidence of pretext.

With regard to Zigelman's remark about Hasham's accent, Zigelman also testified that he had no reason to believe that Hasham's accent would interfere with his ability to supervise. When contrasted with Zigelman's tone and comment that he was not able to understand Hasham's accent and could not see "how did [Hasham] expect to be a supervisor if he can't communicate with people"; again, serious credibility issues for Defendant's main witness, Zigelman, are raised, which could very likely have been one of the foundation blocks for the jury's clear finding of intentional discrimination. Also, as the district court pointed out, the "accent" comment supports an inference of discriminatory intent because accent is generally recognized as a manifestation of national origin and the comment was uttered by the decision maker in this case. Accordingly, we are of the opinion that the trial judge did not abuse its discretion by admitting the remarks which allowed the jury to weigh their significance.

* * *

Notes and Questions

1. Given *Fragante* and *Hasham*, how would you explain to a client whether discrimination based on accent is prohibited national origin discrimination under Title VII?

2. The court seemed to rely heavily on Hasham's superior qualifications to support the jury's finding of pretext. In another national origin case, *Deines v. Texas Department of Protective & Regulatory Services*, 164 F.3d

277, 280 (5th Cir.1999), the court upheld a jury instruction that read, in part, "disparities in qualifications are not enough in and of themselves to demonstrate discriminatory intent unless those disparities are so apparent as virtually to 'jump off the page and slap you in the face.' " Deines argued unsuccessfully that this instruction "essentially elevated his burden of persuasion from the preponderance of evidence standard to a level of clear and convincing evidence." *Id.* Given *Deines,* could plaintiff Hasham have succeeded solely on the basis of superior qualifications or was his other evidence essential?

3. For an analysis of language discrimination claims based on the Equal Protection Clause of the Fourteenth Amendment, *see* Andrew P. Averbach, Note, *Language Classifications and the Equal Protection Clause: When Is Language a Pretext for Race or Ethnicity?,* 74 B.U.L.Rev. 481 (1994).

Chapter 12

DISCRIMINATION BECAUSE OF AGE

A. INTRODUCTION

The Age Discrimination in Employment Act (ADEA), 29 U.S.C. § 621 et seq., protects workers who are at least forty years old against discrimination because of their age. A number of the substantive provisions of the ADEA are patterned after or are similar to provisions in Title VII. As the Supreme Court noted in *McKennon v. Nashville Banner Publishing Co.*, 513 U.S. 352, 358, 115 S.Ct. 879, 884, 130 L.Ed.2d 852 (1995), "[t]he ADEA and Title VII share common substantive features and also a common purpose: 'the elimination of discrimination in the workplace' "(citing Oscar Mayer & Co. v. Evans, 441 U.S. 750, 756, 99 S.Ct. 2066, 2071, 60 L.Ed.2d 609 (1979)). For this reason, courts have relied upon or borrowed from the Title VII jurisprudence in deciding ADEA claims. *See, e.g.,* Madel v. FCI Marketing, Inc., 116 F.3d 1247, 1251 n.2 (8th Cir.1997); Tyler v. Bethlehem Steel Corp., 958 F.2d 1176 (2d Cir.), *cert. denied*, 506 U.S. 826, 113 S.Ct. 82, 121 L.Ed.2d 46 (1992); King v. General Elec. Co., 960 F.2d 617 (7th Cir.1992).

Even though much of the Title VII jurisprudence is pertinent in analyzing ADEA cases, there is an ongoing effort to sort out the similarities and differences between the policies, theories, and analytical approaches underlying the ADEA and Title VII. This chapter explores some of the those similarities and differences, including the applicability of the disparate treatment and disparate impact theories in ADEA claims; the special problems involved in reductions-in-force (RIFs), downsizing, and early retirement incentive plans (ERIPs); and the interrelated problem of waiver of rights under the ADEA.

For a review of the first thirty years of enforcement under the ADEA, see Howard C. Eglit, *The Age Discrimination in Employment Act at Thirty: Where It's Been, Where It Is Today, Where It's Going*, 31 U.Rich.L.Rev. 579 (1997).

B. DISPARATE TREATMENT

Most of the ADEA cases are brought under the disparate treatment theory of discrimination. Former EEOC Vice Chairman, Cathie Shattuck, conducted a survey of plaintiffs seeking relief under the ADEA between 1982 and 1983. The survey disclosed the following profile of the average ADEA plaintiff: a fifty-five-year-old male with twenty years of employment service, earning $32,000 per year in a white-collar job before being terminated by his employer. Cathie A. Shattuck, ADEA Litigation Survey (1984), *reprinted in* Recipients of ADEA Settlements Are Mostly Long–Term, Male Employees, 7 Daily Lab.Rep. (BNA) A–3 (Jan. 12, 1984). (Based on the 1984 salary profile in the Shattuck study, the equivalent income would be a little over $50,000 in 1998 dollars.) Others have suggested a similar profile in which the typical ADEA plaintiff is described as a salaried, nonunion member of management, possibly an executive, supervisor, staff professional, or skilled worker. *See, e.g.,* Samuel Issacharoff & Erica W. Harris, *Is Age Discrimination Really Age Discrimination?: The ADEA's Unnatural Solution*, 72 N.Y.U.L.Rev. 780, 795 (1997). What reasons might explain this typical profile of the ADEA plaintiff?

In *Hazen Paper Co. v. Biggins*, 507 U.S. 604, 609, 113 S.Ct. 1701, 1706, 123 L.Ed.2d 338 (1993), the Supreme Court stated that "[t]he disparate treatment theory is of course available under the ADEA, as the language of that statute makes clear. 'It shall be unlawful for an employer * * * to fail or refuse to hire or to discharge any individual or otherwise discriminate against any individual with respect to his compensation, terms, conditions, or privileges of employment *because of such individual's age.*' 29 U.S.C. § 623(a)(1) (emphasis added)." The Supreme Court has not directly decided whether the analytical scheme of *McDonnell Douglas Corp. v. Green*, 411 U.S. 792, 93 S.Ct. 1817, 36 L.Ed.2d 668 (1973), *Texas Department of Community Affairs v. Burdine*, 450 U.S. 248, 101 S.Ct. 1089, 67 L.Ed.2d 207 (1981), and *St. Mary's Honor Center v. Hicks*, 509 U.S. 502, 113 S.Ct. 2742, 125 L.Ed.2d 407 (1993), is equally applicable to ADEA claims. For example, the Supreme Court observed, in *Reeves v. Sanderson Plumbing Products, Inc.*, 530 U.S. 133, 142, 120 S.Ct. 2097, 2105, 147 L.Ed.2d 105, 116 (2000), discussed in Chapter 3, that "this Court has not squarely addressed whether the *McDonnell Douglas* framework * * * also applies to ADEA actions. Because the parties do not dispute the issue, we shall assume, *arguendo*, that the *McDonnell Douglas* framework is fully applicable here." *See also* O'Connor v. Consolidated Coin Caterers Corp., 571 U.S. 308, 311, 116 S.Ct. 1307, 1310, 134 L.Ed.2d 433 (1996). The lower courts have consistently applied some variant of the *McDonnell Douglas–Burdine–Hicks* analytical framework to ADEA cases. *See, e.g.,* Greene v. Safeway Stores, Inc., 98 F.3d 554, 557–58 (10th Cir.1996); Abdu–Brisson v. Delta Air Lines, 239 F.3d 456 (2d Cir.2001) *cert. denied*, 534 U.S. 993, 122 S.Ct. 460, 151 L.Ed.2d 378 (2001); Russell v. McKinney Hosp. Venture, 235 F.3d 219

(5th Cir.2000); Bresett v. City of Claremont, 218 F.Supp.2d 42 (D.N.H. 2002). Lower courts have also adopted the direct evidence framework suggested in *Price-Waterhouse. See* Fakete v. Aetna, Inc., 308 F.3d 335 (3d Cir.2002). To what extent is this approach affected by *Desert Palace, Inc. v. Costa,* 539 U.S. 90, 123 S.Ct. 2148, 156 L.Ed.2d 84 (2003), discussed Chapter 3?

A typical formulation of the analytical framework the lower courts have adopted for ADEA cases, based on the Title VII disparate treatment cases, requires a plaintiff to establish a prima facie case. To establish a prima facie case, the plaintiff must show that (1) he is within the age group protected under the ADEA; (2) he suffered an adverse employment action or disposition; (3) he was qualified for the position either lost or not gained; and (4) a person younger than the plaintiff was selected for the position over the plaintiff. If the plaintiff establishes a prima facie case, the burden of production of evidence shifts to the employer to present evidence of a legitimate, nondiscriminatory reason for the adverse action taken. If the employer carries its burden of production on a legitimate nondiscriminatory reason, the burdens of production and persuasion return to the plaintiff to produce sufficient evidence from which a jury could find that an employer had intentionally discriminated against the plaintiff in violation of the ADEA. *See, e.g.,* Greene v. Safeway Stores, Inc., 98 F.3d 554, 558–60 (10th Cir.1996); Stein v. National City Bank, 942 F.2d 1062, 1065 (6th Cir.1991) (citing Rose v. National Cash Register Corp., 703 F.2d 225 (6th Cir.) *cert. denied,* 464 U.S. 939, 104 S.Ct. 352, 78 L.Ed.2d 317 (1983)).

Note: O'Connor v. Consolidated Coin Caterers Corp.

In *O'Connor v. Consolidated Coin Caterers Corp.,* 517 U.S. 308, 116 S.Ct. 1307, 134 L.Ed.2d 433 (1996), the Supreme Court considered whether an employee who is fired and replaced by an individual who is also within the age group protected by the ADEA, i.e., forty years of age or older, can establish a prima facie case of age discrimination. The plaintiff in *Consolidated Coin* was fifty-six years old at the time of his discharge and his replacement was forty years of age. Both were protected under the ADEA. The Fourth Circuit held that an ADEA plaintiff must prove, as an element of a prima facie case, that he was replaced by an individual of comparable qualifications who is not within the age group that is protected by the ADEA. The Fourth Circuit was the only court of appeals to adopt such a rule.

The Supreme Court reversed. The Court held that the ADEA "does not ban discrimination against employees because they are aged 40 or older; it bans discrimination against employees because of their age, but limits the protected class to those who are 40 or older." 517 U.S. at 312, 116 S.Ct. at 1310. Justice Scalia, writing for a unanimous Court, stated:

> Perhaps some courts have been induced to adopt the principle urged by [the employer] in order to avoid creating a prima facie case on the basis of thin evidence—for example, the replacement of a 68-year-old by

a 65-year-old. While the [employer's] principle theoretically permits such thin evidence (consider the example above of a 40-year-old replaced by a 39-year-old), as a practical matter it will rarely do so, since the vast majority of age-discrimination claims come from older employees. In our view, however, the proper solution to the problem lies not in making an utterly irrelevant factor an element of the prima facie case, but rather in recognizing that the prima facie case requires *"evidence adequate to create an inference that an employment decision was based on a[n] [illegal] discriminatory criterion. * * * "* In the age-discrimination context, such an inference can not be drawn from the replacement of one worker with another worker insignificantly younger. Because the ADEA prohibits discrimination on the basis of age and not class membership, the fact that a replacement is substantially younger than the plaintiff is a far more reliable indicator of age discrimination than is the fact that the plaintiff was replaced by someone outside the protected class.

Id. at 312–13, 116 S.Ct. at 1310 (emphasis in original).

The Supreme Court did not elaborate on the obvious question of how much younger than the plaintiff a replacement has to be to satisfy the *Consolidated Coin* "substantially younger" standard. Lower courts have responded to this question by adopting differing standards. In *Showalter v. University of Pittsburgh Medical Center,* 190 F.3d 231 (3d Cir.1999), the court noted that there is no "particular age difference that must be shown" but while "[d]ifferent courts have held * * * that a five year difference can be sufficient, * * * a one year difference cannot." *Id.* at 236 (citing Sempier v. Johnson & Higgins, 45 F.3d 724, 729 (3d Cir.1995)). In *Showalter,* the plaintiff was eight years older than one individual who also was protected by the ADEA and sixteen years older than another. The Eighth Circuit has held that a five-year disparity in ages is not substantial enough to support an inference of age discrimination. *See* Schiltz v. Burlington Northern R.R., 115 F.3d 1407 (8th Cir.1997). In *Hartley v. Wisconsin Bell, Inc.,* 124 F.3d 887 (7th Cir.1997), the Seventh Circuit adopted a rule that an age disparity of less than ten years is presumptively insubstantial unless the plaintiff "directs the court to evidence that her employer considered age to be significant." *Id.* at 893. Suppose under the Seventh Circuit's rule the employer had at one time made a statement to the plaintiff that he was "getting too old to do the job." Should that be sufficient? If the plaintiff had evidence that the employer considered age to be significant, should it make any difference that the plaintiff was ten years older than his replacement? *See* Cianci v. Pettibone Corp., 152 F.3d 723 (7th Cir.1998).

As a result of *O'Connor v. Consolidated Coin Caterers,* the Second Circuit now articulates the prima facie case for age discrimination as follow: (1) Plaintiff is a member of the protected class; (2) Plaintiff is qualified for the position; (3) Plaintiff has suffered an adverse employment action; and (4) The circumstances surrounding that action give rise to an inference of discrimination. Abdu–Brisson v. Delta Air Lines, 239 F.3d 456, 466 (2d Cir.2001).

Consider the following in light of Justice Scalia's analysis in *Consolidated Coin Caterers:*

1.   Robert Greene, an executive with Safeway Stores, first became a store manager with Safeway when he was 26 years old. When he was 52 years old, he was discharged and replaced by John King who was 57 years old. Green has now filed an age discrimination claim against Safeway. Because Greene cannot show that he was replaced by a "substantially younger" employee, should his age discrimination claim be dismissed as a matter of law under *Consolidated Coin*? *See* Greene v. Safeway Stores, Inc., 98 F.3d 554, 557–58 (10th Cir.1996).

2.   John Sheehan was an assistant editor in the Chicago office of the *Daily Racing Form*. Five employees were identified as potential candidates for downsizing (or layoff) because the publication had decided to computerize some of its operations. At the time the decision was made, Sheehan was 49 years old. Two other employees were 43 and 44 years old, and the remaining two were 51 and 60 years of age. Sheehan was the only one of the five laid off. Can Sheehan satisfy the "substantially younger" test of *Consolidated Coin*? *See, e.g.*, Sheehan v. Daily Racing Form, Inc., 104 F.3d 940 (7th Cir.), *cert. denied*, 521 U.S. 1104, 117 S.Ct. 2480, 138 L.Ed.2d 989 (1997); Schiltz v. Burlington Northern R.R., 115 F.3d 1407 (8th Cir.1997).

3.   An employer and its union negotiate a contract where retirees no longer receive full health benefits. They agree, however, that those employees who are 50 years of age or older as of the date of the contract may still receive full health benefits when they retire. Employees aged 40–49 years object that this is discrimination against them, based on age. *See* General Dynamics Land Sys. v. Cline, ___ U.S. ___, 124 S.Ct. 1236, 157 L.Ed.2d 1094 (2004) (deciding against the younger employees).

HAZEN PAPER CO. v. BIGGINS

Supreme Court of the United States, 1993.
507 U.S. 604, 113 S.Ct. 1701, 123 L.Ed.2d 338.

JUSTICE O'CONNOR delivered the opinion of the Court.

In this case we clarify the standards for liability and liquidated damages under the Age Discrimination in Employment Act of 1967 (ADEA).

I

Petitioner Hazen Paper Company manufactures coated, laminated, and printed paper and paperboard. The company is owned and operated by two cousins, petitioners Robert Hazen and Thomas N. Hazen. Hazen hired respondent Walter F. Biggins as their technical director in 1977. They fired him in 1986, when he was 62 years old.

Respondent brought suit against petitioners in the United States District Court for the District of Massachusetts, alleging a violation of the ADEA. He claimed that age had been a determinative factor in petitioners' decision to fire him. Petitioners contested this claim, asserting instead that respondent had been fired for doing business with competitors of Hazen Paper. The case was tried before a jury, which rendered a verdict for respondent on his ADEA claim and also found violations of the Employee Retirement Income Security Act of 1974 (ERISA), 29 U.S.C. § 1140, and state law. On the ADEA count, the jury specifically found that petitioners "willfully" violated the statute. Under § 7(b) of the ADEA, 29 U.S.C. § 626(b), a "willful" violation gives rise to liquidated damages.

Petitioners moved for judgment notwithstanding the verdict. The District Court granted the motion with respect to a state-law claim and the finding of "willfulness" but otherwise denied it. An appeal ensued. The United States Court of Appeals for the First Circuit affirmed judgment for respondent on both the ADEA and ERISA counts, and reversed judgment notwithstanding the verdict for petitioners as to "willfulness."

* * *

II

A

The courts of appeals repeatedly have faced the question whether an employer violates the ADEA by acting on the basis of a factor, such as an employee's pension status or seniority, that is empirically correlated with age. *Compare* White v. Westinghouse Electric Co., 862 F.2d 56, 62 (3d Cir.1988) (firing of older employee to prevent vesting of pension benefits violates ADEA); Metz v. Transit Mix, Inc., 828 F.2d 1202 (7th Cir.1987) (firing of older employee to save salary costs resulting from seniority violates ADEA) *with* Williams v. General Motors Corp., 656 F.2d 120, 130, n. 17 (5th Cir.1981) ("Seniority and age discrimination are unrelated. * * * We state without equivocation that the seniority a given plaintiff has accumulated entitles him to no better or worse treatment in an age discrimination suit."), *cert. denied*, 455 U.S. 943, 71 L.Ed.2d 655, 102 S.Ct. 1439 (1982); EEOC v. Clay Printing Co., 955 F.2d 936, 942 (4th Cir.1992) (emphasizing distinction between employee's age and years of service). We now clarify that there is no disparate treatment under the ADEA when the factor motivating the employer is some feature other than the employee's age.

We long have distinguished between "disparate treatment" and "disparate impact" theories of employment discrimination. * * * The disparate treatment theory is of course available under the ADEA, as the language of that statute makes clear. "It shall be unlawful for an employer * * * to fail or refuse to hire or to discharge any individual or otherwise discriminate against any individual with respect to his compensation, terms, conditions, or privileges of employment, *because of such individual's age*." 29 U.S.C. § 623(a)(1) (emphasis added). By contrast, we have never decided whether a disparate impact theory of liability is available under the ADEA, *see* Markham v. Geller, 451 U.S. 945, 68 L.Ed.2d 332, 101 S.Ct. 2028 (1981) (Rehnquist, J., dissenting from denial of certiorari), and we need not do so here. Respondent claims only that he received disparate treatment.

In a disparate treatment case, liability depends on whether the protected trait (under the ADEA, age) actually motivated the employer's decision. The employer may have relied upon a formal, facially discriminatory policy requiring adverse treatment of employees with that trait. Or the employer may have been motivated by the protected trait on an ad hoc, informal basis. Whatever the employer's decisionmaking process, a disparate treatment claim cannot succeed unless the employee's protected trait actually played a role in that process and had a determinative influence on the outcome.

Disparate treatment, thus defined, captures the essence of what Congress sought to prohibit in the ADEA. It is the very essence of age discrimination for an older employee to be fired because the employer believes that productivity and competence decline with old age. As we explained in *EEOC v. Wyoming*, 460 U.S. 226, 75 L.Ed.2d 18, 103 S.Ct. 1054 (1983), Congress' promulgation of the ADEA was prompted by its concern that older workers were being deprived of employment on the basis of inaccurate and stigmatizing stereotypes.

> Although age discrimination rarely was based on the sort of animus motivating some other forms of discrimination, it was based in large part on stereotypes unsupported by objective fact * * *. Moreover, the available empirical evidence demonstrated that arbitrary age lines were in fact generally unfounded and that, as an overall matter, the performance of older workers was at least as good as that of younger workers.

Id. at 231, 103 S.Ct. at 1057–1058. Thus the ADEA commands that "employers are to evaluate [older] employees * * * on their merits and not their age." Western Air Lines, Inc. v. Criswell, 472 U.S. 400, 422, 105 S.Ct. 2743, 2756, 86 L.Ed.2d 321 (1985). The employer cannot rely on age as a proxy for an employee's remaining characteristics, such as productivity, but must instead focus on those factors directly.

When the employer's decision *is* wholly motivated by factors other than age, the problem of inaccurate and stigmatizing stereotypes disappears. This is true even if the motivating factor is correlated with age, as pension status typically is. Pension plans typically provide that an employee's accrued benefits will become nonforfeitable, or "vested," once the employee completes a certain number of years of service with the employer. On average, an older employee has had more years in the work force than a younger employee, and thus may well have accumulated more years of service with a particular employer. Yet an employee's age is analytically distinct from his years of service. An employee who is younger than 40, and therefore outside the class of older workers as defined by the ADEA, *see* 29 U.S.C. § 631(a), may have worked for a particular employer his entire career, while an older worker may have been newly hired. Because age and years of service are analytically distinct, an employer can take account of one while ignoring the other, and thus it is incorrect to say that a decision based on years of service is necessarily "age-based."

The instant case is illustrative. Under the Hazen Paper pension plan, as construed by the Court of Appeals, an employee's pension benefits vest after the employee completes 10 years of service with the company. Perhaps it is true that older employees of Hazen Paper are more likely to be "close to vesting" than younger employees. Yet a decision by the company to fire an older employee solely because he has nine-plus years of service and therefore is "close to vesting" would not constitute discriminatory treatment on the basis of age. The prohibited stereotype ("Older employees are likely to be ___") would not have figured in this decision, and the attendant stigma would not ensue. The decision would not be the result of an inaccurate and denigrating generalization about age, but would rather represent an *accurate* judgment about the employee—that he indeed is "close to vesting."

We do not mean to suggest that an employer *lawfully* could fire an employee in order to prevent his pension benefits from vesting. Such conduct is actionable under § 510 of ERISA, as the Court of Appeals rightly found in affirming judgment for respondent under that statute. But it would not, without more, violate the ADEA. That law requires the employer to ignore an employee's age (absent a statutory exemption or defense); it does not specify *further* characteristics that an employer must also ignore. Although some language in our prior decisions might be read to mean that an employer violates the ADEA whenever its reason for firing an employee is improper *in any respect, see* McDonnell Douglas Corp. v. Green, 411 U.S. 792, 802, 36 L.Ed.2d 668, 93 S.Ct. 1817 (1973) (creating proof framework applicable to ADEA) (employer must have "legitimate, nondiscriminatory reason" for action against employee), this reading is obviously incorrect. For example, it cannot be true that an employer who fires an older black worker because the worker is black thereby violates the ADEA. The employee's race is an improper reason, but it is improper under Title VII, not the ADEA.

We do not preclude the possibility that an employer who targets employees with a particular pension status on the assumption that these employees are likely to be older thereby engages in age discrimination. Pension status may be a proxy for age, not in the sense that the ADEA makes the two factors equivalent, *cf. Metz,* 828 F.2d at 1208 (using "proxy" to mean statutory equivalence), but in the sense that the employer may suppose a correlation between the two factors and act accordingly. Nor do we rule out the possibility of dual liability under ERISA and the ADEA where the decision to fire the employee was motivated both by the employee's age and by his pension status. Finally, we do not consider the special case where an employee is about to vest in pension benefits as a result of his *age,* rather than years of service, and the employer fires the employee in order to prevent vesting. That case is not presented here. Our holding is simply that an employer does not violate the ADEA just by interfering with an older employee's pension benefits that would have vested by virtue of the employee's years of service.

Besides the evidence of pension interference, the Court of Appeals cited some additional evidentiary support for ADEA liability. Although there was no direct evidence of petitioners' motivation, except for two isolated comments by the Hazens, the Court of Appeals did note the following indirect evidence: Respondent was asked to sign a confidentiality agreement, even though no other employee had been required to do so, and his replacement was a younger man who was given a less onerous agreement. In the ordinary ADEA case, indirect evidence of this kind may well suffice to support liability if the plaintiff also shows that the employer's explanation for its decision—here, that respondent had been disloyal to Hazen Paper by doing business with its competitors—is " 'unworthy of credence.' " *Aikens*, 460 U.S., at 716 (quoting *Burdine*, 450 U.S. at 256). But inferring age-motivation from the implausibility of the employer's explanation may be problematic in cases where other unsavory motives, such as pension interference, were present. This issue is now before us in the Title VII context, *see* Hicks v. St. Mary's Honor Center, 970 F.2d 487 (8th Cir.1992), *cert. granted*, 506 U.S. 1042 (1993), 113 S.Ct. 954, 122 L.Ed.2d 111 and we will not address it prematurely. We therefore remand the case for the Court of Appeals to reconsider whether the jury had sufficient evidence to find an ADEA violation.

* * *

JUSTICE KENNEDY, with whom THE CHIEF JUSTICE and JUSTICE THOMAS join, concurring.

* * * [Respondent] has advanced no claim that petitioner's use of an employment practice that has a disproportionate effect on older workers violate the ADEA. As a result, nothing in the Court's opinion should be read as incorporating in the ADEA context the so-called "disparate impact" theory of Title VII * * *. As the Court acknowledges, we have not yet addressed the question whether such a claim is cognizable under the ADEA, and there are substantial arguments that it is improper to carry over disparate impact analysis from Title VII to the ADEA. *See* Markham v. Geller, 451 U.S. 945, 68 L.Ed.2d 332, 101 S.Ct. 2028 (1981) (Rehnquist, J., dissenting from denial of certiorari). It is on the understanding that the Court does not reach this issue that I join in its opinion.

Notes and Questions

1. *The Defense Based on Reasonable Factors Other Than Age (RFOA)*: Section 623(f)(1) of the ADEA provides that an action otherwise prohibited under the ADEA is not an unlawful employment practice "where the differentiation is based on reasonable factors other than age." 29 U.S.C. § 623(f)(1). The RFOA defense has not been relied upon to any substantial degree in ADEA cases, and one reason very well may be the lack of clarity about its substantive content and its role in the order and allocation of the burdens of proof in ADEA cases. The legislative history is not particularly helpful in illuminating the substantive content of the defense. Some courts

hold that the RFOA defense overlaps with the business necessity defense in disparate impact ADEA cases. Other courts have stated that the RFOA defense codifies the business necessity defense in ADEA cases. Still other courts have equated the RFOA defense with the legitimate, nondiscriminatory reason defense. The legislative history and case law are discussed in Howard Eglit, *The Age Discrimination in Employment Act's Forgotten Affirmative Defense: The Reasonable Factors Other Than Age Exception*, 66 B.U.L.Rev. 155 (1986); and Toni J. Querry, Comment, *A Rose by Any Other Name No Longer Smells as Sweet: Disparate Treatment Discrimination and the Age Proxy Doctrine After* Hazen Paper Co. v. Biggins, 81 Cornell L.Rev. 530 (1996).

The Supreme Court did not specifically rely upon the RFOA defense in *Hazen Paper*, but would that defense also support the results the Court reached? If used, what effect would or should it have on the allocation of the burdens of proof in ADEA disparate treatment cases since it is a statutory defense? One of the issues raised in the petition for certiorari in *Western Air Lines, Inc. v. Criswell*, 472 U.S. 400, 105 S.Ct. 2743, 86 L.Ed.2d 321 (1985), was whether, after the plaintiff has established a prima facie case, the burden of persuasion then shifts to the employer to prove that its action was based upon a reasonable factor other than age. *See* 53 U.S.L.W. 3202 (Oct. 2, 1984). The Court declined to grant certiorari on the issue. Western Air Lines, Inc. v. Criswell, 469 U.S. 815, 105 S.Ct. 80, 83 L.Ed.2d 28 (1984).

2. *Overlap Between the ADEA and the Employee Retirement Income Security Act (ERISA)*: *Hazen Paper* held that the conduct at issue is actionable under the Employee Retirement Income Security Act of 1974, 29 U.S.C. §§ 1001–1461, but it would not, without more, violate the ADEA. ERISA is the primary law that governs employees benefits, including private pension plans and fringe benefits. ERISA does not require employers to provide fringe benefits, nor does it specify any level of benefits that must be granted even if the employer chooses to offer them. What ERISA does is to establish minimum standards to protect employees from breaches of benefit promises made by the employer. ERISA is beyond the scope of this book, but it is not unusual for employees who are protected by the ADEA to add an ERISA claim in cases involving benefits, as the plaintiff did in *Hazen Paper*. For a treatment of the potential dual liability under the ADEA and ERISA and related problems, *see* Louis Maslow II, Comment, *Dual Liability: The Growing Overlap of the Age Discrimination in Employment Act and Section 510 of the Employee Retirement Income Security Act*, 58 Alb.L.Rev. 509 (1994).

3. *The Age–Proxy Theory*: The Supreme Court granted certiorari in *Hazen Paper* to resolve what it deemed to be a conflict in the lower courts on the age-proxy theory. As explained by one commentator who questioned whether there was a genuine conflict about the age-proxy theory:

> "Age-proxy theory" refers to a method of proof that permits a finding of age discrimination to be based on an employer's reliance on an age-related factor. As so defined, the proxy theory is a device for proving a disparate treatment claim. There may be cases where an employer's reliance on an age-related factor has an adverse effect on older workers. These cases, however, are properly analyzed under a

disparate impact analysis, not a proxy theory. The thrust of the proxy theory is that the age-related factor is a stand-in for age itself.

Robert J. Gregory, *There Is Life in That Old (I Mean, More "Senior") Dog Yet: The Age–Proxy Theory After* Hazen Paper Co. v. Biggins, 11 Hofstra Lab.L.J. 391, 393 n.14 (1994). What, if anything, remains of the age-proxy theory after *Hazen Paper*? Is there a difference between the age-proxy theory in ADEA cases and pretext analysis in the Title VII disparate treatment circumstantial evidence cases, if age-proxy evidence is deemed to be the equivalent of a "disguised reliance on age"? *See id.* at 396 (citing Howard C. Elgit, 2 Age Discrimination § 16.03A at 2S–97 to 2S–98 (Supp.1992)). Consider also the following case.

SPERLING v. HOFFMANN–LA ROCHE, INC.

United States District Court, District of New Jersey, 1996.
924 F.Supp. 1396.

ACKERMAN, District Court Judge.

[In February 1984, Hoffmann–La Roche discharged or demoted approximately 1,100 employees pursuant to a reduction-in-force, or RIF, known as Operation Turnabout. The plaintiff, Sperling, brought an ADEA class action on behalf of 476 of the affected employees alleging that the discharges or demotions violated their rights under the ADEA. After the Supreme Court decided *Hazen Paper*, and based on plaintiffs' answers to specific interrogatories, Hoffmann La–Roche, relying on the "analytically distinct" doctrine of *Hazen Paper*, filed a motion to dismiss the claims of sixty class members.]

* * *

A. The Individual Claims

Roche argues that the individual disparate treatment claims of sixty plaintiffs must be dismissed because the allegations on which they base their claims of age discrimination, as embodied in their answers to the contention interrogatories, do not state claims of age discrimination after *Hazen Paper*.

* * * [P]laintiffs' answers to the contention interrogatories identified nine factors which Roche allegedly considered in determining who would be fired in Operation Turnabout. Those factors are:

(1) Relatively high salary and/or relatively high salary grade;

(2) Replaced by younger person;

(3) Ample retirement benefits;

(4) Age-related disability;

(5) Proximity to voluntary retirement;

(6) Perceived as less productive and/or less creative;

(7) Perceived as having limited skills and/or ability to acquire skills;

(8) Perceived as over-qualified or over-experienced; and

(9) Perceived as no longer fitting into the organization.

* * *

Roche is not challenging factor 2—replaced by a younger person. In addition, in defining factor nine, plaintiffs provided three alternative definitions for "perceived as no longer fitting into the organization." Roche is not challenging two of the three definitions. Roche argues that, after *Hazen Paper*, the remaining factors (*i.e.*, factors one, three through eight, [and] a portion of factor nine * * *) are not valid bases on which to bring an individual, disparate treatment ADEA claim, and therefore, the plaintiffs who solely allege that they were terminated based on these factors have failed to state a claim of age discrimination. For example, Roche argues that *Hazen Paper* teaches that firing someone because he has a high salary does not violate the ADEA. Therefore, according to Roche, if a plaintiff claimed, via the contention interrogatories, that the only "improper" factor that Roche considered in firing him was his high salary (*i.e.*, factor 1), then that plaintiff's claim must be dismissed because, even if that plaintiff proved that Roche fired him because of his high salary, it did not violate the ADEA. In other words, Roche argues that if a plaintiff only alleges that he was fired because he had a high salary, then that plaintiff has failed to state a cause of action for which relief can be granted under the ADEA.

In response to Roche's motion, plaintiffs argue, among other things, that the theories of age discrimination that are set forth in their contention interrogatories survive *Hazen Paper*. In addition, plaintiffs assert that, even if the factors on which the sixty plaintiffs rely are not viable after *Hazen Paper*, they are not precluded by their answers to the contention interrogatories from raising an additional theory of discrimination that is consistent with *Hazen Paper*.

Thus, in deciding this motion two issues must be addressed. First, it must be determined whether any of the factors that plaintiffs listed in their answers to the contention interrogatories no longer amount to a cause of action under the ADEA after *Hazen Paper*. Second, assuming one or more of the factors on which the plaintiffs rely are no longer viable causes of action under the ADEA, it must be determined whether the individual claims of the plaintiffs who only rely on the invalid factors must be dismissed.

* * *

1. *Plaintiffs' Contentions and* Hazen Paper

* * *

Factor 1—High Salary: A number of the plaintiffs allege that they were terminated because of their relatively high salary or relatively high salary grade. * * *

* * *

Several courts have noted that high salary is similar to years of service in that while, on average, those workers with the highest salaries are older workers, high salary and age are nonetheless analytically distinct, and therefore, termination decisions based on the employee's level of compensation are not violative of the ADEA. Thomure v. Phillips Furniture Company, 30 F.3d 1020, 1024 (8th Cir.1994) (stating that the defendant could " 'take account of one [salary] while ignoring the other [age]' * * * even though there happened to be a correlation between the two in several cases"), *cert. denied*, 115 S.Ct. 1255, 131 L.Ed.2d 135 (1995); Anderson v. Baxter Healthcare Corp., 13 F.3d 1120, 1125–26 (7th Cir.1994) (after noting that the Supreme Court stated in *Hazen Paper* that the ADEA was enacted by Congress because of "its concern that older workers were being deprived of employment on the basis of inaccurate and stigmatizing stereotypes" * * *, and that the Supreme Court held that "when the employer's decision is wholly motivated by factors other than age, the problem of inaccurate and stigmatizing stereotypes disappears * * * [and that] this is true even if the motivating factor is correlated with age, as pension status typically is[,]", the Court of Appeals held that "this rationale applies with equal force to cases where workers are discharged because of salary considerations"); Chiano v. Dimension Molding Corporation, 1993 WL 326687, at *2 n. 3 (N.D.Ill.1993) (stating that "applying the rationale of *Hazen*, if an older worker's salary is based on years of service and not age, the employer does not violate the ADEA by replacing the worker only because of her high salary"); Bornstad v. Sun Company Inc., 1993 WL 257310, at *2 (E.D.Pa.1993) (citing *Hazen Paper* for the proposition that plaintiff's deposition testimony "equating alleged seniority cost-saving motivation with age discrimination" is an approach that is "no longer viable"), *aff'd*, 19 F.3d 642 (3d Cir.1994) (Table). * * *

Therefore, Roche is correct in arguing that a claim made by a plaintiff that Roche fired him because of his high salary, as defined in any of the alternative ways discussed above, does not state a cause of action for which relief can be granted under the ADEA.

As stated above, Roche is not challenging factor 2. Therefore, I will move on to factor 3.

Factor 3—Ample Retirement Benefits: Next, some plaintiffs allege that they were terminated because they had "ample retirement benefits." * * *

* * *

Plaintiffs argue that consideration of this factor violates the ADEA because at Roche an employee's eligibility for retirement benefits is a function of the employee's age. * * * Roche argues that consideration of this factor is not violative of the ADEA because it in no way "implicates the stereotype that older workers are not as competent or productive as younger ones, the stereotype that the ADEA was aimed at outlawing."

* * * [I]n *Hazen Paper*, the Supreme Court held that "an employer does not violate the ADEA just by interfering with an older employee's pension benefits that would have vested by virtue of the employee's years of service." *Hazen Paper*, 507 U.S. at 613, 113 S.Ct. at 1707–08. * * * In *Hazen Paper*, the employer's motive in firing the plaintiff was to prevent plaintiff's pension benefits from vesting. Thus, the employer's decision was wholly motivated by factors that were "analytically distinct" from age, and therefore, "the problem of inaccurate and stigmatizing stereotypes disappeared." *Id.* at 611, 113 S.Ct. at 1706. Because the prohibited stereotype did not figure into the decision, the employer's decision did not violate the ADEA. *See id.* at 611–15, 113 S.Ct. at 1707–08. This is the case even though the motivating factor—pension status—was correlated with age. Pension status is normally based on years of service. * * *

Roche is correct in arguing that reliance on the existence of "ample retirement benefits" in firing a plaintiff is not violative of the ADEA. This is because reliance on this factor does not involve "the problem of inaccurate and stigmatizing stereotypes" "that productivity and competence decline with old age." *See id.* at 611, 113 S.Ct. at 1706. Plaintiffs' definition states that this factor applies where "Roche perceived or presumed that ample retirement benefits providing a 'financial cushion' were then available to said plaintiff." Thus, under this factor, plaintiffs are not alleging that they were fired based on a perception that older workers were less competent or less productive. Rather, plaintiffs are alleging that Roche fired employees who would be better able to absorb the effects of unemployment because of they had "ample retirement benefits." Taking such a factor into consideration when deciding who should be fired does not violate the ADEA. *See* Gokcen v. Babbitt, 999 F.2d 542, 1993 WL 283591 (9th Cir.1993) (table) (holding that ADEA was not violated where "retirement eligibility was considered only to minimize any adverse effect that closure [of the section where plaintiff worked] might have on the [employer] and its employees" and where "nothing in the record suggests the decision [to eliminate plaintiff's position] was partially based on a belief that [plaintiff's] age prevented him from performing [his] duties competently").

That the definition of "ample retirement benefits" also requires that the plaintiff must be at least 50 years old does not detract from this conclusion. First it should be noted that the Supreme Court specifically stated in *Hazen Paper* that it was not "considering the special case where an employee is about to vest in pension benefits as a result of his age, rather than years of service, * * *, and the employer fires the employee in order to prevent vesting." *Hazen Paper*, 507 U.S. at 613, 113 S.Ct. at 1707. Plaintiffs in effect argue that this is such a "special case" because part of the definition of ample retirement benefits is that the employee had to be at least 50 years old and that it should be held that the ADEA is violated in such special cases.

This argument fails because the Supreme Court in *Hazen Paper* clearly stated that "[i]t is *the very essence of age discrimination* for an older employee to be fired because the employer believes that productivity and competence decline with old age," and that "when the employer's decision is wholly motivated by factors other than age, the problem of inaccurate and stigmatizing stereotypes disappear"—even where the motivating factor is correlated with age. *Hazen Paper*, 507 U.S. at 611, 113 S.Ct. at 1706 (emphasis added). Therefore, in this case, even though "ample retirement benefits" clearly is correlated with age, consideration of this factor is not violative of the ADEA because plaintiffs are alleging that Roche fired these plaintiffs because Roche perceived that they had a financial cushion and not because Roche perceived that they were less competent or less productive. Therefore, consideration of this factor would not be within the definition of "the very essence of age discrimination" (*i.e.*, firing someone based on the belief "that productivity and competence decline with old age").

Therefore, a claim by a plaintiff that Roche fired her because she had "ample retirement benefits," as defined above, does not state a cause of action for which relief can be granted under the ADEA.

Factor 4—Age–Related Disability: Next, some plaintiffs claim that they were terminated because they had an "age-related disability." * * *

* * * Thus, the question is whether or not a disability that is "associated" with age is analytically distinct from age.

The Court of Appeals for the Eighth Circuit addressed a similar issue in *Beith v. Nitrogen Products, Inc.*, 7 F.3d 701 (8th Cir.1993). In that case, the defendant fired Beith after the results of a physical examination revealed that Beith had degenerative disc disease and osteoarthritis, precluding him from lifting repetitively more than twenty pounds. Thereafter, Beith brought an age discrimination claim against the defendant. In affirming the judgment for the defendant, the Court of Appeals stated that

> " 'Congress made plain that the age statute was not meant to prohibit employment decisions based on factors sometimes accompanying advancing age, such as declining health or diminished vigor and competence.' " * * * Upon our review of the record, we could discern no evidence that the decision to terminate Beith was other than for his back condition. Because back conditions may be more prevalent in older workers does not alone make the decision an age-based decision.

Id. at 703.

In the case now before the court, the allegation that Roche terminated certain employees due to a disability that was "associated" with age is similarly not violative of the ADEA. Therefore, a claim by a plaintiff that Roche fired her because she had an "age-related disability" does not state a cause of action for which relief can be granted under the ADEA.

Factor 5—Proximity to Retirement: Next, some plaintiffs allege that they were terminated because of their "proximity to retirement." * * *

* * *

The analysis with respect to "proximity to retirement" is the same as for "ample retirement benefits." * * *

Factor 6—Perceived as Less Productive and/or Less Creative: Next, some plaintiffs allege that they were terminated because they were perceived as "less productive and/or less creative." * * *

Roche argues that consideration of this factor is not violative of the ADEA because "terminating an employee because he is perceived to be 'less productive or less energetic' (even if the perception is incorrect) is clearly analytically distinct from assuming that the employee is 'less productive or less energetic' because of his advancing age." Thus, Roche argues that consideration of this factor does not violate the ADEA because the plaintiffs did not tack on the words "because of age" after the allegation that they were terminated because they were perceived to be less energetic and productive.

Roche's argument lacks merit given that Roche's motion is in essence a motion to dismiss. Therefore, I must view plaintiffs allegations liberally and give plaintiffs the benefit of all inferences which may be drawn therefrom. Viewing factor 6 liberally, I conclude that a claim that a plaintiff was terminated because Roche believed that the plaintiff was less productive or less energetic states a cause of action under the ADEA. This is because consideration of stereotypes such as these in making employment decisions is precisely what the ADEA was intended to eradicate. *See Hazen Paper*, 507 U.S. at 609–13, 113 S.Ct. at 1706–07.

Factor 7—Perceived to Have Limited Skills and/or Ability to Acquire Skills: Next, some plaintiffs allege that they were terminated because they were perceived as having limited skills and/or a limited ability to acquire skills. * * *

As in the case of factor 6, viewing factor 7 liberally, I conclude that a claim that a plaintiff was terminated because Roche believed that the plaintiff had limited skills or a limited ability to acquire new skills states a cause of action under the ADEA. Consideration of factors such as these are also the types of stereotypes the ADEA was intended to eradicate from the employment decisionmaking process. *See Hazen Paper*, 507 U.S. at 609–13, 113 S.Ct. at 1706–07.

Factor 8—Perceived as Over–Qualified/Over–Experienced: Next, some plaintiffs allege that they were terminated because * * * they were perceived as being over-qualified and/or over-experienced. * * *

This factor is arguably correlated with age because it is reasonable to assume that persons holding supervisory or managerial positions are older, and also because the years-of-service prong of the definition correlates with age. However, *Hazen Paper* teaches that mere correlation with age is not enough. *Hazen Paper*, 507 U.S. at 609–11, 113 S.Ct. at 1706 ("When an employer's decision is wholly motivated by factors other than age, the problem of inaccurate and stigmatizing stereotypes disappears. This is true even if the motivating factor is correlated with age, as pension status typically is."). Furthermore, being perceived as over-qualified and/or over-experienced is not the equivalent of the denigrating stereotype that competence and productivity decline with age. For these reasons, I find that a claim that Roche made an employment decision based solely on the perception that an employee was over-qualified and/or over-experienced does not state a cause of action under the ADEA. *See* Bay v. Times Mirror Magazines, Inc., 936 F.2d 112, 118 (2d Cir.1991) (pre-*Hazen Paper* decision stating that the ADEA does not forbid "employers from declining to place employees in positions for which they are overqualified on the ground that overqualification may affect performance negatively").

Factor 9—"No Longer Fits into Organization": Next, some plaintiffs allege that they were terminated because Roche believed that they no longer fit into the organization. * * *

* * * Roche argues "[t]hat a plaintiff was considered 'to have been around too long' fails for the same reason * * * factors 6 and 7 fail * * *—because mere statements that somebody is 'less productive' [factor 6] or 'has limited skills' [factor 7] or 'has been around too long' are not actionable unless the reason for that belief is the age of the plaintiff." Roche's argument fails for the same reason it did with respect to factors 6 and 7. This is in effect a motion to dismiss. Therefore, I must view the allegation liberally. After doing so, I conclude that a claim that Roche considered subpart c of factor 9 in terminating a plaintiff states a cause of action under the ADEA.

* * *

Notes and Questions

1. Does *Hazen Paper* provide useful guidelines on determining what factors are helpful in applying the "analytically distinct" test? If not, does *Sperling v. Hoffmann–La Roche*? Does the decision in *Sperling* adequately reflect the Act's stated goals? See the ADEA's statement of Findings and Purpose at 29 U.S.C. § 621.

2. Should *Hazen Paper*'s "analytically distinct" doctrine be equally applicable in analyzing Title VII race discrimination cases? In Title VII sex discrimination cases? If not, why?

3. The court in *Sperling v. Hoffmann–La Roche* held that high salary, ample retirement benefits, age-related disabilities, proximity to retirement, and a perception that an employee is over-qualified or over-experienced do not state a claim for relief under the ADEA, but nevertheless denied Hoffmann–La Roche's motion *in limine* to preclude the plaintiff from introducing evidence on these factors. It is quite obvious, is it not, that Hoffmann–La Roche will object on the ground of relevancy if plaintiffs try to introduce evidence on these factors in the trial on the merits? What arguments can the plaintiffs make that evidence on these factors is relevant to their remaining claims that were left for trial, i.e., that a plaintiff was replaced by a younger person, was perceived as less productive or less creative, or was perceived as having limited skills or ability to acquire skills?

4. *The Cost Justification Defense in ADEA Cases*: The defense that a high-salaried employee who is protected by the ADEA was discharged as a cost-saving measure is another illustration of the cost justification defense that employers have raised in a number of employment discrimination cases. *Sperling v. Hoffmann–La Roche* correctly noted that prior to *Hazen Paper*, the courts generally rejected a broad-based cost-justification defense in ADEA cases. One of the leading cases rejecting the defense was *Geller v. Markham*, 635 F.2d 1027 (2d Cir.1980), *cert. denied*, 451 U.S. 945, 101 S.Ct. 2028, 68 L.Ed.2d 332 (1981). A 55–year-old substitute teacher brought an ADEA claim alleging that the school board's policy of hiring only teachers who have less than five years of experience had a disparate impact on teachers over 40 years of age. The Second Circuit rejected the school board's defense that its policy was justified as a necessary cost-cutting measure in the face of tight budgetary constraints. The court held that

> [t]his cost justification must fail * * * because of the clear rule that a general assertion that the average cost of employing older workers as a group is higher than the average cost of employing younger workers as a group will not be recognized as a differentiation under the terms and provisions of the [ADEA], unless one of the other statutory exceptions applies. * * *

Id. at 1034 (citing 29 C.F.R. § 860.103(h) (1979)). In *Metz v. Transit Mix, Inc.*, 828 F.2d 1202 (7th Cir.1987) (cited approvingly by the Supreme Court in *Hazen Paper*), the Seventh Circuit found an ADEA violation where the employer replaced a high-salaried employee protected by the ADEA with a younger, less-senior, lower-paid employee to save on the salary differential. Relying on *Hazen Paper*, the Seventh Circuit overturned *Metz v. Transit Mix* in *Anderson v. Baxter Healthcare Corp.*, 13 F.3d 1120 (7th Cir.1994):

> [The *Hazen Paper*] rationale applies with equal force to cases where workers are discharged because of salary considerations. Thus, *Hazen Paper Co.* vindicates the dissent in *Metz* which contended that "[w]age discrimination is age discrimination only when wage depends directly on age, so that the use for one is a pretext for the other; high covariance is not sufficient * * *." *Metz*, 828 F.2d at 1212 (Easterbrook, J., dissenting). Compensation is typically correlated with age, just as pension benefits are. The correlation, however, is not perfect. A younger worker who has spent his entire career with the same employer may earn a higher salary than an older worker who has recently been hired by the same employer. "Because age and * * * [compensation levels] are analytically distinct, an employer can take account of one while ignoring the other, and thus it is incorrect to say that a decision based on * * * compensation level is necessarily 'age-based.'" *Hazen*, 113 S.Ct. at 1707. Consequently, Anderson could not prove age discrimination even if he was fired simply because Baxter desired to reduce its salary costs by discharging him.

13 F.3d at 1125–26.

In distinguishing between the problem of costs in Title VII and ADEA cases, Professor Steven J. Kaminshine stated that

> [f]rom Title VII, we are familiar with the maxim that mere cost savings may not be used to justify discrimination. There is, in other words, a

price—a cost—for securing more important remedial and social objectives. To cite but a few examples: employers may not justify discrimination on grounds of customer preference regardless of its profitability; they may not rely on race or gender as crude proxies for performance simply because such proxies may be easy to apply and inexpensive to administer; they may not rely solely on the cheapness of neutral proxies if they operate to target protected groups and are not sufficiently job related; and they must provide women equal pay for equal work even if the market would place a lower value on female labor. These examples illustrate the costs of compliance—employers must forfeit the profits derived from discrimination. But assuming compliance and merit-based selection, blacks and women are not, by their race or gender, uniquely costlier to compensate.

The same cannot be said as easily of workers covered under the ADEA. Seniority and longevity often influence salary and fringe benefit levels. Because these factors correlate with age, older workers can become more costly to compensate than their younger counterparts. This disparity creates significant tension during times of economic stress when employers look to maximize savings by laying off or replacing their costliest workers. The tension exists because the use of salary costs as a criterion for layoffs appears to be both economically rational yet peculiarly burdensome to the older segment of the work force. To the extent that the ADEA prohibits discriminatory discharges out of concern that displaced older workers face unique obstacles in finding employment late in their careers, seniority-related cost comparisons can frustrate that objective. On the other hand, to require employers to ignore such costs as part of an economic cutback may equally frustrate the need for sensible cost-cutting policies.

Steven J. Kaminshine, *The Cost of Older Workers, Disparate Impact, and the Age Discrimination in Employment Act*, 42 Fla.L.Rev. 229, 231–33 (1990). Is a defense based on costs more defensible in ADEA cases than in Title VII race and sex cases? Does *Hazen Paper*, as construed by the courts in *Sperling v. Hoffmann–La Roche* and *Baxter Healthcare*, legitimate a broad-based cost justification defense in ADEA cases? What are the arguments for and against treating a cost-based defense as a reasonable factor other than age (RFOA) under § 623(f)(1) of the ADEA, 29 U.S.C. § 623(f)(1)?

5. ADEA cases are tried before juries. As originally enacted, however, the ADEA was silent on the right to a jury trial. Resolving a split in the circuits, the Supreme Court upheld the right to a jury trial in ADEA cases in *Lorillard v. Pons*, 434 U.S. 575, 98 S.Ct. 866, 55 L.Ed.2d 40 (1978). The same year the Court decided *Pons*, Congress amended the ADEA to provide for the right to a jury trial. 29 U.S.C. § 626(c)(2). Is the issue of whether the employer's justification is "analytically distinct" under the reasoning of *Hazen Paper* a legal issue to be decided by the judge or a fact question to be decided by the jury? Does *Sperling v. Hoffmann–La Roche* suggest an answer? If it is a jury question, what jury instruction is suggested?

6. As noted in *Hazen Paper,* the ADEA provides for the award of liquidated damages when the plaintiff proves a willful violation of the statute, 29 U.S.C. § 626(b). These damages, equal to the compensatory

damages awarded, are not available for a defendant's "negligent mistake concerning the lawfulness of the conduct." Mathis v. Phillips Chevrolet, Inc., 269 F.3d 771 (7th Cir.2001).

7. *Fringe Benefits*: Consistent with *Hazen Paper*, may an employer reduce the fringe benefits package only of employees who are protected by the ADEA? Consider the pre-*Hazen* case of *Finnegan v. Trans World Airlines, Inc.*, 967 F.2d 1161 (7th Cir.1992). In an effort to avoid bankruptcy, TWA cut the wages of its nonunion employees by fourteen percent and reduced some of the employees' benefits, including vacation leave. Vacation leave was capped at four weeks per year, although employees who had sixteen or more years of service previously had been entitled to even more paid vacation. The brunt of the vacation cap thus fell on employees who were protected by the ADEA. In holding that the plaintiffs were not entitled to relief under the ADEA, Judge Richard Posner reasoned:

> Across-the-board cuts in wages and fringe benefits necessitated by business downturns or setbacks are a far cry from the situations that brought the [disparate impact] theory into being. These cuts are not a legacy of deliberate discrimination on grounds of age; they are not the product of inertia or insensitivity. They are an unavoidable response to adversity. Their adverse impact on older workers is unavoidable too, because it is impossible to reduce the costs of fringe benefits without making deeper cuts in the benefits of older workers, simply because, by virtue of being older, they have greater benefits. In this situation no inference of discrimination, whether deliberate or merely inadvertent (but avoidable), can be drawn from the greater impact of curtailing employees' benefits on older workers. Otherwise every time a company tried to reduce its labor costs the federal courts would be dragged in and asked to redesign the reduction so as to shift the burden to some unprotected class of workers—a shift that might incidentally be impossible to accomplish, as it might drive all the younger workers out of the company (the 6-days-a-year vacation problem).

Id. at 1164–65.

8. Local 350, a union, operates a hiring hall for its members. A policy of Local 350 provides that retirees who are receiving a pension are not entitled to referral work; retirees who do not receive a pension are eligible for referrals. Assume that members of Local 350 must be fifty-five years old to be eligible to receive a pension. A retiree of the union who is fifty-seven years of age and is receiving a pension is denied a job referral because of the policy. Are retirees who are over forty protected by the ADEA under the reasoning of *Robinson v. Shell Oil Co.*, 519 U.S. 337, 117 S.Ct. 843, 136 L.Ed.2d 808 (1997) (former employees are protected under Title VII)? *See* EEOC v. Local 350, Plumbers and Pipefitters, 998 F.2d 641 (9th Cir.1992); McKeever v. Ironworkers' Dist. Council, 1997 WL 109569, 73 Fair Empl. Prac.Cas. (BNA) 1000 (E.D.Pa.1997).

9. Should the *Price Waterhouse* rule on mixed-motive or provisions on mixed-motives under the Civil Rights Act of 1991, §§ 703(m) and 706(g)(2)(B), apply to mixed-motive cases in ADEA claims? *See, e.g.*, Lewis v. Young Men's Christian Ass'n, 208 F.3d 1303 (11th Cir.2000). *Lewis* held that the mixed-motive provisions under the 1991 Civil Rights Act do not apply to

ADEA retaliation claims because, although the 1991 Act makes references to other provisions of the ADEA, it did not specifically alter the pre–1991 Act law on retaliation claims under the ADEA. *See also* Donovan v. Milk Marketing Inc., 243 F.3d 584 (2d Cir.2001) (allowing instruction that employer may prevail, even if the jury finds that age was a motivating factor in the plaintiff's discharge, where the jury finds that the plaintiff would have been discharged in any event for his poor performance).

Note: The Bona Fide Occupational Qualification Defense

The bona fide occupational qualification (BFOQ) defense in the ADEA is patterned after a similar provision in Title VII. Section 623(f)(1) provides that an action otherwise prohibited under the ADEA is not an unlawful employment practice "where age is a bona fide occupational qualification reasonably necessary to the normal operation of the particular business." 29 U.S.C. § 623(f)(1). Most of the cases in which the defense is raised involve jobs in which public safety is of paramount concern. *E.g.*, Murnane v. American Airlines, Inc., 667 F.2d 98 (D.C. Cir.1981) (airline pilots), *cert. denied*, 456 U.S. 915, 102 S.Ct. 1770, 72 L.Ed.2d 174 (1982); Usery v. Tamiami Trail Tours, Inc., 531 F.2d 224 (5th Cir.1976) (bus drivers).

Western Air Lines, Inc. v. Criswell, 472 U.S. 400, 105 S.Ct. 2743, 86 L.Ed.2d 321 (1985), is the leading Supreme Court case construing the BFOQ in ADEA cases. *Criswell* involved a challenge to a provision of Western Air Lines' pension plan imposing mandatory retirement on flight engineers at age sixty. A flight engineer is one member of a three-person cockpit team required for the operation of certain aircraft. The flight engineer is responsible for monitoring an instrument panel but does not fly the aircraft unless both the captain and the first officer become incapacitated. *Criswell* rejected Western Air Lines' argument that an employer need only prove a *rational basis in fact* to justify as a BFOQ a facially discriminatory age-based employment policy. Western Airlines' rational basis argument was that the increased risk of psychological and physiological degeneration that occurs with age makes it unsafe to employ older workers as flight engineers.

In rejecting Western Air Lines' argument, the Supreme Court expressly adopted the test of the BFOQ exception that the Fifth Circuit adopted in *Tamiami Trail Tours*. At issue in *Tamiami Trail Tours* was a bus company's policy against hiring persons over the age of forty as intercity bus drivers on the basis of safety considerations; the Fifth Circuit upheld the policy based upon the BFOQ defense. The Supreme Court, in *Criswell*, observed also that the *Tamiami Trail Tours* two-pronged objective test had been approved by every circuit confronting the issue, the EEOC, and implicitly by Congress. 472 U.S. at 415–417, 105 S.Ct. at 2752–53. The first prong of the test requires the employer to prove that the age-related job qualification is "reasonably necessary to the essence of [the employer's] business." *Id.* at 413, 105 S.Ct. at 2751. The second prong requires the employer to prove more than that the qualification is "convenient" or "reasonable," but requires the employer to prove that it is "compelled to rely on age as a proxy for the safety-related qualifications." *Id.* at 414, 105 S.Ct. at 2751. The second prong can be satisfied only if the employer proves that it had a factual basis for believing that "all or substantially all" persons over the age limitation would be "unable to perform safely and efficiently the duties of the job involved," or alternatively, that "age was a legitimate proxy for the safety-related job qualifications" because it is "impossible or highly impractical to deal with older employees on an individualized basis." *Id.* at 414, 105 S.Ct. at 2751–52.

The Supreme Court relied heavily upon the *Criswell* test of BFOQ in *International Union, UAW v. Johnson Controls, Inc.*, 499 U.S. 187, 111 S.Ct. 1196, 113 L.Ed.2d 158 (1991), reproduced in Chapter 6, in construing the BFOQ provision in Title VII involving sex discrimination. *Johnson Controls* and *Criswell* underscore the rule that the BFOQ defense is to be narrowly construed. The Court observed in *Criswell*, however, that in "close cases" when the employer's proof on safety has a credible basis in the factual record, it is not unreasonable to believe that the jury will defer to the employer's judgment. 472 U.S. at 420–21, 105 S.Ct. at 2754.

Firefighters and Law Enforcement Officers: When Congress amended the ADEA in 1986 to prohibit mandatory retirement for most employees, it included an exemption for state and local public safety officers, such as police and firefighters, and for university professors. The exemption expired on December 31, 1993. In October, 1996, President Clinton signed legislation that permanently reinstates the provision in the ADEA that allows state and local governments the option of establishing mandatory age requirements for hiring and retirement for public safety officers, including police officers and firefighters. The legislation is retroactive to December 31, 1993. Section 119 of the Omnibus Consolidated Appropriations Act of 1997, P.L.No. 104–208, 110 Stat. 3009, amending the ADEA. Can the exemption for public safety employees be justified as a BFOQ under *Criswell*?

Note: Reduction-in-Force or Downsizing Cases

During the past several decades, many employers in the United States have adapted to changing economic times by becoming "mean and lean" to compete in the global marketplace. One of the competitive strategies employers use is to downsize or reduce the employer's workforce. For example, in every year between 1988 and 1993, at least one-half of the large and mid-size employers in the United States surveyed by the American Management Association reduced their workforce. Ronald Henkoff, *Getting Beyond Downsizing*, Fortune, Jan. 10, 1994, at 58. Corporate "downsizing" has also been characterized as a "euphemism[] for cost-cutting and lay-offs." Christopher Farrell, et al., *It Won't Take Your Breath Away, But * * **, Business Week, Jan. 10, 1994, at 60. In *Opportunistic Downsizing of Aging Workers: The 1990s Version of Age and Pension Discrimination in Employment*, 48 Hastings L.J. 511, 511 n.1 (1997) (citations omitted), Professor Gary Minda interpreted downsizing as follows:

> The word "downsize" first appeared during the oil crisis of the early 1970s, when automobile executives used "downsizing" to describe the move toward the design of smaller, gas-efficient automobiles. When applied to workers, the word "downsize" has come to signify reduced expectations and reduced employment opportunity. In the labor relations offices of corporate America, downsizing has become a euphemism to soften the hard edge of words like "fired," "dismissed," and "laid

off.'' In the corporate-speak of the 1990s, employees ''are 'downsized,' 'separated,' 'severed,' 'unassigned.' [Employees] are told that their jobs 'are not going forward.' '' In board rooms and chief executive officer (CEO) offices of corporate America, downsizing is a word that summarizes a host of business survival strategies designed to save the corporation from death in the global marketplace. For most American workers, the word symbolizes the permanent loss of a career job. In the print media, the word ''downsize'' is used to characterize a fundamental transformation in the workplace; changes which rival those of the Industrial Revolution of the nineteenth century.

The impact of downsizing is a well-documented phenomena in corporate America. *See, e.g.,* United States Congress, Congressional Budget Office Study: Displaced Worker Trends in the 1980s and Implications for the Future (Feb. 1993) (reporting that ''[e]ach year between 1981 and 1990, an average of 2 million workers lost full-time jobs and were not recalled by their former employers.''); Bureau of Labor Statistics, United States Department of Labor, Worker Displacement During the Mid–1990s (Aug. 22, 1996) (documenting that the most recent job replacement survey shows downsizing and layoffs remain high despite a drop in unemployment rates); Bureau of Labor Statistics, United States Department of Labor, Worker Displacement, Displaced Workers Summary (Aug. 21, 2002), available at *http:// www.bls.gov/cps/* (reporting an increase of displaced workers, from 3.3 million in the 1997–1999 period to 4.0 million for the 1999–2001 period).

Professor Minda further observed that

[a]lthough downsizing may not affect all workers, older workers as a group are particularly vulnerable. The job displacement rates for older workers are higher than average, considering the length of time between jobs as well as the wage loss due to unemployment. * * *

For older workers, anxiety about job loss has a real factual basis. * * * The cost of losing a job in today's economy is thus both significant and persistent for older workers who have a higher displacement rate. For many of these older displaced workers, a good job with promise of long-term job security is a thing of the past.

Minda, *supra,* at 518–19 citing a 1994 study by Ann Huff Stevens and the National Bureau of Economic Research that reported that ''wage loss resulting from displacement is persistent even after re-employment at another job.''

Older workers have relied upon the ADEA to seek relief from adverse employment decisions they suffer as a result of a reduction-in-force (RIF) or downsizing. A typical RIF claim arises under the ADEA in those situations in which an employer restructures its workforce, eliminating one or more jobs. There are two situations under which a RIF case arises, although both follow a restructuring of the workforce. The first is when the employer eliminates the employee's position. In the second situation, rather than layoff the displaced person who formerly held the eliminated position, the displaced person ''bumps'' the plaintiff pursuant to some rule that allows ''bumping.'' *See generally* Robert G. Boehmer, *The Age Discrimination in Employment Act—Reductions in Force as America Grays,* 28 Am.Bus.L.J. 379, 383–84 (1990).

The courts disagree on the analytical framework for determining whether the adverse effects of a RIF or downsizing on older workers constitute a violation of the ADEA; in particular the courts disagree on the showing required to establish a prima facie case. In attempting to develop a coherent analytical framework, the courts have wrestled with how to adjust the *McDonnell Douglas* evidentiary guidelines for RIF cases. The problem is that in a true RIF, the terminated employee is usually meeting the legitimate job performance expectations of the employer and is not replaced after being terminated. *See, e.g.,* Mitchell v. Data Gen. Corp., 12 F.3d 1310, 1315 (4th Cir.1993). In *Coburn v. Pan American World Airways, Inc.*, 711 F.2d 339 (D.C. Cir.), *cert. denied*, 464 U.S. 994, 104 S.Ct. 488, 78 L.Ed.2d 683 (1983), the employer instituted a RIF as one of several cost-cutting measures to improve its precarious financial situation. The plaintiff, who was terminated pursuant to the RIF, was then forty-three years old and had been employed for seventeen years. He brought an action under the ADEA, and the jury ruled in his favor. But the district court entered judgment for the employer on the ground that the plaintiff's evidence did not support the finding of a prima facie case, and, even if it did, the plaintiff failed to prove pretext.

The District of Columbia Court of Appeals affirmed the judgment of the district court but held that a plaintiff can establish a prima facie case with proof that (1) he is a member of the class protected by the ADEA; (2) he was qualified for the job he was doing at the time he was terminated; (3) he was terminated; and (4) the employer retained younger employees whose job responsibilities were substantially the same as that of the plaintiff's former job. The court of appeals rejected the employer's argument that an ADEA plaintiff should be required "to prove something extra to make out a prima facie case" in RIF situations. *Id.* at 343. Because a discharged employee in a RIF case will virtually always be qualified, the employer argued that the plaintiff should be required to prove "direct evidence" of unlawful discrimination. Under *Coburn* the relative qualifications of the plaintiff would not be a factor in deciding whether an inference of unlawful discrimination is established. The court further held that the "exigencies of a reduction-in-force can best be analyzed at the stage where the employer puts on evidence of a nondiscriminatory reason" for the discharge; thus under its analytical approach, courts are to analyze the employer's reason for the RIF on a case-by-case basis. *Id.*

The Fifth Circuit in *Williams v. General Motors Corp.*, 656 F.2d 120 (5th Cir.1981), *cert. denied*, 455 U.S. 943, 102 S.Ct. 1439, 71 L.Ed.2d 655 (1982), adopted a different standard for establishing a prima facie case in RIF cases. In *Williams*, as in *Coburn*, the plaintiff brought an ADEA action after he had been terminated from his salaried supervisory position in a RIF in which the employer terminated approximately 59% of its salaried supervisory staff. *Williams* held that a plaintiff can establish a prima facie ADEA case by showing (1) membership in the protected class; (2) qualification to assume another position at the time of discharge or demotion; (3) circumstantial or direct evidence that the employer intended to discriminate on the basis of age in reaching the employment decision. *Id.* at 129. The court stated that the first two elements have frequently appeared in ADEA cases but the third—which is specifically tailored for RIF cases—is appropriate because the ADEA does not place an affirmative duty on the employer to accord special treatment to workers protected by the ADEA. *Id.* at 129–30. Thus, instead of focusing on whether the employer retained an equally qualified younger employee, the Fifth Circuit considered whether the plaintiff's evidence was sufficient to support an inference that the employer did not treat age neutrally in making its RIF decisions. *Accord* Oxman v. WLS–TV, 12 F.3d 652, 657–58 (7th Cir.1993).

In light of *Consolidated Coin,* discussed earlier in this chapter, the Third Circuit reconsidered the prima facie case involving RIFs in *Showalter v. University of Pittsburgh Medical Center,* 190 F.3d 231 (3d Cir.1999). *Showalter* held that the *Consolidated Coin* "sufficiently younger" standard applied in adjusting the *McDonnell Douglas* prima facie case analytical approach to RIF ADEA cases. The Third Circuit acknowledged that *Consolidated Coin* was not a RIF case, but reasoned that it would be illogical to limit the "substantially younger" standard to non-RIF cases. 190 F.3d at 236.

The Tenth Circuit, in *Stone v. Autoliv ASP, Inc.*, 210 F.3d 1132, 1137 (10th Cir.2000), *cert. denied*, 531 U.S. 876, 121 S.Ct. 182, 148 L.Ed.2d 125 (2000), stated:

> To establish a prima facie case of age discrimination in the RIF context, a claimant affected by a RIF must prove: (1) the claimant is within the protected age group; (2) he or she was doing satisfactory work; (3) the claimant was discharged despite the adequacy of his or her work; and (4) there is some evidence the employer intended to discriminate against the claimant in reaching its RIF decision. * * * The fourth element may be established "through circumstantial evidence that the plaintiff was treated less favorably than younger employees during the [RIF]."

Once the plaintiff established a prima facie case, the employer may advance a nondiscriminatory reason. In most cases, the RIF serves as the nondiscriminating reason. The burden then shifts to the plaintiff to establish pretext. According to the Tenth Circuit,

> There are three common methods used to demonstrate pretext in the RIF context: (1) evidence that the termination of the employee is inconsistent with the employer's RIF criteria; (2) evidence that the employer's evaluation of the employee was falsified to cause termination; or (3) "evidence that the RIF is more generally pretextual."

Stone v. Autoliv ASP, Inc., 210 F.3d 1132, 1140. *See also* Tyler v. Union Oil Co., 304 F.3d 379, 396–92 (5th Cir.2002) (Plaintiffs may show pretext by rebutting particularized evidence of nondiscriminatory reasons for discharge and employer's conscious, unexplained departure from its established RIF process).

Plaintiffs have also utilized the disparate impact model for alleging age discrimination in a RIF. *See* Meacham v. Knolls Atomic Power Lab., 185 F.Supp.2d 193 (N.D.N.Y.2002). Another avenue for challenging a RIF is a disparate treatment claim utilizing statistics to demonstrate a pattern or practice of age discrimination. *See* Adams v. Ameritech Services, Inc., 231 F.3d 414 (7th Cir.2000).

Consider the following issues raised by RIF and downsizing cases under the ADEA:

1.   An initial issue in a RIF or downsizing case is whether, in fact, the employee was terminated as a result of a "true" downsizing or RIF. In *Barnes v. GenCorp Inc.*, 896 F.2d 1457, 1465 (6th Cir.), *cert. denied*, 498 U.S. 878, 111 S.Ct. 211, 112 L.Ed.2d 171 (1990), the Sixth Circuit stated that "[a] work force reduction situation occurs when business considerations cause an employer to eliminate one or more positions," but "[a]n employee is not eliminated as part of work force reduction when he or she is replaced after his or her discharge." The court also stated that "a person is replaced only when another employee is hired or reassigned to perform the plaintiff's duties," but not "when another employee is assigned to perform the plaintiff's duties in addition to other duties, or when the work is redistributed among other existing employees already performing related work." *Id.* The court distinguished *Barnes* in *Brocklehurst v. PPG Industries, Inc.*, 123 F.3d 890, 895 (6th Cir.1997), when it upheld the discharge of an ADEA plaintiff even though his position was not eliminated. *Brocklehurst* held that *Barnes* does not "stand[] for the proposition that a high-level employee may not be found to have been discharged as part of an economically motivated RIF unless that employee's position is eliminated." *Id.* Can *Barnes* and *Brocklehurst* be reconciled?

2.   The analytical approach adopted in *Williams* and *Coburn* has been subjected to much criticism. For example, Professor Minda stated that

> [u]nfortunately, the decisions in cases like *Coburn* and *Williams* have exhibited a lack of judicial understanding about the nature and operation of age discrimination in [the RIF and downsizing context] and consequently, the courts have been unable to develop a workable modification of the *McDonnell Douglas* prima facie case. To develop a workable prima facie standard, the courts must first understand the problem of age discrimination as it is practiced by corporate decision-makers in the era of downsizing.

Gary Minda, *Opportunistic Downsizing of Aging Workers: The 1990s Version of Age and Pension Discrimination in Employment*, 48 Hastings L.J. 511, 544–45 (1997). Professor Minda then argued:

> Because the unique nature of downsizing and RIF does not entail the hiring of replacement workers, a modified formulation of the prima facie case is warranted. The prima facie case for ADEA claims in RIF and downsizing cases should be modified to require the plaintiff to prove that: 1) he or she is forty years old or older; * * * 2) he or she was terminated pursuant to a RIF or downsizing decision; 3) he or she is a late-career employee with firm-specific skills; 4) he or she was permanently laid-off for being too expensive or costly to the firm.

Id. at 567. Under this proposed analysis, a plaintiff should be allowed to present circumstantial evidence that salary or pension was a "proxy" for age and, therefore, age was a motivating factor in the employer's decision. *Id.* The burden of production of evidence would then shift to the employer to show that its "cost containment rationale for downsizing was based on age-neutral considerations which were independent of the salary status of the older workers." *Id.* at 568. The employer could meet its burden with evidence of "technological restructuring, or the elimination of jobs as a result of new technology, reduced market demand for the company's product, and outsourcing and lean manufacturing strategies that do not target older workers by using their salary as a proxy for determining termination." *Id.* at 568–69. In the third stage of the analysis, the plaintiff could establish liability by proving either pretext or the availability of reasonable alternatives that would not result in termination. *Id.* at 569.

A frequently cited student Note, Jessica Lind, *The Prima Facie Case of Age Discrimination in Reduction-in-Force Cases*, 94 Mich.L.Rev. 832 (1995), advocates that the *McDonnell Douglas* prima facie case showing should be reformulated for RIF cases to require the plaintiff to introduce evidence that "1) she is a member of the protected class; 2) she was terminated pursuant to a RIF; 3) her duties were reassigned to a younger, similarly situated employee; and 4) that the younger employee was less qualified than the plaintiff." *Id.* at 845. The Note argues that this proposed modification is more faithful to *McDonnell Douglas* because, at least with respect to the fourth proposed element, all employees are presumably qualified and a consideration of relative qualifications is necessary to protect employers from potential ADEA liability "every time it reduces the size of its workforce." *Id.* at 848.

From a policy and an analytical perspective, which is the better approach, the proposal advocated by Professor Minda or by the student Note? How do they compare to the approaches adopted by the courts in *Coburn*, *Williams* and *Stone*?

3. Is the cost-justification defense more acceptable in the RIF and downsizing cases than in other ADEA cases? If so, why? One court has said that "[t]he ADEA was not intended to protect older workers from the often harsh economic realities of common business decisions and the hardships associated with corporate reorganizations, downsizing, plant closings and relocations." Allen v. Diebold, Inc., 33 F.3d 674, 676 (6th Cir.1994). On the other hand, Congress enacted the ADEA not only to prohibit age discrimination but also to help change attitudes about the capabilities of older workers. As Congress stated in the preamble to the ADEA, "older workers find themselves disadvantaged in their efforts to retain employment, and especially to regain employment when displaced from jobs." 29 U.S.C. § 621(a)(1). Does the quoted language indicate a legislative desire to alter adverse attitudes or does it acknowledge that such attitudes exist and therefore indicate that Congress desires to give older workers protection from the impact of such marketplace prejudices?

4. Because of the unique circumstances in the RIF and downsizing cases, should these cases be analyzed as disparate impact cases? See the section that follows on disparate impact in ADEA cases. *See also* Brendan Sweeney, Comment, *"Downsizing" the Age Discrimination in Employment Act: The Availability of Disparate Impact Liability*, 41 Vill.L.Rev. 1527 (1996).

C. DISPARATE IMPACT

Prior to *Hazen Paper Co. v. Biggins*, 507 U.S. 604, 113 S.Ct. 1701, 123 L.Ed.2d 338 (1993), the lower courts were fairly unanimous in holding that disparate impact claims can be brought under the ADEA.

See, e.g., Massarsky v. General Motors Corp., 706 F.2d 111 (3d Cir.), *cert. denied*, 464 U.S. 937, 104 S.Ct. 348, 78 L.Ed.2d 314 (1983); Pamela S. Krop, Note, *Age Discrimination and the Disparate Impact Doctrine*, 34 Stan.L.Rev. 837 (1982). One of the strongest arguments for allowing disparate impact ADEA claims is that the ADEA's major substantive provisions were derived "in haec verba" from Title VII. *Compare, e.g.*, § 623(a)(2) of the ADEA, 29 U.S.C. § 623(a)(2) *with* § 703(a)(2) of Title VII, 42 U.S.C. § 2000e–2(a)(2). *See, e.g.*, Geller v. Markham, 635 F.2d 1027, 1032 (2d Cir.1980) (citing Lorillard v. Pons, 434 U.S. 575, 584, 98 S.Ct. 866, 55 L.Ed.2d 40 (1978)), *cert. denied*, 451 U.S. 945, 101 S.Ct. 2028, 68 L.Ed.2d 332 (1981)). There is now a split in the circuits over whether *Hazen Paper* sounded the death knell for ADEA disparate impact claims. Some courts, as illustrated in the following case, have relied upon the full range of statutory interpretation techniques to either reject or cast doubt upon the continued viability of the disparate impact theory in ADEA claims.

ELLIS v. UNITED AIRLINES, INC.

United States Court of Appeals, Tenth Circuit, 1996.
73 F.3d 999, *cert. denied*, 517 U.S. 1245, 116 S.Ct. 2500, 135 L.Ed.2d 191 (1996).

EBEL, Circuit Judge.

[Plaintiffs filed an ADEA claim against United Airlines alleging, *inter alia*, that United's age-neutral weight requirement had a disparate impact on employees protected under the ADEA.]

* * *

The following weight chart applied to Plaintiffs as initial job applicants:

Height	Maximum Weight
5′4″	132
5′4 1/4″	133
5′4 1/2″	134
* * *	
5′6″	139
5′6 1/4″	140
5′6 1/2″	141

Had Plaintiffs been hired, they would then have had to keep their weight below the following limits in order to maintain their jobs as flight attendants:

Height	Maximum Weight Age 34 & Younger	35–44	45–54	55 & Older
5′4″	134	137	140	143
5′4 1/4″	135	138	141	144
5′4 1/2″	136	139	142	145
* * *				
5′6″	141	144	147	150

Height	*Maximum Weight* Age 34 & Younger	35–44	45–54	55 & Older
5'6 1/4"	142	145	148	151
5'6 1/2"	143	146	149	152

As the charts reveal, the height/weight requirements for all new job applicants are the same regardless of the applicant's age, while a nine-pound differential exists between the maximum weights for the youngest and oldest employed female flight attendants of a given height. Thus, new job applicants could fail to satisfy the age-neutral weight requirements used for hiring and yet still be within the weight requirement for existing employees of their same age.

* * *

B. Disparate Impact

Plaintiffs claim * * * that United's hiring decisions violated the ADEA because the decisions were based on weight requirements that disparately impacted older job applicants. * * * Whether a disparate impact claim can be brought under the ADEA is, however, an open question. *See Hazen Paper*, 507 U.S. at 610, 113 S.Ct. at 1706 ("[W]e have never decided whether a disparate impact theory of liability is available under the ADEA, and we need not do so here.") (internal citation omitted); Faulkner v. Super Valu Stores, Inc., 3 F.3d at 1428 (explaining that "[t]he Tenth Circuit has never directly addressed whether a disparate impact claim is cognizable under the ADEA," and leaving the question open). Based on our interpretation of the statutory text and congressional intent, we now answer that question and hold that disparate impact claims are not cognizable under the ADEA; thus, we affirm the district court's grant of summary judgment for United on that ground.

Our interpretation begins with the text of the ADEA. The ADEA's core prohibition of discrimination provides, in relevant part, that

> [i]t shall be unlawful for an employer—(1) to fail or refuse to hire or to discharge any individual or otherwise discriminate against any individual with respect to his compensation, terms, conditions, or privileges of employment, *because of such individual's age*; (2) to limit, segregate, or classify his employees in any way which would deprive or tend to deprive any individual of employment opportunities or otherwise adversely affect his status as an employee, *because of such individual's age* * * *.

(Emphasis added.) 29 U.S.C. § 623(a).

Section 623(a)(1), which contains the ADEA's explicit prohibition of discriminatory refusals to hire, specifically proscribes only decisions not to hire *because of* someone's age. The most obvious reading of the clause, "because of such individual's age," is that it prohibits an employer from intentionally treating someone differently based on his or her age. It would be a stretch to read the phrase "because of such individual's age" to prohibit incidental and unintentional discrimination that resulted because of employment decisions which were made for reasons *other than age*. Hazen Paper Co. v. Biggins, 507 U.S. 604, 113 S.Ct. 1701, 1707, 123 L.Ed.2d 338 (1993) ("The ADEA requires the employer to ignore an employee's age * * *; it does not specify further characteristics that an employer must also ignore.").[12]

Admittedly, in *Griggs*, the Supreme Court construed language in Title VII that was nearly identical to that found in Section 623(a) of the ADEA to create a disparate impact theory of discrimination. *Griggs*, 401 U.S. at 431 (holding that employment practices which are neutral in form but which result in discriminatory effects are prohibited unless justified by business necessity). Furthermore, we generally interpret the ADEA in tandem with Title VII because the ADEA was based in substantial part on Title VII. *See* Lorillard v. Pons, 434 U.S. 575, 584, 98 S.Ct. 866, 872, 55 L.Ed.2d 40 (1978) (noting that "the prohibitions of the ADEA were derived *in haec verba* from Title VII") * * *. However, the ADEA differs from Title VII in salient ways that counsel against interpreting the ADEA to recognize disparate impact claims and that reinforce our reading of the text of the ADEA.[13]

First, Section 623(f) of the ADEA provides in relevant part that:

> [i]t shall not be unlawful for an employer, employment agency, or labor organization—(1) to take any action otherwise prohibited under subsections (a), (b), (c), or (e) of this section where age is a bona fide occupational qualification reasonably necessary to the normal operation of the particular business, *or where the differentiation is based on reasonable factors other than age * * ** . (Emphasis added.)

This authorization of actions based on "factors other than age" is similar to section 206(d)(1) of the Equal Pay Act. 29 U.S.C. 206(d)(1).[14]

12. We do not dwell on Section 623(a)(2) because it does not appear to address refusals to hire at all, *see* EEOC v. Francis W. Parker School, 41 F.3d 1073, 1077–78 (7th Cir. 1994), *cert. denied*, 115 S.Ct. 2577, 132 L.Ed.2d 828 (1995). We recognize that the Supreme Court applied language similar to 623(a)(2) in Title VII to job applicants in *Griggs. Griggs*, 401 U.S. at 426–27 & n.1, 91 S.Ct. at 851 & n.1. However, following *Griggs* in 1972, Congress expressly added applicants to the parallel provision in Title VII, *see* 42 U.S.C. § 2000e–2(a)(2), but not to the ADEA, indicating an intent that § 623(a)(2) of the ADEA not apply to applicants as § 623(a)(1) expressly does. Moreover, Section 623(a)(2) concludes with the same phrase as does Section 623(a)(1), and a parallel reading of those two sections would require us to conclude that they are both limited to intentional discrimination.

13. Congress enacted the ADEA before *Griggs*, and, therefore, could not have intended literally to apply *Griggs* to the ADEA by incorporating language from Title VII. Thus, the relevant inquiry is whether the factors that drove the Supreme Court in *Griggs* to recognize disparate impact claims in Title VII apply to the ADEA. However, *Griggs* did not base its holding on the text of Title VII, but rather looked primarily to the larger objectives underlying Congress' enactment of Title VII. *See Griggs*, 401 U.S. at 429–30, 91 S.Ct. at 852–53; Michael C. Sloan, "Disparate Impact in the Age Discrimination in Employment Act," 1995 Wis. L.Rev. 507, 517 (1995) ("[T]he *Griggs* Court did not analyze statutory language to justify its decision, but instead relied on its interpretation of congressional intent and legislative history."). As explained in the text, the ADEA differs from Title VII in these nontextual considerations, as well as in its text and structure.

14. The Equal Pay Act provides, in relevant part, that employers can pay unequal wages to men and women where the pay differential is "based on any other factor than sex * * *." 29 U.S.C. § 206(d)(1).

The Supreme Court interpreted section 206(d)(1) of the Equal Pay Act to preclude disparate impact claims. County of Washington, Ore. v. Gunther, 452 U.S. 161, 170–71, 101 S.Ct. 2242, 2248–49, 68 L.Ed.2d 751 (1981) (distinguishing Title VII on the basis of that provision).

Second, the legislative history of the ADEA suggests it was not enacted to address disparate impact claims. Congress enacted the ADEA in large part on a report it commissioned from the Secretary of Labor, *The Older American Worker: Age Discrimination in Employment* (1965) ("Secretary of Labor Report"). *See* EEOC v. Wyoming, 460 U.S. 226 at 229–31, 103 S.Ct. 1054, 1056–57, 75 L.Ed.2d 18 (tracing legislative history of ADEA and central role of Secretary of Labor Report). That report differentiated between what it termed "arbitrary discrimination" based on age (intentional discrimination based on age stereotypes) and problems resulting from factors that "affect older workers more strongly, as a group, than they do younger employees" (disparate impact) *id.* at 5, 11. The report then recommended that Congress prohibit "arbitrary discrimination," but that factors which "affect older workers" be addressed through programmatic measures to improve opportunities for older workers. *Id.* at 21–25. The ADEA's stated purposes and sections 622 and 623 reflect different approaches for intentional or arbitrary discrimination and the more benign problem of disparate impact.

Third, a comparison of Congress' subsequent amendments to Title VII and to the ADEA further reveals this congressional intent. Specifically, Congress explicitly added a disparate impact cause of action to Title VII in the 1991 Civil Rights Act, *see* Pub.L.No. 102–166, § 105, 105 Stat. 1071, 1074–75 (1991), codified at 42 U.S.C. § 2000e–2(k). However, Congress added no such parallel provision to the ADEA, despite its amendment of other portions of the ADEA, *see, e.g., id.* at § 115, 105 Stat. at 1079 (amending the time period within which an employee may file civil actions); *id.* at § 302(2), 105 Stat. at 1088 (extending coverage of ADEA to congressional employees), thus signalling its intent not to provide for a disparate impact cause of action under the ADEA.

Fourth, the Supreme Court's recent *Hazen Paper* decision further informs our interpretation of the ADEA. The Court, although not expressly ruling on the issue, indicated in dicta that the ADEA only prohibits intentional discrimination. In *Hazen Paper*, the Court addressed a disparate treatment claim against an employer who fired a 62 years old employee just a few weeks before his pension benefits would vest. The Court observed that "[d]isparate treatment captures the essence of what Congress sought to prohibit in the ADEA." *Hazen Paper*, 507 U.S. at 610, 113 S.Ct. at 1706. Even more to the point, the Court said that the ADEA was enacted to prevent older workers from being stigmatized by inaccurate stereotyping and that,

> "When the employer's decision is wholly motivated by factors other than age, the problem of inaccurate and stigmatizing stereotypes

disappears. This is true *even if the motivating factor is correlated with age*, as pension *status typically is*." *Id.* (Emphasis added.)

And, reiterated that theme again later when it said,

> "The law requires the employer to ignore an employee's age * * *; it does not specify further characteristics [like the correlation between age and the likelihood that a worker will qualify for a pension] that an employer must also ignore." *Id.* (Emphasis added.)

Although the Court's holding was technically limited to the disparate treatment claim before it, one cannot read that opinion without receiving the strong impression that the Supreme Court is suggesting that the ADEA does not encompass a disparate impact claim. The Chief Justice and Justices Kennedy and Thomas concurred, noting that "there are substantial arguments that it is improper to carry over disparate impact analysis from Title VII to the ADEA." *Hazen,* 507 U.S. at 618, 113 S.Ct. at 1710.

Fifth, of those courts that have considered the issue since *Hazen,* there is a clear trend toward concluding that the ADEA does not support a disparate impact claim. DiBiase v. SmithKline Beecham Corp., 48 F.3d 719, 732–34 (3d Cir.1995) (holding that there is no disparate impact claim under the ADEA); EEOC v. Francis W. Parker School, 41 F.3d 1073, 1076–77 (7th Cir.1994) (same); Lyon v. Ohio Educ. Ass'n & Professional Staff Union, 53 F.3d 135, 138–39 (6th Cir.1995) (same). *But see,* Mangold v. California Pub. Utilities Comm'n, 67 F.3d 1470, 1474 (9th Cir.1995) (not deciding the issue but referring to earlier Ninth Circuit precedent—one pre-*Hazen* case and one post-*Hazen* case perceiving no conflict between *Hazen* and its decision—that recognize a disparate impact claim under the ADEA); Houghton v. SIPCO, Inc., 38 F.3d 953, 958–59 (8th Cir.1994) (assuming, without analysis, that a disparate impact claim is viable under the ADEA).

Finally, we note that permitting disparate impact age discrimination claims would create several practical problems. In particular, many courts have interpreted the ADEA to prohibit an employer from favoring anyone younger than a protected plaintiff. *See* Rinehart v. City of Independence, Mo., 35 F.3d 1263, 1266 & n. 2 (8th Cir.1994) (noting majority position), *cert. denied,* 514 U.S. 1096, 115 S.Ct. 1822, 131 L.Ed.2d 744 (1995). Accordingly, the line defining the class that is disparately impacted by a challenged policy is an imprecise one, which could be manipulated to either strengthen or weaken the impact of a policy on some age group. As then District Court Judge Higgenbotham remarked,

> the disparate impact analysis in race cases cannot be extended easily to age cases given that the facially neutral factors challenged almost certainly will generate different impacts for different age groups because each point in the life cycle tends to be associated with different distributions. "Unless virtually all facially neutral classifications are to become suspect, the use of nonage factors ought to

enjoy a strong presumption of reasonableness notwithstanding the age-specific differential impacts that inevitably ensue."

Cunningham v. Central Beverage, Inc., 486 F.Supp. 59, 62–63 (N.D.Tex. 1980) (quoting Peter H. Schuck, *The Graying of Civil Rights Law: The Age Discrimination Act of 1975*, 89 Yale L.J. 27, 35–37 (1979)).

Thus, policy considerations add to our analysis of precedent and the ADEA's text, structure, purposes, and legislative history, and confirm our ultimate holding that plaintiffs cannot bring a disparate impact claim under the ADEA. As such, we affirm the district court's grant of summary judgment for United on plaintiff's disparate impact claim on that ground.

* * *

Notes and Questions

1. Other courts of appeals that have rejected or cast doubt upon the applicability of the disparate impact theory in ADEA cases include the First Circuit in *Mullin v. Raytheon Co.*, 164 F.3d 696 (1st Cir.1999); the Third Circuit in *DiBiase v. SmithKline Beecham Corp.*, 48 F.3d 719 (3d Cir.1995); the Fifth Circuit in *Smith v. City of Jackson*, 351 F.3d 183 (5th Cir.2003); the Sixth Circuit, in *Lyon v. Ohio Education Association & Professional Staff Union*, 53 F.3d 135 (6th Cir.1995); the Seventh Circuit, in *EEOC v. Francis W. Parker School*, 41 F.3d 1073 (7th Cir.1994), *cert. denied*, 515 U.S. 1142, 115 S.Ct. 2577, 132 L.Ed.2d 828 (1995); and the Eleventh Circuit in *Adams v. Florida Power Corp.*, 255 F.3d 1322 (11th Cir.2001), *cert. granted*, 534 U.S. 1054, 122 S.Ct. 643, 151 L.Ed.2d 561 (2001), *cert. dismissed* 535 U.S. 228, 122 S.Ct. 1290, 152 L.Ed.2d 345 (2002).

2. The courts of appeals that have continued to recognize that the disparate impact theory is still viable in ADEA claims even after *Hazen Paper* have done so on the basis that *Hazen Paper* did not unequivocally overrule the pre-*Hazen Paper* weight of authority to the contrary. *See, e.g.*, Smith v. Xerox Corp., 196 F.3d 358 (2d Cir.1999); Smith v. City of Des Moines, Iowa, 99 F.3d 1466, 1469–70 (8th Cir.1996); Mangold v. California Pub. Util. Comm'n, 67 F.3d 1470, 1473 (9th Cir.1995). Other courts have assumed, without expressly deciding the issue, that the disparate impact theory applies to the ADEA. *See*, e.g., Koger v. Reno, 98 F.3d 631 (D.C.Cir. 1996). In 1999, the Eighth Circuit reiterated its settled precedent that claims based upon the disparate impact theory are still viable in ADEA case, even while it recognized that the majority of other circuits do not. *See* EEOC v. McDonnell Douglas Corp., 191 F.3d 948 (8th Cir.1999). The Eight Circuit, however, held that a disparate impact ADEA claim cannot be brought on behalf of a subgroup of employees who are within the class protected under the ADEA. The EEOC, as plaintiff, had sought to rely on the disparate impact theory on behalf of only employees who were fifty-five years and older on the ground that McDonnell Douglas's RIF, based on factors such as retirement eligibility, merit raises, and salaries had a greater adverse impact on this subgroup. One of the reasons the Eighth Circuit refused to allow a disparate impact claim for a subgroup was that to do so would require an

employer to attempt "what might well be impossible: to achieve a statistical parity among the virtually infinite number of age subgroups in the work force." *Id.* at 951.

The Supreme Court granted certiorari in *Adams v. Florida Power Corp.*, 534 U.S. 1054, 122 S.Ct. 643, 151 L.Ed.2d 561 (2001), to resolve the circuit split on the applicability of the disparate impact theory to ADEA claims. The Court later dismissed the writ as improvidently granted. 535 U.S. 1028, 122 S.Ct. 1290, 152 L.Ed.2d 345 (2002). In 2004, the Court again agreed to consider the issue. Smith v. City of Jackson, Miss., 351 F.3d 183 (5th Cir.2003), *cert. granted*, ___ U.S. ___, 124 S.Ct. 1724, ___ L.Ed.2d ___ (2004).

3. One of the differences between Title VII and the ADEA is that § 623(a)(2) of the ADEA specifically identifies only "employees," while Title VII in § 703(a)(2), 42 U.S.C. § 2000e–2(a))(2), as amended by Congress in 1972, specifically identifies both "employees and applicants." The *Griggs'* disparate impact theory is grounded in an interpretation of § 703(a)(2) of Title VII. In note 12 of *Ellis v. United Airlines*, the court considered this difference in statutory language, as well as the fact that Congress has not amended the ADEA to specifically apply to "applicants," to be critical to its holding that the disparate impact theory is inapplicable in ADEA claims. Even though technically correct in stating that the Supreme Court in *Griggs* did not specifically refer to § 703(a)(2) as the basis for adopting the disparate impact theory, *Ellis* failed to consider that the Court in *Connecticut v. Teal*, 457 U.S. 440, 448, 102 S.Ct. 2525, 2531, 73 L.Ed.2d 130 (1982), discussed in Chapter 4, clearly stated that the disparate impact theory is based on an interpretation of § 703(a)(2) of Title VII. Should the difference in the definition of the persons protected—*employees* under the ADEA and *employees and applicants* under Title VII—be deemed significant in deciding whether the disparate impact theory applies?

4. Are there countervailing policy reasons—not articulated in *Ellis*— that would support a rule in favor of disparate impact claims under the ADEA?

5. A substantial amount of the scholarly literature on the ADEA has been grounded in law and economics analysis. *See, e.g.,* Christine Jolls, *Hands-Tying and the Age Discrimination in Employment Act*, 74 Tex.L.Rev. 1813 (1996). Arguably, law and economics analysis has had greater influence on the development of ADEA jurisprudence than on the development of Title VII jurisprudence. Two well-known scholars of law and economics, Richard Posner and Frank Easterbrook, formerly law professors at the University of Chicago School of Law, are now judges on the United States Court of Appeals for the Seventh Circuit.

In his book, *Forbidden Grounds: The Case Against Employment Discrimination Laws* (1992), Professor Richard Epstein makes "a frontal assault" on the "social consensus that supports one or another version of the modern antidiscrimination principle." *Id.* at 6. Professor Epstein proposes the repeal of all antidiscrimination laws, including laws prohibiting discrimination on the basis of race, sex, religion, national origin, age, and handicap. *Id.* at 9. His basic premise is that these laws represent an unwarranted interference by the government in the free market. More specifically, he argues that these laws are the "antithesis of freedom of contract, a principle that allows all persons to do business with whomever they please for good reason, bad reason, or no reason at all." *Id.* at 3. An underlying assumption of those who find virtue in markets unfettered by government regulation is that workers and employers will thereby make uncoerced, rational choices guided solely by the goal of maximizing personal gain and that the decisions will be informed by complete, accurate, relevant data. Does your experience confirm the accuracy of this assumption?

For critiques of Professor Epstein's book from a feminist perspective, see Marion Crain, *Rationalizing Inequality: An Antifeminist Defense of the Free Market—A Review of* Forbidden Grounds: The Case Against Employment Discrimination Laws, 61 Geo.Wash.L.Rev. 556 (1993), and Nancy Dowd, *Liberty v. Equality: In Defense of Privileged White Males*, 34 Wm. & Mary L.Rev. 429 (1993) (book review). For a critique of Professor Epstein's book from the perspective of critical race theory, see Richard Delgado, *Rodrigo's Second Chronicle: The Economics and Politics of Race*, 91 Mich. L.Rev. 1183 (1993). *See also* Norman C. Amaker, *Quittin' Time? The Antidiscrimination Principle of Title VII v. The Free Market*, 60 U.Chi.L.Rev. 757 (1993) (book review).

6. One commentator has suggested that the Supreme Court's waffling in *Hazen Paper*, on whether the disparate impact theory is applicable in ADEA cases, "may very well be a conscious effort by the Court to avoid the congressional reversal that has met many of its recent pro-employer decisions by forcing lower courts to reach the more 'palatable' decision to reject disparate impact analysis on their own." Jan W. Henkel, *The Age Discrimination in Employment Act: Disparate Impact Analysis and the Availability of Liquidated Damages After* Hazen Paper Co. v. Biggins, 47 Syracuse L.Rev. 1183, 1185 (1997).

Note: Sex–Plus–Age Claims

In 1996, the Women's Legal Defense Fund prepared two studies for the American Association of Retired Persons. The first study, Volume I, *Employment Discrimination Against Midlife and Older Women: How Courts Treat Sex-and-Age Discrimination Cases* (1996) (hereinafter Midlife and Older Women), examined all court cases decided between 1975 and 1995 that involved claims for sex and age discrimination, and concluded that both judges and lawyers generally have failed to recognize or acknowledge that older women face a unique form of discrimination unlike the type of discrimination that older men and younger women face.

> Midlife and older women make up a steadily increasing share of the American workforce. Yet, too often, they continue to face job discrimination based on both sex and age. To date, however, there has been little research that examines the cumulative or synergistic effect of sex and age on midlife and older women's work opportunities, the form such discrimination may take, or how women's complaints of sex-and-age discrimination are treated in the legal system.

Id. at 1. The courts have been willing, generally, to recognize black women and Asian–American women as a discrete and protected subclass under the theory of either race-plus-sex or national origin-plus-sex. *See, e.g.,* Jefferies

v. Harris County Community Action Ass'n, 615 F.2d 1025 (5th Cir.1980) (black women); Lam v. University of Hawaii, 40 F.3d 1551 (9th Cir.1994) (Asian–American women).

Arnett v. Aspin, 846 F.Supp. 1234 (E.D.Pa.1994), is one of the seminal cases recognizing a sex-plus-age claim. Plaintiff, a female who was more than forty years of age, had been passed over twice for a promotion. Her evidence of sex-plus-age discrimination was that every woman selected for the position had been younger than forty years of age and every man selected had been over forty. The employer sought summary judgment on the ground that plaintiff's sex-plus-age claim had to be treated as two separate claims: one for sex discrimination, the other for age discrimination. The employer argued that it was entitled to summary judgment, as a matter of law, because the evidence showed that *both* younger women and older men had been selected for the at-issue positions. The employer attempted to distinguish the "sex-plus" line of cases, such as *Jefferies*, from Arnett's "age-plus-sex" claim on the ground that Arnett was attempting to combine a subclass based upon two different statutes—Title VII and the ADEA. The court rejected the distinction as insignificant:

> [R]ather than adopt the distinctions suggested by the defendants, I find that the current line drawn between viable and nonviable sex-plus claims is adequate—that the "plus" classification be based on either an immutable characteristic or the exercise of a fundamental right. And, although I have uncovered no other case that recognizes a "sex-plus-age" discrimination claim under Title VII, it is clear that age is an immutable characteristic. For purposes of determining whether the defendants' discriminated against Arnett in violation of Title VII, I find she is member of a discrete subclass of "women over forty." Accordingly, I conclude that Arnett has shown a prima facie case under the *McDonnell Douglas* framework because (1) she is a member of the protected subclass, that is women over forty, (2) she was qualified for and applied for the positions in question, (3) despite her qualifications, she was denied the positions, and (4) other employees outside her protected class were selected, in this case two women under forty.

Id. at 1241. The Women's Legal Defense Fund found that the only other case besides *Arnett* to specifically recognize an "age-plus-sex" claim was *Good v. U.S. West Communications, Inc.*, Civ. No. 93–302–FR, 1995 WL 67672 (D.Ore.1995). 1 Midlife and Older Women 16–19. Other courts require plaintiffs to seek relief separately under the ADEA and Title VII. *E.g.*, Murdock v. B.F. Goodrich, No. 15654, 1992 WL 393158 (Ohio App.1992). Still other courts use a hybrid approach by allowing the fact finder to consider evidence of one claim probative of the other claims. *See, e.g.*, Hoth v. Grinnell College, 23 Fair Empl.Prac.Cas. (BNA) 528 (S.D.Iowa 1980). *See* 1 Midlife and Older Women 19–22.

Among the other findings of the Women's Defense League study were (1) that 52 percent of the plaintiffs in age and sex cases were women in their fifties, and (2) that, of the 81 percent of the "age-plus-sex" claims in which the plaintiff's job was identified, 24 percent involved professional jobs such as professor, teacher, accountant, or nurse, and 21 percent involved executive or managerial positions. 1 *id*. at 4. Twenty-four percent of the defendants in sex and age cases were government employers. 1 *id*. at 5.

In Volume II of the study, *Employment Discrimination Against Midlife and Older Women: An Analysis of Discrimination Charges Filed With the EEOC* (1997), the Women's Legal Defense Fund examined charges of discrimination filed with the EEOC or cross-filed with the EEOC and a state agency by women and men age forty and older during a six-year period from fiscal year 1990 through 1995 (Oct. 1, 1989, through Sept. 30, 1995). Of the approximately 90,000 charges filed by women forty and older during the study period, 21 percent were for sex discrimination only, 24 percent for age discrimination only, and 10 percent were for both. 2 *id*. at 12. The average age of the charging parties was 53. 2 *id*. at 15. About one-third of the white women forty and older who filed discrimination charges made ADEA claims only, whereas only 7 percent of black women complained only of age discrimination. 2 *id*. at 17. One of the recommendations made in Volume II of the study was that the EEOC should develop guidelines for accepting and investigating claims involving multiple categories of discrimination, for example age-plus-sex. 2 *id*. at 31–32.

Consider the following issues that may be raised in "age-plus-sex" discrimination cases:

1.   In *Arnett v. Aspin*, *supra*, the court recognized an "age-plus-sex" claim only with respect to plaintiff's claim brought under Title VII and specifically noted that the claim was not recognized under the ADEA. 846 F.Supp. at 1240. Should it make a difference whether an "age-plus-sex" claim is brought under Title VII or the ADEA? In *Kelly v. Drexel University*, 907 F.Supp. 864 (E.D.Pa.1995), *aff'd*, 94 F.3d 102 (3d Cir.1996), the same judge who decided *Arnett* rejected an "age-plus-disability" claim brought under the ADEA. The court in *Luce v. Dalton*, 166 F.R.D. 457 (S.D.Cal. 1996), relying, in part, on *Kelly*, also rejected an "age-plus-disability" claim brought under the ADEA. The court in *Luce* reasoned that

> Congress has not drafted one statute to govern all claims of employment discrimination, regardless of * * * race, sex, religion, national origin, age, and disability. The factors which Plaintiff seeks to lump together in this lawsuit under the title of "age-plus" theories of discrimination are contained within four separate and distinct statutes: the Age Discrimination in Employment Act, Title VII, the Americans with Disabilities Act, and the Rehabilitation Act. If Congress had intended to allow plaintiffs to mix and match theories of liability for employment discrimination, regardless of whether such claim was based upon race, sex, religion, national origin, age, or disability, it could have amended Title VII to provide protections to older Americans and Americans with disabilities within the confines of that statute. However, Congress chose to pass entirely separate legislation, providing for an entirely different basis for relief to persons who believe they have been discriminated against in employment based upon their age or disability. To allow Plaintiff here to aggregate claims under four completely different statutes, as an extension of the "sex-plus" theories of discrimination, would amount to judicial legislation. * * * [T]he arguments of the courts based upon the interpretation of Title VII's explicit language as barring

discrimination based upon race, sex, national origin, or religion cannot be extended to support "age-plus" theories of discrimination.

In addition, and perhaps more importantly, the "sex-plus" theories of discrimination are based upon a recognition of the unique discriminatory biases against certain subclasses of individuals under Title VII. Unlike African–American or Asian women, there can be no argument that there are unique discriminatory biases against older workers with disabilities or older non-Mormon workers. There is no danger that Plaintiff would be prejudiced by his claims being analyzed according to the unique statutory schemes set up for claims of age discrimination under the ADEA, claims of religious discrimination under Title VII, and claims of disability discrimination under the ADA or Rehabilitation Act.

This Court finds that there does not exist in the law theories of "age-plus-religion" or "age-plus-disability" discrimination under the ADEA as proposed by Plaintiff in this case.

Id. at 461. Does *Hazen Paper Co. v. Biggins*, 507 U.S. 604, 609, 113 S.Ct. 1701, 1706, 123 L.Ed.2d 338 (1993), support the reasoning of the court in *Luce v. Dalton?*

2. To what extent is it likely that the combination of age and sex creates an especially powerful set of stereotypes that potentially limit the employment opportunities of older women? If so, what are some of those stereotypes?

3. In a jurisdiction that endorses the "age-plus-sex" theory of discrimination, how should the jury be instructed on the theory?

4. Employer, Casino Royale, advertises that it is an "upscale gentlemen's club, boasting of providing the finest service, atmosphere, and entertainment. Its facilities include a gourmet restaurant, conference room with office services, a boutique, wide-screen viewing of sports events, and topless dancing." Lindsey, a forty-year old female, was initially hired by the employer as a waitress, but later sought a promotion to a job as a topless dancer. The employer denied her request for the promotion on the ground that she was "too old." Would she have a potential claim under the ADEA? Title VII? Both? *See* Lindsey v. Prive Corp., 987 F.2d 324, 325 (5th Cir.1993).

Note: ADEA Claims Against States

In *Kimel v. Florida Board of Regents*, 528 U.S. 62, 120 S.Ct. 631, 145 L.Ed.2d 522 (2000), the Supreme Court held that the Eleventh Amendment bars private actions under the ADEA against states. A brief discussion of the *Kimel* case is in the *Note, Eleventh Amendment Bar Against Suing State Employers,* found in Chapter 2.

D. SEPARATIONS AND WAIVERS

As the business world becomes more competitive, with mergers and acquisitions, technological advances, and global competition, the focus of many American businesses today is on maintaining profit margins. As one commentator noted,

The quickest way to bolster a company's financial position is to cut costs, and an easy way to cut is to reduce the work force. The most expedient solution of all is to get rid of older employees who because of their long tenure earn more money, are entitled to substantial pensions, and raise the company's tab for health benefits.

Ellen Simon Sacks, *Corporate Downsizing—Or Age Discrimination?*, 28 *Trial* 26, 26 (July 1992). The change in the economic climate and the ADEA's prohibition of mandatory retirement policies have induced employers to look for innovative ways to reduce the ranks of older workers without violating the ADEA. "Downsizing" or reductions-in-force (RIF) and early retirement incentive plans (ERIPs), either through "buy-outs" or other incentives for early retirement, are several of the methods employers have adopted to try to satisfy the mandate of the ADEA and to remain profitable in the highly competitive domestic and international economic markets. Increasingly, a number of employers are persuading their older workers to retire earlier than they could be required to retire under laws such as the ADEA. But as a condition of granting sometimes generous early retirement incentives, employers are requiring employees to sign a waiver of their rights under the ADEA and other laws. These plans are sometimes referred to as the "golden handshake." *See* General Accounting Office, Age Discrimination: Use of Waivers by Large Companies Offering Exit Incentives to Employees, [GAO/HRD–89–87, April 1989] (which reported a steady increase in the use of waivers as an exit incentive in corporate America from 1979 through 1988); Linda C. Messinger, Comment, *Voluntary Acceptance of Early Retirement Offers: Golden Handshake or Gilded Shove?*, 20 Ariz.St.L.J. 797 (1988). May an employer condition a separation package upon a waiver of all ADEA claims? The following case deals with this situation:

OUBRE v. ENTERGY OPERATIONS, INC.

Supreme Court of the United States, 1998.
522 U.S. 422, 118 S.Ct. 838, 139 L.Ed.2d 849.

JUSTICE KENNEDY delivered the opinion of the Court.

An employee, as part of a termination agreement, signed a release of all claims against her employer. In consideration, she received severance pay in installments. The release, however, did not comply with specific federal statutory requirements for a release of claims under the Age Discrimination in Employment Act of 1967 (ADEA). After receiving the last payment, the employee brought suit under the ADEA. The employer claims the employee ratified and validated the nonconforming release by retaining the monies paid to secure it. The employer also insists the release bars the action unless, as a precondition to filing suit, the employee tenders back the monies received. We disagree and rule that, as the release did not comply with the statute, it cannot bar the ADEA claim.

I

Petitioner Dolores Oubre worked as a scheduler at a power plant in Killona, Louisiana, run by her employer, respondent Entergy Operations, Inc. In 1994, she received a poor performance rating. Oubre's supervisor met with her on January 17, 1995, and gave her the option of either improving her performance during the coming year or accepting a voluntary arrangement for her severance. She received a packet of information about the severance agreement and had 14 days to consider her options, during which she consulted with attorneys. On January 31, Oubre decided to accept. She signed a release, in which she "agreed to waive, settle, release, and discharge any and all claims, demands, damages, actions, or causes of action * * * that I may have against Entergy * * * ." In exchange, she received six installment payments over the next four months, totaling $6,258.

The Older Workers Benefit Protection Act (OWBPA) imposes specific requirements for releases covering ADEA claims. OWBPA, 29 U.S.C. §§ 626(f)(1)(B), (F), (G). In procuring the release, Entergy did not comply with the OWBPA in at least three respects: (1) Entergy did not give Oubre enough time to consider her options. (2) Entergy did not give Oubre seven days after she signed the release to change her mind. And (3) the release made no specific reference to claims under the ADEA.

* * * [Oubre] filed this suit against Entergy * * * alleging constructive discharge on the basis of her age in violation of the ADEA * * *. Oubre has not offered or tried to return the $6,258 to Entergy, nor is it clear she has the means to do so. Entergy moved for summary judgment, claiming Oubre had ratified the defective release by failing to return or offer to return the monies she had received. The District Court agreed and entered summary judgment for Entergy. The Court of Appeals affirmed, and we granted certiorari.

II

The employer rests its case upon general principles of state contract jurisprudence. As the employer recites the rule, contracts tainted by mistake, duress, or even fraud are voidable at the option of the innocent party. The employer maintains, however, that before the innocent party can elect avoidance, she must first tender back any benefits received under the contract. If she fails to do so within a reasonable time after learning of her rights, the employer contends, she ratifies the contract and so makes it binding. The employer also invokes the doctrine of equitable estoppel. As a rule, equitable estoppel bars a party from shirking the burdens of a voidable transaction for as long as she retains the benefits received under it. Applying these principles, the employer claims the employee ratified the ineffective release (or faces estoppel) by retaining all the sums paid in consideration of it. The employer, then, relies not upon the execution of the release but upon a later, distinct ratification of its terms.

These general rules may not be as unified as the employer asserts. And in equity, a person suing to rescind a contract, as a rule, is not required to restore the consideration at the very outset of the litigation. Even if the employer's statement of the general rule requiring tender back before one files suit were correct, it would be unavailing. The rule cited is based simply on the course of negotiation of the parties and the alleged later ratification. The authorities cited do not consider the question raised by statutory standards for releases and a statutory declaration making non-conforming releases ineffective. It is the latter question we confront here.

In 1990, Congress amended the ADEA by passing the OWBPA. The OWBPA provides: "An individual may not waive any right or claim under [the ADEA] unless the waiver is knowing and voluntary * * *. [A] waiver may not be considered knowing and voluntary unless at a minimum" it satisfies certain enumerated requirements, including the three listed above. 29 U.S.C. § 626(f)(1).

The statutory command is clear: An employee "may not waive" an ADEA claim unless the waiver or release satisfies the OWBPA's requirements. The policy of the Older Workers Benefit Protection Act is likewise clear from its title: It is designed to protect the rights and benefits of older workers. The OWBPA implements Congress' policy via a strict, unqualified statutory stricture on waivers, and we are bound to take Congress at its word. Congress imposed specific duties on employers who seek releases of certain claims created by statute. Congress delineated these duties with precision and without qualification: An employee "may not waive" an ADEA claim unless the employer complies with the statute. Courts cannot with ease presume ratification of that which Congress forbids.

The OWBPA sets up its own regime for assessing the effect of ADEA waivers, separate and apart from contract law. The statute creates a series of prerequisites for knowing and voluntary waivers and imposes affirmative duties of disclosure and waiting periods. The OWBPA governs the effect under federal law of waivers or releases on ADEA claims and incorporates no exceptions or qualifications. The text of the OWBPA forecloses the employer's defense, notwithstanding how general contract principles would apply to non-ADEA claims.

The rule proposed by the employer would frustrate the statute's practical operation as well as its formal command. In many instances a discharged employee likely will have spent the monies received and will lack the means to tender their return. These realities might tempt employers to risk noncompliance with the OWBPA's waiver provisions, knowing it will be difficult to repay the monies and relying on ratification. We ought not to open the door to an evasion of the statute by this device.

* * *

We reverse the judgment of the Court of Appeals and remand for further proceedings consistent with this opinion.

* * *

[JUSTICE SCALIA dissented in a separate opinion on the ground that there was no "tender back."]

JUSTICE THOMAS, with whom CHIEF JUSTICE REHNQUIST joins, dissenting.

* * * [W]ithout so much as acknowledging the long-established principle that a statute "must 'speak directly' to the question addressed by the common law" in order to abrogate it, the Court holds that the OWBPA abrogates both the common-law doctrine of ratification and the doctrine that a party must "tender back" consideration received under a release of legal claims before bringing suit. Because the OWBPA does not address either of these common-law doctrines at all, much less with the clarity necessary to abrogate them, I respectfully dissent.

* * *

Notes and Questions

1. Congress enacted the OWBPA to overturn the Supreme Court's controversial decision in *Public Employees Retirement System of Ohio v. Betts*, 492 U.S. 158, 109 S.Ct. 2854, 106 L.Ed.2d 134 (1989). Title II of OWBPA on waivers was added later. *See generally* S.Rep.No. 101–263, 101st Cong., 2d Sess. 5 (1990), *reprinted in* 1990 U.S.C.C.A.N. 1509, 1521–22. One of the causes of the controversy over unsupervised waivers in ADEA cases is the Act's hybrid structure. The ADEA is modeled on Title VII, but its enforcement scheme is taken from the Fair Labor Standards Act. Courts have allowed unsupervised waivers of rights under Title VII but have consistently held that unsupervised waivers are prohibited under the FLSA. For a discussion of pre-OWBPA developments on unsupervised waivers under the ADEA in the courts, the EEOC, and Congress, *see* N. Jansen Calamita, Note, *The Older Worker's Benefit Protection Act of 1990: The End of Ratification and Tender Back in ADEA Waiver Cases*, 73 B.U.L.Rev. 639, 641–46 (1993).

2. Prior to OWBPA, the courts of appeals were in disagreement on the proper standard for determining whether waivers of rights under the ADEA were knowing and voluntary. Several courts had adopted a "totality of the circumstances" test as a matter of federal waiver law. Other courts had held that the common law doctrine of contractual ratification of voidable contracts applies to ADEA waivers notwithstanding the enactment of OWBPA; that a release that does not constitute a knowing and voluntary waiver under the OWBPA is not void, but is merely voidable; and that an employee's retention of severance payments constituted a choice not to avoid an invalid release and thus served as a new promise not subjected to the waiver requirements of the OWBPA. *See, e.g.,* Blistein v. St. John's College, 74 F.3d 1459 (4th Cir.1996) (discussing the split in the circuits); Wamsley v. Champlin Refining & Chemicals, Inc., 11 F.3d 534 (5th Cir.1993), *cert. denied*, 514

U.S. 1037, 115 S.Ct. 1403, 131 L.Ed.2d 290 (1995). In enacting the OWBPA, Congress did not adopt either approach, instead it set certain minimum requirements that every release of ADEA rights and claims must meet in order to be deemed knowing and voluntary. The EEOC's position always has been that any waiver not in strict compliance with OWBPA is not enforceable.

3.   The OWBPA makes the validity of a waiver an affirmative defense by providing that "the party asserting the validity of a waiver shall have the burden of proving * * * that a waiver was knowing and voluntary" because all of the minimum requirements of the Act have been satisfied. 29 U.S.C. § 626(f)(3). By making the waiver an affirmative defense, Congress sought to relieve employers from the burden of having to "prove a negative" in the absence of evidence of fraud, duress, or coercion. *See* S.Rep.No. 101–263, 101st Cong., 2d Sess. 35 (1990), *reprinted in* 1990 U.S.C.C.A.N. 1509, 1540. Proof by the employer that all of the statutory minimum requirements have been satisfied shifts the burden to the employee to prove that the waiver was not knowing and voluntary. *Id. See, e.g.*, Griffin v. Kraft Gen. Foods, Inc., 62 F.3d 368 (11th Cir.1995).

Are there arguments open to an employee to support a claim that she did not voluntarily and knowingly waive her rights under the ADEA even if the waiver complies with all of the requirements of the OWBPA? Congress expressly provides in the OWBPA that those standards are the "minimum" that is required for a waiver of rights under the ADEA to be considered voluntary and knowing. 29 U.S.C. § 626(f)(1). In *Bennett v. Coors Brewing Co.*, 189 F.3d 1221 (10th Cir.1999), the court held that under general contract principles, it is well established that a contract is void and unenforceable if procured through fraud. *Id.* at 1229 (citing Restatement (Second) Contracts § 164(1)(1981)). Applying contract principles, the court further held that "non-statutory circumstances such as fraud, duress, or mutual mistake may render an ADEA waiver not 'knowing and voluntary' under the OWBPA." *Id.* The court grounded its rule, in part, on the legislative history of the OWBPA, which stated that "[t]he individual [waiving his rights] * * * *must have acted in the absence of fraud, duress, coercion, or mistake of material fact.*" *Id.* (citing S.Rep.No.263, at 31–32 (1990)), *reprinted in* 1990 U.S.C.C.A.N. 1509, 1537 (emphasis of the court).

4.   The OWBPA establishes a two-tiered scheme on waivers. The first, illustrated in *Oubre*, establishes the statutory floor for waivers involving individuals. The second involves statutory minimum requirements for waivers "requested in connection with an exit incentive or other employment termination program offered to a group or class of employees." 29 U.S.C. § 626(f)(1)(H). Employees subjected to "exit incentive or other employment termination" programs or policies must be given at least forty-five days instead of twenty-one days to consider the agreement containing the waiver. Also, at the commencement of the forty-five day period, the employer must inform each eligible employee in writing "in a manner calculated to be understood" by him, "or by the average individual eligible to participate," as to a description of eligibility factors: the time limits for the exit incentive program, the job titles and ages of all individuals eligible or selected for the program, and the ages of all employees in the same job classifications or

organizational units who are not eligible or who were not selected for the program.

The legislative history of OWBPA reflects congressional intent to prevent employers from unfairly obtaining waivers of ADEA rights from older workers involved in large-scale terminations and layoffs, where the individual employee would not have reason to know or suspect that age may have played a role in the employer's decision or that the program or policy was designed to remove older workers from the workforce. See S.Rep.No. 101–263, 101st Cong., 2d Sess. 32 (1990), *reprinted in* 1990 U.S.C.C.A.N. 1509, 1537–38. The assumption is that individual employees are in a much better position to understand the nature of the action an employer may take against them and can possibly negotiate individually with the employer, but that employees who are offered a standardized benefit package are not free to negotiate.

5. Because the written disclosure requirements of the OWBPA may provide "free discovery" that allows affected employees to evaluate the strengths and weaknesses of a potential age discrimination claim, are the OWBPA waiver requirements likely to discourage massive layoffs or downsizing? What advice would you give an employer to minimize the potential for employees to use the required disclosure to explore potential ADEA claims?

6. How likely is it that employers faced with the stringent waiver provisions of the OWBPA, as interpreted by *Oubre*, will discontinue the use of wholesale layoffs of employees protected by the ADEA? Congress did not believe that they would. In responding to this specific concern, the congressional committees that drafted the OWBPA were not persuaded that the stringent waiver provisions would persuade employers to favor individual layoffs as opposed to mass layoffs. In support of their view, the committees cited the study, General Accounting Office, Age Discrimination: Use of Waivers by Large Companies Offering Exit Incentives to Employees (GAO/HRD–89–87, Apr. 1989), which reported that most companies do not require waivers as part of their exit incentive programs. The committees also reported that exit incentive programs arose long before employers began to use waivers. S.Rep.No. 79 at 13–15. If waivers do not offer employers complete protection from litigation, are they likely to continue to offer handsome monetary incentives to employees protected by the ADEA? If not, is *Oubre* nothing more than a pyrrhic victory for employees?

7. *Oubre* leaves two important questions unanswered. The first is whether an employer who has paid an ADEA claimant money under a waiver agreement that does not comply with the strict requirements of the OWBPA will be allowed to pursue a claim for restitution, recoupment, or set-off in the event that the employee sues the employer under the ADEA. For example, suppose Lois Lane, a sixty-year-old employee of Karo Company, signs a severance package Karo offered to her as part of a downsizing operation. The agreement requires her to waive her rights under the ADEA, but the agreement fails to conform to the requirements of OWBPA. Lane has received a substantial amount of money pursuant to the terms of the agreement. Suppose she sues Karo at a later date under the ADEA and the court allows her to pursue the claim. The case is tried on the merits; the jury

rules in her favor and awards her monetary damages. Under the distinction between void and voidable contracts in *Oubre*, should Karo be entitled to a set-off against her damages award equal to the money it paid her under a nonconforming waiver agreement? Should it make a difference whether the damages the jury awards exceed the amount of money that Karo paid Lane under the nonconforming waiver agreement? *See* Forbus v. Sears Roebuck & Co., 958 F.2d 1036, 1041 (11th Cir.), *cert. denied*, 506 U.S. 955, 113 S.Ct. 412, 121 L.Ed.2d 336 (1992); N. Jansen Calamita, Note, *The Older Worker's Benefit Protection Act of 1990: The End of Ratification and Tender Back in ADEA Waiver Cases*, 73 B.U.L.Rev. 639, 670–72 (1993).

The EEOC has issued regulations, effective January 10, 2001, setting out its views on waivers under the ADEA. 29 C.F.R. § 1625.23 (2002). The regulations adopt the Court's decision in *Oubre* that an employee need not tender back the consideration given for the agreement before filing either a suit in court, a charge with the EEOC, or a charge with a state or local fair employment practice agency. Going beyond *Oubre*, the EEOC takes the position that a provision in a waiver agreement that requires the employer to tender back consideration is unlawful. The EEOC also takes the position that restitution, recoupment, or set-off sought by the employer must be limited to the lesser amount of the award to the prevailing plaintiff or the amount of consideration that the employee received for the waiver.

The second question *Oubre* leaves unanswered is whether the terms of the agreement that are not related to the OWBPA aspects of the employment relationship survive as enforceable provisions. For example, Lois Lane has potential claims against Karo for sexual harassment under Title VII, age discrimination under the ADEA, race discrimination under § 1981, and intentional infliction of emotional distress under state law. Karo and Lane enter into a settlement agreement, and a provision in the agreement requires Lane to waive any and all rights that she may have against Karo that arose in the course of her employment with Karo. The waiver agreement does not comply with the strict provisions of the OWBPA. *Oubre* would not preclude her from subsequently suing Karo under the ADEA; but is the waiver provision enforceable with respect to her claims under Title VII, § 1981, and state law? In *Bennett v. Coors Brewing Co.,* 189 F.3d 1221 (10th Cir.1999), the court held that a failure to tender back severance benefits acts as a waiver to state law claims even where the failure to do so would not affect an ADEA claim that does not comply with the OWBPA.

In *Tung v. Texaco Inc.*, 150 F.3d 206 (2d Cir.1998), a case involving both race and age claims, the court held that the provisions on waiver under OWBPA are limited to the ADEA and are not applicable to Title VII cases. The court held that the "totality of the circumstances" test is to be applied in determining the validity of the waiver in Title VII cases. Under this test, courts consider factors such (1) plaintiff's education and business experience; (2) the amount of time plaintiff had possession of the agreement before signing it; (3) the role of the plaintiff had in deciding the terms of the agreement; (4) the clarity of the agreement; (5) whether the plaintiff was represented by counsel; and (6) whether the consideration given, in exchange for the waiver of claims, exceeds benefits to which the employee was already entitled by law. *Id.* at 208.

8. Assume that the waiver agreement an employer obtains from an ADEA-protected employee is invalid under OWBPA. Under *Oubre*, the employer is precluded from seeking to enforce the waiver agreement in a judicial forum. But should the courts recognize an independent cause of action under the ADEA against the employer by the employee for violating the waiver provisions, or should the employee be limited to raising the invalid waiver agreement as a defense to any action the employer may initiate to recover the consideration given to the employee for the invalid waiver agreement? The courts are divided on this issue. *See* Commonwealth of Mass. v. Bull HN Info. Sys., Inc., 16 F.Supp.2d 90, 106–07 (D.Mass.1998) (discussing the cases).

9. Neither Title VII nor § 1981 has a specific provision on waivers like the ADEA. In *Fleming* v. *United States Postal Service AMF O'Hare*, 27 F.3d 259 (7th Cir.1994), *cert. denied*, 513 U.S. 1085, 115 S.Ct. 741, 130 L.Ed.2d 642 (1995), the Seventh Circuit held that a plaintiff who had settled a Title VII and Rehabilitation Act case for $75,000, but subsequently sought to initiate an action under these statutes for reinstatement, was precluded from doing so unless she demonstrated her willingness and ability to tender back the money. Judge Posner, the author of *Fleming*, based his decision on traditional principles of contract law or, as he described it, a "free market" or "freedom of contract" analysis: "The tender requirement is not a remedy. It is a protection for defendants, although it may * * * benefit plaintiffs in the long run too; a premise of a free-market system is that both sides of the market, buyers as well as sellers, tend to gain from freedom of contract." *Id.* at 261. Judge Posner specifically noted that "[w]hen federal law limits a class of releases, as in cases under the Federal Employers' Liability Act, or the closely parallel Jones Act, or the [ADEA], * * * the common law rule requiring tender as a prerequisite to rescission may have to give way." *Id.* But he said that nothing in either Title VII or the Rehabilitation Act has the kind of limiting provision as in, for example, the ADEA.

Does the Supreme Court's decision in *Oubre* cast doubt on Judge Posner's decision in *Fleming*? The district court, in *Rangel v. El Paso Natural Gas Co.*, 996 F.Supp. 1093 (D.N.M.1998), held that it does. *See also* Cole v. Gaming Entertainment, L.L.C., 199 F.Supp.2d 208 (D. Del.2002).

10. Phillip Morris laid off a number of employees and offered each of them a severance package. The severance package required employees to release the employer from "any and all employment claims" they have had or might have in the future against Phillip Morris. The agreement also required the employees to waive their rights to demand reemployment or any benefits other than those in the severance package. John Adams, a 55–year-old black male employee, was one of the employees affected by the lay-off who accepted the severance package. Some time after Adams left Phillip Morris and while he was still receiving benefits under the agreement, Phillip Morris hired a 30–year-old white female to perform the same job Adams had performed. Suppose that the waiver of claims provision complies with the requirements of OWBPA with respect to any age discrimination claim Adams might have. Should the waiver provision be construed to bar any race or sex discrimination claim Adams may have against Phillip Morris? *See* Adams v. Philip Morris, Inc., 67 F.3d 580 (6th Cir.1995).

11. OWBPA's focus is on unsupervised waiver of rights under the ADEA. Suppose Kate Martin, an employee who is 55 years of age, employs an attorney to advise her on a severance package that has been offered by the employer. Does *Oubre* preclude her attorney from recommending terms of acceptance that do not comply with the waiver requirements of OWBPA? Are there ethical considerations that should counsel an attorney from recommending that a client accept an agreement in which the strict provisions under OWBPA are not followed?

12. For a defense of ERIPs and a criticism of the impact of OWBPA, *see* Samuel Issacharoff & Erica Worth Harris, *Is Age Discrimination Really Age Discrimination?: The ADEA's Unnatural Solution*, 72 N.Y.U.L.Rev. 780 (1997); Erica Worth, Note, *In Defense of Targeted ERIPs: Understanding the Interaction of Life–Cycle Employment and Early Retirement Incentive Plans*, 74 Tex.L.Rev. 411 (1995). *See also* Judith Droz Keyes & Douglas J. Farmer, *Settlement of Age Discrimination Claims—The Meaning and Impact of the Older Workers Benefit Protection Act*, 12 Lab.Law. 261 (1996) (suggesting that the requirements of the OWBPA are too formalistic and rigid, and recommending an approach similar to the "totality of the circumstances" test adopted by some courts prior to the OWBPA).

13. *The High Policymaker Exemption*: Section 631(c) of the ADEA, 29 U.S.C. § 631(c), permits the compulsory retirement of "any employee who has attained 65 years of age and who, for the 2 year period immediately before retirement, is employed in a bona fide executive or high policymaking position" if such individual is entitled to nonforfeitable retirement benefits which equal at least $44,000. *See* Morrissey v. Boston Five Cents Savings Bank, 54 F.3d 27 (1st Cir.1995). The test determining whether an employee occupies an "executive or high policymaking position" is one of function, and it has been held that whether the employee was highly paid is immaterial. Whittlesey v. Union Carbide, 567 F.Supp. 1320 (S.D.N.Y.1983), *aff'd*, 742 F.2d 724 (2d Cir.1984). The EEOC has defined "high policymakers" as "individuals who have little or no line authority but whose position and responsibility are such that they play a significant role in the development of corporate policy." EEOC, Guidelines on Discrimination Because of Age, 29 C.F.R. § 1625.12(e) (1994) (quoting H.R.Rep. No. 950, 95th Cong., 2d Sess. 10 (1978)).

Note: Employee Benefits and Betts

Section 623(a)(1) of the ADEA makes it unlawful to discriminate on the basis of age with respect to "compensation, terms, conditions, or privileges of employment * * *." 29 U.S.C. § 623(a)(1). And, as originally enacted, § 623(f)(2) provided that it was not unlawful under the ADEA for an employer to "observe the terms of * * * any bona fide employee benefit plan such as retirement, pension, or insurance plan" as long as the plan was not "a subterfuge to evade the purposes of" the ADEA. 29 U.S.C. § 623(f)(2). The administrative regulations interpreting § 623(f)(2)—promulgated by the Department of Labor and later affirmed by the EEOC when enforcement of the ADEA was transferred to it—take the position that age-based distinctions in benefit plans be cost-justified in order to qualify for the shelter of the exclusion. *See* 29 U.S.C. § 1625.10(a). The regulations impose the burden of persuasion on the employer to prove that the disparity in benefits is in accordance with the terms of a "bona fide employee benefit plan" and that the plan is not "a subterfuge to evade the purposes of" the ADEA. *Id.* An employer could satisfy its burden of proof with respect to disparity in benefits by showing that the lesser package of benefits to older workers was justified by age-related cost considerations. *Id.* § 1625.10(d).

The Supreme Court rejected that administrative interpretation of "subterfuge" in *United Air Lines v. McMann*, 434 U.S. 192, 98 S.Ct. 444, 54 L.Ed.2d 402 (1977), as applied to benefit plans in effect before the ADEA was passed. The Court in *McMann* defined subterfuge to mean "a scheme, plan, strategem, or artifice of evasion." *Id.* at 203, 98 S.Ct. at 450. Under this definition of subterfuge, the Court held that an employer who based its decision on a pre-ADEA plan could not have possessed the subjective intent to evade the ADEA. Less than a year after *McMann*, Congress amended the ADEA with the intent of overturning the decision. *See* Age Discrimination in Employment Act of 1978, Pub.L.No. 95–256, 92 Stat. 189 (1978).

About twelve years after *McMann*, the Supreme Court revisited the meaning of "subterfuge" in *Public Employees Retirement System v. Betts*, 492 U.S. 158, 109 S.Ct. 2854, 106 L.Ed.2d 134 (1989), and expanded the safe haven for benefit plans. In *Betts*, Ohio's employee retirement system provided substantially lower benefits for disabled employees over sixty years of age than for disabled employees younger than sixty. The plan provided two levels of compensation: "normal" retirement benefits for employees who retired because of age and who had worked at least five years, and "enhanced" retirement benefits for employees who retired because of a disability. Betts retired because of a deteriorating medical condition. But because she was then sixty-one years of age she could collect only the "normal" retirement package rather than the greater retirement package under the "enhanced" program. She then sued under the ADEA claiming discrimination because her employer refused to grant disability retirement benefits because of her age. The Supreme Court found that Betts had not been the victim of unlawful age discrimination because the ADEA did not cover employee benefits unless the plaintiff proved that the denial of benefits was a subterfuge to evade other provisions of the ADEA, e.g., trying to coerce the employee to retire. The Court interpreted "subterfuge" to mean intentional discrimination.

Congress expressed its disappointment with the *Betts* decision with the enactment of OWBPA because it thought it had overturned an earlier Supreme Court decision on the same issue in *McMann*. Under OWBPA, Congress specifically prohibited age discrimination in employment by eliminating the use of the term "subterfuge" and by endorsing the EEOC's cost-based justification defense. For a discussion of the effect of OWBPA in overturning *Betts* and reaffirming the cost-justification rule, see David A. Niles, *The Older Workers Benefit Protection Act: Painting Age–Discrimination Law with a Watery Brush*, 40 Buff.L.Rev. 869 (1992). *See generally* Mark S. Brodin, *Costs, Profits, and Equal Employment Opportunity*, 62 Notre Dame L.Rev. 318 (1987); Steven J. Kaminshine, *The Cost of Older Workers, Disparate Impact, and the Age*

Discrimination in Employment Act, 42 Fla.L.Rev. 229, 231–33 (1990). For two recent cases analyzing the availability of the safe harbor provision of 29 U.S.C. § 623(f)(2)(B)(i), compare *Erie County Retirees Ass'n v. County of Erie*, 220 F.3d 193 (3d Cir.2000), *cert. denied*, 532 U.S. 913, 121 S.Ct. 1247, 149 L.Ed.2d 153 (2001) (covering retirees) with *Gutchen v. Board of Governors of Rhode Island*, 148 F.Supp.2d 151 (D.R.I. 2001).

Note: Hostile Work Environment Claims Under the ADEA

The courts have recognized hostile work environment claims under the ADEA and have adjusted principles established in cases such as *Harris v. Forklift Systems, Inc.*, 510 U.S. 17, 114 S.Ct. 367, 126 L.Ed.2d 295 (1993), for ADEA claims. *See, e.g.*, Crawford v. Medina Gen. Hosp., 96 F.3d 830 (6th Cir.1996); Spence v. Maryland Cas. Co., 995 F.2d 1147 (2d Cir.1993); Sischo–Nownejad v. Merced Community College Dist., 934 F.2d 1104 (9th Cir.1991). Judicial recognition of hostile work environment claims in ADEA cases provides older workers substantial protection because of the possibility that employers might engage in a course of conduct designed to pressure an older worker to quit. If an older worker succumbs to such pressure and quits, he cannot obtain relief, such as back pay or reinstatement, unless he meets the often-difficult burden of proving a claim of constructive discharge. Imposing liability on employers for hostile work environment claims under the ADEA permits older workers to seek relief while they are still employed. *See generally* Julie Vigil, Comment, *Expanding the Hostile Environment Theory to Cover Age Discrimination: How Far Is Too Far?*, 23 Pepp.L.Rev. 565 (1996).

Chapter 13

DISCRIMINATION BECAUSE
OF DISABILITY

A. INTRODUCTION

The elimination of discrimination against individuals with disabilities in transportation, housing, public services, public accommodations, and employment is now a significant component of the national commitment to equality. The two most important federal statutes that prohibit discrimination because of disabilities are the Americans with Disabilities Act of 1990 (ADA), and the Rehabilitation Act of 1973, 29 U.S.C. §§ 701–797(b). Of these two statutes, the ADA is the most comprehensive. The ADA, which President Bush signed into law on July 26, 1990, provides comprehensive civil rights protection to individuals with disabilities, which is similar to the protection against discrimination because of race, color, sex, national origin, and religion that is provided to individuals under the Civil Rights Act of 1964. The ADA is divided into five titles. Title I, which is the subject of this chapter, covers discrimination in employment. Codified at ADA §§ 101–108, 42 U.S.C. §§ 12111–12118, Title I covers essentially the same employers, employment agencies, and labor organizations that Title VII covers, and it incorporates Title VII's administrative exhaustion requirements (discussed in Chapter 2) and remedies (discussed in Chapter 16). ADA § 107, 42 U.S.C. § 12117. Title II extends the prohibition against discrimination on the basis of disabilities to all programs, activities, and services of state and local governments or agencies, regardless of whether these entities receive federal financial assistance. Title II also covers public transportation. Title III prohibits discrimination against individuals with disabilities by privately run places of public accommodation and by public transportation services provided by private entities. Title IV covers telecommunications, and Title V contains several miscellaneous provisions. *See generally* BNA, The Americans with Disabilities Act: A Practical and Legal Guide to Impact, Enforcement and Compliance 63–76 (1990) (a section-by-section analysis of the ADA).

Because it so broadly prohibits discrimination in employment, public services, transportation, and public accommodations, the ADA has been heralded as the twentieth century Emancipation Proclamation and the Bill of Rights for an estimated forty-three million individuals with disabilities. *See, e.g.,* H.R.Rep.No. 101–485, pt.3, at 42 (1990), *reprinted in* 1990 U.S.C.C.A.N. 303, 464–66; 135 Cong.Rec. S10, 789 (daily ed. Sept.7, 1989) (statement of Sen. Kennedy). One commentator has stated that

> [t]he ADA is the most comprehensive piece of disability civil rights legislation ever enacted, and the most important piece of civil rights legislation since the 1964 Civil Rights Act. This legislation will transform the landscape of American society and will have a profound effect on what it means to be disabled.

* * *

From a civil rights perspective, a profound shift in disability public policy occurred in the 1970s. The passage of the first piece of cross-disability civil rights legislation, section 504 of the Rehabilitation Act of 1973, challenged traditional ideas about disability. This legislation, in turn, gave rise to a highly visible and active disability rights movement.

Section 504 of the Rehabilitation Act of 1973 transformed disability public policy in several ways. First, it adopted a cross-disability approach, recognizing that people with different disabilities suffered similar problems in employment, education, and access to society. Second, section 504 used the term "discrimination" for the first time to describe the segregation and exclusion of persons with disabilities. This terminology changed the focus away from the limitations imposed by a disability, and turned it toward the limitations posed by society through attitudinal and architectural barriers. Third, section 504 broadly defined disability to protect those with a current disability, those with a history of disability, or those perceived to have a disability. Finally, and most important, section 504 evidenced Congress' recognition that disability discrimination is a federal civil rights issue. In modeling section 504 on earlier race and sex discrimination statutes, Congress placed disability discrimination firmly within the federal civil rights arena.

Arlene Mayerson, *The Americans with Disabilities Act—An Historic Overview*, 7 Lab.Law. 1, 1–2 (1991). *See generally* Joseph P. Shapiro, No Pity: People with Disabilities Forging a New Civil Rights Movement (1993) (providing a detailed history of the disability rights movement); Bureau of Nat'l Affairs, The Americans with Disabilities Act: A Practical and Legal Guide to Impact, Enforcement and Compliance (1990) (providing a social, legal, and legislative history of the ADA). Beginning in the 1970s, Congress rejected the policy of custodialism for individuals with disabilities, opting instead for a policy of nondiscrimination. *See* Timothy M. Cook, *The Americans with Disabilities Act: The Move to Integration*, 64 Temp.L.Rev. 393 (1991).

Congress's factual findings in the ADA emphasize the need for prohibiting discrimination on the basis of disabilities in American society. For example, Congress found that there were approximately forty-three million Americans with "one or more physical or mental disabilities" and that that number would continue to grow as the population ages. ADA § 2(a)(1), 42 U.S.C. § 12101(a)(1). Congress found also that

> individuals with disabilities are a discrete and insular minority who have been faced with restrictions and limitations, subjected to a history of purposeful unequal treatment, and relegated to a position of political powerlessness in our society, based on characteristics that are beyond the control of such individuals and resulting from stereotypic assumptions not truly indicative of the individual ability of such individuals to participate in, and contribute to, society[.]

Id. § 2(a)(7), 42 U.S.C. § 12101(a)(7). The characterization of individuals with disabilities as a "discrete and insular minority" originates in the famous footnote 4 of *United States v. Carolene Products*, 304 U.S. 144, 152–53 n.4, 58 S.Ct. 778, 783–84 n.4, 82 L.Ed. 1234 (1938): the Supreme Court used the phrase to describe minorities who deserve constitutional protection from discriminatory conduct of governmental actors. *See* Michael L. Perlin, Mental Disability Law: Civil and Criminal § 1.03, at 6 (1989). Congress also enacted the ADA to ensure that the federal government plays a central role in enforcing the "national mandate" of the Act. *Id.* § 2(b)(1), (3), 42 U.S.C. § 12101(b)(1), (3).

Claims arising under the ADA and the Rehabilitation Act have raised and continue to raise a host of difficult and complex issues that are, in many respects, unique to disability jurisprudence. Disability law is one of the most rapidly developing fields in employment discrimination law. Because the case law and scholarly commentary on disability discrimination is so voluminous, only a few selected issues can be treated in a broad-based course on employment discrimination law. Three major themes have emerged in our study of discrimination law: the model or framework for proving discrimination; membership in each protected class; and justification for employer decisions or actions that exclude those members. These themes, as well as a few other selected issues are covered in this chapter. The remainder of this section introduces the statutes covering disability discrimination. Section B of this chapter, covers the definition of "discrimination" under the ADA. Section C explores the definition of disability. Section D focuses on the issues of qualifications, the direct threat defense, and undue hardship. Section E deals briefly with medical inquiries, medical examinations, and medical benefits. As you read through the materials in this chapter, consider whether the ADA has met its initial promise as a transformative piece of civil rights legislation.

The Americans with Disabilities Act of 1990. The ADA broadly prohibits discrimination in employment on the basis of disability by providing that "[n]o covered entity shall discriminate against a qualified individual with a disability because of the disability of such individual in regard to job application procedures, the hiring, advancement, or discharge of employees, employee compensation, job training, and other terms, conditions, and privileges of employment." ADA § 102(a), 42 U.S.C. § 12112(a). In addition to prohibiting discrimination as defined by disparate treatment or disparate impact, the ADA imposes upon employers the affirmative obligation to "make reasonable accommodations to the known physical or mental limitations of a qualified individual" unless doing so "would impose an undue hardship on the operation of the business of the covered entity." ADA § 102(5)(A), 42 U.S.C. § 12112(5)(A). The duty imposed under the ADA to provide reasonable accommodations to qualified individuals with disabilities is the same affirmative obligation that is imposed upon entities that are covered by the Rehabilitation Act. In order to bring an ADA suit, a plaintiff must prove that they are a qualified individual with a disability. Therefore, most suits begin with an examination of whether a plaintiff has a disability. *Id.* § 101(8), 42 U.S.C.§ 12111(8). A "qualified individual with a disability" is defined as "an individual with a disability who, with or without reasonable accommodation, can perform the essential functions of the employment position that such individual holds or desires." Thus, the concept of reasonable accommodation occurs in both the determination of discrimination and the determination of qualifications.

The Rehabilitation Act of 1973. Enacted seventeen years before the ADA, the Rehabilitation Act of 1973 was designed to "promote and expand employment opportunities in the public and private sectors for [individuals with disabilities] and place such individuals in employment." 29 U.S.C. § 701(8). *See* Consolidated Rail Corp. v. Darrone, 465 U.S. 624, 626, 104 S.Ct. 1248, 1250, 79 L.Ed.2d 568 (1984). *See generally* Bureau of Nat'l Affairs, The Americans with Disabilities Act: A Practical and Legal Guide to Impact, Enforcement and Compliance 10–23 (1990). Section 501 of the Rehabilitation Act covers all departments and agencies of the federal government, including the United States Postal Service, and imposes upon them the obligation to develop and implement affirmative action plans for the hiring, placement, and advancement of individuals with disabilities. 29 U.S.C. § 791. Section 503 also covers entities that contract with federal departments or agencies to provide goods and services of more than $2,500. Section 503, like § 501, requires these federal contractors to take affirmative action to employ and promote individuals with disabilities. 29 U.S.C. § 793. Both §§ 501 and 503 have been interpreted to prohibit discrimination as well. *See* Gardner v. Morris, 752 F.2d 1271 (8th Cir.1985) (§ 501); Moon v. Secretary, U.S. Dep't of Labor, 747 F.2d 599 (11th Cir.1984) (§ 503), *cert. denied*, 471 U.S. 1055, 105 S.Ct. 2117, 85 L.Ed.2d 481 (1985). Section 504 covers all entities that receive federal funds, as well as all the programs and activities conducted by federal agencies, and it, too, prohibits discrimination because of disabilities. 29 U.S.C. § 794.

As originally enacted in 1973, the Rehabilitation Act used the term "handicap"; however, Congress amended the Rehabilitation Act in 1992 to substitute the term "disability" for "handicap." *See* Pub.L.No. 102–

569, 102(p) (32), 106 Stat. 4344, 4360 (1992). The change in terminology was intended to reflect a new sensitivity to the impact of descriptive language. The phrase "individual with a disability" was formulated to "convey the message that people are not disabled, but are merely encumbered with disabilities." Brent Edward Kidwell, *The Americans with Disabilities Act of 1990: Overview and Analysis*, 26 Ind.L.Rev. 707, 708 n.5 (1993); *see* H.R.Rep.No. 101–484(II), 101st Cong., 2d Sess. 1, 50–53, *reprinted in* 1990 U.S.C.C.A.N. 303, 332–35. Section 504 of the Rehabilitation Act, 29 U.S.C. § 794(a), provides that "[n]o otherwise qualified individual with a disability in the United States * * * shall, solely by reason of her or his disability, be excluded from the participation in, be denied the benefits of, or be subjected to discrimination under any program or activity receiving federal financial assistance * * *."

Relationship Between the ADA and Rehabilitation Act. The primary focus of this chapter is on Title I of the ADA because it is by far the most comprehensive federal legislation providing protection in the private sector to individuals with disabilities. The materials in this chapter, however, include developments under the Rehabilitation Act because the statutory language and legislative history of both the ADA and the 1992 amendments to the Rehabilitation Act clearly indicate that the legal standards for a finding of unlawful disability discrimination are the same under both statutes. For example, § 504 of the Rehabilitation Act, as amended in 1992, provides that "[t]he standards used to determine whether this section has been violated in a complaint alleging employment discrimination under this section shall be the standards applied under title I of the Americans with Disabilities Act of 1990, * * * as such sections relate to employment." 29 U.S.C. § 794(d). *See also* Francis v. City of Meriden, 129 F.3d 281, 284 n.4 (2d Cir.1997) ("[b]ecause the ADA and the [Rehabilitation Act] are very similar, we look to caselaw interpreting one statute to assist us in interpreting the other.").

Congress directed the EEOC, which has administrative enforcement responsibility over ADA claims, to issue regulations to carry out the mandate of the ADA. ADA § 106, 42 U.S.C. § 12116. In response, the EEOC issued regulations, 29 C.F.R. § 1630, interpretive directives, and guidelines. For a discussion of the EEOC regulations on the ADA, see Elliot H. Shaller & Dean A. Rosen, *A Guide to the EEOC's Final Regulations on the Americans with Disabilities Act*, 17 Empl.Rel.L.J. 405 (1991–1992). The Department of Health and Human Services (HHS) has also promulgated administrative regulations to enforce § 504 of the Rehabilitation Act. 45 C.F.R. § 84.3. Because HHS's regulations were drafted with congressional oversight and approval, the Supreme Court has stated that they are "an important source of guidance on the meaning of the [Rehabilitation Act]." School Bd. of Nassau County v. Arline, 480 U.S. 273, 279, 107 S.Ct. 1123, 1127, 94 L.Ed.2d 307 (1987) (quoting Alexander v. Choate, 469 U.S. 287, 304 n.24, 105 S.Ct. 712, 722 n.24, 83 L.Ed.2d 661 (1985)). Courts utilize both sets of regulations in implementing disability policy.

Notes

1. *Covered Entities*: The ADA uses the phrase "covered entity" to define who is subject to Title I. ADA § 101(2), 42 U.S.C. § 12111(2), defines "covered entity" to mean "an employer, employment agency, labor organization, or joint labor-management committee." "Employer" is further defined in a way that parallels the statutory definition of "employer" under Title VII. *Compare id.* § 102(5)(A), 42 U.S.C. § 12111(5)(A) *with* Title VII, § 701(b), 42 U.S.C. § 2000e–1(b). See Chapter 2. As of July 26, 1994, private employers with fifteen or more employees became subject to the ADA. *Id.*

2. *Federal Employers*: The federal government is specifically excluded from coverage under the ADA. ADA § 101(5)(B), 42 U.S.C. § 12111(5)(B). Congress deemed it unnecessary to extend coverage of the ADA to the federal government in view of the fact that the Rehabilitation Act of 1973 currently protects federal employees from discrimination because of disabilities.

3. *State and Municipal Employers*: In *Board of Trustees of University of Alabama v. Garrett*, 531 U.S. 356, 121 S.Ct. 955, 148 L.Ed.2d 866 (2001), the Supreme Court held that the Eleventh Amendment bars private ADA actions brought against unconsenting states. A brief discussion of *Garrett* is found in the Note, Eleventh Amendment Bar Against Suing State Employers, in Chapter 2.

4. Individuals filing employment discrimination claims under Title I of the ADA, like individuals filing claims under Title VII of the Civil Rights Act of 1964, must first exhaust administrative remedies before the EEOC. See Chapter 2. In fact the ADA specifically provides that the "powers, remedies, and procedures" in Title VII are equally applicable in ADA claims. ADA § 107(a), 42 U.S.C. § 12117(a).

5. There is some dispute over whether public employees may rely upon Title II of the ADA to seek relief from discrimination in employment. The definition of "a qualified individual with a disability" in Title II is broader than the definition under Title I. Title II protects individuals who "with or without reasonable modifications to rules, policies, the removal of architectural, communication, or transportation barriers, or the provisions of auxiliary aids and services, meet the essential eligibility requirements for the receipt of services or the participation in programs or activities provided by a public entity." 42 U.S.C. § 12121(2). Section 802 of the ADA (Title II), 42 U.S.C. § 12132, provides, in pertinent part, that "no qualified individual with a disability shall, by reason of such disability, be excluded from participation in or be denied the benefits of the services, programs, or activities of a public entity, or be subjected to discrimination by any such entity."

"Public entity" is defined to include any state or local government and any department, agency, special purpose district, or other instrumentality of a state or local government. ADA § 801A, 42 U.S.C. § 12131(A)-(B). In *Bledsoe v. Palm Beach County Soil & Water Conservation District*, 133 F.3d 816 (11th Cir.1998), *cert. denied* 525 U.S. 826, 119 S.Ct. 72, 142 L.Ed.2d 57 (1998) the Eleventh Circuit discussed the split of authority on the issue and held that public employees may bring disability-based employment discrimination claims against public entitles as defined in Title II. In *Bledsoe*, the court broadly construed the statutory phrases "services, programs and activities" and "subjected to discrimination by any such entity." In support of its statutory interpretation, the court relied upon the legislative history of the ADA and the Department of Justice regulations promulgated to enforce Title II. The effect of the *Bledsoe* decision is that a public employee who has an ADA employment discrimination claim against a state or local government employer can avoid the administrative exhaustion requirements of Title I and go directly to court to seek relief under Title II. *See generally* Wendy Wilkinson, *Judicially Crafted Barriers to Bringing Suit Under the Americans with Disabilities Act*, 38 S.Tex.L.Rev. 907, 931–33 (1997).

B. THE MEANING OF "DISCRIMINATION" UNDER THE ADA

The definition of discrimination under the ADA includes both the disparate impact and disparate treatment theories of discrimination. *See* ADA § 102(b)(1), (b)(6), (b)(7), 42 U.S.C. § 12112(b)(1), (b)(6), (b)(7). Moreover, the ADA definition of disability discrimination places an affirmative obligation on covered entities to make reasonable accommodations that will allow qualified individuals with disabilities to perform the essential functions of the job that they hold or desire. *Id.* § 102(b)(5)(A), 42 U.S.C. § 12112(5)(A).

Professor Robert Burgdorf, who drafted the first ADA bill, which was introduced in Congress in 1988, has written that

> [d]isability nondiscrimination laws, such as the Americans with Disabilities Act of 1990 (ADA), and the disability rights movement which spawned them have, at their core, a central premise that is both simple and profound. That premise is that people denominated as "disabled" are just people, not different in any critical way from other people. Paradoxically, commentators, enforcement agencies and the courts, which manifest good intentions, have frequently interpreted and applied these laws in ways that reinforce a diametrically opposite premise—that people with disabilities are significantly different, special and need exceptional status and protection. One is reminded of Justice Brandeis's admonition that citizens should be most on guard "when Government's purposes are beneficent" and that the greatest dangers arise from "encroachment by [people] of zeal, well-meaning but without understanding."

Robert L. Burgdorf, Jr., *"Substantially Limited" Protection from Disability Discrimination: The Special Treatment Model and Misconstructions of the Definition of Disability*, 42 Vill.L.Rev. 409, 411 (1997). As you read the cases and materials in this chapter, evaluate them in light of Professor Burgdorf's critique, as well as the continuing debate about the aims of employment discrimination laws. What should be the purpose of the laws prohibiting employment discrimination because of disability? Equal treatment? Equal opportunity? Special treatment? Consider also that Congress stated in the ADA's "Findings and Purpose" that "the Nation's proper goals regarding individuals with disabilities are to assure equality of opportunity, full participation, independent living, and economic self-sufficiency for such individuals * * *." ADA § 2(a)(8), 42 U.S.C. § 12101(a)(8). Does the definition of discrimination in the ADA suggest that Congress intended to do more than simply eradicate discrimination against qualified individuals with disabilities? If so, what might explain the need to go beyond just simply eradicating discrimination on the basis of disability?

RAYTHEON v. HERNANDEZ

Supreme Court of the United States, 2003.
___ U.S. ___, 124 S.Ct. 513, 157 L.Ed.2d 357.

THOMAS, J., delivered the opinion of the Court, in which all other Members joined, except SOUTER, J., who took no part in the decision of the case, and BREYER, J., who took no part in the consideration or decision of the case.

The Americans with Disabilities Act of 1990 (ADA) makes it unlawful for an employer, with respect to hiring, to "discriminate against a qualified individual with a disability because of the disability of such individual." § 12112(a). * * * The United States Court of Appeals for the Ninth Circuit held that an employer's unwritten policy not to rehire employees who left the company for violating personal conduct rules contravenes the ADA, at least as applied to employees who were lawfully forced to resign for illegal drug use but have since been rehabilitated. Because the Ninth Circuit improperly applied a disparate-impact analysis in a disparate-treatment case in order to reach this holding, we vacate its judgment and remand the case for further proceedings consistent with this opinion. * * *

I

Respondent, Joel Hernandez, worked for Hughes Missile Systems for 25 years. On July 11, 1991, respondent's appearance and behavior at work suggested that he might be under the influence of drugs or alcohol. Pursuant to company policy, respondent took a drug test, which came back positive for cocaine. Respondent subsequently admitted that he had been up late drinking beer and using cocaine the night before the test. Because respondent's behavior violated petitioner's workplace conduct rules, respondent was forced to resign. Respondent's "Employee Separation Summary" indicated as the reason for separation: "discharge for personal conduct (quit in lieu of discharge)."

More than two years later, on January 24, 1994, respondent applied to be rehired by petitioner. Respondent stated on his application that he had previously been employed by petitioner. He also attached two reference letters to the application, one from his pastor, stating that respondent was a "faithful and active member" of the church, and the other from an Alcoholics Anonymous counselor, stating that respondent attends Alcoholics Anonymous meetings regularly and is in recovery.

Joanne Bockmiller, an employee in the company's Labor Relations Department, reviewed respondent's application. Bockmiller testified in her deposition that since respondent's application disclosed his prior employment with the company, she pulled his personnel file and reviewed his employee separation summary. She then rejected respondent's application. Bockmiller insisted that the company had a policy against rehiring employees who were terminated for workplace misconduct. Thus, when she reviewed the employment separation summary and found that respondent had been discharged for violating workplace conduct rules, she rejected respondent's application. She testified, in particular, that she did not know that respondent was a former drug addict when she made the employment decision and did not see anything that would constitute a "record of" addiction.

Respondent subsequently filed a charge with the Equal Employment Opportunity Commission (EEOC). Respondent's charge of discrimination indicated that petitioner did not give him a reason for his nonselection, but that respondent believed he had been discriminated against in violation of the ADA.

Petitioner responded to the charge by submitting a letter to the EEOC, in which George M. Medina, Sr., Manager of Diversity Development, wrote:

> The ADA specifically exempts from protection individuals currently engaging in the illegal use of drugs when the covered entity acts on the basis of that use. Contrary to Complainant's unfounded allegation, his non-selection for rehire is not based on any legitimate disability. Rather, Complainant's application was rejected based on his demonstrated drug use while previously employed and the complete lack of evidence indicating successful drug rehabilitation.
>
> The Company maintains it's [sic] right to deny re-employment to employees terminated for violation of Company rules and regulations. * * * Complainant has provided no evidence to alter the Company's position that Complainant's conduct while employed by [petitioner] makes him ineligible for rehire.

This response, together with evidence that the letters submitted with respondent's employment application may have alerted Bockmiller to the reason for respondent's prior termination, led the EEOC to conclude that petitioner may have "rejected [respondent's] application based on his record of past alcohol and drug use." The EEOC thus found that there was "reasonable cause to believe that [respondent] was denied hire to the position of Product Test Specialist because of his disability." The EEOC issued a right-to-sue letter, and respondent subsequently filed this action alleging a violation of the ADA.

Respondent proceeded through discovery on the theory that the company rejected his application because of his record of drug addiction and/or because he was regarded as being a drug addict. See 42 U.S.C. § § 12102(2)(B)-(C). * * * In response to petitioner's motion for summary judgment, respondent for the first time argued in the alternative that if the company really did apply a neutral no-rehire policy in his case, petitioner still violated the ADA because such a policy has a disparate impact. The District Court granted petitioner's motion for summary judgment with respect to respondent's disparate-treatment claim. However, the District Court refused to consider respondent's disparate-impact claim because respondent had failed to plead or raise the theory in a timely manner.

The Court of Appeals agreed with the District Court that respondent had failed timely to raise his disparate-impact claim. *Hernandez v. Hughes Missile Systems Co.,* 298 F.3d 1030, 1037, n.20 (9th Cir.2002). In addressing respondent's disparate-treatment claim, the Court of Appeals proceeded under the familiar burden-shifting approach first adopted by this Court in *McDonnell Douglas Corp. v. Green,* 411 U.S. 792, 93 S.Ct. 1817, 36 L.Ed.2d 668 (1973).[3] First, the Ninth Circuit found that with respect to respondent's prima facie case of discrimination, there were genuine issues of material fact regarding whether respondent was qualified for the position for which he sought to be rehired, and whether the reason for petitioner's refusal to rehire him was his past record of drug addiction.[4] The Court of Appeals thus held that with respect to respondent's prima facie case of discrimination, respondent had proffered sufficient evidence to preclude a grant of summary judgment. Because petitioner does not challenge this aspect of the Ninth Circuit's decision, we do not address it here.

The Court of Appeals then moved to the next step of *McDonnell Douglas,* where the burden shifts to the defendant to provide a legitimate, nondiscriminatory reason for its employment action. Here, petitioner contends that Bockmiller applied the neutral policy against rehiring employees previously terminated for violating workplace conduct rules and that this neutral company policy constituted a legitimate and

3. The Court in *McDonnell Douglas* set forth a burden-shifting scheme for discriminatory-treatment cases. Under *McDonnell Douglas,* a plaintiff must first establish a prima facie case of discrimination. The burden then shifts to the employer to articulate a legitimate, nondiscriminatory reason for its employment action. If the employer meets this burden, the presumption of intentional discrimination disappears, but the plaintiff can still prove disparate treatment by, for instance, offering evidence demonstrating that the employer's explanation is pretextual. See *Reeves v. Sanderson Plumbing Products, Inc.,* 530 U.S. 133, 143, 120 S.Ct. 2097, 147 L.Ed.2d 105 (2000). The Courts of Appeals have consistently utilized this burden-shifting approach when reviewing motions for summary judgment in disparate-treatment cases. See, *e.g., Pugh v. Attica,* 259 F.3d 619, 626 (7th Cir.2001)

(applying burden-shifting approach to an ADA disparate-treatment claim).

4. The Court of Appeals noted that "it is possible that a drug *user* may not be 'disabled' under the ADA if his drug use does not rise to the level of an addiction which substantially limits one or more of his major life activities." 298 F.3d, at 1033–1034, n.9. The parties do not dispute that respondent was "disabled" at the time he quit in lieu of discharge and thus a record of the disability exists. We therefore need not decide in this case whether respondent's employment record constitutes a "record of addiction," which triggers the protections of the ADA. The parties are also not disputing in this Court whether respondent was qualified for the position for which he applied.

nondiscriminatory reason for its decision not to rehire respondent. The Court of Appeals, although admitting that petitioner's no-rehire rule was lawful on its face, held the policy to be unlawful "as applied to former drug addicts whose only work-related offense was testing positive because of their addiction." 298 F.3d, at 1036. The Court of Appeals concluded that petitioner's application of a neutral no-rehire policy was not a legitimate, nondiscriminatory reason for rejecting respondent's application:

> Maintaining a blanket policy against rehire of *all* former employees who violated company policy not only screens out persons with a record of addiction who have been successfully rehabilitated, but may well result, as [petitioner] contends it did here, in the staff member who makes the employment decision remaining unaware of the "disability" and thus of the fact that she is committing an unlawful act * * * Additionally, we hold that a policy that serves to bar the reemployment of a drug addict despite his successful rehabilitation violates the ADA.

In other words, while ostensibly evaluating whether petitioner had proffered a legitimate, nondiscriminatory reason for failing to rehire respondent sufficient to rebut respondent's prima facie showing of disparate treatment, the Court of Appeals held that a neutral no-rehire policy could never suffice in a case where the employee was terminated for illegal drug use, because such a policy has a disparate impact on recovering drug addicts. In so holding, the Court of Appeals erred by conflating the analytical framework for disparate-impact and disparate-treatment claims. Had the Court of Appeals correctly applied the disparate-treatment framework, it would have been obliged to conclude that a neutral no-rehire policy is, by definition, a legitimate, nondiscriminatory reason under the ADA. * * * And thus the only remaining question would be whether respondent could produce sufficient evidence from which a jury could conclude that "petitioner's stated reason for respondent's rejection was in fact pretext." *McDonnell Douglas, supra,* at 804.

II

This Court has consistently recognized a distinction between claims of discrimination based on disparate treatment and claims of discrimination based on disparate impact. The Court has said that " '[d]isparate treatment' * * * is the most easily understood type of discrimination. The employer simply treats some people less favorably than others because of their race, color, religion, sex, or [other protected characteristic]." *Teamsters v. United States,* 431 U.S. 324, 335, n.15, 97 S.Ct. 1843, 52 L.Ed.2d 396 (1977). See also *Hazen Paper Co. v. Biggins,* 507 U.S. 604, 609, 113 S.Ct. 1701, 123 L.Ed.2d 338 (1993) (discussing disparate-treatment claims in the context of the Age Discrimination in Employment Act of 1967). Liability in a disparate-treatment case "depends on whether the protected trait * * * actually motivated the employer's decision." *Id.,* at 610. By contrast, disparate-impact claims "involve employment practices that are facially neutral in their treatment of different groups but that in fact fall more harshly on one group than another and cannot be justified by business necessity." *Teamsters, supra,* at 335–336, n.15. Under a disparate-impact theory of discrimination, "a facially neutral employment practice may be deemed [illegally discriminatory] without evidence of the employer's subjective intent to discriminate that is required in a 'disparate-treatment' case." *Wards Cove Packing Co. v. Atonio,* 490 U.S. 642, 645–646, 109 S.Ct. 2115, 104 L.Ed.2d 733 (1989), superseded by statute on other grounds, Civil Rights Act of 1991, § 105, 105 Stat. 1074–1075, 42 U.S.C. § 2000e–2(k) (1994 ed.).

Both disparate-treatment and disparate-impact claims are cognizable under the ADA. See 42 U.S.C. § 12112(b) (defining "discriminate" to include "utilizing standards, criteria, or methods of administration * * * that have the effect of discrimination on the basis of disability" and "using qualification standards, employment tests or other selection criteria that screen out or tend to screen out an individual with a disability"). Because "the factual issues, and therefore the character of the evidence presented, differ when the plaintiff claims that a facially neutral employment policy has a discriminatory impact on protected classes," *Texas Dept. of Community Affairs v. Burdine,* 450 U.S. 248, 252, n.5, 101 S.Ct. 1089, 67 L.Ed.2d 207 (1981), courts must be careful to distinguish between these theories. Here, respondent did not timely pursue a disparate-impact claim. Rather, the District Court concluded, and the Court of Appeals agreed, that respondent's case was limited to a disparate-treatment theory, that the company refused to rehire respondent because it regarded respondent as being disabled and/or because of respondent's record of a disability.

Petitioner's proffer of its neutral no-rehire policy plainly satisfied its obligation under *McDonnell Douglas* to provide a legitimate, nondiscriminatory reason for refusing to rehire respondent. Thus, the only relevant question before the Court of Appeals, after petitioner presented a neutral explanation for its decision not to rehire respondent, was whether there was sufficient evidence from which a jury could conclude that petitioner did make its employment decision based on respondent's status as disabled despite petitioner's proffered explanation. Instead, the Court of Appeals concluded that, as a matter of law, a neutral no-rehire policy was not a legitimate, nondiscriminatory reason sufficient to defeat a prima facie case of discrimination.[6] The Court of Appeals did not even attempt, in the remainder of its opinion, to treat this claim as one involving only disparate treatment. Instead, the Court of Appeals observed that petitioner's policy "screens out persons with a record of addiction," and further noted that the company had not raised a busi-

---

6. The Court of Appeals characterized respondent's workplace misconduct as merely "testing positive because of [his] addiction." 298 F.3d, at 1036. To the extent that the court suggested that, because respondent's workplace misconduct is related to his disability, petitioner's refusal to re- hire respondent on account of that workplace misconduct violated the ADA, we point out that we have rejected a similar argument in the context of the Age Discrimination in Employment Act. See *Hazen Paper Co. v. Biggins,* 507 U.S. 604, 611, 113 S.Ct. 1701, 123 L.Ed.2d 338 (1993).

ness necessity defense, 298 F.3d, at 1036–1037, and n.19, factors that pertain to disparate-impact claims but not disparate-treatment claims. See, *e.g., Grano v. Department of Development of Columbus,* 637 F.2d 1073, 1081 (6th Cir.1980) ("In a disparate impact situation * * * the issue is whether a neutral selection device * * * screens out disproportionate numbers of [the protected class]"). * * * By improperly focusing on these factors, the Court of Appeals ignored the fact that petitioner's no-rehire policy is a quintessential legitimate, nondiscriminatory reason for refusing to rehire an employee who was terminated for violating workplace conduct rules. If petitioner did indeed apply a neutral, generally applicable no-rehire policy in rejecting respondent's application, petitioner's decision not to rehire respondent can, in no way, be said to have been motivated by respondent's disability.

The Court of Appeals rejected petitioner's legitimate, nondiscriminatory reason for refusing to rehire respondent because it "serves to bar the re-employment of a drug addict despite his successful rehabilitation." 298 F.3d, at 1036–1037. We hold that such an analysis is inapplicable to a disparate-treatment claim. Once respondent had made a prima facie showing of discrimination, the next question for the Court of Appeals was whether petitioner offered a legitimate, nondiscriminatory reason for its actions so as to demonstrate that its actions were not motivated by respondent's disability. To the extent that the Court of Appeals strayed from this task by considering not only discriminatory intent but also discriminatory impact, we vacate its judgment and remand the case for further proceedings consistent with this opinion.

* * *

US AIRWAYS, INC. v. BARNETT

Supreme Court of the United States, 2002.
535 U.S. 391, 122 S.Ct. 1516, 152 L.Ed.2d 589.

JUSTICE BREYER delivered the opinion of the Court.

The Americans with Disabilities Act of 1990 (ADA or Act) prohibits an employer from discriminating against an "individual with a disability" who, with "reasonable accommodation," can perform the essential functions of the job. §§ 12112(a) and (b) (1994 ed.). This case, arising in the context of summary judgment, asks us how the Act resolves a potential conflict between: (1) the interests of a disabled worker who seeks assignment to a particular position as a "reasonable accommodation," and (2) the interests of other workers with superior rights to bid for the job under an employer's seniority system. In such a case, does the accommodation demand trump the seniority system?

In our view, the seniority system will prevail in the run of cases. As we interpret the statute, to show that a requested accommodation conflicts with the rules of a seniority system is ordinarily to show that the accommodation is not "reasonable." Hence such a showing will entitle an employer/defendant to summary judgment on the question—

unless there is more. The plaintiff remains free to present evidence of special circumstances that make "reasonable" a seniority rule exception in the particular case. And such a showing will defeat the employer's demand for summary judgment. Fed. Rule Civ. Proc. 56(e).

I

In 1990, Robert Barnett, the plaintiff and respondent here, injured his back while working in a cargo-handling position at petitioner US Airways, Inc. He invoked seniority rights and transferred to a less physically demanding mailroom position. Under US Airways' seniority system, that position, like others, periodically became open to seniority-based employee bidding. In 1992, Barnett learned that at least two employees senior to him intended to bid for the mailroom job. He asked US Airways to accommodate his disability-imposed limitations by making an exception that would allow him to remain in the mailroom. After permitting Barnett to continue his mailroom work for five months while it considered the matter, US Airways eventually decided not to make an exception. And Barnett lost his job.

Barnett then brought this ADA suit claiming, among other things, that he was an "individual with a disability" capable of performing the essential functions of the mailroom job, that the mailroom job amounted to a "reasonable accommodation" of his disability, and that US Airways, in refusing to assign him the job, unlawfully discriminated against him. US Airways moved for summary judgment. It supported its motion with appropriate affidavits contending that its "well-established" seniority system granted other employees the right to obtain the mailroom position.

The District Court found that the undisputed facts about seniority warranted summary judgment in US Airways' favor. * * * The court said:

> * * * it seems clear that the U.S. Air employees were justified in relying upon the [seniority] policy. As such, any significant alteration of that policy would result in undue hardship to both the company and its non-disabled employees.

An en banc panel of the United States Court of Appeals for the Ninth Circuit reversed. It said that the presence of a seniority system is merely "a factor in the undue hardship analysis." And it held that "[a] case-by-case fact intensive analysis is required to determine whether any particular reassignment would constitute an undue hardship to the employer." US Airways petitioned for certiorari, asking us to decide whether "the [ADA] requires an employer to reassign a disabled employee to a position as a 'reasonable accommodation' even though another employee is entitled to hold the position under the employer's bona fide and established seniority system." * * *

II

In answering the question presented, we must consider the following statutory provisions. First, the ADA says that an employer may not "discriminate against a qualified individual with a disability." 42 U.S.C. § 12112(a). Second, the ADA says that a "qualified" individual includes "an individual with a disability who, *with* or without *reasonable accommodation*, can perform the essential functions of" the relevant "employment position." § 12111(8) (emphasis added). Third, the ADA says that "discrimination" includes an employer's "*not making reasonable accommodations* to the known physical or mental limitations of an otherwise qualified * * * employee, *unless* [the employer] can demonstrate that the accommodation would impose an *undue hardship* on the operation of [its] business." § 12112(b)(5)(A) (emphasis added). Fourth, the ADA says that the term " 'reasonable accommodation' may include * * * reassignment to a vacant position." § 12111(9)(B). The parties interpret this statutory language as applied to seniority systems in radically different ways. In U.S. Airways' view, the fact that an accommodation would violate the rules of a seniority system always shows that the accommodation is not a "reasonable" one. In Barnett's polar opposite view, a seniority system violation never shows that an accommodation sought is not a "reasonable" one. Barnett concedes that a violation of seniority rules might help to show that the accommodation will work "undue" employer "hardship," but that is a matter for an employer to demonstrate case by case. We shall initially consider the parties' main legal arguments in support of these conflicting positions.

A

US Airways' claim that a seniority system virtually always trumps a conflicting accommodation demand rests primarily upon its view of how the Act treats workplace "preferences." Insofar as a requested accommodation violates a disability-neutral workplace rule, such as a seniority rule, it grants the employee with a disability treatment that other workers could not receive. Yet the Act, U.S. Airways says, seeks only "equal" treatment for those with disabilities. See, *e.g.,* 42 U.S.C. § 12101(a)(9). It does not, it contends, require an employer to grant preferential treatment. Cf. H.R.Rep. No. 101–485, pt. 2, p. 66 (1990), U.S.Code Cong. & Admin.News 1990, pp. 303, 348–349; S.Rep. No. 101–116, pp. 26–27 (1989) (employer has no "obligation to prefer *applicants* with disabilities over other *applicants*" (emphasis added)). Hence it does not require the employer to grant a request that, in violating a disability-neutral rule, would provide a preference.

While linguistically logical, this argument fails to recognize what the Act specifies, namely, that preferences will sometimes prove necessary to achieve the Act's basic equal opportunity goal. The Act requires preferences in the form of "reasonable accommodations" that are needed for those with disabilities to obtain the *same* workplace opportunities that those without disabilities automatically enjoy. By definition any special "accommodation" requires the employer to treat an employee with a disability differently, *i.e.,* preferentially. And the fact that the difference in treatment violates an employer's disability-neutral rule cannot by itself place the accommodation beyond the Act's potential reach.

Were that not so, the "reasonable accommodation" provision could not accomplish its intended objective. Neutral office assignment rules would automatically prevent the accommodation of an employee whose disability-imposed limitations require him to work on the ground floor. Neutral "break-from-work" rules would automatically prevent the accommodation of an individual who needs additional breaks from work, perhaps to permit medical visits. Neutral furniture budget rules would automatically prevent the accommodation of an individual who needs a different kind of chair or desk. Many employers will have neutral rules governing the kinds of actions most needed to reasonably accommodate a worker with a disability. See 42 U.S.C. § 12111(9)(b) (setting forth examples such as "job restructuring," "part-time or modified work schedules," "acquisition or modification of equipment or devices," "and other similar accommodations"). Yet Congress, while providing such examples, said nothing suggesting that the presence of such neutral rules would create an automatic exemption. Nor have the lower courts made any such suggestion. Cf. *Garcia-Ayala v. Lederle Parenterals, Inc.*, 212 F.3d 638, 648 (C.A.1 2000) (requiring leave beyond that allowed under the company's own leave policy); *Hendricks-Robinson v. Excel Corp.*, 154 F.3d 685, 699 (C.A.7 1998) (requiring exception to employer's neutral "physical fitness" job requirement).

In sum, the nature of the "reasonable accommodation" requirement, the statutory examples, and the Act's silence about the exempting effect of neutral rules together convince us that the Act does not create any such automatic exemption. The simple fact that an accommodation would provide a "preference"—in the sense that it would permit the worker with a disability to violate a rule that others must obey—cannot, *in and of itself,* automatically show that the accommodation is not "reasonable." As a result, we reject the position taken by U.S. Airways and Justice SCALIA to the contrary.

US Airways also points to the ADA provisions stating that a " 'reasonable accommodation' may include * * * reassignment to a *vacant* position." § 12111(9)(B) (emphasis added). And it claims that the fact that an established seniority system would assign that position to another worker automatically and always means that the position is not a "vacant" one. Nothing in the Act, however, suggests that Congress intended the word "vacant" to have a specialized meaning. And in ordinary English, a seniority system can give employees seniority rights allowing them to bid for a "vacant" position. The position in this case was held, at the time of suit, by Barnett, not by some other worker; and that position, under the U.S. Airways seniority system, became an "open" one. Moreover, U.S. Airways has said that it "reserves the right to change any and all" portions of the seniority system at will. Consequently, we cannot agree with U.S. Airways about the position's vacancy; nor do we agree that the Act would automatically deny Barnett's accommodation request for that reason.

B

Barnett argues that the statutory words "reasonable accommodation" mean only "effective accommodation," authorizing a court to consider the requested accommodation's ability to meet an individual's disability-related needs, and nothing more. On this view, a seniority rule violation, having nothing to do with the accommodation's effectiveness, has nothing to do with its "reasonableness." It might, at most, help to prove an "undue hardship on the operation of the business." But, he adds, that is a matter that the statute requires the employer to demonstrate, case by case.

* * *

These arguments do not persuade us that Barnett's legal interpretation of "reasonable" is correct. For one thing, in ordinary English the word "reasonable" does not mean "effective." * * *

Neither does the statute's primary purpose require Barnett's special reading. The statute seeks to diminish or to eliminate the stereotypical thought processes, the thoughtless actions, and the hostile reactions that far too often bar those with disabilities from participating fully in the Nation's life, including the workplace. See generally §§ 12101(a) and (b). These objectives demand unprejudiced thought and reasonable responsive reaction on the part of employers and fellow workers alike. They will sometimes require affirmative conduct to promote entry of disabled people into the workforce. They do not, however, demand action beyond the realm of the reasonable.

* * *

III

The question in the present case focuses on the relationship between seniority systems and the plaintiff's need to show that an "accommodation" seems reasonable on its face, *i.e.*, ordinarily or in the run of cases. We must assume that the plaintiff, an employee, is an "individual with a disability." He has requested assignment to a mailroom position as a "reasonable accommodation." We also assume that normally such a request would be reasonable within the meaning of the statute, were it not for one circumstance, namely, that the assignment would violate the rules of a seniority system. See § 12111(9) ("reasonable accommodation" may include "reassignment to a vacant position"). Does that circumstance mean that the proposed accommodation is not a "reasonable" one?

In our view, the answer to this question ordinarily is "yes." The statute does not require proof on a case-by-case basis that a seniority system should prevail. That is because it would not be reasonable in the run of cases that the assignment in question trump the rules of a seniority system. To the contrary, it will ordinarily be unreasonable for the assignment to prevail.

A

Several factors support our conclusion that a proposed accommodation will not be reasonable in the run of cases. Analogous case law supports this conclusion, for it has recognized the importance of seniority to employee-management relations. This Court has held that, in the context of a Title VII religious discrimination case, an employer need not adapt to an employee's special worship schedule as a "reasonable accommodation" where doing so would conflict with the seniority rights of other employees. *Trans World Airlines, Inc. v. Hardison,* 432 U.S. 63, 79–80, 97 S.Ct. 2264, 53 L.Ed.2d 113 (1977). The lower courts have unanimously found that collectively bargained seniority trumps the need for reasonable accommodation in the context of the linguistically similar Rehabilitation Act. See *Eckles v. Consolidated Rail Corp.*, 94 F.3d 1041, 1047–1048 (C.A.7 1996) (collecting cases); *Shea v. Tisch,* 870 F.2d 786, 790 (C.A.1 1989); *Carter v. Tisch,* 822 F.2d 465, 469 (C.A.4 1987); *Jasany v. United States Postal Service,* 755 F.2d 1244, 1251–1252 (C.A.6 1985). And several Circuits, though differing in their reasoning, have reached a similar conclusion in the context of seniority and the ADA. See *Smith v. Midland Brake, Inc.,* 180 F.3d 1154, 1175 (C.A.10 1999); *Feliciano v. Rhode Island,* 160 F.3d 780, 787 (C.A.1 1998); *Eckles,* supra, at 1047–1048. All these cases discuss *collectively bargained* seniority systems, not systems (like the present system) which are unilaterally imposed by management. But the relevant seniority system advantages, and related difficulties that result from violations of seniority rules, are not limited to collectively bargained systems.

For one thing, the typical seniority system provides important employee benefits by creating, and fulfilling, employee expectations of fair, uniform treatment. These benefits include "job security and an opportunity for steady and predictable advancement based on objective standards." * * * They include "an element of due process," limiting "unfairness in personnel decisions." Gersuny, Origins of Seniority Provisions in Collective Bargaining, 33 Lab. L.J. 518, 519 (1982). And they consequently encourage employees to invest in the employing company, accepting "less than their value to the firm early in their careers" in return for greater benefits in later years. J. Baron & D. Kreps, Strategic Human Resources: Frameworks for General Managers 288 (1999).

Most important for present purposes, to require the typical employer to show more than the existence of a seniority system might well undermine the employees' expectations of consistent, uniform treatment—expectations upon which the seniority system's benefits depend. That is because such a rule would substitute a complex case-specific "accommodation" decision made by management for the more uniform, impersonal operation of seniority rules. Such management decisionmaking, with its inevitable discretionary elements, would involve a matter of the greatest importance to employees, namely, layoffs; it would take place outside, as well as inside, the confines of a court case; and it might well take place fairly often. Cf. ADA, 42 U.S.C. § 12101(a)(1), (estimating that some 43 million Americans suffer from physical or mental disabilities). We can find nothing in the statute that suggests Congress intended to undermine seniority systems in this way. And we consequently conclude that the employer's showing of violation of the rules of a seniority system is by itself ordinarily sufficient.

B

The plaintiff (here the employee) nonetheless remains free to show that special circumstances warrant a finding that, despite the presence of a seniority system (which the ADA may not trump in the run of cases), the requested "accommodation" is "reasonable" on the particular facts. That is because special circumstances might alter the important expectations described above. Cf. *Borkowski*, 63 F.3d, at 137 ("[A]n accommodation that imposed burdens that would be unreasonable for most members of an industry might nevertheless be required of an individual defendant in light of that employer's particular circumstances"). The plaintiff might show, for example, that the employer, having retained the right to change the seniority system unilaterally, exercises that right fairly frequently, reducing employee expectations that the system will be followed—to the point where one more departure, needed to accommodate an individual with a disability, will not likely make a difference. The plaintiff might show that the system already contains exceptions such that, in the circumstances, one further exception is unlikely to matter. We do not mean these examples to exhaust the kinds of showings that a plaintiff might make. But we do mean to say that the plaintiff must bear the burden of showing special circumstances that make an exception from the seniority system reasonable in the particular case. And to do so, the plaintiff must explain why, in the particular case, an exception to the employer's seniority policy can constitute a "reasonable accommodation" even though in the ordinary case it cannot.

* * *

[The concurring opinion of JUSTICE STEVENS is omitted.]

JUSTICE O'CONNOR, concurring.

I agree with portions of the opinion of the Court, but I find problematic the Court's test for determining whether the fact that a job reassignment violates a seniority system makes the reassignment an unreasonable accommodation under the Americans with Disabilities Act of 1990 (ADA or Act). Although a seniority system plays an important role in the workplace, for the reasons I explain below, I would prefer to say that the effect of a seniority system on the reasonableness of a reassignment as an accommodation for purposes of the ADA depends on whether the seniority system is legally enforceable. * * *

The ADA specifically lists "reassignment to a vacant position" as one example of a "reasonable accommodation." 42 U.S.C. § 12111(9)(B). In deciding whether an otherwise reasonable accommodation involving a reassignment is unreasonable because it would require an exception to a seniority system, I think the relevant issue is whether the seniority system prevents the position in question from being vacant. The word "vacant" means "not filled or occupied by an incumbent [or] possessor." *Webster's Third New International Dictionary* 2527 (1976). In the context of a workplace, a vacant position is a position in which no employee currently works and to which no individual has a legal entitlement. For example, in a workplace without a seniority system, when an employee ceases working for the employer, the employee's former position is vacant until a replacement is hired. Even if the replacement does not start work immediately, once the replacement enters into a contractual agreement with the employer, the position is no longer vacant because it has a "possessor." In contrast, when an employee ceases working in a workplace with a legally enforceable seniority system, the employee's former position does not become vacant if the seniority system entitles another employee to it. Instead, the employee entitled to the position under the seniority system immediately becomes the new "possessor" of that position. In a workplace with an unenforceable seniority policy, however, an employee expecting assignment to a position under the seniority policy would not have any type of contractual right to the position and so could not be said to be its "possessor." The position therefore would become vacant.

Given this understanding of when a position can properly be considered vacant, if a seniority system, in the absence of the ADA, would give someone other than the individual seeking the accommodation a legal entitlement or contractual right to the position to which reassignment is sought, the seniority system prevents the position from being vacant. If a position is not vacant, then reassignment to it is not a reasonable accommodation. The Act specifically says that "reassignment to a *vacant* position" is a type of "reasonable accommodation." § 12111(9)(B) (emphasis added). Indeed, the legislative history of the Act confirms that Congress did not intend reasonable accommodation to require bumping other employees. H.R.Rep. No. 101–485, pt. 2, p. 63 (1990), U.S.Code Cong. & Admin.News 1990, pp. 303, 345 ("The Committee also wishes to make clear that reassignment need only be to a vacant position— 'bumping' another employee out of a position to create a vacancy is not required"); S.Rep. No. 101–116, p. 32 (1989) (same).

Petitioner's Personnel Policy Guide for Agents, which contains its seniority policy, specifically states that it is "*not* intended to be a contract (express or implied) or otherwise to create legally enforceable obligations," and that petitioner "reserves the right to change any and all of the stated policies and procedures in [the] Guide at any time, without advanc[e] notice." Petitioner conceded at oral argument that its seniority policy does not give employees any legally enforceable rights. Because the policy did not give any other employee a right to the position respondent sought, the position could be said to have been vacant when it became open for bidding, making the requested accommodation reasonable.

* * *

JUSTICE SCALIA, with whom JUSTICE THOMAS joins, dissenting.

* * *

The principal defect of today's opinion * * * goes well beyond the uncertainty it produces regarding the relationship between the ADA and the infinite variety of seniority systems. The conclusion that any seniority system can ever be overridden is merely one consequence of a mistaken interpretation of the ADA that makes all employment rules and practices—even those which (like a seniority system) pose no *distinctive* obstacle to the disabled—subject to suspension when that is (in a court's view) a "reasonable" means of enabling a disabled employee to keep his job. That is a far cry from what I believe the accommodation provision of the ADA requires: the suspension (within reason) of those employment rules and practices *that the employee's disability prevents him from observing.*

I

The Court begins its analysis by describing the ADA as declaring that an employer may not "discriminate against a qualified individual with a disability." In fact the Act says more: an employer may not "discriminate against a qualified individual with a disability *because of the disability* of such individual." 42 U.S.C. § 12112(a) (emphasis added). It further provides that discrimination includes "not making reasonable accommodations *to the known physical or mental limitations* of an otherwise qualified individual with a disability." § 12112(b)(5)(A) (emphasis added).

Read together, these provisions order employers to modify or remove (within reason) policies and practices that burden a disabled person "because of [his] disability." In other words, the ADA eliminates workplace barriers only if a disability prevents an employee from overcoming them—those barriers that would not be barriers *but for* the employee's disability. These include, for example, work stations that cannot accept the employee's wheelchair, or an assembly-line practice that requires long periods of standing. But they do not include rules and practices that bear no more heavily upon the disabled employee than upon others— even though an exemption from such a rule or practice might in a sense "make up for" the employee's disability. It is not a required accommodation, for example, to pay a disabled employee more than others at his grade level—even if that increment is earmarked for massage or physical therapy that would enable the employee to work with as little physical discomfort as his co-workers. That would be "accommodating" the disabled employee, but it would not be "making * * * accommodatio[n] *to the known physical or mental limitations*" of the employee, § 12112(b)(5)(A), because it would not eliminate any workplace practice that constitutes an obstacle *because of* his disability.

So also with exemption from a seniority system, which burdens the disabled and nondisabled alike. In particular cases, seniority rules may have a harsher effect upon the disabled employee than upon his co-workers. If the disabled employee is physically capable of performing only one task in the workplace, seniority rules may be, for him, the difference between employment and unemployment. But that does not make the seniority system a disability-related obstacle, any more than harsher impact upon the more needy disabled employee renders the salary system a disability-related obstacle. When one departs from this understanding, the ADA's accommodation provision becomes a standard-less grab bag—leaving it to the courts to decide which workplace preferences (higher salary, longer vacations, reassignment to positions to which others are entitled) can be deemed "reasonable" to "make up for" the particular employee's disability.

Some courts, including the Ninth Circuit in the present case, have accepted respondent's contention that the ADA demands accommodation even with respect to those obstacles that have nothing to do with the disability. Their principal basis for this position is that the definition of "reasonable accommodation" includes "reassignment to a vacant position." § 12111(9)(B). This accommodation would be meaningless, they contend, if it required only that the disabled employee be *considered* for a vacant position. The ADA already prohibits employers from discriminating against the disabled with respect to "hiring, advancement, or discharge * * * and other terms, conditions, and privileges of employment." § 12112(a). Surely, the argument goes, a disabled employee must be given preference over a nondisabled employee when a vacant position appears.

This argument seems to me quite mistaken. The right to be given a vacant position so long as there are no obstacles to that appointment (including another candidate who is better qualified, if "best qualified" is the workplace rule) is of considerable value. If an employee is hired to fill a position but fails miserably, he will typically be fired. Few employers will search their organization charts for vacancies to which the low-performing employee might be suited. The ADA, however, prohibits an employer from firing a person whose disability is the cause of his poor performance without first seeking to place him in a vacant job where the disability will not affect performance. Such reassignment is an accommodation *to the disability* because it removes an obstacle (the inability to perform the functions of the assigned job) arising solely from the disability.

The phrase "reassignment to a vacant position" appears in a subsection describing a variety of potential "reasonable accommodation[s]":

(A) making existing facilities used by employees readily accessible to and usable by individuals with disabilities; and

(B) job restructuring, part-time or modified work schedules, *reassignment to a vacant position,* acquisition or modification of equipment or devices, appropriate adjustment or modifications of examinations, training materials or policies, the provision of qualified readers or interpreters, and other similar accommodations for individuals with disabilities.

§ 12111(9) (emphasis added).

Subsection (A) clearly addresses features of the workplace that burden the disabled *because of* their disabilities. Subsection (B) is broader in scope but equally targeted at disability-related obstacles. Thus it encompasses "modified work schedules" (which may accommodate inability to work for protracted periods), "modification of equipment and devices," and "provision of qualified readers or interpreters." There is no reason why the phrase "reassignment to a vacant position" should be thought to have a uniquely different focus. It envisions elimination of the obstacle of the *current position* (which requires activity that the disabled employee cannot tolerate) when there is an alternate position freely available. If he is qualified for that position, and no one else is seeking it, or no one else who seeks it is better qualified, he *must* be given the position. But "reassignment to a vacant position" does *not* envision the elimination of obstacles to the employee's service in the new position that have nothing to do with his disability—for example, another employee's claim to that position under a seniority system, or another employee's superior qualifications.

Unsurprisingly, most Courts of Appeals addressing the issue have held or assumed that the ADA does not mandate exceptions to a "legitimate, nondiscriminatory policy" such as a seniority system or a consistent policy of assigning the most qualified person to a vacant position.

Even the EEOC, in at least some of its regulations, acknowledges that the ADA clears away only obstacles *arising from* a person's disability and nothing more. According to the agency, the term "reasonable accommodation" means

"(i) [m]odifications or adjustments to a job application process *that enable* a qualified applicant with a disability *to be considered for* the position such qualified applicant desires; or

"(ii) [m]odifications or adjustments to the work environment * * * *that enable* a qualified individual with a disability to perform the essential functions of that position; or

"(iii) [m]odifications or adjustments *that enable* a covered entity's employee with a disability *to enjoy equal benefits and privileges* of employment as are enjoyed by its other similarly situated employees without disabilities." 29 CFR § 1630.2(*o*) (2001) (emphasis added).

See also 29 CFR pt. 1630, App. § 1630.9, p. 364 (2001) ("reasonable accommodation requirement is best understood as a means by which barriers to * * * equal employment opportunity * * * are removed or alleviated").

Sadly, this analysis is lost on the Court, which mistakenly and inexplicably concludes that my position here is the same as that attributed to U.S. Airways. In rejecting the argument that the ADA creates no "automatic exemption" for neutral workplace rules such as "break-from-work" and furniture budget rules, the Court rejects an argument I have not made.

* * *

JUSTICE SOUTER, with whom JUSTICE GINSBURG joins, dissenting.

"[R]eassignment to a vacant position," 42 U.S.C. § 12111(9), is one way an employer may "reasonabl[y] accommodat[e]" disabled employees under the Americans with Disabilities Act of 1990. The Court today holds that a request for reassignment will nonetheless most likely be unreasonable when it would violate the terms of a seniority system imposed by an employer. Although I concur in the Court's appreciation of the value and importance of seniority systems, I do not believe my hand is free to accept the majority's result and therefore respectfully dissent.

Nothing in the ADA insulates seniority rules from the "reasonable accommodation" requirement, in marked contrast to Title VII of the Civil Rights Act of 1964 and the Age Discrimination in Employment Act of 1967, each of which has an explicit protection for seniority. See 42 U.S.C. § 2000e–2(h). ("Notwithstanding any other provision of this subchapter, it shall not be an unlawful employment practice for an employer to [provide different benefits to employees] pursuant to a bona fide seniority * * * system * * *."); 29 U.S.C. § 623(f) (1994 ed.) ("It shall not be unlawful for an employer * * * to take any action otherwise prohibited [under previous sections] * * * to observe the terms of a bona fide seniority system [except for involuntary retirement] * * * "). Because Congress modeled several of the ADA's provisions on Title VII, its failure to replicate Title VII's exemption for seniority systems leaves the statute ambiguous, albeit with more than a hint that seniority rules do not inevitably carry the day.

In any event, the statute's legislative history resolves the ambiguity. The Committee Reports from both the House of Representatives and the Senate explain that seniority protections contained in a collective-bargaining agreement should not amount to more than "a factor" when it comes to deciding whether some accommodation at odds with the seniority rules is "reasonable" nevertheless. H.R.Rep. No. 101–485, pt. 2, p. 63 (1990), U.S.Code Cong. & Admin.News 1990, pp. 303, 345, (existence of collectively bargained protections for seniority "would not be determinative" on the issue whether an accommodation was reasonable); S.Rep. No. 101–116, p. 32 (1989) (a collective-bargaining agreement assigning jobs based on seniority "may be considered as a factor in determining" whether an accommodation is reasonable). * * * The point in this case, however, is simply to recognize that if Congress considered that sort of agreement no more than a factor in the analysis, surely no greater weight was meant for a seniority scheme like the one before us, unilaterally imposed by the employer, and, unlike collective bargaining agreements, not singled out for protection by any positive federal statute.

This legislative history also specifically rules out the majority's reliance on *Trans World Airlines, Inc. v. Hardison,* a case involving a request for a religious accommodation under Title VII that would have broken the seniority rules of a collective-bargaining agreement. We held that such an accommodation would not be "reasonable," and said that our conclusion was "supported" by Title VII's explicit exemption for seniority systems. The committees of both Houses of Congress dealing with the ADA were aware of this case and expressed a choice against treating it as authority under the ADA, with its lack of any provision for maintaining seniority rules. *E.g.,* H.R.Rep. No. 101–485, pt. 2, at 68, U.S.Code Cong. & Admin.News 1990, pp. 303, 350 ("The Committee wishes to make it clear that the principles enunciated by the Supreme Court in *TWA v. Hardison* * * * are not applicable to this legislation."); S.Rep. No. 101–116, at 36 (same).[1]

* * *

* * * I would therefore affirm the Ninth Circuit.

Notes and Questions

1. Consider two views regarding individuals with disabilities: that they are individuals needing special help to overcome discernable differences from the rest of the population and that they are individuals, like everyone else, confronting systemic discrimination. Which view does the Supreme Court adopt in *Raytheon v. Hernandez*?

2. Note the four different positions staked out by the four opinions in *Barnett*. Which position best serves the purposes of the ADA? Who bears the responsibility to make reasonable accommodation—employers or employees?

3. How does the analysis in the majority and concurring opinions in *Barnett* compare with the notion of "reasonable accommodation" found in the religious discrimination cases in Chapter 10? How do these views compare with the notion of "discrimination" found in the affirmative action cases? Given the difference in the basis for prohibiting discrimination (disability versus race, color, religion, sex, or national origin), do these distinctions make sense? Would you support the incorporation of a "reasonable accommodation" standard into the discrimination model for race or sex discrimination?

4. Section 107(a) of the ADA, 42 U.S.C. § 12117(a), provides that

---

1. The House Report singles out Hardison's equation of "undue hardship" and anything more than a "de minimus [*sic*] cost" as being inapplicable to the ADA. By contrast, Hardison itself addressed seniority systems not only in its analysis of undue hardship, but also in its analysis of reasonable accommodation. *Hardison,* 432 U.S., at 81, 84, 97 S.Ct. 2264. Nonetheless, Congress's disavowal of Hardison in light of the "crucial role that reasonable accommodation plays in ensuring meaningful employment opportunities for people with disabilities," H.R.Rep. No. 101–485, pt. 2, at 68, U.S.Code Cong. & Admin.News 1990, pp. 303, 350, renders that case singularly inappropriate to bolster the Court's holding today.

[t]he powers, remedies, and procedures set forth in sections 705, 706, 707, 709, and 710 of the Civil Rights Act of 1964 * * * shall be the powers, remedies, and procedures this title provides to the Commission, to the Attorney General, or to any person alleging discrimination on the basis of disability in violation of any provisions of this Act, * * * concerning employment.

There is a similar provision in § 505(a) of the Rehabilitation Act. 29 U.S.C. § 794(a). The courts have focused on these provisions in shaping the rules on the allocation of the burden of proof under the ADA and the Rehabilitation Act. *See, e.g.*, Barth v. Gelb, 2 F.3d 1180, 1182–84 (D.C.Cir.1993), *cert. denied sub nom*. Barth v. Duffy, 511 U.S. 1030, 114 S.Ct. 1538, 128 L.Ed.2d 190 (1994) (Rehabilitation Act).

5.   The allocation of the burden of proof in ADA cases is discussed in Kevin W. Williams, Note, *The Reasonable Accommodation Difference: The Effect of Applying the Burden Shifting Frameworks Developed Under Title VII in Disparate Treatment Cases to Claims Brought Under Title I of the Americans with Disabilities Act*, 18 Berkeley J.Emp. & Lab.L. 98 (1997). For a critique of the propriety of applying the *McDonnell Douglas* burden-shifting rule in disability discrimination cases, see Lianne C. Knych, Note, *Assessing the Application of* McDonnell Douglas *to Employment Discrimination Claims Brought Under the Americans with Disabilities Act*, 79 Minn. L.Rev. 1515 (1995).

6.   The Fifth Circuit was the first court of appeals to expressly hold that harassment because of disability is cognizable under the ADA. Flowers v. Southern Reg'l Physician Serv., Inc., 247 F.3d 229 (5th Cir.2001). In *Flowers*, the plaintiff, a medical assistant to a physician, alleged that she was harassed and then fired seven months after disclosing that she was HIV-positive. The jury found that her disability was not a motivating factor in her termination, but that she was subjected to disability-based harassment that created a hostile work environment. The court based its ruling on the similarity between Title VII and the ADA, and following *Meritor Savings Bank, FSB v. Vinson*, 477 U.S. 57, 106 S.Ct. 2399, 91 L.Ed.2d 49 (1986), discussed in Chapter 8, held that the phrase "terms, conditions, and privileges of employment" in the ADA should be construed to strike at harassment in the workplace because of disability. The Fourth Circuit also has expressly recognized hostile work environment claims under the ADA. Fox v. General Motors Corp., 247 F.3d 169 (4th Cir.2001).

7.   Specifically excluded from coverage under the ADA are what some might call "sexual behavior disorders" and "gender-identity disorders." *See* ADA §§ 508 (transvestites), 511 (homosexuality and bisexuality), 42 U.S.C. §§ 12208, 12211. Do these exclusions endorse the use of sex-related moral qualifications for employment? For a critical assessment of the exclusions, *see* Adrienne L. Hiegel, Note, *The Americans with Disabilities Act as a Moral Code*, 94 Colum.L.Rev. 1451 (1994).

C. THE MEANING OF "DISABILITY"

SUTTON v. UNITED AIR LINES, INC.

Supreme Court of the United States, 1999.
527 U.S. 471, 119 S.Ct. 2139, 144 L.Ed.2d 450.

JUSTICE O'CONNOR delivered the opinion of the Court.

The Americans with Disabilities Act of 1990 (ADA or Act), prohibits certain employers from discriminating against individuals on the basis of their disabilities. Petitioners challenge the dismissal of their ADA action for failure to state a claim upon which relief can be granted. We conclude that the complaint was properly dismissed. In reaching that result, we hold that the determination of whether an individual is disabled should be made with reference to measures that mitigate the individual's impairment, including, in this instance, eyeglasses and contact lenses. In addition, we hold that petitioners failed to allege properly that respondent "regarded" them as having a disability within the meaning of the ADA.

I

* * * ⌊W⌋e accept the allegations contained in their complaint as true for purposes of this case.

Petitioners are twin sisters, both of whom have severe myopia. Each petitioner's uncorrected visual acuity is 20/200 or worse in her right eye and 20/400 or worse in her left eye, but "[w]ith the use of corrective lenses, each * * * has vision that is 20/20 or better." Consequently, without corrective lenses, each "effectively cannot see to conduct numerous activities such as driving a vehicle, watching television or shopping in public stores," but with corrective measures, such as glasses or contact lenses, both "function identically to individuals without a similar impairment."

In 1992, petitioners applied to respondent for employment as commercial airline pilots. They met respondent's basic age, education, experience, and FAA certification qualifications. After submitting their applications for employment, both petitioners were invited by respondent to an interview and to flight simulator tests. Both were told during their interviews, however, that a mistake had been made in inviting them to interview because petitioners did not meet respondent's minimum vision requirement, which was uncorrected visual acuity of 20/100 or better. Due to their failure to meet this requirement, petitioners' interviews were terminated, and neither was offered a pilot position.

* * * [P]etitioners filed suit * * * alleging that respondent had discriminated against them "on the basis of their disability, or because [respondent] regarded [petitioners] as having a disability" in violation of the ADA. * * *

The District Court dismissed petitioners' complaint for failure to state a claim upon which relief could be granted. Because petitioners could fully correct their visual impairments, the court held that they were not actually substantially limited in any major life activity and thus had not stated a claim that they were disabled within the meaning of the ADA. The court also determined that petitioners had not made allegations sufficient to support their claim that they were "regarded" by the respondent as having an impairment that substantially limits a major life activity. * * * [T]he Court of Appeals for the Tenth Circuit affirmed the District Court's judgment.

The Tenth Circuit's decision is in tension with the decisions of other Courts of Appeals. * * *

II

The ADA prohibits discrimination by covered entities, including private employers, against qualified individuals with a disability. * * * A "qualified individual with a disability" is identified as "an individual with a disability who, with or without reasonable accommodation, can perform the essential functions of the employment position that such individual holds or desires." § 12111(8). In turn, a "disability" is defined as:

"(A) a physical or mental impairment that substantially limits one or more of the major life activities of such individual;

"(B) a record of such an impairment; or

"(C) being regarded as having such an impairment." § 12102(2).

Accordingly, to fall within this definition one must have an actual disability (subsection (A)), have a record of a disability (subsection (B)), or be regarded as having one (subsection (C)).

* * *

[N]o agency has been delegated authority to interpret the term "disability." § 12102(2). * * * The EEOC has, nonetheless, issued regulations to provide additional guidance regarding the proper interpretation of this term. After restating the definition of disability given in the statute, see 29 CFR § 1630.2(g) (1998), the EEOC regulations define the three elements of disability: (1) "physical or mental impairment," (2) "substantially limits," and (3) "major life activities." See id., at §§ 1630.2(h)-(j). Under the regulations, a "physical impairment" includes "[a]ny physiological disorder, or condition, cosmetic disfigurement, or anatomical loss affecting one or more of the following body systems: neurological, musculoskeletal, special sense organs, respiratory (including speech organs), cardiovascular, reproductive, digestive, genitourinary, hemic and lymphatic, skin, and endocrine." § 1630.2(h)(1). The term "substantially limits" means, among other things, "[u]nable to perform a major life activity that the average person in the general population can perform;" or "[s]ignificantly restricted as to the condition, manner or duration under which an individual can perform a particular major life activity as compared to the condition, manner, or duration under which the average person in the general population can perform that same major life activity." § 1630.2(j). Finally, "[m]ajor [l]ife [a]ctivities means functions such as caring for oneself, performing manual tasks, walking, seeing, hearing, speaking, breathing, learning, and working." § 1630.2(i). Because both parties accept these regulations as valid, and determining their validity is not necessary to decide this case, we have no occasion to consider what deference they are due, if any.

The agencies have also issued interpretive guidelines to aid in the implementation of their regulations. For instance, at the time that it promulgated the above regulations, the EEOC issued an "Interpretive Guidance," which provides that "[t]he determination of whether an individual is substantially limited in a major life activity must be made on a case by case basis, without regard to mitigating measures such as medicines, or assistive or prosthetic devices." 29 CFR pt. 1630, App. § 1630.2(j) (1998) (describing § 1630.2(j)). The Department of Justice has issued a similar guideline. See 28 CFR pt. 35, App. A, § 35.104. Although the parties dispute the persuasive force of these interpretive guidelines, we have no need in this case to decide what deference is due.

III

With this statutory and regulatory framework in mind, we turn first to the question whether petitioners have stated a claim under subsection (A) of the disability definition, that is, whether they have alleged that they possess a physical impairment that substantially limits them in one or more major life activities. Because petitioners allege that with corrective measures their vision "is 20/20 or better," they are not actually disabled within the meaning of the Act if the "disability" determination is made with reference to these measures. Consequently, with respect to subsection (A) of the disability definition, our decision turns on whether disability is to be determined with or without reference to corrective measures.

Petitioners maintain that whether an impairment is substantially limiting should be determined without regard to corrective measures. They argue that, because the ADA does not directly address the question at hand, the Court should defer to the agency interpretations of the statute, which are embodied in the agency guidelines issued by the EEOC and the Department of Justice. These guidelines specifically direct that the determination of whether an individual is substantially limited in a major life activity be made without regard to mitigating measures.

Respondent, in turn, maintains that an impairment does not substantially limit a major life activity if it is corrected. It argues that the Court should not defer to the agency guidelines cited by petitioners because the guidelines conflict with the plain meaning of the ADA. The phrase "substantially limits one or more major life activities," it explains, requires that the substantial limitations actually and presently exist. Moreover, respondent argues, disregarding mitigating measures taken by an individual defies the statutory command to examine the effect of the impairment on the major life activities "of such individual." And even if the statute is ambiguous, respondent claims, the guidelines' directive to ignore mitigating measures is not reasonable, and thus this Court should not defer to it.

We conclude that respondent is correct that the approach adopted by the agency guidelines—that persons are to be evaluated in their hypothetical uncorrected state—is an impermissible interpretation of the ADA. Looking at the Act as a whole, it is apparent that if a person is taking measures to correct for, or mitigate, a physical or mental impairment, the effects of those measures—both positive and negative—must be taken into account when judging whether that person is "substantially limited" in a major life activity and thus "disabled" under the Act. The dissent relies on the legislative history of the ADA for the contrary proposition that individuals should be examined in their uncorrected state. Because we decide that, by its terms, the ADA cannot be read in this manner, we have no reason to consider the ADA's legislative history.

Three separate provisions of the ADA, read in concert, lead us to this conclusion. The Act defines a "disability" as "a physical or mental impairment that substantially limits one or more of the major life activities" of an individual. Because the phrase "substantially limits" appears in the Act in the present indicative verb form, we think the language is properly read as requiring that a person be presently—not potentially or hypothetically—substantially limited in order to demonstrate a disability. A "disability" exists only where an impairment "substantially limits" a major life activity, not where it "might," "could," or "would" be substantially limiting if mitigating measures were not taken. A person whose physical or mental impairment is corrected by medication or other measures does not have an impairment that presently "substantially limits" a major life activity. To be sure, a person whose physical or mental impairment is corrected by mitigating measures still has an impairment, but if the impairment is corrected it does not "substantially limi[t]" a major life activity.

The definition of disability also requires that disabilities be evaluated "with respect to an individual" and be determined based on whether an impairment substantially limits the "major life activities of such individual." § 12102(2). Thus, whether a person has a disability under the ADA is an individualized inquiry. *See* Bragdon v. Abbott, 524 U.S. 624, 657, 118 S.Ct. 2196, 141 L.Ed.2d 540 (1998) (declining to consider whether HIV infection is a per se disability under the ADA); 29 CFR pt. 1630, App. § 1630.2(j) ("The determination of whether an individual has a disability is not necessarily based on the name or diagnosis of the impairment the person has, but rather on the effect of that impairment on the life of the individual").

The agency guidelines' directive that persons be judged in their uncorrected or unmitigated state runs directly counter to the individualized inquiry mandated by the ADA. The agency approach would often require courts and employers to speculate about a person's condition and would, in many cases, force them to make a disability determination based on general information about how an uncorrected impairment usually affects individuals, rather than on the individual's actual condition. For instance, under this view, courts would almost certainly find all diabetics to be disabled, because if they failed to monitor their blood sugar levels and administer insulin, they would almost certainly be substantially limited in one or more major life activities. A diabetic whose illness does not impair his or her daily activities would therefore be considered disabled simply because he or she has diabetes. Thus, the guidelines approach would create a system in which persons often must be treated as members of a group of people with similar impairments, rather than as individuals. This is contrary to both the letter and the spirit of the ADA.

The guidelines approach could also lead to the anomalous result that in determining whether an individual is disabled, courts and employers could not consider any negative side effects suffered by an individual resulting from the use of mitigating measures, even when those side effects are very severe. This result is also inconsistent with the individualized approach of the ADA.

Finally, and critically, findings enacted as part of the ADA require the conclusion that Congress did not intend to bring under the statute's protection all those whose uncorrected conditions amount to disabilities. Congress found that "some 43,000,000 Americans have one or more physical or mental disabilities, and this number is increasing as the population as a whole is growing older." § 12101(a)(1). This figure is inconsistent with the definition of disability pressed by petitioners.

Although the exact source of the 43 million figure is not clear, the corresponding finding in the 1988 precursor to the ADA was drawn directly from a report prepared by the National Council on Disability. That report detailed the difficulty of estimating the number of disabled persons due to varying operational definitions of disability. National Council on Disability, Toward Independence 10 (1986). It explained that the estimates of the number of disabled Americans ranged from an overinclusive 160 million under a "health conditions approach," which looks at all conditions that impair the health or normal functional abilities of an individual, to an underinclusive 22.7 million under a "work disability approach," which focuses on individuals' reported ability to work. *Id.*, at 10–11. It noted that "a figure of 35 or 36 million [was] the most commonly quoted estimate." *Id.*, at 10. The 36 million number included in the 1988 bill's findings thus clearly reflects an approach to defining disabilities that is closer to the work disabilities approach than the health conditions approach.

* * *

Regardless of its exact source, however, the 43 million figure reflects an understanding that those whose impairments are largely corrected by medication or other devices are not "disabled" within the meaning of the ADA. The estimate is consistent with the numbers produced by studies performed during this same time period that took a similar functional approach to determining disability. * * *

By contrast, nonfunctional approaches to defining disability produce significantly larger numbers. * * * [T]he 1986 National Council on Disability report estimated that there were over 160 million disabled under the "health conditions approach." Indeed, the number of people with vision impairments alone is 100 million. "It is estimated that more than 28 million Americans have impaired hearing." And there were approximately 50 million people with high blood pressure (hypertension).

Because it is included in the ADA's text, the finding that 43 million individuals are disabled gives content to the ADA's terms, specifically the term "disability." Had Congress intended to include all persons with corrected physical limitations among those covered by the Act, it undoubtedly would have cited a much higher number of disabled persons in the findings. That it did not is evidence that the ADA's coverage is restricted to only those whose impairments are not mitigated by corrective measures.

The dissents suggest that viewing individuals in their corrected state will exclude from the definition of "disab[led]" those who use prosthetic limbs, or take medicine for epilepsy or high blood pressure. This suggestion is incorrect. The use of a corrective device does not, by itself, relieve one's disability. Rather, one has a disability under subsection A if, notwithstanding the use of a corrective device, that individual is substantially limited in a major life activity. For example, individuals who use prosthetic limbs or wheelchairs may be mobile and capable of functioning in society but still be disabled because of a substantial limitation on their ability to walk or run. The same may be true of individuals who take medicine to lessen the symptoms of an impairment so that they can function but nevertheless remain substantially limited. Alternatively, one whose high blood pressure is "cured" by medication may be regarded as disabled by a covered entity, and thus disabled under subsection C of the definition. The use or nonuse of a corrective device does not determine whether an individual is disabled; that determination depends on whether the limitations an individual with an impairment *actually* faces are in fact substantially limiting.

Applying this reading of the Act to the case at hand, we conclude that the Court of Appeals correctly resolved the issue of disability in respondent's favor. As noted above, petitioners allege that with corrective measures, their visual acuity is 20/20, and that they "function identically to individuals without a similar impairment. In addition, petitioners concede that they 'do not argue that the use of corrective lenses in itself demonstrates a substantially limiting impairment.' " Accordingly, because we decide that disability under the Act is to be determined with reference to corrective measures, we agree with the courts below that petitioners have not stated a claim that they are substantially limited in any major life activity.

IV

Our conclusion that petitioners have failed to state a claim that they are actually disabled under subsection (A) of the disability definition does not end our inquiry. Under subsection (C), individuals who are "regarded as" having a disability are disabled within the meaning of the ADA. Subsection (C) provides that having a disability includes "being regarded as having," § 12102(2)(C), "a physical or mental impairment that substantially limits one or more of the major life activities of such individual," § 12102(2)(A). There are two apparent ways in which individuals may fall within this statutory definition: (1) a covered entity mistakenly believes that a person has a physical impairment that substantially limits one or more major life activities, or (2) a covered entity mistakenly believes that an actual, nonlimiting impairment substantially limits one or more major life activities. In both cases, it is necessary that a covered entity entertain misperceptions about the individual—it must believe either that one has a substantially limiting impairment that one does not have or that one has a substantially limiting impairment when, in fact, the impairment is not so limiting. These misperceptions often "resul[t] from stereotypic assumptions often result from stereotypic assumptions not truly indicative of * * * individual ability." *See* 42 U.S.C. § 12101(7). *See also* School Bd. of Nassau Cty. v. Arline, 480 U.S. 273, 284, 107 S.Ct. 1123, 94 L.Ed.2d 307 (1987) ("By amending the definition of 'handicapped individual' to include not only those who are actually physically impaired, but also those who are regarded as impaired and who, as a result, are substantially limited in a major life activity, Congress acknowledged that society's accumulated myths and fears about disability and disease are as handicapping as are the physical limitations that flow from actual impairment").

There is no dispute that petitioners are physically impaired. Petitioners do not make the obvious argument that they are regarded due to their impairments as substantially limited in the major life activity of seeing. They contend only that respondent mistakenly believes their physical impairments substantially limit them in the major life activity of working. To support this claim, petitioners allege that respondent has a vision requirement, which is allegedly based on myth and stereotype. Further, this requirement substantially limits their ability to engage in the major life activity of working by precluding them from obtaining the job of global airline pilot, which they argue is a "class of employment." In reply, respondent argues that the position of global airline pilot is not a class of jobs and therefore petitioners have not stated a claim that they are regarded as substantially limited in the major life activity of working.

Standing alone, the allegation that respondent has a vision requirement in place does not establish a claim that respondent regards petitioners as substantially limited in the major life activity of working. By its terms, the ADA allows employers to prefer some physical attributes over others and to establish physical criteria. An employer runs afoul of the ADA when it makes an employment decision based on a physical or mental impairment, real or imagined, that is regarded as substantially limiting a major life activity. Accordingly, an employer is free to decide that physical characteristics or medical conditions that do not rise to the level of an impairment—such as one's height, build, or singing voice—are preferable to others, just as it is free to decide that some limiting, but not substantially limiting, impairments make individuals less than ideally suited for a job.

Considering the allegations of the amended complaint in tandem, petitioners have not stated a claim that respondent regards their impairment as substantially limiting their ability to work. The ADA does not define "substantially limits," but "substantially" suggests "considerable" or "specified to a large degree." *See* Webster's Third New International Dictionary 2280 (1976) (defining "substantially" as "in a substantial manner" and "substantial" as "considerable in amount, value, or worth" and "being that specified to a large degree or in the main"); *see also* 17 Oxford English Dictionary 66–67 (2d ed.1989) ("substantial": "[r]elating to or proceeding from the essence of a thing; essential"; "of ample or considerable amount, quantity or dimensions"). The EEOC has codified regulations interpreting the term "substantially limits" in this manner, defining the term to mean "[u]nable to perform" or "[s]ignificantly restricted." *See* 29 CFR §§ 1630.2(j)(1)(i), (ii) (1998).

When the major life activity under consideration is that of working, the statutory phrase "substantially limits" requires, at a minimum, that plaintiffs allege they are unable to work in a broad class of jobs. Reflecting this requirement, the EEOC uses a specialized definition of the term "substantially limits" when referring to the major life activity of working:

> "significantly restricted in the ability to perform either a class of jobs or a broad range of jobs in various classes as compared to the average person having comparable training, skills and abilities. The inability to perform a single, particular job does not constitute a substantial limitation in the major life activity of working."

§ 1630.2(j)(3)(i).

The EEOC further identifies several factors that courts should consider when determining whether an individual is substantially limited in the major life activity of working, including the geographical area to which the individual has reasonable access, and "the number and types of jobs utilizing similar training, knowledge, skills or abilities, within the geographical area, from which the individual is also disqualified." §§ 1630.2(j)(3)(ii)(A)(B). To be substantially limited in the major life activity of working, then, one must be precluded from more than one type of job, a specialized job, or a particular job of choice. If jobs utilizing an individual's skills (but perhaps not his or her unique talents) are available, one is not precluded from a substantial class of jobs. Similarly, if a host of different types of jobs are available, one is not precluded from a broad range of jobs.

Because the parties accept that the term "major life activities" includes working, we do not determine the validity of the cited regulations. We note, however, that there may be some conceptual difficulty in defining "major life activities" to include work, for it seems "to argue in a circle to say that if one is excluded, for instance, by reason of [an impairment, from working with others] * * * then that exclusion constitutes an impairment, when the question you're asking is, whether the exclusion itself is by reason of handicap." Indeed, even the EEOC has expressed reluctance to define "major life activities" to include working and has suggested that working be viewed as a residual life activity, considered, as a last resort, *only* "[i]f an individual is not substantially limited with respect to any other major life activity."

Assuming without deciding that working is a major life activity and that the EEOC regulations interpreting the term "substantially limits" are reasonable, petitioners have failed to allege adequately that their poor eyesight is regarded as an impairment that substantially limits them in the major life activity of working. They allege only that respondent regards their poor vision as precluding them from holding positions as a "global airline pilot." Because the position of global airline pilot is a single job, this allegation does not support the claim that respondent regards petitioners as having a substantially limiting impairment. *See* 29 CFR § 1630.2(j)(3)(i) ("The inability to perform a single, particular job does not constitute a substantial limitation in the major life activity of working"). Indeed, there are a number of other positions utilizing petitioners' skills, such as regional pilot and pilot instructor to name a few, that are available to them. Even under the EEOC's Interpretative Guidance, to which petitioners ask us to defer, "an individual who cannot be a commercial airline pilot because of a minor vision impairment, but who can be a commercial airline co-pilot or a pilot for a courier service, would not be substantially limited in the major life activity of working." 29 CFR pt. 1630, App. § 1630.2.

* * *

For these reasons, the decision of the Court of Appeals for the Tenth Circuit is affirmed.

JUSTICE GINSBURG, concurring.

I agree that 42 U.S.C. § 12102(2)(A) does not reach the legions of people with correctable disabilities. The strongest clues to Congress' perception of the domain of the Americans with Disabilities Act (ADA), as I see it, are legislative findings that "some 43,000,000 Americans have one or more physical or mental disabilities," § 12101(a)(1), and that "individuals with disabilities are a discrete and insular minority," persons "subjected to a history of purposeful unequal treatment, and relegated to a position of political powerlessness in our society," § 12101(a)(7). These declarations are inconsistent with the enormously embracing definition of disability petitioners urge. As the Court demonstrates, the inclusion of correctable disabilities within the ADA's domain would extend the Act's coverage to far more than 43 million people. And persons whose uncorrected eyesight is poor, or who rely on daily medication for their well-being, can be found in every social and economic class; they do not cluster among the politically powerless, nor do they coalesce as historical victims of discrimination. In short, in no sensible way can one rank the large numbers of diverse individuals with corrected disabilities as a "discrete and insular minority." I do not mean to suggest that any of the constitutional presumptions or doctrines that may apply to "discrete and insular" minorities in other contexts are relevant here; there is no constitutional dimension to this case. Congress' use of the phrase, however, is a telling indication of its intent to restrict the ADA's coverage to a confined, and historically disadvantaged, class.

JUSTICE STEVENS, with whom JUSTICE BREYER joins, dissenting.

When it enacted the Americans with Disabilities Act in 1990, Congress certainly did not intend to require United Air Lines to hire unsafe or unqualified pilots. Nor, in all likelihood, did it view every person who wears glasses as a member of a "discrete and insular minority." Indeed, by reason of legislative myopia it may not have foreseen that its definition of "disability" might theoretically encompass, not just "some 43,000,000 Americans," but perhaps two or three times that number. Nevertheless, if we apply customary tools of statutory construction, it is quite clear that the threshold question whether an individual is "disabled" within the meaning of the Act—and, therefore, is entitled to the basic assurances that the Act affords—focuses on her past or present physical condition without regard to mitigation that has resulted from rehabilitation, self-improvement, prosthetic devices, or medication. One might reasonably argue that the general rule should not apply to an impairment that merely requires a nearsighted person to wear glasses. But I believe that, in order to be faithful to the remedial purpose of the Act, we should give it a generous, rather than a miserly, construction.

* * *

I

* * *

* * * There are many individuals who have lost one or more limbs in industrial accidents, or perhaps in the service of their country in places like Iwo Jima. With the aid of prostheses, coupled with courageous determination and physical therapy, many of these hardy individuals can perform all of their major life activities just as efficiently as an average couch potato. If the Act were just concerned with their present ability to participate in society, many of these individuals' physical impairments would not be viewed as disabilities. Similarly, if the statute were solely

concerned with whether these individuals viewed themselves as disabled—or with whether a majority of employers regarded them as unable to perform most jobs—many of these individuals would lack statutory protection from discrimination based on their prostheses.

* * *

In my view, when an employer refuses to hire the individual "because of" his prosthesis, and the prosthesis in no way affects his ability to do the job, that employer has unquestionably discriminated against the individual in violation of the Act. Subsection (B) of the definition, in fact, sheds a revelatory light on the question whether Congress was concerned only about the corrected or mitigated status of a person's impairment. If the Court is correct that "[a] 'disability' exists only where" a person's "present" or "actual" condition is substantially impaired, there would be no reason to include in the protected class those who were once disabled but who are now fully recovered. Subsection (B) of the Act's definition, however, plainly covers a person who previously had a serious hearing impairment that has since been completely cured. *See* School Bd. of Nassau Cty. v. Arline, 480 U.S. 273, 281, 107 S.Ct. 1123, 94 L.Ed.2d 307 (1987). Still, if I correctly understand the Court's opinion, it holds that one who continues to wear a hearing aid that she has worn all her life might not be covered—fully cured impairments are covered, but merely treatable ones are not. The text of the Act surely does not require such a bizarre result.

* * *

II

* * *

When faced with classes of individuals or types of discrimination that fall outside the core prohibitions of anti-discrimination statutes, we have consistently construed those statutes to include comparable evils within their coverage, even when the particular evil at issue was beyond Congress' immediate concern in passing the legislation. Congress, for instance, focused almost entirely on the problem of discrimination against African–Americans when it enacted Title VII of the Civil Rights Act of 1964. *See, e.g., United Steelworkers of America v. Weber*, 443 U.S. 193, 202–203, 99 S.Ct. 2721, 61 L.Ed.2d 480 (1979). But that narrow focus could not possibly justify a construction of the statute that excluded Hispanic–Americans or Asian–Americans from its protection—or as we later decided (ironically enough, by relying on legislative history and according "great deference" to the EEOC's "interpretation"), Caucasians. *See McDonald v. Santa Fe Trail Transp. Co.*, 427 U.S. 273, 279–280, 96 S.Ct. 2574, 49 L.Ed.2d 493 (1976).

We unanimously applied this well-accepted method of interpretation last Term with respect to construing Title VII to cover claims of same-sex sexual harassment. Oncale v. Sundowner Offshore Services, Inc., 523 U.S. 75, 118 S.Ct. 998, 140 L.Ed.2d 201 (1998). * * *

* * *

Under the approach we followed in *Oncale* * * * visual impairments should be judged by the same standard as hearing impairments or any other medically controllable condition. The nature of the discrimination alleged is of the same character and should be treated accordingly.

* * *

III

* * *

In the end, the Court is left only with its tenacious grip on Congress' finding that "some 43,000,000 Americans have one or more physical or mental disabilities,"—and that figure's legislative history extrapolated from a law review "article authored by the drafter of the original ADA bill introduced in Congress in 1988." * * *

* * * [I]n mining the depths of the history of the 43 million figure— surveying even agency reports that predate the drafting of any of this case's controlling legislation—the Court fails to acknowledge that its narrow approach may have the perverse effect of denying coverage for a sizeable portion of the core group of 43 million. The Court appears to exclude from the Act's protected class individuals with controllable conditions such as diabetes and severe hypertension that were expressly understood as substantially limiting impairments in the Act's Committee Reports. * * * Given the inability to make the 43 million figure fit any consistent method of interpreting the word "disabled," it would be far wiser for the Court to follow—or at least to mention—the documents reflecting Congress' contemporaneous understanding of the term: the Committee Reports on the actual legislation.

* * *

IV

* * *

* * *[A]lthough I express no opinion on the ultimate merits of petitioners' claim, I am persuaded that they have a disability covered by the ADA. I therefore respectfully dissent.

JUSTICE BREYER, dissenting.

We must draw a statutory line that either (1) will include within the category of persons authorized to bring suit under the Americans with Disabilities Act of 1990 some whom Congress may not have wanted to protect (those who wear ordinary eyeglasses), or (2) will exclude from the threshold category those whom Congress certainly did want to protect (those who successfully use corrective devices or medicines, such as hearing aids or prostheses or medicine for epilepsy). Faced with this dilemma, the statute's language, structure, basic purposes, and history require us to choose the former statutory line, as Justice STEVENS (whose opinion I join) well explains. * * *

Notes and Questions

1. In his dissent in *Sutton*, Justice Stevens relied extensively on the legislative history to support his view that the Suttons were protected under the ADA. In a footnote to his argument based on a review of the legislative history, Justice Stevens commented upon what he deemed to be congressional wisdom in including correctable impairments in the definition of a disability:

> The House's decision to cover correctable impairments under subsection (A) of the statute seems, in retrospect, both deliberate and wise. Much of the structure of the House Reports is borrowed from the Senate Report; thus it appears that the House Committees consciously decided to move the discussion of mitigating measures. This adjustment was prudent because in a case in which an employer refuses, out of animus or fear, to hire an individual who has a condition such as epilepsy that the employer knows is controlled, it may be difficult to determine whether the employer is viewing the individual in her uncorrected state or "regards" her as substantially limited.

Sutton, 527 U.S. at 501 n.2, 119 S.Ct. at 2155 n.2.

2. In a companion case to *Sutton*, *Murphy v. United Parcel Service, Inc.*, 527 U.S. 516, 119 S.Ct. 2133, 144 L.Ed.2d 484 (1999), the Court also dealt with the question of which corrective measures to consider in assessing the level of an individual's impairment. The principal difference between *Sutton* and *Murphy* is that *Sutton* involved individuals who used corrective measures for their myopia and the plaintiff in *Murphy* used medication to control his severe hypertension caused by high blood pressure. Murphy, the plaintiff, had suffered from high blood pressure since his youth, but his physician had testified at trial that, with medication, Murphy's blood pressure could be controlled so that it did not significantly restrict his activity and, in general, he could function normally and engage in activities that other persons normally could perform. A Department of Transportation's (DOT) regulation required that a driver of a commercial vehicle have no current clinical diagnosis of high blood pressure that would likely interfere with his/her ability to operate a commercial vehicle safely.

Without knowing that the DOT had erroneously granted Murphy the appropriate commercial drivers certification, United Parcel hired him as a mechanic, a position that required him to drive commercial vehicles. When a later DOT test revealed that Murphy had high blood pressure, United Parcel fired him on the belief that his blood pressure exceeded the DOT requirement. Murphy then filed suit against United Parcel claiming that he had been discriminated against in violation of his rights under Title I of the ADA. Murphy claimed that he had a disability within the meaning of the same two sections of the ADA on which the sisters in *Sutton* had relied.

In a 7–2 decision, also authored by Justice O'Connor, the Court ruled against Murphy. Applying its decision in *Sutton*, the Court held that Murphy was not disabled because his high blood pressure could be controlled by medication. The Court also rejected Murphy's claim that he was disabled under the "regarded as" prong of the definition of disability because, at most, the only fact that Murphy could prove was that United Parcel regarded him as being unable to perform as a mechanic when that job required driving a commercial vehicle. The Court specifically declined to decide the question whether Murphy was substantially limited in a major life activity even when taking his blood pressure medication.

Justice Stevens, again joined by Justice Breyer, dissented in *Murphy* for the same reasons as he did in *Sutton*.

In a third companion case, *Albertson's v. Kirkingburg*, 527 U.S. 555, 119 S.Ct. 2162, 144 L.Ed.2d 518 (1999), the Court found plaintiff Kirkingburg was not an individual with a disability because his own body system had compensated for his visual disability. In this case, Kinkingburg's brain had developed subconscious mechanisms for coping with his visual impairment (he had monocular vision).

3. It seems intuitively correct, does it not, that individuals with mildly impaired vision or other impairments that are readily correctable with, for example, glasses, contact lenses, or medication, should not be deemed "disabled" for purposes of the ADA? If so, can you suggest a rule other than the one adopted by the Court in *Sutton* that would exclude such individuals?

4. *Sutton* contemplates an individualized determination of each plaintiff's disability claim, given corrective measures. Are courts equipped to make this determination? What should counsel for each party do to facilitate the determination? *See generally* Jeffrey A. Van Detta, *"Typhoid Mary" Meets the ADA: A Case Study of the "Direct Threat" Standard Under the Americans with Disabilities Act*, 22 Harv.J.L. & Pub. Pol'y 849 (1999) (questioning the competency of courts to adequately address the "direct threat" standard under the ADA).

5. Are there times when a plaintiff would be better off not taking corrective measures, such as medication, in order to be considered an individual with a disability? Could a court order a plaintiff to continue (or start) a corrective measure?

6. What if the corrective measure causes an additional or different impairment of a major life activity? In *McAlindin v. County of San Diego*, 192 F.3d 1226 (9th Cir.1999), a post-*Sutton* case, the Ninth Circuit found that the plaintiff, who claimed that even with medication and other treatment his mental impairment still substantially limited his major life activities such as sexual relations, sleeping, and interacting with others, raised an issue of fact about whether he was protected under the ADA.

In the following opinion, the Supreme Court addressed the issue of when a person is substantially limited in performing a major life activity.

TOYOTA MOTOR MFG., KENTUCKY v. WILLIAMS

Supreme Court of the United States, 2002.
534 U.S. 184, 122 S.Ct. 681, 151 L.Ed.2d 615.

JUSTICE O'CONNOR delivered the opinion of the Court.

Under the Americans with Disabilities Act of 1990 (ADA or Act), a physical impairment that "substantially limits one or more * * * major life activities" is a "disability." 42 U.S.C. § 12102(2)(A) (1994 ed.). Respondent, claiming to be disabled because of her carpal tunnel syndrome and other related impairments, sued petitioner, her former employer, for failing to provide her with a reasonable accommodation as required by the ADA. *See* § 12112(b)(5)(A). The District Court granted summary judgment to petitioner, finding that respondent's impairments did not substantially limit any of her major life activities. The Court of Appeals for the Sixth Circuit reversed, finding that the impairments substantially limited respondent in the major life activity of performing manual tasks, and therefore granting partial summary judgment to respondent on the issue of whether she was disabled under the ADA. We conclude that the Court of Appeals did not apply the proper standard in making this determination because it analyzed only a limited class of manual tasks and failed to ask whether respondent's impairments prevented or restricted her from performing tasks that are of central importance to most people's daily lives.

I

Respondent began working at petitioner's automobile manufacturing plant in Georgetown, Kentucky, in August 1990. She was soon placed on an engine fabrication assembly line, where her duties included work with pneumatic tools. Use of these tools eventually caused pain in respondent's hands, wrists, and arms. She sought treatment at petitioner's in-house medical service, where she was diagnosed with bilateral carpal tunnel syndrome and bilateral tendinitis. Respondent consulted a personal physician who placed her on permanent work restrictions that precluded her from lifting more than 20 pounds or from "frequently lifting or carrying of objects weighing up to 10 pounds," engaging in "constant repetitive * * * flexion or extension of [her] wrists or elbows," performing "overhead work," or using "vibratory or pneumatic tools."

* * *

[Later], petitioner placed respondent on a team in Quality Control Inspection Operations (QCIO). QCIO is responsible for four tasks: (1) "assembly paint"; (2) "paint second inspection"; (3) "shell body audit"; and (4) "ED surface repair." Respondent was initially placed on a team that performed only the first two of these tasks, and for a couple of years, she rotated on a weekly basis between them. * * * The parties agree that respondent was physically capable of performing both of these jobs and that her performance was satisfactory.

During the fall of 1996, petitioner announced that it wanted QCIO employees to be able to rotate through all four of the QCIO processes. Respondent therefore received training for the shell body audit job, in which * * * [respondent was required] to hold her hands and arms up around shoulder height for several hours at a time.

A short while after the shell body audit job was added to respondent's rotations, she began to experience pain in her neck and shoulders. Respondent again sought care at petitioner's in-house medical service, where she was diagnosed with myotendinitis bilateral periscapular, an inflammation of the muscles and tendons around both of her shoulder blades; myotendinitis and myositis bilateral forearms with nerve compression causing median nerve irritation; and thoracic outlet compression, a condition that causes pain in the nerves that lead to the upper extremities. Respondent requested that petitioner accommodate her medical conditions by allowing her to return to doing only her original two jobs in QCIO, which respondent claimed she could still perform without difficulty.

* * * On January 27, 1997, respondent received a letter from petitioner that terminated her employment, citing her poor attendance record.

[Respondent filed suit against petitioner alleging that petitioner had violated the ADA by failing to reasonably accommodate her disability and by terminating her employment.] * * *

Respondent based her claim that she was "disabled" under the ADA on the ground that her physical impairments substantially limited her in (1) manual tasks; (2) housework; (3) gardening; (4) playing with her children; (5) lifting; and (6) working, all of which, she argued, constituted major life activities under the Act. Respondent also argued, in the alternative, that she was disabled under the ADA because she had a record of a substantially limiting impairment and because she was regarded as having such an impairment. *See* 42 U.S.C. § 12102(2)(B–C).

After petitioner filed a motion for summary judgment and respondent filed a motion for partial summary judgment on her disability claims, the District Court granted summary judgment to petitioner. The court found that respondent had not been disabled, as defined by the ADA, at the time of petitioner's alleged refusal to accommodate her, and that she had therefore not been covered by the Act's protections. * * * The District Court held that respondent had suffered from a physical impairment, but that the impairment did not qualify as a disability because it had not "substantially limit[ed]" any "major life activit[y]," 42 U.S.C. § 12102(2)(A). The court rejected respondent's arguments that gardening, doing housework, and playing with children are major life activities. Although the court agreed that performing manual tasks, lifting, and working are major life activities, it found the evidence insufficient to demonstrate that respondent had been substantially limited in lifting or working. The court found respondent's claim that she was substantially limited in performing manual tasks to be "irretrievably contradicted by [respondent's] continual insistence that she could perform the tasks in assembly [paint] and paint [second] inspection without difficulty." The court also found no evidence that respondent had had a record of a substantially limiting impairment, or that petitioner had regarded her as having such an impairment.

* * * The Court of Appeals held that in order for respondent to demonstrate that she was disabled due to a substantial limitation in the ability to perform manual tasks at the time of her accommodation request, she had to "show that her manual disability involve[d] a 'class' of manual activities affecting the ability to perform tasks at work." Respondent satisfied this test, according to the Court of Appeals, because her ailments "prevent[ed] her from doing the tasks associated with certain types of manual assembly line jobs, manual product handling jobs and manual building trade jobs (painting, plumbing, roofing, etc.) that require the gripping of tools and repetitive work with hands and arms extended at or above shoulder levels for extended periods of time." In reaching this conclusion, the court disregarded evidence that respondent could "tend to her personal hygiene [and] carry out personal or household chores," finding that such evidence "does not affect a determination that her impairment substantially limit[ed] her ability to perform the range of manual tasks associated with an assembly line job." Because the Court of Appeals concluded that respondent had been substantially limited in performing manual tasks and, for that reason, was entitled to partial summary judgment on the issue of whether she was disabled under the Act, it found that it did not need to determine whether respondent had been substantially limited in the major life activities of lifting or working, or whether she had had a "record of" a disability or had been "regarded as" disabled.

We granted certiorari to consider the proper standard for assessing whether an individual is substantially limited in performing manual tasks. We now reverse the Court of Appeals' decision to grant partial summary judgment to respondent on the issue whether she was substantially limited in performing manual tasks at the time she sought an accommodation. We express no opinion on the working, lifting, or other arguments for disability status that were preserved below but which were not ruled upon by the Court of Appeals.

II

* * * [Under the ADA,] a "disability" is:

"(A) a physical or mental impairment that substantially limits one or more of the major life activities of such individual;

"(B) a record of such an impairment; or

"(C) being regarded as having such an impairment." § 12102(2).

There are two potential sources of guidance for interpreting the terms of this definition—the regulations interpreting the Rehabilitation

Act of 1973 and the EEOC regulations interpreting the ADA. Congress drew the ADA's definition of disability almost verbatim from the definition of "handicapped individual" in the Rehabilitation Act, § 706(8)(B), and Congress' repetition of a well-established term generally implies that Congress intended the term to be construed in accordance with pre-existing regulatory interpretations. *Bragdon* v. *Abbott,* 524 U.S. 624, 631 (1998). As we explained in *Bragdon* v. *Abbott,* Congress did more in the ADA than suggest this construction; it adopted a specific statutory provision directing as follows:

> Except as otherwise provided in this chapter, nothing in this chapter shall be construed to apply a lesser standard than the standards applied under title V of the Rehabilitation Act of 1973 (29 U.S.C. 790 *et seq.*) or the regulations issued by Federal agencies pursuant to such title.

42 U.S.C. § 12201(a).

The persuasive authority of the EEOC regulations is less clear. As we have previously noted, see *Sutton* v. *United Air Lines, Inc.,* 527 U.S. 471, 479 (1999), no agency has been given authority to issue regulations interpreting the term "disability" in the ADA. Nonetheless, the EEOC has done so. *See* 29 CFR §§ 1630.2(g)—(j) (2001). Because both parties accept the EEOC regulations as reasonable, we assume without deciding that they are, and we have no occasion to decide what level of deference, if any, they are due.

To qualify as disabled under subsection (A) of the ADA's definition of disability, a claimant must initially prove that he or she has a physical or mental impairment. *See* 42 U.S.C. § 12102(2)(A). The Rehabilitation Act regulations issued by the Department of Health, Education, and Welfare (HEW) in 1977, which appear without change in the current regulations issued by the Department of Health and Human Services, define "physical impairment," the type of impairment relevant to this case, to mean "any physiological disorder or condition, cosmetic disfigurement, or anatomical loss affecting one or more of the following body systems: neurological; musculoskeletal; special sense organs; respiratory, including speech organs; cardiovascular; reproductive, digestive, genito-urinary; hemic and lymphatic; skin; and endocrine." 45 CFR § 84.3(j)(2)(i) (2001). The HEW regulations are of particular significance because at the time they were issued, HEW was the agency responsible for coordinating the implementation and enforcement of § 504 of the Rehabilitation Act, which prohibits discrimination against individuals with disabilities by recipients of federal financial assistance.

Merely having an impairment does not make one disabled for purposes of the ADA. Claimants also need to demonstrate that the impairment limits a major life activity. See 42 U.S.C. § 12102(2)(A). The HEW Rehabilitation Act regulations provide a list of examples of "major life activities," that includes "walking, seeing, hearing," and, as relevant here, "performing manual tasks." 45 CFR § 84.3(j)(2)(ii).

To qualify as disabled, a claimant must further show that the limitation on the major life activity is "substantia[l]." 42 U.S.C. § 12102(2)(A). * * * According to the EEOC regulations, "substantially limit[ed]" means "[u]nable to perform a major life activity that the average person in the general population can perform"; or "[s]ignificantly restricted as to the condition, manner or duration under which an individual can perform a particular major life activity as compared to the condition, manner, or duration under which the average person in the general population can perform that same major life activity." 29 CFR § 1630.2(j). In determining whether an individual is substantially limited in a major life activity, the regulations instruct that the following factors should be considered: "[t]he nature and severity of the impairment; [t]he duration or expected duration of the impairment; and [t]he permanent or long-term impact, or the expected permanent or long-term impact of or resulting from the impairment." §§ 1630.2(j)(2)(i)-(iii).

III

The question presented by this case is whether the Sixth Circuit properly determined that respondent was disabled under subsection (A) of the ADA's disability definition at the time that she sought an accommodation from petitioner. 42 U.S.C. § 12102(2)(A). The parties do not dispute that respondent's medical conditions, which include carpal tunnel syndrome, myotendinitis, and thoracic outlet compression, amount to physical impairments. The relevant question, therefore, is whether the Sixth Circuit correctly analyzed whether these impairments substantially limited respondent in the major life activity of performing manual tasks. Answering this requires us to address an issue about which the EEOC regulations are silent: what a plaintiff must demonstrate to establish a substantial limitation in the specific major life activity of performing manual tasks.

Our consideration of this issue is guided first and foremost by the words of the disability definition itself. "[S]ubstantially" in the phrase "substantially limits" suggests "considerable" or "to a large degree." See Webster's Third New International Dictionary 2280 (1976) (defining "substantially" as "in a substantial manner" and "substantial" as "considerable in amount, value, or worth" and "being that specified to a large degree or in the main"). * * * The word "substantial" thus clearly precludes impairments that interfere in only a minor way with the performance of manual tasks from qualifying as disabilities. * * *

"Major" in the phrase "major life activities" means important. See Webster's, *supra*, at 1363 (defining "major" as "greater in dignity, rank, importance, or interest"). "Major life activities" thus refers to those activities that are of central importance to daily life. In order for performing manual tasks to fit into this category—a category that includes such basic abilities as walking, seeing, and hearing—the manual tasks in question must be central to daily life. If each of the tasks included in the major life activity of performing manual tasks does not independently qualify as a major life activity, then together they must do so.

That these terms need to be interpreted strictly to create a demanding standard for qualifying as disabled is confirmed by the first section of the ADA, which lays out the legislative findings and purposes that motivate the Act. See 42 U.S.C. § 12101. When it enacted the ADA in 1990, Congress found that "some 43,000,000 Americans have one or more physical or mental disabilities." § 12101(a)(1). If Congress intended everyone with a physical impairment that precluded the performance of some isolated, unimportant, or particularly difficult manual task to qualify as disabled, the number of disabled Americans would surely have been much higher. Cf. *Sutton* v. *United Air Lines, Inc.,* 527 U.S., at 487 (finding that because more than 100 million people need corrective lenses to see properly, "[h]ad Congress intended to include all persons with corrected physical limitations among those covered by the Act, it undoubtedly would have cited a much higher number [than 43 million disabled persons in the findings").

We therefore hold that to be substantially limited in performing manual tasks, an individual must have an impairment that prevents or severely restricts the individual from doing activities that are of central importance to most people's daily lives. The impairment's impact must also be permanent or long-term. See 29 CFR §§ 1630.2(j)(2)(ii)-(iii) (2001).

It is insufficient for individuals attempting to prove disability status under this test to merely submit evidence of a medical diagnosis of an impairment. Instead, the ADA requires those "claiming the Act's protection * * * to prove a disability by offering evidence that the extent of the limitation [caused by their impairment] in terms of their own experience * * * is substantial." *Albertson's, Inc.* v. *Kirkingburg, supra,* at 567 (holding that monocular vision is not invariably a disability, but must be analyzed on an individual basis, taking into account the individual's ability to compensate for the impairment). That the Act defines "disability" "with respect to an individual," 42 U.S.C. § 12102(2), makes clear that Congress intended the existence of a disability to be determined in such a case-by-case manner. * * *

An individualized assessment of the effect of an impairment is particularly necessary when the impairment is one whose symptoms vary widely from person to person. Carpal tunnel syndrome, one of respondent's impairments, is just such a condition. While cases of severe carpal tunnel syndrome are characterized by muscle atrophy and extreme sensory deficits, mild cases generally do not have either of these effects and create only intermittent symptoms of numbness and tingling. Studies have further shown that, even without surgical treatment, one quarter of carpal tunnel cases resolve in one month, but that in 22 percent of cases, symptoms last for eight years or longer. When pregnancy is the cause of carpal tunnel syndrome, in contrast, the symptoms normally resolve within two weeks of delivery. Given these large potential differences in the severity and duration of the effects of carpal tunnel syndrome, an individual's carpal tunnel syndrome diagnosis, on its own, does not indicate whether the individual has a disability within the meaning of the ADA.

IV

The Court of Appeals' analysis of respondent's claimed disability suggested that in order to prove a substantial limitation in the major life activity of performing manual tasks, a "plaintiff must show that her manual disability involves a 'class' of manual activities," and that those activities "affec[t] the ability to perform tasks at work." Both of these ideas lack support.

The Court of Appeals relied on our opinion in *Sutton* v. *United Air Lines, Inc.,* for the idea that a "class" of manual activities must be implicated for an impairment to substantially limit the major life activity of performing manual tasks. But *Sutton* said only that *"[w]hen the major life activity under consideration is that of working*, the statutory phrase 'substantially limits' requires * * * that plaintiffs allege that they are unable to work in a broad class of jobs." 527 U.S., at 491 (emphasis added). Because of the conceptual difficulties inherent in the argument that working could be a major life activity, we have been hesitant to hold as much, and we need not decide this difficult question today. In *Sutton,* we noted that even assuming that working is a major life activity, a claimant would be required to show an inability to work in a "broad range of jobs," rather than a specific job. *Id.,* at 492. But *Sutton* did not suggest that a class-based analysis should be applied to any major life activity other than working. Nor do the EEOC regulations. In defining "substantially limits," the EEOC regulations only mention the "class" concept in the context of the major life activity of working. 29 CFR § 1630.2(j)(3) (2001) ("With respect to the major life activity of *working*[,] [t]he term *substantially limits* means significantly restricted in the ability to perform either a class of jobs or a broad range of jobs in various classes as compared to the average person having comparable training, skills and abilities"). Nothing in the text of the Act, our previous opinions, or the regulations suggests that a class-based framework should apply outside the context of the major life activity of working.

While the Court of Appeals in this case addressed the different major life activity of performing manual tasks, its analysis circumvented *Sutton* by focusing on respondent's inability to perform manual tasks associated only with her job. This was error. When addressing the major life activity of performing manual tasks, the central inquiry must be whether the claimant is unable to perform the variety of tasks central to most people's daily lives, not whether the claimant is unable to perform the tasks associated with her specific job. Otherwise, *Sutton*'s restriction on claims of disability based on a substantial limitation in working will be rendered meaningless because an inability to perform a specific job always can be recast as an inability to perform a "class" of tasks associated with that specific job.

There is also no support in the Act, our previous opinions, or the regulations for the Court of Appeals' idea that the question of whether an impairment constitutes a disability is to be answered only by analyzing the effect of the impairment in the workplace. * * *

Even more critically, the manual tasks unique to any particular job are not necessarily important parts of most people's lives. As a result, occupation-specific tasks may have only limited relevance to the manual task inquiry. In this case, "repetitive work with hands and arms extended at or above shoulder levels for extended periods of time," the manual task on which the Court of Appeals relied, is not an important part of most people's daily lives. The court, therefore, should not have considered respondent's inability to do such manual work in her specialized assembly line job as sufficient proof that she was substantially limited in performing manual tasks.

At the same time, the Court of Appeals appears to have disregarded the very type of evidence that it should have focused upon. It treated as irrelevant "the fact that [respondent] can * * * tend to her personal hygiene [and] carry out personal or household chores." Yet household chores, bathing, and brushing one's teeth are among the types of manual tasks of central importance to people's daily lives, and should have been part of the assessment of whether respondent was substantially limited in performing manual tasks.

The District Court noted that at the time respondent sought an accommodation from petitioner, she admitted that she was able to do the manual tasks required by her original two jobs in QCIO. In addition, according to respondent's deposition testimony, even after her condition worsened, she could still brush her teeth, wash her face, bathe, tend her flower garden, fix breakfast, do laundry, and pick up around the house. The record also indicates that her medical conditions caused her to avoid sweeping, to quit dancing, to occasionally seek help dressing, and to reduce how often she plays with her children, gardens, and drives long distances. But these changes in her life did not amount to such severe restrictions in the activities that are of central importance to most people's daily lives that they establish a manual-task disability as a matter of law. On this record, it was therefore inappropriate for the Court of Appeals to grant partial summary judgment to respondent on the issue whether she was substantially limited in performing manual tasks, and its decision to do so must be reversed.

* * *

Notes and Questions

1. In the *Williams* case, the district court rejected plaintiff's arguments that gardening, doing housework, and playing with children are major life activities. Did the Supreme Court agree with the district court? If not, how did the Supreme Court treat this question? Do you agree with the Supreme Court's characterization of major life activities in *Williams*? In *Chenoweth v.*

Hillsborough County, 250 F.3d 1328 (11th Cir.2001), *cert. denied*, 534 U.S. 1131, 122 S.Ct. 1071, 151 L.Ed.2d 973 (2002), the court rejected plaintiff's claim that driving was a major life activity. It stated:

> Major life activities are enumerated by EEOC regulation as "functions such as caring for oneself, performing manual tasks, walking, seeing, hearing, speaking, breathing, learning and working." 29 C.F.R. § 1630.2(i). Although this enumeration is not exhaustive, driving is not only absent from the list but is conspicuously different in character from the activities that are listed. It would be at the least an oddity that a major life activity should require a license from the state, revocable for a variety of reasons including failure to insure. We are an automobile society and an automobile economy, so that it is not entirely farfetched to promote driving to a major life activity; but millions of Americans do not drive, millions are passengers to work, and deprivation of being self-driven to work cannot be sensibly compared to inability to see or to learn.

Id. at 1329–30.

2. In determining whether a condition qualifies as a disability, consider the facts in *Equal Employment Opportunity Commission v. United Parcel Service*, 249 F.3d 557 (6th Cir.2001), *cert. denied*, 535 U.S. 904, 122 S.Ct. 1203, 152 L.Ed.2d 141 (2002):

> The record at the time of the summary judgment motion showed that Woods had been a driver in the company's Austin district since January 1984. Without question, he was a "qualified individual" for ADA purposes: his record at UPS was unblemished and he later received positive letters of recommendation from his supervisor in Texas. In 1988, Woods began developing serious allergic reactions that grew progressively worse over time. By 1994, these reactions were quite severe and constant, including fever, swollen eyes, nasal congestion, fever blisters, rashes, lung congestion, fatigue and depression, making it difficult for him to breathe, eat, and sleep. According to his doctors, Woods was allergic to the pollen of a plant, Mountain Cedar, which is specific to central Texas and unique in causing allergic rhinitis. Because the pollen is found only in a particular area of the country, Woods' doctors advised him that relocation might be the only solution when other treatments failed.

> * * * [As an accommodation, Woods sought a transfer to the Kentucky area where he had lived previously and had not suffered from allergies.] One physician pointed out that numerous medications prescribed for Woods's condition "had been ineffective" but that alternatives were unavailable because they would cause sedation, an unsafe condition for a professional driver. * * *

> * * *

> The EEOC insists that Woods was disabled while in Texas because his allergies were so severe as to impair his ability to breathe and to care for himself. There is testimony in the record which indicates that Woods's reactions to the allergen were steadily worsening, and that by the time he requested the transfer he rarely left home and spent nearly

all of his non-working hours in bed. His wife assumed responsibility for his correspondence and household duties, while he suffered with severe nasal and bronchial congestion, swollen eyes and nose, rashes and fever blisters over large areas of his body, fatigue, fever, and depression. UPS counters that Woods cannot be viewed as disabled because he was able to work his regular hours without accommodation while in Texas, and because he was admittedly no longer disabled once he moved to northern Kentucky.

Id. at 560–61, 562–63.

Given the Court's decisions in *Sutton* and *Williams*, what are the best arguments that the parties can make about whether Mr. Woods does or does not suffers from a "disability" as defined by the ADA?

3.   *Obesity as a Disability*: *Cook v. Rhode Island Department of Mental Health, Retardation & Hospitals*, 10 F.3d 17 (1st Cir.1993), cited in *Sutton*, is one of the leading cases holding that morbid obesity is a physical disability. The *Cook* case arose under the Rehabilitation Act and involved a plaintiff who was 5'2 tall and weighted 320 pounds. She had been previously employed as an institutional attendant for mentally retarded residents, but upon reapplying in 1988 the employer rejected her application on the ground that her "morbid obesity compromised her ability to evacuate patients in case of an emergency and put her at a greater risk of developing serious ailments." *Id.* at 21. The First Circuit held that a "jury could plausibly have found that plaintiff had a physical impairment" based on medical evidence "that morbid obesity is a physiological disorder involving a dysfunction of both the metabolic system and the neurological appetite-suppressing signal system," or that, although not disabled, she was regarded as disabled by the employer. *Id.* at 23. Judge Selya, who wrote the court's opinion, observed that "[i]n a society that all too often confuses 'slim' with 'beautiful' or 'good,' morbid obesity can present formidable barriers to employment." *Id.* at 28. For treatment of the topic of obesity as a disability, *see* Jane Byeff Korn, *Fat*, 77 B.U.L.Rev. 25 (1997); Karen M. Kramer & Arlene B. Mayerson, *Obesity Discrimination in the Workplace: Protection Through a Perceived Disability Claim Under the Rehabilitation Act and the Americans with Disabilities Act*, 31 Cal.W.L.Rev. 41 (1994). *See also* Cassista v. Community Foods, 5 Cal.4th 1050, 22 Cal.Rptr.2d 287, 856 P.2d 1143 (1993) (weight may qualify as a protected "handicap" or "disability" under state law).

4.   *Treatment as a Disability*. What if a medical condition is not itself a "disability" under the ADA, but in the prudent judgment of medical professionals, the *treatment* of the medical condition is a disability? Should the treatment be protected under the ADA? Consider the following: Mandy Christian has a condition known as hypocholesterolemia, which essentially means that she has a very high cholesterol count. Her doctor has recommended a treatment known as pheresis, i.e., periodically draining her blood from her body, removing the cholesterol, and then returning the blood to her body. The treatment would require her to take two days off each month. She has asked her employer to accommodate her pheresis treatments by allowing her to take the necessary time off each month. The employer has refused her request. Assume that hypocholesterolemia is not itself considered a disability. How would you analyze Christian's claim under the ADA? Consider also

that cancer in many instances is not disabling, at least in the early stages, but aggressive treatment in the early stages may provide a cure or otherwise enhance the possibility of remission. *See* Christian v. St. Anthony Med. Ctr., 117 F.3d 1051 (7th Cir.1997), *cert. denied*, 523 U.S. 1022, 118 S.Ct. 1304, 140 L.Ed.2d 469 (1998). Would Christian be entitled to medical leave under the Family and Medical Leave Act? The FMLA is covered in Chapter 6, Section D.

5. Articulate the definition of disability for an individual who is "regarded as" having a disability.

D. QUALIFICATIONS, DIRECT THREAT, AND UNDUE HARDSHIP

1. QUALIFICATION STANDARDS

The ADA prohibits discrimination "against" a qualified individual with a disability. Section 12111(8) defines a "qualified individual with a disability" as "an individual with a disability who, with or without reasonable accommodation, can perform the essential functions of the employment position that such individual holds or desires." The ADA does not define the "essential functions" of a job, but does provide that "the employer's judgment as to what functions of a job are essential" shall be given "consideration," and if a written job description is prepared "before advertising or interviewing applicants for the job," it "shall be considered evidence of the essential functions of the job." ADA § 101(8), 42 U.S.C. § 12111(8). The term "essential functions," however, is defined generally in the ADA regulations promulgated by the EEOC.

Essential functions—

(1) *In general.* The term essential functions means the fundamental job duties of the employment position the individual with a disability holds or desires. The term "essential functions" does not include the marginal functions of the position.

(2) A job function may be considered essential for any of several reasons, including but not limited to the following:

(i) The function may be essential because the reason the position exists is to perform that function;

(ii) The function may be essential because of the limited number of employees available among whom the performance of that job function can be distributed; and/or

(iii) The function may be highly specialized so that the incumbent in the position is hired for his or her expertise or ability to perform the particular function.

(3) Evidence of whether a particular function is essential includes, but is not limited to:

(i) The employer's judgment as to which functions are essential;

(ii) Written job descriptions prepared before advertising or interviewing applicants for the job;

(iii) The amount of time spent on the job performing the function;

(iv) The consequences of not requiring the incumbent to perform the function;

(v) The terms of a collective bargaining agreement;

(vi) The work experiences of past incumbents in the job; and/or

(vii) The current work experience of incumbents in similar jobs.

29 C.F.R. § 1630.2(n). Plainly, the considerations set out in this regulation are fact-intensive. Usually no single listed factor will be dispositive, and the regulations themselves state that the evidentiary examples provided are not meant to be exhaustive.

Although the ADA prohibits "qualification standards, employment tests or other selection criteria that screen out or tend to screen out an individual with a disability or a class of individuals with disabilities," it allows these if they are "job-related for the position in question" and "consistent with business necessity." 42 U.S.C. § 12112(b)(6). In *Albertson's v. Kirkingburg*, 527 U.S. 555, 119 S.Ct. 2162, 144 L.Ed.2d 518 (1999), the Supreme Court discussed both the meaning of "disability" and the meaning of a "qualified individual" under the ADA. The Court framed the qualification standard issue as whether an employer who requires as a job qualification that an employee meet an otherwise applicable federal safety regulation must, in an action brought under the ADA, justify enforcing that regulation solely because its standard may be waived in an individual case. Justice Souter delivered the opinion for the unanimous court on this issue. The plaintiff, Kirkingburg, and the federal government argued that an employer should not be allowed to adopt even facially neutral regulatory standards that are subject to waiver unless shown to be mandated by business necessity. The government further argued that an employer should not be allowed to impose a safety regulation that has a disparate impact on individuals with a disability unless the employer proves that safety concerns are necessary to avoid a direct threat to the safety of others. The Court rejected the arguments of Kirkingburg and the government and held than an employer is not required to justify its enforcement of an otherwise applicable federal safety regulation solely because that standard may have been waived experimentally in an individual case, even though the safety regulation would have a disparate impact on disabled individuals.

An issue that a number of courts have addressed is whether the doctrine of judicial estoppel precludes an individual from claiming that she is an individual eligible for the protection of the ADA when she has sought or received disability benefits from a source other than the ADA. Judicial estoppel, sometimes known as the doctrine of preclusion of inconsistent positions, prevents a party from gaining an advantage by taking incompatible positions in different forums. It is an equitable doctrine that is intended to protect the integrity of the judicial process by preventing litigants from "playing fast and loose" with the courts. Rissetto v. Plumbers & Steamfitters Local 343, 94 F.3d 597, 600–03 (9th Cir.1996). Though termed "judicial estoppel" the doctrine applies whether the prior position was taken in a judicial or administrative proceeding. *Id.* at 604. *See generally* Eric A. Schreiber, Comment, *The Judiciary Says, You Can't Have It Both Ways: Judicial Estoppel—A Doctrine Precluding Inconsistent Positions*, 30 Loy.L.A.L.Rev. 323 (1996).

The issue of judicial estoppel arises in disability discrimination law, for example, when an individual seeks benefits under the Social Security Act and later seeks relief also under either the ADA or the Rehabilitation Act. The Social Security Act is designed to provide a guaranteed level of income to individuals with disabilities when it has been determined that they are incapable of gainful employment. *See generally* 42 U.S.C. §§ 1381, 1382(a)(3)(B). Judicial estoppel also can arise in the context of claims brought under workers' compensation statutes, which are designed to provide for prompt and fair settlements of employee claims against employers for occupational injuries and illnesses. *See generally* 1 Arthur Larson, The Law of Workmen's Compensation § 1–1.10 (1994). The issue may also be raised in the context of benefits under employer-provided disability insurance plans, which are contractual rather than statutory. The purpose of employer-provided disability benefits is to provide partial wage replacement for employees who are unable to work because of illness, injury, or disease. The meaning of "disability" under these different remedial schemes is not necessarily the same. *See, e.g.,* Whitbeck v. Vital Signs, Inc., 116 F.3d 588 (D.C.Cir.1997).

The majority of the courts of appeals rule that a employee may qualify for disability benefits and still be a qualified individual with a disability for the purposes of the ADA. The Supreme Court, in *Cleveland v. Policy Management Systems Corporation*, 526 U.S. 795, 119 S.Ct. 1597, 143 L.Ed.2d 966 (1999), agreed as well. The reasoning of the Ninth Circuit in *Johnson v. Oregon*, 141 F.3d 1361 (9th Cir.1998) (collecting cases) is typical:

* * *

It is possible, due to the different definitions of disability employed by various agencies, to qualify for disability benefits and to satisfy the ADA's definition of a qualified person with a disability. The distinct purposes of the ADA, Social Security, and disability insurance inform the different definitions of disability employed. * * *

The ADA requires a highly fact-specific analysis of whether a particular, disabled individual can perform a certain job with (or without) reasonable accommodation. EEOC Enforcement Guidance, EEOC Notice No. 915.002, February 12, 1997, II.A. This accords with the ADA's goals: to prevent discrimination and further work opportunities for those with disabilities. *See* 42 U.S.C. § 12101(b)(1) * * *.

Swanks v. Washington Metro. Area. Transit Auth., 116 F.3d 582, 584 (D.C.Cir.1997) (discussing statute). *But see* McNemar v. Disney Store, Inc., 91 F.3d 610 (3d Cir. 1996), *cert. denied*, 519 U.S. 115, 117 S. Ct. 958, 136 L.Ed.2d 845 (1997) (dismissing ADA claim of employee who had stated he was disabled on application for social security benefits).

In contrast, the SSA, through a generalized assessment, determines whether an individual is disabled and unable to work. The Social Security Act does not take into account an individual's ability to work with accommodation. *See Swanks*, 116 F.3d at 585 (reviewing federal regulations). Thus, where "a claimant had no accommodation in his or her past work, a Social Security Administration determination that the claimant cannot do past work says nothing about the claimant's ability to perform his or her job with reasonable accommodation." *Id.* This has led the SSA to conclude: "The ADA and the disability provision of the Social Security Act have different purposes, and have no direct application to one another." *Id.* at 586 (quoting Daniel L. Skoler, Assoc. Comm'r, Soc. Sec. Admin., Disabilities Act Info. Memo at 3 (June 2, 1993) (No. SG3P2)). *See also*, Anne E. Beaumont, Note, *This Estoppel Has Got to Stop: Judicial Estoppel and the Americans with Disabilities Act*, 71 N.Y.U.L.Rev. 1529 (1996).

Notes and Questions

1. How does the definition of a "qualified" individual under the ADA differ from a "qualified" individual under the other employment discrimination statutes you have studied?

2. Recall the definition of a "disability" under *Sutton* and *Williams*. The ADA prohibits discrimination against a "qualified" individual with "disability." How large is the protected class?

2. QUALIFICATION STANDARDS AND THE DIRECT THREAT DEFENSE

The ADA provides that "[t]he term 'qualification standards' may include a requirement that an individual shall not pose a direct threat to the health or safety of other individuals in the workplace." ADA § 103(b), 42 U.S.C. § 12113(b). The ADA defines the phrase "direct threat" to mean "a significant risk to the health or safety of others that cannot be eliminated by reasonable accommodation." The EEOC regulations provide:

> The determination that an individual poses a "direct threat" shall be based on an individual's present ability to safely perform the essential functions of the job. This assessment shall be based on a reasonable medical judgment that relies on the most current medical knowledge and/or on the best available objective evidence. In deter-

mining whether an individual would pose a direct threat, the factors to be considered include:

(1) The duration of the risk;

(2) The nature and severity of the potential harm;

(3) The likelihood that the potential harm will occur; and

(4) The imminence of the potential harm.

29 C.F.R. § 1630.2(r). These factors parallel the factors the Supreme Court endorsed in *School Board of Nassau County v. Arline*, 480 U.S. 273, 107 S.Ct. 1123, 94 L.Ed.2d 307 (1987), a case brought under the Rehabilitation Act. The Rehabilitation Act does not have a provision similar to the "direct threat" provision in the ADA, but the courts have endorsed the "direct threat" principle as being applicable in the Rehabilitation Act cases. In *Arline*, the Court held that the issue of the threat to others posed by an employee with a communicable disease was properly analyzed as a question of whether the individual was "otherwise qualified." *Id.* at 287, 107 S.Ct. at 1130. *Arline* held that a person with an infectious disease who poses a significant risk of communicating the disease to others is not "otherwise qualified" to perform his or her job. *Id.* at 287 n.16, 107 S.Ct. at 1131 n.16.

In *Bragdon v. Abbott*, 524 U.S. 624, 118 S.Ct. 2196, 141 L.Ed.2d 540 (1998), the Supreme Court applied the direct threat standard under Title II of the ADA. When plaintiff Sidney Abbot, who had been infected with HIV, sought dental care, her dentist refused to fill her cavity. After finding that HIV infection constituted a disability, the Court turned to the dentist's contention that he did not have to treat plaintiff because her infectious condition posed a direct threat to his safety. The Court adopted the analysis of *Arline* and emphasized that, in order to qualify as a defense under the direct threat standard, a risk must be both significant and based on medical or other objective evidence.

Notes and Questions

1. There is a split of authority on which party bears the greater burden of proof on the existence of a "direct threat" to the health and safety of others in the workplace. Why is the allocation of the burden of proof a problem? First, it could be argued that, as a statutory defense, it is an affirmative defense that should impose the burden of proof on the employer. *See* Rizzo v. Children's World Learning Ctrs., Inc., 84 F.3d 758, 764 (5th Cir.1996) ("As with all affirmative defenses, the employer bears the burden of proving that the employee is a direct threat."). Second, however, the question of whether a plaintiff poses a "direct threat" is intimately related to the element of a prima facie case that requires the plaintiff to prove that she is a qualified individual with a disability who can perform the essential functions of the job, with or without reasonable accommodation. *See* EEOC v. Amego, Inc., 110 F.3d 135, 142–44 (1st Cir.1997); Moses v. American Nonwovens, Inc., 97 F.3d 446, 447 (11th Cir.1996), *cert. denied*, 519 U.S. 1118, 117 S.Ct. 964, 136 L.Ed.2d 849 (1997). Which of the two views on the

allocation of the burden of proof on "direct threat" do you believe is more consistent with the mandate of the ADA and the Rehabilitation Act?

2. What advice would you give an employer who wishes to assert the direct threat defense on the basis of a good faith belief that an employee poses a "significant risk to the health or safety of others"? *See* 42 U.S.C. § 12182(b)(3).

3. Section 103(d)(1) of the ADA, 42 U.S.C. § 12113(d)(1), requires the Secretary of Health and Human Services to "review" and "publish a list of" all "infectious and communicable diseases which may be transmitted through handling the food supply," to "publish the methods by which such diseases are transmitted," and to "widely disseminate" the information "to the general public." If an individual has an infectious or communicable disease that appears on the list, an employer "may refuse to assign or continue to assign such individual to a job involving food handling" if the disease "cannot be eliminated by reasonable accommodation." ADA § 103(d)(2), 42 U.S.C. § 12113(d)(2). The most recent list published pursuant to § 103(d)(1) by the Centers for Disease Control and Prevention, 68 F.R. 62809–10 42426 (Nov. 6, 2003), does not include AIDS. Consider the following:

Sharp was hired by a grocery store to work in the produce department. Because they use sharp instruments, such as knives, to prune produce for display, produce department employees are subject to bleeding from nicks and cuts to their hands. Several months after his employment began, Sharp informed his employer that he has AIDS. The employer asked Sharp to provide medical information from his own doctor or to submit to a medical examination by a doctor selected by the employer; in either case, the employer agreed to pay for the medical examination. After waiting a reasonable period of time for Sharp to comply with its request, the employer discharged him. Does Sharp have any rights under the ADA?

What if, after learning about his AIDS, the employer had offered Sharp a job in another department of the grocery store, which did not involve working with sharp instruments, but Sharp had insisted on keeping his current job because AIDS was not on the § 103(d) list of infectious and communicable diseases. Suppose that the employer then had discharged Sharp when he refused to accept the alternative job in which he would have received the same pay and worked the same hours. If Sharp had sought your advice on whether to pursue an ADA claim, what advice would you have given him? Why? *See* EEOC v. Prevo's Family Market, Inc., 135 F.3d 1089 (6th Cir.1998).

4. *The Special Problem of Health Care Workers*: Franz Polo was employed as an operating room technician until his employer, the Medical Center, received information that Polo has "full blown" AIDS. As part of his duties, Polo occasionally had to place his hands into a patient's body cavities in the presence of sharp instruments. In the past, he had sustained needle sticks and minor lacerations while assisting in surgeries. Upon learning about Polo's HIV-positive status, the Medical Center created a new full-time job for him as a cart/instrument coordinator, with responsibility for ensuring that the appropriate surgical instruments were ready for surgical operations. How would you evaluate Polo's claim for discrimination on the basis of

having a disability? Would your evaluation change if Polo instead had been a pharmacist in the Medical Center's pharmacy? *See* In the Matter of Westchester County Medical Center, [Sept. 1991–May 1994 Transfer Binder] Empl.Prac.Dec. (CCH) ¶ 5340 (Decision & Order of Admin. Law Judge, U.S. Dep't of Health & Human Serv., Departmental Appeals Board, Apr. 20, 1992).

On facts similar to these, the Sixth Circuit issued a divided decision in *Estate of Mauro v. Borgess Medical Center*, 137 F.3d 398 (6th Cir.1998), *cert. denied* 525 U.S. 815, 119 S.Ct. 51, 142 L.Ed.2d 39 (1998). The majority found that Mauro's continued employment as a surgical technician posed a direct threat to the health and safety of others, and the court affirmed the ruling of the lower court against Mauro's estate. The dissenting judge found that the case presented a jury issue; thus the lower court should not have granted summary judgment in favor of the Medical Center. *See also* EEOC v. Prevo's Family Market, Inc., 135 F.3d 1089 (6th Cir.1998).

The Centers for Disease Control has issued a report on recommendations for HIV-positive health care workers. *See* 40 Morbidity & Mortality Weekly Report (July 12, 1991). The report states that the risk of transmission of HIV from an infected health care worker to a patient is very small, and it recommends allowing HIV-positive health care workers to continue performing surgical procedures, provided that they follow safety precautions outlined in the report. The report differentiates between two types of invasive procedures, which it labels as "exposure-prone" procedures and "general invasive" procedures. General invasive procedures range from insertions of intravenous lines to most types of surgery. Exposure-prone procedures are those that pose a greater risk of percutananeous (skin-piercing) procedures.

5. For an article on the "direct threat" standard, *see* Steven H. Winterbauer, *The Direct Threat Defense: Striking a Balance Between the Duties to Accommodate and to Provide a Safe Workplace*, 23 Empl.Rel.L.J. 5 (1997).

––––––––––

The statutory language of the ADA deals with a threat to the health or safety of *others*. The EEOC promulgated a regulation that expanded on this statutory language to permit a qualification standard that requires covered individual not to pose a direct threat to his or her *own* health or safety, in addition to the health or safety of others. The application of this expanded qualification was challenged in the following case:

CHEVRON U.S.A. v. ECHAZABAL

Supreme Court of the United States, 2002.
536 U.S. 73, 122 S.Ct. 2045, 153 L.Ed.2d 82.

JUSTICE SOUTER delivered the opinion of the Court.

A regulation of the Equal Employment Opportunity Commission authorizes refusal to hire an individual because his performance on the job would endanger his own health, owing to a disability. The question in this case is whether the Americans with Disabilities Act of 1990 permits the regulation. We hold that it does.

I

Beginning in 1972, respondent Mario Echazabal worked for independent contractors at an oil refinery owned by petitioner Chevron U.S.A. Inc. Twice he applied for a job directly with Chevron, which offered to hire him if he could pass the company's physical examination. *See* 42 U.S.C. § 12112(d)(3). Each time, the exam showed liver abnormality or damage, the cause eventually being identified as Hepatitis C, which Chevron's doctors said would be aggravated by continued exposure to toxins at Chevron's refinery. In each instance, the company withdrew the offer, and the second time it asked the contractor employing Echazabal either to reassign him to a job without exposure to harmful chemicals or to remove him from the refinery altogether. The contractor laid him off in early 1996.

Echazabal filed suit, ultimately removed to federal court, claiming, among other things, that Chevron violated the Americans With Disabilities Act in refusing to hire him, or even to let him continue working in the plant, because of a disability, his liver condition. Chevron defended under a regulation of the Equal Employment Opportunity Commission permitting the defense that a worker's disability on the job would pose a "direct threat" to his health, see 29 CFR § 1630.15(b)(2) (2001). Although two medical witnesses disputed Chevron's judgment that Echazabal's liver function was impaired and subject to further damage under the job conditions in the refinery, the District Court granted summary judgment for Chevron. It held that Echazabal raised no genuine issue of material fact as to whether the company acted reasonably in relying on its own doctors' medical advice, regardless of its accuracy.

* * *

II

Section 102 of the Americans with Disabilities Act of 1990 prohibits "discriminat[ion] against a qualified individual with a disability because of the disability * * * in regard to" a number of actions by an employer, including "hiring." 42 U.S.C. § 12112(a). The statutory definition of "discriminat[ion]" covers a number of things an employer might do to block a disabled person from advancing in the workplace, such as "using qualification standards * * * that screen out or tend to screen out an individual with a disability." § 12112(b)(6). By that same definition as well as by separate provision, § 12113(a), the Act creates an affirmative defense for action under a qualification standard "shown to be job-related for the position in question and * * * consistent with business necessity." Such a standard may include "a requirement that an individual shall not pose a direct threat to the health or safety of other individuals in the workplace," § 12113(b), if the individual cannot perform the job safely with reasonable accommodation, § 12113(a). By regulation, the EEOC carries the defense one step further, in allowing an employer to screen out a potential worker with a disability not only for risks that he would pose to others in the workplace but for risks on the job to his own health or safety as well: "The term 'qualification standard' may include a requirement that an individual shall not pose a direct threat to the health or safety of the individual or others in the workplace." 29 CFR § 1630.15(b)(2) (2001).

Chevron relies on the regulation here, since it says a job in the refinery would pose a "direct threat" to Echazabal's health. In seeking deference to the agency, it argues that nothing in the statute unambiguously precludes such a defense, while the regulation was adopted under authority explicitly delegated by Congress, 42 U.S.C. § 12116, and after notice-and-comment rulemaking. Echazabal, on the contrary, argues that as a matter of law the statute precludes the regulation, which he claims would be an unreasonable interpretation even if the agency had leeway to go beyond the literal text.

* * *

A

As for the textual bar to any agency action as a matter of law, Echazabal says that Chevron loses on the threshold question whether the statute leaves a gap for the EEOC to fill. Echazabal recognizes the generality of the language providing for a defense when a plaintiff is screened out by "qualification standards" that are "job-related and consistent with business necessity" (and reasonable accommodation would not cure the difficulty posed by employment). 42 U.S.C. § 12113(a). Without more, those provisions would allow an employer to turn away someone whose work would pose a serious risk to himself. That possibility is said to be eliminated, however, by the further specification that " 'qualification standards' may include a requirement that an individual shall not pose a direct threat to the health or safety of other individuals in the workplace." § 12113(b); *see also* § 12111(3) (defining "direct threat" in terms of risk to others). Echazabal contrasts this provision with an EEOC regulation under the Rehabilitation Act of 1973, antedating the ADA, which recognized an employer's right to consider threats both to other workers and to the threatening employee himself. Because the ADA defense provision recognizes threats only if they extend to another, Echazabal reads the statute to imply as a matter of law that threats to the worker himself cannot count.

The argument follows the reliance of the Ninth Circuit majority on the interpretive canon, *expressio unius exclusio alterius*, "expressing one item of [an] associated group or series excludes another left unmentioned." *United States* v. *Vonn*, 535 U.S. 55, 65, 122 S.Ct. 1043, 1050, 152 L.Ed.2d 90, 104 (2002) (slip op., at 8). The rule is fine when it applies, but this case joins some others in showing when it does not.

The first strike against the expression-exclusion rule here is right in the text that Echazabal quotes. Congress included the harm-to-others provision as an example of legitimate qualifications that are "job-related and consistent with business necessity." These are spacious defensive categories, which seem to give an agency (or in the absence of agency action, a court) a good deal of discretion in setting the limits of permissible qualification standards. That discretion is confirmed, if not magnified, by the provision that "qualification standards" falling within the limits of job relation and business necessity "may include" a veto on those who would directly threaten others in the workplace. * * *

* * *

Strike two in this case is the failure to identify any such established series, including both threats to others and threats to self, from which Congress appears to have made a deliberate choice to omit the latter item as a signal of the affirmative defense's scope. The closest Echazabal comes is the EEOC's rule interpreting the Rehabilitation Act of 1973, a precursor of the ADA. That statute excepts from the definition of a protected "qualified individual with a handicap" anyone who would pose a "direct threat to the health or safety of other individuals," but, like the later ADA, the Rehabilitation Act says nothing about threats to self that particular employment might pose. 42 U.S.C. § 12113(b). The EEOC nonetheless extended the exception to cover threat-to-self employment, 29 CFR § 1613.702(f) (1990), and Echazabal argues that Congress's adoption only of the threat-to-others exception in the ADA must have been a deliberate omission of the Rehabilitation Act regulation's tandem term of threat-to-self, with intent to exclude it.

But two reasons stand in the way of treating the omission as an unequivocal implication of congressional intent. The first is that the EEOC was not the only agency interpreting the Rehabilitation Act, with the consequence that its regulation did not establish a clear, standard pairing of threats to self and others. * * * It would be a stretch, then, to say that there was a standard usage, with its source in agency practice or elsewhere, that connected threats to others so closely to threats to self that leaving out one was like ignoring a twin.

Even if we put aside this variety of administrative experience, however, and look no further than the EEOC's Rehabilitation Act regulation pairing self and others, the congressional choice to speak only of threats to others would still be equivocal. * * * Instead of making the ADA different from the Rehabilitation Act on the point at issue, Congress used identical language, knowing full well what the EEOC had made of that language under the earlier statute. Did Congress mean to imply that the agency had been wrong in reading the earlier language to allow it to recognize threats to self, or did Congress just assume that the agency was free to do under the ADA what it had already done under the earlier Act's identical language? There is no way to tell. Omitting the EEOC's reference to self-harm while using the very language that the

EEOC had read as consistent with recognizing self-harm is equivocal at best. No negative inference is possible.

There is even a third strike against applying the expression-exclusion rule here. It is simply that there is no apparent stopping point to the argument that by specifying a threat-to-others defense Congress intended a negative implication about those whose safety could be considered. When Congress specified threats to others in the workplace, for example, could it possibly have meant that an employer could not defend a refusal to hire when a worker's disability would threaten others outside the workplace? If Typhoid Mary had come under the ADA, would a meat packer have been defenseless if Mary had sued after being turned away? See 42 U.S.C. § 12113(d). *Expressio unius* just fails to work here.

B

Since Congress has not spoken exhaustively on threats to a worker's own health, the agency regulation can claim adherence under the rule in *Chevron*, 467 U.S., at 843, so long as it makes sense of the statutory defense for qualification standards that are "job-related and consistent with business necessity." 42 U.S.C. § 12113(a). Chevron's reasons for calling the regulation reasonable are unsurprising: moral concerns aside, it wishes to avoid time lost to sickness, excessive turnover from medical retirement or death, litigation under state tort law, and the risk of violating the national Occupational Safety and Health Act of 1970, as amended, 29 U.S.C. § 651 *et seq.* Although Echazabal claims that none of these reasons is legitimate, focusing on the concern with OSHA will be enough to show that the regulation is entitled to survive.

Echazabal points out that there is no known instance of OSHA enforcement, or even threatened enforcement, against an employer who relied on the ADA to hire a worker willing to accept a risk to himself from his disability on the job. In Echazabal's mind, this shows that invoking OSHA policy and possible OSHA liability is just a red herring to excuse covert discrimination. But there is another side to this. The text of OSHA itself says its point is "to assure so far as possible every working man and woman in the Nation safe and healthful working conditions," § 651(b), and Congress specifically obligated an employer to "furnish to each of his employees employment and a place of employment which are free from recognized hazards that are causing or are likely to cause death or serious physical harm to his employees," § 654(a)(1). Although there may be an open question whether an employer would actually be liable under OSHA for hiring an individual who knowingly consented to the particular dangers the job would pose to him, there is no denying that the employer would be asking for trouble: his decision to hire would put Congress's policy in the ADA, a disabled individual's right to operate on equal terms within the workplace, at loggerheads with the competing policy of OSHA, to ensure the safety of "each" and "every" worker. Courts would, of course, resolve the tension if there were no agency action, but the EEOC's resolution exemplifies the substantive choices that agencies are expected to make when Congress leaves the intersection of competing objectives both imprecisely marked but subject to the administrative leeway found in 42 U.S.C. § 12113(a).

Nor can the EEOC's resolution be fairly called unreasonable as allowing the kind of workplace paternalism the ADA was meant to outlaw. It is true that Congress had paternalism in its sights when it passed the ADA, see § 12101(a)(5) (recognizing "overprotective rules and policies" as a form of discrimination). But the EEOC has taken this to mean that Congress was not aiming at an employer's refusal to place disabled workers at a specifically demonstrated risk, but was trying to get at refusals to give an even break to classes of disabled people, while claiming to act for their own good in reliance on untested and pretextual stereotypes. Its regulation disallows just this sort of sham protection, through demands for a particularized enquiry into the harms the employee would probably face. The direct threat defense must be "based on a reasonable medical judgment that relies on the most current medical knowledge and/or the best available objective evidence," and upon an expressly "individualized assessment of the individual's present ability to safely perform the essential functions of the job," reached after considering, among other things, the imminence of the risk and the severity of the harm portended. 29 CFR § 1630.2(r) (2001). The EEOC was certainly acting within the reasonable zone when it saw a difference between rejecting workplace paternalism and ignoring specific and documented risks to the employee himself, even if the employee would take his chances for the sake of getting a job.

Finally, our conclusions that some regulation is permissible and this one is reasonable are not open to Echazabal's objection that they reduce the direct threat provision to "surplusage," see *Babbitt* v. *Sweet Home Chapter, Communities for Great Ore.,* 515 U.S. 687, 698 (1995). The mere fact that a threat-to-self defense reasonably falls within the general "job related" and "business necessity" standard does not mean that Congress accomplished nothing with its explicit provision for a defense based on threats to others. The provision made a conclusion clear that might otherwise have been fought over in litigation or administrative rulemaking. It did not lack a job to do merely because the EEOC might have adopted the same rule later in applying the general defense provisions, nor was its job any less responsible simply because the agency was left with the option to go a step further. A provision can be useful even without congressional attention being indispensable.

Accordingly, we reverse the judgment of the Court of Appeals and remand the case for proceedings consistent with this opinion.

Notes and Questions

1. The Court in *Echazabal* did not consider whether an individual who poses a direct threat to himself can be a "qualified individual" who can perform the "essential functions" of the employment position.

2. Do you agree with the Court that the EEOC regulation does not represent the type of workplace paternalism that the ADA was meant to

outlaw? Does the requirement that the direct threat to self be significant and based upon an individualized assessment satisfy this concern?

3.   Can you reconcile the approach to workplace paternalism taken by the Court in *Echazabal* with its approach in *Dothard v. Rawlinson* and *International Union, United Automobile Workers v. Johnson Controls*, reproduced in Chapter 6? Recall that in *Dothard*, the Court indicated that safety risks to a female prison guard herself would not satisfy a BFOQ defense to sex discrimination under Title VII. 433 U.S. at 335, 97 S.Ct. at 2730. In *Johnson Controls*, the Court struck down the employer's gender-based fetal-protection policy, concluding that Title VII's BFOQ provision, as amended by the Pregnancy Discrimination Act, "prohibit[s] an employer from discriminating against a woman because of her capacity to become pregnant unless her reproductive potential prevents her from performing the duties of her job." 499 U.S. at 206, 111 S.Ct. at 1207.

4.   What arguments might be available to plaintiffs and employers in the following cases based on the "direct threat" rule?

a.   Moses, an employee in a butcher shop, has applied for a vacancy as a butcher. Butchers operate heavy machinery, including very powerful band saws. Moses has epilepsy and is subject to seizures. He is on medication to control his epileptic seizures. Is Moses "qualified" for the job under the ADA? Can the employer refuse to hire him as a butcher? How would your arguments be affected if the evidence showed that, although Moses is an epileptic, he has never suffered a seizure and that he does not regularly take his prescribed medication? *See* Moses v. American Nonwovens, Inc., 97 F.3d 446 (11th Cir.1996), *cert. denied*, 519 U.S. 1118, 117 S.Ct. 964, 136 L.Ed.2d 849 (1997).

b.   Victoria Rizzo is employed by Children's Learning Center as a teacher's aide. The Learning Center is a day care center for children between the ages of three and five. Until recently, her job functions have included driving a van to transport the children on various outings to museums, zoos, and parks. Usually she has driven the van alone because the regular teachers have used other means of transportation for the outings. In addition, sometimes she has been alone in the classroom with children. Rizzo has a hearing impairment that requires the use of hearing aids, and her hearing has continued to deteriorate over time, requiring that she be fitted with more powerful hearing aids. Several parents whose children are enrolled in the Learning Center have complained to the director about Rizzo. They are concerned about Rizzo's ability to hear sirens on emergency vehicles, e.g., fire trucks, ambulances, or police vehicles, and to hear children who may be choking in the rear of the van. The Learning Center has a job available preparing food in the kitchen for the children and staff. Rizzo could easily do the job, but it involves different hours and less pay. The director of the Learning Center would like to transfer Rizzo to this position, and he has asked you for your advice on what he should do. What advice would you give him and why? *See* Rizzo v. Children's World Learning Ctrs., Inc., 84 F.3d 758 (5th Cir.1996).

c.   Would the outcome of the analysis in these cases be different if they were analyzed under the "essential functions" test instead of the "direct threat" standard? Consider the following: Palmer was employed as a court liaison but has been diagnosed as having a delusional (paranoid) disorder and he suffers from depression. He stated to another employee, "Look, if you don't leave me alone, I'm going to throw you out of the window." He later telephoned his supervisor and called her a "bitch." He told another worker that he was "so sick" of his supervisor that he "could just kill her" and that "she would be better off dead." The employer discharged Palmer on the ground that his conduct constituted a pattern of abusive behavior. *See* Palmer v. Circuit Court of Cook County, 117 F.3d 351 (7th Cir.1997), *cert. denied*, 522 U.S. 1096, 118 S.Ct. 893, 139 L.Ed.2d 879 (1998).

5. For an in-depth examination of a range of issues involving the "direct threat" standard under the ADA, see Jeffrey A. Van Detta, *"Typhoid Mary" Meets the ADA: A Case Study of the "Direct Threat" Standard Under the Americans with Disabilities Act*, 22 Harv.J.L. & Pub. Pol'y 849 (1999).

3. REASONABLE ACCOMMODATION AND UNDUE HARDSHIP

In what way does the concept of "undue hardship" interact with the "reasonable" portion of "reasonable accommodation?" The following case looks at the requirement of undue hardship in more detail:

VANDE ZANDE v. WISCONSIN DEPARTMENT OF ADMINISTRATION

United States Court of Appeals for the Seventh Circuit, 1995.
44 F.3d 538.

POSNER, Chief Judge.

* * *

The more problematic [disability] case is that of an individual who has a vocationally relevant disability—an impairment such as blindness or paralysis that limits a major human capability, such as seeing or walking. In the common case in which such an impairment interferes with the individual's ability to perform up to the standards of the workplace, or increases the cost of employing him, hiring and firing decisions based on the impairment are not "discriminatory" in a sense closely analogous to employment discrimination on racial grounds. The draftsmen of the [Americans with Disabilities] Act knew this. But they were unwilling to confine the concept of disability discrimination to cases in which the disability is irrelevant to the performance of the disabled person's job. Instead, they defined "discrimination" to include an employer's "not making reasonable accommodations to the known physical or mental limitations of an otherwise qualified individual with a disability who is an applicant or employee, unless * * * [the employer] can demonstrate that the accommodation would impose an undue hardship on the operation of the * * * [employer's] business." 42 U.S.C. § 12112(b)(5)(A).

The term "reasonable accommodations" is not a legal novelty, even if we ignore its use in the provision of Title VII forbidding religious discrimination in employment. It is one of a number of provisions in the employment subchapter that were borrowed from regulations issued by the Equal Employment Opportunity Commission in implementation of the Rehabilitation Act of 1973, 29 U.S.C. §§ 701 *et seq.* * * * Indeed, to a great extent the employment provisions of the new Act merely generalize to the economy as a whole the duties, including that of reasonable accommodation, that the regulations under the Rehabilitation Act imposed on federal agencies and federal contractors. We can therefore look to the decisions interpreting those regulations for clues to the meaning of the same terms in the new law.

It is plain enough what "accommodation" means. The employer must be willing to consider making changes in its ordinary work rules, facilities, terms, and conditions in order to enable a disabled individual to work. The difficult term is "reasonable." The plaintiff in our case, a paraplegic, argues in effect that the term just means apt or efficacious. An accommodation is reasonable, she believes, when it is tailored to the particular individual's disability. A ramp or lift is thus a reasonable accommodation for a person who like this plaintiff is confined to a wheelchair. Considerations of cost do not enter into the term as the plaintiff would have us construe it. Cost is, she argues, the domain of "undue hardship" (another term borrowed from the regulations under the Rehabilitation Act)—a safe harbor for an employer that can show that it would go broke or suffer other excruciating financial distress were it compelled to make a reasonable accommodation in the sense of one effective in enabling the disabled person to overcome the vocational effects of the disability.

These are questionable interpretations both of "reasonable" and of "undue hardship." To "accommodate" a disability is to make some change that will enable the disabled person to work. An unrelated, inefficacious change would not be an accommodation of the disability at all. So "reasonable" may be intended to qualify (in the sense of weaken) "accommodation," in just the same way that if one requires a "reasonable effort" of someone this means less than the maximum possible effort, or in law that the duty of "reasonable care," the cornerstone of the law of negligence, requires something less than the maximum possible care. It is understood in that law that in deciding what care is reasonable the court considers the cost of increased care. * * * Similar reasoning could be used to flesh out the meaning of the word "reasonable" in the term "reasonable accommodations." It would not follow that the costs and benefits of altering a workplace to enable a disabled person to work would always have to be quantified, or even that an accommodation would have to be deemed unreasonable if the cost exceeded the benefit however slightly. But, at the very least, the cost could not be disproportionate to the benefit. Even if an employer is so large or wealthy—or, like the principal defendant in this case, is a state, which can raise taxes in order to finance any accommodations that it must make to disabled employees—that it may not be able to plead "undue *hardship*," it would not be required to expend enormous sums in order to bring about a trivial improvement in the life of a disabled employee. If the nation's employers have potentially unlimited financial obligations to 43 million disabled persons, the Americans with Disabilities Act will have imposed an indirect tax potentially greater than the national debt. We do not find an intention to bring about such a radical result in either the language of the Act or its history. The preamble actually "markets" the Act as a cost saver, pointing to "billions of dollars in unnecessary expenses resulting from dependency and nonproductivity." The savings will be illusory if employers are required to expend many more billions in accommodation than will be saved by enabling disabled people to work.

The concept of reasonable accommodation is at the heart of this case. The plaintiff sought a number of accommodations to her paraplegia that were turned down. The principal defendant as we have said is a state, which does not argue that the plaintiff's proposals were rejected because accepting them would have imposed undue hardship on the state or because they would not have done her any good. The district judge nevertheless granted summary judgment for the defendants on the ground that the evidence obtained in discovery, construed as favorably to the plaintiff as the record permitted, showed that they had gone as far to accommodate the plaintiff's demands as reasonableness, in a sense distinct from either aptness or hardship—a sense based, rather, on considerations of cost and proportionality—required. On this analysis, the function of the "undue hardship" safe harbor, like the "failing company" defense to antitrust liability is to excuse compliance by a firm that is financially distressed, even though the cost of the accommodation to the firm might be less than the benefit to disabled employees.

This interpretation of "undue hardship" is not inevitable—in fact probably is incorrect. It is a defined term in the Americans with Disabilities Act, and the definition is "an action requiring significant difficulty or expense." The financial condition of the employer is only one consideration in determining whether an accommodation otherwise reasonable would impose an undue hardship. The legislative history equates "undue hardship" to "unduly costly." These are terms of relation. We must ask, "undue" in relation to what? Presumably (given the statutory definition and the legislative history) in relation to the benefits of the accommodation to the disabled worker as well as to the employer's resources.

So it seems that costs enter at two points in the analysis of claims to an accommodation to a disability. The employee must show that the accommodation is reasonable in the sense both of efficacious and of proportional to costs. Even if this prima facie showing is made, the employer has an opportunity to prove that upon more careful consideration the costs are excessive in relation either to the benefits of the accommodation or to the employer's financial survival or health. In a classic negligence case, the idiosyncrasies of the particular employer are irrelevant. Having above-average costs, or being in a precarious financial situation, is not a defense to negligence. One interpretation of "undue hardship" is that it permits an employer to escape liability if he can carry the burden of proving that a disability accommodation reasonable for a normal employer would break him.

Lori Vande Zande, aged 35, is paralyzed from the waist down as a result of a tumor of the spinal cord. Her paralysis makes her prone to develop pressure ulcers, treatment of which often requires that she stay at home for several weeks. * * * We hold that Vande Zande's pressure ulcers are a part of her disability, and therefore a part of what the State of Wisconsin had a duty to accommodate—reasonably.

Vande Zande worked for the housing division of the state's department of administration for three years, beginning in January 1990. The housing division supervises the state's public housing programs. Her job was that of a program assistant, and involved preparing public information materials, planning meetings, interpreting regulations, typing, mailing, filing, and copying. In short, her tasks were of a clerical, secretarial, and administrative assistant character. In order to enable her to do this work, the defendants, as she acknowledges, "made numerous accommodations relating to the plaintiff's disability." As examples, in her words, "they paid the landlord to have bathrooms modified and to have a step ramped; they bought special adjustable furniture for the plaintiff; they ordered and paid for one-half of the cost of a cot that the plaintiff needed for daily personal care at work; they sometimes adjusted the plaintiff's schedule to perform backup telephone duties to accommodate the plaintiff's medical appointments; they made changes to the plans for a locker room in the new state office building; and they agreed to provide some of the specific accommodations the plaintiff requested in her October 5 "Reasonable Accommodation Request."

But she complains that the defendants did not go far enough in two principal respects. One concerns a period of eight weeks when a bout of pressure ulcers forced her to stay home. She wanted to work full time at home and believed that she would be able to do so if the division would provide her with a desktop computer at home (though she already had a laptop). Her supervisor refused, and told her that he probably would have only 15 to 20 hours of work for her to do at home per week and that she would have to make up the difference between that and a full work week out of her sick leave or vacation leave. In the event, she was able to work all but 16.5 hours in the eight-week period. She took 16.5 hours of sick leave to make up the difference. As a result, she incurred no loss of income, but did lose sick leave that she could have carried forward indefinitely. She now works for another agency of the State of Wisconsin, but any unused sick leave in her employment by the housing division would have accompanied her to her new job. Restoration of the 16.5 hours of lost sick leave is one form of relief that she seeks in this suit.

She argues that a jury might have found that a reasonable accommodation required the housing division either to give her the desktop computer or to excuse her from having to dig into her sick leave to get paid for the hours in which, in the absence of the computer, she was unable to do her work at home. No jury, however, could in our view be permitted to stretch the concept of "reasonable accommodation" so far. Most jobs in organizations public or private involve team work under supervision rather than solitary unsupervised work, and team work under supervision generally cannot be performed at home without a substantial reduction in the quality of the employee's performance. This will no doubt change as communications technology advances, but is the situation today. Generally, therefore, an employer is not required to accommodate a disability by allowing the disabled worker to work, by himself, without supervision, at home. This is the majority view, illustrated by *Tyndall v. National Education Centers, Inc.*, 31 F.3d 209, 213–14 (4th Cir.1994), and *Law v. United States Postal Service*, 852 F.2d 1278 (Fed.Cir.1988) (per curiam). The District of Columbia Circuit disagrees. Langon v. Dep't of Health & Human Serv., 959 F.2d 1053, 1060–61 (D.C.Cir.1992); Carr v. Reno, 23 F.3d 525, 530 (D.C.Cir.1994). But we think the majority view is correct. An employer is not required to allow disabled workers to work at home, where their productivity inevitably would be greatly reduced. No doubt to this as to any generalization about so complex and varied an activity as employment there are exceptions, but it would take a very extraordinary case for the employee to be able to create a triable issue of the employer's failure to allow the employee to work at home.

And if the employer, because it is a government agency and therefore is not under intense competitive pressure to minimize its labor costs or maximize the value of its output, or for some other reason, bends over backwards to accommodate a disabled worker—goes further than the law requires—by allowing the worker to work at home, it must not be punished for its generosity by being deemed to have conceded the reasonableness of so far-reaching an accommodation. That would hurt rather than help disabled workers. Wisconsin's housing division was not required by the Americans with Disabilities Act to allow Vande Zande to work at home; even more clearly it was not required to install a computer in her home so that she could avoid using up 16.5 hours of sick leave. It is conjectural that she will ever need those 16.5 hours; the expected cost of the loss must, therefore, surely be slight. An accommodation that allows a disabled worker to work at home, at full pay, subject only to a slight loss of sick leave that may never be needed, hence never missed, is, we hold, reasonable as a matter of law.

* * *

Her second complaint has to do with the kitchenettes in the housing division's building, which are for the use of employees during lunch and coffee breaks. Both the sink and the counter in each of the kitchenettes were 36 inches high, which is too high for a person in a wheelchair. The building was under construction, and the kitchenettes not yet built, when the plaintiff complained about this feature of the design. But the defendants refused to alter the design to lower the sink and counter to

34 inches, the height convenient for a person in a wheelchair. Construction of the building had begun before the effective date of the Americans with Disabilities Act, and Vande Zande does not argue that the failure to include 34–inch sinks and counters in the design of the building violated the Act. She could not argue that; the Act is not retroactive. But she argues that once she brought the problem to the attention of her supervisors, they were obliged to lower the sink and counter, at least on the floor on which her office was located but possibly on the other floors in the building as well, since she might be moved to another floor. All that the defendants were willing to do was to install a shelf 34 inches high in the kitchenette area on Vande Zande's floor. That took care of the counter problem. As for the sink, the defendants took the position that since the plumbing was already in place it would be too costly to lower the sink and that the plaintiff could use the bathroom sink, which is 34 inches high.

Apparently it would have cost only about $150 to lower the sink on Vande Zande's floor; to lower it on all the floors might have cost as much as $2,000, though possibly less. Given the proximity of the bathroom sink, Vande Zande can hardly complain that the inaccessibility of the kitchenette sink interfered with her ability to work or with her physical comfort. Her argument rather is that forcing her to use the bathroom sink for activities (such as washing out her coffee cup) for which the other employees could use the kitchenette sink stigmatized her as different and inferior; she seeks an award of compensatory damages for the resulting emotional distress. We may assume without having to decide that emotional as well as physical barriers to the integration of disabled persons into the workforce are relevant in determining the reasonableness of an accommodation. But we do not think an employer has a duty to expend even modest amounts of money to bring about an absolute identity in working conditions between disabled and nondisabled workers. The creation of such a duty would be the inevitable consequence of deeming a failure to achieve identical conditions "stigmatizing." That is merely an epithet. We conclude that access to a particular sink, when access to an equivalent sink, conveniently located, is provided, is not a legal duty of an employer. The duty of reasonable accommodation is satisfied when the employer does what is necessary to enable the disabled worker to work in reasonable comfort.

* * *

Notes and Questions

1.   The EEOC regulations promulgated to implement the ADA provide that

[t]o determine the appropriate reasonable accommodation it may be necessary for the covered entity to initiate an informal, interactive process with the qualified individual with a disability in need of the accommodation. This process should identify the precise limitations

resulting from the disability and potential reasonable accommodations that could overcome those limitations.

29 C.F.R. § 1630.2(*o*)(3). The regulations also state that "[t]he appropriate reasonable accommodation is best determined through a flexible, interactive process that involves both the employer and the qualified individual with a disability." 29 C.F.R. pt. 1630 app. § 1630.9.

2.   One of the most common criticisms of the ADA is that its reasonable accommodation requirement will impose substantial costs on employers that will outweigh the benefits, particularly for small businesses. The argument about costs and benefits is cast primarily in law and economics terms. *See, e.g.*, Max Schulz, *Disability Rules Moving in on Smaller Businesses*, Wash. Times, Aug. 28 1994, at B3; Ron A. Vassel, Note, *The Americans with Disabilities Act: The Cost, Uncertainty and Inefficiency*, 13 J.L. & Com. 397 (1994). A study commissioned by Sears, Roebuck and Co. indicated that 69% of the reasonable accommodations provided by Sears cost nothing; that 28% cost less than $1,000; and only 3% cost more than $1,000. The average cost of accommodations was less than $50 compared to the average costs of $1,800 to $2,400 that Sears incurred for terminating and replacing an employee. Peter David Blanck, *Transcending Title I of the Americans with Disabilities Act: A Report on Sears, Roebuck and Co.*, 20 Mental & Physical Disability Rep. 278 (1996). And, a 1994 report from the President's Committee on Employment of People with Disabilities found that between October, 1992, and the study's end, 68% of the accommodations made for workers with disabilities cost $500 or less. *See* Steven B. Epstein, *In Search of a Bright Line: Determining When an Employer's Financial Hardship Becomes "Undue" Under the Americans with Disabilities Act*, 48 Vand.L.Rev. 391, 394 n.11 (1995) (discussing the Committee's data).

3.   Taylor, a manager for an investment company, told his supervisor, Mick James, that he was suffering from bipolar disorder, a form of mental depression. Taylor also informed James that he was "okay," and the only help he needed was for James to reduce Taylor's work performance objectives and to learn about the symptoms of the disorder in order to facilitate communication with Taylor. James did nothing. Did Taylor's conversation with James trigger an obligation by the employer to initiate an informal investigation into the need for reasonable accommodations for Taylor? *See* Taylor v. Principal Fin. Group, Inc., 93 F.3d 155 (5th Cir.), *cert. denied*, 519 U.S. 1029, 117 S.Ct. 586, 136 L.Ed.2d 515 (1996).

4.   What obligation, if any, does the ADA impose on an employer, who has been found liable for "regarding" an employee as having a disability when it is proven that the employee does not, in fact, have a disability as defined by the Act? Several courts have held that when an employer has violated the ADA under the "regarded as" prong of the definition of a "disability," it is, nevertheless, obligated to remedy the violation by attempting to make a reasonable accommodation. *See* Katz v. City Metal Co., 87 F.3d 26 (1st Cir.1996); Chandler v. City of Dallas, 2 F.3d 1385 (5th Cir.1993), *cert. denied*, 511 U.S. 1011, 114 S.Ct. 1386, 128 L.Ed.2d 61 (1994). The First Circuit in *Katz* held that one of the purposes of the ADA was to protect individuals who are not substantially disabled but are wrongly perceived to be so. If the decision in *Katz* is the correct interpretation of the statute, what

is a reasonable accommodation for an individual, who is regarded as having a physical or mental disability, but who actually has no such disability? If no accommodation is required, what relief would be appropriate? *See* Deane v. Pocono Med. Ctr., 142 F.3d 138 (3d Cir.1998) (en banc).

5. If a law firm hires as an associate a recent law school graduate who is wheelchair-bound, what accommodations would you expect the firm to make in order to comply with the ADA? What if the new associate is a quadriplegic? *See* Monica Bay, *Attorneys with Disabilities Get Organized*, The Recorder (San Francisco), Oct. 6, 1992, at 17.

6. *Reasonable Accommodation in the Unionized Sector*: Unions fall within the definition of the term "covered entity" under § 101(2) of the ADA, 42 U.S.C. § 12111(2). Thus, like employers, unions are now statutorily obligated to refrain from discriminating against individuals with disabilities and to make reasonable accommodations for individuals who are within the class protected under the ADA. Many of these issues are explored in Joanne Jocha Ervin, *Reasonable Accommodation and the Collective Bargaining Agreement Under the Americans with Disabilities Act of 1990*, 1991 Det. C.L.Rev. 925; Jerry M. Hunter, *Potential Conflicts Between Obligations Imposed on Employers and Unions by the National Labor Relations Act and the Americans with Disabilities Act*, 13 N.Ill.U.L. Rev. 207 (1993); Mary K. O'Melveny, *The Americans with Disabilities Act and Collective Bargaining Agreements: Reasonable Accommodations or Irreconcilable Conflicts?*, 82 Ky.L.J. 219 (1994); Robert W. Pritchard, *Avoiding the Inevitable: Resolving the Conflicts Between the ADA and the NLRA*, 11 Lab. Law. 375 (1996), Rose Daly–Rooney, Note, *Reconciling Conflicts Between the Americans with Disabilities Act and the National Labor Relations Act to Accommodate People with Disabilities*, 6 DePaul Bus.L.J. 387 (1994). William McDevitt, *Seniority Systems and the Americans with Disabilities Act: The Fate of "Reasonable Accommodation" After Eckles*, 9 St. Thomas L.Rev. 359 (1997) (discussing a union's responsibility to fairly represent employees with disabilities during bargaining); Condon A. McGlothlen & Gary N. Savine, Eckles v. Consolidated Rail Corp.: *Reconciling the ADA with Collective Bargaining Agreements: Is This the Correct Approach?*, 46 DePaul L.Rev. 1043 (1997) (same).

E.   MEDICAL INQUIRIES, MEDICAL EXAMINATIONS, AND MEDICAL BENEFITS

1.   MEDICAL INQUIRIES AND EXAMINATIONS

Prior to the enactment of the ADA, it was a common practice for many employers to include medical examinations and health history questionnaires as part of the employment application. Also, fairly candid discussions between employers and employees about health concerns was the norm. The ADA imposes a series of restrictions on an employer's use of medical examinations and inquiries in three situations: at the application stage ("pre-offer stage"), after individuals have been offered a job ("entering employees" or "post-offer stage"), and for current or "existing employees." ADA § 102(d), 42 U.S.C. § 1211(d). *See* Norman–Bloodsaw v. Lawrence Berkeley Lab., 135 F.3d 1260 (9th Cir.1998); Chai Feldblum, *Medical Examinations and Inquiries Under the Americans with Disabilities Act: A View from the Inside*, 64 Temple L.Rev. 521 (1991) (discussing the legislative history of the provisions on medical examinations and inquiries). The EEOC has issued enforcement guidance to assist employers in understanding and complying with the ADA's limitations on medical inquiries and medical examinations. EEOC, Guidance on Preemployment Disability–Related Inquiries and Medical Examinations Under the Americans with Disabilities Act (Oct. 1995) (Guidance on Preemployment Inquiries), *reprinted* in BNA, Americans with Disabilities Act Manual, at 70:1103. *See* Susan Alexander, *Preemployment Inquiries and Examination: What Employers Need to Know About the New EEOC Guidelines*, 45 Lab.L.J. 667 (1994).

Pre-Offer Stage: Section 102(d)(2)(A) of the ADA, 42 U.S.C. § 12112(d)(2)(A), provides that unless otherwise expressly allowed, an employer may not conduct "a medical examination or make inquiries of a job applicant as to whether such applicant is an individual with a disability or as to the nature or severity of such disability." Although screening of applicants generally must be based on nonmedical factors, the ADA permits employers to discuss medical issues with job applicants in three rather narrow situations. The first, found in ADA § 102(d)(2)(B), 42 U.S.C. § 12112(d)(2)(B), allows an employer to "make preemployment inquiries into the ability of an applicant to perform job-related functions," provided the inquiry is made of all applicants for the particular job. Second, an employer may ask an applicant to demonstrate how she or he would perform the essential functions of the job for which the applicant is applying. Third, an employer may ask an applicant with an obvious or a known disability what accommodation is required. For example, an applicant using a wheelchair may be asked how he would perform the essential functions of the job position, but he may not be asked how long he has used a wheelchair or how the disability occurred. *See* EEOC Guidance on Preemployment Inquiries.

Post-Employment Stage—"Entering Employees": An "entering employee" is an individual who has received a job offer but has not yet started to work. As for "entering employees," ADA § 102(d)(2)(B)(3), 42 U.S.C. § 12112(d)(2)(B)(3), provides that an employer "may require a medical examination after an offer of employment has been made to a job applicant and prior to the commencement of the employment duties of such applicant, and may condition an offer of employment on the results of such examination," provided certain conditions are met. The conditions are that (1) all entering employees must have the same medical examination regardless of whether they have a disability; (2) the employer keeps the medical information on separate forms, in separate medical files, and treats it as a "confidential medical record," and (3) the employer uses the results of any examination only to comply with the ADA. *Id.* As to the confidentiality provision, the ADA allows the employer to disclose medical information to supervisors and managers who have a "need to know" of necessary restrictions on the employee's duties and "necessary accommodations," to first aid and safety personnel who "need to know" should emergency treatment of the employee become necessary, and to government officials who need the information to investigate compliance with the ADA. *Id.* Based upon the information obtained in a medical examination, an offer of employment cannot be withdrawn unless it is (1) related to the individual's job and (2) necessary for the conduct of the employer's business. An offer of employment also can be withdrawn if the entering employee's disability would constitute a "direct threat" to the health and safety of the employee and others and no reasonable accommodation is available.

Current or "Existing Employees": The ADA § 102(d)(4), 42 U.S.C. § 12112(d)(4), prohibits an employer from requiring current employees to submit to a "medical examination" or to "make inquiries of an employee as to whether such employee is an individual with a disability or as to the nature or severity of the disability, unless such examination or inquiry is shown to be job-related and consistent with business necessity." The EEOC has construed § 102(d)(4) of the ADA, 42 U.S.C. § 12112(d)(4), to permit an employer "to make inquiries or require medical examinations (fitness for duty exams) when there is a need to determine whether an employee is still able to perform the essential functions of his or her job." 29 C.F.R. pt. 1630, app. § 1630.14(c). The courts generally have deferred to the EEOC's interpretation of § 102(d)(4), because the EEOC has taken the position that if an employee suffers an injury or arguably has a "serious health condition" that appears to affect the employee's ability to perform the essential functions of a job, a medical examination is deemed to be job related and consistent with business necessity. *See* Porter v. U.S. Alumoweld Co., Inc., 125 F.3d 243 (4th Cir.1997) (citing the EEOC Technical Manual on the Employment Provisions of the ADA).

Drug Testing: Drug testing is not prohibited under the ADA because the statute provides that the term "qualified individual with a disability" excludes "any employee or applicant who is currently engaging in the illegal use of drugs." ADA § 104(a), 42 U.S.C. § 12114(a). Nevertheless, the ADA provides that nothing in the statute "shall be construed to exclude as a qualified individual with a disability an individual who * * * has successfully completed a supervised drug rehabilitation program and is no longer engaging in" the use of illegal drugs, or has been "successfully" rehabilitated and "is no longer engaging in" the use of illegal drugs. *Id.* § 104(b)(1), 42 U.S.C. § 12114(b)(1).

The Ninth Circuit's decision in *Collings v. Longview Fibre Co.*, 63 F.3d 828 (9th Cir.1995), *cert. denied*, 516 U.S. 1048, 116 S.Ct. 711, 133 L.Ed.2d 666 (1996), illustrates how most courts interpret the term "currently" in the phrase "currently engaging in the illegal use of drugs." In *Collings*, eight employees sued under the ADA after they had been discharged for illegal drug use. The employees admitted they had used illegal drugs in the weeks before their termination, but they argued that they were protected under the ADA because, at the time of discharge, they were drug-free and were enrolled in a rehabilitation program. The Ninth Circuit rejected the argument relying, in substantial part, on the EEOC regulations that interpret "currently engaging" in illegal drug use to mean an illegal use of drugs "that has occurred recently enough to indicate that the individual is actively engaged in such conduct." *Id.* at 833 (citing 29 C.F.R. § 1630.3 app.). Other courts have reached a similar conclusion. *See, e.g.,* Shafer v. Preston Mem'l Hosp. Corp., 107 F.3d 274, 278 (4th Cir.1997) (ordinary meaning of "currently" does not require that drug user "have heroin syringe in his arm or a marijuana bong to his mouth at the exact moment contemplated"); McDaniel v. Mississippi Baptist Med. Ctr., 877 F.Supp. 321, 327 (S.D.Miss.1994) (Congress contemplated "a drug free period of some considerable length"), *aff'd,* 74 F.3d 1238 (5th Cir.1995) (table decision).

The ADA treats alcohol users differently from users of illegal drugs because alcohol is not a "drug" within the meaning of the statute, *see* ADA § 101(6)(B), 42 U.S.C. § 12111(6)(b), and an alcoholic is not automatically excluded from ADA protection because of "current" alcohol use. *See* Mararri v. WCI Steel, Inc., 130 F.3d 1180 (6th Cir.1997) (although alcoholism is a disability protected under the ADA, the discharge of an alcoholic employee was upheld when he failed to live up to the terms of an agreement to be tested and treated for his alcoholism). If a former alcoholic has been successfully rehabilitated, can he still qualify as an "individual with a disability" under the ADA or the Rehabilitation Act? Is a rehabilitated alcoholic analogous to an individual with a disability that can be corrected or controlled by mediative procedures? If a rehabilitated alcoholic can no longer be considered an "individual with a disability," does it lead to the anomalous result of affording ADA protection to alcoholics who continue to drink alcohol, but not those who are recovering? *See* Burch v. Coca–Cola Co., 119 F.3d 305 (5th Cir.1997) (ADA protection is limited to alcoholic-induced mental or physical impairments that substantially limit major life activities), *cert. denied,* 522 U.S. 1084, 118 S.Ct. 871, 139 L.Ed.2d 768 (1998).

Genetic Testing: On January 20, 1998, the Department of Labor, the Equal Opportunity Commission, the Department of Health and Human Services, and the Department of Justice issued a report of a study of genetic information in the workplace. Genetic Information in the Workplace, *reprinted in* 49 Lab.L.J. 867 (1998). The report was, in substantial part, a response to the Human Genome Project, which is attempting to identify the 50,000 to 100,000 or so genes that make up the human genome. Genetic technology, including genetic testing, has the potential to identify specific individuals who have a particular genetic trait for disabilities or disorders, such as Huntington's disease, breast cancer, sickle cell anemia, and epilepsy. There are currently two types of genetic testing that can be done in the workplace: screening for specific inherited diseases and screening for susceptibility to diseases that might be aggravated by conditions or substances in the workplace. As genetic technology increases, the possibility for discrimination on the basis of disabilities increases. Although a number of states have enacted specific legislation prohibiting genetic testing, presently there is only one federal law that speaks directly to the issue, the Health Insurance Portability and Accountability Act of 1996, Pub.L. No. 104–191, Sec. 101, § 702, 110 Stat. 1936, 1945–46 (codified at 29 U.S.C. § 1182 (2000)). HIPAA prohibits group health insurance plans from using any health-status-related factor, including genetic information, as a basis for denying or limiting eligibility for coverage or for charging individuals more for coverage. What arguments could be made for or against the position that the ADA or Rehabilitation Act prohibits genetic screening and testing in the workplace? Melinda B. Kaufmann, *Genetic Discrimination in the Workplace: An Overview of Existing Problems,* 30 Loy.U.Chi.L.J. 393 (1999) (discussing the legal and ethical ramifications of using genetic information to screen job applicants and monitor employees.)

The ADA and the FMLA: The limitations on medical examinations and inquiries under the ADA must be considered in light of the employer's obligations under the Family and Medical Leave Act of 1993 (FMLA), 29 U.S.C. § 2601 et seq., which is covered in Chapter 6, section D. Under the FMLA, an employee is eligible for FMLA leave because of "a serious health condition that makes the employee unable to perform the functions of the position." 29 U.S.C. § 2612(a)(1)(D). The FMLA requires the employee to notify the employer of the reasons and necessity for FMLA leave. If the employer is on notice that a FMLA leave might be appropriate, but the information the employer has received from the employee is not sufficient for the employer to determine whether the employee qualifies for a FMLA leave, then the employer has to make further inquiries. To substantiate the reasons for the requested FMLA leave, the employer can require the employee to provide medical certification from his doctor using FMLA forms.

It is possible that an employer's inquiry about the "serious health condition" of an employee pursuant to the employee's request for a FMLA leave, might violate the restrictions on medical inquiries under the ADA for "current or existing employees." Does this pose a dilemma for the employer? For example, suppose that an employee has a "serious health condition" that qualifies for a leave under the FMLA and the medical condition would also be considered a "disability" under the ADA. May the employer request a medical report certifying that the employee is medically fit to return to work if that request seeks more medical information about the employee than the employer could lawfully obtain under the ADA? *See, e.g.,* Porter v. U.S. Alumoweld Co., Inc., 125 F.3d 243 (4th Cir.1997); Albert v. Runyon, 6 F.Supp.2d 57 (D.Mass. 1998). The regulations promulgated by the Department of Labor, which has responsibility for enforcing the FMLA, provide that, following a FMLA leave, a "fitness-for duty" certification under the FMLA "need only be a simple statement of an employee's ability to return to work." 29 C.F.R. § 825.310(c).

Questions

1. Daisy Bates applied for a job in a bakery for which the employer had advertised a vacancy. The bakery's application form asks various questions about educational background and work experience. In addition, it has the following questions: "Have you ever received worker's compensation or disability income?" "Do you have any physical defects which would preclude you from performing certain jobs?" "If yes, describe." In response to these questions, Bates described workers' compensation payments she had received for third-degree burns to her hand and foot, surgery to her elbow, and a sprained shoulder. After completing the application and other parts of the screening process, Bates was told by the interviewer that she was the most qualified applicant for the job. Bates later learned that the job was awarded to another applicant. Assuming that Bates is fully qualified for the position and that she would not be able to prove that she has a disability within the meaning of the ADA, would she have an ADA claim against the employer? *See* Armstrong v. Turner Indus. Ltd., 950 F.Supp. 162 (M.D.La.1996), *aff'd*, 141 F.3d 554, (5th Cir.1998). *See also* Jeff Barge, *Job Interview Can Bring ADA Liability*, 82 A.B.A.J. 34 (Mar. 1996); *Illegal Questions Brings $150,000 Punitive Damage Award*, Disability Compliance Bulletin (Apr. 10, 1997).

2. An employer, Resort, Inc., has adopted the following policy:

Employees must report, without qualification, all drugs present within their body systems. Further, they must remain free of drugs while on the job. They must not use, possess, conceal, manufacture, distribute, dispense, transport, or sell drugs while on the job, in Resort vehicles or on Resort's properties. Additionally, prescribed drugs may be used only to the extent that they have been reported and approved by an employee supervisor and that they can be taken by the employee without risk of sensory impairment and/or injury to any person, employee, or customer of Resort.

Is the policy lawful under the ADA? *See* Roe v. Cheyenne Mountain Conference Resort, Inc., 124 F.3d 1221, 1226 (10th Cir.1997).

3. An employer has a practice of making offers of employment conditioned upon the applicant agreeing to submit to a medical examination. In the course of the medical examination, each applicant, who has received an offer of employment, completes a detailed medical history questionnaire and is required to provide blood and urine samples. The questionnaire asks, *inter alia*, whether the applicant has any of sixty-one listed medical conditions, including sickle cell anemia, venereal disease, and, in the case of female applicants, menstrual disorders. The blood and urine samples of all applicants are tested for syphilis, sickle cell traits, and genetic traits. The blood and urine samples of women are tested for pregnancy, and the blood samples of men are tested for prostate gland disorders. The tests on blood and urine samples are conducted without any prior or subsequent notice to applicants that these particular tests will be or have been performed. Does the practice of the employer violate the ADA? Title VII? Both? Neither? *See* Norman–Bloodsaw v. Lawrence Berkeley Lab., 135 F.3d 1260 (9th Cir.1998).

2. MEDICAL BENEFITS

The ADA has several provisions that affect health, disability, and other employee benefits. First, § 102 of the ADA, 42 U.S.C. § 12112, broadly prohibits discrimination because of disability. Health insurance and other benefits fall within the meaning of "terms, conditions, and privileges of employment" under § 102. *See* Ford v. Schering–Plough Corp., 145 F.3d 601, 604 (3d Cir.1998); Lewis v. Aetna Life Ins. Co., 982 F.Supp. 1158, 1160–61 (E.D.Va.1997). The EEOC's regulations also state that the ADA prohibits an employer from discriminating against a qualified individual with a disability in regard to "[f]ringe benefits available by virtue of employment, whether or not administered by the [employer]," 29 C.F.R. § 1630.4(f). Second, § 101, 42 U.S.C. § 12111, contains a statutory cost-justification defense that is not found in other federal employment discrimination statutes. For example, § 101(10)(A)-(B) provides that "[t]he term 'undue hardship' means an action requiring significant difficulty or expense, when considered in light of * * * factors" such as "the nature and cost of the accommodation," "the overall financial resources of the facility," and "the overall financial resources of the covered entity." Third, § 501(c), 42 U.S.C. § 12201(c), frequently referred to as the safe-harbor provision of the ADA, permits insurance companies and benefit managers to continue their risk-assessment practices so long as these practices are not "used as a subterfuge to evade the purposes of [titles] I and III" of the ADA. Fourth, § 102(2), 42 U.S.C. § 12112(b)(2), defines discrimination to include "participating in a contractual or other arrangement or relationship that has the effect of subjecting a covered entity's qualified applicant or employee with a disability to the discrimination prohibited by [the ADA]."

The ADA's broad prohibition against disability discrimination can conflict with the general practice of the insurance industry and self-insured employers to limit coverage or benefits for certain conditions or classes of conditions. One commentator has described the problem as follows:

> Spiraling health care costs and the concomitant increases in the costs of medical and other insurance coverages have led insurers and employers to make great efforts to reduce coverage costs. This is often accomplished by increasing premiums and employee contributions for the cost of coverage, limiting various coverages (such as those for substance abuse and mental health disorders), or eliminating coverages altogether. Additionally, insurance companies providing group and individual coverages not only limit coverage for particular types of treatments (such as cosmetic surgery and experimental treatment), they often underwrite insurance risks as well. For example, based upon a prospective insured's medical history, an insurer may decline to provide the coverage requested, may limit or eliminate coverage for the prospective insured's known medical conditions, or may charge the prospective insured a higher than standard premium for the coverage requested. Insureds and employees have contested these efforts by claiming that the actions of their actual or prospective insurers or of their employers violate the statutory protections embodied in the Americans with Disabilities Act.

Daniel A. Engel, *The ADA and Life, Health, and Disability Insurance: Where Is the Liability?* 33 Tort & Ins.L.J. 227, 227 (1997). *See also* Monica E. McFadden, *Insurance Benefits Under the ADA: Discrimination or Business as Usual?*, 28 Tort & Ins.L.J. 480 (1993); Susan Nanovic Flannery, *Employer Health–Care Plans: The Feasibility of Disability–Based Distinctions Under ERISA and the Americans with Disabilities Act*, 12 Hofstra Lab.L.J. 211 (1995); Bonnie Poitras Tucker, *Insurance and the ADA*, 46 DePaul L.Rev. 915 (1997).

One of the major categories of cases involving claims of disability-based discrimination with respect to benefits is that in which the employer or its insurance carrier provides less coverage for mental disabilities than for physical disabilities. This category of cases has raised several issues that have divided the courts. The first issue involves standing. Title I protects only individuals with disabilities who, with or without reasonable accommodation, can perform the essential functions of the job. ADA § 101(8), 42 U.S.C. §§ 12111(8). Does an employee who is unable to perform the essential functions of her job have standing under Title I to challenge her employer's policy of providing different benefits coverage for mental and physical impairments? Several courts of appeals have held that individuals who became unable to work because of mental disabilities do not have standing to sue under Title I when their disability benefits are about to terminate. Parker v. Metropolitan Life Ins. Co., 875 F.Supp. 1321 (W.D.Tenn.1995), *aff'd in part and rev'd in part*, 99 F.3d 181 (6th Cir.1996) (*Parker I*), *reh'g en banc*, 121 F.3d 1006 (6th Cir.1997) (*Parker II*), *cert. denied*, 522 U.S. 1084, 118 S.Ct. 871, 139 L.Ed.2d 768 (1998); EEOC v. CNA Insurance Co., 96 F.3d 1039 (7th Cir.1996); Beauford v. Father Flanagan's Boys' Home, 831 F.2d 768 (8th Cir.1987) (ADA should be interpreted the same as the Rehabilitation Act, which does not provide protection for employees who are no longer able to do their jobs), *cert. denied* 485 U.S. 938, 108 S.Ct. 1116, 99 L.Ed.2d 277 (1988); Gonzales v. Garner Food Services, Inc., 89 F.3d 1523 (11th Cir.1996), *cert. denied sub nom.* Wood v. Garner Food Services, Inc. 520 U.S. 1229, 117 S.Ct. 1822, 137 L.Ed.2d 1030 (1997). The Third Circuit, in *Ford v. Schering–Plough Corp.*, 145 F.3d 601 (3d Cir. 1998), ruled in favor of standing on the ground that the plaintiff had been "injured in fact" by the denial of benefits. *Id.* 604–05 (citing Simon v. Eastern Ky. Welfare Rights Org., 426 U.S. 26, 38, 96 S.Ct. 1917, 1924, 48 L.Ed.2d 450 (1976)). *See also* Castellano v. City of New York, 142 F.3d 58 (2d Cir.1998) (ruling in favor of standing).

A second major issue is whether, under Title I of the ADA, employers may provide more generous long-term benefits for physical disabilities than for mental disabilities. A number of courts of appeals have held that Title I does not bar employers from providing different long-term benefits for mental and physical disabilities. *See* EEOC v. Staten Island Savings Bank, 207 F.3d 144 (2d Cir.2000) (collecting cases). Adopting the reasoning of other courts of appeals, the Second Circuit in *Staten Island Savings Bank* held that although § 102(b) of Title I, 42 U.S.C. § 12112(b), defines discrimination to include participating in a relationship that has the effect of subjecting a qualified individual with a disability to discrimination, that section does not provide an unambiguous answer as to whether an employer can offer long-term disability plans that provide differing levels of coverage for different disabilities. The court observed that it has long been insurance industry practice to distinguish between physical and mental conditions and that if Congress had intended to prohibit the practice it would have spoken more plainly to effectuate a radical departure from the practice. The court then considered whether the Mental Health Parity Act, codified primarily at 29 U.S.C. § 1185a and 42 U.S.C. § 300gg–5, dictated a different outcome. The Mental Health Parity Act limits the right of health insurance plans to provide lower benefits for mental conditions than they do for physical conditions. Agreeing with other circuits that had considered the issue, the Second Circuit noted that "Congress' passage of the Mental Health Parity Act suggests Congress believed that the ADA neither governs the content of insurance policies nor requires parity between physical and mental conditions." *Id.* at 152, (citing Parker v. Metropolitan Life Ins. Co., 121 F.3d 1006, 1018 (6th Cir.1997)). The developments on discrimination because of disability in providing different levels of long-term disability for physical and mental conditions are explored and criticized in Andrea K. Short, *Eradicating Discrimination Among Individuals with Disabilities in Employer–Provided, Long–Term Disability Benefit Plans,* 56 Wash. & Lee L.Rev. 1341 (1999).

Questions

Is infertility a disability? Is so, should an employer be permitted to provide less coverage for infertility than for other diseases and impairments under its employee benefits health plan? *See* Krauel v. Iowa Methodist Med. Ctr., 95 F.3d 674 (8th Cir.1996); Deborah K. Dallmann, Note, *The Lay View of What "Disability" Means Must Give Way to What Congress Says It Means: Infertility as a "Disability" Under the Americans with Disabilities* Act, 38 Wm. & Mary L.Rev. 371 (1996).

Chapter 14

UNION LIABILITY

A. INTRODUCTION

Union liability for unlawful discrimination under Title VII is integrally related to the duties imposed on unions under the federal labor laws and the role that unions play in collective bargaining and grievance arbitration. Long before Title VII was enacted, the Supreme Court recognized that the Railway Labor Act (RLA), 45 U.S.C. § 151 et seq., bars labor unions from engaging in invidious discrimination on the basis of race when they act in their role as statutory representative. In *Steele v. Louisville & Nashville Railroad*, 323 U.S. 192, 65 S.Ct. 226, 89 L.Ed. 173 (1944), a railway union that was the exclusive representative for a bargaining unit of locomotive firemen excluded all black firemen from membership in the union and bargained with the railroad to restrict the employment and promotion of black workers. Without limiting the union's right to restrict its membership on the basis of race, the Supreme Court held that the union violated the duty of fair representation by discriminating against the black firemen in its bargaining demands with the employer. The Court held:

> [T]he Railway Labor Act imposes upon the statutory representative of a craft at least as exacting a duty to protect equally the interests of the members of the craft as the Constitution imposes upon a legislature to give equal protection to the interests of those for whom it legislates. Congress has seen fit to clothe the bargaining representative with powers comparable to those possessed by a legislative body both to create and restrict the rights of those whom it represents, but it has also imposed on the representative a corresponding duty. We hold that the language of the Act * * * expresses the aim of Congress to impose on the bargaining representative of a craft or class of employees the duty to exercise fairly the power conferred upon it in behalf of all those for whom it acts, without hostile discrimination against them.

> This does not mean that the statutory representative of a craft is barred from making contracts which may have unfavorable effects on some of the members of the craft represented. Variations in the

terms of the contract based on differences relevant to the authorized purposes of the contract in conditions to which they are to be applied, such as differences in seniority, the type of work performed, the competence and skill with which it is performed, are within the scope of the bargaining representation of a craft, all of whose members are not identical in their interest or merit. Without attempting to mark the allowable limits of differences in the terms of contracts based on differences of conditions to which they apply, it is enough for present purposes to say that the statutory power to represent a craft and to make contracts as to wages, hours and working conditions does not include the authority to make among members of the craft discriminations not based on such relevant differences. Here the discriminations based on race alone are obviously irrelevant and invidious. Congress plainly did not undertake to authorize the bargaining representative to make such discriminations.

Id. at 202–03, 65 S.Ct. at 232.

The same day that the *Steele* case was decided, the Supreme Court determined that the duty of fair representation should also be read into the National Labor Relations Act (NLRA), 29 U.S.C. § 151 et seq., because the duty derives from the union's status as the exclusive bargaining agent for all employees in the bargaining unit. *See* Wallace Corp. v. NLRB, 323 U.S. 248, 65 S.Ct. 238, 89 L.Ed. 216 (1944). Subsequently, in *Ford Motor Co. v. Huffman*, 345 U.S. 330, 73 S.Ct. 681, 97 L.Ed. 1048 (1953), the Court made clear that labor organizations have a wide range of reasonableness in their choice of bargaining positions in representing a diverse membership. Unlike *Steele*, neither *Wallace* nor *Ford v. Huffman* involved racial discrimination, and from the inception of the duty of fair representation it was not restricted to race. Nevertheless, during the first twenty years of its existence, the duty was used primarily, though not always effectively, in race cases. *See* Neil M. Herring, *The "Fair Representation" Doctrine: An Effective Weapon Against Union Racial Discrimination?*, 24 Md.L.Rev. 113 (1964). In *Vaca v. Sipes*, 386 U.S. 171, 87 S.Ct. 903, 17 L.Ed.2d 842 (1967), the Supreme Court held that the duty of fair representation does not give individual employees an "absolute right" to have their grievances arbitrated, but requires only that a union process the grievances of employees in a manner that is not arbitrary, discriminatory, or in bad faith. *See, e.g.*, Woods v. Graphic Communications, 925 F.2d 1195, 1203 (9th Cir.1991) (holding that a union's "intentional and knowing failure to file grievances on behalf of [a black member] concerning racial harassment" is a "primary violation" of its duty of fair representation). Discriminatory conduct by a union on the basis of race, religion, sex, or national origin may constitute a breach of the union's duty of fair representation, an unfair labor practice under § 8(b) of the NLRA, *see, e.g.*, Hughes Tool Co., 147 N.L.R.B. 1573 (1964), and also may subject a union to liability under Title VII. *See* Martin v. Local 1513, IAMAW, 859 F.2d 581 (8th Cir.1988); Farmer v. ARA Servs., Inc., 660 F.2d 1096 (6th Cir.1981).

B.   UNION LIABILITY UNDER TITLE VII AS A "LABOR ORGANIZATION"

A union is subject to liability under Title VII in two capacities: as an "employer" under § 703(a) and as a "labor organization" under § 703(c). A union's responsibilities to its own employees under § 703(a) are the same as any other "employer" covered by Title VII. But what are the unlawful employment practices of unions as "labor organizations"? The historical experiences with the duty of fair representation suggest one possible framework for thinking about § 703(c). Consider the reach of § 703(c) as interpreted by the Supreme Court in the following case:

GOODMAN v. LUKENS STEEL CO.

Supreme Court of the United States, 1987.
482 U.S. 656, 107 S.Ct. 2617, 96 L.Ed.2d 572.

JUSTICE WHITE delivered the opinion of the Court.

In 1973, individual employees of Lukens Steel Company (Lukens) brought this suit on behalf of themselves and others, asserting racial discrimination claims under Title VII * * * and 42 U.S.C. § 1981 against their employer and their collective-bargaining agents, the United Steelworkers of America and two of its local unions (Unions). * * *

* * *

[After a 32–day trial in 1980], the District court proceeded to find that the company had violated Title VII in several significant respects, including the discharge of employees during their probationary period, the toleration of racial harassment by employees, initial job assignments, promotions, and decisions on incentive pay. The court also found that in these identical ways the company had also violated § 1981, a finding the court could not have made without concluding that the company had intentionally discriminated on a racial basis in these respects.

Similarly, the Unions were found to have discriminated on racial grounds in violation of both Title VII and § 1981 in certain ways: failing to challenge discriminatory discharges of probationary employees; failure and refusal to assert racial discrimination as a ground for grievances; and toleration and tacit encouragement of racial harassment.

* * *

The Unions contend that the judgment against them rests on the erroneous legal premise that Title VII and § 1981 are violated if a union passively sits by and does not affirmatively oppose the employer's racially discriminatory employment practices. It is true that the District Court declared that "mere union passivity in the face of employer discrimination renders the union liable under Title VII and, if racial animus is properly inferrable, under § 1981 as well." We need not discuss this rather abstract observation, for the court went on to say that the evidence proves "far more" than mere passivity.[11] As found by the court, the facts were that since 1965, the collective-bargaining contract contained an express clause binding both the employer and the Unions not to discriminate on racial grounds; that the employer was discriminating against blacks in discharging probationary employees, which the Unions were aware of but refused to do anything about by way of filing proffered grievances or otherwise; that the Unions had ignored grievances based on instances of harassment which were indisputably racial in nature; and that the Unions had regularly refused to include assertions of racial discrimination in grievances that also asserted other contract violations.[12]

In affirming the District Court's findings against the Unions, the Court of Appeals also appeared to hold that the Unions had an affirmative duty to combat employer discrimination in the workplace. But it, too, held that the case against the Unions was much stronger than one of mere acquiescence in that the Unions deliberately chose not to assert claims of racial discrimination by the employer. It was the Court of Appeals' view that these intentional and knowing refusals discriminated against the victims who were entitled to have their grievances heard.

The Unions submit that the only basis for any liability in this case under Title VII is § 703(c)(3), which provides that a Union may not "cause or attempt to cause an employer to discriminate against an individual in violation of this section," and that nothing the District Court found and the Court of Appeals accepted justifies liability under this prohibition. We need not differ with the Unions on the reach of § 703(c)(3), for § 703(c)(1) makes it an unlawful practice for a Union to "exclude or to expel from its membership, *or otherwise to discriminate against*, any individual because of his race, color, religion, sex, or national origin." (Emphasis added.) Both courts below found that the Unions had indeed discriminated on the basis of race by the way in which they represented the workers, and the Court of Appeals expressly held that "[t]he deliberate choice not to process grievances also violated § 703(c)(1) of Title VII." The plain language of the statute supports this conclusion.

The Court of Appeals is also faulted for stating that the Unions had violated their duty of fair representation, which the Unions assert has no

---

11. * * * The District Court noted that it was the company, not the Unions, which pressed for a nondiscrimination clause in the collective-bargaining agreement. The District Court found that the Unions never took any action over the segregated locker facilities at Lukens and did not complain over other discriminatory practices by the company. The District Court found that when one employee approached the president of one of the local unions to complain about the segregated locker facilities in 1962, the president dissuaded him from complaining to the appropriate state agen-

cy. The District Court, however, found "inconclusive" the evidence offered in support of the employees' claim that the Unions discriminated against blacks in their overall handling of grievances under the collective-bargaining agreement.

12. The District Court also found that although the Unions had objected to the company's use of certain tests, they had never done so on racial grounds, even though they "were certainly chargeable with knowledge that many of the tests" had a racially disparate impact.

relevance to this case. But we do not understand the Court of Appeals to have rested its affirmance on this ground, for as indicated above, it held that the Unions had violated § 703.

The Unions insist that it was error to hold them liable for not including racial discrimination claims in grievances claiming other violations of the contract. The Unions followed this practice, it was urged, because these grievances could be resolved without making racial allegations and because the employer would "get its back up" if racial bias was charged, thereby making it much more difficult to prevail. The trial judge, although initially impressed by this seemingly neutral reason for failing to press race discrimination claims, ultimately found the explanation "unacceptable" because the Unions also ignored grievances which involved racial harassment violating the contract covenant against racial discrimination but which did not also violate another provision. The judge also noted that the Unions had refused to complain about racially based terminations of probationary employees, even though the express undertaking not to discriminate protected this group of employees, as well as others, and even though, as the District Court found, the Unions knew that blacks were being discharged at a disproportionately higher rate than whites. In the judgment of the District Court, the virtual failure by the Unions to file any race-bias grievances until after this lawsuit started, knowing that the employer was practicing what the contract prevented, rendered the Unions' explanation for their conduct unconvincing.[13]

As we understand it, there was no suggestion below that the Unions held any racial animus against or denigrated blacks generally. Rather, it was held that a collective-bargaining agent could not, without violating Title VII and § 1981, follow a policy of refusing to file grievable racial discrimination claims however strong they might be and however sure the agent was that the employer was discriminating against blacks. The Unions, in effect, categorized racial grievances as unworthy of pursuit and, while pursuing thousands of other legitimate grievances, ignored racial discrimination claims on behalf of blacks, knowing that the employer was discriminating in violation of the contract. Such conduct, the courts below concluded, intentionally discriminated against blacks seeking a remedy for disparate treatment based on their race and violated both Title VII and § 1981. As the District Court said: "A union which intentionally avoids asserting discrimination claims, either so as not to antagonize the employer and thus improve its chances of success on

---

13. The District Court also rejected the Unions' argument that much of the workers' case involved discrimination by the company in making initial job assignments, and that it had no control over those assignments. The court found that once hired, new employees were entitled to the protection of the collective-bargaining agreement, including the protection afforded by the nondiscrimination clause:

To require blacks to continue to work in lower paying and less desirable jobs, in units disparately black, is to discriminate against them in violation of the collective bargaining agreement (and, of course, also in violation of Title VII). It is very clear, on the record in this case, that the defendant unions never sought to avail themselves of this rather obvious mechanism for protecting the interests of their members.

other issues, or in deference to the perceived desires of its white membership, is liable under both Title [VII] and § 1981, regardless of whether, as a subjective matter, its leaders were favorably disposed toward minorities."

The courts below, in our view, properly construed and applied Title VII and § 1981. Those provisions do not permit a union to refuse to file any and all grievances presented by a black person on the ground that the employer looks with disfavor on and resents such grievances. It is no less violative of these laws for a union to pursue a policy of rejecting disparate-treatment grievances presented by blacks solely because the claims assert racial bias and would be very troublesome to process.

[T]he judgment of the Court of Appeals is affirmed.

[JUSTICE BRENNAN, joined by JUSTICES MARSHALL and BLACKMUN, concurred in the part of the Court's opinion reproduced above and dissented from a part of the opinion not reproduced here. JUSTICE O'CONNOR filed an opinion concurring in the judgment in part and dissenting in part.]

[JUSTICE POWELL, joined by JUSTICES SCALIA and O'CON-NOR, concurred with a part of the Court's decision not reproduced here and dissented from the part reproduced above. Justice Powell's dissent included the following observations on a union's obligations under Title VII.]

* * *

The Court does not reach the question whether a union may be held liable under Title VII for "mere passivity" in the face of discrimination by the employer, because it agrees with the courts below that the record shows more than mere passivity on the part of the Unions. I disagree with that conclusion, and so must consider whether the judgment can be affirmed on the ground that Title VII imposes an affirmative duty on unions to combat discrimination by the employer.

The starting point for analysis of this statutory question is, as always, the language of the statute itself. Section 703(c), the provision of Title VII governing suits against unions, does not suggest that the union has a duty to take affirmative steps to remedy employer discrimination. Section 703(c)(1) makes it unlawful for a union "to exclude or to expel from its membership, or otherwise to discriminate against, any individual because of his race, color, religion, sex, or national origin." This subsection parallels § 703(a)(1), that applies to employers. This parallelism, and the reference to union membership, indicate that § 703(c)(1) prohibits direct discrimination by a union against its members; it does not impose upon a union an obligation to remedy discrimination by the *employer*. Moreover, § 703(c)(3) specifically addresses the union's inter-action with the employer, by outlawing efforts by the union "to cause or attempt to cause an employer to discriminate against an individual in violation of this section." If Congress had intended to impose on unions a duty to challenge discrimination by the employer, it hardly could have chosen language more ill-suited to its purpose. First, "[t]o say that the union 'causes' employer discrimination simply by allowing it is to stretch the meaning of the word beyond its limits." 1 A. Larson & L. Larson, Employment Discrimination, § 44.50, p. 9–40 (1985). Moreover, the language of § 703(c)(3) is taken *in haec verba* from § 8(b)(2) of the National Labor Relations Act (NLRA), 29 U.S.C. § 158(b)(2). That provision of the NLRA has been held not to impose liability for passive acquiescence in wrongdoing by the employer. Indeed, well before the enactment of Title VII, the Court held that even encouraging or inducing employer discrimination is not sufficient to incur liability under § 8(b)(2). Electrical Workers v. NLRB, 341 U.S. 694, 703, 71 S.Ct. 954, 959, 95 L.Ed. 1299 (1951).

In the absence of a clear statement of legislative intent, the Court has been reluctant to read Title VII to disrupt the basic policies of the labor laws. *See* Trans World Airlines, Inc. v. Hardison, 432 U.S. 63, 79, 97 S.Ct. 2264, 2274, 53 L.Ed.2d 113 (1977). Unquestionably an affirmative duty to oppose employer discrimination could work such a disruption. A union, unlike an employer, is a democratically controlled institution directed by the will of its constituents, subject to the duty of fair representation. Like other representative entities, unions must balance the competing claims of its constituents. A union must make difficult choices among goals such as eliminating racial discrimination in the workplace, removing health and safety hazards, providing better insurance and pension benefits, and increasing wages. The Court has recognized that "[t]he complete satisfaction of all who are represented is hardly to be expected." Ford Motor Co. v. Huffman, 345 U.S. 330, 338, 73 S.Ct. 681, 686, 97 L.Ed. 1048 (1953). For these reasons unions are afforded broad discretion in the handling of grievances. Union members' suits against their unions may deplete union treasuries, and may induce unions to process frivolous claims and resist fair settlement offers. The employee is not without a remedy, because union members may file Title VII actions directly against their employers. Alexander v. Gardner–Denver Co., 415 U.S. 36, 94 S.Ct. 1011, 39 L.Ed.2d 147 (1974). I therefore would hold that Title VII imposes on unions no affirmative duty to remedy discrimination by the employer.

* * *

Notes and Questions

1. The facts of the *Goodman* case present a classic intra-union struggle between a "minority" group—black steelworkers—and a union hierarchy that supported the interests of the "majority" of its members—its traditional white constituency. But the Court in *Goodman* observed that "there was no suggestion below that the Unions held any racial animus against or denigrated blacks generally." If racial animus did not motivate the unions in the choices they made about which grievances they would process, what was their motivation? What did the district court in *Goodman* say about the relevance of racial animus to its analysis?

Professor Elizabeth Iglesias made the following observations about the Supreme Court's analysis in *Goodman*:

> Initially, what is most curious about *Goodman* is not so much what it holds but what it fails or refuses to hold. The plaintiffs in *Goodman* raised two additional issues which the majority opinion intentionally left unaddressed. First, the Court refused to decide whether the unions had, and consequently had violated, an affirmative duty under Title VII to challenge the employer's racially discriminatory employment practices. Although both lower courts held that unions do have this duty, the Supreme Court refused "to discuss this rather abstract observation" because the case against the unions was based on more than "mere passivity." The unions had intentionally and knowingly chosen not to challenge the employer's racially discriminatory actions and were therefore liable for their own affirmative misconduct.
>
> The Court's opinion also skirted the issue of fair representation and the scope of a union's obligation to challenge an employer's racially discriminatory practices under the [duty of fair representation]. The unions argued that the DFR "had no relevance to the case." The majority simply avoided the issue by stating that the unions' liability was established under Section 703 of Title VII.

Elizabeth M. Iglesias, *Structures of Subordination: Women of Color at the Intersection of Title VII and the NLRA. NOT!*, 28 Harv.C.R.-C.L.L.Rev. 395, 448 (1993). Why do you think the majority refused to address these two issues? Is the answer found in Justice Powell's dissent?

2. *Acquiescence*: Before *Goodman*, some lower courts had ruled that a union may be liable for "acquiescing" in an employer's racially discriminatory conduct. *See, e.g.*, Bonilla v. Oakland Scavenger Co., 697 F.2d 1297, 1304 (9th Cir.1982), *cert. denied*, 467 U.S. 1251, 104 S.Ct. 3533, 82 L.Ed.2d 838 (1984). For a post-*Goodman* case relying on the acquiescence theory, see *Woods v. Graphic Communications*, 925 F.2d 1195, 1200 (9th Cir.1991). What exactly is "acquiescence"? One court has held that "[m]ere inaction does not constitute acquiescence." York v. American Tel. & Tel. Co., 95 F.3d 948, 956 (10th Cir.1996). Rather, "[a]cquiescence requires: 1) knowledge that prohibited discrimination may have occurred, and 2) a decision not to assert the discrimination claim." Catley v. Graphic Communications Int'l Union, Local 277–M, 982 F.Supp. 1332, 1343 (E.D.Wis.1997) (citing *York*, 95 F.3d. at 956–57). *See also* Johnson v. Palma, 931 F.2d 203, 209 (2d Cir.1991) (ruling that "the refusal to proceed with [a] grievance process because of a company policy amounts to more than mere passivity"). "Liability by way of acquiescence" has also been rejected by several lower courts since *Goodman*. *See, e.g.*, Martin v. Local 1513, IAMAW, 859 F.2d 581, 584 (8th Cir.1988); *Catley*, 982 F.Supp. at 1343–44. What are the policy arguments for and against recognition of an acquiescence theory of union liability in discrimination cases? Is liability for acquiescence in discrimination different from "an affirmative duty to insure compliance with Title VII"? *See* Romero v. Union Pac. R.R., 615 F.2d 1303, 1310 (10th Cir.1980).

At a minimum, does a union have an affirmative obligation to investigate any complaints of unlawful discrimination that are brought by members of the bargaining unit? *See* Wilson v. Myers, 823 F.2d 253 (8th Cir.1987).

Consider the following: An employee who believes that she has been subjected to sexual harassment by co-workers complains to her union shop steward. The shop steward, however, does not investigate and does not report the complaints to the employer. Subsequently, the employee files a Title VII sexual harassment charge against the employer and the union. At this point, the employer learns for the first time about the alleged harassment. Assuming that the elements of a sexual harassment claim are satisfied, is the union liable for the harassment? *See* Thorn v. Amalgamated Transit Union, 305 F.3d 826, 832 (8th Cir.2002) ("[N]owhere in [Title VII] do we find language imposing upon unions an affirmative duty to investigate and take steps to remedy employer discrimination."). Should the union's failure to report the harassment, which deprived the employer of an opportunity to remedy the harassment in a timely fashion, relieve the employer of liability under Title VII? Should employers, in negotiating collective bargaining agreements, seek to include specific provisions obligating union representatives to report immediately to management all employee complaints about sexual harassment? Should unions offer their shop stewards training in how to investigate complaints of sexual harassment?

3. *The Duty of Fair Representation and Discrimination During Contract Negotiations*: Under Justice Powell's dissenting view in *Goodman*, Title VII does not impose an affirmative obligation on a union to remedy the unlawful discrimination of an employer because the duty of fair representation requires that unions have "broad discretion" to make the "difficult choices" needed to resolve the "competing claims" of their "constituents." In *Air Line Pilots Association (ALPA) v. O'Neill*, 499 U.S. 65, 111 S.Ct. 1127, 113 L.Ed.2d 51 (1991), the Supreme Court held that the duty of fair representation permits unions substantial freedom to accommodate the competing claims of groups of employees during contract negotiations. The decision upheld the settlement of a strike by pilots against Continental Airlines, which provided that the pilots who returned to work during the strike were allocated more captain positions than the pilots who had refused to work throughout the strike. Applying the *Vaca v. Sipes* tripartite standard for evaluating claims of breach of the duty of fair representation (i.e., whether the union's conduct was arbitrary, discriminatory, or in bad faith), the Supreme Court held that a union's conduct during contract negotiations is "arbitrary only if, in light of the factual and legal landscape at the time of the union's action, the union's behavior is so far out of a 'wide range of reasonableness' as to be irrational." *Id.* at 67, 111 S.Ct. at 1130. In response to the plaintiffs' claim that "discrimination" between striking pilots and working pilots breached the union's duty of fair representation, the Court stated:

> If we are correct in our conclusion that it was rational for ALPA to accept a compromise between the claims of the two groups of pilots * * *, some form of allocation was inevitable. A rational compromise on the initial allocation of positions was not invidious "discrimination" of the kind prohibited by the duty of fair representation.

Id. at 81, 111 S.Ct. at 1137.

In light of the Supreme Court's rationale in *Goodman* and in *Air Line Pilots*, consider whether the union has engaged in illegal discrimination under Title VII in the following case: The Food Workers Union represents grocery store employees in a large urban area, including employees of the Gourmet Store chain. Under a master labor agreement with the grocers, all meat department employees are classified according to their skill-level and duties. Meat cutters, who are permitted to perform all functions in the meat department, must have completed an apprenticeship and vocational training. Meat wrappers, who need no specialized training, are assigned only to tasks requiring little skill, such as weighing and wrapping meat, and cleaning machinery. From 2000 to 2003, all meat cutters employed by Gourmet Stores were male and all meat wrappers were female. During this period, the union-negotiated wage for meat cutters was two dollars an hour more than the wage for wrappers.

During the course of contract negotiations between the union and the grocers, the following events occurred: (1) a head meat cutter at a Gourmet Store called a wrapper an "old woman" and a "wench," and when she complained to him, he said she was a "women's libber" who was "going to go to the union"; (2) the union rejected the proposal by a female union member to bargain for layoff protection for a fixed ratio of meat wrappers to meat cutters; (3) the president of the union said to a group of meat cutters, "Isn't it great we're going to be rid of all the meat wrappers by the end of this year?"; and (4) when female union members attempted to speak at union meetings, male union members would "boo" and make so much noise that the wrappers' contract proposals could not be effectively presented. In the collective bargaining agreement eventually negotiated, the union did not obtain any improvements in the job security or other employment terms of the meat wrappers because it did not bargain as vigorously for the wrappers as it did for the cutters. Shortly after the contract was ratified, Gourmet Stores began to eliminate the jobs of the meat wrappers but not the meat cutters, whose jobs were protected by the new contract. If the meat wrappers brought a Title VII claim against the union for violating § 703(c), do you think they would prevail? *See* Carter v. United Food & Commercial Workers, 963 F.2d 1078 (8th Cir.1992) (sex discrimination claim); Considine v. Newspaper Agency Corp., 43 F.3d 1349 (10th Cir.1994) (age discrimination claim). Do the meat wrappers have a viable claim that the union violated its duty of fair representation?

4. *Union Membership Policies*: Read §§ 703(c)(1) and (2) of Title VII and consider how these provisions might apply in the following case: In 1998, a union of steamship clerks had about 100 active members, all of whom were white. The clerks, who are former longshoremen, check cargo inventories on ships arriving in Boston harbor. Shippers hire clerks exclusively through the union. The clerks are highly paid and the job is considered one of the most coveted positions that dock workers can obtain. In 1999, the union adopted a formal membership policy under which only individuals sponsored by a union member could be considered for membership in the union. Over the next five years, the union added 30 new members, all of whom were white and were related by blood or marriage to existing members. During this period the relevant labor pool in the Boston area was comprised of approximately 20% blacks and 5% Latinos. The EEOC has brought a Title VII claim challenging the union's membership policy on behalf of a group of black and Latino longshoremen who have been unable to

obtain sponsors for union membership. The union has made the following arguments: (1) that there is no evidence that any individual black or Latino longshoreman applied for and was denied membership, (2) that the membership policy is the most efficient method for recruiting individuals with the necessary job qualifications, (3) that the new members recruited were carrying on a family tradition of working as steamship clerks, and (4) that nepotism, in any event, is not the same as discrimination.

How would you evaluate the claim that the union's membership policy is a violation of Title VII? *See* EEOC v. Steamship Clerks Union, Local 1066, 48 F.3d 594 (1st Cir.), *cert. denied*, 516 U.S. 814, 116 S.Ct. 65, 133 L.Ed.2d 27 (1995). Can the membership policy be justified under the disparate treatment rationale of *EEOC v. Consolidated Service Systems*, 989 F.2d 233 (7th Cir.1993), in Chapter 3? If the membership policies are challenged under a disparate impact analysis does the union have a viable business necessity defense? *See* Alexander v. Local 496, Laborers' Int'l Union of N. Am., 177 F.3d 394, 405–07 (6th Cir.1999) (striking down under disparate impact analysis a union's facially neutral "work-in-the-calling" rule and its practice of limiting employment referrals to union members only), *cert. denied*, 528 U.S. 1154, 120 S.Ct. 1158, 145 L.Ed.2d 1070 (2000). For a critique of the role of Title VII and the NLRA in the integration of racially segregated union locals in the South during the 1960s and 1970s, see Iglesias, *supra* Note 1, at 408–15.

5. *Retaliation Claims Against Unions*: For twenty years, Samuel Johnson, a black male, was an employee of a battery manufacturer that has a collective bargaining agreement with a local union. Recently, Johnson, who is a member of the union, was fired for habitual tardiness. He filed a timely charge with the EEOC, alleging that his employer discriminated against him on the basis of race. In addition, he asked his union to pursue a grievance, claiming that his discharge violated the nondiscrimination clause in the collective bargaining agreement. The union refused to process his grievance unless he first withdrew his EEOC complaint. Under "pressure" from the union, Johnson then withdrew his EEOC complaint. Section 704(a) of Title VII prohibits a union from retaliating against a member because he has filed a charge with the EEOC. 42 U.S.C. § 2000e–3(a). (See the discussion of retaliation claims in Chapter 15.) Would Johnson have a prima facie case of union retaliation in these circumstances? If so, would the union be able to establish a legitimate, nondiscriminatory reason for its action if it is able to prove that it was relying on a company policy of not proceeding with a discrimination grievance while the same discrimination claim was pending before the EEOC? *See* Johnson v. Palma, 931 F.2d 203 (2d Cir.1991).

6. *Sexual Harassment Claims*: As one court has noted, the holding of *Goodman v. Lukens Steel* "applies equally to sex discrimination as to the race discrimination at issue in *Goodman*." EEOC v. Regency Architectural Metals Corp., 896 F.Supp. 260, 269 (D.Conn.1995) (finding a violation of Title VII where the union, "in deference to the perceived desires of its male membership," intentionally avoided asserting the plaintiff's "colorable claim" of creating a hostile work environment). Would Title VII claims against unions based on sexual harassment be more difficult to prove than the paradigmatic case of race discrimination found in *Goodman*? (See the discussion of sexual harassment in Chapter 8).

In *Marquart v. Lodge 837, International Association of Machinists and Aerospace Workers*, 26 F.3d 842 (8th Cir.1994), the court described the elements of a prima facie case of hostile environment sexual harassment against a union. The plaintiff must allege (1) that she is a member of a protected group—women, (2) that male employees and union members "harassed her because she was a woman," (3) that "the harassment affected her conditions of employment by creating a hostile work atmosphere," and (4) that "the [u]nion knew about this harassment but refused to process her complaint because the individuals who harassed her were favored male members of the Union." *Id.* at 853. What if the union also failed to process the sexual harassment grievances of its male members? Does the plaintiff have to show that the union treated her less favorably than "similarly situated" male employees? *See* Catley v. Graphic Communications Int'l Union, Local 277–M, 982 F.Supp. 1332, 1343 (E.D.Wis.1997). What if there are no "similarly situated" male employees with complaints of sexual harassment? In light of the Supreme Court's decision in *Oncale v. Sundowner Offshore Services, Inc.*, 523 U.S. 75, 118 S.Ct. 998, 140 L.Ed.2d 201 (1998), in Chapter 8, how would you articulate the elements of a prima facie case of same-sex sexual harassment against a union?

Would the union be liable for sexual harassment if the plaintiff failed to file a grievance with the union? *See* Carter v. Chrysler Corp., 173 F.3d 693, 704 (8th Cir.1999) (affirming summary judgment for the union where the plaintiff never requested that the union file a grievance about her sexual and racial harassment claims). *See also Catley*, 982 F.Supp. at 1342–43. In *Catley*, the court ruled that, under Title VII, a prima facie case of sex discrimination against a union requires evidence that "1) the employer violated the collective bargaining agreement with respect to her; 2) the union let the breach go unrepaired, thereby breaching its own duty of fair representation; and 3) some evidence indicates that gender animus motivated the union." *Id.* at 1340 (citing Greenslade v. Chicago Sun–Times, Inc., 112 F.3d 853, 866 (7th Cir.1997)). In light of *Goodman*, is the court in *Catley* correct in including evidence of "gender tainted motivation" as one of the elements of a prima facie Title VII case against a union? *See Catley*, 982 at 1341; *Greenslade*, 112 F.3d at 867. If the complainant does file a grievance with her union, is she precluded from seeking judicial relief under Title VII? See the discussion of *Alexander v. Gardner–Denver Co.* in Chapter 18.

7. Professor Marion Crain asserts that "many unions themselves are far from blameless in the perpetuation of sexualized work environments." Marion Crain, *Women, Labor Unions, and Hostile Work Environment Sexual Harassment: The Untold Story*, 4 Tex.J. Women & L. 9, 13 (1995). She also critiques judges and labor arbitrators for their implicit roles in perpetuating sex-based hostile work environment harassment. *See id.* at 45–46. With respect to the role of Title VII jurisprudence, she writes:

> The invisibility of unions in Title VII hostile work environment cases from unionized workplaces has far-reaching significance. The fact that there is little or no discussion of a union's obligation to represent female victims of harassment or to prevent workplace sexual harassment by its male members suggests that unions have no such obligation, and assumes that unions will and should align themselves with the interests of their male members, particularly where men constitute a

> majority in the bargaining unit. As such, sexual harassment in the workplace becomes the employer's legal problem and the victim's practical problem. The union becomes, at best, a passive bystander or, at worst, a recalcitrant which can be counted upon to uphold the status quo while representing the interests of the harasser(s).

Id. at 12. What role should unions be required to play in policing or resolving sexual harassment grievances in the unionized workplace? Can unions effectively deal with hostile environment complaints that are brought against co-workers who are members of the same bargaining unit as the complainant? When co-workers are involved, both harassment victims and alleged harassers have a right to invoke the grievance procedures under the collective bargaining agreement. *See* Thorn v. Amalgamated Transit Union, 305 F.3d 826, 833 (8th Cir.2002) ("When the employer investigates a sexual harassment claim by one union member against another, the union has a statutory duty to fairly represent both in their disciplinary dealings with the employer."). Is this problematic for the union? Is arbitration (discussed in Chapter 18) an effective alternative forum for resolving hostile environment disputes brought against either supervisors or co-workers? *See generally,* Crain, *supra* at 45–61; Sally E. Barker & Loretta K. Haggard, *A Labor Union's Duties and Potential Liabilities Arising Out of Coworker Complaints of Sexual Harassment,* 11 St. Louis U.Pub.L.Rev. 135 (1992); Sally E. Barker, *Union Duties and Potential Conflicts Arising Out of Complaints of Sexual Harassment,* in A.B.A. Ctr. for Continuing Legal Educ., National Institute on Sexual Harassment: A Multi–Disciplined View of the New Generation of Sexual Harassment Policies and Procedures and A Trial of a Sexual Harassment Case (Oct. 15–18, 1997).

    8. *Union Liability for Harassment During a Strike*: In *Dowd v. United Steelworkers of America,* 253 F.3d 1093 (8th Cir.2001), the court affirmed a jury verdict against a union for the racial harassment experienced by black employees who crossed the picket line during a strike. The plaintiffs faced "racial slurs and threats of physical violence each time they drove into and out of the plant." *Id.* at 1102. The court held that the offensive conduct on the picket line outside the plaint "affect[ed] the working atmosphere inside the plant." *Id.* Moreover, sufficient evidence supported the jury's conclusion that the union was responsible for the hostile work environment. Not only was the racial harassment "directly connected to a union-sponsored activity—the strike," but "at least one union steward participated in the harassment," while "others stood silently by," and "the union's president exhibited discriminatory animus." *Id.* at 1103.

    9. *Preemption Defenses to State Law Claims in Harassment Cases*: Plaintiffs who bring statutory discrimination claims based on a hostile environment theory may also seek recovery under state law causes of action, particularly tort theories such as intentional infliction of mental distress, assault, or battery. Awards for compensatory or punitive damages under state law claims are not subject to the statutory caps on damages for Title VII claims. Civil Rights Act of 1991, 42 U.S.C. § 1981a(b)(3). A state law claim based on contract or tort theories may be preempted by federal law under two circumstances: (1) if the state law claim requires interpretation of the collective bargaining agreement, it will be preempted by § 301 of the Labor Management Relations Act; or (2) if the state law claim is based on

conduct of the union that is clearly or arguably a violation of the National Labor Relations Act and does not fall within one of a few narrow exceptions to NLRA preemption, it will be preempted because of the primary subject matter jurisdiction of the NLRB. *See, e.g.,* Anspach v. Tomkins Indus., Inc., 817 F.Supp. 1499, 1512–14 (D.Kan.1993), *aff'd,* 51 F.3d 285 (10th Cir.1995) (unpublished table decision).

10. *Discrimination on the Basis of Disabilities*: The Americans with Disabilities Act of 1990 (ADA), discussed in Chapter 13, extends nondiscrimination protection, as well as rights to reasonable workplace accommodations, to disabled individuals who are otherwise qualified to perform the particular job. Professor Ann Hodges has observed,

> As is the case with most employee protective legislation, unions were among the supporters of the ADA, but Congress appears to have given little thought to the implications of the ADA for the unionized workplace. Unlike the Rehabilitation Act of 1973 * * *, after which it was patterned, the ADA covers labor organizations. But in contrast to Title VII of the Civil Rights Act, which also covers labor organizations, the ADA does not contain language expressly defining the nondiscrimination obligations of unions. Thus, there is no statutory blueprint for applying the ADA in the unionized workplace.

Ann C. Hodges, *The Americans With Disabilities Act in the Unionized Workplace*, 48 U. Miami L.Rev. 567, 567–68 (1994). Is *Goodman v. Lukens Steel*—a Title VII case—a helpful guide to interpreting union obligations under the ADA? When a disabled individual seeks a "reasonable accommodation" under the ADA that conflicts with the collectively bargained seniority rights of co-workers, how should the conflict be resolved? *See* US Airways, Inc. v. Barnett, 535 U.S. 391, 122 S.Ct. 1516, 152 L.Ed.2d 589 (2002), in Chapter 13.

11. *Dual Capacities of Unions*: A union can be sued under Title VII either as a "labor organization" or as an "employer," depending on the nature of the claim. When Title VII was enacted in 1964, labor organizations that operated a hiring hall or had 100 or more members were covered by the Act. As a result of the 1972 amendments, Title VII now covers any "labor organization" that has fifteen or more members or operates a hiring hall. Title VII, § 701(e), 42 U.S.C. § 2000e(e). A labor organization can be sued in its capacity as an "employer" if it meets the jurisdictional requirements of a Title VII employer, i.e., if it has "fifteen or more employees for each working day in each of twenty or more calendar weeks in the current or preceding year." Title VII, § 701(b), 42 U.S.C. § 2000e(b). One court has noted that "[m]any labor organizations have fewer than 14 employees but thousands of members." Dowd v. United Steelworkers of Am., 253 F.3d 1093, 1099–1100 (8th Cir.2001). But who are the "employees" of a union? Can union stewards be "employees"? *See* Daggitt v. United Food & Commercial Workers Int'l Union, Local 304A, 245 F.3d 981, 986–89 (8th Cir.2001). Assume that a labor union is sued by black members for intentional racial discrimination during contract negotiations. If the union has less than fifteen employees but more than 500 members, is it potentially liable for compensatory and punitive damages up to $300,000 per complaining party? *See* 42 U.S.C. § 1981a(b)(3), which caps damages according to the number of "employees" of the "respon-

dent." *See Dowd*, 253 F.3d at 1100; *id.* at 1104–05 (Hansen, J., dissenting in part).

Note: Title VII and the NLRA's Exclusivity Principle

In *Emporium Capwell Co. v. Western Addition Community Organization*, 420 U.S. 50, 95 S.Ct. 977, 43 L.Ed.2d 12 (1975), two black employees were discharged for engaging in picketing and boycott activities in protest of their employer's racially discriminatory practices. Prior to the discharge, the two employees had received written warnings that they could be discharged if they continued their picketing and adverse publicity about the employer. The employees were covered by a collective bargaining agreement that contained a no-strike or lockout clause, a nondiscrimination clause, and a grievance and arbitration provision for processing claimed violations of the contract. Before the employees resorted to the boycott and picketing activities, a group of black employees had presented a list of grievances, including claims of racial discrimination, to the union representatives; furthermore, the company and union had agreed to "look into the matter" of discrimination and see what needed to be done.

A local civil rights association filed charges with the National Labor Relations Board (NLRB) on behalf of the discharged employees claiming that the employer had interfered with the employees' rights under § 7 of the NLRA to engage in concerted activity "for the purpose of collective bargaining or other mutual aid or protection." 29 U.S.C. § 157. The NLRB found that the employees' conduct was not protected under the NLRA because they were, in effect, attempting to bargain directly with their employer on the issue of racial discrimination. The Board held that such bargaining circumvented the efforts to remedy discrimination undertaken by their union, which had the statutory authority under § 9(a) of the NLRA to act as the exclusive representative of all the employees in the bargaining unit. 29 U.S.C. § 159(a).

The Court of Appeals reversed and remanded, arguing that, because racial discrimination holds a "unique status" under both the NLRA and Title VII, the Board should determine "whether the union was actually remedying the discrimination to the *fullest extent possible*, by *the most expedient and efficacious means*." 420 U.S. at 59–60, 95 S.Ct. at 983. The Supreme Court reversed, upholding the Board's findings and conclusions. In response to the argument that the "unique status" of racial discrimination should permit an exception to the exclusivity principle, Justice Marshall wrote for the Court:

> Against [a] background of long and consistent adherence to the principle of exclusive representation tempered by safeguards for the protection of minority interests, respondent urges this Court to fashion a limited exception to that principle: employees who seek to bargain separately with their employer as to the elimination of racially discriminatory employment practices peculiarly affecting them,[15] should be free

---

15. As respondent conceded at oral argument, the rule it espouses here would necessarily have equal application to any identifiable group of employees—racial or religious groups, women, etc.—that reasonably believed themselves to be the object of

from the constraints of the exclusivity principle of § 9(a). Essentially because established procedures under Title VII or, as in this case, a grievance machinery, are too time consuming, the national labor policy against discrimination requires this exception, respondent argues, and its adoption would not unduly compromise the legitimate interests of either unions or employers.

Plainly, national labor policy embodies the principles of nondiscrimination as a matter of highest priority, and it is a commonplace that we must construe the NLRA in light of the broad national labor policy of which it is a part. These general principles do not aid respondent, however, as it is far from clear that separate bargaining is necessary to help eliminate discrimination. Indeed, as the facts of this litigation demonstrate, the proposed remedy might have just the opposite effect. The collective-bargaining agreement involved here prohibited without qualification all manner of invidious discrimination and made any claimed violation a grievable issue. The grievance procedure is directed precisely at determining whether discrimination has occurred. That orderly determination, if affirmative, could lead to an arbitral award enforceable in court. Nor is there any reason to believe that the processing of grievances is inherently limited to the correction of individual cases of discrimination. Quite apart from the essentially contractual question of whether the Union could grieve against a "pattern or practice" it deems inconsistent with the nondiscrimination clause of the contract, one would hardly expect an employer to continue in effect an employment practice that routinely results in adverse arbitral decisions.

The decision by a handful of employees to bypass the grievance procedure in favor of attempting to bargain with their employer, by contrast, may or may not be predicated upon the actual existence of discrimination. An employer confronted with bargaining demands from each of several minority groups would not necessarily, or even probably, be able to agree to remedial steps satisfactory to all at once. Competing claims on the employer's ability to accommodate each group's demands, e.g., for reassignments and promotions to a limited number of positions, could only set one group against the other even if it is not the employer's intention to divide and overcome them. Having divided themselves, the minority employees will not be in position to advance their cause unless it be by recourse seriatim to economic coercion, which can only have the effect of further dividing them along racial or other lines. Nor is the situation materially different where, as apparently happened here, self-designated representatives purport to speak for all groups that might consider themselves to be victims of discrimination. Even if in actual bargaining the various groups did not perceive their interests as divergent and further subdivide themselves, the employer would be bound to bargain with them in a field largely pre-empted by the current collective-bargaining agreement with the elected bargaining representative. * * * The potential for conflict between the minority and other employees in this situation is manifest. With each group able to enforce its conflicting demands—the incumbent employees by resort

invidious discrimination by their employer. As seemingly limited by the Court of Appeals, however, such a group would have to give their elected representative an opportunity to adjust the matter in some way before resorting to self-help.

to contractual processes and the minority employees by economic coercion—the probability of strife and deadlock is high; the likelihood of making headway against discriminatory practices would be minimal.

Emporium Capwell, 420 U.S. at 65–69, 95 S.Ct. at 986–88. For a critique arguing that *Emporium Capwell* "legitimate[s] the submergence and demobilization of minorities within the broader collectivity controlled by a white majority," see Elizabeth M. Iglesias, *Structures of Subordination: Women of Color at the Intersection of Title VII and the NLRA. NOT!*, 28 Harv.C.R.-C.L.L.Rev. 395, 416 (1993); *see generally id.* at 415–31.

How do the principles of majority rule and exclusivity affect the responsibility unions should bear for discrimination in the workplace? Can the processes of collective bargaining and grievance arbitration offer employees fairer, quicker, and more creative solutions to discriminatory employment practices than Title VII? Or than self-help? In light of the limits that *Emporium Capwell* imposes on minority groups in a unionized workplace, what role can or should a union play in ensuring that all members of a particular bargaining unit work in an environment free from unlawful discrimination? Is it enough that the union does not violate its duty of fair representation, the NLRA, or one of the antidiscrimination statutes? Or should unions be expected (if not legally required) to play a more active role in promoting nondiscrimination policies—to "provide voice and muscle to enforce workers' public law rights"? *See* Robert J. Rabin, *The Role of Unions in the Rights–Based Workplace*, 25 U.S.F.L.Rev. 169, 171 (1991). For that matter, are unions capable of adapting to the new demands that are placed on them by an increasingly diverse workforce? *See generally* Marion Crain & Ken Matheny, *Labor's Identity Crisis*, 89 Cal.L.Rev. 1767 (2001); Molly S. McUsic & Michael Selmi, *Postmodern Unions: Identity Politics in the Workplace*, 82 Iowa L.Rev. 1339 (1997). A labor historian has observed that

labor's leaders remain overwhelmingly white, male, and less than successful in forging links among unions, women's groups, and communities of color. The change in race and gender of union membership obviously does not guarantee policy change in and of itself * * *. Moreover, the demographic shift in labor's base has resulted as much from the loss of white men as members as from dynamic organizing among white women or among minority workers, male and female. But whatever the source of the shift in membership, the lag in leadership, and the precarious position of unions generally, the recomposition of the labor movement raises unprecedented possibilities * * *.

David Roediger, *What if Labor Were Not White and Male? Recentering Working–Class History and Reconstructing Debate on the Unions and Race*, 51 Int'l Lab. & Working–Class Hist. 72, 76 (Spring 1997). Considering *Emporium Capwell* as well as the Supreme Court's treatment of union liability for discrimination under Title VII in *Goodman v. Lukens Steel*, would you agree with Roediger's last statement above? *See* Ruben J. Garcia, *New Voices at Work: Race and Gender Identity Caucuses in the U.S. Labor Movement*, 54 Hastings L.J. 79 (2002) (discussing *Emporium Capwell, id.* at 125–33, and "empirical research suggesting that members of identity caucuses do not find exclusive union representation problematic," *id.* at 133). *See also* Marion Crain, *Colorblind Unionism*, 49 UCLA L.Rev. 1313 (2002) (arguing for race-conscious and identity-based union organizing and bargaining unit determination).

Chapter 15

RETALIATION

A. INTRODUCTION

Protection against retaliation because an individual has participated in enforcement proceedings or has opposed unlawful employment practices is considered essential to the effective enforcement of laws prohibiting discrimination in employment. As one court has observed,

> [t]he ability to seek enforcement and protection of one's right to be free of [unlawful] discrimination is an integral part of the right itself. A person who believes he has been discriminated against because [of an unlawful reason] should not be deterred from attempting to vindicate his rights because he fears his employer will punish him for doing so. Were we to protect retaliatory conduct, we would in effect be discouraging the filing of meritorious civil rights suits and sanctioning further discrimination against those persons willing to risk their employer's vengeance by filing suits. [Laws prohibiting discrimination in employment] would become meaningless if an employer could fire an employee for attempting to enforce his rights under [those statutes].

Goff v. Continental Oil Co., 678 F.2d 593, 598 (5th Cir.1982). Protection against retaliation is an integral part of the right to equality:

> [A]n employee who is punished for seeking administrative or judicial relief, regardless of the merits of his initial claim, has failed to secure that right to equal treatment which constitutes the fundamental promise of [laws prohibiting discrimination in employment]. When a complainant experiences retaliation for the assertion of a claim to even-handed treatment, he remains under a handicap not faced by his colleagues.

Choudhury v. Polytechnic Inst. of New York, 735 F.2d 38, 43 (2d Cir.1984).

1. STATUTORY PROVISIONS

Title VII and the ADEA contain almost identical provisions that make it an unlawful employment practice to discriminate against any individual because that individual has *opposed* any practice made unlawful under these statutes or because he has *participated* in any manner in proceedings to enforce these statutes. Title VII, § 704(a), 42 U.S.C. § 2000e–3(a); ADEA, § 4(d), 29 U.S.C. § 623(d). The ADA, § 503, 42 U.S.C. § 12203(a), also prohibits retaliation because of an individual's "opposition" to unlawful practices or "participation" in enforcement proceedings. In addition, § 503(b) of the ADA, 42 U.S.C. § 12203(b), makes it unlawful to "coerce, intimidate, threaten, or interfere" with any individual based on the exercise of rights under the ADA, or because an individual has "aided or encouraged any other individual in the exercise or enjoyment of" rights provided under the ADA. Protection from retaliation in Equal Pay Act cases is provided in the Fair Labor Standards Act, 29 U.S.C. § 215(a)(3).

Prior to the Supreme Court's decision in *Patterson v. McLean Credit Union*, 491 U.S. 164, 109 S.Ct. 2363, 105 L.Ed.2d 132 (1989), the lower courts were uniform in holding that retaliation claims were cognizable under § 1981, even absent specific statutory authorization. *See, e.g.*, Goff v. Continental Oil Co., 678 F.2d 593 (5th Cir.1982); Choudhury v. Polytechnic Inst. of New York, 735 F.2d 38 (2d Cir.1984); Setser v. Novack Inv. Co., 638 F.2d 1137 (8th Cir.), *modified on other grounds*, 657 F.2d 962 (en banc), *cert. denied*, 454 U.S. 1064, 102 S.Ct. 615, 70 L.Ed.2d 601 (1981). In *Patterson*, the Supreme Court held that racial harassment claims cannot be brought under § 1981, but Congress overturned *Patterson* in the Civil Rights Act of 1991. As a result of the Civil Rights Act of 1991, retaliation claims are again cognizable under § 1981. *See* H.R.Rep. 102–40(II), at 37, *reprinted in* 1991 U.S.C.C.A.N. 549, 730–31; Thomas v. Exxon, U.S.A., 943 F.Supp. 751, 762–63 (S.D.Tex.1996), (collecting cases), *aff'd*, 122 F.3d 1067 (5th Cir.1997).

Legislative history on both the scope and extent of protection under the participation and opposition clauses is practically nonexistent. Thus, the federal judiciary has played a significant role in the development of the law on retaliation. *See, e.g.*, Hochstadt v. Worcester Found. for Experimental Biology, 545 F.2d 222, 230 (1st Cir.1976). And, as is the case with many other subjects in employment discrimination law, much of the jurisprudence of retaliation under other statutes prohibiting discrimination has relied on Title VII cases. *See e.g.*, Passer v. American Chem. Soc'y, 935 F.2d 322, 330 (D.C.Cir.1991) (ADEA); Morgan v. Hilti, Inc., 108 F.3d 1319, 1324–25 (10th Cir.1997) (ADA and FMLA); Cross v. Cleaver, 142 F.3d 1059 (8th Cir.1998) (state human rights statute).

2.   ANALYTICAL FRAMEWORK FOR RETALIATION CLAIMS

LOVE v. RE/MAX OF AMERICA, INC.

United States Court of Appeals for the Tenth Circuit, 1984.
738 F.2d 383.

SEYMOUR, Circuit Judge.

Linda Love brought this action against RE/MAX of America, Inc. (RE/MAX) pursuant to 42 U.S.C. § 2000e et seq. (1976) (Title VII), and

29 U.S.C. § 201 et seq. (1982) (Fair Labor Standards Act) as modified by 29 U.S.C. § 206(d) (1982) (Equal Pay Act). Love alleged that RE/MAX violated Title VII by discriminating against her on the basis of sex, violated the Equal Pay Act by failing to give her equal pay for equal work, and retaliated against her in violation of both Title VII and the Fair Labor Standards Act. After a trial to the bench, the judge rendered an oral decision in which he determined that RE/MAX had not discriminated against Love or violated the Equal Pay Act with respect to her salary. However, the court decided that Love's discharge by RE/MAX was retaliatory and directed an award of damages and attorneys fees. RE/MAX appeals and we affirm.

I

The claim of retaliatory discharge is based on the following undisputed facts. Love was hired by RE/MAX in February 1978 as director of advertising. She was named vice president for advertising in February 1979, but was not given a raise in pay until April 1979. During this time Love discovered that male vice presidents had received larger starting salaries than she. In December 1979, Love was told that her projects were unacceptably over budget, and that if she went over budget again she would be fired. Love agreed to keep costs down. In March 1980, Love learned that male employees of RE/MAX in positions she believed were comparable to hers had been given substantial raises the previous November although she had not. Love asked the company president, Gail Main, for a performance review and indicated her desire for a pay raise. She was told at the end of March that the company was not happy with her work and that she would not get a raise. On April 18, 1980, Love wrote a memo to the president requesting a raise. She attached a copy of the Equal Pay Act to the memo. Within two hours the chief executive officer of RE/MAX, Dave Liniger, went to her office with the memo and fired her.

The district court found that Love had made a legitimate good faith assertion of a statutory right by sending the memo and attaching to it a copy of the Equal Pay Act. The court held that Love was entitled to recover for retaliation because one of the dominant reasons for her discharge was the assertion of that statutory right. The court did not specify whether it found retaliation under the Fair Labor Standards Act, Title VII, or both.

On appeal, RE/MAX contends that the claim of discriminatory retaliation should be analyzed exclusively under the Title VII standards set out in McDonnell Douglas Corp. v. Green, 411 U.S. 792, 802, 36 L. Ed. 2d 668, 93 S. Ct. 1817 (1973), and its progeny, and that the district court misapplied the McDonnell Douglas test. Love argues that the court's decision is sustainable if it is correct under the Fair Labor Standards Act. We need not resolve this dispute because in our view Love met the standards for proving retaliation under either Act.

II

Title VII provides in pertinent part:

It shall be an unlawful employment practice for an employer to discriminate against any of his employees * * * *because [the employee] has opposed any practice made an unlawful employment practice* by this subchapter, or because he has made a charge, testified, assisted, or participated in any manner in an investigation, proceeding, or hearing under this subchapter.

42 U.S.C. § 2000e–3(a) (emphasis added). This circuit applies to retaliation claims the approach to Title VII suits established in *McDonnell Douglas*. See Burrus v. United Telephone Co., 683 F.2d 339 (10th Cir.), *cert. denied*, 459 U.S. 1071, 74 L. Ed. 2d 633, 103 S. Ct. 491 (1982). In *Burrus* we held that the elements of a prima facie case of retaliation are: (1) protected opposition to Title VII discrimination or participation in a Title VII proceeding; (2) adverse action by the employer subsequent to or contemporaneous with such employee activity; and (3) a causal connection between such activity and the employer's action. Id. at 343.

RE/MAX argues that under the language of the statute, opposition is not protected unless the conduct opposed is in fact unlawful. Given the district court's finding that RE/MAX did not discriminate against Love on the basis of sex, RE/MAX contends that Love's good faith belief was not legally sufficient to state a retaliation claim under the opposition clause. Every circuit that has considered the issue, however, has concluded that opposition activity is protected when it is based on a mistaken good faith belief that Title VII has been violated. * * * We agree that a good faith belief is sufficient.

RE/MAX also argues that the district court committed reversible error by improperly shifting to it the burden of proving the absence of retaliatory motive. As discussed in *Burrus*,

If a prima facie case is established, then the burden of production shifts to the defendant to articulate a legitimate, nondiscriminatory reason for the adverse action. * * * The defendant need not prove the "absence of retaliatory motive, but only produce evidence that would dispel the inference of retaliation by establishing the existence of a legitimate reason." * * * If evidence of a legitimate reason is produced, the plaintiff may still prevail if she demonstrates the articulated reason was a mere pretext for discrimination. The overall burden of persuasion remains on the plaintiff.

683 F.2d at 343.

We are not persuaded that the district court misunderstood the nature of the burden of production that shifts to a defendant in a Title VII case. Indeed, after observing that the facts were very close on the disparate treatment claim, the court found the evidence to be "inconclusive" and denied Love relief on that claim. * * * We believe the court's resolution of the disparate treatment claim indicates that the judge properly placed on Love the overall burden of persuasion in the Title VII claims.

RE/MAX contends alternatively that the record does not support the trial court's decision. RE/MAX argues that Love did not present a prima facie case because the evidence does not establish that she asserted her rights in good faith or that a causal connection existed between her conduct and the employer's action. RE/MAX further argues that Love failed to rebut its legitimate business reasons with sufficient evidence of pretext.

Once the trial court declines to dismiss a Title VII claim for failure to make a prima facie case and the defendant proceeds to present evidence of a legitimate business reason, the court then must decide the ultimate fact issue—"which party's explanation of the employer's motivation it believes." United States Postal Service Board of Governors v. Aikens, 460 U.S. 711, 103 S. Ct. 1478, 1482,75 L. Ed. 2d 403 (1983). In some cases a "plaintiff's initial evidence, combined with effective cross-examination of the defendant, will suffice to discredit the defendant's explanation." Texas Department of Community Affairs v. Burdine, 450 U.S. 248, 255 n.10, 67 L. Ed. 2d 207, 101 S.Ct. 1089 (1981).

In deciding that Love had asserted her rights in good faith, the trial court found that RE/MAX, and particularly Mr. Liniger, "would put up with more from men in the company than from women." * * * The court further found that "the looseness and the lack of precision of managerial concepts has caused an atmosphere to exist in which any sensitive thinking woman would consider that there was discrimination," and that "she would see other vice-presidents and consider that she was sharing the same or even greater moments of pressure than they were and think that she should be paid to the extent that they should." The court found that Love's feeling of gender discrimination also was justified by "the churlish remarks that were made around the office."

With respect to a causal connection between the protected activity and the adverse employment action, the evidence shows that Liniger fired Love within two hours of receiving her memo containing a raise request and a copy of the Equal Pay Act. "The causal connection may be demonstrated by evidence of circumstances that justify an inference of retaliatory motive, such as protected conduct closely followed by adverse action." Burrus, 683 F.2d at 343. Love demonstrated to the satisfaction of the trial court that the reasons offered by RE/MAX for her termination were unconvincing "afterthoughts," * * * and not worthy of belief.

We may set aside these determinations on appeal only if they are clearly erroneous. Fed. R. Civ. P. 52(a); see Aikens, 103 S. Ct. at 1482–83.

* * *

We have carefully reviewed the entire record and we are not left with a definite and firm conviction that a mistake has been made. The finding of unlawful retaliation by RE/MAX is sustainable under Title VII.

* * *

In sum, we affirm the trial court's decision that Love was illegally discharged in retaliation for the good faith assertion of her statutory rights.

Notes and Questions

1.   As in *Love v. Re/Max,* the courts have adjusted the burden-shifting scheme of *McDonnell Douglas v. Green* for retaliation cases. First, the plaintiff must establish a prima facie case of retaliation. The plaintiff must prove (1) that she was engaged in statutorily protected activity; (2) that she suffered an adverse employment action at the hands of the employer; and (3) that a causal link exists between the protected activity and the adverse action. The prima facie case establishes a rebuttable presumption of unlawful retaliatory motive. Assuming the plaintiff establishes a prima facie case, the burden then shifts to the employer to rebut the presumption of unlawful retaliation by articulating a legitimate, nondiscriminatory reason for the adverse action it took against the plaintiff. The plaintiff then has the ultimate burden of proving pretext, i.e., that the adverse action was motivated by retaliatory animus. *See, e.g.,* Holt v. KMI–Continental, Inc., 95 F.3d 123, 130 (2d Cir.1996) (Title VII), *cert. denied,* 520 U.S. 1228, 117 S.Ct. 1819, 137 L.Ed.2d 1027 (1997); Berman v. Orkin Exterminating Co., Inc., 160 F.3d 697, 701–02 (11th Cir. 1998); Folkerson v. Circus Circus Enter., 107 F.3d 754, 755 (9th Cir. 1997) (Title VII); Holt v. JTM Indus., Inc., 89 F.3d 1224, 1225–26 (5th Cir.1996) (ADEA), *cert. denied,* 520 U.S. 1229, 117 S.Ct. 1821, 137 L.Ed.2d 1029 (1997); McNely v. Ocala Star–Banner Corp., 99 F.3d 1068, 1073, 1075–77 (11th Cir.1996) (ADA), *cert. denied,* 520 U.S. 1228, 117 S.Ct. 1819, 137 L.Ed.2d 1028 (1997).

2.   *Causation*: The causal link can be established by showing that the protected conduct and the adverse employment action are not wholly unrelated. *See* Fierros v. Texas Dep't of Health, 274 F.3d 187, 191 (5th Cir.2001); Pennington v. City of Huntsville, 261 F.3d 1262, 1265–66 (11th Cir.2001); Hunt–Golliday v. Metropolitan Water, 104 F.3d 1004, 1014 (7th Cir.1997) (citing Simmons v. Camden County Bd. of Educ., 757 F.2d 1187, 1189 (11th Cir.1985)). An employer's proven lack of knowledge that the employee engaged in protected activity, however, has been found to be fatal to a prima facie showing of causation. *See, e.g.,* Sanchez v. Denver Publ. Sch., 164 F.3d 527, 533–34 (10th Cir.1998); Smith v. Riceland Foods, 151 F.3d 813, 818 (8th Cir.1998).

The causation element can be established several ways. One way is through direct evidence of retaliatory animus. *See* Stone v. City of Indianapolis, 281 F.3d 640, 644 (7th Cir.2002); DeCintio v. Westchester County Med. Ctr., 821 F.2d 111, 115 (2d Cir.1987), *cert. denied,* 484 U.S. 965, 108 S.Ct. 455, 98 L.Ed.2d 395 (1987). Another is through proof that other employees who engaged in protected activity were also subjected to adverse employment action. *DeCintio,* 821 F.2d at 115. A third way is with evidence of a close temporal proximity between the adverse action and protected activity in which the plaintiff engaged. In some cases a time lapse of two months or less has been found to satisfy the causal link. *E.g.*, Evans v. Houston, 246 F.3d 344, 354 (5th Cir.2001) (five days); Miller v. Fairchild Indus., Inc., 797 F.2d 727, 731–32 (9th Cir.1986) (two months); Womack v. Munson, 619 F.2d 1292, 1296 (8th Cir.1980) (twenty days), *cert. denied*, 450 U.S. 979, 101 S.Ct. 1513, 67 L.Ed.2d 814 (1981). The Supreme Court has suggested that a three- or four-month time lapse may be insufficient, and has found that a twenty-month delay, by itself, is "no causality at all." Clark County School Dist. v. Breeden, 532 U.S. 268, 273–74, 121 S.Ct. 1508, 149 L.Ed.2d 509 (2001) (per curiam). As the temporal distance between the protected activity and the adverse employment action increases the less likely it is that the causal element can be established. *See, e.g.*, McKenzie v. Illinois Dep't of Transp., 92 F.3d 473, 485 (7th Cir.1996). But the fact that a substantial period of time has elapsed between the protected conduct and the adverse employment action will not necessarily defeat a finding of causation:

> Our research reveals that other cases which permit claims of retaliation after * * * long periods of time each involve additional circumstances which raised suspicion about the legitimacy of the employer's acts. *See, e.g.*, Moss v. Southern Ry. Co., 41 FEP 553, 1986 WL 10510 (N.D.Ga. 1986) (one-year time span between expression and retaliation did not defeat plaintiff's claim where termination was disproportionately severe for minor error); Ross v. Kansas Comm'n on Civil Rights, 45 FEP 1476, 1985 WL 17574 (D.Kan.1985) (one-year time span did not defeat plaintiff's claim in light of plaintiff's prior outstanding job performance); Shirley v. Chrysler First, Inc., 970 F.2d 39 (5th Cir.1992) (plaintiff's verdict affirmed, despite fourteen-month time span between expression and retaliation, where retaliation occurred two months after the EEOC dismissed the complaint).

McKenzie, 92 F.3d at 485; *but see* Filipovic v. K & R Express Sys., Inc., 176 F.3d 390, 398–99 (7th Cir.1999) (four-month delay is a "substantial time lapse"); Cooper v. City of North Olmsted, 795 F.2d 1265, 1272 (6th Cir.1986) (fact that plaintiff was discharged four months after filing a discrimination claim was "insufficient to support an inference of retaliation").

An increasing number of courts are holding, however, that temporal proximity alone is not sufficient to show a causal link. The Third Circuit, in *Robinson v. City of Pittsburgh*, 120 F.3d 1286, 1302 (3d Cir.1997), noting a split in its cases on the issue, questioned whether "temporal proximity" alone should be sufficient to satisfy the causation element, absent unusual facts suggestive of retaliatory motive. *See also* Little v. BP Exploration & Oil Co., 265 F.3d 357, 363–64 (6th Cir. 2001); Feltmann v. Sieben, 108 F.3d 970, 977 (8th Cir.1997) (temporal proximity alone is not sufficient to establish causal link). Even if temporal proximity is not sufficient by itself to prove a causal link, should temporal proximity be enough to show causal connection as part of a prima facie case of retaliation? Should a showing of temporal proximity allow the claim to survive summary judgment? *See* Stone v. City of Indianapolis, 281 F.3d 640, 644 (7th Cir.2002) ("mere temporal proximity between the filing of the charge of discrimination and the action alleged to have been taken in retaliation for that finding will rarely be sufficient in and of itself to create a triable issue").

3. Can an employee prevail on a retaliation claim merely by making out a prima facie case of retaliation followed by a showing that the employer's articulated reasons for allegedly retaliating were pretextual? What if the employee can only show that the employer was lying about his reasons for the alleged retaliation? Should *St. Mary's Honor Center v. Hicks*, 509 U.S. 502, 113 S.Ct. 2742, 125 L.Ed.2d 407 (1993), reproduced in Chapter 3, apply in analyzing retaliation claims? *See, e.g.*, Dea v. Washington Suburban Sanitary Comm'n, 11 Fed.Appx. 352, 366–67 (4th Cir.2001) (yes); Woodson v. Scott Paper Co., 109 F.3d 913, 920 n.2 (3d Cir.) (yes), *cert. denied*, 522 U.S. 914, 118 S.Ct. 299, 139 L.Ed.2d 230 (1997). Should *Hicks* or even *McDonnell-Douglas* be applicable to retaliation cases if the prima facie burden is substantial, as it might be if temporal proximity is not sufficient to establish a causal connection in the prima facie case?

4. *Mixed-Motive Retaliation Cases*: Should the statutory provision on mixed-motive cases under the Civil Rights Act of 1991, 42 U.S.C. § 2000e–2(m), apply to retaliation cases? Courts have held that the mixed-motive proof scheme outlined in *Price Waterhouse* is available to Title VII plaintiffs bringing retaliation claims. *See, e.g.*, Matima v. Celli, 228 F.3d 68, 80–81 (2d Cir.2000); Kubicko v. Ogden Logistics Servs., 181 F.3d 544, 553 n. 8 (4th Cir.1999); Medlock v. Ortho Biotech Inc., 164 F.3d 545, 549–51 (10th Cir.1999). Mixed-motive cases are discussed in Chapter 3. Under § 703(m) of Title VII, 42 U.S.C. § 2000e–2(m), as amended by the 1991 Civil Rights Act, an unlawful employment practice is established when the plaintiff demonstrates that an impermissible factor, e.g., race or sex, was "a motivating factor for any employment practice, even though other factors also motivated the practice." The section also provides that while an employer proving mixed motivation escapes liability for money damages, a court may nonetheless grant the plaintiff attorney's fees, injunctive relief (not including reinstatement or promotion), and declaratory relief. However, courts have held that these mixed-motive damages provisions under the 1991 Civil Rights Act are not applicable in retaliation cases. *See, e.g.*, Matima v. Celli, 228 F.3d 68, 81 (2d Cir.2000); Norbeck v. Basin Elec. Power Coop., 215 F.3d 848, 852 (8th Cir.2000); Lewis v. YMCA, 208 F.3d 1303, 1305–06 (11th Cir.2000); Woodson v. Scott Paper Co., 109 F.3d 913, 933–35 (3d Cir.), *cert. denied*, 522 U.S. 914, 118 S.Ct. 299, 139 L.Ed.2d 230 (1997); Tanca v. Nordberg, 98 F.3d 680, 682–83 (1st Cir.1996), *cert. denied*, 520 U.S. 1119, 117 S.Ct. 1253, 139 L.Ed.2d 330 (1997). In *Woodson v. Scott Paper*, for example, the Third Circuit held that the 1991 Civil Rights Act's provisions on mixed-motive cases are inapplicable because (1) the provisions on mixed motives do not refer specifically to retaliation or to the general provision under Title VII on retaliation, and (2) the general rule is that "where Congress includes particular language in one section of a statute but omits it from another section of the same Act, it is generally presumed that Congress acts intentionally and purposely in the disparate inclusion and exclusion." 109 F.3d at 933–34.

The Supreme Court in *Costa v. Desert Palace*, Chapter 3, Section B.3, held that the Civil Rights Act of 1991 should be applied broadly based on the language of the statute; accordingly the Court rejected an approach to mixed-motive cases that relied on the distinction between direct and indirect evidence. Does *Costa* suggest that temporal proximity could or should provide a causal link in retaliation cases? After *Costa* should the Civil Rights Act of 1991 apply broadly to include retaliation cases, because they, like direct evidence, are not expressly mentioned or excluded in the statutory language of the Act?

5. *Employer Liability*: Should an employer be strictly liable for retaliatory conduct engaged in by its agents? Are the retaliation cases sufficiently analogous to the harassment cases such that agency principles should control? In *Cross v. Cleaver*, 142 F.3d 1059, 1070 (8th Cir.1998), a retaliation case, the Eighth Circuit rejected the "knew or should have known" test some courts had used to determine employer liability in hostile work environment harassment cases; it adopted instead the strict liability test imposed in the quid pro quo harassment cases. *Id.* The Supreme Court in *Burlington Industries, Inc. v. Ellerth*, 524 U.S. 742, 118 S.Ct. 2257, 141 L.Ed.2d 633 (1998), and *Faragher v. City of Boca Raton* 524 U.S. 775, 118 S.Ct. 2275, 141 L.Ed.2d 662 (1998), Chapter 8, Section C.1, resolved the conflict in the circuit courts over the appropriate standard for employer liability in cases of sexual harassment by supervisory employees. Do *Ellerth* and *Faragher* affect the standard for employer liability in retaliation cases? Should they?

B.   SCOPE OF PROTECTED ACTIVITY

Two kinds of activities are protected under the anti-retaliation provisions of Title VII. The *participation clause* prohibits retaliation because an individual "has made a charge, testified, assisted, or participated in any manner in an investigation, proceeding, or hearing" to enforce laws prohibiting discrimination in employment. Title VII, § 704(a), 42 U.S.C. § 2000e–3(a). The *opposition clause* prohibits retaliation because an employee or applicant "has opposed any practice made an unlawful employment practice" by Title VII. *Id.* The Sixth Circuit in *Booker v. Brown & Williamson Tobacco Co.*, 879 F.2d 1304 (6th Cir. 1989), discussed the rationale for the distinction between the participation and opposition clauses:

> The distinction between employee activities protected by the participation clause and those protected by the opposition clause is significant because federal courts generally have granted less protection for opposition than participation in enforcement proceedings. The "exceptionally broad protection" of the participation clause extends to persons who have "participated in any manner" in Title VII proceedings. Protection is not lost if the employee is wrong on the merits of the charge, nor is protection lost if the contents of the charge are malicious and defamatory as well as wrong. Thus, once the activity in question is found to be within the scope of the participation clause, the employee is generally protected from retaliation. However, the fact an employee files a complaint or a charge does not create any right on the part of the employee "to miss work, fail to perform assigned work, or leave work without notice," unless absence from work is necessitated by proceedings that occur subsequent to the filing of a complaint or charge. Still, while the absence

may be excused, the employee is generally required to provide notice to his employer that the reason for his absence is a proceeding recognized by [Title VII].

On the other hand, " 'the opposition clause' does not protect all 'opposition' activity." Courts are required "to balance the purpose of [Title VII] to protect persons engaging reasonably in activities opposing * * * discrimination, against Congress' equally manifest desire not to tie the hands of employers in the objective selection and control of personnel * * *. The requirements of the job and the tolerable limits of conduct in a particular setting must be explored." Hochstadt v. Worcester Found. for Experimental Biology, 545 F.2d 222, 231 (1st Cir.1976). "There may arise instances where the employee's conduct in protest of an unlawful employment practice so interferes with the performance of his job that it renders him ineffective in the position for which he was employed. In such a case, his conduct, or form of opposition, is not covered * * *." Rosser v. Laborers' Int'l Union, 616 F.2d 221, 223 (5th Cir.), *cert. denied*, 449 U.S. 886, 101 S.Ct. 241, 66 L.Ed.2d 112 (1980). An employee is not protected when he violates legitimate rules and orders of his employer, disrupts the employment environment, or interferes with the attainment of his employer's goals.

Id. at 1312.

Although the participation clause covers a narrower range of activities than the opposition clause covers, it provides greater protection to those activities. The courts, however, have not always clearly delineated "whether a particular claim is cognizable under the 'participation' or the 'opposition' clause." Laughlin v. Metropolitan Wash. Airports Auth., 952 F.Supp. 1129, 1133 n. 9 (E.D.Va.1997) (quoting Croushorn v. Board of Trustees of Univ. of Tenn., 518 F.Supp. 9, 22 n.8 (M.D.Tenn.1980)). As one court noted, the opposition clause is "often relied upon in cases in which application of the 'participation' clause to the employee's conduct is considered dubious." *Croushorn*, 518 F.Supp. at 24.

1. THE PARTICIPATION CLAUSE

The courts have broadly construed the protection afforded by the participation clause. The paradigm case in which such protection is extended is the filing of a charge with the EEOC. *See, e.g.*, Woodson v. Scott Paper Co., 109 F.3d 913, 920 (3d Cir.), *cert. denied*, 522 U.S. 914, 118 S.Ct. 299, 139 L.Ed.2d 230 (1997). The types of activities covered by the participation clause have been described as follows:

An employee who files charges with the EEOC or with a similar state agency is protected by § 704(a) from employer retaliation. * * *

In addition * * * § 704(a) also protects employees who participate in a Title VII investigation, proceeding, or hearing on their own behalf or on behalf of another. An employee is protected if the employee encourages co-workers to enforce their Title VII rights, refuses to sign an inaccurate affidavit on behalf of the employer, testifies on behalf of a co-worker, aids the state or federal investigating authority, participates in a conciliation meeting on behalf of a co-worker, submits affidavits on behalf of co-workers to the EEOC, or submits nonconfidential documentary evidence to an agency investigating a discrimination complaint. An employer is liable for retaliation if the employer promulgates a rule prohibiting employees from cooperating in Title VII investigations without prior supervisory approval, coercively interviews employees under circumstances that could render their testimony involuntary, or fails to prevent harassment of an employee by co-workers who give the employer notice that they intend to engage in harassment of the employee.

R. Bales, *A New Standard for Title VII Opposition Cases: Fitting the Personnel Manager Double Standard into a Cognizable Framework*, 35 S.Tex.L.Rev. 95, 104–05 (1994) (citing cases).

The participation clause protects employees and applicants from retaliation regardless of the underlying merits of the claim. The leading case on this point is the Fifth Circuit's decision in *Pettway v. American Cast Iron Pipe Co.*, 411 F.2d 998 (5th Cir.1969). In *Pettway*, Peter Wrenn, one of a group of black employees who had previously filed a charge with the EEOC, sent a letter to the EEOC complaining about the racially discriminatory practices of the employer. The letter suggested that a company official had bribed an EEOC official in order to influence that official to make a no-cause finding on the prior charge that the black employees had filed. The employer discharged Wrenn after the EEOC sent it a copy of his letter. The employer's ground for discharge was that Wrenn had made malicious and untrue statements about the employer in his letter to the EEOC. The Fifth Circuit, in *Pettway*, held that "where, disregarding the malicious material contained in a charge (or * * * other communication with EEOC sufficient for EEOC purposes, or in a proceeding before EEOC) the charge otherwise satisfies the liberal requirements of a charge, the charging party is exercising a protected right under [Title VII]." *Id.* at 1007. The court found that Wrenn's letter was protected conduct under Title VII, even if a trial court agreed that Wrenn's letter contained misstatements and potentially libelous statements. The court in *Pettway* left open the possibility that the employer could seek relief for damage to its reputation in state court on a state cause of action for libel if malice could be proven. *Id.* at 1007 n.22. ("We in no way imply that an employer is preempted by Section 704(a) from vindicating his reputation through resort to a civil action for malicious defamation.").

Notes and Questions

1. Wilson, a female security officer at a private university, made claims of sexual harassment against a male co-employee. After meeting with Wilson and the alleged harasser, her supervisor concluded that Wilson had exaggerated her claims and asked Wilson to sign a statement that she had "lied and

maliciously maligned her fellow officer." After she signed the statement, Wilson requested a copy; her supervisor refused to give her a copy, but allowed her to copy it by hand. In copying the statement, Wilson paraphrased it. Subsequently, she obtained a lawyer to represent her on a sexual harassment claim. When the lawyer presented Wilson's hand-copied statement to her supervisor, he concluded that the statement was a misrepresentation of the original. He then discharged her for misrepresentation. Wilson has now filed a Title VII action alleging that she was discharged in retaliation for making false charges of sexual harassment. Should *Pettway* control? The Sixth Circuit ruled against Wilson on the ground that *Pettway* is inapposite because *"Pettway* only protects employees from retaliation for misrepresentations made in certain documents or statements in EEOC proceedings." Wilson v. UT Health Ctr., 973 F.2d 1263, 1268 (5th Cir.1992), *cert. denied sub. nom* Hurst v. Wilson, 507 U.S. 1004, 113 S.Ct. 1644, 123 L.Ed.2d 266 (1993). Do you agree with the result in *Wilson?*

2. Warren and Clover, two employees, were each asked questions pursuant to internal investigations regarding sexual harassment complaints filed against other workers at their respective workplaces. Warren falsely responded that she had seen a co-worker engage in sexually harassing activity. Clover falsely stated her reasons for being late to the investigational interrogation. Clover's employer was conducting an investigation because it had received notice that a charge had been filed with the EEOC. Warren's employer, however, was conducting an internal investigation pursuant to a strictly internal complaint, with no EEOC involvement whatsoever. When both Warren and Clover were terminated for lying, they each filed retaliation claims alleging that they had been fired for their participation in internal investigations regarding Title VII claims. At the time of their terminations, however, neither Warren nor Clover knew that Title VII charges had been filed. Does the participation clause protect either employee?

The Eleventh Circuit ruled against Warren, maintaining that the participation clause "protects proceedings and activities which occur in conjunction with or after the filing of a formal charge with the EEOC; it does not include participating in an employer's internal, in-house investigation, conducted apart from a formal charge with the EEOC." EEOC v. Total Sys. Servs., Inc., 221 F.3d 1171, 1174 (11th Cir.2000). The court, however, ruled in favor of Clover, stating that "[b]ecause the information the employer gathers as part of its investigation in response to the notice of discrimination will be utilized by the EEOC, it follows that an employee who participates in the employer's process of gathering such information is participating, in some manner, in the EEOC's investigation." Clover v. Total Sys. Servs., Inc., 176 F.3d 1346, 1353 (11th Cir. 1999).

3. Because of the growing number of defamation suits brought by individuals against their former employers, many employers are adopting "no comment" policies in order to reduce their chances of being sued. Under a "no comment" policy, a referring employer refuses to disclose to prospective employers any information other than the employee's dates of employment and the positions he held. *See generally* Robert S. Adler & Ellen R. Peirce, *Encouraging Employers to Abandon Their "No Comment" Policies Regarding Job References: A Reform Proposal*, 53 Wash. & Lee L.Rev. 1381 (1996). Suppose an employer, Zerkon, has adopted a "no comment" policy. A

female employee of Zerkon is discharged and files a charge of discrimination with the EEOC claiming the discharge occurred because of her sex. The charge is served on Zerkon by the EEOC, so the employer is aware she has filed the charge. The employee then seeks employment with Alpha which informs her that she will be employed if Zerkon gives a full accounting of her prior employment. Alpha calls Zerkon for a job reference, but the only information Zerkon provides is the dates of her employment and the jobs she held. Does she have a claim for retaliation against Zerkon for not providing more information? *See* Sparrow v. Piedmont Health Sys. Agency, Inc., 593 F.Supp. 1107 (M.D.N.C.1984).

4.   Suppose that a plaintiff makes defamatory and untrue statements about the employer in the charge filed with the EEOC. Should the employer be allowed to bring a common law action for defamation in state court? Courts have held that a Title VII retaliation claim can be based on a defamation action that is filed in bad faith, motivated by retaliatory animus. *See* Harmar v. United Airlines, Inc., No. 95–C–7665, 1996 WL 199734, at *1 (N.D.Ill.1996) (collecting cases). What factors would be relevant in determining whether the employer has satisfied the good faith standard in filing the defamation suit? Recall that, in *St. Mary's Honor Center v. Hicks*, 509 U.S. 502, 521, 113 S.Ct. 2742, 2754, 125 L.Ed.2d 407 (1993), reproduced in Chapter 3, Section B.1, Justice Scalia said that "Title VII is not a cause of action for perjury; we have other civil and criminal remedies for that."

5.   Merritt, a male, and Moore, a female, worked for the same employer, Dillard Paper Company. Both male and female employees working at the company told off-color jokes, made sexually explicit comments, used profanity of a sexual nature, and circulated sexually suggestive cartoons and articles in the office. Moore, who did not participate in this activity, filed a claim of hostile work environment harassment in federal court. Counsel for Dillard took Merritt's deposition in which he admitted that he and other males engaged in a variety of sexually harassing activities. Dillard and Moore settled the sexual harassment claim before trial. Subsequently Dillard terminated Merritt for engaging in sexually harassing conduct. Does Merritt have a Title VII claim for retaliation? *See* Merritt v. Dillard Paper Co., 120 F.3d 1181 (11th Cir.1997).

6.   Suppose an employer has a good faith basis for believing that the employee engaged in criminal conduct while on the job, and this conduct would be a violation of the state's criminal law. The employer does not, however, inform the district attorney of the criminal conduct until after the plaintiff has filed a charge of discrimination with the EEOC. Should the plaintiff have a claim for retaliation based on the act of the employer in informing the district attorney of the criminal conduct? *See* Berry v. Stevinson Chevrolet, 74 F.3d 980 (10th Cir.1996).

2.   THE OPPOSITION CLAUSE

Regarding the scope of protected activity under the opposition clause, the court in *Sumner v. United States Postal Service*, 899 F.2d 203, 209 (2d Cir.1990), observed,

> In addition to protecting the filing of formal charges of discrimination, § 704(a)'s opposition clause protects as well informal protests

of discriminatory employment practices, including making complaints to management, writing critical letters to customers, protesting against discrimination by industry or by society in general, and expressing support of co-workers who have filed formal charges.

Unlawful or illegal activity engaged in by employees is not protected conduct. For example, in *Green v. McDonnell Douglas Corp.*, 463 F.2d 337 (8th Cir.1972), *vacated on other grounds*, 411 U.S. 792, 93 S.Ct. 1817, 36 L.Ed.2d 668 (1973), the court held that participation in an unlawful "stall-in" demonstration blocking access to an employer's business is not protected under Title VII. In fact, in *McDonnell Douglas*, reproduced in Chapter 3, the Supreme Court held that the employer's reliance on Green's participation in the "stall-in" was a legitimate nondiscriminatory reason for refusing to hire Green.

Misappropriation or unauthorized copying and distribution of an employer's documents, particularly confidential documents, is not protected activity under the opposition clause, even if the employee's intent is to substantiate her own claim of unlawful employment discrimination or to assist her co-worker in a claim of unemployment discrimination. *See* McKennon v. Nashville Banner, Chapter 3, Section B.4; Douglas v. DynMcDermott Petroleum Operations Co., 144 F.3d 364 (5th Cir.1998); Laughlin v. Metropolitan Wash. Airports Auth., 952 F.Supp. 1129 (E.D.Va.1997). Conduct is not necessarily protected under the opposition clause simply because it is not otherwise unlawful:

> Congress certainly did not mean to grant sanctuary to employees to engage in political activity for women's liberation on company time, and an employee does not enjoy immunity from discharge for misconduct merely by claiming that at all times she was defending the rights of her sex by "opposing" discriminatory practices. An employer remains entitled to loyalty and cooperativeness from employees:
>
> > "Management prerogatives * * * are to be left undisturbed to the greatest extent possible. Internal affairs * * * must not be interfered with except to the limited extent that correction is required in discrimination practices."

Hochstadt v. Worcester Found. for Experimental Biology, 545 F.2d 222, 230 (1st Cir.1976) (citation omitted). *See also* Matima v. Celli, 228 F.3d 68, 79 (2nd Cir. 2000); Robbins v. Jefferson County School Dist., 186 F.3d 1253, 1260 (10th Cir. 1999). In *Armstrong v. Index Journal Co.*, 647 F.2d 441 (4th Cir.1981), the court stated that the opposition clause "was not intended to immunize insubordinate, disruptive or nonproductive behavior at work. * * * An employer must retain the power to discipline and discharge disobedient employees." *Id.* at 448. For a discussion of a broad range of issues posed by the opposition clause, *see* Edward C. Walterscheid, *A Question of Retaliation: Opposition Conduct as Protected Expression Under Title VII of the Civil Rights Act of 1964*, 29 B.C.L.Rev. 391 (1988).

PAYNE v. McLEMORE'S WHOLESALE & RETAIL STORES

United States Court of Appeals for the Fifth Circuit, 1981.
654 F.2d 1130, *cert. denied*, 455 U.S. 1000, 102 S.Ct. 1630, 71 L.Ed.2d 866 (1982).

SAM D. JOHNSON, Circuit Judge.

This is a Title VII action alleging that in early 1971, defendant McLemore's Wholesale & Retail Stores, Inc. failed to rehire plaintiff Charles Payne because of his participation in activities protected by section 704(a) of the Civil Rights Act of 1964. * * *

* * *

[I]t appears that plaintiff began his employment with defendant about May or June of 1966. Plaintiff originally worked in McLemore's fertilizer plant. The operation of the plant was seasonal in nature since the demand for fertilizer was dependent upon the farmers' planting seasons. During the first two years of plaintiff's employment with defendant, he was laid off for three months each year during the seasonal decline in work. In later years, during the off-season plaintiff was not laid off, but was instead shifted to positions in other parts of the defendant's operations. As a result, during his employment with McLemore's, plaintiff worked as a fertilizer plant operator, a truck driver, a warehouse worker, a dock worker, and a farm store porter.

In November 1970, plaintiff was once again laid off due to the seasonal business decline. Two other black employees and two white employees were laid off at the same time. About a month later, plaintiff became involved in the formation and organization of the Franklin Parish Improvement Organization, a nonprofit civil rights organization. The formation of the Improvement Organization was precipitated by an incident involving two black children who were turned away from a public swimming pool. The organization was interested in improving social conditions of blacks in Franklin Parish, and it focused especially on the need to get blacks hired in retail stores in money-handling and supervisory positions in order to improve the treatment that blacks received while shopping in stores. Shortly after its formation, the members of the organization decided to boycott several retail businesses, including those of defendant in Winnsboro. Plaintiff organized and implemented the boycott and was actively involved in picketing McLemore's Jitney Jungle Food Stores. Defendant knew of plaintiff's involvement in the boycott and picketing. Moreover, the boycott and picketing were effective and defendant's business suffered as a result.

In previous years when he had been laid off, plaintiff had always gone back to work for defendant when the work picked back up. In the year of the boycott, however, he was not recalled or rehired. * * *

On June 17, 1976, plaintiff filed this action in federal district court alleging that defendant's failure to rehire plaintiff was a result of plaintiff's race and his civil rights activity. In its answer, McLemore's denied that it had committed any discriminatory actions, and asserted that the reason the plaintiff was not rehired was because he failed to reapply for a position with McLemore's after he was laid off. The district court held that plaintiff did reapply for his job, but that he was not rehired because of his participation in boycotting and picketing activities. The court further found that participation in the boycott and picketing was protected activity under section 704(a) of Title VII; in other words, the district court concluded that the boycott and picketing were in opposition to an unlawful employment practice of the defendant. * * *

The opposition clause of section 704(a) of Title VII provides protection against retaliation for employees who oppose unlawful employment practices committed by an employer. * * *

In this case, plaintiff contends that he was not rehired in retaliation for his boycott and picketing activities which were, according to plaintiff, in opposition to unlawful employment practices committed by McLemore's. Plaintiff asserted that the unlawful employment practices his boycott and picketing activities were intended to protest were McLemore's discrimination against blacks in hiring and promotion—specifically, McLemore's failure to employ blacks in money-handling, clerking, or supervisory positions. * * *

* * * The first element of the prima facie case—statutorily protected expression—requires conduct by the plaintiff that is in opposition to an unlawful employment practice of the defendant. Thus, for the plaintiff to prove that he engaged in statutorily protected expression, he must show that the boycott and picketing activity in which he participated was in opposition to conduct by McLemore's that was made unlawful by Title VII. According to the plaintiff, the purpose of the boycott and picketing was to oppose McLemore's discrimination against blacks in hiring and promotion. Plaintiff's complaint stated that the Franklin Parish Improvement Organization "engaged in the peaceful boycotting of Winnsboro stores, among them McLemore's Jitney Jungle Food Stores, which had refused to employ blacks except in a few menial positions." * * * [T]here is substantial evidence to support the district court finding that the purpose of the boycott and picketing was to oppose defendant's discrimination against blacks in certain employment opportunities—an unlawful employment practice under section 703(a)(1).

Defendant argues, however, that plaintiff failed to establish his prima facie case because he failed to *prove* that defendant had committed any unlawful employment practices. Plaintiff responds that he was not required to *prove* the actual existence of those unlawful employment practices; instead, he asserts that it was sufficient to establish a prima facie case if he had a *reasonable belief* that defendant had engaged in the unlawful employment practices. We agree with plaintiff and conclude that it was not fatal to plaintiff's section 704(a) case that he failed to prove, under the *McDonnell Douglas* criteria for proving an unlawful employment practice under section 703(a)(1), that McLemore's discriminated against blacks in retail store employment opportunities.

The Ninth Circuit was apparently the first appellate court to decide whether the opposition clause of section 704(a) required proof of actual discrimination. Sias v. City Demonstration Agency, 588 F.2d 692 (9th Cir.1978). In *Sias*, the plaintiff alleged that he was discharged by the City Demonstration Agency * * * in retaliation for his opposition to acts of racial discrimination by the City of Los Angeles. The City did not deny that plaintiff "was discharged for writing a letter of grievance to the Regional Administrator of the Department of Housing and Urban Development (HUD). Rather, it contend[ed] that, inasmuch as the trial court made no finding of actual discrimination, it [could not] be held to have violated" section 704(a). The Ninth Circuit concluded that "[s]uch a narrow interpretation * * * would not only chill the legitimate assertion of employee rights under Title VII but would tend to force employees to file formal charges rather than seek conciliation or informal adjustment of grievances." The *Sias* court quoted extensively from *Hearth v. Metropolitan Transit Commission*, 436 F.Supp. 685 (D.Minn.1977), which held that "as long as the employee had a reasonable belief that what was being opposed constituted discrimination under Title VII, the claim of retaliation does not hinge upon a showing that the employer was in fact in violation of Title VII." *Id.* at 688. The *Hearth* court went on to state:

> But this Court believes that appropriate informal opposition to perceived discrimination must not be chilled by the fear of retaliatory action in the event the alleged wrongdoing does not exist. It should not be necessary for an employee to resort immediately to the EEOC or similar State agencies in order to bring complaints of discrimination to the attention of the employer with some measure of protection. The resolution of such charges without governmental prodding should be encouraged.

> The statutory language does not compel a contrary result. The elimination of discrimination in employment is the purpose behind Title VII and the statute is entitled to a liberal interpretation. When an employee reasonably believes that discrimination exists, opposition thereto is opposition to an employment practice made unlawful by Title VII even if the employee turns out to be mistaken as to the facts.

Id. at 688–89 (footnote omitted), *quoted in* Sias, 588 F.2d at 695. The Seventh Circuit has also adopted this position. Berg v. La Crosse Cooler Co., 612 F.2d 1041 (7th Cir.1980). In *Berg*, the plaintiff was discharged when she challenged her employer's failure to provide pregnancy benefits as sex-based discrimination. After she was fired, the United States Supreme Court ruled that a disability benefits plan does not violate Title VII because of its failure to cover pregnancy related disabilities. General Electric Co. v. Gilbert, 429 U.S. 125, 97 S.Ct. 401, 50 L.Ed.2d 343 (1976). The Seventh Circuit held that where the employee opposed a practice that she reasonably believed was an unlawful employment practice under Title VII, her opposition was protected from retaliatory discharge even where the practice was later determined not be an unlawful employment practice. The court concluded that to interpret the opposition clause to require proof of an actual unlawful employment practice

> undermines Title VII's central purpose, the elimination of employment discrimination by informal means; destroys one of the chief means of achieving that purpose, the frank and nondisruptive exchange of ideas between employers and employees; and serves no redeeming statutory or policy purposes of its own. Section 2000e–3(a) plays a central role in effectuating these objectives. By protecting employees from retaliation, it is designed to encourage employees to call to their employers' attention discriminatory practices of which the employer may be unaware or which might result in protracted litigation to determine their legality if they are not voluntarily changed.

612 F.2d at 1045.

* * *

The Ninth Circuit recognized that the "considerations controlling the interpretation of the opposition clause are not entirely the same as those applying to the participation clause," and that the opposition clause "serves a more limited purpose" than does the participation clause. *Sias*, 588 F.2d at 695. However, interpreting the opposition clause to require proof of an actual unlawful employment practice would "chill the legitimate assertion of employee rights under Title VII," *id.*, just as surely as would interpreting the participation clause to require a truthful charge. On the other hand, interpreting the opposition clause to protect an employee who reasonably believes that discrimination exists "is consistent with a liberal construction of Title VII to implement the Congressional purpose of eliminating discrimination in employment." *Id.*

* * *

To effectuate the policies of Title VII and to avoid the chilling effect that would otherwise arise, we are compelled to conclude that a plaintiff can establish a prima facie case of retaliatory discharge under the opposition clause of section 704(a) if he shows that he had a reasonable belief that the employer was engaged in unlawful employment practices.[11] While the district court made no explicit finding that plaintiff's

---

11. The First Circuit has adopted a somewhat different test than have the Seventh and Ninth Circuits. The First Circuit has not explicitly decided whether a section 704(a) plaintiff must "demonstrate that he harbored a 'reasonable belief' of discriminatory employer behavior" or whether the plaintiff must show that he harbored a " 'conscientiously held belief' of such misconduct." Monteiro v. Poole Silver Co., 615 F.2d 4, 8 (1st Cir.1980) (footnote omitted). The *Monteiro* court found that "[u]nder either standard the employer's conduct being non-discriminatory in fact—the plaintiff must show that his so-called opposition was in response to some *honestly held*, if mistaken, feeling that discriminatory practices existed." *Id.* (emphasis added). Thus, according to that court, if a reasonable person might have believed that the employer was engaged in unlawful employment practices, but the plaintiff actually did not in good faith hold such a belief, then the plaintiff's opposition conduct is unprotected. *Id.* at 8

opposition was based upon a reasonable belief that McLemore's hiring and promotional policies violated Title VII, such a finding is implicit and is sufficiently supported by evidence in the record. Thus, plaintiff established that he reasonably believed that defendant McLemore's discriminated against blacks in employment opportunities. Moreover, plaintiff showed that his boycott and picketing activities were in opposition to this unlawful employment practice. Defendant's failure to rehire was undoubtedly an adverse employment action. Finally, there was evidence to support an inference that defendant's failure to rehire plaintiff was causally related to plaintiff's boycott and picketing activities. The burden then shifted to the defendant to "rebut the presumption of discrimination by producing evidence" of a legitimate, nondiscriminatory reason for its failure to rehire plaintiff.

Defendant McLemore's steadfastly maintained at trial that the *only* reason plaintiff was not rehired was because he failed to reapply for a position with defendant. * * *

* * *

* * * The trial court found "as a fact that Mr. Payne did reapply for his position with the defendant corporation." There is, therefore, substantial evidence in the record to support the district court's conclusion that the defendant's explanation for its failure to rehire the plaintiff was merely pretextual. * * *

Now on appeal, for the first time, defendant contends that even if plaintiff's activity was in opposition to unlawful employment practices of defendant, plaintiff's actions were not protected by section 704(a) because the *form* of plaintiff's opposition was not covered by the statute. It is well-established that not all activity in opposition to unlawful employment practices is protected by section 704(a). Hochstadt v. Worcester Found. for Experimental Biology, 545 F.2d 222, 229–34 (1st Cir.1976). Certain conduct—for example, illegal acts of opposition or unreasonably hostile or aggressive conduct—may provide a legitimate, independent, and nondiscriminatory basis for an employee's discharge. *Id.* at 229. "There may arise instances where the employee's conduct in protest of an unlawful employment practice so interferes with the performance of his job that it renders him ineffective in the position for which he was employed. In such a case, his conduct, or form of opposition, is not covered by § 704(a)." Rosser v. Laborers' Int'l Union, Local 438, 616 F.2d 221, 223 (5th Cir.), *cert. denied*, 449 U.S. 887, 101 S.Ct. 241, 66 L.Ed.2d 112 (1980). In order to determine when such a situation exists, the court must engage in a balancing test: "[T]he courts have required that the employee conduct be reasonable in light of the circumstances, and have held that 'the employer's right to run his business must be

n.6. We need not decide here whether it is necessary to adopt a good faith requirement in addition to the reasonable belief requirement since, in the case before this Court, the plaintiff believed—reasonably and in good faith—that McLemore's was engaged in unlawful employment practices, and plaintiff's opposition conduct was in response to this belief.

balanced against the rights of the employee to express his grievances and promote his own welfare.'" Jefferies v. Harris County Community Action Assoc., 615 F.2d 1025, 1036 (5th Cir.1980) (quoting *Hochstadt*, 545 F.2d at 233).

It appears that a number of cases have assumed that it is part of defendant's rebuttal burden to show that the form of plaintiff's opposition was unprotected by the statute. *See, e.g., Rosser*, 616 F.2d at 223–24; *Jeffries*, 615 F.2d at 1035–37; *Hochstadt*, 545 F.2d at 229–34. If the defendant took an adverse employment action against the plaintiff because of opposition conduct by the plaintiff that was outside the protection of the statute, then the defendant may have had a legitimate, nondiscriminatory reason to justify its actions. Thus, in the case before this Court, if the *form* of plaintiff's activities placed them outside the protection of section 704(a), then the defendant may have had a legitimate, nondiscriminatory reason for its failure to rehire the plaintiff. However, if the form of plaintiff's activities was the nondiscriminatory reason for the defendant's failure to rehire the plaintiff, it was the defendant's responsibility to introduce evidence to that effect at trial. In *Rosser*, for example, plaintiff was a dues posting clerk with the defendant union, and her immediate supervisor was the union's secretary-treasurer. Ms. Rosser was nominated to run against her supervisor for the secretary-treasurer position at the request of some black union members who felt that the union discriminated against its black members. Although Ms. Rosser was subsequently disqualified from the race, she was discharged two days after her supervisor was re-elected. She brought a Title VII action, alleging that her candidacy was in opposition to practices made unlawful by Title VII, and that she was discharged in violation of section 704(a). The district court granted the union's motion for summary judgment on the ground "that the form of Mrs. Rosser's opposition, an attempted political ouster, was not protected by the statute and the union thus had a valid defense to her prima facie case" of discrimination. 616 F.2d at 223. The Fifth Circuit affirmed, finding that Ms. Rosser did make out a prima facie case of discrimination, but that "the union had a valid defense since the chosen form of her opposition, a political challenge, [was] not protected under Title VII." *Id.* at 224.

In *Gonzalez v. Bolger*, 486 F. Supp. 595 (D.D.C.1980), the plaintiff, a former post office employee, brought an employment discrimination suit pursuant to section 704(a) alleging that he was discharged unlawfully in retaliation for his exercise of rights protected by Title VII. The district court made the following findings:

> At trial, plaintiff presented a *prima facie* case of retaliatory discrimination, by showing that he engaged in protected activities, that his employer was aware of the protected activities, and that he was subsequently discharged, within a relatively short time interval after his performance of the activities. This series of events is

sufficient to enable a court to infer retaliatory motivation, absent further explanation from the employer. * * *

* * *

In rebuttal, however, defendant presented substantial proof, through testimony and documentary exhibits, that plaintiff's insubordination and disruptive outbursts were in fact the cause for his termination. These reasons, if accepted on the proof as a whole, would constitute a valid non-discriminatory explanation for defendant's action.

Id. at 601–602. Since the court further found that plaintiff failed to establish that defendant's proffered justification was in fact pretextual, the court concluded that "[b]ecause plaintiff exceeded the limits of reasonable opposition activity on a continuing basis and his dismissal is attributable to these transgressions, the Court is forced to conclude that his termination was not pretextual, but rather was for valid non-discriminatory reasons." *Id.* at 601. The *Gonzalez* court clearly placed the burden on defendant to show as part of its rebuttal burden, that the "plaintiff's excessive conduct was the cause for his termination." *Id.* at 603.

Similarly, in *Hochstadt* the plaintiff claimed that her discharge violated section 704(a). The court in that case formulated the issue as whether plaintiff's hostile conduct "afforded an independent, nondiscriminatory basis for her discharge, or whether it was protected 'opposition' conduct under section 704(a) * * *." 545 F.2d at 229. This characterization of the issue indicates that the plaintiff's participation in activity unprotected by section 704(a) can provide the employer with a legitimate, nondiscriminatory reason for its employment actions. The *Hochstadt* court concluded that plaintiff's "serious acts of disloyalty, which damaged the employer's interests and were of an excessive nature which was not warranted as a response to any conduct of the [employer]" provided the employer with a legitimate, nondiscriminatory basis for discharging the plaintiff. *Id.* at 234.

* * * Here, the defendant failed to offer *any* evidence at trial that its legitimate and nondiscriminatory reason for not rehiring the plaintiff was that plaintiff had engaged in hostile, unprotected activity that was detrimental to the employer's interests.

* * *

Since plaintiff made out his prima facie case of discrimination under section 704(a), and since the only explanation offered by the defendant for the failure to rehire the plaintiff was correctly determined to be pretextual, the judgment of the district court for plaintiff is

AFFIRMED.

Notes and Questions

1. What is the difference, if any, between the *Payne* "reasonable belief" standard and the First Circuit's "honestly held" or "good faith" belief standard? Should it make a difference whether the mistaken belief is one of law or fact? *See* Wolf v. J.I. Case Co., 617 F.Supp. 858 (E.D.Wis.1985). Can an employee have a "reasonable belief" that Title VII prohibits discrimination based on sexual orientation? *See* Martin v. New York State Dep't of Correctional Servs., 224 F. Supp.2d 434, 448 (N.D.N.Y.2002) (yes); Hamner v. St. Vincent Hosp. & Health Care Ctr., Inc., 224 F.3d 701, 706–07 (7th Cir.2000) (no). What about sexual harassment on the basis of sexual orientation after the *Oncale* case, which was covered in Chapter 8?

2. In *Hochstadt v. Worcester Foundation for Experimental Biology*, 545 F.2d 222 (1st Cir.1976), plaintiff—Dr. Hochstadt—and her husband, both microbiologists, were offered employment with the same employer. The husband received a salary of $24,000, and Dr. Hochstadt received a salary of $18,000. Over a three-year period, the following occurred: at periodic meetings to discuss policies, recruitment practices, and the direction of research, Dr. Hochstadt raised questions about her salary being lower than similarly situated male employees. She also commissioned a covert affirmative action survey, invited a newspaper reporter to examine confidential salary information, misused secretarial and copying services, and ran up a substantial personal bill on the employer's telephone. In July, 1973, Dr. Hochstadt filed a charge with the state human rights agency claiming wage discrimination on the basis of sex. In 1974, while the claim was pending, the employer criticized her for poor work performance and for having poor relations with other scientists. Finally, after a grant application was denied, allegedly because of Dr. Hochstadt's performance, the employer discharged her. Using a balancing test, the court of appeals ruled against Dr. Hochstadt on her Title VII retaliation claim. On one side of the scales, the court placed management's prerogatives—to expect loyalty and cooperation from its employees and to be able to discipline employees for disruptive behavior; and on the other side were employees' rights—to be free from retaliation when they assert statutory claims under Title VII.

How would you decide the following cases under the *Hochstadt* balancing test?

a. A black nurse was discharged because she publicly complained about the treatment of black patients at the hospital where she worked. The discharge occurred after she expressed her complaints at a news conference that took place away from the hospital. After the news conference, she refused to cooperate with a hospital fact-finding commission comprised of black community leaders who were appointed to investigate allegations of discriminatory treatment of black patients. Before she held the news conference, she had met with hospital officials several times to express her complaints, but they seemed disinterested in her comments.

b. Bob Morris, who had been a manager eighteen years, was discharged after he participated in an informal investigation of a claim of sexual harassment asserted by a female employee. The investigation was made pursuant to the employer's internal policies for investigating claims of on-the-job harassment. The testimony Morris gave in the internal investigation supported the female employee's allegation of sexual harassment. The employer discharged the male harasser at the conclusion of the investigation because the evidence presented, including Morris's statements, supported the female employee's claim. Has Morris engaged in activity that is protected under the opposition clause? The participation clause? Both? Neither? *See* Morris v. Boston Edison Co., 942 F.Supp. 65 (D.Mass.1996).

3. INDIVIDUALS PROTECTED FROM RETALIATION

a. *Former employees*: Section 704(a) of Title VII specifically covers "employees" and "applicants for employment." 42 U.S.C. § 2000e–3(a). Are former employees covered? In *Robinson v. Shell Oil Co.*, 519 U.S. 337, 117 S.Ct. 843, 136 L.Ed.2d 808 (1997), the Supreme Court resolved a split in the circuits on whether former employees are covered. Shell Oil had discharged Robinson, the plaintiff, in 1991. Robinson then filed a charge of racial discrimination with the EEOC claiming that his termination was racially motivated. While the charge was pending before the EEOC, Robinson applied for a position with Metropolitan Life Insurance Co. Metropolitan had indicated to Robinson that it would hire him contingent upon a favorable employment reference from Shell. Shell, using Metropolitan's reference form, rated Robinson as "poor" in all areas. Robinson then filed a second charge with the EEOC against Shell Oil alleging that Shell Oil had given him a negative job reference in retaliation for his having filed the first charge with the EEOC. The Fourth Circuit held that former employees are not within the class protected from retaliation because the plain language of § 704(a) applies only to "employees" and "applicants for employment." A unanimous Supreme Court reversed. The Court held that although the language of § 704(a) is ambiguous, former employees are protected from retaliatory conduct.

> Finding that the term "employees" in § 704(a) is ambiguous, we are left to resolve that ambiguity. The broader context provided by other sections of the statute provides considerable assistance in this regard. * * * [S]everal sections of the statute plainly contemplate that former employees will make use of the remedial mechanisms of Title VII. Indeed, § 703(a) expressly includes discriminatory "discharge" as one of the unlawful employment practices against whic Title VII is directed. Insofar as § 704(a)expressly protects employees from retaliation for filing a "charge" under Title VII, and a charge under § 703(a) alleging unlawful discharge would necessarily be brought by a former employee, it is far more consistent to include former employees within the scope of "employees" protected by § 704(a).

> In further support of this view, petitioner argues that the word "employees" includes former employees because to hold otherwise would effectively vitiate much of the protection afforded by § 704(a). This is also the position taken by EEOC. According to EEOC,

exclusion of former employees from protection of § 704(a) would undermine the effectiveness of Title VII by allowing the threat of post-employment retaliation to deter victims of discrimination from complaining to EEOC, and would provide a perverse incentive for employers to fire employees who might bring Title VII claims.

Those arguments carry persuasive force given their coherence and their consistency with a primary purpose of antiretaliation provisions: Maintaining unfettered access to statutory remedial mechanisms.

519 U.S. at 344, 117 S.Ct. at 848.

b. *Third-party reprisals*: *DeMedina v. Reinhardt*, 444 F.Supp. 573 (D.D.C.1978), is the leading case holding that individuals can be victims of retaliation under the theory of third-party reprisal. The plaintiff in *DeMedina* claimed the employer retaliated against her—refused to employ her—because her husband, who worked for the employer, had participated in protected activity by speaking out about the discriminatory treatment of the employer's minority employees. The employer moved to dismiss her retaliation claim on the ground that only employees (or applicants) who actually engage in protected conduct can seek relief from retaliatory conduct. In rejecting the employer's argument, the court held that

[w]hile the language of [§ 704(a)] indicates that Congress did not expressly consider the possibility of third-party reprisals—*i.e.*, discrimination against one person because of a friend's or relative's protected activities—the very clear intent of Congress would be undermined by the construction defendant suggests. * * * Since tolerance of third-party reprisals would, no less than the tolerance of direct reprisals, deter persons from exercising their protected rights under Title VII, the Court must conclude, as has the only other court to consider the issue, *Kornbluh v. Stearns & Foster Co.*, 73 F.R.D. 307, 312 (N.D.Ohio 1976), that section [704(a)] proscribes the alleged retaliation of which plaintiff complains.

444 F.Supp. at 580. The court also rejected the employer's argument that even if its action was proscribed retaliatory action, the husband rather than the plaintiff was the only person who could seek relief:

Such a construction of Title VII would produce absurd and unjust results, for while plaintiff's husband might be in a position to seek injunctive relief to prohibit future reprisals against his spouse, he would not be in a position to seek back pay and/or retroactive promotion based on his spouse's employment denial. Thus, unless the plaintiff herself is permitted to seek relief based on the denial of her employment application, the "make whole" purpose of Title VII would be frustrated.

Id.

Should the *DeMedina* third-party reprisal rule extend to the activity of employees who are not related to each other? In *EEOC v. Ohio Edison*

Co., 7 F.3d 541 (6th Cir.1993), the employer had discharged Whitfield, a black employee. Shortly thereafter, the employer made an offer to reinstate Whitfield but withdrew the offer when a black management employee complained that Whitfield had been the victim of racial discrimination and told the employer that Whitfield had planned to sue the employer for racial discrimination. Whitfield then filed a charge of discrimination with the EEOC. Whitfield and the black manager were not related. EEOC brought suit on behalf of Whitfield alleging that by withdrawing the offer of reinstatement, the employer had retaliated against Whitfield because of the protected activity engaged in by the black manager.

The Sixth Circuit held that the antiretaliation provision should be broadly construed to include within its protection not only the protected activity of the employee but also *"his representative"* who has opposed any unlawful employment practice. *Id.* at 545–46. The court found that the reasoning in *DeMedina* supported its holding. *Id.* at 544, 545–46. *See also Millstein v. Henske,* 722 A.2d 850, 854–55 (D.C.Ct.App.1999) ("no court applying the extended reprisal doctrine has applied it to the bare relationship of co-employees").

The Fifth Circuit, in *Holt v. JTM Industries, Inc.,* 89 F.3d 1224 (5th Cir.1996), *cert. denied,* 520 U.S. 1229, 117 S.Ct. 1821, 137 L.Ed.2d 1029 (1997), rejected the *DeMedina* third-party reprisal rule to the extent that it confers on a plaintiff automatic standing to sue for retaliation when his relative or friend, rather than the plaintiff himself, has engaged in protected activity. The plaintiffs in *Holt* were a married couple who worked for the same employer in Texas. The wife filed a charge of age discrimination with the EEOC. Shortly after receiving notice that the wife had filed a charge, the employer first placed the husband on administrative leave and later offered him a job in another location— Atlanta, Georgia. The husband took the Atlanta job but quit several weeks later. Both the husband and wife then filed age and retaliation claims against the employer. Under the rule in *Holt,* only those applicants and employees who themselves have engaged in protected activity have standing to sue for retaliation. *See also* Smith v. Riceland Foods, Inc., 151 F.3d 813, 819 (8th Cir.1998) (following *Holt*); Fogleman v. Mercy Hosp., Inc., 283 F.3d 561 (3d Cir.2002) (following *Holt* in an ADA case).

Which of the two views on standing, the Sixth Circuit's view in *Ohio Edison* or the Fifth Circuit's view in *Holt,* do you believe is the better view? If you agree with the majority view in *Holt,* then how do you respond to the concerns of the court in *DeMedina*?

Note: Adverse Employment Action That Triggers a Retaliation Claim

An individual seeking relief because of retaliation must prove that she has suffered an adverse employment action. The range of adverse actions that constitute retaliatory conduct, if found to be causally linked to protected activity, includes not only the most obvious adverse actions, such as a discharge or refusal to hire, but also negative evaluations, suspensions, harassment, unfavorable job assignments, imposition of work assignments that would be intolerable to a reasonable person, and diminution of benefits. *See generally* Douglas E. Ray, *Title VII Retaliation Cases: Creating a New Protected Class*, 58 U.Pitt.L.Rev. 405, 414–22 (1997) (citing cases).

Most circuits have taken an expansive approach to the definition of adverse employment action. *See,e.g.,* Schobert v. Illinois Dep't of Transp., 304 F.3d 725, 733 (7th Cir.2002) (undesirable assignments and being blamed for others mistakes); Burke v. Gould, 286 F.3d 513, 522 (D.C.Cir.2002) (removal of supervisory duties, reassignment, and poor performance evaluation); Von Gunten v. Maryland, 243 F.3d 858, 866 (4th Cir.2001); Ray v. Henderson, 217 F.3d 1234, 1241 (9th Cir.2000) (eliminating employee involvement program, eliminating flexible start time, instituting a security lock-down procedure, and decreasing pay); Hernandez–Torres v. Intercontinental Trading, 158 F.3d 43, 47 (1st Cir.1998); Wideman v. Wal–Mart, 141 F.3d 1453, 1456 (11th Cir.1998) (improperly being listed as absent, denial of lunch break, soliciting negative statements about employee from coworkers, reprimands, suspension, denial of work, and delayed medical treatment); Berry v. Stevinson Chevrolet, 74 F.3d 980, 984–86 (10th Cir.1996) (malicious prosecution). However, two circuits require an adverse action on an "ultimate employment decision." *See,e.g.,* Bradley v. Widnall, 232 F.3d 626, 632 (8th Cir.2000); Mattern v. Eastman Kodak Co., 104 F.3d 702 (5th Cir.), *cert. denied,* 522 U.S. 932, 118 S.Ct. 336, 139 L.Ed.2d 260 (1997).

One court has claimed that the "ultimate employment decision" doctrine serves a fundamental policy of employment laws by precluding " 'an irritable, chip-on-the-shoulder employee' " from relying on "minor and even trivial employment actions" as a basis for bringing an employment discrimination claim. Smart v. Ball State Univ., 89 F.3d 437, 441 (7th Cir.1996) (citation omitted). *See also* Williams v. Bristol–Myers Squibb Co., 85 F.3d 270, 274 (7th Cir.1996) ("purely lateral transfer * * * that does not involve a demotion in form or substance" is not an adverse employment action); Ledergerber v. Stangler, 122 F.3d 1142, 1144 (8th Cir.1997) (finding no retaliatory adverse employment action where, in response to plaintiff's expressions of concern about the employer's affirmative action policies, the employer changed the staffing of the employees that the plaintiff supervised but made no changes in her salary, benefits, responsibility, title, or office location). Judge Bean, dissenting in *Ledergerber,* 122 F.3d at 1145–46, cited a number of cases in which the courts have found that, even where the employee does not suffer a loss of rank or pay, the loss of intangibles such as public respect, unofficial "in-house" title, or a prestigious position, constitute an adverse employment action.

In deciding whether a refusal to transfer a plaintiff to another position can be retaliatory conduct, the court in *Randlett v. Shalala*, 118 F.3d 857, 861–62 (1st Cir.1997), stated:

> The central issue is HHS' refusal to transfer Randlett to the Boston office. The district court said that this was "not a[n] adverse action cognizable by federal law * * *."

The more difficult [question] is the legal question: what types of employer actions adverse to the employee can, where improperly motivated, give rise to a Title VII complaint. * * *

The statute [Title VII] itself says that an employer may not "discriminate" against an employee or applicant "because [the employee or applicant] has made a charge * * * or participated in any manner" in a Title VII investigation or proceeding. Elsewhere, the statute lists actions that can constitute discrimination, specifying a refusal to hire, a discharge, or any discriminatory treatment with respect to "compensation, terms, conditions, or privileges of employment." Arguably the two sections should be read together.

Under *Randlett,* a court looks to the kind of conduct that would be covered by the relevant statutory language, e.g., "terms, conditions, or privileges of employment" in § 703(a)(1) of Title VII, to determine whether the adverse action taken against the plaintiff is retaliatory conduct. Is the *Randlett* approach broader or narrower than the "ultimate employment decision" approach?

Is an "ultimate employment decision" like a "tangible employment action" that serves to establish strict liability for employers in sexual harassment cases? The Supreme Court in *Burlington Industries, Inc. v. Ellerth,* and *Faragher v. City of Boca Raton,* covered in Chapter 8, Section C.1, defined a tangible employment action as "a significant change in employment status, such as hiring, firing, failing to promote, reassignment with significantly different responsibilities, or a decision causing a significant change in benefits." *Ellerth,* 524 U.S. 742, 761, 118 S.Ct. 2257, 2268, 141 L.Ed.2d 633 (1998). Does the fact that an employer may still be liable for sexual harassment that falls below the "tangible employment action" line suggest that employers may be liable for retaliatory action that falls below the "ultimate employment decision" line? Is it fair to compare the two standards? *See* Manning v. Metropolitan Life Ins. Co., 127 F.3d 686, 692 (8th Cir.1997) (requiring, in a retaliation case, that there be a "tangible change in duties or working conditions that constituted a material employment disadvantage").

*

Part IV

RELIEF

Chapter 16

REMEDIES

A. INTRODUCTION

Two separate but related issues are involved in every employment discrimination case. The first concerns substantive liability: whether a defendant has discriminated against an individual or a class of individuals in violation of the applicable law. The second involves a determination of the appropriate forms of relief to redress the substantive violation: for example, whether a proven victim of unlawful employment discrimination is entitled to reinstatement, promotion, back pay, front pay, preliminary injunctions, or attorney's fees. As one federal judge observed, attorneys tend to devote considerably less attention to appropriate forms of relief although the scope and nature of relief often is the most important phase of an employment discrimination case. Charles R. Richey, *A Federal Trial Judge's Reflections on the Preparation for and Trial of Civil Cases*, 52 Ind.L.J. 111, 112 (1976). Anyone involved with employment discrimination cases must be as familiar with the law on relief as they are with the law on substantive liability. In commenting upon a defense strategy that ignores remedies, particularly monetary damages, the court in *Avitia v. Metropolitan Club of Chicago, Inc.*, 49 F.3d 1219, 1230 (7th Cir.1995), observed,

> When a defendant goes for broke, staking it all on convincing the jury to award zero damages—fearing otherwise a compromise verdict—it risks being hit with a verdict much larger than if it had offered the jury an alternative estimate of damages to the plaintiff's. It should not expect the appellate court to relieve it of the consequences of its gamble.

The focus of Part IV is on relief in employment discrimination cases. Chapter 16 covers some of the basic substantive and procedural rules governing the award of legal and equitable relief, e.g., reinstatement, back pay, front pay, compensatory damages, punitive damage, and attorney's fees. Chapter 17 examines the use of affirmative action as a remediation policy for achieving equality in the workplace. For a comprehensive treatment of the topics covered in Chapter 16 (except for attorney's fees), see Robert Belton, Remedies in Employment Law (1992) [hereinafter Belton, Remedies].

Statutory Provisions: Each of the federal statutes covered in these materials, except § 1981, has a specific provision on relief. Section 706(g)(1) of Title VII, 42 U.S.C. § 2000e–5(g)(1), provides that upon a finding of unlawful discrimination, a "court may enjoin the [defendant] from engaging in [the] unlawful employment practice, and order such affirmative action as may be appropriate, which may include, but is not limited to, reinstatement or hiring of employees, with or without back pay * * *, or any other equitable relief as the court deems appropriate." Section 107 of the ADA, 42 U.S.C. § 12117, provides that the same forms of relief available under Title VII are also available under the ADA. The Rehabilitation Act incorporates the remedies available under § 706(g) of Title VII with respect to claims against the federal government and federal grantees. 29 U.S.C. §§ 791, 794. The Civil Rights Act of 1991 provides for limited compensatory and punitive damages under Title VII, the ADA, and the Rehabilitation Act. 42 U.S.C. § 1981a(a)(1)–(2). The ADEA incorporates many of the remedial schemes of the Fair Labor Standards Act of 1938, 29 U.S.C. § 201. Like the FLSA, § 626(b) of the ADEA, 29 U.S.C. § 626(b), provides for "such legal or equitable relief as may be appropriate to effectuate the purposes" of the ADEA, "including judgments compelling employment, reinstatement or promotion." The ADEA also incorporates the FLSA provisions that permit awards of liquidated damages, which are recoverable only for willful violations. *See* 29 U.S.C. § 216(b). The Equal Pay Act, which is an amendment to the FLSA, provides for both legal and equitable relief, including reinstatement, promotion, and "the payment of wages lost and an additional equal amount as liquidated damages." *Id.* The Equal Pay Act, like the ADEA, permits recovery of liquidated damages only for willful violations. Liquidated damages under the Equal Pay Act and the ADEA has a special meaning that is set in Section G of this chapter. Section 1981 does not have a specific provision on relief, but in *Johnson v. Railway Express Agency, Inc.*, 421 U.S. 454, 460, 95 S.Ct. 1716, 1720, 44 L.Ed.2d 295 (1975), the Supreme Court held that legal and equitable relief, including compensatory and punitive damages, can be recovered under § 1981.

B. BASIC REMEDIAL PRINCIPLES

The Supreme Court enunciated the two basic remedial principles governing employment discrimination cases—make-whole (damages) and rightful place relief (equitable relief)—in the leading cases of *Albemarle Paper Co. v. Moody*, 422 U.S. 405, 95 S.Ct. 2362, 45 L.Ed.2d 280 (1975), and *Franks v. Bowman Transportation Co.*, 424 U.S. 747, 96 S.Ct. 1251, 47 L.Ed.2d 444 (1976).

ALBEMARLE PAPER CO. v. MOODY

Supreme Court of the United States, 1975.
422 U.S. 405, 95 S.Ct. 2362, 45 L.Ed.2d 280.

JUSTICE STEWART delivered the opinion of the Court.

[Relying on a disparate impact theory, the plaintiffs brought a Title VII race discrimination class action challenging the employer's high school diploma and general ability testing requirements, as well as its seniority system negotiated under a collective bargaining agreement. The district court found the seniority system to be unlawful under Title VII and enjoined its use. The district court, however, rejected the plaintiffs' claim for back pay.]

* * *

These consolidated cases raise [an] important question[] under Title VII of the Civil Rights Act of 1964. * * * When employees or applicants for employment have lost the opportunity to earn wages because an employer has engaged in an unlawful discriminatory employment practice, what standards should a federal district court follow in deciding whether to award or deny backpay? * * *

* * *

II

Whether a particular member of the plaintiff class should have been awarded any backpay and, if so, how much, are questions not involved in this review. The equities of individual cases were never reached. Though at least some of the members of the plaintiff class obviously suffered a loss of wage opportunities on account of Albemarle's unlawfully discriminatory system of job seniority, the District Court decided that *no* backpay should be awarded to *anyone* in the class. The court declined to make such an award on two stated grounds: the lack of "evidence of bad faith non-compliance with the Act," and the fact that "the defendants would be substantially prejudiced" by an award of backpay that was demanded contrary to an earlier representation and late in the progress of the litigation. * * *

* * *

The petitioners contend that the statutory scheme provides no guidance, beyond indicating that backpay awards are within the District Court's discretion. We disagree. It is true that backpay is not an automatic or mandatory remedy; like all other remedies under the Act, it is one which the courts "may" invoke. * * * The power to award backpay was bestowed by Congress, as part of a complex legislative design directed at a historic evil of national proportions. A court must exercise this power "in light of the large objectives of the Act." That the court's discretion is equitable in nature, hardly means that it is unfettered by meaningful standards or shielded from thorough appellate review. In *Mitchell v. DeMario Jewelry*, 361 U.S. 288, 292, 80 S.Ct.332, 4 L.Ed.2d 323 (1960), this Court held, in the face of a silent statute, that district courts enjoyed the "historic power of equity" to award lost wages to workmen unlawfully discriminated against under § 17 of the Fair Labor Standards Act of 1938. The Court simultaneously noted that "the statutory purposes [leave] little room for the exercise of discretion not to order reimbursement." 361 U.S. at 296, 80 S.Ct. at 337.

* * *

The District Court's decision must therefore be measured against the purposes which inform Title VII. As the Court observed in *Griggs v. Duke Power Co.*, 401 U.S. 424, 429–30, 91 S.Ct. 849, 853, 28 L.Ed.2d 158 (1971), the primary objective was a prophylactic one:

> It was to achieve equality of employment opportunities and remove barriers that have operated in the past to favor an identifiable group of white employees over other employees.

Backpay has an obvious connection with this purpose. If employers faced only the prospect of an injunctive order, they would have little incentive to shun practices of dubious legality. It is the reasonably certain prospect of a backpay award that "provido[s] the spur or catalyst which causes employers and unions to self-examine and to self-evaluate their employment practices and to endeavor to eliminate, so far as possible, the last vestiges of an unfortunate and ignominious page in this country's history." United States v. N.L. Industries, Inc., 479 F.2d 354, 379 (8th Cir.1973).

It is also the purpose of Title VII to make persons whole for injuries suffered on account of unlawful employment discrimination. This is shown by the very fact that Congress took care to arm the courts with full equitable powers. For it is the historic purpose of equity to "secur[e] complete justice." Brown v. Swann, 10 Pet. 497, 503, 9 L.Ed. 508 (1836). "[W]here federally protected rights have been invaded, it has been the rule from the beginning that courts will be alert to adjust their remedies so as to grant the necessary relief." Bell v. Hood, 327 U.S. 678, 684, 66 S.Ct. 773, 777, 90 L.Ed. 939 (1946). Title VII deals with legal injuries of an economic character occasioned by racial or other antiminority discrimination. The terms "complete justice" and "necessary relief" have acquired a clear meaning in such circumstances. Where racial discrimination is concerned, "the [district] court has not merely the power but the duty to render a decree which will so far as possible eliminate the discriminatory effects of the past as well as bar like discrimination in the future." Louisiana v. United States, 380 U.S. 145, 154, 85 S.Ct. 817, 822, 13 L.Ed.2d 709 (1965). And where a legal injury is of an economic character,

> [t]he general rule is, that when a wrong has been done, and the law gives a remedy, the compensation shall be equal to the injury. The latter is the standard by which the former is to be measured. The

injured party is to be placed, as near as may be, in the situation he would have occupied if the wrong had not been committed.

Wicker v. Hoppock, 6 Wall. 94, 99, 18 L.Ed. 752 (1867).

The "make whole" purpose of Title VII is made evident by the legislative history. The backpay provision was expressly modeled on the backpay provision of the National Labor Relations Act. Under that Act, "[m]aking the workers whole for losses suffered on account of an unfair labor practice is part of the vindication of the public policy which the Board enforces." Phelps Dodge Corp. v. NLRB, 313 U.S. 177, 197, 61 S.Ct. 845, 854, 85 L.Ed. 1271 (1941). We may assume that Congress was aware that the Board, since its inception, has awarded backpay as a matter of course—not randomly or in the exercise of a standardless discretion, and not merely where employer violations are peculiarly deliberate, egregious, or inexcusable. Furthermore, in passing the Equal Employment Opportunity Act of 1972, Congress considered several bills to limit the judicial power to award backpay. These limiting efforts were rejected, and the backpay provision was re-enacted substantially in its original form. A Section-by-Section Analysis introduced by Senator Williams to accompany the Conference Committee Report on the 1972 Act strongly reaffirmed the "make whole" purpose of Title VII:

> The provisions of this subsection are intended to give the courts wide discretion exercising their equitable powers to fashion the most complete relief possible. In dealing with the present section 706(g) the courts have stressed that the scope of relief under that section of the Act is intended to make the victims of unlawful discrimination whole, and that the attainment of this objective rests not only upon the elimination of the particular unlawful employment practice complained of, but also requires that persons aggrieved by the consequences and effects of the unlawful employment practice be, so far as possible, restored to a position where they would have been were it not for the unlawful discrimination.

118 Cong. Rec. 7168 (1972). As this makes clear, Congress' purpose in vesting a variety of "discretionary" powers in the courts was not to limit appellate review of trial courts, or to invite inconsistency and caprice, but rather to make possible the "fashion[ing] [of] the most complete relief possible."

It follows that, given a finding of unlawful discrimination, backpay should be denied only for reasons which, if applied generally, would not frustrate the central statutory purposes of eradicating discrimination throughout the economy and making persons whole for injuries suffered through past discrimination.[14] The courts of appeals must maintain a consistent and principled application of the backpay provision, consonant with the twin statutory objectives, while at the same time recognizing

---

14. It is necessary, therefore, that if a district court does decline to award back-pay, it carefully articulate its reasons.

that the trial court will often have the keener appreciation of those facts and circumstances peculiar to particular cases.

* * *

FRANKS v. BOWMAN TRANSPORTATION CO.

Supreme Court of the United States, 1976.
424 U.S. 747, 96 S.Ct. 1251, 47 L.Ed.2d 444.

JUSTICE BRENNAN delivered the opinion of the Court.

[Plaintiffs brought a Title VII class action against the employer, Bowman Transportation, and several labor unions challenging various racially discriminatory employment practices, including the denial of employment to blacks in over-the-road (OTR) truck driving jobs. After plaintiffs prevailed on the substantive liability issue, the district court permanently enjoined the defendants from perpetuating their discriminatory employment practices. But the court declined to grant the unnamed members of the class seniority status retroactive to the dates they had applied for the OTR jobs that had been denied to them on the basis of race. The court of appeals affirmed the district court's denial of any form of seniority relief, holding that such relief was barred, as a matter of law, by § 703(h) of Title VII, 42 U.S.C. § 2000e–2(h). Section 703(h) provides, *inter alia*, that it shall not be an unlawful employment practice for an employer to apply different conditions of employment pursuant to a bona fide seniority system.]

* * *

This case presents the question whether identifiable applicants who were denied employment because of race after the effective date and in violation of Title VII may be awarded seniority status retroactive to the dates of their employment applications.

* * *

III

* * *

We begin by repeating the observation of earlier decisions that in enacting Title VII of the Civil Rights Act of 1964, Congress intended to prohibit all practices in whatever form which create inequality in employment opportunity due to discrimination on the basis of race, religion, sex, or national origin, and ordained that its policy of outlawing such discrimination should have the "highest priority," Newman v. Piggie Park Enterprises, Inc., 390 U.S. 400, 402, 88 S.Ct. 964, 966, 19 L.Ed.2d 1263 (1968). Last Term's *Albemarle Paper Co. v. Moody*, 422 U.S. 405, 95 S.Ct. 2362, 45 L.Ed.2d 280 (1975), consistently with the congressional plan, held that one of the central purposes of Title VII is "to make persons whole for injuries suffered on account of unlawful employment discrimination." * * * "The provisions of [§ 706(g)] are intended to give the courts wide discretion exercising their equitable powers to fashion the most complete relief possible. * * * [T]he Act is intended to make the victims of unlawful employment discrimination whole, and * * * the attainment of this objective * * * requires that persons aggrieved by the consequences and effects of the unlawful employment practice be, so far as possible, restored to a position where they would have been were it not for the unlawful discrimination." Section-by-Section Analysis of H.R. 1746, accompanying the Equal Employment Opportunity Act of 1972—Conference Report, 118 Cong. Rec. 7166, 7168 (1972). This is emphatic confirmation that federal courts are empowered to fashion such relief as the particular circumstances of a case may require to effect restitution, making whole insofar as possible the victims of racial discrimination in hiring.[21] Adequate relief may well be denied in the absence of a seniority remedy slotting the victim in that position in the seniority system that would have been his had he been hired at the time of his application. It can hardly be questioned that ordinarily such relief will be necessary to achieve the "make-whole" purposes of the Act.

* * *

Seniority systems and the entitlements conferred by credits earned thereunder are of vast and increasing importance in the economic employment system of this Nation. * * * "More than any other provision of the collective-[bargaining] agreement * * * seniority affects the economic security of the individual employee covered by its terms." Aaron, *Reflections on the Legal Nature and Enforceability of Seniority Rights*, 75 Harv.L.Rev. 1532, 1535 (1962). "Competitive status" seniority also often plays a broader role in modern employment systems, particularly systems operated under collective-bargaining agreements:

> Included among the benefits, options, and safeguards affected by competitive status seniority, are not only promotion and layoff, but also transfer, demotion, rest days, shift assignments, prerogative in scheduling vacation, order of layoff, possibilities of lateral transfer to avoid layoff, "bumping" possibilities in the face of layoff, order of recall, training opportunities, working conditions, length of layoff endured without reducing seniority, length of layoff recall rights will withstand, overtime opportunities, parking privileges, and, in one plant, a preferred place in the punch-out line.

---

21. It is true that backpay is the only remedy specifically mentioned in § 706(g). But to draw from this fact and other sections of the statute any implicit statement by Congress that seniority relief is a prohibited, or at least less available, form of remedy is not warranted. Indeed, any such contention necessarily disregards the extensive legislative history underlying the 1972 amendments to Title VII. The 1972 amendments added the phrase speaking to "other equitable relief" in § 706(g). * * * The Reports of both Houses of Congress indicated that "rightful place" was the intended objective of Title VII and the relief accorded thereunder. *Ibid.*; H.R. Rep. No. 92–238, p. 4 (1971). * * * [R]ightful-place seniority, implicating an employee's future earnings, job security, and advancement prospects, is absolutely essential to obtaining this congressionally mandated goal.

Stacy, *Title VII Seniority Remedies in a Time of Economic Downturn*, 28 Vand.L.Rev. 487, 490 (1975) (footnotes omitted).

* * *

IV

We are not to be understood as holding that an award of seniority status is requisite in all circumstances. The fashioning of appropriate remedies invokes the sound equitable discretion of the district courts. Respondent Bowman attempts to justify the District Court's denial of seniority relief for petitioners as an exercise of equitable discretion, but the record is its own refutation of the argument.

Albemarle Paper, supra, at 416, 95 S.Ct. at 2371, made clear that discretion imports not the court's " 'inclination, but * * * its judgment; and its judgment is to be guided by sound legal principles.' " Discretion is vested not for purposes of "limit[ing] appellate review of trial courts, or * * * invit[ing] inconsistency and caprice," but rather to allow the most complete achievement of the objectives of Title VII that is attainable under the facts and circumstances of the specific case. 422 U.S. at 421, 95 S.Ct. at 2373. Accordingly the District Court's denial of any form of seniority remedy must be reviewed in terms of its effect on the attainment of the Act's objectives under the circumstances presented by this record. No less than with the denial of the remedy of backpay, the denial of seniority relief to victims of illegal racial discrimination in hiring is permissible "only for reasons which, if applied generally, would not frustrate the central statutory purposes of eradicating discrimination throughout the economy and making persons whole for injuries suffered through past discrimination." *Ibid.*

The District Court stated two reasons for its denial of seniority relief for the unnamed class members. The first was that those individuals had not filed administrative charges under the provisions of Title VII with the Equal Employment Opportunity Commission and therefore class relief of this sort was not appropriate. We rejected this justification for denial of class-based relief in the context of backpay awards in *Albemarle Paper*, and for the same reasons reject it here. This justification for denying class-based relief in Title VII suits has been unanimously rejected by the courts of appeals, and Congress ratified that construction by the 1972 amendments. *Albemarle Paper*, 422 U.S. at 414 n.8, 95 S.Ct. at 2370 n.8.

The second reason stated by the District Court was that such claims "presuppose a vacancy, qualification, and performance by every member. There is no evidence on which to base these multiple conclusions." * * *

We read the District Court's reference to the lack of evidence regarding a "vacancy, qualification, and performance" for every individual member of the class as an expression of concern that some of the unnamed class members (unhired black applicants whose employment applications were summarized in the record) may not in fact have been actual victims of racial discrimination. That factor will become material however only when those persons reapply for OTR positions pursuant to the hiring relief ordered by the District Court. Generalizations concerning such individually applicable evidence cannot serve as a justification for the denial of relief to the entire class. Rather, at such time as individual class members seek positions as OTR drivers, positions for which they are presumptively entitled to priority hiring consideration under the District Court's order, evidence that particular individuals were not in fact victims of racial discrimination will be material. But petitioners here have carried their burden of demonstrating the existence of a discriminatory hiring pattern and practice by the respondents and, therefore, the burden will be upon respondents to prove that individuals who reapply were not in fact victims of previous hiring discrimination. Only if this burden is met may retroactive seniority—if otherwise determined to be an appropriate form of relief under the circumstances of the particular case—be denied individual class members.

Respondent Bowman raises an alternative theory of justification. Bowman argues that an award of retroactive seniority to the class of discriminatees will conflict with the economic interests of other Bowman employees. Accordingly, it is argued, the District Court acted within its discretion in denying this form of relief as an attempt to accommodate the competing interests of the various groups of employees.

We reject this argument for two reasons. First, the District Court made no mention of such considerations in its order denying the seniority relief. As we noted in *Albemarle Paper*, 422 U.S. at 421 n.14, 95 S.Ct. at 2373 n.14, if the district court declines, due to the peculiar circumstances of the particular case, to award relief generally appropriate under Title VII, "[i]t is necessary * * * that * * * it carefully articulate its reasons" for so doing. Second, and more fundamentally, it is apparent that denial of seniority relief to identifiable victims of racial discrimination on the sole ground that such relief diminishes the expectations of other, arguably innocent, employees would if applied generally frustrate the central "make whole" objective of Title VII. These conflicting interests of other employees will, of course, always be present in instances where some scarce employment benefit is distributed among employees on the basis of their status in the seniority hierarchy. But, as we have said, there is nothing in the language of Title VII, or in its legislative history, to show that Congress intended generally to bar this form of relief to victims of illegal discrimination, and the experience under its remedial model in the National Labor Relations Act points to the contrary. Accordingly, we find untenable the conclusion that this form of relief may be denied merely because the interests of other employees may thereby be affected. "If relief under Title VII can be denied merely because the majority group of employees, who have not suffered discrimination, will be unhappy about it, there will be little hope of correcting the wrongs to which the Act is directed." United States v. Bethlehem Steel Corp., 446 F.2d 652, 663 (2d Cir.1971).

* * *

Accordingly, the judgment of the Court of Appeals affirming the District Court's denial of seniority relief to [unnamed class members] is reversed * * *.

Notes

1. *Moody* and *Franks* limit a trial court's discretion to deny relief upon finding a Title VII violation because the statutory prohibition of employment discrimination is designed to serve two purposes: deterrence and compensation. The deterrence principle is effectuated by the *rightful place theory of relief* enunciated in *Franks*. Under this theory, a court is to award successful plaintiffs the "terms, conditions, or privileges" of employment they would have had with the defendant but for unlawful employment discrimination. The compensatory principle is effectuated by the *make-whole theory of relief* enunciated in *Moody*. Under this theory, successful plaintiffs are entitled to monetary compensation to remedy the economic harm they have suffered in the past or may suffer in the future as a consequence of the defendant's unlawful employment discrimination. *See generally* Robert Belton, *Harnessing Discretionary Justice in the Employment Discrimination Cases: The* Moody *and* Franks *Standards*, 44 Ohio St.L.J. 571 (1983).

2. *Moody* and *Franks* establish a rebuttable presumption, known as the "presumptive entitlement" rule, which allows victims of unlawful employment discrimination to be awarded whatever remedies are necessary to achieve rightful place and make-whole relief. In *City of Los Angeles Department of Water & Power v. Manhart*, 435 U.S. 702, 719, 98 S.Ct. 1370, 1381, 55 L.Ed.2d 657 (1978), the Supreme Court stated that the presumption is "seldom overcome." Moreover, trial courts must make findings of fact to justify the denial of complete make-whole and rightful place relief. *See* note 14 in *Moody*; *see also* Weaver v. Amoco Prod. Co., 66 F.3d 85 (5th Cir.1995) (vacating a district court's award of front pay and remanding for review of the remedy where district court failed to articulate its reasons for concluding that reinstatement was not feasible).

3. In the remedial phase of a discrimination trial, the plaintiff has a relatively light burden under *Moody* and *Franks* of establishing her "presumptive entitlement" to a particular form of relief such as back pay or reinstatement. Once the plaintiff has met her burden, the defendant has the heavier burden of proof, i.e., the burdens of persuasion and production, to demonstrate that the plaintiff should get no relief or only limited relief. *Teamsters v. United States*, 431 U.S. 324, 97 S.Ct. 1843, 52 L.Ed.2d 396 (1977), was a pattern and practice case, but its rule on the allocation of the burden of proof also applies in individual cases:

> [I]ndividual relief does not arise until it has been proved that the employer has followed an employment policy of unlawful discrimination. The force of that proof does not dissipate at the remedial stage of the trial. * * *

* * * The [plaintiffs] need only show that an alleged individual discriminatee unsuccessfully applied for a job and therefore was a potential victim of the proved discrimination. As in *Franks*, the burden then rests on the employer to demonstrate that the individual applicant was denied an employment opportunity for lawful reasons.

431 U.S. at 361–62 (citing *Franks*, 424 U.S. at 773 n.32, 96 S.Ct. at 1268 n.32). *See also* Taylor v. Teletype Corp., 648 F.2d 1129, 1136–38 (8th Cir.) (Title VII), *cert. denied*, 454 U.S. 969, 102 S.Ct. 515, 70 L.Ed.2d 386 (1981); Graefenhain v. Pabst Brewing Co., 870 F.2d 1198, 1208–09 (7th Cir.1989) (ADEA); Thomlison v. City of Omaha, 63 F.3d 786, 789–90 (8th Cir.1995) (Rehabilitation Act and Title VII).

C. REINSTATEMENT

A reinstatement order in a discharge case (or instatement in a refusal to hire case) is an affirmative injunction directing the defendant to re-employ (or employ) the plaintiff in the job or position that she had or would have had but for the discriminatory conduct of the employer. District Judge Weinfeld's discussion of the reinstatement remedy has been quoted frequently:

Like the other remedies available under Title VII, reinstatement is not mandatory upon a finding that an employee has been discriminatorily discharged, but is an equitable remedy whose appropriateness depends upon the discretion of the court in the light of the facts of each individual case. However, since the purpose of reinstatement is to make the plaintiff whole for the injury she has suffered, it, like back pay, should be denied only for reasons which, if applied generally would not frustrate the central statutory purposes of eradicating discrimination throughout the economy and making persons whole for injuries suffered through past discrimination.

EEOC v. Kallir, Philips, Ross, Inc., 420 F.Supp. 919, 926 (S.D.N.Y.1976), *aff'd*, 559 F.2d 1203 (2d Cir.), *cert. denied*, 434 U.S. 920, 98 S.Ct. 395, 54 L.Ed.2d 277 (1977).

Reinstatement serves several objectives: (1) it recreates the employment relationship as it would have existed but for unlawful employment discrimination; (2) it prevents future economic loss to the plaintiff; (3) it allows an employer to demonstrate good faith compliance with the law to other employees; and (4) it prevents the employer from trying to get rid of employees, at any cost, who assert their rights under laws prohibiting discrimination in employment. *See* Darnell v. City of Jasper, 730 F.2d 653 (11th Cir.1984); Belton, Remedies § 7.4 (collecting cases). One court in an ADEA case has stated that "[a]fter all discharge is 'the industrial equivalent of capital punishment.'" Metz v. Transit Mix, Inc., 828 F.2d 1202, 1209 (7th Cir.1987) (citing Complete Auto Transit, Inc. v. Reis, 451 U.S. 401, 421, 101 S.Ct. 1836, 68 L.Ed.2d 248 (1981) (quoting M. Jay Whitman, Wild Cat Strikes: The Union's Narrowing Path to Rectitude?, 50 Ind.L.Rev. 472, 481 (1975)). Reinstatement is particularly appropriate in retaliatory discharge cases. Donnellon v. Fruehauf Corp., 794 F.2d

598, 602 (11th Cir.1986). Nevertheless, the rule that prevailing plaintiffs are presumptively entitled to reinstatement is contrary to the common law rule against enforcing personal service contracts. *See, e.g.*, Henry v. Lennox Indus., Inc., 768 F.2d 746 (6th Cir.1985). Why do courts order reinstatement in discrimination cases when the general rule is that courts will not order specific performance of personal service contracts?

1. RECONSTRUCTED HISTORY DOCTRINE

To determine a plaintiff's rightful place, particularly in class actions, courts may need to apply the "reconstructed history" doctrine. The Supreme Court laid the foundation for this doctrine in *Teamsters v. United States*, 431 U.S. 324, 372, 97 S.Ct. 1843, 1873, 52 L.Ed.2d 396 (1977):

> After the victims [of discrimination] have been identified, the court must, as nearly as possible, " 'recreate the conditions and relationships that would have been had there been no' " unlawful discrimination. *Franks*, 424 U.S. at 769, 96 S.Ct. at 1266. This process of recreating the past will necessarily involve a degree of approximation and imprecision. * * *

> Moreover, after the victims have been identified and their rightful place determined, the District Court will again be faced with the delicate task of adjusting the remedial interests of discriminatees and the legitimate expectations of other employees innocent of any wrongdoing.

The reconstructed history doctrine requires that courts first reconstruct the job or jobs the discriminatee would have had but for discrimination and, second, balance the competing interests of any "innocent employees" who currently hold the contested positions. The reconstructed history rule may require courts to conduct *"Teamsters"* or minihearings. *See* Segar v. Smith, 738 F.2d 1249, 1289–90 (D.C.Cir.1984), *cert. denied sub nom.* Meese v. Segar, 471 U.S. 1115, 105 S.Ct. 2357, 86 L.Ed.2d 258 (1985). *Teamsters* hearings are a series of mini-trials in the remedial phase of a class action in which members of the class put on evidence in support of their claims to individualized relief. The *Teamsters* hearings can be very time consuming, particularly in large class actions. *See, e.g.*, Jenson v. Eveleth Taconite Co., 130 F.3d 1287, 1290 (8th Cir.1997) (the special master on relief produced a 416–page report and recommendation), *cert. denied sub nom.* Oglebay Norton Co. v. Jenson, 524 U.S. 953, 118 S.Ct. 2370, 141 L.Ed.2d 738 (1998). The length, difficulty, and complexity of *Teamsters* mini-hearings strongly support settlement in class action employment discrimination cases. *See, e.g.*, Steve Watkins, The Black O: Racism and Redemption in an American Corporate Empire (1997) (a behind-the-scenes chronicle of the events that led to the settlement of a major race discrimination class action employment case against Shoney's). District courts, however, have discretion to award relief without *Teamsters* hearings in class action cases in which unlawful discrimination has so thoroughly permeated the workplace that any attempt to reconstruct individualized employment histories would "drag the court into a quagmire or hypothetical judgment" and would result in "mere guesswork." *See* Segar v. Smith, 738 F.2d 1249, 1289–90 (D.C.Cir.1984), *cert. denied sub nom.* Meese v. Segar, 471 U.S. 1115, 105 S.Ct. 2357, 86 L.Ed.2d 258 (1985); Hartman v. Wick, 678 F.Supp. 312, 336–37 (D.D.C.1988).

The reconstructed history doctrine may be used in individual cases as well. *See, e.g.*, Kyriazi v. Western Elec. Co., 476 F.Supp. 335 (D.N.J. 1979); Machakos v. Meese, 647 F.Supp. 1253 (D.D.C.1986), *aff'd*, 859 F.2d 1487 (D.C.Cir.1988). In *Kyriazi*, for example, the plaintiff, a female, was first employed by Western Electric in 1965; she was discharged in 1971. Between 1965 and 1971, she had been promoted and transferred several times. The court found that she had been denied promotions because of her sex prior to her discharge in 1971. To provide an appropriate reinstatement remedy, the court used the employment history of a similarly situated male employee—his qualifications, his promotions, and the average time between his promotions—to determine the highest position the plaintiff would have obtained but for the unlawful sex discrimination. In addition, the court used the plaintiff's reconstructed history and the salary of the male comparator to calculate the plaintiff's back pay award.

2. SPECIAL CIRCUMSTANCES THAT REBUT ENTITLEMENT TO REINSTATEMENT

Reinstatement may be denied if the employer is able to prove special or exceptional circumstances. *See* Rosario–Torres v. Hernandez–Colon, 889 F.2d 314, 323–24 (1st Cir.1989). The two situations in which courts have deemed appropriate in which to deny reinstatement are (1) when an innocent employee currently occupies the at-issue job and should not be bumped, and (2) when hostility or animosity between the plaintiff and employer would make an amicable and productive working relationship impossible.

a. *The innocent employee/no-bumping rule*: When the position that the plaintiff would presumptively be entitled to be awarded is occupied by another employee, and that employee is deemed to be an "innocent victim," i.e., an individual who played no role in the employer's discriminatory treatment of the plaintiff, the courts have held that the "innocent employee" should not be bumped to effectuate a reinstatement order. The "innocent employee" rule is based, in substantial part, on the potentially unsettling "domino" effect that bumping might have on employees who had no role in the employer's discriminatory conduct. *See* Patterson v. American Tobacco Co., 535 F.2d 257 (4th Cir.), *cert. denied*, 429 U.S. 920, 97 S.Ct. 314, 50 L.Ed.2d 286 (1976). The Supreme Court has endorsed the innocent victim doctrine. *See* Franks v. Bowman Transp. Co., 424 U.S. 747, 96 S.Ct. 1251, 47 L.Ed.2d 444 (1976); Firefighters Local Union 1784 v. Stotts, 467 U.S. 561, 104 S.Ct. 2576, 81 L.Ed.2d 483 (1984). The EEOC position on the "innocent employee" doctrine is found in EEOC, "Policy Statement on Remedies and Relief for Individual Cases of Unlawful Discrimination," *reprinted in* Fred W. Alvarez & Barbara Lipsky, *Remedies for Individual Cases of Unlawful Employment Discrimination: A Law Enforcement Perspective*, 3 Lab.Law. 199, app. at 232–37 (1987). The "no-bumping" rule may also apply if bumping would require the employer to violate a seniority provision of a collective bargaining agreement. *See e.g.*, Milton v. Scrivner, Inc., 53 F.3d 1118, 1125 (10th Cir.1995) ("reasonable accommodation" under the ADA cannot defeat seniority rights under a collective bargaining agreement); Eckles v. Consolidated Rail Corp., 94 F.3d 1041, 1047–48 (7th Cir.1996) (collecting cases upholding the same rule under the Rehabilitation Act), *cert. denied*, 520 U.S. 1146, 117 S.Ct. 1318, 137 L.Ed.2d 480 (1997). See also U.S. Airways, Inc. v. Barnett, 535 U.S. 391, 393, 122 S.Ct. 1516, 152 L.Ed.2d 589 (2002) ("[T]o show that a requested accommodation conflicts with the rules of a seniority provision is ordinarily to show that the accommodation is not 'reasonable.' ").

Bumping innocent employees is considered an extraordinary remedy that may be ordered only if necessary to achieve rightful place relief. The Eleventh Circuit, in *Walters v. City of Atlanta*, 803 F.2d 1135, 1150 (11th Cir.1986), identified four factors that courts should consider in determining whether an innocent employee should be bumped: (1) Is there evidence of repeated acts of discrimination by the employer? (2) Was the plaintiff the victim of retaliation? (3) Is a unique position involved? and (4) Are there other employment opportunities for the bumped employee? *Walters* upheld the bumping of a director of a museum to effectuate a reinstatement order because the position was found to be unique. The District of Columbia Court of Appeals also ordered bumping when a unique position was at stake in *Lander v. Lujan*, 888 F.2d 153, 155–58 (D.C.Cir.1989) (high-level administrative position was unique).

Bumping an incumbent employee may also be appropriate when an employer violates a court decree ordering reinstatement, *see* Spagnuolo v. Whirlpool Corp., 717 F.2d 114 (4th Cir.1983), or when an employer breaches a settlement agreement on reinstatement, *see* Brewer v. Muscle Shoals Bd. of Educ., 790 F.2d 1515 (11th Cir.1986). One court ordered the responsibilities of the at-issue position to be shared between the plaintiff and the innocent employee. Sebastian v. Texas Dep't of Corrections, 541 F.Supp. 970, 978 (S.D.Tex.1982) (holding that, if job sharing does not work out, the incumbent must be displaced, if necessary, in order to reinstate the plaintiff).

     b.   *Hostility or animosity*: Evidence of hostility or animosity between the plaintiff and the employer that would make it impossible for them to have a harmonious working relationship may be sufficient to rebut the presumption that the plaintiff is entitled to reinstatement. *See* EEOC v. Kallir, Philips, Ross, Inc., 420 F.Supp. 919, 926–27 (S.D.N.Y. 1976) (leading case), *aff'd*, 559 F.2d 1203 (2d Cir.), *cert. denied*, 434 U.S. 920, 98 S.Ct. 395, 54 L.Ed.2d 277 (1977); McIntosh v. Jones Truck Lines, Inc., 767 F.2d 433 (8th Cir.1985) (reinstatement denied where hostility between parties occurred prior to suit). *But see* Taylor v. Teletype Corp., 648 F.2d 1129, 1139 (8th Cir.) (rejecting employer's argument that reinstatement must be set aside because of hostility engendered by the filing of discrimination case), *cert. denied*, 454 U.S. 969, 102 S.Ct. 515, 70 L.Ed.2d 386 (1981).

c. *The "presently qualified" rule*: A plaintiff seeking reinstatement must be "presently qualified" as a condition precedent to reinstatement. Locke v. Kansas City Power & Light Co., 660 F.2d 359, 368–69 (8th Cir.1981). Past performance in a higher position may satisfy the "presently qualified" rule. Pecker v. Heckler, 801 F.2d 709 (4th Cir.1986).

Notes and Questions

1. Is the no-bumping rule consistent with the make-whole and rightful place theories enunciated by the Supreme Court in *Moody* and *Franks*? Who should have the greater interest in appealing to the "Chancellor's conscience" under the reasoning of the Supreme Court in *Moody*—the plaintiff who has proven that she is the victim of unlawful employment discrimination or the "innocent employee"? *See* Larry M. Parsons, Note, *Title VII Remedies: Reinstatement and the Innocent Incumbent Employee*, 42 Vand. L.Rev. 1441 (1989). For a treatment of the "innocent employee" problem under the National Labor Relations Act, see J. Freedley Hunsicker, Jr., Jonathan A. Kane, Peter D. Walther, Jr., NLRB Remedies for Unfair Labor Practices 129–42 (1986). For a brief discussion of the contrast between reinstatement rights under Title VII and the NLRA, see Leroy D. Clark, *The Future Civil Rights Agenda: Speculation on Litigation, Legislation, and Organization*, 38 Cath.U.L.Rev. 795, 815–16 (1989).

2. Should the preferences of the parties be given any weight in a court's determination of whether to order reinstatement? What if a plaintiff who has been discriminatorily discharged prefers not to be reinstated? Or what if an employer would prefer the court to order front pay instead of reinstatement? What should the court do in these situations? Should the court's decision on these issues turn on whether the position at issue is a low-level, routine, skilled or semi-skilled job, or a high-level, policy-making or supervisory position? *See, e.g.*, Blim v. Western Elec. Co., 731 F.2d 1473, 1478–79 (10th Cir.), *cert. denied sub nom*. AT & T Technologies v. Blim, 469 U.S. 874, 105 S.Ct. 233, 83 L.Ed.2d 161 (1984).

3. Suppose a plaintiff has prevailed on her claim that she was constructively discharged because of sexual harassment under the hostile work environment theory. What arguments would you make that she should or should not be reinstated? Should her preferences be determinative in this category of cases? If she should be reinstated, are there additional remedial measures the court should order?

4. What problems are there, if any, with the "presently qualified" rule for reinstatement in ADA cases? *See, e.g.*, Thomlison v. City of Omaha, 63 F.3d 786 (8th Cir.1995).

5. Congress has legislatively overruled the presumptive reinstatement rule in mixed-motive cases in which the defendant proves the "same decision" defense. Title VII, §§ 703(m), 706(g)(2)(B), 42 U.S.C. §§ 2000e–2(m), –5(g)(2)(B). And, in *McKennon v. Nashville Banner*, 513 U.S. 352, 115 S.Ct.

879, 130 L.Ed.2d 852 (1995), reproduced in Chapter 3, the Supreme Court, endorsed a strong presumption against reinstatement in after-acquired evidence cases when the employer proves that the later-acquired legitimate nondiscriminatory reason is of such severity that it justifies a decision in favor of the employer.

Note: Other Forms of Injunctive Relief

Reinstatement and monetary damages are the forms of relief that courts have ordered most frequently in employment discrimination cases. The courts, however, have been willing to consider and order a wider range of remedies when necessary to effectuate the rightful place and make-whole principles of *Moody* and *Franks*. In some instances, declaratory relief might be the only remedy that would be appropriate. *See* Mitchell v. OsAir, Inc., 629 F.Supp. 636 (N.D.Ohio 1986) (the court found discrimination, but also found plaintiff had been discharged for lawful reasons). "[D]eclaratory relief simply declares the rights of the parties or expresses the court's opinion on a question of law without any party to do anything," and in employment discrimination cases this form of relief "is likely to provide no more than a statement which says that the defendant violated plaintiff's right * * * because of * * * race or sex." Belton, Remedies § 8.2. Word-of-mouth recruiting has been enjoined where the practice has an adverse impact on the employment opportunities of a protected class and cannot be justified under the business necessity doctrine. *See, e.g.,* United States v. Georgia Power Co., 474 F.2d 906 (5th Cir.1973). What arguments would you make in support of an injunction against the word-of-mouth recruiting practice at issue in *EEOC v. Consolidated Services Systems*, 30 F.3d 58 (7th Cir.1994), reproduced in Chapter 3, Section B, if a court would have found in favor of the EEOC under the disparate impact theory?

A plaintiff might be entitled to an injunction directing the employer to expunge from its employment records any negative references about the plaintiff that were recorded in retaliation against the plaintiff. *See, e.g.,* Sherkow v. Wisconsin Dep't of Pub. Instruction, 630 F.2d 498 (7th Cir.1980). In order to advise employees of the measures an employer needs to take to comply with the law, a court may require an employer to post notices on employee bulletin boards of the court's remedial order. *See, e.g.,* Mead v. United States Fidelity & Guar. Co., 442 F.Supp. 114, 137 (D.Minn.1977). In addition, to remedy unlawful retaliation, a court may require the employer to inform its staff by memorandum or letter of any court orders regarding the substance of any letters of recommendation to the plaintiff's prospective employers. *See, e.g.,* Ross v. Beaumont Hosp., 678 F.Supp. 680, 684 (E.D.Mich.1988). Similarly, a court may order the employer to refrain from disclosing to subsequent employers any adverse actions the employer took in retaliation against a plaintiff. *See, e.g.,* Jaquette v. Black Hawk County, 710 F.2d 455, 456–57 (8th Cir.1983); EEOC v. Eazor Express Co., 499 F.Supp. 1377, 1390 (W.D.Penn.1980), *aff'd*, 659 F.2d 1066 (3d Cir.1981) (table).

D. FRONT PAY

Where special or exceptional circumstances warrant a denial of reinstatement, the courts generally award the employee front pay. Front pay is often considered an alternative to or substitute for reinstatement. *See, e.g.*, Avitia v. Metropolitan Club of Chicago, 49 F.3d 1219, 1232 (7th Cir.1995); Anderson v. Phillips Petroleum Co., 861 F.2d 631 (10th Cir.1988). The courts have adopted a variety of definitions of front pay. For example, the Seventh Circuit has defined front pay as "the difference (after proper discounting to present value) between what the plaintiff would have earned in the future had he been reinstated at the time of trial and what he would have earned in the future in his next best employment." *Avitia*, 49 F.3d at 1231. In *Lander v. Lujan*, 888 F.2d 153, 159 (D.C.Cir.1989), then-Judge Ruth Bader Ginsburg, concurring in a Title VII case, referred to an award of front pay as "rightful place" relief because it avoids any unfairness resulting from "bumping" an incumbent out of a position when a court orders the employer to promote the plaintiff immediately.

Even though none of the federal statutes prohibiting employment discrimination specify front pay as a remedy, the overwhelming weight of judicial opinion is that front pay can be awarded under Title VII, ADEA, ADA, the Rehabilitation Act, and § 1981. *See* Belton, Remedies § 10.3 (collecting cases). For example, prior to the Civil Rights Act of 1991, many courts found the statutory authority to award front pay—as an alternative to reinstatement—in the catchall phrase in § 706(g)(1) of Title VII: "any other equitable *relief* the court deems appropriate." *See* Hudson v. Reno, 130 F.3d 1193, 1203 & n. 6 (6th Cir.1997). Front pay generally is not awarded in an Equal Pay Act case because back pay and an injunction to equalize the wages of males and females usually provides adequate relief.

Front pay is awarded to harmonize back pay awards, the plaintiff's presumptive entitlement to reinstatement, and the policy of protecting innocent victims through a no-bumping rule, with the make-whole and rightful place theories of relief under *Moody* and *Franks*. For example, in one of the leading cases on front pay, the Fourth Circuit stated that

> although Congress did not intend [Title VII] to be used as a vehicle for displacing incumbents, it did not leave the victims of discrimination without a remedy. * * *
>
> * * *
>
> To satisfy [the] objectives [of laws prohibiting discrimination in employment], back pay must be allowed [to a victim of discrimination] from [the date of the occurrence of the discriminatory act] * * * until he [achieves his rightful place]. Some employees who have been victims of discrimination will be unable to move immediately into jobs to which their seniority and ability entitle them. The back pay award should be fashioned to compensate them until they can obtain a job commensurate with their status. This may be accomplished by allowing back pay for a period commencing at the time the employee was unlawfully denied a position until the date of the judgment * * *. This compensation should be supplemented by an award equal to the estimated present value of lost earnings that

are reasonably likely to occur between the date of the judgment and the time when the employee can assume his new [rightful place] position.

Patterson v. American Tobacco Co., 535 F.2d 257, 269 (4th Cir.), *cert. denied*, 429 U.S. 920, 97 S.Ct. 314, 50 L.Ed.2d 286 (1976). *See also* Koyen v. Consolidated Edison Co., 560 F.Supp. 1161, 1168 (S.D.N.Y. 1983) (rejecting arguments that front pay awards lack specific statutory authority and are too speculative). Plaintiffs generally are not entitled to both front pay and reinstatement because this would provide a windfall to the plaintiff. *See* Suggs v. Servicemaster Educ. Food Management, 72 F.3d 1228, 1234–35 (6th Cir.1996). Front pay is likely to be awarded in cases where a plaintiff cannot be reinstated because the position is staffed by an "innocent victim," because of hostility or antagonism between the plaintiff and the employer, or because the plaintiff in an ADEA case is likely to retire in the near future. *See, e.g.*, McKnight v. General Motors Corp., 908 F.2d 104, 115–16 (7th Cir.1990) (hostility or antagonism between employer and plaintiff may preclude reinstatement), *cert. denied*, 499 U.S. 919, 111 S.Ct. 1306, 113 L.Ed.2d 241 (1991); Wildman v. Lerner Stores, Corp., 771 F.2d 605, 616 (1st Cir. 1985) (adopting rule that "[f]uture damages should not be awarded unless reinstatement is impracticable or impossible"); Davis v. Combustion Eng'g, Inc., 742 F.2d 916, 922 (6th Cir.1984) (plaintiff's probable retirement within a few years justifies an award of front pay rather than reinstatement).

Two issues are involved in awards of front pay: first is whether front pay should be awarded; if the answer is affirmative, the second issue is what amount should be awarded. The courts appear to be fairly uniform in holding that the trial judge rather than the jury decides whether to award front pay. The courts are divided, however, on whether the judge or the jury should determine the amount of the award. The split in the courts turns on whether front pay is considered legal or equitable relief. If it is legal relief, then the jury should decide both issues. If it is deemed to be equitable relief, then the court, sitting without a jury, decides both issues, even though the court may impanel an advisory jury to determine the amount of the award. *See* Newhouse v. McCormick & Co., 110 F.3d 635 (8th Cir.1997). What difference should it make whether a judge or jury determines these two issues?

The elements used to determine the amount of front pay are generally the same as those used in determining back pay. *See* Buckley v. Reynolds Metals Co., 690 F.Supp. 211 (S.D.N.Y.1988) (using wages, and pension, health, and life insurance benefits to determine front pay). *See* Section E, *infra*. The amount awarded as front pay is not included in calculating liquidated damages in ADEA cases because front pay does not fall within the meaning of "amounts owing" under § 216(b) of the Fair Labor Standards Act. *See* Cooper v. Asplundh Tree Expert Co., 836 F.2d 1544, 1556–57 (10th Cir.1988).

In Pollard v. E.I. du Pont de Nemours & Co., 532 U.S. 843, 121 S.Ct. 1946, 150 L.Ed.2d 62 (2001), the Supreme Court upheld the authority of lower courts to award front pay under § 706(g) of Title VII:

> * * * Although courts have defined "front pay" in numerous ways, front pay is simply money awarded for lost compensation during the period between judgment and reinstatement or in lieu of reinstatement.

> * * *

> * * * [T]he original language of § 706(g) authorizing backpay awards was modeled after the same language in the NLRA. This provision in the NLRA has been construed to allow awards of backpay up to the date of reinstatement, even if reinstatement occurred after the judgment. Accordingly, backpay awards made for the period between the date of judgment and the date of reinstatement, which today we call front pay awards under Title VII, were authorized under § 706(g).

> As to front pay awards that are made in lieu of reinstatement, we construe § 706(g) as authorizing these awards as well.

Id. at 846, 853, 121 S.Ct. at 1948, 1952.

Front pay not the same as "future pecuniary losses": The Civil Rights Act of 1991 provides for "future pecuniary losses" as an element of compensatory damages. The lower courts split over the issue of the relationship, if any, between a front pay award that is available under § 706(g) of Title VII, and "future pecuniary losses" that are recoverable as part of compensatory damages. The Supreme Court resolved the circuit split in *Pollard, supra.* The issue before the Court was "whether a front pay award is an element of compensatory damages under the Civil Rights Act of 1991." *Id.* at 845. In an opinion written for a unanimous Court by Justice Thomas (with Justice O'Connor not participating), the Court held front pay is not an element of compensatory damages within the meaning of the term "future pecuniary losses" of a compensatory damages award now available under Title VII. As a result of this ruling, front pay is not subject to the statutory caps in Title VII compensatory damages awards. The Court relied on essentially two lines of reasoning. First, based on a statutory interpretation, the Court found that front pay awards were authorized by Congress before the 1991 provision allowing compensatory damages. Second, the Court found that Congress had made clear in the 1991 Civil Rights Act that its decision to provide compensatory (and punitive) damages were designed to provide "additional remedies to deter harassment and intentional discrimination in the workplace" *Id.* at 852 (citing the Civil Rights Act of 1991).

The issue whether a plaintiff's claim falls within the front pay theory or falls within compensatory damages in the form of "future pecuniary losses" may, at times, be difficult to decide. Consider the following: Plaintiff brings an ADA claim and alleges that her employer so exacerbated her disability that she is permanently disabled for the remainder of her actuarial life. The jury finds in favor of the plaintiff on her ADA claim, and now plaintiff wants to obtain monetary damages for the remainder of her actuarial life. Is the claim properly characterized as one for "front pay" or for "future pecuniary losses"? This issue was raised but not decided in Swiech v. Gottlieb Memorial Hospital, 2003 WL 21183887 (N.D.Ill. 2003).

Front pay is specifically excluded in mixed-motive cases under the 1991 Act. Title VII, § 706(g)(B), 42 U.S.C. § 2000e–5(g)(B).

E. BACK PAY

The theory of back pay, based upon the *Moody* make-whole principle, is to compensate victims of unlawful employment discrimination for the economic losses they have suffered from the date of the occurrence of the discriminatory act to the date of the entry of judgment on liability or until the date the plaintiff finds comparable employment. The period for which back pay is computed is generally based on the reconstructed history rule for determining rightful place for reinstatement discussed in Section C. 1. of this chapter. *See* Thorne v. City of El Segundo, 802 F.2d 1131 (9th Cir.1986). As a general rule, the beginning date is the date of the occurrence of the discriminatory act, e.g., discharge, refusal to hire, or failure to promote. *See* Velazquez v. Chardon, 736 F.2d 831 (1st Cir.1984). Back pay cannot extend to more than two years prior to the filing of a charge with the EEOC. *See, e.g.,* Title VII, § 706(g), 42 U.S.C. § 2000e–5(g). The ending date varies depending upon the circumstances of the particular case, but the general rule is that it is the date of the entry of judgment on liability. *See* Henry v. Lennox Indus., Inc., 768 F.2d 746 (6th Cir.1985). Other potential cut-off dates include the date on which the plaintiff's income from a new job exceeds the income she would have received "but for" the discrimination, *see* Darnell v. City of Jasper, 730 F.2d 653 (11th Cir.1984); the date the plaintiff removed herself from the labor market, *see* Brady v. Thurston Motor Lines, Inc., 753 F.2d 1269 (4th Cir.1985); or the date of normal retirement, *see* Fite v. First Tennessee Produc. Credit Assoc., 861 F.2d 884 (6th Cir.1988).

1. COMPUTING BACK PAY

The courts have adopted two basic rules on back pay awards: first, "unrealistic exactitude is not required," and second, any doubt as to the amount "should be resolved against the discriminating employer." Pettway v. American Cast Iron Pipe Co., 494 F.2d 211, 268 (5th Cir.1974). The courts have also used a variety of methods for computing back pay awards, and this variety is consistent with the view announced by the Supreme Court in *Moody* that courts have broad discretion in computing back pay. In the usual case, the courts first determine what jobs, pay, and benefits the plaintiff would have received but for discrimination (under the reconstructed history approach), and then compute the amount of back pay. *See, e.g.,* EEOC v. Korn Indus., 662 F.2d 256 (4th Cir.1981). Other methods include:

a. *The hypothetical employee*: Under this approach the court constructs a "hypothetical employee" and follows her as she advances up the employment ladder to the highest position she would have had "but for" discrimination, taking into account, for example, her qualifications and the length of time before she would have been promoted. *See* White v. Carolina Paperboard Corp., 564 F.2d 1073 (4th Cir.1977).

b. *The Woolworth formula*: This formula, first adopted by the NLRB in *F.W. Woolworth*, 90 N.L.R.B. 289 (1950), determines back pay for each quarter the employee works. The quarterly periods begin on the first day of January, April, July, and October. Because of the duty to mitigate damages, quarterly calculations of the amount of backpay reduces the windfall to the employer (and the incentive for delay) that results if the plaintiff eventually finds a better paying job. *See* Darnell v. City of Jasper, 730 F.2d 653 (11th Cir.1984).

c. *The average employee approach*: Under this approach, the courts base gross back pay on the actual wages of a group of employees who are similarly situated to the plaintiff. *See* Merriweather v. Hercules, Inc., 631 F.2d 1161 (5th Cir.1980).

2. ELEMENTS INCLUDED IN BACK PAY

The elements used in computing back pay include but are not limited to wages, salary, bonuses, commissions, raises, and fringe benefits, e.g., sick pay, vacation pay, pension benefits, health benefits, stock purchase benefits, bonuses (including the cost of the missed Christmas turkey or ham). *See* Pettway v. American Cast Iron Pipe Co. 494 F.2d 211 (5th Cir.1974); Rasimas v. Michigan Dep't of Mental Health, 714 F.2d 614 (6th Cir.1983), *cert. denied*, 466 U.S. 950, 104 S.Ct. 2151, 80 L.Ed.2d 537 (1984); Catlett v. Missouri State Highway Comm'n, 627 F.Supp. 1015 (W.D.Mo.1985), *aff'd in part, rev'd in part*, 828 F.2d 1260 (8th Cir.1987), *cert. denied*, 485 U.S. 1021, 108 S.Ct. 1574, 99 L.Ed.2d 889 (1988); Buckley v. Reynolds Metals Co., 690 F.Supp. 211 (D.C.N.Y. 1988) (dental and vision insurance).

Notes and Questions

1. Suppose two women apply for the same job and each is successful in proving that she was rejected because of unlawful sex discrimination. Should the court order reinstatement or back pay to one, both, or neither? *See* Catlett v. Missouri Highway & Transp. Comm'n, 828 F.2d 1260 (8th Cir. 1987) (reinstatement cannot be awarded to a number of discriminatees greater than the number of vacant positions), *cert. denied*, 485 U.S. 1021, 108 S.Ct. 1574, 99 L.Ed.2d 889 (1988). Several commentators who have examined this problem identify the three positions courts have adopted on this issue: (1) only the most qualified employee is entitled to relief; (2) both of the plaintiffs are entitled to relief; and (3) a division of the monetary relief between the plaintiffs. Daniel J. Winters & Steven J. Pearlman, *Musical Chairs and Multiple Plaintiffs: Employment Discrimination Actions Where Multiple Plaintiffs Are Denied the Same Position*, 28 Empl.Rel.L.J. 7 (2003). Which do you believe is the better approach?

2. Should the back pay award include a cost of living adjustment? An inflation factor? Based on *Moody*, could an argument be made that they should be included?

3. *Duty to Mitigate Damages*: Title VII and the ADA impose on victims of discrimination a statutory duty to mitigate damages: "Interim earnings or amounts earnable with reasonable diligence by the person or persons discriminated against shall operate to reduce the back pay otherwise allowable." 42 U.S.C. § 2000e–5(g); 42 U.S.C. § 12117(a). The courts have also read a duty to mitigate damages into the ADEA, the Equal Pay Act, and § 1981. *See, e.g.*, Maxfield v. Sinclair Int'l, 766 F.2d 788, 793–95 (3d Cir.1985) (ADEA), *cert. denied*, 474 U.S. 1057, 106 S.Ct. 796, 88 L.Ed.2d 773 (1986); Piva v. Xerox Corp., 654 F.2d 591, 598–99 (9th Cir.1981) (Equal Pay Act). The failure to mitigate damages is an affirmative defense on which the employer bears the burden of proof—both the burden of the production of evidence and the burden of persuasion. Generally, the plaintiff's duty to mitigate is not an onerous burden; the plaintiff is required only to try to find a "substantially equivalent" position or to use "reasonable diligence" to try to find a job that is the same or substantially equivalent in responsibilities, working conditions, and status to the job discriminatorily denied. Success in the plaintiff's efforts to find another position is not essential. Sellers v. Delgado Community College, 839 F.2d 1132, 1138 (5th Cir.1988). Moreover, the courts have held that the plaintiff is required only to make a good faith reasonable effort. *See e.g.*, Brooks v. Woodline Motor Freight, Inc., 852 F.2d 1061 (8th Cir.1988).

a. Should the concept of reasonableness include the obligation to relocate in a different geographical area?

b. And under what circumstances should a plaintiff be expected to "lower his or her sights" when substantially equivalent employment is not available?

c. Should a plaintiff be denied back pay if she refuses to accept a job that has less responsibility or pay than the job that the employer discriminatorily denied her?

4. Suppose an employer has denied jobs to several female applicants and there is a strong basis for believing that the employer did so solely because they are female. Later the employer offers the women jobs, but does not include compensation for the economic loss they suffered between the date they were first rejected and the date they received the job offers. Should the women be required to accept the job offers pursuant to the duty to mitigate damages? *Ford Motor Co. v. EEOC*, 458 U.S. 219, 102 S.Ct. 3057, 73 L.Ed.2d 721 (1982), held that, absent special circumstances, an offer of employment to a rejected applicant tolls the accrual of back pay if the employer makes an unconditional offer of the job denied, even if the offer does not include all the relief that the plaintiff is entitled to receive. What are some special circumstances that would make the *Ford Motor* unconditional offer rule inapplicable?

5. *Set-Offs Against Back Pay*: A defendant is entitled to certain set-offs against the amount of back pay a court ultimately decides should be awarded to the plaintiff. These set-offs include, for example, the plaintiff's income earned in mitigation of damages, as well as "moonlight" earnings—earnings

from a second job—but only if the plaintiff could not have held the supplemental job at the same time as the job he lost because of discrimination. *See, e.g.*, Bing v. Roadway Express, Inc., 485 F.2d 441, 454 (5th Cir.1973) (the leading case).

6. *Collateral Source Doctrine*: Are defendants entitled to a set-off for income that plaintiffs receive from collateral sources? Some of the most obvious collateral sources are social security, unemployment compensation, welfare benefits, and disability income. Some courts hold that benefits received from a source collateral to the discriminatory conduct of the employer may not be used to reduce back pay awards. *See, e.g.*, Craig v. Y & Y Snacks, Inc., 721 F.2d 77 (3d Cir.1983); *see also* NLRB v. Gullet Gin Co., 340 U.S. 361, 364, 71 S.Ct. 337, 339, 95 L.Ed. 337 (1951) (back pay award not to be reduced by amount received under unemployment benefits). Others hold that district courts have discretion to set off collateral source income against a back pay award. *See, e.g.*, Dailey v. Societe Generale, 108 F.3d 451 (2d Cir.1997). For a discussion of the problem of applying the collateral source doctrine to front pay, see Eric Pearson, Note, *Collateral Benefits and Front Pay: A Rule of No Offset Encourages Agency Recoupment*, 69 U.Chi. L.Rev. 1957 (2002).

7. *Doctrine of Laches*: The defendant is likely to raise the laches defense either because of a delay caused when the EEOC administrative process has consumed a substantial amount of time beyond the statutory period of six months or because of delays that have occurred during litigation. A successful laches defense either cuts off back pay or limits the amount awarded. *Moody* adopted a two-pronged test for the laches defense: unreasonable delay and prejudice to defendant. The defendant has the burden of proof on both prongs. *See* Jeffries v. Chicago Transit Auth., 770 F.2d 676 (7th Cir.1985), *cert. denied*, 475 U.S. 1050, 106 S.Ct. 1273, 89 L.Ed.2d 581 (1986).

8. *Ability to Pay*: Should the ability of a defendant to pay a monetary award be a factor in determining whether to award back pay or other forms of monetary relief, or in determining the amount to be awarded? Generally the courts have held that ability to pay is not relevant. *See* EEOC v. Rath Packing Co., 787 F.2d 318 (8th Cir.) (but court disallowed an award of prejudgment interest for that reason), *cert. denied*, 479 U.S. 910, 107 S.Ct. 307, 93 L.Ed.2d 282 (1986).

9. *Interest*: Prejudgment interest is intended to compensate the plaintiff for the loss of an opportunity to invest her wages at the going rate of interest. The courts are unanimous in holding that trial courts have discretion to award prejudgment interest. Several courts, relying on *Moody*'s make-whole theory, have adopted a strong presumption in favor of prejudgment interest. *See, e.g.*, Chamberlin v. 101 Realty, Inc., 915 F.2d 777 (1st Cir.1990); Davis v. Construction Materials, 558 F.Supp. 697 (N.D.Ala.), *aff'd*, 720 F.2d 1293 (11th Cir.1983). The courts have not adopted a uniform standard for determining the rate of prejudgment interest. For a list of prejudgment rates used by various courts, *see* Belton, Remedies § 15.11 (1998 Supplement).

Postjudgment interest is now mandatory under federal law. 28 U.S.C. § 1961 (1986), and the rate of interest is tied to federal interest rates.

Congress amended Title VII, § 717, 42 U.S.C. § 2000e–16, to make the federal government subject to the same interest rates as are applied to nonpublic parties.

10. *Right of Contribution Between Employers and Unions*: In *Northwest Airlines, Inc. v. Transport Workers Union*, 451 U.S. 77, 90–91, 101 S.Ct. 1571, 1580–81, 67 L.Ed.2d 750 (1981), the Supreme Court held that an employer is not entitled to contribution for the back pay award from the union even if the union is also found to be liable for the unlawful discrimination.

F. COMPENSATORY AND PUNITIVE DAMAGES

1. COMPENSATORY DAMAGES

Compensatory and punitive damages have been available in § 1981 employment discrimination cases since the Supreme Court decided *Johnson v. Railway Express Agency, Inc.*, 421 U.S. 454, 95 S.Ct. 1716, 44 L.Ed.2d 295 (1975). The Civil Rights Act of 1991 now makes compensatory and punitive damages available under Title VII and the ADA but only in disparate treatment cases not involving mixed-motive claims. 42 U.S.C. § 1981a, §§ 703(m) and 706(g)(2)(b) of Title VII, 42 U.S.C. §§ 2000e–2(m), and 2000e–5(g)(2)(b). The expansion of monetary relief in the 1991 Act was, in substantial part, Congress' response to the argument that it was patently unfair to deny the right to recover compensatory and punitive damages for claims of sex or disability discrimination when such damages are recoverable in race discrimination claims brought under § 1981.

The Civil Rights Act of 1991, however, places caps on the amounts that can be awarded as compensatory and punitive damages, depending upon the size of the employer's workforce:

—Employers with more than 14 but fewer than 101 employees: $50,000.

—More than 100 but fewer than 201: $100,000.

—More than 200 but fewer than 501: $200,000.

—More than 500: $300,000.

See 42 U.S.C. § 1981a(b)(3).

Compensatory damages are defined under the Civil Rights Act of 1991 to include "future pecuniary losses, emotional pain, suffering, inconvenience, mental anguish, loss of enjoyment of life, and other nonpecuniary losses." 42 U.S.C. § 1981a(b)(3). The Act also provides that the caps are not to apply to § 1981 claims. *Id.* § 1981a(b)(4). The EEOC has issued a policy statement that the following are recoverable as compensatory damages: injury to professional standing, injury to character and reputation, injury to credit standing, loss of health, and aggravation of preexisting emotional difficulties if further deterioration is caused by the employer's conduct (e.g., victim of incest who brings a sexual harassment claim). EEOC, Enforcement Guidance No. 915.002, *Compen-*

satory and Punitive Damages Available Under Section 102 of the Civil Rights Act of 1991, [Sept. 1991—May 1994 Transfer Binder] Empl. Prac.Dec. (CCH) ¶ 5360, at 6225 (July 14, 1992).

a. Do the caps Congress placed on compensatory and punitive damages under Title VII violate a plaintiff's Seventh Amendment right under the Constitution because they usurp the jury's fact-finding function? The court in *Madison v. IBP, Inc.*, 257 F.3d 780 (8th Cir.2001), *cert. granted, judgment vacated*, 536 U.S. 919, 122 S.Ct. 2583, 153 L.Ed.2d 773 (2002) (remanding for reconsideration in light of *National R.R. Passenger Corp. v. Morgan*, 536 U.S. 101, 122 S.Ct. 2061, 153 L.Ed.2d 106 (2002), held that they do not because Congress's power to create the Title VII cause of action carries the constitutional authority to set limits for its recovery.

b. What arguments could you make that the caps on recovery for compensatory and punitive damages under Title VII violate the Equal Protection Clause of the Constitution of the United States because they limit the amount of monetary recovery for women, but under 42 U.S.C. § 1981, racial and ethnic minorities might recover more than the Title VII caps? Do the two statutes make distinctions based on sex? In thinking about this question, should it make a difference whether the issue is raised by a black female or a white female? A male or a female? And if so, which standard should apply—rational basis or strict scrutiny? In *Lansdale v. Hi–Health Supermart Corp.*, 314 F.3d 355 (9th Cir.2002), the plaintiff argued that Congress violated the separation of powers provision of the Constitution because the caps invade the province of the jury and that the caps violate the Equal Protection Clause of the Constitution. The court rejected both arguments. The court rejected the separation of powers argument on the ground that the Supreme Court has held that when Congress creates a statutory right it has discretion to define the right, to assign the burdens of proof, and to prescribe remedies. *Id.* at 357 (citing Hemmings v. Tidyman's Inc., 285 F.3d 1174, 1200–02)(citing Northern Pipeline Constr. Co. v. Marathon Pipe Line Co., 458 U.S. 50, 83, 102 S.Ct. 2858, 73 L.Ed.2d 598 (1982)). The court rejected the Equal Protection argument on the ground that Congress is not required to resolve every facet of a societal problem when it enacts legislation. *Id.* at 358.

c. Do the statutory caps apply in a case in which a plaintiff seeks relief from employment discrimination under both federal and state law, the state law claim is virtually identical to the federal law claim, and the state law does not impose a limit on damages? In *Gagliardo v. Connaught Laboratories, Inc.*, 311 F.3d 565 (3d Cir.2002), the plaintiff sued under the ADA and a similar Pennsylvania state law. The jury returned a general verdict in favor of the plaintiff for $2,000,000 in compensatory damages and $500,000 in punitive damages but did not apportion the damages award between the federal and state law claims. The trial court, pursuant to the employer's motion to alter or amend the judgment, applied the federal cap to only the punitive damages, thus lowering the punitive damages to $300,000, and allocated all of the compensatory damages to the state law claims. One of the issues presented to the court of appeals is whether the trial court erred in not applying the federal caps applies to the entire award, here, $2,500,000 where the jury has not allocated the award between the federal and state claims. Relying on two other cases raising essentially the same issue—Passantino v. Johnson & Johnson, 212 F.3d 493 (9th Cir.2000), and Martini v. Fed. Nat'l Mortgage Ass'n, 178 F.3d 1336 (D.C.Cir.1999)—the Third Circuit held that the district court did not abuse its discretion in allocating the entire compensatory award to the state law claim. In reaching that decision, the court relied, in part, on 42 U.S.C. § 12201(b), which provides that the ADA is not to be construed to limit rights or remedies available to discriminatee under state laws. *Id.* at 571.

2. PUNITIVE DAMAGES

The Civil Rights Act of 1991 provides that punitive damages may be recovered against a defendant (other than any government agency or political subdivision) if the plaintiff proves that the defendant engaged in an unlawful employment practice "with malice or with reckless indifference to the federally protected rights" of the plaintiff. 42 U.S.C. § 1981a(b)(1). This is essentially the same standard adopted by the Supreme Court in § 1983 litigation in *Smith v. Wade*, 461 U.S. 30, 55, 103 S.Ct. 1625, 1640, 75 L.Ed.2d 632 (1983) ("reckless or callous indifference to the federally protected rights of others"). Conduct more egregious than intentional discrimination is required to support an award of punitive damages, but the courts have generally rejected a standard requiring a showing of "extraordinarily egregious" conduct. Factors to be considered in determining the amount of punitive damages include the nature and the severity of the discriminatory conduct, the duration and frequency of the conduct, and the financial status of the employer. *See* EEOC, Enforcement Guidance No. 915.002, *Compensatory and Punitive Damages Available Under Section 102 of the Civil Rights Act of 1991*, [Sept. 1991—May 1994 Transfer Binder] Empl.Prac.Dec. (CCH) ¶ 5360, at 6228 (July 14, 1992) (collecting cases brought under § 1981). Evidence about a defendant's net worth is highly relevant on the issue of the amount to be awarded as punitive damages. *See* Rodgers v. Fisher Body Div., GMC, 739 F.2d 1102 (6th Cir.1984), *cert. denied*, 470 U.S. 1054, 105 S.Ct. 1759, 84 L.Ed.2d 821 (1985).

a. In *Kolstad v. American Dental Association,* 527 U.S. 526, 119 S.Ct. 2118, 144 L.Ed.2d 494 (1999), the Supreme Court resolved a conflict between the circuits on the burden a plaintiff must carry to prove malice or recklessness. The Court granted certiorari to address the issue of "the circumstances under which a jury may consider a request for punitive damages under § 1981(a)(b)(1)." *Id.* at 533, 119 S.Ct. at 2123. The Court construed the statutory structure as requiring two separate standards for recovery of compensatory and punitive damages:

The very structure of § 1981a suggests a congressional intent to authorize punitive awards in only a subset of cases involving intentional discrimination. Section 1981a(a)(1) limits compensatory and punitive awards to instances of intentional discrimination, while § 1981a(b)(1) requires plaintiffs to make an additional "demonstrat[ion]" of their eligibility for punitive damages. Congress plainly sought to impose two standards of liability—one for establishing a right to compensatory damages and another, higher standard that a plaintiff must satisfy to qualify for a punitive award.

Id. at 534, 119 S.Ct. at 2124.

Having concluded that Congress intended to impose a higher standard for an award of punitive damages in statutory employment discrimination cases, the Court then set out to define what that standard should be. The Court squarely rejected the lower court's standard that punitive damages can be awarded only upon a showing of extraordinary egregious conduct. Egregious conduct may certainly be "evidence of the requisite mental state [but] § 1981a does not limit plaintiffs to this form of evidence, and the section does not require a showing of egregious or outrageous discrimination independent of the employer's state of mind." *Id.*, 119 S.Ct. at 2124. Based upon its reading of congressional intent, the Court held that the statutory standards of "malice" or "reckless indifference to federally protected rights of an aggrieved individual" require proof that an employer had "guilty" knowledge that it "may be acting in violation of federal law," rather than proof that the employer was aware that it was "engaging in unlawful discrimination." *Id.* at 535, 119 S.Ct. at 2124. The Court variously characterized the terms "malice" or "reckless indifference" as imposing an obligation on a plaintiff to prove that the employer's conduct was not only the result of intentional discrimination, but also was "motivated by evil motive or intent or callous indifference to rights of others," or showed a "subjective consciousness of a risk of injury or illegality," or showed "knowledge of falsity or reckless disregard of the truth." 119 S.Ct. at 2125.

The Court then attempted to shed light on the types of situation in which a plaintiff proves intentional discrimination but where the requisite malice or reckless indifference may not be present:

In some instances, the employer may simply be unaware of the relevant prohibition. There will be cases, moreover, in which the employer discriminates with the distinct belief that its discrimination is lawful. The underlying theory of discrimination may be novel or otherwise poorly recognized, or an employer may reasonably believe that its discrimination satisfied the bona fide occupational qualification defense or other statutory exception to liability.

119 S.Ct. at 2125.

b. The more controversial and difficult holding in *Kolstad* is Part II, where the majority of the Court reached out to decide an issue not presented for review in the granting of certiorari. 119 S.Ct. at 2127. In Part II, the Court held that in addition to proving malice or reckless indifference under its newly crafted test for punitive damages, there must be some basis for imputing liability to the employer for the award. 119 S.Ct. at 2127. Observing that "[i]n express terms, Congress has directed federal courts to interpret Title VII based on agency principles" (citing Burlington Industries, Inc. v. Ellerth, 524 U.S. 742, 754, 118 S.Ct. 2257, 141 L.Ed.2d 633 (1998)), reproduced in Chapter 8, the Court cited to the following provisions of Restatement (Second) of Agency which cover the extent to which an agent's misconduct may be imputed to an employer for purposes of awarding punitive damages:

"Punitive damages can properly be awarded against a master or other principal because of an act by the agent, if but only if:

"(a) the principal authorized the doing and manner of the act, or

"(b) the agent was unfit and the principal was reckless in employing him, or

"(c) the agent was employed in a managerial capacity and was acting in the scope of employment, or

"(d) the principal or a managerial agent of the principal ratified or approved the act."

Id. at 542, 119 S.Ct. at 2128 (quoting Restatement (Second) of Agency § 217(C)(1957)).

The Court also clearly rejected a straightforward application of the Restatement (Second) of Agency "scope of employment" rule for several reasons. First, the Court thought doing so would "penalize those employees who educate themselves and their employees of Title VII's prohibitions"; second, the rule would "[d]issuade employees form implementing programs or policies to prevent discrimination in the workplace" because the primary objective of Title VII is prophylactic, *i.e.,* "not to provide redress but to avoid harm" (citing Faragher v. Boca Raton, 524 U.S. 775, 806, 118 S.Ct. 2275, 141 L.Ed.2d 662 (1998)); and third, "[t]he purposes underlying Title VII are similarly advanced where employers are encouraged to adopt antidiscrimination policies and to educate their personnel on Title VII's prohibitions." *Id.* at 543–34, 119 S.Ct. at 2129. Based on these concerns, the Court then held that "an employer may not be vicariously liable for the discriminatory decisions of managerial agents where these decisions are contrary to the employer's good faith efforts to comply with Title VII." 119 S.Ct. at 2129 (citing Kolstad v. American Dental Association, 139 F.3d at 974 (Tatel, J., dissenting)).

The Court observed that the Restatement (Second) of Agency contemplates employer liability for punitive damages where an employee is serving in a "managerial capacity" and is "acting in the scope of employment." 119 S.Ct. at 2128. The Court recognized, however, that it was unable to find a "good definition of what constitutes a 'managerial capacity.'" *Id.* But in making the determination whether an employee is employed in a "managerial capacity," the Court instructed the lower court to "review the type of authority that the employer has given to the employee, the amount of discretion the employee has in what is done and how it is accomplished." *Id.* Looking to examples provided in the Restatement (Second) of Torts, the Court stated that employees need not be "top management, officers, or directors" to be acting "in a managerial capacity." *Id.* Under principles from the Restatement (Second) of Agency, however, an employee may be found in some situations to have been "acting in the scope of employment" even if the employee engages in acts "specifically forbidden" by the employer. *Id.*

One court has stated that a Title VII plaintiff must prove the following to support an award of punitive damages: (1) the employer acted with malice or reckless indifference, an inquiry that focuses on the state of mind of the actor; (2) the employee causing or permitting the unlawful discrimination was employed in a managerial capacity; (3) the managerial employee was acting within the scope of employment; and (4) the managerial employee's unlawful discrimination was not contrary to the employer's good faith efforts to comply with Title VII. Miller v. Kenworth of Dothan, Inc., 82 F.Supp.2d 1299, 1306 (M.D.Ala.2000).

c. In *Lowery v. Circuit City Stores, Inc.,* 206 F.3d 431 (4th Cir. 2000), the Fourth Circuit suggested that *Kolstad* instructs the following series of questions that are relevant in assessing the evidence to determine whether the employer is liable for punitive damages:

We must first ask whether the record contains sufficient evidence for a reasonable juror to find that in intentionally refusing to promote the plaintiff to the position at issue, the decision maker did so in the face of a perceived risk that her decision would violate federal law. If the answer is no, [the court] should [not award punitive damages]. If the answer is yes and * * * the decision maker was not a principal, we should next ask whether a reasonable juror could find the decision maker served the employer in a managerial capacity. Again, if the answer is no [then the court should not award punitive damages]. However, if the answer is yes, we must ask whether a reasonable juror could find that the decision maker acted within the scope of her employment in making the challenged decision. If the answer is no, [then no punitive damages]. Finally, if the answer to this question is yes, we must ask whether a reasonable juror could only conclude that [the employer] engaged in a good-faith effort to comply with [federal law]. If the answer to this question is yes, [the employer] prevails. If the answer is no, [the plaintiff is entitled to punitive damages].

Id. at 443.

d. What constitutes a "good faith effort to comply with Title VII" under the Supreme Court's newly crafted rule on employer liability for punitive damages is likely to be one of the most contentious issues in punitive damages litigation. The Court failed to provide any guidance on its new standard. The Court's decisions in *Burlington Industries, Inc. v. Ellerth* and *Faragher v. Boca Raton,* reproduced in Chapter 8, may provide a useful starting point to flesh out the reach and limits of the *Kolstad* good faith test. The good faith defense is explored in *EEOC v. Wal–Mart Stores, Inc.,* 187 F.3d 1241 (10th Cir.1999).

e. Juries are not to be informed of the caps on damages, but a court must reduce the amounts awarded as compensatory and punitive damages if the jury's award exceeds the statutory caps. *See, e.g.*, Hudson v. Reno, 130 F.3d 1193, 1198–1201 (6th Cir.1997), *cert. denied*, 525 U.S. 822, 119 S.Ct. 64, 142 L.Ed.2d 50 (1998). And the courts uniformly hold that the caps apply to the aggregate of all claims brought by a single plaintiff and not to each individual claim on which the plaintiff prevails, *id.* at 1200; that is, the total of both compensatory and punitive damages cannot exceed the caps for each plaintiff. *See* Suggs v. Servicemaster Educ. Food Management, 72 F.3d 1228 (6th Cir.1996); Hogan v. Bangor & Aroostook R.R., 61 F.3d 1034, 1037 (1st Cir.1995).

f. The courts are split over whether punitive damages can be awarded absent an award of compensatory damages. The split is summarized in Salitros v. Chrysler Corp., 306 F.3d 562 (8th Cir.2002):

> Chrysler attacks the jury's award of punitive damages on several grounds. First, Chrysler contends that punitive damages could not be awarded at all because the jury did not award compensatory damages.

> The federal courts are split several ways over the issue of whether federal law generally, and 42 U.S.C. § 1981a specifically, allow an award of punitive damages without a supporting award of actual or nominal damages.

> The most austere position is that taken by the Fourth Circuit in a Fair Housing Act case, that an award of punitive damages cannot stand without compensatory damages. *People Helpers Found. v. Richmond*, 12 F.3d 1321, 1327 (4th Cir.1993). The court summarized the common law rule as holding that "punitive damages are not appropriate in cases where a plaintiff has failed to demonstrate actionable harm." *Id.* The court held that the wide currency of the common-law rule made it reasonable to apply the rule in federal cases in which the statute was silent on the subject: "[W]e are persuaded by the law of a majority of the states, the reasoning behind the law, and the federal case law applying the rule in the absence of statutory language to the contrary that punitive damages are not recoverable in this circumstance." *Id.* Our Circuit long ago rejected the notion that compensatory damages, as opposed to nominal damages, were prerequisite to an award of punitives. *Goodwin v. Circuit Court of St. Louis County*, 729 F.2d 541, 548 (8th Cir.1984).

> Other courts have held that only where there has been a violation of *constitutional* rights, may punitive damages be awarded without an award of compensatory or nominal damages. In *Louisiana ACORN Fair Housing v. LeBlanc*, 211 F.3d 298, 303 (5th Cir.2000), *cert. denied*, 532 U.S. 904, 121 S.Ct. 1225, 149 L.Ed.2d 136 (2001), this rule led to reversal of an award of punitive damages in a Fair Housing Act case, because a violation of the Fair Housing Act did not amount to a constitutional violation. In *Alexander v. Riga*, 208 F.3d 419, 430 (3d Cir.2000), *cert. denied*, 531 U.S. 1069, 121 S.Ct. 757, 148 L.Ed.2d 660 (2001), the Third Circuit articulated the same rule, but reached the opposite result, reversing the district

court for failing to submit punitive damages to the jury in a Fair Housing Act case in which no actual damages were awarded. *See Searles v. Van Bebber*, 251 F.3d 869, 880–81 (10th Cir.2001) ("We note that, as a general rule, punitive damages may be recovered for constitutional violations without a showing of compensable injury."), *cert. denied*, 536 U.S. 904, 122 S.Ct. 2356, 153 L.Ed.2d 179 (2002). We have, in fact, held that liability for nominal damages follows automatically from a finding of certain constitutional violations, *Risdal v. Halford*, 209 F.3d 1071, 1072 (8th Cir.2000), and this would support a rule permitting punitive damages upon the finding of such violations. *See Goodwin*, 729 F.2d at 548 (punitive damages permitted in case where nominal, but not actual, damages awarded). However, no one has argued that retaliation for activity protected under the ADA is a constitutional violation, and so this rule would not be applicable in our case.

In the First and Eleventh Circuits, punitive damages may be awarded under section 1981a if there was an award of backpay, but no compensatory or nominal damages. *EEOC v. W & O, Inc.*, 213 F.3d 600, 615 (11th Cir.2000); *Provencher v. CVS Pharmacy*, 145 F.3d 5, 12 (1st Cir.1998). The First Circuit cited the reasoning of the Seventh Circuit in an earlier case that back pay is compensatory in function, and in fact represents the most direct economic loss in an employment discrimination case. *Provencher*, 145 F.3d at 11–12 (citing *Hennessy v. Penril Datacomm Networks, Inc.*, 69 F.3d 1344, 1352 (7th Cir.1995)). Therefore, the First Circuit held that an award of backpay should be sufficient to support an accompanying award of punitive damages. *Id.* However, the First Circuit has held that without compensatory or nominal damages or backpay, an award of punitives cannot stand. *Kerr-Selgas v. American Airlines, Inc.*, 69 F.3d 1205, 1214–15 (1st Cir.1995). The Eleventh Circuit reserved this question. *W & O*, 213 F.3d at 615 n. 5.

The most liberal position is that section 1981a does not require any other sort of damages to be awarded as a prerequisite to punitive damages. The Seventh Circuit held that section 1981a permits awards of punitive damages without compensatory damages or back pay, reasoning from "federal common law" in section 1983 cases. *Timm v. Progressive Steel Treating, Inc.*, 137 F.3d 1008, 1010 (7th Cir.1998). The Second Circuit also held that an award of actual or nominal damages is not a prerequisite to punitive damages, citing the plain language of section 1981a, which does not mention such a prerequisite, and the lack of a uniform common law rule on the subject. *Cush-Crawford v. Adchem Corp.*, 271 F.3d 352, 357–59 (2d Cir.2001).

Id. at 575–74.

Notes and Questions

1. Should the after-acquired evidence defense bar an award of compensatory or punitive damages? The EEOC has taken the position that broad

relief, including compensatory and punitive damages, can be awarded in after-acquired evidence cases. *See EEOC Guidance on After–Acquired Evidence*, 1995 Daily Lab.Rep. (BNA) 241, at d29 (Dec. 15, 1995). Do you agree with the EEOC's position?

2.　In *West v. Gibson,* 527 U.S. 212, 119 S.Ct. 1906, 144 L.Ed.2d 196 (1999), the Court resolved a split in the circuits on the issue whether the EEOC has the legal authority to require federal agencies to pay compensatory damages when they discriminate against federal applicants and employees in violation of Title VII. In a 5–4 decision written by Justice Breyer, the Court held that the EEOC has the authority to order federal agencies to pay compensatory damages. Justice Breyer relied upon the language, purpose, and history of the 1972 amendments to Title VII and the Civil Rights Act of 1991 to support his decision. The Court also reasoned that to deny the EEOC the authority to award compensatory damages against federal agencies would undermine the remedial scheme of Title VII by forcing into court employment discrimination claims that the EEOC might otherwise have resolved. Justice Kennedy, joined by Chief Justice Rehnquist, and Justices Scalia and Thomas, dissented on the ground that the EEOC cannot award compensatory damages against federal agencies because nothing in the statutory scheme of Title VII supports a clear and unambiguous waiver of the United States' sovereign immunity to compensatory damages.

The lower court had held that a federal applicant or employee need not exhaust administrative remedies before the EEOC because the EEOC did not have the authority to award compensatory damages. Gibson v. Brown, 137 F.3d 992 (7th Cir.1998), *vacated on other grounds sub nom.* West v. Gibson, 527 U.S. 212, 119 S.Ct. 1906, 144 L.Ed.2d 196 (1999). The Supreme Court refused to decide the exhaustion issue (which the plaintiff Gibson asked it to decide) because it fell outside of the issue on which certiorari had been granted. The Court remanded the issue of whether the claim of compensatory damages had been properly raised in the EEOC administrative process, and if so, then directed the lower court to decide the exhaustion issue. On remand, the Seventh Circuit held that failure to exhaust is a precondition to suing in courts rather than a jurisdictional requirement. Gibson v. West, 201 F.3d 990 (7th Cir.2000). Gibson ultimately lost because the court found that he had not raised the claim of compensatory damages in a timely fashion.

3.　A claim for compensatory damages that includes damages for emotional or mental distress may form the basis for the employer to demand that the plaintiff submit to a Rule 35 mental examination. Are there special problems posed by Rule 35 examinations in harassment cases in which emotional or psychological distress is claimed? For a discussion of the problem in employment discrimination cases, *see* Richard A. Bales & Priscilla Ray, *The Availability of Rule 35 Mental Examinations in Employment Discrimination Cases*, 16 Rev.Litig. 1 (1997).

4.　The statutory caps on compensatory and punitive damages under the Civil Rights Act of 1991 are not applicable to claims brought under § 1981, even if the § 1981 claim is joined with a claim that would be subject to the caps. *See* Kim v. Nash Finch Co., 123 F.3d 1046, 1067 (8th Cir.1997).

5. The Supreme Court has held that there are substantive and procedural constitutional limitations on punitive awards that state courts can award because the Constitution provides an upper limit on punitive damages so that a person has "fair notice not only of the conduct that will subject him to punishment but also the severity of the penalty that * * * may be imposed." BMW of North America, Inc. v. Gore, 517 U.S. 559, 574 116 S.Ct. 1589, 134 L.Ed.2d 809 (1996). *Gore* instructs courts reviewing punitive damages awards to consider three guideposts: (1) reprehensibility of defendant's conduct; (2) the disparity between the actual and potential harm suffered by the plaintiff and the punitive damages award; and (3) the difference between the punitive damages awarded by the jury and the civil penalties authorized or imposed in comparable cases. 517 U.S. at 575. In *State Farm Mutual Automobile Insurance Co. v. Campbell*, 538 U.S. 408, 123 S.Ct. 1513, 155 L.Ed.2d 585 (2003), the Court addressed the *Gore* guidepost in more considerable detail. *Gore* and *State Farm* appear to be equally applicable to statutory employment discrimination claims. *See* Ross v. Kansas City Power & Light Co., 293 F.3d 1041, 1048–49 (8th Cir.2002).

6. Compensatory and punitive damages can be awarded in race discrimination cases brought under § 1981 so recovery of these kinds of damages must be sought under § 1981 and not under Title VII where a plaintiff relies both on § 1981 and Title VII. *See* Lowery v. Circuit City Stores, Inc., 206 F.3d 431 (4th Cir.2000).

7. In *National R.R. Passenger Corp. v. Morgan*, 536 U.S. 101, 122 S.Ct. 2061, 153 L.Ed.2d 106 (2002), the Supreme Court held that because hostile work environment claims are deemed to be continuing violations, a successful plaintiff in a hostile work environment claim can recover damages for that portion of a hostile environment claim that falls outside of the period for filing a timely charge with the EEOC. Does this mean that a successful plaintiff in a hostile work environment case can recover *both* compensatory and punitive damages for the portion of the hostile work environment claim that falls outside of the period for filing a timely charge with the EEOC? *See* Madison v. IBP, Inc., 330 F.3d 1051 (8th Cir.2003) (on remand from the Supreme Court for reconsideration in light of *Morgan*). *Morgan* is inapplicable to race discrimination claims brought under Section 1981.

8. *The Availability of Compensatory and Punitive Damages in Class Actions*: The courts are split on whether compensatory and punitive damages can be recovered in class actions brought under Rule 23(b)(2) of the Federal Rules of Civil Procedure. In Allison v. Citgo Petroleum Corp., 151 F.3d 402 (5th Cir.1998), the court ruled against class certification in which compensatory and punitive damages are sought. The Second Circuit reached the opposite result in *Robinson v. Metro–North Commuter Railroad Co.*, 267 F.3d 147 (2d Cir.2001). This issue is explored in W. Lyle Stamps, *Getting Title VII Back on Track: Leaving Allison Behind the Robinson Line*, 17 BYU J.Pub.L. 411 (2003).

G.   LIQUIDATED DAMAGES

Liquidated damages under the Equal Pay Act and the ADEA are an additional amount awarded that is equal to the back pay award. 29

U.S.C. §§ 216(b), 626(b). (The term "liquidated damages" has a different meaning here than in contract law.) *See, e.g.,* Avitia v. Metropolitan Club of Chicago, Inc., 49 F.3d 1219 (7th Cir.1995) (Equal Pay Act case). Set-offs should be made before liquidated damages are determined. *See* Bhaya v. Westinghouse Elec. Corp., 624 F.Supp. 921 (E.D.Pa.1985), *vacated & remanded on other grounds*, 832 F.2d 258 (3d Cir.1987), *cert. denied*, 488 U.S. 1004, 109 S.Ct. 782, 102 L.Ed.2d 774 (1989).

Liquidated damages are recoverable in ADEA cases if the evidence supports a finding of a willful violation. 29 U.S.C. § 626(b). In *Trans World Airlines v. Thurston*, 469 U.S. 111, 105 S.Ct. 613, 83 L.Ed.2d 523 (1985), the Supreme Court resolved a conflict between the circuits on the standard of willfulness. The Court adopted a test requiring proof that the employer "knew or showed reckless disregard" whether the conduct was prohibited by the ADEA standard. *Id.* at 126, 105 S.Ct. at 624. This standard of willfulness was not met in *Thurston* because the policy at issue—the employer's refusal to permit less senior flight engineers who reached the age of sixty to bump other employees in order to avoid layoff—was adopted after consultation with counsel. In a later case, *McLaughlin v. Richland Shoe*, 486 U.S. 128, 108 S.Ct. 1677, 100 L.Ed.2d 115 (1988), the Court held that even if an employer acted unreasonably, but not recklessly, in determining its statutory obligation, such conduct would not be "willful" under the *Thurston* standard.

Thurston involved an ADEA challenge to a policy that was discriminatory on its face, but the lower courts had adopted differing standards of willfulness in ADEA disparate treatment cases. In *Hazen Paper Co. v. Biggins*, 507 U.S. 604, 113 S.Ct. 1701, 123 L.Ed.2d 338 (1993), reproduced in Chapter 12, the Supreme Court, in a unanimous decision, resolved the split in the circuits and held that the *Thurston* standard applies in disparate treatment ADEA cases.

Should both liquidated damages and prejudgment interest be awarded? The courts were in conflict on this issue before *Thurston*. After *Thurston*, most courts now hold that both forms of monetary relief cannot be awarded because liquidated damages are punitive in nature and generally prejudgment interest is not awarded on punitive damages. *See* Lindsey v. American Cast Iron Pipe Co., 810 F.2d 1094 (11th Cir.1987).

H. TAXATION OF AWARDS

Monetary awards that are recoverable under the *Moody* make-whole theory of relief include back pay, front pay, compensatory damages, punitive damages, liquidated damages, and prejudgment and post-judgment interest. Which of these items of monetary recovery should be subject to taxation under federal and state income tax laws has become an important and complex subject in employment discrimination law. The Supreme Court's decision in *United States v. Burke*, 504 U.S. 229, 112 S.Ct. 1867, 119 L.Ed.2d 34 (1992), was a major decision that ushered in the movement toward taxation of damages in employment discrimination law. In *Burke*, the Supreme Court held that back pay awards under Title VII are not excludable from taxable income because Title VII, prior to the Civil Rights Act of 1991, provided only for back pay and other equitable relief, not a "tort-type personal injury" recovery that would be excludable from gross income under the Internal Revenue Code. The decision in *Burke* arose in a Title VII case that was settled before 1991. In the Civil Rights Act of 1991, Congress amended Title VII, the ADA, and the Rehabilitation Act to allow compensatory and punitive damages.

Following *Burke*, the Internal Revenue Service first issued a ruling that provided that all the damages received under Title VII after the 1991 Act were excludable from gross income, but the Service later rescinded that ruling. In 1995, in *Commissioner v. Schleier*, 515 U.S. 323, 115 S.Ct. 2159, 132 L.Ed.2d 294, the Supreme Court held that neither back pay nor liquidated damages recovered under the ADEA were excludable from gross income. And in *O'Gilvie v. United States*, 519 U.S. 79, 117 S.Ct. 452, 136 L.Ed.2d 454 (1996), the Court held that punitive damages received in a tort action for personal injuries were not excludable from taxable gross income.

On August 20, 1996, President Clinton signed into law the Small Business Job Protection Act of 1996, Pub.L.No. 104–188, § 1605, 110 Stat. 1755, 1838 (codified at 26 U.S.C. § 104(a)), which amends the Internal Revenue Code to provide that all punitive damages are now taxable and that damages for emotional distress are excludable only if recovered for physical sickness or physical injury. The post-*Burke* developments in tax law make it clear that most monetary awards recovered in employment discrimination cases will be treated as taxable income. These monetary awards, whether received as a result of a judicial order or through a settlement, pose significant compliance problems for the recipients and potential ethical problems for their attorneys. For a discussion of some of these problems, *see* Laura A. Quigley, *IRS Nips at Damages Awards; Attorneys Confront Conflicts*, Nat'l L.J., Mar. 17, 1997, at B8; Douglas A. Kahn, *Compensatory and Punitive Damages for a Personal Injury: To Tax or Not to Tax?*, 2 Fla.Tax Rev. 327 (1994). *See also* Robert W. Wood, Taxation of Damage Awards and Settlement Payments, ch.3 (2d ed.1998).

In *United States v. Cleveland Indians Baseball Co.*, 532 U.S. 200, 121 S.Ct. 1433, 149 L.Ed.2d 401 (2001), the Supreme Court held that taxes on an award of back pay should be calculated as of the year the award is actually paid, and not the year it was earned. The Court agreed with the position of the IRS on this issue.

Questions

1. Should an "income tax bite" component be included in damage awards now that they are subject to federal taxation? *See* Sears v. Atchison, Topeka & Santa Fe Ry., 749 F.2d 1451 (10th Cir.1984) (yes), *cert. denied sub nom.* United Transp. Union v. Sears, 471 U.S. 1099, 105 S.Ct. 2322, 85

L.Ed.2d 840 (1985). If this component is included, what potential problems do you foresee?

2. Attorney's fees, as discussed in the next section, are recoverable under substantially all of the federal statutes prohibiting discrimination in employment. Suppose the parties to an employment discrimination lawsuit decide to settle the case and the employer is willing to agree to a handsome recovery, but is willing to issue only a single check in the amount of $500,000 to cover both the plaintiff's monetary recovery and attorney's fees. You represent the plaintiff in this situation.

a. Do you envision any ethical problems in simultaneously negotiating a settlement on behalf of your client and the amount of your attorney's fees? The Third Circuit, in *Prandini v. National Tea Co.*, 557 F.2d 1015 (3d Cir.1977), was one of the first circuits to adopt an ironclad rule barring fee negotiation until after the settlement of the merits of a case. In *Evans v. Jeff D.*, 475 U.S. 717, 106 S.Ct. 1531, 89 L.Ed.2d 747 (1986), the Supreme Court rejected the *Prandini* rule, unanimously approving the simultaneous negotiation of attorney's fees and the plaintiff's recovery.

b. What are the tax consequences for the client when her attorney's fees are awarded by a court or obtained through settlement? In *Jeff D.*, the Supreme Court adopted the view that Congress vested the entitlement to fees in the parties rather than in their counsel. *See also* Freeman v. B & B Assocs., 790 F.2d 145 (D.C.Cir.1986) (attorneys do not have standing to sue adversary parties for fees).

I. ATTORNEY'S FEES

1. ENTITLEMENT TO FEES

Traditionally, all parties involved in litigation in the United States are obligated to bear their own costs and attorney's fees. This is the so-called American no-fee rule. The American courts, particularly the federal courts, have carved out certain exceptions to the no-fee rule. One of the exceptions is the "private attorney general" rule. This exception empowers courts to impose the costs of litigation and attorney's fees on the losing party in litigation that is deemed to vindicate important public policy. *See, e.g.*, Newman v. Piggie Park Enterprises, Inc., 390 U.S. 400, 88 S.Ct. 964, 19 L.Ed.2d 1263 (1968). In *Alyeska Pipeline Service Co. v. Wilderness Society*, 421 U.S. 240, 95 S.Ct. 1612, 44 L.Ed.2d 141 (1975), the Supreme Court limited the application of the private attorney general doctrine to cases in which Congress has specifically enacted a statutory fee-shifting provision. A fee-shifting statute empowers a court to require one party to pay the other party's attorney's fees or attorney's fees and costs.

All of the major federal statutes prohibiting discrimination in employment have fee-shifting provisions. For example, § 706(k) of Title VII provides that a "court, in its discretion, may allow the prevailing party, other than the [EEOC] or the United States, a reasonable attorney's fee (including expert fees) as part of the costs * * *." The ADA, § 107, 42 U.S.C. § 12117, incorporates the fee-shifting provision of Title VII. Fees and costs for claims brought under § 1981 and the Fourteenth Amendment Equal Protection Clause are recoverable under the Civil Rights Attorney's Fees Awards Act of 1976, 42 U.S.C. § 1988. Fees can be awarded to a "prevailing plaintiff" or a "prevailing defendant" under Title VII, § 1981, or the ADA. But only "prevailing plaintiffs" are entitled to benefit from the fee-shifting provision in Equal Pay Act cases because the statute on fees provides that a court "shall * * * allow a reasonable attorney's fee to be paid by the defendant, and costs of the action." 29 U.S.C. § 216(b). *See* Horner v. Mary Institute, 613 F.2d 706 (8th Cir.1980). The ADEA incorporated the Fair Labor Standards Act provision on fees (the same statutory provision as is applicable in Equal Pay Act cases), but some courts have allowed prevailing defendants to recover fees and costs in ADEA cases where a court finds that the plaintiff litigated the case in bad faith. *See, e.g.*, Turlington v. Atlanta Gas Light Co., 135 F.3d 1428, 1437 (11th Cir.1998) (citing other circuits that allow fees under the bad faith rule).

2. STANDARDS FOR AN AWARD OF FEES

CHRISTIANSBURG GARMENT CO. v. EEOC

Supreme Court of the United States, 1978.
434 U.S. 412, 98 S.Ct. 694, 54 L.Ed.2d 648.

JUSTICE STEWART delivered the opinion of the Court.

Section 706(k) of Title VII of the Civil Rights Act of 1964 provides:

"In any action or proceeding under this title the court, in its discretion, may allow the prevailing party * * * a reasonable attorney's fee * * *."

The question in this case is under what circumstances an attorney's fee should be allowed when the defendant is the prevailing party in a Title VII action—a question about which the federal courts have expressed divergent views.

* * *

In *Newman v. Piggie Park Enterprises*, 390 U.S. 400, 88 S.Ct. 964, 19 L.Ed.2d 1263, the Court considered a substantially identical statute authorizing the award of attorney's fees under Title II of the Civil Rights Act of 1964. In that case the plaintiffs had prevailed, and the Court of Appeals had held that they should be awarded their attorney's fees "only to the extent that the respondents' defenses had been advanced 'for purposes of delay and not in good faith.'" We ruled that this "subjective standard" did not properly effectuate the purposes of the counsel-fee provision of Title II. Relying primarily on the intent of Congress to cast a Title II plaintiff in the role of "a 'private attorney general,' vindicating a policy that Congress considered of the highest priority," we held that a prevailing plaintiff under Title II "should ordinarily recover an attorney's fee unless special circumstances would render such an award unjust." We noted in passing that if the objective of Congress had been to permit the award of attorney's fees only against defendants who had acted in bad faith, "no new statutory provision would have been necessary," since even the American common-law rule allows the award of attorney's fees in those exceptional circumstances.

In *Albemarle Paper Co. v. Moody*, 422 U.S. 405, 95 S.Ct. 2362, 45 L.Ed.2d 280, the Court made clear that the *Piggie Park* standard of awarding attorney's fees to a successful plaintiff is equally applicable in an action under Title VII of the Civil Rights Act. It can thus be taken as established, as the parties in this case both acknowledge, that under § 706(k) of Title VII a prevailing plaintiff ordinarily is to be awarded attorney's fees in all but special circumstances.

III

* * *

The company contends that the *Piggie Park* criterion for a successful plaintiff should apply equally as a guide to the award of attorney's fees to a successful defendant. Its submission, in short, is that every prevailing defendant in a Title VII action should receive an allowance of attorney's fees "unless special circumstances would render such an award unjust." The respondent Commission, by contrast, argues that the prevailing defendant should receive an award of attorney's fees only when it is found that the plaintiff's action was brought in bad faith. We have concluded that neither of these positions is correct.

A

* * * The terms of § 706(k) provide no indication whatever of the circumstances under which either a plaintiff or a defendant should be entitled to attorney's fees. And a moment's reflection reveals that there are at least two strong equitable considerations counseling an attorney's fee award to a prevailing Title VII plaintiff that are wholly absent in the case of a prevailing Title VII defendant.

First, as emphasized so forcefully in *Piggie Park*, the plaintiff is the chosen instrument of Congress to vindicate "a policy that Congress considered of the highest priority." Second, when a district court awards counsel fees to a prevailing plaintiff, it is awarding them against a violator of federal law. As the Court of Appeals clearly perceived, "these policy considerations which support the award of fees to a prevailing plaintiff are not present in the case of a prevailing defendant." A successful defendant seeking counsel fees under § 706(k) must rely on quite different equitable considerations.

But if the company's position is untenable, the Commission's argument also misses the mark. It seems clear, in short, that in enacting § 706(k) Congress did not intend to permit the award of attorney's fees to a prevailing defendant only in a situation where the plaintiff was motivated by bad faith in bringing the action. * * *

B

The sparse legislative history of § 706(k) reveals little more than the barest outlines of a proper accommodation of the competing considerations we have discussed. * * * The Court of Appeals for the District of Columbia Circuit seems to have drawn the maximum significance from the Senate debates when it concluded:

> [From these debates] two purposes for § 706(k) emerge. First, Congress desired to "make it easier for a plaintiff of limited means to bring a meritorious suit" * * *. But second, and equally important, Congress intended to "deter the bringing of lawsuits without foundation" by providing that the "prevailing party"—be it plaintiff or defendant—could obtain legal fees.

Grubbs v. Butz, 179 U.S. App. D.C. 18, 20, 548 F.2d 973, 975.

The first federal appellate court to consider what criteria should govern the award of attorney's fees to a prevailing Title VII defendant was the Court of Appeals for the Third Circuit in *United States Steel Corp. v. United States*, 519 F.2d 359. There a District Court had denied a fee award to a defendant that had successfully resisted a Commission demand for documents, the court finding that the Commission's action had not been " 'unfounded, meritless, frivolous or vexatiously brought.' " The Court of Appeals concluded that the District Court had not abused its discretion in denying the award. A similar standard was adopted by the Court of Appeals for the Second Circuit in *Carrion v. Yeshiva University*, 535 F.2d 722. In upholding an attorney's fee award to a successful defendant, that court stated that such awards should be permitted "not routinely, not simply because he succeeds, but only where the action brought is found to be unreasonable, frivolous, meritless or vexatious." *Id.* at 727.

To the extent that abstract words can deal with concrete cases, we think that the concept embodied in the language adopted by these two Courts of Appeals is correct. We would qualify their words only by pointing out that the term "meritless" is to be understood as meaning groundless or without foundation, rather than simply that the plaintiff has ultimately lost his case, and that the term "vexatious" in no way implies that the plaintiff's subjective bad faith is a necessary prerequisite to a fee award against him. In sum, a district court may in its discretion award attorney's fees to a prevailing defendant in a Title VII case upon a finding that the plaintiff's action was frivolous, unreasonable, or without foundation, even though not brought in subjective bad faith.

In applying these criteria, it is important that a district court resist the understandable temptation to engage in post hoc reasoning by concluding that, because a plaintiff did not ultimately prevail, his action must have been unreasonable or without foundation. This kind of hindsight logic could discourage all but the most airtight claims, for seldom can a prospective plaintiff be sure of ultimate success. No matter how honest one's belief that he has been the victim of discrimination, no matter how meritorious one's claim may appear at the outset, the course of litigation is rarely predictable. Decisive facts may not emerge until discovery or trial. The law may change or clarify in the midst of litigation. Even when the law or the facts appear questionable or unfavorable at the outset, a party may have an entirely reasonable ground for bringing suit.

That § 706(k) allows fee awards only to prevailing private plaintiffs should assure that this statutory provision will not in itself operate as an incentive to the bringing of claims that have little chance of success. To take the further step of assessing attorney's fees against plaintiffs simply because they do not finally prevail would substantially add to the risks inhering in most litigation and would undercut the efforts of Congress to promote the vigorous enforcement of the provisions of Title VII. Hence, a plaintiff should not be assessed his opponent's attorney's fees unless a court finds that his claim was frivolous, unreasonable, or groundless, or that the plaintiff continued to litigate after it clearly became so. And, needless to say, if a plaintiff is found to have brought or continued such a claim in bad faith, there will be an even stronger basis for charging him with the attorney's fees incurred by the defense.

V

* * * [T]he judgment of the Court of Appeals upholding the decision of the District Court is affirmed.

Notes and Questions

1. It appears that *Christiansburg Garment* establishes a strong, but rebuttable, presumption in favor of awards of attorney's fees for prevailing plaintiffs and a corresponding rebuttable presumption against awards of attorney's fees for prevailing defendants.

a. Are you persuaded by the Court's reasoning in *Christiansburg Garment* that different standards should control awards of attorney's fees to prevailing plaintiffs and prevailing defendants?

b. Do the separate standards strike the appropriate balance between the policy of discouraging frivolous litigation and encouraging private enforcement of civil rights laws?

2. In *Hensley v. Eckerhart*, 461 U.S. 424, 437, 103 S.Ct. 1933, 1941, 76 L.Ed.2d 40 (1983), the Supreme Court observed that "[a] request for attorney's fees should not result in a second major litigation. Ideally, of course, litigants will settle the amount of a fee." Disputes about attorney's fees awards have become a major issue in civil rights litigation, and a substantial number of cases have reached the Supreme Court. What might account for the significant amount of time spent on litigating attorney's fees in civil rights cases?

3. There have been only a few cases in which courts have found special circumstances sufficient to deny fees to prevailing plaintiffs. *See, e.g.*, Phelps v. Hamilton, 120 F.3d 1126 (10th Cir.1997). In *Marquart v. Lodge 837, International Association of Machinists & Aerospace Workers*, 26 F.3d 842, 848–49 (8th Cir.1994), the Eighth Circuit, after critically examining the

Christiansburg Garment standards for awards of fees to prevailing defendants, noted that prevailing defendants should be awarded fees only in the narrowest of circumstances. *See generally* Michael J. McNamara, Note, *Judicial Discretion and the 1976 Civil Rights Attorney's Fees Awards Act: What Special Circumstances Render an Award Unjust?*, 51 Fordham L.Rev. 320 (1982).

4. In *Hensley v. Eckerhart*, 461 U.S. 424, 433, 103 S.Ct. 1933, 1939, 76 L.Ed.2d 40 (1983), the Court held that

> [a] plaintiff must be a "prevailing party" to recover an attorney's fee under § 1988. The standard for making this threshold determination has been framed in various ways. A typical formulation is that "plaintiffs may be considered 'prevailing parties' for attorney's fees purposes if they succeed on any significant issue in litigation which achieves some of the benefit the parties sought in bringing suit." Nadeau v. Helgemoe, 581 F.2d 275, 278–79 (1st Cir.1978). This is a generous formulation that brings the plaintiff only across the statutory threshold. It remains for the district court to determine what fee is "reasonable."

Hensley did not completely resolve the issue on the standard for determining prevailing plaintiff status.

The Supreme Court revisited the issue in *Texas State Teachers Association v. Garland Independent School District*, 489 U.S. 782, 109 S.Ct. 1486, 103 L.Ed.2d 866 (1989), to reject the "central issue" test that the Fifth Circuit had adopted. *Garland* also seemed to endorse the "catalyst" theory for determining prevailing party status. The catalyst theory holds that a plaintiff is the prevailing party if his lawsuit is a substantial factor in bringing about the employer's compliance with the law. In a more recent case, *Farrar v. Hobby*, 506 U.S. 103, 113 S.Ct. 566, 121 L.Ed.2d 494 (1992), the Supreme Court held that a civil rights plaintiff who received only nominal damages was entitled to prevailing party status. But the Court nevertheless sanctioned a rule that would limit the fee award. As a result of *Farrar*, the lower courts are split on the issue of whether the catalyst theory survives *Farrar*. *Compare* S–1 and S–2 v. State Board of Education, 21 F.3d 49, 51 (4th Cir.) (en banc), *cert. denied*, 513 U.S. 876, 115 S.Ct. 205, 130 L.Ed.2d 135 (1994) (catalyst theory does not survive *Farrar*) *with* Beard v. Teska, 31 F.3d 942, 951 (10th Cir.1994) (catalyst theory does survive *Farrar*).

5. In *Buckhannon Board & Care Home, Inc. v. West Virginia Department of Health & Human Resources*, 532 U.S. 598, 121 S.Ct. 1835, 149 L.Ed.2d 855 (2001), in a 5–4 decision written by Justice Rehnquist, the Court rejected the catalyst theory as a basis for obtaining prevailing party status. The catalyst theory allowed the plaintiff to obtain fees as a prevailing party if a court were to decide that the plaintiff's lawsuit was deemed to be the "catalyst" for a defendant's voluntary change in its conduct after the lawsuit was filed. Buckhannon held that the term "prevailing party" requires that a plaintiff obtain a judgment or similar form of judicial relief as a predicate for attorney's fees.

6. *Calculating a Reasonable Fee*: Prior to *Hensley*, the courts had adopted various standards for determining what constitutes a reasonable fee.

See Hensley, 461 U.S. at 429–34, 103 S.Ct. at 1937–40. *Hensley* endorsed the "lodestar" method that is now the predominant method for calculating a reasonable fee. As explained by the Supreme Court in *Hensley*,

> [t]he most useful starting point for determining the amount of a reasonable fee is the number of hours reasonably expended on the litigation multiplied by a reasonable hourly rate. This calculation provides an objective basis on which to make an initial estimate of the value of a lawyer's services. The party seeking an award of fees should submit evidence supporting the hours worked and rates claimed. Where the documentation of hours is inadequate, the district court may reduce the award accordingly.

Id. at 433, 103 S.Ct. at 1939.

7. *Reasonable Number of Hours*: The first step under the lodestar approach is to ascertain the number of hours "reasonably expended." Under *Hensley*, excessive, redundant, or otherwise unnecessary hours should be excluded from the calculation. 461 U.S. at 434, 103 S.Ct. at 1939–40. *Hensley* thus requires fees claimants to exercise billing judgment. Billing judgment requires the fees claimant to exclude hours that would be unreasonable to bill to paying clients. Time spent in administrative proceedings before the EEOC are compensable because exhaustion of administrative procedures is required. *See* New York Gaslight Club, Inc. v. Carey, 447 U.S. 54, 100 S.Ct. 2024, 64 L.Ed.2d 723 (1980). Reasonable hours also includes time spent by law clerks and paralegals even though their time is compensated at a lower hourly rate than the time spent by an attorney. *See* Missouri v. Jenkins, 491 U.S. 274, 109 S.Ct. 2463, 105 L.Ed.2d 229 (1989).

One court has identified three categories of questions that arise in litigation over whether the number of hours are reasonable or excessive:

> (1) factual questions about whether the lawyer actually worked the hours claimed or is padding the account; (2) legal questions about whether the work performed is sufficiently related to the points on which the client prevailed as to be compensable; and (3) mixed questions about whether the lawyer used poor judgment in spending too many hours on some part of the case or by unnecessarily duplicating the work of co-counsel.

Coulter v. Tennessee, 805 F.2d 146, 150–51 (6th Cir.1986), *cert. denied*, 482 U.S. 914, 107 S.Ct. 3186, 96 L.Ed.2d 674 (1987).

Suppose an attorney who represented a prevailing party failed to exercise billing judgment by substantially padding the hours, requested an unreasonable hourly rate, billed the client for hours spent on other services, and agreed to split the fee with the client. Should a fee be allowed? Are there other sanctions that would be appropriate? *See* Keener v. Department of the Army, 136 F.R.D. 140 (M.D.Tenn.1991), *aff'd in unreported opinion*, 956 F.2d 269 (6th Cir.1992).

Some courts have held that fees will be denied to a prevailing party if contemporaneous time records are not kept. *See* Grendel's Den, Inc. v. Larkin, 749 F.2d 945, 952 (1st Cir.1984); Ramos v. Lamm, 713 F.2d 546, 553 (10th Cir.1983); New York State Ass'n of Retarded Children, Inc. v. Carey, 711 F.2d 1136, 1147 (2d Cir.1983).

8. *Reasonable Hourly Rate*: Unlike attorneys with major law firms, many public interest attorneys, small practitioners, legal services attorneys, and some civil rights attorneys do not have established hourly billing rates. What standard should determine the reasonable hourly rate for this category of attorney? In *Blum v. Stenson*, 465 U.S. 886, 104 S.Ct. 1541, 79 L.Ed.2d 891 (1984), the Supreme Court adopted the prevailing market rate standard. The "prevailing market rate" is broadly defined as "those [rates] prevailing in the community for similar services by lawyers of reasonably comparable skill, experience and reputation." *Id.* at 896, 104 S.Ct. at 1547. The prevailing market rate is applicable regardless of whether the plaintiff is represented by private or nonprofit counsel.

9. *Enhancement to the Lodestar*: In *City of Burlington v. Dague*, 505 U.S. 557, 562, 112 S.Ct. 2638, 2641, 120 L.Ed.2d 449 (1992), the Court held that the lodestar method has "become the guiding light of our fee-shifting jurisprudence," establishing a "strong presumption" that this method yields a "reasonable" fee. Whether a lodestar amount should be increased because of a contingency or risk-of-loss factor was not ultimately decided until *Dague*. Lower courts prior to *Dague* had often used a contingency factor or risk multiplier to enhance the lodestar on the ground that many lawyers who represent civil rights claimants risk not getting a fee at all because civil rights plaintiffs simply do not have the resources to pay fees. If the plaintiff prevailed on the merits, then the attorney would petition for fees; otherwise the attorney was not paid. Earlier Supreme Court cases tended to support an upward adjustment based upon the contingency factor, but in *Dague*, a majority of the Court held that contingency enhancement is never appropriate. *Id.* at 566, 112 S.Ct. at 2643.

10. For a comprehensive treatment of attorney's fees under fee-shifting statutes, *see, e.g.*, Mary Francis Derfner & Authur Wolf, Court Awarded Attorney Fees (1997) (3 vols.); Alba Conte, Attorney Fee Awards (2d ed.1993); Martin A. Schwartz & John E. Kirklin, 2 Section 1983 Litigation: Claims, Defenses and Fees (1991).

11. Is a plaintiff who recovers both damages and attorney's fees in an employment discrimination case required to include both the damages and the fees in gross income for income tax purposes if the attorney must also report his attorney's fees in his gross income? If so, is this double taxation of attorney's fees good public policy? This problem was illustrated in powerful way in a New York Times article. The plaintiff, a police officer brought a sex discrimination and sexual harassment case. She was eventually awarded $300,000, attorney's fees of $850,000, and costs in the amount of $100,000. Under current law, she is responsible for paying income taxes on both her award and the attorney's fees award, which combined is over $1 million dollars. Her attorney says that the plaintiff "loses every penny of the award * * * plus she will end up owing the Internal Revenue Service $99,000." Adam Liptak, *Tax Bill Exceeds Award to Officer in Sex Bias Suit*, N.Y. Times, Aug. 11, 2002, at A 12.

There is currently a split among the circuits on this issue. Some courts of appeals hold that a client may exclude contingency fees from gross income. Other courts of appeals and the Tax Court hold that contingency fees must be included in gross income. If contingency fees are not excludable from a client's income, fees are potentially subject to double taxation: once to the plaintiff as part of the total monetary recovery the plaintiff receives (damages and attorney's fees); and once to the plaintiff's attorney as income for services rendered. *See, e.g.*, Campbell v. C.I.R., 274 F.3d 1312, 1314 (10th Cir.2001) (collecting cases), *cert. denied sub nom.* Hukkanen–Campbell v. C.I.R., 535 U.S. 1056 , 122 S.Ct. 1915, 152 L.Ed.2d 824 (2002); Cornelius Cowles, *To Include or Exclude? The Circuit Court Split on Double Taxation of Contingent Fees*, 28 Mar.Vt.B.J. 25 (2002). In *Campbell*, the Tenth Circuit, which ruled that contingency fees are includable in gross income, recognized that the outcome depends, in substantial part, on the "unique provisions of a particular state's attorney lien statute." *Id.* at 1314. Although the court recognized also that a uniform rule on the issue "is desirable," it held that it is the responsibility of Congress and not the courts to correct the problem. *Id.*

Legislation has been introduced in Congress on several occasions to eliminate "double-taxation" of attorney's fees. See H.Rept. No. 108–126; Marcia Coyle, *Bill to Remove Tax on Awards May See Action*, N.Y.L.J., Aug. 19, 2002, at 3. See generally, Stephen D. Feldman, Comment, *Exclusion of Contingent Attorney's Fees from Gross Income*, 68 U.Chi.L.Rev. 1309 (2001).

Note: Insuring Against Employment Discrimination Claims

Employers commonly obtain insurance to protect themselves against the numerous claims that might be made against them that arise in the course of doing business. The more traditional of these insurance policies are directors and officers (D & O) policies and comprehensive general liability (CGL) policies. Employers, concerned about liability for their employment decisions, including liability for unlawful employment discrimination, increasingly have begun to seek more effective insurance coverage against these claims because of the mixed results in coverage under the more traditional D & O and CGL policies. The move toward insurance against employment discrimination claims is fueled not only by the growing number of statutory and common law claims now available to applicants and employees, but also by the headline-grabbing, multimillion dollar verdicts and settlements in employment discrimination cases. For example, in *Weeks v. Baker & McKenzie*, 76 Fair Empl.Prac.Cas. (BNA) 1219, 63 Cal.App.4th 1128, 74 Cal.Rptr.2d 510 (1998), a California court affirmed a multimillion dollar award in a sexual harassment case, and Texaco settled a race discrimination claim reported to be worth about $176 million, *see* Roberts v. Texaco, Inc., 979 F.Supp. 185, 191 n. 6 (S.D.N.Y.1997). Also, attorney's fees in successful employment discrimination cases can be substantial. *See, e.g.*, Darryl Van Duch, *Merrill Deal Paves Way for New ADR*, Nat'l L.J., May 18, 1998, at B1, B4 (noting multimillion dollar payments for legal fees provided in settlements of class action employment discrimination suits).

A new type of insurance now available to defendants is called Employment Practices Liability Insurance (EPLI). EPLI policies are specifically drafted to cover employment discrimination claims. For a recent comprehensive treatment of insurance coverage of employment discrimination claims under traditional policies and EPLI policies, see

Francis J. Mootz, III, *Insurance Coverage of Employment Discrimination Claims*, 52 U.Miami L.Rev. 1 (1997).

As a matter of policy, should defendants be permitted to obtain insurance for employment discrimination claims? If so, should they be allowed to insure against all types of claims, e.g., disparate impact (nonintentional) and disparate treatment (intentional) claims, including, for example, claims of sexual harassment and retaliation? What about employment discrimination claims based upon the Equal Protection Clause or the Freedom of Religion Clauses of the Constitution? Should employers be allowed to insure against all types of monetary remedies, e.g., punitive damages or liquidated damages that are punitive in nature? Can such insurance coverage introduce an additional overseer (the insurance carrier) with a stake in curbing violations of antidiscrimination laws? Consider also that insurance is but one form of risk management that prudent employers use to protect their profit margins in a competitive economy.

Chapter 17

AFFIRMATIVE ACTION

A. INTRODUCTION

In the efforts of the United States government to implement its policies on equal employment opportunity, perhaps no issue has generated more controversy and so little agreement than the appropriateness of affirmative action as a remedy for discrimination in both public and private employment. As one commentator has explained:

> To its critics, affirmative action is both a euphemism for discrimination against white men and a system that bureaucratizes the entire society at the cost of meritocratic decision making; it is a symbol for all that has gone wrong with American society since the sixties. To its supporters, it is a first step towards remedying the crime of slavery and eliminating the discriminatory preferences that have guaranteed white men the easiest paths to wealth and power; it is a symbol of justice, and a promise of a future of hope.

David Benjamin Oppenheimer, *Distinguishing Five Models of Affirmative Action*, 4 Berkeley Women's L.J. 42, 42 (1988–89). These competing perspectives on affirmative action derive, in part, from the different experiences of many blacks and whites. Consider the following hypothetical workers, one white and one black, described by Professor David Chang:

> Imagine a white person. He is of moderate means, attended suburban schools, and has worked hard to become a police officer. Today he is unemployed, however, because the government, his employer, has adopted an affirmative action program. Suffering from a governmental choice to cure the lingering effects of historic injustices, he is an "innocent victim" of the racial discrimination pervasive in America's past. He believes this is unfair. He hopes it is unconstitutional.

> Now imagine a black person. He is poor, attended inner city schools, and has worked hard because he wants to become a police officer. He will not achieve this goal, however, because he cannot pass the government's qualifying test. Suffering from a governmental choice not to address the lingering effects of historic injustices,

he, also, is an "innocent victim" of the racial discrimination in America's past. He believes this is unfair. He hopes it is unconstitutional.

David Chang, *Discriminatory Impact, Affirmative Action, and Innocent Victims: Judicial Conservatism or Conservative Justices*, 91 Colum.L.Rev. 790, 790–91 (1991). Similar stories can be told with respect to sex discrimination.

This chapter explores affirmative action as a means of implementing equality in the workplace. The remainder of this section discusses the meaning of affirmative action and provides a brief history of the evolution of affirmative action as a remedy for discrimination. Although the major focus of this chapter is on affirmative action in the workplace under statutes prohibiting discrimination in employment, Section B of this chapter briefly examines the legality of affirmative action under the Fifth and Fourteenth Amendments because constitutional equal protection analysis provides the background for analyzing affirmative action under Title VII. It also applies directly to public employers and to court-ordered remedial affirmative action. Section C, which is the heart of this chapter, deals with the propriety of using affirmative action to prohibit discrimination in the workplace. *Griggs v. Duke Power Co.*, reproduced in Chapter 4, has become a focal point of attempts to define the political and legal contours of affirmative action. *See, e.g.*, Alfred W. Blumrosen, *The Legacy of* Griggs: *Social Progress and Subjective Judgments*, 63 Chi.-Kent L.Rev. 1, 6 (1987) ("*Griggs* provides the underlying justification for race conscious affirmative action programs under Title VII.").

The United States Commission on Civil Rights defines affirmative action as "any measure, beyond simple termination of a discriminatory practice, adopted to correct or compensate for past or present discrimination or to prevent discrimination from recurring in the future." United States Commission on Civil Rights, Statement on Affirmative Action 2 (1977). Commentators have expanded on this definition:

> The term "affirmative action," although embodying a variety of concepts, generally can be used to describe any plan or program designed to redress past unlawful discrimination, or its present effects, against women or racial and ethnic minorities by considering such characteristics in allocating "public or private economic or other resources or opportunities in our society," particularly by increasing participation of these groups in the work force and in government programs.

Michael K. Braswell, Gary A. Moore & Stephen L. Poe, *Affirmative Action: An Assessment of Its Continuing Role in Employment Discrimination Policy*, 57 Alb.L.Rev. 365, 366 (1993) (citations omitted). The relationship between the principle of equality and the policy of affirmative action is complex. Consider the following observation:

> The affirmative action concept embodies a policy decision that some forms of race-conscious remedies are necessary to improve the social and economic status of blacks in our society. That policy decision, however, cannot be isolated from the history that gave rise to the

affirmative action concept. When viewed in light of that history—decades of blatant public and private discrimination against blacks *as a group*—the underlying premise of affirmative action is manifest: If the chasm between "equality" as an abstract proposition and "equality" as a reality is to be bridged, something more is needed than mere prohibitions of positive acts of discrimination and the substitution of passive neutrality. That something more, the affirmative action concept dictates, must include race-conscious remedies.

Robert Belton, *Discrimination and Affirmative Action: An Analysis of Competing Theories of Equality and* Weber, 59 N.C.L.Rev. 531, 534 (1981).

Professor David Oppenheimer has identified five models of affirmative action:

> [S]trict quotas favoring women or minorities (Model I); preference systems in which women or minorities are given some preference over white men (Model II); self-examination plans in which the failure to reach expected goals within expected periods of time triggers self-study, to determine whether discrimination is interfering with a decisionmaking process (Model III); outreach plans in which attempts are made to include more women and minorities within the pool of persons from which selections are made (Model IV); and, affirmative commitments not to discriminate (Model V).

Oppenheimer, *supra*, at 42. Model IV is sometimes referred to as the "pool problem"; its purpose is to eliminate the "good old boy" network—meaning the informal network of white males—as the basis for defining the pool of candidates for a particular job. Which of the models of affirmative action described by Professor Oppenheimer is the most controversial? Which is the least controversial? Why?

The premise of affirmative action is that it provides a remedy for the past and continuing effects of a long history of societal race and sex discrimination in a broad range of activities, including employment. The phrase "societal discrimination" is frequently used in the legal literature on affirmative action, but scholars and other commentators rarely attempt to define the concept. On several occasions, the Supreme Court has acknowledged the existence of societal discrimination, without attempting to articulate its precise meaning. For example, in *City of Richmond v. J.A. Croson Co.*, 488 U.S. 469, 109 S.Ct. 706, 102 L.Ed.2d 854 (1989), Justice O'Connor, writing for the plurality, observed that "the sorry history of both private and public discrimination in this country has contributed to a lack of opportunities for black entrepreneurs * * *." 488 U.S. at 499, 109 S.Ct. at 724. In *Wards Cove Packing Co. v. Atonio*, 490 U.S. 642, 662, 109 S.Ct. 2115, 2127, 104 L.Ed.2d 733 (1989), reproduced in Chapter 4, Justice Blackmun, in dissent, criticized the Court's decision by questioning whether "the majority still believes that race discrimination * * * against nonwhites * * * is a problem in our society." Justice White, who wrote the majority opinion in *Wards*

Cove, responded, "Of course, it is unfortunately true that race discrimination exists in our country." *Id.* at 650 n.4, 109 S.Ct. at 2121 n.4. And, in *Adarand Constructors, Inc. v. Pena*, 515 U.S. 200, 237, 115 S.Ct. 2097, 2117, 132 L.Ed.2d 158 (1995), Justice O'Connor, for the majority, observed that "[t]he unhappy persistence of both the practice and lingering effects of racial discrimination against minority groups in this country is an unfortunate reality, and the government is not disqualified from acting in response to it." In *Wygant v. Jackson Board of Education*, 476 U.S. 267, 276, 106 S.Ct. 1842, 1848, 90 L.Ed.2d 260 (1986), the Court also acknowledged the reality of past "societal discrimination," but concluded that the concept was "too amorphous" to justify remediation.

In *Grutter v. Bollinger*, 539 U.S. 306, 123 S.Ct. 2325, 156 L.Ed.2d 304 (2003), the Supreme Court discussed the effect of societal discrimination on the ability of students to be admitted to law school. It stated "By virtue of our Nation's struggle with racial inequality, [underrepresented minority students] are both likely to have experiences of particular importance to the Law School's mission, and less likely to be admitted in meaningful numbers on criteria that ignore those experiences." *Id.*, 123 S.Ct. 2325, 2344. As part of this analysis, it stated that the presence of societal discrimination affects a person's viewpoint, thereby making them valuable in creating a diverse student body ("Just as growing up in a particular region or having particular professional experiences is likely to affect an individual's views, so too is one's own unique experience of being a racial minority in a society, like our own, in which race unfortunately still matters." *Id.*, 123 S.Ct. 2325, 2341.) Justice O'Connor concluded her opinion with the following sentiment, "It has been 25 years since Justice Powell first approved the use of race to further an interest in student body diversity in the context of public higher education. Since that time, the number of minority applicants with high grades and test scores has indeed increased. * * * We expect that 25 years from now, the use of racial preferences will no longer be necessary to further the interest approved today." *Id.*, 123 S.Ct. 2325, 2346. Do you agree with Justice O'Connor's conclusion?

So what is "societal discrimination"? One commentator stated that it is "nothing more than an accumulation of wrongs on the part of governmental and private entities that cannot be identified with particularity at the present time." Robert Allen Sedler, *Beyond* Bakke: *The Constitution and Redressing the Social History of Racism*, 14 Harv.C.R.-C.L.L.Rev. 133, 157 (1979). Another explanation is that it

> is caused by broad social factors and attitudes, and is manifested by general patterns of inequality. The legal significance of the concept is that it is not ascribed to a particular entity, such as an employer, university, or governmental unit. Rather it is the result of pervasive racism, which has affected the structure and expectations of society * * *. Where discrimination can be tied to a specific source it is legally actionable under various substantive theories, including several titles of the 1964 Civil Rights Act, constitutional guarantees,

and the Reconstruction Statutes. On the other hand, societal discrimination is a justification for voluntary affirmative action, rather than a basis for legal liability and corrective relief.

Nancy E. Dowd, Note, Bakke *and* Weber: *The Concept of Societal Discrimination*, 11 Loy.U.Chi.L.J. 297, 297–98 (1980).

Notes and Questions

1. How would you define "affirmative action?" Is it "reverse discrimination?" And if it is "reverse discrimination," how do you define "reverse discrimination"? See also the cases discussed in Chapter 3.

2. How would you evaluate the claim that minorities and women suffer from the effects of "societal discrimination" today? What about Asian–Americans, Latinos/as, persons with disabilities, or persons over forty years of age? Consider the observation of Justice John Marshall Harlan in 1896:

> The white race deems itself to be the dominant race in this country. And so it is, in prestige, in achievements, in education, in wealth and in power. So, I doubt not, it will continue to be for all time, if it remains true to its great heritage, and holds fast to the principles of constitutional liberty.

Plessy v. Ferguson, 163 U.S. 537, 559, 16 S.Ct. 1138, 1146, 41 L.Ed. 256 (1896) (Harlan, J., dissenting).

3. How does your perspective on the causes of race or sex discrimination influence your views on "affirmative action," "societal discrimination," and "reverse discrimination"? Consider the following argument by Professor Alan Freeman:

> The concept of "racial discrimination" may be approached from the perspective of either its victim or its perpetrator. From the victim's perspective, racial discrimination describes those conditions of actual social existence as a member of a perpetual underclass. This perspective includes both the objective conditions of life—lack of jobs, lack of money, lack of housing—and the consciousness associated with those objective conditions—lack of choice and lack of human individuality in being forever perceived as a member of a group rather than as an individual. The perpetrator perspective sees racial discrimination not as conditions, but as actions, or series of actions, inflicted on the victim by the perpetrator. The focus is more on what particular perpetrators have done or are doing to some victims than it is on the overall life situation of the victim's class.

> The victim, or "condition," conception of racial discrimination suggests that the problem will not be solved until the conditions associated with it have been eliminated. To remedy the condition of racial discrimination would demand affirmative efforts to change the condition. The remedial dimension of the perpetrator perspective, however, is negative. The task is merely to neutralize the inappropriate conduct of the perpetrator.

* * *

The perpetrator perspective presupposes a world composed of atomistic individuals whose actions are outside of and apart from the social fabric and without historical continuity. From this perspective, the law views racial discrimination not as a social phenomenon, but merely as the misguided conduct of particular actors.

Alan David Freeman, *Legitimizing Racial Discrimination Through Antidiscrimination Law: A Critical Review of Supreme Court Doctrine*, 62 Minn. L.Rev. 1049, 1052–54 (1978).

4. *Innocent Victim*: One argument against affirmative action as a remedy for discrimination is that it infringes upon the rights of "innocent victims." *See, e.g.*, William Van Alstyne, *Rites of Passage: Race, the Supreme Court, and the Constitution*, 46 U.Chi.L.Rev. 775 (1979). Which of the two hypothetical workers, described by Professor Chang, *supra*, is an "innocent victim"? Professor Michel Rosenfeld has argued that "affirmative action designed to remedy the present effects of past discrimination does not take away from 'innocent' whites anything that they have rightfully earned," but only denies them "the [undeserved] increased prospects of success gained through the unjust treatment of blacks." Michel Rosenfeld, *Decoding* Richmond: *Affirmative Action and the Elusive Meaning of Constitutional Equality*, 87 Mich.L.Rev. 1729, 1790 (1989). Do you agree? *See generally* Belton, *supra*, at 121–29 (discussing the "innocent victim").

In an internal report for the Department of Labor, Professor Alfred Blumrosen concluded that "reverse discrimination" cases accounted for between 1% and 3% of some 3,000 reported employment discrimination cases between 1990 and 1994 and that a high percentage of cases were dismissed by the federal courts. Alfred W. Blumrosen, Draft Report on Reverse Discrimination Commissioned by Labor Department: How Courts Are Handling Reverse Discrimination Claims, 1995 Daily Lab.Rep. (BNA) 56 d22 (Mar. 23, 1995). Professor Paul Burstein, a sociologist, reached the same conclusion. Paul Burstein, *"Reverse Discrimination" Cases in the Federal Courts: Legal Mobilization by a Countermovement*, 32 Soc.Q. 511 (1991).

5. In evaluating an affirmative action plan, how would you distinguish between a quota, a goal, and a timetable? In *Local 28, Sheet Metal Workers' International Association v. EEOC*, 478 U.S. 421, 106 S.Ct. 3019, 92 L.Ed.2d 344 (1986). Justice O'Connor relied on the following distinctions between a *quota* and a *goal*:

> [A] quota "would impose a fixed number or percentage which must be attained, or which cannot be exceeded," and would do so "regardless of the number of potential applicants who meet necessary qualifications." * * * By contrast, a goal is "a numerical objective, fixed realistically in terms of the number of vacancies expected, and the number of qualified applicants available in the relevant job."

Id. at 495–96, 106 S.Ct. 3060 (quoting Department of Labor and EEOC, Memorandum: Permissible Goals and Timetables in State and Local Government Employment Practices (Mar. 23, 1973), *reprinted* in 2 CCH Employment Practices ¶ 3776, at 3856).

6. Do you agree with Justice Blackmun's view that "[i]n order to get beyond racism, we must first take account of race"? Regents of the Univ. of

Cal. v. Bakke, 438 U.S. 265, 407, 98 S.Ct. 2733, 2807, 57 L.Ed.2d 750 (1978). What about the argument of Professor Van Alstyne that "one gets beyond racism by getting beyond it now: by a complete, resolute, and credible commitment never to tolerate * * * differential treatment of other human beings by race"? William Van Alstyne, *Rites of Passage: Race, the Supreme Court, and the Constitution*, 46 U.Chi.L.Rev. 775, 809 (1979). Can the two views be harmonized?

Note: Evolution of Affirmative Action as a Remedy

Although affirmative action appears to be a relatively recent remedy for discrimination, the argument has been made that its historical roots can be traced back to developments in the immediate aftermath of the ratification of the Thirteen, Fourteenth, and Fifteenth Amendments. For example, after a detailed review of historical materials, Professor Eric Schnapper argued that "[f]rom the closing days of the Civil War until the end of civilian Reconstruction some five years later, Congress adopted a series of social welfare programs whose benefits were expressly limited to blacks." Eric Schnapper, *Affirmative Action and the Legislative History of the Fourteenth Amendment*, 71 Va.L.Rev. 753, 754 (1985). For example, the Freedman's Bureau was established by Congress in 1866 to provide special protection and assistance to newly freed slaves. *Id.* at 755–75. Much of the legislative material on which Professor Schnapper based his argument was included in the NAACP Legal Defense and Educational Fund, Inc., brief submitted in support of the affirmative action program at issue in *Regents of the University of California v. Bakke*, 438 U.S. 265, 98 S.Ct. 2733, 57 L.Ed.2d 750 (1978). Justice Thurgood Marshall relied on some of this historical material in his separate opinion in *Bakke*. *See id.* at 387–402, 98 S.Ct. at 2797–2805. *See also* Schnapper, *supra*, at n.*; James E. Jones, Jr., *The Genesis and Present Status of Affirmative Action in Employment: Economic, Legal, and Political Realities*, 70 Iowa L.Rev. 901, 903–04 (1985).

More recently, the use of affirmative action as a remedy for discrimination has been associated with Presidential Executive Orders. In 1961, President Kennedy issued Executive Order No. 10,925, which required federal contractors to "take affirmative action to ensure that applicants are employed, and that employees are treated during employment, without regard to their race, creed, color or national origin." Executive Order No. 10,925, 3 C.F.R. 448, 450 (1959–1963 Compilation). President Kennedy borrowed the phrase "affirmative action" from the 1935 National Labor Relations Act which delegated to the National Labor Relations Board the authority to remedy unfair labor practices by ordering "such affirmative action" as was necessary to "effectuate the policies" of the statute. *See* Hugh Davis Graham, *The Origins of Affirmative Action: Civil Rights and the Regulatory State*, 523 Annals Am.Acad.Pol. & Soc.Sci., Sept. 1992, at 50, 53–54.

In 1964, Congress enacted Title VII. Several provisions are directly relevant to the use of affirmative action as a remedy for discrimination. First, § 703(j), 42 U.S.C. § 2000e–2(j), provides that nothing in Title VII shall be interpreted to require any employer, employment agency, [or] labor organization * * * to grant preferential treatment to any individual or to any group because of the race, color, religion, sex, or national origin of such individual or group [in order to correct any imbalance between the employer's work force and the relevant labor market].

Section 706(g)(1), 42 U.S.C. § 2000e–5(g)(1), authorizes the courts, in devising remedies for unlawful violations of Title VII, to "order such affirmative action as may be appropriate." Prior to the enactment of Title VII, affirmative action as a remedy for discrimination generally was limited to the federal government and federal contractors under the Executive Orders; Title VII extended the use of affirmative action to the private sector work force.

In 1965, shortly after the effective date of Title VII, President Johnson replaced President Kennedy's Executive Order 10,925 with Executive Order No. 11,246, which requires federal agencies to establish and maintain affirmative action programs. 3 C.F.R. 339 (1964–65 Comp.). It also requires federal contractors to adopt affirmative action policies for employment decisions regarding applicants and employees. In October 1965, the Office of Contract Compliance (now called the Office of Contract Compliance Programs (OFCCP)) was established in the Department of Justice and delegated the responsibility for administering Executive Order No. 11,246.

On December 22, 1994, Senator Robert Dole requested the Congressional Research Service to compile a list of every federal statute, regulation, program, and executive order that grants a preference to individuals on the basis of race, sex, national origin, or ethnic background. The report identified over 160 such programs. *See* 141 Cong.Rec. S3929–01 (Mar. 15, 1995). The Justice Department, on June 28, 1995, issued a preliminary legal guidance on the implications of Supreme Court cases for federal affirmative action programs. President Clinton directed that a review be made of federal governmental affirmative action programs. See Affirmative Action Review: Report to the President (July 19, 1995). The Report became the basis of the "Mend it, don't end it" speech on affirmative action delivered by President Clinton on July 19, 1995.

The history of affirmative action under the Executive Orders is discussed in James E. Jones, Jr., *The Genesis and Present Status of Affirmative Action in Employment: Economic, Legal, and Political Realities*, 70 Iowa L.Rev. 901 (1985), and *Twenty-One Years of Affirmative Action: The Maturation of the Administrative Enforcement Process Under the Executive Order 11,246 as amended*, 59 Chi.-Kent L.Rev. 67 (1982).

B. EQUAL PROTECTION CHALLENGES TO AFFIRMATIVE ACTION PLANS

The Equal Protection Clause of the Fourteenth Amendment and the equal protection component of the Due Process Clause of the Fifth

Amendment require reasonableness in legislative and administrative classifications. With most governmental classifications, the standard equal protection analysis inquires whether laws that treat persons or groups differently serve a legitimate governmental interest. "To provide content, equal protection came to be seen as requiring 'some rationality in the nature of the class singled out,' with 'rationality' tested by the classification's ability to serve the purposes intended by the legislative or administrative rule." Lawrence H. Tribe, American Constitutional Law 1440 (2d ed.1988) (quoting Rinaldi v. Yeager, 384 U.S. 305, 308–09, 86 S.Ct. 1497, 1499, 16 L.Ed.2d 577 (1966)); *see generally id.* at 1439–54.

The Supreme Court has adopted three standards of review in equal protection jurisprudence, ranging from deferential to strict. Strict scrutiny applies when a governmental rule, law, or policy creates a suspect classification, such as race, or burdens a fundamental right. *See, e.g.,* Loving v. Virginia, 388 U.S. 1, 11, 87 S.Ct. 1817, 18 L.Ed.2d 1010 (1967) (striking down state law prohibiting interracial marriage); Kramer v. Union Free Sch. Dist. No. 15, 395 U.S. 621, 89 S.Ct. 1886, 23 L.Ed.2d 583 (1969) (applying equal protection to restrictions on the right to vote). Under strict scrutiny, the Court will uphold the law or policy only if it is necessary to achieve some compelling governmental interest. The means to achieve that end must be narrowly tailored and the Court will always consider whether the same purpose can be achieved with less burdensome means. *See, e.g.,* City of Cleburne v. Cleburne Living Ctr., Inc., 473 U.S. 432, 440, 105 S.Ct. 3249, 3254, 87 L.Ed.2d 313 (1985). An intermediate standard applies heightened scrutiny, which requires an exceedingly persuasive justification when the legislation or policy affects a quasi-suspect classification such as gender. To survive judicial review under this intermediate standard, the law or policy must substantially further an important state interest. *See, e.g.,* United States v. Virginia, 518 U.S. 515, 116 S.Ct. 2264, 135 L.Ed.2d 735 (1996) (striking down, under heightened scrutiny, a male-only admission policy at a state-supported institution of higher education). Rational basis scrutiny, the most deferential of the three standards, applies in all other instances when the courts review government laws or policies. Under this level of review, the Court will uphold a law or policy as long as it is rationally related to a legitimate state interest. *See, e.g.,* Schweiker v. Wilson, 450 U.S. 221, 230, 101 S.Ct. 1074, 1080, 67 L.Ed.2d 186 (1981).

Beginning with its 1978 decision in *Regents of the University of California v. Bakke,* 438 U.S. 265, 98 S.Ct. 2733, 57 L.Ed.2d 750 (1978), the Supreme Court has wrestled with two issues involving the constitutionality of the use of affirmative action plans as a remedy for racial discrimination. The first is what standard of review should be applied when these plans are challenged on equal protection grounds. The second is whether the same standard of equal protection review applies to the laws of both federal and state or local governments. In *Adarand Constructors, Inc. v. Pena,* 515 U.S. 200, 115 S.Ct. 2097, 132 L.Ed.2d 158 (1995), the Court considered whether "the Federal Government's practice of giving general contractors on government projects a financial incentive to hire subcontractors controlled by 'socially and economically disadvantaged individuals,' and in particular, the Government's use of race-based presumptions in identifying such individuals, violate[d] the equal protection component of the Fifth Amendment's Due Process Clause." *Id.* at 204. With regard to the standard of review to be used, the Court began by reviewing its prior cases:

> Most of the [Equal Protection Clause cases prior to *Bakke*] involved classifications burdening groups that have suffered discrimination in our society. In 1978, the Court confronted the question whether race-based governmental action designed to *benefit* such groups should also be subject to "the most rigid scrutiny." *Regents of University of California v. Bakke*, 438 U.S. 265, 98 S.Ct. 2733, 57 L.Ed.2d 750 (1978), involved an equal protection challenge to a state-run medical school's practice of reserving a number of spaces in its entering class for minority students. The petitioners argued that "strict scrutiny" should apply only to "classifications that disadvantage 'discrete and insular minorities.' " *Id.* at 287–88, 98 S.Ct. at 2747 (opinion of Powell, J.) (citing United States v. Carolene Products Co., 304 U.S. 144, 152 n. 4, 58 S.Ct. 778, 784 n. 4, 82 L.Ed. 1234 (1938)). Bakke did not produce an opinion for the Court, but Justice Powell's opinion announcing the Court's judgment rejected the argument. In a passage joined by Justice White, Justice Powell wrote that "[t]he guarantee of equal protection cannot mean one thing when applied to one individual and something else when applied to a person of another color." 438 U.S. at 289–90, 98 S.Ct. at 2748. He concluded that "[r]acial and ethnic distinctions of any sort are inherently suspect and thus call for the most exacting judicial examination." *Id.* at 291, 98 S.Ct. at 2748. On the other hand, four Justices in *Bakke* would have applied a less stringent standard of review to racial classifications "designed to further remedial purposes," *see id.* at 359, 98 S.Ct. at 2783 (Brennan, White, Marshall, and Blackmun, JJ., concurring in judgment in part and dissenting in part). And four Justices thought the case should be decided on statutory grounds. *Id.* at 411–12, 421, 98 S.Ct. at 2809–10, 2815 (Stevens, J., joined by Burger, C.J., and Stewart and Rehnquist, JJ., concurring in judgment in part and dissenting in part).

* * *

In *Wygant v. Jackson Board of Education*, 476 U.S. 267, 106 S.Ct. 1842, 90 L.Ed.2d 260 (1986), the Court considered a Fourteenth Amendment challenge to another form of remedial racial classification. The issue in *Wygant* was whether a school board could adopt race-based preferences in determining which teachers to lay off. Justice Powell's plurality opinion observed that "the level of scrutiny does not change merely because the challenged classification operates against a group that historically has not been subject to governmental discrimination," *id.* at 273, 106 S.Ct. at 1846, and stated the two-part inquiry as "whether the layoff provision is supported by a compelling state purpose and whether the means chosen to accomplish that purpose are narrowly tailored." *Id.* at 274, 106 S.Ct. at 1847. In other words, "racial classifications of any sort must be subjected to 'strict scrutiny.'" *Id.* at 285, 106 S.Ct. at 1852 (O'Connor, J., concurring in part and concurring in judgment). The plurality then concluded that the school board's interest in "providing minority role models for its minority students, as an attempt to alleviate the effects of societal discrimination," *id.* at 274, 106 S.Ct. at 1847, was not a compelling interest that could justify the use of a racial classification. It added that "[s]ocietal discrimination, without more, is too amorphous a basis for imposing a racially classified remedy," *id.* at 276, 106 S.Ct. at 1848, and insisted instead that "a public employer * * * must ensure that, before it embarks on an affirmative-action program, it has convincing evidence that remedial action is warranted. That is, it must have sufficient evidence to justify the conclusion that there has been prior discrimination," *id.* at 277, 106 S.Ct. at 1848–49. Justice White concurred only in the judgment, although he agreed that the school board's asserted interests could not, "singly or together, justify this racially discriminatory layoff policy." *Id.* at 295, 106 S.Ct. at 1858. Four Justices dissented, three of whom again argued for intermediate scrutiny of remedial race-based government action. *Id.* at 301–02, 106 S.Ct. at 1861–62 (Marshall, J., joined by Brennan and Blackmun, JJ., dissenting).

The Court's failure to produce a majority opinion in *Bakke, Fullilove,* and *Wygant* left unresolved the proper analysis for remedial race-based governmental action. *See* United States v. Paradise, 480 U.S. at 166, 107 S.Ct. at 1063 (plurality opinion of Brennan, J.) ("[A]lthough this Court has consistently held that some elevated level of scrutiny is required when a racial or ethnic distinction is made for remedial purposes, it has yet to reach consensus on the appropriate constitutional analysis"); Sheet Metal Workers v. EEOC, 478 U.S. 421, 480, 106 S.Ct. 3019, 92 L.Ed.2d 344 (1986) (plurality opinion of Brennan, J.). Lower courts found this lack of guidance unsettling. * * *

Id., at 218–221. After discussing *Richmond v. J.A. Croson Co.,* 488 U.S. 469, 109 S.Ct. 706, 102 L.Ed.2d 854 (1989), the Court concluded as follows:

Despite lingering uncertainty in the details, however, the Court's cases through *Croson* had established three general propositions with respect to governmental racial classifications. First, skepticism: " '[a]ny preference based on racial or ethnic criteria must necessarily receive a most searching examination,'" *Wygant,* 476 U.S. at 273, 106 S.Ct. at 1847 (plurality opinion of Powell, J.); *Fullilove,* 448 U.S. at 491, 100 S.Ct. at 2781 (opinion of Burger, C. J.). * * * Second, consistency: "the standard of review under the Equal Protection Clause is not dependent on the race of those burdened or benefited by a particular classification," *Croson,* 488

U.S. at 494, 109 S.Ct. at 722 (plurality opinion); *id.* at 520, 109 S.Ct. at 735 (Scalia, J., concurring in judgment). * * * And third, congruence: "[e]qual protection analysis in the Fifth Amendment area is the same as that under the Fourteenth Amendment," *Buckley v. Valeo*, 424 U.S. at 93, 96 S.Ct. at 670. * * * Taken together, these three propositions lead to the conclusion that any person, of whatever race, has the right to demand that any governmental actor subject to the Constitution justify any racial classification subjecting that person to unequal treatment under the strictest judicial scrutiny. * * *

* * *

* * * [W]e hold today that all racial classifications, imposed by whatever federal, state, or local governmental actor, must be analyzed by a reviewing court under strict scrutiny. In other words, such classifications are constitutional only if they are narrowly tailored measures that further compelling governmental interests. To the extent that *Metro Broadcasting* is inconsistent with that holding, it is overruled.

* * *

Our action today makes explicit what Justice Powell thought implicit in the *Fullilove* lead opinion: federal racial classifications, like those of a State, must serve a compelling state interest, and must be narrowly tailored to further that interest. *See Fullilove*, 448 U.S. at 496, 100 S.Ct. at 2783–84 (concurring opinion).

Id. at 223–227, 235.

Notes and Questions

1. The fundamental issue at stake in the Supreme Court's equal protection jurisprudence is how to harmonize a color- or sex-blind theory of equality with the reality of the present and continuing effects of societal discrimination. Does the strict scrutiny test accommodate both of these concerns? *See, e.g.*, Brent E. Simmons, *Reconsidering Strict Scrutiny*, 2 Mich.J.Race & Law, 51 (1996); K.G. Jan Pillai, *Phantom of the Strict Scrutiny*, 31 New Eng.L.Rev. 397 (1997). *See also* Neil Gotanda, *A Critique of "Our Constitution Is Color–Blind*," 44 Stan.L.Rev. 1, 2 (1991) (arguing that the Supreme Court's use of "color-blind Constitutionalism * * * legitimates and thereby maintains, the social, economic and political advantages that whites hold over other Americans"). Justice Thomas suggested in *Adarand* that the government would never have a compelling reason to enact race-specific legislation. *Adarand*, 515 U.S. at 240–41, 115 S.Ct. at 2119 (Thomas, J., concurring).

2. If a government employer adopted an affirmative action plan in order to remedy the present effects of past racial discrimination, what kind of evidence of a compelling state interest would it have to produce to satisfy the equal protection standard of *Adarand*? Consider the following observation of the Court in *Croson*:

In *Wygant*, 476 U.S. 267, 106 S.Ct. 1842, 90 L.Ed.2d 260 (1986), four Members of the Court applied heightened scrutiny to a race-based system of employee layoffs. Justice Powell, writing for the plurality, * * * drew a distinction between "societal discrimination" which is an inadequate basis for race-conscious classifications, and the type of identified discrimination that can support and define the scope of race-based relief. The challenged classification in that case tied the layoff of minority teachers to the percentage of minority students enrolled in the school district. The lower court upheld the scheme, based on the theory that minority students were in need of "role models" to alleviate the effects of prior discrimination in society. This Court reversed, with a plurality of four Justices reiterating the view expressed by Justice Powell in *Bakke* that "[s]ocietal discrimination, without more, is too amorphous a basis for imposing a racially classified remedy." *Wygant*, 476 U.S. at 276, 106 S.Ct. at 1848.

City of Richmond v. J.A. Croson Co., 488 U.S. 469, 497, 109 S.Ct. 706, 723–24, 102 L.Ed.2d 854 (1989). The Court in *Croson* stated that allowing a race-based plan on the basis of societal discrimination, without "particularized findings" of unlawful discrimination would allow " 'remedies that are ageless in their reach into the past, and timeless in their ability to affect the future.' " *Id.* at 498, 109 S.Ct. at 724 (citing *Wygant*, 476 U.S. at 276, 106 S.Ct. at 1848). The Court rejected the "role model" argument in *Wygant* because "the statistical disparity between students and teachers had no probative value in demonstrating the kind of prior discrimination in hiring and promotion that would justify race-based relief" and "the role model theory had no relation to some basis for believing that a constitutional or statutory violation had occurred." *Id.* at 497–98, 109 S.Ct. at 724.

In *Shaw v. Hunt*, 517 U.S. 899, 116 S.Ct. 1894, 135 L.Ed.2d 207 (1996), the Court stated that two conditions must be present to satisfy the compelling governmental interest prong of the strict scrutiny test. First, "the discrimination must be 'identified discrimination,' " *Id.* at 1902 (quoting *Croson*, 488 U.S. at 499, 500, 505, 507, 509, 109 S.Ct. at 724–25, 725, 728, 729, 730). Second, the state entity "must have had a 'strong basis in evidence' to conclude that remedial action was necessary '*before* it embarks on an affirmative-action program.' " 517 U.S. at 910, 116 S.Ct. at 1903 (quoting *Wygant*, 476 U.S. at 277, 106 S.Ct. at 1848 (plurality opinion) (emphasis added by *Shaw* Court)).

For an analysis of the compelling governmental interest test in equal protection jurisprudence, see Lori Jayne Hoffman, *Fatal in Fact: An Analysis of the Application of the Compelling Governmental Interest Leg of Strict Scrutiny in* City of Richmond v. J.A. Croson, 70 B.U.L.Rev. 889 (1990) (noting that few, if any, affirmative action cases have been upheld under the constitutional strict scrutiny test). For an analysis of the "narrowly tailored" prong of strict scrutiny review, see Ian Ayers, *Narrow Tailoring*, 43 UCLA L.Rev. 1781 (1996).

3. In *Grutter v. Bollinger*, 539 U.S. 306, 123 S.Ct. 2325, 156 L.Ed.2d 304 (2003), the Supreme Court applied strict scrutiny in reviewing the admissions policy at the University of Michigan Law School, which sought to achieve a diverse student body by, among other things, enrolling a "critical

mass of underrepresented minority students." The Court stated "we have never held that the only governmental use of race that can survive strict scrutiny is remedying past discrimination. * * * Today we hold that the Law School has a compelling interest in attaining a diverse student body." *Id.* at 123 S.Ct. 2325, 2339. In finding that diversity can be a compelling governmental interest, it deferred to the Law School's judgment that such diversity is essential to its educational mission. The Law School supported its judgment by putting forth concrete testimony and well-documented studies showing the benefits of critical mass diversity. Several major American businesses and military leaders filed amicus briefs also documenting the real benefits of exposure to widely diverse people, culture, ideas and viewpoints. In finding that diversity can be a compelling state interest, the Court implicitly overruled *Hopwood v. Texas*, 78 F.3d 932 (5th Cir. 1996).

The Court went on to find that the Law School's policy, although race-conscious, was narrowly tailored to meet its purpose because the program was flexible enough to ensure that each applicant would be "evaluated as an individual" and that an applicant's race or ethnicity would not be "the defining feature of his or her application." *Grutter v. Bollinger*, 123 S.Ct. 2325, 2343. The Law School sufficiently considered workable race-neutral alternatives, such as a lottery, and showed that these alternatives would sacrifice academic quality. The Court concluded that "the Law School's race-conscious admission policy did not unduly harm nonminority applicants" because the Law School considers all pertinent elements of diversity in addition to race and ethnicity. *Id.*, 123 S.Ct. 2325, 2346. It noted that the Law School "can (and does) select nonminority applicants who have greater potential to enhance student body diversity over underrepresented minority applicants." *Id.*, 123 S.Ct. 2325, 2345.

In a companion case, *Gratz v. Bollinger,* 539 U.S. 244, 123 S.Ct. 2411, 156 L.Ed.2d 257 (2003), the Court found that the admissions policy used by the University of Michigan's College of Literature, Science and Arts (LSA) violated the equal protection clause because it was not narrowly tailored to meet the compelling government interest in diversity. The LSA policy, which awarded twenty points (out of 150 total points) on a selection index to every applicant from an underrepresented minority group, did not provide individualized consideration and the effect of making race or ethnicity "decisive for virtually every minimally qualified underrepresented minority applicant." *Id.*, 123 S.Ct. 2411, 2428.

4. The federal program at issue in *Adarand* benefitted women as well as minorities. The Court, however, did not address whether strict scrutiny should apply to affirmative action plans adopted to benefit women. When laws and policies that have sex-based classifications are challenged on equal protection grounds, the Supreme Court has applied intermediate scrutiny rather than the more stringent standard of strict scrutiny. *See, e.g.,* United States v. Virginia, 518 U.S. 515, 116 S.Ct. 2264, 135 L.Ed.2d 735 (1996). Does this fact support the proposition that gender-based affirmative action policies are more likely to be upheld than race-based affirmative action plans? Justice Stevens raised this possibility in his dissenting opinion in *Adarand*:

[T]he Court may find that its new "consistency" approach to race-based classifications is difficult to square with its insistence upon rigidly separate categories for discrimination against different classes of individuals. For example, as the law currently stands, the Court will apply "intermediate scrutiny" to cases of invidious gender discrimination and "strict scrutiny" to cases of invidious race discrimination, while applying the same standard for benign classifications as for invidious ones. If this remains the law, then today's lecture about "consistency" will produce the anomalous result that the Government can more easily enact affirmative-action programs to remedy discrimination against women than it can enact affirmative-action programs to remedy discrimination against African–Americans—even though the primary purpose of the Equal Protection Clause was to end discrimination against the former slaves.

515 U.S. at 247, 115 S.Ct. at 2122. Should the same constitutional standard of review apply to race and sex claims?

5. Does strict scrutiny apply to judicial decrees that impose affirmative action as a remedy after a finding of unlawful employment discrimination? In *United States v. Paradise*, 480 U.S. 149, 107 S.Ct. 1053, 94 L.Ed.2d 203 (1987), the lower court entered a judicial decree directing the employer, the Alabama Department of Public Safety, to hire one black trooper for each white trooper until the number of black troopers constituted approximately 25% of the state trooper work force. The lower court entered its affirmative action decree because the employer had failed to comply with an earlier remedial decree that did not have an affirmative action component. The case had been filed under the Equal Protection Clause of the Fourteenth Amendment. The Court, in an opinion written by Justice Brennan, found that the race-specific decree satisfied the "compelling state interest" prong of strict scrutiny. The Court also found that the one-for-one promotion requirement was narrowly tailored to serve a compelling state interest. Justice O'Connor, with whom Chief Justice Rehnquist and Justice Scalia joined, dissented. She agreed that the state had a compelling interest in remedying its own past and present racial discrimination in employment in the department, but she was of the view that the district court had erred in imposing the hiring ratios without first considering the effectiveness of alternative possibilities under the "narrowly tailored" prong of the strict scrutiny test.

6. Must beneficiaries of affirmative action plans demonstrate that they have been victims of discrimination? The Supreme Court has construed § 706(g) of Title VII, 42 U.S.C. § 2000e–2(g)(1), as granting the courts broad authority to order race- or sex-based affirmative action relief after making a finding of unlawful employment discrimination. *In Local 93, International Association of Firefighters v. City of Cleveland*, 478 U.S. 501, 106 S.Ct. 3063, 92 L.Ed.2d 405 (1986), the Court considered whether § 706(g) precludes the entry of a consent decree which contains an affirmative action provision that may provide relief for individuals who have not been found to be actual victims of a defendant's discriminatory practices. In an opinion by Justice Brennan, six members of the Court held that it does not. The Court read § 706(g) as a limitation solely on court orders and not on consent decrees because consent decrees are not "orders" within the meaning of that section. Justice Rehnquist, in a dissent joined by Chief Justice Burger, argued that

consent decrees are "orders" under § 706(g) and that only specific, identified victims of discrimination are entitled to relief.

7. *Collateral Attack on Affirmative Action Consent Decrees:* A consent decree is "a settlement agreement among the parties to a lawsuit, signed by the court and entered as a judgment in the case." Maimon Schwarzschild, *Public Law by Private Bargain: Title VII Consent Decrees and the Fairness of Negotiated Institutional Reform*, 1984 Duke L.J. 887, 894. Consent decrees are entered in many cases, including employment discrimination cases, but this is particularly true in class-action employment discrimination cases. Class action cases can not be settled, however, without court approval. *See* Fed.R.Civ.P. 23.

Prior to the Supreme Court's decision in *Martin v. Wilks*, 490 U.S. 755, 109 S.Ct. 2180, 104 L.Ed.2d 835 (1989), the parties in employment discrimination cases frequently entered into consent decrees that contained affirmative action provisions. *Martin v. Wilks* was a race discrimination case involving the Birmingham fire department. The parties—the black firefighters and the employer—settled the case, which had an affirmative action provision for the benefit of the black plaintiffs. After the parties settled the case, white firefighters were invited to participate in the "fairness" hearing that courts generally conduct before entering the consent decree as the judgment. The white plaintiffs refused to participate in the "fairness" hearing; nevertheless, the court eventually approved the consent decree. Later, the white firefighters brought a collateral attack against the consent decree by filing a separate Title VII lawsuit alleging that the race-specific provisions of the decree discriminated against them because of their race. The issue before the Supreme Court was whether the white firefighters could collaterally attack the consent decree. The Supreme Court held that they could. The effect of *Martin v. Wilks* was to "open the floodgates" for lawsuits by whites or males on every then-extant consent decree that contained an affirmative action provision. *See* William B. Gould, IV, *The Supreme Court and Employment Discrimination Law in 1989: Judicial Retreat and Congressional Response*, 64 Tul.L.Rev. 1485, 1514 n.124 (1990).

Congress overturned *Martin v. Wilks* in the Civil Rights Act of 1991. Title VII § 703(n), 42 U.S.C. § 2000e–2(n). Section 703(n) makes it more difficult for a nonparty to use a collateral attack to challenge a litigated or consent judgment where he or she has had notice of the proposed disposition of the case and a reasonable opportunity to present objections, or where his or her interests were adequately represented by another party in the litigation. For a discussion of *Martin v. Wilks* and Congress' response in the Civil Rights Act of 1991, *see, e.g.*, Susan S. Grover, *The Silenced Majority:* Martin v. Wilks *and the Legislative Response*, 1992 U.Ill.L.Rev. 43 (1992); Andrea Catania & Charles A. Sullivan, *Judging Judgments: The 1991 Civil Rights Act and the Lingering Ghost of* Martin v. Wilks, 57 Brook.L.Rev. 995 (1992).

8. For a provocative discussion of the merits, and the viability after *Adarand* of affirmative action on the basis of relative economic disadvantage, see Deborah C. Malamud, *Class-Based Affirmative Action: Lessons and Caveats*, 74 Tex.L.Rev. 1847 (1996).

C. AFFIRMATIVE ACTION UNDER FEDERAL ANTIDISCRIMINATION STATUTES

1. AFFIRMATIVE ACTION AND TITLE VII'S EQUALITY PRINCIPLE

UNITED STEELWORKERS OF AMERICA v. WEBER

Supreme Court of the United States, 1979.
443 U.S. 193, 99 S.Ct. 2721, 61 L.Ed.2d 480.

JUSTICE BRENNAN delivered the opinion of the Court.

Challenged here is the legality of an affirmative action plan—collectively bargained by an employer and a union—that reserves for black employees 50% of the openings in an in-plant craft-training program until the percentage of black craftworkers in the plant is commensurate with the percentage of blacks in the local labor force. The question for decision is whether Congress, in Title VII left employers and unions in the private sector free to take such race-conscious steps to eliminate manifest racial imbalances in traditionally segregated job categories. We hold that Title VII does not prohibit such race-conscious affirmative action plans.

I

In 1974, petitioner United Steelworkers of America (USWA) and petitioner Kaiser Aluminum & Chemical Corp. (Kaiser) entered into a master collective-bargaining agreement covering terms and conditions of employment at 15 Kaiser plants. The agreement contained, *inter alia*, an affirmative action plan designed to eliminate conspicuous racial imbalances in Kaiser's then almost exclusively white craft-work forces. Black craft-hiring goals were set for each Kaiser plant equal to the percentage of blacks in the respective local labor forces. To enable plants to meet these goals, on-the-job training programs were established to teach unskilled production workers—black and white—the skills necessary to become craftworkers. The plan reserved for black employees 50% of the openings in these newly created in-plant training programs.

This case arose from the operation of the plan at Kaiser's plant in Gramercy, La. Until 1974, Kaiser hired as craftworkers for that plant only persons who had had prior craft experience. Because blacks had long been excluded from craft unions,[1] few were able to present such credentials. As a consequence, prior to 1974 only 1.83% (5 out of 273) of the skilled craftworkers at the Gramercy plant were black, even though the work force in the Gramercy area was approximately 39% black.

Pursuant to the national agreement Kaiser altered its craft-hiring practice in the Gramercy plant. Rather than hiring already trained

---

1. Judicial findings of exclusion from crafts on racial grounds are so numerous as to make such exclusion a proper subject for judicial notice [Citations omitted.]

outsiders, Kaiser established a training program to train its production workers to fill craft openings. Selection of craft trainees was made on the basis of seniority, with the proviso that at least 50% of the new trainees were to be black until the percentage of black skilled craftworkers in the Gramercy plant approximated the percentage of blacks in the local labor force.

During 1974, the first year of the operation of the Kaiser–USWA affirmative action plan, 13 craft trainees were selected from Gramercy's production work force. Of these, seven were black and six white. The most senior black selected into the program had less seniority than several white production workers whose bids for admission were rejected. Thereafter one of those white production workers, respondent Brian Weber (hereafter respondent), instituted this class action in the United States District Court for the Eastern District of Louisiana.

The complaint alleged that the filling of craft trainee positions at the Gramercy plant pursuant to the affirmative action program had resulted in junior black employees' receiving training in preference to senior white employees, thus discriminating against respondent and other similarly situated white employees in violation of §§ 703(a) and (d) of Title VII. The District Court held that the plan violated Title VII * * *. A divided panel of the Court of Appeals for the Fifth Circuit affirmed * * *. We granted certiorari. We reverse.

II

* * * The only question before us is the narrow statutory issue of whether Title VII *forbids* private employers and unions from voluntarily agreeing upon bona fide affirmative action plans that accord racial preferences in the manner and for the purpose provided in the Kaiser–USWA plan. * * *

Respondent argues that Congress intended in Title VII to prohibit all race-conscious affirmative action plans. Respondent's argument rests upon a literal interpretation of §§ 703(a) and (d) of the Act. Those sections make it unlawful to "discriminate * * * because of * * * race" in hiring and in the selection of apprentices for training programs. Since, the argument runs, *McDonald v. Santa Fe Trail Transp. Co.*, 427 U.S. 273, 96 S.Ct. 2574, 49 L.Ed.2d 493 (1976), settled that Title VII forbids discrimination against whites as well as blacks, and since the Kaiser–USWA affirmative action plan operates to discriminate against white employees solely because they are white, it follows that the Kaiser–USWA plan violates Title VII.

Respondent's argument is not without force. But it overlooks the significance of the fact that the Kaiser–USWA plan is an affirmative action plan voluntarily adopted by private parties to eliminate traditional patterns of racial segregation. In this context respondent's reliance upon a literal construction of §§ 703(a) and (d) and upon *McDonald* is misplaced. It is a "familiar rule, that a thing may be within the letter of the statute and yet not within the statute, because not within its spirit, nor within the intention of its makers." *Holy Trinity Church v. United States*, 143 U.S. 457, 459, 12 S.Ct. 511, 512, 36 L.Ed. 226 (1892). The prohibition against racial discrimination in §§ 703(a) and (d) of Title VII must therefore be read against the background of the legislative history of Title VII and the historical context from which the Act arose. Examination of those sources makes clear that an interpretation of the sections that forbade all race-conscious affirmative action would "bring about an end completely at variance with the purpose of the statute" and must be rejected. United States v. Public Utilities Comm'n, 345 U.S. 295, 315, 73 S.Ct. 706, 718, 97 L.Ed. 1020 (1953).

Congress' primary concern in enacting the prohibition against racial discrimination in Title VII of the Civil Rights Act of 1964 was with "the plight of the Negro in our economy." 110 Cong. Rec. 6548 (1964) (remarks of Sen. Humphrey). * * *

* * * [I]t was clear to Congress that "[t]he crux of the problem [was] to open employment opportunities for Negroes in occupations which have been traditionally closed to them," 110 Cong. Rec. 6548 (1964) (remarks of Sen. Humphrey), and it was to this problem that Title VII's prohibition against racial discrimination in employment was primarily addressed.

It plainly appears from the House Report accompanying the Civil Rights Act that Congress did not intend wholly to prohibit private and voluntary affirmative action efforts as one method of solving this problem. The Report provides:

> No bill can or should lay claim to eliminating all of the causes and consequences of racial and other types of discrimination against minorities. There is reason to believe, however, that national leadership provided by the enactment of Federal legislation dealing with the most troublesome problems *will create an atmosphere conducive to voluntary or local resolution of other forms of discrimination.*

H.R.Rep.No. 914, 88th Cong., 1st Sess., pt. 1, p.18 (1963). (Emphasis supplied.)

Given this legislative history, we cannot agree with respondent that Congress intended to prohibit the private sector from taking effective steps to accomplish the goal that Congress designed Title VII to achieve. The very statutory words intended as a spur or catalyst to cause "employers and unions to self-examine and to self-evaluate their employment practices and to endeavor to eliminate, so far as possible, the last vestiges of an unfortunate and ignominious page in this country's history," *Albemarle Paper Co. v. Moody*, 422 U.S. 405, 418, 95 S.Ct. 2362, 2372, 45 L.Ed.2d 280 (1975), cannot be interpreted as an absolute prohibition against all private, voluntary, race-conscious affirmative action efforts to hasten the elimination of such vestiges. It would be ironic indeed if a law triggered by a Nation's concern over centuries of racial injustice and intended to improve the lot of those who had "been excluded from the American dream for so long," 110 Cong. Rec. 6552 (1964) (remarks of Sen. Humphrey), constituted the first legislative prohibition of all voluntary, private, race-conscious efforts to abolish traditional patterns of racial segregation and hierarchy.

Our conclusion is further reinforced by examination of the language and legislative history of § 703(j) of Title VII.[5] Opponents of Title VII raised two related arguments against the bill. First, they argued that the Act would be interpreted to *require* employers with racially imbalanced work forces to grant preferential treatment to racial minorities in order to integrate. Second, they argued that employers with racially imbalanced work forces would grant preferential treatment to racial minorities, even if not required to do so by the Act. *See* 110 Cong. Rec. 8618–8619 (1964) (remarks of Sen. Sparkman). Had Congress meant to prohibit all race-conscious affirmative action, as respondent urges, it easily could have answered both objections by providing that Title VII would not require or *permit* racially preferential integration efforts. But Congress did not choose such a course. Rather, Congress added § 703(j) which addresses only the first objection. The section provides that nothing contained in Title VII "shall be interpreted to *require* any employer * * * to grant preferential treatment * * * to any group because of the race * * * of such * * * group on account of" a *de facto* racial imbalance in the employer's work force. The section does not state that "nothing in Title VII shall be interpreted to *permit*" voluntary affirmative efforts to correct racial imbalances. The natural inference is that Congress chose not to forbid all voluntary race-conscious affirmative action. •

The reasons for this choice are evident from the legislative record. Title VII could not have been enacted into law without substantial support from legislators in both Houses who traditionally resisted federal regulation of private business. Those legislators demanded as a price for their support that "management prerogatives, and union freedoms * * * be left undisturbed to the greatest extent possible." Section 703(j) was proposed by Senator Dirksen to allay any fears that the Act might be interpreted in such a way as to upset this compromise. The section was designed to prevent § 703 of Title VII from being interpreted in such a way as to lead to undue "Federal Government interference with private businesses because of some Federal employee's ideas about racial balance or racial imbalance." * * * Clearly, a prohibition against all voluntary, race-conscious, affirmative action efforts would disserve these ends. Such a prohibition would augment the powers of the Federal Government and diminish traditional management prerogatives while at the same time impeding attainment of the ultimate statutory goals. In view of this legislative history and in view of Congress' desire to avoid undue federal regulation of private businesses, use of the word "require" rather than the phrase "require or permit" in § 703(j) fortifies the

---

5. * * * Section 703(j) speaks to substantive liability under Title VII, but it does not preclude courts from considering racial imbalance as evidence of a Title VII violation. *See Teamsters v. United States*, 431 U.S. 324, 339–340, n. 20, 97 S.Ct. 1843, 1856, 52 L.Ed.2d 396 (1977). Remedies for substantive violations are governed by § 706 (g), 42 U.S.C. § 2000e–5(g).

conclusion that Congress did not intend to limit traditional business freedom to such a degree as to prohibit all voluntary, race-conscious affirmative action.

We therefore hold that Title VII's prohibition in §§ 703(a) and (d) against racial discrimination does not condemn all private, voluntary, race-conscious affirmative action plans.

III

We need not today define in detail the line of demarcation between permissible and impermissible affirmative action plans. It suffices to hold that the challenged Kaiser–USWA affirmative action plan falls on the permissible side of the line. The purposes of the plan mirror those of the statute. Both were designed to break down old patterns of racial segregation and hierarchy. Both were structured to "open employment opportunities for Negroes in occupations which have been traditionally closed to them."[8]

At the same time, the plan does not unnecessarily trammel the interests of the white employees. The plan does not require the discharge of white workers and their replacement with new black hirees. Nor does the plan create an absolute bar to the advancement of white employees; half of those trained in the program will be white. Moreover, the plan is a temporary measure; it is not intended to maintain racial balance, but simply to eliminate a manifest racial imbalance. Preferential selection of craft trainees at the Gramercy plant will end as soon as the percentage of black skilled craftworkers in the Gramercy plant approximates the percentage of blacks in the local labor force.

We conclude, therefore, that the adoption of the Kaiser–USWA plan for the Gramercy plant falls within the area of discretion left by Title VII to the private sector voluntarily to adopt affirmative action plans designed to eliminate conspicuous racial imbalance in traditionally segregated job categories. * * *

JUSTICE POWELL and JUSTICE STEVENS took no part in the consideration or decision of these cases.

JUSTICE REHNQUIST, with whom THE CHIEF JUSTICE joins, dissenting.

* * *

The operative sections of Title VII prohibit racial discrimination in employment *simpliciter*. Taken in its normal meaning, and as understood by all Members of Congress who spoke to the issue during the legislative debates, this language prohibits a covered employer from considering race when making an employment decision, whether the race be black or white. Several years ago, however, a United States District Court held that "the dismissal of white employees charged with misap-

---

8. This is not to suggest that the freedom of an employer to undertake race-conscious affirmative action efforts depends on whether or not his effort is motivated by fear of liability under Title VII.

propriating company property while not dismissing a similarly charged Negro employee does not raise a claim upon which Title VII relief may be granted." *McDonald v. Santa Fe Trail Transp. Co.*, 427 U.S. 273, 278, 96 S.Ct. 2574, 2578, 49 L.Ed.2d 493 (1976). This Court unanimously reversed, concluding from the "uncontradicted legislative history" that "[T]itle VII prohibits racial discrimination against the white petitioners in this case upon the same standards as would be applicable were they Negroes * * *." *Id*. at 280, 96 S.Ct. at 2579.

We have never wavered in our understanding that Title VII "prohibits *all* racial discrimination in employment, without exception for any group of particular employees." *Id*. at 283 (emphasis in original). In *Griggs v. Duke Power Co.*, 401 U.S. 424, 431, 91 S.Ct. 849, 853, 28 L.Ed.2d 158 (1971), our first occasion to interpret Title VII, a unanimous Court observed that "[d]iscriminatory preference, for any group, minority or majority, is precisely and only what Congress has proscribed." And in our most recent discussion of the issue, we uttered words seemingly dispositive of this case: "It is clear beyond cavil that the obligation imposed by Title VII is to provide an equal opportunity for *each* applicant regardless of race, without regard to whether members of the applicant's race are already proportionately represented in the work force." Furnco Construction Corp. v. Waters, 438 U.S. 567, 579, 98 S.Ct. 2943, 2951, 57 L.Ed.2d 957 (1978) (emphasis in original).[1]

* * *

Thus, by a *tour de force* reminiscent not of jurists such as Hale, Holmes, and Hughes, but of escape artists such as Houdini, the Court eludes clear statutory language, "uncontradicted" legislative history, and uniform precedent in concluding that employers are, after all, permitted to consider race in making employment decisions. * * *

II

Were Congress to act today specifically to prohibit the type of racial discrimination suffered by Weber, it would be hard pressed to draft language better tailored to the task than that found in § 703(d) of Title VII:

> It shall be an unlawful employment practice for any employer, labor organization, or joint labor-management committee controlling apprenticeship or other training or retraining, including on-the-job training programs to discriminate against any individual because of his race, color, religion, sex, or national origin in admission to, or employment in, any program established to provide apprenticeship or other training.

42 U.S.C. § 2000e–2(d). Equally suited to the task would be § 703(a)(2), which makes it unlawful for an employer to classify his employees "in any way which would deprive or tend to deprive any individual of

---

1. Our statements in *Griggs* and *Furnco Construction*, patently inconsistent with to- day's holding, are not even mentioned, much less distinguished, by the Court.

employment opportunities or otherwise adversely affect his status as an employee, because of such individual's race, color, religion, sex, or national origin." 42 U.S.C. § 2000e–2(a)(2).

Entirely consistent with these two express prohibitions is the language of § 703(j) of Title VII, which provides that the Act is not to be interpreted "to require any employer * * * to grant preferential treatment to any individual or to any group because of the race * * * of such individual or group" to correct a racial imbalance in the employer's work force. Seizing on the word "require," the Court infers that Congress must have intended to "permit" this type of racial discrimination. Not only is this reading of § 703(j) outlandish in the light of the flat prohibitions of §§ 703(a) and (d), but * * * it is also totally belied by the Act's legislative history.

Quite simply, Kaiser's racially discriminatory admission quota is flatly prohibited by the plain language of Title VII. This normally dispositive fact, however, gives the Court only momentary pause. An "interpretation" of the statute upholding Weber's claim would, according to the Court, " 'bring about an end completely at variance with the purpose of the statute.' " To support this conclusion, the Court calls upon the "spirit" of the Act, which it divines from passages in Title VII's legislative history indicating that enactment of the statute was prompted by Congress' desire " 'to open employment opportunities for Negroes in occupations which [had] been traditionally closed to them.' " But the legislative history invoked by the Court to avoid the plain language of §§ 703(a) and (d) simply misses the point. To be sure, the reality of employment discrimination against Negroes provided the primary impetus for passage of Title VII. But this fact by no means supports the proposition that Congress intended to leave employers free to discriminate against white persons. In most cases,"[l]egislative history * * * is more vague than the statute we are called upon to interpret." Here, however, the legislative history of Title VII is as clear as the language of §§ 703(a) and (d), and it irrefutably demonstrates that Congress meant precisely what it said in §§ 703(a) and (d)—that no racial discrimination in employment is permissible under Title VII, not even preferential treatment of minorities to correct racial imbalance.

* * *

IV

Reading the language of Title VII, as the Court purports to do, "against the background of [its] legislative history * * * and the historical context from which the Act arose," one is led inescapably to the conclusion that Congress fully understood what it was saying and meant precisely what it said. Opponents of the civil rights bill did not argue that employers would be permitted under Title VII voluntarily to grant preferential treatment to minorities to correct racial imbalance. The plain language of the statute too clearly prohibited such racial discrimination to admit of any doubt. They argued, tirelessly, that Title VII would be interpreted by federal agencies and their agents to require unwilling employers to racially balance their work forces by granting preferential treatment to minorities. Supporters of H. R. 7152 responded, equally tirelessly, that the Act would not be so interpreted because not only does it not require preferential treatment of minorities, it also does not *permit* preferential treatment of any race for any reason. It cannot be doubted that the proponents of Title VII understood the meaning of their words, for "[s]eldom has similar legislation been debated with greater consciousness of the need for 'legislative history,' or with greater care in the making thereof, to guide the courts in interpreting and applying the law." Title VII: Legislative History, at 444.

To put an end to the dispute, supporters of the civil rights bill drafted and introduced § 703(j). Specifically addressed to the opposition's charge, § 703(j) simply enjoins federal agencies and courts from interpreting Title VII to require an employer to prefer certain racial groups to correct imbalances in his work force. The section says nothing about voluntary preferential treatment of minorities because such racial discrimination is plainly proscribed by §§ 703(a) and (d). Indeed, had Congress intended to except voluntary, race-conscious preferential treatment from the blanket prohibition of racial discrimination in §§ 703 (a) and (d), it surely could have drafted language better suited to the task than § 703(j). It knew how. * * *

* * *

Our task in this case, like any other case involving the construction of a statute, is to give effect to the intent of Congress. To divine that intent, we traditionally look first to the words of the statute and, if they are unclear, then to the statute's legislative history. Finding the desired result hopelessly foreclosed by these conventional sources, the Court turns to a third source—the "spirit" of the Act. But close examination of what the Court proffers as the spirit of the Act reveals it as the spirit animating the present majority, not the 88th Congress. For if the spirit of the Act eludes the cold words of the statute itself, it rings out with unmistakable clarity in the words of the elected representatives who made the Act law. It is *equality*. * * *

There is perhaps no device more destructive to the notion of equality than the *numerus clausus*—the quota. Whether described as "benign discrimination" or "affirmative action," the racial quota is nonetheless a creator of castes, a two-edged sword that must demean one in order to prefer another. In passing Title VII, Congress outlawed *all* racial discrimination, recognizing that no discrimination based on race is benign, that no action disadvantaging a person because of his color is affirmative. With today's holding, the Court introduces into Title VII a tolerance for the very evil that the law was intended to eradicate, without offering even a clue as to what the limits on that tolerance may be. We are told simply that Kaiser's racially discriminatory admission quota "falls on the permissible side of the line." By going not merely *beyond*, but directly against Title VII's language and legislative history, the Court has sown the wind. Later courts will face the impossible task of reaping the whirlwind.

Notes and Questions

1. The disagreement between Justice Brennan and Justice Rehnquist about the proper construction of § 703(j) is a debate about what vision of equality Congress intended to express in Title VII. This is also the same debate that is at the heart of the controversy over the meaning of equal protection under the Constitution. How would you describe the different visions of workplace equality advocated by Justices Brennan and Rehnquist in *Weber*?

2. In *Weber*, the analysis in both Justice Brennan's majority opinion and Justice Rehnquist's dissent is grounded in *Griggs v. Duke Power Co.*, although Justice Brennan never cites *Griggs* in his opinion. In footnote 1 of Justice Rehnquist's dissent in *Weber*, Justice Rehnquist argued that *Griggs* flatly prohibits race-based affirmative action. Does *Griggs* support the conflicting views of equality that are reflected in the opinions of Justices Brennan and Rehnquist in *Weber*?

3. Would the *Griggs* disparate impact theory survive under Justice Rhenquist's analysis of the affirmative action plan in *Weber*? In light of the fact that Congress codified the *Griggs* disparate impact theory in the Civil Rights Act of 1991, does Justice Rehnquist's construction of *Griggs* in *Weber* continue to have any validity?

4. In *Connecticut v. Teal*, 457 U.S. 440, 102 S.Ct. 2525, 73 L.Ed.2d 130 (1982), reproduced in Chapter 4, a case involving the bottom-line defense, Justice Brennan construed Title VII as protecting individuals and not groups. Is Justice Brennan's construction of § 703(j) in *Weber* consistent with his opinion for the Court in *Connecticut v. Teal*?

5. *Weber* established a three-pronged test to determine whether a voluntarily adopted affirmative action plan survives a challenge under Title VII. First, the purpose of the plan must be to remedy traditional patterns of discrimination. Second, the plan must not unduly trammel the interests of applicants and employees who are not beneficiaries of the plan. Third, the plan must be temporary, that is, it must be in effect only so long as it is necessary to eradicate traditional patterns of discrimination. See Chris Engels, *Voluntary Affirmative Action in Employment for Women and Minorities Under Title VII of the Civil Rights Act: Extending Possibilities for Employers to Engage in Preferential Treatment to Achieve Equal Employment Opportunity*, 24 J. Marshall L.Rev. 731 (1991); Nancy E. Dowd, Bakke *and* Weber: *The Concept of Societal Discrimination*, 11 Loy.U.Chi.L.J. 297, 297–98 (1980).

In his concurring opinion in *Weber*, Justice Blackmun questioned whether the Court's three-pronged test might be overly broad because it would legitimate an affirmative action plan under Title VII even when the plan is designed to remedy societal discrimination. He asserted that an "arguable violation" theory would provide a more legitimate justification for a voluntary affirmative action plan under Title VII:

In his dissent from the decision of the United States Court of Appeals for the Fifth Circuit, Judge Wisdom pointed out that this litigation arises from a practical problem in the administration of Title VII. The broad prohibition against discrimination places the employer and the union on what he accurately described as a "high tightrope without a net beneath them." If Title VII is read literally, on the one hand they face liability for past discrimination against blacks, and on the other they face liability to whites for any voluntary preferences adopted to mitigate the effects of prior discrimination against blacks.

* * *

The "arguable violation" theory has a number of advantages. It responds to a practical problem in the administration of Title VII not anticipated by Congress. It draws predictability from the outline of present law and closely effectuates the purpose of the Act. Both Kaiser and the United States urge its adoption here. Because I agree that it is the soundest way to approach this case, my preference would be to resolve this litigation by applying it and holding that Kaiser's craft training program meets the requirement that voluntary affirmative action be a reasonable response to an "arguable violation" of Title VII.

* * *

The Court, however, declines to consider the narrow "arguable violation" approach and adheres instead to an interpretation of Title VII that permits affirmative action by an employer whenever the job category in question is "traditionally segregated." The sources cited suggest that the Court considers a job category to be "traditionally segregated" when there has been a societal history of purposeful exclusion of blacks from the job category, resulting in a persistent disparity between the proportion of blacks in the labor force and the proportion of blacks among those who hold jobs within the category.

"Traditional segregated job categories," where they exist, sweep more broadly than the class of "arguable violations" of Title VII. The Court's expansive approach is somewhat disturbing for me because, as Mr. Justice Rehnquist points out, the Congress that passed Title VII probably thought it was adopting a principle of nondiscrimination that would apply to blacks and whites alike.

Weber, 443 U.S. at 209–13, 99 S.Ct. at 2730–32 (Blackmun, J., concurring). What options are open to employers and unions that face the kind of "high tightrope without a net beneath them" described by Justice Blackmun? What advice would you give to an employer or union in this situation?

6. Employers were highly critical of the affirmative action remedy prior to *Weber*, but over time many became strong supporters of affirmative action. The response of the business community to affirmative action is discussed in Note, *Rethinking* Weber: *The Business Response to Affirmative Action*, 102 Harv.L.Rev. 658 (1989).

2. EVALUATING THE LEGITIMACY OF AFFIRMATIVE ACTION UNDER TITLE VII

JOHNSON v. TRANSPORTATION AGENCY, SANTA CLARA COUNTY, CALIFORNIA

Supreme Court of the United States, 1987.
480 U.S. 616, 107 S.Ct. 1442, 94 L.Ed.2d 615.

JUSTICE BRENNAN delivered the opinion of the Court.

Respondent, Transportation Agency of Santa Clara County, California, unilaterally promulgated an Affirmative Action Plan applicable, *inter alia*, to promotions of employees. In selecting applicants for the promotional position of road dispatcher, the Agency, pursuant to the Plan, passed over petitioner Paul Johnson, a male employee, and promoted a female employee applicant, Diane Joyce. The question for decision is whether in making the promotion the Agency impermissibly took into account the sex of the applicants in violation of Title VII of the Civil Rights Act of 1964. The District Court * * * held that respondent had violated Title VII. The Court of Appeals for the Ninth Circuit reversed. We granted certiorari. We affirm.[2]

I

A

In December 1978, the Santa Clara County Transit District Board of Supervisors adopted an Affirmative Action Plan (Plan) for the County Transportation Agency. The Plan implemented a County Affirmative Action Plan, which had been adopted, declared the County, because "mere prohibition of discriminatory practices is not enough to remedy the effects of past practices and to permit attainment of an equitable representation of minorities, women and handicapped persons." Relevant to this case, the Agency Plan provides that, in making promotions to positions within a traditionally segregated job classification in which women have been significantly underrepresented, the Agency is authorized to consider as one factor the sex of a qualified applicant.

In reviewing the composition of its work force, the Agency noted in its Plan that women were represented in numbers far less than their proportion of the County labor force in both the Agency as a whole and in five of seven job categories. Specifically, while women constituted 36.4% of the area labor market, they composed only 22.4% of Agency employees. Furthermore, women working at the Agency were concentrated largely in EEOC job categories traditionally held by women: women made up 76% of Office and Clerical Workers, but only 7.1% of

---

2. No constitutional issue was either raised or addressed in the litigation below. We therefore decide in this case only the issue of the prohibitory scope of Title VII. Of course, where the issue is properly raised, public employers must justify the adoption and implementation of a voluntary affirmative action plan under the Equal Protection Clause. *See* Wygant v. Jackson Board of Education, 476 U.S. 267, 106 S.Ct. 1842, 90 L.Ed.2d 260 (1986).

Agency Officials and Administrators, 8.6% of Professionals, 9.7% of Technicians, and 22% of Service and Maintenance Workers. As for the job classification relevant to this case, none of the 238 Skilled Craft Worker positions was held by a woman. The Plan noted that this underrepresentation of women in part reflected the fact that women had not traditionally been employed in these positions, and that they had not been strongly motivated to seek training or employment in them "because of the limited opportunities that have existed in the past for them to work in such classifications." The Plan also observed that, while the proportion of ethnic minorities in the Agency as a whole exceeded the proportion of such minorities in the County work force, a smaller percentage of minority employees held management, professional, and technical positions.[4]

The Agency stated that its Plan was intended to achieve "a statistically measurable yearly improvement in hiring, training and promotion of minorities and women throughout the Agency in all major job classifications where they are underrepresented." As a benchmark by which to evaluate progress, the Agency stated that its long-term goal was to attain a work force whose composition reflected the proportion of minorities and women in the area labor force. Thus, for the Skilled Craft category in which the road dispatcher position at issue here was classified, the Agency's aspiration was that eventually about 36% of the jobs would be occupied by women.

* * *

The Agency's Plan thus set aside no specific number of positions for minorities or women, but authorized the consideration of ethnicity or sex as a factor when evaluating qualified candidates for jobs in which members of such groups were poorly represented. One such job was the road dispatcher position that is the subject of the dispute in this case.

B

On December 12, 1979, the Agency announced a vacancy for the promotional position of road dispatcher in the Agency's Roads Division. Dispatchers assign road crews, equipment, and materials, and maintain records pertaining to road maintenance jobs. The position requires at minimum four years of dispatch or road maintenance work experience for Santa Clara County. * * *

Twelve County employees applied for the promotion, including Joyce and Johnson. Joyce had worked for the County since 1970, serving as an account clerk until 1975. She had applied for a road dispatcher position in 1974, but was deemed ineligible because she had not served as a road maintenance worker. In 1975, Joyce transferred from a senior account clerk position to a road maintenance worker position, becoming the first

---

4. While minorities constituted 19.7% of the County labor force, they represented 7.1% of the Agency's Officials and Administrators, 19% of its Professionals, and 16.9% of its Technicians.

woman to fill such a job. During her four years in that position, she occasionally worked out of class as a road dispatcher.

Petitioner Johnson began with the County in 1967 as a road yard clerk, after private employment that included working as a supervisor and dispatcher. He had also unsuccessfully applied for the road dispatcher opening in 1974. In 1977, his clerical position was downgraded, and he sought and received a transfer to the position of road maintenance worker. He also occasionally worked out of class as a dispatcher while performing that job.

Nine of the applicants, including Joyce and Johnson, were deemed qualified for the job, and were interviewed by a two-person board. Seven of the applicants scored above 70 on this interview, which meant that they were certified as eligible for selection by the appointing authority. The scores awarded ranged from 70 to 80. Johnson was tied for second with a score of 75, while Joyce ranked next with a score of 73. A second interview was conducted by three Agency supervisors, who ultimately recommended that Johnson be promoted. * * * At the time, the Agency employed no women in any Skilled Craft position, and had never employed a woman as a road dispatcher. The Coordinator recommended to the Director of the Agency, James Graebner, that Joyce be promoted.

Graebner, authorized to choose any of the seven persons deemed eligible, thus had the benefit of suggestions by the second interview panel and by the Agency Coordinator in arriving at his decision. After deliberation, Graebner concluded that the promotion should be given to Joyce. As he testified: "I tried to look at the whole picture, the combination of her qualifications and Mr. Johnson's qualifications, their test scores, their expertise, their background, affirmative action matters, things like that * * *. I believe it was a combination of all those."

The certification form naming Joyce as the person promoted to the dispatcher position stated that both she and Johnson were rated as well qualified for the job. The evaluation of Joyce read: "Well qualified by virtue of 18 years of past clerical experience including 3 1/2 years at West Yard plus almost 5 years as a [road maintenance worker]." The evaluation of Johnson was as follows: "Well qualified applicant; two years of [road maintenance worker] experience plus 11 years of Road Yard Clerk. Has had previous outside Dispatch experience but was 13 years ago." Graebner testified that he did not regard as significant the fact that Johnson scored 75 and Joyce 73 when interviewed by the two-person board.

Petitioner Johnson filed a complaint with the EEOC alleging that he had been denied promotion on the basis of sex in violation of Title VII. * * *

* * *

II

* * *

The assessment of the legality of the Agency Plan must be guided by our decision in *Weber*.[6] * * *

* * *

In reviewing the employment decision at issue in this case, we must first examine whether that decision was made pursuant to a plan prompted by concerns similar to those of the employer in *Weber*. Next, we must determine whether the effect of the Plan on males and nonminorities is comparable to the effect of the plan in that case.

The first issue is therefore whether consideration of the sex of applicants for Skilled Craft jobs was justified by the existence of a "manifest imbalance" that reflected underrepresentation of women in "traditionally segregated job categories." In determining whether an imbalance exists that would justify taking sex or race into account, a comparison of the percentage of minorities or women in the employer's work force with the percentage in the area labor market or general population is appropriate in analyzing jobs that require no special expertise or training programs designed to provide expertise, *see* Teamsters v. United States, 431 U.S. 324, 97 S.Ct. 1843, 52 L.Ed.2d 396 (1977) (comparison between percentage of blacks in employer's work force and in general population proper in determining extent of imbalance in truck driving positions), or training programs designed to provide experience, *see* Steelworkers v. Weber, 443 U.S. 193, 99 S.Ct. 2721, 61 L.Ed.2d 480 (1979). Where a job requires special training, however, the comparison should be with those in the labor force who possess the relevant qualifications. *See* Hazelwood School District v. United States, 433 U.S. 299, 97 S.Ct. 2736, 53 L.Ed.2d 768 (1977). The requirement that the "manifest imbalance" relate to a "traditionally segregated job category" provides assurance both that sex or race will be taken into account in a manner consistent with Title VII's purpose of eliminating the effects of employment discrimination, and that the interests of those employees not benefiting from the plan will not be unduly infringed.

---

6. Justice Scalia's dissent maintains that the obligations of a public employer under Title VII must be identical to its obligations under the Constitution, and that a public employer's adoption of an affirmative action plan therefore should be governed by *Wygant*. This rests on the following logic: Title VI embodies the same constraints as the Constitution; Title VI and Title VII have the same prohibitory scope; therefore, Title VII and the Constitution are coterminous for purposes of this case. The flaw is with the second step of the analysis, for it advances a proposition that we explicitly considered and rejected in *Weber*. As we noted in that case, Title VI was an exercise of federal power "over a matter in which the Federal Government was already directly involved," since Congress "was legislating to assure federal funds would not be used in an improper manner." 443 U.S. at 206 n.6, 99 S.Ct. at 2729 n.6. "Title VII, by contrast, was enacted pursuant to the commerce power to regulate purely private decisionmaking and was not intended to incorporate and particularize the commands of the Fifth and Fourteenth Amendments. Title VII and Title VI, therefore, cannot be read *in pari materia*." *Ibid*. This point is underscored by Congress' concern that the receipt of any form of financial assistance might render an employer subject to the commands of Title VI rather than Title VII. * * *

A manifest imbalance need not be such that it would support a prima facie case against the employer, as suggested in Justice O'Connor's concurrence, since we do not regard as identical the constraints of Title VII and the Federal Constitution on voluntarily adopted affirmative action plans. Application of the "prima facie" standard in Title VII cases would be inconsistent with *Weber*'s focus on statistical imbalance,[10] and could inappropriately create a significant disincentive for employers to adopt an affirmative action plan. *See Weber*, 443 U.S. at 204, 99 S.Ct. at 2727–28 (Title VII intended as a "catalyst" for employer efforts to eliminate vestiges of discrimination). A corporation concerned with maximizing return on investment, for instance, is hardly likely to adopt a plan if in order to do so it must compile evidence that could be used to subject it to a colorable Title VII suit.[11]

It is clear that the decision to hire Joyce was made pursuant to an Agency plan that directed that sex or race be taken into account for the purpose of remedying underrepresentation. The Agency Plan acknowledged the "limited opportunities that have existed in the past," for women to find employment in certain job classifications "where women have not been traditionally employed in significant numbers." As a result, observed the Plan, women were concentrated in traditionally female jobs in the Agency, and represented a lower percentage in other job classifications than would be expected if such traditional segregation had not occurred. Specifically, 9 of the 10 Para–Professionals and 110 of the 145 Office and Clerical Workers were women. By contrast, women

---

10. The difference between the "manifest imbalance" and "prima facie" standards is illuminated by *Weber*. Had the Court in that case been concerned with past discrimination by the employer, it would have focused on discrimination in hiring skilled, not unskilled, workers, since only the scarcity of the former in Kaiser's work force would have made it vulnerable to a Title VII suit. In order to make out a prima facie case on such a claim, a plaintiff would be required to compare the percentage of black skilled workers in the Kaiser work force with the percentage of black skilled craft workers in the area labor market.

Weber obviously did not make such a comparison. Instead, it focused on the disparity between the percentage of black skilled craft workers in Kaiser's ranks and the percentage of blacks in the area labor force. Such an approach reflected a recognition that the proportion of black craft workers in the local labor force was likely as minuscule as the proportion in Kaiser's work force. The Court realized that the lack of imbalance between these figures would mean that employers in precisely those industries in which discrimination has been most effective would be precluded from adopting training programs to increase the percentage of qualified minorities. Thus, in cases such as *Weber*, where the employment decision at issue involves the selection of unskilled persons for a training program, the "manifest imbalance" standard permits comparison with the general labor force. By contrast, the "prima facie" standard would require comparison with the percentage of minorities or women qualified for the job for which the trainees are being trained, a standard that would have invalidated the plan in *Weber* itself.

11. In some cases, of course, the manifest imbalance may be sufficiently egregious to establish a prima facie case. However, as long as there is a manifest imbalance, an employer may adopt a plan even where the disparity is not so striking, without being required to introduce the nonstatistical evidence of past discrimination that would be demanded by the "prima facie" standard. *See, e.g.*, Teamsters v. United States, 431 U.S. 324, 339, 97 S.Ct. 1843, 1856, 52 L.Ed.2d 396 (1977) (statistics in pattern and practice case supplemented by testimony regarding employment practices). Of course, when there is sufficient evidence to meet the more stringent "prima facie" standard, be it statistical, nonstatistical, or a combination of the two, the employer is free to adopt an affirmative action plan.

were only 2 of the 28 Officials and Administrators, 5 of the 58 Professionals, 12 of the 124 Technicians, none of the Skilled Craft Workers, and 1—who was Joyce—of the 110 Road Maintenance Workers. The Plan sought to remedy these imbalances through "hiring, training and promotion of * * * women throughout the Agency in all major job classifications where they are underrepresented."

As an initial matter, the Agency adopted as a benchmark for measuring progress in eliminating underrepresentation the long-term goal of a work force that mirrored in its major job classifications the percentage of women in the area labor market.[13] Even as it did so, however, the Agency acknowledged that such a figure could not by itself necessarily justify taking into account the sex of applicants for positions in all job categories. For positions requiring specialized training and experience, the Plan observed that the number of minorities and women "who possess the qualifications required for entry into such job classifications is limited." The Plan therefore directed that annual short-term goals be formulated that would provide a more realistic indication of the degree to which sex should be taken into account in filling particular positions. The Plan stressed that such goals "should not be construed as 'quotas' that must be met," but as reasonable aspirations in correcting the imbalance in the Agency's work force. These goals were to take into account factors such as "turnover, layoffs, lateral transfers, new job openings, retirements and availability of minorities, women and handicapped persons in the area work force who possess the desired qualifications or potential for placement." The Plan specifically directed that, in establishing such goals, the Agency work with the County Planning Department and other sources in attempting to compile data on the percentage of minorities and women in the local labor force that were actually working in the job classifications constituting the Agency work force. From the outset, therefore, the Plan sought annually to develop even more refined measures of the underrepresentation in each job category that required attention.

As the Agency Plan recognized, women were most egregiously underrepresented in the Skilled Craft job category, since none of the 238 positions was occupied by a woman. In mid–1980, when Joyce was selected for the road dispatcher position, the Agency was still in the process of refining its short-term goals for Skilled Craft Workers in accordance with the directive of the Plan. This process did not reach fruition until 1982, when the Agency established a short-term goal for that year of 3 women for the 55 expected openings in that job category— a modest goal of about 6% for that category.

We reject petitioner's argument that, since only the long-term goal was in place for Skilled Craft positions at the time of Joyce's promotion, it was inappropriate for the Director to take into account affirmative

---

13. Because of the employment decision at issue in this case, our discussion henceforth refers primarily to the Plan's provisions to remedy the underrepresentation of women. Our analysis could apply as well, however, to the provisions of the plan pertaining to minorities.

action considerations in filling the road dispatcher position. The Agency's Plan emphasized that the long-term goals were not to be taken as guides for actual hiring decisions, but that supervisors were to consider a host of practical factors in seeking to meet affirmative action objectives, including the fact that in some job categories women were not qualified in numbers comparable to their representation in the labor force.

By contrast, had the Plan simply calculated imbalances in all categories according to the proportion of women in the area labor pool, and then directed that hiring be governed solely by those figures, its validity fairly could be called into question. This is because analysis of a more specialized labor pool normally is necessary in determining underrepresentation in some positions. If a plan failed to take distinctions in qualifications into account in providing guidance for actual employment decisions, it would dictate mere blind hiring by the numbers, for it would hold supervisors to "achievement of a particular percentage of minority employment or membership * * * regardless of circumstances such as economic conditions or the number of available qualified minority applicants * * *." Sheet Metal Workers v. EEOC, 478 U.S. 421, 495, 106 S.Ct. 3019, 3060, 92 L.Ed.2d 344 (1986) (O'Connor, J., concurring in part and dissenting in part).

The Agency's Plan emphatically did *not* authorize such blind hiring. It expressly directed that numerous factors be taken into account in making hiring decisions, including specifically the qualifications of female applicants for particular jobs. Thus, despite the fact that no precise short-term goal was yet in place for the Skilled Craft category in mid–1980, the Agency's management nevertheless had been clearly instructed that they were not to hire solely by reference to statistics. The fact that only the long-term goal had been established for this category posed no danger that personnel decisions would be made by reflexive adherence to a numerical standard.

Furthermore, in considering the candidates for the road dispatcher position in 1980, the Agency hardly needed to rely on a refined short-term goal to realize that it had a significant problem of underrepresentation that required attention. Given the obvious imbalance in the Skilled Craft category, and given the Agency's commitment to eliminating such imbalances, it was plainly not unreasonable for the Agency to determine that it was appropriate to consider as one factor the sex of Ms. Joyce in making its decision.[14] The promotion of Joyce thus satisfies the first requirement enunciated in *Weber*, since it was undertaken to further an affirmative action plan designed to eliminate Agency work force imbalances in traditionally segregated job categories.

---

14. In addition, the Agency was mindful of the importance of finally hiring a woman in a job category that had formerly been all male. The Director testified that, while the promotion of Joyce "made a small dent, for sure, in the numbers," nonetheless "philosophically it made a larger impact in that it probably has encouraged other females and minorities to look at the possibility of so-called 'non-traditional' jobs as areas where they and the agency both have samples of a success story."

We next consider whether the Agency Plan unnecessarily trammeled the rights of male employees or created an absolute bar to their advancement. In contrast to the plan in *Weber*, which provided that 50% of the positions in the craft training program were exclusively for blacks, and to the consent decree upheld last Term in *Firefighters v. Cleveland*, 478 U.S. 501, 106 S.Ct. 3063, 92 L.Ed.2d 405 (1986), which required the promotion of specific numbers of minorities, the Plan sets aside no positions for women. The Plan expressly states that "[t]he 'goals' established for each Division should not be construed as 'quotas' that must be met." Rather, the Plan merely authorizes that consideration be given to affirmative action concerns when evaluating qualified applicants. As the Agency Director testified, the sex of Joyce was but one of numerous factors he took into account in arriving at his decision. The Plan thus resembles the "Harvard Plan" approvingly noted by Justice Powell in *Regents of University of California v. Bakke*, 438 U.S. 265, 316–319, 98 S.Ct. 2733, 2761–63, 57 L.Ed.2d 750 (1978), which considers race along with other criteria in determining admission to the college. As Justice Powell observed: "In such an admissions program, race or ethnic background may be deemed a 'plus' in a particular applicant's file, yet it does not insulate the individual from comparison with all other candidates for the available seats." *Id*. at 317, 98 S.Ct. at 2762. Similarly, the Agency Plan requires women to compete with all other qualified applicants. *No* persons are automatically excluded from consideration; *all* are able to have their qualifications weighed against those of other applicants.

In addition, petitioner had no absolute entitlement to the road dispatcher position. Seven of the applicants were classified as qualified and eligible, and the Agency Director was authorized to promote any of the seven. Thus, denial of the promotion unsettled no legitimate, firmly rooted expectation on the part of petitioner. Furthermore, while petitioner in this case was denied a promotion, he retained his employment with the Agency, at the same salary and with the same seniority, and remained eligible for other promotions.

Finally, the Agency's Plan was intended to *attain* a balanced workforce, not to maintain one. The Plan contains 10 references to the Agency's desire to "attain" such a balance, but no reference whatsoever to a goal of maintaining it. The Director testified that, while the "broader goal" of affirmative action, defined as "the desire to hire, to promote, to give opportunity and training on an equitable, non-discriminatory basis," is something that is "a permanent part" of "the Agency's operating philosophy," that broader goal "is divorced, if you will, from specific numbers or percentages."

The Agency acknowledged the difficulties that it would confront in remedying the imbalance in its work force, and it anticipated only gradual increases in the representation of minorities and women. It is thus unsurprising that the Plan contains no explicit end date, for the Agency's flexible, case-by-case approach was not expected to yield success in a brief period of time. Express assurance that a program is only temporary may be necessary if the program actually sets aside positions according to specific numbers. *See, e.g., Firefighters*, 478 U.S. at 510, 106 S.Ct. at 3069 (4–year duration for consent decree providing for promotion of particular number of minorities); *Weber*, 443 U.S. at 199, 99 S.Ct. at 2725 (plan requiring that blacks constitute 50% of new trainees in effect until percentage of employer work force equal to percentage in local labor force). This is necessary both to minimize the effect of the program on other employees, and to ensure that the plan's goals "[are] not being used simply to achieve and maintain * * * balance, but rather as a benchmark against which" the employer may measure its progress in eliminating the underrepresentation of minorities and women. *Sheet Metal Workers*, 478 U.S. at 477–78, 106 S.Ct. at 3051. In this case, however, substantial evidence shows that the Agency has sought to take a moderate, gradual approach to eliminating the imbalance in its work force, one which establishes realistic guidance for employment decisions, and which visits minimal intrusion on the legitimate expectations of other employees. Given this fact, as well as the Agency's express commitment to "attain" a balanced work force, there is ample assurance that the Agency does not seek to use its Plan to maintain a permanent racial and sexual balance.

III

In evaluating the compliance of an affirmative action plan with Title VII's prohibition on discrimination, we must be mindful of "this Court's and Congress' consistent emphasis on 'the value of voluntary efforts to further the objectives of the law.'" *Wygant*, 476 U.S. at 290, 106 S.Ct. at 1855 (O'Connor J., concurring in part and concurring in judgment) (quoting *Bakke*, 438 U.S. at 364, 98 S.Ct. 2785–86). The Agency in the case before us has undertaken such a voluntary effort, and has done so in full recognition of both the difficulties and the potential for intrusion on males and nonminorities. The Agency has identified a conspicuous imbalance in job categories traditionally segregated by race and sex. It has made clear from the outset, however, that employment decisions may not be justified solely by reference to this imbalance, but must rest on a multitude of practical, realistic factors. It has therefore committed itself to annual adjustment of goals so as to provide a reasonable guide for actual hiring and promotion decisions. The Agency earmarks no positions for anyone; sex is but one of several factors that may be taken into account in evaluating qualified applicants for a position.[17] As both

---

17. Justice Scalia's dissent predicts that today's decision will loose a flood of "less qualified" minorities and women upon the work force, as employers seek to forestall possible Title VII liability. The first problem with this projection is that it is by no means certain that employers could in every case necessarily avoid liability for discrimination merely by adopting an affirmative action plan. Indeed, our unwillingness to require an admission of discrimination as the price of adopting a plan has been prem-

ised on concern that the potential liability to which such an admission would expose an employer would serve as a disincentive for creating an affirmative action program. A second, and more fundamental, problem with Justice Scalia's speculation is that he ignores the fact that

> [i]t is a standard tenet of personnel administration that there is rarely a single, "best qualified" person for a job. An effective personnel system will bring before the selecting official several fully-quali-

the Plan's language and its manner of operation attest, the Agency has no intention of establishing a work force whose permanent composition is dictated by rigid numerical standards.

We therefore hold that the Agency appropriately took into account as one factor the sex of Diane Joyce in determining that she should be promoted to the road dispatcher position. The decision to do so was made pursuant to an affirmative action plan that represents a moderate, flexible, case-by-case approach to effecting a gradual improvement in the representation of minorities and women in the Agency's work force. Such a plan is fully consistent with Title VII, for it embodies the contribution that voluntary employer action can make in eliminating the vestiges of discrimination in the workplace. * * *

* * *

JUSTICE O'CONNOR, concurring in the judgment.

* * *

I concur in the judgment of the Court in light of our precedents. I write separately, however, because the Court has chosen to follow an expansive and ill-defined approach to voluntary affirmative action by public employers despite the limitations imposed by the Constitution and by the provisions of Title VII, and because Justice Scalia's dissent rejects the Court's precedents and addresses the question of how Title VII should be interpreted as if the Court were writing on a clean slate. The former course of action gives insufficient guidance to courts and litigants; the latter course of action serves as a useful point of academic discussion, but fails to reckon with the reality of the course that the majority of the Court has determined to follow.

In my view, the proper initial inquiry in evaluating the legality of an affirmative action plan by a public employer under Title VII is no different from that required by the Equal Protection Clause. In either case, consistent with the congressional intent to provide some measure of protection to the interests of the employer's nonminority employees, the employer must have had a firm basis for believing that remedial action was required. An employer would have such a firm basis if it can point to a statistical disparity sufficient to support a prima facie claim under Title VII by the employee beneficiaries of the affirmative action plan of a pattern or practice claim of discrimination.

* * *

fied candidates who each may possess different attributes which recommend them for selection. Especially where the job is an unexceptional, middle-level craft position, without the need for unique work experience or educational attainment and for which several well-qualified candidates are available, final determinations as to which candidate is "best qualified" are at best subjective.

Brief for the American Society for Personnel Administration as *Amicus Curiae* 9.

This case provides an example of precisely this point. Any differences in qualifications between Johnson and Joyce were minimal, to say the least. The selection of Joyce thus belies Justice Scalia's contention that the beneficiaries of affirmative action programs will be those employees who are merely not "utterly unqualified."

The *Weber* view of Congress' resolution of the conflicting concerns of minority and nonminority workers in Title VII appears substantially similar to this Court's resolution of these same concerns in *Wygant v. Jackson Board of Education*, 476 U.S. 267, 106 S.Ct. 1842, 90 L.Ed.2d 260 (1986), which involved the claim that an affirmative action plan by a public employer violated the Equal Protection Clause. In *Wygant*, the Court was in agreement that remedying past or present racial discrimination by a state actor is a sufficiently weighty interest to warrant the remedial use of a carefully constructed affirmative action plan. The Court also concluded, however, that "[s]ocietal discrimination, without more, is too amorphous a basis for imposing a racially classified remedy." *Id.* at 276, 106 S.Ct. at 1848. Instead, we determined that affirmative action was valid if it was crafted to remedy past or present discrimination by the employer. Although the employer need not point to any contemporaneous findings of actual discrimination, I concluded in *Wygant* that the employer must point to evidence sufficient to establish a firm basis for believing that remedial action is required, and that a statistical imbalance sufficient for a Title VII prima facie case against the employer would satisfy this firm basis requirement. * * *

The *Wygant* analysis is entirely consistent with *Weber*. * * *

* * *

In sum, I agree that respondents' affirmative action plan as implemented in this instance with respect to skilled craft positions satisfies the requirements of *Weber* and of *Wygant*. Accordingly, I concur in the judgment of the Court.

JUSTICE WHITE, dissenting.

* * * My understanding of *Weber* was, and is, that the employer's plan did not violate Title VII because it was designed to remedy the intentional and systematic exclusion of blacks by the employer and the unions from certain job categories. That is how I understood the phrase "traditionally segregated jobs" that we used in that case. The Court now interprets it to mean nothing more than a manifest imbalance between one identifiable group and another in an employer's labor force. As so interpreted, that case, as well as today's decision, * * * is a perversion of Title VII. I would overrule *Weber* and reverse the judgment below.

JUSTICE SCALIA, with whom THE CHIEF JUSTICE joins, and with whom JUSTICE WHITE joins * * *, in parts I and II, dissenting.

* * *

II

The most significant proposition of law established by today's decision is that racial or sexual discrimination is permitted under Title VII when it is intended to overcome the effect, not of the employer's own discrimination, but of societal attitudes that have limited the entry of certain races, or of a particular sex, into certain jobs. Even if the societal attitudes in question consisted exclusively of conscious discrimination by other employers, this holding would contradict a decision of this Court rendered only last Term. *Wygant v. Jackson Board of Education*, 476 U.S. 267, 106 S.Ct. 1842, 90 L.Ed.2d 260 (1986), held that the objective of remedying societal discrimination cannot prevent remedial affirmative action from violating the Equal Protection Clause. While Mr. Johnson does not advance a constitutional claim here, it is most unlikely that Title VII was intended to place a *lesser* restraint on discrimination by public actors than is established by the Constitution. * * *

* * *

It is unlikely that today's result will be displeasing to politically elected officials, to whom it provides the means of quickly accommodating the demands of organized groups to achieve concrete, numerical improvement in the economic status of particular constituencies. Nor will it displease the world of corporate and governmental employers (many of whom have filed briefs as *amici* in the present case, all on the side of Santa Clara) for whom the cost of hiring less qualified workers is often substantially less—and infinitely more predictable—than the cost of litigating Title VII cases and of seeking to convince federal agencies by nonnumerical means that no discrimination exists. In fact, the only losers in the process are the Johnsons of the country, for whom Title VII has been not merely repealed but actually inverted. The irony is that these individuals—predominantly unknown, unaffluent, unorganized—suffer this injustice at the hands of a Court fond of thinking itself the champion of the politically impotent. I dissent.

Notes and Questions

1. Justices Brennan and Scalia disagreed about whether the equal protection strict scrutiny test applies to a public employer even when its affirmative action plan is challenged solely under Title VII. Justice Brennan argued that the test is not the same; Justice Scalia argued that it is. Should the standard of review be the same for both public and private employers? *See* George Rutherglen & Daniel R. Ortiz, *Affirmative Action Under the Constitution and Title VII: From Confusion to Convergence*, 35 UCLA L.Rev. 467 (1988). What problems do you envision if Justice Scalia's view prevailed? If Justice Scalia's view were to prevail, would it mean that the Court would have to overturn *Washington v. Davis*, 426 U.S. 229, 96 S.Ct. 2040, 48 L.Ed.2d 597 (1976), where the Court refused to apply Title VII disparate impact analysis to employment discrimination cases brought under the equal protection component of the Fifth Amendment.

2. Justice Brennan and Justice O'Connor disagreed about the applicable standard for the first prong of *Weber*. Justice Brennan adopted the "manifest imbalance" standard; Justice O'Connor advocated the "firm basis in fact for believing that remedial action is necessary" test. What do you think is at the bottom of their disagreement? Is it about the meaning of

discrimination? Is it about the appropriateness of societal discrimination as a justification for affirmative action? Is it about whether affirmative action plans adopted by government employers should be subject to the same level of scrutiny under both the Constitution and Title VII? Relying on her opinion in *Wygant*, Justice O'Connor argues that this initial inquiry is the same for a public employer whether the affirmative action plan is challenged under Title VII or the Equal Protection Clause. Is there any substantive difference between these two standards?

It is clear, is it not, that under Justice Brennan's view, an employer could rely upon societal discrimination to satisfy the "manifest imbalance" test? Justice White, who dissented in *Johnson*, would overrule *Weber* because he viewed *Weber*'s first prong—traditionally segregated jobs or manifest imbalance—to mean only intentional discrimination and not societal discrimination. *Johnson*, 480 U.S. at 657, 107 S.Ct. at 1465. Could a public employer satisfy the first prong of *Weber* under Justice O'Connor's view by relying on evidence of societal discrimination? Does her decision in *Weber* suggest that a private employer or union could rely on evidence of societal discrimination to satisfy the first prong of *Weber*? For a discussion of some of the difficulties with the "manifest imbalance" prong, see David D. Meyer, Note, *Finding a "Manifest Imbalance": The Case for a Unified Statistical Test for Voluntary Affirmative Action Under Title VII*, 87 Mich.L.Rev. 1986 (1989).

3. Justice O'Connor apparently did not disagree with Justice Brennan's treatment and analysis of the "unduly trammel" and "temporary nature" prongs of *Weber*.

4. Suppose the plaintiff in *Johnson v. Transportation Agency* had brought his claim solely under the Fourteenth Amendment Equal Protection Clause instead of under Title VII? What is the likelihood that the result would have been different? If the outcome would have been different, does this mean that Title VII and the Equal Protection Clause embrace different visions of workplace equality?

5. Suppose an employer—public or private—voluntarily adopts an affirmative action plan for persons of color and women but fails to follow that plan with respect to individuals in the beneficiary class. For example, suppose the employer in *Johnson v. Transportation Agency* had failed to follow its affirmative action plan, and Paul Johnson, the male, rather than Diane Joyce, the female, had been awarded the job, even though both were equally qualified and all other facts remained the same. Would a member of a beneficiary class under an affirmative action plan, like Diane Joyce, who arguably should have been awarded an employment opportunity pursuant to the plan, have a claim for discrimination if the employer had failed to follow its plan? Should an employer's failure to follow its own affirmative action plan be sufficient, standing alone, to establish a prima facie case of employment discrimination? If not, what would constitute relevant evidence of discriminatory intent? *See* Liao v. TVA, 867 F.2d 1366, *cert. denied sub nom.* Liao v. Dean, 494 U.S. 1078, 110 S.Ct. 1806, 108 L.Ed.2d 937 (1990). If an employer is not obligated to follow its own affirmative action plan, does it mean that only nonbeneficiaries can sue the employer when it adopts such a plan?

6. For a case study of *Johnson*, see Melvin I. Urofsky, Affirmative Action on Trial: Sex Discrimination in *Johnson v. Santa Clara* (1997).

7. In her article, *Civil Rights Perestroika: Intergoup Relations After Affirmative Action*, 86 Calif.L.Rev. 1251 (1998), Linda Hamilton Krieger raises and responds to questions that permeate much of the debate about affirmative action:

> What might we expect if every institution in the nation—every college and university, every corporation, every state and local public agency, and every arm and organ of the federal government—suddenly prohibited its employees from considering the race, sex, or national origin of applicants or employees in hiring, contracting, promotion, or admission to educational programs? What would happen if every employment and admissions decision maker was told simply to "be colorblind," to base his or her decision only on "considerations of merit"? Would they do it? Could they do it? Could we identify those who did not do it, whose decisions were tainted by intergroup bias?

> The answers to these questions are, quite simply, "no," "no," and "no." Perhaps constitutions can be colorblind. Perhaps official government or corporate policies can be colorblind. But human beings living in a society in which history, ideology, law, and patterns of social, economic, and political distribution have made race, sex, and ethnicity salient, cannot be colorblind. The "colorblindness" approach to nondiscrimination will prove ineffective because it provides neither a framework for enabling people to recognize the effects of race, gender, or national origin on their perceptions and judgments, nor the tools required to help them counteract those effects. Indeed, a color blindness-centered interpretation of the nondiscrimination principle, coupled with well-meaning people's awareness that they do categorize along racial and ethnic lines, may exacerbate the very intergroup anxiety and ambivalence that lead to what social psychologist refer to as aversive racism.

> Furthermore, decision makers cannot base selection decisions only on colorblind considerations of merit for the simple reason that merit has a color. Conceptions of merit are socially and politically constructed and are shaped by the same ingroup preferences that give rise to other subtle forms of intergroup bias. Affirmative action preferences have, in many ways, diverted our attention from the biases inherent in the construction of merit. But if preferences are eliminated, this problem and the inequities it generates will soon rise in sharp relief.

> Finally, there is substantial reason to doubt that remaining law enforcement tools, particularly the adjudication of individual disparate treatment cases, will prove effective in identifying and remedying subtle but pervasive forms of intergroup bias. For a variety of reasons, reliance on individual disparate treatment adjudication can be expected to result in the serious underidentification of discrimination by judicial decision makers, victims, and private fact finders.

Id. at 1276–77. Do you agree with the responses that Professor Krieger gives to the questions that she raises? If not, how would you respond to the questions?

8.   Assume the following facts:

The Piscataway School Board decided to lay off one of the teachers in the Business Education Department of the high school. State law required that public schools lay off teachers on the basis of seniority and gave school boards discretion to make lay off decisions only in the case of a tie in seniority. There were only two teachers in the Piscataway high school Business Education Department: one, Debra Williams, is black; the other, Sharon Taxman, is white. Both Williams and Taxman had the same seniority standing because both had started working at the high school on the same day nine years earlier. The Board determined that both were equally qualified in their "classroom performance, evaluations, volunteerism, and certifications."

In previous decisions regarding lay off of employees with equal seniority, none of which had involved employees of different races, the Board had broken the tie through a random process which included drawing numbers out of a container, drawing lots or having a lottery. In deciding whether to lay off Taxman or Williams, the Board made a discretionary decision to rely on its affirmative action policy even though it was not bound to do so. The Board chose to lay off Taxman and to retain Williams. The president of the Board testified that Williams was retained over Taxman in order to provide a role model for students and to promote understanding and tolerance of persons of different backgrounds.

The affirmative action plan had not been adopted to achieve any remedial purpose, i.e., to remedy prior racial discrimination or to correct an imbalance of minorities in the school system. Statistical evidence showed that the percentage of black teachers in the job category that included all teachers exceeded the percentage of blacks in the available work force. The Affirmative Action plan stated, "In all cases, the most qualified candidate will be recommended for appointment. However, when candidates appear to be of equal qualification, candidates meeting the criteria of the affirmative action program will be recommended."

How should a court decide the case? Is the answer different after *Grutter v. Bollinger, supra*? For a pre-*Grutter* opinion, see *Taxman v. Board of Education of Township of Piscataway*, 91 F.3d 1547 (3d Cir.1996) (en banc), *cert. granted,* 521 U.S. 1117, 117 S.Ct. 2506, 138 L.Ed.2d 1010 (1997), *cert. dismissed*, 522 U.S. 1010, 118 S.Ct. 595, 139 L.Ed.2d 431 (1997). Is the rationale supporting "diversity" as a goal of affirmative action equally compelling in the contexts of both education and employment? For analyses of racial diversity as a governmental goal, *see generally* Andy Portinga, *Racial Diversity as a Compelling Governmental Interest*, 75 U.Det. Mercy L.Rev. 73 (1997); Robert J. Donahue, Note, *Racial Diversity as a Compelling Governmental Interest*, 30 Ind. L.Rev. 523 (1997).

9.   Suppose an employer adopts an affirmative action plan designed to establish a racially, sexually, and ethnically diverse management team in order to develop strategies for marketing its products to a racially,

sexually, and ethnically diverse clientele? Would the plan survive scrutiny under *Weber* and *Johnson*? Recall that in *Wygant v. Jackson Board of Education*, 476 U.S. 267, 276, 106 S.Ct. 1842, 1848, 90 L.Ed.2d 260 (1986), the Supreme Court rejected the argument that the "role model" rationale was a sufficiently compelling interest to support an affirmative action plan governing teacher layoffs in an educational institution.

10.   The Glass Ceiling Commission, created by Congress in the Civil Rights Act of 1991, has issued a report that supports affirmative action in the workplace for minorities and women. *See* Glass Ceiling Commission, Good for Business: Making Full Use of the Nation's Human Capital (Mar. 1995).

11.   Studies have indicated that "white women have benefited the most from affirmative action." Evelyn Hu–DeHart, *Affirmative Action: Some Concluding Thoughts*, 68 U.Colo.L.Rev. 1209, 1212 (1997); Heidi Hartmann, *Who Has Benefited from Affirmative Action in Employment?*, *in* The Affirmative Action Debate 77 (George E. Curry ed. 1996). Can you explain this result?

Note: Affirmative Action and the Civil Rights Act of 1991

Congress overturned or modified a number of the Supreme Court employment discrimination decisions that the Court handed down during its 1988 Term because it viewed the Court's decisions as weakening the scope and effectiveness of laws prohibiting discrimination in employment. *See* Mark S. Brodin, *Reflections on the Supreme Court's 1988 Term: Employment Discrimination Decisions and the Abandonment of the Second Reconstruction*, 31 B.C.L.Rev. 1 (1989) (discussing the cases). The *Griggs* disparate impact theory, which is one of the major underpinnings of affirmative action, was the subject of extensive scrutiny during the congressional debates that led to the enactment of the 1991 Civil Rights Act. Ultimately, Congress codified the *Griggs* disparate impact theory in the 1991 Act. Title VII § 703(k)(1)(A), 42 U.S.C. § 2000e–2(k)(1)(A). Although Congress did not directly address in the 1991 Act the status of the Court's affirmative action analysis in *Johnson* and *Weber*, two provisions of the Act raise questions about the continued vitality of *Weber* and *Johnson*. The first is Title VII § 703(m), 42 U.S.C. § 2000e–2(m). Section 703(m), which is discussed in Chapter 3, provides that

> [e]xcept as otherwise provided in this title, an unlawful employment practice is established when the complaining party demonstrates that race, color, religion, sex, or national origin was a motivating factor for any employment practice, even though other factors also motivated the practice.

Some have argued that § 703(m) "sounded the death knell" or was the "killer provision" for affirmative action under Title VII because affirmative action, by definition, specifically considers race or sex as one factor. *See* Fred Barnes, *Last Laugh*, New Republic, Dec. 16, 1991, at 9; *Uncivil Rites*, New Republic, Dec. 16, 1991, at 9. The second provision is § 116, which provides that "[n]othing in the amendments * * * shall be construed to affect court-ordered remedies, affirmative action, or conciliation agreements, that are in accordance with the law." Pub.L. No. 102–166, § 116, 105 Stat. 1071 (1991).

The Ninth Circuit, in *Officers for Justice v. Civil Service Commission*, 979 F.2d 721 (9th Cir.1992), *cert.denied*, 507 U.S. 1004, 113 S.Ct. 1645, 123 L.Ed.2d 267 (1993), was the first court of appeals to address the impact of the 1991 Civil Rights Act on affirmative action. In rejecting the argument that the 1991 Act sounded the death knell for affirmative action, the Ninth Circuit, construing §§ 703(m) and 116 together, stated:

> The City asserts, and the Union does not dispute, that the savings clause of section [703(m)—"except as otherwise provided by law"] encompasses section 116 of the 1991 Act. * * * The Union argues that the phrase "in accordance with law" refers to the law as amended by the 1991 Act and that because section [703(m)] prohibits the use of race as a motivating factor, "even though other factors also motivated the practice," the race conscious promotions at issue in this case are not "in accordance with law."

> The Union's reading of the 1991 Act is predicated on an internal inconsistency: that Congress sought to protect affirmative action in section 116 while outlawing it in section [703(m)]. Such an interpretation should be "avoided if alternative interpretations consistent with the legislative purpose are available." The City properly argues that a more natural reading of the phrase "in accordance with law" is that affirmative action programs that were in accordance with law prior to passage of the 1991 Act are unaffected by the amendments. The language of the statute is clear, and the City's interpretation is consistent with that language.

Id. at 725 (citations omitted). The EEOC has taken the position that the 1991 Act does not change the law on affirmative action under Title VII and declared that its 1979 guidelines on affirmative action under Title VII remain in effect. *See* 29 C.F.R. pt. 1608.

Commentators who have addressed the legal status of affirmative action after the 1991 Civil Rights Act have reached conflicting conclusions. Some commentators have argued that the 1991 Civil Rights Act supports the continued legitimacy of the Court's construction of Title VII in *Weber* and *Johnson*. These commentators argue that Congress did not expressly overrule *Johnson* and *Weber* in the 1991 Act as it had done with other Supreme Court decisions; therefore, the phrase, "in accordance with law," could only refer to *Johnson* and *Weber*. *See, e.g.*, Charles R. Lawrence, III & Mari J. Matsuda, We Won't Go Back: Making the Case for Affirmative Action (1997); Alfred W. Blumrosen, *Society in Transition IV: Affirmation of Affirmative Action Under the Civil Rights Act of 1991*, 45 Rutgers L.Rev. 903 (1993); Robert A. Sedler, *Employment Equality, Affirmative Action, and the Constitutional Political Consensus*, 90 Mich.L.Rev. 1315 (1992) (book review). Others have advanced the argument that Congress laid the foundation in the 1991 Civil Rights Act for the Supreme Court to overturn *Johnson* and *Weber*. *See, e.g.*, Nelson Lund, *The Law of Affirmative Action in and After the Civil Rights Act of 1991: Congress Invites Judicial Reform*, 6 Geo.Mason L.Rev. 87 (1997).

Notes

1. The Rehabilitation Act of 1973 expressly requires federal agencies to implement affirmative action plans for the hiring, placement, and advancement of persons with disabilities. 29 U.S.C. § 791(b).

2. For the most part, remedial affirmative action plans have focused on discrimination against blacks and women. Should groups other than blacks and women be included in the dialogue on affirmative action? There is a growing body of scholarship that proposes including other groups in the legal and policy debates on affirmative action. *See, e.g.*, Jeffrey S. Byrne, *Affirmative Action for Lesbians and Gay Men: A Proposal for True Equality of Opportunity and Workplace Diversity*, 11 Yale L. & Pol'y Rev. 47 (1993); Laura M. Padilla, *Intersectionality and Positionality: Situating Women of Color in the Affirmative Action Dialogue*, 66 Fordham L.Rev. 843 (1997); John E. Sanchez, *Religious Affirmative Action in Employment: Fearful Symmetry*, 1991 Det.C.L.Rev. 1019; Frank H. Wu, *Neither Black Nor White: Asian Americans and Affirmative Action*, 15 B.C. Third World L.J. 225 (1995); Wayne R. Farnsworth, Note, *Bureau of Indian Affairs Hiring Preferences After* Adarand Constructors, Inc. v. Pena, 1996 B.Y.U.L.Rev. 503; Harvey Gee, Comment, *Changing Landscapes: The Need for Asian Americans to Be Included in the Affirmative Action Debate*, 32 Gonz.L.Rev. 621 (1996–1997); Barry Bennett Kaufman, Note, *Preferential Hiring Policies for Older Workers Under the Age Discrimination in Employment Act*, 56 S.Cal. L.Rev. 825 (1983).

3. A number of studies have compared affirmative action policies in the United States to similar policies in other countries. *See, e.g.*, Kevin A. Burke, *Fair Employment in Northern Ireland: The Role of Affirmative Action*, 28 Colum.J.L. & Soc.Probs. 1 (1994) (discussing religious discrimination in Northern Ireland); M. Varn Chandola, *Affirmative Action in India and the United States: The Untouchable and Black Experience*, 3 Ind. Int'l & Comp. L.Rev. 101 (1992) (comparing compensatory discrimination in India with affirmative action in the United States); Alan M. Katz, *Benign Preferences: An Indian Decision & the* Bakke *Case*, 25 Am.J.Comp.L. 611 (1977) (comparing *Bakke* with an Indian decision); Deidre A. Grossman, Comment, *Voluntary Affirmative Action Plans in Italy and the United States: Differing Notions of Gender Equality*, 14 Comp.Lab.L.J. 185 (1993) (comparing affirmative action in Italy and the United States). The Canadian constitution explicitly recognizes and protects affirmative action. See, e.g., Ruth Colker, *Hypercapitalism: Affirmative Protections for People With Disabilities, Illness and Parenting Responsibilities Under United States Law*, 9 Yale J.L. & Feminism 213 (1997).

Part V

ALTERNATIVE DISPUTE RESOLUTION

Chapter 18

ALTERNATIVE DISPUTE RESOLUTION

A. INTRODUCTION

Alternative dispute resolution (ADR) has been defined as "a set of practices and techniques that aim (1) to permit legal disputes to be resolved outside the courts for the benefit of all disputants; (2) to reduce the cost of conventional litigation and the delays to which it is ordinarily subject; or (3) to prevent legal disputes that would otherwise likely be brought to the courts." Jethro K. Lieberman & James F. Henry, *Lessons from the Alternative Dispute Resolution Movement*, 53 U.Chi.L.Rev. 424, 425–26 (1986). Commonly used ADR methodologies include (1) arbitration, (2) mediation, (3) early neutral evaluation, (4) neutral fact-finding, (5) mini-trials, (6) and summary jury trials. *See generally* Laura Cooper, Dennis Nolan & Richard Bales, *ADR in the Workplace* (West 2002); Thomas D. Lambros, *The Summary Jury Trial and Other Alternative Methods of Dispute Resolution: A Report to the Judicial Conference of the United States Committee on the Operation of the Jury System*, 103 F.R.D 461 (1984).

Mediation is commonly used by the EEOC to attempt to resolve some meritorious employment discrimination charges prior to litigation. *See* E. Patrick McDermott et al., *An Evaluation of the Equal Employment Opportunity Commission's Mediation Program*, <*http://www.eeoc.gov/mediate/report*>, at Part IV.C (Sept. 20, 2000). In recent years, proposals have surfaced for modifying and expanding mediation of employment discrimination claims. *See, e.g.,* Michael Z. Green, *Proposing a New Paradigm for EEOC Enforcement After 35 Years: Outsourcing Charge Processing by Mandatory Mediation*, 105 Dick.L.Rev. 305 (2001); Michael J. Yelnosky, *Title VII, Mediation, and Collective Action*, 1999 U.Ill.L.Rev. 583 (1999).

Arbitration is one of the most widely used ADR methods. The parties to an arbitration agreement consent to have their disputes resolved by a neutral third-party in a process that, for the most part, is less formal, less costly, and less time-consuming than litigation. The parties waive their rights to bring a lawsuit and agree to be bound by the arbitrator's decision—the "arbitral award." Generally the arbitrator makes a final, binding determination, although the parties may agree to a nonbinding award. For the most part, arbitration resembles an adjudicative process. In most other ADR methodologies, such as mediation and negotiated settlements, the third-party neutral is a facilitator, not an adjudicator; the parties are free to agree or not, and either party can resort to judicial processes if they cannot reach an agreement.

In arbitration, to resolve the parties' dispute, the arbitrator will hold a hearing to determine the facts and hear arguments from opposing sides. Procedural rules governing the arbitrator's conduct of the hearing can be defined in the arbitration agreement, but the general practice is that there is no, or very limited, prehearing discovery, the rules of evidence do not apply, and there may be no record of the proceedings. The parties may be represented by attorneys who prepare witnesses, present arguments, and submit briefs; although non-lawyers, such as union business agents in labor arbitrations, often will represent employees.

Arbitrators are not required to have legal training, and many arbitrators are nonlawyers. Arbitrators, however, generally develop considerable expertise in a specialized field of commercial or labor disputes. Although arbitrators essentially function as judges, arbitral awards are not judicial opinions, though they may, at times, resemble such opinions. If the parties require the arbitrator to submit a written opinion, it can be brief with limited analysis. This is primarily because the role of the arbitrator is to resolve the particular dispute between the parties, not to apply external rules of law. Thus, arbitrators are not constrained by stare decisis, but must find the rationale for resolving the dispute within the four corners of the parties' contract or from the past practices and course of dealing between the parties.

Arbitration awards are binding only on the parties who have agreed to the process and have no precedential effect on the disputes of third parties. Courts are reluctant to overturn arbitral awards, and a party can obtain judicial review of an arbitral award in only very limited circumstances, such as when the arbitrator makes an award that is clearly illegal or is the result of fraud, egregious error, mistake, or misconduct.

B.   ARBITRATION OF EMPLOYMENT DISCRIMINATION CLAIMS IN NONUNION WORKPLACES

1.   ARBITRABILITY

May an employer in a nonunion workplace require an employee to agree, as a condition of employment, to submit all statutory claims of employment discrimination to arbitration? This question has raised complex legal and policy issues in the wake of the following 1991 Supreme Court decision, *Gilmer v. Interstate/Johnson Lane Corp.* Predispute arbitration agreements, like the one at issue in *Gilmer*, are executed at the outset of the parties' relationship, before conflicts develop and disputes arise. As one commentator noted, "pre-dispute agreements dominate the case law on arbitration because, as a general matter, if both parties agree to use arbitration after the nature of a claim is known, the agreement is made with full awareness of the implications of arbitration." Jordan L. Resnick, Note, *Beyond* Mastrobuono: *A Practitioners' Guide to Arbitration, Employment Disputes, Punitive Damages, and the Implications of the Civil Rights Act of 1991,* 23 Hofstra L.Rev. 913, 915, n.5 (1995).

GILMER v. INTERSTATE/JOHNSON LANE CORP.

Supreme Court of the United States, 1991.
500 U.S. 20, 111 S.Ct. 1647, 114 L.Ed.2d 26.

JUSTICE WHITE delivered the opinion of the Court.

The question presented in this case is whether a claim under the Age Discrimination in Employment Act of 1967 (ADEA) can be subjected to compulsory arbitration pursuant to an arbitration agreement in a securities registration application. The Court of Appeals held that it could, and we affirm.

I

Respondent Interstate/Johnson Lane Corporation (Interstate) hired petitioner Robert Gilmer as a Manager of Financial Services in May 1981. As required by his employment, Gilmer registered as a securities representative with several stock exchanges, including the New York Stock Exchange (NYSE). His registration application, entitled "Uniform Application for Securities Industry Registration or Transfer," provided, among other things, that Gilmer "agree[d] to arbitrate any dispute, claim or controversy" arising between him and Interstate "that is required to be arbitrated under the rules, constitutions or by-laws of the organizations with which I register." Of relevance to this case, NYSE Rule 347 provides for arbitration of "[a]ny controversy between a registered representative and any member or member organization arising out of the employment or termination of employment of such registered representative."

Interstate terminated Gilmer's employment in 1987, at which time Gilmer was 62 years of age. After first filing an age discrimination charge with the Equal Employment Opportunity Commission, Gilmer subsequently brought suit in the United States District Court for the Western District of North Carolina, alleging that Interstate had discharged him because of his age, in violation of the ADEA. In response to Gilmer's complaint, Interstate filed in the District Court a motion to compel arbitration of the ADEA claim. In its motion, Interstate relied upon the arbitration agreement in Gilmer's registration application, as well as the Federal Arbitration Act (FAA), 9 U.S.C. § 1 *et seq.* The District Court denied Interstate's motion, based on this Court's decision in *Alexander v. Gardner–Denver Co.*, 415 U.S. 36, 94 S.Ct. 1011, 39 L.Ed.2d 147 (1974), and because it concluded that "Congress intended to protect ADEA claimants from the waiver of a judicial forum." The United States Court of Appeals for the Fourth Circuit reversed, finding "nothing in the text, legislative history, or underlying purposes of the ADEA indicating a congressional intent to preclude enforcement of arbitration agreements." We granted certiorari, to resolve a conflict among the Courts of Appeals regarding the arbitrability of ADEA claims.

II

The FAA was originally enacted in 1925, and then reenacted and codified in 1947 as Title 9 of the United States Code. Its purpose was to reverse the longstanding judicial hostility to arbitration agreements that had existed at English common law and had been adopted by American courts, and to place arbitration agreements upon the same footing as other contracts. Its primary substantive provision states that "[a] written provision in any maritime transaction or a contract evidencing a transaction involving commerce to settle by arbitration a controversy thereafter arising out of such contract or transaction * * * shall be valid, irrevocable, and enforceable, save upon such grounds as exist at law or in equity for the revocation of any contract." 9 U.S.C. § 2. The FAA also provides for stays of proceedings in federal district courts when an issue in the proceeding is referable to arbitration, § 3, and for orders compelling arbitration when one party has failed, neglected, or refused to comply with an arbitration agreement, § 4. These provisions manifest a "liberal federal policy favoring arbitration agreements." Moses H. Cone Memorial Hospital v. Mercury Construction Corp., 460 U.S. 1, 24, 103 S.Ct. 927, 74 L.Ed.2d 765 (1983).[12]

It is by now clear that statutory claims may be the subject of an arbitration agreement, enforceable pursuant to the FAA. Indeed, in recent years we have held enforceable arbitration agreements relating to claims arising under the Sherman Act, 15 U.S.C. § 1–7; § 10(b) of the Securities Exchange Act of 1934, 15 U.S.C. § 78j(b); the civil provisions of the Racketeer Influenced and Corrupt Organizations Act (RICO), 18 U.S.C. § 1961 *et seq.*; and § 12(2) of the Securities Act of 1933, 15 U.S.C. § 77l(2). *See* Mitsubishi Motors Corp. v. Soler Chrysler–Plymouth, Inc., 473 U.S. 614, 105 S.Ct. 3346, 87 L.Ed.2d 444 (1985); Shearson/American Express Inc. v. McMahon, 482 U.S. 220, 107 S.Ct. 2332, 96 L.Ed.2d 185

---

12. Section 1 of the FAA provides that "nothing herein contained shall apply to contracts of employment of seamen, railroad employees, or any other class of workers engaged in foreign or interstate commerce." 9 U.S.C. § 1. Several *amici curiae* in support of Gilmer argue that section excludes from the coverage of the FAA all "contracts of employment." Gilmer, however, did not raise the issue in the courts below; it was not addressed there; and it was not among the questions presented in the petition for certiorari. In any event, it would be inappropriate to address the scope of the § 1 exclusion because the arbitration clause being enforced here is not contained in a contract of employment. * * * Unlike the dissent, we choose to follow the plain language of the FAA and the weight of authority, and we therefore hold that § 1's exclusionary clause does not apply to Gilmer's arbitration agreement. Consequently, we leave for another day the issue raised by *amici curiae.*

(1987); Rodriguez de Quijas v. Shearson/American Express, Inc., 490 U.S. 477, 109 S.Ct. 1917, 104 L.Ed.2d 526 (1989). In these cases we recognized that "[b]y agreeing to arbitrate a statutory claim, a party does not forgo the substantive rights afforded by the statute; it only submits to their resolution in an arbitral, rather than a judicial, forum." *Mitsubishi*, 473 U.S. at 628, 105 S.Ct. at 3354.

Although all statutory claims may not be appropriate for arbitration, "[h]aving made the bargain to arbitrate, the party should be held to it unless Congress itself has evinced an intention to preclude a waiver of judicial remedies for the statutory rights at issue." In this regard, we note that the burden is on Gilmer to show that Congress intended to preclude a waiver of a judicial forum for ADEA claims. If such an intention exists, it will be discoverable in the text of the ADEA, its legislative history, or an "inherent conflict" between arbitration and the ADEA's underlying purposes. Throughout such an inquiry, it should be kept in mind that "questions of arbitrability must be addressed with a healthy regard for the federal policy favoring arbitration." *Moses H. Cone*, 460 U.S. at 24, 103 S.Ct. at 941.

III

Gilmer concedes that nothing in the text of the ADEA or its legislative history explicitly precludes arbitration. He argues, however, that compulsory arbitration of ADEA claims pursuant to arbitration agreements would be inconsistent with the statutory framework and purposes of the ADEA. Like the Court of Appeals, we disagree.

A

Congress enacted the ADEA in 1967 "to promote employment of older persons based on their ability rather than age; to prohibit arbitrary age discrimination in employment; [and] to help employers and workers find ways of meeting problems arising from the impact of age on employment." 29 U.S.C. § 621(b). To achieve those goals, the ADEA, among other things, makes it unlawful for an employer "to fail or refuse to hire or to discharge any individual or otherwise discriminate against any individual with respect to his compensation, terms, conditions, or privileges of employment, because of such individual's age." *Id.* § 623(a)(1). This proscription is enforced both by private suits and by the EEOC. * * *

As Gilmer contends, the ADEA is designed not only to address individual grievances, but also to further important social policies. We do not perceive any inherent inconsistency between those policies, however, and enforcing agreements to arbitrate age discrimination claims. It is true that arbitration focuses on specific disputes between the parties involved. The same can be said, however, of judicial resolution of claims. Both of these dispute resolution mechanisms nevertheless also can further broader social purposes. The Sherman Act, the Securities Exchange Act of 1934, RICO, and the Securities Act of 1933 all are designed to advance important public policies, but, as noted above, claims under those statutes are appropriate for arbitration. "[S]o long as the prospective litigant effectively may vindicate [his or her] statutory cause of action in the arbitral forum, the statute will continue to serve both its remedial and deterrent function." *Mitsubishi*, 473 U.S. at 637, 105 S.Ct. at 3359.

We also are unpersuaded by the argument that arbitration will undermine the role of the EEOC in enforcing the ADEA. An individual ADEA claimant subject to an arbitration agreement will still be free to file a charge with the EEOC, even though the claimant is not able to institute a private judicial action. Indeed, Gilmer filed a charge with the EEOC in this case. In any event, the EEOC's role in combating age discrimination is not dependent on the filing of a charge; the agency may receive information concerning alleged violations of the ADEA "from any source," and it has independent authority to investigate age discrimination. Moreover, nothing in the ADEA indicates that Congress intended that the EEOC be involved in all employment disputes. Such disputes can be settled, for example, without any EEOC involvement.[3] Finally, the mere involvement of an administrative agency in the enforcement of a statute is not sufficient to preclude arbitration. For example, the Securities Exchange Commission is heavily involved in the enforcement of the Securities Exchange Act of 1934 and the Securities Act of 1933, but we have held that claims under both of those statutes may be subject to compulsory arbitration. *See* Shearson/American Express Inc. v. McMahon, 482 U.S. 220, 107 S.Ct. 2332, 96 L.Ed.2d 185 (1987); Rodriguez de Quijas v. Shearson/American Express, Inc., 490 U.S. 477, 109 S.Ct. 1917, 104 L.Ed.2d 526 (1989).

Gilmer also argues that compulsory arbitration is improper because it deprives claimants of the judicial forum provided for by the ADEA. Congress, however, did not explicitly preclude arbitration or other nonjudicial resolution of claims, even in its recent amendments to the ADEA. "[I]f Congress intended the substantive protection afforded [by the ADEA] to include protection against waiver of the right to a judicial forum, that intention will be deducible from text or legislative history." *Mitsubishi*, 473 U.S. at 628, 105 S.Ct. 3354. Moreover, Gilmer's argument ignores the ADEA's flexible approach to resolution of claims. The EEOC, for example, is directed to pursue "informal methods of conciliation, conference, and persuasion," which suggests that out-of-court dispute resolution, such as arbitration, is consistent with the statutory scheme established by Congress. In addition, arbitration is consistent with Congress' grant of concurrent jurisdiction over ADEA claims to state and federal courts, *see* 29 U.S.C. § 626(c)(1) (allowing suits to be brought "in any court of competent jurisdiction"), because arbitration agreements,"like the provision for concurrent jurisdiction, serve to ad-

---

3. In the recently enacted Older Workers Benefit Protection Act, Pub. L. 101–433, 104 Stat. 978, Congress amended the ADEA to provide that "[a]n individual may not waive any right or claim under this Act unless the waiver is knowing and voluntary." Congress also specified certain conditions that must be met in order for a waiver to be knowing and voluntary.

vance the objective of allowing [claimants] a broader right to select the forum for resolving disputes, whether it be judicial or otherwise." *Rodriguez de Quijas*, 490 U.S. at 483, 109 S.Ct. at 1921.

B

In arguing that arbitration is inconsistent with the ADEA, Gilmer also raises a host of challenges to the adequacy of arbitration procedures. Initially, we note that in our recent arbitration cases we have already rejected most of these arguments as insufficient to preclude arbitration of statutory claims. Such generalized attacks on arbitration "res[t] on suspicion of arbitration as a method of weakening the protections afforded in the substantive law to would-be complainants," and as such, they are "far out of step with our current strong endorsement of the federal statutes favoring this method of resolving disputes." *Rodriguez de Quijas*, 490 U.S. at 481, 109 S.Ct. at 1920. Consequently, we address these arguments only briefly.

Gilmer first speculates that arbitration panels will be biased. However, "[w]e decline to indulge the presumption that the parties and arbitral body conducting a proceeding will be unable or unwilling to retain competent, conscientious and impartial arbitrators." *Mitsubishi*, 473 U.S. at 634, 105 S.Ct. at 3357–58. In any event, we note that the NYSE arbitration rules, which are applicable to the dispute in this case, provide protections against biased panels. The rules require, for example, that the parties be informed of the employment histories of the arbitrators, and that they be allowed to make further inquiries into the arbitrators' backgrounds. In addition, each party is allowed one peremptory challenge and unlimited challenges for cause. Moreover, the arbitrators are required to disclose "any circumstances which might preclude [them] from rendering an objective and impartial determination." The FAA also protects against bias, by providing that courts may overturn arbitration decisions "[w]here there was evident partiality or corruption in the arbitrators." 9 U.S.C. § 10(b). There has been no showing in this case that those provisions are inadequate to guard against potential bias.

Gilmer also complains that the discovery allowed in arbitration is more limited than in the federal courts, which he contends will make it difficult to prove discrimination. It is unlikely, however, that age discrimination claims require more extensive discovery than other claims that we have found to be arbitrable, such as RICO and antitrust claims. Moreover, there has been no showing in this case that the NYSE discovery provisions, which allow for document production, information requests, depositions, and subpoenas, will prove insufficient to allow ADEA claimants such as Gilmer a fair opportunity to present their claims. Although those procedures might not be as extensive as in the federal courts, by agreeing to arbitrate, a party "trades the procedures and opportunity for review of the courtroom for the simplicity, informality, and expedition of arbitration." *Mitsubishi*, 473 U.S. at 628, 105 S.Ct. at 3354. Indeed, an important counterweight to the reduced discovery in

NYSE arbitration is that arbitrators are not bound by the rules of evidence.

A further alleged deficiency of arbitration is that arbitrators often will not issue written opinions, resulting, Gilmer contends, in a lack of public knowledge of employers' discriminatory policies, an inability to obtain effective appellate review, and a stifling of the development of the law. The NYSE rules, however, do require that all arbitration awards be in writing, and that the awards contain the names of the parties, a summary of the issues in controversy, and a description of the award issued. In addition, the award decisions are made available to the public. Furthermore, judicial decisions addressing ADEA claims will continue to be issued because it is unlikely that all or even most ADEA claimants will be subject to arbitration agreements. Finally, Gilmer's concerns apply equally to settlements of ADEA claims, which, as noted above, are clearly allowed.[4]

It is also argued that arbitration procedures cannot adequately further the purposes of the ADEA because they do not provide for broad equitable relief and class actions. As the court below noted, however, arbitrators do have the power to fashion equitable relief. Indeed, the NYSE rules applicable here do not restrict the types of relief an arbitrator may award, but merely refer to "damages and/or other relief." The NYSE rules also provide for collective proceedings. But "even if the arbitration could not go forward as a class action or class relief could not be granted by the arbitrator, the fact that the [ADEA] provides for the possibility of bringing a collective action does not mean that individual attempts at conciliation were intended to be barred." Nicholson v. CPC Int'l, Inc., 877 F.2d 221, 241 (3d Cir.1989) (Becker, J., dissenting). Finally, it should be remembered that arbitration agreements will not preclude the EEOC from bringing actions seeking class-wide and equitable relief.

C

An additional reason advanced by Gilmer for refusing to enforce arbitration agreements relating to ADEA claims is his contention that there often will be unequal bargaining power between employers and employees. Mere inequality in bargaining power, however, is not a sufficient reason to hold that arbitration agreements are never enforceable in the employment context. Relationships between securities dealers and investors, for example, may involve unequal bargaining power, but we nevertheless held in *Rodriguez de Quijas* and *McMahon* that agreements to arbitrate in that context are enforceable. As discussed above, the FAA's purpose was to place arbitration agreements on the same footing as other contracts. Thus, arbitration agreements are enforceable

---

4. Gilmer also contends that judicial review of arbitration decisions is too limited. We have stated, however, that "although judicial scrutiny of arbitration awards necessarily is limited, such review is sufficient to ensure that arbitrators comply with the requirements of the statute" at issue. Shearson/American Express Inc. v. McMahon, 482 U.S. 220, 232, 107 S.Ct. 2332, 2340, 96 L.Ed.2d 185 (1987).

"save upon such grounds as exist at law or in equity for the revocation of any contract." 9 U.S.C. § 2. "Of course, courts should remain attuned to well-supported claims that the agreement to arbitrate resulted from the sort of fraud or overwhelming economic power that would provide grounds 'for the revocation of any contract.' " *Mitsubishi*, 473 U.S. at 627, 105 S.Ct. at 3354. There is no indication in this case, however, that Gilmer, an experienced businessman, was coerced or defrauded into agreeing to the arbitration clause in his registration application. As with the claimed procedural inadequacies discussed above, this claim of unequal bargaining power is best left for resolution in specific cases.

IV

In addition to the arguments discussed above, Gilmer vigorously asserts that our decision in *Alexander v. Gardner–Denver Co.*, 415 U.S. 36, 94 S.Ct. 1011, 39 L.Ed.2d 147 (1974), and its progeny—*Barrentine v. Arkansas–Best Freight System, Inc.*, 450 U.S. 728, 101 S.Ct. 1437, 67 L.Ed.2d 641 (1981), and *McDonald v. West Branch*, 466 U.S. 284, 104 S.Ct. 1799 80 L.Ed.2d 302 (1984)—preclude arbitration of employment discrimination claims. Gilmer's reliance on these cases, however, is misplaced.

In *Gardner-Denver*, the issue was whether a discharged employee whose grievance had been arbitrated pursuant to an arbitration clause in a collective-bargaining agreement was precluded from subsequently bringing a Title VII action based upon the conduct that was the subject of the grievance. In holding that the employee was not foreclosed from bringing the Title VII claim, we stressed that an employee's contractual rights under a collective-bargaining agreement are distinct from the employee's statutory Title VII rights:

> In submitting his grievance to arbitration, an employee seeks to vindicate his contractual right under a collective-bargaining agreement. By contrast, in filing a lawsuit under Title VII, an employee asserts independent statutory rights accorded by Congress. The distinctly separate nature of these contractual and statutory rights is not vitiated merely because both were violated as a result of the same factual occurrence.

415 U.S. at 49–50, 94 S.Ct. at 1020.

We also noted that a labor arbitrator has authority only to resolve questions of contractual rights. *Id.* at 53–54, 94 S.Ct. at 1022–23. The arbitrator's "task is to effectuate the intent of the parties" and he or she does not have the "general authority to invoke public laws that conflict with the bargain between the parties." *Id.* at 53, 94 S.Ct. at 1022. By contrast, "in instituting an action under Title VII, the employee is not seeking review of the arbitrator's decision. Rather, he is asserting a statutory right independent of the arbitration process." *Id.* at 54, 94 S.Ct. at 1022. We further expressed concern that in collective-bargaining arbitration "the interests of the individual employee may be subordinated to the collective interests of all employees in the bargaining unit."[5] *Id.* at 58 n.19, 94 S.Ct. at 1024 n.19.

Barrentine and *McDonald* similarly involved the issue whether arbitration under a collective-bargaining agreement precluded a subsequent statutory claim. In holding that the statutory claims there were not precluded, we noted, as in *Gardner-Denver*, the difference between contractual rights under a collective-bargaining agreement and individual statutory rights, the potential disparity in interests between a union and an employee, and the limited authority and power of labor arbitrators.

There are several important distinctions between the *Gardner-Denver* line of cases and the case before us. First, those cases did not involve the issue of the enforceability of an agreement to arbitrate statutory claims. Rather, they involved the quite different issue whether arbitration of contract-based claims precluded subsequent judicial resolution of statutory claims. Since the employees there had not agreed to arbitrate their statutory claims, and the labor arbitrators were not authorized to resolve such claims, the arbitration in those cases understandably was held not to preclude subsequent statutory actions. Second, because the arbitration in those cases occurred in the context of a collective-bargaining agreement, the claimants there were represented by their unions in the arbitration proceedings. An important concern therefore was the tension between collective representation and individual statutory rights, a concern not applicable to the present case. Finally, those cases were not decided under the FAA, which, as discussed above, reflects a "liberal federal policy favoring arbitration agreements." *Mitsubishi*, 473 U.S. at 625, 105 S.Ct. at 3353. Therefore, those cases provide no basis for refusing to enforce Gilmer's agreement to arbitrate his ADEA claim.

V

We conclude that Gilmer has not met his burden of showing that Congress, in enacting the ADEA, intended to preclude arbitration of claims under that Act. Accordingly, the judgment of the Court of Appeals is [a]ffirmed.

[JUSTICE STEVENS, with whom JUSTICE MARSHALL joined, dissented on the grounds that the Court should have reached the question whether employment contracts are excluded from the FAA. He was of the opinion that they should be.]

5. The Court in *Alexander v. Gardner-Denver Co.*, 415 U.S. 36, 94 S.Ct. 1011, 39 L.Ed.2d 147 (1974), also expressed the view that arbitration was inferior to the judicial process for resolving statutory claims. That "mistrust of the arbitral process," however, has been undermined by our recent arbitration decisions. *McMahon*, 482 U.S. at 231–232. "[W]e are well past the time when judicial suspicion of the desirability of arbitration and of the competence of arbitral tribunals inhibited the development of arbitration as an alternative means of dispute resolution." Mitsubishi Motors Corp. v. Soler Chrysler–Plymouth, Inc., 473 U.S. 614, 105 S.Ct. 3346, 87 L.Ed.2d 444 (1985).

Notes and Questions

1. *Gilmer* is the first Supreme Court decision to hold that statutory employment discrimination claims can be subjected to mandatory arbitration. Competing policy objectives lie at the core of *Gilmer*: (1) the enforcement of contractual rights generally; (2) the enforcement of compulsory arbitration under the FAA; and (3) the elimination of employment discrimination pursuant to the federal antidiscrimination laws. Does *Gilmer* give more weight to one or more of the competing policy considerations than to others? In thinking about these questions, consider the issues raised in the notes that follow.

a. In a line of pre-*Gilmer* cases, the Supreme Court recognized that Congress, in enacting Title VII, had declared a strong public policy that the elimination of discrimination is to be accorded the "highest priority." *See, e.g.*, Franks v. Bowman Transp. Co., 424 U.S. 747, 763, 96 S.Ct. 1251, 1263, 47 L.Ed.2d 444 (1976) (citing Newman v. Piggie Park Enterp., Inc., 390 U.S. 400, 402, 88 S.Ct. 964, 966, 19 L.Ed.2d 1263 (1968)). And, in *Alexander v. Gardner–Denver Co.*, 415 U.S. 36, 44–45, 94 S.Ct. 1011, 1018, 39 L.Ed.2d 147 (1974), the Court stated that "final responsibility for enforcement of Title VII is vested with federal courts" because the provisions of the act "make plain that federal courts have been assigned plenary powers to secure compliance with Title VII."

b. Concern about the "litigation explosion" in the federal courts has helped to fuel the development of a variety of ADR techniques. *See* Roberto L. Corrada, *The Arbitral Imperative in Labor and Employment Law,* 47 Cath.U.L.Rev. 919 (1998). Although the number of employment discrimination cases filed in federal district courts has declined slightly since 1997 (see *<http://www.uscourts.gov/recenttrends2001>*), a substantial increase in filings had been noted in the prior decade. For example, in November 1988, in response to increased public and professional concern with the congestion of the federal courts, the delay and expense of litigation, and the expansion of federal rights, Congress created a Federal Courts Study Committee to examine the "litigation explosion." The Committee reported that since 1969 the number of private employment discrimination cases filed in the federal courts had increased by more than 2,000%—from under 400 cases in 1970 to almost 7,500 cases in 1989. The Committee recommended that Congress authorize a five-year test program to allow the EEOC to arbitrate employment discrimination cases with the consent of both parties. *See* Judicial Conference of the U.S., Report of the Federal Courts Study Committee 19, 60–61 (Apr. 1990).

c. Title VII requires a judge to assign a case for a hearing "at the earliest practicable date and to cause the case to be in every way expedited." 42 U.S.C. § 2000e–5(f)(5). However, in 1989 the median time between filing a claim in court and its final disposition in the district court was eight months, and for cases that actually went to trial the average time was fourteen months. In addition, 10% of cases that went to trial took over thirty-six months until final disposition. *See* Clyde Summers, *Effective Remedies for Employment Rights: Preliminary Guidelines and Proposals,* 141 U.Pa.L.Rev. 457, 483–84 (1992) (citing 1989 Director of Admin. Off. U.S.

Cts. Ann. Rpt.). These statistics are based on pre–1991 cases, when jury trials were unavailable in Title VII cases, and thus do not reflect the additional time involved in jury trials. When considered in light of the EEOC administrative exhaustion requirements (see Chapter 2), a plaintiff in an employment discrimination case can expect to wait two, three, or more years before her claim is finally resolved. Of course, if the case is appealed, as it will be in many instances, the delay between the filing of the administrative charge and final judicial disposition is even longer. The ordeal—financial, psychological, and emotional—from the perspective of an individual plaintiff is chronicled in Eugene Goodman, All the Justice I Could Afford (1983). Goodman was the plaintiff in *Goodman v. Heublein, Inc.*, 645 F.2d 127 (2d Cir.1981), an ADEA case. *See also* Nan Robertson, The Girls in the Balcony: Women, Men, and the New York Times (1992) (a class-action sex discrimination claim against the *New York Times*); Ann Branigar Hopkins, So Ordered: Making Partner the Hard Way (1996) (a sex discrimination claim against an accounting firm). For a comparison of costs in arbitration versus litigation and an examination of how the courts of appeals approach the issue, *see* Michael H. LeRoy & Peter Feuille, *When Is Cost an Unlawful Barrier to Alternative Dispute Resolution? The Ever Green Tree of Mandatory Employment Arbitration,* 50 UCLA L.Rev 143 (2002).

2. Two books that explore the history, policy, and law on arbitration of statutory employment discrimination claims are Richard A. Bales, Compulsory Arbitration: The Grand Experiment in Employment (1997), and Vern E. Hauck, Arbitrating Race, Religion, and National Origin Discrimination Grievances (1997). *See also* Joseph R. Grodin, *Arbitration of Employment Discrimination Claims: Doctrine and Policy in the Wake of* Gilmer, 14 Hofstra L.J. 1 (1996); Samuel Estreicher, *Predispute Agreements to Arbitrate Statutory Employment Claims,* 72 N.Y.U.L.Rev. 1344 (1997).

CIRCUIT CITY STORES, INC. v. ADAMS

Supreme Court of the United States, 2001.
532 U.S. 105, 121 S.Ct. 1302, 149 L.Ed.2d 234.

JUSTICE KENNEDY delivered the opinion of the Court.

Section 1 of the Federal Arbitration Act (FAA) excludes from the Act's coverage "contracts of employment of seamen, railroad employees, or any other class of workers engaged in foreign or interstate commerce." 9 U.S.C. § 1. All but one of the Courts of Appeals which have addressed the issue interpret this provision as exempting contracts of employment of transportation workers, but not other employment contracts, from the FAA's coverage. A different interpretation has been adopted by the Court of Appeals for the Ninth Circuit, which construes the exemption so that all contracts of employment are beyond the FAA's reach, whether or not the worker is engaged in transportation. * * * We now decide that the better interpretation is to construe the statute, as most of the Courts of Appeals have done, to confine the exemption to transportation workers.

I

In October 1995, respondent Saint Clair Adams applied for a job at petitioner Circuit City Stores, Inc., a national retailer of consumer electronics. Adams signed an employment application which included the following provision:

"I agree that I will settle any and all previously unasserted claims, disputes or controversies arising out of or relating to my application or candidacy for employment, employment and/or cessation of employment with Circuit City, exclusively by final and binding arbitration before a neutral Arbitrator. By way of example only, such claims include claims under federal, state, and local statutory or common law, such as the Age Discrimination in Employment Act, Title VII of the Civil Rights Act of 1964, as amended, including the amendments of the Civil Rights Act of 1991, the Americans with Disabilities Act, the law of contract and the law of tort."

Adams was hired as a sales counselor in Circuit City's store in Santa Rosa, California.

Two years later, Adams filed an employment discrimination lawsuit against Circuit City in state court, asserting claims under California's Fair Employment and Housing Act * * * and other claims based on general tort theories under California law. Circuit City filed suit in the United States District Court for the Northern District of California, seeking to enjoin the state-court action and to compel arbitration of respondent's claims pursuant to the FAA, 9 U.S.C. §§ 1–16. The District Court entered the requested order. Respondent, the court concluded, was obligated by the arbitration agreement to submit his claims against the employer to binding arbitration. An appeal followed.

* * * [T]he Court of Appeals [for the Ninth Circuit] held the arbitration agreement between Adams and Circuit City was contained in a "contract of employment," and so was not subject to the FAA. Circuit City petitioned this Court, noting that the Ninth Circuit's conclusion that all employment contracts are excluded from the FAA conflicts with every other Court of Appeals to have addressed the question. * * * We granted certiorari to resolve the issue.

II

A

* * * The FAA's coverage provision, § 2, provides that

[a] written provision in any maritime transaction or a contract evidencing a transaction involving commerce to settle by arbitration a controversy thereafter arising out of such contract or transaction, or the refusal to perform the whole or any part thereof, or an agreement in writing to submit to arbitration an existing controversy arising out of such a contract, transaction, or refusal, shall be valid, irrevocable, and enforceable, save upon such grounds as exist at law or in equity for the revocation of any contract.

9 U.S.C. § 2.

* * *

The instant case, of course, involves not the basic coverage authorization under § 2 of the Act, but the exemption from coverage under § 1. The exemption clause provides the Act shall not apply "to contracts of employment of seamen, railroad employees, or any other class of workers engaged in foreign or interstate commerce." 9 U.S.C. § 1. * * *

B

Respondent, at the outset, contends that we need not address the meaning of the § 1 exclusion provision to decide the case in his favor. In his view, an employment contract is not a "contract evidencing a transaction involving interstate commerce" at all, since the word "transaction" in § 2 extends only to commercial contracts. This line of reasoning proves too much, for it would make the § 1 exclusion provision superfluous. If all contracts of employment are beyond the scope of the Act under the § 2 coverage provision, the separate exemption for "contracts of employment of seamen, railroad employees, or any other class of workers engaged in * * * interstate commerce" would be pointless. The proffered interpretation of "evidencing a transaction involving commerce," * * * would be inconsistent with *Gilmer v. Interstate/Johnson Lane Corp.*, 500 U.S. 20, 111 S.Ct. 1647, 114 L.Ed.2d 26 (1991), where we held that § 2 required the arbitration of an age discrimination claim based on an agreement in a securities registration application, a dispute that did not arise from a "commercial deal or merchant's sale." * * * If, then, there is an argument to be made that arbitration agreements in employment contracts are not covered by the Act, it must be premised on the language of the § 1 exclusion provision itself.

Respondent, endorsing the reasoning of the Court of Appeals for the Ninth Circuit that the provision excludes all employment contracts, relies on the asserted breadth of the words "contracts of employment of * * * any other class of workers engaged in * * * commerce." Referring to our construction of § 2's coverage provision in *Allied-Bruce* [Terminix Cos. v. Dobson, 513 U.S. 265, 115 S.Ct. 834, 130 L.Ed.2d 753 (1995)]— concluding that the words "involving commerce" evidence the congressional intent to regulate to the full extent of its commerce power— respondent contends § 1's interpretation should have a like reach, thus exempting all employment contracts. The two provisions, it is argued, are coterminous; under this view the "involving commerce" provision brings within the FAA's scope all contracts within the Congress' commerce power, and the "engaged in * * * commerce" language in § 1 in turn exempts from the FAA all employment contracts falling within that authority.

This reading of § 1, however, runs into an immediate and, in our view, insurmountable textual obstacle. Unlike the "involving commerce" language in § 2, the words "any other class of workers engaged in * * * commerce" constitute a residual phrase, following, in the same sentence, explicit reference to "seamen" and "railroad employees." Construing the residual phrase to exclude all employment contracts fails to give independent effect to the statute's enumeration of the specific categories of workers which precedes it; there would be no need for Congress to use the phrases "seamen" and "railroad employees" if those same classes of workers were subsumed within the meaning of the "engaged in * * * commerce" residual clause. The wording of § 1 calls for the application of the maxim *ejusdem generis*, the statutory canon that "[w]here general words follow specific words in a statutory enumeration, the general words are construed to embrace only objects similar in nature to those objects enumerated by the preceding specific words." Under this rule of construction the residual clause should be read to give effect to the terms "seamen" and "railroad employees," and should itself be controlled and defined by reference to the enumerated categories of workers which are recited just before it; the interpretation of the clause pressed by respondent fails to produce these results.

Canons of construction need not be conclusive and are often countered, of course, by some maxim pointing in a different direction. The application of the rule *ejusdem generis* in this case, however, is in full accord with other sound considerations bearing upon the proper interpretation of the clause. For even if the term "engaged in commerce" stood alone in § 1, we would not construe the provision to exclude all contracts of employment from the FAA. Congress uses different modifiers to the word "commerce" in the design and enactment of its statutes. The phrase "affecting commerce" indicates Congress' intent to regulate to the outer limits of its authority under the Commerce Clause. See, *e.g.*, *Allied-Bruce*, 513 U.S., at 277. The "involving commerce" phrase, the operative words for the reach of the basic coverage provision in § 2, was at issue in *Allied-Bruce*. That particular phrase had not been interpreted before by this Court. Considering the usual meaning of the word "involving," and the pro-arbitration purposes of the FAA, *Allied-Bruce* held the "word 'involving,' like 'affecting,' signals an intent to exercise Congress' commerce power to the full." *Ibid.* Unlike those phrases, however, the general words "in commerce" and the specific phrase "engaged in commerce" are understood to have a more limited reach. In *Allied-Bruce* itself the Court said the words "in commerce" are "often-found words of art" that we have not read as expressing congressional intent to regulate to the outer limits of authority under the Commerce Clause. *Id.* at 273.

It is argued that we should assess the meaning of the phrase "engaged in commerce" in a different manner here, because the FAA was enacted when congressional authority to regulate under the commerce power was to a large extent confined by our decisions. When the FAA was enacted in 1925, respondent reasons, the phrase "engaged in commerce" was not a term of art indicating a limited assertion of congressional jurisdiction; to the contrary, it is said, the formulation came close to expressing the outer limits of Congress' power as then understood. Were this mode of interpretation to prevail, we would take into account the scope of the Commerce Clause, as then elaborated by the Court, at the date of the FAA's enactment in order to interpret what the statute means now.

* * *

In sum, the text of the FAA forecloses the construction of § 1 followed by the Court of Appeals in the case under review, a construction which would exclude all employment contracts from the FAA. While the historical arguments respecting Congress' understanding of its power in 1925 are not insubstantial, this fact alone does not give us basis to adopt, "by judicial decision rather than amendatory legislation," *Gulf Oil, supra,* at 202, 95 S.Ct. 392, an expansive construction of the FAA's exclusion provision that goes beyond the meaning of the words Congress used. While it is of course possible to speculate that Congress might have chosen a different jurisdictional formulation had it known that the Court would soon embrace a less restrictive reading of the Commerce Clause, the text of § 1 precludes interpreting the exclusion provision to defeat the language of § 2 as to all employment contracts. Section 1 exempts from the FAA only contracts of employment of transportation workers.

C

As the conclusion we reach today is directed by the text of § 1, we need not assess the legislative history of the exclusion provision. * * *

* * *

III

Various *amici,* including the attorneys general of 22 States, object that the reading of the § 1 exclusion provision adopted today intrudes upon the policies of the separate States. They point out that, by requiring arbitration agreements in most employment contracts to be covered by the FAA, the statute in effect pre-empts those state employment laws which restrict or limit the ability of employees and employers to enter into arbitration agreements. It is argued that States should be permitted, pursuant to their traditional role in regulating employment relationships, to prohibit employees like respondent from contracting away their right to pursue state-law discrimination claims in court.

It is not our holding today which is the proper target of this criticism. The line of argument is relevant instead to the Court's decision in *Southland Corp. v. Keating,* 465 U.S. 1, 104 S.Ct. 852, 79 L.Ed.2d 1 (1984), holding that Congress intended the FAA to apply in state courts, and to pre-empt state antiarbitration laws to the contrary. *See id.,* at 16, 104 S.Ct. 852.

The question of *Southland's* continuing vitality was given explicit consideration in *Allied-Bruce,* and the Court declined to overrule it. 513 U.S., at 272, 115 S.Ct. 834; see also *id.,* at 282, 115 S.Ct. 834 (O'CONNOR, J., concurring). * * * In *Allied-Bruce* the Court noted that Congress had not moved to overturn *Southland,* see 513 U.S., at 272, 115

S.Ct. 834; and we now note that it has not done so in response to *Allied-Bruce* itself.

Furthermore, for parties to employment contracts not involving the specific exempted categories set forth in § 1, it is true here, just as it was for the parties to the contract at issue in *Allied-Bruce*, that there are real benefits to the enforcement of arbitration provisions. We have been clear in rejecting the supposition that the advantages of the arbitration process somehow disappear when transferred to the employment context. See *Gilmer*, 500 U.S., at 30–32, 111 S.Ct. 1647. Arbitration agreements allow parties to avoid the costs of litigation, a benefit that may be of particular importance in employment litigation, which often involves smaller sums of money than disputes concerning commercial contracts. These litigation costs to parties (and the accompanying burden to the Courts) would be compounded by the difficult choice-of-law questions that are often presented in disputes arising from the employment relationship, and the necessity of bifurcation of proceedings in those cases where state law precludes arbitration of certain types of employment claims but not others. The considerable complexity and uncertainty that the construction of § 1 urged by respondent would introduce into the enforceability of arbitration agreements in employment contracts would call into doubt the efficacy of alternative dispute resolution procedures adopted by many of the Nation's employers, in the process undermining the FAA's proarbitration purposes and "breeding litigation from a statute that seeks to avoid it." *Allied-Bruce, supra,* at 275, 115 S.Ct. 834. The Court has been quite specific in holding that arbitration agreements can be enforced under the FAA without contravening the policies of congressional enactments giving employees specific protection against discrimination prohibited by federal law; as we noted in *Gilmer*, " '[b]y agreeing to arbitrate a statutory claim, a party does not forgo the substantive rights afforded by the statute; it only submits to their resolution in an arbitral, rather than a judicial, forum.' " 500 U.S., at 26, 111 S.Ct. 1647 (quoting *Mitsubishi Motors Corp. v. Soler Chrysler–Plymouth, Inc.,* 473 U.S. 614, 628, 105 S.Ct. 3346, 87 L.Ed.2d 444 (1985)). *Gilmer,* of course, involved a federal statute, while the argument here is that a state statute ought not be denied state judicial enforcement while awaiting the outcome of arbitration. That matter, though, was addressed in *Southland* and *Allied-Bruce,* and we do not revisit the question here.

* * *

For the foregoing reasons, the judgment of the Court of Appeals for the Ninth Circuit is reversed, and the case is remanded for further proceedings consistent with this opinion.

* * *

JUSTICE SOUTER, with whom JUSTICE STEVENS, JUSTICE GINSBURG, and JUSTICE BREYER join, dissenting.

Section 2 of the Federal Arbitration Act (FAA or Act) provides for the enforceability of a written arbitration clause in "any maritime transaction or a contract evidencing a transaction involving commerce," 9 U.S.C. § 2, while § 1 exempts from the Act's coverage "contracts of employment of seamen, railroad employees, or any other class of workers engaged in foreign or interstate commerce." Whatever the understanding of Congress's implied admiralty power may have been when the Act was passed in 1925, the commerce power was then thought to be far narrower than we have subsequently come to see it. As a consequence, there are two quite different ways of reading the scope of the Act's provisions. One way would be to say, for example, that the coverage provision extends only to those contracts "involving commerce" that were understood to be covered in 1925; the other would be to read it as exercising Congress's commerce jurisdiction in its modern conception in the same way it was thought to implement the more limited view of the Commerce Clause in 1925. The first possibility would result in a statutory ambit frozen in time, behooving Congress to amend the statute whenever it desired to expand arbitration clause enforcement beyond its scope in 1925; the second would produce an elastic reach, based on an understanding that Congress used language intended to go as far as Congress could go, whatever that might be over time.

In *Allied-Bruce Terminix Cos. v. Dobson*, 513 U.S. 265, 130 L.Ed.2d 753, 115 S. Ct. 834 (1995), we decided that the elastic understanding of § 2 was the more sensible way to give effect to what Congress intended when it legislated to cover contracts "involving commerce," a phrase that we found an apt way of providing that coverage would extend to the outer constitutional limits under the Commerce Clause. The question here is whether a similarly general phrase in the § 1 exemption, referring to contracts of "any * * * class of workers engaged in foreign or interstate commerce," should receive a correspondingly evolutionary reading, so as to expand the exemption for employment contracts to keep pace with the enhanced reach of the general enforceability provision. If it is tempting to answer yes, on the principle that what is sauce for the goose is sauce for the gander, it is sobering to realize that the Courts of Appeals have, albeit with some fits and starts as noted by JUSTICE STEVENS * * * overwhelmingly rejected the evolutionary reading of § 1 accepted by the Court of Appeals in this case. * * * A majority of this Court now puts its imprimatur on the majority view among the Courts of Appeals.

The number of courts arrayed against reading the § 1 exemption in a way that would allow it to grow parallel to the expanding § 2 coverage reflects the fact that this minority view faces two hurdles, each textually based and apparent from the face of the Act. First, the language of coverage (a contract evidencing a transaction "involving commerce") is different from the language of the exemption (a contract of a worker "engaged in * * * commerce"). Second, the "engaged in * * * commerce" catchall phrase in the exemption is placed in the text following more specific exemptions for employment contracts of "seamen" and "railroad employees." The placement possibly indicates that workers who are excused from arbitrating by virtue of the catchall exclusion must resemble seamen and railroad workers, perhaps by being employees who actually handle and move goods as they are shipped interstate or internationally.

Neither hurdle turns out to be a bar, however. The first objection is at best inconclusive and weaker than the grounds to reject it; the second is even more certainly inapposite, for reasons the Court itself has stated but misunderstood.

A

Is Congress further from a plenary exercise of the commerce power when it deals with contracts of workers "engaged in * * * commerce" than with contracts detailing transactions "involving commerce?" The answer is an easy yes, insofar as the former are only the class of labor contracts, while the latter are not so limited. But that is not the point. The question is whether Congress used language indicating that it meant to cover as many contracts as the Commerce Clause allows it to reach within each class of contracts addressed. In *Allied-Bruce* we examined the 1925 context and held that "involving commerce" showed just such a plenary intention, even though at the time we decided that case we had long understood "affecting commerce" to be the quintessential expression of an intended plenary exercise of commerce power. *Allied-Bruce, supra,* at 273–274; *see also* Wickard v.Filburn, 317 U.S. 111, 87 L. Ed. 122, 63 S. Ct. 82 (1942).

Again looking to the context of the time, I reach the same conclusion about the phrase "engaged in commerce" as a description of employment contracts exempted from the Act. When the Act was passed (and the commerce power was closely confined) our case law indicated that the only employment relationships subject to the commerce power were those in which workers were actually engaged in interstate commerce. *Compare* The Employers' Liability Cases, 207 U.S. 463, 496, 498, 52 L. Ed. 297, 28 S. Ct. 141 (1908) (suggesting that regulation of the employment relations of railroad employees "actually engaged in an operation of interstate commerce" is permissible under the Commerce Clause but that regulation of a railroad company's clerical force is not), *with* Hammer v. Dagenhart, 247 U.S. 251, 271–276, 62 L. Ed. 1101, 38 S. Ct. 529 (1918) (invalidating statute that had the "necessary effect" of "regulating the hours of labor of children in factories and mines within the States"). Thus, by using "engaged in" for the exclusion, Congress showed an intent to exclude to the limit of its power to cover employment contracts in the first place, and it did so just as clearly as its use of "involving commerce" showed its intent to legislate to the hilt over commercial contracts at a more general level. That conclusion is in fact borne out by the statement of the then-Secretary of Commerce, Herbert Hoover, who suggested to Congress that the § 1 exclusion language should be adopted "if objection appears to the inclusion of workers' contracts in the law's scheme." Sales and Contracts to Sell in Interstate and Foreign Commerce, and Federal Commercial Arbitration: Hearing on S. 4213 and S. 4214 Before a Subcommittee of the Senate Committee on the Judiciary, 67th Cong., 4th Sess., 14 (1923) (hereinafter Hearing on S. 4213 et al.).

* * *

B

The second hurdle is cleared more easily still, and the Court has shown how. Like some Courts of Appeals before it, the majority today finds great significance in the fact that the generally phrased exemption for the employment contracts of workers "engaged in commerce" does not stand alone, but occurs at the end of a sequence of more specific exemptions: for "contracts of employment of seamen, railroad employees, or any other class of workers engaged in foreign or interstate commerce." Like those other courts, this Court sees the sequence as an occasion to apply the interpretive maxim of *ejusdem generis*, that is, when specific terms are followed by a general one, the latter is meant to cover only examples of the same sort as the preceding specifics. Here, the same sort is thought to be contracts of transportation workers, or employees of transporters, the very carriers of commerce. And that, of course, excludes respondent Adams from benefit of the exemption, for he is employed by a retail seller.

Like many interpretive canons, however, *ejusdem generis* is a fallback, and if there are good reasons not to apply it, it is put aside. E.g., Norfolk & Western R. Co. v. Train Dispatchers, 499 U.S. 117, 129, 113 L. Ed. 2d 95, 111 S. Ct. 1156 (1991). * * * There are good reasons here. As Adams argued, it is imputing something very odd to the working of the congressional brain to say that Congress took care to bar application of the Act to the class of employment contracts it most obviously had authority to legislate about in 1925, contracts of workers employed by carriers and handlers of commerce, while covering only employees "engaged" in less obvious ways, over whose coverage litigation might be anticipated with uncertain results. It would seem to have made more sense either to cover all coverable employment contracts or to exclude them all. In fact, exclusion might well have been in order based on concern that arbitration could prove expensive or unfavorable to employees, many of whom lack the bargaining power to resist an arbitration clause if their prospective employers insist on one. * * * And excluding all employment contracts from the Act's enforcement of mandatory arbitration clauses is consistent with Secretary Hoover's suggestion that the exemption language would respond to any "objection * * * to the inclusion of workers' contracts."

* * *

Nothing stands in the way of construing the coverage and exclusion clauses together, consistently and coherently. * * *

* * *

JUSTICE STEVENS, with whom JUSTICE GINSBURG and JUS-
TICE BREYER join, and with whom JUSTICE SOUTER joins as to
Parts II and III, dissenting.

* * *

III

Times have changed. Judges in the 19th century disfavored private
arbitration. The 1925 Act was intended to overcome that attitude, but a
number of this Court's cases decided in the last several decades have
pushed the pendulum far beyond a neutral attitude and endorsed a
policy that strongly favors private arbitration. * * * The strength of that
policy preference has been echoed in the recent Court of Appeals
opinions on which the Court relies. * * * In a sense, therefore, the Court
is standing on its own shoulders when it points to those cases as the
basis for its narrow construction of the exclusion in § 1. There is little
doubt that the Court's interpretation of the Act has given it a scope far
beyond the expectations of the Congress that enacted it. *See, e.g.,*
Southland Corp. v. Keating, 465 U.S. 1, 17–21, 104 S. Ct. 852, 79 L.Ed.2d
1 (1984). * * *

It is not necessarily wrong for the Court to put its own imprint on a
statute. But when its refusal to look beyond the raw statutory text
enables it to disregard countervailing considerations that were expressed
by Members of the enacting Congress and that remain valid today, the
Court misuses its authority. As the history of the legislation indicates,
the potential disparity in bargaining power between individual employees and large employers was the source of organized labor's opposition to
the Act, which it feared would require courts to enforce unfair employment contracts. That same concern, as JUSTICE SOUTER points out,
* * * underlay Congress' exemption of contracts of employment from
mandatory arbitration. When the Court simply ignores the interest of
the unrepresented employee, it skews its interpretation with it own
policy preferences.

This case illustrates the wisdom of an observation made by Justice
Aharon Barak of the Supreme Court of Israel. He has perceptively noted
that the "minimalist" judge "who holds that the purpose of the statute
may be learned only from its language" has more discretion than the
judge "who will seek guidance from every reliable source." Judicial
Discretion 62 (Y. Kaufmann transl. 1989). A method of statutory interpretation that is deliberately uninformed, and hence unconstrained, may
produce a result that is consistent with a court's own views of how
things should be, but it may also defeat the very purpose for which a
provision was enacted. That is the sad result in this case.

* * *

Notes and Questions

1. The Court in *Circuit City* seems to suggest that employment discrimination claims generally should be treated like "garden variety" tort claims. Recall that the Court stated that "employment litigation * * * often involves smaller sums of money than disputes concerning commercial contracts." Should employment discrimination claims be considered less worthy of judicial resources than commercial claims? *Circuit City* involved only discrimination and tort claims brought under state law. Is it right that the FAA should preempt any state anti-arbitration laws and policies in cases involving only state claims? Does it matter for purposes of preemption that the dispute over arbitrability of state claims was pursued in a federal court?

2. There has been a vigorous debate about mandatory employment arbitration since *Gilmer. See, e.g.,* Martin H. Malin, *Privatizing Justice But by How Much? Questions* Gilmer *Did Not Answer,* 16 Ohio St.J.Disp.Res. 589, 590–600 (2001) [hereinafter Malin, *Privatizing Justice*]. Those who question arbitration's validity point to the concerns addressed in the *Gilmer* case, including the problem of resolving disputes involving public values and rights in a private setting (*e.g.,* Private arbitration awards are not generally available to the public, making it difficult to chart developments and the progress of employment discrimination law.) Also, arbitral processes do not generally afford the same discovery as the courts, inhibiting access to information that may be critical for vindicating statutory rights. Moreover, the fact that employers are "repeat" players in the arbitral process, whereas an individual employee will use arbitration only once, raises concerns about possible arbitrator bias in favor of employers.

a. Substantial questions still abound regarding the voluntariness of employee agreements to arbitrate, since employers generally have much greater bargaining power. *See, e.g.,* David E. Feller, *Putting* Gilmer *Where It Belongs: The FAA's Labor Exemption,* 18 Hofstra Lab. & Emp.L.J. 253 (2000); Martin H. Malin & Robert F. Ladenson, *Privatizing Justice: A Jurisprudential Perspective on Labor and Employment Arbitration from the* Steelworkers Trilogy *to* Gilmer, 44 Hastings L.J. 1187 (1993) [hereinafter Malin & Ladenson, *Privatizing Justice: A Jurisprudential Perspective*]. The EEOC has declared, "agreements that mandate binding arbitration of employment discrimination claims as a condition of employment are contrary to the fundamental principles evinced in [the nation's employment discrimination] laws." *See* EEOC Policy Statement on Mandatory Binding Arbitration of Employment Discrimination Disputes as a Condition of Employment, <www.eeoc.gov> (July 10, 1997).

b. Professor Katherine Stone has advanced the view that a predispute arbitration agreement is a modern-day version of the "yellow dog contract." Katherine Van Wezel Stone, *Mandatory Arbitration of Individual Employment Rights: The Yellow Dog Contract of the 1990s,* 73 Denv.L.Rev. 1017 (1996). Employers used so-called yellow dog contracts primarily in the late nineteenth and early twentieth centuries to avoid unionization. The employer required an applicant, as a condition of employment, to sign a contract stating that he was not then, nor would he become, a member of a labor union. Several states recognized the coercive nature of such contracts and enacted legislation outlawing them on the grounds of public policy. Congress also enacted legislation outlawing them in the railroad industry. The Supreme Court struck down both the federal and state statutes on the ground that they interfered with the substantive due process right of freedom of contract. *See* Adair v. United States, 208 U.S. 161, 28 S.Ct. 277, 52 L.Ed. 436 (1908); Coppage v. Kansas, 236 U.S. 1, 35 S.Ct. 240, 59 L.Ed. 441 (1915). Finally, in 1932, with the enactment of the Norris–LaGuardia Act, 29 U.S.C. § 102, Congress denied the federal courts jurisdiction to issue injunctions to enforce yellow dog contracts.

c.   Those who support mandatory arbitration claim that many of the issues surrounding arbitrability can be raised and addressed in the arbitration proceeding itself, and arbitration is more efficient, faster, and less costly than proceeding through court. *See, e.g.,* Mark Berger, *Can Employment Law Arbitration Really Work?* 61 U.M.K.C.L.Rev. 693 (1993); Samuel Estreicher, *Saturns for Rickshaws: The Stakes in the Debate Over Predispute Employment Arbitration Agreements,* 16 Ohio St.J.Disp.Res. 559 (2001). Other commentators have explored ways in which arbitration might be molded to achieve the benefits of arbitration while avoiding the disadvantages. *See, e.g.,* Roberto L. Corrada, *Claiming Private Law for the Left: Exploring* Gilmer's *Impact and Legacy,* 73 Denv.L.Rev. 1051 (1996); Dennis O. Lynch, *Conceptualizing Forum Selection as a "Public Good": A Response to Professor Stone,* 73 Denv.L.Rev. 1071 (1996); Calvin William Sharpe, *Integrity Review of Statutory Arbitration Awards,* 54 Hastings L.J. 311 (2003).

d.   In *Cole v. Burns International Security Services, Inc.,* 105 F.3d 1465 (D.C.Cir.1997), the court concluded:

> We acknowledge the concerns that have been raised regarding arbitration's ability to vindicate employees' statutory rights. However, for all of arbitration's shortcomings, the process, if fairly conducted, is not necessarily inferior to litigation as a mechanism for the resolution of employment disputes. As the Dunlop Commission recognized:
>
>> Litigation has become a less-than-ideal method of resolving employees' public law claims. As spelled out in the Fact Finding Report, employees bringing public law claims in court must endure long waiting periods as governing agencies and the overburdened court system struggle to find time to properly investigate and hear the complaint. Moreover, the average profile of employee litigants * * * indicates that lower-wage workers may not fare as well as higher-wage professionals in the litigation system; lower-wage workers are less able to afford the time required to pursue a court complaint, and are less likely to receive large monetary relief from juries. Finally, the litigation model of dispute resolution seems to be dominated by "ex-employee" complainants, indicating that the litigation system is less useful to employees who need redress for legitimate complaints, but also wish to remain in their current jobs.
>
> Commission on the Future of Worker–Management Relations, Report and Recommendations at 30. Arbitration also offers employees a guarantee that there will be a hearing on the merits of their claims; no such

guarantee exists in litigation where relatively few employees survive the procedural hurdles necessary to take a case to trial in the federal courts. As a result, it is perhaps misguided to mourn the Supreme Court's endorsement of the arbitration of complex and important public law claims. Arbitrators, however, must be mindful that the Court's endorsement has been based on the assumption that "competent, conscientious, and impartial arbitrators" will be available to decide these cases. *Mitsubishi Motors*, 473 U.S. at 634, 105 S.Ct. at 3357.

Id. at 1487–88.

e. After *Gilmer* and *Circuit City,* most employment arbitration agreements signed by individuals will be covered by the FAA and, therefore, will be enforceable. What are the implications of *Gilmer* and *Circuit City* for the future development of employment discrimination law in light of the fact that these decisions have the effect of replacing public processes with private ones, and replacing judges with private parties (arbitrators), to resolve employment discrimination claims? In light of *Gilmer* and *Circuit City*, in what circumstances can courts refuse to enforce these agreements?

3. Subsequent to *Gilmer*, a number of employers adopted mandatory pre-dispute arbitration policies by including such policies in individual contracts of employment, employee handbooks, or other employment-related documents such as application forms. *See, e.g.,* Nghiem v. NEC Elec., Inc., 25 F.3d 1437 (9th Cir.1994) (policy found in employment contract and employee handbook), *cert. denied*, 513 U.S. 1044, 115 S.Ct. 638, 130 L.Ed.2d 544 (1994). The Supreme Court has acknowledged the strong trend in favor of including mandatory pre-dispute arbitration agreements in employment contracts. *See* EEOC v. Waffle House, 534 U.S. 279, 296 n.11, 122 S.Ct. 754, 765 n. 11, 151 L.Ed.2d 755, 770 (2002) (indicating that a greater percentage of the work force is becoming subject to arbitration agreements as a condition of employment). The American Arbitration Association estimates that "more than 3.5 million employees are covered" by arbitration agreements designating [AAA] to administer arbitration proceedings. *Voluntary Arbitration in Worker Disputes Endorsed by 2 Groups*, Wall St.J., June 20, 1997, at B2 (quoted in *Waffle House,* 534 U.S. at 296 n. 11). Pre-dispute mandatory arbitration agreements are "often boilerplate provisions in employment contracts at Fortune 500 companies and are the norm in industries such as financial services, health care, engineering, and information technology." Christine M. Reilly, *Achieving Knowing and Voluntary Consent in Pre–Dispute Mandatory Arbitration Agreements at the Contracting Stage of Employment,* 90 Cal.L.Rev. 1203, 1208 (2002).

4. The arbitration provisions of most employment agreements can be utilized by the employer or the employee; however, employees are more likely to want a chance to present their claims to a jury. As a result, the employer is generally the party seeking to enforce an arbitration agreement. Studies examining arbitral disputes involving employment and commercial claims from 1992–1995 have shown that an employer who is a repeat player in an arbitration scheme has a substantially greater chance of prevailing in arbitration than does an employee. *See* Lisa B. Bingham, *Is There a Bias in Arbitration of Nonunion Employment Disputes? An Analysis of Actual Cases*

and Outcomes, 6 Intl.J. Conflict Mgmt. 369 (1995); Lisa B. Bingham, *Employment Arbitration: The Repeat Player Effect,* 1 Employee Rts. & Emp. Pol'y J. 189 (1997); Lisa B. Bingham, *On Repeat Players, Adhesive Contracts, and the Use of Statistics in Judicial Review of Employment Arbitration Awards,* 29 McGeorge L.Rev. 223 (1998). *See also* Malin, *Privatizing Justice, supra* Note 2, at 601–605. An informal survey of employment discrimination arbitrations in the securities industry concluded that employers have been relatively successful in defending employment discrimination claims in arbitration proceedings. Stuart H. Bompey & Andrea H. Stempel, *Four Years Later: A Look at Compulsory Arbitration of Employment Discrimination Claims After* Gilmer v. Interstate/Johnson Lane Corp., 21 Emp.Rel.L.J. 21 (1995). Another survey reported that, in 1994, plaintiffs won 43.3% of jury trials in employment discrimination litigation, but only 22.1% of the bench trials, and that the median judgment in the jury-tried cases was $102,000 compared to only $36,000 in bench-tried cases. 6 Emp.Discrim.Rep. (BNA) at 511 (Apr. 17, 1996) (reporting on survey conducted by the Lawyer's Committee for Civil Rights Under Law). However, other studies show that employees fare better in arbitration than in court generally. *See* Lewis Maltby, *Private Justice: Employment Arbitration and Civil Rights,* 30 Colum.Hum.Rts.L.Rev. 29, 46 (1998) (citing other studies showing employees prevail more often in arbitration than in court).

5. *Gilmer* involved the ADEA and *Circuit City* involved state employment discrimination claims. Should these cases serve as precedents favoring arbitration in other areas of statutory status discrimination like the Americans with Disabilities Act (ADA), Section 1981, or Title VII? *See, e.g.,* EEOC v. Waffle House, reproduced below (ADA); Johnson v. Circuit City Stores, Inc., 148 F.3d 373 (4th Cir.1998), *affirmed,* 203 F.3d 821 (4th Cir.), *cert. denied,* 530 U.S. 1276, 120 S.Ct. 2744, 147 L.Ed.2d 1008 (2000) (§ 1981); Desiderio v. National Ass'n of Sec. Dealers, 191 F.3d 198 (2d Cir.1999), *cert. denied,* 531 U.S. 1069, 121 S.Ct. 756, 148 L.Ed.2d 659 (2001) (Title VII). Should subsequent amendments to Title VII (the Civil Rights Act of 1991) and to the ADEA (the Older Worker Benefits and Protection Act (OWBPA)) affect the arbitrability analysis? With respect to Title VII and the Civil Rights Act of 1991, every court of appeals has held that § 118 of the Civil Rights Act of 1991 does not evince a congressional intent to preclude predispute arbitration agreements. *See* EEOC v. Luce, Forward, Hamilton & Scripps, 345 F.3d 742 (9th Cir. 2003) (en banc) (explicitly overruling *Duffield,* and collecting cases).

With respect to the OWBPA, the analysis is a little less clear, given the special purpose of the amendments in preventing casual waivers of ADEA claims, ostensibly including the right to a jury trial. The OWBPA (29 U.S.C. § 626(f)) was enacted to resolve a conflict among the circuits on the standard for determining whether ADEA claimants have knowingly and voluntarily waived rights under the ADEA. *See* Chapter 12, Section D. The OWBPA thus imposes strict requirements for a valid waiver of statutory rights under the ADEA. The Supreme Court apparently found the OWBPA inapposite in *Gilmer* because there was no indication in the record that the plaintiff, an experienced businessman, had been coerced or defrauded into agreeing to the arbitration provision. Does *Gilmer* hint that inequality of bargaining power, in some limited circumstances, may be a basis for not enforcing an arbitration agreement? In light of the Court's decision in *Oubre v. Entergy Operations, Inc.*, 522 U.S. 422, 118 S.Ct. 838, 139 L.Ed.2d 849 (1998), *see* Chapter 12, Section D, what do you think the outcome in *Gilmer* would have been if the plaintiff had raised an OWBPA claim?

6. Should *Gilmer* and *Circuit City* control the resolution of employment discrimination claims that are based on the Constitution? What if the claims are wholly constitutional? For example, suppose a public employer adopts a policy requiring as a condition of employment that employees agree to submit to mandatory arbitration any and all disputes arising out of the employment relationship. A female employee has a claim for sex discrimination and wishes to seek relief under the Equal Protection Clause of the Fourteenth Amendment. Is the dispute arbitrable? What if she also brings a Title VII claim? What if the arbitration clause expressly covers claims based on the Constitution? *See generally* Edward Brunet, *Arbitration and Constitutional Rights*, 71 N.C. L. Rev. 81 (1992).

7. After *Gilmer* and *Circuit City,* may an employer refuse to employ an applicant who refuses to sign a predispute arbitration agreement or discharge an employee who refuses to sign the agreement? Would the applicant or employee have a claim for retaliation, the claim being that they engaged in statutorily protected activity because of a good faith belief that they could not lawfully be required to sign the agreement? *See, e.g.*, Weeks v. Harden Mfg. Corp., 291 F.3d 1307 (11th Cir.2002).

Gilmer and *Circuit City* dealt with discrimination claims brought by individual employees. Can an arbitration agreement eliminate or modify the EEOC's statutorily authorized right to pursue judicial relief for an individual employee in an employment discrimination case based on Title VII or the ADA? The Supreme Court addressed this issue in the following ADA case.

EEOC v. WAFFLE HOUSE, INC.

Supreme Court of the United States, 2002.
534 U.S. 279, 122 S.Ct. 754, 151 L.Ed.2d 755.

JUSTICE STEVENS delivered the opinion of the Court.

The question presented is whether an agreement between an employer and an employee to arbitrate employment-related disputes bars the Equal Employment Opportunity Commission (EEOC) from pursuing victim-specific judicial relief, such as backpay, reinstatement, and damages, in an enforcement action alleging that the employer has violated Title I of the Americans with Disabilities Act of 1990 (ADA).

I

In his application for employment with respondent, Eric Baker agreed that "any dispute or claim" concerning his employment would be "settled by binding arbitration."[1] As a condition of employment, all prospective Waffle House employees are required to sign an application containing a similar mandatory arbitration agreement. Baker began working as a grill operator at one of respondent's restaurants on August 10, 1994. Sixteen days later he suffered a seizure at work and soon thereafter was discharged. Baker did not initiate arbitration proceedings, nor has he in the seven years since his termination, but he did file a timely charge of discrimination with the EEOC alleging that his discharge violated the ADA.

After an investigation and an unsuccessful attempt to conciliate, the EEOC filed an enforcement action against respondent in the Federal District Court for the District of South Carolina, pursuant to § 107(a) of the ADA, and § 102 of the Civil Rights Act of 1991. Baker is not a party to the case. The EEOC's complaint alleged that respondent engaged in employment practices that violated the ADA, including its discharge of Baker "because of his disability," and that its violation was intentional, and "done with malice or with reckless indifference to [his] federally protected rights." The complaint requested the court to grant injunctive relief to "eradicate the effects of [respondent's] past and present unlawful employment practices," to order specific relief designed to make Baker whole, including backpay, reinstatement, and compensatory damages, and to award punitive damages for malicious and reckless conduct.

Respondent filed a petition under the Federal Arbitration Act (FAA), 9 U.S.C. § 1 *et seq.*, to stay the EEOC's suit and compel arbitration, or to dismiss the action. Based on a factual determination that Baker's actual employment contract had not included the arbitration provision, the District Court denied the motion. The Court of Appeals granted an interlocutory appeal and held that a valid, enforceable arbitration agreement between Baker and respondent did exist. The court then proceeded to consider "what effect, if any, the binding arbitration agreement between Baker and Waffle House has on the EEOC, which filed this action in its own name both in the public interest and on behalf of Baker." After reviewing the relevant statutes and the language of the contract, the court concluded that the agreement did not foreclose the enforcement action because the EEOC was not a party to the contract, and it has independent statutory authority to bring suit in any federal district court where venue is proper. Nevertheless, the court held that the EEOC was precluded from seeking victim-specific relief in court

---

1. The agreement states:

"The parties agree that any dispute or claim concerning Applicant's employment with Waffle House, Inc., or any subsidiary or Franchisee of Waffle House, Inc., or the terms, conditions or benefits of such employment, including whether such dispute or claim is arbitrable, will be settled by binding arbitration. The arbitration proceedings shall be conducted under the Commercial Arbitration Rules of the American Arbitration Association in effect at the time a demand for arbitration is made. A decision and award of the arbitrator made under the said rules shall be exclusive, final and binding on both parties, their heirs, executors, administrators, successors and assigns. The costs and expenses of the arbitration shall be borne evenly by the parties."

because the policy goals expressed in the FAA required giving some effect to Baker's arbitration agreement. * * *

Several Courts of Appeals have considered this issue and reached conflicting conclusions. We granted the EEOC's petition for certiorari to resolve this conflict, and now reverse.

* * *

II

Congress has directed the EEOC to exercise the same enforcement powers, remedies, and procedures that are set forth in Title VII of the Civil Rights Act of 1964 when it is enforcing the ADA's prohibitions against employment discrimination on the basis of disability. 42 U.S.C. § 12117(a) (1994 ed.). Accordingly, the provisions of Title VII defining the EEOC's authority provide the starting point for our analysis.

When Title VII was enacted in 1964, it authorized private actions by individual employees and public actions by the Attorney General in cases involving a "pattern or practice" of discrimination. 42 U.S.C. § 2000e–6(a) (1994 ed.). The EEOC, however, merely had the authority to investigate and, if possible, to conciliate charges of discrimination. See *General Telephone Co. of Northwest v. EEOC*, 446 U.S. 318, 325, 100 S.Ct. 1698, 64 L.Ed.2d 319 (1980). In 1972, Congress amended Title VII to authorize the EEOC to bring its own enforcement actions; indeed, we have observed that the 1972 amendments created a system in which the EEOC was intended "to bear the primary burden of litigation," *id.*, at 326, 100 S.Ct. 1698. Those amendments authorize the courts to enjoin employers from engaging in unlawful employment practices, and to order appropriate affirmative action, which may include reinstatement, with or without backpay. Moreover, the amendments specify the judicial districts in which such actions may be brought. They do not mention arbitration proceedings.

In 1991, Congress again amended Title VII to allow the recovery of compensatory and punitive damages by a "complaining party." 42 U.S.C. § 1981a(a)(1) (1994 ed.). The term includes both private plaintiffs and the EEOC, § 1981a(d)(1)(A), and the amendments apply to ADA claims as well, §§ 1981a(a)(2), (d)(1)(B). As a complaining party, the EEOC may bring suit to enjoin an employer from engaging in unlawful employment practices, and to pursue reinstatement, backpay, and compensatory or punitive damages. Thus, these statutes unambiguously authorize the EEOC to obtain the relief that it seeks in its complaint if it can prove its case against respondent.

Prior to the 1991 amendments, we recognized the difference between the EEOC's enforcement role and an individual employee's private cause of action in *Occidental Life Ins. Co. of Cal. v. EEOC*, 432 U.S. 355, 97 S.Ct. 2447, 53 L.Ed.2d 402 (1977), and *General Telephone, supra*. *Occidental* presented the question whether EEOC enforcement actions are subject to the same statutes of limitations that govern individuals' claims. After engaging in an unsuccessful conciliation process, the EEOC filed suit in Federal District Court, on behalf of a female employee, alleging sex discrimination. The court granted the defendant's motion for summary judgment on the ground that the EEOC's claim was time barred; the EEOC filed suit after California's 1–year statute of limitations had run. We reversed because "under the procedural structure created by the 1972 amendments, the EEOC does not function simply as a vehicle for conducting litigation on behalf of private parties," 432 U.S., at 368, 97 S.Ct. 2447. To hold otherwise would have undermined the agency's independent statutory responsibility to investigate and conciliate claims by subjecting the EEOC to inconsistent limitations periods.

In *General Telephone*, the EEOC sought to bring a discrimination claim on behalf of all female employees at General Telephone's facilities in four States, without being certified as the class representative under Federal Rule of Civil Procedure 23. 446 U.S., at 321–322, 100 S.Ct. 1698. Relying on the plain language of Title VII and the legislative intent behind the 1972 amendments, we held that the EEOC was not required to comply with Rule 23 because it "need look no further than § 706 for its authority to bring suit in its own name for the purpose, among others, of securing relief for a group of aggrieved individuals." *Id.*, at 324, 100 S.Ct. 1698. In light of the provisions granting the EEOC exclusive jurisdiction over the claim for 180 days after the employee files a charge, we concluded that "the EEOC is not merely a proxy for the victims of discrimination and that [its] enforcement suits should not be considered representative actions subject to Rule 23." *Id.*, at 326, 100 S.Ct. 1698.

Against the backdrop of our decisions in *Occidental* and *General Telephone*, Congress expanded the remedies available in EEOC enforcement actions in 1991 to include compensatory and punitive damages. There is no language in the statute or in either of these cases suggesting that the existence of an arbitration agreement between private parties materially changes the EEOC's statutory function or the remedies that are otherwise available.

* * *

IV

The Court of Appeals based its decision on its evaluation of the "competing policies" implemented by the ADA and the FAA, rather than on any language in the text of either the statutes or the arbitration agreement between Baker and respondent. It recognized that the EEOC never agreed to arbitrate its statutory claim, * * * and that the EEOC has "independent statutory authority" to vindicate the public interest, but opined that permitting the EEOC to prosecute Baker's claim in court "would significantly trample" the strong federal policy favoring arbitration because Baker had agreed to submit his claim to arbitration. To effectuate this policy, the court distinguished between injunctive and victim-specific relief, and held that the EEOC is barred from obtaining the latter because any public interest served when the EEOC pursues "make whole" relief is outweighed by the policy goals favoring arbitration. Only when the EEOC seeks broad injunctive relief, in the Court of Appeals' view, does the public interest overcome the goals underpinning the FAA.

If it were true that the EEOC could prosecute its claim only with Baker's consent, or if its prayer for relief could be dictated by Baker, the court's analysis might be persuasive. But once a charge is filed, the exact opposite is true under the statute—the EEOC is in command of the process. The EEOC has exclusive jurisdiction over the claim for 180 days. During that time, the employee must obtain a right-to-sue letter from the agency before prosecuting the claim. If, however, the EEOC files suit on its own, the employee has no independent cause of action, although the employee may intervene in the EEOC's suit. 42 U.S.C. § 2000e–5(f)(1). In fact, the EEOC takes the position that it may pursue a claim on the employee's behalf even after the employee has disavowed any desire to seek relief. The statute clearly makes the EEOC the master of its own case and confers on the agency the authority to evaluate the strength of the public interest at stake. Absent textual support for a contrary view, it is the public agency's province—not that of the court— to determine whether public resources should be committed to the recovery of victim-specific relief. And if the agency makes that determination, the statutory text unambiguously authorizes it to proceed in a judicial forum.

Respondent and the dissent contend that Title VII supports the Court of Appeals' bar against victim-specific relief, because the statute limits the EEOC's recovery to "appropriate" relief as determined by a court. * * *

* * *

The Court of Appeals wisely did not adopt respondent's reading of § 706(g). Instead, it simply sought to balance the policy goals of the FAA against the clear language of Title VII and the agreement. While this may be a more coherent approach, it is inconsistent with our recent arbitration cases. The FAA directs courts to place arbitration agreements on equal footing with other contracts, but it "does not require parties to arbitrate when they have not agreed to do so." * * * Because the FAA is "at bottom a policy guaranteeing the enforcement of private contractual arrangements," *Mitsubishi Motors Corp. v. Soler Chrysler–Plymouth, Inc.*, 473 U.S. 614, 625, 105 S.Ct. 3346, 87 L.Ed.2d 444 (1985), we look first to whether the parties agreed to arbitrate a dispute, not to general policy goals, to determine the scope of the agreement. *Id.*, at 626, 105 S.Ct. 3346. While ambiguities in the language of the agreement should be resolved in favor of arbitration, * * * we do not override the clear intent of the parties, or reach a result inconsistent with the plain text of the contract, simply because the policy favoring arbitration is implicated. "Arbitration under the [FAA] is a matter of consent, not coercion." Here there is no ambiguity. No one asserts that the EEOC is a party to the contract, or that it agreed to arbitrate its claims. It goes without saying that a contract cannot bind a nonparty. Accordingly, the proarbitration policy goals of the FAA do not require the agency to relinquish its statutory authority if it has not agreed to do so.

Even if the policy goals underlying the FAA did necessitate some limit on the EEOC's statutory authority, the line drawn by the Court of Appeals between injunctive and victim-specific relief creates an uncomfortable fit with its avowed purpose of preserving the EEOC's public function while favoring arbitration. For that purpose, the category of victim-specific relief is both overinclusive and underinclusive. For example, it is overinclusive because while punitive damages benefit the individual employee, they also serve an obvious public function in deterring future violations. See *Newport v. Fact Concerts, Inc.*, 453 U.S. 247, 266–270, 101 S.Ct. 2748, 69 L.Ed.2d 616 (1981) ("Punitive damages by definition are not intended to compensate the injured party, but rather to punish the tortfeasor * * *, and to deter him and others from similar extreme conduct"); Restatement (Second) of Torts § 908 (1977). Punitive damages may often have a greater impact on the behavior of other employers than the threat of an injunction, yet the EEOC is precluded from seeking this form of relief under the Court of Appeals' compromise scheme. And, it is underinclusive because injunctive relief, although seemingly not "victim-specific," can be seen as more closely tied to the employees' injury than to any public interest. * * *

The compromise solution reached by the Court of Appeals turns what is effectively a forum selection clause into a waiver of a nonparty's statutory remedies. But if the federal policy favoring arbitration trumps the plain language of Title VII and the contract, the EEOC should be barred from pursuing any claim outside the arbitral forum. If not, then the statutory language is clear; the EEOC has the authority to pursue victim-specific relief regardless of the forum that the employer and employee have chosen to resolve their disputes. Rather than attempt to split the difference, we are persuaded that, pursuant to Title VII and the ADA, whenever the EEOC chooses from among the many charges filed each year to bring an enforcement action in a particular case, the agency may be seeking to vindicate a public interest, not simply provide make-whole relief for the employee, even when it pursues entirely victim-specific relief. To hold otherwise would undermine the detailed enforcement scheme created by Congress simply to give greater effect to an agreement between private parties that does not even contemplate the EEOC's statutory function.[11]

11. If injunctive relief were the only remedy available, an employee who signed an arbitration agreement would have little incentive to file a charge with the EEOC. As a greater percentage of the work force becomes subject to arbitration agreements as a condition of employment, see Voluntary Arbitration in Worker Disputes Endorsed by 2 Groups, Wall St. J., June 20, 1997, p. B2 (reporting that the American Arbitration Association estimates "more than 3.5 million employees are covered" by arbitration agreements designating it to administer arbitration proceedings), the pool of charges from which the EEOC can choose cases that best vindicate the public interest would likely get smaller and become distorted. We have generally been re-

V

It is true, as respondent and its *amici* have argued, that Baker's conduct may have the effect of limiting the relief that the EEOC may obtain in court. If, for example, he had failed to mitigate his damages, or had accepted a monetary settlement, any recovery by the EEOC would be limited accordingly. * * * As we have noted, it "goes without saying that the courts can and should preclude double recovery by an individual." *General Telephone*, 446 U.S., at 333, 100 S.Ct. 1698.

But no question concerning the validity of his claim or the character of the relief that could be appropriately awarded in either a judicial or an arbitral forum is presented by this record. Baker has not sought arbitration of his claim, nor is there any indication that he has entered into settlement negotiations with respondent. It is an open question whether a settlement or arbitration judgment would affect the validity of the EEOC's claim or the character of relief the EEOC may seek. The only issue before this Court is whether the fact that Baker has signed a mandatory arbitration agreement limits the remedies available to the EEOC. The text of the relevant statutes provides a clear answer to that question. They do not authorize the courts to balance the competing policies of the ADA and the FAA or to second-guess the agency's judgment concerning which of the remedies authorized by law that it shall seek in any given case.

Moreover, it simply does not follow from the cases holding that the employee's conduct may affect the EEOC's recovery that the EEOC's claim is merely derivative. We have recognized several situations in which the EEOC does not stand in the employee's shoes. See *Occidental*, 432 U.S., at 368, 97 S.Ct. 2447 (EEOC does not have to comply with state statutes of limitations); *General Telephone*, 446 U.S., at 326, 100 S.Ct. 1698 (EEOC does not have to satisfy Rule 23 requirements); *Gilmer*, 500 U.S., at 32, 111 S.Ct. 1647 (EEOC is not precluded from seeking classwide and equitable relief in court on behalf of an employee who signed an arbitration agreement). And, in this context, the statute specifically grants the EEOC exclusive authority over the choice of forum and the prayer for relief once a charge has been filed. The fact that ordinary principles of res judicata, mootness, or mitigation may apply to EEOC claims, does not contradict these decisions, nor does it render the EEOC a proxy for the employee.

The judgment of the Court of Appeals is reversed, and the case is remanded for further proceedings consistent with this opinion.

[JUSTICE THOMAS, joined by THE CHIEF JUSTICE and JUSTICE SCALIA, dissented.]

Notes and Questions

1. What effect, if any, is *Waffle House* likely to have on the trend toward arbitration in employment discrimination disputes in light of the fact

luctant to approve rules that may jeopardize the EEOC's ability to investigate and   select cases from a broad sample of claims. * * *

that the EEOC filed less than two percent of the 21,032 employment discrimination lawsuits filed in court in 2000? *See Waffle House*, 534 U.S. 279, 290 n. 7, 122 S.Ct. 754, 762 n.7, 151 L.Ed.2d 755 (2002).

2. Do the holding and rationale of *Waffle House* suggest any potential barriers to obtaining victim-specific relief in a case brought by the EEOC for employees who have signed arbitration agreements?

3. The ADEA has a different enforcement scheme than Title VII and the ADA. Because the Court in *Waffle House* relied so heavily on the statutory enforcement scheme of Title VII, should the decision in *Waffle House* apply equally to ADEA cases?

4. The only question the Court addressed in *Waffle House* was whether the existence of a pre-dispute arbitration agreement—under which no arbitration process had been initiated—limits the authority of the EEOC to seek victim-specific relief for an employee who has agreed to submit his employment discrimination claim to arbitration. Assuming that Baker, the employee in *Waffle House,* first pursued his ADA claim under the arbitration agreement and that the arbitrator had found against Baker on the merits, should the EEOC be barred from seeking specific relief for Baker in a lawsuit it later files under its independent statutory authority? Does the majority opinion suggest what the outcome should be? If the EEOC is later allowed to seek specific relief for Baker in court, what impact would a later judicial decision have on Baker's earlier arbitration?

2. THE ARBITRATION AGREEMENT

Due Process: It seems clear that if statutory employment discrimination claims are arbitrable, arbitration agreements cannot be used to circumvent substantive rights. In the absence of statutory standards, however, what procedures are at least minimally required in order to allow an employee to vindicate a statutory employment discrimination claim? More importantly, how do courts ensure that appropriate procedures are reflected in arbitration agreements? What is the basis for requiring specific procedures in arbitration agreements? Is it the statutes themselves? Is it some notion of minimal fairness or due process? In *Halligan v. Piper Jaffray, Inc.*, 148 F.3d 197 (2d Cir.1998), *cert. denied*, 526 U.S. 1034, 119 S.Ct. 1286, 143 L.Ed.2d 378 (1999), the Second Circuit specifically recognized the public controversy over whether arbitration has proven to be fair to employees as ostensibly envisioned by the Supreme Court in *Gilmer*:

> In the aftermath of *Gilmer*, * * * mandatory binding arbitration of employment discrimination disputes as a condition of employment has caused increased controversy. Attention has focused on, among other things, whether additional procedural requirements are necessary to ensure that employees will be able, in the words of *Gilmer*, to "effectively * * * vindicate" their statutory rights in arbitration. 500 U.S. at 28, 111 S.Ct. 1647. * * * The major independent arbitration agencies have formulated due process standards for the adjudication of these disputes. *See, e.g.,* National Academy of Arbitrators, Guidelines on Arbitration of Statutory Claims Under

Employer–Promulgated Systems (Statement adopted May 21, 1997); American Arbitration Association, National Rules for the Resolution of Employment Disputes (1996, as amended 1997); JAMS/ENDIS-PUTE, Six Principles of Neutrality and Fairness for Employment Dispute Resolution Practice (1995). Industry self-regulatory organizations (SRO's) like the NASD have been singled out for criticism because, among other reasons, the role they play in determining the pool of available arbitrators and selecting the arbitrators who will hear a particular discrimination claim against a member firm of the SRO calls into question the impartiality of the arbitrators selected.

Id. at 202.

In *Morrison v. Circuit City Stores, Inc.,* 317 F.3d 646, 653 (6th Cir.2003), the court indicated that "the Supreme Court has emphasized that 'federal statutory claims may be the subject of an arbitration agreement * * * enforceable pursuant to the FAA because the agreement only determines the choice of forum' ". (*citing* EEOC v. Waffle House, Inc., 534 U.S. 279, 295 n.10, 122 S.Ct. 754, 770 n.10, 151 L.Ed.2d 755, 765 n. 10 (2002)). The Supreme Court has acknowledged as much in interpreting the FAA in other statutory contexts: "By agreeing to arbitrate a statutory claim, a party does not forgo the substantive rights afforded by the statute; it only submits to their resolution in an arbitral, rather than a judicial, forum." Mitsubishi Motors Corp. v. Soler Chrysler–Plymouth, Inc., 473 U.S. 614, 628, 105 S.Ct. 3346, 3355, 87 L.Ed.2d 444, (1985).

What procedural safeguards must an employer provide in an arbitration agreement that covers federal statutory claims to allow an employee to effectively vindicate statutory rights? Chief Judge Harry Edwards of the D.C. Circuit Court of Appeals, who is a former labor law professor and labor arbitrator, authored one of the leading opinions on this issue in *Cole v. Burns International Security Services,* 105 F.3d 1465 (D.C.Cir. 1997). He interpreted *Gilmer* as requiring at least the following: (1) a neutral arbitrator; (2) more than minimal discovery; (3) a written award; (4) an opportunity in the arbitration proceeding to obtain all the remedies that would be available if the plaintiff were successful in a court action; and (5) a requirement that the employee must not be obligated to pay either unreasonable costs or any of the arbitrator's fees or expenses. *Id.* at 1482. *See also* Malin, *Privatizing Justice, supra* Note 2, page 953, at 601–22 (2001).

Notes and Questions

1. May an employer require a shorter statute of limitations in an arbitration agreement than is provided under federal law for initiating a claim of employment discrimination? Under Title VII, for example, a charging party has either 180 or 300 days within which to file a charge with the EEOC. *See, e.g.,* National R.R. Passenger Corp. v. Morgan, 536 U.S. 101, 122 S.Ct. 2061, 153 L.Ed.2d 106 (2002), Chapter 2, Section C. Suppose an employer, in an arbitration agreement, requires employees to initiate the

mandatory arbitration process for federal employment discrimination claims within four months after the claim occurs? *See, e.g.*, Soltani v. Western & Southern Life Ins. Co., 258 F.3d 1038 (9th Cir.2001) (applying a reasonableness standard in upholding a six-month statute of limitations in an arbitration agreement in a claim for wrongful discharge based on state law even though the state law limitations period for contract claims was longer). What if the employer, in an arbitration agreement, imposes a more generous limitations period than Title VII, say one year, but makes that limit hard and fast so that continuing violations are effectively cutoff at the one-year mark as well? *See* Ingle v. Circuit City Stores, Inc., 328 F.3d 1165 (9th Cir.2003).

2. May an employer, in an arbitration agreement, place caps on compensatory and punitive damages that are lower than the caps available under Title VII and the ADA? *See* Ingle v. Circuit City Stores, Inc., 328 F.3d 1165 (9th Cir.2003); Paladino v. Avnet Computer Techs., Inc., 134 F.3d 1054 (11th Cir.1998); Alcaraz v. Avnet, Inc., 933 F.Supp. 1025 (D.N.M.1996).

3. In addition to the D.C. Circuit in the *Cole* case discussed above, several other courts of appeals have held that a compulsory pre-dispute arbitration agreement that requires an employee to pay a portion of an arbitrator's fees is unenforceable under the FAA. Shankle v. B–G Maintenance Mgmt. of Colorado, 163 F.3d 1230 (10th Cir.1999) (arbitrator charged $250 per hour; $125 per hour for travel time; and $45 per hour for each hour of paralegal time); *Paladino*, 134 F.3d 1054.

4. In *Green Tree Financial Corp.–Alabama v. Randolph*, 531 U.S. 79, 121 S.Ct. 513, 148 L.Ed.2d 373 (2000), a case not involving employment discrimination law, the Supreme Court addressed the question whether an arbitration agreement is unenforceable when it imposes costs on both parties but does not specify the amount of those costs. The Court recognized that the existence of large arbitration costs could effectively preclude a person from vindicating her federal statutory rights in an arbitral forum. In *Green Tree*, the Court, relying on *Gilmer*, placed the burden on the person alleging excessive arbitration costs to prove the likelihood that the costs would be prohibitively expensive. Plaintiffs may be entitled to some discovery on the issue of whether costs of arbitration are likely effectively to preclude them from vindicating their federal rights in arbitration. *See* Blair v. Scott Specialty Gases, 283 F.3d 595 (3d Cir.2002).

In *Morrison v. Circuit City Stores, Inc.*, 317 F.3d 646 (6th Cir. 2003), the Sixth Circuit applied *Green Tree* to employment arbitration agreements that included cost-splitting provisions for arbitration fees and costs. In forging a standard consistent with *Green Tree,* the court focused on the deterrent component of antidiscrimination laws. In order for the deterrent aspect of these laws to work, the court opined, a useful standard must take into account any chilling effect on not only a particular individual but also other similarly situated individuals prior to arbitration. *Post hoc* judicial review of arbitration cases and the appropriateness of costs and cost-splitting provisions are inadequate when viewed from a deterrent perspective for two reasons. First, judicial review of arbitration awards is narrow and it is not clear whether it can adequately protect statutory rights. *Id.* at 662. Second, allowing *post hoc* judicial review of arbitration awards places plaintiffs in a

Catch–22 situation: "[T]hey cannot claim, in advance of arbitration, that the risk of incurring arbitration costs would deter them from arbitrating their claims because they do not know what the costs will be, but if they arbitrate and actually incur costs, they cannot then argue that the costs deterred them because they have already arbitrated their claims." *Id.* at 662–63. In addition, according to the *Morrison* court, if a "cost-splitting provision would deter a substantial number of potential litigants, then that provision undermines the deterrent effect of the anti-discrimination statutes. Thus, in order to protect the statutory rights at issue, the reviewing court must look to more than just the interests and conduct of a particular plaintiff." *Id.* at 663. The remedial function of antidiscrimination laws, on the other hand, is directed more toward the rights of particular wronged individuals.

Combining these two themes, the *Morrison* court held that "potential litigants must be given an opportunity, prior to arbitration on the merits, to demonstrate that the potential costs of arbitration are great enough to deter them *and* similarly situated individuals from seeking to vindicate their federal statutory rights in the arbitral forum." *Id.* (emphasis added). The reviewing court should define similarly situated individuals by "job description and socioeconomic background." *Id.* It should also use "average or typical arbitration costs" in its assessment because "that is the kind of information that potential litigants will take into account in deciding whether to bring their claims in the arbitral forum." *Id.* at 664. According to the court, "the issue is not 'the fact that [the] fees would be paid to the arbitrator,' but rather whether the 'overall cost of arbitration' from the perspective of the potential litigant, is greater than 'the cost of litigation in court.'" *Id.* at 664 (*citing Bradford v. Rockwell Semiconductor Sys., Inc.,* 238 F.3d 549, 556 (4th Cir.2001)). Likewise, the Fourth and Fifth Circuits have adopted the view that the decision whether an employee can be required to pay a part of the arbitrator's fees is to be decided on a case-by-case basis. *See Bradford v. Rockwell Semiconductor Sys., Inc.,* 238 F.3d 549 (4th Cir. 2001) (finding that fee-splitting provision requiring employee to pay half of the arbitrator's fees and costs is enforceable, but adopting a case-by-case approach rather than a *per se* rule against all fee-splitting); *Williams v. Cigna Fin. Advisors, Inc.,* 197 F.3d 752, 763–65 (5th Cir.1999), *cert. denied,* 529 U.S. 1099, 120 S.Ct. 1833, 146 L.Ed.2d 777 (2000).

Does *Green Tree* reject the per se rule on allocation of costs adopted by the court in *Cole*? Might an arbitrator be unduly influenced by the fact that his or her fees are provided solely by the employer, especially if the arbitrator hopes to get repeat business from that employer? *See* Lisa B. Bingham, *On Repeat Players, Adhesive Contracts, and the Use of Statistics in Judicial Review of Employment Awards,* 29 McGeorge L.Rev. 223 (1998).

5.   In light of the fact that there are no statutory requirements that arbitrators receive training in law or even have expertise in the subject matter being arbitrated, what arguments might be available to challenge the qualifications of an arbitrator? *See* Paul L. Edenfield, *No More the*

*Independent and Virtuous Judiciary: Triaging Antidiscrimination Policy in a Post-*Gilmer *World,* 54 Stan.L.Rev. 1321, 1339–45 (2002).

6.   Should the fact that Congress has now provided for jury trials in certain disparate treatment cases under the Civil Rights Act of 1991 be sufficient to preclude enforcement of agreements to arbitrate employment discrimination claims? *See* Nghiem v. NEC Elec., Inc., 25 F.3d 1437, 1441 (9th Cir.), *cert. denied,* 513 U.S. 1044, 115 S.Ct. 638, 130 L.Ed.2d 544 (1994) (no).

7.   What about attorney's fees? Can an employer require that an employee pay his or her own attorney's fees in arbitration? *See* McCaskill v. SCI Mgmt. Corp., 298 F.3d 677 (7th Cir.2002) (holding that an agreement requiring arbitration of Title VII claims is unenforceable if it limits an employee's ability to recover attorney's fees).

8.   Can an arbitration agreement preclude employee class actions seeking to vindicate claims of systemic discrimination against an employer? What if the agreement is silent on the issue of class actions? In *Bazzle v. Green Tree Fin. Corp.,* 351 S.C. 244, 569 S.E.2d 349 (2002), *vacated & remanded,* 539 U.S. 444, 123 S.Ct. 2402, 156 L.Ed.2d 414 (2003), a commercial arbitration case, the Bazzles and their class members had utilized Green Tree Financial to assist in financing home improvements. Class members signed various documents, including one with an arbitration clause stating, in part, "this contract * * * will be resolved by binding arbitration by an arbitrator selected by us with the consent of you." Green Tree Financial argued the singular language of the clause precluded class-wide arbitration. The South Carolina Supreme Court found that, although South Carolina state law, like federal law, generally favors arbitration, the United States Supreme Court has accepted common-law rules of contract construction even in a case involving arbitration issues (see Mastrobuono v. Shearson Lehman Hutton, Inc., 514 U.S. 52, 115 S.Ct. 1212, 131 L.Ed.2d 76 (1995)), noting that any ambiguous language should be "construed liberally and interpreted strongly in favor of the non-drafting party." 569 S.E.2d at 358. According to the South Carolina court, the fact that the arbitration clause was silent regarding class-wide arbitration created an ambiguity, on independent state grounds, and, therefore, should be construed against Green Tree as the drafting party. The court held that "class-wide arbitration may be ordered when the arbitration agreement is silent if it would serve efficiency and equity, and would not result in prejudice," *id.* at 360, and therefore upheld the *Bazzle* arbitrator's decision to certify a class. *id.* at 361–62. A divided U.S. Supreme Court, however, reversed and remanded the South Carolina decision, holding that "the question whether the agreement forbids class arbitration is for the arbitrator to decide." *Green Tree Fin. Corp. v. Bazzle,* 539 U.S. 444, 123 S.Ct. 2402, 2407, 156 L.Ed.2d 414, 422 (2003).

For a more complete discussion of issues relating to class actions in the arbitration context, see Jean R. Sternlight, *As Mandatory Binding Arbitration Meets the Class Action, Will the Class Action Survive?,* 42

Wm. & Mary L.Rev. 1 (2000); Samuel Estreicher & Michael J. Puma, *Arbitration and Class Actions after* Bazzle, 58 Disp.Resol.J. (Aug/Oct 2003).

Contract Formation: For an arbitration agreement between an employer and an employee to be enforced, there must first be a contract between the parties. Contract formation requires offer, acceptance, and consideration. Regarding consideration, what exactly does the employee get out of the arbitral agreement? Is there consideration even though there is no benefit to the employee? Does the job itself supply consideration for the agreement? Certainly express language of agreement in a written contract between the parties should be enforceable, but what if there is no express agreement by the employee? Or, what if the express language is buried in the agreement or is otherwise vague and difficult to comprehend? Can a contractual agreement exist even if assent by the employee can only be inferred by her actions? Can agreement be inferred by employee silence?

CIRCUIT CITY STORES, INC. v. NAJD

United States Court of Appeals for the Ninth Circuit, 2002.
294 F.3d 1104.

O'SCANNLAIN, Circuit Judge.

* * *

I

Circuit City Stores ("Circuit City") hired Monir Najd as a sales associate in 1985. In 1995, Circuit City instituted the "Associate Issue Resolution Program" at Najd's store of employment. As part of the program, Circuit City distributed a packet of materials to the store's employees, which included a "Dispute Resolution Agreement" (the "DRA"). The DRA provided that "any and all employment-related legal disputes, controversies or claims of an Associate arising out of, or relating to, * * * employment or cessation of employment with Circuit City * * * shall be settled exclusively by final and binding arbitration." The store's current employees were allowed to opt out of the DRA by returning a form to Circuit City's corporate headquarters. Najd acknowledged receipt of the packet in writing and did not exercise his right to opt out.

In February 1997, Alex Khorsand became Najd's supervisor. According to Najd, Khorsand continually harassed him on the basis of his ethnicity, culminating in his termination in February 1998. Najd filed suit against Circuit City and Khorsand in California Superior Court, alleging various common law torts and a violation of California's Fair Employment and Housing Act ("FEHA"), Cal. Gov't Code § 12940(a).

Circuit City responded by filing a petition in federal district court under the Federal Arbitration Act ("FAA"), seeking to stay the state court action and to compel arbitration of Najd's claims.

* * *

VI

Najd also claims that the DRA is not a valid contract because he never assented to it and it lacks consideration. Neither *Ahmed* [283 F.3d 1198 (9th Cir.2002)] nor *Adams III* [279 F.3d 889 (9th Cir.2002)] explicitly addressed these issues, and thus we proceed to consider them in turn.

Section 2 of the FAA provides that arbitration agreements "shall be valid, irrevocable, and enforceable, save upon such grounds that exist at law or in equity for the revocation of any contract." 9 U.S.C. § 2. Hence, generally applicable contract defenses, such as lack of consideration and mutual assent, may invalidate an arbitration agreement. * * * The parties agree that we look to California contract law to determine the DRA's validity * * *. Najd argues that the DRA is not supported by adequate consideration because Circuit City is not required to submit any of its claims against employees to arbitration. However, Circuit City's promise to be bound by the arbitration process itself serves as adequate consideration. *See Armendariz,* 6 P.3d at 692. * * * In other words, Circuit City's promise to submit to arbitration and to forego the option of a judicial forum for a specified class of claims constitutes sufficient consideration.[3]

Alternatively, Najd claims that he did not assent to the DRA because he did not affirmatively opt in to the program. "As a general rule, silence or inaction does not constitute acceptance of an offer." Golden Eagle Ins. Co. v. Foremost Ins. Co., 20 Cal. App. 4th 1372, 25 Cal. Rptr. 2d 242, 251 (Ct. App. 1993). However, "where circumstances or the previous course of dealing between the parties places the offeree under a duty to act or be bound, his silence or inactivity will constitute his assent." Beatty Safway Scaffold, Inc. v. B.H. Skrable, 180 Cal. App. 2d 650, 4 Cal. Rptr. 543, 546 (Ct. App. 1960).

Najd and Circuit City were not two typical parties contracting at arm's length. Rather, Najd, as employee of Circuit City, acknowledged receipt of the DRA in writing and was asked to review it within the course of his employment. In other circumstances acceptance by silence may be troubling, and explicit consent indispensable. Here, however, where the import of Najd's silence was as apparent as if he signed his consent, we may infer assent. The acknowledgment form that Najd signed clearly set out in writing the significance of his failure to opt out and described in detail the mechanism by which he could express his disagreement. The explicit opportunity to review the agreement with an attorney highlighted the legal effect of the agreement. Circuit City communicated in detail and in writing the effect of Najd's acceptance on his right to bring claims against his employer. Also, Circuit City made clear that opting out of the agreement would have no effect on the

---

3. In *Armendariz*, the California Supreme Court held a similar agreement substantively unconscionable in part because the agreement only required the employee to submit his claims to arbitration. 6 P.3d at 692–94. However, the court also concluded that the employer's promise to be bound by the arbitration process supplied adequate consideration. 6 P.3d at 692.

employment relationship. Finally, Najd had thirty days to review the agreement and mull over whether to opt out of it. When, as here, inaction is indistinguishable from overt acceptance, we may conclude that the parties have come to agreement. Thus, the circumstances of this case permit us to infer that Najd assented to the DRA by failing to exercise his right to opt out of the program. * * * In sum, we uphold the validity of the DRA.

* * *

Notes and Questions

1. In the case of waiver of forum for statutory employment discrimination claims, should ordinary contract law principles apply? Should an arbitration clause regarding such claims only be enforced if employee acceptance is "knowing and voluntary"? After all, a standard of "clear and unmistakable" is erected by the Supreme Court in *Wright v. Universal Maritime Service, see infra* Section C.1 of this chapter, for a union's waiver of statutory antidiscrimination rights of employees in a collective bargaining unit. Is there a good reason for a distinction between waiver standards in nonunion and unionized settings? In *Prudential Ins. Co. v. Lai*, 42 F.3d 1299 (1994), *cert. denied*, 516 U.S. 812, 116 S.Ct. 61, 133 L.Ed.2d 24 (1995), the Ninth Circuit held that Title VII requires that an employee knowingly agree to submit disputes under the statute to arbitration. In *Lai*, female employees filed a claim in state court alleging that their employer had engaged in sexual harassment and sexual discrimination in violation of state law. The employer then filed an independent action in federal court to compel mandatory arbitration of the claims under an agreement plaintiffs had signed when applying for employment. The Ninth Circuit held that the employees were not bound by the arbitration agreement because they had not knowingly agreed to waive their statutory rights to a judicial forum. The court based its decision on evidence relating to the arbitration agreement which showed that when the employees were hired and signed some forms containing the arbitration agreement, (1) they were told only that they were applying to take a required test; (2) they were directed to sign the relevant forms without being given an opportunity to read the documents; (3) they were not advised about the arbitration agreement in the documents they signed; (4) they were not given a copy of the documents containing the actual terms of the arbitration agreement; and (5) the documents containing the arbitration agreement did not describe the types of disputes that would be subject to arbitration. For two differing views on the question of waiver standards, *compare* Dennis R. Nolan, *Employment Arbitration After* Circuit City, 41 Brandeis L.J. 853 (2003) (most courts do not require "knowing and voluntary") *and* Stephen J. Ware, *Employment Arbitration and Voluntary Consent*, 25 Hofstra L.Rev. 83 (1996) (contract law question regarding assent is whether an agreement is voluntary or coerced) *with* William W. Fick, *Gnawing at* Gilmer: *Giving Teeth to "Consent" in Employment Arbitration Agreements*, 17 Yale L. & Pol'y Rev. 965 (1999) (standard for consent in arbitration of employment discrimination claims should be "knowing and voluntary").

2.   Can an employee be held to an agreement to arbitrate if she fails to expressly agree, but continues to work and receive a paycheck? Is the action of continuing to work sufficient to infer assent to terms of an employment agreement, including an agreement to waive a right to a judicial forum for statutory employment discrimination claims?

3.   *Contracts of Adhesion:* Contracts of adhesion are generally standardized contracts, drafted by the party who possesses superior bargaining strength, that offer to the other party only the opportunity to accept the terms and conditions of the contract on a "take-it-or-leave-it" basis. The economically weaker party has no realistic opportunity to bargain over individual terms. *See* Black's Law Dictionary 40 (6th ed. 1990); Todd D. Rakoff, *Contracts of Adhesion: An Essay in Reconstruction*, 96 Harv.L.Rev. 1173, 1177 (1983) (listing seven characteristics of adhesion contracts). Insurance contracts are prototypical contracts of adhesion. In those instances in which employment is offered on a "take-it-or-leave-it" basis and is conditioned on the applicant's agreement to a pre-dispute arbitration provision that waives judicial resolution of all employment discrimination claims, should the courts refuse to enforce the arbitration provision? *See* Justice Stevens' dissent in *Gilmer*, 500 U.S. at 36, 111 S.Ct. at 1657; Armendariz v. Foundation Health Psychcare Servs., Inc., 24 Cal.4th 83, 99 Cal.Rptr.2d 745, 6 P.3d 669 (2000) (holding that an employment arbitration agreement is an unlawful contract of adhesion if it fails to preserve substantial statutory rights); Mago v. Shearson Lehman Hutton, Inc., 956 F.2d 932 (9th Cir.1992) (finding that the arbitration agreement used in the security industry is not a contract of adhesion even though the form containing the agreement is standardized for the industry).

MORRISON v. CIRCUIT CITY STORES, INC.,

United States Court of Appeals for the Sixth Circuit, 2003.
317 F.3d 646.

MOORE, Circuit Judge.

These cases, consolidated for purposes of en banc review, involve the interaction in the employment context of the Federal Arbitration Act ("FAA"), 9 U.S.C. § 1 et seq., with federal anti-discrimination laws, such as Title VII of the Civil Rights Act of 1964. Both of the employees involved, Lillian Pebbles Morrison and Mark F. Shankle, were required to sign arbitration agreements as conditions of their employment, Morrison with Circuit City Stores, Inc. ("Circuit City"), and Shankle with the Pep Boys–Manny, Moe & Jack, Inc. ("Pep Boys"). Morrison and Shankle both sought to sue their former employers in court for discrimination after termination. In Morrison's case, the district court held that the arbitration agreement was enforceable and thus stayed Morrison's lawsuit pending arbitration. In Shankle's case, the district court held the agreement unenforceable and stayed arbitration pending litigation. We ordered a consolidated en banc hearing to address the important issues presented in these cases regarding mandatory arbitration agreements in the employment context.

* * *

On July 10, 1995, Plaintiff–Appellant Morrison, an African–American female with a bachelor's degree in engineering from the U.S. Air Force Academy and a master's degree in administration from Central Michigan University, submitted an application for a managerial position at a Circuit City store in Cincinnati, Ohio. As part of the application process, Morrison was required to sign a document entitled "Dispute Resolution Agreement." This document contained an arbitration clause that required resolution of all disputes or controversies arising out of employment with Circuit City in an arbitral forum. The application provided that Circuit City would not consider any application for employment unless the arbitration agreement was signed, that all applicants were required to arbitrate any legal dispute relating to their employment with Circuit City, including all state and federal statutory claims, contract claims, and tort claims, that all arbitrations would occur before a neutral arbitrator, and that all such arbitrations would be final and binding. Applicants could withdraw their consent to the arbitration agreement within three days of signing the application, but such action would also constitute withdrawal of their application for employment at Circuit City.

The Circuit City arbitration agreement also provided that all arbitrations were to proceed according to the "Circuit City Dispute Resolution Rules and Procedures." These rules and procedures addressed a variety of arbitral matters, including the time limitations for filing a request for arbitration, the limitation on remedies available to plaintiffs in the arbitral forum, filing fees, the payment of arbitration costs, discovery, and attorney fees. * * *

Morrison began her employment at Circuit City on or about December 1, 1995. Two years later, on December 12, 1997, she was terminated. Morrison alleges that her termination was the result of race and sex discrimination. She filed this lawsuit on December 11, 1998, in Ohio state court, alleging federal and state claims of race and sex discrimination, a violation of Ohio public policy, and a promissory estoppel claim. Circuit City removed the case to federal court and then moved to compel arbitration and to dismiss Morrison's claims. The district court granted Circuit City's motion, rejecting Morrison's arguments that the arbitration agreement was unenforceable under federal and state law.

Morrison's appeal followed. Because the arbitration was not stayed below, however, in April 2000, Morrison and Circuit City participated in an arbitration hearing on her claims, and on July 14, 2000, the arbitrator issued an award. Neither Morrison nor Circuit City has sought to vacate, modify, or correct the award, and the period in which judicial review of the arbitrator's award might have been sought has expired. For this reason, Circuit City moved this court to dismiss this appeal as moot. We denied that motion on January 17, 2002.[2]

---

2. Even though Morrison's case has been arbitrated, the claims she raises in this appeal are not moot because this court could still grant effectual relief in the present case, if we were to determine that the arbitration agreement was in fact unen-

The case was originally argued before a hearing panel on January 26, 2001. A majority of the active judges of the court voted to rehear the case en banc, the court issued an order for rehearing en banc on October 17, 2001, and the consolidated rehearing * * * was held on March 20, 2002.

* * *

We review de novo an order compelling arbitration. Floss v. Ryan's Family Steak Houses, Inc., 211 F.3d 306, 311 (6th Cir.2000), *cert. denied*, 531 U.S. 1072, 148 L. Ed. 2d 664, 121 S. Ct. 763 (2001).[11] In deciding whether to compel arbitration of a federal statutory claim, we first consider whether the statutory claim is generally subject to compulsory arbitration. If the claim is not exempt from arbitration, we must then consider whether the arbitration agreement is valid. *See id.* Because we have previously held that Title VII claims may be heard in an arbitral forum, *see* Willis v. Dean Witter Reynolds, Inc., 948 F.2d 305, 309 (6th Cir.1991), we proceed to the second step in the review process, *i.e.*, determining whether the Circuit City arbitration agreement is valid and enforceable.

Under section 2 of the FAA, an arbitration agreement is "valid, irrevocable, and enforceable, save upon such grounds as exist at law or in equity for the revocation of any contract." 9 U.S.C. § 2. We review the enforceability of an arbitration agreement according to the applicable state law of contract formation. First Options of Chicago, Inc. v. Kaplan, 514 U.S. 938, 943–44, 131 L.Ed.2d 985 115 S.Ct. 1920, (1995). In Morrison's case, we apply the Ohio law of contract formation, as Morrison was employed by Circuit City in the state of Ohio, and the parties have agreed that Ohio law applies. *See* * * * (Arbitration Agreement) (stating that "the Arbitrator shall apply the substantive law of the State in which the Associate is or was predominantly employed").

B.   Enforceability of the Agreement

Morrison * * * argues that the arbitration agreement is unenforceable because it is unsupported by consideration and because there is no mutuality of obligation. Morrison argues that there was no mutuality of obligation or consideration for the arbitration agreement because Circuit

---

forceable and thus arbitration should never have taken place. *Cf.* Church of Scientology v. United States, 506 U.S. 9, 113 S.Ct. 447, 121 L.Ed.2d 313 (1992) (holding that appeal of IRS summons was not moot even though subject of summons had already turned over the evidence at issue because court could still order some partial relief). As discussed *infra*, however, we ultimately hold that, although the challenged provisions are unenforceable, they are also severable from the agreement. Given that these provisions were not enforced in Morrison's arbitration, the arbitration proceeded as though the provisions were in fact unen-

forceable and severed. For this reason, we affirm the district court's order on these grounds.

11. In *Green Tree Financial Corp.-Alabama v. Randolph*, 531 U.S. 79, 89, 148 L.Ed.2d 373, 121 S.Ct. 513 (2000), the Supreme Court unanimously held that a district court order compelling arbitration and dismissing all the claims before the court is immediately appealable under 9 U.S.C. § 16(a)(3). After *Green Tree*, our jurisdiction in the present appeal is clearly established.

City had the power to alter or terminate the agreement on December 31 of each year upon giving thirty days' notice to its employees. We conclude, however, that the Circuit City arbitration agreement was supported by sufficient consideration and a mutuality of obligation. In making this determination, we look to Ohio law. Although the Ohio Supreme Court has not yet addressed this question, two courts of appeals have addressed related questions. The first is *Harmon v. Philip Morris, Inc.*, 120 Ohio App.3d 187, 697 N.E.2d 270 (Ohio Ct.App.1997). In *Harmon*, the court ruled that an arbitration agreement requiring employees to submit their claims to arbitration but imposing no reciprocal obligation on the employer, and giving the employer the right to amend or terminate the arbitration program "at any time," lacked consideration because it "neither offered a benefit to its employees nor incurred any detriment by modifying the terms of the employment relationship." *See Harmon*, 697 N.E.2d at 272. The Circuit City agreement is identical to the agreement at issue in *Harmon* in that it requires employees to submit their disputes to arbitration but makes no similar demand on the employer. * * * Accordingly, the only question is whether the Circuit City's timing provision, which allows Circuit City to amend unilaterally the agreement only on a specified date, is enough of a limitation to constitute consideration.

The second relevant Ohio case, *Century 21 American Landmark, Inc. v. McIntyre*, 68 Ohio App.2d 126, 427 N.E.2d 534 (Ohio Ct.App. 1980), may provide some insight on this question. In that case, the court stated that "a contract is illusory only when by its terms the promisor retains an unlimited right to determine the nature or extent of his performance; the unlimited right, in effect, destroys his promise and thus makes it merely illusory." *Century 21*, 427 N.E.2d at 536–37. Although the court did not define the sorts of limits that would be relevant to such an inquiry, it found a limit sufficient when a homeowner's unilateral power to terminate a home sale contract "arose only upon the happening of an event, i.e. a repair order resulting from [a third-party inspection of the home], over which the [homeowner] had no control." *Century 21*, 427 N.E.2d at 537. This could suggest that Ohio courts would consider a unilateral right to amend or terminate a contract "unlimited" whenever the power lies entirely within the amending or terminating party's control and subject only to that party's decision to amend or terminate.

We are hesitant to divine such a principle from the Ohio courts on the basis of this single decision, when that decision itself expresses no such principle and is equally consistent with an opposing interpretation. Although we cannot be certain how Ohio courts will proceed, we conclude that Ohio courts would find consideration sufficient and the contract enforceable. We do this in part based on the Restatement (Second) of Contracts, which considers a thirty-days-notice provision sufficient to constitute consideration. The Restatement suggests that when A promises B to act as B's agent for three years on certain terms, and B agrees but reserves the power to terminate the agreement on thirty days notice, "B's agreement is consideration, since he promises to continue the agency for at least thirty days." Restatement (Second) of Contracts § 77 cmt. b, illus. 1 (1979). In contrast, if B reserves the right to terminate "at any time," the agreement lacks consideration, "since it involves no promise" by B. *Id.* at cmt. a, illus. 2. Accordingly, the Restatement suggests that Circuit City's promise to maintain the arbitration agreement for at least thirty days, and until the end of each calendar year, constitutes sufficient consideration. So although the Ohio courts do not appear to have addressed this issue, we adopt a position that is consistent with their decisions and endorsed by the Restatement. *See also Harmon,* 697 N.E.2d at 272 (noting that under Ohio law, "a detriment to the promisee" such as "forbearance * * * by the promisee" may constitute consideration).

Further, the present case is distinguishable from *Floss*, in which we concluded that an arbitration agreement was unenforceable because the employer had "unfettered discretion in choosing the nature of [the arbitral] forum" and could alter the applicable rules and procedures without any notice to or consent from employees. *Floss,* 211 F.3d at 315–16; *see also Hooters of Am., Inc. v. Phillips,* 173 F.3d 933, 938–40 (4th Cir.1999) (holding that an arbitration agreement was invalid because, *inter alia*, the employer could modify the rules at any time without notice). Unlike in *Floss*, in this case Circuit City had the authority to alter the agreement on only one day of each year and had to provide its employees with thirty days' notice before doing so.

* * *

Notes and Questions

1. Can arbitration agreements be so one-sided in favor of the employer as to present constructive issues of assent or mutuality, or constructive breach of agreement? In *Hooters of America, Inc. v. Phillips*, 173 F.3d 933 (4th Cir.1999), a Title VII sexual harassment case, the employer conditioned eligibility for raises, transfers, and promotions upon an employee's willingness to sign an agreement to arbitrate all employment-related disputes. The agreement also provided that resolution of disputes would be made pursuant to rules promulgated by the employer, but the employees were not given a copy of the rules at the time they signed the arbitration agreement. After the plaintiff took steps to seek judicial relief, Hooters filed a motion to compel arbitration. The district court denied the motion and the Fourth Circuit affirmed. The Fourth Circuit held that the plaintiff was not required to submit her sexual harassment claim to arbitration because "Hooters set up a dispute resolution process so utterly lacking in the rudiments of even-handedness * * *[,] [it] breached its agreement to arbitrate." *Id.* at 935. The agreement allowed Hooters, but not its employees, to bring suit in court to vacate or modify an arbitral award when Hooters could show, by the preponderance of evidence, that the [arbitration] panel exceeded its authority. The agreement required employees to notify the company of any claim, including the nature of the claim, the specific acts or omissions which

formed the basis of the claim, as well as a list of all fact witnesses with a brief summary of all facts known to each. Hooters was not required, however, to file any responsive pleading, notice of its defenses, or lists of witnesses. The arbitrators were to be chosen from a list created exclusively by Hooters, and it could place on the list arbitrators with existing financial or familial relationships with the company. *Id.* Employees were forbidden to raise in arbitration any matter not raised in the initial notice, and Hooters, but not its employees, was allowed to audio or videotape the arbitration proceedings. *Id.* at 938–39.

2. Is an agreement to arbitrate sufficient to satisfy the consideration requirement for a contract? *See* Tinder v. Pinkerton Sec., 305 F.3d 728, 736 (7th Cir.2002) (holding that employee's continued work past the effective date of the arbitration agreement coupled with employer's agreement to be bound by arbitration is sufficient for consideration). Is there consideration if virtually all of the obligations of the agreement are shouldered by the employee? *See* Michalski v. Circuit City Stores, Inc., 177 F.3d 634 (7th Cir.1999) (finding sufficient consideration if employer agrees to be bound by the arbitral result); Johnson v. Circuit City Stores, Inc., 148 F.3d 373 (4th Cir.1998), *affirmed,* 203 F.3d 821 (4th Cir.), *cert. denied,* 530 U.S. 1276, 120 S.Ct. 2744, 147 L.Ed.2d 1008 (2000); Gibson v. Neighborhood Health Clinics, Inc., 121 F.3d 1126 (7th Cir.1997) (finding insufficient consideration if employer is not bound by arbitration); Smith v. Chrysler Fin. Corp., 101 F.Supp.2d 534 (E.D.Mich.2000); Jenkins v. United Healthcare, 82 Fair Emp.Prac.Cas. 984 (D.C.2000). What if the arbitration agreement is with a third party arbitration service that simply obligates it to provide an arbitration in case of a dispute and does not spell out any other terms regarding the arbitration? *See* Penn v. Ryan's Family Steak Houses, Inc., 269 F.3d 753 (7th Cir.2001); Floss v. Ryan's Family Steak Houses, Inc., 211 F.3d 306 (6th Cir.2000), *cert. denied,* 531 U.S. 1072, 121 S.Ct. 763, 148 L.Ed.2d 664 (2001) (in both cases, agreements with a third party arbitration service that did not detail arbitral procedures in advance failed for indefiniteness and lack of mutuality).

Contract Defenses: Once an arbitral agreement has been formed as a contract between the employer and employee, is there any way to have the contract set aside? An exception to the general rule that arbitration agreements are enforceable is found in § 2 of the FAA: arbitration agreements can be challenged on "such grounds as exist at law or in equity for the revocation of any contract." 9 U.S.C. § 2. Because these grounds are matters of state law, the rules will vary from state to state. The grounds on which courts may invalidate a contract include fraud, duress, mistake, and unconscionability. *See, e.g.,* First Options of Chicago, Inc. v. Kaplan, 514 U.S. 938, 944, 115 S.Ct. 1920, 1924, 131 L.Ed.2d 985 (1995) (ruling that "[w]hen deciding whether the parties agreed to arbitrate a certain matter * * * courts generally * * * should apply ordinary state-law principles that govern the formation of contracts"); Haskins v. Prudential Ins. Co. of Am., 230 F.3d 231 (6th Cir.), *cert. denied,* 531 U.S. 1113, 121 S.Ct. 859, 148 L.Ed.2d 773 (2001). *Gilmer* recognized that, pursuant to FAA § 2, "fraud or overwhelming economic power" could provide grounds for revocation of an agreement to arbitrate and that such cases should be "left for resolution in specific cases." *Gilmer*, 500 U.S. at 33, 111 S.Ct. at 1656. Even though state contract law applies to determine the validity of an arbitration agreement, the FAA has been construed to prohibit states from enacting laws that apply only to arbitration agreements. *See* Doctor's Assocs., Inc. v. Casarotto, 517 U.S. 681, 116 S.Ct. 1652, 134 L.Ed.2d 902 (1996) (the Federal Arbitration Act preempts a Montana law that required contracts with an arbitration provision to set out the arbitration clause on the first page of the contract, typed in underlined capital letters). What circumstances would constitute "fraud or overwhelming economic power" sufficient to provide grounds for revoking an agreement to arbitrate a claim of employment discrimination? What about mistake or unconscionability? The following case of *Circuit City II*, on remand from the Supreme Court, illustrates an approach to unconscionability under the § 2 exception.

CIRCUIT CITY STORES, INC. v. ADAMS

United States Court of Appeals for the Ninth Circuit, 2002.
279 F.3d 889, *cert. denied*, 535 U.S. 1112, 122 S.Ct. 2329, 153 L.Ed.2d 160.

D.W. NELSON, Circuit Judge.

* * *

A. *Applicable Law*

* * *

Adams argues that the DRA [Circuit City's Dispute Resolution Agreement] is an unconscionable contract of adhesion. Because Adams was employed in California, we look to California contract law to determine whether the agreement is valid. *See* Ticknor v. Choice Hotels Int'l, Inc., 265 F.3d 931 (9th Cir.2001) (applying Montana law to decide whether arbitration clause was valid).

Under California law, a contract is unenforceable if it is both procedurally and substantively unconscionable. Armendariz v. Found. Health Psychcare Svcs., Inc., 24 Cal.4th 83, 99 Cal.Rptr.2d 745, 6 P.3d 669, 690 (2000). When assessing procedural unconscionability, we consider the equilibrium of bargaining power between the parties and the extent to which the contract clearly discloses its terms. Stirlen v. Supercuts, Inc., 51 Cal.App.4th 1519, 60 Cal.Rptr.2d 138, 145 (1997). A determination of substantive unconscionability, on the other hand, involves whether the terms of the contract are unduly harsh or oppressive. *Id.*

B. *The DRA and Unconscionability*

The DRA is procedurally unconscionable because it is a contract of adhesion: a standard-form contract, drafted by the party with superior bargaining power, which relegates to the other party the option of either adhering to its terms without modification or rejecting the contract entirely. *Id.* at 145–46 (indicating that a contract of adhesion is procedurally unconscionable). Circuit City, which possesses considerably more bargaining power than nearly all of its employees or applicants, drafted the contract and uses it as its standard arbitration agreement for all of its new employees. The agreement is a prerequisite to employment, and job applicants are not permitted to modify the agreement's terms—they must take the contract or leave it. *See Armendariz,* 99 Cal.Rptr.2d 745, 6 P.3d at 690 (noting that few applicants are in a position to refuse a job because of an arbitration agreement).

The California Supreme Court's recent decision in *Armendariz* counsels in favor of finding that the Circuit City arbitration agreement is substantively unconscionable as well. In *Armendariz,* the California court reversed an order compelling arbitration of a FEHA discrimination claim because the arbitration agreement at issue required arbitration only of employees' claims and excluded damages that would otherwise be available under the FEHA. *Armendariz,* 99 Cal.Rptr.2d 745, 6 P.3d at 694. The agreement in *Armendariz* required employees, as a condition of employment, to submit all claims relating to termination of that employment—including any claim that the termination violated the employee's rights—to binding arbitration. *Id.* at 675. The employer, however, was free to bring suit in court or arbitrate any dispute with its employees. In analyzing this asymmetrical arrangement, the court concluded that in order for a mandatory arbitration agreement to be valid, some "modicum of bilaterality" is required. *Id.* at 692. Since the employer was not bound to arbitrate its claims and there was no apparent justification for the lack of mutual obligations, the court reasoned that arbitration appeared to be functioning "less as a forum for neutral dispute resolution and more as a means of maximizing employer advantage." *Id.*

The substantive one-sidedness of the *Armendariz* agreement was compounded by the fact that it did not allow full recovery of damages for which the employees would be eligible under the FEHA. *Id.* at 694. The exclusive remedy was back pay from the date of discharge until the date of the arbitration award, whereas plaintiffs in FEHA suits would be entitled to punitive damages, injunctive relief, front pay, emotional distress damages, and attorneys' fees.

We find the arbitration agreement at issue here virtually indistinguishable from the agreement the California Supreme Court found unconscionable in *Armendariz.* Like the agreement in *Armendariz,* the DRA unilaterally forces employees to arbitrate claims against the employer. The claims subject to arbitration under the DRA include "any and all employment-related legal disputes, controversies or claims *of an Associate* arising out of, or relating to, an Associate's application or candidacy for employment, employment or cessation of employment with Circuit City." (emphasis added). The provision does not require Circuit City to arbitrate its claims against employees. Circuit City has offered no justification for this asymmetry, nor is there any indication that "business realities" warrant the one-sided obligation. This unjustified one-sidedness deprives the DRA of the "modicum of bilaterality" that the

California Supreme Court requires for contracts to be enforceable under California law.

And again as in *Armendariz,* the asymmetry is compounded by the fact that the agreement limits the relief available to employees. Under the DRA, the remedies are limited to injunctive relief, up to one year of back pay and up to two years of front pay, compensatory damages, and punitive damages in an amount up to the greater of the amount of back pay and front pay awarded or $5,000. By contrast, a plaintiff in a civil suit for sexual harassment under the FEHA is eligible for all forms of relief that are generally available to civil litigants—including appropriate punitive damages and damages for emotional distress. *See* Commodore Home Sys., Inc. v. Superior Court of San Bernardino County, 32 Cal.3d 211, 185 Cal.Rptr. 270, 649 P.2d 912, 914 (1982). The DRA also requires the employee to split the arbitrator's fees with Circuit City. This fee allocation scheme alone would render an arbitration agreement unenforceable. *Cf.* Cole v. Burns Intern. Security Svcs., 105 F.3d 1465 (D.C.Cir.1997) (holding that it is unlawful to require an employee, through a mandatory arbitration agreement, to share the costs of arbitration). But the DRA goes even further: it also imposes a strict one year statute of limitations on arbitrating claims that would deprive Adams of the benefit of the continuing violation doctrine available in FEHA suits. *See, e.g.,* Richards v. CH2M Hill, Inc., 26 Cal.4th 798, 111 Cal.Rptr.2d 87, 29 P.3d 175, 176 (2001). In short, and just like the agreement invalidated by the California Supreme Court in *Armendariz,* the DRA forces Adams to arbitrate his statutory claims without affording him the benefit of the full range of statutory remedies.

In addition, our decision is entirely consistent with federal law concerning the enforceability of arbitration agreements. The Supreme Court, in *Gilmer v. Interstate/Johnson Lane Corp.,* 500 U.S. 20, 26, 111 S.Ct. 1647, 114 L.Ed.2d 26 (1991), held that "[b]y agreeing to arbitrate a statutory claim, [an employee] does not forgo the substantive rights afforded by the statute; [he] only submits to their resolution in an arbitral, rather than a judicial forum." While the Court in *Gilmer* affirmed that statutory rights can be resolved through arbitration, the decision also recognized that the arbitral forum must allow the employee to adequately pursue statutory rights. *Id.* at 28, 111 S.Ct. 1647.

Courts have since interpreted *Gilmer* to require basic procedural and remedial protections so that claimants can effectively pursue their statutory rights. *See, e.g., Cole,* 105 F.3d at 1482 (listing five basic requirements that an arbitral forum must meet). We note that here, Circuit City's arbitration agreement fails to meet two of *Cole's* minimum requirements: it fails to provide for all of the types of relief that would otherwise be available in court, or to ensure that employees do not have to pay either unreasonable costs or any arbitrators' fees or expenses as a condition of access to the arbitration forum. *Id.*

Nor does our decision run afoul of the FAA by imposing a heightened burden on arbitration agreements. Because unconscionability is a defense to contracts generally and does not single out arbitration agreements for special scrutiny, it is also a valid reason not to enforce an arbitration agreement under the FAA. Indeed, the Supreme Court has specifically mentioned unconscionability as a "generally applicable contract defense[ ]" that may be raised consistent with § 2 of the FAA. *Doctor's Assocs.*, 517 U.S. at 687, 116 S.Ct. 1652.

Our conclusion here is further buttressed by this Circuit's recent opinion in *Ticknor.* The majority in *Ticknor* looked to Montana law and found an asymmetrical arbitration clause (similar to the one at issue here) unconscionable and unenforceable. *Ticknor,* 265 F.3d at 942. The majority was careful to explain that the FAA did not stand as a bar to the court's holding because the FAA does not preempt state law governing the unconscionability of adhesion contracts. *Id.* at 935; *see also id.* at 941 (overruling, so far as they are inconsistent with that conclusion, *Cohen v. Wedbush, Noble, Cooke, Inc.,* 841 F.2d 282, 286 (9th Cir.1988), and *Bayma v. Smith Barney, Harris Upham & Co.,* 784 F.2d 1023 (9th Cir.1986)). We follow *Ticknor* in concluding that the result we reach today is fully consistent with the FAA.

C.   *Severability*

Under California law, courts have discretion to sever an unconscionable provision or refuse to enforce the contract in its entirety. *See* Cal. Civ.Code § 1670.5(a). In deciding whether to invalidate the contract,

> [c]ourts are to look to the various purposes of the contract. If the central purpose of the contract is tainted with illegality, then the contract as a whole cannot be enforced. If the illegality is collateral to the main purpose of the contract, and the illegal provision can be extirpated from the contract by means of severance or restriction, then such severance and restriction are appropriate.

Armendariz, 99 Cal.Rptr.2d 745, 6 P.3d at 696.

In this case, as in *Armendariz,* the objectionable provisions pervade the entire contract. In addition to the damages limitation and the fee-sharing scheme, the unilateral aspect of the DRA runs throughout the agreement and defines the scope of the matters that are covered. Removing these provisions would go beyond mere excision to rewriting the contract, which is not the proper role of this Court. *See id.* at 125, 99 Cal.Rptr.2d 745, 6 P.3d 669. Therefore, we find the entire arbitration agreement unenforceable.

* * *

Notes and Questions

1. Does *Circuit City II* set a reasonable standard for challenging arbitration agreements using traditional contractual defenses? Does the case comport with unconscionability doctrine as it is understood in general contract law analysis? Does the court apply unconscionability too

broadly? Can an unconscionability claim be made in any arbitration agreement challenge now? *See* Dennis R. Nolan, *Employment Arbitration After* Circuit City, 41 Brandeis L.J. 853, 856–59 (2003) (discussing the Ninth Circuit's use of contract avoidance principles as a sword (in *Circuit City II*) to void arbitration agreements rather than as a shield (in *Armendariz*) to protect weaker contracting parties).

2.   Suppose one of the non-English speaking employees in *Garcia v. Spun Steak*, 998 F.2d 1480 (9th Cir. 1993), see Chapter 11, Section C, had been required as a condition of employment to sign an arbitration agreement. Assume further that this employee now believes that he was discriminated against because of his national origin. Should the employee be allowed to challenge the arbitration agreement on the ground of procedural unconscionability under *Circuit City II* if he proves that the employer neither translated the agreement into Spanish nor explained it to him in Spanish? *See* Prevot v. Phillips Petroleum Co., 133 F.Supp.2d 937 (S.D.Tex.2001). What other illustrations of procedural unconscionability can you think of?

3.   Should an arbitration agreement be deemed unconscionable because the employer exerts undue control over the process for selecting the arbitrator? If so, what role should the employee have in the selection of the arbitrator? *See* Hooters of Am., Inc. v. Phillips, 173 F.3d 933 (4th Cir.1999). *See also* Malin, *Privatizing Justice, supra* Note 2, page 953, at 601–613.

4.   If only parts of an arbitration agreement are unconscionable, should the entire agreement be unenforceable? If not, under what circumstances may the offending provisions be severed from the remainder of the agreement? In *Circuit City Stores, Inc. v. Adams,* above, the court refuses to sever the unconscionable provisions because they pervade the contract so much as to be essential to the agreement of the parties. *Compare* Ingle v. Circuit City Stores, Inc., 328 F.3d 1165 (9th Cir.2003) (refusing to sever the unconscionable provisions and enforce the remainder due to the "numerous provisions" in the Circuit City agreement that were found to be unconscionable), *petition for cert. filed*, 72 U.S.L.W. 3309 (U.S. Oct. 20, 2003)(No. 03–604), *and* Ferguson v. Countrywide Credit Indus., 298 F.3d 778 (9th Cir.2002) (same) *with* Morrison v. Circuit City Stores, Inc., 317 F.3d 646, 675 (6th Cir.2003) (severing unconscionable provisions and enforcing remainder of arbitration agreement where unconscionable provisions had not been applied in earlier arbitration).

5.   Plaintiff is employed by an employer at one of its facilities in New Hampshire. He signs an arbitration agreement which provides, among other things, that the terms of the agreement are to be construed and enforced in accordance with the laws of California, and that the actual arbitration proceeding, if invoked, would take place in California. Plaintiff is discharged and files suit in federal district court in New Hampshire. The employer moves to compel the plaintiff to abide by the arbitration agreement. The plaintiff objects on the ground that it is too

expensive for him to travel to California to arbitrate the claim, thus making the arbitral forum inaccessible to him. Should the court grant the motion to compel arbitration? Should it make a difference whether the plaintiff is an experienced business-person like the plaintiff in *Gilmer*, or a low-level employee? *See e.g.*, Klinedinst v. Tiger Drylac, U.S.A., 2001 WL 1561821 (D.N.H.2001) (unpublished).

3. THE ARBITRAL RESULT

COLE v. BURNS INTERNATIONAL SECURITY SERVICES

United States Court of Appeals for the District of Columbia Circuit, 1997.
105 F.3d 1465.

EDWARDS, Circuit Judge.

* * *

4. *Judicial Review*

The final issue in this case concerns the scope of judicial review of arbitral awards in cases of this sort, where an employee is compelled as a condition of employment to arbitrate statutory claims. Cole has argued that the arbitration agreement is unconscionable, because any arbitrator's rulings, even as to the meaning of public law under Title VII, will not be subject to judicial review. Cole is wrong on this point.

Judicial review of arbitration awards covering statutory claims is necessarily focused, but that does not mean that meaningful review is unavailable. * * *

* * *

The Supreme Court has * * * indicated that arbitration awards can be vacated if they are in "manifest disregard of the law." *See* First Options of Chicago, Inc. v. Kaplan, 514 U.S. 938, 115 S.Ct. 1920, 1923, 131 L.Ed.2d 985 (1995) (citing Wilko v. Swan, 346 U.S. 427, 436–37, 74 S.Ct. 182, 98 L.Ed.168 (1953), *overruled on other grounds in* Rodriguez de Quijas v. Shearson/American Express, Inc., 490 U.S. 477, 109 S.Ct. 1917, 104 L.Ed.2d 526 (1989)). Although this term has not been defined by the Court, and the circuits have adopted various formulations, we believe that this type of review must be defined by reference to the assumptions underlying the Court's endorsement of arbitration. As discussed above, the strict deference accorded to arbitration decisions in the collective bargaining arena may not be appropriate in statutory cases in which an employee has been forced to resort to arbitration as a condition of employment. Rather, in this statutory context, the "manifest disregard of law" standard must be defined in light of the bases underlying the Court's decisions in *Gilmer*-type cases.

Two assumptions have been central to the Court's decisions in this area. First, the Court has insisted that, " '[b]y agreeing to arbitrate a statutory claim, a party does not forego the substantive rights afforded by the statute; it only submits to their resolution in an arbitral, rather than a judicial, forum.' " *Gilmer*, 500 U.S. at 26, 111 S.Ct. at 1652 (quoting *Mitsubishi*, 473 U.S. at 628, 105 S.Ct. at 3354) (alteration in original). Second, the Court has stated repeatedly that, " 'although judicial scrutiny of arbitration awards necessarily is limited, such review is sufficient to ensure that arbitrators comply with the requirements of the statute' at issue." *Gilmer*, 500 U.S. at 32 n.4, 111 S.Ct. at 1655 n.4 (quoting *McMahon*, 482 U.S. at 232, 107 S.Ct. at 2340). These twin assumptions regarding the arbitration of statutory claims are valid only if judicial review under the "manifest disregard of the law" standard is sufficiently rigorous to ensure that arbitrators have properly interpreted and applied statutory law.

The value and finality of an employer's arbitration system will not be undermined by focused review of arbitral legal determinations. Most employment discrimination claims are entirely factual in nature and involve well-settled legal principles. * * * In fact, one study done in the 1980s found that discrimination cases involve factual claims approximately 84% of the time. *See* Michele Hoyman & Lamont E. Stallworth, *The Arbitration of Discrimination Grievances in the Aftermath of* Gardner–Denver, 39 Arb. J. 49, 53 (Sept. 1984). As a result, in the vast majority of cases, judicial review of legal determinations to ensure compliance with public law should have no adverse impact on the arbitration process.[7] Nonetheless, there will be some cases in which novel or difficult legal issues are presented demanding judicial judgment. In such cases, the courts are empowered to review an arbitrator's award to ensure that its resolution of public law issues is correct. Indeed, at oral argument, Burns conceded the courts' authority to engage in such review. Because meaningful judicial review of public law issues is available, Cole's agreement to arbitrate is not unconscionable or otherwise unenforceable.

* * *

Notes and Questions

1. The statutory grounds for vacatur of arbitration awards are narrow and strictly construed by the courts. The FAA provides that awards may be vacated where

(1) the award was procured by corruption, fraud or undue means.

(2) there was evident partiality or corruption in the arbitrators * * *.

(3) the arbitrators were guilty of misconduct in refusing to postpone the hearing, upon sufficient cause shown, or in refusing to hear evidence pertinent and material to the controversy; or of any other misbehavior by which the rights of any party have been prejudiced.

---

7. The Hoyman/Stallworth study of arbitral awards in discrimination cases found that, even in cases where de novo review was available under *Gardner-Denver*, only 1.2% of all discrimination cases were reversed by the courts. *See* Hoyman & Stallworth, 39 Arb. J. at 55.

(4) the arbitrators exceeded their powers, or so imperfectly executed them that a mutual, final, and definite award upon the subject matter submitted was not made.

9 U.S.C. §§ 10(a)(1)–(4). Additionally, the FAA provides that an arbitral award may be corrected or modified where

(1) there was an evident miscalculation of figures.

(2) the arbitrators have issued an award on an issue not submitted to them.

(3) the award is imperfect in a manner or form not affecting the merits of the controversy.

9 U.S.C. § 11.

The courts have also crafted additional grounds for vacating or modifying arbitration awards. These non-statutory grounds include (1) the arbitrator's manifest disregard of the law; (2) the award conflicts with a strong public policy; (3) the award is arbitrary and capricious; (4) the award is completely irrational; or (5) the award fails to draw its essence from the underlying contract. *See* Williams v. Cigna Fin. Advisors, Inc., 197 F.3d 752, 757–58 (5th Cir.1999), *cert. denied*, 529 U.S. 1099, 120 S.Ct. 1833, 146 L.Ed.2d 777 (2000) (citing Gabriel M. Wilner, 1 Domke on Commercial Arbitration § 34:07 at 14 (Rev.ed.1998)).

2. The "manifest disregard of the law" test, which is discussed in *Cole v. Burns International Security Services*, above, has been invoked as a basis to vacate arbitral awards in statutory employment discrimination cases. *See, e.g.,* Halligan v. Piper Jaffray, Inc., 148 F.3d 197 (2d Cir. 1998), *cert. denied*, 526 U.S. 1034, 119 S.Ct. 1286, 143 L.Ed.2d 378 (1999). The courts have not, however, developed a uniform analytical framework for applying the "manifest disregard of the law" test, especially in the context of arbitration of statutory employment discrimination claims. In *Halligan*, for example, the court, in cautioning that the "manifest disregard" standard is severely limited, stated that it means more than error or misunderstanding with respect to the law. To modify or vacate an award, a court must find both (1) the arbitrator knew of a legal governing principle yet refused to apply it or ignored it altogether, and (2) the law ignored by the arbitrator was well defined, explicit, and clearly applicable to the case. *Id.* at 202 (citing DiRussa v. Dean Witter Reynolds, Inc., 121 F.3d 818, 821 (2d Cir.1997), *cert. denied*, 522 U.S. 1049, 118 S.Ct. 695, 139 L.Ed.2d 639 (1998); Michael P. O'Mullan, Note, *Seeking Consistency in Judicial Review of Securities Arbitration: An Analysis of the Manifest Disregard of the Law Standard*, 64 Fordham L.Rev. 1121 (1995)). In *DiRussa*, an ADEA case, the court held that the "manifest disregard" test was more stringent than the "clearly erroneous" standard and that it had not been satisfied where the arbitrator had failed to award attorney's fees to the prevailing party in the arbitration. *See also* Pike v. Freeman, 266 F.3d 78 (2d Cir.2001). Other courts have been more expansive about applying the "manifest disregard" standard in the nonunion employment discrimination, *Gilmer*-type, case context. *See, e.g.,* Cole v. Burns Int'l Sec. Serv., 105 F.3d 1465

(D.C.Cir. 1997); Williams v. CIGNA Fin. Advisors, 197 F.3d 752 (5th Cir.1999), *cert. denied,* 529 U.S. 1099, 120 S.Ct. 1833, 146 L.Ed.2d 777 (2000) (applying a test suggested in Ian R. MacNeil et al, 2 Federal Arbitration Law § 40.7.2.6, at 40:95 (1994): First, where on the basis of the information made available to the court it is not manifest that the arbitrators acted contrary to the applicable law, the award should be upheld. Second, where, on the basis of the information available to the court, it is manifest that the arbitrators acted contrary to the applicable law, the award should be upheld unless it would result in significant injustice, taking into account all of the circumstances of the case, including the powers of arbitrators to judge norms appropriate to the relations between the parties); DeGaetano v. Smith Barney, Inc., 983 F.Supp. 459 (S.D.N.Y.1997) (manifest disregard for arbitrator to fail to award attorney's fees to prevailing employee). *But see* Dennis R. Nolan, *Employment Arbitration After* Circuit City, 41 Brandeis L.J. 853, 877–80 (2003) (most courts reaching the "standard of review" question have favored the narrower view of the manifest disregard standard).

3.   May parties contractually agree to a particular standard of review? *See* Hughes Training Inc. v. Cook, 254 F.3d 588 (5th Cir.2001) (yes).

4.   If a "manifest disregard of the law" standard is inadequate to safeguard important statutory rights prohibiting employment discrimination, what should the standard be instead? *See* Calvin William Sharpe, *Integrity Review of Statutory Arbitration Awards,* 54 Hastings L.J. 311 (2003) (suggesting courts first review the correctness, on facts and law, of the arbitral result and then proceed to review the arbitral rationale only if the result is incorrect); Norman S. Poser, *Judicial Review of Arbitration Awards: Manifest Disregard of the Law,* 64 Brook.L.Rev. 471 (1998) (proposing that arbitral awards should be vacated if they show extraordinary lack of fidelity to, or egregious departure from, established law); Malin & Ladenson, *Privatizing Justice: A Jurisprudential Perspective, supra* Note 2.a, page 953 (arguing for heavy deference to arbitral factfinding but de novo review of arbitral statutory legal interpretations).

C. ARBITRATION OF EMPLOYMENT DISCRIMINATION CLAIMS IN UNIONIZED WORKPLACES

Employers and unions have long used arbitration to resolve grievances that arise under collective bargaining agreements. Typically, the collective bargaining agreement will provide for a multi-stage grievance procedure that culminates in binding arbitration. The arbitration provisions of the agreement provide a method for selecting a third-party neutral as arbitrator. The grievance process is initiated when an employee files a written grievance. As the exclusive representative of the employees in the bargaining unit, the union is responsible for handling the grievance through all stages, including representing the employee at the arbitration hearing. Many employee grievances are settled at early stages of the grievance process and never go to arbitration. More importantly, the union is not obligated to accept every grievance; as long as the union does not violate the duty of fair representation, it is free to exercise considerable discretion in determining which employee grievances warrant adjustment through the collective bargaining agreement's grievance and arbitration process, though the employee is generally free to adjust their grievances with the employer directly if the union chooses not to take up a claim. *See* Vaca v. Sipes, 386 U.S. 171, 87 S.Ct. 903, 17 L.Ed.2d 842 (1967). The duty of fair representation (DFR) is discussed in Chapter 14. For a comprehensive treatment of the arbitration process, see Elkouri and Elkouri: How Arbitration Works (Alan Miles Ruben, ed., 7th ed.2003).

The union arbitral process has been used to vindicate employment discrimination claims. Questions have arisen regarding the use of these processes to decide statutory claims of discrimination. In *Alexander v. Gardner–Denver*, 415 U.S. 36, 94 S.Ct. 1011, 39 L.Ed.2d 147(1974), the plaintiff, a black employee, alleged that he had been discharged because of his race. He had filed a grievance contesting his discharge under the grievance-arbitration provision of the collective bargaining agreement and also had filed an action under Title VII in federal court. The union processed the grievance through arbitration. Without discussing plaintiff's claim of racial discrimination, the arbitrator concluded that the plaintiff had been discharged for just cause. Following the arbitration decision, the employer moved for summary judgment on the Title VII claim. The district court granted the motion, and the court of appeals affirmed. On certiorari, the Supreme Court reversed, holding that an employee does not forfeit his rights under Title VII by first pursuing binding arbitration of a union grievance. The Court reasoned that the contractual rights granted unions under a collective bargaining agreement and the individual rights granted to employees under Title VII are "distinctly separate." *Id.* at 50, 94 S.Ct. at 1020.

The Court concluded that Title VII confers individual rights upon employees that "can form no part of the collective-bargaining process since waiver of these rights would defeat the paramount congressional purpose behind Title VII." *Id.* at 51, 94 S.Ct. at 1021. The Court continued:

> [W]e think it clear that there can be no prospective waiver of an employee's rights under Title VII. It is true, of course, that a union may waive certain statutory rights related to collective activity, such as the right to strike. These rights are conferred on employees collectively to foster the processes of bargaining and properly may be exercised or relinquished by the union as collective-bargaining agent to obtain economic benefits for union members. Title VII, on the other hand, stands on plainly different ground; it concerns not majoritarian processes, but an individual's right to equal employment opportunities. Title VII's strictures are absolute and represent a congressional command that each employee be free from discriminatory practices. Of necessity, the rights conferred can form no part of the collective-bargaining process since waiver of these rights

would defeat the paramount congressional purpose behind Title VII. In these circumstances, an employee's rights under Title VII are not susceptible of prospective waiver.

Id. at 51–52, 94 S.Ct. at 1021 (citations omitted). The Court drew a clear distinction between employee rights arising from a statute and employee rights arising from a collective bargaining agreement. It noted that where an employee's claim is based on a collective bargaining agreement, courts should defer to the arbitrator's decision. However, different considerations apply where a claim is based on a statute like Title VII, which is designed to provide minimum substantive guarantees to employees.

Of more relevance outside of collective bargaining was the Court's articulation of the view that arbitration was inappropriate for resolving Title VII claims. This conclusion rested on four grounds: (1) that labor arbitrators lack the expertise and authority competently to resolve Title VII claims; (2) that arbitral factfinding procedures fail adequately to protect employees' rights under Title VII; (3) that arbitrators are not required to issue written opinions; and (4) that because unions have exclusive control over the manner and extent to which an individual employee's grievance is pursued, unions and employers can discriminate jointly without suffering adverse legal consequences if arbitration is an employee's exclusive remedy.

In *Gilmer v. Interstate/Johnson Lane Corp*, 500 U.S. 20, 111 S.Ct. 1647, 114 L.Ed.2d 26 (1991), reproduced in this Chapter, Section B.1, the Court held that a claim under the Age Discrimination in Employment Act could be subjected to compulsory arbitration pursuant to an arbitration agreement in a securities registration application of the employee. Prior to *Gilmer*, lower courts widely interpreted *Gardner-Denver* as holding that employees who asserted statutory discrimination claims were entitled to litigate their claims in court, regardless of any predispute agreement to arbitrate. *See, e.g.*, Rosenfeld v. Department of Army, 769 F.2d 237, 239 (4th Cir.1985) ("The plain lesson of *Alexander v. Gardner–Denver Co.* * * * is that Congress entrusted the ultimate resolution of questions of discrimination to the federal judiciary."); Utley v. Goldman Sachs & Co., 883 F.2d 184 (1st Cir.1989), *cert. denied*, 493 U.S. 1045, 110 S.Ct. 842, 107 L.Ed.2d 836 (1990); EEOC v. Children's Hosp. Med. Ctr., 719 F.2d 1426 (9th Cir.1983).

Several years after *Gilmer* and decades after *Gardner-Denver*, the Supreme Court in *Wright v. Universal Maritime Service Corp.*, 525 U.S. 70, 119 S.Ct. 391, 142 L.Ed.2d 361 (1998), was presented with an opportunity to clarify its position on arbitration of statutory claims in the unionized workplace. The *Wright* case presented the following question: whether a collective bargaining agreement's general arbitration clause requires an employee to use an internal grievance process to contest an alleged Americans with Disabilities Act violation? The Supreme Court held that the collective bargaining agreement's general arbitration clause failed to meet the required "clear and unmistakable" standard for union-negotiated waivers of statutory rights. The Court refused to decide, however, whether there should be a presumption of arbitrability under the Federal Arbitration Act for such claims and whether a proper waiver would be enforceable.

The facts of *Wright* involved a longshoreman, Caesar Wright, who injured his right heel and back while working. The injury was severe enough to allow him to receive both social security disability and workers' compensation benefits. A contested workers' compensation claim resulted in a settlement award to Wright of $250,000 and an additional $10,000 in attorney's fees. Almost three years after his injury, Wright returned to work. As a member of the Stevedores Union, Wright applied for work through his union hiring hall. He worked for ten days with no employer complaints about his labor, but when the companies for whom he was working discovered that he had settled a permanent disability claim, they refused to employ him any further on the grounds that he was not qualified to work due to his disability. Although the union disputed the employers' claim, it ultimately advised Wright to hire an attorney who could press a claim under the Americans with Disabilities Act. Wright filed a charge with the EEOC and then sued the Union and six employers in federal district court. The district court adopted the magistrate's recommendation and report which concluded that the claim should be dismissed for failure to exhaust, meaning, of course, that Wright should have first grieved his claim through the collective bargaining agreement's arbitration process. The Court of Appeals for the Fourth Circuit affirmed the district court's action.

The Supreme Court noted a tension between two cases. The Supreme Court's 1974 decision in *Alexander v. Gardner–Denver,* discussed above, and the Court's 1991 decision in *Gilmer v. Interstate/Johnson Lane Corp.,* reproduced in this chapter, Section B.1. While the *Gardner-Denver* decision held that Title VII rights are not susceptible to prospective waiver in a collective bargaining agreement, the *Gilmer* decision held that a right to a judicial forum can be waived in an individual contract. Respondents maintained that the Court should apply a presumption of arbitrability. The Court refused to do so because labor law's presumption of arbitrability arises out of arbitrator expertise in handling contractual, not statutory, claims. The Court refused to decide whether a presumption of arbitrability could be premised alternatively on the Federal Arbitration Act, stating that the point had not been made below and was not relied upon by the Fourth Circuit in its decision. Because there was no presumption of arbitrability, the Court required that any agreement to arbitrate statutory claims must be "clear and unmistakable." The Court held that the general arbitration provisions in this case were too general to meet the standard of a clear and unmistakable waiver of statutory rights. The Court found that the arbitration clause's applicability to "matters under dispute" could be read to mean only disputes *under the contract* (i.e., the collective bargaining agreement) and not statutory disputes like one involving the ADA.

*

Index

References are to Pages

†

0–314–14709–8

9 780314 147097